The Encyclopedia of Jazz in the Seventies

by **LEONARD FEATHER**
and **IRA GITLER**

THE
ENCYCLOPEDIA
OF
JAZZ
IN THE SEVENTIES

Introduction by QUINCY JONES

Quartet Books
London, Melbourne, New York

To Jane and Lorraine
and
To Mary Jo and Fitz

Copyright © 1976 by Leonard Feather and Ira Gitler
First published in Great Britain
by Quartet Books Ltd. 1978
A member of the Namara Group
27 Goodge Street, London W1P 1FD

ISBN 0 7043 2175 0

Authors' Prefaces

The Encyclopedia of Jazz in the '70s is the third in a series of books, each in its way autonomous. The others are *The Encyclopedia of Jazz* (previously known as *The New Encyclopedia of Jazz*), published in 1960 and covering men, women and events in jazz history from the beginning until that time; and *The Encyclopedia of Jazz in the '60s*, covering events through mid-1966 and published late in that year. The present work is an examination of the ten-year period since the preparation of the previous volume.

Even more than during the compilation of the earlier books, the lines between jazz and other idioms became vague and arbitrary. This was particularly true of the borders between jazz and rock, and of those between jazz and free music or black music. Certain artists, protesting that they did not wish to be classified as jazz musicians, asked to be excluded from the new work. In many cases we acceded to their wishes; however, in some instances their association with jazz seemed to have been established so firmly at one time or another within the jazz community that they were included. Stix Hooper, leader of a group that was known for many years as the Jazz Crusaders, is a case in point.

Ira Gitler, an associate since the inception of the entire series (research on an early *Encyclopedia of Jazz* began with his help in 1954), has now become a full collaborator. It is no exaggeration to state that, given the enormous complexity of this job, it could not have been done without the knowledge and dedication Ira applied to completing it.

Frankie Nemko, who began as my secretary but who in the course of the work became a full-fledged editorial associate, brought to her part of the work a rare combination of familiarity with the subject, enthusiasm and painstaking accuracy. Ira and I are both grateful for her help.

Among the many friends and newly found correspondents around the world who gladly gave their time in enabling us to make this as complete a collection of facts as was reasonably possible, the following were particularly helpful: Joachim Berendt, Pawel Brodowski, Jan Byrczek, Philippe Carles, Roger Coterell, Stanley Crouch, Jim Crockett, Stanley Dance, Edmond Devoghelaere, Gudrun Endress, Gretchen Horton, Randi Hultin, Kiyoshi Koyama, Floyd Levin, Mike Mantler, Dennis H. Matthews, Mark Miller, Moscatelli Nello, John Norris, Arrigo Polillo, Charles Suber, Eric Vogel and Nils Winther.

I recall with a mixture of gratitude and sadness the many constructive notes sent me by the late Ralph J. Gleason, a man who loved jazz and was determined to offer help unselfishly to anyone of us who shared his concern.

As in the last volume, it is necessary to apologize to those whose biographies were submitted but for reasons of space could not be included; and to others on whom material proved difficult or impossible to obtain. Fortunately the latter were in a small minority and included none of the truly significant, established figures.

This is not simply a book dealing with artists who came to prominence during the past decade. Those who died after the previous book went to press, and the many others who were still a part of the jazz scene as this latest volume was being wrapped up, all are included in the pages that follow. Eubie Blake has a place in *The Encyclopedia of Jazz in the '70s* no less important than that of Jon Faddis.

For this edition we were determined to obtain the finest possible illustrations and to avoid conventional, press-agent photographs, Veryl Oakland (during the past ten years, and continuing into the mid-'70s, an important photo contributor to *down beat; Jazz Magazine* (Paris); *Swing Journal* (Tokyo); *Billboard; Guitar Player; Contemporary Keyboard*; and *Rolling Stone*) was unstintingly helpful in supplying lists, making up prints and availing us of his very special artistry. He is the photographer most abundantly represented, but we were fortunate also to have the cooperation of David D. Spitzer and others.

Finally, a reminder: although this book is self-sufficient, in the sense that it includes brief recapitulations of the pre-1966 careers of almost all the performers listed in the previous volumes, it is rather the combination of all three books that is intended to provide the most complete series possible. Together, they form what we believe is the most comprehensive reference set covering the 75 tumultuous years in which jazz has been a sturdy, ever-growing art form.

Leonard Feather
North Hollywood, Calif.

I can only second the words of my colleague and add our thanks to the help received from Jeff Atterton, Len Dobbin, Marta Jones, Arthur Levy, (especially) Dan Morgenstern, Stanley Sands, Don Schlitten, David Spewack, Jane Welch and Krzysztof Zagrodzki.

I am already aware of the book's value. It helped greatly itself in its own completion.

We acknowledge, with special thanks, the discriminating and devoted assistance given to us in connection with the manifold details of this book by Tony Outhwaite of Horizon Press.

Ira Gitler
New York City

Contents

Illustrations

Introduction by Quincy Jones

It is impossible for me to look back over the past eventful decade in modern music, or to speculate about what the future may hold, without recalling an answer I gave to a question Leonard Feather asked me many years ago. I was one of a group of musicians he approached for a concluding chapter in *The Book of Jazz*, in an attempt to predict what jazz would be like in 1984.

I'd like to recall some of the observations I made at that time, back in 1957: "How many attitudes," I said, "will be changed if jazz goes just where we want it to? If backgrounds for television shows and other situations like that become what we now call 'hip' and earn acceptance by every layman—will it still be progressive music or will it then become just popular music? In other words, if jazz becomes so widely used and accepted, then isn't it likely that it will just be considered popular music and the critics will go some place else and find something farther out, more esoteric?

"Concerning the blending of classical and jazz forms, I don't go for it too much today—this business of jazz musicians' trying to compete with Hindemith and Stravinsky. There's really no competition at all. And the 12-tone scale may be new to us, but it's quite old-fashioned to the classical composer, so what we do with it is really a joke. It sounds very amateurish to try to write atonal things without any conception of basic composition, just for the sake of trying to be far out. That's not progress. It's like a classical composer hanging out in nightclubs for a couple of nights and then trying to play bebop piano.

"What I hope will happen, though, is that sym-phony musicians' training in the future will have them better informed as to what has happened in jazz, so that when the guys are making a strong attempt to bring these two things together and combine the techniques, the orchestras will be better equipped.

"Eventually I think the two groups will simply be musicians—like for instance in Sweden, where a guy is just as familiar with a Ravel string quartet as he is with Lunceford's *For Dancers Only*. It will be wonderful if we get to a place where all the groups are speaking one another's language.

"This is my ultimate in the future of jazz. If there has to be a fusion of classical music and jazz, I think it will come in the day when there are capable soloists inside the symphony orchestra—when they have the same backgrounds. When everybody in the symphony orchestra can sit down and build, and have the same subtlety and looseness of rhythm. But it would have to come from the roots, and everybody in the orchestra would have to have those roots. If that happened, they would satisfy just as much as Duke Ellington—and that would be my idea of the perfect future for jazz."

In reviewing these observations of mine, Leonard mentioned that I had touched on a point he felt was very relevant: that jazz has been subjected to a Law of Diminishing Repute. He pointed out that by 1957, for example, scores of trumpet players were capable of performances that would have seemed fantastic in 1943, just as Dizzy Gillespie's first bebop records were around that time. But after all the time that had passed since bop began, a solo by, say, Lee

Morgan, objectively, must be judged in terms of the listener's awareness of earlier contributions by Gillespie and the other pioneers of the 1940's. Jazz in the next twenty-five years, he concluded, would continue along these lines: "The innovation of today will be the cliché of tomorrow."

Well, here we are now, not too far away from the 1984 that seemed so distant to us when we talked and wrote about it then; and some of the points made then have turned out to be very germane to the contemporary scene.

In order to get a clear perspective of what progress has been made, of what sounds are really yesterday's innovations and today's cliches, it's important to bear in mind that many of the things people tend to think of as new have really been around for quite a while. It would be difficult for me to state that I have heard many new, actual, organic innovative approaches toward music of *any* kind in the past ten years.

We heard some of the most sophisticated sounds imaginable back at the end of the '40's and the beginning of the '50's. My mind used to get torn off every time I'd hear Bird or Fats Navarro or Clifford Brown. I haven't been slapped in the head on that level in a long time.

Let's deal with the situation element by element. Velocity? We won't even get into that, because there's nobody alive who's playing faster than Art Tatum was playing back then. Or Dizzy, or Bird, Ray Brown, Max Roach.

Harmony? In terms of avant garde harmonic concepts there are none, really; in jazz that is our least innovative area, because the classical composers had raked the total realm of harmonic innovations a hundred years before we even touched this area.

Melodically I haven't heard that much, aside from some experiments with twelve tone improvisation, which in any case musicians have always been experimenting with on both sides, from Lukas Foss to a lot of jazz musicians. Polytonality is nothing new; neither is serial music.

Rhythmically you have people today like Billy Cobham, who really understands what polyrhythms are all about. But it's very difficult to call that new, if you sit down and listen to forty or fifty African records. That's been an African tradition for centuries. The so-called "new" time signatures also are no brainchildren of the '70's; they were in African

music and classical music centuries ago.

All right, then; we've eliminated velocity, harmonic structure, melody, rhythm, time signatures; so what do you have left that is strongly progressive? The fusion of styles, and the use of technology. And here the role played by electronics immediately comes to mind.

Actually, the year 1953 locked up the incubation period for the granddaddies of electronics. Specifically, there was Charlie Christian, who established the electric guitar in 1939; and in 1953, when I was twenty years old and playing in Lionel Hampton's orchestra, Monk Montgomery was playing fender bass—the first musician ever to use one.

Those two instruments turned the whole thing around. The rest were just supplementary items—the echoplexes, and so forth. Basically, the thrust of evolution was motivated by the electric guitar and fender bass. When the bass was amplified, it was necessary to deal with a totally different concept of the function of the bass.

Once the bottom of the rhythm section began to become filled out with such strong, predominant sounds, and the focus went down to the basement, our perspective of what happened on top with ad lib improvisation was completely turned around. The guitar and bass played a vital part in determining the function of a jazz group. I know that the synthesizers constitute a pervasive force today, but those things are accouterments. The rhythm section does not function off of a synthesizer, which is just a color, rather than the backbone of the rhythm section. The synthesizer is not so much a musical instrument as a controller of sound.

One facet of the scene that has changed appreciably in the past ten years is that of communication. I think my generation came out of a school that said to hell with the public. I remember feeling a certain joy, when I was seventeen, hearing a layman tell me he didn't understand what I was doing. It was fashionable, and the highest compliment in the world, to be outside. But now you have musicians who are eager to get through to the people; men like Herbie Hancock and Billy Cobham. Cobham has studied his drums, he's listened to Max and all the jazz greats, as well as to the rock cats, and he feels he doesn't have to be self-conscious about his playing, because he can outplay anyone on either side of the fence. So he plays to express himself, to get it all out. He wants to communicate, and he succeeds.

Another aspect in which there has been a notable change in recent years is the self-respect among musicians. In the early years of jazz, of course, it was considered anything but respectable. Black musicians in particular went through such a brainwashing process that they weren't considered complete musicians until they had just about abandoned their roots and were able to play Opus Number So-and-So. Everything was judged by European art music standards.

Even at the black universities in this country black music isn't allowed, or wasn't until comparatively recently. Cannonball Adderley once told me he had the same problem when he was teaching school. It was completely forbidden to become involved in the blues or jazz or boogie woogie. Howard University stopped using Handel and other European music for their commencements only as recently as ten or fifteen years ago. Black music wasn't allowed in the schools, and that applied to eighty per cent of the black colleges and universities in America.

In doing some research on the history of black music I came across a book that included an astonishing example of how people's minds were manipulated in this country. The book is called *Discovering Music*, and it was part of a series called *War Department Educational Manual*, printed by the United States Armed Forces Institute of Madison, Wisconsin. The authors are Howard D. McKinney and W. R. Anderson. The book is described as a course in music appreciation, and was published in 1944. In the course of a chapter labeled *The Adventurous Conquest*, there is a paragraph that reads: "Some may start with an enthusiasm for music of the jazz type but they cannot go farther, for jazz is peculiarly of an inbred feeble stock race, incapable of development. In any case, the people for whom it is meant could not understand it if it did develop. Jazz is sterile; it is all right for fun or as a mild anodyne like tobacco, but its lack of rhythmical variety necessitated by its special purpose, its brevity, its repetitiveness and lack of sustained development, together with the fact that commercial reasons prevent its being as a rule very well written, all mark it as a side issue having next to nothing to do with serious music, and consequently it has proved itself entirely useless as a basis for developing the tastes of the amateur. The ambitious listener might better start from

the level of Chopin's melodious piano music or Grieg's northern pieces.''

That is an illustration of how our armed forces were being indoctrinated thirty-odd years ago, but it also indicates the entire attitude that has prevailed in American society, one that has been tremendously difficult to overcome. Today, more than ever, in any discussion of jazz, the problem arises of defining the word itself. If you were to stop the man on the street and ask what the word means to him, you would be given so many different answers that it would blow your mind; because we are dealing with endless areas of styles, pictures, associations, and, above all, stereotypes. The word has so many meanings that ultimately it has none at all. Even students who have infinitely more understanding of the music than the writers of the quotation above have difficulty in drawing the line between jazz and other forms. For example, how could you separate the Third Stream concert works of John Lewis from what the authors call "serious music"?

On another level, if you were to take Charlie Parker's solo on *Stella By Starlight* and put the Stevie Wonder rhythm section underneath it, it would still be jazz. By the same token, how do you classify Stevie Wonder's *Too High*? It cannot be called rhythm and blues. He plays polytonal chords and jazz figures along with rhythm and blues licks; it is a total fusion. Harmonically, melodically, and every other way, it really has a jazz base, but it is performed by artists who are categorized as rhythm and blues.

Jazz is the stepchild of many matriarchal types of music such as gospel, the blues, and spirituals; yet, somehow it attained a position in which it could influence and swallow up anything with which it came into contact, from quadrilles to Stravinsky, to Country and Western. Whatever it came next to, it could eat alive. Consequently, it has always had an incredible number of influences around it, but its roots have remained planted where the mother elements come from.

The chord changes, and melodic ideas in rhythm and blues are developing every day. More and more the fusion is showing that basically all these forms stem from one source. John Coltrane's sound brings the same kind of message as the cat who was singing the field hollers back in slavery days. It is a continuation of a life style, and the remarkable thing about every form of artistic evolution is that no matter which direction is taken—avant garde, sophisticated, crude, blues, emotional basis or intellectual basis—it is still in many ways a sociological basis that provides the fundamental determination; and there were sociological reasons for the attitudes behind the music appreciation course that found jazz sterile and incapable of development.

Actually, it has developed so far and so dynamically that today there are probably more categories within the category of jazz itself than in any other music.

I don't envy Leonard Feather and Ira Gitler their role in putting this book together. Ten years ago there was a whole different set of circumstances. The typical musician today is not isolated in an ivory tower. He has listened to and been a part of many other forms of music. He has been affected by instant communication, by the dynamics of society over these past turbulent years. I have always felt that if I had the choice of picking a particular time to be around, especially as a musician, I would not want to trade this particular spot that I have. It covered the end of what was called the swing period, the birth of modern jazz, and all the subsequent developments. It meant a great deal to me, when I decided to take a few months off and write some music based on the Afro-American heritage, to be able to get on the telephone and call Duke Ellington to straighten

out any conflict I might find in the history books. That was a real luxury. This is a golden age we are living in, because we have been able to feel the impact made by the personalities and musical influences of what is really the first team.

I remember being particularly conscious of this one night at the Monterey Jazz Festival when a group of us got together and we were all sitting under a blanket. Louis Armstrong was there, and Roy Eldridge, and Dizzy: three generations of music sitting right under that blanket! We didn't think anything about it at the time, other than that we were happy to be alive, but obviously that can't happen twenty years from now.

It is difficult to explain, to anyone who has not experienced Charlie Parker or Dizzy Gillespie or Louis Armstrong or Duke Ellington or Billy Eckstine or Count Basie, just what that person represents as a total human being in the hierarchy of a great tradition. That has been one of the greatest joys of my life, to have known and been around these people, to have been influenced by them, and to have lived through the different eras they symbolize. All these great figures, and the artists who have come up more recently as an outgrowth of their influences, are represented in the pages of *The Encyclopedia of Jazz In The '70s*. That's the biggest talent blanket of them all.

Brentwood, Calif.

The practitioner as preacher:
The best of the Blindfold Test

The Blindfold Test, which I inaugurated in 1946 in *Metronome*, and which has been appearing regularly in *down beat* since 1951, was based on the premise that the musician has the right to function as a critic of his own art form, and that a listener, given no prior information concerning the record he is listening to, will be unencumbered by any prejudice.

The main objective of these interviews is the eliciting of an honest reaction to the music—the soloists, composition, arrangement, recording. The guessing of the artists' identities has always been a secondary consideration; this is pointed out to the blindfoldee before he is interviewed.

The following excerpts, all from tests conducted during the decade before this book went to press, were chosen on the basis of their general interest, without regard to the positive or negative character of the comments. The ratings indicate outstanding (five stars), very good (four), good (three), fair (two) and poor (one).

The excerpts are reproduced through the cooperation of Jack Maher, editor, and Charles Suber, publisher, of *down beat*, and by permission of Maher Publications.

The date after the artist's name before each comment indicates the year in which the interview was first published.

BAND LEADERS

Don Ellis. *Passacaglia and Fugue* (from *Live at Monterey*, Pacific Jazz). Ellis, trumpet; Tom Scott, alto.

Michel Legrand (1967): I like it very much, but—I wonder, is it an old album? . . . There was a little touch of the bebop in there.

Is that an organized band which plays every day? It sounds to me like—like the way Lalo Schifrin works—a studio band. But the composition, and the way it was orchestrated, I found very interesting. Interesting construction.

Who is the trumpet player? And also the alto at the beginning? I liked them . . . it could have been Phil Woods. Four stars.

Woody Herman. *The Sound of Music* (from *My Kind of Broadway*, Columbia). Herman, leader, alto saxophone; Raoul Romero, arranger.

Cannonball Adderley (1967): Well, taken as good sounding dance music, I think that that's five stars. It's good to hear Woody Herman sounding like he did years ago; in fact, I really do get nostalgic about bands. . . . I had the feeling that this was the same caliber, the same scope of things that Woody did in the *Summer Sequence* period, and it felt like Ralph Burns to me . . . It is not adventurous jazz, but there's room for everything, and I'm happy to know that Woody is still doing that sort of thing—maybe his music will survive as a result of his being able to play music for just ordinary folks.

As far as big bands and what it takes for them to survive, vive le Woody Herman!

Dave Brubeck. *World's Fair* (from *Time Changes*, Columbia).

Don Ellis (1967): There is nothing like a nice relaxed 13! . . . Dave Brubeck has been playing these time things as a group longer than anyone else, but they don't seem to be very free within the time yet . . . They haven't gotten to the point yet where they can really mess with the time. . . . It seems they should be much further into it, given the amount of time they have been doing it.

This is the first time I heard them playing in 13, and they played it all the way through.

I noticed Dave was having a little trouble keeping his left hand right on the rhythm, but he came out okay. . . . I'm just sorry that Dave and his group haven't been able to develop a more flowing thing, to get a little more imaginative. But the piece is nice; let's give them four stars.

Andrew Hill. *Spectrum* (from *Point of Departure*, Blue Note). Hill, piano, composer; Eric Dolphy, bass clarinet; Anthony Williams, drums.

Don Ellis (1967): One thing that Eric Dolphy always had was a sense of the dramatic. In a blindfold test we did a few years back I commented that I liked what Eric did . . . He tends to repeat licks that you have heard him do a hundred times before. In this particular track he seemed to be very creative, seemed to stay away from those.

One very valuable lesson that the avant-gardist can learn from Eric is that the sense of urgency—the sense of drama that he has in his playing, the violent contrast that he would sometimes use—this immediately gives it more direction.

I would like to comment on the drummer, who could have been Tony Williams. This particular style of drumming, breaking up the time into different fragments, can be very effective, but it also can be very deadly, particularly behind the piano solo . . . I felt that the time lost its intensity.

For me the most interesting section was the 5/4 section that they got into. But just to repeat an abbreviated form of the beginning at the end was sort of a copout, compositionally. The piece . . . should have built someplace . . . There were some good moments, especially Eric's playing. I give it 3 ½ stars.

Oliver Nelson. *Cascades* (from *Blues and the Abstract Truth*, Impulse). Nelson, composer; Freddie Hubbard, trumpet; Bill Evans, piano; Paul Chambers, bass; Roy Haynes, drums.

Stan Kenton (1966): The reason I asked to hear the first portion of that record again was that at first I thought there were some cross-rhythms going on that would be very interesting . . . when I listened again I didn't think it was anything strange I heard—there were just time hassles going on. They were awfully disturbing. . . . But it did have an interesting sound.

I liked the trumpet player very much. I wasn't too impressed with the piano. He's tasty, but suffers from the same fault of a lot of modern pianists—they get into one idiom and they keep it going, and there are so many possibilities.

Especially during the piano solo, the bass and the drummer were very listless, there was not much energy coming from them . . . I didn't feel that during the trumpet solo, because I believe the trumpet had more assertion.

Inasfar as the little composition idea on the end, I feel that sometimes these little modal effects can be carried too far; after it's said once or twice, then they should go ahead and spice it with something else. It gets to be a boring thing, and you finally feel that you want to stop the record and say, "What else is new?"

Three stars, I guess.

Duke Ellington. *Artistry in Rhythm* (from *Will Big Bands Ever Come Back?*, Reprise). Kenton, composer; unidentified arranger.

Stan Kenton (1966): I think I have to say that this affects me in a very personal way. It's like the master of us all said, "Stan, don't take yourself too seriously. After all, you know, you do have a sense of humor; the world will turn whether you push it or not." And I think in essence it kind of says, "Regardless of all your screaming and hollering, we still like you anyway."

I think it's beautiful. And he is the master too. I'd have to give it four stars.

I don't know whose arrangement it is . . . There were ideas that were very pleasing.

BASS

Charles Mingus. *Chazz Fingers No. 2*, (from *Mingus Revisited*, Trip Jazz). Mingus, composer, bass.

Don Ellis: I love Mingus' spirit, his writing, everything about him . . . he has the jazz spirit, and yet the avant-garde, and yet the old . . . you can hear the Duke Ellington, some Gil Fuller . . . he just brings everything together. And that's one of my favorite things, to mix a lot of elements together.

PIANO

Art Tatum. *I Would Do Anything For You* (from *Art Tatum Masterpieces*, MCA). Tatum, piano; Tiny Grimes, guitar; Slam Stewart, bass. Recorded 1944.

Earl "Fatha" Hines: That's a nice record. I wouldn't give it five. There's so many of them doing those same passages, it's hard to tell. Peterson does it . . . it's confusing me. The bass player is Slam and I think the guitar was Tiny Grimes. But who was on piano? Was that made just recently?

It's a nice record; they stick close to the melody. But there's nothing to get excited about. I'd give it three.

Chick Corea. *Earth Juice* (from *Where Have I Known You Before*, Polydor). Corea, piano; Stanley Clarke, bass; Al DiMeola, guitar; Lenny White, drums; comp. by group.

Lonnie Liston Smith (1975): That was definitely Stanley Clarke; since there was no piano solo, it must have been Stanley's date. I like that for a lot of different reasons. He's greatly John McLaughlin influenced, but that particular composition will give creative music, improvisational music, more exposure because of its overall rhythmic concept, and the electric guitar; so that will appeal more to the young kids. I've found that once they are exposed, they really enjoy the music.

BASS

Eddie Harris. *Superfluous* (from *Instant Death*, Atlantic). Harris, electric sax, composer; Rufus Reid, bass.

Al McKibbon (1972): The bass player, I think, is Richard Davis, because he's the only one I know outside of Charlie Mingus who'd have that much nerve . . .

BIG BANDS

Stan Kenton. *Artemis* (from *Adventures in Time*, Capitol). Kenton, piano.

Howard Rumsey (1966): That's a Kenton band and a two-star record. There's nobody listening to that kind of music. . . . This is dear Stan carrying on his tradition as the Wagner of American jazz and he's hung with it and he'll never be able to get away from it, and it's okay with me. In another 30 years there might be a place for that band; but as it is right now it's just hanging out here with no particular reason.

The piano sounded like an attempt to sound delicate, but it didn't come out that way. Very mediocre. Jeepers creepers.

Don Ellis. *Ferris Wheel.* (from *The New Don Ellis Band Goes Underground*, Columbia). Ellis, trumpet, composer, arranger.

Doc Severinsen (1970): It's got to be Don Ellis. Now that's a perfect example of the utilization of a big band in today's bag. They've forgotten all about Glenn Miller and Les Brown and all that, and they've just gone to what it should be.

. . . . Great arrangement, beautifully recorded, great playing. . . . Five stars!

Don Ellis. *Open Beauty* (from *Electric Bath*, Columbia). Ellis, composer, trumpet.

Bill Evans (1968): It's possibly the Don Ellis orchestra, but it doesn't matter. I would give it about four stars for imaginative sound adventure in music, and perhaps 1 ½ stars for the actual musical content.

To me, of course, the musical content is always primary, and although this is something that can attract one's attention immediately, in 20 years' time it's not going to mean a thing as far as novelty is concerned.

Don Ellis. *Freedom Dance* (from *Live in 3⅔ 4 Time*, Pacific Jazz).

Dave Holland (1968): I think his preoccupation with time signatures is a bit of a gimmick. There's a record I heard where he does these very slick announcements about it . . . "Now, ladies and gentlemen, we'd like to do a little old thing in 12¾ . . ." and it seems he's so knocked out with that that maybe he's losing sight of what music really is. . . . I'd give it three.

Duke Ellington. *Blood Count* (from *And His Mother Called Him Bill*, RCA). Johnny Hodges, alto saxophone; Billy Strayhorn, composer.

Duke Pearson (1968): It had to be Duke Ellington. This is the most beautiful band in the world. . . . I can remember as a teenager going to school proms and hearing this kind of music, not wanting to hear any other kind of music. . . . With music like this you can relive memories, pleasant things happening to you. That was Johnny Hodges on alto; couldn't be anyone else.

I think that's a Billy Strayhorn tune. It had to be, because of its melodic structure, even though Duke could have written it himself. . . . I loved it—I can give this one 20, 50 stars.

Oliver Nelson. *Flute Salad* (from *Sound Pieces*, Impulse). Nelson, composer, arranger.

Thad Jones (1968): That was a Billy Byers arrangement, and what impressed me most was the use of flutes and French horn backgrounds. It was a very lush and beautiful sound and always moves. He manages to keep the harmonic structure very interesting. As a matter of fact, Billy is one of my favorite arrangers anyway. I'd rate that at least 4½.

Mel Lewis: I don't think it's Byers, but I think it was definitely made out here on the West Coast, because of all the flutes—using all the flutes like that, bass flute, alto flute, and I have a feeling it's either Johnny Williams or Mancini. . . . It was a good chart, simple, good melody.

Thad Jones: That's what makes it so complex; it's such a simple thing, but so well constructed.

Mel Lewis: Thad knows more about the voicing and construction; he can hear something more than I would that way. I would rate it a little differently, too. I'd rate it about three.

Lionel Hampton. *Thai Silk* (from *Newport Uproar*, RCA Victor). Hampton, vibes, composer; Jerome Richardson, lead alto sax.

Thad Jones (1968): I loved the reed section, it had a good quality. I don't know if that was a regular band of Hampton's or not. It was probably a band that got together for that particular occasion—Newport possibly? And for a live performance like that, I thought it was recorded exceptionally well.

I really liked it, and I'll go along with another five stars. For the quality of the recording, and for the musicianship.

Mel Lewis (1968): We have a few ex-Hamptonites in our band, and I know they really didn't have much time to get themselves together for this. It sounded like they didn't really know the chart that well, but they played the hell out of it, because they're pros, and it had that kind of feeling. Not like a band that's been together for a long time, but like a band that could do about as good as you would want at very, very short notice. So, I'd go along with the high rating, just because of the circumstances.

Count Basie. *Switch in Time* (from *Basie Straight Ahead*, Dot). Al Aarons, trumpet; Eric Dixon, tenor saxophone; Harold Jones, drums; Sam Nestico, composer, arranger.

Stix Hooper (1970): At first I thought it was Ted Heath, and then it sounded like Louis Bellson . . . could be one of those bands made up of studio musicians. Trumpet player sounded a little like Charlie Shavers, tenor player a bit like Budd Johnson. I kind of liked his sound. The drummer could have been Bellson. . . . I'd give it three stars for the arrangement.

Woody Herman. *Keep on Keepin' On* (from *Light My Fire*, Cadet). Richard Evans, composer, arranger; Sal Nistico, tenor saxophone.

Gene Ammons (1970): I'm pretty sure that was my man Woody Herman. Being an alumnus of Woody's band, I'm pretty partial to the band as a whole. I came up in the middle of the big band era; consequently big bands are really my first love. I've always liked the sound of all the brass and the feeling that five reeds can get in a band of the type that Woody has—and always has had down through the years.

The tune sounds pretty original, and it was really swinging as only Woody can do. The tenor player sounded like Sal Nistico, who's a very dear friend of mine.

So there's nothing bad I can say about Woody and the band and Sal and everybody—so I'll have to give it five stars.

Count Basie. *Love Me Or Leave Me* (from *Super Chief*, Columbia). Buck Clayton, Shad Collins, trumpets; Lester Young, tenor sax; Jo Jones, drums; recorded 1939.

Harold Jones (1972): This to me is where we came from. I probably wasn't born when this was played. But because of something like that, when you start rating them, I just call that top echelon in giving it stars, because nothing came before that.

CLARINET

Jimmie Noone. *I Know That You Know* (from *Jimmie Noone & Earl Hines at the Apex Club*, Decca). Noone, clarinet; Hines, piano; Joe Poston, alto saxophone.

Barney Bigard (1969): I couldn't miss knowing who that was, because he was one of my favorites—the great, great Jimmie Noone.

Noone was a great influence for me—I stole a lot from him! I used to go and listen to him at the Apex Club in Chicago every night, and I'd get a lot of ideas from him. He was a great friend of mine, too. He helped me quite a bit.

I'd give it four stars.

Oliver Nelson. *Ja-Da* (from *The Spirit of '67*, Impulse). Pee Wee Russell, clarinet; Nelson, arranger.

Roland Kirk (1968): I think that was Oliver Nelson and Pee Wee Russell, and I'd like to commend Pee Wee Russell for keeping an open mind about music. He seems to keep up with a lot of the new music and techniques and still be playing his style.

I've known about Pee Wee for quite some years, and I've tried to talk to him the same as I have with some of the others. But some of these people are reluctant to talk with you, being younger than them. Like I called Barney Bigard the last time I was out here, and talked with him. I don't think he was too familiar with who I was, but I just wanted him to know that I enjoyed his clarinet playing.

I don't really want to mess around with stars, but if you want a rating, I'd give it four for good listening.

COMBOS

Supersax. *If I Should Lose You* (from *Supersax Plays Bird With Strings*, Capitol.)

Terry Gibbs (1975): Five stars for the effort those guys put into really getting the feel of Charlie Parker—Med Flory and Buddy Clark. By the way, Supersax actually started in my band, with Joe Maini. I feel very close to this whole thing.

Every one of them deserves five stars . . . it's not easy to play, you have to know Charlie Parker. I've seen some of the bars written on paper . . . I saw one bar on *Don't Blame Me* that took up a whole page, that I wouldn't want to read at all if I knew how to read it!

Chico Hamilton. *Jim-Jeannie* (from *The Dealer*, Impulse). Hamilton, drums, composer; Larry Coryell, guitar.

Gabor Szabo (1969): I'm pretty sure that's Chico Hamilton and his organization. . . . The first impression I got was that the unison line at the beginning was somewhat out of tune—it was unmusical and disturbing. I don't always care if somebody isn't right on pitch, because that's secondary, usually, for me. But here it bothered me.

I imagine that was a Chico Hamilton composition, because I recognize that theme, having been with Chico for about 3½ years. Toward the end it became worse and more disturbing, this chaos and frenzy.

I would rate it two stars, and that's only because I know two of the musicians, and Joe Beck I regard as a very good young guitar player. It was all very disturbing to me, with a lack of taste.

Miroslav Vitous. *Infinite Search* (from *Infinite Search*, Embryo). Vitous, bass, composer; Herbie Hancock, piano; Jack DeJohnette, drums.

Terry Gibbs (1970): They're three good players . . . I'll give it three stars, but maybe it should deserve more. . . . The electric piano guy was playing all right notes, made sense to me.

A lot of the new players seem to start with John Coltrane, and to me a good player should be able to do anything; Coltrane would have been able to sit in with the Dukes of Dixieland and swing the hell out of it. I don't think a lot of the newer guys would be able to play a basic 12-bar blues without getting off into some wild tangent, whereas some of the older players from the John Coltrane era can play out, but also play in.

Modern Jazz Quartet. *The Golden Striker* (from *No Sun In Venice*, Atlantic).
Don Ellis (1972): When I was in college I remember going down to Storyville in Boston and hearing them do a ballad, and I'd never heard an instrumental group do a ballad so they got the whole audience so connected . . . you could hear everybody go "Ooh!", it was so incredibly beautiful.

Weather Report. *Tears* (from *Weather Report*, Columbia).
Phil Woods (1971): I like that kind of direction, the thing that Miles introduced, with the longer lines; and I like the feeling of the record. The looseness with the way jazz composers are treating songs now, there's a certain elasticity within the form that I find very intriguing, although it can be overdone.

DRUMS

Buddy Rich. *Love and Peace* (from *Buddy & Soul*, World Pacific). Joe Sample, arr.
Stix Hooper (1970): I'll have to give that four stars for the arrangement! . . . . Of course that was Buddy on drums with his style that's very well known. It was a Joe Sample arrangement; my friend from the rhythm section of the Jazz Crusaders.
I respect Buddy Rich for what he's done as a technician, but I don't think that he's done anything creative. . . . He is, of course, a phenomenal drummer. He has one of those fantastic techniques that you just don't get in a music school; you have to have it from birth, it's inbred. But if he's not playing under fiery circumstances, he's not able to project, as far as I'm concerned. . . . With him everything is very mechanical and he plays in one bag.
Leonard Feather: Who would you say is the most creative big band drummer?
Hooper: It's hard to say who is the *most* creative. I haven't heard many; Harold Jones plays very tastefully, so did Sonny Payne. . . . Also Mel Lewis—these guys play within the context of each tune, arrangement and composition.

VIOLIN

Mahavishnu Orchestra. *Awakening* (from *The Inner Mounting Flame*, Columbia). Jerry Goodman, violin.

Jean-Luc Ponty (1973): Of course, Mahavishnu . . . and what can I say? A big record and a great crew . . . I didn't like Jerry Goodman when I heard him with The Flock. I mean I was admiring his talents on the violin because he is really talented to play with his instrument, but I didn't feel he was really together with the group. But since he play with Mahavishnu, I really love his playing . . . he is playing in a very different way, looking for another kind of sound. . . .

DRUMS

Mahavishnu John McLaughlin. *The Awakening* (from *The Inner Mounting Flame*, Columbia); Billy Cobham, drums.
Bobby Colomby (1972): That's Cobham, I think, on drums, and he's incredible. I think if he's ever recorded right he's going to frighten every other drummer out of playing. . . .

Buddy Rich-Max Roach. *Figure Eights* (from *Rich vs. Roach*, Mercury). Rich, drums (left channel); Roach, drums (right channel).
Elvin Jones (1966): Drums aplenty! That's an interesting way to make a drum record—just two cats playing eight bars apiece.
It sounded like Louie Bellson to me on the left channel—and Buddy Rich, maybe, on the right. Or maybe not. Maybe it was Louie over there, too, 'cause they sound so much alike.
The bass drum work was sort of reminiscent of some of the things that Max has introduced. . . . I think if they had taken a chorus apiece at some point, it would have progressed a little bit more, so that the bass drum pattern would have developed . . . it knocked me out, though . . . five stars.

Louie Bellson. *The Diplomat Speaks* (from *Live at the Summit*, Roulette). Bellson, composer, drums.
Elvin Jones (1966): Now this time it's *got* to be Louie Bellson! Louie with Duke Ellington's orchestra. Years ago, when Louie was with Duke the first time . . . I was introduced to him . . . Louie gave me a pair of sticks—I still have them.
Five stars or ten!—you can't beat that. It sounds like Louie's tune. . . . That was some solo he developed—the graduation was so nice.

Count Basie. *Good Time Blues* (from *Basie in Sweden*, Roulette). Basie, piano; Louie Bellson, drums.
Buddy Rich (1967): What can you say about him that hasn't been said by everybody in the world? I'm sure that was Mr. Basie. And as far as I'm concerned, Mr. Basie can do no wrong in anything he ever does or anything he ever will do. He's got all the taste in the world; the band

sounds beautiful. And I think that was Louie Bellson on drums. The sound was much cleaner and more articulate than Sonny Payne.

Just for being Basie, I give it five stars.

Thad Jones-Mel Lewis. *Mean What You Say* (from *The Jazz Orchestra*, Solid State). Jones, fluegelhorn, composer; Lewis, drums; Richard Davis, bass.

Buddy Rich (1967): I'll take a guess. I'd say that's the new Thad Jones-Mel Lewis band. Mel has a very distinctive style. He's one of the three or four best big-band drummers. He knows how to accompany a big band, and he has the ability to swing a big band.

I guess that was Thad playing trumpet or fluegelhorn. . . . I would demand more from the composition. . . . I think the band could have done more with something a little less contrived.

The rhythm section—I don't know if that was Richard Davis on the bass or not, but whoever it was sure gets a beautiful sound. . . . In general it's very well-done . . . three stars.

COMPOSERS

Modern Jazz Quartet. *Odds Against Tomorrow* (from *Odds Against Tomorrow*, United Artists).

Henry Mancini (1967): That was early Modern Jazz Quartet . . . I think a thing John Lewis wrote. . . . It's a beautiful mood piece.

I like John's film music. He did a wonderful score for *Odds Against Tomorrow*, but he hasn't done anything recently . . . one of the reasons might be the group is New York based.

If you want to write concert music . . . you go to New York. But I wish he'd write more for films; he has such a wonderful dramatic feeling that is rare in a jazz writer. Four stars.

DRUMS

Chico Hamilton. *The Dealer* (from *The Dealer*, Impulse). Hamilton, drums, composer; Arnie Lawrence, alto saxophone; Richard Davis, bass.

Shelly Manne (1967): That was a jazz, rock, rhythm and blues, bossa nova record, if you could combine them all. The record is more of a mood record to me than anything else. I think they could have made more use of dynamics.

The alto player sounds like a good saxophone player; a replaced bop saxophone player in today's mood. The bass player is doing something that bothers me a little bit nowadays in a lot of bass players—they play effects rather than musical content in their solos.

To give a comment as a jazz record, I don't like the record; as a commercial record, I don't think I'm qualified to say, but I would just give it two stars.

ELLINGTON

Duke Ellington. *Aristocracy A La Jean Lafitte* (from *New Orleans Suite*, Atlantic).

Michel Legrand (1972): I saw Duke so many times in concert, and heard almost everything he did. There are some marvelous, some bad, some mediocre. But what I like, it's like Charlie Chaplin; not one thing, it's the whole career, the whole person, everything he represents and everything he is.

Duke Ellington. *Ebony Rhapsody* (from *Daybreak Express*, RCA Victor). Ellington, arranger, piano; Franz Liszt, composer; recorded 1934.

Benny Carter (1971): An excellent record; it certainly has stood the test of time, which I think is really the criterion for excellence. It sounds as good today as it did when it was first recorded. Actually it sounds better now, because you've got more to compare it with . . . when you compare it with some of the trash that we've been hearing—like the old saying, "Jazz, what sins are committed in thy name?"—and this is really real music.

Duke Ellington. *Agra* (from *Far East Suite*, RCA). Ellington, Billy Strayhorn, composers, arrangers.

Clare Fischer (1967): That's wild! I'll start off with five stars and work backwards from there. Now there, to me, is the most perfect band in existence, whether you're thinking of it orchestrationally or in terms of Duke's immensely creative writing. I can't think of anybody I admire more than this man; nobody could even be compared with him, except Billy Strayhorn.

Duke does something with this same old tired instrumentation of trumpets, trombones, and saxophones, and he has a perfect way of utilizing the men's specific sounds. Anything he plays is a work of art. The band is out of tune, for instance, and it doesn't even matter. They almost have their own brand of intonation.

Now that is the kind of record I like. Why didn't you play more things like that?

Duke Ellington and Earl Hines. *House of Lords* (from *The Jazz Piano*, RCA). Hines, Ellington, pianos; bass and drums unidentified.

Toshiko Akiyoshi (1966): It's two pianos, I guess. Certain places came out very dry but kind of interesting. But I enjoyed it more because they seemed to have fun in doing it. But musically, I strongly question something like this. I didn't hear anything happen rhythmically or melodically or dynamic-wise.

One star, I guess . . . but such a big difference between two stars and one—I hate to give it only one.

FLUTE

Hubert Laws. *Miss Thing* (from *The Laws of Jazz*). Laws, flute; Bobby Thomas, composer.

Prince Lasha (1968): Yes, that's Herbie Mann's ensemble. I can't recognize right off the rhythm section, but I do know that he was out front, and I think the arrangement is by Herbie Mann also.

I'd only give that two stars, because I didn't get too much from it. Just about one line, so to speak, of the rhythm, and a few bars of the flute emphasized, and then back to the original theme.

Sonny Simmons: Yes, I think it was Herbie Mann. I'm also not acquainted with the personnel, but it was a regular run-of-the-mill, 16-bar, 8-bar blues. It grooves you a little. . . . Not really my kind of music . . . 1½ stars.

Herbie Mann. *Nirvana* (from *Nirvana*, Atlantic). Mann, flute; Bill Evans, piano.

Charles Lloyd (1966): It's my feeling that music should take people on a trip, and that approach—getting back to the modal kind of playing, the whole concept of using the ecclesiastical modes and using scales as a point of departure—really requires a kind of delving into.

The flute player, he's a better flute player than I am, in terms of handling the instrument—sounded like maybe Paul Horn—but I think the commitment should be to the music. If you're going to play something modal, try to find some way of opening it up. I want to be touched when I hear music! Two-and-a-half stars.

Herbie Mann. *Claudia Pie* (from *Muscle Shoals Nitty Gritty*, Embryo). Mann, flute, composer.

Yusef Lateef (1970): It sounded restful. As for the flute player, I can only guess; I think it was David Fathead Newman. No further comment.

Yusef Lateef. *Bamboo Flute Blues* (from *Psychicemotus*, Impulse). Lateef, composer, bamboo flute.

Mike Nock (1970): Yusef uses space much more than most people do. Like the way the drums kept on with that high hat crash—that was really nice. I worked steady with him for about a year, although I was associated with him for two years, maybe longer. That was a really beautiful experience for me, because Yusef has a basic kind of attitude that I have . . . he likes to play a variety of music, which is the kind of thing I dig to do, too. So we really had a ball together . . . and, of course, his flute playing—bamboo flute, yeah! I'd give that four stars.

Paul Horn. *Alap in Raga Bhairay* (from *Paul Horn In Kashmir*, World Pacific).

Rahsaan Roland Kirk (1968): That was Paul Horn, a beautiful flute player, reed player; I have nothing against what he's doing musically, because in his playing he has a

lot of ability. The only thing I would say—not just to him, but to all who are doing this—there's so much music going on here in America that can be extended.

Indians tell me that in order to play these ragas, they require so much study for so many years. I've talked to several people like Ravi Shankar and they tell me they stay with the masters for 10 to 15 years. But now it's got so everybody goes to this guy Mahashoka, or whatever his name is, and pays him, and then he tells everybody that they're tuned into the Indian thing within three or four months. I can't understand it.

It just seemed to me like Paul was playing what he'd play on a regular record but with the Indian context with the sitar and everything. . . . There's things over here that we could really elevate and commercialize to extend our music—not just black music, not just white music, but our music—and put it on such a level that people can't come and tear it up like the way they've separated us. The Indian music—the Beatles' music—and all this, it's beautiful; I'm just saying that American music should be elevated . . . I'm just saying not to let these fads upset us.

Sam Rivers. *Detour Ahead* (from *A New Conception*, Blue Note). Rivers, flute, soprano and tenor saxophones.

James Moody (1968): The only time I ever understood anything on that record was when the tenor player finally came in. At the beginning the idea would come to me and then fade . . . I guess I'm old fashioned and I'm still learning about music. I'm not too hip to all these new things going on, but I'm trying to learn.

Whoever the guy is playing flute, he put in some time to learn the instrument, but it didn't really do anything for me. Just one star.

Charles Lloyd. *Third Floor Richard* (from *Of Course, Of Course*, Columbia). Lloyd, flute, composer; Ron Carter, bass; Tony Williams, drums.

Herbie Mann (1968): That sounded like the Japanese flute player I worked with in Japan recently, Sadao Watanabe. I'm not sure, but he has the same upper register sound, a little out of tune.

It's a nice old kind of blues, straight time, but the drummer and the bass player weren't together. . . . It was a nice record, but if it was Sadao, he's playing much better now. I've got to give it 2½ stars.

Herbie Mann. *Uskudar* (from *Impressions of the Middle East*, Atlantic). Mann, flute.

Stanley Turrentine (1967): That was Herbie Mann. He didn't kill me. I don't know what he was trying to do. He didn't play anything on it, to me. It didn't do anything. You better ask him what he was trying to do!

Leonard Feather: Does this have any relationship to jazz, do you think?

Turrentine: There's that word again—jazz! It has such

a wide scope. To my conception of jazz, it didn't feel like it, to me. I didn't feel anything with that. I think that with jazz you should be able to feel a certain amount of emotion, but there's nothing happening to me. I can't give it anything.

GUITAR

George Barnes-Bucky Pizzarelli. *Honeysuckle Rose* (from *Guitars Pure and Honest*, A & R Records).

Gabor Szabo (1975): The spirit was marvelous, especially one player—I don't know which, and wouldn't even make a guess. He had a chord passage there playing with some very fast and moving things . . . it could have been Joe Pass . . . five stars. Both players really played very excitingly and with control of their instrument and the situation.

Herb Ellis-Joe Pass. *Seven Come Eleven* (from *Seven Come Eleven*, Concord Jazz).

Lee Ritenour (1975): That was another five star record . . . just virtuoso guitar playing with Herb Ellis and Joe Pass. When I see Herb and Joe performing at a club, it's totally different than hearing them on record. They've played together for quite a while and Herb began to sound a little more like Joe, and Joe began to loosen up and sound more like Herb, in that Texas-blues kind of thing. On record it's very hard to differentiate between the two players.

Chuck Wayne-Joe Puma. *Lester Leaps In* (from *Interactions*, Choice).

Larry Coryell (1974): That's definitely a five star record. I think every young guitarist should take note of what they were doing. When one was soloing, the other would go into fantastically perfect accompaniment. The balance between the two players was just incredible. I heard some electronic effects in there, some wah-wah or something . . . it was definitely two older guitarists who have a commanding knowledge of bop.

John McLaughlin. *Marbles* (from *Devotion*, Douglas). McLaughlin, guitar, composer.

Gabor Szabo (1971). All I can say is they mixed up space and rock and some monotonous exciting *Peter Gunn*-type background, and how can you miss? But no stars.

Bill Harris. *Well, You Needn't* (from *Caught In The Act*, Jazz Guitar). Harris, unaccompanied guitar.

Kenny Burrell (1967): It's either Bill Harris or Charlie Byrd. Probably Bill Harris. . . .

Certain things about it annoyed me . . . either it wasn't recorded close enough, or it seemed like the guitarist was overplaying the instrument to get the tone out

of it. . . . With that particular style, the finger style, sometimes you have a problem in rhythm.

For effort, being that I know what he was doing, I'll give it three stars.

Joe Pass. *Sometime Ago* (from *Simplicity*, World Pacific). Pass, guitar.

Wes Montgomery (1967): I don't know who that was . . . but it was beautiful. In fact, I couldn't concentrate on who it might be, because of listening to it! It's *beautiful*. I like all of it—I like the lines, I like the phrases, the guitar player has beautiful tone, he phrases good, and everybody's sort of, like together.

It's really together. I'd give that four stars right away.

George Benson. *Benny's Back* (from *The George Benson Cookbook*, Columbia). Benson, guitar, composer; Bennie Green, trombone; no bass listed.

Wes Montgomery (1967): It has a fresh sound . . . seems like it lost a little bit of fire at the end. But naturally, the guitar solo was out of sight! It sounded like Georgie Benson. I think it rates three stars anyway.

Sounded like Al Grey on trombone, but I'm not sure. The group sounded like it was baritone, organ, trombone, guitar, electric bass, and drums. You know, I think the electric bass is getting more popular; it's moving out of rock-and-roll into jazz.

PIANO

Ahmad Jamal. *New Rhumba* (from *Inspiration*, Cadet Records). Jamal, piano, composer.

Walter Bishop, Jr. (1974): Ahmad is a virtuoso pianist, yet he uses space. It's very hard to do if you have that kind of technique; very hard to use space, because the inclination is to want to fill it up and show what you can do. He's always had impeccable taste, and for a man with that kind of technical ability, he made a whole thing out of understatement. In fact, he hipped Miles to space. . . .

Oscar Peterson. *Travelin' On* (MPS). Peterson, piano.

Hampton Hawes (1969): Well, that has to be Oscar Peterson. I know jazz has gone through all kinds of changes, but I don't see how you could possibly say anything like this is out of date. He is one artist who really has great command of the piano, and I can think of hardly anyone else living who has this much technique and talent. . . . That was a wonderful, exciting performance, brilliantly played. . . . Five stars.

Miles Davis. *Mlle. Mabry* (from *Filles De Kilimanjaro*, Columbia). Davis, trumpet, composer; Chick Corea, piano.

Hampton Hawes (1969): It sounded like Miles at first, but I really am not sure. . . . There's three good piano players that experiment with electric piano; Herbie Hancock, Chick Corea and Joe Zawinul, and to my knowledge, since this instrument has just been brought into the jazz scene, it's very difficult to distinguish between them, because the sound is the same, whereas on a regular piano, you can usually detect a guy's touch. The electric piano blurs some of the lines. I feel, however, that as time goes on it will be much easier to distinguish each player as they begin getting different sounds out of the instrument.

I'd have liked it if they had changed from that definite beat that was going through the whole tune . . . a little more flavored; that's why I give it four stars instead of five.

Oscar Peterson. *Who Can I Turn To* (from *My Favorite Instrument*, MPS). Peterson, solo piano.

Bill Evans (1970): That's beautiful! . . . I suspect this is Oscar Peterson . . . Oscar does surprise me at times. It's almost as if Tatum had come back to life. Even some of the harmonic angle that Art would throw into a tune just by some little change in between, as an afterthought; Oscar gets that going too. And it's gorgeous, it's perfect in its own way, so I have to say five stars.

Herbie Hancock. *Jessica* (from *Fat Albert Rotunda*, Warner Bros.). Hancock, composer, arranger, piano; Johnny Coles, fluegelhorn; Garnett Brown, trombone; Buster Williams, bass; Tootie Heath, drums; Joe Henderson, flute.

Joe Zawinul (1970): A million stars! . . . Herbie. That's a beautiful record. Herbie Hancock is a really complete musician; his playing and writing are equally balanced. In this band he has now, Johnny Coles is really fitting into it beautifully . . . melodic and lyrical playing. And I think I heard Garnett play the melody—great!

Roy McCurdy: Well, I agree with Joe, very beautiful and sensitive. I liked the things that Buster Williams was playing on bass, long notes, beautiful things. And Tootie played very well, very sensitively, and Joe Henderson on flute . . . fantastic. . . . All the stars you can give.

McCoy Tyner. *Inception* (from *Inception*, Impulse). Tyner, piano, composer; Art Davis, bass; Elvin Jones, drums.

Chick Corea (1970): That makes me feel best of all, and the reason for that is that there's such a strong belief in that kind of music. The strength of that kind of belief is what's carrying the world along at this moment. The stronger we can believe in our own universes (how we each see things as individuals), the clearer the other two universes become (the physical universe and other people's universes). And when that universe is very strong, no matter what it is—now that happens to be one particular viewpoint, but the fact that the belief is so strong and the purpose so clear and so high, that it just takes

all the other things and makes them fit together and provides a point out there that everyone can safely relate to.

That strength is the thing that keeps us all going, and it's saying we all have that strength, and all we have to do is make it more real. The more we have to rely on other people's viewpoints, the shakier and more vague our own become. Therefore our degree of self-determinism is lowered, but through seeing the beauty of the strength of a viewpoint, it makes us believe more in our own viewpoints.

McCoy and Elvin; that was one of McCoy's earlier efforts.

Cannonball Adderley. *The Scavenger* (from *In Person*, Capitol). Adderley, soprano saxophone; Joe Zawinul, piano, composer.

Herbie Hancock (1969): That's Joe's composition. Joe is the only one I can think of—besides Miles, who shapes all the tunes that come into his band and sometimes they wind up similar in shape, or within the same general open conception as Joe's.

Joe was the first person I met when I came to New York. His whole being has gone through such a metamorphosis since then. He had certain kinds of insecurities at that time, which since *Mercy, Mercy* have completely disappeared. He's a European piano player, his roots are not in the music which comes out of America—and he's white, too. Maybe this was the source of the insecurities he had, and then he writes one of the greatest soul pieces of today's music; that completely washed all those other things away.

That is something everybody should hear and buy. Five stars.

Cecil Taylor. *Tales (8 Whisps)* (from *Unit Structures*, Blue Note). Taylor, piano, composer.

Les McCann (1969): Take it off—that's enough! . . . I would like to say about Cecil Taylor, if he's serious about his music, that's all right. It's different, it's just not my groove, but what gets me is that there are so many other guys copying, and call it some name like avant garde which has nothing to do with feeling, as far as I'm concerned. In my opinion that's what jazz is all about; swing and feeling! I've got to sit down and figure out what the hell he's doing, and that's a big waste of time when I can be listening to, say, Wynton Kelly burn. So I would say minus 30.

VIOLIN

Eddie Lang-Joe Venuti. *Stringin' the Blues* (from *Stringin' the Blues*, Columbia). Lang, guitar; Venuti, violin. Recorded 1927.

Jean-Luc Ponty (1969): I think this was Eddie South. This is more difficult for me to find because I think at that period the sound of the violin was not really similar. Maybe because at that time they didn't play with an amplifier. It also was maybe Django on guitar.

I like very much the chord changes on the guitar, and the sound. I'm not especially excited by the violin here. Maybe because I'm too young to really appreciate. Three stars for both of them.

PIANO

Herbie Hancock. *Fat Mama* (from *Fat Albert Rotunda*, Warner Bros.). Hancock, piano, composer.
Al Kooper (1971): None of that moves me emotionally —which is what I like about music. That would be nice to sweep the house to, or something like that.

Herbie Hancock. *The Eye of the Hurricane* (from *Maiden Voyage*, Blue Note). Hancock, piano, composer; Freddie Hubbard, trumpet; George Coleman, tenor saxophone; Ron Carter, bass; Tony Williams, drums.
Randy Weston (1966): I want to take a wild guess on the composer—I would say Freddie Hubbard.

I would say Freddie on trumpet, George Coleman on saxophone, probably Tony Williams on drums, Herbie Hancock, and most likely Ron Carter. They are all excellent musicians. I think they played very well on this composition. . . . I'd give it four stars.

Willie (The Lion) Smith & Don Ewell. *A Porter's Love Song* (from *Grand Piano*, Exclusive). Smith and Ewell, pianos.
George Shearing (1967): I have a theory about two-piano jazz. It's far too muddy to come off, and I don't think this is any exception. It's very kinda thick and very logey. Because of this fact, I don't know who the pianists are.

. . . I like a lot of the Fats Waller idiosyncrasies in it, but I don't really think it comes off, because there's an awful lot of close chord positions used way down low in the bass, which kinda muddy it up, and I don't think it's light and airy enough to really swing. . . . One or two stars. I don't know who it is.

Bill Evans. *Spring is Here* (from *Bill Evans at Town Hall*, Verve). Evans, piano.
George Shearing (1967). One of my favorite piano players, Bill Evans. He shows the greatest respect for a ballad; he shows the greatest desire for musical organization; shows the greatest respect for the piano as an instrument; wants only to make it sound like a piano; beautiful sustained quality, beautiful sound; well organized and beautiful sense of harmony.

As many stars as you can give it. . . .

Martial Solal. *Jordu* (from *Solal*, Milestone). Solal, piano; Guy Pederson, bass; Daniel Humair, drums.
Oscar Peterson (1967): I find this very disjointed— primarily because the cohesion I have come to expect from different trios is not evident here. If I were to look at it from the aspect of a solo piano performance, I would have to classify it as the type of piano which is something for everyone.

I particularly didn't like the background for the bass solo . . . I would give it two stars. I think it's Martial Solal.

Earl Hines. *Save It, Pretty Mama* (from *Here Comes Earl "Fatha" Hines*, Contact). Hines, piano.
Oscar Peterson (1967): That sounds like a group in the cocktail bar at an airport. It started off as if it was going to develop into some sort of musical growth, but somewhere it sort of dissipated. I can't give it any stars. I don't even know who it is, either.

Thelonious Monk. *Well, You Needn't* (from *Genius of Modern Music*, Blue Note). Monk, piano, composer. Recorded 1951.
Pete Robinson (1971): . . . he doesn't play a piano like a piano, it's rather an extension of himself. His influence on me isn't in terms of the style that I'm playing, just that I listen to him a lot and I dig him. Monk is beautiful.

Ramsey Lewis. *Function at the Junction* (from *Goin' Latin*, Cadet). Lewis, piano.
Oscar Peterson (1967): The pitiful part of all this is that playing in this particular vein, it's very hard to distinguish between one of, say, six pianists. I think you tend to lose a lot of your own identity. I couldn't tell who this is; because it could be someone who honestly plays this way, in which case I'm sorry for him; or it is someone who can really play, but has decided to prostitute himself for that particular bag at the moment, and if that be the case, they're doing it well enough—or bad enough—so that I still couldn't tell.

I'll give it a half a star for the fact that all the technicians came in and all the musicians showed up.

Mary Lou Williams. *45° Angle* (from *The Jazz Piano*, RCA). Williams, piano; drums and bass unidentified.
Toshiko Akiyoshi (1966): It's so hard to tell who the piano player is, because I can't hear the particular touch . . . the balance is pretty bad.

He has a good percussive left hand; his playing is traditional, in a way, but modern. . . . It's good, it's an enjoyable performance, but the drummer is a little too overpowering. Very unimaginative. Very heavy on the sock cymbal. . . . Two stars.

McCoy Tyner. *Desert Cry* (from *Sama Layuca*, Milestone).

Les McCann(1975): I found that didn't go anywhere. I don't know who it was playing. It was like they had an idea about something, and rather than play what they were really feeling, they played what they thought was the thing to do. I'd give that two stars.

ROCK

Kai Winding. *You've Lost That Lovin' Feelin'*, (from *The 'In' Instrumentalists*, Verve). Winding, trombone; Gary Chester, Jack Jennings, percussion; Garry Sherman, arr.

Shelly Manne (1966): That leaves me absolutely cold for many reasons. . . . This had no swing, and they're using two drummers, with a real heavy rock-and-roll-influenced beat. When drummers used to play with that feeling in the old days you just called them "leadfoots."

Sounds to me like some a&r man had a jazzman under contract and thought he'd try to make a hit. I don't think one good thing has come from rock and roll. Whatever good things you find in it were there long before, in rhythm and blues—the old records of Peetie Wheatstraw, the Devil's Son-in-law; Roosevelt Sykes; Bessie Smith—all that influence was there many years ago. Rock and roll has taken all those things and blown them out of proportion into a grotesque, crude way of playing . . . I give this absolutely zero.

The Beatles. *The Fool on the Hill* (from *Magical Mystery Tour*, Capitol). John Lennon, Paul McCartney, composers.

Larry Coryell (1968): I've been told that this particular tune was written about the Maharishi. I don't know whether this is true or not; it's a nice fantasy, I suppose, but the lyrics are beautiful. The intellectual and emotional content of all the lyrics the Beatles do I've always identified with, and become personally involved in all their work.

They're still the best of all the rock 'n' roll groups. It's fantastic, they're so different than all the rest. . . . They always stuck to rock, or non-jazz. I really don't believe in mixing the two. . . . Five stars.

Gary Burton: I'd like to say in addition that the Beatles are models for recording sessions these days. . . . The records they've made for the past couple of years have been so well produced that this in itself sets them apart from all the other products available.

This being their most recent record, it's obvious how skillfully it can be done. That, in itself, becomes an art.

I'd rate it five stars too.

Beatles. *When I'm Sixty-Four* (from *Sgt. Peppers Lonely Lonely Hearts Club Band*, Capitol). John Lennon, solo voice.

George Shearing (1967): That can be only one of two groups. It's either the Winchester Cathedral Variety Band from England, or the Beatles. I happen to think that some of the Beatle compositions are extremely clever. Whether this is the Winchester Cathedral Group or the Beatles, this is really not one of the clever ones, for my taste anyhow. It's what it's supposed to be—1920's . . . I just don't happen to like that.

If it's the Beatles, . . . the soloist is probably John Lennon. I like his voice immensely, he has a very nice voice; he's in tune, he has some range. . . . No comment about stars at all.

ALTO SAX

Dewey Redman. *Interconnection* (from *The Ear of the Behearer*, Impulse). Redman, alto saxophone, composer; Ted Daniel, trumpet; Jane Robertson, cello.

Woody Herman (1974): Well, that's fairly avant-garde. There's some good players, like the trumpeter and the string player. But it should have a title like *The Madness of Youth*, because when I hear extreme things played by very well equipped people, the only thing they seem to forget completely is that these tapes and records will live forever, and at some time in their life they're going to hear these things again—at another point in their development—and the embarrassment must be complete!

Anthony Braxton. *To Artist Murray De Pillars* (from *For Alto*, Delmark).

Phil Woods (1971): That was terrible. I can't imagine the ego of a person thinking they can sustain a whole performance by themselves, when they can't really play the saxophone well. . . . It should be called "the trill is gone." I'm sure he hasn't studied the saxophone. This doesn't bother me, there's a lot of primitives that play and get a lot of exciting music; but this is such an ego trip, that you can think you're that much of a bitch that you can do a solo album.

Eddie Harris. *It's Crazy* (from *Plug Me In*, Atlantic). Harris, amplified saxophone, composer.

Sonny Criss (1968): It sounds like something Eddie Harris would do. . . . I just have nothing to say about amplified saxophone, because I just don't dig it. . . . The most important thing in jazz, I think, as far as an instrumentalist is concerned, is the sound, whether you are a drummer, pianist, bassist—sound—personal sound, an identifying thing. You hear one or two notes and you know who you're listening to. I don't have to hear 12 bars of Johnny Hodges to know it's Johnny Hodges, or Benny Carter or Ben Webster. Sometimes it's not the notes they play that's so important.

I realize that this electrified thing is in vogue now, but as the music changes, I think one has to choose the best and let the rest go by. It's even difficult to rate this. According to the standards I've held over the years, I'd rate it two stars.

Eric Kloss. *The Girl With the Fall in Her Hair* (from *Sky Shadows,* Prestige). Kloss, alto saxophone; Pat Martino, composer.

Frank Strozier (1969): I enjoyed the record. It sounded like it might have been John Handy and I like him, but it was so much of the same stuff you're hearing today—just go for broke on one scale.

I have nothing against one scale; I love it, but it's just a crutch for so many musicians today. I think that the caliber of a lot of musicians who are doing well today, or have records out, is just not up to the caliber of, say, a few years ago, simply because of these modes. You can get away with so much—who's to say you're wrong?

Eric Dolphy. *Miss Ann* (from *Far Cry*, Prestige). Eric Dolphy, alto saxophone, composer.

Herbie Hancock (1969): It's Eric's tune—I used to play it with him. . . . I worked with Eric for about a month. That was my first experience playing—avant garde, quote unquote. Eric called me to work at the Village Gate to take Jaki Byard's place. I didn't know what I was supposed to play, whatever I wanted, and certain things started happening in my mind as the music started to form, and I found out some things that I wasn't even aware of before. About rule-breaking—that was the first thing I figured, that you have to break some rules in order to make the music fit.

I just like Eric . . . there's a certain kind of feeling, happy feeling that's generated through all of the angular kind of sounds that he plays. It swings in a different sort of way than most people think of swinging.

I'll have to judge this on the standards of jazz at that particular point in the history of jazz, and I'd say 3½ stars.

Mills Blue Rhythm Band. *Blue Rhythm Blues* (from *Big Bands!* Onyx). Stan Getz, alto sax; Lucky Thompson, tenor sax; recorded 1947.

Stan Getz (1973): (After few bars of alto solo, Getz exclaims "Bird?", after a few more, "No!") Is that the Blue Mills Rhythm Band? Is that me playing alto? I haven't heard this since we made it . . . Lucky Thompson? I played alto because they needed an alto player and I needed the money—it was that simple.

Play that again, please . . . the two alto players are a little out of tune and I'm the one who's causing it.

Tribute To Charlie Parker. Wee (RCA Victor). Howard McGhee, trumpet; J.J. Johnson, trombone; Sonny Stitt, tenor saxophone; Harold Mabern, piano; Arthur Harper Jr., bass; Max Roach, drums.

Cannonball Adderley (1967): I want to tell you, that's kind of interesting. Of course I recognized J.J. Johnson and I thought I recognized Sonny Stitt. The trumpet player sounded a bit like Howard McGhee, but I got the feeling it was a swing trumpet player who branched over

into modern jazz, strongly influenced by Dizzy Gillespie.

It sounded like Max Roach playing drums. The other guys, I don't know.

The sound is new, but everybody played pretty much like the cats were playing 15 years ago. This is all right with me. I don't agree with the theory some people have that jazz musicians have to continue to change. I think that they should grow within their own thing.

Overall, I just say three stars. I especially like J.J.'s solo and Max's solo.

Eric Dolphy. *Miss Ann* (Limelight). Dolphy, composer, alto saxophone.

John Handy (1966): It's not my favorite alto player. . . . That was Eric Dolphy, I'm sure; he had a lot of command of technique on his instrument, and at times—well, to be frank, I liked him very much when he was with Chico Hamilton and had a chance to play, when they gave him blowing space and the more traditional chord changes.

The kind of things that he did in his later years I didn't like much. Many of them, to me, were just erratic, didn't make any sense.

It's not something I'd buy. One star.

Yusel Lateef. *Feelin' All Right* (from *A-Flat, G-Flat and C*, Impulse). Lateef, alto saxophone, composer.

Joe Zawinul (1967): I don't really know what to say about this. This is a beautiful bebop thing, which I love very much. The performance I didn't like too much. I don't think it had too much life and spirit.

It sounded to me like whoever was playing the saxophone had some kind of the Detroit influence of playing. I would define the Detroit influence—for instance, I worked a long time with Yusef, and Yusef used to be a great influence on some of the musicians in Detroit . . . I would say about two-and-a-half stars.

Esquire All-American 1946 Award Winners. *Gone With The Wind* (from *Esquire's All-American Hot Jazz*, RCA). Johnny Hodges, also saxophone; Don Byas, tenor saxophone.

Cannonball Adderley (1967): You know, it's not often that you can sit and listen to a group of soloists play the melody and not get bored; but when they happen to be Don Byas and Johnny Hodges, it's all right. I had the feeling that I'd like to hear Ben Webster play it after Johnny, yet a third time.

For the soloists five stars.

SOPRANO SAX

John Coltrane. *Chim Chim Cheree* (from *The JC Quartet Plays*, Impulse). Coltrane, soprano saxophone; Elvin Jones, drums.

Buddy Rich (1967): Yeah, well. What can I say about that? They had a slight accident there in the beginning, by letting the melody slip through. I imagine they had great difficulty in keeping the snake in the basket.

I don't want to venture a guess as to whether that's a soprano saxophone or a flute. I really can't quite comprehend what they were doing, except they managed to start the thing together and finish together, and I think I'd have to give it two stars for bravery beyond the call of duty.

The drummer might be Max, it might be Roy Haynes, it might even be Tony Williams, although I'm not too familiar with Tony's playing. . . . It certainly wasn't jazz as I know jazz, and it wasn't really anything. It might have been Charles Lloyd.

Cannonball Adderley. *Gunjah* (from *Accent on Africa*, Capital). Adderley, soprano saxophone; David Axelrod, composer; H.B. Barnum, arranger.

Tom Scott (1970): That's from the Cannonball Adderley album called *Accent on Africa*. He just represents one of the greatest jazzmen of all time. I love the idea of him doing an African album, because the instruments have such a great sound, and all that percussion and everything. But . . . H.B. Barnum is the wrong cat for this album, to me, as the arranger. He doesn't have the harmonic sense that comes anywhere near Cannonball. . . . It's almost like a Broadway show, instead of being hip and up to the kind of thing that Cannonball should have behind him. . . . To Cannonball I'd always give five stars, but to the arrangement I'd only give one.

Tom Scott. *Naima* (from *The Honeysuckle Breeze*, Impulse). Scott, soprano saxophone with electronic octave divider; John Coltrane, composer.

Roland Kirk (1968): It was a boy out here on the coast named Scott, playing saxella, an instrument copied off the manzello, and it's a hard instrument to play in tune. This sounds out of tune to me. . . . When he was going into the changes, it kept me on eggshells. It didn't make me lay back and relax and drink my beer and say, "Yeah, that guy's really sailing through them changes," because the tune is not that hard.

It's a beautiful tune, I mean it's hard to interpret it the way that Trane wrote it. . . . That octave thing kept me unrelaxed because people used to get on to me about being out of tune, and they make these electric things—I played one of them—and you still have to *think* in tune to play one of them.

TENOR SAX

John Coltrane. *Mr. P.C.* (from *Giant Steps*, Atlantic). Coltrane, tenor saxophone; Paul Chambers, bass; Tommy Flanagan, piano; Art Taylor, drums.

Gato Barbieri (1974): I remember this tune Coltrane wrote for Paul Chambers—we used to call it for the Communist Party, because in Argentina it's called Partida Communista, P.C., so we always made a joke of it.

That period was an important part of my life . . . I have to give the record five stars. John was about to leap into the era of the great quartet with McCoy and Elvin. Art Taylor played very good, but sometimes he would leave Trane a little bit alone. He'd play mostly the rhythm and wouldn't give Coltrane enough dynamics.

I remember in Buenos Aires I was looking for something different; then I heard one tune by Trane with McCoy and Elvin, on which John played tenor and soprano . . . and I heard something very different in that rhythm section.

Charles Lloyd. *European Fantasy* (from *Charles Lloyd in Europe*, Atlantic). Lloyd, tenor saxophone, composer; Keith Jarrett, piano; Cecil McBee, bass; Jack DeJohnette, drums.

Gabor Szabo (1969): That was Charles Lloyd in concert. . . . There is a lot of humor, and this is the part I enjoyed the most about it. His tone and phrasing and everything sounds like a real old, corny saxophone player, and yet his playing is a way-out type of music.

It just proves how different my musical convictions are since I left Charles. I went in a completely different direction, and I find great satisfaction and release in playing more disciplined music and find all the freedom within those sometimes even rigid disciplinary forms.

There are absolutely no musical rules to be followed and no ways to judge the form—or even the musicianship, because you cannot tell how good a musician is from something like this. . . . The only way I can judge this kind of thing is through the energy level, and I feel there's a great amount of energy being released, and if everything clicks, then some music will come out of it—this time it did.

Ornette Coleman. *Enfant* (from *Ornette on Tenor*, Atlantic). Coleman, tenor saxophone; Don Cherry, pocket trumpet; Jimmy Garrison, bass; Ed Blackwell, drums.

John Klemmer (1969): I thought that was crazy. I'm sure it was Ornette on tenor, an earlier recording, with Don Cherry on trumpet. I think whether or not people care for Ornette is a matter of taste, but he's always done something that's interesting.

I was a little skeptical of Ornette when I first heard him, but I delved into his music and played some of his tunes, and I really dig him.

What I look mostly for in players is somebody trying to do something with imagination, of course with the prerequisite of knowing what they're doing and studying for it. Five stars.

Pharoah Sanders. *Aum* (from *Tauhid*, Impulse). Sanders, tenor saxophone, composer.

Zoot Sims (1970): Take it off, I don't want to hear any more of that. . . . If that represents the sounds of our time, well, I don't like it.

You've got to be who you are . . . maybe that's who he is, but it just doesn't get to me. I like beauty, and I don't see any beauty in that, because the world is mad in the first place, so why allow art to make it seem madder? I don't think we should dwell on what's already going on.

Music should be *exciting*, and make you clap your hands. But this represents—chaos! . . . We've got enough chaos out there on the freeway; we don't need music to give us more chaos.

John Klemmer. *All The Children Cried* (from *All The Children Cried*, Cadet). Klemmer, tenor saxophone, composer.

Yusef Lateef (1970): I don't know who that was. The tenor player made me think of the player with Shelly Manne—with the long hair, you know. . . . (John Gross, L.F.).

It was interesting enough. Sounded contemporary. No, let me change that—what is the other expression? Current. It sounded current. I've heard similar music recently.

Duke Ellington. *Chelsea Bridge* (from *Concert in the Virgin Islands*, Reprise). Paul Gonsalves, tenor saxophone; Billy Strayhorn, composer.

Eddie (Lockjaw) Davis (1967): Well, that was Paul Gonsalves—to me one of the most underrated saxophone players that we have. He has all the qualities that one could desire—such as tonal quality, technique, creative ability—and it seems a tragedy that the public doesn't hear more of him especially when he's performing at his height, which is in concert. He always takes care of business—excellent saxophonist, really. So therefore give it five stars. To me, that was a collector's item.

Albert Ayler. *Bells* (from *Love Cry*, Impulse). Ayler, tenor saxophone, composer.

Jerome Richardson (1968): Well, what do you want me to say about that? It sounds like a club date tenor player trying to get into the jazz thing. I wonder what they were doing—I don't know whether they were trying to fool somebody or not. If that was their version of avant garde, they'd better do a little listening.

I haven't the slightest idea who it was. The tenor player, I could give a wild guess—I'd guess it was Don Ellis' band. I'll give it one star for effort.

Archie Shepp. *In a Sentimental Mood* (from *Live in San Francisco*, Impulse). Shepp, tenor saxophone.

Eddie (Lockjaw) Davis (1967): Please take that off—discontinue that. I have one word for that—tragedy.

It seems unbelievable that a man with such potential

talent—you can hear that in this saxophonist . . . I wouldn't underrate him—he puts me in mind of a frustrated musician who has failed to gain recognition through his genuine talents, and in order to attract such, he goes, shall we say, abstract. Just like a revolt.

Now it's a process of elimination as to describe who that is. I would take a guess it's Archie Shepp.

I couldn't classify it as entertainment; it's like fighting—it's like a challenge. This is really a good record for the *Blindfold Test*. Challenge—tell me who I am! It's very sad that he's let such talent go so far astray. I couldn't even rate this.

Eddie (Lockjaw) Davis. *On a Clear Day* (from *Lock the Fox*, RCA Victor). Davis, tenor saxophone.

Booker Ervin (1967): I know exactly who it was from the first note; it was Lockjaw. No one could imitate Lockjaw. I didn't recognize the name of the tune right off.

I've been liking Jaws a long time—he's one of my favorite tenor players. I've never heard anybody imitate him—it sounds like he plays backwards!

I'd give that three stars for Jaws, because he's one of my favorites.

Ben Webster. *Accent on Youth* (from *Warm Moods*, Reprise). Webster, tenor saxophone; Johnny Richards, arranger, conductor.

Stanley Turrentine (1967). Give it all you got! If you've got more than five, give it more than that. That Ben Webster—he's the most lyrical tenor player I've ever heard in my life. He has always been an influence on me. I love this album. . . .

As far as the overall playing and writing were concerned, I thought it was good. It complemented Ben. Ben has always been my favorite—I like the sound he gets. . . . Just about anything Ben plays knocks me out.

Albert Ayler. *Holy Ghost* (from *The New Wave in Jazz*, Impulse). Ayler, tenor saxophone; Joel Freedman, cello.

Oliver Nelson (1967). Of course, that was a very highly charged performance. I suppose this—the kind of music I just heard—would be typical of the new wave or whatever.

There was little melodic organization, but toward the end they did something very startling. They played the melody. . . . And they tried to play it in unison, and the ending was conventional.

If I have to object to anything about this music, it's mainly lacking in texture, and naturally I would feel that way, being an orchestrator and arranger. The same intensities are used.

As to form; well, everybody just plays. It was a live performance, and the audience seemed pleased. . . . I guess you would call it chaos—out of it, somebody is going to have enough talent to integrate whatever is happening with this kind of music.

Give the cellist four stars, but I'd rather not rate the record as a whole.

Stan Getz. *Keep Me In Your Heart* (from *Voices*, Verve). Getz, tenor saxophone; Claus Ogerman, arranger.

Oscar Peterson (1967): I would sooner own five albums like this than 100,000 of the others, because we're speaking of true creativity, musical honesty. Stan Getz, without becoming maudlin, is definitely a genius in my book.

When persons with that kind of talent put their hand or their heart or mind to material . . . it has even greater importance.

I would have to give this five stars for everything—for voices, which were beautifully done behind him, and certainly for Stan.

Gato Barbieri. *Tupac Amaru* (from *Fenix*, Flying Dutchman).

John Klemmer (1972): I enjoyed the overall texture of the group, but I really did, after a while, find it fairly monotonous . . . the concept of modality, I think, has to be treated with more care than the approach to changes, to harmonic movement. . . . I think to be a success it must reach an emotional climax, or even more so a rhythmic climax.

Gato Barbieri. *Milorga Triste* (from *Viva Emiliano Zapata*, Impulse).

Grover Washington, Jr. (1975): Unmistakably Gato Barbieri . . . five stars. What can I say? Most of his music reminds me of going back into when I was trying to play classical music, the romantic and impressionistic music. It just moves me. I haven't found one thing that I haven't liked by Gato.

John Coltrane. *Welcome* (from *Kulu Se Mama*, Impulse).

John Klemmer (1972): One of the things I really loved about John's music was his ballad sense. Even though they're playing out of tempo there's still a feeling of jazz.

SINGERS

Blossom Dearie. *I'm Shadowing You* (from *Blossom Dearie Sings*, Daffodil).

Joe Williams (1974): Blossom has that smart New York thing, entertainment thing . . . light and yet she can do things that have great depth too. She's a part of that very special group: Mabel Mercer, Bobby Short, Ellis Larkins. That very special sophisticated, continental, international set type of entertainer that is very, very refreshing. I love her sound.

I understand she's also a favorite of Miles, who used to insist that she come into the Vanguard when he was there.

Lonnie Liston Smith. *Naima* (from *Cosmic Funk*, Flying Dutchman). Smith, keyboards; Donald Smith, vocal; John Coltrane, composer.

Chick Corea: I don't know who that singer was. An interesting thing about him is that his voice is—I guess this has happened to me before—I listen to a singer, I don't know who it is and because it's a very beautiful rendition of a melody, the singer transcends gender . . . I can't tell whether it's a man or woman. I got that it was a man toward the end . . . but it could have been a woman with a husky voice.

Diana Ross. *Good Morning Heartache* (from *Lady Sings The Blues*, Motown).

Carmen McRae (1973): . . . As far as Diana singing this song, that is not her song. I'm sorry. *I* sing it better than she does, so consequently I'm not giving her any stars. I'll give her E. for the great effort she made.

Miriam Makeba. *U-Mngoma* (from *Makeba!*, Reprise).

Sarah Vaughan (1969): That was Miriam Makeba. The rhythm was too much! I like Miriam very much. . . . The language barrier doesn't necessarily make much difference, but I'd like to know the story on what's happening here.

When I go overseas it seems like they can understand me a little better than I can understand them if they came here . . . it seems like everybody speaks English over there, but not many people here speak Xhosa! I liked the record except, as I say, I don't know what it was about. I'd give it two stars.

Ella Fitzgerald. *Taking A Chance On Love* (from *Ella's Golden Favorites*, Decca). Fitzgerald, vocal. Recorded in 1940.

Vernon Duke (1966): To me, the first part, before she doubled the tempo, was immeasurably superior to the rest. The rest of it was well sung, too, of course, but the slow part was very touching to me. An excellent performance anyway—first rate.

It has to be a Negro singer. It's not Sarah Vaughan; it's not Ella Fitzgerald. Who is it?

Mose Allison. *Seventh Son* (from *The Best of Mose Allison*, Atlantic).

Jimmy Witherspoon (1972): . . . he can sing the blues! This is an art form that was started by blacks, but anybody's entitled to learn this if they dig it. And he can feel it, you can tell. He grew up listening to black artists.

Tony Bennett. *Fly Me to the Moon* (from *Songs for the Jet Set*, Columbia).

Joe Williams (1967): Five stars—nobody's gonna do that any better! Really, that's Tony Bennett at his warmest and best. It's a great arrangement and beautifully recorded.

When you buy a record of Tony Bennett's, you're getting Tony Bennett and Tony Bennett's ideas along with the people who love Tony and are inspired by him—and who inspire him. He tries to surround himself with this kind of person, which is why he is such a fine artist.

Ray Charles. *In the Heat of the Night* (from the original sound track, United Artists). Quincy Jones, composer; Alan and Marilyn Bergman, lyrics.

Joe Williams (1967): The president of the Soul Society . . . brother Ray Charles. Give him four stars for that one. As far as I'm concerned, he is by far the greatest exponent of blues and feeling and what we call soul.

If he's feeling good, he really makes you feel better than anyone else, and if he's feeling bad, he can make you cry. His musical taste for the thing he does is impeccable.

Horace Silver. *Won't You Open Up Your Senses* (from *Total Response*, Blue Note). Silver, piano, composer; Andy Bey, vocal.

Jon Hendricks (1972): It was Andy Bey . . . with Horace Silver's Quintet. Of course, Horace's own composition and lyrics. This is very significant to me, because I remember when I was Horace's lyricist. He was fooling around with lyrics and I gave him some encouragement, like "Go ahead, write your own," and I never thought he'd really do that. I wouldn't mind, except that he does it so well.

TRUMPET

Ornette Coleman. *Freeway Express* (from *The Empty Foxhole*, Blue Note). Coleman, trumpet, composer; Charles Haden, bass; Ornette Denardo Coleman, drums.

Freddie Hubbard (1968): That was Ornette Coleman on trumpet. . . . I think Ornette is neglecting the basics of playing trumpet. I love his alto, he knocks me out, but the trumpet—I don't think he should play that in public.

I didn't get anything out of it. Being a trumpet player I can't rate it. As far as the drummer is concerned, it just sounded like a little kid fooling around, and knew nothing about the drums.

I could have done what Ornette is doing when I was five.

There's a whole lot of guys can do that, who know nothing about trumpet. Why should a guy study for years —*study* trumpet—then see a guy come out on trumpet, and he gets a lot of popularity, like this—it doesn't make sense.

Encyclopedia of Jazz All Stars. *Twelve Tone Blues* (from

The Sound of Feeling, Verve). Nat Adderley, cornet; Ron Carter, bass; Leonard Feather, composer; Oliver Nelson, conductor, arranger.

Nat Adderley (1969): That's a helluva tune, a hell of an arrangement, the solos are a bitch. . . . I'm not an egotist or an illusionist, but my solo was greatly in context with the tune, and Ron Carter is a bitch! But the way it was played, the general feeling—the tune is out, the way the arrangement is. Now, played with a small group, straight without the changes moving in that direction, it could be like a regular bebop tune. But in this context with that arrangement, it's a five star record—I don't care who played it or who wrote it!

John Carter-Bobby Bradford. *Abstractions For Three Lovers* (from *Flight for Four*, Flying Dutchman). Bradford, trumpet; Carter, composer, alto saxophone; Tom Williamson, bass; Bruz Freeman, drums.

Freddie Hubbard (1970): It sounded a little bit like Don Cherry on trumpet for a minute—I don't know who they are. I recognized Richard Davis on bass and he's one of the greatest.

When guys do this sort of thing, a lot of times I think they lose the feeling—the free form thing. You have to be careful, because it bogs down and people lose interest. There has to be some feeling to keep a person's interest. And in this arrangement I didn't get the message. But I'll give it two stars because they're trying something different.

Art Farmer. *Didn't We* (from *Gentle Eyes*, Mainstream). Farmer, flugelhorn. Recorded in Vienna with strings.

Woody Shaw (1972): That's Chet Baker on flugelhorn. I'm not very impressed with it. It's a little complacent, a little too plush. . . . Still it's some of the best playing I've heard Chet Baker do. Actually, my favorite flugelhornist is Art Farmer.

Louis Armstrong. *Love, You Funny Thing* (from *V.S.O.P.*, Epic). Armstrong Big Band with Zilner Randolph, trumpet and arranger; recorded Chicago, 1932.

Barney Bigard (1971): Oh, man! I know Louis must have been drug with that band! I think it was the old Los Angeles Cotton Club band that was run by Les Hite, and I imagine Louis would turn in his grave to hear that band behind him.

Ornette Coleman. *The Circle With A Hole In The Middle* (from *The Art of the Improvisers*, Atlantic). Coleman, alto sax, composer; Don Cherry, cornet.

Donald Byrd (1971): "The trumpet and saxophone are well established instruments . . . when I think back to how old they are and what's been done, I don't think you have to necessarily distort it . . . the same thing could have been done very honestly if they were more proficient. . . . To play strange lines, atonal lines, you don't have to distort it. . . .

Jackie McLean. *Demon's Dance* (from *Demon's Dance*, Blue Note). McLean, composer, alto sax; Woody Shaw, trumpet.

Ted Curson (1971): I've heard Woody Shaw around Paris before he came back to New York, and he was playing very nice trumpet. But I think he's wasting his time imitating Freddie Hubbard because he doesn't really have the chops for that.

Dizzy Gillespie. *Lover, Come Back to Me* (from *Dizzy Gillespie*, RCA Victor). Gillespie, trumpet, arranger. Recorded in 1948.

Louie Bellson (1967): How high can you go with the stars—is there a limit? I was going to say that that's one of the greatest trumpet players of all time, and I'm not just saying it because he's sitting here. I say it all the time. In fact, I bring his name up at my drum clinics all the time.

It's interesting to listen to one of Dizzy's early big bands; everything even today is so modern. It's like Ellington—when you hear something Duke did 20 years ago, it's got all those traces of all the modern things in it.

Gerald Wilson. *Carlos* (from *The Golden Sword*, Pacific Jazz). Jimmy Owens, trumpet; Wilson, composer.

Jack Sheldon (1967): It sounded like Donald Byrd to me, with Stan Kenton. I give it four stars because it was such a big sound.

On second thought, I don't believe it was Stan Kenton; although it could have been his band with this trumpet player added as guest soloist or something.

The orchestration was very Mexican, and I liked that. Very well done.

VIBES

Roy Ayers. *Stoned Soul Picnic* (from *Stoned Soul Picnic*, Atlantic). Ayers, vibes; Hubert Laws, flute; Gary Bartz, alto saxophone; Herbie Hancock, piano; Ron Carter, bass; Grady Tate, drums; Laura Nyro, composer; Charles Tolliver, trumpet.

Tommy Vig (1969): This is the thing I really don't like; I would say it's bad and phony and ugly, except for the vibes solo, which shows good talent and good technique and swing—I don't know who it was; it reminded me of Terry Gibbs a little bit and I hope none of my friends are involved in this. I don't like the tune, arrangement or their conception—none of them have merit or truth or high artistic aims or anything—I just dislike everything about it.

All the components that this consists of, like let's say the rock rhythm or this half-rock rhythm, individually I

don't like them. But, put together like this, it's *very* bad . . . I wouldn't rate this at all.

Terry Gibbs. *Norwegian Wood* (from *Reza*, Dot). Gibbs, marimba.

Bobby Hutcherson (1967): First of all, this is somebody trying to get a hit. I'm trying to think who would be doing that; it's difficult to tell.

It sounds more like a marimba than a xylophone, because it has a higher pitch to it. It doesn't have very much to do with jazz, and I'm not very much of an AM listener on the radio.

To rate this musically, just one star.

Terry Gibbs. *Oge* (from *Take It From Me*, Impulse).

Milt Jackson (1975): One thing about most other vibes players—not to put them down—but you really have to experiment a while to get a sound. . . . The context of the piece is very good, but the sound . . . too much of a clanking sound. It goes back again to the instrument being so mechanical you gotta try and work with it to get the best from it.

Gary Burton. *The Sunset Bell* (from *Alone At Last*, Atlantic). Burton, unaccompanied vibes.

Lionel Hampton (1972): Was that supposed to be jazz? If you want me to comment on the jazz, I don't hear any. I know that's Gary Burton, and I'm quite sure he's striving for something new, but I wouldn't put that in the class of jazz like Bags, Hutcherson, Ayers . . . maybe he's got a new thing, and more power to him.

Milt Jackson. *Extraordinary Blues* (from *Milt Jackson & Big Brass*, Riverside). Jackson, vibraharp.

Bobby Hutcherson (1967): Bags has a way of playing so that he takes you up to the top of the instrument and gets hung up in playing these notes, and you hear them up there, and he lets the rhythm section hang below him, and that's a helluva feeling.

I've heard him recorded a lot better than this. But sometimes you hear a record like this, and you think it might be someone else; then in a few seconds it hits you, and you know it just can't be anybody else but him. He hangs it up in the sky . . . it just lays there.

I'd rate that 5 stars—a million stars for Bags!

MILES

Miles Davis. *Put Your Little Foot Right Out* (from *Jazz Track* (Columbia). Davis, trumpet; recorded 1958.

Benny Carter (1971): Having heard so little of what Miles is doing today, although I do have his album *Bitches Brew*, it's difficult for me to compare, but I do prefer what I've just listened to. That's one of the loveliest things I've heard . . . I would think it's from the mid-1950s. Five stars.

Miles Davis. *Bitches Brew* (from *Bitches Brew*, Columbia). Davis, fluegelhorn, composer.

Clark Terry (1972): This was probably one of the most controversial records and jazz personalities of the past century. The way he's been ostracized and criticized—and probably rightly so in many instances—but I suppose in his case he's a man who likes to stay abreast of things. . . . I only think this record can be considered jazz because Miles is on it, but I don't think that some of the stuff on it is. To me jazz has to stimulate . . . this is not necessarily stimulating. It's something to listen to as far as new sounds are concerned, but it could just as easily have been background for a scene in a jungle movie . . . an Australian setting with the foo birds running around and the kangaroos making love to each other. I'm not necessarily putting it down; it's different.

Miles Davis. *Black Satin* (from *On The Corner*, Columbia).

Doc Severinsen (1973):

Feather: It's very interesting that it took you quite some time to even figure out that it was a trumpet.

Severinsen: My feeling is that what Miles was doing there with the trumpet could probably have been done more effectively with an electric guitar. Maybe he's frustrated by the fact that it isn't a guitar. Sometimes I feel that way. I'll say to myself, "Oh, hell, why don't I play the guitar, it'd be so much easier."

Feather: Do you think Miles' playing on this record required as much technical expertise on the trumpet as some of the things he was doing earlier?

Severinsen: I don't really know. It's hard for me to say, because the whole thing was concealed quite a bit. I couldn't tell exactly what he was doing. There's a technique of using that pedal . . . it's very inventive, very creative; what you'd expect of Miles. He's not going in to play Bop City again.

I really don't think that the trumpet, and his use of it, is as effective for that kind of thing as, for some reason I think, a violin would have been, or a guitar. It's the Mahavishnu type of approach.

Miles Davis. *Orbits* (from *Miles Smiles*, Columbia). Davis, trumpet; Wayne Shorter, tenor saxophone, composer; Herbie Hancock, piano.

Herbie Mann (1968): Miles is one of my influences—Miles and Ray Charles—not so much in playing, but in the fact that he's very true to himself; he's very believable and he's his own person, and I try to set that standard for myself.

I've heard the group play fantastically and I'd give this four stars for *almost* fantastically. I think this is from *Miles Smiles*. Wayne, Herbie, Tony, and Ron are the

tightest there is in the business, because they all listen to each other all the time. That's the beautiful thing about it.

Miles Davis. *ESP* (from *Miles Davis' Greatest Hits*, Columbia). Davis, composer, trumpet; Wayne Shorter, co-composer.

Freddie Hubbard (1970): They sound like they just came off a road trip. You know, you just come off the road and you decide you want to do a date when you get back, instead of relaxing a couple of weeks.

It seems like I heard another cut of this, because this one doesn't have the drive that I know Miles has. It was smooth, a beautiful arrangement, but I don't think his chops worked that day. But five stars for Miles, although it's not one of the best performances I've heard of his. That composition was nice—linear, floating—but it didn't kill me.

Miles Davis. *The Sorcerer* (from *The Sorcerer*, Columbia). Davis, trumpet; Wayne Shorter, tenor saxophone; Herbie Hancock, piano, composer; Tony Williams, drums.

Bobby Bryant (1969): I think Miles is much more pleasing on the slower things, in a little different setting than the avant garde setting. There gets to be a certain sameness about his performances that sort of leaves me cold.

He still is Miles and deserves a great deal of credit for his lyricism. The composition just doesn't call for lyricism, and I think lyricism is his really good suit, really where he's strong. The sameness which is occurring on his recent records I don't like. . . . Three stars.

Miles Davis. *It Never Entered My Mind* (from *Three Decades of Jazz*—1949-'59, Blue Note). Davis, trumpet; Horace Silver, piano; Percy Heath, bass; Art Blakey, drums. (Recorded 3/6/54).

Dizzy Gillespie (1970): That was Miles. I've made a sort of analysis—not being too much concerned with what people *say* Miles is, but with his own personality.

He is shy, for one thing. You'd never think it, but I've been watching him for so many years . . . I think that the reasons for some of his actions are a natural result of his being shy.

As for his music, Miles' has a deep, deep, deep spiritual value to it. It's far deeper than mine, which is a part of me I expect to be developed due to the Bahai faith, and I think my music is going to be affected by this too.

Miles and I played several times together at the Village Gate and a place in Harlem, and the last time he came up to me afterwards and said, "How'd you like it?" So I said, "What is it? Explain it to me." Well, it seems they have a basic melody and they work around that. I guess you have to know the basic tune. . . .

Feather: It's not so much a tune as a mode, isn't it?

Gillespie: I don't know . . . but I'd like to spend some time having him explain it to me because I'd like to know what it is he's doing.

It reminded me so much of Ornette Coleman—I never listened to him too much to this point. But when Bernard Stollman gave me one of his Town Hall concerts, I was alone when I put on the record, and I could follow the chords he was playing. It was difficult stuff, very complex and highly enjoyable. And that's when I really started listening closely to what he was doing.

Going back to the record just played, I couldn't hear too much of that rhythm section, with Miles playing out there. But I'd rate it five stars.

Miles Davis. *Riot* (from *Nefertiti*, Columbia).

Chuck Mangione: I think Miles Davis is really the most important jazz musician that we've had, as far as being a leader in musical directions. Unlike somebody like Dizzy Gillespie, who established a direction and a style, and has been able to play it for these many years because of its utter uniqueness. It's like the music of the great classical composers which will always live.

Miles has always made so many important contributions to music. His playing as well has changed drastically in such a relatively short time. I really love his music. Everything he does is valid, just because I believe him to be one of the most honest and creative musicians around. I see no reason to dislike what I heard.

Miles Davis. *Honky Tonk* (from *Get Up With It*, Columbia). Davis, trumpet, composer; Keith Jarrett, Herbie Hancock, keyboards; Steve Grossman, soprano sax; Michael Henderson, bass; John McLaughlin, guitar; Billy Cobham, drums; Airto Moreira, percussion.

Blue Mitchell: This one I can't make no contact with at all. I don't know any of the personnel. I don't particularly like the arrangement; it doesn't sound like a composition, it just sounds like somebody blowing . . . trying to kill some time till the set's over. I hope it ain't nobody I know. . . . They are probably some good players, if you put 'em with the right group.

Miles Davis. *Red China Blues* (from *Get Up With It*, Columbia).

Horace Silver: It ain't my particular cup of tea, to tell the truth. I wouldn't venture forth to buy it. I doubt if it was given to me that I'd play it. I'd keep it, but probably wouldn't play it that much. He might say the same thing of my new material! We all have to open our minds, stretch forth, take chances and venture out musically to try to arrive at something new and different, and he's doing it—and I give him credit for that.

MILES AT THE MICROPHONE

In an introduction to a blindfold test conducted with Miles Davis in 1968, I commented:

Four years ago, the last time Miles Davis was blindfolded, I remarked that he was "unusually selective in his listening habits." The only record that drew a favorable reaction was one by Stan Getz and Joao Gilberto, which brought a five-star rave. Everything else was put down in varying degrees; Les McCann, Rod Levitt, Sonny Rollins, Eric Dolphy, Cecil Taylor; even his early favorite Clark Terry and his idol Duke Ellington.

Visiting Miles in his Hollywood hotel suite, I found strewn around the room records or tape cartridges by James Brown, Dionne Warwick, Tony Bennett, the Byrds, Aretha Franklin and the Fifth Dimension.

1. Freddie Hubbard. **On the Que-Tee** (from **Backlash**, Atlantic). Hubbard, trumpet, composer.

MD: I don't dig that kind of s---, man, just a straight 32 bars, I mean whatever it is. The time they were playing was too tight, you know. It's formal, man, and scales and all that. . . . No kind of sound, straight sound—no imagination. They shouldn't even put that out.

Freddie's a great trumpet player, but if he had some kind of other direction to go . . . if you place a guy in a spot where he has to do something else, other than what he can do, so he can do *that*. He's got to have something that challenges his imagination, far above what he thinks he's going to play, and what it might lead into, then above *that*, so he won't be fighting when things change.

That's what I tell all my musicians; I tell them be ready to play what you know and play *above* what you know. Anything might happen above what you've been used to playing—you're ready to get into that, and above that, and take that out.

But this sounds like just a lead sheet.

LF: Do you think he's capable of more than that?

MD: Yes, if he's directed, because he must have other imagination, other than this. I wouldn't even put that s--- on record.

2. Thad Jones-Mel Lewis. **Bacha Feelin'** (from **Live at the Village Vanguard**, Solid State). Jones, fluegelhorn; Garnett Brown, trombone, composer; Joe Farrell, tenor saxophone; Roland Hanna, piano; Richard Davis, bass; Lewis, drums.

MD: It's got to be Thad's big band. . . . I don't understand why those guys have to push themselves and say "Wow! wee!" and all that, during an arrangement, to make somebody think it's more than what it is, when it ain't nothing. I like the way Thad writes, but I also like the way he plays when he writes. I like when he plays his tunes, without all that stuff—no solos, you know. It's nothing to play off of.

LF: There was a long tenor solo on that.

MD: Yes, but it was nothing; they didn't need that, and the trombone player should be shot.

LF: Well, who do you think wrote that?

MD: I don't really know, but I don't like those kind of arrangements. You don't write arrangements like that for white guys . . . (humming). That ain't nothing.

In the first place, a band with that instrumentation f---s up an arrangement—the saxophones particularly. They could play other instruments, but you only get one sound like that. On that arrangement, the only one that rates is the piano player. He's something else. And Richard Davis. The drummer just plays straight, no shading. I couldn't stand a band like that for myself. It makes me feel like I'm broke and wearing a slip that doesn't belong to me, and my hair's combed the wrong way; it makes me feel funny, even as a listener.

Those guys don't have a musical mind—just playing what's written. They don't know what the notes mean.

LF: Have you heard that band much in person?

MD: Yes, I've heard them, but I don't like them. I like Thad's arrangements, but I don't like the guys pushing the arrangements, and shouting, because there's nothing happening. It would be better if they recorded the shouts at the end—or at least shout in tune!

3. Archie Shepp. **The Funeral** (from **Archie Shepp in Europe**, (Delmark). Don Cherry, cornet; John Tchicai, alto saxophone; Shepp, tenor saxophone. (Recorded 1963).

MD: You're putting me on with that! . . . I know who it is—Ornette, f---ing up the trumpet and the alto. I don't understand that jive at all. The guy has nice rhythm on saxophone.

People are so gullible—they go for that—they go for something they don't know about.

LF: Why do you think they go for it?

MD: Because they feel it's not hip *not* to go for it. But if something sounds terrible, man, a person should have enough respect for his own mind to say it doesn't sound good. It doesn't to me, and I'm not going to listen to it. No matter how long you listen to it, it doesn't sound any good.

Anyone can tell that guy's not a trumpet player—it's just notes that come out, and every note he plays, he looks serious about it, and people will go for it—especially white people. They go for anything. They want to be hipper than any other race, and they go for anything ridiculous like that.

LF: Actually, you got that one wrong—it wasn't Ornette. It was an Archie Shepp date with John Tchicai on alto and Don Cherry on trumpet.

MD: Well, whoever it is, it sounds the same—Ornette sounds the same way. That's where Archie and them got that s--- from; there sure ain't nothing there.

4. Fifth Dimension. **Prologue, The Magic Garden** (from **The Magic Garden, Soul City**). Jim Webb, composer, arranger.

MD: That record is planned, you know. It's like when I do things, it's planned and you lead into other things. It makes sense. It has different sounds in the voicing, and they're using the stereo—they can sure use stereo today, coming out from different sides and different people making statements and things like that. That's the way you should record!

Yeah, that's a nice record; it sounds nice. I liked the composition and the arrangement. It's Jim Webb and the Fifth Dimension. It could be a little smoother—they push it too hard for the singers. You don't have to push that hard. When you push, you get a raggedy edge, and an edge gives another vibration.

I liked the instrumental introduction too. We did things like that on **Porgy and Bess**—just played parts of things.

I told Diahann Carroll about an idea I had for her to record, based on things like that. There are certain tunes—parts of tunes—that you like, and you have to go through all the other s--- to get to that part—but she can just sing that part. She could sing it in any kind of musical form—18th century, today's beat, and she can say the statement over and make the background change the mood and change the time. They could also use her as an instrument; instead of the strings under her, she could be *in* the strings, and have her coming out from each side of the stereo. She told me to set it up for her, and I was trying to do it for her.

Jimmy Webb would be great for her. I think Wayne could do it for her, too; but I told her to get a guy like Mel to put the story together.

LF: Which Mel?

MD: Mel Torme. And you could have the music in between, to change the mood to whatever mood she wanted to sing in. She was interested, and insisted that I produce it, but I don't want to get involved in that end of it.

5. The Electric Flag. **Over-Lovin' You** (from **A Long Time Comin'**, Columbia). Barry Goldberg, Mike Bloomfield, composers.

MD: Who was that? Leave that record here, it's a nice record. I like guys that get into what they're supposed to be singing, and the guys that play behind it really get into what *they're* doing—when the mood changes they go right in it. It makes the record smooth; makes it mean something.

It's a pleasure to get a record like that, because you know they're serious no matter what they do . . . I liked the rhythm on that. I mean, if you're going to do something like that, man, you've got to *do* it. You know what I mean? If you're going to play like that, play like that—*good*—but don't jive around.

I like to cop myself—I don't like to miss. I like to get into the meat of things, and sometimes it don't happen and sometimes it does; when it does, it feels great, and it makes up for the times when it doesn't. But if you know it's going to happen one night, it keeps you going.

6. Sun Ra. **Brainville** (from **Sun Song**, Delmark). Dave Young, trumpet; Sun Ra, composer. (Recorded in 1956).

MD: That's gotta come from Europe. We wouldn't play no s--- like that. It's so sad. It sounds funny to me. Sounds like a 1935 arrangement by Raymond Scott. They must be joking—the Florida A&M band sounds better than that. They should record them, rather than that s---. They've got more spirit than that. That ain't nothing.

Why put that on record? What does that do? You mean there's somebody around here that feels like that? Even the white people don't feel that sad.

LF: Do you think that's a white group?

MD: The trumpet player didn't sound white. . . . I

don't know, man. You know, there's a little thing that trumpet players play to make a jazz sound, that if you don't have your own sound, you can hear an adopted jazz sound, which is a drag, especially in the mute. I mean you can tell when a guy's got his own thing.

People should have good friends to tell them, "Man, that ain't it, so don't play trumpet," you know what I mean? Or "Don't play drums, 'cause you don't have anything." I'd rather have that said to me than go on playing trumpet when it doesn't sound like I want it to sound. I know he doesn't want it to sound like that, so he should work at it, or play another instrument—a lower instrument.

When an arrangement's tight like that, you have to play every chord, because the background parts when they record, like they play them single, instead of making it smooth—and it's hard to play like that. You have to play each chord, then play the other chords or you never connect anything, and in between it's just blank.

To me it's just like canned music. Even canned music sounds good sometimes, but not s--- like this.

7. Don Ellis. **Alone** (from **Electric Bath,** Columbia). Ellis, trumpet; Hank Levy, composer.

MD: Who's that supposed to be? It's too straight, man. You know, you'd be surprised, this trumpet player probably can play, he sounds all right, but with a strong rhythm like that—if you have a straight rhythm like that, the band has to play against the rhythm, because the rhythm is never gonna change, and that's very hard to do. The best way to do that is for the rhythm to play real soft.

You don't need a trumpet in something like that. It was just one of those major, minor, major. . . .

It's a kind of mood tune. I would play it slower, and have the band way down, so they could have got some kind of feeling into it. You could tell they don't feel like playing this. Somebody was impressed with 5/4 time, but what difference does that make? What's so great about a whole number in 5/4? In our group we change the beat around and do all kind of things with time, but not just to say, "Look at me, I'm playing 5/4!" There's nothing there, but I guess the critics will have something to write about.

LF: It was Don Ellis. Have you ever heard him?

MD: Yeah. I heard him. He's no soloist. I mean, he's a nice guy and all that, but to me he's just another white trumpet player. He can't play in a chord, can't play with any feeling; that's the reason I guess they use all that time s---.

Anybody can make a record, and try to do something new, to sell; but to me a record is more than something new, and I don't care how much it sells. You have to capture some feeling—you can't just play like a f---ing machine. You can't even turn on with any kind of dope and get any feeling to play if you don't have it in your heart. No matter what you do, it won't make you play any better. You are what you are, no matter what you do. I can be loud and no good, soft and no good, in 7/8 and no good. You can be black and no good, white and no good. . . . A guy like Bobby Hackett plays what he plays with feeling, and you can put him into any kind of thing and he'll do it.

8. Al Hirt. **Goin' To Chicago Blues** (from **Live at Carnegie Hall,** RCA). Hirt, trumpet.

MD: It's Al Hirt. I think he's a very good trumpet player. For anyone that feels that way, I guess he hits them. He's a good trumpet player, but that's some corny-ass s--- he plays here.

They want him to be fat and white and funny and talented, but he ain't. They want something that looks good on television; fat, with a beard, and jovial and jolly. He's like a white Uncle Tom. And he's a nice guy; it's a drag. You know, white folks made Negroes tom a long time ago by giving them money. To do this in front of some white people, to pay you to have that kind of personality, like him, it's tomming. I can't see why a guy like Al Hirt . . . I guess if he was thin he wouldn't do that.

Harry James is a good trumpet player, and he never did tom or no s--- like that. Harry had some feeling.

For a guy to shake his unattractive body and think somebody thinks it's funny—it ain't funny, it's disgusting. He can't entertain me like that; he can entertain some corny ofays, but all the colored folks I know would say, "Oh, f---! I don't want to hear that!"

Introduction to biographies

The principal intention of this book is to provide factual information concerning the most important musicians, singers, composers and arrangers who were a part of the jazz world at some time during the decade prior to press time (mid-1976). In addition, we have included biographies of many others who, though history has not yet had time to judge them, seem likely to make a durable contribution to the music.

Because of the world-wide proliferation of jazz and, in particular, its immense popularity in Japan, a number of artists have been included whose names may be unfamiliar to the American reader. In many instances we have relied on the assurance of experts in Europe, and of Kiyoshi Koyama, editor of *Swing Journal*, that they were worthy of inclusion.

The discographies are selective, and wherever possible represent the personal choices of the musicians.

The brevity or length of a biography should not be in-terpreted as necessarily relating to the importance of the artist. The number of jobs held, the length of the career, the quantity of information supplied or available, along with many other factors, helped determine the space devoted to each listing.

Because of an increasing tendency of contemporary musicians to double on many instruments it can be assumed that in virtually all cases the newer pianists play electric as well as acoustic keyboard and, in many cases, clavinet, synthesizers, etc.; similarly bassists play electric as well as upright bass. Whether they are so listed or not, it may also be assumed that the vast majority of instrumentalists who have come to prominence in the past decade are also composers.

As supplementary reading the authors suggest John Chilton's *Who's Who Of Jazz* (musicians born before 1920) and Irwin Stambler's *Encyclopedia Of Pop, Rock and Soul*.

Pepper Adams (*Veryl Oakland*)

Cannonball Adderley *(Fantasy Records)*

Nat Adderley (*Veryl Oakland*)

Barry Altschul (*Randi Hultin*)

Louis Armstrong and Joe Glaser (*Sam Shaw*)

Toshiko Akiyoshi (*Veryl Oakland*)

Mose Allison (*David D. Spitzer*)

Chet Baker (*Veryl Oakland*)

Svend Asmussen (*Veryl Oakland*)

Gary Bartz (*Veryl Oakland*)

Louie Bellson (*Veryl Oakland*)

Gato Barbieri
(*David D. Spitzer*)

George Benson (*CTI Records*)

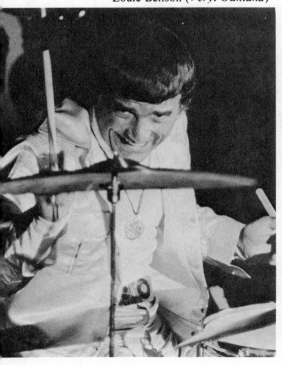

Clark Terry and Eubie Blake (*Randi Hultin*)

Art Blakey (*David D. Spitzer*)

Paul Bley (*David D. Spitzer*)   Dee Dee Bridgewater (*Veryl Oakland*)   Cecil Bridgewater (*David D. Spitzer*)

Lester Bowie (*David D. Spitzer*)

Roy Brooks
(*David D. Spitzer*)

Walter Booker (*Veryl Oakland*)

Garnett Brown (*David D. Spitzer*)

Ruby Braff and George Barnes (*Veryl Oakland*)

Dave Brubeck (*David D. Spitzer*)

Olive Brown   Kenny Burrell (*Veryl Oakland*)   Milt Buckner (*David D. Spitzer*)

Gary Burton (*Veryl Oakland*)   Donald Byrd (*Veryl Oakland*)   Betty Carter (*Veryl Oakland*)

Benny Carter (*Veryl Oakland*)

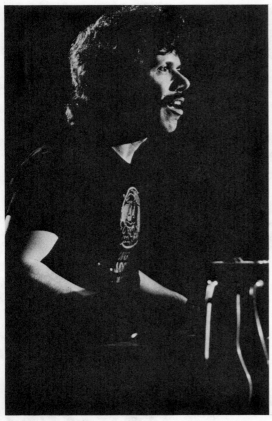

Chick Corea (*Veryl Oakland*)

Billy Cobham (*Veryl Oakland*)

Ron Carter (*CTI Records*)

Stanley Clarke
(*Veryl Oakland*)

Johnny Coles (*Veryl Oakland*)

Abbreviations

ABC   American Broadcasting Co.
acc.   accompanied, accompanying, accompanist
addr.   address
AFM   American Federation of Musicians
app.   appeared, appearing, appearance
a & r   artists and repertoire
arr.   arranged, arranger, arrangement
ASCAP   American Society of Composers, Authors and
    Publishers
Atl.   Atlantic
Aud. Fid.   Audio Fidelity
b.   born
B&B   Black and Blue
BBC   British Broadcasting Corporation
Beth.   Bethlehem
Bl. Lion   Black Lion
BN   Blue Note
BS&T   Blood, Sweat & Tears
bro.   brother
Bruns.   Brunswick
ca.   about
Cam.   Camden
Cap.   Capitol
CAPS   Creative Artists Program Service
CBA   Collective Black Artists
CBS   Columbia Broadcasting System
Chiaro   Chiaroscuro
cl., clar.   clarinet
CNE   Canadian National Exposition
Cobble.   Cobblestone
Col.   Columbia
Coll.   college
Comm.   Commodore
comp.   composed, composer, composition
cond.   conductor, conducting, conducted
cons.   conservatory
cont.   continued
Contemp.   Contemporary
CUNY   City University of New York
d.   died
deb.   debut
Del.   Delmark
Diff. Drum.   Differant Drummer
DSC   Dutch Swing College
educ.   educated, education
Elek.   Elektra
Fant.   Fantasy
fav., favs.   favorite, favorites
feat.   featured, featuring
Fly. Dutch.   Flying Dutchman
Folk.   Folkways
Font.   Fontana
GNP   Gene Norman Presents
Gr. Mer.   Groove Merchant
gp.   group
hca.   harmonica
harm.   harmony
incl.   included, including
infl.   influence, influenced
instr.   instrument
JATP   Jazz at the Philharmonic
Jazzl.   Jazzland
JF   jazz festival
JCOA   Jazz Composers Orchestra Association
JP   jazz party
KC   Kansas City

LA   Los Angeles
LACC   Los Angeles City College
Lond.   London
LV   Las Vegas
LP   long playing record
Main.   Mainstream
MCA   Music Corporation of America
Merc.   Mercury
Mile., Milest.   Milestone
MJF   Monterey Jazz Festival
MJQ   Modern Jazz Quartet
MMO   Music Minus One
mod.   modern
Mon.-Ever.   Monmouth-Evergreen
mos.   months
mus. dir.   musical director
MUSE   Brooklyn Children's Museum
NARAS   National Academy of Recording Arts and
    Sciences
NAJE   National Association of Jazz Educators
NBC   National Broadcasting Company
NEA   National Endowment for the Arts
Nemp.   Nemperor
NJF   Newport Jazz Festival
NJF-NY   Newport Jazz Festival-New York
NO   New Orleans
NOJF   New Orleans Jazz Festival
NYJRC   New York Jazz Repertory Company
NYC   New York City
orch.   orchestra
Pac. Jazz   Pacific Jazz
Para.   Paramount
pl.   played, plays, playing
Pres.   Prestige
Prest.   Prestige
publ.   publication, published
RCA   Radio Corporation of America; RCA Victor
RCI   Radio Canada International
rec.   recorded, recordings
repl.   replaced, replacing
Repr.   Reprise
ret.   returned, returning
r & b   rhythm and blues
Rivers.   Riverside
Roul.   Roulette
r & r   rock and roll
Sack.   Sackville
Sav.   Savoy
sch.   school
SF   San Francisco
SS   Solid State
st.   started
Steeple.   SteepleChase
stud.   studied, studying
SUNY   State University of New York
symph.   symphony
tpt.   trumpet
trom.   trombone
UA   United Artists
U., Univ.   University
Van., Vang.   Vanguard
vln.   violin
WB, War. Bros.   Warner Brothers
w.   with
Wor. Pac.   World Pacific
yr., yrs.   year, years

For further biographical information covering earlier periods, with respect to any artist whose name is followed by an asterisk (*), see *The Encyclopedia of Jazz* (1960) and/or *The Encyclopedia of Jazz in the Sixties* (1966) Horizon Press.

Biographies

A.A.C.M. see Abrams, Muhal Richard.

AARONS, ALBERT N. (AL), *trumpet, fluegelhorn*; b. Pittsburgh, Pa., 3/23/32. Stud. privately in Pitts., '47-50; Chicago, '51-3; Wayne State U., Detroit, '55-7. Pl. w. Y. Lateef, '56-7, Barry Harris, '57, Flame & Frolic Showbars, Detr., '58-60, Wild Bill Davis, '61, Basie, '61-9. Settling in LA, he played on TV series w. Della Reese, '69-70; Flip Wilson, '70-4; Burt Bacharach, '71; Bill Cosby, '72; Nancy Wilson, '74-5; Q. Jones, various occasions. Also worked w. Henry Mancini for TV shows and concert apps., '71, and with many big jazz bands in clubs in LA area.

Infls: Clifford Brown, D. Gillespie, L. Armstrong. Aarons is part owner and co-founder of the Legend record label.

LPs: w. Basie on various labels; w. Frank Wess, *Southern Comfort* (Roulette); w. R. Brown/M. Jackson, *Memphis Blues* (Impulse); w. Buddy Collette, *Now and Then* (Legend); *Sarah Vaughan and the Jimmy Rowles Quintet* (Mainstream).

ABDULLAH, SHAKUR (Charles Weaver), *percussion, drums*; b. Cleveland, Ohio, 3/22/40. Self-taught, but was insp. by Candido, Juno Lewis, J. Coltrane, Jack Costanza, Ch. Parker, Clifford Brown, Max Roach, A. Ayler, Dupree Bolton. Pl. w. many groups in LA area: Owen Marshall quintet; Abbey Lincoln Quintet; Walter Bishop Jr. Quintet; Gene Russell Quartet; Enmedio Saracho Quintet; Calvin Keys Quintet; Troy Robinson big band; H. Tapscott big band, '72-4. Chico Hamilton, '74- . Film sound tracks w. Tapscott, Hamilton. Fests: Newport West; Ch. Parker Fest; Festival in Black; Watts Festival. Comps: *Sufi Dance; Love; Dance of the Wives; Raga Allah; N.Y. Mornings.*

LPs: w. Marshall, *The Naked Truth* (Aditi Records); w. Bishop, *4th Cycle;* w. Russell, *Talk To My Lady* (Black Jazz); w. Hamilton, *Peregrinations* (BN).

ABENE, MICHAEL CHRISTIAN JOSEPH (MIKE), *piano, composer*; also *keyboards*; b. Brooklyn, N.Y., 7/2/42. Father pl. guitar, had own band. Pl. w. Farming-dale High School band and Newport Youth Band under Marshall Brown. Informal arr. & piano lessons w. John LaPorta, Wally Cirillo. Comp. major at Manhattan Sch. of Mus. for two yrs. before going on the road w. Maynard Ferguson at age 18. Experience at Cork 'N Bib on L.I. w. Clark Terry, Jimmy Nottingham, etc. in early '60s. With Don Ellis, '60-1; M. Ferguson, '61-5. Also worked in LV w. B. Rich, H. Edison, G. Auld, '63. From '65-7 pl. at Half Note w. Al Cohn-Zoot Sims; Bill Berry-Richie Kamuca; R. Braff. Writing and pl. jingles from '66. Wrote arrs. for Joe Shepley-Burt Collins-Mike Abene 11-piece band. Own duo at Bradley's in NYC, '72-5. TV: many apps. on *Love of Life* soap opera as solo, trio pianist; *Dial M For Music; Jazz Adventures.* Fests: NJF w. Farmingdale band; Newport Youth Band; Ferguson. NJF-NY '75 w. Sylvia Syms. Arrs: *Maryann; I Believe to My Soul* in LP *The Blues Roar* w. Ferguson on Mainstream; *Lennon-McCartney Live* w. Collins-Shepley Galaxy on MTA; comp. & arr. *Time, Space and the Blues* for Collins-Shepley Galaxy and pl. on album (MTA). Other LPs w. Ferguson (Main.).

ABERCROMBIE, JOHN L., *guitar*; also *bass*; b. Portchester, N.Y., 12/16/44. Started on guitar at 14; some private lessons but mostly self-taught until he att. Berklee Coll. of Mus., '62-6, where he stud. guitar w. Jack Petersen; theory, harmony. Worked w. Johnny Hammond, '67-8; Dreams, '69; Chico Hamilton, '70; Jeremy Steig; Gil Evans; Gato Barbieri, '71-3; Billy Cobham, Jan. '74-Jan. '75. During that time he also pl. w. Jack De Johnette, touring Europe w. him. W. De Johnette; gigs w. own trio & quartet, '75. A dextrous guitarist who mixes rock flavorings w. jazz in a most sensitive, unaffected manner.

Infl: Jim Hall, Bill Evans, Sonny Rollins, Coltrane. TV: film of Montreux JF. Fest: Montreux w. Hamilton, '71; Antibes w. Gil Evans; NJF-NY; Montreux w. Barbieri, '74. Won DB Critics poll, TDWR, '75. Comp: *Timeless; Ralph's Piano Waltz; Remembering; Love Song.* LPs: *Timeless;* w. De Johnette, Dave Holland,

Gateway (ECM); w. Barbieri (Fly. Dutch); *Dreams* (Col.); Cobham (Atl.).

ABNEY, JOHN DONALD (DON), * *piano*; b. Baltimore, Md., 3/10/23. Principal employment during '60s in Universal Studios w. Stanley Wilson. On the road w. own trio, '69-71. Joined Pearl Bailey in L. Bellson's band for her TV series in '71, then went on tour, incl. Middle East and London, '73, remaining with her until '74. Conducted for Rosemary Clooney in Lake Tahoe, Cal., '70. Joined Jack Jones, '75.

LP: w. Benny Carter, *Additions to Further Definitions* (Imp.).

ABRAMS, MUHAL RICHARD, *piano, composer, leader; also clarinet, cello*; b. Chicago, Ill., 9/19/30. Studying piano from age 17. Four yrs. at Chicago Musical Coll.; then self-taught. Began playing professionally in '48. Wrote for King Fleming band, '50. First pianist w. MJT+3, '55, also arranging and composing for group. Formed big band, the Experimental Band, in Chicago '61. Members incl. Eddie Harris, Victor Sproles. In '65 he founded the AACM, the Association for the Advancement of Creative Music which, besides enjoying an independent existence, gave rise to the Art Ensemble of Chicago. In addition to serving as director of the AACM, Abrams has been active as a pianist on the Chicago scene for over two decades, often accompanying visiting soloists who traveled there for club work without their own rhythm sections. Early infl: Nat Cole; William E. Jackson, King Fleming, Art Tatum, James P. Johnson. "Only Cecil Taylor and Don Pullen," wrote Ray Townley, "each in their own distinctive way, approximates his sense of line structure and use of space. But Abrams also is deeply rooted in the Harlem stride school. Traces of Willie "The Lion" Smith, James P. Johnson, and later stylists such as Art Tatum and the incomparable Bud Powell can be gleaned from his playing."

Abrams explains: "My playing was instinctively governed by rhythm even before I left school but I couldn't see it yet. After I got away from the classroom routine my playing began to gain something of its own personality."

He has long been an "elder statesman" and "guru" to Chicago's modern musicians. Joseph Jarman said, "Until I had the first meeting with Richard Abrams, I was 'like all the rest' of the 'hip' ghetto niggers; I was cool, I took dope, I smoked pot, etc. I did not care for the life that I had been given. In having the chance to work in the Experimental Band with Richard and the other musicians there, I found the first something with meaning/reason for doing . . ."

Won DB Critics poll as pianist, TDWR, '74. Comp: *Ballad For New Souls; March of the Transients; The Bird Song; No Land's Man.* LPs: solo (Why Not); duo, *Sight Song* (Black Saint); *Levels and Degrees of Light; Things to Come From Those Now Gone; Young in Heart, Wise in Time* (Del.); *Creative Construction Company* (Muse); w. Art Ensemble of Chicago, *Fanfare For the Warriors* (Atl.); w. A. Braxton, *Three Compositions*;

w. J. Jarman, *As If It Were the Seasons* (Del.); w. MJT+3 (Argo); w. Marion Brown, *Sweet Flying Earth* (Imp.); w. E. Harris, *Excursions; Eddie Harris Sings the Blues* (Atl.).

ADAMS, GEORGE RUFUS, *tenor sax; also flute, bass clarinet*; b. Covington, Ga., 4/29/40. Piano at 11; alto sax in junior high for a yr., then tenor sax. Stud. at David T. Howard HS, Atlanta; pl. w. David Hudson HS Band. Won a scholarship to Clark Coll. where he stud. w. Wayman Carver whom he says was a "guide to taste and style." A Music major and Education minor, he was asst. band dir. during last semester. Pl. bassoon in orch. Began pl. on local clubs at 16 in Lathonia, Ga. Blues experience w. house band pl. before shows of Jimmy Red, Howlin' Wolf, Elmo James, Lightnin' Hopkins. Pl. behind Sam Cooke, Hank Ballard in Atlanta a few yrs. later. Moved to Ohio '63, traveling w. organ gps. such as Eddie Baccus; Bill Doggett; Hank Marr. To NYC spring '68, working w. the Flamingoes; Roy Haynes Hip Ensemble; Gil Evans; Art Blakey. From '73 w. Charles Mingus. Infl: Charlie Parker, Coltrane, Ben Webster. TV: Euro. w. Mingus; *Like It Is* w. Leon Thomas; educ. TV w. Haynes. Fest: NJF-NY w. Haynes, '72; Mingus, '73; Perugia; Umbria; Newport fall tour of Europe w. Mingus, '75. Comp: *Full Moon; Flowers For a Lady.* Adams says he got his "roots from church music and r&b from south side of Chicago." LPs: *George Adams and Jazz Encounters; Suite For Swingers* (Horo); w. Mingus, *Changes I; Changes II; Mingus Moves* (Atl.); w. Haynes, *Senyah* (Main.); w. Evans, *There Comes a Time* (RCA).

ADAMS, PARK (PEPPER), * *baritone sax*; b. Highland Park, Mich., 10/8/30. One of the many, fine, young musicians who peopled the Detroit jazz scene in the early 1950s before he moved to NYC in '56. Played w. Maynard Ferguson, Benny Goodman and, most often, his old Detroit colleague Donald Byrd. A charter member of the Thad Jones-Mel Lewis orch. from Dec. 65, he has toured Europe and Japan with them; solo appearances in Europe and Canada w. local musicians. As part of David Amram's group he has also performed with the Philadelphia Orch., the Toronto and American Symphs., and the Rochester Phil., recording Amram's *Triple Concerto* with the latter for RCA.

Won DB Critics' Poll, TDWR '67; Playboy All-Stars' All Stars '75. LPs: *Ephemera* (Zim or Spotlite); *Encounter* (Prestige); *Mean What You Say* (Milestone); *Plays Charles Mingus* (Workshop); w. Amram, *No More Walls* (RCA Victor); Jones-Lewis (Solid State, Blue Note, Philadelphia Int., Horizon).

ADDERLEY, JULIAN EDWIN (CANNONBALL), * *alto and soprano sax, composer*; b. Tampa, Fla., 9/15/28. The Adderley Quintet maintained a stable personnel throughout the middle and late 1960s, with Nat Adderley, Joe Zawinul, Roy McCurdy and Vic Gaskin (later repl. by Walter Booker). Zawinul's comp. *Mercy Mercy Mercy* became the title tune for an album released in March 1967. The album and single both were among the most successful and best-selling jazz records of all time. During the next few years Adderley enjoyed unprecedented success, playing an areas normally hospitable only to rock performers.

In addition to playing alto sax in a style that showed the strong influence on him of younger musicians and the new developments in jazz, Adderley began doubling most effectively on soprano sax. He was also acclaimed for his role as an articulate spokesman for the music, and for his involvement in a variety of extracurricular activities.

He became a member of the committee of the National Endowment for the Arts; a member of the Black Academy of Arts and Letters; served on the board of governors of NARAS; was a member of Florida A & M University's Hall of Fame; and a member of the jazz advisory panel for the John F. Kennedy Center for the Performing Arts. He produced albums with other artists whose careers he helped foster, conducted seminars at many colleges, and served on the advisory board for Harvard University's Artist in Residence program (later posthumously renamed the Julian Cannonball Adderley Artist in Resident Program).

Keenly interested in electronic developments, Adderley incorporated some of these elements into his recordings, sometimes adding rock musicians to his personnel. On Zawinul's departure from the group (see ZAWINUL, JOSEF), George Duke joined the quintet, repl. by Hal Galper and then by Michael Wolff. The personnel remained otherwise unchanged.

While on tour in Indiana, Adderley suffered a massive stroke 7/13/75. He was taken to a hospital in Gary, Ind., where he died 8/8/75.

An album entitled *Big Man*, based on the legend of John Henry, for which all the music was composed by the Adderley brothers with Joe Williams in the title role, was released two months after Cannonball's death. He considered it one of the major achievements of his career and had hoped to see it presented as a Broadway musical or television special.

Julian Adderley's compositions included *Pretty Paul; The Steam Drill; Marabi; Sticks; Sack O' Woe; Introduction to a Samba; Domination; Sermonette; Primativo; Savior* (with lyrics by his wife, Olga James Adderley); *Them Dirty Blues*; and a three part work entitled *Suite Cannon*, comprising *The King & I; Time In;* and *For Melvin Lastie.*

Adderley as an individual and the quintet as a group won innumerable polls, starting with "new star" awards in 1956 and '59.

Motion pictures: *Play Misty For Me; Soul to Soul; Save The Children.* Television: Adderley served as host for 13 weeks in 1972 on a series entitled *90 Minutes.* He played very little on these programs, confining his role mainly to interviews with guests from all walks of life. He had an acting role in one sequence of *Kung Fu.* Playing apps. on *David Frost Show; Tonight; Nancy Wilson Show; Playboy After Dark* etc.

Festivals: Newport, Monterey, Montreux, Cannes,

Pori, Hampton; Alaska Festival of Music, June 1975. In the fall of 1972 the Adderley Quintet played concerts in Budapest and Belgrade, as well as in many Western European cities, as part of the "Newport Jazz Festival in Europe" package show.

Publications: *Play Saxophone Like Cannonball Adderley*, Robbins Music Corp.

LPs: Adderley was under contract to Capitol from 1963-73, then signed with Fantasy. In addition to recording with his own group as an instrumental unit, he joined with many singers and instrumentalists, among them Nancy Wilson, Lou Rawls, Wes Montgomery, Eddie Vinson, Sergio Mendes, all of whom are heard in the anthological album *Cannonball Adderley and Friends* (Cap.); *Best of; Black Messiah; Country Preacher; Happy People; Mercy Mercy Mercy; The Price You Got To Pay To Be Free; Soul of the Bible; Soul Zodiac; Walk Tall/Quiet Nights* (Capitol). *Inside Straight; Love, Sex & The Zodiac; Pyramid; Phoenix; Big Man* (Fantasy); *Adderley & Eight Giants; Adderley In New Orleans* (Milestone); *Somethin' Else* w. Miles Davis (Blue Note). Earlier sessions w. Davis (Col.) and w. own groups (Mercury, Limelight, Trip). *Cannonball w. Coltrane* was made for Limelight and reissued on Archive of Folk and Jazz Music.

Other LPs as sideman w. Nat Adderley; J. Zawinul; Joe Williams; Gene Ammons; Dave Axelrod; Johnny Guitar Watson et al.

ADDERLEY, NATHANIEL (NAT),* *cornet, composer;* b. Tampa, Fla., 11/25/31. Continued to play in the quintet of his brother (see above) and therefore his career ran almost parallel, except when he recorded with his own units. After Cannonball's death the group became inactive. Adderley, himself, went to Germany for TV apps. in Jan. '76. On his own album, *You, Baby,* he used the Varitone attachment with success but usually did not seek help for the natural electricity of his charged attack. Comp: *Electric Eel; New Orleans; Halftime,* co-written w. Cannon; *59 Go and Pass; Contant 19.* LPs: *You, Baby; Calling Out Loud* (A&M); *Natural Soul; Scavenger* (Mile.); *Double Exposure* (Prest.); *Soul of the Bible* (Cap.); w. Charlie Byrd, *Top Hat* (Fant.); *Newport in New York, The Jam Sessions* (Cobble.); w. Cannonball (see above).

ADDERLEY, NATHANIEL JR. (NAT), *piano, composer; also acoustic guitar, flute, clarinet;* b. Quincy, Fla., 5/22/55. Son of Nat Adderley. Studied at Manhattan Sch. of Mus. for three yrs.; Juilliard for six; HS of Mus. & Art; Yale U. Received the Merit Scholarship for five yrs. Won Wycoff Male Chorus Competition, '71; placed first in the Piano Competition for the Bergen (NJ) Philharmonic Orch., '70. Pl. w. Bergen Phil. '70. Performed on WNYC radio for the Piano Teachers Congress of NYC, '70; app. on *Take a Giant Step,* CBS-TV, '71. Fest: MJF, '70. At age 11 had first comp., *I'm On My Way,* rec. by Cannonball Adderley. Other comps: *The Price You Gotta Pay to Be Free; Red, Black and Green.* LPs: w. Natural Essence, *In Search of Happiness* (Fant.);

w. C. Adderley (Cap.); movie score for *The Honey Baby* (RCA).

AIRTO (pr. **Eye-***ear***-toe**) (**Airto Guimorva Moreira**), *percussion, drums, singer*; b. Itaiopolis, S. Brazil, 8/5/41. Stud. acoustic guitar, piano 1948-50. As a child, was on radio program starting at age six, pl. in combos at 12. Went to Sao Paulo and Rio when he was 16; spent three years playing cabarets all over Brazil. After working with the Sambalanco Trio, formed his own group at 22 feat. Hermeto Pascoal. With the latter, he later assembled the Quarteto Novo. Moving to Los Angeles, he stud. w. Moacir Santos 1968-9, then went to New York. Came to prominence through records with Miles Davis 1970. Played his first official U.S. job with Lee Morgan in Brooklyn Feb. 1971. From then until Nov. '74, living in New York, Airto became one of the busiest percussionists on the new music scene, in constant demand for records. Part of original Return to Forever w. C. Corea, '72. Among the dozens of leaders with whom he recorded and/or toured were Stan Getz, Cannonball Adderley, Gato Barbieri and additional recordings with Miles Davis. For a while worked with trio featuring Don Friedman, Reggie Workman. Own group's debut in April '73. Moving to Berkeley, Ca. with his wife, singer Flora Purim (q.v.), he recorded with her and made albums under his own name.

Airto names among his early influences musicians of many backgrounds: Gil Evans, Bill Evans, Ray Charles, Miles Davis, Antonio Carlos Jobim, Pascoal, Wes Montgomery, John Coltrane, Ravi Shankar. Made movie or TV sound tracks with Gary McFarland, Quincy Jones, Michel Legrand, Herbie Hancock, Oliver Nelson et al.

LPs: *Natural Feelings; Seeds On The Ground* (Buddah); *Free; Fingers* (CTI), *Virgin Land* (Salvation); w. M. Davis, *at Fillmore East; Live-Evil* (Col.); w. Corea, *Return to Forever* (ECM); *Light As a Feather* (Poly.); w. Getz (Col.); w. Cannonball Adderley (Cap.)

AKIYOSHI, TOSHIKO,* *composer, piano*; b. Dairen, Manchuria, 12/12/29. To U.S. 1956; studied and worked in Boston; played and wrote in NYC during '60s; frequent return visits to Japan with her then husband, Charles Mariano (since divorced). Own radio program in NYC 1967-8. Debut as composer-conductor, playing solo and with trio and big band at Town Hall, Oct. '67. Clubs in Greenwich Village, '67-71. Own quartet at Expo 70 in Japan, 1970. Carnegie Hall concert and Japanese tour with quartet featuring husband Lew Tabackin, 1971. In 1972 she and Tabackin moved to Los Angeles, where they formed a 16 piece band, also gigging locally with a quartet. Appeared as piano soloist in 1973 MJF. An LP she rec. in Hollywood w. Tabackin was highly acclaimed in Japan, where it won the Swing Journal Silver Award in '74.

Ms. Akiyoshi, while less active as pianist in recent years, was greatly respected for her original compositions and arrangements. Among them are *Sumie; Long Yellow Road; Henpecked Old Man; American Ballad; Memory.*

Publ: *Originals by Toshiko Akiyoshi*, Berklee College of Music, Boston. LPs: Toshiko Akiyoshi-L. Tabackin big band, *Kogun* (RCA Japan); *Top of the Gate* (Takt, Japan).

ALBAM, EMMANUEL (MANNY),* *composer*; b. Samana, Dominican Republic, 6/24/22. Continued as an active arranger on the New York scene for artists such as Carmen McRae, Buddy Rich, Stan Getz, Gerry Mulligan, Clark Terry, Dick Hyman and Chuck Mangione. Also served as musical director for Solid State Records. Participated in many college clinics and festivals as clinician and adjudicator. Organized arranger's workshops at Eastman School; also teaches at Glassboro St. Coll.; and is co-ordinator for jazz in the prison system for New York state.

TV: arranger-composer for *Around The World Of Mike Todd; Four Clowns;* for NET, *Glory Trail; Artists USA; Chicago Picasso.* Comps. incl. *The Horns (And Voices) Of A Dilemma* for Chorus, Wind Ensemble and Jazz Band; *Afro-Dizzyac* for Dizzy Gillespie; *Country Man* for Dakota Staton; arr. *Suite For Jazz Piano and Orchestra* (a Billy Taylor comp.) for Utah Symph.

LPs: *Soul Of The City; Brass On Fire* (Solid State), *Jazz Goes To The Movies* (Impulse); LPs w. Coleman Hawkins (Impulse); O'Donnel Levy (Groove Merchant).

ALBANY, JOE,* (**Joseph Albani**),* *piano*; b. Atlantic City, N.J., 1/24/24. Sisters are classical pianist, operatic soprano. Worked in 1940s w. Benny Carter, Ch. Parker, Geo. Auld, Lester Young; free-lanced in LA. For the next 25 years Albany became a legend, in and out of obscurity. He was heard on one album with Warne Marsh on Riverside in 1957; was in SF in '59; w. Ch. Mingus in NY '63; Russ Morgan in LV '64. In 1971 some tapes he had sent to English critic Mark Gardner were released in Britain. After making one album for US release, Albany left for Europe Dec. '72, rec. an LP in Copenhagen '73 and a duo set with bassist Niels Pedersen in '74. Returned briefly to US in summer of '74 and again in spring of '75 to settle in LA again.

LPs: *Proto-Bopper* (Revelation); *Birdtown Birds; Two's Company* (Steeple).

ALDEBERT, LOUIS J., *singer, piano, composer*; b. Ismailia, Egypt, 6/8/31. Stud. in Port Said, '43; later in Paris, where he pl. in jazz clubs w. D. Byas, '55; S. Grappelli, '57; and many others during next decade. As singer, was member of the Blue Stars, '55-6, and Double Six of Paris, '60-1, '63-5. With this group he toured Canada in '60 and visited US in '63. The Double Six broke up in '65; Aldebert and his wife, singer Monique Aldebert left in '67 for LV, where they sang for a year in a vocal group in the Casino de Paris show. In Feb. '69 they moved to LA, where they app. at numerous clubs and occasionally gave coll. concerts, leading a duo or a quartet, enlarging in late '74 to a sextet.

Aldebert and his wife (q.v.) are the composers of many charming songs, among them *Life's A Mockingbird; Do It With A Smile;* they have also arranged vocal versions of jazz instrumentals such as Bill Evans' *The Dolphin* and

D. Reinhardt's *Nuages.* Fests: Antibes, Lugano, Montreal, San Remo.

LPs: w. Double Six of Paris, *Swingin' & Singin'; Sing Ray Charles*; w. M. Aldebert, arr. by M. Legrand (Philips); others on European labels.

ALDEBERT, MONIQUE (Monique Dozo), singer; b. Monaco, 5/5/31. Mus. stud. in Monte Carlo and Paris. Pro. debut in '47 w. Bernard Peiffer. Many club engagements in Paris w. Django Reinhardt, Roger Guérin, Bobby Jaspar, Don Byas; concert w. Bill Coleman, '66. Sang w. Double Six of Paris, early '60s. For many years she was active in studio work, making numerous commercials, movies, TV, radio shows. Her career in LV and LA ran parallel with that of her husband, Louis Aldebert (q.v.). She has also recorded on her own for Philips with arrs. by M. Legrand, and took part in André Hodeir's LP of *Anna Livia Plurabelle* on Epic. Sang in English version of movie *Umbrellas of Cherbourg.* Sound track for L. Schifrin's music, film *Kelly's Heroes,* '70.

An academically trained musician, she has a well developed jazz feeling and light, attractive timbre, singing unison or duo in both English and French, with her husband.

LPs: w. Double Six of Paris, *Swingin' & Singin'; Sing Ray Charles* (Philips); w. Q. Jones (Pathe-Marconi).

ALEXANDER, MONTGOMERY BERNARD (MONTY), piano; b. Kingston, Jamaica, 6/6/44. Studied privately, '50-9, w. three different teachers. TO US '62. Played in Miami where he was heard by Jilly Rizzo who hired him for his club, Jilly's in NYC. Continued to lead own trio except for work w. Milt Jackson-Ray Brown group in early '70s. Infl: Nat Cole, Oscar Peterson, Ahmad Jamal, Ray Brown, Milt Jackson, Sonny Rollins. Fest: Monterey; Concord; San Diego. Doug Ramsey characterized his playing as "a mix that is spiced with something more common to jazz horn players than to pianists, a rhythmic concept charged by the dance music of the Caribbean islands," and talked of his "piquantly hesitant placement of notes at precisely the correct strategic spots behind the beat."

LPs: *Rass; Here Comes the Sun; We've Only Just Begun* (BASF); *Alexander the Great; Spunky* (Pac. Jazz); *Zing* (RCA); *This is Monty Alexander; Taste of Freedom* (MGM); w. Milt Jackson, *That's the Way It Is* (Imp.).

ALEXANDER, ELMER (MOUSEY),* drums; b. Gary, Ind., 6/29/22. European tour w. Georgie Auld '60, So. America w. Benny Goodman '61; Goodman sextet '66-67, European concerts and Carnegie Hall w. Goodman '72. Active as jingle contractor in NYC '62-65; Sweden and Czechoslovakia w. Paul Anka '66. From '65 many apps. w. Al Cohn-Zoot Sims at Half Note; own trio at Plaza 9 '68-69; own quartet at Half Note '74. W. Clark Terry big band '69-72; other gigs in '72 w. Sonny Stitt, Lee Konitz, James Moody, Sy Oliver big band tour of Europe '73; Doc Severinsen on *Tonight* Show '73. In July suffered a heart attack, followed by a second one in August which bedded him for the remainder of that year.

Resumed pl. in spring '74 w. Sims, Terry. App. at Dick Gibson's Colorado Jazz Party intermittently from '67. Odessa Jazz Party '71, '75; NJF '68. LPs: w. Gene Krupa, *Percussion King* (Verve), Clark Terry big band live at Carnegie Hall (Etoile); w. Lee Konitz, *Spirits* (Milestone); w. Goodman, *Live in Copenhagen* (London); *Colorado Jazz Party* (MPS/BASF).

ALI, RASHIED,* drums; b. Philadelphia, Pa. 7/1/35. Well known in avant garde circles in NYC from 1963. Rec. and pl. w. John Coltrane '65-7. In '68 toured in Europe with his own quartet, also pl. w. S. Rollins. Records and jobs w. Jackie McLean, Alice Coltrane, Bud Powell, '69. Concert w. own quartet, Carnegie Recital Hall, '70; various colleges and clubs, '71. In summer of '72, organizer of New York Jazz Musicians' Festival. Under a grant from National Endowment for the Arts, introduced his *New Directions In Jazz* suite.

Continued workshops, concepts and occasional lectures in mid-70s, incl. memorial concert for Coltrane at New York Jazz Museum. Opened restaurant-club, Studio 77/Ali's Alley w. own group in residence, '74.

TV: *Free Time; Jazz Set; Soul; Positively Black.* Festivals: NJF, '71-2; New York Jazz Musicians' Festival, '72. LPs w. Coltrane: *Expressions, Interstellar Space, Concert in Japan* (Impulse); *Duo Exchange, Rashied Ali Quintet, New Directions in Modern Music* (Survival).

Addr: Studio 77/Ali's Alley, 77 Greene St., New York, N.Y. 10012.

ALKE, BJORN, bass, composer; also piano, violin; b. Sundsvall, Sweden, 4/15/38. Stud. w. private violin teacher for four yrs.; three yrs. at music high school in Stockholm. Pl. w. Lars Gullin, Bernt Rosengren, Eje Thelin and other prominent Swedish jazzmen. Fests: Antibes w. Thelin, '63; Pori; Kongsberg, '75; several in Sweden, '64-75. Won *Orkester Journalen* poll on bass, '65. Comp: *Hommage à Bud; Gun; Bossa Noja; Coma.* Infl: Tatum, Miles Davis, Paul Chambers, Gil Evans, Bud Powell, but says that "Lars Gullin, Powell and Dexter Gordon are the ones I have learnt most from, concerning music and way of living." LPs: *Jazz Sverige;* w. Gullin, *Portrait of My Pals* (SSX); w. Rosengren, *Notes From Underground.*

ALLAN, JAN, trumpet; also piano; b. Falun, Sweden, 11/7/34. Father violinist and bassist during '20s and '30s. Stud. piano privately from six years old, switching to trumpet later. Pro. engagements w. Lars Gullin-Rolf Billberg, '54-55; Carl-Henrik Norin, '55-7; Allan-Billberg quintet '60-3; Jan Allen orch., '63-8; Harry Arnold; The Swedish Radio Jazz Group, '68-75. Won Golden Record from *Orkester Journalen,* for *Ceramics,* best jazz recording, '70. Many fest. apps. throughout Europe, as well TV in Germany, Denmark, Sweden etc. Infls: Fats Navarro, Miles Davis, Clifford Brown, Coltrane et al. Allan has concurrent career as Elementary Particle Physicist at Stockholm U.

LPs: *Jan Allan '70* (MCA); *Swedish Radio Jazz Group* (SR); others w. Gullin; own quartet (Sonet); J. Johansson-G. Riedel; Monica Zetterlund (SR); *Greetings and*

Salutations, Swedish Radio Jazz Group w. Thad Jones (Four Leaf Clover).

ALLEN, HENRY JR. (RED), * *trumpet, singer*; b. Algiers, La., 1/7/08. Prominent in '30s w. Luis Russell, Fletcher Henderson, Lucky Millinder, Louis Armstrong; in '40s with own sextet, and in '50s leading various groups, also working as soloist and touring Europe as sideman w. K. Ory in '59. During '60s he visited England several times, freelanced around NY, toured Britain again in Feb. '67, but by then was seriously ill and died in NYC, 4/17/67. Allen's searing, heated style, first noted by critics during L. Armstrong's heyday, established him as possibly the most important new trumpet artist after Armstrong. LPs: *Memorial Album* (Prest.); French RCA.

ALLEN, STEVE, * *songwriter, piano, vibes, leader*; b. New York City, 12/26/21. Presented many jazz artists on his TV shows in the '50s and '60s. Produced series of 26 half hour TV programs, *Jazz Scene USA*, each feat. a well known combo or singer, '61-2. Series had limited exposure in US but was shown extensively overseas. In later years, though busy with many other projects, incl. a series of books, Allen maintained occasional contact with jazz, frequently using Terry Gibbs as leader of groups for night clubs and concerts. Wrote jazz-oriented score for MGM film, *A Man Called Dagger*. LPs: An album of Allen's compositions was recorded by Chet Baker on Beverly Hills Records.

ALLISON, MOSE JOHN JR., * *piano, singer, composer*; b. Tippo, Miss., 11/11/27. A solo performer for many years, Allison continued to work in a trio context, singing and playing in night clubs and at concerts. As Ben Sidran wrote, "He is one of the few performing pros who has both survived the fickle moods of the record buying public and maintained his following through live gigs at small clubs." Comps: *Parchman Farm; Young Man; Everybody Cryin' Mercy; Look What You Made Me Do; I Don't Worry About a Thing; Powerhouse; Hello There Universe.*

LPs: Atlantic; earlier sessions, mainly as pianist, on Prestige.

ALLYN, DAVID, * *singer*; b. Hartford, Conn., 7/19/23. Sang w. the Boyd Raeburn band of the mid-1940s and rec. some much admired ballads for Discovery w. Johnny Richards. In '58 rec. LP of Jerome Kern songs w. Johnny Mandel arrs. for World Pac. From that time to late '67 he app. at clubs, etc. in LA, SF, LV and NYC incl. the Crescendo w. S. Kenton '60; Basin St. East and Lake Tahoe w. C. Basie, '64. Also worked Playboy Club circuit, '60-4. App. at Playboy JF in Chi., '59. TV: *The World of Lenny Bruce*, '59; *Tonight Show*, '63; *Today Show*; Merv Griffin; Mike Douglas, '67. Comps: *She Is My Star; Kim (was); A Swing For Joey; Pleasant Dreams*. From '68 Allyn has done rehabilitation counseling for drug addicts at Phoenix House and Halfway House in NYC; Addiction Services in Hartford; and, in the '70s for the VA in LA. He ret. to rec., '75 acc. only by Barry Harris in an LP, *Don't Look Back* (Xanadu).

ALMEIDA, LAURINDO, * *guitar, composer*; b. Sao Paolo, Brazil, 9/2/17. Primarily a concert guitarist, Almeida from the late 1960s appeared in recitals w. his wife, soprano Deltra Eamon, and in many others alone and w. symphony orchs. In '74-5 he made jazz appearances with the L.A. Four: himself, Ray Brown, Shelly Manne, Bud Shank. He toured New Zealand, Australia and Mexico with this combo in '75.

Awards: DB movie poll winner for underscoring *The Old Man And The Sea*; won Oscar for scoring *The Magic Pear Tree*. Six time winner and 13 time nominee for NARAS (Grammy) awards in various classical, pop, jazz categories.

Movie and TV scores: *A Star Is Born; Goya; Death Takes A Holiday*; John Steinbeck's *Flight* etc. Some underscoring for *Viva Zapata; On A Clear Day; The Godfather; Lost Horizon* etc.

Publs: *Guitar Tutor In Three Courses* (Criterion Music, 6124 Selma Ave., Hollywood, CA 90028); *Contemporary Moods for Guitar* (Robbins Music Corp., 1775 Broadway, NYC 10019); *Popular Brazilian Music*, arrs. for two guitars and rhythm (Gwyn Publishing Co., Box 5900, Sherman Oaks, CA 91413); *Laurindo Almeida Guitar Method*, (Gwyn Publishing).

LPs: Many classical and bossa nova albums on Capitol; Almeida-Ray Brown duo (Century City Records); LA Four (Concord); solo albums, and duos with Deltra Eamon (Orion, P.O. Box 24332, Los Angeles, CA 90024).

Complete catalogue of pieces arr. or transcribed for solo guitar publ: (Brazilliance Music, 4101 Witzel Dr., Sherman Oaks, CA 91423).

ALMOND, JOHN, *saxophones, flute, keyboards, vibes*; b. Enfield, Middlesex, England, 7/20/46. Father a drummer; private lessons on saxophone; while in high school began professional career. Working with Nite Sounds, Wally Johnson band, also pl. flute, clarinet. Freelanced with own combo; first records during year w. Tony Knight's Chess Men. Two years w. Zoot Money, 18 months w. Alan Price Set, which became Paul Williams Set; joined John Mayall June '69 and played with him that year at NJF.

Leaving Mayall, Almond formed his own group, Mark-Almond, with guitarist Jon Mark. Together they enjoyed extensive acceptance in pop and folk circles. After breakup of Mark-Almond group, Almond toured in Billy Joel's band in '75. A superior jazzman on all instruments, Almond has listened attentively to Eddie Lockjaw Davis, Y. Lateef, R.R. Kirk. Own jazz LP: *Hollywood Blues*, by Johnny Almond Music Machine (Deram-London). LPs with J. Mayall on Polydor; Mark-Almond LPs on Blue Thumb. In '75 Mark-Almond LPs on Columbia.

ALTSCHUL, BARRY, *drums*; b. Bronx, NYC, 1/6/43. Stud. w. Charlie Persip, Sam Ulano, Lee Konitz. Frequent app. w. Paul Bley trio, 1964-70; Jazz Composers' Guild Orch., '64-8; Carmell Jones-Leo Wright in Europe, '68; Sonny Criss, Hampton Hawes, Cal., '69;

Tony Scott, NYC, '69; Chick Corea, '70-2 in US and Europe; also domestic and foreign jobs w. Anthony Braxton; Sam Rivers.

Spent much time in Europe from late '60s, working with David Holland, John Surman, Babs Gonzales, Steve Lacy, Jimmy Owens, Karl Berger, J.R. Monterose, Johnny Griffin, Gato Barbieri, Slide Hampton, and own group. US appearances with Andrew Hill, David Liebman, Mike Nock, Paul Winter, Roswell Rudd, Gary Peacock, Robin Kenyatta.

In '75 teaching and writing a conceptual study book for drums.

An eclectic and adaptable performer, Altschul has appeared on LPs w. Rivers (Impulse); Braxton; Rudd; Andrew Hill (Arista); Buddy Guy (Vanguard); Corea (Blue Note, ECM); Bley (Milestone, ESP, BYG, Polydor, Fontana, Debut); Liebman (ECM); etc.

ALTSCHUL, MIKE, *woodwinds*; b. Los Angeles, Ca., 12/27/45. Educ: S. Park El. Sch., '51-7; Bret Harte Jr. High, '57-60; Washington High, '60-3; CSULA, '63-7. Toured w. S. Kenton, '67-9. During '69 he pl. w. Don Ellis briefly, then w. Gerald Wilson, with whom he was still working in the mid-'70s, as well as Duke Pearson and Frank Zappa '71-5. Altschul has also pl. w. B. Bryant, L. Bellson, Willie Bobo, Nat Adderley, C. Mangione, Bill Holman, T. Gibbs and Carole King. Has worked in studio orchs. on TV: *Sonny & Cher Show; Bill Cosby Show; Dinah Shore Show* and others. Fests: Monterey w. Bryant and Adderley, '69; Montreux, w. King, '73; Concord, w. Wilson, '75.

LPs: Kenton (Cap.); *Don Ellis Goes Underground* (Col.); *Hot Rats; Grand Wazoo* w. Zappa (Bizarre); *Fantasy; Music; Rhymes & Reasons*, w. King (Ode).

ALVIS, HAYES, * *bass, tuba*; b. Chicago, Ill. 6/1/07. Pl. w. E. Hines, D. Ellington, B. Carter, L. Armstrong, many small groups off and on, but was also active in interior decorating business; studied dentistry and held a pilot's license. Among his last apps. were European tours w. J. McShann, '70 and Tiny Grimes, '71. Alvis died 12/30/72 in NYC.

AMBROSE, BERT, * *leader*; b. London, England, 1897. Heyday in swing era as leader of band considered by many to be Britain's best big band. From 1966 Ambrose devoted his time to managing the singer Kathy Kirby. He collapsed in a TV studio and died 6/12/71 in Leeds Infirmary.

AMBROSETTI, FLAVIO, * *alto, soprano saxes, composer*; b. Lugano, Switz., 10/8/19. Early exp. in Swiss combos. Pl. in Italy, France. Orig. inspiration C. Hawkins, then C. Parker. In '60s and '70s working in Europe mostly w. own quintet feat. his son Franco, pianist George Gruntz, drummer Daniel Humair and a variety of bassists.

This was nucleus for The Band, an orch. of Americans and Europeans which toured Europe in '72. TV: Italy, Switz., Yugoslavia, Belgium, France, Holland; US at Monterey Fest. '67. Other fests: Prague, '66; Pori, '67; Ljubljana, '70; Bologna, '73. Grad. w. engineering degree

from Politecnicum, Zurich '45, he has been general manager of family wheel co. for more than 25 yrs. Comp: *Gentiliano Serenade; Looking Forward; Our Suite Dig; Age of Prominence; El Comendador (Nebulosa).* LPs: (Dire); Ljubljana Jazz Fest. (Helidon); *The Band-Alpine Power Plant* (MPS).

AMBROSETTI, FRANCO, * *trumpet, fluegelhorn, composer*; also *piano, drums*; b. Lugano, Switzerland, 12/10/41. Played w. father Flavio Ambrosetti's gp.; in Zurich w. own gp. in early-mid-'60s. Won first prize for trumpet at Vienna Int. Jazz Competition, '66. From that time continued working w. father's quintet and w. his own gp. incl. George Gruntz, Daniel Humair, Ron Mathewson. In '72, w. father, Gruntz and Humair, formed big band called The Band, touring in Europe and doing TV shows. The Band's MPS rec. won as best jazz rec. in Italy, '73. Fest: MJF w. father's gp., '67; other fests. in Italy, Switz., Austria, Yugo., France, Finland, '67-73. Comp: *Pistrophallobus; Blues for Ursula; Cameroon Talk; In Memory of Eric.*

Master's Degree in Economics from U. of Basle; works as manager of family co. which produces wheels for various vehicles in a large area of the European market. LPs: *Steppenwolf* (PDU); other quartet dates (Horo, Dire); co-leader, *The Band*; sideman on *From Sticksland With Love* (MPS-BASF).

AMMONS, EUGENE (GENE OR JUG), * *tenor saxophone*; b. Chicago, Ill., 4/14/25. His father was the pioneer boogie woogie pianist Albert Ammons. Gene played in the Billy Eckstine band at age 19, left him in '48 and worked w. W. Herman in '49. In the '50s he was often feat. in a two tenor combo w. S. Stitt. His career was interrupted by narcotics problems, culminating in a seven year prison sentence ending in '69, after which he resumed touring, backed by a rhythm section. His big sound and driving beat established him as one of the giants of modern tenor saxophone. Ammons became ill in the spring of '74, was hospitalized in Chicago with cancer in July, and died of pneumonia 7/23/74.

TV: *Just Jazz*, PBS, '71. LPs: More than 30 albums on Prestige, among them *Goodbye; Brasswind; And Friends at Montreux; Big Bad Jug; Chase* w. D. Gordon; *Soul Summit* w. Stitt; *Chicago Concert*, w. J. Moody; *My Way, Velvet Soul, Boss Tenor*; reissue, *Juganthology*, etc; also *Mingus and Friends* (Col.).

AMRAM, DAVID WERNER III, * *composer, French horn* also *Pakistani flute, piano, singer, guitar, bouzoukie, dumbeg*; b. Philadelphia, Pa., 11/17/30. This musical renaissance man was continually active as a classical composer, utilizing elements in his works, and as a player-writer mixing folk, classical and Middle Eastern elements into his essentially jazz-based performances. First composer-in-residence at NY Phil.; pl. w. Freddie Redd at Casey's, '66; conducted Houston Symph., pl. jazz concert in second half of program, '67; pl. Fillmore East w. Mingus, J. Steig, '68; Village Gate w. George Barrow, '69. In '70 Amram formed a quartet, incl. Pepper Adams, with which he pl. coll. circuit. Premiered his

Triple Concerto at Phil. Hall and also pl. w. Mary Lou Williams in her *Mass*, '71. Cond. Brooklyn Philharmonia, w. his quartet as part of orch., in free concerts for over 30,000 children in NYC; perf. *Triple Concerto* w. Phila. Symph., '72. Pl. at Five Spot, Village Vanguard, St. James Infirmary, concerts, etc., '74-5. Workshops at coll., high schools, parks on a world-wide basis. Amram strives to "bring the jazz experience to folk festivals and symphony concerts, where I end the concert with a jam session involving the audience, singing and make up lyrics and music on the spot to show that spontaneity is a natural blessing to all."

Amram's biography, *Vibrations*, pub. by Viking, '68, was later issued in paperback by Compass. Pl. in film, *Pull My Daisy*, for which he wrote title song with lyrics by Kerouac and Allen Ginsberg. Fests: Phila. Folk; Mariposa Folk; Kennedy Center; also concerts at Wolftrap Farm; South St. Seaport; Jazz on the River. Comps. *Triple Concerto for Woodwind, Brass, Jazz Quintet and Symphony; Bassoon Concerto; Horn Concerto; Violin Concerto; Trio for Tenor Sax, Horn and Bassoon;* Bi-Centennial piece for oboe, mezzo-soprano and orch., based on American Indian writings called *Trail of Beauty*, commissioned by Phila. Orch.; *Ballad For Red Allen; Tompkins Square Park Consciousness Expander; The Fabulous Fifties; Horn and Hardart Succotash Blues*. His classical works are publ. by C.F. Peters, 373 Park Ave. South, New York, N.Y. 10010. LPs: *No More Walls; Subway Night; Triple Concerto* (RCA); w. Mary Lou Williams (Mary); cond. for Hannibal Marvin Peterson, *Children of the Fire* (Sunrise).

ANDERS, JORGE, *saxophones, clarinet, composer;* b. Lanus, Buenos Aires, Argentina, 4/18/39. Father was first violinist in Belgian symph. orch. Clarinet in '55; tenor sax in '60. Pl. trad. jazz w. Argentine jazz octet, '61. In '63 pl. at international jazz fest. w. B. Shank. Has led own quartet and orch., feat. orig. comps. such as *Blackman; El Justiciero; La Vuelta Del Elefanton (Big Elephant's Comeback); El Marques*. Anders plays in a modern, driving style and has reached a definite sound that identifies his playing.

ANDERSEN, ARILD, *bass;* b. Oslo, Norway, 10/27/45. Priv. stud. w. George Russell. First pro. engagement w. Jan Garbarek quartet, '67-73; also acc. singer Karin Krog from '67. Toured Africa, France s. S. Getz, '70; USA, '74. Worked in U.S. w. Sam Rivers, Paul Bley, '73-4. Leading own group '74- . Fests: Berlin Jazztage, '68; Montreux, '68, 72; Antibes, '70; many other European fests. incl. Cascais '75. Was voted Musician of the Year in Norway, '69. Infls: Bley, Jon Christensen, Garbarek.

LPs: *Afric Pepperbird; Sart; Triptykon; Clouds In My Head* (ECM); *There Is No Energy Crisis* (Imp.); w. R. Rudd, *Flexible Flyer* (Arista); w. D. Cherry, *Eternal Rhythm* (MPS); *Joy* (Sonet); *Listen to the Silence* (Concept).

ANDERSON, WILLIAM ALONZO (CAT),* *trumpet, fluegelhorn;* b. Greenville, S.C., 9/12/16. The veteran high note specialist, first prominent with Duke Ellington's orchestra from 1944, spent most of the 1960s back in the band after a two-year absence (1959-61). Leaving for the last time in Jan. 1971, he made his home in the San Fernando Valley and became active in Hollywood studios. TV: *Duke Ellington: We Love You Madly;* Julie Andrews, Merv Griffin shows. Movies: *Lady Sings The Blues* etc. Many records; occasional gigs with own groups, playing Ellington alumni concerts, and pl. w. Bill Berry band. Festivals: Newport, Monterey, Concord. Toured as first trumpet, also asst. conductor and later conductor, of band for *Ice Capades* show, 1974-5. LPs for French labels with own gps. and w. Claude Bolling; many others w. Ellington, Johnny Hodges et al (q.v.) w. L. Bellson (Pablo); w. B. Berry (Beez); *Newport in New York, The Jam Sessions* (Cobble).

Publ: *Cat Anderson Trumpet Method* (Gwyn Publ. Co., P.O. Box 5900, Sherman Oaks, Calif. 91413).

ANDERSON, JOHN JR.,* *trumpet, composer;* b. Birmingham, Ala., 1/31/21. Anderson, who pl. during the '40s and '50s w. Benny Carter, Earl Bostic, and who in '59-60 was a trumpeter and arranger for C. Basie, later toured w. Ray Charles and the Ike and Tina Turner Revue. He rec. an album with his big band in '70 for the Tangerine label. On 8/17/74, in Birmingham, he suffered a stroke and died the following day.

ANDRE, WAYNE, *trombone;* also *baritone horn;* b. Manchester, Conn., 11/17/31. Stud. at Hartt School of Music, '48-9; Berklee, '49-50, Manhattan School of Music, '58-61, and several private teachers. Pl. w. Charlie Spivak orch., '50; Sauter-Finegan, '55; W. Herman, '56. In '56-7, worked w. Kai Winding septet, for which he composed *Nutcracker* and arr. *The Preacher*. With Gerry Mulligan Concert Jazz Band, '60.

In '61-5, Andre was a member of a CBS staff orch., NYC. Side ventures incl. a USSR tour w. B. Goodman, '62, Thad Jones-Mel Lewis orch., '66, Clark Terry big band, '67. NJF-NY '73 w. M. Legrand; G. Mulligan.

A dependable section man and occasional soloist, Andre was heard in albums w. Winding on Columbia and A & M, as well as w. Liza Minelli, soloing on *More Than You Know* on her album *Liza With a Z*. Comp. *Ayo* for Bill Watrous LP, '74.

ARCHEY, JAMES (JIMMY),* *trombone;* b. Norfolk, Va., 10/12/02. The veteran of many names bands (King Oliver, Luis Russell, Benny Carter) died in Amityville, L.I., N.Y., 11/16/67 after a long illness. His last major job was a European tour w. the NO All Stars, Feb. '66.

ARMSTRONG, LILIAN HARDIN (LIL),* *piano, singer, composer;* b. Memphis, Tenn., 2/3/1902 (Her birth date was variously given from 1898 to 1903, but 1902 was confirmed by Mrs. Armstrong). Was married to Louis Armstrong from 1924, when they were both playing in King Oliver's band; they were separated in the early '30s. She played on and wrote music for many of Armstrong's Hot Five and Hot Seven records. In later years stud. extensively in Chicago and N.Y., led various bands and combos. She was still living in Chicago, in the house she and Armstrong had bought in 1927, and was playing at a *Tribute to Louis Armstrong* concert at Chicago's Civic Center Plaza, when she collapsed and died of a heart attack, 7/27/71.

ARMSTRONG, DANIEL LOUIS (SATCHMO or POPS),* *trumpet, singer, leader*; b. New Orleans, La., 7/4/00. In 1966, Armstrong and his group still were active on a full time basis, pl. a summer season that year at Jones Beach Marine Theatre. Armstrong was ill for two months in the spring of '67 but shortly afterward resumed his schedule, pl. concerts in Dublin, Antibes, St. Tropez and Majorca. Early in '68, after a few American engagements, Armstrong and his All Stars pl. at the San Remo Festival. In June they appeared at the New Orleans JF, then immediately went back to Britain. After a series of successful concerts, the band returned home. During that year Armstrong was represented on record with one of his popular hits, *What A Wonderful World*. In Sept. he was taken seriously ill and was confined to Beth Israel hospital in NYC. Released in Jan. '69, he soon became ill again, re-entering the hospital in February for two months. By June, when his perennial manager, Joe Glaser, died, Armstrong was out of the hospital and attended the funeral. His public appearances for the rest of the year were limited mostly to guest shots. During '69 the film *Hello Dolly!* was released, featuring Armstrong in a scene w. Barbra Streisand.

Although under doctors' orders not to play trumpet, in '70 Armstrong made numerous TV apps. as singer, and recorded two vocal albums, *Louis and His Friends* and a country/western set. He talked and sang at a special 70th birthday concert held at the Shrine Auditirium in LA, and the following week app. in a *Salute to Satch* tribute at NJF. By Sept. he was well enough to resume playing. He app. in Las Vegas, co-starring in a show w. Pearl Bailey. In October, he flew to London to sing and play at a benefit concert.

During early '71 he continued appearing occasionally, but after playing for two weeks at the Empire Room of the Waldorf-Astoria, he suffered a heart attack and returned to the hospital March 15. On May 6 he was allowed to go home, but his health was precarious, and early in the morning of 7/6/71 he died in his sleep at his home in Corona, Long Island.

Armstrong's role as the most important improvising musician in the 70 year history of jazz was not to be forgotten or neglected. Immediately after his death, memorial albums began appearing and tributes were given to him all over the world, and his widow, Mrs. Lucille Armstrong, found herself in a position of roving ambassador, making many apps. in the U.S. and overseas as a representative of jazz, of Satchmo, and of everything he stood for. She was chairperson of the Louis Armstrong Arts and Cultural Memorial Organization; in '74 she traveled through eastern Europe under the auspices of the State Dept., showing films of Armstrong and answering questions from fans. She served as a consultant on TV films, articles, books etc., dealing w. Louis' history and

was present at the unveiling, in the summer of '74, of a bust of her late husband, in the Jardins de Cimiez, Nice, site of the Nice JF.

Posthumous Honors: On the 73rd anniversary of Armstrong's birth, the name of Singer Bowl in Queens, N.Y., was changed to Louis Armstrong Memorial Stadium. To celebrate the occasion, a benefit concert was held, proceeds of which went to charities selected by Mrs. Armstrong.

In June-July '75, the New York Jazz Repertory Orchestra's concert program dedicated to Armstrong's music toured the Soviet Union as part of a cultural exchange between the U.S. and USSR. Dick Hyman, pianist and musical director, transcribed many of Armstrong's original solos and arr. them for the trumpet section.

A carefully documented book entitled *Louis: The Louis Armstrong Story*, by Max Jones and John Chilton, was published late in '71 by Little, Brown & Co. It includes many reproductions of Armstrong's long typewritten letters to friends, as well as photographs, a chronology (from which much of the above information was culled) and a list of Armstrong's film appearances.

The availability of Armstrong's records has fluctuated greatly, but late in 1975 the following were still listed in the U.S. catalogues: *Hello Dolly!; At The Crescendo* (MCA); *Best Of; Definitive Album; Louis Armstrong; w. Dukes of Dixieland* (Audiofidelity); *Disney Songs the Satchmo Way* (Buena); *I Will Wait For You* (Bruns.); *Louis "Satchmo" Armstrong* (Archive of Folk & Jazz); *Mame* (Pickwick); *Verve's Best Choice* (Verve); *What A Wonderful World* (ABC); *w. His Friends* (Amsterdam); *July 4, 1900/July 6, 1971* (RCA); *The Genius of Louis Armstrong* (Col.).

ARNET, JAN, *bass*; b. Prague, Czechoslovakia, 1934. Stud. piano, violin, trombone, 1945-52; bass, theory, '57-60. Between 1958 and '65 rec. on more than 100 LPs w. Zdenek Bartak big band; Karel Vlach band; SH Quintet (winner of Czech jazz critics' poll, '63-4); Reduta Quintet, '65 in Austria, West Germany, Egypt. After working w. Leo Wright, Booker Ervin, Nathan Davis et al. in West Germany and France, came to U.S. in 1966, working as producer, arranger, conductor and performer. Pl. w. Elvin Jones; Tony Scott; Howard McGhee; Attila Zoller; Sonny Stitt, '66-7; US and Mexico w. Chico Hamilton, '68-9; Art Blakey, '69-70. Has written articles and lectured; commentator for US Information Agency's Voice of America.

ARNOLD, HORACEE (pron. Hor-as) E.,* *drums, composer*; also *piano, acoustic guitar*; b. Wayland, Ky., 9/25/37. Pl. in Louisville and LA in '50s; NYC in '60s w. Mingus; R.R. Kirk; Barry Harris; Bud Powell. Studied comp. w. Heiner Stadler; classical guitar w. Hy Gubernik; Ralph Towner, '66-9. Formed gp., The Here and Now Company, which then incl. Karl Berger, Robin Kenyatta, Sam Rivers, for concerts and workshops in Young Audiences series at high schools throughout NYC; concert at Whitney Museum. From '69-72 worked as coordinator for Jazzmobile and perf. in concert w. own gp. Pl. w. Chick Corea; Stan Getz, '72. Concerts and lecture-demonstrations in Summer Jazz Camp series, '74; high schools and colls. w. Here and Now, '75. Infl: Corea, Zawinul, Ellington, Albeniz, de Falla, Kodaly, Ravel, Debussy, W. Shorter.

TV: *The People; Round Trip,* CBS; *Peter Pan,* Metromedia. Fest: NJF-NY at Apollo Theatre, '73; Concord. Grant from National Endowment for the Arts, '74-5.

Comp: *Tales of the Exonerated Flea; Sing Nightjar; Puppett of the Seasons; Benzele Windows; Chinnereth II; Euroaquilo Silence; Delicate Evasions.* LPs: *Tales of the Exonerated Flea; Tribe* (Col.); w. Corea, *Is; Sundance* (SS); w. Kenyatta, *Until* (Vortex); w. H. Masekela (Merc.).

ART ENSEMBLE OF CHICAGO. Group formed in the fall of 1968 by Joseph Jarman, Roscoe Mitchell, Lester Bowie and Malachi Favors which played and lived in France, '69-71, and has since pl. concerts and clubs in the US. Its performances are a mixture of theatricality and music: the stage filled with instruments from bass saxophones to banjos, fender bass to log drums, bike horns, gongs and whistles to tenor saxes and flutes; the players in grass skirts, faces painted in African ceremonial designs; wearing straw boaters or a hard hat. Jarman, commenting on painting faces, says: "A lot of people like to suggest this has to do with a militant attitude, when in fact it is a tribal attitude. The mask in African culture, functions to alleviate human beings so the spiritual aspects of things can come out."

David Spitzer wrote: "The members of the group produce musical sounds which run the gamut from the traditional to the absurd and the surreal. They also include valid, humorous, vocal discourses and cries, as well as atypical sounds produced on traditional instruments."

Concerts & Fests: Int. Fest. Amougies, Belgium; Rotterdam Int. Pop Fest.; Jazz-Beat Fest. '71, Aarhus, Denmark; Fest. of Chateauvallon, France; Baden-Baden Free Jazz Fest.; Museum of Modern Art, Paris; Nat. Gallery of Art, Berlin; French Ministry of Culture tours, '70-1; U. of Wisconsin; Notre Dame; Chicago; Indiana; Stanford; Antioch; Wayne State; Malcolm X Coll.; Ohio State; Michigan State; Washington U.; Lenox Arts Center, Mass.; Ann Arbor Blues & Jazz Fest. '72; NJF-NY, '73; Montreux, '74; Grande Maison de O.R.T.F., Paris '74; six-city tour of Japan, '74. Apps. on Radio Denmark; Stockholm Radio; Organisation Radio Television Francaise.

Awards: Record of the Year, '70, Academie de Jazz Francaise for *People in Sorrow*; Album of the Year, *Melody Maker* '73-4 for *Baptizum; Melody Maker; Jazz Podium; Jazz Hot; Jazz Magazine* polls; DB Critics' poll, combo TDWR, '71.

LPs: *People in Sorrow; Les Stances a Sophie* (Nessa); *Reese and the Smooth Ones; A Jackson in Your House; Message to Our Folks* (Byg); *Spiritual* (Poly.); *Tutankhamun* (Freedom), same as *The Paris Session* (Aris-

ta); *Home* (Galloway); *Certain Blacks; Phase One; Art Ensemble w. Fontella Bass; Chi-Congo* (America); *Baptizum; Fanfare for the Warriors* (Atl.); *Live at Mandel Hall* (Delmark/Trio).

ARVANITAS, GEORGES,* *piano, organ*; b. Marseilles, France, 6/13/31. Played w. Donald Byrd et al in Paris early '60s. To U.S. in '64; spent nine months w. Y. Lateef, '65. After returning to France, where he led trio, back to U.S. for six months working w. Lloyd Price. Own trio at Cameleon in Paris, '66-7; Chat Qui Peche club, '68-70. His rhythm section backed many visiting Americans incl. L. Konitz, Dexter Gordon, H. Mobley. During early '70s Arvanitas played concerts w. Clark Terry, B. Webster, Robin Kenyatta; toured Japan w. Michel Legrand, '72; Italy, first w. Sonny Criss, later w. S. Stitt. His trio, w. Jacky Samson on bass and Charles Saudrais on drums, was organized in September '65 and was still working together in '75.

Publ: *Piano Jazz,* transcription for piano, ed. Paul Beuscher, 27 Boulevard Beaumarchais, Paris 11ᵉ. Own LPs on European labels; also, *Anita O'Day In Berlin* (BASF).

ASH, MARVIN (Marvin Ashbaugh),* *piano*; b. Lamar, Colo., 10/4/14. The veteran pianist, well known in LA in the '40s, died 8/21/74 in Encino, Cal.

ASHBY, HAROLD KENNETH,* *tenor saxophone*; b. Kansas City, Mo., 3/27/25. After working with Mercer Ellington and often subbing in Duke Ellington's band, Ashby became a regular member of the senior Ellington's orchestra 7/5/68 at the NJF. Touring with the band on its various overseas bookings, including Europe, Japan, Australia in '70, USSR, '71, Africa, '73, Ashby was also featured in his own album *Born To Swing* on Master Jazz in '72.

He remained with the orch. under Mercer Ellington's direction, after Duke's death, still playing in the full-toned style reminiscent of his predecessors in the band, Ben Webster and Paul Gonsalves. LPs w. Ellington: *My People* (Flying Dutchman); *70th Birthday Concert, Togo Brava Suite* (UA); *New Orleans Suite* (Atl.); *Third Sacred Concert* (RCA); w. M. Ellington, *Continuum* (Fant.).

ASHBY, IRVING C.,* *guitar*; b. Somerville, Mass., 12/29/20. Former Lionel Hampton, King Cole and Oscar Peterson guitarist; devoted most of the late '60s and early '70s to private teaching. In '69 left Los Angeles, moved to Perris, Cal. and, in semi-retirement, became active in landscape design, sign painting, teaching orchestra and guitar at high school; also in '71 at U. of Cal., Riverside.

Publ: *Guitar Work Book* (Trebla Publ. Co., Rt. 1, Box 146, Perris, Ca. 92370). LPs: *California Guitar* w. Mundell Lowe (Famous Door); *The Bosses* w. Count Basie and Joe Turner (Pablo).

ASMUSSEN, SVEND,* *violin*; b. Copenhagen, Denmark, 2/28/16. Ranking alongside S. Grappelli as one of Europe's first great jazz violinists, he toured for many years as a member of a pop vocal-instrumental unit known as the Swe-Danes, feat. singer Alice Babs. After Babs left the group in '61, Asmussen cont. touring with the third member, guitarist Ulrik Neumann. In '66, he led his own quintet at the Tivoli in Copenhagen. From '67 he toured Sweden with this group, app. at MJF, traveled through the Far East and Africa, and rec. a celebrated album, *Violin Summit*, w. Stuff Smith, Grappelli and Jean-Luc Ponty (MPS).

From '69-72 Asmussen was reunited w. Babs, touring Scandinavia with her. Asmussen experimented with amplified violin and brought strong rock infls. into his jazz work. He was heard in concerts with a group feat. Ed Thigpen on drums, and two Scandinavian musicians on organ and fender bass. To Brazil w. Babs, Jan. '74. From '74, w. clarinetist Putte Wickman and pianist Ivan Renliden, pl. concerts in many churches throughout Sweden and Denmark, with repertoire incl. Bach, Telemann, Mozart and improv. on hymns and folk themes. In Sept. '75 Asmussen returned to the U.S. to make his second app. at the MJF.

LP: *Yesterday and Today*, w. Toots Thielemans (A & M).

ASSUNTO, FRANK JOSEPH,* *trumpet, leader*; b. New Orleans, La., 1/29/32. Co-founder and leader (with his brother Fred) of the Dukes of Dixieland. Died in NO, 2/25/74, after a brief illness.

ASSUNTO, JACOB (PAPA JAC),* *trombone, banjo*; b. Lake Charles, La., 11/1/05. His two sons, Fred and Frank, leaders of Dukes of Dixieland, died in '66 and '74 respectively. Not long after the death of the latter he retired to Metairie, La., where he devoted part of his time to teaching.

AUGER, BRIAN, *organ, keyboards*; b. London, England, 7/18/39. No formal tuition. Started in London, 1962, at Ronnie Scott's and other clubs. Freelance pianist, '63. Put together band incl. John McLaughlin, Rick Laird, '64. The following year began pl. organ. In '65-6 he pl. with Steam Packet feat. Julie Driscoll. Again feat. with Ms. Driscoll in Brian Auger and the Trinity, '67-9. From '70, leader of Oblivion Express, with which he frequently visited U.S. Numerous TV and jazz fest. appearances, incl. Montreux, Berlin, Frankfurt.

Won *Melody Maker* piano and new star sections, '64. Trinity won *Melody Maker* poll, '68. Auger names McCoy Tyner, John Coltrane, Herbie Hancock as original inspirations. LPs: Polydor (Britain); Atlantic, RCA (USA).

AULD, GEORGIE (John Altwerger),* *tenor, alto, soprano saxes*; b. Toronto, Ontario, Canada, 5/19/19. First prominent in '30s w. Bunny Berigan, Artie Shaw, and '40s w. Benny Goodman and Shaw. During '60s and '70s freelanced in Los Angeles. In '67 joined Tony Martin as conductor and soloist, touring Europe and S. America. Enjoying his greatest individual successes in Japan, Auld by '75 had toured there a dozen times, and had recorded some 15 albums in Japan, many of them great popular hits. In Los Angeles, however, he remained in relative

obscurity, playing as sideman on Flip Wilson and other TV shows.

LPs: None of his many albums as a leader were available in '75; however, he was heard in many reissues w. Berigan, Shaw (RCA), Goodman (Columbia) etc.

AURA (a.k.a. AURA LEE, Aura Urziceanu), *singer*; also *violin, percussion*; b. Bucharest, Romania, 12/14/46. Stud. classical violin from '61-4 with her father, Ion Urziceanu, concert master of the Bucharest Symph. Classical voice training w. Florica Orascu, '63-7. Stud. at Bucharest Conserv., '65-7. Toured U.S.S.R., Poland, Israel, '65 w. Jancsi Korossy trio. With Bucharest Jazz Quintet, '66-9. In Canada, '70, worked w. Phil Nimmons and w. drummer Ron Rully. Married Rully and settled in Canada, '71. In '72, she made several apps. w. D. Ellington, incl. a NJF-NY Carnegie Hall concert, for which she was widely praised. Returned to Europe, '73, working w. Art Farmer, Slide Hampton. In Toronto, w. Gene DiNovi trio, '74. Toured w. Q. Jones, '74-5 in U.S. and Japan.

Infls: Fitzgerald, Vaughan, McRae, Nancy Wilson; Ellington, Rully, Q. Jones, L. Schifrin. In '71 she won the European Reporters' Press Prize in Brussels as most promising singer, and Europe Cup at Knokke, Belgium. Winner of polls annually in Romania, from '71. App. on own TV specs. in Bucharest.

Aura, who has an extraordinarily pure sound and remarkable range, is one of the most individual jazz oriented vocal stylists to emerge during the early '70s.

LPs: several in Europe, incl. some arranged and conducted by Rully for Electrachord.

AUSTIN, LOVIE,* *piano, composer*; b. Chattanooga, Tenn., 9/19/1887. The one-time leader of the Blues Serenaders, who made her first record in 1923 with Ida Cox and her last in Chicago 9/1/61, died in Chicago 7/10/72.

AUTREY, HERMAN,* *trumpet*; b. Evergreen, Ala., 12/4/04. Key sideman w. Fats Waller in '30s; pl. w. Saints & Sinners in '60s, touring Europe w. them in '67, '69. Free-lancing in NYC in mid-'70s, occasionally subbing at Jimmy Ryan's. LPs: w. Saints & Sinners (MPS, Sack.); in Albert McCarthy's *Swing Today* series (Eng. RCA); Fats Waller reissue (Bluebird).

AXELROD, DAVID, *composer*; b. Los Angeles, Ca., 4/17/36. Mostly self-taught. Stud. informally w. Gerald Wiggins; harmony and comp. w. Mauro Bruno, '59; harmony at UCLA, '60-1. Infl. by O. Coleman, M. Davis, Gil Evans, Ch. Mingus, T. Monk, H. Silver, G. Wiggins.

From the late '50s, Axelrod was principally known as the producer of jazz albums for a series of companies, but later he shifted the focus of his work to composing and arranging. Among his works are *Songs of Innocence; Earth Rot; The Contemporary Messiah; The Auction; Seriously Deep*, all rec. by leading artists.

In '70, Axelrod conducted his comp. *Tensity* for the C. Adderley quintet and orch. at the MJF. The sound track album of *Easy Rider*, in which his *Mass In F. Minor* was heard, was awarded a gold record. Benny Carter and others have attested to the growth of Axelrod's talent as a writer capable of mixing many contemporary idioms.

LPs: *Tensity* w. Adderley (Capitol); *Double Exposure* w. N. Adderley (Prestige); *Brasswind* w. G. Ammons (Prestige); *Northern Windows* w. H. Hawes (Fantasy); *The Way It Was, The Way It Is* w. Lou Rawls (Capitol).

AYERS, ROY E. JR.,* *vibes, singer;* b. Los Angeles, Cal., 9/10/40. After working w. Gerald Wilson, Jack Wilson, and as co-leader with Hampton Hawes in the early '60s, Ayers led a quartet, '65-6, before touring w. Herbie Mann from '66-70. He then formed his own group, Roy Ayers Ubiquity. Toured Japan, Europe, '71. Festivals: NJF, 67, '73; Montreux, '71. Composed sound track for film *Coffy* (also released as Polydor LP). Developing many attractive new sound effects through the use of electronics, Ayers enjoyed growing popularity in the '70s, his many Polydor albums reaching a wide rock and jazz audience. Early LPs on Atlantic: *Virgo Vibes; Stoned Soul Picnic; Daddy Bug.* LPs on Polydor: *Ubiquity,* '70; *He's Coming,* '71; *Ubiquity Live at Montreux,* '72; *Red, Black and Green,* '73; *Virgo Red, Change Up The Groove,* '74. Won DB awards, '66, '71.

AYLER, ALBERT,* *tenor, soprano, alto saxophones, bagpipes, composer;* b. Cleveland, Ohio, 7/13/36. A prominent figure in the free jazz of the '60s, Ayler stirred strong controversy with his concerts, recordings and compositions. In the late '60s his music reverted somewhat towards a more blues rooted style, using themes suggesting r & b infl.

On 11/25/70 Ayler's body was found floating in the East River, NYC. The circumstances of his death were never cleared up. Critic Joachim Berendt found "the joyous air of the folk musician" in Ayler's work. Michael Cuscuna wrote: "The music of Albert Ayler remains among the most unique and haunting in the history of black American music . . . of all the players of the 1960s avant garde, including the geniuses, the competent musicians, and the lame hucksters, Ayler's music seemed to evoke the strongest reaction, be it pro or con . . . (he offered) simple, unforgettable melodies, such as *Ghosts,* which many feel to be the anthem of 1960s black music. After stating a theme, he would pursue improvisational variations and developments, twisting his saxophone out of the grip of European music fundamentals."

LPs: *My Name is Albert Ayler; Introducing Albert Ayler* (Fant.); *Spiritual Unity; Bells; N.Y. Eye & Ear Control; Spirits Rejoice* (ESP); *First Recordings* (GNP); *In Greenwich Village; Reevaluation: The Impulse Years; Last Album; Love Cry; Music Is The Healing Force; New Grass* (Imp.); *Vibrations* (Arista-Freedom).

AYOUB, NICHOLAS (NICK), *tenor sax, composer;* also *oboe, flute, clarinet;* b. Three Rivers, Que., Canada, 9/7/26. Son Jimmy is drummer with rock gp. Mahogany Rush. Studied saxophone w. Arthur Romano; oboe w. Romano, Harold Gomberg. Received Premier Prix from Montreal Conserv. of Mus. for classical saxophone '52. At 17 pl. w. Maynard Ferguson's band. He was also in the Johnny Holmes band that incl. Oscar Peterson. Pl. at Emanon Jazz Society Meetings w. baritone saxophonist Freddie Nichols. Worked w. Butch Watanabe in '50s. Own quintet for concerts and clubs in Montreal. Active in recs., jingles, and for CBC-TV. Professor of classical saxophone, jazz improvisation, and director of the jazz band at Montreal Conserv. of Mus. Infl: Webster, Getz, Parker, Coltrane. TV: soloist and w. own quintet for CBC; member of Canadian all-star jazz orch. sponsored by Timex '57. Fest: Montreal JF opposite Duke Ellington '65; Dawson Coll.; Concordia U. '75. Comp.: *Concertino for Jazz Band; Pillsville; Love of Three Flutes; Montreal East; Montreal West; Time Compulsion, Lynn's Tune; Little Nicky; Abstraction; Walkin' Home.* LPs: *Montreal Jazz Scene* (RCA Victor, Can.); *Canadian Talent Library; Nick Ayoub Plays Bossa Nova* (Trans Canada).

BABS, ALICE (Alice Nilson), *singer;* b. Kalmar, Sweden, 1/26/24. Father Jean Nilson, pianist and composer; husband Nils Ivar Sjöblom, lyricist; daughter Titti Breitholtz, singer. Stud. w. Prof. Ragnar Hulthen, Royal Swedish Academy of Mus., from '56. Estab. as Sweden's most popular vocalist; actress with leading parts in a dozen Swedish films; TV star throughout Europe etc., she also app. at Cocoanut Grove in '60s as single and w. Swe-Danes trio, making several recs. in Hollywood. She met D. Ellington in '63; a few weeks later he called her to record with him in Paris. LP was released under the title *Serenade to Sweden* (European Reprise—never available in US). During next decade she made many apps. w. Ellington, among them one on her birthday in '67 in Malmo, Sweden, and several at Ellington's Sacred Concerts, incl. the premiere of the second Sacred Concert at the Cathedral of St. John the Divine, NYC, '68. Fests: Paris, '49; Newport, '73. Infls: Ivie Anderson, Billie Holiday, Ellington. Honors: Royal Court Singer, appointed by King of Sweden in '72, the only non-opera singer given that title. Member of Royal Swedish Academy of Music, '74.

Ellington once said of Alice Babs: "This voice, ladies and gentlemen, embodies all the warmth, joy, life, rhythm and tragedy that, for me, is the innermost secret of jazz." Babs' extraordinary purity of sound and remarkable range are exquisitely showcased in his albums. LPs w. Ellington: *Second Sacred Concert* (Fant.); *Third Sacred Concert* (RCA). Others: *Alice & Wonderband* (Decca); *Music with a Jazz Flavour; Alice Babs Serenading Duke Ellington* (Swedish Society Discofil).

BACSIK (pron. Bott-chik), ELEK, *violin, violectra, guitar;* b. Budapest, Hungary, 5/22/26. A gypsy, he was originally self-taught on violin, but later prepared for a career as a concert artist at the Budapest Conservatory. At an early age he taught himself guitar and was established as Hungary's leading jazz guitarist. After three years in the Army, he lived in Vienna, later Switzerland, Lebanon, Italy, Spain, Portugal and Paris, playing with many visiting American jazzmen in '59-66. To U.S., '66; toured with gypsy band, settled in LA for a while, moving in '67 to Las Vegas. For the next seven years he remained in obscurity until Bob Thiele heard him at the Sahara, where he was in the orch. backing Thiele's wife, Teresa Brewer. Soon afterward, he made his first album for the Bob Thiele label. Fest: NJF-NY, '74.

A true eclectic who has absorbed much of the essence of American jazz, Bacsik has a predilection for the bebop era, and is a good friend of Dizzy Gillespie, with whom he rec. in the early '60s.

LPs: *I Love You; Bird and Dizzy* (Bob Thiele Music); *Dizzy on the French Riviera* w. Gillespie (Philips).

BACULIS, ALPHONSE (AL), *clarinet*; also *saxophone, piano*; b. Montreal, Que., Canada, 11/21/30. Wife and sister-in-law both singers; brother-in-law is composer Ron Collier. Studied at McGill U., '48-51; theory & comp. w. Marvin Duchow, Istvan Anhalt, '52-6. Played w. Canadian All Stars which rec. for Discovery (long out of print) '55. Worked w. many Montreal gps. From '58 has been occupied mainly with writing, comp. & arrs. for TV and films; pl. w. studio orchs.; writing and conducting jazz shows. Infl: Parker, Gillespie, Tristano, Schoenberg, Webern, Hindemith, Stravinsky, Bartok. Won clarinet division of Canadian jazz poll for more than five years in '50s. LPs: w. Al Baculis Singers, hits from *Anne of Green Gables* and other Canadian shows (Dominion); transcriptions and records for CBC.

BADINI, GERARD,* *tenor sax, clarinet*; b. Paris, France, 4/16/31. From '58 concentrated more on tenor than clarinet. Mostly studio work in '60s, '70s. Toured Europe, Africa, Middle East w. Claude Bolling. Founded Les Swingers w. Francois Guin (q.v.), touring Africa, '70, '72. Pl. in Europe w. R. Eldridge; P. Gonsalves; D. Ellington; L. Hampton. Own gp., The Swing Machine, from '73. Pl. clubs in US w. Bobby Hackett, Aaron Bell, '74. Infl: Ellington, Parker, Gonsalves, Lockjaw Davis. TV: many shows w. Bolling; did music for shorts, *Noir et Blanc*; soundtracks w. Bolling; M. Legrand. Fest: Montreux; Nice; Antibes; Warsaw; Prague; Dakar; Pescara. Comp: a ballet illustrating the history of jazz, *Jungle is Not So Virgin As People Said*, excerpts of which were recorded on the Polish label Muza. LPs: *Swing Machine; Swing Machine* w. *Sam Woodyard* (B&B); *Swingers in the Groove; Paul Gonsalves in Paris* w. *the Swingers* (Barclay); Anderson, Bolling & Co; others w. Bolling (Philips); w. Jacques Denjean (Poly.); w. Duke Ellington and Alice Babs (Reprise).

BAILEY, ERNEST HAROLD (BENNY),* *trumpet*; b. Cleveland, Ohio, 8/13/25. Played w. D. Gillespie; L. Hampton in '40s; Q. Jones in '59-60, after having pl. in Swedish Radio Band, '57-9. Returned briefly to US '60 but once again moved to Sweden. Then worked w. Berlin Radio Band for two yrs.; Max Greger band for five yrs.

in Munich before settling in Geneva to play w. the Radio Swiss Romande orch. With Clarke-Boland Big Band from early '60s to band's breakup in '73. Fest: major Euro. fest. incl. Montreux '69 w. Les McCann and Eddie Harris; Pori '71 w. Red Mitchell; Middleheim '74 w. Boland small gp. A fine lead player and excellent soloist in the Gillespie-Navarro tradition. LPs: *Midnight in Europe* (MCE); w. L. McCann-E. Harris, *Swiss Movement* (Atl.); also see Clarke-Boland.

BAILEY, WILLIAM C. (BUSTER),* *clarinet*; b. Memphis, Tenn., 7/19/02. Joined Louis Armstrong All-Stars, '65, remaining until his death, in Brooklyn, 4/12/67. Bailey, one of the first major jazz clarinetists with a thorough academic background in music, was a prolific recording artist. He can be heard on albums w. Fletcher Henderson, Bessie Smith, Lionel Hampton, Red Allen et al. LPs: *All About Memphis* (Master Jazz).

BAILEY, COLIN,* *drums*; b. Swindon, England, 7/9/34. After touring Australia, pl. in US since 1961; worked with Victor Feldman, B. Goodman, Terry Gibbs; many groups in SF, LA. Toured w. G. Shearing '66-7; during next five years, jazz work w. Chet Baker, Ray Brown, Joe Pass; concerts w. Joao Gilberto. In '73-4 traveled w. Vic Damone. Many jazz jobs with Gibbs, R. Kellaway, Pass, Feldman, '73-5. Subbed often in *Tonight Show* TV band.

LPs: Sinatra-Jobim (Reprise); *New Look* w. Shearing (Capitol); *Almaville* w. Vince Guaraldi (WB); *Simplicity* w. Pass (World Pacific). Publs: *Bass Drum Control; Modern Drum Solos for the Drum Set*, (Try Publishing Co., 854 N. Vine St., Hollywood, CA 90028).

BAILEY, SAMUEL DAVID (DAVE),* *drums, educator*; b. Portsmouth, Va., 2/22/26. Known for his work w. Gerry Mulligan; Billy Taylor; Clark Terry-Bob Brookmeyer gps. Continued pl. w. Terry from '66-9. An accomplised pilot and former AAF officer, he gave up music to fly a Lear jet for lawyer F. Lee Bailey, '69-73. Billy Taylor then asked him to take his place w. the Jazzmobile, and from '73 Bailey has been executive director administrating all aspects from the summer street concerts in New York's five boroughs to the students Workshop. Additionally, he teaches drums in the Workshop.

In the winter of '75 he became actively involved as president of the Consortium of Jazz Organizations, 16 jazz arms in the New York area, which hopes to serve as a nucleus of a national jazz organization focussing on the artistic and business needs of the musician. In the summer of '75 he also headed the Citizens Committee to Save Jazz Radio, Inc., a group battling to preserve WRVR-FM's full-time jazz policy.

Toward the end of the year he was considering adding active playing to his schedule. LPs: w. Terry, *It's What's Happenin'* (Imp.); w. Terry-Brookmeyer (Main.).

BAILEY, DEREK, *guitar*; b. Sheffield, England, 1/29/32. Grandfather, professional pianist-banjoist; uncle, George Wing, professional guitarist. Bailey states: "After 10 years working as a guitar player in the entertainment industry I have since 1963 pursued the ideal of free improvisation. During this period I have had the good fortune to work with most of the leading German blasters, American groovers, Dutch acrobats and English kaleidoscopists in this field." Publ: *Improvisation: Its Nature and Practice in Music* (Latimer Press, 14 W. Central St., London, W.C.1, England). LPs: solo; duo w. Evan Parker (Incus); duo w. Han Bennink (ICP); duo w. Anthony Braxton (Emanem).

BAILEY, DONALD ORLANDO,* *drums, harmonica, trombone*; b. Phila., Pa., 3/26/33. Best known as drummer w. organist Jimmy Smith's trio for eight years. Freelanced in LA from mid-60s w. Jack Wilson, Hampton Hawes, Freddie Hubbard, Joe Pass, Gene Ammons, Bobby Hutcherson, Gerald Wilson, Jimmy Rowles, and innumerable others. During '70s, harmonica soloist at jazz and rock concerts, sometimes billed under name "Harmonica Man." Also played hca. w. Bill Cosby; assisted Sonny Terry in movie sound track for *Buck and the Preacher*. One of the most respected and tasteful freelance drummers on LA scene.

LPs: w. Hampton Hawes (Contemporary, Vault); Harold Land (Contemp., Mainstream); Blue Mitchell (Mainstream); Dave Frishberg (Seeds); Mundell Lowe (Famous Door).

BAILEY, PEARL,* *singer*; b. Newport News, Va., 3/29/18. The former dancer and one time Cootie Williams orch. vocalist began her career as a prominent stage performer in *St. Louis Woman*, 1946. Married Louie Bellson, '52. Many other shows, Las Vegas appearances etc. Acclaimed for her performance in *Hello Dolly* on Broadway in '67-9. Own TV series on ABC, '70. Several movies over the years incl. *Porgy and Bess; Carmen Jones; That Certain Feeling; All The Fine Young Cannibals*. Sang at Concord Jazz Fest., '74. LPs: *Pearl's Pearls* (RCA). Many others on Roulette.

BAKER, CHESNEY H. (CHET),* *trumpet, fluegelhorn, singer*; b. Yale, Okla., 12/23/29. Came to fame w. Gerry Mulligan Quartet 1952-3. From '59-64 was in Europe, where he was in frequent trouble with the law due to narcotics problems. Baker then lived in NYC and LA until 1968; then, in SF, he was the victim of a beating by hoodlums, suffering severe injuries that included the loss of his teeth. For two years he stopped playing. Controlling his dope addiction through the use of methadone, he made a slow comeback, gigging in New York '74-5 and returning to prominence on records through his own album and a reunion concert w. Mulligan. According to John S. Wilson, Baker in 1974 had developed "more range and assertiveness within the wistfully ruminative style with which he has always been associated."

LPs: Mulligan-Baker Carnegie Hall Concert, vols. 1 & 2; *She Was Too Good To Me*; w. Jim Hall, *Concierto* (CTI); *Comin' On; Groovin'; Smokin'* (Prestige); *Baker's Holiday* (Trip).

BAKER, DAVID NATHANIEL,* *cello, composer, educator*; also *trombone, piano, bass*; b. Indianapolis, Ind., 12/21/31. Played w. Kenton; M. Ferguson in '50s; Q. Jones; G. Russell in '60s: all as trombonist. Problems w.

his jaw forced him to switch to cello in '62 but in the '70s he was playing both instruments. Teaching at Indiana U. from '66; active as teacher, clinician, lecturer at univs. throughout the US; National Stage Band Camps. Headed Newport Educational Series for Rutgers U., '72-5. As cellist, pl. at Radio City Jam Session, NJF-NY '73. An educator who is able to combine the theoretical with the practicality of experience.

Comp: *Sonata for Cello and Piano*, rec. by Janos Starker (Col.); *Le Chat Qui Peche, A suite for Orchestra, Jazz Quartet and Soprano*, rec. by Louisville Symph., Jamey Aebersold and Linda Anderson (First Edition); *Levels, for Solo Bass Viol, Jazz Band, String Quartet, Flute Quartet and Horn Quartet* perf. by Bernard Turetzky and nominated for Pulitzer Prize; *The Soul of '76 for Jazz Band*, commissioned by J.C. Penney for the Bicentennial, the music and a record given to every high school in the US by the company; *Black American Cantata*, presented annually by Voice of America on death anny. of M.L. King.

Hundreds of pieces for jazz ensemble and big band publ. by *down beat*; for string orch. publ. by William Lewis & Sons; jazz rock series publ: (New Sounds in Modern Music, 315 W. 53rd St., NYC). Chairman, NEA '74.

Comps. for NET series, *Black Frontier*; for NET series, *The Trial of Captain Henry Flipper*; *Son Mar*, theme music for *Black Experience*, WTTV, Indianapolis.

Textbook publ: *Developing Improvisational Technique, Based on the Lydian Concept; Dev. Improv. Facility with the II, V, VII Progression; Dev. Improv. Facility with the Turnback; Arr. & Comp. for the Small Ensemble; Jazz Improv.; Jazz Styles & Analysis—Trombone; Contemporary Techniques for the Trombone: A Revolutionary Approach to Dealing with the Problems of Music in the 20th Century; Advanced Jazz Improvisation*, (*down beat* Workshop Publs., 222 West Adams St., Chi., Ill. 60606). Contributed over 100 transcribed solos of various recordings by jazzmen for *down beat*.

Books in Progress: *Black Music Now, A Source Book for the 20th Century* (Kent State); *A History of Jazz* (Prentice-Hall); *Contemporary Black Music* (Harper and Row).

LPs: *Black America* (Univ. of Illinois Press); *Concerto for Violin & Jazz Band; Concerto for Flute & Jazz Band* (Coronet); cello w. Nathan Davis; trombone w. Toots Thielemans, *The Big Time* (Segue); bass trombone w. Bill Evans-George Russell, *Living Time* (Col.); trombone w. Russell (Mile.).

BAKER, PETER (GINGER), *drums*; b. Lewisham, England, 8/19/40. As young boy in London, pl. dr. while in secondary school during early 1950s, and was attracted to blues and jazz. First pro. jobs in '56. In early '60s perf. w. Alexis Korner and Graham Bond gps. Formed Cream in '66 w. Eric Clapton and Jack Bruce. This gp. won gold awards for all its albums; disbanded '68. In '69, w. Clapton, Stevie Winwood and Rick Grech, formed Blind Faith; pl. concerts throughout U.K. and U.S. In '70, on breakup of Blind Faith, Baker organized Air Force, which pl. Afro-jazz flavored music.

Baker's first idol was Baby Dodds; his style developed from trad. through dance bands to bebop and thence to blues-rock. His recent African-inspired sound was much admired by many African musicians, such as Guy Warren and the Ghanaian broadcaster and percussionist Michael Eghan, who said of Baker: "He's the most African sounding drummer in Europe." However, Elvin Jones, on hearing Baker's solo in *Do What You Like*, said: "Nothing happening. Cat's got delusions of grandeur with no grounds. They should make him an astronaut and lose his ass." LPs: w. Cream, *Heavy Cream; Off The Top* (Poly.).

BAKER, KENNETH (KENNY),* trumpet; b. Withersnea, Yorks., England, 3/1/21. Pro. debut in London, '39. In recent years, studio work w. J. Parnell; occ. quartet gigs on BBC Jazz Club. Rec. recreations of swing era hits under the late Ted Heath's name. Max Jones observed in '75 that "the years have not diminished Baker's fire or technical fluency. He has maintained the highest musical standards and his enthusiasm for jazz in the mainstream idiom."

LP: *Sensational Trumpet of Kenny Baker* (Decca).

BAKER, HAROLD J. (SHORTY),* trumpet; b. St. Louis, Mo., 5/26/14. Gained early fame with Fate Marable, Erskine Tate, Don Redman in '30s. Teddy Wilson, Andy Kirk, Mary Lou Williams (his wife), '40s; Ellington, '30s, '40s and '50s. Freelanced in NYC until illness sidelined him. After undergoing surgery in '65, returned to work, but died of cancer 11/8/66 in NYC.

BALABAN, LEONARD J. (RED), bass; also *singer, tuba, tenor guitar, banjo*; b. Chicago, Ill., 12/22/29. Father, Barney Balaban, headed the famed theatre chain Balaban & Katz. Stud. informally: tuba w. Wm. Cramer at Florida State U. '66-7; bass w. Milt Beisiegel of New Haven Symph., '71-3. From '55-67 pl. w. dance bands in Fla.; own gps. under name Balaban & Cats from '50s. Also in cattle business in Fla., '62-7. Moved to NYC '67, working off and on w. Wild Bill Davison from that time. Also pl w. Max Kaminsky; Blues Alley, Wash., D.C. w. Tony Parenti, '72; gig w. Dukes of Dixieland, '74. Balaban & Cats app. regularly on Sundays at Your Father's Mustache, '70-2 and throughout the NY, NJ, Conn. area '70-5. In '75 Balaban purchased a club at 144 W. 54th Street and opened it in March as Eddie Condon's, w. Balaban & Cats as the house band. Regular members incl. Herb Hall, Vic Dickenson and El Polcer. From '70 many musicians have been hired by Balaban to augment the Cats from time to time, among them Ruby Braff, Bobby Hackett, Al Cohn, Zoot Sims, Budd Johnson, Teddy Wilson, Gene Krupa and Condon.

Infl: Louis Armstrong, Wellman Braud, Bob Casey, Bing Crosby, Freddie Green, Condon, Singleton Palmer. Fest: NJF-NY '75 for Hudson River boatride. LP: *A Night at the New Eddie Condon's* (Classic Jazz); *Bits and Pieces of Balaban & Cats; A Night at the Town House* (Balaban & Cats).

BALES, BURTON F. (BURT),* piano, singer; b. Stevensville, Mont., 3/20/16. Worked w. many trad. groups from early '40s incl. Lu Watters, Bunk Johnson, Turk Murphy. Based in SF, he pl. at Pier 23 as solo pianist from '54-66. In '66 he went to electronics school, graduating in '69 as electronic technician. Returned to active performing in '75, pl. mainly solo. Bales, who had a band at the first MJF in '58, and returned there the following year, acc. Lizzie Miles, is feat. in a solo LP, released in '75 on Euphonic Records, from tapes made in the mid-50s.

BARBARIN, PAUL,* drums; b. New Orleans, La., 5/5/01. Early work w. Luis Russell, Amos White, Fats Pichon, King Oliver. Toured w. L. Armstrong in '30s. In '55 Barbarin formed his own band app. in NYC, LA and other major U.S. cities. It was while leading this group known as Onward Brass Band in the Proteus Carnival parade (the prelude to the Mardi Gras festival) in New Orleans, that he collapsed and died of a heart attack, 2/10/69.

BARBER, JOHN WILLIAM (BILL),* tuba; b. Hornell, N.Y., 5/21/20. A member of the Claude Thornhill orchestra of the late '40s and the original Miles Davis nonet which made the historic "Birth of the Cool" sessions, Barber has been teaching instrumental music in the Long Island public school system from 1960. Plays summers with the Goldman Band and many free-lance jobs incl. concerts, commercials, brass ensembles, banjo bands and German festivals. Also active as a clinician, for events like the New York Brass Conference For Scholarships Jan. '75. LPs w. Miles Davis (Cap., Col.), Gil Evans (Wor. Pac., Imp.).

BARBER, DONALD CHRISTOPHER (CHRIS),* trombone, leader; b. London, England, 4/17/30. Made seven tours of U.S. in early '60s. Still active since then, but no longer prominent in U.S.

BARBIERI, LEANDRO J., (GATO),* tenor sax, composer; b. Rosario, Argentina, 11/28/34. Uncle pl. tenor sax. Gato first attracted to jazz by Charlie Parker record. Stud. at Infancia Desvalida, Rosario, 1944; clarinet for five years with private teacher in Buenos Aires, where his family moved; also stud. alto sax, composition. Pl. in Lalo Schifrin's orch., '53. At age 20 took up tenor sax.

After several years of prominence in Buenos Aires, Barbieri spent seven months in Brazil; then, in '62, he and his Italian-born wife left for Rome, where his reputation as a jazzman grew rapidly. He played with Ted Curson and Jim Hall, met Don Cherry in Paris, '65, and was closely associated with him during next two years. In '65, at Cherry's urging, he went to New York for the first time and recorded *Complete Communion* with Cherry. Around the same time, he came under the influence of movie makers, notably Bernardo Bertolucci and Gianni Amico, sketching some music for the latter's *Notes for a Film on Jazz*.

Gradually Barbieri became aware of the need to blend his freedom as a jazz musician with his South American roots. He began listening to authentic tango music and expressed himself in a new and more provocative manner. In Nov. '69 he recorded *The Third World*, his first American LP as a leader, for Flying Dutchman. Soon afterward, he returned to Argentina to extend his experiments in the cross-fertilization of idioms.

During the early '70s Barbieri was firmly established as a major new voice, traveling internationally. In '72 he won the DB poll (TDWR), made his first app. at the NJF, and composed sound track for the film *Last Tango In Paris*, which won him a Grammy award. He also appeared briefly in the movie.

Among his other fest. apps. were Montreux, '71, '73, Bologna, '65, '74, Newport, '73, 74. Barbieri's most personal characteristics are a driving, impassioned style and grainy tone that gave his sound immediate identification. Nat Hentoff has attested to "The life-affirming, surging spirit of his performances, with their supple range of colors, rhythms, soaring melodies . . . Gato, in sum, is among the least abstract of musicians, because he is so explosively, specifically alive." The qualities of his work, both as instrumentalist and composer, were best set in context from 1973, when he began recording and touring with a newly assembled group of S. American musicians, mainly from Argentina and Brazil. Some critics felt that by '74 he was weakening his artistic potential by pursuing a course more like an aspiring pop-star.

LPs: *The Third World; Fenix; El Pampero* (recorded live at Montreux Festival); *Under Fire; The Legend of Gato Barbieri; Bolivia* (w. Lonnie Liston Smith); *Yesterdays* (Flying Dutchman); *Last Tango In Paris* (United Artists); *Chapter One: Latin America; Chapter Two: Hasta Siempre; Chapter Three: Viva Emiliano Zapata* (Impulse).

BAREFIELD, EDWARD EMANUEL (EDDIE),* *clarinet, saxes, composer*; b. Scandia, Iowa, 12/12/09. Major association w. Cab Calloway from '34 as player, arranger, musical director. Broadway pit band work in '60s. Pl. in Jazz Giants '67; toured w. own band in Africa, summer '69; w. Saints & Sinners in Europe later that year. Heading up rehearsal bands for Local 802. Concert w. own gp. at NY Jazz Museum, '74; gigs at Seafood Playhouse, summer '75. LPs: in *Swing Today* series (Brit. RCA); *Eddie Barefield's Bearcats* (Major-Minor).

BARKER, DANIEL (DANNY),* *guitar, banjo*; b. New Orleans, La., 1/13/09. Played w. James P. Johnson, Cab Calloway, Benny Carter during big band era. After freelancing in NYC in early '60s, returned to NO '65. A Grand Marshall for the NO Jazzfest '69, he led the Congo Square Brass Band in street parade. In '70s pl. on Bourbon St.; leading and coaching Fairview Baptist Church Christian Brass Band. Co-authored book w. Jack Buerkle, *Bourbon Street Black* (see bibliography).

BARNES, GEORGE,* *guitar*; b. Chicago Heights, Ill., 7/17/21. After Carl Kress' death in June '65, ended their duo, Barnes freelanced until he formed a new guitar team w. Bucky Pizzarelli, which endured from '69-'72. In '73 Barnes and cornetist Ruby Braff debuted their quartet at the NJF-NY, and app. at fests. in the U.S. and Europe.

Concert tour w. T. Bennett, '73-4; also TV app. w. Bennett. The Barnes-Braff quartet was voted best new group of the year by *Hi-Fidelity* mag., '75 but disbanded during that summer. Comps: *Something Tender; Suite For Octette; It's Like The Fourth of July; Frolic for Basses*. Barnes and his daughter, Alexandra, are collaborators in song. Publs: *The George Barnes Guitar Method* (Wm. J. Smith); *How To Play The Guitar* (Music Minus One, 43 W. 61st St., NYC); *The Great George Barnes Guitar Course*, Cassette & LP (Prentice-Hall, Nat. Inst. of Ed., 24 Rope Ferry Rd., Waterford, Conn.); *How to Arrange for the Guitar* (Peer International, 1740 B'way, NYC 10019).

LPs: *Guitars Pure and Honest*, w. Pizzarelli (Mercury); *Swing Guitars*, w. G. Barnes quartet (Famous Door); w. Braff-Barnes Quartet: *Carnegie Hall Concert* (Chiaroscuro); *Play George Gershwin; Play Rodgers and Hart* (Concord); *To Fred Astaire, With Love* (RCA).

BARNET, CHARLES DALY (CHARLIE),* *saxophones, leader, composer*; b. NYC, 10/26/13. Greatest years as bandleader 1939-45, with style often inspired by Ellington. Semi-retired in later years, but assembled a band that appeared in Hollywood, Las Vegas and New York, winter of '66-7. Taped hour-long TV concert in color and stereo, '67, still unreleased in '75.

Festivals: NJF, '69; Canadian Exposition, Toronto, '72. Led band at Disneyland, '72. Early LPs reissued on RCA; '67 band on Vault available through Creative World Inc.

BARONE, GARY, *trumpet, fluegelhorn, drums*; b. Detroit, Mich., 12/12/41. Father, Joe Barone, pl. tpt. w. Bob Crosby; brother, Mike, is trombonist. BA from Mich. State U. 1964; San Fernando Valley State Coll. '65-7. During latter period, also pl. w. Stan Kenton, and w. LA Neophonic '66. Gigs with Gerald Wilson, '68-9; Bud Shank, '69; Shelly Manne, '69-73; Mike Barone, '67-70; Frank Zappa, '72; Willie Bobo, '74- ; Frank Strazzeri et al. TV and movie rec. w. L. Schifrin, D. Grusin, Tom Scott. LPs w. Kenton-LA Neophonic (Cap.); w. Manne, *Outside; Alive in London* (Contemp.); *Mannekind* (Mainstream).

BARONE, MICHAEL (MIKE), *trombone, composer*; b. Detroit, Mich., 12/27/36. Raised in Cleveland. Stud. w. father, also w. musicians in Cleve. Symph. & NY Phil. Some guitar and Schillinger studies. Army 1956-9; in West Point Band; to Europe, where he led service band. Settled in LA late '59, working w. Si Zentner, Louie Bellson, and for several years off and on w. Gerald Wilson. Studio work w. L. Schifrin, D. Grusin, Tom Scott; wrote theme music w. Chuck Barris for several daytime TV series, also comp. TV commercials and numerous jazz-oriented arrs. for *Tonight Show* band.

In 1967 Barone led the first big band to play at Donte's, gigging there occasionally through 1970. In 1970s he became more active as comp.-arr. His *Breakthrough* was rec. by Bellson in LP of that name; *Spirit of '76* rec. by Emil Richards; *Just Messin' Around* by Tom Scott. Many stage band arrs. for schools, publ.

by (Mike Barone Music, Box 35216, Los Angeles, Calif. 90035).

LPs: In late '60s Barone and F. Rosolino were assoc. with a series of LPs for Liberty under the name *Trombones Unlimited.*

BARRON, WILLIAM JR. (BILL),* *tenor, soprano saxophones, flute, composer, educator;* b. Philadelphia, Pa., 3/27/27. Active in NYC w. Cecil Taylor; Philly Joe Jones; Ted Curson in late '50s and first half of '60s. In '70s led own quartet and also app. w. brother, Kenny, in Barron Brothers gp. From '68-74, however, main occupation was Director of Jazz Workshop at MUSE (Bedford Lincoln Neighborhood Museum operated by the Brooklyn Children's Museum); presented bi-monthly concert series; taught improvisation, composing, arranging, theory and reeds; directed and wrote for the small ensemble and big band; initiated and moderated *The Anthology of Black Classical Music* on radio station WNYC. During the spring term '74 he was an Adjunct Associate Professor at City Coll., CUNY, teaching *Improvisation Using Embellishments.* From Sept. '75, Assistant Professor of Music and Dir. of Afro-American Music at Wesleyan U.; co-ordinator of Jazz Workshop at NEW MUSE (the Community Museum of Brooklyn). Holds a BA in Comp., Combs Coll. of Mus., Phila.; Doctorate in Education from U. of Mass. at Amherst. Participated in National Conf. of Black American Mus. (part of "Black Expo"), Chicago '71. Panelist on music theory for CBA Symposium '72. Fest: Kongsberg w. Y. Lateef, '66; *An Academy of Improvisation* at NJF-NY; *First Music Awakening* workshops, Kingsborough Community Coll.; U. of Mass., '74. TV: interview, *Inside Bedford Stuyvesant,* WNET, '70; w. T. Curson, WNET, '72. Received comp. grant from National Endowment. Comps: *Ode to An Earthgirl; Motivation; Hold Back Tomorrow.* LPs: *Motivation* (Savoy); w. C. Mingus, *Mingus Revisited* (Trip).

BARRON, KENNETH (KENNY),* *piano, composer, educator;* also *bass, tuba;* b. Philadelphia, Pa., 6/9/43. Played w. James Moody, Roy Haynes in early '60s; then w. Dizzy Gillespie, '62-6. In '66-70, worked w. Freddie Hubbard; Jimmy Owens; as accompanist for singer Esther Marrow; and w. Stanley Turrentine at Minton's. From '70 a regular member of the Yusef Lateef quartet, also working intermittently w. Milt Jackson; Jimmy Heath; gigs w. Stan Getz, '74; Buddy Rich in small gp. at Buddy's Place, '75. Taught piano at Jazzmobile Workshop, NYC, '72-3. From '73 full-time instructor at Rutgers Univ., Livingston campus, teaching theory, keyboard harmony, piano. ". . . Barron is a pormanteau pianist," wrote Neil Tesser, "summing and summoning up in one style a highly accurate picture of what has gone before, and where it has all led."

TV: *Positively Black,* NBC, w. Lateef; Ron Carter; *Like It Is,* ABC, w. E. Marrow. Fest: Bologna; Kongsberg w. Lateef, '73; Newport, R.I. w. Getz, '75. Comp: *Peruvian Blue; The Procession; Two Areas; In the Meantime; Dreams; Morning Glory; Revelation; A Flower;* *Sunset; Dawn; Swamp Demon; Delores Street.*

LPs: *Peruvian Blue; Sunset to Dawn;* w. Albert Heath, *Kwanza;* w. Moody, *Feelin' It Together* (Muse); w. G. Benson, *Bad Benson* (CTI); w. Joe Henderson, *Tetragon; The Kicker* (Mile.); w. Jimmy Heath. *The Gap Sealer* (Cobble.); w. Hubbard, *High Blues Pressure;* w. Owens-Barron, *You Had Better Listen* (Atl.); w. Rich (Groove Merchant); w. Lateef (Atl.).

BARTKOWSKI, CZESLAW, *drums;* also *piano, percussion;* b. Lodz, Poland, 4/19/43. Att. music coll. in Wroctaw, Poland. Worked w. Krzysztof Komeda quintet, '63-5; Zbigniew Namyslowski quartet, '63-6; Czeslaw Niemen Enigmatic, '68-70; Michal Urbaniak, '71-4; trio w. Wojciech Karolak & Namyslowski, '73-4. In '74 he became part of Namyslowski's new quintet. He also performed in a trio w. Tomasz Stanko & Adam Makowicz, formed in '75 and continued to be part of the Polish Jazz Radio big band which he first joined in '73. Fests: all major European events; also Tauranga (New Zealand). NJF-NY w. Urbaniak; Cascais (Portugal) w. Namyslowski quintet, '74. Comp: *Suggestion; Blues,* rec. by Makowicz in *Unit* on Muza. LPs: own album for Muza; *Unit* w. Makowicz; *Mainstem* w. Jan Wroblewski (Muza); w. Namyslowski, *Lola* (Decca); w. Urbaniak, *Inactin; Paratyphus B* (Intercord); *Super Constellation* (CBS); *Fusion; Atma* (Col.).

BARTZ, GARY LEE, *saxophones, composer, singer;* b. Baltimore, Md., 9/26/40. Father ran local jazz club where Bartz pl. as teenager. Acquired an alto sax at 11. At 17, went to NYC, studied at Juilliard for three semesters, jammed w. F. Hubbard, L. Morgan, P. Sanders. Back in Baltimore, stud. at Peabody Cons. Professional debut w. Max Roach-Abbey Lincoln group, followed by a stint w. Art Blakey, '65-6. Worked w. Roach again, '68-9, also w. McCoy Tyner and Blue Mitchell during same period. Originally org. his own combo known as Ntu Troop (the word means the unification of all things spiritual and physical, in the Bantu philosophy) in '69 and began making a series of recordings with this unit, but joined Miles Davis in Aug. '70 and remained with him through late '71.

In his notes to an early album cut by Bartz in 1967, Orrin Keepnews observed: "This is, at its core, melodic jazz; and it is basically happy music. There is much complexity and thought here; but there is also a distinct feeling of pleasure." He noted that Louis Jordan and Sonny Rollins were among Bartz's early influences. Bartz, however, in a statement some years later, after the rise of the Ntu Troop to international popularity, declared that he was not playing jazz, but American music, adding that "I'm trying to decategorize things with and about myself."

In addition to traveling with the group and appearing at major festivals, Bartz was involved in such outside ventures as the writing of theme and score for an ABC-TV special, *About Time,* aired in late '72. Though he has done much of his best work on alto and soprano saxes, Bartz also has been heard on records playing sopranino sax, electric piano, percussion, and singing. His reputation as a creative artist and writer grew with the release, in 1974, of the *Singerella* album (see below). He has app. at many fests. incl. Kongsberg, '73; Montreux, '73; Berkeley, '74. Won DB and Melody Maker polls on alto sax, '72.

LPs: *Libra; Another Earth; Harlem Bush Music-Taifa; Harlem Bush Music—Uhuru; Home* (Milestone); *Follow The Medicine Man; I've Known Rivers* (live at Montreux); *Ju-Ju Street Songs; Singerella—A Ghetto Fairytale* (Prest.); w. Davis, *Live-Evil* (Col.).

BASCOMB, WILBUR ODELL (DUD), * trumpet; b. Birmingham, Ala., 5/16/16. The featured trumpet soloist with the Erskine Hawkins orchestra of the 30's and 40's was occupied as a busy free-lancer during the 60's and early 70's until his death, 12/25/72, NYC. Played in off-Broadway production *Cindy* '66; pit orch. for *Purlie* '70. Concerts and European tours w. Buddy Tate '68, '70. Led own sextet for gig in Toronto '68. Played on sound tracks for *It's A Mad, Mad, Mad World; Midnight Cowboy; Legend of Nigger Charlie.* His son, bassist, Wilbur Jr., worked with him and also was with the Billy Taylor band on the David Frost TV show '72.

LPs: *Unbroken* w. Buddy Tate (MPS), Erskine Hawkins Reunion (Stang).

BASIE, WILLIAM (COUNT), * leader, piano, organ, composer; b. Red Bank, N.J., 8/21/04. A bandleader since '35, when he was discovered in Kansas City by John Hammond, Basie during the '60s and '70s broadened his popularity by rec. and appearing in concerts with such singers as F. Sinatra and T. Bennett. During these years the band's personnel changed more frequently than it had in the past. In '69, it comprised Gene Goe, Sonny Cohn, Al Aarons, Oscar Brashear, trumpets; Bill Hughes, Grover Mitchell, Richard Boone, Frank Hooks, trombones; Marshal Royal, Bobby Plater, Eddie Davis, Eric Dixon, Charlie Fowlkes, saxophones; Freddie Green, guitar; Norman Keenan, bass; Harold Jones, drums. Within the next couple of years most of these musicians had left the band, though some, incl. Fowlkes, Hughes and Dixon, returned after absences of varying lengths. Green was the only sideman who had remained with Basie almost continuously since the late '30s.

An important development was the addition to Basie's arr. staff of Sammy Nestico (q.v.), whose original comps. formed the basis for several of the orchestra's most musically interesting albums. An unusual venture was the band's tentative attempt to incorporate avant garde and other unconventional elements in the album *Afrique*, rec. in late '70 w. O. Nelson as arr. and conductor. On this occasion, the band was augmented by Hubert Laws on flute, Buddy Lucas on harmonica and John B. Williams on elect. bass. The title tune was Basie's first and only rec. in 7/4 time.

Beginning in early '70, the band made a series of annual cruises on the Queen Elizabeth II, and additionally took part in a Caribbean cruise, Showboat 2, aboard the Rotterdam, Dec. '74. In '75, after freelancing for many years on a variety of labels, Basie began rec. regularly for Norman Granz's Pablo Records. The result was a collection of LPs that showed him in several different and challenging settings, in sharp contrast to the uninspired pairings with such artists as the Mills Bros. and various other singers, vocal groups etc. that had marked too much of his LP activity for several years. The personnel in late '75 comprised: Pete Minger, Frank Szabo, Dave Stahl, Bobby Mitchell, Sonny Cohn, trumpets; Al Grey, Curtis Fuller, Bill Hughes, Mel Wanzo, trombones; Danny Turner, Bobby Plater, altos; Jimmy Forrest, tenor; Eric Dixon, tenor & flute; Charlie Fowlkes, baritone; Freedie Green, guitar; John Duke, bass; Butch Miles, drums.

In '74, Basie's 70th birthday was celebrated in a banquet attended by many of his friends and old associates, at the Waldorf-Astoria Hotel, NYC. In the fall of '75 the orch. took part in concerts w. F. Sinatra at the Uris Theatre, NYC, Palladium, London. In recent years, Basie has made his home in Freeport, Bahamas.

LPs: *Basie Big Band; Satch & Josh,* w. O. Peterson; *For The First Time* w. Basie Trio; *Basie Jam* w. H. Edison, Z. Sims, Eddie Davis, J.J. Johnson et al; *Basie Jam Session at the Montreux Jazz Festival, '75* w. R. Eldridge, L. Bellson, Milt Jackson, Johnny Griffin, Niels-Henning Orsted Pedersen et al (Pablo); *Afrique* (Fl. Dutchman); *Basic Basie* (MPS); *Basie's In The Bag* (Bruns.); *Best of; Echoes of an Era; Echoes of an Era, Vocal Years; Fantail; Kansas City Suite/Easin' It; Kid From Red Bank*; w. Eckstine; w. Vaughan (Roulette); *Board of Directors,* w. Mills Bros; *Standing Ovation; Straight Ahead* (Dot); *Broadway Basie's Way* (Com.); *Hits of 50s and 60s* (Repr.); *Kansas City 7* (Imp.); *Meets Bond* (Solid); *Newport Years*; w. J. Williams (Verve); *16 Great Perf.* w. Mills Bros (ABC); *Songs of Bessie Smith,* w. Teresa Brewer (Fl. Dutchman).

BASS, LEE ODDIS III (MICKEY), *bass, composer; also piano, brass, flute;* b. Pittsburgh, Pa., 5/2/43. Mother was a singer; grandmother, a piano teacher, taught him and cousins barbershop harmony. Studied bass in high school and privately w. William Lewis for several years in Pitts. Pl. in All City High School orch. Attended Howard U., Coll. of Fine Arts, 1961-3, majoring in Music Ed.; NYU, '67-8. First job in NYC w. Hank Mobley at Theresa Hotel, '64; then worked w. Bennie Green at Birdland; briefly w. Jackie McLean; Art Blakey; Sonny Rollins. With Bobby Timmons, '65; Gloria Lynne from '65 for three yrs; Blakey; Carmen McRae, '67; Gloria Lynne, '68; Billy Eckstine, '68-9; Blakey, '70; Freddie Freddie Hubbard; Miriam Makeba; Blakey again. Teaches bass and jazz improvisational technique at High School of the Arts, Wash., D.C.; and for Jazzmobile in NYC. Own group on Sundays at Doctor Generosity's; also w. Duke Jordan at Churchill's, NYC, '76. Own weekly record show on WBAI-FM. Infl: C. Parker, M. Davis, J. Coltrane. TV: Today w. Frank Foster; NBC Special for National Council of Churches w. David Amram; Billy Eckstine Show w. F. Hubbard; American and Japanese apps. w. Blakey. Fests: NJF-NY w. Hubbard, '71; Blakey, '73. Comps: *Sweat; A Chant Bu; One For Trane; Mickey's Tune; Meditations; Gayle's Groove; Soul Sock 'N Jamboree; Siempre Me Amor.* Wrote arrs. for NYU Stage Band; Jaki Byard's big band. Composing jazz string quartet, '76. LPs: w. Blakey, *Buhaina; Anthenagin* (Prest.); w. Curtis Fuller, *Smokin'* (Main.).

BASSO, GIANNI,* *tenor saxophone;* b. Asti, Italy, 5/24/31. Educ. Conservatorio di Asti. Frequent partnership w. Oscar Valdambrini from '50s. Worked with many visiting leaders in Italy, incl. M. Ferguson, D. Goykovich, Slide Hampton, C. Baker, P. Woods, K. Clarke, Sal Nistico, G. Mulligan, F. Rosolino, B. Collette, C. Candoli, Lars Gullin. Film: *La Prima Notte di Quiete* w. Ferguson. Numerous jazz fests. throughout Europe. LPs: w. own group; eight w. Valdambrini; others with S. Hampton, Baker, Collette, Rosolino.

BAYETÉ (Todd Cochran), *piano, keyboards, composer;* b. San Francisco, Cal., 9/3/51. Began playing at three; priv. studies from age six. During high school was enrolled in corresp. course from Trinity College, England, obtaining B.M. in '70 after eight years of study. Additional educ. under a scholarship at San Jose State U. Bayeté was only 17 when he began working w. John Handy, remaining with the group for about a year. He spent most of the next two years w. B. Hutcherson and H. Land, leaving their group to form his own combo. He also did sound track work w. Herbie Hancock.

Bayeté made an immediate impression both as pianist and composer in the Hutcherson-Land album *Head On.* His strong keyboard style suggested a McCoy Tyner influence, and his compositions were fresh and texturally original. Evaluating his music, he said: "It involves contemporary harmonic and basic ethnic rhythms, and it calls for an understanding of the Afro-American experience." He was inspired by Hutcherson, with whom, he said, he felt his closest and most spiritual relationship, and was also infl. by William Fischer.

Fests: Concord, Berkeley, and a tribute to Miles Davis at MJF. LPs: *Seeking Other Beauty; Worlds Around The Sun* (Pres.) *Iapetus* w. Hadley Caliman (Mainstream); *Head On* w. Hutcherson (Blue Note).

BEAL, EDDIE,* *piano, composer;* b. Redlands, Cal., 6/13/10. Best known as songwriter, talent scout and vocal coach. To Viet Nam with Christy Minstrels, '69. Two road tours as pianist/conductor for L. Rawls, '70. Own gp. Playboy Club, Century City, '73, and Desert Inn, LV, '74. In Dec. '74 and Jan. '75, he was feat. pianist in concert w. T. Dorsey band under direction of M. McEachern, pl. throughout Florida and other southern states. Also went on a Sitmar cruise with the orch. Film: App. as pianist in *Sparkle.* TV: *Sanford & Son.* Best known comps: *Softly,* rec. by Georgia Carr, S. Kenton; *All Because of You,* rec. by Kenton, D. Washington; *Skoot* (written with E. Garner), rec. by Kenton, MJQ; *Let Your Love Walk In,* rec. by Kenton.

BEAN, FLOYD R.,* *piano, composer;* b. Ladora, Iowa, 8/30/04. Played w. Bix Beiderbecke in Davenport, '23;

later w. Bunny Berigan; Jack Jenney as sidemen in various bands. In '30s and '40s w. Bob Crosby; Boyd Raeburn; Sidney Bechet. In '50s w. Muggsy Spanier, Georg Brunis in Chicago. Cont. to pl. in Chi. until '64 when he moved to Cedar Rapids, Iowa where he died 3/9/74.

BECK, GORDON, *piano, electric piano, composer;* b. London, England, 9/16/36. Three years classical piano tuition from age 12-15. Began prof. career in 1961; names Ch. Parker, B. Powell, B. Evans, H. Hancock, P. Woods, Delius, Ravel as infls. From '62-66 w. groups of Tony Kinsey, Tubby Hayes; acc. Annie Ross. In '69 own trio backed Helen Merrill, Joe Henderson, Lee Konitz, Phil Woods et al at Ronnie Scott Club. From '69-72 extensive touring of Europe and U.S. w. P. Woods quartet with whom he app. at NJF, '71. Other jazz fests in Montreux and throughout Europe. In '73 was member of Piano Conclave. In '73-75 own group "Gyroscope."

Several of Beck's comps. have been recorded, incl. *The Day When The World Comes Alive,* Cleo Laine (RCA); *Here Comes The Mallet Man; Tying Up Loose Ends,* Gary Burton (Polydor); *The Meeting,* P. Woods (Embryo). Other comps. include a suite for seven piece orch. for BBC radio.

BECK, JOE, *guitar;* b. Phila., Pa., 7/29/45. First professional work with Paul Winter, '64; Charles Lloyd, '64; Gary McFarland, 64-6; Chico Hamilton, '67; Gil Evans, '67-70. Left the music business in '71 to become a dairy farmer; returned to New York and musical activity '73. Beck has also worked with Peggy Lee, Lena Horne, Gene Ammons, Jimmy Smith, Maynard Ferguson, Buddy Rich, Woody Herman, Joe Farrell. LPs: *Joe Beck* (Kudu); *Penny Arcade; Upon This Rock,* w. Farrell (CTI); tracks in *The Guitar Album,* rec. live at Town Hall Concert, Aug. '71 (Col.); w. David Sanborn (WB).

BECKERHOFF, ULI, *trumpet, fluegelhorn, piano;* b. Muenster, W. Germany, 12/6/47. Began playing in high school. Stud. in Muenster and Cologne, also w. Manfred Schoof, '68-70, and others. Pl. with several big bands in Bremen, Dortmund, Cologne. From '72 worked with Jazztrack Quintet. In '73 and '74 pl. at J.E. Berendt's New Jazz Meeting in Baden-Baden, with C. Mariano, A. Mangelsdorff, Marvin Peterson et al. Worked with German All Stars Globe Unity Orch., Joachim Kuhn. In '71 won first prize with an international quartet in Holland.

LP: *First Call,* w. Jazztrack Quintet.

BELL, SAMUEL, AARON,* *bass, tuba, trumpet, piano, composer;* b. Muskogee, Okla., 4/24/22. Prominent as bassist with many N.Y. groups in '50s, also Duke Ellington, '60-2. Played in pit bands. Composed for off-Broadway theatre, '69-72. Resident composer La Mama Experimental Theatre, '70-3. Asst. Prof., Essex College, Newark, N.J., '70-5 teaching theory, arr., comp. M.Ed. degree, Columbia U. May '75. Mus. Dir., Elmsford Dinner Theatre, '74-5. Pl. at NJF '73 w. Paul Jeffrey; '74 w. Corky Corcoran.

Comps: *Watergate Sonata* for piano; *Rondo Schizo* for clarinet and piano; *Frugal Fugue* for small combo. LPs:

Duke Meets Coltrane; Duke Meets the Hawk (Impulse).

BELLSON, LOUIE PAUL (**Louis Balassoni**),* *drums, composer, leader*; b. Rock Falls, Ill., 7/26/24. Drummer in many name bands incl. B. Goodman, T. Dorsey, H. James; toured w. D. Ellington, '51-3 and again '65-6. After rejoining James for a while, he organized his own Hollywood-based big band, which played together intermittently; however, he frequently fronted other bands as mus. dir. for his wife, Pearl Bailey.

As composer, his wide ranging activities included *The London Suite*, which he recorded with a specially assembled band in London; the first movement, written in collaboration with Jack Hayes, is the well known *Carnaby Street*, which was the theme for the Pearl Bailey TV show. Bellson also wrote words and music for *I Need Your Key*, sung by James Brown in a King album backed by Bellson's orch; *The Marriage Vows*, perf. at LV Jazz Fest. '62; *Symphony in Americana*, premiered by 60 piece orch. in LV; and *Composition for Piano and Orchestra*, presented in concert by a 55 piece orch. in Washington, D.C.

Universally admired and respected as a musician who combines enthusiasm and a driving beat with an astonishing technique, incl. the use of two bass drums, Bellson was described by Ellington as "The world's greatest drummer . . . Louie Bellson has all the requirements for perfection in his craft."

During '70s, has played and talked at many clinics in schools and colleges. Publs. incl. two sight reading books (Belwin Music, Inc., NYC); Method Book (Try Publ., 854 Vine St., Hollywood, CA. 90028); three drum method books (Robbins Music, NYC).

LPs: *Explosion* (Pablo); *Breakthrough* (Proj. 3); *Louie Rides Again* (Percussion Power, 5109 Nagle Ave., Sherman Oaks, Cal. 91403); w. Basie; Trumpet Kings; Oscar Peterson: all at Montreux '75 (Pablo).

BENEKE, TEX, * *tenor sax, singer, leader*; b. Fort Worth, Tex, 2/12/14. The former (1938-42) Glenn Miller soloist continued to assemble orchestras for concert and dance dates at which he played music in the Miller style. Though the band was not officially sanctioned by Miller's estate, it usually included singers and instrumentalists who had worked in the original Miller organization.

BENFORD, THOMAS P. (TOMMY),* *drums*; b. Charleston, W. Va., 4/19/05. With older brother, Bill, a noted tuba player, learned music at the Jenkins Orphanage in S. Carolina. Toured w. Orphanage band, incl. England, 1914. Several perfs. in London before World War I forced return to US. Stud. drums w. Steve and Herbert Wright. First pro. job w. Green River Minstrel Show in '20. Pl. w. Marie Lucas, Edgar Hayes, Charlie Skeet, Bill Benford, F. Waller, D. Ellington in '20s. To Europe w. Eddie South, '32 where he worked also w. Freddie Taylor, '36-7; Willie Lewis, '38-41. In US w. Noble Sissle, '43; Snub Mosley, '46-8; Bob Wilber, 48-9; Jimmy Archey, '50-2, incl. tour of Germany and Switzerland, '52. In '50s also pl. w. Rex Stewart, M. Spanier; subbed in Geo. Lewis band and pl. in house bands at

Central Plaza and Jimmy Ryan's. Worked w. Freddy Johnson, '59. To Europe w. *Jazz Train* under dir. of Eddie Barefield, '60-1. Pl. w. Joe Thomas, Edmond Hall, Danny Barker, NYC, '63, then w. Saints and Sinners. Dec. '68 w. Franz Jackson. Benford, who played w. Jelly Roll Morton in the '20s, is not active on a fulltime basis but app. w. pianist Bob Greene's World of Jelly Roll Morton recreation of the Red Hot Peppers in concert at the NJF-NY, '73, and at Alice Tully Hall, '73-4. The veteran drummer, who rec. extensively in Europe in the '30s w. South, C. Hawkins, Benny Carter and D. Reinhardt, can be heard w. Greene in *The World of Jelly Roll Morton* (RCA).

BENJAMIN, JOSEPH RUPERT (JOE),* *bass*; b. Atlantic City, N.J. 11/4/19. Veteran bassist, who pl. his first major date w. D. Ellington at a 1951 Metropolitan Opera House concert, and was intermittently associated w. Ellington over the years as copyist, sideman and employee of Ellington's publ. co. Benjamin died 1/26/74 in Livingstone, N.J., of a heart attack, some weeks after suffering injuries in an automobile accident. LP: w. Ellington, *Eastbourne Performance* (RCA).

BENNETT, MAX,* *bass*; b. Des Moines, Iowa, 5/24/28. Confined mainly to studio work in LA through '72, also with big bands led by Mike Barone, Bud Brisbois, Jack Daugherty. Became original member of Tom Scott's L.A. Express in late '72, touring throughout '74 with this group and singer Joni Mitchell. Also w. Crusaders during '73 and rec. with them. Composed songs and lyrics rec. by Peggy Lee; instr. for L.A. Express.

LPs: w. L.A. Express (A & M); *Class of '71* w. Daugherty (A & M); *Scratch* w. Crusaders (Blue Thumb).

BENNETT, TONY (**Anthony Dominick Benedetto**), *singer*; b. Queens, L.I., N.Y., 8/3/26. Discovered by Pearl Bailey and Bob Hope; began recording 1950 and was heard in series of best-selling hit singles such as *Because of You; Cold Cold Heart; Tender is the Night*. After a fallow period, Bennett's career was revived with a 1962 hit, *I Left My Heart in San Francisco*. His association with jazz has been marked by the use of such musicians as pianist John Bunch; cornetists Bobby Hackett and Ruby Braff; saxophonists Zoot Sims and Al Cohn. He recorded two albums w. Basie band in the mid-1950s and toured in concerts with Duke Ellington, Woody Herman. One of the best jazz-influenced singers in the classic pop tradition, he was heard at his best in a duo album w. Bill Evans, late '75 (Fantasy). Formed own record co., Improv, '75, planning to feature himself in a variety of pop and jazz settings. Other LPs: Columbia.

BENSON, GEORGE,* *guitar, singer*; b. Pittsburgh, Pa., 3/22/43. After three yrs. w. Jack McDuff, formed own gp. and has toured w. it from '65. His unit that rec. for Col. included Ronnie Cuber on baritone and Lonnie Smith, organ. In the '70s he became affiliated w. Creed Taylor, first at A&M Records, then w. Taylor's CTI label, in productions that surrounded the guitarist with large orchestral arrs. designed to bring him to a wider audience. Many felt that Taylor was trying to fit Benson into the slot vacated by the late Wes Montgomery. Although the albums did enjoy commercial success, Benson demonstrated that despite the format he was still his own man. He toured w. the CTI concert package, utilizing his singing both with words and in a wordless technique that he blended with his guitar. When he participated in the TV tribute to John Hammond on NET, as part of the house gp., he again showed his link to Charlie Christian especially when specifically asked to do so in accompanying Benny Goodman. Fest: NJF-NY, '73, '75. Comps: *The Shape of Things That Are and Were; Footin' It; The Borgia Stick.*

LPs: *Body Talk; White Rabbit; Bad Benson; Beyond the Blue Horizon* (CTI); *Other Side of Abbey Road; Shape of Things; Tell It Like It Is* (A&M); *Cookbook; Willow Weep For Me; Spirituals to Swing, 30th Anniversary* (Col.); *Jaki Byard With Strings* (Prest.); w. M. Davis, *Miles in the Sky* (Col.).

BERGER, KARL HANS, *piano, vibes*; also *percussion, composer*; b. Heidelberg, Germany, 3/30/35. Stud. Heidelberg Conserv., '48-54; musicology, philosophy, Univ. of Berin, '55-63; earned Ph.D., '63. Based in Paris, he worked w. Don Cherry, '65-6. Later moved to NYC, working w. Roswell Rudd, Steve Lacy, Marion Brown, David Izenzon, Horacee Arnold, Sam Rivers. School and coll. concerts through Young Audiences Inc., '67-71. Berger led his own groups off and on from '66, making several tours to Europe and Canada. Assoc. w. JCOA. Infls: J.S. Bach, Bud Powell, O. Coleman, Ing Rid (his wife, a singer).

Berger, in '71, was founder, w. Coleman, of Creative Music Foundation Inc. Dir. of Creative Music Studio, Woodstock, N.Y. and similar studio at Haropa Inst., Boulder, Colo. Comp. and leader for *Karl Berger & Friends: Music Universe.* Won DB Critics Poll, TDWR, as vibraphonist in '68, and again in '71, '74, '75. TV: many apps on German TV network and Danish TV in Copenhagen. Fests: Prague, Molde, Pori, Antibes, Frankfurt, Berlin. Publs: *Thesis on Music Ideology* (Osteuropa Institut, Berlin). Comps: *Cycles of the Birth of the New World; Space In Time; Silence in Sound; From Now On; Tune In; With Silence; We Are You.* Berger is one of the most scholarly as well as most gifted artists of the jazz-oriented avant-garde school.

LPs: *From Now On* (ESP); *Tune In* (Milest.); *With Silence* (Enja) *We Are You* (Calig.); *Peace Church Concerts* (CMC); *When Fortune Smiles,* w. J. McLaughlin, J. Surman, D. Holland (Pye); w. Cherry, *Symphony for Improvisers* (BN); *Eternal Rhythm* (MPS); w. L. Konitz, *Lee Konitz Duets* (Milest.).

BERK, RICHARD ALAN (DICK), *drums*; b. San Francisco, Cal., 5/22/39. Educ. Berklee College w. Alan Dawson, '59-60. After local work, moved to NYC, '58. Many night clubs w. Nick Brignola, Ted Curson-Bill Barron, Ch. Mingus, W. Bishop Jr., F. Hubbard, M. Allison, Monty Alexander. Moved to LA, '68; Monterey Fest. and tours w. G. Szabo, George Duke. Numerous concerts and fests. in U.S. and Europe. Regular member

of Cal Tjader quintet from '70, also gigging with Milt Jackson, Ray Brown, touring Japan with G. Auld etc. After settling in LA, took up acting; seen in play *Idiot's Delight* w. J. Lemmon, also roles in movies *Bummer; Mad Mad Movie Makers*; and TV series *Emergency.*

LPs: w. Don Friedman (Riverside); Jean-Luc Ponty (Liberty-UA); Curson (Audio-Fidelity, Atlantic, Fontana); M. Jackson (Impulse); Tjader (Fantasy).

BERK, LAWRENCE, *educator, composer, arranger, piano*; b. Boston, Mass., 12/10/08. Classmate of Harry Carney in HS. Stud. w. Joseph Schillinger, '33-9. Comp., arr. for many network radio shows. Founder and president of Berklee Coll. of Music, '45, then known as Schillinger House, now recognized as the largest independent, non-profit, accredited, degree-granting college of music in the world.

Inspired by the school's jazz-oriented curriculum were such alumni as Q. Jones, G. Burton, G. McFarland, K. Jarrett, Rick Laird, C. Mariano, A. Broadbent, Mike Gibbs, Geo Mraz, Toshiko Akiyoshi, G. Szabo, Arif Mardin, Jan Hammer, Lennie Johnson, Pat LaBarbera, Sadao Watanabe, Bill Chase, Dick Nash, J. Zawinul, Lin Biviano, M. Vitous, Steve Marcus, Yasuo Arakawa, Ernie Watts, Dusko Gojkovic, Kurt Jaernberg, Allan Ganley, Gene Cherico, Jake Hanna, Bill Berry.

In developing the scope of educational opportunities at Berklee, Berk initiated significant and innovative concepts in jazz methodology that have been acclaimed by educators throughout the world.

BERRY, WILLIAM R. (BILL),* *trumpet, fluegelhorn, vibes, composer, leader*; b. Benton Harbor, Mich., 9/14/30. Pl. w. Duke Ellington, '62. With Merv Griffin TV show band from '64 in NYC and from '70 in LA. Member of all star group at White House for Ellington's 70th birthday party, '69. Concerts and TV shows dedicated to Ellington.

In '71 Berry formed the L.A. Big Band, a West Coast equivalent of the Thad Jones-Mel Lewis orch., comprising freelance musicians, many of them alumni of Ellington, Basie, Kenton, gigging in local clubs and at Concord Summer Fest. Berry also composed a Sacred Concert for choir and jazz band presented '73. Other comps: *Betty; Bloose; A Little Song for Mex; Sho* (recorded by Bill Watrous). Grant for jazz comp. from NEA, '70.

LPs: w. Ellington (Columbia, Reprise), Jones-Lewis (UA); *Once Upon A Time* w. Earl Hines (Impulse); *Profiles* w. Gary McFarland (Impulse). Live album, *Hot and Happy,* with own band for Beez Records (23033 Bryce St., Woodland Hills, CA. 91364) in '75.

BERRY, EMMETT,* *trumpet*; b. Macon, Ga., 7/23/16. Veteran of the Fletcher and Horace Henderson bands in the '30s; Teddy Wilson, Eddie Heywood, Count Basie, etc. in '40s. Pl. w. Peanuts Hucko, '66; Wilbur DeParis, '67; Big Chief Moore, '68; Buddy Tate, '69. In the '70s he left music and retired to Cleveland, Ohio due to ill health.

BERT, EDDIE,* *trombones*; b. Yonkers, N.Y., 5/16/22. From '66 to '68 played w. Elliot Lawrence orch. for Broadway shows: *Golden Boy, Apple Tree, Golden Rain-*

bow. Member of Bobby Rosengarden orch. for Dick Cavett ABC-TV show '68-72; Thad Jones-Mel Lewis orch. '67-March '72 incl. European tours; Charles Mingus orch. March-Aug. '72. With Sy Oliver from '73; also member of NYJRC '74-75 for Carnegie Hall concerts. *Eddie Bert Trombone Method* published by (Charles Colin, 315 W. 53rd St., N.Y., N.Y. 10019).

LPs w. Jones-Lewis (Solid State, Blue Note); Mingus (Columbia); Olatunji (Paramount).

BEY, ANDREW W. JR. (**ANDY**), *singer, piano, composer*; b. Newark, N.J., 10/28/39. His sisters, Salome and Geraldine, with whom he worked for 10 years as Andy & The Bey Sisters, are still active as singers. Started playing piano by ear at three; attended Arts High School of Music & Art in Newark. Studied piano w. Sanford Gold in '65 for a year. Voice coaching from Nat Jones and Romney Fell but basically a self-taught vocalist. During early 50's appeared on TV as a "Startime Kid" with Connie Francis, etc. With Louis Jordan at Apollo Theatre '53; to Europe w. his sisters in '58 for 16 months in France, England, Germany, Spain and Belgium. Has worked and recorded with Max Roach, Gary Bartz, Horace Silver, Duke Pearson and William Fischer. Nine months as vocalist with Thad Jones-Mel Lewis in '70s. Also w. Umajo Ensemble led by Mtume. Inspired and influenced by Coltrane, Ella Fitzgerald, Miles Davis, Art Tatum, Charlie Parker, Sarah Vaughan, Billie Holiday, Nat Cole, Sonny Rollins, Aretha Franklin, Ray Charles and Dinah Washington. Comp. *Celestial Blues*, recorded w. Gary Bartz' *Uhuru* on Milestone and his own album, *Experience And Judgement*, on Atlantic. Other LPs: *Healin' Feelin'* w. Horace Silver (BN); *Children of Forever* w. Stanley Clarke (Polydor); Mtume (Strata-East).

BERTONCINI, GENE, *guitar*; b. New York City, 4/6/37. Started lessons at age nine; first job at 16. With his brother, an accordionist, pl. children's TV series. After high school, entered Notre Dame, majoring in architecture, but returned to music in NYC after graduation. Worked w. Mike Mainieri, Buddy Rich. After service in Marine Corps, was active for years in television with Merv Griffin; Skitch Henderson on the *Tonight* show, etc. Abandoned his TV career to concentrate on further studies, later becoming active in a broad variety of areas, pl. w. Metropolitan Opera Orch., acc. Tony Bennett, Morgana King, Nancy Wilson, and playing innumerable pop and jazz record dates. Characterized by Georgia Urban in *Different Drummer* as "one of the most versatile men on the instrument . . . a vital part of the jazz world . . . he is destined to become one of the most respected guitarists."

LPs w. Hubert Laws, *Rite of Spring; Afro-Classic; Carnegie Hall* (CTI); w. Clark Terry, *More* (Cameo); w. T. Bennett, *I've Gotta Be Me* (Col.); w. Nancy Wilson, *But Beautiful* (Cap.); w. Wayne Shorter, *Odyssey of Iska* (Blue Note); w. Ron Carter, *Blues Farm* (CTI); w. L. Schifrin, *Marquis de Sade* (Verve); w. Earl Coleman, *Love Songs* (Atl.).

BICKERT, EDWARD ISAAC (**ED**),* *guitar*; b. Hochfeld, Manitoba, Canada, 11/29/32. Prominent in Toronto jazz circles w. Moe Koffman, Phil Nimmons, Ron Collier in '50s, he continued to pl. w. these leaders in the '60s & '70s, also app. w. Rob McConnell's Boss Brass and acc. visiting mus. like Paul Desmond, Frank Rosolino, Ch. McPherson in clubs. Active studio man who makes many apps. on CBC-TV. Fest: Belvedere King-Size Jazz Fest., Canada, '74. Bickert's reputation is mainly local but he is highly regarded by the Americans who have pl. w. him. LPs: *Collages* (MPS); w. Desmond, *Pure Desmond* (CTI); *Moe Koffman Live at George's* (GRT); w. McConnell, *Best Damn Band in the Land* (UA).

BIGARD, LEON ALBANY (**BARNEY**),* *clarinet, composer*; b. New Orleans, 3/3/06. Best known as co-composer of *Mood Indigo*, soloist w. Ellington, '28-42, L. Armstrong '46-52, '53-5, '60-1. Occasional freelance work in LA, incl. gigs w. Rex Stewart, '66; Armstrong 70th birthday concert, '70; Dick Gibson jazz parties in Colorado, '71, 72, '73; toured colleges, high schools w. Art Hodes, Wild Bill Davison, Eddie Condon, '71. Received keys to city from Mayor of New Orleans during jazz fest. April '72. Numerous fests. in U.S. and overseas, '74-5, incl. NJF, Nice, Pescara, San Sebastian, Bordeaux. In addition to many early LPs with Armstrong, Ellington, heard more recently in *Bucket's Got A Hole In It* (Delmark); *Stars of Jazz* (Jazzology), and w. Legends of Jazz (Crescent Jazz); also own LP on French RCA. In '75, toured Switzerland with New Ragtime Jazzband; film, *Musical Biography of Barney Bigard* for presentation on French TV.

BIG MAYBELLE (**Mabel Smith**),* *singer*; b. Jackson, Tenn., 1924. Best known for her 1958 appearance at NJF and in the film *Jazz on a Summer's Day* produced at the festival, the blues singer died 1/23/72 in Cleveland, Ohio after a long illness. LPs: *The Gospel Soul of Big Maybelle* (Bruns.); *Last of Big Maybelle* (Para.).

BISHOP, WALTER JR.,* *piano, composer*; b. New York City, 10/4/27. Member of many pioneer bop groups led by Parker, M. Davis, Pettiford, T. Gibbs, Blakey. Extensive studies in late '60s w. Ida Elkan, Rudolph Schramm, Hall Overton and, after move to Cal. in 1970, w. Lyle (Spud) Murphy, Albert Harris. Gigs, recs. w. many LA combos incl. Supersax, Blue Mitchell. Taught privately, 1972-5; pl., lectured at LA colleges with own gp., "4th Cycle." Publ.: *A Study In 4ths* (Don Sickler, 254 West 44th St., New York, N.Y. 10036).

Comps: *Coral Keys* rec. by F. Hubbard; *Waltz for Sweetie* rec. by Joe Henderson; *Soul Village* rec. by B. Mitchell; *Sweet Rosa* w. own gp.

LPs: Own gps. (Black Jazz; Muse; Prestige); also w. Supersax (Cap.); Blue Mitchell (Main.); many reissues w. Ch. Parker (Verve, etc.).

BLACK ARTHUR (**Arthur Murray Blythe**), *alto, soprano saxophones, composer*; b. Los Angeles, Cal., 7/5/40. Stud. w. former J. Lunceford saxophonist Kirt Bradford; David Jackson, a tenor saxophonist and composer, who worked w. Lenny McBrowne, Ray Charles. Based in LA, he pl. w. H. Tapscott, '63-73; Owen Marshall, '67; Stanley Crouch and the Black Music Infinity, '67-73. Moving to NYC in '74, worked w. Leon Thomas, Ted Daniel and the Energy Band; Julius Hemphill; Chico Hamilton. Visited Cal. briefly w. Hamilton in summer of '75. Infls: Coltrane, Ellington, T. Monk, Ch. Parker, Harold Land, Daniel Jackson, E. Dolphy. Film sound tracks (playing): *Sweet Jesus Preacher; As Above, Also Below; Coonskin.* Fests: Watts, '67 w. Marshall; Cal. State w. Tapscott, '68; Coltrane Fest, '69, w. Crouch; Billie Holiday Fest., '71, w. Tapscott; Ch. Parker Fest, '72, w. Tapscott. The Coltrane, Holiday and Parker fests. were given in the black community of LA and were organized by Quincy Troupe.

In '75 Blythe observed: "I am presently working out ways of arranging that would make use of multi-phonics in reed voicings. I had discovered those things around 1961 before I heard Coltrane do them." Comps: *The Bitter Suite; The Grip; Illusions; Shadows; Metamorphosis.*

LPs: w. Tapscott, *The Giant Is Awakening* (Fl. Dutchman); w. Azar Lawrence, *Bridge to the New Age* (Prest.); w. Hamilton, *Peregrinations* (BN); others w. Hemphill (Arista); *Now Is Another Time; Past Spirits,* w. Crouch.

BLACKBURN, LOU,* *trombone;* also *bass trombone, flute, schalmei;* b. Rankin, Pa. 11/12/22. Active as studio musician in Hollywood and w. Onzy Matthews, Gerald Wilson, B. Bryant, S. Kenton's Neophonic orch., N. Riddle and Cocoanut Grove band, backing many singers, '66-70. Moved to Berlin, Oct. '70; worked w. radio orch. there and w. Kurt Edelhagen band. Mus. Dir. for the German prod. of *Catch My Soul* at Theater des Westens. Remained w. theater orch. also freelancing in Germany, until July '73. Formed a group, Mombasa, feat. African musicians in Sept. '73, playing mixture of African and Western music built on polyrhythms, written and arr. by Blackburn. Toured extensively in Europe, '74-5. Fests: Monterey w. Ch. Mingus, T. Monk, B. Bryant; German fests. since '73. Motion pic. work w. D. Amram, Q. Jones, J.J. Johnson. Many TV shows, incl. specs. w. Sinatra, The Supremes, Milton Berle.

LPs: *New Frontier; Two Note Samba* (Imperial-Liberty); *Monterey Jazz Festival,* w. Mingus (Fant.).

BLACKWELL, EDWARD B. (ED), *drums;* b. New Orleans, La., 1927. Playing in late '40s in NO. Met Ornette Coleman when the latter visited there in '49. To LA '51 and in mid-'50s maintained close contact w. Coleman. Returned to NO in late '50s before moving to NYC, '60, replacing Billy Higgins in Coleman's quartet. Played at Five Spot w. Eric Dolphy-Booker Little quintet, '61. w. Randy Weston, '65-7 incl. African tour. Gigs w. Mose Allison. Back w. Coleman '67-8; and again in '70s. App. w. him at NJF-NY, '72. Pl. in "free jazz" set in Radio City jam session at NJF-NY '73. Took ill with a kidney ailment in '74 and benefits to raise money for his treatment were held in NYC; NO; Baton Rouge, La.; England; Denton Coll., and Western Coll., both in Ohio. Artist-in-residence at Wesleyan U., fall '75. Original infls.

were early NO drummers Baby Dodds, Zutty Singleton, Paul Barbarin. His melodic concept coupled with his roots makes Blackwell the most musical drummer to emerge from the avant garde of the '60s. LPs: w. Coleman, *Science Fiction* (Col.); *Friends and Neighbors* (Fly. Dutch.); *Free Jazz* (Atl.); w. Don Cherry, *Relativity Suite* (JCOA); *Symphony For Improvisers; Where Is Brooklyn* (BN); w. A. Shepp, *Magic of Ju Ju* (Imp.); w. A. Heath, *Kawaida* (Trip); *The Great Concert of Eric Dolphy* (Prest.).

BLAIR, JOHN, *vitar, singer, composer;* b. Toledo, Ohio, 11/8/43. Raised in San Diego, Cal. Began studying violin at age 10 and made prof. debut at 16 w. San Diego Symph. Won a Musical Merit Scholarship an international musicians' award given to 100 students chosen for the Pablo Casals festival in Puerto Rico. Received scholarship to Eastman School in Rochester, N.Y. where he earned Bachelor of Music. Pl. w. Air Force Strolling Strings at White House during Kennedy and Johnson administrations. Further studies at Curtis Institute in Phila. To NYC '64 where he began to play jazz, pop, rock and soul with a variety of people incl. Richie Havens, Johnny Mathis, James Brown, Stevie Wonder, Horace Silver, Bobby Womack, Isaac Hayes and Alice Coltrane.

Plays the vitar, a solid body electric instrument made for him by Lee Larison of the Boston Symph. It combines violin, viola and guitar, has a built-in fuzztone, and volume controls for each of its five strings. This gives it synthesizer-like qualities.

Blair, who names John Coltrane as his main influence, made an unscheduled, unannounced appearance at one of the Radio City Music Hall jam sessions of the NJF-NY '72. At NJF-NY '73 he again again pl. at the Radio City jam and w. his own quintet on a concert w. the gps. of John Mayall and Chuck Mangione at Philharmonic Hall. A fourth degree Black Belt, he operates the American Natural Style Karate School in Manhattan.

TV: *David Frost; To Tell the Truth; New York Illustrated; Black News; Black Journal; Tonight.* Comp: *Southern Love; Sunburst; I Sent My Son; Canadian Rock Lady; Tower of Fantasy; Searchin' Uptown; Hot Pants.* LPs: *Southern Love* (Col.); *Newport in New York, The Jam Sessions, Vols. 1 & 2* (Cobble.).

BLAKE, JAMES HUBERT (EUBIE),* *composer, piano;* b. Baltimore, Md. 2/7/1883. After many years of intermittent activity, Blake returned to prominence as a result of a two record album produced by John Hammond for Columbia in '69. In '72 he started his own record company, Eubie Blake Music, and appeared at the Newport-New York and Berlin Jazz Fests. In Feb. '73, shortly after traveling by train to LA for radio and TV shows and lectures, he was honored by ASCAP in NYC Feb. 7, his 90th birthday. The following May he made his first plane flight, to record five numbers for QRS Music Rolls in Buffalo, N.Y. Other appearances during that year incl. Boston Pops with Arthur Fiedler; fests. in Switzerland, Denmark, Norway; many concerts and TV shows. In '74 he taped a biographical film, *Reminiscing with Sissle and*

Blake, in Tampa, Fla., with his old vaudeville partner Noble Sissle. Later that year he played a Carnegie Hall concert with Benny Goodman, a jazz fest. in Nice, and a Scott Joplin fest. in Sedalia, Miss. In Sept. '74 made his first app. at MJF.

Blake's best known comps. are *I'm Just Wild About Harry* and *Memories Of You*. A lavishly illustrated book, also entitled *Reminiscing with Sissle and Blake*, by Robert Kimball and William Bolcom, was publ. in '72 by Viking Press (625 Madison Ave., N.Y. 10022).

LPs: *The Eighty-Six Years of Eubie Blake* (Columbia); Eubie Blake Vol. I (feat. Ivan Harold Browning); *Rags To Classics* (solo piano); *Eubie Blake and his friends Edith Wilson & Ivan Harold Browning; Sissle & Blake; Eubie Blake/Live Concert; Eubie Blake Introducing Jim Hession* (Eubie Blake Music, 284-A Stuyvesant Ave., Brooklyn, N.Y. 11221).

BLAKE, RAN,* *piano, keyboards, composer*; b. Springfield, Mass. 4/20/35. Co-director of Community Services Dept. of the New England Conservatory of Music, '68; Production Manager and Music Director, '69-72; Recruiter for Admissions Dept., '68-73. Governor's Task Force, Committee on Accessibility to the Arts, '71; Metropolitan Cultural Alliance, '72; Member of New England Conserv. faculty (improvisation), '69-73; Chairman, Third Stream Music Dept., '73. Author of book on vocal improvisation for Macmillan. LPs: *Ran Blake Plays Solo Piano* (ESP); *The Newest Sound Around*, with singer Jeanne Lee (RCA); *Blue Potato and Other Outrages* (Milestone).

BLAKENEY, ANDREW (ANDY), *trumpet*; b. Quitman, Miss., 6/10/1898. In 1925 Blakeney pl. for two weeks in Chicago with King Oliver, and in the late '20s moved to California and worked locally. With Les Hite in early '30s, later with Charlie Echols. From '35-9 lived and worked in Hawaii, first w. drummer Monk McFay, then w. own band. During '40s, back in Cal., worked w. Kid Ory, and led own band for many years. During the 60's and '70s Blakeney freelanced in the LA area, and in '73 joined Barry Martyn's Legends of Jazz. With this group he toured Europe twice and made many appearances throughout U.S., incl. fests. in NO, Sacramento, '74 and Monterey, '75.

LPs: w. Legends of Jazz (Crescent Jazz Prods.).

BLAKEY, ART (Abdullah Ibn Buhaina),* *drums, leader*; b. Pittsburgh, Pa., 10/11/19. Formed Jazz Messengers in '55 (he first used the name for a big band and small group he led in '47) and has been at its head from that time. Sometimes it has been a sextet but most often a quintet. From the late '60s through the first half of the '70s the personnel has incl., among others, Woody Shaw, Olu Dara, Bill Hardman, trumpet; Billy Harper, Carter Jefferson, David Schnitter, tenor saxophone; and Cedar Walton, piano.

As with Blakey-led groups of the past, the '70s Messengers are dedicated to vibrant, hard-swinging music propelled by Blakey, considered by many to be the most "soulful" of the drum masters to have expanded percus-

sion horizons in the bop and hard-bop periods. In portions of '71-72 he took a hiatus from his group to tour with Dizzy Gillespie, Thelonious Monk, Sonny Stitt et al in The Giants of Jazz. Blakey appeared w. them at the NJF-NY '72, and also took part in the Radio City Music Hall Jam Session at the same fest. From '73-5 the Messengers were featured at NJF-NY and in '74 Blakey was also part of a historic drum battle among Max Roach, Buddy Rich and Elvin Jones at a Radio City jam.

With both the Messengers and the Giants of Jazz, Blakey toured in Europe and Japan. In '75 the Messengers made many NYC apps. at a variety of clubs especially the Top of the Gate. LPs: *Child's Dance; Buhaina; Anthenagin* (Prest.); *Like Someone in Love; Roots & Herbs* (BN); reissues (Milest.; Trip); w. *Giants of Jazz* (Atl.); *Newport in New York, The Jam Sessions, Vols. 3&4* (Cobble.); *Sonny Stitt with Art Blakey and The Jazz Messengers* (Poly.).

BLANKE, TOTO, *guitar*; also *bass, drums, bouzoukie*; b. Paderborn, W. Germany, 9/16/39. Stud. classical guitar. Professional debut '69 with own trio. From '70 feat. w. Jasper van't Hof quartet, founded with Pierre Courbois. Toured Europe '73 w. Jeremy Steig; concerts w. Steig, Joachim Kuhn, Randy Brecker, and solo recitals. As soloist, winner of Loosdrecht Fest., Holland, '69.

BLATNY, DR. PAVEL,* *composer, piano, organ*; b. Brno, Czech., 9/14/31. Prominent Czech composer whose works have been widely played by Gustav Brom; Prague radio jazz orch.; Kurt Edelhagen; Erwin Lehn; Brussels Radio Big Band; Copenhagen Radio Big Band; Don Ellis; and many others in England, Austria, Holland, Sweden, Finland, etc. App. at jazz festivals in Prague, '64-74; Stuttgart '68-70; Jazz Labor Ruhrgebiet, '68-9; Amsterdam, '69; Graz '74. From '74 chief of the music dept. of TV Station Brno. Teacher at Remscheider Jazz Kurse '68, '70. Member of the Int. Soc. for Jazz Research, Graz, Austria. Publ: scores of jazz comp. (Supraphon, Palackeho 1, Prague 1, Czech.); Subeditions (Edition Modern Music, Munich, Germany). Comp: *Pour Ellis; Study for Quartertone Trumpet; 10' 30''; For Eric; Suite for Gustav Brom; In Modo Classico Suite for String Quartet and Jazz Orchestra*. LPs: *Third Stream Compositions; Czechoslovakian Jazz* (Supraphon); w. Brom, *Swinging the Jazz* (Saba).

BLEY, CARLA,* *composer, piano*; b. Oakland, Cal., 5/11/38. In '66 Ms. Bley undertook her second European tour of concerts, radio and TV apps. She spent '67 writing *A Genuine Tong Funeral*, a suite commissioned by G. Burton and rec. Nov. '67 for RCA. Divorced Paul Bley, married Michael Mantler. Began work on *Escalator Over The Hill*, which she characterized as a chronotransduction, together with lyricist Paul Haines. Commissioned by harpsichordist Antoinette Vischer to write composition, *Untitled Piece in 8 Layers*.

Perf. and rec. as pianist with the Jazz Composers' Orch., '68-9. Commissioned by Charlie Haden to write an album of revolutionary songs. Arr., comp. for, perf. on Haden's *Liberation Music Orchestra* (Impulse), Apr.

'69. *Escalator* released on JCOA Records Mar. '72. In that year Ms. Bley won the DB critics' poll for the third time in TDWR category. She has since lectured, done film scoring (for Jodorowski's *Holy Mountain*, w. Don Cherry and members of JCOA); received French Oscar du Disque de Jazz for '73.

She started her own record company, WATT, with Michael Mantler and created a newspaper for the New Music Distribution Services that had been launched by JCOA. Rec. *Tropic Appetites*, '73-4 with Mantler, G. Barbieri, Dave Holland et al. Her comp., *3/4*, feat. K. Jarrett as soloist, was presented Mar. '74 at Alice Tully Hall, NYC.

LPs: See above. Addr: JCOA, 6 W. 95th St., NYC 10025.

BLEY, PAUL,* *piano, synthesizer, composer*; b. Montreal, Quebec, Canada, 11/10/32. After pl. w. Charles Mingus; Ornette Coleman, Don Cherry and w. his own gp. in Calif. in the '50s, he went to NYC where, in the '60s, he again worked w. Mingus, and w. Jimmy Giuffre; Don Ellis; Sonny Rollins; Gary Peacock; and was a member of the Jazz Composers' Guild, which evolved into the Jazz Composers Orchestra Association. Divorced from Carla Bley, he teamed up with Annette Peacock, Gary Peacock's former wife, who sang with him, sometimes utilizing the synthesizer with her voice much as he was doing with the piano, up until early '73. "I find myself in a period of historical transition between acoustic and electric instruments," said Bley, "so this reflected in my music. In terms of what improvisation is going to be about, there is no other place for it to go, except to electronics."

Bley's modus operandi is to take a synthesizer, an electric piano, clavinet, and an acoustic piano with pickup, and stack the three keyboards on top of each other. "By playing all those keyboards simultaneously," he explains, "you literally run off one keyboard onto another. And I find I don't have any problem at all making the jumps musically, that the combined instrument itself doesn't become the detractor from the music."

Michael Levin, reviewing *The Paul Bley Synthesizer Show*, makes the point that the synthesizer "has a totally constant sound . . . elements of tone and touch which distinguish individual artists are absent" and to recognize the player "one can rely only on the stream of ideas." He concludes that on "*Parks*, set in a swinging four . . ." Bley plays "a reedily voiced single-line solo which works well, modifying it as he goes into a more slurred oscillator-keyed tone . . . . the ideas are good and he plays superbly—but the contribution of the synthesizer, save for some guitar-like pedal shadings, is not that distinctive."

Bley also continued to play and record on acoustic piano. In the early '70s he divided his time between Europe and the U.S. In '73-5 he made two tours of Europe, pl. solo piano for fests and TV. In '75 he formed his own production company in partnership w. Carol Goss (Improvising Artists Inc., 26 Jane St., New York,

N.Y. 10014) and began releasing recordings of his own and other artists (Sam Rivers-Dave Holland; Ran Blake) on the IAI label. Comp: *Started; Harlem; Summer; Later; Upstairs; Carla; Mating of Urgency; Meeting; Capricorn; Mr. Joy; The Archangel; Nothing Ever Was, Anyway; Gary; Snakes; Parks.* LPs: *Alone Again; Quiet Song; Turning Point; Virtuoso* (IAI); *Ballads; Open to Love* (ECM); *Blood* (Fontana); *Paul Bley-NHOP* (Steeple.); *Scorpio; Synthesizer Show* (Milest.); *Copenhagen & Haarlem* (Arista); *Ramblin'* (Byg); Paul Bley-Annette Peacock, *I'm the One* (RCA).

BLOOD, SWEAT AND TEARS. see Colomby, Bobby.

BOBO, WILLIE (William Correa),* *timbales, percussion, singer*; b. New York, N.Y., 2/28/34. After working as sideman for Latin and jazz groups, formed own band in LA 1966 and during the next decade was seen at numerous Latin and jazz clubs, concert halls. In 1970 began to sing *Dindi*, a Brazilian song that became his first popular vocal record. App. in Venezuela at International Song Fest.; Monterey as guest star w. Cal Tjader; Latin Jazz Fest. at Madison Sq. Garden; to Ghana as guest w. Santana for filming of *Soul to Soul*.

Bobo gained additional recognition as an actor-musician on the Bill Cosby comedy TV series. Though entertainment-oriented, his combo achieved an effective blend of Latin music, soul and jazz improvisation.

LPs: *Evil Ways; Spanish Grease* (Verve); *Latin Beat* (Trip); *Do What You Want To Do* (Sussex).

BOHANNON, STEVE, *drums, organ*; b. 1947. Son of trombonist Hoyt Bohannon. Worked w. S. Kenton; pl. organ w. Howard Roberts quartet, but was best known as drummer w. Don Ellis orch. His career came to a tragically early end when a car in which he was a passenger collided with a truck near Victorville, Cal., 10/21/68. He was killed outright.

LPs: w. Ellis (Pac. Jazz).

BOHANON, GEORGE ROLAND JR.,* *trombone*; also *euphonium, flute, tenor sax, piano, bass*; b. Detroit, Mich., 8/7/37. First prominent in '60s w. Chico Hamilton quintet. Later became interested in record production and worked as contractor for sessions. Also pl. w. Ujima Ensemble from '72. TV work w. Bill Cosby, Nancy Wilson. NJF '70 w. Bunions Bradford (Cosby). LPs w. G. Ammons; H. Hawes; Patrice Rushen; D. Axelrod (Fant.); *Brass Fever* (Imp.); and with many pop artists. Toured Europe w. Carole King, '73 and '74.

BOLAND, FRANCOIS (FRANCY),* *composer, leader, piano*; b. Namur, Belgium, 11/6/29. Co-leader w. K. Clarke from '62 of the Clarke-Boland big band, which incl. U.S. expatriates and European musicians. The band achieved a unique reputation, rec. LPs w. guest stars such as Lockjaw Davis, S. Getz, J. Griffin, but due to the loss of such key players as Derek Humble and Ake Persson, Clarke and Boland disbanded in '73. At the Middelheim Fest. in '74 Boland pl. w. a sextet incl. his son Chris on guitar and Benny Bailey on trumpet.

LPs: *All Smiles; Big Band Sound; Fellini 712; All Blues; More Smiles; Latin Kaleidoscope; Sax No End;*

Faces (MPS); *Off Limits; Rue Chaptal; Volcano* (Poly.); *At Her Majesty's Pleasure* (Black Lion); *Open Door* (Muse); *Change of Scene* w. Stan Getz (Euro. Verve).

BOLLING, CLAUDE,* *leader, piano, composer*; b. Cannes, France, 4/10/30. Own big band for recs. '56; apps. and/or recs. w. Bill Coleman, Sidney Bechet, Don Byas, Kenny Clarke, Cat Anderson, Paul Gonsalves, Sam Woodyard, Buck Clayton, L. Hampton, etc. In recent yrs. worked in studios as comp.-arr. and leader. Acc. prominent French singers Sacha Distel, Mireille Mathieu, Mouloudji, Juliette Greco, Charles Trenet, Darion Moreno, Henri Salvador; also Brigitte Bardot, Liza Minelli. Occasional apps. as pianist-leader of Show Biz Band, an Ellington/Basie-styled outfit. Wrote music for films: *Borsalino; Catch Me a Spy.* TV: *To Bix or Not to Bix.* Musical Comedy: *Monsieur Pompadour.* Did shows for Jerry Lewis; Distel. Led vocal gp., Les Parisiennes. Awards: Grand Prix du Disque six times. In late '75 Columbia released his *Suite for Flute and Jazz Piano* feat. himself and flutist Jean-Pierre Rampal. Other LPs: *Original Jazz Classics*; w. Cat Anderson, *Anderson, Bolling & Co.* (Philips); *With the Help of My Friends* (Biram); w. big band, *Swing Session; Jazz Party* (French RCA).

BONANO, JOSEPH (SHARKEY),* *trumpet, singer*; b. Milneburg, La., 4/9/04. Best known through a series of recordings made in New Orleans and New York, '36-7. In later years he returned home and in 1969 he appeared at the New Orleans Jazz Festival. After a long illness Bonano died in New Orleans, 3/27/72.

BONNER, JOSEPH LEONARD (JOE), *piano, composer*; also *tuba*; b. Rocky Mount, N.C., 4/20/48. Grandfather was in minstrel shows; mother sang; father pl. violin. Studied music from elementary school, through junior high, Booker Washington HS, Virginia State Coll. Pl. w. local jazz gps. while att. Va. State. With Roy Haynes, '70-1; Freddie Hubbard, '71-2; Pharoah Sanders, '72-4; also Thad Jones-Mel Lewis; Harold Vick; Max Roach; Leon Thomas; Billy Harper. Forming own gp. TV: w. Max Roach & J.C. White Singers, *Soul*, NET, '72. Fest: NJF w. Hubbard, '71; NJF-NY w. Sanders, '72; Pori; Perugia w. Harper, '75. Infl: McCoy Tyner, Herbie Hancock, Mingus, Charles Lloyd, Hubbard, Sanders, Vick, Lee Morgan, Miles Davis. Neil Tesser has described his style as one of "colors, new hues and primal pigments blended and juxtaposed, occasionally clashed, into an essentially harmonious whole. It is a style, not of the realists or the classicists . . . but of the impressionists."

Comp: *The Little Chocolate Boy; Love Dance; Celebration; Ode to Trane; Healing Song; The Golden Lamp.* LPs: *The Lifesaver* (Muse); w. Harper, *Black Saint* (Black Saint); Vick, *Don't Look Back* (Strata-East); Harold Alexander, *Raw Root* (Atl.); Sanders (Imp.).

BOOKER, WALTER M. JR.,* *bass*; b. Prairie View, Texas, 12/17/33. Early work in Washington, D.C., then in NYC from '64 w. D. Byrd, T. Monk, A. Farmer, S. Getz. Booker toured with the C. Adderley quintet during that group's final seven years of existence, traveling frequently abroad and app. on all the band's albums; also in film *Play Misty For Me*, and on TV shows w. Nancy Wilson et al.

LPs: see ADDERLEY, JULIAN and NAT; also *Revelation*, w. S. Rollins (Imp.).

BOONE, RICHARD, *trombone, singer*; b. Little Rock, Ark., 2/23/30. Began singing at age five in Baptist church. In 1946, won talent contest and toured for a month w. Lucky Millinder's band. Army, 1948-53, pl. w. Special Service orch. Studied music at Philander Smith College, Little Rock, '53. To LA, studio work and club dates w. Gerald Wilson, Dolo Coker, Sonny Criss, Dexter Gordon, Teddy Edwards. Toured w. Della Reese, 1961-6. Joined Count Basie, June 1966, staying three years; during that time became known for an individual, humor-tinged vocal style in which he alternately sang straight and yodeled or scatted the blues. In 1969, rec. own album for the short-lived Nocturne label in LA. Starting in 1970, many tours in Europe as singer and trombonist, living much of the time in Copenhagen. Favs: Tony Bennett, C. McRae, S. Vaughan, B. Eckstine. Won DB Critics poll, TDWR, '67, '72. LPs w. Basie (Verve, Dot).

BOWIE, LESTER, *trumpet, fluegelhorn, Kelphorn, singer, percussion, composer*; b. Frederick, Md., 10/11/41. Raised in Little Rock, Ark., and St. Louis, Mo. Began pl. 1946; from age ten took part in school and religious music activities. At 16 led youth group. Following military service in Texas, worked w. r & b bands around South and Midwest, also gigged w. wife, singer Fontella Bass, and w. Frank Foster. Made r & b sessions for Chess Records and occasionally played jazz jobs.

Around 1965 Bowie began to gain recognition as one of a group of creative artists in Chicago who organized the AACM (Association for the Advancement of Creative Music). Later a group that had recorded under the names of Bowie and Roscoe Mitchell (also incl. Malachi Favors) evolved into the Art Ensemble of Chicago, a cooperative unit that became, according to Michael Cuscuna, "one of the most powerful, dynamic and unique groups of the new music (and the old music too)." Bowie also helped form BAG (Black Artist Group) and the Great Black Music Orch. in St. Louis.

The Art Ensemble was heard in Europe in 1969, playing concerts and recording with considerable success. Bowie recorded with Archie Shepp, Sunny Murray, Jimmy Lyons, Cecil Taylor and others, also wrote, conducted and recorded *Gettin' to Know Y'All* with the 50-piece Baden Baden Free Jazz Orch., and again in 1970 at the Frankfurt JF. Toured Senegal, '74, performing with local drummers. Comp: *Theme De Yoyo; Jazz Death; Barnyard Scuffel Shuffel.*

Bowie, whom Joachim Berendt described as "a Cootie Williams of the avant garde with his growl solos," also became a major contributor to the visual, comedic and dramatic aspects of the Art Ensemble. Early infl: Louis Armstrong, Kenny Dorham.

LPs w. Art Ensemble of Chicago on Prestige, Atlantic;

Arista; own LP: *Fast Last!* (Muse); many others on European labels with above-named artists.

BOWN, PATRICIA ANNE (PATTI),* *piano*; b. Seattle, Wash., 7/26/31. Played w. Q. Jones on Euro. tour of show, *Free and Easy*. Freelance in NYC from early '60s. Solo piano at Needle's Eye in early '70s; Half Note, '74. In orch. for Broadway musical *Purlie*, '72-4. Concerts w. NYJRC, '74-5. Jam sessions at NJF-NY, '74-5. Rec. movie scores w. Q. Jones. LPs: w. S. Stitt (Cadet); O. Nelson (Fly. Dutch.); Aretha Franklin (Atl); James Brown, etc.

BRACKEEN, JOANNE (Joanne Grogan), *piano, composer*; b. Ventura, Calif., 7/26/38. A few private lessons but essentially self-taught. Worked in Calif. w. Teddy Edwards, D. Gordon, C. Lloyd, '59; Freddie McCoy, late '60s; Woody Shaw in '69; Dave Liebman, '69, '74; Art Blakey, '70-2; Joe Henderson, '72-5; Joe Farrell; Sonny Red, '73; Sonny Stitt; Horacee Arnold; Stan Getz, '75; also many engagements w. own duo at West Boondock, NYC, '72-5, The Surf Maid, NYC, '74-5. Comps: *Snooze; Images; Sri-C; Zulu; 6-ate*. LPs: *Vital Views*; w. Toots Thielemans, *Captured Alive* (Choice); w. McCoy (Prest.)

BRADFORD, BOBBY LEE, *cornet, trumpet, composer*; b. Cleveland, Miss., 7/19/34. Stud. Lincoln High, Dallas, '49-52; Sam Houston Coll., Austin, '52-3; U. of Texas, '59-60; Houston-Tillotson Coll., '62-3. In addition to being in and out of teaching, principally at Cal. State Coll., Pasadena City Coll., Claremont Colls., Bradford pl. w. Ornette Coleman, '53-4 and '61-3; w. Q. Jones in NYC, '62; from '66-71 co-led a combo with saxophonist John Carter, mainly in LA. Played Watts Fest., '71; Brussels Fest., '73. Won DB poll, TDWR, '73.

Comps: *Woman; Song For The Unsung; Love's Dream; Eye of the Storm; Comin' On; Room 408*. LPs: *Flight for Four* (Flying Dutchman); *Seeking* (Revelation); *Love's Dream* (Emanem); w. Coleman, *Science Fiction* (Columbia).

BRADFORD, PERRY,* *singer, piano*; b. Montgomery, Ala., 2/14/1893. A pioneer producer and artist on early recs. First man to arr. session for a black singer, Mamie Smith, in 1920. He became successful publisher, entrepreneur and rec. consultant in '20s. Numerous rec. dates w. L. Armstrong, Johnny Dunn, Willie The Lion Smith, James P. Johnson et al. His autobiography, *Born with the Blues* was publ. in '65. Bradford died 4/22/70 in Queens, N.Y.

BRAFF, REUBEN (RUBY),* *cornet*; b. Boston, Mass., 3/16/27. After building a reputation around Boston, he found that because he played in a classic style he was not in demand in the late '50s. Even when he did begin to work more regularly in the '60s, he did not record very much. In the '70s, however he became more active in all areas, touring as featured soloist w. Tony Bennett, '71-3; co-leading a popular and successful quartet w. guitarist George Barnes. '73-5, that also toured w. Bennett in '73-4. After Braff and Barnes broke up in the summer of '75 he free-lanced in NYC, subbing for Roy Eldridge at

Jimmy Ryan's on several occasions. Made NYJRC Tribute to Louis Armstrong tour of Europe, fall '75. Writing arrs. to enable him to work within quartet, sextet or octet contexts. Braff's mellow, melodic style had fully matured by the '70s to a point where the seeming ease with which his music was made was matched by its easy-listening quality.

Film: *This Funny World* w. Bennett, unreleased. TV: Mike Douglas; *Today*; many Euro. apps. Fest: NJF-NY; Colo. JP; Concord. Comp: *Everything's George; With Time to Love; People's Choice*. LPs: w. Braff-Barnes Quartet, *Carnegie Hall Concert* (Chiaro.); *Play Gershwin; Play Rodgers and Hart* (Concord); *To Fred Astaire, With Love* (RCA). *Plays Louis Armstrong* (Byg); w. Ellis Larkins, *Grand Reunion* (Chiaro.); w. George Wein, *Newport All Stars* (Atl.); *George Wein is Alive and Well in Mexico* (Col.).

BRAND, ADOLPH JOHANNES (DOLLAR) (Abdullah Ibrahim),* *piano, composer*; also *Indian-African flute, soprano sax, cello*; b. Capetown, So. Africa, 10/9/34. Playing in Europe in early and mid-'60s, he was discovered by Duke Ellington who encouraged him to come to the US in '65. After pl. w. Elvin Jones, '66, he free-lanced before returning to Africa in '68. He has been back and forth to the US five times between then and Jan. '76. Lived in Swaziland, '71-3; Capetown & Johannesburg, '73-5; Capetown, '75. In addition he has spent much time in Europe, particularly Scandinavia, and toured Japan and Australia in '73. Most of his apps. are as solo pianist but in '74 he took a 10-piece band, a similar personnel to the one that rec. *African Space Program*, on tour in Germany, Italy and Switzerland. He has also pl. in Holland; Canada, '74; London, '75. When he performs in anything but a solo setting, his wife, singer Sathima (Bea Benjamin) often appears with him. Has pl. bamboo flute from '67; cello from '68; soprano sax from '71. Fest: produced two in Swaziland; pl. at Nancy, '73; Antibes, '75; Bergamo; Berlin; Kongsberg; Musicforum, Austria; concert in Boswil, Switzerland. TV: Austria; Holland; three different projects in '60s and '70s w. Erik Moseholm and Danish Radio Big Band. His conversion to Islam in '68 has helped him "to rediscover a sense of the natural" and subsequently led him into the study of karate and acupuncture. Won DB Critics poll, TDWR, '75. Comp: *The Aloe and the Wildrose; Salaam; Anatomy of a South African Village; Tintiyana; The Dream; Tariq; African Sun; Bra Joe From Kilimanjaro; Sunset in Blue; Kippi; Monk From Harlem; The Pilgrim; Jabulani; Easter Joy*. LPs: *Manenberg; African Herbs* (As-Shams, Kohinoor, Kort Street, Johannesburg, South Africa); *Ode to Duke Ellington; Memories* (Japanese Philips); *African Sketchbook; African Space Program* (Enja); *This is Dollar Brand* (Bl. Lion); *Peace; Dollar Brand + 3 with Kippi Moeketsi* (Soultown); *African Piano; Ancient Africa* (Japo); *Sangoma* (Sack.); *Anatomy of a South African Village* (Spectator); w. Gato Barbieri, *Hamba Kahle* (Togetherness); *Confluence* (Freedom); Elvin Jones, *Midnight Walk* (Atl.).

BRASHEAR, OSCAR, *trumpet, fluegelhorn*; also *piccolo trumpet, cornet, piano*; b. Chicago, Ill., 8/18/44. Mother a church pianist. Stud. DuSable HS, Wright Jr. Coll., Roosevelt U.; priv. lessons w. Ch. Allen. Pl. w. Morris Ellis big band, Latin groups, record dates, jingles, '62-6; W. Herman, '67; C. Basie '68-9. Freelanced in Chi. w. S. Stitt, G. Ammons, D. Gordon, J. Moody, '70. From '71 very active in LA w. Gerald Wilson, H. Land, O. Nelson, S. Manne, Q. Jones, H. Silver, Duke Pearson band. Infls: J. Coltrane, F. Hubbard, Clifford Brown, W. Shorter, McCoy Tyner, H. Hancock, Miles Davis, A. Blakey. Fests: Newport w. Basie; Monterey w. Jones, W. Herman etc.

Brashear emerged in the mid-'70s as a spirited, exceptionally fluent soloist, considered by some critics to be a latter day Clifford Brown.

LPs: w. Land, *Damisi* (Mainstr.); w. J. Henderson, *Canyon Lady* (Milestone); w. S. Manne *Hot Coles* (Fl. Dutchman); Moacir Santos, *Carnival of the Spirits*; w. Hutcherson, *Head On* (BN); w. C. Adderley, *Big Man* (Fantasy); w. Earth, Wind & Fire, *Head to the Sky* (Col.); others w. Eddie Harris, Groove Holmes, H. Silver, H. Hawes et al; *Brass Fever* (Imp.).

BRASS COMPANY. see Hardman, Bill.

BRAUD, WELLMAN,* *bass*; b. St. James, La., 1/25/1891. Best known as bassist with Ellington orch. 1926-35. After leaving Ellington, took over direction of Spirits of Rhythm, then formed own trio in '37 until '41. During '40s and '50s primarily involved in business ventures in Harlem, but toured Europe in '56 with Kid Ory. Braud died of a heart attack 10/29/66 at his LA home.

BRAXTON, ANTHONY, *alto sax, clarinet, bass clarinet, sopranino, flute, composer*; b. Chicago, Ill., 6/4/45. First studies w. Jack Gell at Chi. Sch. of Mus.; then at Chi. Mus. Coll.; philosophy under Dr. Zabeet at Roosevelt U. At 17, met Roscoe Mitchell who turned his attention from strictly classical music to jazz. Early infl: Paul Desmond, Warne Marsh, Eric Dolphy, Coltrane. Became involved w. AACM through Mitchell in '66 began pl. "free-jazz" w. them at Lincoln Center in Chicago. Earned a great part of his living as a chess hustler. Pl. w. Art Ensemble of Chicago in Europe '69. Became part of Circle, a gp. w. Chick Corea, Dave Holland and Barry Altschul in NYC '70, pl. w. it there and in France, Feb. '71. From a point several months later, when Circle disbanded, Braxton has led his own groups, traveling between Europe and the US until Sept. '74 when he moved to Woodstock, N.Y., pl. in the US, Canada and Europe with Kenny Wheeler, Holland and Altschul. In '70-1 he came to the US w. Musica Elettronica Viva an Italian group which plays contemporary classical and improvised music. He also app. in duo w. guitarist Derek Bailey at London's Wigmore Hall. In May '72 he was heard in concert at Town Hall; and (solo) at Carnegie Hall; in July '73 at Chateau Le Rault, France; Oct. '74, Burton Auditorium, Toronto.

Braxton, who names as additional infls., Lee Konitz, Ornette Coleman, Cecil Taylor and Stockhausen had been quoted to the effect that his "interest in music is scientific. I'm interested in 'functionalism' " he said, "in the sense that I can try out different systems in an attempt to discover the basis for a new life. I'm interested in tapping anything that hints of that vibration but hasn't been there before."

Later, he modified this intellectualism. "The basis upon which I am building music is still math," he explained, "but it's changing. I'm starting to accept feeling again. At one point I consciously wanted to eliminate feeling from my music—in the beginning when I was heavily into John Cage. To play music with feeling the approach is different. You must deal more with the 'is' than the 'how.' I've found that mathematics as a *total* basis for my music is interesting, but it's not what's happening."

His compositions are represented by mathematical diagrams rather than titles. A typical one is:

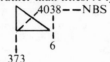

They are written structures that can be used constantly as reference points. "The diagrams," says Braxton, "have to do with the implications of what structural approach was taken, and also with vibrational flows."

In several of his albums, particularly *In the Tradition*, he plays standards and jazz originals by Warne Marsh, Mingus and Charlie Parker. *You Stepped Out of a Dream* from his *Five Pieces 1975* LP is cited by writer Robert Palmer as evidence refuting critical opinion that Braxton "lacks authenticity as a jazzman." Others felt that here his lack of swing and flow in his phrasing underlined the original criticism. Barry McRae, discussing his "free" solos, said that they "dispensed with any suggestion that his organizational mind might make his music clinical."

TV: Italy, Germany, France. Fests: Montreux; Pescara; Antibes. Film: wrote score for *Paris Streets*, commissioned by M.I.T.; *Un Coup de Franc*, France. LPs: *Five Pieces 1975; New York Fall 1974* (Arista); *In the Tradition* (Steeple.); *Three Compositions; For Alto*; Anthony Braxton & Joseph Jarman, *Together Alone* (Del.); Anthony Braxton & Derek Bailey, *Duo 1; Duo 2* (Emanem); w. Circle, *Paris Concert* (ECM); *Circle 1 & 2* (CBS-Sony).

BREAU, LEONARD (LENNY), *guitar*; b. Auburn, Maine, 8/5/41. Parents both singers. Began playing country music; came to prominence in Winnipeg. To Toronto, '64, pl. w. own trio, singer Don Franks et al. Briefly in LA in mid-60s, led trio at Shelly's Manne Hole, where he rec. a live album. Again led own combo and worked with singers in Toronto, '70-2. In semi-retirement in Winnipeg, '73-5. Living Killaloe, Ont., '75, performing only occasionally. Movies: *Toronto Jazz*, '64, for Nat'l Film Board of Canada. Rec. live for Radio-Canada's *Jazz Canadiana* and *Jazz Radio-Canada*. Infl.

by Bill Evans, Chet Atkins and Tal Farlow, Breau is a gifted musician little known outside Canada.

LPs: *Guitar Sounds; Live at Shelly's Manne-Hole* (RCA).

BRECKER, MIKE, *tenor saxophone*; also *flute, soprano sax, drums, piano*; b. Phila. Pa., 3/29/49. Father and sister are pianists. Brother, Randy, is trumpeter (see below). Stud. w. Vince Trombetta, '65-9 and Joe Allard. Pl. with Edwin Birdsong, '70; Dreams, '70-3; James Taylor, '73; Horace Silver, '73-4; Billy Cobham from '74; also in Japan w. Yoko Ono, '74. Own LP: *The Brecker Brothers* (Arista). Others incl. *Journey* w. Arif Mardin (Atl.), *In Pursuit of the 27th Man* w. Silver (Blue Note), *Mind Games* w. J. Lennon (Apple); and albums w. Hal Galper, J. Taylor, Carly Simon, Don Sebesky.

BRECKER, RANDY, *trumpet*; also *piano, drums*; b. Phila., Pa., 11/27/45. Brother is saxophonist Mike Brecker. Stud. Indiana U. '63-5, as well as w. David Baker and several other private teachers. Pl. w. Blood, Sweat & Tears, '66; H. Silver, '67, '69, '73; Janis Joplin, '68; Duke Pearson and Clark Terry big bands, '68; Stevie Wonder; Art Blakey, '70; Dreams '71-2; James Taylor, '71; Larry Coryell; Deodato; Johnny & Edgar Winter, '73; Billy Cobham, '73-4; Mike Longo; Idris Muhammad, '74.

Won DB poll, TDWR, '69. Own LP: *Brecker Brothers* (Arista). Others w. Muhammad (CTI); Silver, Pearson (Blue Note); Longo (Groove Merchant); Hal Galper (Mainstream); Coryell (Vanguard); Cobham (Atl.).

BREEDEN, PROF. HAROLD LEON,* *educator, clarinet, saxophones, bassoon*; b. Guthrie, Okla., 10/3/21. Best known for his work at NTSU, one of whose Lab bands performed, under his direction, at the White House in June '67, the first such appearance by a large Univ. jazz group. D. Ellington and S. Getz appeared as guests with the band. In '72 Breeden organized a celebration, at NTSU, of the 25th anniversary of jazz education at that institution. One of his student units was the official big band at Montreux JF, '70, also touring Germany. Breeden was adjudicator for the U.S. high school competition in Montreux in '71 and '72; conducted all star band for Jazz Internationale, '72 in London and Paris. Has also acted as clinician/judge at innumerable U.S. colleges. Visiting prof. of music for Houston public schools, Jan. '75 under a grant from the National Endowment for the Arts.

Breeden, who has long been established as one of the pioneers in jazz education, was listed in *Outstanding Educators of America* in '71.

BREWER, TERESA (Theresa Brewer), *singer*; b. Toledo, Ohio, 5/7/31. No formal mus. educ., but was a child prodigy, winning a Major Bowes contest at age six. She became a major pop star while in her teens, her biggest hit being *Music! Music! Music!* in 1950. Became interested in contemporary music through her four daughters by first marriage, and was encouraged to work in jazz settings just before and after her marriage in 1972 to producer Bob Thiele. Her jazz-oriented LPs were enthusi-

astically endorsed by critic Nat Hentoff, who called them "a triumph . . . this is a matured, still growing musician who decided some years ago to take jazz, and herself as a communicator of jazz, seriously. Singers with this quality of pungent flavor and crackling swing are rare in any generation."

LPs: *Singing A Doo Dah Song; Teresa Brewer In London With Oily Rags* (Amsterdam); *It Don't Mean a Thing* w. D. Ellington Orch.; *The Songs of Bessie Smith* w. Count Basie Orch., arr. Thad Jones; *What a Wonderful World* w. Bobby Hackett (Fl. Dutchman).

BRIDGEWATER, CECIL VERNON, *trumpet, composer*; b. Urbana, Ill. 10/10/42. Ex-wife is singer Dee Dee Bridgewater; brother saxophonist Ron Bridgewater. Stud. at U. of Ill., '60-4 and '68-9; pl. in U. of Ill. Jazz Band, European tour, '68, Russian tour, '69. Pl. w. H. Silver, '70. From '70-5 Bridgewater was principally known for his work in the Thad Jones-Mel Lewis orch., touring the U.S., Europe, USSR and Japan. He worked w. M. Roach frequently, '71-5, in Europe, U.S., Africa; also during early '70s w. A. Blakey, Harold Vick, Frank Foster, Randy Weston, Jimmy Heath, D. Gillespie's big band, Joe Henderson, Roy Brooks, Sam Rivers, Buddy Terry, Bridgewater Generations.

Bridgewater has had extensive experience as a teacher, giving private lessons and working for Henry Street Settlement, Jazzmobile Workshop, Greenhaven Prison, clinics at high schools and colleges.

LPs: w. Jones-Lewis, *Potpourri* (Philadelphia Int'l.); *Today's Man*, w. Ch. McPherson, *The Loud Minority*, w. Frank Foster, *Awareness*, w. Buddy Terry (all on Mainstream); *United States of Mind*, w. H. Silver (Blue Note); *Lift Every Voice And Sing*, w. Roach (Atl.); *Generations*, Cecil & Ron Bridgewater (Strata-East).

BRIDGEWATER, DENISE (DEE DEE), *singer*; b. Memphis, Tenn., 5/27/50. Family moved to Flint, Mich. while she was a toddler. Father pl. trumpet. She sang as a child but took it up seriously in early teens. Own trio in junior high school; then sang w. father's gp. at local dances. Went to Mich. State U. '68. Sang w. saxist Andy Goodrich for a year. He took her to fest. at U. of Illinois '69. Four months later John Garvey invited her to tour Russia w. Illinois band. Met husband Cecil Bridgewater (see above) and came to NYC w. him. Featured vocalist w. Thad Jones-Mel Lewis orch. '72-4, touring Europe and Japan. App. as a single at Hopper's, NYC, '76. Studied w. Roland Hanna "because I want to be a musician/singer. I want to know what I'm singing and I want to understand what the musicians are playing so that I can work better with them."

Of her wordless singing on *The Great One* in *Suite For Pops* Thad Jones said: "There's never anything written out for her. She is so musical that she goes her own way and we know she isn't going anywhere we are not."

Early infl: Nina Simone, Lena Horne, Gloria Lynne, Nancy Wilson. Won Tony Award for her performance in Broadway musical *The Wiz* '75; TDWR, DB Critics poll, '75. TV: *Woman Alive*, PBS, '76.

LPs: w. Jones-Lewis, *Suite For Pops* (Horizon); w. Heiner Stadler, *Ecstasy* (Labor).

BRIGHT, RONNELL, * *piano, composer*; b. Chicago, Ill., 7/3/30. First prominent as accompanist with singers, incl. Sarah Vaughan in '50s, Nancy Wilson in mid-60s. Occasional appearances as movie and TV actor, incl. *They Shoot Horses Don't They; Lepke; Sanford & Son; Don Adams Special; Mannix; The Jeffersons.* Pianist in George Wyle orch. on Flip Wilson TV Show, '70-4. High school music teacher '74-5. Staff vocal arr., Carol Burnett TV series, '74-5.

As songwriter, Bright composed *Be A Sweet Pumpkin,* rec. by Blue Mitchell, Bill Henderson and others; *Cherry Blossom,* rec. by H. Silver, C. Tjader; *Tender Loving Care* and *Satisfy* and several others all rec. by N. Wilson. Bright's best jazz-oriented work in recent years was his stint with Supersax, '73-4.

LPs: *Supersax Plays Bird* (Capitol); others with Nancy Wilson et al.

BROADBENT, ALAN, *composer, piano*; b. Auckland, New Zealand, 4/23/47. Studied at Royal Trinity College of Music, Auckland, '54-60; Berklee Coll. of Music, '66-9; piano privately with Lennie Tristano, '67-9; then toured w. Woody Herman orch. '69-72, gaining a reputation for his special extended works perf. by the band, notably *Blues In The Night Suite* and *Variations on A Scene,* latter introduced by the Herman band with the Houston Symph. Joined John Klemmer group '75.

Won first prize for *Sonata for Violincello and Piano,* Boston Public Library Music Assn., '69; DB Critics' Poll, TDWR, '72. Influenced by Lester Young, Tristano, Bud Powell, Ch. Parker, Ellington, Gil Evans, John Mandel, Broadbent became the first New Zealand born musician to achieve international stature in jazz.

LPs w. Herman: *Woody* (Cadet); *Brand New Woody; Giant Steps; Thundering Herd* (Fant.).

BROM, GUSTAV, *clarinet, composer, leader*; also *saxophone, violin*; b. Velke Levary, Czech., 5/22/21. His son, Gustav Brom, Jr., b. 1/2/46, pl. trombone w. Brom's orch. Brom stud. at Moravan Music School, Kromeriz; private stud. w. Prof. Horak at Brno Conserv. Pl. in student orch. until '40. From that time he has led his own band starting with six members which grew to 12 by '42, thereby making it one of the oldest European big bands. Soloists who have made guest apps. with the orch. incl. M. Ferguson, T. Curson, D. Goykovich, A. Mangelsdorff, P. Herbolzheimer, H. Koller, B. Bailey. Brom has also collaborated w. Ray Conniff in western Europe. Infl: Ellington, Lunceford, Kenton. His band has app. on innumerable European TV programs and has done the music for feature length films as well as TV films. From early '60s he has app. at fest. in England and on the continent, incl. Manchester, Nuremberg, Molde, Prague, Warsaw and Ljubljana. Brom has won the Jaroslav Jezek prize; Int. Jury prize, Prague JF; and also made a Laureate of Jazz Music at Prague, '68. Comp: *Dance Songs; Dreaming in Two; Adele; The Evening Guest.* LPs: Supraphon, incl. one w. Maynard Ferguson; MPS.

BRÖTZMANN, PETER, *tenor sax*; also *alto, baritone, bass saxophones, clarinet*; b. Remscheid, W. Germany, 3/6/41. Studied painting at the art academy in Wuppertal; self-taught on clarinet and saxophone. Began pl. jazz at 18 w. dixieland school band and cont. w. several amateur dixie/swing groups. With Jazz Realities—Carla Bley and Mike Mantler '66; then w. Don Cherry, Steve Lacy and European avant-garde musicians all over the continent at festivals and concerts. Own trio from '68 with pianist Fred van Hove and drummer Han Bennink. Also worked w. Nam June Paik, Tonas Schmit and the Fluxus movement. Comps. incl. *Machine Gun; Drunken in the Morning Sunrise; Der Alte Mann Bricht Sein Schweigen.* A member of Free Music Production, a musicians' organization which produces records, concerts and festivals in association with like groups such as Instant Composers Poll (Holland) and Incus (Eng.). LPs w. own trio, *Machine Gun; Balls* (Free Music Production); trio plus Albert Mangelsdorff; Globe Unity Orch. Live in Wuppertal (Free Music Production).

BROOKMEYER, ROBERT (BOB), * *valve trombone, piano, composer*; b. Kansas City, Kansas, 12/19/29. Worked in NYC on Merv Griffin TV show and w. Thad Jones-Mel Lewis orch. until '68, when he moved to Cal. Becoming almost inactive in jazz, he was with various TV series, incl. Della Reese Show, '69-70. Reunited w. Jones-Lewis at MJF, '71, and w. Gerry Mulligan at NJF-NY, '73. Rejoined Jones-Lewis on tour Jan. '75.

Comps: *ABC Blues,* rec. by Jones-Lewis; *Blues Suite,* rec. by own gp. on Atl. Among his best arrs. for Jones-Lewis are *Willow Tree; Samba Con Getchu; St. Louis Blues.*

LPs: *Gloomy Sunday and Other Bright Moments* (Verve); *Brookmeyer & Friends* w. Getz, Hancock, G. Burton, R. Carter, E. Jones (Col.); also two with Jones-Lewis (UA), three with Clark Terry (Mainstream), and *Age of Steam* w. Mulligan (A & M).

BROOKS, ROY, *drums*; also *piano, vibes, marimba*; b. Detroit, Mich., 9/3/38. As teenager was inspired to take up drums through listening to Elvin Jones at Bluebird. Played w. Yusef Lateef, Barry Harris et al at El Sino; New Music Society sessions at World Stage coffee house. Worked w. Beans Bowles at Lavert's Lounge. To LV w. the Four Tops. Joined Horace Silver '59, remaining with him into '64. With Lateef '67-70; Pharoah Sanders; James Moody '70-2; Wes Montgomery; Sonny Stitt; Jackie McLean; Dexter Gordon; Dollar Brand; Four Tops; Charles Mingus '72-3. Formed own gp. The Artistic Truth; also active with M'Boom re: percussion, a seven-man ensemble. Infl: C. Parker, M. Roach, J. Coltrane, E. Jones, A. Blakey, K. Clarke. TV: *Today; Tonight; Like It Is; Positively Black; Dial M for Music.* Fest: NJF; MJF; Watts; many European fests. Comp: *Eboness; Five For Max; The Smart Set.* His solos are shaped with melodic contours which he sometimes enhances by blowing through rubber tubing, inflating his drums, thereby varying the pitch. LPs: *Roy Brooks Beat* (Jazz Workshop); *The Free Slave* (Muse); *Ethnic Expres-*

sions (Imhotep); w. Silver, *Horacescope; Doin' the Thing* (Blue Note); w. Stitt, *Constellation* (Cobble.); w. C. McPherson, *McPherson's Mood* (Prest.); w. R. Garland, *Auf Wiedersehen* (MPS); w. D. Brand, *African Space Program* (Enja).

BROWN, GARNETT,* *trombone, composer*; b. Memphis, Tenn., 1/31/36. Early experience w. C. Hamilton, Geo. Russell. Spent 13 yrs. as freelance arranger/composer, jazz and commercial artist in NYC. Many apps. at NJF w. M. Legrand, Benny Carter, Billy Taylor, Diana Ross, NYJRC. Comps: *Pieces of Miles; Ornette*, extended works written for *75 Years Of Jazz*, presented by NYJRC, Apr. '75.

In July '75 Brown moved to LA, where he pl. in the band for the show *Purlie*, and worked in TV, film and commercial recordings. Awards: DB Readers Poll, TDWR, '67; Readers Poll in main trombone category, '74; Ebony All Star Band, '73-4.

During his yrs. in NYC, Brown app. w. Thad Jones-Mel Lewis, Herbie Hancock, Johnny Richards, Billy Taylor, O. Nelson, Duke Pearson, Frank Foster, L. Hampton, Deodato.

LPs: *Jazz For A Sunday Afternoon*, Vols. 2, 4; w. Jones-Lewis, *Live at the Village Vanguard; Monday Night* (Solid State); w. Russell, *The Outer View* (Rivers.); w. R. Kirk, *Slightly Latin* (Limelight); w. Booker Ervin, *Heavy!!!*; w. Teddy Edwards, *It's All Right* (Prest.); w. Jack Wilson, *Easterly Winds*; w. Foster *Manhattan Fever*; w. D. Pearson, *Introducing Duke Pearson's Big Band; Now Hear This* (BN); w. Doug Carn, *Spirit of the New Land* (Black Jazz); w. B. Cobham, *Crosswinds* (Atl.); w. Hancock, *Fat Albert Rotunda* (WB); *Brass Fever* (Imp.).

BROWN, LAWRENCE,* *trombone*; b. Lawrence, Kansas, 7/3/05. Member of Duke Ellington orch., '32-51, and again '60-Jan. '70. He then settled in Washington, D.C., where he was appointed by Pres. Nixon to the Advisory Committee for Kennedy Center; also served on Board of Directors as member of consultant firm, One America. In '72 Brown returned to Cal., where he had been raised, and took a job as recording agent for Local 47 of the Amer. Fed. of Mus., in Hollywood. He completely gave up playing after leaving Ellington orch. His unique legato style and smooth sound can be heard in his own LP, *Inspired Abandon* (Imp.). Other albums w. Ellington on many labels; also w. Jackie Gleason, *Torch with a Blue Flame* (Cap.).

BROWN, LESTER RAYMOND (LES),* *leader, clarinet*; b. Reinerton, Pa., 3/14/12. A bandleader since '38, Brown remained active in the late '60s and '70s, best known through his numerous tours and TV shows w. Bob Hope.

BROWN, MARION,* *alto sax, composer*; b. Atlanta, Ga., 9/8/35. After playing and recording w. Archie Shepp, John Coltrane and leading his own gp. in the mid-'60s in NYC, he went to Europe for concerts and recs. in Holland, France. Returning to US he was, in the mid-'70s at Wesleyan U. in Conn., working on his Masters in

Ethnomusicology. As part of his thesis, he was exploring the possibilities of such instruments as the Ghanian atenteben; Japanese shakuhachi; bamboo flutes; notched bamboo flutes. Stud. So. Indian flute w. P. Vishwanathan. Also investigating history of Afro-American fife and drumming in Miss. & Ga. Comp: *Similar Limits; Sound Structure; Improvisation; QBIC; Porto Novo; Geechee Reflections.*

LPs: *Porto Novo* (Arista); own quartet; *Why Not* (ESP); *Geechee Reflections; Sweet Earth Flying; Three for Shepp* (Imp.); w. Elliott Schwartz, *Soundways* (BCMP).

BROWN, MARSHALL RICHARD,* *valve trombone, euphonium, bass trumpet, composer*; b. Framingham, Mass., 12/21/20. First known as educator, and as organizer of Newport Youth Band, '59. Toured w. Ruby Braff and other mainstream groups in '60s. Eddie Condon, '66-7, R. Eldridge, '68-70. From '71 to '74 played and toured w. Lee Kontiz quintet, in addition to composing and arranging most of the book. Appeared w. Konitz at NJF, '72. Arr. and conducted for Maxine Sullivan LP, '75. Own gp. at Willy's, Greenwich Village, '75.

LPs: *The Lee Konitz Duets; Peacemeal* w. L. Konitz quartet (Milestone).

BROWN, OLIVE, *singer*; also *cocktail drums*; b. St. Louis, Mo., 8/30/22. Sang at Sanctified Church, but acquired early knowledge of and feeling for the blues. Worked in the '40s w. Earl Bostic, Cecil Scott at Small's Paradise, NYC; w. Todd Rhodes in Detroit. Spent three years off and on w. T. Buckner band. In Chicago, was feat. singer in cabarets. Sang at Club Moonglow, Buffalo, N.Y. w. C.Q. Price's band, '58. Worked mostly in Texas, '58-60, w. Don Albert and others. During '60s she rec. twice in NYC, but the sessions were never released. In later years she earned a substantial following in Canada, working in Toronto with leading U.S. mainstream musicians.

Brown sang at several jazz and blues festivals in '70s, incl. Cotton Fest. in Memphis, Tenn., '72; St. Louis Ragtime Fest., '73. Comps: *A Woman's Lament; Monkey on My Back*. Infls: Ethel Waters, Bessie Smith, Louis Armstrong, and (for mannerisms and direction) Hildegarde.

Though inadequately represented on record, Olive Brown has a powerfully convincing voice, bringing to her blues performances in particular a conviction and authenticity that reflects strongly the Bessie Smith influence.

LP: *Olive Brown and Her Blues Chasers* (Jim Taylor Presents, 12311 Gratiot Ave., Detroit, Mich. 48205).

BROWN, RAYMOND H. (RAY), *fluegelhorn, trumpet, composer, arranger*; b. Oceanside, N.Y., 11/7/46. Father a music educator for many years, initiated school stage bands in N.Y., '39. B.M. from Ithaca Coll., '64-8; also four summers at Lake Shore Music Score Camp run by father. Arr. and pl. for U.S. Army field band, '68-71. Worked w. S. Kenton, pl. in band and serving as improvisation clinician, Sep. '71 to Nov. '72. With Bill Watrous band in N.Y., '73-4; guest soloist at Lincoln Center

w. Ithaca Coll. jazz workshop. Led own rehearsal band in NYC, '73-5. Received NEA grant to write work for own band, Mar. '75. Teacher of improv. in nine N.J. schools through grant from N.J. State Council on the Arts. On faculty of Five Towns Coll. in Merrick, N.Y., '74-5, teaching arranging, improv., brass.

Publ: *An Introduction to Jazz Improvisation* by Ray and Steve Brown, publ. by (Creative World, Inc., P.O. Box 35216, Los Angeles, Ca. 90035). Also 15 comps. for stage band. Comps: *Mi Burrito; Call Me Mister; Clyde's Glides; Double Fault Blues; Afterthoughts*. LPs: *National Anthems of the World; Stan Kenton Live at Butler University; Stan Kenton and the Four Freshmen* (all on Creative World).

BROWN, RAYMOND MATTHEWS (RAY),* *bass*; b. Pittsburgh, Pa., 10/13/26. From Jan. '66, when he left the O. Peterson trio after an association that had lasted more than 15 years, Brown became intensely active in a variety of assignments in LA. He produced jazz concerts for the Hollywood Bowl, wrote instruction books, rec. on freelance basis with hundreds of artists, and became Quincy Jones' manager. His TV work incl. regular apps. as a member of the orch. on the Merv Griffin show.

At the beginning of '74 Brown joined the L.A. Four, whose other members were Laurindo Almeida, Shelly Manne and Bud Shank. This group toured in Australia and New Zealand, app. in Mexico and Canada, as well as clubs and fests. in Cal. Publ: *Ray Brown Bass Book I* (Ray Brown Music Co., P.O. Box 1254, Hollywood, Ca. 90028).

Despite the multiplicity of his other chores as businessman, publisher etc., Brown remained one of the most gifted, flexible and influential bass players in jazz, still frequently winning polls and constantly in demand for jazz jobs as well as commercial work.

LPs: *This One's for Blanton*, duo album w. D. Ellington; *Duke's Big 4* (Pablo); *That's The Way It Is; Memphis Jackson; Just The Way It Had To Be*, w. M. Jackson (Imp.); *Walking In Space* and others w. Q. Jones (A & M); *Seven Come Eleven; Jazz/Concord* w. Herb Ellis, Joe Pass; *Soft Shoe*; L.A. Four (Concord Jazz).

BROWN, RUTH,* *singer*; b. Portsmouth, Va., 1/30/28. First nationally prominent as r & b singer with her hit record *Mama He Treats Your Daughter Mean*, recorded in Dec. 1952. Continued to play theatres and clubs, including 3½ years on Playboy Club circuit in mid-1960s. Living in Deer Park, N.Y., she worked as teacher in pre-school program and was participant in International Art of Jazz clinics in Long Island. Occasionally worked in clubs, mainly Sonny's Place in Seaford, L.I. Made her first West Coast app. in a decade playing the role of Mahalia Jackson in the production *Selma*, in Hollywood, 1975-6.

Brown's record of *Miss Brown's Blues*, on the short-lived Skye label in 1969, was a masterpiece of emotional blues singing and a reminder that she has long been one of the modern underrated artists in the interpretation of authentic blues. The album, now hard to obtain, was en-

titled *Black Is Brown and Brown Is Beautiful*. Other LPs: *Ruth Brown '65* (Mainstream); *Big Band Sound of Thad Jones/Mel Lewis Featuring Miss Ruth Brown* (Solid State); *The Real Ruth Brown* (Cobblestone); new album on London, 1976.

BROWN, SAMUEL T. (SAM), *guitar*; also *bass*; b. Baltimore, Md., 1/19/39. Father was operatic tenor who pl. violin, piano, flute, cornet. St. pl. piano at four; mandolin at six. Began pl. on weekly TV show at 12; also w. high school dance band on guitar. Joined paratroopers at 17 for three yrs., the last two in band where he learned to read. Stud. classical guitar w. Joe Fava in Det., '58-60; Mannes Coll. of Mus., NYC, '60-1; class. gtr. w. Leonid Bolotine, '60-3; harm. & theory w. Fred Wurle; master classes w. Julian Bream and Gustavo Lopez. Played w. Miriam Makeba, '61-4; Astrud Gilberto, incl. Japanese tour, '65; Ella Fitzgerald, '65-6; Ars Nova, '66-68; Gary Burton; Keith Jarrett, '69-71; Ron Carter, '71; Herbie Mann, '74; Dave Matthews band from '74; Sundays at Gregory's w. Al Haig, '75. Has also pl. concerts and/or gigs w. Stan Getz; Hubert Laws; Jimmy Owens; Charlie Haden; Joe Farrell; etc.

Infl: Django Reinhardt, Andres Segovia, Tal Farlow, Johnny Smith, Bill Evans, Coltrane, Ravi Shankar. TV: Ed Sullivan w. Makeba, Harry Belafonte; *Tonight* w. Fitzgerald; Vic Damone; *Electric Village* w. Ars Nova; *Jazz Special* w. Burton. Arr. albums for Carly Simon; Makeba. Comp: *My Hoss Knows the Way; Sunrise Highs; Dance of the Windchimes; Love Will Find a Way*. Fest: NJF-NY w. Burton; Getz; Mulligan. LPs: w. *Gary Burton & Keith Jarrett*; w. Jarrett, *Expectations; Treasure Island*; w. H. Mann, *First Light*; w. Ars Nova, *Sunshine & Shadows* (Atl.); w. Jeremy Steig, *Wayfaring Stranger* (SS); w. C. Haden, *Liberation Music Orch.* (Imp.); w. Bill Evans, *From Left to Right* (MGM); *Makeba Sings* (RCA); w. David Matthews, *Live at the Five Spot* (Muse).

BROWN, GERALD (SONNY), *drums*; b. Cincinnati, Ohio, 4/20/36. Began on drums that belonged to George Russell; Russell's mother gave them to Brown. Studied at Woodward High School in Cincinnati; Cincinnati Conserv. of Mus. Army '53-6. Played in Cincinnati, Chicago, Detroit and other midwestern locations w. Eddie Vinson; Amos Milburn; Dinah Washington; and various Gospel groups, '56-60. To NYC '61, working w. Frank Foster; Randy Weston; Ray Bryant in early '60s; Kenny Burrell for a year in mid-60s; Jon Hendricks, '63-4. Made gigs w. a wide variety of NY musicians incl. Clifford Jordan; Sonny Rollins; Curtis Fuller; Coleman Hawkins; Zoot Sims; Lee Konitz; Archie Shepp; and Sam Rivers. With New York Bass Choir from '68. Made Scandinavian tour w. Joe Henderson and Ron Carter, '70. In '75 playing mostly w. Rahsaan Roland Kirk w. whom he has been associated, off and on, from '57. Lecturer at Mark Twain JHS, August '68; staff member of YDA program in Harlem, '68-73; teaching at P.S. 139, Bronx, '69-70; Jazzmobile Workshop, '72; Jazz Interactions Workshop, I.S. 44, '73; pl. for critics symposium, Smithsonian Institute,

Wash., D.C., Sept. '74. Infl: Donald Linder, Jo Jones, Sonny Greer, Chris Columbus, Blakey, Roach, Roy Haynes, Philly Joe Jones, Elvin Jones.

TV: *Tonight; Today; Soul.* Fest: House drummer at MJF, '63-4; NJF-NY w. Bass Choir; Babs Gonzales. LPs: w. Mingus, *Let My Children Hear Music* (Col.); w. Richard Davis (Muse); K. Burrell (Prest.); A. Zoller (Embryo); R.R. Kirk (Atl.); R. Bryant (Sue); NY Bass Choir; NY Brass Co.; *Decendants of Mike & Phoebe* (Strata-East).

BRUBECK, CHRIS, *trombone, bass, composer*; also *keyboards, bass guitar*; b. Los Angeles, Cal., 3/19/52. Father, Dave Brubeck; brothers, Darius and Danny Brubeck. Studied at Interlochen Arts Academy w. trombone teacher and head of stage band, Dave Sporney; Univ. of Michigan, '71-4. Pl. w. Addiss & Crofut, '70. Own gp., New Heavenly Blue, '70-1; w. Darius Brubeck Ensemble; Two Generations of Brubeck from '72; own gp. Sky King, from '74. "Chris is one of those humorous trombone players," says his father. "He's never heard Bill Harris, but he reminds me very much of Bill."

TV: Mike Douglas; Merv Griffin; *AM America; Today*; PBS. Fest: NJF-NY; Alaska; Ravinia; Ann Arbor Blues. Comp: *Bright Day; For God's Sake Elizabeth; The Coming of the Rhino; Silver Eyes; New Heavenly Blue; Love You Tonight; Raft Song; Where Are You Tonight; Pegleg Back in 35*; opera, *The Rise and Demise of Tucker P. Fudpucker.* Publ: Derry Music Co.

LPs: *Educated Homegrown* (RCA); *New Heavenly Blue* (Atl.); *Sky King*; w. Dave Brubeck, *Summit Sessions* (Col.); *Truth is Fallen; Two Generations of Brubeck; Brother the Great Spirit Made Us All* (Atl.)

BRUBECK, DANIEL (DANNY), *drums, percussion, tabla, squeeze drum*; b. Oakland, Cal., 5/4/55. Father, Dave Brubeck; brothers, Chris and Darius. Rec. on finger cymbals w. father at age 10. Studies at Interlochen Academy of the Arts; No. Carolina School of the Arts, '72. Played w. Darius Brubeck Ensemble '73; Two Generations of Brubeck from '72; when Dave is not present the gp. is called Earthrise. Infl: Joe Morello; Alan Dawson. Some people see a stylistic resemblance to Sid Catlett, although Brubeck had never heard him. Fest: Alaska; NJF-NY; White Mountain; Ravinia. LPs: w. Dave Brubeck, *Two Generations of Brubeck; Brother the Great Spirit Made Us All* (Atl.); *Summit Sessions* (Col.).

BRUBECK, DAVID DARIUS, *keyboards, composer*; also *synthesizer, guitar, veena, sarod, trumpet*; b. San Francisco, Cal., 6/14/47. Son of Dave Brubeck; brothers, Chris and Danny. Named after Darius Milhaud. Piano lessons to age 14; harm. w. Gordon Smith at Mills Coll., '65-7; w. Milhaud in Aspen, '62; comp. w. Donald Martino at Yale, '63-4. B.A. from Wesleyan U., '69. Stud. ethnomusicology, majoring in Indian music but grad. cum laude in History of Religions. Stud. Ind. mus. w. Dagar, Ragu, Narayanaswami, Nageswara Rao, Maryvonne Pointer, Robert E. Brown; graduate counterpoint w. Richard K. Winslow; comp. privately w. Robert Jordan Fritz, '69-71. His Darius Brubeck Ensemble toured

as part of Two Generations of Brubeck on a world-wide basis from '72; also jobs as a separate entity in US and Canada. Sideman on occasion w. Maruga; Fritz. Co-produced New Heavenly Blue album w. brother, Chris, '70. Infl: Dave Brubeck, Dolphy, Jimi Hendrix, Milhaud, Webern, Stravinsky, Bartok, Ives, George Martin, Keith Jarrett, Corea. Fests: NJF-NY, '73-5. Presented lecture series, *Understanding Jazz*, for Conn. Cent. of Cont. Ed.; awarded ind. artist grant in comp. by Conn. Comm. on the Arts. Comps: *Tin Sink; Temptation Boogie; Sky-Scape; Earthrise; Pneuma Hagion*; tunes and score for *American Vaudeville Tent-Show*; score for *Evening of Poetry & Jazz* w. Don Taylor, Joanne Woodward; arrs. of *Blue Rondo a La Turk, Three to Get Ready* for full orch. LPs: *Two Generations of Brubeck; Brother, the Great Spirit Made Us All* (Atlantic); *Chaplin's Back* (Paramount); *Maruga* (Origin).

BRUBECK, DAVID WARREN (DAVE),* *piano, composer*; b. Concord, Calif., 12/6/20. December 26, 1967 saw the formal finish of the Dave Brubeck quartet in which he and Paul Desmond had played together from 1951. A new quartet, with Gerry Mulligan, Jack Six and Alan Dawson began performing and recording the following year. From '72 the trio, without Mulligan, toured with Brubeck's sons (q.v.) as Two Generations of Brubeck, Mulligan and Desmond joining the entourage for special concert and festival appearances. Eventually Chris and Danny Brubeck replaced Six and Dawson, making a world tour '74.

As in the first half of the '60s Brubeck concerned himself with the writing of extended works: the cantatas, *The Gates of Justice; Truth is Fallen; Song of Bethlehem*; an oratorio, *The Light in the Wilderness*; and an ethnic panoramic tone poem, *They All Sang Yankee Doodle*. The latter was performed by the New Haven Symphony in May '75; as a concerto for two pianos in Westport, Conn. in June '75; and, with the composer at the piano, by the Dallas Symphony in July '75.

Jazz comp: *Happy Anniversary; The Duke; Blessed Are the Poor; Forty Days; Elementals; Indian Song; Circadian Disrhythmia; The Holy One; Knives.*

Film: Paul Mazursky's *Next Stop Greenwich Village* used recordings of the early '50s Brubeck quartet on the sound track.

TV: Johnny Carson; Mike Douglas; Merv Griffin; *AM America; Today*; Dedication of Louis Armstrong Stadium at NJF-NY, NET; *Timex Special; Look Up and Live.* Fest: Berlin; Alaska; White Mountain; Ravinia; Blossom; Monterey; Antibes; Warsaw; Saratoga; NO; Mexico; Mar Y Sol; NJF-NY w. Mulligan & Desmond, '72; solo piano pl. the music of J. Van Heusen, '73; w. Two Generations, '73, '75. Poll: Group won *Playboy*, '66-8; Brubeck won piano '66-71; elected to *Playboy* Hall of Fame, '66.

LPs: *Summit Sessions; Blues Roots; Brubeck in Amsterdam; Last Time I Saw Paris; Live at the Berlin Philharmonic* (Col.); *Brubeck & Mulligan in Cincinnati; The Light in the Wilderness; The Gates of Justice* (Decca);

Truth Is Fallen; The Last Set at Newport; Two Generations of Brubeck; We're All Together Again For the First Time; Brother the Great Spirit Made Us All (Atl.); *Duets 1975/Desmond-Brubeck* (Horizon); reissues: *The Art of Dave Brubeck, The Fantasy Years* (Atl.); *Dave Brubeck's All-Time Greatest Hits* (Col.).

BRUCE, JOHN SYMON ASHER (JACK), *bass, singer, composer*; also *keyboards, synthesizer, harmonica*; b. Bishopbriggs, Lanarkshire, Scotland, 5/14/43. Won a scholarship to Royal Scottish Acad. of Mus. at age 17, stud. cello and comp. Pl. bass w. jazz bands in Glasgow area clubs during this period and met Alexis Korner, Ginger Baker, Dick Heckstall-Smith and Graham Bond. Joined the latter three in the Graham Bond Organization; then worked w. John Mayall's Bluesbreakers; Manfred Mann; Cream; Tony Williams Lifetime; West, Bruce and Laing. Pl. in a short-lived gp. w. Carla Bley, '75. LPs: *Out of the Storm* (RSO); own gp.; w. Cream; w. Tony Williams (Poly.); West, Bruce and Laing (Col.).

BRUNIS, GEORG (George Brunies),* *trombone*; b. New Orleans, La., 2/6/1900. Made first rec. w. NO Rhythm Kings, '22. Toured for 12 years w. clarinetist Ted Lewis. Settling in Chicago in '40s he spent the rest of his life gigging locally and rec. with many jazz artists incl. Eddie Condon; the latter's *Windy City Seven Commodores* is said to be Brunis' fav. session, and can be found in *Eddie Condon/Bud Freeman* on Atl. Brunis died in Chicago, 11/19/74.

BRYAN, MIKE,* *guitar*; b. Byhalia, Miss., 1916. Bryan pl. guitar in B. Goodman's orch. during the period when Ch. Christian was a member of the Goodman sextet; was active in the '60s as the producer of a series of TV jazz films, feat. Armstrong, Ellington, Condon et al. Made for the Goodyear Co., the films were only seen outside the U.S. Bryan later resumed playing; toured Viet Nam w. Martha Raye. He died of leukemia in LA, 8/20/72.

BRYANT, BOBBY, *trumpet, fluegelhorn, composer*; b. Hattiesburg, Miss., 5/19/34. Played tenor sax and trumpet with local bands during his teens. After moving to Chicago, stud. from '52-7, earning bachelor's degree in music education with trumpet major from Cosmopolitan School of Music. While in Chicago, pl. with various small bands, Latin combos, Red Saunders etc. Also led band for touring show starring singer Billy Williams.

Bryant traveled as lead trumpeter w. Vic Damone from '60-5, working throughout the U.S., Canada, Philippines, Puerto Rico. Settling in LA, he worked w. Gerald Wilson, O. Nelson and hundreds of recording groups in pop, r & b and other areas; also as staff musician at NBC-TV. He led a combo and occasionally a big band locally in clubs and on records; comp. and arr. for Damone, Peggy Lee, L. Rawls, B. Goodman, Marlena Shaw and many other singers. Led band on Bill Cosby TV comedy series, and played as sideman in numerous other TV shows. Feat. soloist on sound tracks of movies *A Day With The Boys; Assault On A Queen;* and *Winning.* Dir. of Mus. for *What It Is*, 10 segs. on black history for NBC-TV.

As a soloist and leader Bryant makes an imposing fig-

ure, combining elements of Cat Anderson, M. Ferguson and D. Ellis with a touch of the blues added. A brilliant composer and performer, he was prevented by economic conditions from gaining the success he deserved with his own orch.

LPs: *Swahili Strut; Ain't Doing Too B-a-d, Bad* (Cadet); *Big Band Blues* (Vee-Jay). Others by band, such as *Earth Dance* and *Hair*, both on Wor. Pac., were deleted.

BRYANT, RAPHAEL (RAY),* *piano, composer*; b. Philadelphia, Pa., 12/24/31. Continued to work w. own trio or as solo pianist. Appeared in the latter context at the Montreux Jazz Fest., '72. A recording of his performance, *Alone at Montreux*, was issued on Atlantic. Comp: *Blues #2; Blues #3; Changes; Cubano Chant; Little Susie; Slow Freight.* Other LPs: Pablo; Cadet; reissue on Prest.; w. Z. Sims (Pablo).

BRYANT, ROYAL G. (RUSTY), *tenor and alto saxophones, leader*; b. Huntington, W. Va., 11/25/29. Raised in Columbus from 1935. Father, a mortician and amateur musician, bought him trumpet, later alto sax. At 13, pl. w. Archie (Stomp) Gordon band. U.S. Navy 1948-9; stationed in Boston, where he heard Sam Rivers, Jaki Byard, Nat Pierce band and others who were influential. Back in Columbus, briefly joined Tiny Grimes; then opened w. own gp. at Carolyn Club for five years. Began recording for Dot and had several hit singles, notably *Night Train.* Placed emphasis on honking pre-rock style. From '56-8 his girl vocalist was Nancy Wilson. Later the band was heard throughout the midwest and east, often under the leadership of organist Hank Marr.

Bryant made a comeback under his own name when he resumed recording as a leader in 1969, for Prestige. LPs: *Until It's Time For You To Go; For the Good Times; Friday Night Funk; Wild Fire; Soul Liberation; Fire Eater; Night Train Now!; Rusty Bryant Returns* (Prestige). Earlier LPs: *America's Greatest Jazz; Jazz Horizons* (Dot).

BRYDEN, BERYL, *singer*; b. Norwich, England, 5/11/26. To London 1945. Sang w. Geo. Webb's Dixielanders and other trad. gps. In Paris in '53 and '54, sang at Vieux Colombier and was feat. w. Lionel Hampton at Olympia. Later in Holland, Germany; long assoc. w. Fatty George band, then w. Tremble Kids in Zurich. During these years, busy radio, TV, recording schedule. In 1960s, pl. Antibes Fest., toured Far East; Africa 1965. First visit to NY 1970; in Australia '71-2 w. Graeme Bell. A loyal devotee of early jazz forms, she attended the NOJF in '73 as a visitor. Innumerable jazz festivals around the Continent, and rec. w. more than 20 bands in eight countries, from a Freddy Randall date in London, 1948, to an LP w. Piccadilly Six in Zurich, '75. Others on Esquire, Decca, Supraphon, Col., Pye, Muza etc.

BUCKNER, MILTON (MILT),* *organ, piano, composer*; also *trombone, vibes*; b. St. Louis, Mo., 7/10/15. With L. Hampton in '40s and early '50s, Buckner popularized "locked-hands" piano style (both hands pl. parallel chord patterns) which he originated in Detroit, '34, to "give

Don Cox five-piece orch. more depth." Own organ trio from '52. W. I. Jacquet, A. Dawson at Lennie's-On-the-Turnpike, '66. European tours: w. Jacquet, R. Eldridge, '66; w. B. Tate, Wallace Bishop, '67; Jo Jones; MPS record tour, '69; L. Hampton, '71. TV: Global Shows, Toronto, '74. Fests: NJF, '68, '70-5; Nice, '74-5; MJF, '70. Comp: *Hamp's Boogie Woogie; Slide Hamp, Slide; Overtime; The Lamplighter; Mighty Low; Count's Basement; Jumping at the Zanzibar; Mighty High; Rockin' With Milt.* LPs: *Play Chords* (MPS/BASF); *Blues For Diane* (Jazz Odyssey); *Midnight Mood, Rockin' Hammond* (Cadet); w. Jacquet (Prestige); Tate (B & B); *Newport in New York, The Jam Sessions, vols. 1 & 2* (Cobblestone).

BUCKNER, THEODORE GUY (TED),* alto sax; b. St. Louis, Mo., 12/14/13. The veteran alto saxophonist, brother of pianist Milt Buckner, continued to be active in the Detroit area and was associated with the revised edition of McKinney's Cotton Pickers. He died in April 1976 in Detroit.

BUCKNER, JOHN EDWARD (TEDDY),* trumpet; b. Sherman, Tex., 7/16/09. Has led his own small band since the late '50s, mostly in LA area. Worked regularly in New Orleans Square at Disneyland from mid '60s; also occasional concerts at Pilgrimage Theatre etc.; night club gigs at Donte's, Times Restaurant. In '75, did sound track work for *Louis Armstrong: Chicago Style,* a TV film, ABC.

LPs: *Teddy Buckner All Stars* (D.J.); *Midnight In Moscow* (GNP-Crescendo); *On Sunset Strip* (D.J.).

BUDIMIR, DENNIS MATTHEW,* guitar; b. Los Angeles, Ca., 6/20/38. Played w. Harry James, C. Hamilton, B. Shank, Peggy Lee, Julie London, Gerald Wilson and many others in LA area. For more than a decade worked mainly as studio musician w. Q. Jones, L. Schifrin, M. Paich, D. Grusin, D. Ellis, Joe Williams, G. Melle et al.

Won DB Critics' Poll, TDWR, '71. LPs: *Second Coming; Session with Albert; Sprung Free!* (Revelation).

BUDWIG, MONTY,* bass; b. Pender, Neb. 12/26/29. Well known for many years for jazz associations w. Goodman, Herman, and west coast groups in '50s, '60s. Cont. freelance studio and night club work in '70s. Concord Jazz Fest., '71 and Australian tour '73, w. Goodman. S. America, '74 w. Carmen McRae. Best LPs: *Jazz Gunn* w. S. Manne (Atl.); *Manne That's Gershwin,* w. Manne (Capitol); *Summer Night* w. Mike Wofford trio (Milestone); Sarah Vaughan & J. Rowles trio (Mainstream).

BUNCH, JOHN L. JR.,* piano, conductor; b. Tipton, Ind., 12/1/21. Own duo for 44 weeks at Luigi II in NYC, '65-6; w. Buddy Rich big band, '66. Became accompanist-mus. dir. for Tony Bennett in late '66, remaining until late '72. In this capacity cond. the bands of Basie, Ellington, Herman, Rich, the LA Philharmonic and Cleve. Orch. Worked mostly w. B. Goodman sextet '73, incl. European tour in Dec.; Rich septet, '74, incl. European tour in Oct. Bunch also led own trio or duo at Bradley's, NYC and Anchorage Hotel, Antigua, BWI,

'73-5. App. on many TV shows incl. *This Is Music*—13 Tony Bennett specials, filmed in London and seen in US; Tom Jones; Pearl Bailey; Jonathan Winters; Dean Martin. Comp: *Why You; Feathers;* arrs. for Herman, Goodman. Fest: Concord JF w. Rich, '74. LPs: own sextet (Famous Door); w. Bennett (Col., MGM); Cal Tjader (MGM); Rich; Sammy Davis-Rich (Reprise); Jane Harvey; Eddie Barefield (RCA); Joe Venuti-Zoot Sims (Chiaro.).

BUNKER, LAWRENCE BENJAMIN (LARRY),* drums, vibes; b. Long Beach, Cal., 11/4/28. Busy in studios since '50s, he has continued to maintain an association with jazz. Along with apps. with the LA Phil. under Zubin Mehta, and other symph. orchs., he app. at Shelly's Manne Hole w. Z. Sims, Dave Grusin; at Donte's w. Howard Roberts, Clare Fischer, Mike Barone, O. Nelson, B. Shank and many others. At Ojai Fest. pl. music of Stravinsky under Pierre Boulez, '71; music of Messiaen, '72; in '75, Brahms, Schoenberg, under Michael Tilson Thomas. Bunker also has fulfilled numerous film and TV assignments w. Q. Jones, L. Schifrin, O. Nelson, Pat Williams, Tom Scott, Grusin, G. Mulligan, John Mandel. As an avocation, he collects and restores antiques, also custom makes instruments and auxiliary equipment for the perf. of contemporary music.

LPs: w. Gary Burton, *Time Machine; Something's Coming* (RCA); w. Q. Jones, *Smackwater Jack* (A & M); w. Williams, *Threshold* (Cap.); w. Dominic Frontiere, *On Any Sunday*—movie sound track (Bell); w. 5th Dimension, *Stone Soul Picnic* (Liberty).

BURNS, DAVID (DAVE), trumpet; fluegelhorn; also piano; b. Perth Amboy, N.J., 3/5/24. Studied privately w. Nicholan Morrisey from ages nine to 13; Thomas Ippolito, 13-17; two yrs., off and on, w. Carmine Caruso. Worked w. Savoy Sultans, '41-3. Led an AAF Band, '43-5. With Dizzy Gillespie's big band, '46-9; Duke Ellington, '50-2; James Moody, '52-7. From '57-60 app. w. a variety of small gps. in NYC; then w. Billy Mitchell-Al Grey sextet, '61-4; Willie Bobo, '64-6; combo work at Minton's; James Moody at Half Note; Leon Bibb TV show, NBC, '66-8. Moved to Long Island and pl. w. Mitchell in "*Project Read,*" '69. From '70 working w. International Art of Jazz, pl. concerts, lecturing and cond. "rap sessions" on all levels from elementary school to coll. Also teaching improvisation on all instr. in own studio in Freeport, L.I. One of the earliest of Gillespie's disciples in the '40s.

Other infl: Armstrong, Eldridge. TV: Milton Berle show w. Ellington; Sammy Davis show w. Johnny Brown sextet. Films: *Sweet Love Bitter* w. Dick Gregory; *Jivin' in Bebop* w. Gillespie; w. Ellington for Universal, '50. Fest: NJF. Comp: *Common Touch; C.B. Blues; Be's That Way; Automation; Toe Tappin'; Rigor "Mortez"; Livin' Through It All.* Own LPs: *Warming Up; Dave 'Burns';* w. Bill English (Vang.); w. Arthur Taylor, *A.T.'s Delight;* w. George Wallington (Blue Note); w. Gillespie (Prest., RCA Vict.); w. Ray Brown-Milt Jackson (Savoy); w. W. Bobo (Roulette); Mitchell-Grey (Argo);

w. Eddie Jefferson, *Body and Soul*; w. Moody (Prest.); w. Dexter Gordon (unreleased) for BN.

BURRELL, HERMAN DAVIS II (DAVE), *piano, composer*; also *clarinet, vibes*; b. Middletown, Ohio, 9/10/40. Mother a singer, organist, pianist, choir director. Studied under Dr. Barbara Smith at U. of Hawaii where he was Music Major '58-60. Grad. from Boston Conserv. of Mus. and Berklee Coll of Mus., '61-5, majoring in Performance, Arr. & Comp. He has performed in Hawaii, Europe, Japan, Algeria, Surinam and all over the US and Canada as a soloist, w. own duos, trios, quartet; Archie Shepp; Marion Brown; and the 360 Degree Music Experience w. Grachan Moncur III and Beaver Harris. Pl. many concerts for prisoners; coll. concerts, also lecturing as artist-in-residence. Fest: NJF-NY, Radio City jam session, '73; NJF-NY w. Shepp, '71-2; NJF w. Sunny Murray Spiritual Infinity; NJF in Japan concert tour w. Shepp; Molde; Pori w. 360 Degree; Mednarodni, Yugo., Ann Arbor Blues & Jazz Fest. w. Shepp; Baden-Baden Free Jazz Meeting; Paris Int. JF. Pan-African Cultural Fest. in Algiers w. Shepp-led avant garde all stars. Pl. w. Rastafarian musicians in Kingston, Jamaica; w. Haitian percussionists in Port-au-Prince where he performed and rec. a West African voodoo ceremony. Received grants from NEA to adapt Haitian folk music to a Jazz Suite which he performed in Central Park, NYC; to write music to the theme of a book by Edgar White, *Crucifado*. In the Sahara Desert wrote music for a French film co. illustrating Black American musicians pl. and discussing music with nomadic Touareg musicians. Other comp: *A.M. Rag (Margie Pargie); Blue Notes On the Black and White Keys; Polynesian Suite; Sketches of Harlem; Echo; Japan; My March; After Love; Answer; Epilogue; East Side Colors*. Arrs. for Shepp; Pharoah Sanders; Marion Brown; 360 Degree Experience. Also *La Vie de Boheme*, based on Puccini's *La Boheme*. Publ: (360 Music Co., 269 W. 72nd St., N.Y., N.Y. 10023).

Infl: Jelly Roll Morton, Ellington, Monk, Bud Powell, boogie woogie, Coltrane, Shepp, Moncur, Max Roach, Prokofiev, Puccini, Rimsky-Korsakoff. TV: *Like It Is* w. Shepp; 360 Degree; sound track for *Witherspoon*, Black Drama Repertory Workshop, CBS; documentary, *Jazz in New York Today*, filmed for Rome TV in NYC. Music Instructor at Queens Col, NYC, '71-73. LPs: own trio (Black Saint); quartet (Horo); w. S. Cowell; *Only Me; Dreams; Questions and Answers* (Trio); *High* (Douglas); *La Vie De Boheme; Echo* (Byg); w. Sanders; Brown (Imp.); Shepp (Imp.; Black Saint; Arista; Big; American) Moncur; Murray; Clifford Thornton (Byg); Alan Silva (ESP); w. 360 Degree Exp., *From Ragtime to No Time* (360°).

BURRELL, KENNETH EARL (KENNY),* *guitar, composer, singer*; b. Detroit, Mich., 7/31/31. Prominent since the mid-1950s, occasionally as sideman with D. Gillespie, B. Goodman et al, but most often leading his own groups, Burrell by the 1960s was occupied with NYC studio work, along with clubs and concerts. He undertook his first tour of California in 1967, and his initial

European tour, with his own group, in '69. During that year he also started his own club, The Guitar. In '70 he took his combo on a tour of Japan, and returned there the following year. Also in '71 he began a series of college seminars in the U.S.

Burrell began recording for Fantasy in 1972, traveled in both Eastern and Western European countries, visited Japan, New Zealand and Australia, then Europe, with the Newport All Stars, and relocated in California. From '73 he became active in LA studio work along with many festivals, clubs, concerts, seminars and clinics. He was appointed executive director of Guitar Player Productions in '74. Japan again in '75; *Tribute to Duke Ellington* album, '75.

In addition to winning innumerable *down beat* polls, Burrell has placed first on guitar in Japan's *Swing Journal* poll and the London *Melody Maker* poll for the past several years. He won the first *Ebony* Magazine music poll.

Publs: *Jazz Guitar* (Elliott Music Co. Inc., 144 Jolind Rd., Paoli, Pa. 19301).

Comps: *Ode to 52nd St.*, title work of LP (Cadet); *Asphalt Canyon Suite*, title work of LP (Verve); *Sausalito Nights; Be Yourself* etc.

LPs: *Introducing; Burrell, Vol. 2* (BN); *Best; Blue Moods; Crash; Out of This World; Quintet*, feat. Coltrane; *All Day Long & All Night Long*, feat. Byrd, Waldron, Mobley (Prest.); *Both Feet on the Ground; 'Round Midnight; Up The Street* (Fant.); *Cool Cookin'* (Chess); *God Bless The Child* (CTI); *Guitar Forms* (Verve); *Man At Work; Ode to 52nd Street; Tender Gender* (Cadet); w. S. Rollins, *Alfie* (Imp.).

BURROWS, DONALD VERNON (DON), *clarinet, composer*; also *saxophones, flutes, fife*; b. Sydney, Australia, 8/8/28. Stud. at Sydney Conservatorium, '46-8. First rec. date at age 16 in dixieland group. Over the past 30 years, innumerable apps. in concerts, fests. and often on TV as sideman, leader, soloist, MC and lecturer. Burrows, who has led combos and bands of every kind, pl. dance halls and night clubs in the '40s and '50s, radio shows from the '40s, TV from late '50s, is an admirable clarinetist and Australia's best known jazz musician. Insp. by B. Goodman, B. De Franco, Ellington, G. Mulligan, Ch. Parker, G. Burton. Toured New Zealand, '60 on same show w. Oscar Peterson trio; toured Australia, '72 in program w. Burton, C. Byrd. Took part in the world's first satellite telecast, Montreal Expo '67. Mus. Dir. on Australian show at Expo 70 in Osaka, Japan; pl. at NJF-NY, '72. Toured Southeast Asia for Australian Dept. of Foreign Affairs, '74. Burrows has won many awards incl. Australian music mag. polls, gold record for his album *Just The Beginning*; Album of the Year award, '74 for *Don Burrows Quartet at Sydney Opera House*. In '72 Queen Elizabeth awarded him the MBE for services to jazz. In '73 the Australian Prime Minister appointed him to Council for the Arts and he was successful in helping establish Australia's first jazz studies program at Sydney Conservatorium, where he teaches.

Burrows' quartet has app. w. symph. orchs. in a series of concerts since '66. Comps: sound track for movie *2000 Weeks*, and for dozens of documentaries and TV programs, background music for stage, radio and TV plays, as well as originals for a dozen albums.

LPs: *Don Burrows Quartet at Sydney Opera House* (Mainstream); others on Australian labels: *The Jazz Sounds of the Don Burrows Quartet; On Camera* (Col.); *Jazz Australia* (CBS); *Just The Beginning; Australia and all that Jazz* (Cherry Pie).

BURTON, GARY, * *vibes, composer, educator;* b. Anderson, Ind., 1/23/43. First prominent in '63 w. G. Shearing and S. Getz, '64-6, he formed his own quartet in '67 w. Larry Coryell, guitar; Bob Moses, drums; and Steve Swallow, bass. Swallow was still w. him in '75 and Moses had rejoined. From '70 Burton has also pl. solo concerts and recorded w. other prominent jazzmen (see LPs below). Between '71-5 he toured in Japan, Australia, England and the Continent, incl. Communist-bloc countries. As an educator he has been a permanent staff member at the Berklee Coll. Mus. from '71 but also presents lecture-seminar-concert programs w. his quartet at univs. all over the U.S. Consultant in instr. design for Musser Co. Fest: NJF, '64-75; MJF, Montreux, Berlin, '66-73. Won first place in DB Readers poll, '68-74; Critics poll, '72, '74-5; DB Jazzman of the Year, '68. Publ: Introduction to *Jazz Vibes; Solo Book; Four Mallet Studies* (Creative Music, Chicago). Comps: *The Sunset Bell; Leroy the Magician; Walter L.; Dreams; Response; Brownout; Boston Marathon.*

The harmonic richness of Burton's four-mallet forays showed most graphically his original Bill Evans influence, but he has continued to deepen and widen his personal expression by using challenging material that is extremely contemporary, without yielding to the excesses of the avant garde or the pursuit of the rock dollar. He won a Grammy for his solo album, *Alone At Last*, on Atlantic. Other LPs: *New Quartet; Ring; Seven Songs For Quartet & Chamber Orch.* (ECM); *In the Public Interest* (Poly.); *Good Vibes; Throb* (Atl.); *In Concert; Lofty Fake Anagram; Duster* (RCA); *Paris Encounter* w. S. Grappelli (Atl.); *Crystal Silence* w. C. Corea; *Matchbook* w. Ralph Towner; *Hotel Hello* w. S. Swallow (ECM); *Genuine Tong Funeral* w. Carla Bley (RCA); w. K. Jarrett (Atl.).

BURTON, WILLIAM RON, *piano, composer;* also *organ;* b. Louisville, Ky., 2/10/34. Private lessons at 13 for four yrs. First prof. job at 18 w. local gps. of Tommy Walker; Edgar "Eggeye" Brooks. Roland Kirk came through Louisville in '53 and for next six yrs. Burton went out w. him to Nashville, Indianapolis, Cincinnati, Milwaukee and Chicago. Spent eight mos. on own in NYC, '60; then w. Chris Powell in Syracuse, '60-1. Returned to Louisville, leaving as organist w. George Adams trio, '64-5. Met Norris Jones (Sirone), Ron Hampton, Lloyd McNeil in Atlanta and pl. in gp. w. them, '65-6. Freelanced in NYC '66, joining R.R. Kirk, '67. Through '72 pl. clubs, concerts, major US and Euro. fests. w. him. From '72 w. Piano Choir; own gp. From '74 w. Michael

Carvin; gigs w. Stanley Turrentine; Leon Thomas; Carlos Garnett. Infl: Peterson, Lloyd Glenn, Garner, Bud Powell, H. Silver, Red Garland, K. Drew, Richard Abrams, Andrew Hill. TV: w. Kirk, documentary on Martin Luther King, *March to Freedom*, Westinghouse Broad.; *Soul*, PBS; w. Ray Ore and the Creative Connoisseurs, Channel 50, Trenton, N.J. Comp: *Seven Points; African Sunrise; Desert Trot; Fertility Dance.* LPs: *The Cosmic Twins;* w. Dick Griffin, *The Eighth Number* (Strata-East); w. Kirk, (Atl.); Michael Carvin (Steeple.); Grubbs Bros. (Cobble.).

BUSH, LEONARD WALTER (LENNIE), * *bass;* b. London, England, 6/6/27. Pro. since '44. Mainly active in studios in recent years w. J. Parnell et al. Occ. jazz gigs at Ronnie Scott's Club w. C. Terry, Z. Sims, J. Pass, B. Webster, C. McRae, A. O'Day et al. Three Euro. tours w. B. Goodman, '71-2, incl. rec.

BUSHKIN, JOE, * *piano, songwriter;* b. 11/17/16. After living some years in Hawaii, Bushkin moved to Santa Barbara, Cal. Except for a brief tenure at a hotel in Palm Springs, Cal., in 1970, he remained in virtual retirement, raising thoroughbred horses in Santa Barbara, Calif. He came to NYC in November '75 to play an engagement at Michael's Pub. At the same time his daughters were winning prizes at the National horse show, Madison Square Garden.

BUSHLER, HERB, *bass;* also *piano;* b. New York City, 3/7/39. Two yrs. of piano study, '47-9; then taught self tuba until "damned thing got too heavy." Took up bass, doubling Fender from '65. Bushler, who has app. as soloist w. Toronto, Phila., Cinci., American, Brooklyn and Roch. symphonies, has also worked w. a variety of groups, some concurrently, such as Ted Curson '65; Fifth Dimension, '69; Paul Winter, '71-3; Gil Evans, '67-74; Tony Williams, '73; Blossom Dearie, '71-3; David Amram, '70- . Also active in '70s w. Billy Harper, Joe Chambers, Coleridge Perkinson, Howard Johnson Substructure and Joe Farrell. Infl: Coleridge Perkinson. Arrs. for singer Gerri Granger. Cond. Negro Ensemble Co. prod: *Song of the Lusitanian Bogey*, '68; *Man Better Man*, '74; pl. piano for prod. of Behan's *The Hostage*, '62. Fest: Newport, Newport West, Lugano w. Curson, Evans, T. Williams, Montego Joe. LPs: Farrell (CTI); G. Evans (Ampex, Atl.); *Living Time* w. B. Evans-G. Russell (Col.); Dearie (Daffodil); Amram (RCA); Curson (Atl.); Teresa Brewer w. Ellington (Fly. Dutch.).

BUTLER, FRANK, * *drums;* b. Kansas City, Mo., 2/18/28. Worked for short period w. J. Coltrane, Miles Davis; mainly active in LA area w. Harold Land, Jimmy Rowles, Terry Gibbs, Teddy Edwards, Conte Candoli, Gerald Wilson, Lorez Alexandria. Infrequently heard in 1970s; worked for a while as drug abuse counsellor in Youth Outreach Program for LA County Health Dept. Festivals: Monterey; Black Fest. of Arts. LP: w. Teddy Edwards, *Feelin's* (Muse); w. Miles Davis, *Seven Steps to Heaven* (Col.).

BUTTERFIELD, CHARLES WILLIAM (BILLY), * *trumpet, fluegelhorn;* b. Middleton, Ohio, 1/14/17. Featured soloist w. Bob Crosby, Shaw and Goodman bands in '30s and '40s. After many years on NYC studio scene moved to Va., where he led own band in late '50s-early '60s. Living in Fla. during '60s, working w. own units until he became charter member of World's Greatest Jazzband, '68, with which he toured in US, Europe, England, So. America, So. Africa and Australia. Returned to Fla. '72, gigging on own and w. Flip Phillips. TV and fests. w. WGJ incl. NJF, NOJF, Berlin. Many apps. at Colo. Jazz Party, '60s, '70s. LPs: *Bobby, Billy and Brazil* w. B. Hackett (MGM); w. WGJ (Proj. 3, Atl., World Jazz); *Swing That Music* w. Dutch Coll. Swing Band; *In a Mellow Tone* w. own sextet (DCS); *Rapport* w. D. Wellstood (77).

BUTTS, JAMES H. (JIMMY), *bass, singer;* b. New York City, 1917. Started on piano at high school. Bass w. Dr. Sausage and the Five Pork Chops, 1937. Pl. w. Chris Columbus '39-43, except for brief stint w. Les Hite spring '41. After pl. w. Doc Wheeler's Sunset Royals and Don Redman, worked up comedy act w. Wilbur Kirk. In Sept. 1944 was member of Tiny Grimes rec. group that incl. Ch. Parker (latter's first combo session). Later worked w. Trummy Young, Art Hodes, Buddy Tate, Josh White, own trio; joined Dud Bascomb, '48. Teamed w. bassist-pianist Doles Dickens 1952-7; then spent 11 years w. Juanita Smith in duo act for hotels, lounges. In '68 started gp. w. vocalist-wife Edye Byrde, who pl. cocktail drums; they have worked various restaurants and hotels in NY and NJ. LP: reissue, Charlie Parker (Arista).

BYARD, JOHN A. (JAKI),* *piano, composer, educator;* also *saxophones, trumpet, bass, trombone, guitar, drums;* b. Worcester, Mass., 6/15/22. Played w. Maynard Ferguson in early '60s, then moved to NYC and joined Charles Mingus. Toured Europe w. him, '68, '70. Played and rec. w. Rahsaan Roland Kirk but most of his NYC apps. have been as a solo pianist at Top of the Gate, late '60s; and in a duo setting during a long run of Sundays at Bradley's, '74-5. In '74-5 he was guest cond. of Sinclair Acey's Music Complex in a Sunday series at the Five Spot. Byard has also pl. in Australia; Japan, '71; Japan; China, '72.

From '69 teaching comp. & arr., piano at New England Conservatory; from '71 at SE Mass. U.; Elmo Lewis Sch. of Fine Arts, Boston; from '75 Julius Hartt Sch. of Mus., Hartford, Conn. Also taught at City Coll., CUNY during early '70s. From '71 he has also conducted seminars at many institutions such as Bismarck JC in No. Dakota; U. of Pitts.; Smithsonian Inst.; Howard U.; and the Hotchkiss School.

A versatile performer who is at home in every style from ragtime to freedom, and a strong communicator of emotion with more than a modicum of wit. Won DB Critics' Poll, TDWR, '66, '71.

Fest: Molde '67; San Sebastian; Barcelona '75: all w. C. Terry; NO '69; Colo. JP '71; Toulon '74; Nice '75. Comp: *Falling Rains of Life; Cat's Cradle Conference Rag; Hazy Eve; The Hollis Stomp; Seasons; New Orleans Strut; Top of the Gate Rag; Spanish Tinge; Sp.*

Tinge #2; Sp. Tinge #3; To Bob Vatel of Paris; Tribute to Jimmy Slide; Aluminum Baby.

LPs: *There'll Be Some Changes Made* (Muse); *Duet* w. E. Hines (MPS); *Sunshine of My Soul; Solo Piano; Freedom; On the Spot; Jaki Byard With Strings; The Jaki Byard Experience* (Prest.); also in France on Futura; Japan on JVC; w. Al Cohn-Zoot Sims, *Body and Soul;* w. Phil Woods, *Musique Du Bois* (Muse); w. RR Kirk (Atl.); w. Mingus (Prest., Fant.); Bobby Jones (Cobble.).

BYAS, CARLOS WESLEY (DON),* *tenor saxophone;* b. Muskogee, Okla., 10/21/12. Prominent in the U.S. w. C. Basie, later w. small groups on 52nd St., Byas settled in Europe after touring there w. Don Redman's band in '46. He lived in France, then in Holland. Returning to the U.S. in June '70, he app. at NJF. In early '71 he toured Japan w. A. Blakey, then returned to Holland. Byas died of lung cancer in Amsterdam, 8/24/72.

One of the last of the great ballad-oriented tenor saxophonists in the Hawkins tradition, Byas also was among the first of his generation to ally himself with the bebop movement in jazz, pl. w. Gillespie in '44 at the Onyx Club, NYC.

TV: *Just Jazz,* PBS, '71. Comp: *Orgasm.*

LPs: *In Paris* (Pres.); *Anthropology* (Black Lion); *Le Grand* (MJR); *Free & Easy* (Savoy); *Midnight at Mintons* (Onyx); *Don Byas* (GNP); *Don Byas Meets Ben Webster* (Pres.); *April In Paris* (Battle).

BYERS, WILLIAM MITCHELL (BILLY),* *composer, trombone;* b. Los Angeles, Cal., 5/1/27. After working extensively w. Q. Jones in the late '50s and early '60s, Byers moved to S. Cal. and was active principally as an arranger for films, TV, records and night club acts, for Jones (until '70), C. Basie, F. Sinatra (with whom he toured Japan and Europe as a sideman in '74), D. Ellington, H. Edison, T. Dorsey band (directed by M. McEachern), Sammy Davis, B. Eckstine, Peggy Lee and numerous pop artists. With Marvin Hamlisch he did orchestration for movies *The Sting* and *The Way We Were.* TV: wrote occasional episodes for *Streets of San Francisco; Barnaby Jones* etc. Served as judge at college lab band contests. Wrote music for film *Hauser's Memory;* also originals for *Basie Land* and arrangements for *More Hits of the 50s and 60s,* both for Basie.

LPs: *Impressions of Duke Ellington* (Merc.); *More Hits of the 50s and 60s; Basie Land* (Verve).

BYRD, CHARLES L. (CHARLIE),* *guitar, composer;* b. Suffolk, Va., 9/16/25. The sensitive, versatile artist continued to present programs with a mix of jazz, Latin American and classical music. He appeared several times at the NJF-NY in the '70s and also toured Australia. Commenting on Byrd's album with Aldemaro Romero, Barry Ulanov remarked that his playing on *Romance* "evokes two Segovias, the Renaissance Spanish city and the great classical guitarist."

LPs: *Top Hat; Byrd By the Sea; Crystal Silence; Tambu* w. C. Tjader (Fant.); *Stroke of Genius; Onda Nueva* w. A. Romero; *For All We Know; Delicately; Let Go; Let It Be; More Brazilian; Sketches of Brazil;* three tracks in *The Guitar Album*, rec. live at Town Hall Aug. '71 (Col.); reissue, *Latin Byrd* (Mile.).

BYRD, DONALD,* *trumpet, fluegelhorn, educator, composer*; b. Detroit, Mich., 12/9/32. Established himself in NYC w. Art Blakey, Max Roach, etc.; then led own gps. in '60s while furthering his post-graduate studies and becoming active as an educator. Received Masters in Music Education from Manhattan School of Music. In '71 received Ph.D. in college teaching and administration from Columbia U. Sch. of Education. Concerned with the history and culture of Afro-American music, he is one of the leading ethnomusicologists. He was the Chairman of the Black Music Dept. at Howard U., Wash., D.C. when in '73 he recorded an album originally designed for the late Lee Morgan. Issued under the title *Black Byrd* on Byrd's long time affiliate Blue Note, it became the biggest selling album in the company's 35 year history and put Byrd full into the pop-soul market. His subsequent albums were in the same direction, using currently fashionable rhythms and electronic effects. Some of his Howard students became his sidemen (see Kevin Toney; Joe Hall) and he also produced an LP of them as a group, the Black Byrds (in which he does not play) for Fantasy. Whether he was playing in a club or a college concert, Byrd lectured at various campuses on education, black music, and law as it pertains to music and musicians. (By '75 he had completed two yrs. of Law school.) These lectures were usually combined with a music workshop.

Some musicians and critics accused Byrd of selling out in his new approach and offered that as a college professor he should have been influencing his students to pursue a less "commercialized" route but he said at the time: "One of the things I'm trying to do is to get people involved, and to dramatize through any means possible the plight of black musicians in *academia*. You would think in this day and age that would have changed with respect to black music, that it would have achieved some degree of acceptance in the university, but the truth is, until we get an integrated view of things with respect to black music, nothing is going to happen."

Although he left Howard, in late '75 he was again teaching, this time at No. Carolina Central Coll. Comp: *I Love the Girl; Estavanico; Essence; The Dude*.

LPs: *Places and Spaces; Stepping Into Tomorrow; Street Lady; Black Byrd; Ethiopian Knights; Fancy Free; Slow Drag; Blackjack* (BN).

BYRNE, WILLIAM E. JR. (BILL), *saxophones*; also *clarinet, flute*; b. Stamford, Conn., 4/26/42. Educ: Oakland H.S., '55-9; SF State Coll. '60-5; BA degree in mus. (clarinet major), '65. Started pl. professionally around Oakland-SF area until he joined the Army in '66, where he served in NORAD commanders. On his discharge, worked briefly w. Harry James in U.S. and Europe. Since late '70 has been freelancing in LA TV and rec. studios. Often member of the orchs. of B. Berry, L. Bellson, T. Gibbs, N. Hefti. Infl: Ch. Parker. Fests: Belvedere JF, Canada, w. Bellson and Supersax; Concord,

w. Berry, '74; Concord Pavillion w. C. Mangione orch., '75.

LPs: *Louie Rides Again*, w. Bellson (Pablo); *Chase The Clouds Away*, w. Mangione (A & M); w. Berry (Beez).

CABLES, GEORGE ANDREW, *piano, keyboards, composer*; b. Brooklyn, N.Y., 11/14/44. Stud. High Sch. of Perf. Arts 1958-62; Mannes College '63-5. Worked with Art Blakey, Max Roach; joined Sonny Rollins, '69; Joe Henderson, '69-71; Freddie Hubbard, '71- . Has also written for choirs, East Harlem Protestant Parish.

Comps: *Think On Me*, which he rec. w. Woody Shaw in *Blackstone Legacy* (also rec. by Woody Herman); *Ebony Moonbeams; Lost Dreams; Camel Rise*, rec. w. Hubbard; also rec. by B. Hutcherson; *Love Song*, rec. by Hutcherson.

Infl: Wynton Kelly, Miles Davis, Coltrane, Buddy Montgomery, H. Hancock as pianists and composers; McCoy Tyner. Festivals: Newport, Monterey, many foreign concert and fest. apps.

LPs: Rec. in Japan as leader, comp. & arr. (Myuh). As sideman, w. Hubbard, *Polar AC; Keep Your Soul Together* (CTI); *High Energy; Liquid Love* (Col.); w. Woody Shaw, *Blackstone Legacy* (Contemp.); w. Henderson *Black is the Color; In Pursuit of Blackness; If You're Not Part of the Solution* (Mile.); w. Blakey, *Child's Dance* (Prest.); w. Joe Chambers, *The Almoravid* (Muse).

CACERES, ERNEST (ERNIE),* *clarinet, baritone sax*; b. Rockport, Tex., 11/22/11. Played w. J. Teagarden; G. Miller; B. Goodman; W. Herman; and B. Hackett. After working w. B. Butterfield in Va., '62, settled in San Antonio, app. occasionally w. Jim Cullum's Happy Jazz Band. Pl. at Dick Gibson's Colorado JP in Aspen, Vail in '60s. Died in San Antonio, 1/10/71. LP: *Ernie and Emilio Caceres* (Audiophile).

CAIN, JACQUELINE RUTH (JACKIE),* *singer*; b. Milwaukee, Wisc., 5/22/28. Sang on TV commercials, many of which were produced and written by her husband Roy Kral (q.v.) and also appeared with him in their group, Jackie & Roy, on TV, in nightclubs and at festivals. Among the latter apps. were Munich, Toulon, Loosdrecht '71; CTI Summer Jazz at Hollywood Bowl '71; MJF '73, NJF-NY '74, Reno JF '75. Other concerts at Town Hall '71, '73, Carnegie Hall '72. App. at Ronnie Scott's in London early '75. LPs: *Changes; Lovesick* (Verve); *Grass* (Capitol); *Time and Love; A Wilder Alias* (CTI).

CALDWELL, ALBERT (HAPPY),* *tenor sax*; also *clarinet, flute*; b. Chicago, Ill., 7/25/03. Although his regular non-music job is with City College of the City Univ. of

N.Y., he cont. to gig as a member of the New Amsterdam Mus. Assoc., N.Y.'s oldest black mus. org., and for many Masonic Lodges, Eastern Star chapters, of one of which he is a past master. Honored by the Overseas Jazz Club at jazz concert in which he app. w. own group, Feb. '75. Visited Sweden and Copenhagen Youth Center, Denmark, '75, for playing and participation in seminars. Active in Senior Citizens entertainment program. Preparing book on chords.

LP: w. Clyde Bernhardt, *More Blues and Jazz from Harlem* (Saydisc).

CALIMAN, HADLEY, *tenor saxophone*; also *flute, bass clarinet, soprano sax*; b. Idabel, Okla., 1/12/32. Stud. at high school, also three years of theory at Pomona State Coll., S.F. Conservatory. Insp. by L. Young, D. Gordon, J. Coltrane and Joe Henderson, Caliman was heard with bands and combos in the LA area in the '60s and mainly in SF in the '70s. In addition to leading his own group, he was heard with B. Bryant, Gerald Wilson, M. Santamaria, D. Ellis, Willie Bobo, Big Black, Luis Gasca, Eddie Henderson, Jon Hendricks. Concord and Berkeley Jazz Fests.

Although Caliman won a DB poll in the TDWR category some years ago, he has not yet achieved the acclaim he deserves as a soloist who combines mainstream characteristics with the infl. of J. Coltrane.

LPs: *Hadley Caliman; Iapetus* (Mainstream); *Live and Swinging* and others w. Wilson (Wor. Pac.); others w. H. Hawes, Patrice Rushen, Azar Lawrence, F. Purim (Fant.); *Hollywood Blues,* w. Johnny Almond (Deram-London).

CALLENDER, GEORGE (RED), * *tuba, bass*; b. Richmond, Va., 3/6/18. Though employed regularly as TV staff musician, and later as a freelance in TV and rec. studios, Callender continued his jazz activities from time to time. In '73 he became part owner, along with B. Collette, Grover Mitchell, Al Aarons, Al Viola and L. Vinnegar of Legend Record Co. Feat. on *Hawaii Five-O,* w. Nancy Wilson, '69; was member of Carol Burnett show orch. through '69; Flip Wilson show, '70-4, incl. bit apps. on camera; Sammy Davis show, '74. Pl. bass and tuba at Dick Gibson's jazz party, '74, '75. His hit song, *Primrose Lane,* was used as a theme on the Henry Fonda show, *Smith Family.* Other songs incl. *Pastel,* rec. by E. Garner, I. Jacquet; 12 orig. tunes on own album *Swinging Suite,* reissued in '75.

LPs: *Basin-Street Brass; Callender Speaks Low and Swinging; Now and Then* w. Collette (Legend); earlier albums, many deleted, incl. *Big Fat Brass* w. Billy May (Cap.); *The Lowest* (MGM-Metro); tuba on Ray Charles LPs (ABC).

CAMPISE, ANTHONY S. (TONY), *flute, alto, tenor sax*; also all *reeds, flutes* and *oboe*; b. Houston, Tex., 1/22/43. Stud. alto sax, clarinet w. Hal Tennyson, '56-62; improvisation w. Jerry Coker in Houston and Cal., '61-3; flute w. Byron Hester betw. '63-71; oboe w. Barbara Hester, '67-9; also improvisation briefly w. L. Kon-

itz. Attended music schools at Sam Houston U., U. of Houston, Houston Baptist Coll. and Monterey Penninsula Coll. Pl. in Houston w. Don Cannon, '62-5; Paul Schmitt, '67-71; Young Audience Jazz Ensemble, '69-75; Gulf Coast Giants of Jazz, '70-3. Three seasons of musicals at Houston Music Theatre, '72-4. Lead alto and flute w. Stan Kenton from '74.

Infls: Ch. Parker, J. Coltrane, Konitz, L. Tristano, E. Dolphy. Fests: Corpus Christi; Longhorn '73; NJF-NY w. Kenton, '74. LPs: w. Kenton, *Kenton Plays Chicago; Fire, Fury and Fun* (Creative World).

CANDIDO (Candido Camero), * *bongo, conga drums*; b. Regal, Havana, Cuba, 4/22/21. Well known from the '50s when he came to US and began playing w. Dizzy Gillespie; Stan Kenton; and Billy Taylor. Continued as an extremely active freelance in both jazz and Latin music working w. his own gps. and w. such personalities as Sonny Rollins; Elvin Jones; and Tony Bennett on a world wide basis. TV: w. Bennett; Lionel Hampton; Charo on Mike Douglas Show. Fest: NJF-NY w. S. Kenton '75. LPs: *Drum Fever* (Poly.); *The Thousand Finger Man* (SS); *Beautiful* (UA); w. Randy Weston, *Tanjah* (Poly.); David Amram, *No More Walls* (RCA).

CANDOLI, SECONDO (CONTE), * *trumpet*; b. Mishawaka, Ind., 7/12/27. Remained w. Shelly Manne gp. from '66-72; also active in Hollywood studios. App. once a month w. Kenton Neophonic Orch. at LA Music Center, '67-9. From '70-4 member of staff orch. on Flip Wilson TV show; also app. w. own gp. or others at local clubs. In '72 joined Supersax, and in that year visited England with gp., but working mostly local jobs. Since '68 has been with NBC-TV *Tonight* show band, making several LPs with Doc Severinsen. Candoli has also busied himself with coll. clinics at Indiana U., Purdue, Notre Dame, Chicago State. In '75 to Holland, Germany, Italy for club, radio, TV apps. and occasional concerts. Fests: Monterey '73 w. Candoli Brothers; Concord, '74 w. Bill Berry band.

LPs: *Monk's Blues,* w. T. Monk (Col.); *Supersax Plays Bird; Salt Peanuts* w. Supersax; *Supersax Plays Bird With Strings* (Cap.); w. F. Strazzeri, *View From Within* (Creative World); w. T. Edwards, *Feelin's* (Muse); w. Bill Berry (Beez).

CANDOLI, WALTER JOSEPH (PETE), * *trumpet*; b. Mishawaka, Ind., 6/28/23. The former big band musician (Herman, Kenton, Basie, Barnet) devoted most of his time in later years to studio work in Hollywood, rec. w. M. Legrand, Q. Jones, H. Mancini, Peggy Lee, I. Stravinsky. Regular member of band on Merv Griffin and *Tonight* shows. From '72, teamed with wife Edie Adams in night club act, also in several theatrical musicals. Films: pl. trumpet solos for scores of *Save The Tiger* and *Prisoner of Second Ave.* Candoli also conducts coll. music seminars. Fests: Monterey, '73 w. Candoli Bros.

CAPP, FRANK, * *drums*; b. Worcester, Mass., 8/20/31. Former name band drummer (Kenton, Hefti, Billy May);

a prominent studio musician in LA for more than 20 years. TV with Merv Griffin, Steve Allen, etc.; movies w. A. Previn, P. Rugolo, H. Mancini; records w. Ben Webster, Terry Gibbs, Bud Shank, B. Kessel, and about 20 albums w. Previn. Fests: Monterey; Concord. LPs: *Percussion Tribute to the Big Bands* (ten-album series: Kimberley); w. Bob Florence, *Here & Now* (Liberty).

CARDOSO, RUI, *alto sax, flute, composer*; b. Portugal, Jan. 1939. Played w. jazz and jazz-rock gps. related, for the most part, to Lisbon's Hot Club of Portugal. Turned professional in '71, working in clubs and as film composer; pop arranger. In '75 he joined forces with Araripa (Emilio Robalo, piano; Jose Eduardo, bass; Joao Heitor, drums), app. at the Cascais Fest. in November.

CARISI, JOHN E. (JOHNNY),* *composer, trumpet, fluegelhorn*; b. Hasbrouck Heights, N.J., 2/23/22. A member of the ensemble faculty, Manhattan School of Music from 1969; adjunct lecturer at Queens Coll. 1971-73. Orchestrated Anita Loos-Ralph Blane musical, *Something About Anne*, choreographed by his wife, dancer Gemze de Lappe; piece commissioned by Gerry Mulligan for baritone saxophone and woodwind ensemble performed by Wilder Winds at Town Hall and Kennedy Arts Center; comps. for National Jazz Ensemble concerts at Wolf Trap Farm and Alice Tully Hall in '70s; arrs. for Ten Wheel Drive; works for tuba virtuoso Harvey Phillips, professor of music at the Univ. of Indiana, '75. As trumpeter pl. w. Brew Moore at Joey Archer's Sports Corner and the Limelight in NYC, '69-70. LPs: arrs. for *Urbie Green's Big Beautiful Band* (Project 3); six comps., nine arrs. for Marvin Stamm *Machinations* (Verve).

CARLTON, LARRY EUGENE, *guitar*; also *fender bass, arranger*; b. Torrance, Cal., 3/2/48. Stud. w. Slim Edwards from age 6 to 14; music major, LA Harbor Coll., '66-68; music major Cal-State U., Long Beach, '68-70. In '68 pl. at Disneyland w. Bill Elliott, toured w. 5th Dimension, rec. first solo album for Uni. In Dec. '69 became musical director of NBC children's show. Perf. on camera as co-star, Larry Guitar, as well as writing much of music used on show. From '70 Carlton played on literally thousands of rec. sessions, TV shows, movies, commercial jingles. Along with this work, he became a member of the Crusaders, '73. Won NARAS award as Most Valuable Guitar Player, '73, '74.

Comps: *The Well's Gone Dry*, rec. by Crusaders; *Free Way*, rec. by Carlton. Favorites: J. Pass, B.B. King, B. Kessel, Louie Shelton. Own LPs: on ABC-Blue Thumb; w. Crusaders: *Crusaders I; 2nd Crusade; Unsung Heroes; Scratch; Southern Comfort* (ABC-Blue Thumb); w. Tom Scott and L.A. Express (Ode).

CARN, DOUG (aka ABDUL RAHIM IBRAHIM), *organ, keyboards, oboe, saxophone, synthesizer, singer, composer*; b. New York City, 7/14/48. Piano lessons at 5 with mother; alto sax at 9, organ at 13. Oboe and composition, Jacksonville U., '65-7; completed studies at Georgia State Coll., '67-9.

Carn has led his own group almost continuously since the age of 13; however, he has worked briefly w. Lou Donaldson, S. Turrentine, Irene Reid. He first achieved widespread acceptance in jazz circles with his albums for the Black Jazz label. In '75 he worked with the Philadelphia Community Coll. choir, expanding vocal writing techniques.

Carn says: "I am a devout, orthodox Muslim by faith. I strive to express the Islamic Ideal of Oneness of God (Allah) as manifested through creation—music being only one aspect of that creation."

Comps: Carn wrote lyrics, music and/or arrs. for many of the works on his Black Jazz albums, among them *Moonchild; Infant Eyes; Arise and Shine; Blue In Greene; Revelation; Time Is Running Out; Jihad; Adam's Apple; Higher Ground; Western Sunrise*; and J. Coltrane's *Naima*. LPs: *The Doug Carn Trio* (Savoy); *Infant Eyes; Spirit of the New Land; Revelation; Adam's Apple* (Black Jazz); two w. Earth, Wind & Fire (WB).

CARNEY, HARRY HOWELL,* *baritone sax, bass clarinet, clarinet*; b. Boston, Mass., 4/1/10. Joined Duke Ellington Orch. at the age of 16 and was established during the early '30s as the first outstanding jazz soloist on baritone sax, a distinctive anchor man of the Ellington reed section. Carney was still a member of the Ellington orch. at the time of the leader's death, despite illness. He played with the band under the direction of Mercer Ellington during the next few months, but was intermittently absent, suffering from phlebitis. He died in New York, 10/8/74.

The sound of Harry Carney was one of the most vital and irreplaceable in the Ellington orchestral structure. He was to the baritone sax what Coleman Hawkins had been to the tenor; a virtual inventor of the instrument in terms of its jazz use. With the deep, full sonority that was the essence of his sound, he made the band instantly recognizable, perhaps more than any other individual.

LPs: see Ellington and J. Hodges.

CARR, IAN,* *trumpet, fluegelhorn, composer*; b. Dumfries, Scotland, 4/21/33. Continued w. Rendell-Carr quintet until Oct. '69 when he formed Nucleus. This group won first prize Montreux JF, '70; also pl. at NJF in same year. Nucleus has app. at all major Euro. JF, as well as countless TV apps. In '71 gave 16 min. perf. w. visuals of an extended work, *Solar Plexus*, presented on BBC2 TV. Won first place in sm. gp. category, '71-2 in MM polls.

Carr, a prolific composer, wrote *Will's Birthday Suite*, dedicated to William Shakespeare; organized and comp. mus. for Sam Wanamaker's Annual Concert in honor of Shakespeare's birthday. Publs: *Music Outside* (Latimer New Dimensions); in '75 Carr was researching biog. of Miles Davis for same publisher.

Many listeners and critics have agreed that Nucleus has been a seminal influence on jazz-rock groups in Europe and elsewhere.

LPs: *Elastic Rock; We'll Talk About It Later; Solar Plexus; Belladonna; Labyrinth; Roots; Under The Sun; Snakehips Etcetera; Alleycat* (Vertigo).

CARRY, GEORGE DORMAN (SCOOPS),* *alto saxophone, clarinet*; b. Little Rock, Ark., 1/23/15. Best known for his work in the Earl Hines orch. in the '30s and '40s, Carry in '43 became a lawyer. He died 8/4/70 in Chicago after a long illness. His most famous rec. solo is *Jelly Jelly* w. Hines (RCA-Bluebird).

CARTER, BENNETT LESTER (BENNY),* *composer, alto saxophone*; also *trumpet*; b. New York City, 8/8/07. Led own bands in U.S. and Europe during '30s; gave up traveling in mid-40s to settle in Cal., where he was actively involved in writing for motion pictures and later for television. During '60s appeared occasionally in public, touring in Europe, Australia and Japan.

TV assignments incl. *Bob Hope Presents*, '65-8; segs. for *Ironside, Name of the Game, Banyon, Sarah Vaughan Special.* Film scores: *A Man Called Adam*, '66; *Buck and the Preacher*, '72. Many arrs. for Pearl Bailey during '60s and '70s; others for Rod McKuen, Debbie Reynolds and Ray Charles. A record of *Busted*, by Charles, arr. by Carter, won a Grammy award in '63.

During the '70s Carter aligned himself with the world of jazz education. He was an artist-in-residence at Baldwin-Wallace Coll. in '70. In '72 he gave seminars at two Univs. in Colorado, and Eisenhower Coll. in Seneca Falls, N.Y. In '73 he was visiting lecturer at Princeton, where he also perf. in concerts; the following year he received an Honorary Doctorate of Humanities from Princeton. That same year he gave a seminar and app. in concert at Cornell.

Also during '74 Carter became associated with Maria Muldaur, assembling an all star jazz orch. for some of her records and for several concerts. They appeared together at the NJF, '75. Carter wrote the score for *Louis Armstrong: Chicago Style*, a TV movie in '75.

Along with all these activities Carter continued to play periodically, visiting Europe almost every year, concentrating on the alto saxophone and hardly ever playing trumpet. Despite the infrequency of his playing, he remained possibly the most eloquent and melodically appealing saxophonist in jazz. Among the most famous works in his long career as a composer are *Blues In My Heart; When Lights Are Low; Take My Word; Blue Interlude; Cow Cow Boogie*; also *Kansas City Suite* for Count Basie, and many other instrumental works.

LPs: *Further Definitions; Additions to Further Definitions* (Imp.); *Waitress in A Donut Shop*, w. Muldaur (Repr.); *With Love*, w. Joe Williams (Temponic); *Carmen*, w. C. McRae (Temponic); *Greatest Jazz Concert in the World* (Pablo).

CARTER, BETTY,* *singer*; b. Flint, Mich., 5/16/30. One of the few real jazz singers in terms of improvisation and feeling, she continued to appear in clubs, concerts and college dates backed by her own trio. In '72 she was heard at Antioch Coll.; Goddard Coll.; Rutgers U. Tam Fiofori, reviewing a concert at Judson Hall in NYC, '70, wrote: Betty Carter draws the listeners into her songs, so much that on the one level one is and becomes aware of the triteness of some of the lyrics . . . (plastic-gloss Broadway-Hollywood-type-material). On the other level, the listener also becomes aware of and feels the fresh-airiness of her voice injecting new meaning and life into these songs . . ." LPs: two albums on own label, Bet-Car (Bet-Car Productions, North Plainfield, N.J.).

CARTER, CHARLES JR. (CHUCK),* *drums*; b. St. Louis, Mo., 7/12/39. Cousin of Gerald Wilson. Father a drummer. Self-taught. Pl. w. L. Vinnegar, Teddy Edwards, '61-3; Paul Horn quintet and G. Wilson big band, '64-5. Many other associations since then, incl. F. Hubbard, Ray Brown, Milt Jackson. Worked w. Herb Geller in Berlin, '66; Letta Mbulu, '67; Hugh Masekela, '70-1. Traveling w. E. Garner, '74-5. Favs: Max Roach, Elvin Jones, Philly Joe Jones.

LPs: *Portraits; On Stage* w. G. Wilson (Wor. Pac.); *Glass of Water*, w. Vinnegar (Legend); others w. Masekela.

CARTER, JOHN WALLACE, *clarinet, saxophones, flute*; b. Fort Worth, Texas, 9/24/29. B.A. from Lincoln U., Mo., '49; M.Mus. Educ., U. of Colo., and NTSU, '56; Cal. State U., L.A., '61. Insp. by Parker, Young, Coltrane. Played throughout Southwest in late '40s, early '50s with jazz and blues groups. West coast in early '60s, organized quartet w. Bobby Bradford, '65, involved in much lecture-demonstration-concert activity in first part of '70s. Won DB award as most promising combo. Group disbanded '73, when Carter put together his own ensemble. Played in Europe, '73. Teaching: public schools, Ft. Worth and LA; college level, Cal. State, Dominguez Hills. Fests: Pl. w. Ornette Coleman group and conducted fest. orch. in Coleman's music in LA '65.

LPs: *Seeking; Secrets* (Revelation); *Flight for Four; Self Determination Music* (Flying Dutchman).

CARTER, RONALD LEVIN (RON),* *bass, cello, composer*; also *violin; clarinet, trombone, tuba*; b. Ferndale, Mich., 5/4/37. Worked w. C. Hamilton, C. Adderley, E. Dolphy, J. Byard, etc. in early '60s. Joined Miles Davis '63 and pl. w. him to '68. With NY Bass Choir from '69; Lena Horne's NYC apps., '70-4; Michel Legrand from '71; NY Jazz Quartet from '72; own quartet from '75. Free-lance work w. S. Turrentine; H. Laws; L. Hampton; J. Henderson. Carter also pl. as soloist, and accompanist for Laws, G. Benson et al, on CTI concert tour packages from '70. With CTI to Europe, '72; Japan, '71, '72, '73. Europe w. F. Gulda, '69, '70; Japan w. NYJQ, '74. Won DB Readers' Poll, '73-5.

In Carter's new quartet he also plays piccolo bass ("It's about three-quarters the size of a three-quarter bass . . . tuned like a cello upside-down.) backed by bassist Buster Williams. "My objective," he says, "is to re-investigate acoustic sounds and to give the public a viable listening option not at their command recently."

TV: Leon Bibb, NBC, '70-3; *Positively Black*; Howard Cosell show, '75. Fest: Mont. JF w. M. Davis, '67; house bassist, '73; NJF-NY, Concord w. NYJQ, '74. Publ: *Building a Jazz Bass Line, Vols. 1 & 2* (Charles Hansen, 1860 Broadway, N.Y., N.Y. 10023). Comp: *De Samba; Little Waltz; Arkansas; El Noche Sol; Sabado Sombre-*

ro. LPs: *Anything Goes* (Kudu); *Blues Farm; All Blues; Spanish Blue* (CTI); *Uptown Conversation* (Embryo); *NY Jazz Quartet, Live in Japan* (Salvation); *Magic,* reissue of earlier material w. Dolphy (Prest.); w. Davis, *Sorcerer; Nefertiti; Miles in the Sky* (Col.); w. M. Tyner, *Trident; Alone Together* (Mile.); w. Legrand, *Live at Jimmy's* (RCA); w. H. Silver, *Silver 'n Brass* (BN); w. F. Gulda, *Euro-Jazz Orch., 1970* (MPS); w. Laws; F. Hubbard; M. Jackson; Don Sebesky; Grover Washington (CTI); Roberta Flack; Aretha Franklin (Atl.); *Jaki Byard With Strings* (Prest.).

CARVER, WAYMAN,* *saxophones, flute;* b. Portsmouth, Va., 12/25/05. The noted music educator died in Atlanta, Ga., 5/6/67. He was the first artist ever to record jazz solos on flute, originally with Spike Hughes' orchestra in 1933 (London Records LL 1387) and later as a member of Chick Webb's orchestra.

CARVIN, MICHAEL, *drums;* b. Houston, Tex., 12/12/44. Father, Henry Carvin, one of Houston's top drummers, began teaching him at early age. After high school moved to LA and att. LACC. Joined Earl Grant's big band '65 and traveled for two yrs. in U.S., Europe & Japan before becoming a member of the 266th Div. Army Band for a two-yr. Vietnam tour of duty. Ret. to LA in '68. House drummer for Motown, '68-9. Worked w. The Four Tops; Martha and the Vandellas, '68; Eddie Khan, '68-70; B.B. King, '68-9; Monk Montgomery, '69; Abbey Lincoln; George Duke; Woody Shaw; Henry Franklin, '70; Walter Bishop; Hugh Masekela, '70-1; Jimmy Smith; Gerry Mulligan; Thelma Houston; Doug Carn; Hampton Hawes; Dexter Gordon in Copenhagen, '71; Bobby Hutcherson, '71-2; Lonnie Liston Smith; Bayete, '72; Freddie Hubbard; Pharoah Sanders; Larry Young, '73; McCoy Tyner; Atmosphere, '74; Jackie McLean, '72-5. Founder and instructor, Creative Artists Development Center, NYC. Also taught at Artists Collective, Hartford, Conn., under McLean; Grant Music Center, LA, under Henry Grant; Community Learning Center, Oakland, under Charles Moffett; as artist-in-residence for elementary schools in Hartford; Vallekilde Music Clinics, Denmark, summer '74. Infl: Henry Carvin, Art Blakey, Max Roach, B. Hutcherson, J. McLean, Jo Jones, Elvin Jones, Coltrane. Comp: *Comahlee Ah; Hump; Voodoo Woman; Osun, The Camel.* TV: *Barbara McNair Show,* '69-70. Publ: *Something For All Drummers* (Arual Publ. Co., 507 5th Ave., New York, N.Y. 10017). LPs: *The Camel; Antiquity,* duo w. McLean; w. McLean, *New York Calling;* w. Billy Gault, *When Destiny Calls* (Steeple.); w. P. Sanders, *Elevation* (Imp.); w. L.L. Smith, *Expansions* (Fly. Dutch.); w. Atmospheres, *Voyage to Uranus* (Cap.); w. Jimmy Smith (MGM); w. Doug Carn; Henry Franklin (Black Jazz); w. M. Montgomery (Chisa); w. Bayete (Prest.); w. C. McBee (Strata-East).

CARY, RICHARD DURANT (DICK),* *trumpet, composer, piano, mellophone* etc.; b. Hartford, Conn., 7/10/16. First prominent as trad. pianist w. Armstrong, Condon et al, he moved to Cal. and during '60s became very active

as composer/arranger and pl. trumpet, alto horn. Working with rehearsal gps., built library of close to 1000 arrs. Dance band and concert dates feat. Abe Most in swing era recreations. Wrote for and rehearsed a brass quintet, for which a suite he wrote was pl. at an LA museum concert. Also working w. gp. feat. eight reeds and rhythm, and pl. horn in a woodwind quintet. From 1970, led nine piece band for jazz concerts in LA parks and schools.

Publ: *Brass Quintets* (Maggio Music, 12044 Vanowen, No. Hollywood, Ca.). Stage band originals for Don Rader catalogue. Films: *Great Gatsby* sound track. TV: *The Jazz Show,* KNBC; various jingles; Dick Van Dyke Special.

LPs: piano w. Condon on *Midnight in Moscow* (Epic); w. Barney Bigard for European RCA.

CASTLEMAN, JEFFRY ALAN, *bass;* b. Los Angeles, 1/27/46. Stud. at U. of Cal. Riverside, pvt. teachers incl. Ralph Pena. Prof. debut at 18 w. Si Zentner in LV. Worked off and on w. L. Bellson for two years, also a year w. Joe Castro Trio. Joined Duke Ellington, late 1967, and remained with the band until mid-'69, when he married Trish Turner, Ellington's vocalist; both he and Ms. Turner then settled in LA. Castleman went on the road for a few months w. Sarah Vaughan, also w. Tony Bennett. Gigs w. Shelly Manne, 1971-3; since then, mostly commercial work in LA on fender bass. He played the latter occasionally with Ellington, the first bassist ever to do so. On upright bass he was praised by Duke as "the greatest bassist since Jimmy Blanton."

LPs w. Ellington-F. Sinatra (Reprise); w. Ellington, *Yale Concert* (Fantasy); *Second Sacred Concert* (Prestige); w. Earl Hines, J. Hodges, *Swing's Our Thing* (Verve). Five trio numbers written and recorded by Ellington w. Castleman and drummer Sam Woodyard had still not been released in 1975.

CASTRO, JOSEPH (JOE),* *piano, composer;* b. Miami, Ariz., 8/15/27. For many years has devoted his time between commercial work, accompanying singers on tour or in Las Vegas, and jazz activities. In latter capacity, his jazz trio was feat. with Honolulu Symph., '66; he played at Beverly Hills Hotel, '67-8; trio around LA, '69. From '70, arr. and cond. for commercial artists in LV, but arr. for Joe Williams, Count Basie and Al Hibbler, '73. From '70-4 wrote and cond. film projects for Sutherland Educational Associates, using Buddy Collette, Jack Sheldon, Frank Rosolino et al.

Own big band LP with all star LA personnel (Clover); quartet w. Teddy Edwards (Contemporary).

CASTRO NEVES, OSCAR (Carlos Oscar de Castro Neves), *guitar, keyboards, composer;* b. Rio de Janeiro, Brazil, 5/15/40. A triplet, born into a family of amateur musicians, he was self-taught until, in LA, he stud. composing w. Albert Harris and Paul Glass. Began pl. cavaquinho (Brazilian ukulele) at age five. Considered to be one of the group of musicians and composers who, w. A.C. Jobim et al, originated the bossa nova movement in the late '50s. To NYC for first Carnegie Hall bossa nova concert, Nov. '62, after which he worked in LA w. L.

Schifrin, D. Gillespie, L. Almeida/B. Shank. Returned to Brazil, organized classical concert series. Back to U.S., '67, directing vocal quartet, The Girls from Bahia, for records and TV. After a third visit to U.S. with this group, he settled in LA in '68. Worked w. Paul Winter Consort, '69-70, arranging and touring. Lead and rhythm guitar player, also arr. w. S. Mendes group, '71- . Has also pl. in U.S. w. Q. Jones, John Mandel, John Pisano, Almeida, L. Ritenour, D. Grusin.

LPs: w. J. Gilberto (Orpheon); Flora Purim (Fant.); Girls from Bahia (WB); Almeida (Daybreak); Getz/Gilberto (Col.).

CATHERINE, PHILIP, *guitar*; b. London, England, 10/27/42. English mother, Belgian father. Insp. by D. Reinhardt, Rene Thomas. Pl. w. Lou Bennett, '59. During '60s, w. Jack Sels, Fats Sadi, and on Belgian radio. In '70s turned to rock-jazz; worked w. J.L. Ponty, Dec. '70-June '72, then stud. for a year at Berklee in Boston. At end of '73 he started a group called Pork Pie w. Ch. Mariano. Recent infls. are J. McLaughlin, L. Coryell. LPs on Warner Bros., Atl.; also w. L. Bennett (RCA); w. Sels, *Relax* (Vogel); *Placebo* (EMI); T. Thielemans; Mariano (Keytone); Pork Pie (MPS); Chris Hinze (CBS); H. Geller (Atl.).

CEROLI, NICK,* *drums*; b. Warren, Ohio, 12/22/39. In late '50s, early '60s worked in Chicago, Las Vegas and LA w. Lionel Hampton, Gerald Wilson, Terry Gibbs, S. Kenton. W. Tijuana Brass from '65 to '69; then w. Steve Lawrence-Eydie Gorme, '71; Vikki Carr, '72; subbed on *Tonight* show for year and a half, then regularly on Merv Griffin show. Studio work in LA, also pl. w. Zoot Sims, Clark Terry locally, as well as other jazz groups. Publ: *Modern Approach To Independence, Vols. I & II* (Try Publ., Hollywood, Ca.). LPs: w. Kenton Neophonic Orch. (Capitol); w. Pete Jolly, *Give A Damn* (A & M).

CHAMBERS, HENDERSON CHARLES,* *trombone*; b. Alexandria, La., 5/1/08. A prominent sideman w. many big bands from the '30s, he worked w. Ray Charles for two yrs. before playing w. C. Basie '64-6. Helped in the organization of a rehearsal band w. Edgar Battle in NYC before he died there of a heart attack, 10/19/67.

CHAMBERS, JOSEPH ARTHUR (JOE),* *drums, composer*; also *piano*; b. Stoneacre, Va., 6/25/42. Brother Steve is classical comp. Studied at Phila. Conserv. and American U., Wash., D.C. Pl. w. JFK Quintet in Wash., '60-3; then in NYC w. E. Dolphy; F. Hubbard; L. Donaldson; J. Giuffre; A. Hill. Associated w. Bobby Hutcherson from '65, he played w. him, '67-70. In the '70s he worked w. Donald Byrd; Jeremy Steig but has concentrated on writing. His suite, *The Almoravid*, including the title piece; *Gazelle Suite; Medina;* and *Jihad* was performed by the NYJRC at Carnegie Hall, '74. Other comp: *Mirrors; Dialog; Idlewild.*

Gary Giddins wrote of his playing: "The enormous potency—bordering on ferocity—combined with complete authority and tonal clarity . . . has made him one of the more distinctive percussion voices in recent years. His is a hard style but not a busy one. Force is touched by sim-

plicity. However complex his rhythms, his playing is sensitive and to the point."

LPs: *The Almoravid* (Muse); w. Hill, *One For One;* w. Hutcherson (BN); w. C. Mingus, *Charles Mingus and Friends* (Col.).

CHAMBERS, PAUL LAURENCE DUNBAR JR.,* *bass*; b. Pittsburgh, Pa., 4/22/35. Played with Miles Davis, '55-60. Then he teamed with two other Davis alumni, Wynton Kelly and Jimmy Cobb to form a trio, which at one time backed W. Montgomery. Chambers later freelanced in NYC w. Tony Scott, Barry Harris and others. Afrer several months' illness, he died in a NYC hospital 1/4/69. One of the greats and a strong influence on his contemporaries.

LPs: *Paul Chambers* (Epitaph); *High Step; Bass on Top; Whims of Chambers* (BN); *East/West Controversy* (Xanadu); *Just Friends* (Trip); w. Davis, *Tallest Trees; Collector's Items; Workin' & Steamin'* (Pres.); *Kind of Blue; Round About Midnight; Someday My Prince Will Come; Porgy & Bess* (Col.); w. Coltrane, *Giant Steps* (Atl.); *Bull's Eye,* w. Barry Harris (Pres.); *Peace Piece and Other Pieces,* w. Bill Evans; *Keep It Movin',* w. W. Kelly (Milest.).

CHARLES, RAY (Ray Charles Robinson),* *singer, piano, composer, organ, alto saxophone*; b. Albany, Ga., 9/23/32. Established via records as r & b, blues and gospel/jazz star from 1954. Broadened his audience in 1960s through use of pop and country-western songs, large orchestral backgrounds with strings etc.

Using a theatrical presentation involving his female vocal group, the Raeletts, and other acts, Charles covered a wide range of styles, including jazz, and using a big band that generally included a number of outstanding sidemen, with baritone saxophonist Leroy Cooper as music director in recent years.

The Charles show has spent a substantial proportion of its time overseas. In 1969, for example, there were visits to Mexico and to 22 European cities; in 1970, 27 concerts in Europe, others in four South American countries, Mexico, the Bahamas, Canada and Japan. The European tours have continued annually, as well as return trips to Japan almost every year. During 1975 Charles was seen in England, France, Belgium, Germany, Switzerland, Spain, New Zealand, Australia, Indonesia, Singapore, Japan and Canada.

TV: Frequent guest shots on shows starring Glen Campbell, Della Reese, Smothers Brothers, Bill Cosby, Barbra Streisand, Flip Wilson, Dinah Shore et al. Specials: *Switched-on Symphony*, 1970; *NBC Follies,* '73; *Cotton Club '75,* '74.

In 1971 Charles' annual U.S. tour included a visit to Houston for the world premiere of Quincy Jones' *Black Requiem* (see JONES, QUINCY).

LPs: *My Kind of Jazz*, 1970, and *Jazz Number II*, 1973, both featuring the band, were released on Charles' own Tangerine label. Pop and other albums, not basically jazz, incl. *Crying Time*, winner of two Grammy awards for best r & b recording of 1966 (ABC); *Ray's Moods;*

Ray Charles, A Man and His Soul; Ray Charles Invites You To Listen; A Portrait of Ray; I'm All Yours Baby; Doing His Thing; Love Country Style; Volcanic Action of My Soul; A 25th Anniversary in Show Business Salute to Ray Charles; A Message From The People; Through the Eyes of Love (ABC); Come Live With Me; Renaissance (Crossover).

CHASE, BILL, trumpet, composer, leader; b. Boston, Mass., 1935. Came to prominence as lead trumpeter w. M. Ferguson, S. Kenton, and most notably in early and mid '60s w. W. Herman. Chase attained national stature after organizing a nine piece jazz-rock group, known as Chase, with a distinctive instrumentation comprising four trumpets, organ, rhythm section and vocalist. The band's first LP, released early in '71, enjoyed widespread acceptance and was voted the number one pop album of the year in the DB Readers' poll.

The momentum of this album was not followed up; Bill Chase's suite Ennea, on his next album, disappointed the public and the group underwent an extended hiatus. After reorganizing and starting a comeback tour, Chase was killed, along with three members of his band, in a plane crash, outside Jackson, Minn., 8/9/74. LPs: Pure Music; Ennea (Epic).

CHEATHAM, ADOLPHUS ANTHONY (DOC),* trumpet; b. Nashville, Tenn., 6/13/05. With Cab Calloway; Teddy Wilson, Benny Carter, Teddy Hill, McKinney's Cotton Pickers bands in 30s; Eddie Heywood in '40s; Machito, Wilbur DeParis, in '50s; to Africa w. Herbie Mann, '60. Own band at International, NYC, '60-5. Played w. Benny Goodman; Ricardo Rey, '67; to London w. Top Brass tour, fall '67; Ricardo Rey, '68-70, incl. So. American tour, '68. Worked in show Two Gentlemen of Verona, '71; Red Balaban & Cats, '72-4; Countsmen; Sy Oliver, '74. Fest: NJF-NY, dedication of Louis Armstrong Stadium, '73; Cab Calloway, '73; Teddy Wilson, '74. Grande Parade du Jazz, Nice '75. Carnegie Hall concerts w. NYJRC, also Russian tour w. L. Armstrong tribute. Publ: Ad Lib Chord Reading (B. Feldman & Co. Ltd., London). LPs: Doc Cheatham (Jezebel); Doc Cheatham Prescribes (Jazzways); From Dixieland to Swing (Music Minus One); w. Clyde Bernhardt, More Blues From Harlem (Saydisc); w. Earl Hines; Buck Clayton (Chiaro.); Sammy Price (B&B); Countsmen (Eng. RCA).

CHERICO, EUGENE V. (GENE),* bass; b. Buffalo, N.Y., 4/15/35. Continued working w. S. Getz through '66; traveling w. Peter Nero, '66-70. In 1970 was working locally in LA area w. F. Strazzeri, F. Rosolino, L. Bellson, Dick Grove, Toshiko, R. Norvo, C. McRae, Peggy Lee. Toured w. F. Sinatra in fall of '73; also w. Nancy Wilson, incl. visit to Venezuela. Several concerts w. G. Mulligan, '74. During much of '70s was busy in LA studios. App. at Concord JF w. T. Gibbs, '73. Wrote and pl. bass theme on segment of Rod Serling's Night Gallery. Other TV apps: Streets of San Francisco; Barnaby Jones; Marcus Welby; The Pearl Bailey Show.

LPs: Louie Rides Again, w. Bellson (Percussion

Power, 5109 Nagle Ave., Sherman Oaks, Ca. 91403); Hey, Now, Hey, w. Aretha Franklin (Atl.); Kogun, w. Toshiko (RCA); Big Bad & Beautiful, w. Grove (FPM Records, 12754 Ventura Blvd., Studio City, Ca. 91604).

CHERRY, DONALD E. (DON),* trumpet, composer; also flute, bamboo flute, percussion; b. Oklahoma City, Okla., 11/18/36. After Ornette Coleman's quartet disbanded in the early '60s, Cherry played briefly w. Steve Lacy; and Sonny Rollins. In the summer of '63 he was a founding member of the New York Contemporary Five w. Archie Shepp and John Tchicai, playing and rec. in Europe before it broke up early in '64. Returned to Europe w. Albert Ayler and by the end of the year had formed his own gp. in Paris w. Gato Barbieri. It remained more or less intact until the fall of '66, rec. in Europe and New York. In '65 Cherry rec. w. George Russell at a concert in Stuttgart; in '66 w. Giorgio Gaslini in Milan. During the last part of the '60s he commuted between Europe and the US. Settling in Sweden in '71, he and his artist wife, Moki, on vocals and percussion, presented a series of concerts in a specially constructed tent at the Museum of Modern Art in Stockholm. Excerpts from this series were issued under the title Organic Music Society on the Swedish label Caprice Riks. In July '73 Cherry appeared at an outdoor concert in Central Park at the NJF-NY under the heading Organic Music Theatre. He and wife festooned the stage with multi-colored banners and several children were incorporated in the OMT's performance. Barry McRae's description of the Caprice Riks album in Jazz Journal fits the NJF-NY set. "The music is very much international in flavour," he wrote. "To produce music beyond category and owing its tradition to no one particular ethnic source would seem to be Cherry's current aim. Within this context he still includes moments of pure jazz trumpet but these are only appropriate interludes and are not the raison d'être of the music. As a highly prejudiced jazz follower, I regret this step, but I must concede that Cherry's music remains highly appealing. It can only be hoped that, if he has truly found his niche in Europe, the odd trip to America might find him in a record studio with jazzmen of equal stature reminding the world that here is one of the finest horn men the music ever produced."

Film: soundtrack for New York Eye and Ear Control by Michael Snow; music for Alexander Jodorowsky's Holy Mountain.

Comp: Relativity Suite; Symphony For Improvisers; Manhattan Cry; Lunatic; Om Nu; Complete Communion; Elephantasy; Taste Maker; The Thing; There is the Bomb, Unite.

LPs: Human Music (Fly. Dutch.); Mu First Part; Mu Second Part; Don Cherry; Blue Lake (Byg); Eternal Rhythm (MPS); Relativity Suite (JCOA); Actions/Penderecki-Don Cherry (Philips); Complete Communion; Symphony For Improvisers; Where Is Brooklyn? (BN); Togetherness (Durium); The Jazz Composer's Orchestra; Escalator Over the Hill (JCOA); w. O. Coleman, Crisis (Imp.); Clifford Jordan in the World

(Strata-East); Charlie Haden, *Liberation Music Orchestra* (Imp); *G. Gaslini, Ensemble* (Ital. RCA); Sunny Murray, *Sunny's Time Now* (Jihad); *George Russell Sextet at Beethoven Hall, Vols. I & II* (Saba); Albert Ayler, *Ghosts* (Debut); *New York Eye and Ear Control* (ESP); New York Contemporary Five (Fontana; Sonet; Savoy); w. A. Heath, *Kawaida* (Trip).

CHIASSON, WARREN, * *vibes, composer*; also *piano, percussion*; b. Cheticamp, N.S., Canada, 4/17/34. Raised and educ. in Sydney, N.S. where his family moved when he was five. Stud. guitar, violin, tromb.; then xylophone at coll., vibes from '57. Joined George Shearing, July '59, remaining through '61, incl. Australian tour, '60. Own gps. in NYC, '62-3. In house band at Dupont Pavilion, NY World's Fair, '64-5; piano for gigs w. dance bands, '65; w. Grachan Moncur III in Mont., NYC '67. In '68-70 hosted weekly sessions at Signs of Zodiac, NYC, backing guest soloists w. his quartet. Back w. Shearing, off and on, Nov. '72-Aug. '74. Gigs w. Chet Baker, '74. Solo vibes at Gregory's, NYC, Jan.-May '75. Toured w. Roberta Flack, '75. Orig. infl: L. Tristano, P. Bley. TV: many apps. on CBC; *Jazz Adventures*, PBS, May '74. Fests: NJF; MJF w. Shearing '59-60; NJF-NY w. Baker, '75. Comps: *Bossa Nova Scotia; Bedouin; Magic Lantern; September; Paula; My Own; A Shanty for Peggy; Para Siempre; Festival*. Publ: *The Contemporary Vibist* (Charles H. Hansen, 1842 West Ave., Miami Beach, Fla. 33139).

Chiasson's vibes work is marked by harmonic subtlety, a light, dancing quality and mastery of multi-mallet techniques. LPs: *Quartessence* (Van Los); w. Harold Vick, *Straight Up* (RCA); w. Shearing, *Satin Affair; San Francisco Scene; Satin Brass* (Cap.).

CHICAGO. Originally formed as Chicago Transit Authority in mid-'60s out of such Chicago gps. as The Missing Links, The Exceptions, The Majestics and The Big Thing. Played at bars at colleges in Chicago area mixing jazz, blues, rock and classical influences and helped to pioneer use of brass arrangements within rock, along with such gps. as Blood, Sweat & Tears, Electric Flag. Moved to LA, pl. The Shrine, LA; Fillmore West & East. Shortened name to Chicago, '69. Its eight LPs on Columbia have each sold in excess of $1,000,000. Personnel consists of Robert Lamm, keyboards, vocals, who moved to Chicago at age 15 from his native Brooklyn; comp: *Saturday in the Park*. Own LP: *Skinny Boy* (Col.); James Pankow, trombone, composer, who had own jazz quintet while majoring in music at Quincy Coll. in Ill.; worked w. Bobby Christian; Ted Weems; Bill Russo's Chicago Jazz Ensemb.; formed own gp. at DePaul U. where he met drummer Danny Seraphine; woodwind player Walt Parazaider; guitarist Terry Kath. Other members include Lee Loughnane, trumpet; Peter Cetera, bass, steel guitar; and later addition Laudir De Oliveira, percussion. Group's producer is former bassist (Mothers of Invention) James William Guercio who also attended music courses at DePaul. Guercio's film, *Electra Glide in Blue*, incl. cameo perfs. by Loughnane and Parazaider.

CHISHOLM, GEORGE, * *trombone*; also *bass trumpet, euphonium, vibes, piano* etc.; b. Glasgow, Scotland, 3/29/15. One of Britain's first great jazzmen, he app. annually in the '70s at London's Festival Hall in tributes to L. Armstrong; pl. jazz concerts and fests. around the country, incl. Ireland, sometimes w. own group. The latter was also heard extensively on radio. Feat. in *Jazz At The Ronnie Scott Club* TV series, '71. LPs: Led own gp. in '73 for album on Rediffusion-International.

CHITTISON, HERMAN, * *piano*; b. Flemingsburg, Ky., 1909. The Art Tatum-influenced pianist, who lived in Europe during most of the 1930s, later became a favorite in New York's East Side supper clubs. Chittison died 3/8/67 in Cleveland, Ohio.

CHRISTENSEN, JON, *drums*; b. Oslo, Norway, 3/20/43. Self-taught. First worked with singer Karin Krog in 1964, app. at Antibes Fest. With Steve Kuhn, '67-70; also Jan Garbarek quartet, '69-73. In '73 the group became known as Jan Garbarek-Bobo Stenson Quartet and Christensen continued pl. with the group. Tours w. Eberhard Weber-Charlie Mariano, '75. Has made many TV apps. in Europe, notably w. S. Getz at Antibes; G. Russell in Oslo, Stockholm; K. Jarrett, Oslo, Bremen, Hanover; and w. Garbarek-Stenson. Since '64 Christensen has pl. w. many visiting American jazzmen, incl. Dexter Gordon, Bud Powell, S. Rollins. Has won many European awards, both as number one drummer and for recs. Infls: Kuhn, Gordon, Tony Williams, Garbarek, Russell, Stenson, Palle Danielson.

LPs: *Watch What Happens*, w. Kuhn (MPS); *The Essence of George Russell* (Concept); *Belonging*, w. Jarrett; *Witchi-Tai-To*, w. Garbarek-Stenson; *Solstice*, w. Ralph Towner (ECM).

CHRISTIAN, EMILE JOSEPH, * *trombone, bass*; b. New Orleans, La., 4/20/1895. Trombonist w. Original Dixieland Jazz Band, 1918-20; later spent many years in Europe. Returning home to NO, Christian continued to gig in clubs and fests. He died 12/3/73 in NO.

CHRISTIE, RONALD KEITH, * *trombone*; b. Blackpool, England, 1/6/31. Alumnus of H. Lyttelton, J. Dankworth, Ted Heath bands; three tours of Euro. w. B. Goodman, '70-2, incl. rec. Pl. w. Kenny Wheeler and other big bands. Led own quintet for broadcasts, jazz clubs, concerts. Film: pl. on *Alfie* sound track w. R. Scott et al. Concerts, TV w. Ray Conniff. Jazz Workshop in Germany w. Euro. All Stars. Reincarnation of Jelly Roll Morton Red Hot Peppers, w. Twyla Tharpe Dance Found. for TV, concerts, rec.

CHRISTIE, LYNDON VAN (LYN), *bass, composer*; also *trumpet, synthesizer*; b. Sydney, Australia, 8/3/28. Father pl. sax and was president of mus. union in Christchurch, N.Z.; mother pl. piano; one brother, drums; another, bassoon. Self-taught until he came to NYC, '65, and joined Nat. Orchestral Assoc. for symph. training. Received grant from assoc. to stud. w. Homer Mensch of N.Y. Phil. & Juilliard, '68-9. First jobs w. parents' dance band while in high school; then weekly radio broadcasts w. big bands led by Martin Winiata, Julian Lee. Grad.

from Otago Medical Sch., spent some yrs. interning at hospital and then went into general practice. Pl. infrequently during this time. Left New Zealand and ret. to Sydney, '61, to practice medicine but soon became involved w. music. Led own quartet at club and on Aust. radio & TV. To NYC, '65 to "expand musical experience" but spent first two yrs. as chief resident at Yonkers General Hospital. Then undertook full-time music career as busy free-lance. Principal bass w. Westchester Phil.; Northeastern Penna. Phil.; Ridgefield Symphonette. Duos w. Eddie Thompson, Jaki Byard, David Lahm, Patti Bown, Lance Hayward, Roland Hanna, Freddie Redd, Pat Rebillot, Mike Abene, Dick Katz, etc.; combo work w. Jeremy Steig, Tal Farlow, Don Heckman, Paul Winter, Al Cohn-Zoot Sims, Chet Baker, Daphne Hellman, Ahmad Jamal, Ted Curson, Clark Terry, Chico Hamilton; big bands incl. Jones-Lewis, B. Rich, Dick Cone, Bob Rosengarden. During '73-4 led band incl. Randy Brecker for concerts at NYU and other colleges. Toured Japan w. Toshiko, '71; Germany w. A. Zoller, '71, '74. Pl. Colo. Jazz Party, '71-3. Infl: Blanton, R. Brown, Pettiford, P. Chambers, Vitous, LaFaro, S. Stewart, S. Clarke. TV: Aust. Broad. Comm., '61-5; w. Leon Bibb on *Something New,* '69; *Our American Musical Heritage,* '72; w. Marlena Shaw on *Positively Black,* '75, all NBC. Comp: *In Vino Veritas; Minnesota Thins; Beedies; A Place Within; Orpheus and Eurydice; Australian Jazz Suite; Portraits of Peace; Pagan Festival.* Teaches priv. and has given bass and electronic mus. workshops in Scranton, Pa. school district gifted student prog. and at Univ. of Scranton. Complements bowing with keening vocal style. LPs: *Hope For Tomorrow* w. Don Friedman (East Wind); others in Japan w. Toshiko; *Colorado Jazz Party* (BASF); w. M. Mainieri, *Insight* (SS); Austr. albums: w. Judy Bailey, *You and the Night and the Music* (CBS); w. Errol Buddle, *The Wind* (HMV).

CHRISTLIEB, PETER (PETE), *tenor saxophone;* also *flute, clarinet, bass clarinet;* b. Los Angeles, Cal., 2/16/45. Mother an operatic soprano; father a bassoonist in motion picture and TV work, and authority on double reed instruments. Stud. violin from '51-7; tenor sax in high school with priv. teacher. Pl. in jazz band at Venice H.S. and gained important infl. and training here, with a second priv. teacher. Stud. improvisation w. Ralph Lee; further studies w. Bob McDonald, Valley State and LACC. Pl. w. Jerry Gray, '63-4; Chet Baker, '64; Si Zentner, '65; W. Herman, '66; L. Bellson, '67- .

From the late '60s Christlieb doubled between jazz and a busy career in the studios. First motion pic. in band backing Elvis Presley. Frequent member of D. Severinsen orch. on *Tonight* show. Christlieb's background, besides direct study, was an environment that brought Stravinsky, Boulez, Stockhausen and many other famous composers into his parents' home as visitors. He is a tenor soloist of rare fluency, capable of strong, dynamic up tempo work and of warm, sensitive ballad performances. Infls: Parker, Mulligan, Sims, Getz, Rollins,

Coltrane, C. Adderley, Clifford Brown.

LPs: *Jazz City* (R.A.H.M.P., 3311 Scadlock Ln., Sherman Oaks, Cal. 91403); w. Bellson, *Explosion* (Pablo); *Breakthrough* (Proj. 3); *Louie Rides Again* (Percussion Power, 5109 Nagle Ave., Sherman Oaks, Cal. 91403); w. Q. Jones, *Body Heat* (A & M); w. M. Legrand-S. Vaughan (Mainstream).

CHRISTY, JUNE, * *singer;* b. Springfield, Ill., 11/20/25. The former (1945-9) Stan Kenton vocalist went into semi-retirement in the late 1960s. Living in the San Fernando Valley, she emerged occasionally for night club engagements in North Hollywood and San Francisco. Guest app. w. Kenton at NJF-NY, '72.

LPs w. Kenton (Creative World).

CHURCHILL, SAVANNAH, * *singer;* b. New Orleans, La., 8/21/19. Best known as vocalist with Benny Carter band 1942-4, she died in Brooklyn, N.Y., 4/19/74.

CIRILLO, WALLACE JOSEPH (WALLY), * *piano, synthesizer, composer;* b. Huntington, N.Y. 2/4/27. Educ: Two masters of music degrees, major in comp. under Vittorio Gianinni, '58; major in mus. educ., '60 Manhattan School of Music, NYC; experimental comp. w. John Cage at New School, NYC. Infls: "Everyone from Pinetop Smith to Karlheinz Stockhausen." In '50s perf. own comps. at Carnegie Hall and Museum of Modern Art, NYC, w. Jazz Composers Workshop. Comp. and perf. first 12-tone jazz work, *Trans-Season,* '54 (Savoy Records); also in '50s wrote three symphs., chamber works, sonata for flute and piano, numerous avant garde and electronic jazz works. Moving to Boca Raton, Fla., '61, pl. w. Phil Napoleon, '64; Flip Phillips, Ira Sullivan et al. In Miami w. Terry Gibbs, '72; Anita O'Day, '73. Coll. concerts and TV in duo with guitarist Joe Diorio, '72-5. Teacher of improvisation and piano at U. of Miami, Miami-Dade Jr. Coll. and Florida Int'l. U., '75.

LPs: w. Joe Diorio (Spitball); w. John La Porta (Fantasy, Debut); J.J. Johnson-Kai Winding (Savoy); Charles Mingus (Savoy, Debut); Johnny Mathis (Columbia) etc.

CLARK, WALTER JR. (BUDDY), * *bass, arranger;* b. Kenosha, Wis., 7/10/29. Studies and early jobs in Chicago. Toured with many name bands early '50s; moved to LA, freelanced in studios, clubs. Pl. MJF w. Med Flory, '58. Active throughout '60s as studio bassist; recs., TV jingles etc.; also occasional trips w. Peggy Lee since '56. Co-founder w. Flory (q.v.) of Supersax, '72. Frequent sub for Ray Brown on Merv Griffin TV show, '71- . Broke w. Flory and was no longer w. Supersax in late '75.

Supersax, most of whose arrs. were transcribed by Flory or Clark from solos on old Ch. Parker records and orchestrated for five saxophones, won a Grammy award in '73 for the Best Jazz Performance by a group. In addition to rec., and app. at Donte's and other LA clubs. Supersax pl. Monterey, Concord Fests. '73, made a cross-Canada tour, '74 and a tour of Japan, early '75. Clark's arrs. for the band incl. *Ko-Ko; Parker's Mood; Night in Tunisia; Hot House; Kim.*

LPs: *Supersax Plays Bird; Salt Peanuts; Supersax Plays Bird with Strings* (Cap.).

CLARK, CHARLES E., *bass, cello*; b. Chicago, Ill., 3/11/45. Studied w. Wilbur Ware; classical bass w. Davis Bethe and Joseph Guastefeste, first bassist of the Chi. Symph. Began prof. in '63. Played w. Richard Abrams' Experimental Big Band. In '65 became one of the founding members of the Association for the Advancement of Creative Musicians, subsequently performing w. many AACM gps., most particularly Joseph Jarman; and violinist Leroy Jenkins. He was also a member, on scholarship, of the Chicago Civic Orch., the Chicago Symphony's official training orch. On his way home from a Civic Orch. rehearsal, he was stricken with a cerebral hemorrhage and died almost instantly, 4/15/69. The Civic Orch. established a scholarship in his name, to be awarded annually to a young, talented black musician.

DB commented of the "power and youthful exuberance of his playing, both arco and pizzicato. Clark," they wrote, "was also a gifted cellist." LPs: w. Abrams, *Levels and Degrees of Light*; w. Jarman, *Song For; As If It Were the Seasons* (Delmark).

CLARKE, KENNETH SPEARMAN (KENNY, KLOOK),* *drums*; b. Pittsburgh, Pa., 1/9/14. With Francy Boland (q.v.), co-led the Clarke-Boland Big Band until it disbanded in '73. He continued to teach and play in Paris, also touring w. a small group, which often incl. guitarist Jimmy Gourley; Lou Bennett or Eddy Louiss on organ. "No doubt the man remains a giant;" Burt Korall wrote of Clarke in *down beat*, "he has forgotten more than most drummers will ever know about moving and shaping music. Beguiling brush work, always a primary Clarke asset, his 1-1-1-1-1 sound on the ride cymbal—indeed his mastery of the entire kit in the service of the music—make for pleasure and provocation for the listener and certainly for his sidemen." One of the sidemen was British drummer Kenny Clare, who gave the band dual percussion.

In October '72 Clarke made one of his rare visits to the US to participate in the Duke Ellington Fellowship program at Yale Univ. With the Clarke-Boland band he played many European fests. but at Montreux '73 he appeared as the "house" drummer, pl. and rec. w. Dexter Gordon, Gene Ammons, etc. Comp: *The Wildman.* TV: many Euro. apps.; Montreux '73 seen on PBS in US. LPs: see Boland; *Paris Bebop Sessions* (Prest.); *Gene Ammons and Friends at Montreux*; Dexter Gordon, *Blues a la Suisse*; w. D. Gillespie, *The Giant* (Prest.); w. Bud Powell, *Bud in Paris* (Xanadu).

CLARKE, STANLEY M., *bass, composer*; b. Philadelphia, Pa., 6/30/51. Studied in early school years; also at Phila. Mus. Acad. w. Ed Arian, Neil Courtney. Early experience with rock groups in and around Philadelphia in late 1960s. Six months w. Horace Silver, 1970; then a year w. Joe Henderson, followed by stints w. Pharoah Sanders, Stan Getz. He then joined Chick Corea and remained with him when Corea organized his new group, Return to Forever.

Clarke, who started out playing violin, later, took up cello before switching to bass. A master of both the acoustic and electric instruments, he says: "The difference between the Fender and the 'real' bass is that one bass is made of wood and has more of a natural sound. The other bass is made out of steel and it's made to be used through electronic things, like amplifiers, which have a more synthetic sound. I personally like both of the sounds, they both fit well in different situations."

Polls: DB Critics, TDWR, '73-4 on acoustic bass; '74 on electric bass; DB Reader's poll '74-5. Infl: Blanton, Pettiford, Chambers, La Faro, Coltrane, M. Davis. Fest: Many apps. at NJF-NY & European events. Comp: *Children of Forever; Unexpected; Bass Folk Song; Butterfly Dreams; Vulcan Princess; Yesterday Princess; Lopsy Lu; Power; Life Suite; Blue; Quiet Afternoon; Light As A Feather.* LPs: *Stanley Clarke; Journey to Love;* (Nemporer); *Children of Forever* (Polydor); w. Corea (Polydor); Norman Connors (Cobblestone, Buddah); Getz (Columbia); D. Gordon (Prestige); J. Farrell (CTI); P. Sanders (Imp.).

CLARKE, TERENCE MICHAEL (TERRY),* *drums, percussion*; b. Vancouver, B.C., Canada, 8/20/44. Early exp. w. local gps. and w. B. Kessel, V. Guaraldi. Pl. w. John Handy at Both/And Club in SF, cont. w. him in U.S. & Can. through March. '67. Joined Fifth Dimension, Oct. '67, touring w. them in U.S., Can. & Europe until '70 when he settled in Toronto, becoming active in TV and rec. A reg. member of Rob McConnell's Boss Brass; also pl. w. gps. of Moe Koffman, Guido Basso, Sonny Greenwich, Ed Bickert, Ted Moses and Lenny Breau. Acc. visiting soloists such as Jim Hall, Blue Mitchell, James Moody, Paul Desmond, etc. in Toronto clubs. TV: *Bell Telephone Hour* w. Handy '66, NBC; numerous variety shows w. Fifth Dimension; CBC *Bandwagon* w. Basso; *Music to See* w. Moses. Fests: MJF '65-6; Costa Mesa '66 w. Handy. LPs: w. Handy, *Live at the Monterey Jazz. Fest.; The 2nd John Handy Album; Spirituals to Swing 30th Anniv. Concert* (Col.); w. McConnell, *Best Damn Band in the Land* (UA); w. Greenwich, *Sunsong*; w. Moses, *Sidereal Time* (Radio Canada Int.); w. Koffman, *Plays Bach; Vivaldi, The Four Seasons; Solar Explorations* (GRT); w. Jim Hall (Horizon).

CLAYTON, WILBUR (BUCK),* *trumpet, composer*; b. Parsons, Kansas, 11/12/11. The former Count Basie star was a busy free-lance in NYC during the '50s and '60s, also making trips to Switzerland, Australia, Japan and, especially, England. He followed this pattern into the '70s until problems with his embouchure forced him to give up the trumpet in '72. He worked in the insurance department of Local 802 but in '73 left to devote himself to writing and arranging. In '74 and '75 groups of all star soloists recorded his compositions and arrs. in a jam session format for Chiaroscuro, recreating the atmosphere of similar dates for Columbia in the '50s. Fest: NO, '69. Comps: *Sidekick; Change For a Buck; The Duke We Knew; Boss Blues; Case Closed; Easy Blue; Rockaway.* LPs: *Buck Clayton Jam Session; Jam Session, Vol. 2* (Chiaro.); *Le Vrai Buck Clayton* (77); *Spirituals to Swing, 30th Anniversary* (Col.); also wrote all material for Humphrey Lyttelton-Buddy Tate, *Kansas City Woman* (Bl. Lion).

CLEVELAND, JAMES (JIMMY),* trombone. composer; b. Wartrace, Tenn. 5/3/26. An alumnus of the L. Hampton and Q. Jones bands, Cleveland extended his work in commercial TV and recording areas, first in NYC in mid and late '60s, then in Calif. Member of regular band on Della Reese, Pearl Bailey, Bill Cosby, Music Scene and Merv Griffin shows. Along with these activities he continued to play jazz, at NJF 1966-8; MJF, '69; Concord, '70, and gigs in Hollywood etc. w. small combos. Comps: *Little Beaver; Count 'Em; Jimmy's Tune; Jimmy's Old Funky Blues.*

LPs: Many excellent albums, as leader and sideman in 1950s and early '60s, were deleted; some reissues on Trip. Cleveland has rec. w. Gil Evans, Q. Jones, O. Nelson, Wes Montgomery, D. Gillespie, Miles Davis, C. Adderley, L. Schifrin, Michel Legrand.

COATES, JOHN FRANCIS JR., *piano*; also *vibes*; b. Trenton, N.J., 2/17/38. Father a jazz pianist and music teacher. Studies at Mannes and Dalcroze music schools, NYC; Rutgers Univ., New Brunswick, N.J.; privately, '45-56, w. Urana Clarke. After high school grad., '56, joined Charlie Ventura for two yrs. Returned to matriculate at Rutgers. Since grad. he has confined most of his playing to the Deer Head Inn, a jazz club in the small town of Delaware Water Gap, Pa., pl. occasional concerts elsewhere. Musicians such as Al Cohn, Phil Woods, Zoot Sims have pl. w. him at the Deer Head. Infl: John Coates Sr., Art Tatum. TV apps. w. Ventura, Barry Miles, Bernard Peiffer. Comps: 100 choral arrs; several orig. comps. for chorus; two mus. comedies; 50 songs "which are important to me for use in my jazz playing." Coates is composer-arranger-editor for Shawnee Press, Inc., Delaware Water Gap, Pa. LPs: *The Jazz Piano of John Coates, Jr.* (Omnisound); *Portrait* (Savoy); vibes w. Peiffer (Polydor).

COBB, ARNETT,* *tenor sax*; b. Houston, Tex., 8/10/18. Popular extrovert soloist in Lionel Hampton orch. in '40s. Toured w. own band from '47 but inactive at different times due to illness; auto crash. Own bands in Houston, '60s but illness once again prevented him from playing for long periods. Active again in '70, he traveled from Houston to NYC to play w. Illinois Jacquet at Town Hall, July '73. LP: *Jazz at Town Hall* w. Jacquet (JRC).

COBB, WILBUR JAMES (JIMMY),* *drums*; b. Washington, D.C., 1/20/29. A member of Miles Davis' quintet & sextet, '58-63, he then pl. w. Paul Chambers and Wynton Kelly in trio under Kelly's name that also acc. Wes Montgomery, '65-6. When Montgomery left to form his own gp., the trio cont. to work together, and after Chambers' death in '69, Cobb and Kelly were still a team until Cobb joined Sarah Vaughan in '71. Film: soundtrack for *Seven Days in May* w. David Amram. TV: w. Sarah Vaughan at Wolf Trap Farm, PBS. Fests: w. Vaughan at NJF-NY, '74-5.

LPs w. Vaughan (Mainstream).

COBHAM, WILLIAM C. (BILLY); *drums, composer, leader*; b. Panama, 5/16/44. At age three he and his mother joined father, William Sr., a pianist who had preceded them to NYC. Began fooling around w. timbales at age two. By age eight was sitting-in w. father publicly. Infl. by the many local parades in Brooklyn joined Boy Scouts in order to pl. drums. In drum corps., '56-8. Entered the High Sch. of Music & Art '59 and got first complete drum set. Pl. w. Jazz Samaritans which incl. George Cables and Clint Houston. Other schoolmates were Larry Willis, Bobby Colomby, Jimmy Owens, Eddie Gomez.

After high School was in the Army, pl. w. Military Ocean Terminal Base Band at Brooklyn Army Terminal; band at Ft. Dix, N.J. w. Grover Washington. While still in the Army, through the last half of '67, worked w. Billy Taylor trio at Hickory House; gigged w. the NY Jazz Sextet (Hubert Laws, Tom McIntosh, Owens, etc.); taught and served as a clinician for Jazzmobile; and paired w. Chris White in Rhythm Associates, pl. practice seminar rehearsals for bassists and drummers.

In '68, after his Army discharge, Cobham was hired by Horace Silver and pl. w. his quintet, Feb.-Oct. incl. a European tour. Then he became extremely active in recs. for film (*Shaft*), TV (*Mission Impossible*) and jingles. Pl. w. S. Turrentine; K. Burrell. Formed jazz-rock fusion band Dreams in '69 and remained w. it through '70. During this time made several important recs. w. Miles Davis. In spring '71 rec. w. John McLaughlin and shortly thereafter became a member of the newly-formed Mahavishnu Orchestra. When they disbanded on Jan. 1, '73 he began rec. under his own name. Formed own band in Feb. '74 for clubs, concerts, European tour, summer '74, pl. Montreux JF; Rainbow Theatre in London. Returned to Europe, May '75, for six wks. In Sept. assembled a new quartet called Spectrum, after the title of his first rec. as a leader, with George Duke, keyboards; John Scofield, guitar; Doug Rauch, bass.

As a producer he has been responsible for Airto's *Virgin Land* (Salvation); and David Sancious' *Forest of Feelings* (CBS).

Early infl: Erroll Garner, Billy Eckstine, Miles Davis, Tito Puente, Stan Levey, Sonny Payne, Jo Jones, Gus Johnson. Fest: NJF w. Silver, '68; NJF-NY w. Mahavishnu, '72. Won DB Readers poll, '73-5. Comp: *Spanish Moss; Savannah the Serene; Storm; Flash Flood; The Pleasant Pheasant; Heather; Crosswind; Panhandler; Solarization.* LPs: *A Funky Thide of Sings; Shabazz; Total Eclipse; Crosswinds; Spectrum* (Atl.); *Dreams*; w. Mahavishnu, *The Inner Mounting Flame; Birds of Fire*; w. M. Davis, *Jack Johnson; Live-Evil; Big Fun; Get Up With It; Bitches Brew* (Col.); w. J. McLaughlin, *My Goal's Beyond* (Douglas); w. H. Silver, *Serenade to a Soul Sister; You Got to Take a Little Love* (BN); also w. George Benson; Ron Carter; Deodato; Freddie Hubbard; Randy Weston; Milt Jackson; H. Laws; Don Sebesky; S. Turrentine; G. Washington (CTI).

COCHRAN, TODD (See BAYETÉ)

COE, ANTHONY GEORGE (TONY),* *tenor saxophone, clarinet*; also *bass clarinet, soprano sax, flute, basset horn, composer*; b. Canterbury, England, 11/29/34. Four years w. J. Dankworth, '66-9; Clarke-Boland band from '69 until its breakup in '73. In '70 he also worked w. Matrix, a group that pl. chamber music and jazz-oriented works, some written by Coe. Has led own combo off and on for fests. and broadcasts. In '75 his first major comp., *Zeitgeist*, was perf. Movies, recordings w. H. Mancini incl. *Return of The Pink Panther*. Infl. by B. Bigard; on tenor by Hawkins, Webster, Gonsalves; in comp. by Schoenberg, Berg.

Own LP w. Brian Lemon Trio (77 Records); others w. P. Seamen (Decibel); Clarke-Boland (Poly., MPS, Bl. Lion).

COHN, ALVIN GILBERT (AL),* *tenor sax, composer*; b. Brooklyn, N.Y., 11/24/25. Writer for TV specials such as award-winning *Anne Bancroft Show* and *S'Wonderful, S'Marvelous, S'Gershwin*, '69-70, and for annual *Tony Award* show. Chief arr. for Broadway musicals *Raisin*, '73 and *Music, Music, Music* '74. Pl. solos on the soundtrack of film *Lenny*. Although he concentrated on writing, he continued to app. in clubs and concerts w. his longtime sidekick, Zoot Sims, and w. his own quartet in Toronto, Wash., D.C., N.J., NYC, and Pennsylvania's Pocono Mts. where he makes his home. With Sims, toured Scandinavia, '74. Own gp. at NY Jazz Museum; guest apps. w. Balaban & Cats at Eddie Condon's, '75. Though underrated by the public his playing is much admired by fellow musicians. Fests: NJF w. Sims, '66; NJF-NY w. W. Herman alumni, '72; Molde, '75; Colo. Jazz Party, '68-72, '74-5. Comp: *Mama Flosie; The Underdog* (a.k.a. *Ah-Moore*); *Mr. George; The Note; You 'N' Me*. LPs: *Play It Now* (Xanadu); *Broadway 1954* (Prest.); *Too Heavy For Words* w. J. Moody (MPS); w. Sims, *Body and Soul* (Muse) & *You 'N' Me* (Trip); *Colorado Jazz Party* (MPS); w. J. Rushing, *The You and Me That Used to Be* (RCA); w. Tony Bennett (Col.); w. Bill Watrous; John Bunch (Famous Door); w. Sonny Berman (Onyx).

COHN, GEORGE THOMAS (SONNY),* *trumpet, fluegelhorn*; b. Chicago, Ill., 3/14/25. Heard with many bands in Chicago from mid-'40s; later w. L. Bellson, Erskine Hawkins. Joined C. Basie orch, '60 and during next 15 years toured the world with the band. For details of travels see BASIE, COUNT.

LPs: *Jazz at the Santa Monica Civic '72* w. Basie, Fitzgerald (Pablo); *Basie and Sinatra Live at the Sands* (Reprise); *Standing Ovation; Basie Straight Ahead* (Daybreak); *Afrique* w. Basie (Flying Dutchman).

COKER, CHARLES MITCHELL (DOLO),* *piano*; also *alto sax*; b. Hartford, Conn., 11/16/27. Raised in S. Carolina, pl. his first pro. jobs in and around Phila. Moved to LA, '60, led own trio at Club Casbah, Memory Lane, Club Libra through '72. Has also worked w. Herb Ellis, Blue Mitchell, Supersax, S. Stitt, Red Rodney, L. Konitz and Sahib Shihab at a variety of LA area clubs.

Title I Concerts at over 80 schools in Unified School District w. S. Criss, '73, '74. Pl. w. Jack Sheldon, Richard Boone, D. Gordon, '74; the groups of Harry Edison and T. Edwards, '75; Redd Foxx Show in concert, '70s. Coker is also active as piano teacher and vocal coach. TV: *Rosey Grier Show*, '68; *In Name Only*, Screen Gems, '69; *Della Reese Show*, '69; *Festival In Black*, KCET, '71; *Black Omnibus*, '73; *Lucy Show; Sanford & Son*. Fests: Watts Summer Jazz Fest., '70-2. Comps: *Lovely Lisa; Field Day; Affair in Havana*.

LPs: *Superbop*, w. Rodney; *Feelin's*, w. Edwards (Muse); *I've Got A Right To Sing*, w. Boone (Nocturne).

COKER, HENRY,* *trombone*; b. Dallas, Tex., 12/24/19. Best known through association w. Count Basie band, '52-63. Toured w. Ray Charles, '66-71. Sound track work for film *Lady Sings The Blues*, '72. Gigged in LA area from '71, also rejoined Basie for four months in '73.

LPs w. Basie on various labels; also Teresa Brewer-Basie (Flying Dutchman); *My Kind of Jazz Part I* and *My Kind of Jazz Part III*, w. Charles (Crossover).

COLE, WILLIAM R. (COZY),* *drums*; also *tympani, vibes*; East Orange, N.J., 10/17/09. Continued to lead his own combo through 1968. Joined Jonah Jones quartet '69. Operated Krupa & Cole Drum School from '54 until Krupa's death in '73. App. at NJF '73 w. Cab Calloway reunion band; Nice fest. '74. Pub: *Modern Drum Technique; Gene Krupa & Cozy Cole Drum Book*, both w. (Mills Music, 1619 Broadway, NYC); *Cozy Cole, William V. Kessler Modern Studies for Drums* (BMI). LPs: *A Cozy Conception of Carmen* (MGM); *Drum Beat for Dancing Feet* w. guests Krupa, Ray McKinley, Panama Francis (Coral); *Topsy* (Love); w. Jo Jones, Zutty Singleton (Jazz Odyssey).

COLEMAN, WILLIAM JOHNSON (BILL),* *trumpet, singer*; b. Paris, Ky., 8/4/04. Living in France from the end of '48. Toured in England as a soloist, '66 and '67. Featured at Jazz Expo, London, '69. Other fest: Nice '74; Montreux w. S. Grappelli. LPs: Bill Coleman & Guy Lafitte, *Mainstream at Montreux*; w. Ben Webster (Black Lion); *Nice 1974, Tribute to Count Basie* (Eng. RCA).

COLEMAN, EARL,* *singer*; b. Port Huron, Mich., 8/12/25. Sang w. E. Hines; J. McShann in '40s. Rec. w. Charlie Parker. In mid-'60s app. w. Billy Taylor; Frank Foster big band in NYC; one-nighters at the Playboy Club. To LA late '68, working at Redd Foxx's club. Remained in LA through late '75, except for a trip back to NYC '69. At Foxx's '70; Parisian Room; Donte's; Baked Potato; one nighters w. Bill Berry; Gerald Wilson bands. When Wilson subbed for Ellington band at Biltmore, Coleman sang Ellingtonia w. him. Assembled a gp. to present a half-hour musical eulogy to Duke at Museum of Science & Industry, broadcast on KBCA. Working in Cincinnati, St. Louis in late '75. Leonard Feather described his bass-baritone sound as having "a searing intensity, at times almost an anguish, that bespeaks his rare depth of understanding born of a long and bitter life experience. LPs: *Love Songs* (Atl.); Parker reissue (Spotlite); reissue of '40s material w. Fats Navarro, *Bebop Revisited*, Vol. 1 (Xanadu).

COLEMAN, GEORGE,* *tenor saxophone*; also *alto sax*; b. Memphis, Tenn., 3/8/35. Pl. and rec. w. Miles Davis quintet, '63-4; L. Hampton, Ch. McPherson, L. Morgan, Elvin Jones, Shirley Scott, '65-73. Toured Europe three months, '74, as leader, also w. S. Hampton. Comp. music for bands of all sizes, perf. in concerts, clubs, colleges, '74-5. Playing and conducting concerts presented by Jazzmobile w. own octet. Also pl. w. Cedar Walton quartet '75. NEA Grant. Comp: *Revival of the Fittest; Little Miss Half-Steps*.

LPs: w. Roach (Mercury); Davis (Columbia); H. Hancock, H. Silver, E. Jones, Jimmy Smith, Lee Morgan (Blue Note); Harold Mabern (Prestige); S. Hampton (Strand); S. Scott (Chess); Elvin Jones (Enja).

COLEMAN, ORNETTE,* *alto sax, composer*; also *tenor sax, trumpet, violin, shenai*; b. Ft. Worth, Tex., 3/19/30. After moving from California and appearing at the Five Spot in NYC, '59, with Don Cherry in the quartet that helped alter the face of jazz, Coleman has made Manhattan his base of operations. His mid-'60s trio of David Izenzon and Charles Moffett gave way to a quartet format again, this time with Dewey Redman; Charlie Haden; and either Ed Blackwell or Ornette's son Denardo on drums. His album, *Science Fiction*, reunited him with many of his cohorts incl. Cherry, Bobby Bradford, Billy Higgins, etc. As the '70s moved toward mid-decade Coleman tended to maintain a low profile, concentrating on writing and doing most of his playing at his own Artist House (131 Prince St.) in the Soho section of Manhattan. In '67 he played at the Village Theater with quartet and the Philadelphia Woodwind Quintet; In '69 Don Cherry rejoined him briefly for a quintet concert at the Loeb Student Center of NYU. The quartet with Redman was on stage with a symphony orchestra at the NJF-NY '72 for a performance of his *Skies of America* written with what he describes as his "harmelodic theory." The texture of the orchestral writing, he says, comes from "The total collective blending of the transposed and nontransposed instruments using the same intervals."

Gary Giddins, reviewing a recording of *Skies of America*, noted: "These formulations give the impression of a more complicated and radical music than the ear actually hears—the work is readily approachable and can be enjoyed without the footnotes."

Whitney Balliett in '67 found that Coleman's "feet remain firmly in the old blues and his head is full of celestial things—a balanced presence that could offset a great deal of the malarkey that afflicts the rest of the 'new thing.' "

Even in the '70s, however, not everyone was totally convinced of Coleman's credibility. Charles Mingus was quoted by Balliett in '71 as saying: "But I feel sorry about jazz. The truth has been lost in the music. All the different styles and factions went to war with each other, and it hasn't done any good. Take Ornette Coleman."

"Mingus sang half a chorus of *Body and Soul* in a loud, off-key voice," wrote Balliett, "drowning out the jukebox. It was an uncanny imitation."

"That's all he does," said Mingus. "Just pushing the melody out of line here and there. Trouble is, he can't play it straight."

Joachim Berendt, commenting on *Skies of America*, wrote: "At the time of the refined string sounds of such composers as Ligeti and Penderecki, Coleman writes simply, almost naively, for the symphony orchestra—using parallel lines and a host of parallel and duplicated voices. The more astonishing how rich and expressive the effects that he produces! Ornette Coleman remains a jazz musician—even when composing for symphony orchestra. The symphony orchestra, to him, is an enlarged 'horn' on which he improvises."

Berendt also described Coleman at the '71 Berlin Jazz Days as the musician who "in the early sixties revolutionized jazz" but here was "simply making 'beautiful music': clear, singing, wonderfully balanced alto lines."

In '74 Coleman played at San Francisco's Keystone Corner in '74; visited France in the summer of '75; and played at the Five Spot, NYC, in that same year. His new group consisted of James "Blood" Ulmer, guitar; Haden; Denardo; and Barbara Huey, percussion.

Coleman received Guggenheim Fellowships for composition in '67 and '74. DB Awards: Jazzman of the Year, '66, '71; Hall of Fame, '69; *At the Golden Circle, Vol. 1*, Record of the Year in Critics and Readers polls. '66; alto sax, Critics poll, '67, '72-4; Readers poll, '72-4.

Comp: *Broken Shadows; Comme Il Faut; Space Jungle; Trouble in the East; Forms and Sounds; Civilization Day; Love and Sex; Street Woman; Atavism; Rock the Clock; Law Years; All My Life*. LPs: *Skies of America; Science Fiction* (Col.); *Friends and Neighbors* (Fly. Dutch.); *At 12; Crisis* (Imp.); *The Empty Foxhole; At the Golden Circle, Vols. 1&2*; w. J. McLean, *New and Old Gospel* (BN); reissue, *Best* (Atl.).

COLES, JOHN (JOHNNY),* *trumpet*; b. Trenton, N.J., 7/3/26. After pl. w. George Coleman at NJF '66 and as sideman for Hunter Coll. jazz concerts continued to freelance until he became one of the original members of the Herbie Hancock sextet '68. W. Ray Charles orch. '69-70 before joining Duke Ellington and remaining until Duke's death. Rejoined Charles May '74. Recorded sound track for Bill Cosby's Fat Albert TV series '69. LPs: *Katumbo* (Mainstream); *The Prisoner* w. Hancock (Blue Note); *The Great Concert of Charles Mingus* (Prestige); *Guitar Forms* w. Kenny Burrell; *Look To the Rainbow* w. Astrud Gilberto (Verve); several albums w. Ellington.

COLLETTE, WILLIAM MARCELL (BUDDY),* *saxes, flute, clarinet, piano, composer*; b. Los Angeles, Cal., 8/6/21. Prominent since '40s in both jazz and studio work. Gave courses on music writing for TV and motion pics., also directed stage band, for three years at Cal. State U., LA. Has written everything from TV jingles and industrial film music to a three part fugue for nine instruments, and a suite for harp and flute using 12 tone system. Collette also helped start a record company, Legend, in '73, and in '75 was serving as President. Fest. apps. at Monterey etc.; occasional gigs leading quintet in jazz clubs.

LPs: *Now and Then* (Legend); *Basin Street Brass* w. Red Callender (Legend); *Blue Sands* w. C. Hamilton (Wor. Pac.).

COLLIER, GRAHAM, *bass, composer*; b. Tynemouth, England, 2/21/37. Father was drummer for silent movies. Stud. Berklee Coll., '61-3 w. Herb Pomeroy, William Curtis. While there pl. w. Jimmy Dorsey band led by Lee Castle. Returned to England late '63, formed own band '64; concerts and clubs; also first British jazz group to tour schools extensively presenting lecture concerts for children. Collier is also active in comp. for TV commercials, documentary films, stage. Inspirations: Duke Ellington, Gil Evans, Charles Mingus. Publs: *Inside Jazz* (Quartet, 27 Goodge St., London W.I.), *Jazz* (Cambridge Univ. Press, Cambridge, England). Fests: Antibes; Montreux '71.

LPs: *Darius; Midnight Blue* (Mosaic Records); *Mosaics* (Philips).

COLLIER, RON, *composer*; also *trombone*; b. Coleman, Alberta, Canada, 7/3/30. Mother & father amateur mus.; wife, sister & brother-in-law prof. mus. Stud. arr. & comp. w. Gordon Delamont, '51-5; orchestration & comp. w. George Russell, Hall Overton, '62-3. Had own quintet and tentet in '50s & '60s. Resident composer at Humber Coll. Won stage band jazz competition, open class, for Canada w. Humber Coll. Band. App. at Toronto Jazz Fest.; Stratford Music Fest.; Expo '67. Wrote music for feature films: *A Fan's Notes; Face Off; Paperback Hero.* Worked and collaborated w. Ellington on his ballet, *The River* and symphony, *Celebration.* Comps: *The City,* suite for orch.; *Carnival,* for orch., narrator and solo fluegelhorn; *Requiem for J.F.K.; Aurora Borealis,* ballet. LPs: *Duke Ellington, North of the Border in Canada with the Ron Collier Orch.* (Decca), reissued as *Collages* (MPS); w. Moe Koffman, *Solar Explorations* (GRT).

COLLINS, BURTON I. (BURT),* *trumpet*; also *fluegelhorn, piccolo trumpet*; b. Bronx, N.Y., 3/27/31. Feat. sideman w. Woody Herman, Johnny Richards in '50s; became a busy, free-lance studio man in NYC during the '60s and '70s. Pl. w. pit bands for Broad. shows, *Bye Bye Birdie,* '60; *How to Succeed in Business,* '61-2. Did many club dates, '63-4; jazz soloist w. band on Les Crane TV Show, ABC, '65. Other TV: specials w. Victor Borge; Jonathan Winters. Fests: Randall's Island in early '60s w. C. Adderley big band; J. Richards orch. In '75 pl. w. bands of Dave Matthews; Lee Konitz. LPs: w. Collins-Shepley Galaxy, *Time, Space and the Blues; Lennon/McCartney Live* (MTA); *Introducing Duke Pearson; Now Hear This* w. Pearson (Blue Note); *Live at the Five Spot* w. Matthews (Muse).

COLLINS, JOHN ELBERT,* *guitar, banjo*; b. Montgomery, Ala., 9/20/13. After the death in 1965 of Nat King Cole, with whom he had worked since '59, Collins spent six years with Bobby Troup's quartet in locations in

and around LA. Other engagements w. F. Sinatra, Sammy Davis, Nancy Wilson, Neal Hefti. In '75 he was chosen to participate in the NEA Jazz Oral History Project of the Smithsonian Institution. Led own quartet feat. Jimmy Jones on piano, '74-5.

LPs: w. E. Fitzgerald, *Thirty by Ella* (Cap.); w. Lorez Alexandria, *Didn't We* (Pzazz).

COLLINS, RUDOLPH ALEXANDER (RUDY),* *drums*; b. New York City, 7/24/34. In 1967-68 toured w. Ray Bryant, Kenny Burrell and, briefly, Woody Herman; six mos. in house band at Raleigh Hotel in Catskill Mts., then w. Junior Mance, Lloyd Price, Harry Belafonte '69; Broadway and off-Broadway show work, incl. *Hair* and *Purlie;* clubs w. Bill Russell, Morris Nanton trios, '70-71; Jimmy Neeley, Dave Rivera, Earl Hines trios '72, also gigs at Steer Inn on Long Island '72; Apollo Theatre w. Reuben Phillips house band, tours w. Monty Alexander, Sam "The Man" Taylor (Japan), NYC clubs w. Dakota Staton, Duke Pearson, Lee Konitz '73; Randy Weston, Bernie Leighton, Count Basie, incl. Toronto JF '74; toured the US and Canada w. Cleo Laine and John Dankworth '74 and TV special w. them '75. Other TV apps. w. Gillespie '71, Weston '74. Teaching drums at Brooklyn Children's Museum from '69. LPs: *Tanjah* w. Weston (Polydor); *Live at the Village Gate* w. Mance (Atlantic); *This Is Billy Butler;* Gene Ammons (Prest.).

COLOMBY, ROBERT WAYNE (BOBBY), *drums*; b. New York, N.Y., 12/20/44. Began listening to jazz at age 15 through brothers Jules, a trumpeter, and Harry, both of whom later managed T. Monk. Pl. w. Jon Hendricks, Odetta, Eric Anderson. Founder member in '68 of Blood, Sweat & Tears, the first group to achieve int'l stature and commercial success with an amalgam of rock and jazz elements, which drew young musicians away from a strictly guitar-oriented format by their use of horns. TV: *In Concert; Midnight Special; Up Beat; Live in Scandinavia Special; In Concert* (London), plus many other European, Australian and Japanese apps. Fests: Newport, Montreux, Longhorn. LPs: w. B.S.&T. (Col.).

COLTRANE, ALICE,* *piano, composer*; also *organ, harp*; b. Detroit, Mich., 8/27/37. After pl. w. the Terry Gibbs quartet in the early '60s, under her maiden name of Alice McLeod, she joined John Coltrane in '66 and was married to him later that year. Following his death in '67 she began leading her own group for clubs, concerts and recordings. The various musicians who have app. with her in these capacities incl. P. Sanders, A. Shepp, O. Coleman, Carlos Ward and Frank Lowe. In the '65-7 period she toured extensively in the U.S. and Japan w. J. Coltrane. With her own group she pl. at the Village Vanguard; as a soloist at Carnegie Hall, '71; but since she moved to Cal. in '72 her public apps. have been sporadic.

Originally a Bud Powell-oriented pianist, she was later greatly infl. by McCoy Tyner. She has a strong interest in "all religions of the world" and "a deep appreciation for spiritual music-meditative music."

Imamu Baraka described her relation to Coltrane's

music as "a vector, a further earth exploration." Bill Cole has called her playing "vibrant, fresh, innovative and uncompromising . . . her right hand is very light and dextrous on the organ, while her left plays unyielding chords that give strong drone feelings." DB reviewer Will Smith, while praising her piano and organ solos, said that her harp work, "no matter how lovely it can be, is quite lightweight," and called her string writing "super saccharine, often corny and terribly repetitive."

Fests: Newport, w. J. Coltrane, '66. Her albums contain many of her original compositions. She names *Journey in Satchidananda* and *Blue Nile* as her most important.

LPs: *Lord of Lords; World Galaxy; Universal Consciousness; Journey in Satchidananda; Ptah the El Daoud; Huntington Ashram Monastery; Monastic Trio* (Imp.); w. J. Coltrane, *Infinity* (rec. in mid-'60s, completed '72); *Concert in Japan; Live at the Village Vanguard Again; Cosmic Music; Expression* (Imp.); *Illuminations*, w. C. Santana (Col.); *The Elements* w. J. Henderson (Milest.).

COLTRANE, JOHN WILLIAM,* *tenor, soprano saxes, composer, leader*; also *bass clarinet, flute*; b. Hamlet, N.C., 9/23/26. From the end of '65, when both McCoy Tyner and Elvin Jones left his group, the music of Coltrane continued more deeply into the religious expression he had begun earlier with *A Love Supreme*. Retained were saxophonist Pharoah Sanders and drummer Rashied Ali. Tyner's replacement was Alice McLeod who became Mrs. John Coltrane. Other drummers were hired on different jobs to complement Ali.

In July '66 Coltrane toured Japan for two weeks, playing 17 concerts before capacity audiences. Following the tour bassist Jimmy Garrison, the last remaining member of his most famous quartet, left after expressing dissatisfaction with the direction of the music. Back in New York, for an engagement at the Vanguard, Ali brought in a supporting cast of several percussionists on bells, tambourines, congas, triangles, etc. Coltrane occasionally did some primitive yodeling, described by C.O. Simpkins as "sometimes . . . high and screaming. Other times . . . deep and thudding, with him striking his chest as though it were a resonant drum."

Coltrane began studying the conga and practiced with his wife. He took to hiring large ensembles, many of whom were drummers, to accompany him, as in an appearance at the Front Room in Newark. When his fans requested his older numbers he replied, "We're not playing that kind of thing anymore."

Early in '67 he again played at the Vanguard and, in April played a concert at the opening of Olatunji's Center of African Culture in Harlem. In June there was a recurrence of "stomach trouble" which had been plaguing him since the previous year. (Many pictures taken on the Japanese tour show him holding his hand over the right part of his abdomen.) This liver ailment continued to worsen and, after hospitalization, he died on July 17, 1967.

He was already considered one of the major innovators in the history of jazz. Long after his death Coltrane continued to be a pervasive influence on contemporary music and musicians, not only jazz and saxophonists, but rock and players of all instruments. He affected music in several ways: harmonically-melodically; rhythmically; tonally; and in terms of form. Saxophonists such as Wayne Shorter, Joe Farrell and Charles Lloyd, to name just three, received much inspiration from him; other reedmen like Pharoah Sanders, Archie Shepp, Albert Ayler and John Gilmore, after drawing on him for inspiration, later helped shape his final period with their interpretations. He had already popularized the soprano among modern saxophonists.

Gordon Kopulos, writing in *down beat* in '71, pointed out: "It is irrelevant if the Beatles ever heard John Coltrane. It is important that some three years before they impacted on the American scene, Trane was already playing *India*. Four years after their first success, the Beatles transiently flirted with the music of Ravi Shankar, and an overnight cult sprang up. A sitar solo was even grafted on to a Beatles tune. The closing refrain of *No Time* by The Guess Who is remarkably similar in form to the repetitive device Trane used in so many of his solos. *Vehicle* by the Ides of March sounds embarrassingly like a slightly altered lift from *Blue Train*."

Some of his critics and fellow musicians felt that he had had a detrimental effect on the music by surrounding himself with, and encouraging, lesser musicians.

Whitney Balliett, in *The New Yorker*, wrote: "But born poets like Coltrane sometimes misjudge the size of their gifts, and in trying to further them, to ennoble them, they fall over into sentimentality or the maniacal. Coltrane did both, and it is ironic that these lapses, which were mistakenly considered to be musical reflections of our inchoate times, drew his heaviest acclaim. People said they heard the dark night of the Negro in Coltrane's wildest music, but what they really heard was a heroic and unique lyrical voice at the mercy of its own power."

He won DB Critics poll & Readers poll, '66. In '75 books on his life by C.O. Simpkins and J.C. Thomas were published (see bibliography).

Comp: *Naima; Cousin Mary; Spiral; Countdown; Giant Steps; Mr. P.C.; Syeeda's Song Flute; Alabama; Ogunde; Moment's Notice; Blue Train; A Love Supreme; Trane's Blues; Spiritual; Crescent; Manifestation; Reverend King; Lord Help Me to Be; The Sun; Expression; Impressions; Father, Son and Holy Ghost.*

LPs: *Kulu Se Mama; Meditations; Expression; Live at the Village Vanguard Again; Om; Cosmic Music; Selflessness; Transition; Live in Seattle; Sun Ship; Infinity; Live—Concert in Japan; The Africa/Brass Sessions, Vol. II; Interstellar Space* (Imp.); *Alternate Takes* (Atl.); *High Step* w. Paul Chambers, incl. reissue and unissued material (BN); reissues on Imp.; Prest.; Atl.; Trip; BN.

COLYER, KEN,* *trumpet*; also *guitar*; b. Gt. Yarmouth, Norfolk, England, 4/18/28. Pro. since '40s, leading own group frequently from '53. Many tours of Europe, also U.S. and Canada in '75; pl. w. Canadian band at NO

Jazz and Heritage Fest. Numerous other trad. fests., riverboat gigs etc. TV in Germany; BBC Jazz Club etc. Colyer has long been dedicated to NO style jazz.

LP: *I Want To Be Happy*, rec. in Germany (Happy Bird).

CONDON, ALBERT EDWIN (EDDIE),* *guitar*; b. Goodland, Ind., 11/16/04. Illness precluded Condon from more than occasional activity during the '60s. In '67 he made what turned out to be his final California appearance, leading a group for one night at Disneyland. Co-led World's Greatest Jazzband II w. Kai Winding at Roosevelt Grill, '69. Toured high schools and colls. w. Art Hodes, Wild Bill Davison and B. Bigard, '71. Was the subject of a tribute, in which he himself appeared briefly, at NJF-NY, Carnegie Hall, July '72, surrounded by many musicians who had played at his Town Hall concerts in the '40s. Condon died Aug. 4, 1973 in a New York hospital. The use of his name in connection with a night club, which had flourished from '49-58 on West Third Street in NYC, and from '58-67 on East 56th Street, was revived early in '75 when a third club known as Eddie Condon's opened on West 54th Street, feat. jazz musicians, some of whom had been assoc. w. Condon and his earlier clubs. The new premises were under the management of bassist Red Balaban.

Book: *Eddie Condon's Scrapbook of Jazz*, by Condon and Hank O'Neal (St. Martin's Press, N.Y.). Publ. four months after Condon's death, this collection of reminiscences, photographs, reproductions of record labels, album covers, articles by Condon, cartoons, paintings etc., captures the essence of his era. Earlier books: *We Called It Music*, w. Thomas Sugrue (Henry Holt, 1947); *Eddie Condon's Treasury of Jazz* w. Richard Gehman (Dial Press, 1956).

LPs: *Eddie Condon & Co. Vol. 1—Gershwin Program (1941-1945)* (Decca); *The Eddie Condon Concerts*, Town Hall 1944-45, feat. Pee Wee Russell; *The Eddie Condon Concerts*, Town Hall 1944; *Jazz at the New School* (Chiaroscuro); *Eddie Condon's World of Jazz* (Col.); *The Commodore Years, Eddie Condon & Bud Freeman* (Atl.); *The Best of Eddie Condon* (MCA).

CONNELL, WILL, JR., *alto saxophone*; also *flute, clarinet, piano*; b. Los Angeles, Cal., 11/22/38. Stud. at LA City Coll. Freelanced and led own groups in LA: wrote for and pl. w. H. Tapscott. Took part in various Watts Festivals and Festival in Black.

Comps: *Fatisha; Shakti (Mountain Song)*. Connell was the uncredited composer, arranger and orchestrator on at least one motion picture.

LPs: w. Azar Lawrence, *Bridge Into the New Age* (Prest.).

CONNERS, GENE (MIGHTY FLEA), *trombone*; b. Birmingham, Ala., 1930. Mother led the Gospel Harmonettes. Started on trombone at seven. Played in New Orleans funeral bands from '44 w. Bunk Johnson and others. After four years in Navy, lived in LA, rec. w. Ray Charles, Wynonie Harris, Dinah Washington et al. Best known for his work w. Johnny Otis, with whom he app.

in clubs and visited Europe. His frenetic style earned him popularity with r & b audiences.

LPs w. J. Otis (Epic, Blues Spectrum); Shuggie Otis (Epic).

CONNIFF, RAY,* *composer, trombone*; b. Attelboro, Mass., 11/6/16. Mainly a popular music personality, but continued to play occasional jazz trombone in a Dixieland group as part of his vocal-group show and on records. Winner of many awards, gold albums etc. Tours of Europe, Japan. In '74, set a precedent as first U.S. pop artist to rec. in Soviet Union, using Russian singers and musicians.

LPs: (incl. jazz tracks): *Concert in Stereo Live at the Sahara/Tahoe* (Col.); others on Col.

CONNOR, CHRIS,* *singer*; b. Kansas City, Mo., 11/8/27. The former Stan Kenton vocalist of the '50s who toured successfully as a single in the '50s and early '60s, was intermittently active in the late '60s-early '70s but surfaced at the Half Note and then pl. the Maisonette at the St. Regis Hotel, NYC. LP: *Sketches* (Stanyan).

CONNORS, WILLIAM A. (BILL), *guitar*; b. Los Angeles, Ca., 9/24/49. Self-taught. Infl. by many classical guitarists, composers and jazz musicians. Pl. w. Mike Nock, '72 in SF, S. Swallow, '73 in SF. Traveled w. C. Corea, '74, incl. European tour.

LPs: *Theme to the Guardian*, solo album (ECM); *Hymn of the Seventh Galaxy*, w. Corea (Polydor).

CONNORS, NORMAN (Norman Connor Jr.), *drums, composer*; also *percussion, vibes*; b. Phila., Pa., 3/1/47. Studied comp., theory, harmony at Settlement House in Phila.; percussion at Music City; vibes, drums, tympani w. Gilbert Stanton; private drum and perc. lessons from ages five to 15; at Temple Univ., '65-9; perc. major at Juilliard, '67-8. First insp. by Lex Humphries, he began prof. while in high school, gigging locally, sometimes w. own groups. To NYC, '66, were he pl. w. Marion Brown, Archie Shepp, Sun Ra, Sam Rivers, Jackie McLean, Carlos Garnett, Jack McDuff and Pharoah Sanders. In '72 he formed his own group, rec. and touring with it in the U.S. and abroad. Fest: NJF-NY, '73-74; Phila. '73-4; Berkeley; Howard U.; Montreux, '74; Pori; Paris; Berlin; Japan, '75. Infl: Roach, Blakey, T. Williams, E. Jones, Parker, Coltrane, M. Davis, Sanders, Hancock. Awarded grants from CAPS, '73; National Endowment For the Arts, '74. "Music, vocals and dance are all a part of the Norman Connors concept," he says. "Like a ritual." His comp. incl. *Spirit of a Pisces*, a work for dance; *Brazilian Sketches*, a filmscore; other comp., rec. w. his group: *The Dance of Magic; Black Lightnin'; Drums Around the World*. LPs: *Dance of Magic; Dark of Light; Love From the Sun; Slewfoot; Saturday Night Special* (Buddah); w. Sanders (Impulse); Garnett (Muse); Shepp; Rivers (Imp.).

CONOVER, WILLIS CLARK, JR., *broadcaster, concert producer, narrator, writer, editor*; b. Buffalo, N.Y., 12/18/20. From 1939 has broadcast jazz and classical popular music in Washington and Manhattan, most notably in his *Music USA* programs for the Voice of America, worldwide from December '54. Musicians in Eastern Europe and the USSR call him the source of their own jazz activities. Has traveled in more than 40 countries.

In the '40s Conover helped desegregate officially-segregated Washington: requiring that blacks be admitted, he assembled groups of musicians and presented them in local night-clubs. Began Saturday-midnight concerts at the Howard Theater. In '51 helped drummer Joe Timer organize a big band, which over several years performed in local clubs and on TV, then recorded an album for Brunswick. In Manhattan in the early '60s Conover and Lalo Schfrin rehearsed an all-star band, a precursor of the Thad Jones-Mel Lewis Orchestra. In '70 he and Bill Berry presented a new band at the Roosevelt Grill. When Berry left with the Merv Griffin Show for the West Coast, where he organized his L.A. Band, Al Cohn directed the New York Band; later Bill Watrous assumed its leadership.

Conover emceed the Newport Jazz Festivals for more than a decade beginning in '51. Produced and narrated the New Orleans International Jazz Festival of 1969. He has presented concerts at New York's Town Hall, Carnegie Hall, Avery Fisher Hall, and Whitney Museum, and was responsible for 30 concerts at the John F. Kennedy Center for the Performing Arts. In '69 he produced and narrated the White House concert celebrating Duke Ellington's 70th birthday. Established and chaired the jazz panel for the National Endowment for the Arts, raising the annual allotment for jazz to a quarter of a million dollars. Serves on the State Department Cultural Presentations subcommittee for jazz and on the board of trustees for the Berklee College of Music. At the U. of Maryland in the '70s conducted accredited summer courses in jazz appreciation for elementary and high school music-teachers.

Publ: *Lovecraft at Last* (Carrollton Clark, 1975), a memoir of his teenage association with the writer H. P. Lovecraft; editor of *Science-Fantasy Correspondent*, a literary journal.

COOK, HERMAN (JUNIOR),* *tenor sax*; b. Pensacola, Fla., 7/22/34. After leaving Horace Silver in '64, pl. w. Blue Mitchell in quintet through '69. In '70s was teacher at Berklee Coll. in Boston. Pl. w. Freddie Hubbard, '73-5. Pl. w. Elvin Jones; then free-lancing in NYC incl. gigs at Boomer's; also w. Keno Duke Contemporaries; George Coleman Octet; co-led quintet w. Louis Hayes, '75-6. LPs: w. Hubbard, *Keep Your Soul Together* (CTI); w. Mitchell, *The Thing to Do; Down With It; Bring It Home to Me* (BN); w. Barry Harris, *Luminescence*; w. Don Patterson, *Opus De Don* (Prest.).

COOPER, BOB,* *tenor saxophone*; also *all reeds, woodwinds*; b. Pittsburgh, Pa., 12/6/25. During '70s working in LA with big bands of Bill Holman, T. Vig, Ed Shaughnessy, T. Gibbs; also composed contemporary 12-tone woodwind quintet. Fests: Kansas City w. Ray Brown, Herb Ellis; Concord w. B. Kessel. Comps: *Sax Therapy*, for Shaughnessy band.

LP: w. Vig (Creative World).

COOPER, GEORGE (BUSTER),* *trombone*; b. St. Petersburg, Fla., 4/4/29. During '50s worked w. L. Hampton; 2 years w. B. Goodman; co-leader of Cooper Brothers quintet backing Josephine Baker at Olympia Theatre, Paris for one year. Traveled w. D. Ellington orch., '62-9, then moved back to St. Petersburg, formed quartet w. brother, bassist Steve Cooper. Began jazz class at New Coll., Sarasota, Fla. for one year. Moved to LA July '73, freelancing there with various bands and combos, incl. Ellington alumni groups. Toured S. Africa w. Monk Montgomery latter part of '74. Fests: Newport, Monterey, Colo. JP, Oslo etc.

LPs: *Triple Play*, w. J. Hodges; *The Popular Duke Ellington* (RCA); *Outskirts of Town* w. Prestige Blues Swingers; *Smooth Sailing* w. Arnett Cobb (Prestige); *Claude Bolling & Co.* w. Cat Anderson (Philips); *Swing's Our Thing* w. Hodges & Hines (Verve).

COOPER, JEROME, *drums, composer*; also *piano, percussion*; b. Chicago, Ill, 12/14/46. Studied w. Oliver Coleman, '58-63; Capt. Walter Dyett at Du Sable HS, '63-5; Loop Jr. Coll., '67-8. Worked w. Oscar Brown Jr. in Chi., '68; Rahsaan Roland Kirk, '70-1, incl. Euro. tour; Dizzy Reece in Paris & Italy; Noah Howard; Clifford Jordan, Paris; Lou Bennett, W. Africa, '70; Steve Lacy, France, Germany, NYC, '70-1; Robin Kenyatta, Italy, France, Virginia, '71-2; Art Ensemble of Chicago, Paris, '71; Alan Silva, Paris, NYC, '71-2; George Adams; Sam Rivers; Karl Berger, NYC, '73; Andrew Hill; Anthony Braxton, '74; Maurice McIntyre w. whom he had pl. in Chi. & Nashville, Tenn. in '68-9, again in NYC, '75. From '71 w. Revolutionary Ensemble w. Sirone, L. Jenkins, app. w. it several times at Five Spot, fall '75. He says, "In order to play multidirectional group improvised music there are certain basic concepts and ideas in which we had to develop: that there is no leader; that each individual is a leader in his or her own right; that all musical instruments are solo instruments in their own right. This creative music has gotten to the point, or should I say has always been religious music (Black Classical Music)."

Infl: Roscoe Mitchell, Art Blakey, Max Roach, Walter Dyett, Anthony Williams. TV: France w. R.R. Kirk; *Today* w. Chad Mitchell. Fest: Berlin, '71; Ann Arbor, '73. Comp: *Positive-Negative; Reaction; Invasion; Chinese Rock*. LPs: w. Revolutionary Ensemble (India Navigation, ESP, Re, A&M); w. S. Lacy (Futura); A. Silva (Byg); C. Thornton (Bates); A. Braxton (Arista).

COPELAND, RAY M.,* *trumpet, fluegelhorn, composer*; b. Norfolk, Va., 7/17/26. Concerts at Univ. of California w. Randy Weston sextet in fall '66; lectured and performed w. Marian McPartland in Suffolk County public school concerts '68-69. Toured Africa w. Weston for US State Dept. Jan.-April '67, Europe w. T. Monk Nov. '68, Morocco w. Weston May '70, Europe, incl. Rumania, Yugoslavia w. *Musical Life of Charlie Parker* Oct.-Nov. '74. NJF w. Weston '73. Broadway show credits: *No, No, Nanette* '70, *Two Gentlemen of Verona* '72 incl. cast albums. Pl. History of Jazz concerts w. Orch. Da Camera in Nassau & Suffolk County schools '71-73; for International Art of Jazz in same school system '72-74. Active as adjudicator and clinician Villanova U. '72, in Pa. and Del. high schools '73-74; as teacher Pratt Inst. '68, Wilmington (Del.) School of Music & N.J. high school system '73, Jazzmobile Workshop, Fordham U. '74. His *Classical Jazz Suite in Six Movements* premiered at Lincoln Center Mar. '70. *The Ray Copeland Method and Approach to the Creative Art of Jazz Improvisation* pub. by Kaercea Music Enterprises, Inc. (110-21 195th St., St. Albans, N.Y., 11412), has been demonstrated by its author at the New York Conf. for Brass Scholarships and other mus. educ. conclaves '74. Stud. soundtrack, clicktrack writing and scoring for films. LPs: w. Weston, *African Cookbook* (Atlantic); *Tanjah* (Polydor); *Gloria Coleman Sings & Swings Organ* (Mainstream).

CORCORAN, GENE PATRICK (CORKY),* *tenor sax*; also *clarinet, English horn*; b. Tacoma, Wash., 7/28/24. Rejoined H. James '74 after an illness had kept him away from the band for which he first went to work in 1949. He no longer plays in the sax section but is feat. as a soloist. When James is not working, Corcoran fronts his own small combos in Las Vegas. App. at NJF-NY w. James, '74; concert with own group at N.Y. Jazz Museum, '74.

LPs: *Something*, w. own small group (RCS); *Everywhere*, w. own big band (C.C.); *In A Relaxed Mood*, w. James (Dot).

COREA, ARMANDO ANTHONY (CHICK),* *piano, composer*; also *organ, synthesizer*; b. Chelsea, Mass., 6/12/41. After working as a sideman in the first half of the '60s w. Mongo Santamaria, Willie Bobo, Blue Mitchell and Herbie Mann, he started to lead his own gps. for rec. and in-person performances. In '68 he became associated w. Miles Davis, adding textural layers on a variety of electric keyboards as well as on acoustic piano, for such albums as *In A Silent Way; Bitches' Brew, Live at the Fillmore East* and *Live/Evil.*

In '70 formed Circle with Anthony Braxton, Dave Holland and Barry Altschul but by late '71 was w. the Stan Getz quartet. With Stanley Clarke and Airto from the Getz group he formed Return to Forever along w. Airto's wife, Flora Purim and Joe Farrell in '72, touring Japan in that year. In '73 Bill Connors, Lenny White and percussionist Mingo Lewis joined the group with Clarke as the only holdover. It became more electrified, rock-oriented at a high decibel level and increasingly popular. Bob Stein wrote: "Necessarily the writing is less delicate than that on the earlier Return to Forever albums, but it is still bright despite the cumbersome additions of much electronic equipment."

On the other hand as a solo pianist and composer Corea has been described by Joachim Berendt as "the romanticist of the contemporary jazz piano, not only as a pianist, but also as a composer. Critics have compared his affable piano pieces with the nineteenth century piano music of Schumann, Mendelssohn, Schubert, or Rubenstein—but failed to notice the imminent tension with which Corea 'fills' his romanticism. This 'filling' of ro-

manticism with tension is, in many ways, a real challenge to the music in the seventies."

For many years Corea has been involved in the study of Scientology. He feels it has helped increase his awareness in all aspects of life, including music.

TV: *Rock Concert*, PBS. Fest: many international fests., incl. Montreux, and tours; NJF-NY '73-4. Publ: *Forever Songbook, Vol. 1* (Litha Music, 146 Manetto Hill Rd., Huntington, N.Y. 11743).

Awards: Jazzman of the Year; Pianist of the Year, *Swing Journal*, '72; *Piano Improvisations*, Album of the Year, *Swing Journal*, '72. DB Readers poll, composer, '73-4; piano, '73; electric piano, '75; DB Critics poll, composer, TDWR, '73. Return to Forever won Album of the Year from *Swing Journal*, '72; *Jazz Forum*; NY *Times*, '73.

Comp: *Spain; La Fiesta; Sometime Ago; 500 Miles High; Song For Thad; Song For Lee Lee; A New Place; Departure From Planet Earth; Windows; Gemini; I Don't Know; Samba Yanta; Bossa; Steps-What Was; Matrix; Now He Sings, Now He Sobs; Now He Beats the Drum, Now He Stops; The Law of Falling and Catching Up; Straight Up and Down; Tones For Joan's Bones; Litha; Guijira; Crystal Silence; Children's Song; What Games Shall We Play Today; Señor Mouse; Desert Air; Trio For Flute, Bassoon and Piano.*

LPs: *Hymn of the Seventh Galaxy; Light As a Feather; Where Have I Known You* (Poly.); *Return to Forever*; w. Circle, *Paris Concert* (ECM); *Circle 1&2* (CBS-Sony); *Is; Now He Sings, Now He Sobs* (SS); *Circling In* (BN); *Inner Space* (Atl.); *Piano Improvisations Vols. 1&2* (ECM); *Sundance* (Gr. Merch.); w. Gary Burton, *Crystal Silence* (ECM); *Jazz For a Sunday Afternoon* (SS); w. Getz, *Captain Marvel*; w. Davis (Col.); Joe Farrell (CTI).

CORYELL, LARRY, *guitar, composer, singer, leader*; b. Galveston, Tex., 4/2/43. Family moved to state of Washington when he was seven. Began playing in rock and roll gp. at 15. Did some private studying but mostly self-taught. Worked in Seattle. Moved to NYC '65 and joined Chico Hamilton. Played w. Free Spirits, an early jazz-rock fusion, and then toured w. Gary Burton, '67-8. Pl. briefly w. Herbie Mann, '69, before forming own gp. called Foreplay w. Steve Marcus and Mike Mandel. He also rec. an album, *Spaces*, w. John McLaughlin, Chick Corea, Miroslav Vitous and Billy Cobham. Formed The Eleventh House in '73, traveling extensively incl. four European concert tours. and one in Japan, Feb. '74. In Sept. '75 pl. acoustic solo concert w. Steve Khan at Carnegie Hall. Steve Lake, writing in *Melody Maker*, said: "To describe Coryell the guitarist as merely agile or inventive would be to do him a serious disservice. He is amazing. Truly everyman's guitarist, able to suggest shades of Montgomery, Hendrix, Reinhardt and Shankar in less time than it takes to say it, and always sounding like himself anyway . . ."

Fest: NJF-NY '73-4; in '73 fest. also pl. in blues set at Radio City jam session. Comp: *The Restful Mind; Ann*

Arbor; After Later; Lady Coryell; Foreplay; Scotland I; Birdfingers; Low-Lee-Tah; Theme For a Dream.

LPs: *Level One* (Arista); *The Restful Mind; Introducing the Eleventh House; Real Great Escape; Offering; Spaces; Lady Coryell; At the Village Gate; Coryell* (Vang.); *Barefoot Boy* (Fly. Dutch.); *Fairyland* (Mega); w. H. Mann, *Memphis Underground* (Atl.); w. G. Burton, *Duster; In Concert* (RCA); w. C. Hamilton, *The Dealer* (Imp.).

COSBY, WILLIAM H. JR. (BILL), *percussion;* b. Philadelphia, Pa., 7/12/37. The TV personality, though not a prof. musician, has led jazz and r & b groups in occasional club and fest. apps, usually billing himself as Bunions Bradford Funeral and Marching Band. Comps: *Camille; Train to Memphis.* LP: *Bill Cosby Really Sings* (Partee).

COVA, ALYRIO LIMA, *percussion;* b. Salvador-Bahia, Brazil, 12/18/49. Started pl. accordion at age six for three years, then percussion in religious ceremonies. Moved to Rio de Janeiro, '61 and began pl. regular drums. Mus. educ: Pro-Art School of Music, Rio, '69-70; Inst. River, Rio, '71-2; Brazilian Sinfonic Dept. of Teaching, '72-3; Berklee Coll., Boston, '74; New England Conserv. of Mus., '74-5. While in Rio pl. Brazilian music initially, then switched to jazz-rock and avant garde. Experiments with different sounds. During '68-71 pl. with American group, Soma. To U.S., '73 and pl. w. Webster Lewis ensemble. In Dec. '74 he joined Weather Report, touring the U.S. and Europe.

Cova is a graduate from IBM school in computer systems and analysis and also grad. Brazilian Inst. of Art in Composition of Media. He worked for two years at the Brazilian Center of Physics and Aero-space development. Infls: Harry Partch; Lalo Schifrin; John Coltrane; Wayne Shorter; J. Zawinul; Miles Davis et al. Many TV progs. in Brazil, both jazz and educ.

LPs: w. Weather Report, *Tale Spinnin'* (Col.); *Avisk Grapoc,* w. Morocco Art Ensemble (Nat'l Rec. of Morocco).

COVINGTON, WARREN, * *trombone, leader, arranger, singer;* b. Philadelphia, Pa., 8/7/21. Cont. to lead his own orchs., using different personnel, in six areas: New York, Wilmington, Del., Champaign, Ill., Denton, Tex., Austin, Tex. and Springfield, Mo., utilizing college bands such from North Texas St. and the Univ. of Texas. Toured England for 22 concerts in March '74 with a nostalgia package of his own design feat. former big band players such as Pee Wee Erwin, Chris Griffin, Bernie Privin, Johnny Mince, Skeets Herfurt and Sy Oliver. The Tommy Dorsey orientation was further emphasized by Oliver's wife Lil Clark, one of the orig. Clark Sisters, who sang lead with Covington and the Pied Pipers. Also active as studio mus. in NYC and as jingle contractor for Glenn Osser; member of NYJRC '74 season. Planning Warren Covington Supper Club East in Ocean City, Md. fall '75. Movies: sound track work for *Barbarella; Everything You Wanted to Know About Sex;* and *The Godfather.* Publ: *Sentimental Trombone, Toy Trombone, Tipsy*

Trombone (Belwyn-Mills, Lynbrook, L.I., N.Y.). LPs: *Hits of the 60's* (Re-Car); own band and w. Jo Stafford & the Pied Pipers (Readers Digest); Freddie Hubbard; George Benson (CTI); Allman Bros. (Capricorn); Perry Como (RCA Victor).

COWELL, STANLEY A., *piano, composer;* also *organ, kalimba;* b. Toledo, Ohio, 5/5/41. Took up piano at four. Art Tatum pl. at his house two yrs. later. Studied piano w. Emil Danenberg; comp. w. Richard Hoffman at Oberlin, BM '62; Mozarteum Academy, Salzburg, Austria, '60-1; U. of Wichita, '62-3; comp. w. Ingolf Dahl, USC, '63-4. MM in Piano, U. of Mich. '66. As a teenager sat in w. Yusef Lateef. While at Oberlin worked w. R.R. Kirk; at USC w. Curtis Amy, Ray Crawford in LA. Worked w. bassist Ron Brooks trio in Ann Arbor, Mich.; w. Charles Moore's Detroit Contemporary Four. Played w. R.R. Kirk; Gene McDaniels, '66; Marion Brown, '66-7; Max Roach, '67-70; Miles Davis; Herbie Mann, '68; Bobby Hutcherson-Harold Land, '68-71; Stan Getz, '69; Music Inc. w. Charles Tolliver, '69-73. Gloria Lynne, '70; subbing w. Thad Jones-Mel Lewis from '70; Donald Byrd, '73; Clifford Jordan from '74; Sonny Rollins, '74-5; Heath Bros. quartet from '75.

At age 14 feat. soloist w. Toledo Youth Orch.; feat. soloist w. American Youth Symph., Santa Monica, Cal., '64; composer-performer in *New Detroit,* for double sextet and flute, premiered at U. of Mich. Creative Arts Fest., '67. As accompanist for Max Roach and Abbey Lincoln, he was also panelist at Int. Fest. of Mus., Shiraz, Iran, '69. Has toured in most European countries; Africa; Brazil and Japan. Founder and organizer of the Piano Choir from '71; incorporator and founding member of Collective Black Artists, Inc. Conducted CBA Ensemble, '73-4. From '72 president of Strata-East Records, musician-owned label. A musical dir. of NYJRC, '74. Consultant to Oberlin Coll. Afro-American Mus. Studies curriculum, '71-2.

"Listening to his stride work on Marion Brown's *Spooks,* his free, rockish contributions to the *DeJohnette Concept,* or his thick-textured, straight-ahead work within Gary Bartz' *Another Earth,* one realizes the wide scope of Cowell's musicianship," wrote Michael Cuscuna in '69. His contributions in the '70s have served to illustrate his continuing maturity and versatility.

Infl: Tatum, Ellington, Cecil Taylor, McCoy Tyner. TV: taped half-hour w. Piano Choir in Boston for NET. Fest: NJF-NY; Antibes; Pori; Molde; Montreux; Japan.

Won DB Critics Poll, TDWR, '70. CAPS grant for comp., '73. Comp: *Conversation for Nine Instruments; Sonata for Piano; Illusion Suite; Killers; Departure #1; Abstrusions; Effi; Equipoise; Abscretions; Brilliant Circles; Blues For the Viet Cong; Wedding March; Stealin' Gold.* LPs: w. own trio, *Blues For the V.C.* (Poly.); *Stanley Cowell* (Byg); *Illusion Suite* (ECM); solo, *Musa/Ancestral Dreams* (Strata-East); w. own sextet, *Brilliant Circles* (Arista); w. C. Tolliver's Music Inc., *Live at the Domicile* (Enja); *The Ringer* (Arista); *Music Inc.; Live in Tokyo; Live at Slugs* (Strata-East); w. Hutcherson, *Now* (BN); w. DeJohnette; Bartz (Mile.); Roach, *Members Don't Get Weary* (Atl.); Marion Brown, *Three For Shepp*; (Imp.), *Why Not* (ESP); duo w. Dave Burrell, *Questions/Answers* (Trio); w. The Piano Choir, *Handscapes*; w. C. Jordan, *Glass Bead Games*; w. Mtume, *Alkebu-Lan* (Str.-East); w. Oliver Nelson at Montreux (Fly. Dutch.).

COX, IDA, * singer; b. Knoxville, Tenn., 1889. A successful blues recording artist from 1923, Cox in the '40s went into semi-retirement, returning to record an album for Riverside in '61. After a long illness she died 11/10/67 in her home town. She is well remembered for a recording date produced by John Hammond in '39 for which she was acc. by Ch. Christian, James P. Johnson, Hot Lips Page and Edmond Hall among others. She is heard on one track on *From Spirituals To Swing* (Vanguard).

CRANSHAW, MELBOURNE R. (BOB), * bass, bass guitar; also *piano, drums*; b. Evanston, Ill., 12/10/32. Played w. the MJT+3 in '50 and came w. it to NYC in '60. Worked w. Sonny Rollins; Carmen McRae; Joe Williams; Junior Mance in early '60s. Active in NY studios from mid-'60s and has performed w. Bobby Scott; Quincy Jones; Charles Aznavour; Mary Lou Williams; Billy Taylor. Toured in Europe and Japan w. Ella Fitzgerald and Oscar Peterson. Reunited for gigs w. Rollins in '70s. Own trio, pl. at Hopper's, Greenwich Village, '75. Rec. soundtracks for *Anderson Tapes, The Pawnbroker* w. Q. Jones. TV: David Frost show w. B. Taylor orch.; *Sesame Street, Electric Company*, NET, from their inception; *Saturday Night Live*, NBC. Theater: *Jesus Christ, Superstar; Sergeant Pepper*. Fest: NJF-NY w. Taylor, '72; house bassist for Prestige artists at Montreux '73; Montreux and other Euro. fests. w. Rollins, '74. One of the top acoustic bassists, Cranshaw is also one of the few to transcend many of the negative characteristics of the electric bass. LPs: *Gene Ammons and Friends at Montreux*; w. Dexter Gordon, *Blues a la Suisse* (Prest.); w. S. Rollins, *The Cutting Edge*, (Mile.); w. H. Silver (BN); J. Moody (Vang.); B. Rich (Gr. Mer.); B. Taylor (Bell); J. McDuff (Cadet); E. Garner (Lond.).

CRAWFORD, BENNIE ROSS JR. (HANK), * alto sax; also *piano, tenor, baritone sax, composer*; b. Memphis, Tenn., 12/21/34. Continued to lead his blues-oriented small band in the US, Canada, Europe and Japan. Fest. apps. at Monterey, Amsterdam, London, Munich, Berlin, Copenhagen, Stockholm, Honolulu, Tokyo. Film: *Appelez-Moi Lise*, Montreal. TV: *Black Omnibus*, LA; *Black Journal*, NYC. Comps: *Jana; Groovy Junction; Dig These Blues; Stoney Lonesome*. LPs: *Help Me Make It Through the Night; We Got A Good Thing Going; Wildflower; Don't You Worry Bout A Thing* (Kudu); *Mr. Blues Plays Lady Soul; After Hours; the Art of; the Best of* (Atlantic).

CREACH, JOHN (PAPA JOHN), violin, singer; b. Beaver Falls, Pa., 5/28/17. One of ten children, he started on violin in 1928. To Chicago in '34, stud. w. symph. musicians. Spent seven yrs. touring midwest and Canada with a trio called The Chocolate Music Bars. In early

'40s began playing pop music in cocktail lounges. Also traveled around Tennessee and Mississippi w. Roy Milton and other r & b gps.

In '43 he began pl. electric violin. Two years later, Creach moved to Cal. and started a new trio, working Palm Springs and Newport Beach. For seven years he pl. with a gp. called The Shipmates on the S.S. *Catalina*, traveling between LA and Catalina Island. From '68-70 he was a resident at the Parisian Room in LA.

Early in '70, through a friendship with Joey Covington, who had become the drummer w. Jefferson Airplane, he rec. with that group in SF and in Oct. '70 became a regular member. Soon afterward, he also began to rec. and tour w. Hot Tuna, a spinoff gp. Under the auspices of the Airplane, Creach formed his own combo, Zulu, later known as Midnight Sun. He continued to rec. and perf. w. the Airplane.

Despite his strong rock associations in recent years, Creach is an accomplished jazz violinist; in addition, he is given to sentimental interpretations of such songs as *Danny Boy*. His albums display him in an exceptionally broad cross section of styles.

LPs: *I'm the Fiddle Man* (Buddah); *Filthy!; Playing My Fiddle For You; Papa John Creach*; others w. Jefferson Airplane; Hot Tuna (all on Grunt).

CRISS, WILLIAM (SONNY), * alto, soprano saxophones; b. Memphis, Tenn., 10/23/27. Leader and sideman in LA during late '40s and '50s; Europe, '62-5. Continuing to freelance in LA, he devoted much of his time from '70-4 to working with children, welfare recipients, alcoholics and drug addicts, offering a series of concerts for young people during the Hollywood Bowl summer program, '71-2. He received an award for his contribution to and influence on the youth of So. LA. During '73 he was in Europe, pl. concerts, radio, TV. On returning to U.S., continued pl., teaching and lecturing, but returned to continent in '74, headquartering in Paris and touring Italy. In '75 he recorded for Xanadu and Muse labels, his first albums in several years; then signed w. Impulse. Fests: Newport, '68.

LPs: *Up, Up & Away; This Is Criss; Rocking In Rhythm; Sonny's Dream; The Beat Goes On; Portrait of Sonny Criss; I'll Catch The Sun* (Prest.); *Crisscraft* (Muse); *Saturday Morning* (Xanadu).

CROMBIE, ANTHONY JOHN (TONY), * drums, composer; b. London, England, 8/27/25. Led many bands from '54 in Britain, Israel; numerous Euro. tours w. jazz and pop artists, incl. Tony Bennett, Jack Jones. Acc. C. Hawkins, B. Webster, J. Witherspoon, J.J. Johnson et al for their apps. at Ronnie Scott's Club. Own group on BBC Jazz Club. Crombie comps. incl. *So Near So Far*, rec. by Miles Davis; *Debs Delight*, rec. by P. Gonsalves; *Child's Fancy*, rec. by R. Nance; *That Tune; Restless Girl*, rec. by S. Grappelli. Extensive TV writing, incl. background mus. for series, *Man from Interpol*, which was rec. on Top Rank label.

CROSBY, GEORGE ROBERT (BOB), * singer, leader; b. Spokane, Wash., 8/23/13. Younger brother of Bing

Crosby. Led dixieland oriented swing band '35-42. Since then, has reappeared frequently leading groups of various sizes from small Bob Cats combo to full ensemble in the style of the orig. orch., incl. many apps. at Disneyland, '60s and '70s. Concerts throughout U.S. in '72, '73, '74 as part of Big Band Cavalcade. NJF-NY '75 w. Bobcats. Comps: *Until; Silver and Gold; March of the Bob Cats; The Wonderful World of You.* LPs: *Live at the Rainbow Grill; Mardi Gras Parade* (Monmouth Evergreen); *Big Band Cavalcade* (RCA); also *Swinging Years* series for Readers Digest LP project.

CROUCH, STANLEY, *drums, poet, critic, composer, educator;* b. Los Angeles, Calif., 12/14/45. Cousin, Sam Crouch, pl. keyboards; another cousin, Andre Crouch, important in black gospel music. Eight weeks of piano lessons as child; half a semester of theory in high school; essentially self-taught. Began pl. in '66. Worked w. LA underground pianist Raymond King. Pl. at Watts Summer Fest., '67, w. Owen Marshall, King and Black Arthur. Started co-op gp., The Quartet, '67, which later incl. Black Arthur, Bobby Bradford. Gp. name changed to Stanley Crouch and Black Music Infinity: flutist James Newton, bassist Mark Dresser and tenor saxist David Murray came into band. Recorded, adding Bradford, David Baker, Charles Tyler, '73. Premiered his *Ellington Suite* at Pomona Coll., Nov. '74. To NYC '75, pl. w. Dresser and Murray in latter's trio. Infl: Mingus, Ellington, Monk, O. Coleman, Sunny Murray, Milford Graves, Roach, Blakey, Ed Blackwell. Has "developed a style based on bent and sustained tones and exceptional textural variety in hopes of moving drums as far as Ayler took the saxophone."

Crouch's book of poetry, *Ain't No Ambulances For No Nigguhs Tonight* was publ. in '70. Worked as a playwright and actor under Jayne Cortez, '65-7. Taught at Claremont Coll., '69-75 as instructor in drama, literature, jazz history. Articles for *Players Magazine; Village Voice.* Comp: *Future Sallie's Time; Chicago For Bobby Seale; The Confessions of Father None; Flying Through Wire; Attica in Black September; Noteworthy Lady.* LPs: *Now Is Another Time; Past Spirits,* which he plans to release as bicentennial underground note.

CRUSADERS. Formerly Jazz Crusaders. see Hooper, Stix.

CUBER, RONALD EDWARD (RONNIE), *baritone sax;* also *soprano sax, flute, bass clarinet;* b. Brooklyn, N.Y., 12/25/41. Father pl. accordion; mother piano. Studied clarinet at age nine; tenor sax at Alexander Hamilton H.S. Auditioned on tenor for Marshall Brown's Newport Youth Band. There were too many tenors but he was given the baritone chair, '59. Played w. Maynard Ferguson, '63-5; George Benson, '66-7; Lionel Hampton, '68; Woody Herman, '69, incl. Euro. tour; White Elephant, '70-1; King Curtis and Aretha Franklin, '71-2. Working w. Eddie Palmieri from '72; Bobby Paunetto from '75. Much studio work in '70s for which he studied flute w. Danny Bank, '72; took up bass clarinet. A hard-swinging soloist with a big, cutting sound. Infl: Hank

Mobley, Coltrane, Harold Land, Pepper Adams, Cecil Payne. Fest: NJF w. Newport Youth Band; Ferguson; Herman. Has written arrs. for Palmieri. Won DB Critics' Poll, TDWR, '66.

LPs: *The George Benson Cookbook; It's Uptown* w. Benson; *Spirituals to Swing,* 1967, tracks w. Benson (Col.); *Willow Weep For Me,* reissue of material from first two Benson LPs (French CBS); w. Ferguson (Main); *Paunetto's Point* w. Paunetto (Pathfinder).

CULLAZ, ALBERT (ALBY), *bass;* b. Paris, France, 5/25/41. Brother is guitarist Pierre Cullaz; father music critic-producer, Maurice Cullaz. Took up bass at 17. Pl. in France and throughout continent w. Jean-Luc Ponty, Johnny Griffin, D. Gordon, Eddy Louiss, S. Grappelli, Philly Joe Jones, Walter Davis Jr., Rene Urtreger, René Thomas, D. Gillespie, Art Taylor, H. Mobley, S. Hampton, Kenny Clarke et al. Won Django Reinhardt Jazz Academy prize, '72.

LPs: w. Michel Graillier Trio (Saravatt); w. Mobley (BN); Jef Gilson (SFP); Jean Bonal Free Sound (PES).

CULLAZ, PIERRE, *guitar;* also *cello;* b. Paris, France, 7/21/35. Brother of Alby Cullaz (see above). Took up guitar in '49. Worked w. Michel Hausser, Art Simmons in late '50s; Eddy Louiss, '64-5; Guitars Unlimited, '65-7; Claude Bolling and other big bands. Mus. for films w. M. Legrand. A versatile soloist equally at home in contemporary classical and jazz settings.

LPs: w. Andre Persiany, *Swinging Here and There; Andre Persiany Plays Count Basie* (Pathe-Marconi); w. S. Vaughan-Q. Jones (Mercury); Guitars Unlimited (Barclay); w. Sir Charles Thompson; Buck Clayton (Vogue); Guy Lafitte (Musidisc).

CURNOW, ROBERT, *composer, arranger, trombone, bass, piano;* b. Easton, Pa., 11/1/41. Extensive studies at Mich. State U., '64-7; arr. and comp. w. Russ Garcia and Johnny Richards, '61-3; trombone w. Buddy Baker. Toured w. S. Kenton for nine months in '63. Later gigged w. L. Hampton, Warren Covington, B. Goodman, Sammy Davis et al. Spent much time cond. coll. bands, incl. jazz ensemble at Notre Dame, '64-70.

Curnow is best known as a writer with Kenton, for whom he arranged such LPs as the double set of 38 national anthems, '72; *Kenton Plays Chicago,* '74, and *7.5 On The Richter Scale* (Creative World). He was appointed producer for many Kenton albums, and was general manager and director of a & r for Kenton's Creative World Records office. Infls: J.J. Johnson, F. Rosolino, Bill Harris, Bill Holman. Curnow is a distinguished educator with many scholastic honors to his credit.

CURSON, THEODORE (TED),* *trumpet, piccolo trumpet, fluegelhorn;* b. Philadelphia, Pa., 6/3/35. Spent much time in Europe during late '60s and early '70s pl. concerts, clubs and esp. fests. all over the continent. Member of the Schauspielhaus theatre orch., Zurich, '73 where he pl. in perf. of *Marat/Sade* and *Threepenny Opera.* Clubs in Paris and NYC w. Chris Woods, Andrew Hill, Lee Konitz, Kenny Barron, Nick Brignola. Pl. and lectured at campuses of U. of Cal.; Vallekilde Mus.

Ornette Coleman (*David D. Spitzer*)

Larry Coryell (*Veryl Oakland*)

Ted Curson

Andrew Cyrille (*Veryl Oakland*)

Richard Davis (*David D. Spitzer*)

Miles Davis (*Veryl Oakland*)

George Duke (*Veryl Oakland*)

Harry "Sweets" Edison and Plas Johnson (*Veryl Oakland*)

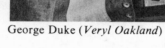

Eddie "Lockjaw" Davis (*Veryl Oakland*)

Paul Desmond (*CTI Records*)

Raul De Souza (*Milestone Records*)

Jerry Dodgion (*David D. Spitzer*)

Bill Evans (*Veryl Oakland*)

Teddy Edwards (*Veryl Oakland*)

Don Ellis (*Veryl Oakland*)

Joe Farrell (*CTI Records*)

Herb Ellis (*Veryl Oakland*)

Duke Ellington (*Veryl Oakland*)

Mercer Ellington (*Rolf Zieger*)

110

Maynard Ferguson (*David D. Spitzer*)

Leonard Feather, Dizzy Gillespie and Mundell Lowe
(*Ray Avery's Rare Records*)

Ella Fitzgerald and Norman Granz (*Phil Stern*)

Sonny Fortune (*Veryl Oakland*)

Carl Fontana and Jake Hanna (*Veryl Oakland*)

Curtis Fuller (*David D. Spitzer*)

Stan Getz (*David D. Spitzer*)

Carlos Garnett (*Veryl Oakland*)

Slim Gaillard and Slam Stewart (*Veryl Oakland*)

Larry Gales (*Veryl Oakland*)

Sch., Denmark; and U. of Vermont. Sponsored first U.S. app. of Arne Domnerus group from Sweden, NYC, winter '74. Won New Star Award DB Critics Poll '66; first foreign musician to be awarded grant from Finnish govt. at Pori Fest. '73. Wrote music (*Tears for Dolphy*) for film *Teorama*; app. in film, *Notes for a Film on Jazz* w. G. Barbieri, Aldo Romano; TV apps: *Jazz Set* (U.S.); *Live From Club Severine* (France); Pori Int. Jazz Fest. Band (Finland). Comps: *Typical Ted; The Leopard; Sugar 'N Spice; Reava's Waltz; Airi's Tune; Cracklin' Bread*. Publ: *The New Thing: Nine Originals By Ted Curson*, book of piano arrs. (Nosruc Pub., 130 Arlington Ave., Jersey City, N.J. 07305). LPs: *Tears for Dolphy* (Fontana); *Ode to Booker Ervin* (EMI); *Cattin' Curson; Pop Wine* (Futura); *Ted Curson Meets Blue Sun* (CBS Denmark); *Quicksand* (Atl.); *Urge*, w. Ervin (Fontana).

CURTIS, KING (Curtis Ousley), *saxophones, composer*; b. Fort Worth, Tex., 1935. Played w. Lionel Hampton; rec. w. Nat Adderley, Wynton Kelly, but was mainly known as a major r & b figure, acc. many singers. He was mus. dir. of a TV series *Soul*, for which he wrote the theme *Soulful 13*. Other comps: *Soul Serenade; Instant Groove; Memphis Soul Stew*. Curtis died 8/14/71 of stab wounds suffered in a fight w. a man in front of a building owned by Curtis in NYC.

LPs: *Jazz Groove* (Prestige); *King Curtis Live at Fillmore West* (Atl.); *King Curtis & Jack Dupree Blues at Montreux* (Atl.).

CUTSHALL, ROBERT DEWEES (CUTTY), * *trombone*; b. Huntington County, Pa., 12/29/11. Best known for early work with Benny Goodman, later regular job for many years w. Eddie Condon, gigs w. Peanuts Hucko et al, Cutshall was an original member of the group organized in Denver as The Nine Greats of Jazz, which soon evolved into the World's Greatest Jazzband; but before the latter group was to make its first album, Cutshall, while working with Condon in Toronto, died 8/16/68 of a heart attack. His exceptional, Teagarden-inspired work can be heard on a number of LPs w. Condon, as well as on dates w. Wild Bill Davison, Yank Lawson, Geo. Wettling, Boyce Brown.

CYRILLE, ANDREW CHARLES, *drums*; b. Brooklyn, N.Y., 11/10/39. Stud. w. Lennie McBrowne and others, '52-7; matriculated at Juilliard, '58; Stud. briefly w. Philly Joe Jones, '58; Tony Columbia, '67. Early exp. w. Nellie Lutcher, Roland Hanna, Illinois Jacquet, Olatunji, '59-61; Walt Dickerson, Bill Barron, Rahsaan Roland Kirk, '62-3. From '64-6 w. J. Giuffre, Cedar Walton et al.

Cyrille's most important assoc. has been w. Cecil Taylor, in whose unit he worked from '64, in addition to taking up many other duties intermittently, among them the following: '67, w. S. Turrentine; G. Bartz; J. Mance; Benny Powell; G. Moncur; '68-9, Ghanaian musician Joe Mensah; Voices Inc.; '70, own quintet; '71 formed perc. trio w. Milford Graves and Rashied Ali, Dialogue of the Drums; staff percussionist Wyandanch Jr. H.S., and Jazz Interactions teaching prog., artist-in-residence, Antioch

Coll.; '71-3, comp., arr. and perf. w. 19 percussionists own comps. at Harlem Cultural Center in NYC; toured, perf. in Europe, Japan with C. Taylor; '74, perf. and was videotaped, concert of orig. works w. M. Graves, hosted radio prog. feat. music from around the world in NYC; '75, cont. to work w. Taylor; formed another band under own direction, Andrew Cyrille & MAONO.

Comps: *What About; Rhythmical Space; Rims and Things; The Soul Is The Music; Aural Coordination*. LPs: w. C. Hawkins, *The Hawk Relaxes*; w. Walt Dickerson, *Relativity* (Prest.); w. Bill Barron, *Hot Line* (Savoy); *Jazz Composers Orchestra* (JCOA); w. Marion Brown, *Afternoon of a Georgia Faun* (ECM); w. Cecil Taylor, *Conquistador* (Blue Note); w. Jimmy Lyons, *Lazy Afternoons*; w. Grachan Moncur, *New Africa*; own group, *What About* (all on BYG/Actuel); *Dialogue of the Drums* (IPS); own group, *Bulu Akisakila Kutala* (Trio Records).

DAHLANDER, NILS-BERTIL (BERT), * *drums*; b. Gothenburg, Sweden, 5/13/28. Divided his time between U.S. and Scandinavia from '54. From '66, living in Aspen, Colo., he played with small groups, worked w. Peanuts Hucko in Denver. To Finland, Sweden, '74, playing in Stockholm w. Alice Babs; house band in Swedish TV Jan. to May '75. Pl. Colo. JP several times in '60s, '70s.

DAILEY, ALBERT PRESTON (AL), * *piano, composer*; b. Baltimore, Md., 6/16/38. After pl. w. own trio at Bohemian Caverns in Wash., D.C., '63-4 came to NYC and worked w. D. Gordon; R. Haynes; H. Mobley; A. Farmer; S. Vaughan through '66. With Woody Herman; Art Blakey, '68-9; C. Mingus; Joe Williams; Betty Carter; Thad Jones-Mel Lewis in early '70s; Sonny Rollins, off and on, '70-3; Milt Jackson, '72-3; Stan Getz, '73-5; Blakey, '75. Received NEA Grant to write *Africa Suite* for voices and electronic instruments, '75. TV w. Getz; Herman. Fest: MJF w. Herman; NJF-NY '73-4; Euro. fests. w. Getz. Resourceful player whose compositional abilities show up in his solos.

Comp: *The Day After the Dawn; Bittersweet Waltz; Encounter; A Lady's Mistake*. LPs: *The Day After the Dawn* (Col.); w. Azar Lawrence (Prest.); Getz w. Joao Gilberto (Col.); F. Hubbard (Atl.); J. Williams w. Jones-Lewis (SS).

DALY, WARREN JAMES, *drums, composer*; b. Sydney, Australia, 8/22/46. Stud. w. several teachers in Sydney, Roy Burns in Honolulu, Bob Tilles in Chicago, Henry Adler in NYC. Started in rock during late '50s; switched to jazz in '65. Pl. w. Col Nolan trio in Sydney, '65; Bill Barratt big band, '66. After working as staff drummer on a Sydney TV station, he toured the U.S. in late '67 w. Kirby Stone Four, later working w. Si Zentner and Glenn

Miller orchestras, the latter under Buddy De Franco. Following tours with other U.S. bands, he returned to Australia in late '68, and in early '69, w. trombonist Ed Wilson (q.v.), he formed the Daly-Wilson big band. In '69-70, Daly also pl. in Don Burrows quartet in Sydney. During the next few years the Daly-Wilson orch. acquired great prestige domestically, touring Australia eight times, and was voted Band of the Year in '72 in Australia's *Music Maker* magazine poll.

In Oct. '75, after pl. engagements in the Soviet Union, the band app. in LV and at Donte's in N. Hollywood. Daly comp. and/or co-arr. w. Wilson many numbers for the band, incl. *W.D. and H.O. Blues; El Boro; My Goodness.*

LPs: *Live at the Cell Block* (EMI); *Featuring Kerrie Biddell* (Festival); *On Tour; Featuring Marcia Hines* (WB). All albums released in the U.S. on G.R.C. Elephant label. The band received a gold record award for *On Tour.*

D'ANDREA, FRANCO, *piano;* b. Merano, Italy, 3/8/41. Self-taught, first on trumpet, clarinet, sax. Piano at 17. Pl. w. Nunzio Rotondo, '63; Gato Barbieri, '64-5 and occasionally since then. Formed Modern Art Trio, '68; member of Perigeo group from '72. Numerous TV, fest. apps. in Italy, France etc. w. Charles Tolliver, Jean-Luc Ponty, Barbieri, et al. Radio, clubs and/or concerts with many U.S. musicians in Italy, incl. M. Roach, Dexter Gordon, Lucky Thompson, Slide Hampton, Hank Mobley, Frank Rosolino, Conte Candoli.

LPs: Some 35 albums, starting in '64 with L. Konitz, Johnny Griffin, Modern Art Trio, and several with Perigeo, incl. *Genealogia* (RCA). The Perigeo LP *Abbiamo Tutti Un Blues Da Piangere* won the Italian Discographical Critics' Prize, '73.

DANIELS, EDWARD KENNETH (EDDIE),* *saxophones, clarinets, flutes;* b. Brooklyn, N.Y. 10/19/41. From '66-73 w. T. Jones-M. Lewis orch., then w. Bobby Rosengarden band on Dick Cavett TV show, '72-4. Busy freelancer in TV and rec. work, NYC. Daniels, with a Master's degree in clarinet from Juilliard, has stud. classical flute since '67, and is highly proficient on alto, baritone and tenor saxes, the latter being his main instrument. An intense, fiery player reflecting the influences of Rollins and Coltrane. Won DB Critics' Poll, TDWR, '68, on clarinet. NJF-NY w. Rosengarden, '72; Radio City jam session, '73-4.

LPs: *A Flower For All Seasons* (Choice); *The Return of Don Patterson* (Muse); others w. Jones-Lewis (SS, BN).

DANISH RADIO BIG BAND. Founded in '64. Consists of five trumpets; five trombones; five saxes; and rhythm. First leader was Ib Glindemann. His main inspiration was Stan Kenton and an early highlight for the band was a concert w. Kenton as guest leader, '66. In '67 Gene Roland was staff arranger, and that fall Maynard Ferguson gave a concert with it.

From '68 many visiting musicians have performed or been associated w. the band incl: Ted Curson; Booker

Ervin; Frank Foster; Art Farmer; Babs Gonzales; Johnny Griffin; Burton Greene; Slide Hampton; Joe Henderson; Jimmy Heath; Freddie Hubbard; Chuck Israels; Clifford Jordan; Lee Konitz; Yusef Lateef; Oliver Nelson; George Russell; Charlie Shavers; Lucky Thompson; Charles Tolliver; Clark Terry; Mary Lou Williams and Phil Woods; also Danish residents such as Kenny Drew; Dexter Gordon and Ben Webster; and Europeans such as Monica Zetterlund; Karin Krog; Alice Babs; Bengt Hallberg; Mike Gibbs; and Mike Westbrook.

Among the band's members are trumpeters Allan Botchinsky, Idrees Sulieman; trombonist Richard Boone; saxophonists Jasper Thilo, Bent Jaedig; pianist Ole Kock Hansen; bassist Niels Henning Orsted Pedersen; drummer Bjarne Rostvold; vibist Finn Ziegler; and percussionist Kasper Winding.

DANISH RADIO JAZZGROUP. Started in Oct. '61 w. nine musicians. Within next five yrs. expanded to 12. Led by bassist Erik Moseholm until '66 when he became producer on Danish radio. Saxophonist Ray Pitts took it over for a couple of yrs., followed by Palle Mikkelborg. From '73 pianist Torben Kjaer has been in charge.

The Radio Jazzgroup has pl. experimental jazz and given opportunities to Danish writers as well as arranger-composers such as Dollar Brand; Mike Gibbs; Graham Collier; Jan Johanssen; Bengt Hallberg; and George Russell. 45 Danish and 25 foreign arrs. had contributed to the repertory which consists of 600 pieces of music. 20 have been recorded on 3 LPs and one EP. The group has toured in Denmark, Poland and Germany. Personnel incl: Erik Tschenter, Lars Togeby, Poul Chr. Nielsen, trumpets; Peter Westh, Flemming Andreasen, trombones; Michael Hove, Bent Jaedig, Svend Baring, saxes; Thomas Clausen, piano; Torben Munk, guitar; Bo Stief, bass; Alex Riel, drums.

DANKWORTH, JOHN PHILIP WILLIAM,* *alto saxophone, clarinet, composer;* b. Woodford, London, England, 9/20/27. Continuing his career as a composer and arranger, Dankworth was involved with the following films as composer/music dir.: *Morgan; A Suitable Case For Treatment; The Idol,* '66; *Fathom; Accident; The Last Safari,* '67; *Salt & Pepper; The Magus; I Love You, I Hate You,* '68; *The Last Grenade,* '69; *Perfect Friday; The Engagement; 10 Rillington Place,* '70. TV: comp. themes for *Tomorrow's World; The Frost Report* for BBC-1, '66; *Pippa; The Helicopter; Ooh La La* for BBC-2, '68; *Bird's Eye View,* BBC-2, '69; *The Enchanted House,* Granada TV, '70; *The Canterbury Tales; The Open University,* BBC-2, '71. Other musical works: *Tom Sawyer's Saturday* for Farnham Fest., '67; many other classical and semi-classical works, incl. a piano concerto for small chamber orch. for Westminster Fest., '72.

Along with his studio work, Dankworth continued to record occasionally with specially assembled orchs., and to tour regularly with his wife, singer Cleo Laine (q.v.). His buoyant alto sax, exceptionally fluent clarinet, ingenious arrangements and occasional original lyrics contributed significantly to the success of their joint appearances, which incl. triumphant concerts in the U.S. from '72.

LPs: *Movies 'N' Me* (RCA); *Full Circle* (Philips); Johnny Dankworth-Billy Strayhorn (Roul.); w. Cleo Laine, *Live at Carnegie Hall; I Am A Song* (RCA); *Portrait* (Philips); as arr. on *A Beautiful Thing* (RCA).

DARENSBOURG, JOSEPH (JOE),* *clarinet, soprano sax;* b. Baton Rouge, La., 7/9/06. Veteran of F. Marable riverboat bands. 10 years w. Kid Ory, '44-54. World travels as member of Louis Armstrong combo, '61-4. Frequent gigs at Disneyland, '65-9. Led own band in LA '70-3; joined Legends of Jazz for concerts and tours, '73-5. Filmed movie of his life, in London, Aug. '74. During this time, pl. w. Chris Barber and several other trad. bands in England. Fests: Newport, Monterey, Sacramento, New Orleans and many in Europe.

LPs: *Hello Dolly* w. Armstrong (Kapp); *The Real Ambassadors,* w. Armstrong (Col.); w. Legends of Jazz (Crescent Jazz).

DARIN, ROBERT (BOBBY),* *singer;* b. Bronx, N.Y. 5/14/36. Many hit records from late 1950s, his version of *Mack the Knife* sold over two million records. Switched to folk/rock idiom in '71. Darin died in Los Angeles following open heart surgery 12/20/73. From the jazz standpoint, his best LP by far was *Darin Sings Ray Charles* (Atco).

DASEK, RUDOLF, *guitar, composer;* b. Prague, Czech., 8/27/33. Graduated from State Conserv. of Mus., Prague, '66. Pl. w. all conserv. ensembles. In '64 formed own trio w. G. Mraz, pl. regularly with Carmell Jones, Leo Wright, etc. Formed System Tandem, a duo w. reedman Jiri Stivin, '72. Infl: Keith Jarrett, Jim Hall. Fest: Bilzen; Nuremberg; Ost-West Fest., Altena; Ljubljana; Jazz Jamboree Warsaw; Prague; Pori; Balver Hohle, West Germany. Comp: series of folklore-inspired fashanks: *Burial Mounds; Blow!; Tandem; One, Two, Free.* LPs: *Fairytale for Beritka* w. own trio; *B & S* w. Slide Hampton and Vaclav Zahradnik Big Band; *Concert in Ljubljana* w. System Tandem; *5 Hits to Arrow* (Supraphon).

DASH, ST. JULIAN BENNETT,* *tenor sax;* b. Charleston, S.C., 4/9/16. Member of Erskine Hawkins orch. for many years off and on from 1938; later inactive in music except for reunion recording w. Hawkins and small combo date in early '70s on Master Jazz; also tour of Europe in late '72. Dash died in NYC 2/24/74. LP: w. J. Rushing, *Who Was It Sang That Song* (Master Jazz).

DAUNER, WOLFGANG,* *keyboards, synthesizer, composer; also trumpet, percussion;* b. Stuttgart, Germany, 12/30/35. With his own trio and quintet he app. at all the important German jazz fests. '67-70; tours with German all stars in S. America, '69; Asia, '71. Fest. apps. w. Jean-Luc Ponty, '70-1, L. Coryell, '72. Danish, Finnish, Swiss, Portuguese fests. '72-3; w. own quintet at Berlin Jazztage, '74. From '70 Dauner led radio jazz group in Stuttgart and has rec. with guest soloists such as C. Corea, Ponty, M. Urbaniak. He has conducted many workshops for children about creativity and improvisa-

tion in music, and in '74 had his own TV show, *Glotzmusik,* for children. Infl: John Cage. Won German Sounds poll, '72, '73. Comps: *Dream Talk; Dämmerung; Dauneraschingen; Sketch Up And Downer; The Primal Scream; Yin.* LPs: *Free Action* (MPS); *Für . . .* (Calif); also several others on European labels.

DAVERN, JOHN KENNETH (KENNY),* *soprano sax, clarinet;* b. Huntington, L.I., N.Y., 1/7/35. Gigs w. Ruby Braff, At Nick's w. Pee Wee Erwin '60; own group At Nick's '61; Eddie Condon's all stars, one month w. Ted Lewis at Roseland '62; toured for a year w. Dukes of Dixieland and rec. for Columbia w. Clara Ward '63; pl. w. Wild Bill Davison, Bud Freeman, Shorty Baker in Toronto and at Metropole, Central Plaza, NYC '64. After leaving NYC w. Jackie Gleason entourage for Florida, pl. a month in Miami w. Phil Napoleon '65. From '65 through '68 alternated between the Ferryboat in Brielle, N.J. w. Dick Wellstood, Ed Hubble, and Gaslight Club (NYC) w. George Wettling, Charlie Queener. Cont. to work around NY metropolitan area '69-71. Five weeks in Durban, So. Africa as singer, New Orleans w. Wild Bill Davison '72. From '72-74 several apps. at Michael's Pub, NYC w. Wellstood; also Odessa, Texas Jazz Party, Dick Gibson's Colo. Jazz Party. Toured Europe w. Erwin, Hubble, etc. '74; Grande Parade du Jazz, Nice '73, '75; NYJRC concerts, Newport-NY JF '74-75. App. in film *The Hustler;* on Broadway in *Marathon '33.* Won DB Int. Critics Poll on sop. sax new star '73.

Davern, who switched his main concentration from clarinet to soprano in the late '60s, formed a corporate group w. Bob Wilber called Soprano Summit in '75.

LPs: *Soprano Summit* (World Jazz); w. Dick Wellstood (Seeds, Chiaroscuro); *The Music of Jelly Roll Morton* w. Dick Hyman (Columbia); *Jazz at the New School* (Chiaroscuro); Marva Josie-Earl Hines (Thimble).

DAVIS, CHARLES,* *baritone, soprano saxes, composer;* b. Goodman, Miss., 5/20/33. Heard with many NY gps., as well as w. his own quintet in the '60s, he later worked w. Elvin Jones and, for a time in '72, w. the Cedar Walton-Hank Mobley quintet called Artistry in Music. Free-lancing in NYC at Boomer's, etc. in mid-'70s. LPs: Strata-East; w. Walton-Mobley, *Breakthrough* (Cobble.); w. Kenny Dorham, *Memorial Album* (Xanadu); w. Roswell Rudd, *Numatik Swing Band* (JCOA); w. Archie Shepp, *Kwanza* (Imp.)

DAVIS, EDDIE (LOCKJAW),* *tenor sax;* b. New York City, 3/2/22. From 1966-73 the rough-toned, extrovert saxophonist was featured w. Count Basie. He also participated in European tours apart from the band, '68, '73, '74: '73 as part of Norman Granz troupe w. Ella Fitzgerald; '74 w. George Wein tour, *The Musical Life of Charlie Parker.* Moved to Las Vegas 1973. Pl. w. Zoot Sims at Jazz Medium in Chi., Feb. '75. Fests: NJF w. Basie, Fitzgerald; Cascais, Portugal '74; Nice.

LPs: *Love Calls* (RCA Victor); *Cookbook* (Prestige); *Ella Live at Newport, Carnegie Hall* (Columbia); others on many labels w. Basie (q.v.); *Basie Jam; Dizzy at Montreux* (Pablo).

DAVIS, JEFFREY HAYES (JEFF), *trumpet, fluegelhorn*; b. St. Albans, N.Y., 12/19/52. Grandfather, Ovie Alston, was trumpet player and singer w. Claude Hopkins. Mother, Jean Alston Davis, sang w. Alston band; still working NY area in mid-70s. Davis stud. at H.S., later earned BM at Berklee, where he pl. in Phil Wilson, Herb Pomeroy ensembles and stud. w. Wes Hensel, Gary Burton and Andy McGhee. Pl. jazz and lead trumpet w. L. Hampton, '72-4; lead trumpet w. W. Herman, '75, incl. apps. w. Caterina Valente, Tony Bennett.

DAVIS, MILES DEWEY, * *trumpet, fluegelhorn, composer, leader*; b. Alton, Ill., 5/25/26. The Herbie Hancock-Ron Carter-Tony Williams rhythm section that had been with Davis from '63, and saxophonist Wayne Shorter, who joined him late in '64, continued through to the fall of '68 when Chick Corea and Dave Holland replaced Hancock and Carter. This quintet, which had recorded *E.S.P.* in '65, made a series of albums in the following years that, like *E.S.P.*, used no standards, show tunes, etc. which up to then had always been part of the Davis repertoire. Most of the material came from within the group or were jazz originals like *Freedom Jazz Dance* by Eddie Harris, or *Gingerbread Boy* by Jimmy Heath. Both these songs were on *Miles Smiles*, recorded in '66. This was followed by *Sorcerer* and *Nefertiti*, both taped in '67. *Miles in the Sky*, done in '68, added George Benson's guitar for one number and was notable for Hancock's use of electric piano. In '68 *Filles De Kilimanjaro* again used electric piano by Hancock, on one session, and Chick Corea.

Hancock, Corea and Joe Zawinul all pl. electric keyboards on *In A Silent Way*, '69, and John McLaughlin was also present. The long pieces are dreamlike "head music" kind of a "soft rock" using some of the harmonic freedom engendered by the avant garde of the '60s.

With *Bitches' Brew*, rec. later in '69, he moved toward a harder, more electrified jazz-avant-rock expression and continued this trend with *A Tribute to Jack Johnson; Live at the Fillmore East*, '70; *Live-Evil*, '71; and *On the Corner*, '72. The attitude of Bill Cole, in his book *Miles Davis: A Musical Biography* (Wm. Morrow), echoes that of many of Davis' critics in this period. Calling *Bitches' Brew* "and its lineage" backward steps, he wrote: "The only piece on the collection of *Bitches' Brew* which hints at any strength coming from Miles is *Sanctuary*, but as stunning as it is, it is only a repeated statement. The music since then has been just other variations of this new theme. Miles plays very little, using as many aids as possible, taking advantage of the rhythm actually to cover his sometimes very sad solos." He calls *On the Corner* "an insult to the intellect of the people."

Will Smith in *down beat* mentioned the "supposedly hypnotic but ultimately static rhythm"; claimed that Davis did not play enough; and that his electronic amplifier made people think his trumpet was a guitar. In the '70s Davis made use of a wah-wah pedal attachment for his trumpet; on his tribute to Duke Ellington, the album entitled *Get Up With It*, he is heard at the keyboard.

Quincy Jones defended Davis against his detractors with: "I think you have to trust the same mojo that led you into the first style and go from there. It's fortunate that Miles is flexible enough to have given us the kind of contrast that separates *Miles Ahead* from *Jack Johnson*. I think he's blessed to have that scope, that range."

Davis' reaction to his critics was harsher. "I don't play rock, he told Frederick D. Murphy in *Encore* magazine. "Rock is a white word. And I don't like the word jazz that white folks dropped on us. We just play *Black*. We play what the day recommends. It's 1975. You don't play 1955 music or that straight crap like *My Funny Valentine* . . . That's the old nostalgic junk written for white people."

While controversy, never a stranger, swirled around him Davis, long a living legend, had already left indelible marks as an influence; an incubator for leaders.

In October '72 Davis broke both his legs when he crashed while driving his car in New York City. They continued to give him much pain in the years following the accident. At the end of '75 he was hospitalized for hip trouble but was recuperating at home in January '76.

Davis won the DB Critics poll, '66-70; Readers poll, '66-72, '75; his group won Critics and Readers polls, '66-71; he was voted Jazzman of the Year, '69-71. *Miles Smiles* won in both polls, '67; *Bitches' Brew* in '70; *Filles De Kilimanjaro* won Readers poll, '69.

Comp: *E.S.P.; Eighty-One; Agitation; Circle; Country Son; Stuff; Frelon Brun; Filles De Kilimanjaro; Petits Machins; Mademoiselle Mabry; Bitches' Brew; Yesternow; He Loved Him Madly.*

LPs: *Miles Smiles; Sorcerer; Nefertiti; Filles De Kilimanjaro; Miles in the Sky; In a Silent Way; Bitches' Brew; At the Fillmore; A Tribute to Jack Johnson; Live-Evil; On the Corner; In Concert; Jazz at the Plaza; Big Fun; Get Up With It* (Col.); *In Tokyo* (CBS-Sony); reissues, *Basic Miles* (Col.); *Dig; Collector's Items; Tallest Trees; Workin' & Steamin'* (Prest.); *Miles Davis* (UA); *The Complete Birth of the Cool* (Cap.); w. C. Adderley, *Something Else* (BN).

DAVIS, NATHAN TATE, * *educator, composer, saxophones, flute*; b. Kansas City, Kansas, 2/15/37. U.S. Army in Berlin as musician, arranger, '60-2. From '62-9 played in Europe w. Kenny Clarke, D. Byrd, E. Dolphy; stud. comp. w. André Hodeir. Comp.-arr.-soloist for Paris radio show *Jazz Aux Champs Elysées*. During late '60s, became increasingly active as student and teacher of jazz and ethnomusicology in France, Belgium, W. Germany. Joined U. of Pittsburgh as asst. prof. of music and dir. of jazz studies, '69. During hiatus from college, returned to Europe each summer. Received Ph.D. from Wesleyan U. in ethnomusicology. Traveled to Brazil, made field recordings. In '75, after five years of holding annual jazz seminars at Pittsburgh U., he wrote: "I am still a world citizen trying to balance between a career as jazz musician and scholar."

Davis joined Segue Records as artist and vice pres. of a & r, '70. Lps for several European labels; also *Makatuka* (Segue).

DAVIS, QUIN HALL, *saxophones, clarinet, flute*; b. Artesia, Cal., 3/12/44. Stud. w. Lennie Niehaus, '60-3; Long Beach State Coll., '62-6. Traveled w. Si Zentner, '65; Buddy Rich, Jan. to Apr. '67. After Army service, rejoined Rich, June '69, remaining until Mar. '70. Feat. w. S. Kenton orch. July '70 to Jan. '73. Three months later he joined H. James. Fests: Newport, Monterey, w. Rich; others, also many coll. clinics w. Kenton.

LPs: w. Kenton, *Live at Redlands University; Live at Butler University; Live at Brigham Young University* (Creative World).

DAVIS, RICHARD,* *bass, composer*; b. Chicago, Ill., 4/15/30. His great versatility was in evidence early in his career through his work w. such diverse gps. as Benny Goodman, Sarah Vaughan; symphony jobs w. Igor Stravinsky, Leonard Bernstein. In early '60s was part of Booker Little-Eric Dolphy quintet; also gigs and recs. w. Al Cohn-Zoot Sims; Andrew Hill; James Moody. With the Thad Jones-Mel Lewis orch., '66-71, incl. Russian tour, '72. A member of the NY Bass Choir from '69. Continued to be one of the busiest free-lance musicians in NYC during '70s. App. w. NY Philharmonic '73; w. L. Bernstein and Philharmonic, '75. Jobs w. Helen Merrill; Novella Nelson; Nancy Harrow; Roland Hanna; TV special w. Barbra Streisand; own gp. for college dates, '75. Fest: NJF-NY, '72-4; MJF w. John Lewis, '74-5. Film: sound track for *Holy Mountain*. TV: *Like It Is*, ABC, w. Bass Choir; Black Journal, NET. Polls: DB Critics, '66, TDWR; '67-74; DB Readers, '68-72. Comp: *Dealin'; What'd You Say; Julie's Rag Doll; Blues For Now; Sweet'n; Sorta*. Publ: *Walking On Chords* (RR&R Music Publ., P.O. Box 117, Planetarium Sta., N.Y., N.Y. 10024). Davis' hobby is horsemanship and he has showed in Dressage and Jumper Hunter Divisions. Devoted to Nichiren Shoshu Buddhism. LPs: *Philosophy of the Spiritual* (Buddah); *Epistrophy & Now's the Time; Dealin'; With Understanding* (Muse); *Muses for Richard Davis* (BASF); w. Bobby Hackett (Fly. Dutch); Phil Woods (Muse); Jimmy Raney (MPS); Jones-Lewis (BN, SS); Jaki Byard; Eric Kloss (Prestige); Bobby Jones (Cobble.).

DAVIS, WALTER JR.,* *piano, composer*; b. Richmond, Va., 9/2/32. Active around Newark, N.J. before joining Max Roach in early '50s; then w. D. Gillespie; D. Byrd; Art Blakey through '50s. From '60 has led own trio (sometimes duo). Visited and pl. in India '69. Also pl. w. Sonny Rollins, April '73-April '74; Art Blakey, '75; '73-5 app. in several NYC concerts w. own trio and trios of Barry Harris, Cedar Walton. TV: *Focus* w. Betty Carter, Wash., D.C. Fest: NJF-NY w. Rollins, '74; Blakey, '75; Antwerp; Naarden; Toulon. Also is painter and costume designer.

Comp: *Ronnie's a Dynamite Lady; Backgammon; Uranus; Illumination; Gypsy Folk Tales; Greasy; Davis Cup; A Million Or More Times*. Comp. publ: (Karmic

Music, 434 Hudson St., New York, N.Y. 10014). LPs: w. Rollins, *Horn Culture* (Milestone); w. Sonny Criss, *This Is Criss; Portrait of Sonny Criss* (Prest.); w. A. Shepp, *Attica Blues; Way Ahead* (Imp.); *There's A Trumpet in My Soul* (Arista).

DAVIS, WILLIAM STRETHEN (WILD BILL),* *organ, piano, composer*; b. Glasgow, Mo., 11/24/18. The pioneer jazz organist has led his own trio from '51. He continued w. his annual summer job at the Little Belmont in Atlantic City, N.J. In addition, he subbed on piano in the Ellington band, '69, when Duke had a hand ailment. In the '70s he also played in France, recording for the Black and Blue label in the process. Appeared in organ concerts at the NJF-NY, '73-4 Jazz cruise on S.S. Rotterdam w. Jimmy Tyler band, summer '75. Own LP: *Impulsions*; LPs w. Illinois Jacquet; Buddy Tate; Al Grey; Slam Stewart; Floyd Smith (B&B).

DAVISON, WILLIAM EDWARD (WILD BILL),* *cornet, leader*; b. Defiance, Ohio, 1/5/06. Professional in Chicago bands from 1927, Milwaukee, '33-40, NYC from '40. Toured in U.S. extensively, '60s; England and continent, '64. Lived in LA for a year in late '60s, but spent much of his time on the road, esp. on several tours to Europe and Australia. Between '65 and '75 he app. with over 100 different bands, made more than 20 albums (mostly overseas) and discussed with audiences the blend of dixieland, Chicago and New Orleans jazz styles from historical and technical standpoints. Played annually at jazz parties in Odessa, Tex.; Aspen, Colo., '65-6; Big Horn JF, '72; Detroit JF, '73-4; Nice, France, fest. summer of '74. Toured U.S. w. E. Condon, A. Hodes, B. Bigard, '71.

Davison, who at times has played trumpet, bass trumpet, valve trombone, mellophone, banjo, guitar and mandolin, was still playing in his 70th year with the same vigor he demonstrated during his first years of NY prominence in the '40s. In '73-5 he was based in Washington, D.C., but worked only occasionally.

American LPs on Big Horn, Chiaroscuro, Fat Cat, Jazzology. Canadian LP on Sackville. European LPs on Swiss Philips with Wolverines Jazz Band; and Danish Horekiks w. Fessors Big City Band; also many re-releases in England and on continent.

DAWSON, ALAN,* *drums*; also *vibes*; b. Marietta, Pa., 7/14/29. A faculty member of the Berklee Coll. of Music in Boston from '57, he has also been active as drummer for visiting soloists to Boston clubs; as a clinician for the Fibes Drum Co.; and from '68-74, a member of the Dave Brubeck quartet, for tours, concerts and fests. Fests: NJF; MJF; Colo. JP. TV: special, *The Light in the Wilderness* w. Brubeck. Publ: *A Manual For The Modern Drummer; Blues and Odd Time Signatures*.

A strong, sensitive drummer with rock-steady time, Dawson is also a resourceful soloist. LPs w. Brubeck, *We're All Together Again For the First Time; The Last Set At Newport* (Atl.); *Blues Roots; Compadres; Live at the Berlin Philharmonic* (Col.); w. Phil Woods; Terry Gibbs (Muse); Sonny Stitt (Cobble.); Jimmy Raney

(MPS); Colo. Jazz Party (MPS/BASF); Al Cohn (Xanadu).

DEARIE, BLOSSOM,* *singer, piano, composer*; b. East Durham, N.Y., 4/28/26. Early experience in vocal gps. w. Woody Herman, Alvino Rey bands in '40s. To Paris in '52 where she teamed w. Annie Ross and formed own vocal gp. The Blue Stars. Returned to U.S. in '58 and established herself as an exceptional, intimately swinging nightclub singer, accompanying her vocals at the head of her own trio. Whitney Balliett wrote: "She is an elegant, polite, and often funny improviser, who lights the songs she sings by carefully altering certain tones and by using a subtle, intense rhythmic attack."

In the '70s she app. mainly in NYC, LA, and London at Ronnie Scott's with a repertory that incl. many of her own songs such as: *I'm Shadowing You; I Like You, You're Nice; Hey John; Sweet Georgie Fame.*

Own LPs: *Blossom Dearie Sings; Blossom Dearie 1975* (Daffodil Records, Box 21N, East Durham, N.Y. 12423); also one track w. King Pleasure in *The Source* (Prest.).

DE BREST, JAMES (SPANKY),* *bass*; b. Philadelphia, Pa., 4/24/37. Worked with small combos incl. Art Blakey, Jay Jay Johnson, also rec. w. Ray Draper. After a long illness, DeBrest died in Philadelphia 3/2/73.

DEDRICK, LYLE F. (RUSTY),* *trumpet, composer*; b. Delevan, N.Y., 7/12/18. Playing and writing for jazz-oriented studio recs., TV, jingles, industrial shows, club dates, pit bands and concerts. W. Urbie Green '67; the Free Design, as mus. dir., '69-70; Lionel Hampton '70-71. Since '71 he has been a member of the jazz dept. of the Manhattan Sch. of Mus. and has been writing originals and arrs. primarily for the educational field. Jazz fest. apps. on Long Island and Dick Gibson Colo. Jazz Party '74. Comps. incl. *The Modern Art Suite* and *Suite for Alto Saxophone and Trumpet.* LPs: *Many Facets, Many Friends* (Monmouth-Evergreen); *Kites Are Fun* w. Free Design (Project 3); *Back Home Again* w. Lee Wiley; *Harold Arlen in Hollywood; Sullivan, Shakespeare & Hyman* (Mon.-Ever.); *Big Band Hits* w. Enoch Light (Project 3).

DEEMS, BARRETT B., *drums*; b. Springfield, Ill., 3/1/13. Traveled w. Louis Armstrong 1954-8, then worked in Chicago, where he played w. Bill Reinhardt at Jazz Ltd. July 1966-Jan. '70. From Feb. '70-, w. Joe Kelly Gaslight Band. Periodic app. subbing in World's Greatest Jazzband 1971-5. TV: Timex All Star Jazz Show, NYC, 1972. During '70s rec. several LPs w. Art Hodes. Earlier LPs w. Armstrong (Col., MCA).

DE FAUT, VOLTAIRE (VOLLEY),* *clarinet, saxophones*; b. Little Rock, Ark., 3/14/04. Known for his work w. the NORK and Jean Goldkette in the '20s, De Faut, one of the first Chicagoans to master the NO clarinet style, later was staff mus. on WGN, Chi. and also active as a dog-breeder. Gigged intermittently from mid-'40s, rec. w. Art Hodes, '53. In last perfs. used electronic amplification device on his clarinet. He died in So. Chicago Heights, 4/29/73.

DE FRANCO, BONIFACE FERDINAND LEONARDO (BUDDY), *clarinet*; also *bass clarinet, composer*; b. Camden, N.J., 2/17/23. With many big bands in 1940s; Count Basie Septet 1950, own big band '51, then led quartets through '50s and co-led combo w. Tommy Gumina in early '60s. From 1966 until 1/18/74 he toured the world as nominal leader of the Glenn Miller orchestra, a job that afforded him few chances to display his unique, bop-inspired improvisational talent to jazz audiences. De Franco, who starting in 1947 won the DB poll as #1 clarinetist 19 times, then returned to jazz, touring Canada with a quintet in a jazz festival. Settling in Panama City, Florida, he went out on occasional club jobs w. jazz combos, played stage band clinics and writing stage band arrs. and instruction books, such as *Buddy De Franco on Jazz Improvisation*, (Famous Solos Ent., Dept. A, Box 567, Saddle River, N.J. 07458). Original arrs. publ. by Creative Artists and Pacific Palisades Music. Played Colo. Jazz Party, and in Sweden, Sept. '75.

LP on bass clarinet (Vee Jay). On clarinet: *Free Sail* (Choice). LP incl. transcriptions of his solos for students on Famous Solos Ent. (address above). Many earlier albums deleted; LPs w. Miller band available in England, Japan.

DE GRAAFF, REIN, *piano, composer*; b. Groningen, Holland, 10/24/42. Private lessons from age 10 for four yrs. In '64, trumpeter Nedly Elstak instructed him more fully about chord changes. Pl. w. Jenna Meinema, '57. Formed own trio and quartet, '60. To Germany, '63, where he pl. w. Jazzopators; also in Switzerland. Pl. locally while stationed w. Dutch Army at NATO base in Germany, '63. Met tenor saxophonist Dick Vennik in Amsterdam, '64, and became associated w. him in de Graaff-Vennik quartet from '64. Visited US, fall '67 and sat in w. gps. of Lee Morgan; Hank Mobley; Elvin Jones. Worked w. Rene Thomas, '73-4. Acc. many visiting soloists incl. Cecil Payne; Mobley; Red Rodney; Clifford Jordan; and expatriates, Johnny Griffin; Tony Scott; Don Byas; Dexter Gordon; Leo Wright; Carmell Jones. Infl: H. Silver, B. Powell, Barry Harris, C. Walton, M. Tyner, Mobley, K. Dorham, Milt Jackson. Dutch TV: from '64 w. own gp.; Benny Bailey, '72; C. Terry, '75. Fest: Loosdrecht; Laren; Pescara; Zurich; Comblain-la-tour; Reims; Hammerfeld; Middleheim; Dunkirk. Writing reviews and articles for Dutch mags., *Oor; Jazz Wereld* from '70. Comp: *Cornish Pixie; Time Machine; Modal Soul; Voodoo Dance; Point of No Return.* LPs: *Minor Moods* (Nowa); *Departure* (BASF); *Point of No Return* (Universe); w. J.R. Monterose, *Body and Soul* (Munich); w. R. Thomas, *TPL* (Vogel).

DE JOHNETTE, JACK, *drums, composer, melodica*; also *piano, saxophone*; b. Chicago, Ill., 8/9/42. Stud. classical piano for ten years with Viola Burns; grad. of American Conservatory of Music, Chicago; music major at Wilson Jr. College. Influenced by records of C. Parker, D. Gillespie, Billie Holiday, Louis Jordan. On joining high school concert band he worked briefly as bassist before taking up drums. He was first inspired by Max Roach, later by Philly Joe Jones and Elvin Jones. During his Chicago years he worked with groups of every genre, from T-Bone Walker and other blues bands to the free jazz of such musicians as Richard Abrams and Roscoe Mitchell. Visiting NYC early in '66 he was spotted by organist John Patton, whose group he joined. Later came engagements with Jackie McLean, singers Betty Carter and Abbey Lincoln, and Charles Lloyd, with whose quintet he toured for more than two years.

DeJohnette then worked around NYC. At one time or another he played with John Coltrane, Thelonious Monk, Freddie Hubbard, Bill Evans, Keith Jarrett and Chick Corea. During part of '68 he was with Stan Getz.

His best known association was with Miles Davis, whom he joined in the spring of '70. During the next two years, in addition to recording some of Davis' most significant albums, DeJohnette became a leader in his own right on LPs, and was heard more frequently doubling on melodica, piano, clavinet and organ and occasional vocals. In summer of '71 he organized a combo, known as Compost, for concert tours and clubs in the U.S. and overseas. Later he led other groups; in '75 he formed quartet with Alex Foster, saxophone; John Abercrombie, guitar; and Peter Warren, bass.

Like many musicians who came to prominence in the '60s originally as drummers, DeJohnette is a complete and adaptable musician with considerable talent as a composer. By the late '60s he had listened extensively to rock groups and was strongly influenced by some of them. Among his most representative albums is *The DeJohnette Complex* (Milestone). This includes his two Requiem compositions, in memory of the Kennedys, Malcolm X and Martin Luther King.

LPs: w. Bill Evans, *Live At Montreux* (Verve); w. Lloyd, *Forest Flower; Dream Weaver* (Atlantic); w. Davis, *Bitches' Brew; Live At Fillmore; Live-Evil* (Columbia); w. Joe Henderson, *Power To The People* (Milestone); w. F. Hubbard, *Straight Life; Joe Farrell Quartet* (CTI); w. Miroslav Vitous, *Infinite Search* (Embryo); *Keith Jarrett-Jack DeJohnette* (ECM); own groups *The DeJohnette Complex; Have You Heard* (Milestone); *Sorcery* (Prestige); w. Compost, *Take Off Your Body; Life Is Round* (Columbia).

DE LA ROSA, FRANK (Francisco Estaban Jr.), bass; b. El Paso, Tex., 12/26/33. Father and brother, Oscar, both musicians. Stud. LA Conservatory of Music and Fine Arts w. Sam H. Rice, '56-8. Worked w. Latin groups until '59, then moved to Las Vegas, where he played in many casino bands. Moving back to LA May '65, became more active in jazz. Pl. w. D. Ellis '66-8; Sweets Edison, '68-9; E. Fitzgerald, '69-72; Don Menza '72-5; Don Piestrup, '72-5; Mayo Tiana, '72-5; S. Vaughan, '74-5. Has app. at Monterey, Newport and most leading European jazz fests. A clean-toned, dependable artist much respected for his work on upright bass.

LPs: w. D. Ellis (Pacific Jazz); E. Fitzgerald (MPS-BASF) etc.

DE MERLE, LESTER WILLIAM (LES), drums, composer; also percussion, piano; b. Brooklyn, N.Y., 11/4/46. Stud. drums and perc. w. Bob Livingston, NYC, '60-5; harmony, theory at Berklee w. Alf Clausen. At 16 worked w. L. Hampton for nine months while still in school. In '65 w. Billy Williams Revue; Connie Haines; Lee Castle-Jimmy Dorsey band, '66. Formed first group, '67 w. R. Brecker, Arnie Lawrence, also gigging around NYC w. J. Farrell, L. Konitz, Garnett Brown, W. Bishop Jr. until '70s. Moved to LA, '71; started group, Transfusion, and in '72 opened Cellar Theatre, home base for Transfusion and showcase for young artists. NJF, '74, w. H. James.

Publ: *Jazz-Rock Fusion*, Vols. I & II (Try Pubs., 854 Vine St., Hollywood, Ca. 90038). LPs: *Spectrum* (UA); *Arizona Slim* sound track w. Paul Beaver.

DEODATO, EUMIR DE ALMEIDA, piano, composer; also guitar, bass, synthesizer; b. Rio de Janeiro, Brazil, 6/22/42. Self-taught. Insp. by Gil Evans, J. Coltrane, Miles Davis, Glenn Miller, S. Kenton, Ravel, Debussy, Moussorgsky, Stevie Wonder. Prof. debut in Brazil w. Astrud Gilberto, Luis Bonfa. His first comp., *Spirit of Summer*, won top honors at Rio Song Fest., where he also received three awards as best arranger. Left Brazil, '67, spent three years off and on in U.S. From '70 spent most of his time in studios where he enjoyed a reputation as arranger for albums feat. R. Flack, F. Sinatra, A. Franklin, B. Midler, W. Montgomery, S. Turrentine, A.C. Jobim, L. Bonfa, A. Gilberto etc. He also wrote scores for two prize-winning movies, *Bahia*; and *The Reporter*, and for *The Adventurers; Target Risk; Gentle Rain; The Girl From Ipanema*; and *Twiggy Special*. Other comps. incl. *The Legend of The Amazon Bird; Super Strut*. Deodato achieved sudden national prominence in the U.S. in '73 when his jazz-rock arr. of *Also Sprach Zarathustra* (the theme from *2001*) became a best selling record. On the strength of it he won many awards, incl. a Grammy, *Billboard* listing as top jazz artist, *Playboy*, etc. Toured U.S. and Canada, '73 and '74; also Italy, Venezuela, Japan, Philippines, Hawaii, '74.

Later rock and jazz arrs. incl. *Rhapsody In Blue; Moonlight Serenade*. LPs: *Prelude; Deodato 2; Deodato/Airto In Concert* (CTI); *Donato + Deodato* (Muse); *Whirlwinds; Artistry* (MCA).

DE PARIS, SIDNEY,* trumpet; b. Crawfordsville, Ind., 5/30/05. Prominent in 1930s w. McKinney's Cotton Pickers, Don Redman; w. Benny Carter 1940-41, then off and on w. brother Wilbur's combo from '43. De Paris died in NYC 9/14/67. LP: *De Paris Dixie* (BN).

DE PARIS, WILBUR,* trombone; b. Crawfordsville, Ind., 1/11/00. During 1930s and '40s pl. w. Benny Carter, Teddy Hill, Louis Armstrong, Ella Fitzgerald, Roy Eldridge, Duke Ellington. Led successful traditionalist small band that played for a decade at Jimmy Ryan's in NYC, also toured Africa for State Dept. in

1957. Less active after death of brother Sidney, but played a few dates w. new group in 1972. Died in NYC 1/3/73.

DESMOND, PAUL,* *alto sax*; b. San Francisco, Calif., 11/25/24. When the Dave Brubeck quartet, of which he had been a member from its inception in '51, broke up in Dec. '67 Desmond entered a period of little musical activity. He began writing a book about his experiences with the working title, *How Many of You Are There in the Quartet?* In the mid-'70s he reported that it was proceeding at "a glacial pace." A chapter appeared in *Punch.*

In '69 appeared at the New Orleans Jazz Festival and recorded for A&M. He was reunited with Brubeck in The Two Generations of Brubeck in '72, playing at NJF-NY and touring for George Wein in Europe, Australia and Japan. He continued to make guest appearances with them in concerts and fests. like NJF-NY '73 and '75. As a single he played at the MJF, '75. Rarely a club performer, he worked at the new Half Note with his own group, '74, and with a Canadian rhythm section on three different occasions at Bourbon Street in Toronto, '74-5. In June '75 he and Brubeck, with Dave's sons, played for the Jazz Cruise on the S.S. Rotterdam. Out of this came an album of Brubeck-Desmond duets, one of which resulted from a BBC-TV shipboard taping; the rest, inspired by this, from a September studio date. This, and his recs. for CTI, as leader and sideman, show that the years have deepened his bittersweet lines. Among Desmond's other TV apps. was the Timex jazz show, '72.

He was summoned to Hollywood in the fall of '75 to tape a soundtrack for Paul Mazursky's film, *Next Stop Greenwich Village,* but it was later decided to use in addition some of the old recordings of the Brubeck quartet of the early '50s, the time in which the movie is set. Comp: *Wendy; Take Ten; North By Northeast.* LPs: *Skylark; Pure Desmond* (CTI); *Bridge Over Troubled Water; From the Hot Afternoon; Summertime* (A&M); *Duets 1975/Brubeck-Desmond* (Horizon); w. Don Sebesky, *Giant Box;* w. Jim Hall, *Concierto* (CTI).

DE SOUZA, JOÃO JOSÉ PEREIRA (RAUL), *half-bass trombone;* also *composer, trumpet, bass, tuba, flute saxophone, percussion;* b. Rio de Janeiro, Brazil, 8/23/34. Self-taught except for studies at Berklee Coll. of Music in Boston. Started on trombone while in teens. Spent five and a half years in Brazilian Air Force. Played with many groups incl. three of his own in Brazil, Mexico City. One of his Brazilian combos, Impacto 8, made an LP in '68. De Souza worked with Sergio Mendes in Brazil and Europe, '63-4. In '65-6, after traveling in Europe with a Brazilian group, he played w. Kenny Clarke at the Blue Note club in Paris. Soon after, spent three and a half years in Mexico City. First came to U.S. in Aug. '73, after which he played frequently w. Airto.

Infl. by J.J. Johnson, whom he heard on records in '59, De Souza was voted Brazil's best trombonist in various polls between '67 and '71. His style suggested an inspired extension of Johnson.

Comp: *Water Buffalo.* LPs: *Colors* (Milestone); *Bossa Rio,* w. Mendes (Philips); *Stories To Tell* w. F. Purim (Milestone); others w. Azar Lawrence (Milestone) et al.

DEUCHAR, JAMES (JIMMIE),* *trumpet, fluegelhorn, mellophonium;* b. Dundee, Scotland, 6/26/30. Pl. w. Ronnie Scott and Tubby Hayes, '60-66; Kurt Edelhagen as soloist and arr.; K. Clarke-F. Boland big band from '65-71; ret. to England in '71, began arr. for BBC. Moved back to Scotland early '70s.

Comps: *Portrait of Elvin; Drum In* (for Edelhagen); *U.K. Suite* (for Clarke-Boland). LPs: w. Clarke-Boland on Atl., MPS, Col.

DE VEGA, HENRY (HANK), *clarinet, saxes, flute* etc.; b. El Paso, Tex., 8/4/30. In 1949 began studies at LA Cons. of Mus., interrupted by service in USAF band, 1950-53. Pl. baritone sax, rec. w. Roy Porter bebop band, '49-50; brief stints w. J. Otis, Ike Carpenter, Harry James. Hotel bands in LV, '53-4; Benny Carter, '55; joined Lionel Hampton '55 and was seriously injured in a bus accident that involved the entire band. After a long recuperation, he resumed LV work, '60-65; free-lanced around LA, '65-8; pl. w. Gerald Wilson orch., '68- . Exhibiting artist in mixed media painting; working at USC, supervisor, reproduction services. LPs: *Everywhere; California Soul; Eternal Equinox* w. Wilson (Pac. Jazz); *Things Ain't What They Used To Be* w. Wilson, Ella Fitzgerald (Reprise).

DICKENSON, VICTOR (VIC),* *trombone, composer;* also *singer;* b. Xenia, Ohio, 8/6/06. Pl. w. big bands of Claude Hopkins in '30s; Benny Carter, Count Basie, Eddie Heywood's small gp. in '40s; Red Allen; Ed Hall gps. in '50s; Wild Bill Davison, early '60s. From '63-68 w. Saints & Sinners; then '68-70 w. Bobby Hackett w. whom he had been associated in '51 and '56. Joined World's Greatest Jazzband spring '70, pl. w. them into '72. With Hackett again '73, pl. at Americana, NYC '74; Toronto; New England. From March '75 pl. w. Balaban & Cats at Eddie Condon's. One of the great trombone stylists in the history of the music, he displayed his usual fluency, warmth and unique wit in the '70s. Won DB Critics poll, '71-4. TV: *Just Jazz,* PBS, '71 w. Hackett. Fest: Pescara; San Sebastian, '74; Nice, '74-5; NJF-NY, several times in '70s, incl. Newport Hall of Fame, '75; Colorado JP annually. Comp: *Alone; Constantly; I'll Try.* LPs: w. Hackett, *Live at the Roosevelt Grill* (Chiaro.); *Plus Vic Dickenson* (Proj. 3); *Buck Clayton Jam Session* (Chiaro.); w. WGJ (Atl., World Jazz); w. Balaban & Cats, *A Night at the New Eddie Condon's* (Classic Jazz); also represented in Albert McCarthy's *Swing Today* series (Eng. RCA).

DICKERSON, DWIGHT LOWELL, *piano;* also *singer;* b. Los Angeles, Ca., 12/26/44. Stud. Berklee, '65; also privately w. Ray Santisi, Mrs. Margaret Chaloff in Boston; Cal State U., LA, '73. Played with innumerable small combos, among them Sergio Mendes' Bossa Rio, '69-70; Bola Sete, '70-1; Charles Owens, '71; Calvin Keys, '72; James Moody, '72; Larry Gales from '72; Bobby Bryant, '72; Ch. Lloyd, '73; Leroy Vinnegar, '73-4; Red Holloway, Freddie Hill, B. Hutcherson, '74; Sahib Shihab, '74-5; S. Criss, '74-5.

Dickerson, who has a BA from Cal State, is at home in many settings, as is evidenced by his LPs: *Alegria*, w. Bossa Rio (Blue Thumb); *Shebaba*, w. Sete (Fantasy); *I Stand Alone*, w. Owens (Vault); *Free Again*, w. G. Ammons & B. Bryant Big Band (Prestige); *Glass of Water*, w. Vinnegar (Legend).

DIORIO, JOSEPH LOUIS (JOE), *guitar, composer*; b. Waterbury, Conn., 8/6/36. Stud. at Berdice School of Music, '49-54, subsequently self-taught. Established through records and/or gigs in early and mid-60s w. Eddie Harris, S. Stitt, Bennie Green, Bunky Green, Nicky Hill, and with many other leading jazzmen in Chicago from '60-9. Moving to Florida, composed and played music for a TV documentary, worked on local TV shows. To Washington, '71 for House of Sounds Fest. at JFK Center w. Ira Sullivan, perf. as duo.

In '75 Diorio also was studying drawing and painting at two Miami Univs., and was writing several books for guitar. A highly capable all around artist on both electric and classical guitar.

LPs: *Exodus to Jazz* w. Eddie Harris (Veejay); *Play Back*, w. Sam Lazar (Cadet); *My Main Man*, w. S. Stitt (Cadet); *Rapport*, co-leader w. Wally Cirillo (Spitball).

DITMAS, BRUCE, *drums*; also *percussion, synthesizers*; b. Atlantic City, N.J., 12/12/46. Grew up in Miami, Fla. Father, who pl. trombone w. Art Mooney; Claude Thornhill, Jerry Wald in '40s, is very active in Miami, primarily w. hotel show bands. Began on piano but switched to drums at 10. Studied for seven yrs. w. Tony Crisetello in Miami. Att. Stan Kenton Clinics at Indiana U.; Michigan State, '62, '63. Various jazz gigs at 15, mostly w. Ira Sullivan; hotel show bands in Miami Beach; then w. Sullivan, '62-4, then two yrs. w. Judy Garland, moving home base to NYC. Between '66-70 pl. w. Barbra Streisand; Della Reese; Leslie Uggams; Yolande Bavan; Sheila Jordan; Jack Reilly trio. With Gil Evans orch. from '71; Trevor Koehler from '71 until his death in '75; Enrico Rava from '71. Pit band for *Promises, Promises*; Joe Newman quartet; and Jazz Interactions orch. for L. Armstrong tribute w. Thad Jones; Johnny Coles, '71. Worked w. Stardrive; Atmospheres w. Clive Stevens; Steve Kuhn; Albert Dailey; Hammerline w. Koehler; Future Shock w. Brecker bros., '72; helped form The New Wilderness Preservation Band for series of concerts at Peace Church; w. Evans at Vanguard, Village Gate, Bitter End, '72-3, and NYJRC concerts, '73-4. Pl. w. Paul Bley; Lee Konitz; Chet Baker; Koehler, '74; Evans; Rava, in US and Europe; Barry Miles, '75. Early infl: Roach, Blakey, Elvin Jones. Fav: Jack DeJohnette. Other infl: Lenny White, Billy Hart, Evans, Koehler. Film: *The Cage*. TV: Merv Griffin; *Today; Take a Giant Step; Look Up and Live*; European shows w. Evans. Fest: NJF-NY, LA, SF; Montreux; Antibes; others in Denmark, Italy, Switz. LPs: w. Evans (RCA, Atl., Nippon Phonogram); w. S. Kuhn (Cobble.); J. Coles (Main.); Stardrive (Elektra); Wavy Gravy (Just Sunshine).

DIXON, ERIC,* *tenor sax, flute, composer*; b. Staten Island, N.Y., 3/28/30. A veteran of the Count Basie reed section from '62, he left in '72 to operate a restaurant on Staten Island w. his wife called The Meeting Place, but rejoined in summer '75. Recorded an LP for Master Jazz in '74 entitled *Eric's Edge* incl. his own comp: *Background Blues; Whisper M&I; The Meeting Place; Blues For Ilean; Eric's Edge*. LP: w. Basie (Pablo).

DODGION, DOTTIE (Dorothy Giaimo), *drums*; b. Brea, Cal., 9/23/29. Father a prof. drummer in SF; husband is Jerry Dodgion. Mainly self-taught. Pl. w. Nick Esposito, Ch. Mingus in SF. To NYC, worked w. Benny Goodman, '61; Marian McPartland, '64; Billy Mitchell-Al Grey Quintet. Toronto club w. Wild Bill Davison; Las Vegas w. Carl Fontana, Gus Mancuso; college tours w. Eugene Wright; Half Note, NYC, w. Al Cohn-Zoot Sims, then joined Ruby Braff Quartet, app. at Concord JF '72. Living in LA, '75, gigged w. Mancuso, Wright. Insp. by Sid Catlett, Jo Jones and later drummers; a sensitive drummer who fits into every modern jazz context.

LPs: w. Braff; Davison (Chiaroscuro).

DODGION, JERRY,* *alto sax*; also *flute, soprano sax*; b. Richmond, Calif., 8/29/32. Played w. Gerald Wilson, Benny Carter, Red Norvo in '50s. Moved to NYC '61 where he occ. teamed w. wife, drummer Dottie Dodgion, in quartet. Made tours of So. America, Russia w. Benny Goodman. A charter member of the Thad Jones-Mel Lewis orch. from late '65, he took over lead alto chair when Jerome Richardson left in '71. Through '75 he had made six European, three Japanese tours w. them and one of Soviet Union, '72. A busy NYC free-lance he has rec. w. Basie, Ruby Braff, Richard Davis, Goodman, H. Hancock, Blue Mitchell, O. Nelson and D. Amram, also making concert apps. w. Amram. Wrote arr. of Marian McPartland's *Ambiance* for Jones-Lewis *Potpourri* album on Phila. Int. Fests: see Jones-Lewis. LPs: see Jones-Lewis; also *The Phantom; Now Hear This; Introducing Duke Pearson*, all w. Pearson; *Fancy Free* w. D. Byrd (BN); w. D. Amram, *No More Walls* (RCA).

DOGGETT, WILLIAM BALLARD (BILL),* *organ, piano, composer*; b. Philadelphia, Pa., 2/6/16. Long popular in jazz and r & b circles, Doggett continued to pl. colleges, night clubs and one-nighters throughout the U.S. and Canada. He rec. w. Della Reese in '66, but for the most part was heard leading his own combo. He was also personal manager for recording artist Edwin Starr. In recent years Doggett has been teamed for many engagements with the Ink Spots.

Fests: Juan-les-Pins, '66; Antwerp, Nice, '71. Publ: *Honky-Tonk*, instrumental version (Islip Mus. Publ. Co., 120 W. Bayberry Rd., Islip, N.Y. 11751).

LPs: on King, Sue, ABC etc.; w. Ella Fitzgerald, *Rhythm is Our Business* (Verve).

DOLDINGER, KLAUS,* *tenor, soprano sax*; also *clarinet, keyboards, synthesizer, mellotron*; b. Berlin, Germany, 5/12/36. After his assoc. in '63-4 in a jazz workshop with visiting Americans such as Kenny Clarke, J. Griffin, Benny Bailey, Max Roach, Donald Byrd, did much touring with own quintet in N. Africa, Middle East and Scandinavia, '64; S. America for West German Gov't., '65. In '70 formed Motherhood, which from '71 was known as Passport. Many European fests. and TV apps., also TV in Hong Kong, Tokyo, Rio de Janeiro. Toured U.S. w. own combo Apr. 1975. Insps. and infls. Sidney Bechet, Ch. Parker, Coltrane, O. Coleman, G. Evans, Miles Davis. Won several German jazz and rock polls. Comps: *Eternal Spiral; Looking Thru; Cross Collateral; Will-O-The-Wisp; Jazz Concertino* for jazz quartet and symph. orch. Publ: book of comps. for Passport (Muz, 8 Munchen, Leopoldstr. 38).

LPs: *Doldinger Jubilee Concert; Looking Thru; Cross Collateral* (Atco); *Passport et al/Doldinger Jubilee '75* (Atl.).

DONAHUE, SAM KOONTZ,* *tenor sax, trumpet, leader*; b. Detroit, Mich., 3/8/18. Own band in 1930s; later pl. w. Goodman, James, Krupa. Fronted Tommy Dorsey "ghost band" 1961-5; later settled in Reno, Nev., where he died 3/22/74.

DONALD, BARBARA KAY, *trumpet*; also *piano, voice, saxophone, trombone*; b. Minneapolis, Minn., 2/9/42. Started playing cornet at nine. Moved to LA; cont. studying horn and voice through HS and at Valley State Coll. Veteran Little Benny Harris later became her teacher. At 18, went on the road w. own group; toured w. Chuck Cabot big band and with various rock groups. Freelanced in LA w. D. Gordon, Gene Russell, Stanley Cowell, Burt Wilson. In '62 she married Norwegian pianist Ole Calmeyer; divorced in '65, married Sonny Simmons (q.v.) and has worked with him ever since. Moved to NYC, '66; back to SF, '70 and LA, '75. Donald has also pl. w. Mike White, Clifford Jordan, Richard Davis, Smiley Winters, Prince Lasha, Billy Higgins, R.R. Kirk, Charles Moffett, Tony Scott, Lonnie Liston Smith, Cecil McBee, Clifford Jarvis, John Hicks, and in '65 w. J. Coltrane.

Donald says she is "still struggling to become accepted as a woman artist, and fighting this planet's low conception of music."

LPs: w. Simmons, *Staying on Watch; Music of the Spheres* (ESP); *Manhattan Egos* (Arhoolie); *Ruma Suma; Burning Spirits* (Contemp.); w. Winters, *Smiley Ect.* (Arhoolie); *Les Oublies De Jazz Ensemble* (Touche).

DONALDSON, ROBERT STANLEY (BOBBY),* *drums*; b. Boston, Mass., 11/29/22. An alumnus of many name groups incl. Edmond Hall, Sy Oliver, B. Goodman, Andy Kirk, Donaldson later worked as a studio musician. He died of a heart attack 7/2/71 in NYC.

DONALDSON, LOU,* *alto sax*; b. Badin, N.C., 11/1/26. Concentrating on blues-based, funky material he continued to lead his small combo (organ, trumpet, guitar, drums) in small clubs in the East. In '67 he left the Cadet label, where he had been under contract from '63, to return to his former, long time affiliate Blue Note. His basic repertoire was described by Bob Porter as combining " 'down-home' melodies with New Orleans r&b drums." This is intermixed w. some ballads and an oc-

casional Charlie Parker song, reflecting his active participation in small gp. jazz of the early '50s w. Art Blakey, Clifford Brown et al. Donaldson is an outspoken critic of the avant garde. He says: "The guys say they are searching but actually all they need to find is a good saxophone or trumpet teacher and their search would be over because they would teach them how to play it." LPs: *Sophisticated Lou* feat. him pl. ballads with strings; w. quintet, *Alligator Boogaloo; Hot Dog; Everything I Play is Funky*, etc. (BN); *Fried Buzzard*, etc. (Cadet).

DONATO, MICHEL ANDRE, *bass*; also *piano*; b. Montreal, Quebec, Canada, 8/25/42. Father, Ronald pl. tenor sax; uncle Maurice Donato, piano. Stud. at Mont. Cons., '60-3; otherwise self-taught. From '62-9 pl. w. Pierre Leduc; Lee Gagnon; Nick Ayoub; Ron Proby; Art Roberts, Sonny Greenwich, Brian Barley; Carmen McRae; Jacques Brel; Charles Aznavour; Michel Legrand; member of Mont. Symph., '64. In Toronto from '70 w. Lenny Breau; Moe Koffman; Bernie Senensky; Don Thompson; Sonny Greenwich; Alvin Pall; Claude Ranger; clubs w. Benny Carter; Art Farmer; Milt Jackson; Dave McKenna; studio work pl. jingles. World tour w. O. Peterson, '73-4. Infl: LaFaro, Pettiford, P. Heath, Mingus, Gary Karr. TV: *Everything Goes* w. Koffman; *Jazz En Liberte*, '65-70; CBC Chamber Orch. on radio. Fests: Pitts., NJF-NY w. Peterson, '73; Belvedere "King-Size" in Can. w. Koffman, L. Bellson big band, '74. LPs: w. Peterson (Japan. Col.); Don Thompson; S. Greenwich (Sack.); *The Montreal Scene* w. Ayoub (Can. RCA); *Jazzzz* w. Gagnon (Barclay); *Beloved Gift* w. Senensky; others w. Herbie Spanier, Art Maiste, Pierre Nadeau (RCI).

DORHAM, McKINLEY HOWARD (KENNY),* *trumpet, composer*; b. Fairfield, Tex., 8/30/24. Graduate of innumerable name groups of 1940s and '50s, incl. Gillespie, Eckstine, Hampton, Mercer Ellington; founder member of Art Blakey's Jazz Messengers. Replaced the late Clifford Brown in Max Roach quintet, '56-8. Later freelanced extensively, visiting Europe often, also teaching and composing. Successful partnership w. Joe Henderson, '62-3, and later w. Hank Mobley. Attended NYU graduate school of music in late '60s. In failing health in later years, Dorham continued playing sporadically until shortly before his death of kidney failure 12/5/72 in NYC. His *Fragments of An Autobiography* was published in *Music '70, down beat*'s annual for '69.

A superior composer and a brilliant trumpeter who forged a style of his own out of the influences of Gillespie, Navarro and Miles Davis. Comp: *Una Mas; Blue Spring; Lotus Blossom* (also known as *Asiatic Raes*); *Trompeta Toccata; Whistle Stop; Epitaph; Blue Bossa; Dead End*. Dorham is represented on many LPs, the best of them under his own name or w. Blakey, almost all on Blue Note. Rec. w. Ch. Parker, Th. Monk, O. Nelson, T. Dameron, J.J. Johnson, S. Rollins, H. Silver, S. Stitt, C. Walton, Cecil Taylor, Joe Henderson; also *Kenny Dorham Memorial Album* (Xanadu); *Ease It* (Muse); w. Cecil Payne, *Zodiac* (Strata-East); *1959*; w. Barry

Harris, *Bull's Eye* (Prest.); reissue, *Max Roach + 4* (Trip).

DOROUGH, ROBERT LROD (BOB),* *piano, singer, composer*; also *vibes, harmonica, saxophone*; b. Cherry Hill, Ark., 12/12/23. Early work as accompanist for Sugar Ray Robinson. In Paris at Mars Club, '54-5. After many years leading combos in NYC, Chicago and LA, became active in record and jingle production, also producing and composing for TV. Played at Bradley's, NYC in mid-70s; SF & LA, Aug.-Sept., '75. Wrote *Multiplication Rock*, a series of animated films designed for children, seen on ABC-TV, '72-5. Other comps: *Grammar Rock; America Rock; Comin' Home Baby; Winds of Heaven; Nothing Like You.*

Dorough is well known for his rec. as vocalist and composer w. M. Davis in '62, when he was heard on *Blue Xmas* in *Jingle Bell Jazz*; and '67 on *Nothing Like You* in *Sorcerer* (both Col.). His hip, quavery vocal style and bop infl. piano are much admired by a number of jazz musicians. Own LPs: *Just About Everything* (Focus); *Multiplication Rock* (Cap.); *Disguises* (Laissez Faire); w. *Children of All Ages* (Differant Drummer); w. Bobby Jones (Cobble.).

DOTSON, DENNIS, *trumpet, fluegelhorn*; b. Jacksonville, Tex., 6/18/46. Self-taught. Pl. w. Edgar Winter in Houston, 1968. Spent five years in LV playing casino shows, also w. Carl Fontana, Red Rodney, Sam Noto. Joined Woody Herman, 1975. LP: *Children of Lima* w. Herman (Fantasy).

DRAPER, RAYMOND ALLEN (RAY),* *tuba, composer*; also *valve trombone, baritone horn, bass trumpet, keyboards, vocals*; b. New York, N.Y., 8/3/40. Prominent in LA from '64, where he lived in Venice, working w. Big Black, '66-7; rec. sound tracks w. Q. Jones; pl. w. Horace Tapscott. Formed nine piece rock group, Red Beans & Rice, '68, staying together for a year and a half.

In '69 Draper moved to London and became music director for Ronnie Scott Directions. Comp., arr., rec. w. ten piece band, Sweetwater Canal. Toured Europe as leader w. Arthur Conley show, and w. A. Shepp, D. Cherry, Dr. John. Rec. w. Mick Jagger, Eric Clapton, Michael Henderson, Walter Davis Jr. Pl. Montreux JF, '70.

Returned to U.S. w. Dr. John cont. to work with him until '72. He then became involved in teaching theory and harmony, recording studio techniques etc. at the Univ. of the Streets and Wesleyan U., Middletown, Conn. Received grant for comp. from NEA, '73-4. Worked w. Cathy Chamberlain's Rag & Roll Revue, '74-5. Moved back to LA and rejoined Dr. John, '75. Films: *Amougee*, filmed in Belgium; *Jazz on a Summer's Day*, made at Newport JF; sang *Lay Your Love On Me* for *Last Summer*. TV: *Jazz Set* (PBS). Comps: *Fugue for Brass Ensemble; Filide; Happiness & Mess Around.*

LPs: *Red Beans & Rice* (Epic); w. Big Black, *Elements of Now* (Uni); *Sonny's Dream* w. S. Criss (Prest.); *Sun, Moon & Herbs* w. Dr. John (Atl.); *Who Knows What Tomorrow's Gonna Bring*, w. Jack McDuff (BN).

DRESSER, MARK, *bass*; b. Los Angeles, Calif., 9/26/52. Lessons from Gary Karr; studied for a long time w. Bertram Turetzsky. Pl. rock as a teenager. Then studied and pl. w. David Baker at U. of Indiana, '70-1. Through Turetzsky met Stanley Crouch in summer of '72 and has pl. w. him from that time. With San Diego Symph., '73-5; David Murray-Butch Morris Ensemble; Murray trio & quintet; Leo Smith; Ice Follies band under dir. of Cat Anderson, '75. Has also pl. w. Bobby Bradford; Black Arthur; James Newton; Charles Tyler. To NYC summer '75; then moved to New Haven. Infl: Mingus, P. Chambers, Pettiford, W. Ware, C. Haden, Ellington, Rollins, M. Favors, B. Bradford. Dance has become imp. infl. after working w. improvising dancers. Fest: Studio Rivbea JF w. Murray quintet, '75. LPs: two albums w. Crouch, '73, as yet unreleased.

DREW, KENNETH SIDNEY (KENNY),* *piano, composer*; b. New York City, 8/28/28. After important early playing w. Lester Young, Ch. Parker et al, was active on the West Coast scene; toured w. Dinah Washington; Buddy Rich. Moved to Europe, '61, settling in Copenhagen, '64. Married to daughter of the late Leo Mathisen, well known Danish jazz pianist. Began playing at Montmartre Jazzhus w. Dexter Gordon and such visiting soloists as K. Dorham, J. Griffin, H. Mobley, J. Henderson, S. Rollins, Y. Lateef and, also, B. Webster. Formed ongoing alliance w. bassist Niels-Henning Orsted Pedersen in duo, trio combinations. Duo concept started in '66 when they were chosen to represent Denmark for the European Broadcasting Union. Fest: major European fests.; Tangier, '72. Comps: *Suite for Big Band* for Danish Radio; *Dark Beauty; Blues Inn; Largo; Come Summer; Serenity; Sunset; Duo Trip*. British critic Mark Gardner wrote: "As a pianist Kenny Drew has certainly matured greatly in the past 13 years. He always had unusual technical facility, but all that is now harnessed to a probing musical mind and a deeper realization of his individuality."

Own publ. co.: Shirew Publ., Aboulevarden 18, 2200. Copenhagen N., Denmark.

LPs: solo album, *Everything I Love; Duo; Duo 2; Dark Beauty*; w. Jackie McLean, *Live at Montmartre; Ghetto Lullaby*; w. McLean-D. Gordon, *The Meeting; The Source*; w. Gordon, *The Apartment*; w. Ken McIntyre, *Hindsight*; w. J. Griffin, *Blues for Harvey* (SteepleChase); w. D. Gillespie, *Giant*; w. G. Ammons, *Goodbye* (Prest.); *Violin Summit* (MPS).

DROOTIN, ALBERT M. (AL), *clarinet*; also *saxes, flute*; b. Boston, Mass., 12/24/16. Family all pro. mus. for many generations. Father taught him clarinet. Jam sessions at Ken Club w. brother Buzzy (q.v.); then to NYC, joining Bud Freeman '40. Muggsy Spanier, '41; Boyd Raeburn, '42; army band; then ret. to Boston and freelanced. House band at Mahogany Hall, '51-3; Savoy, Hi-Hat, other local clubs; formed trio w. soprano sax, banjo at Gaslite Room, '59; continued to gig around Boston for 14 years, then formed Drootin Bros. Band '73 (see Drootin, Buzzy).

LPs w. Al Donahue, Raeburn, Storyville gp. etc., deleted.

DROOTIN, BENJAMIN (BUZZY),* *drums*, b. Russia, 4/22/20. Veteran of traditional style gps.; during mid-1960s toured w. B. Hackett, J. Teagarden, E. Condon, Roy Eldridge, Dukes of Dixieland, Newport All Stars. Bandleader at El Morocco, NYC, '66 (only jazz mus. ever to hold this job); traveled w. Jazz Giants (Wild Bill Davison et al) '67-9; formed own gp., B.D.'s Jazz Family, w. Herman Autry, Benny Morton, '69-70; free-lanced around NYC, '71-2; in '73 returned to Boston, where he was raised, to join brother Al and nephew Sonny in Drootin Brothers Band, house gp. at Scotch 'n' Sirloin '73-5. Fest: NJF-NY, '73.

TV: *Buzzy's Jazz Family* on PBS network. Drootin Bros. Band on New England Network's *Good Morning* show. *Today, Tonight* shows w. Dukes of Dixieland.

LPs: *Great Moments at Newport Festival* (RCA); *Jazz Giants* w. Davison; *Old Tyme Modern* w. Herb Hall (Sackville); *Jazz Ultimate* w. Hackett, Teagarden (Capitol); *Braff* w. Ruby Braff (Epic).

DUDEK, GERHARD ROCHUS (GERD), *tenor saxophone*; also *soprano sax, clarinet, flute, shennai*; b. Gr. Dobern, Germany, 9/28/38. Brother, Ossi Dudek, pl. trumpet w. SFB Radio Band in Berlin. Private clarinet lessons in Siegen, '54, then music school there. Worked in brother's big band until '58. W. Berlin Jazz Quintet, '60-4. From that time has pl. w. Kurt Edelhagen Orch. in Cologne, also touring Russia w. Edelhagen; Manfred Schoof quintet; Globe Unity Orch.; w. George Russell at Berlin Fest.; Wolfgang Dauner; Albert Manglesdorff quintet; Four For Jazz; Don Cherry; and own groups. Fests: Antibes, Molde, Montreux. Infl: Coltrane, Coleman, M. Davis, C. Parker, Cherry, A. Ayler. LPs: w. Schoof, *Voices* (CBS); w. T. Honda quartet, *Flying to the Sky*, Trio jazz series (Japan); w. Joachim Kuhn, *This Way Out*; w. Baden Baden Free Jazz Orch., *Gittin' To Know Y'All* (MPS).

DUDZIAK, URSZULA, *singer*, also *percussion, synthesizer, composer*; b. Straconka, Poland, 10/22/43. Stud. piano at music school in Zielona-Gora. Inspired by Miles Davis, K. Komeda, Wayne Shorter, Billie Holiday, Ella Fitzgerald. Married to Michal Urbaniak, with whose group she traveled throughout Europe from 1965. Jazz festivals in Warsaw 1969-72; Molde, '71; Pescara, '72; various others in France etc. before coming to US in 1974. Composer of music for ballet (New York Dance Collective), 1974.

Ms. Dudziak's innovative abilities came to the attention of the American public in a unique album, *Newborn Light*, in which she was accompanied only by pianist Adam Makowicz. Though not the first singer to achieve startling effects through the use of electronic devices such as tape-echo, she was the first to achieve prominence with this rare genre of wordless singing.

Among her original works (most of them largely unplanned and improvised rather than composed) are *Dear Christopher Komeda; Ballad; Darkness and Newborn*

Light; Bandi and Bamse, the latter two in collab. w. Makowicz.

LPs: *Newborn Light* (Col.); *Fusion, Atma* w. Urbaniak (Col.); *Journey* w. Arif Mardin (Atl.).

DUKE, GEORGE, *keyboards, synthesizer, composer*; b. San Rafael, Cal., 1/12/46. Extensive studies throughout school years. BM in comp. from SF Conservatory, '67; MA from Cal. State, SF. Pl. at Half Note club, SF, '65-7. From '66-70 Duke's trio also traveled w. a vocal group, The Third Wave, for which he wrote most of the material. The trio toured Mexico in '68; worked in SF backing D. Gillespie, B. Hutcherson, H. Land, K. Dorham et al. In '69, pl. w. J-L. Ponty, after which the trio broke up; Duke spent eight months w. D. Ellis band. He began assoc. w. F. Zappa on records, and joined Zappa's Mothers of Invention, '70. After touring w. C. Adderley quintet, '71-2, he returned to the Zappa group, '73-5. Co-led group w. B. Cobham, '75. During '73-5 Duke began working on various occasions with his own group w. Leon Ndugu Chancler or Chester Thompson, drums; Tom Fowler or Al Johnson, bass. Films and TV: Zappa's *2000 Motels* sound track. While pl. with the Third Wave, app. on *Hollywood Palace*. With Ellis on Ed Sullivan show.

Fests: Monterey, '68 w. Third Wave; Monterey, '69, Newport, '70, w. Ponty; Newport, '71, Berlin, '72 w. Adderley. Comps: *Tzina*, a six scene, two act opera, which was his MA thesis; *Giant Child Within Us—Ego*; arr. album, *Here and Now* for Third Wave.

Duke is a musician of rare versatility. In addition to developing a compelling jazz style, he has worked with equal success in the worlds of pop, rock, Latin and avant garde music. He names Ravel, Stravinsky, Stockhausen, Herbie Hancock, Ahmad Jamal, Miles Davis, L. McCann and Zappa among his sources of inspiration.

LPs: *Faces in Reflection; Feel; The Aura Will Prevail; I Love The Blues; She Heard My Cry* (BASF); *Jean-Luc Ponty Experience*, with Geo. Duke Trio (Liberty); w. Cobham, *Crosswinds*; w. Stanley Clarke, *Journey To Love* (Atl.); w. Eddie Henderson, *Sunburst* (BN); w. Adderley (Cap., Fantasy); w. Airto, *Virgin Land* (CTI); w. Flora Purim, *Butterfly Dreams; Stories To Tell* (Milestone); w. Zappa (Discreet).

DUKE, KENO, *drums*; b. St. Michaels, Barbados, W.I., 8/24/27. Stud. under Prof. C.B. Cooding-Edgehill in marching band on Barbados, '38; w. Prof. Auskist at Red Hook Music Centre, Brooklyn, N.Y., '40-2; at U.S. Navy Music Annex, Balboa, Canal Zone, '46-8. Pl. w. U.S. Navy Band in Panama; Atlantic Submarine Fleet Band; Navy Band, Portsmouth, N.H.; then worked w. Bunny Richardson in Boston and New Hampshire area, '56-8. Was member of Joe Gordine big band, along w. J. Richardson, Thad Jones, Willie Bobo, Eddie Jones in NYC area, '58-9. Worked at Keynote Music Club, Brooklyn, w. Sonny Red, B. Timmons, Paul West, '60-1; Needle's Eye, NYC, w. Joe Carroll, Johnny Hartman, '73. Formed the Contemporaries in '70 for a series of Sundays at the Village Vanguard. They have since performed at Amherst, Holyoke and Wm. Patterson State colleges and for the Jazzmobile. The front line has incl., at various times, Clifford Jordan, Julius Watkins, F. Strozier, Junior Cook and George Coleman. Duke, who was a disc jockey for Armed Forces radio, has his own record show on WHBI in NYC and is a faculty member of the Henry St. Settlement House Music School. Infl: Sid Catlett, Max Roach, Philly Joe Jones. TV: *Jazz Set* on PBS w. Contemporaries, '72. Comp: *3 MB; Sense of Values; Bajan-Bajan; Little "D"; Nschi I; Crest of the Wave.* LPs: *Reasons in Tonality; Sense of Values* (Strata-East).

DUNBAR, EARL THEODORE (TED), *guitar, composer;* also *trumpet, valve trombone;* b. Port Arthur, Tex., 1/17/37. Orig. self-taught. Pl. in Lincoln High marching and dance bands and was student dir. of latter. From '55-9 pl. trumpet & guitar in Texas Southern U. concert and jazz bands. Grad. in '59 with pharmacy degree and is licensed in Tex., Ind. & N.Y. Stud. Lydian Concept w. David Baker in Indianapolis, '63. Worked w. Arnett Cobb in Houston, '56-8; Joe Turner, '58; Don Wilkerson, '57-59; David Baker Ensemb., '61-3; subbed for Wes Montgomery for four mos. in his trio, '62-3; Ret. to Tex. from Ind. in '64, working w. Red Garland, Fathead Newman, Billy Harper, James Clay in Dallas, '64-5. Moved to NYC '66. Pl. w. Broadway pit bands for *Big Time Buck White; To Live Another Summer;* w. N.Y. Shakespeare Fest.: *Two Gentlemen of Verona; Sambo.* From 1968 has done school concerts w. Andrew Frierson; Billy Mitchell; Seldon Powell's Orch. Da Camera; Jazzmobile w. Billy Taylor, Jimmy Heath, McCoy Tyner. Worked w. Ron Jefferson Choir, '69-70; Larry Ridley '70; Gil Evans, '70-3; Tony Williams Lifetime, '71-2; Sonny Rollins; Newport Jazz Ens. w. G. Wein; trio w. Ron Carter, Ben Riley, '73; Grady Tate '73, 74; Billy Harper Sextet; Joe Newman Quartet, '74-5; Roy Haynes; F. Wess, '74; F. Foster big band & combo, '73-5; duo w. Richard Davis, '75. Member of the N.Y. Jazz Rep. Co. and also perf. w. Nat. Jazz Ens. Pl. school concerts on the islands of St. Thomas, St. John & St. Croix w. Harold Ousley for West Indian Gov. Cultural Program. Film: rec. soundtrack for *Fortune and Men's Eyes;* Japanese movie w. G. Evans. TV: staff member for Leon Bibb Show, NBC; apps. on *Soul; Positively Black; Like It Is; Black Journal.* Euro. perfs. w. T. Williams. Fests: NJF w. Bill Cosby; NJF-NY Radio City Jam Session, '72; NJF West (LA & Oak.), NJF-NY w. Gil Evans, '73. Infls: Wes Montgomery, T-Bone Walker, B.B. King, Ellington, M. Davis, T. Monk, Clifford Brown, George Russell, D. Baker, Tony Williams, H. Silver, Oscar McNeil (high school bandmaster). Comps: *Two Areas; You Say You Saw What; Hang In There; A New Machine for Pedro; Oh I'm Just Heah; Mrs. Frankenstein You're Hurt; Turn-back I'm Scared; Tonal Search.*

Dunbar has been able to combine his strong Texas blues background with his further studies in a style that contains the strengths of both. He is an assistant professor of Music at Livingston Coll. of Rutgers U. in New Brunswick, N.J.; staff guitar instructor for Jazzmobile &

Jazz Interaction workshops; and has taught at seminars, music camps and Nat. Band Camp (DeKalb, Ill.). Publs: *A System of Tonal Convergence for Improvisers, Arrangers & Composers; Jazz Guitar By Ted Dunbar* (Dunte Pub. Co., 6 Lake Ave. #5B, East Brunswick, N.J. 08816).

LPs: *Svengali* w. G. Evans; *House of David* w. David Newman (Atl.); *Peruvian Blue* w. Kenny Barron; *The Return of Don Patterson; Kwanza* w. Al Heath (Muse); also w. T. Williams (Polydor); Charles McPherson; Charles Williams; Curtis Fuller (Mainstream); McCoy Tyner; Lou Donaldson (Blue Note).

DUNCAN, HENRY (HANK),* piano; b. Bowling Green, Ky., 10/26/96. Featured as solo pianist at Nick's in Greenwich Village for most of the club's final decade (through 1963), Duncan was a pioneer of stride piano. After a long illness he died in NYC 6/7/68.

DUNLOP, FRANCIS (FRANKIE),* *drums, singer;* b. Buffalo, N.Y., 12/6/28. After serving as Thelonious Monk's drummer for much of the early '60s, he pl. w. Sonny Rollins '66-7; free-lanced around NYC incl. subbing in pit bands for Broadway shows *The Me Nobody Knows* and *Promises, Promises,* '67-9; own groups and sub drummer w. *Purlie,* '69-70. App. w. own jazz pantomime and mimicry act in NYC, LA and Santa Monica, '70-1; pl. Broadway show *Inner City* '71-3; toured w. Earl Hines '73-4; worked w. various groups at resort hotels in Catskill and Pocono Mts., '74-5. LPs: *Alfie* w. Rollins (Impulse); also w. Monk (Columbia); Richard Davis (Muse, Polydor); Leo Wright (Vortex).

DURHAM, EDDIE,* *composer, guitar, trombone;* b. San Marcos, Tex., 8/19/06. Played and arr. for J. Lunceford; C. Basie in '30s. Led own bands and cont. writing for other gps. as well in '50s-60s. Pl. trombone and guitar w. B. Tate band '69. In mid '70s co-leading a small group w. trumpeter Franc Williams two nights a week at West End Cafe, NYC, concentrating more on trombone than previously. LP: w. *Swing Today* series (Brit. RCA).

DUTCH SWING COLLEGE BAND. This popular Holland-based group was founded in 1945, w. Peter Schilperoort as leader and clarinetist. The group has app. at innumerable fests., the first of which took place in '48 in Knokke, Belgium. Toured England, '49. Many international travels w. leading Amer. musicians as feat. attraction, incl. S. Bechet, '49-50, '53-4; Hot Lips Page, '51; Albert Nicholas, '54. Schilperoort left the band in Sept. '55; his place as clarinetist was taken by Jan Morks, and the band's pianist, Joop Schrier, became the leader. Schilperoort returned and again assumed musical leadership in '59. The band's personnel in the early '60s incl. Oscar Klein, trumpet; Dick Kaart, trombone, et al. In later years J. Witherspoon, J. Venuti, Teddy Wilson and Billy Butterfield were among the many U.S. stars to tour with the band, which cont. to enjoy popularity throughout Western Europe in traditionalist-oriented circles. Many LPs on Dutch Philips.

DUVIVIER, GEORGE B.,* *bass, composer;* b. New York City, 8/17/20. Played w. C. Hawkins; L. Millinder; J.

Lunceford; Sy Oliver in '40s. Backed many singers in '50s, mainly Lena Horne w. whom he made several European trips. Also pl. in NYC w. Bud Powell; T. Gibbs. His credits are so extensive that they are impossible to list. He has traveled and/or rec. w. more than 80 singers from Kate Smith to Sinatra; over 65 instrumentalists, rec. on every major label. Rec. sound tracks for such films as *Requiem For a Heavyweight; Serpico; Experiment in Terror; The Godfather.* Rec. jingles for more than 80 separate commercial products, app. in a "I'd Rather Fight Than Switch" commercial complete w. black eye.

Apps. w. Boston Pops; Brooklyn Philharmonia; NY Phil.; Chicago and Phila. Orchs; Cleveland and Rochester Orchs.

Duvivier says: "For good measure see if this 'one-nighter' can be topped for distance—Los Angeles to Monaco to Los Angeles for a command performance."

TV: three yrs. on staff w. B. Rosengarden orch. for Dick Cavett Show, ABC, in '70s; on call for *Today; Tonight*, NBC; *Ed Sullivan; Camera 3*, CBS. Fest: NJF; NJF-NY; Colo. JP.

Although occupied, for the most part, with studio work, Duvivier, in his jazz apps. and recs., shows all the attributes of a master bassist in time, tone and feeling.

LPs: w. Barry Harris, *Vicissitudes* (MPS); w. C. Terry, *It's What's Happenin'* (Imp.); w. Joe Venuti-Zoot Sims (Chiaro.); *Soprano Summit* w. Wilber-Davern (World Jazz).

EARLAND, CHARLES, *organ, composer*; also *soprano sax*; b. Philadelphia, Pa., 5/24/41. Schoolmates were Pat Martino, Lew Tabackin. Early mus. training on alto sax. Pl. tenor sax w. Jimmy McGriff at age 17. Several yrs. later led own band. Made switch to organ in '63 and led own quartet. Pl. w. Lou Donaldson, '68-Dec. '69. Formed trio and rec. *Black Talk* LP which became a hit and enabled him to start touring US in mid-'70. Began doubling on soprano sax, '73. Pl. at NJF-NY, '73-4. Comps: *Black Talk*, incl. in soundtrack of film *Fritz the Cat; Auburn Delight; Cause I Love Her; Never Ending Melody; Asteroid; Brown Eyes; Morgan; Tyner; Van Jay.* Bob Porter wrote that "Earland's style reveals perhaps the best walking-bass line among organists and a unique second type of bass line that creates a rolling, long-meter feeling on rock tunes."

LPs: *Leaving This Planet; Charles the III; Live at the Lighthouse; Intensity; Black Drops; Black Talk; Soul Story* (Prestige); w. Donaldson, *Say It Loud; Hot Dog; Everything I Play is Funky* (Blue Note).

ECKSTINE, WILLIAM CLARENCE (BILLY),* *singer, trumpet, valve trombone, guitar*; b. Pittsburgh, Pa., 7/8/14. Sang w. E. Hines band '39-43. Led own orch. feat. Gillespie, Parker, Blakey, Miles Davis et al, '44-7.

Popular since late '40s as single, but has often teamed up with name bands. Was host of monthly TV series, *The Jazz Show*, in LA '71 and part of '72. Toured Europe w. G. Wein package feat. tribute to Ch. Parker, late '74. Though primarily known as a ballad singer, he has had many jazz associations and is a competent instrumentalist. Pl. role in movie, *Let's Do It Again*, w. Bill Cosby, 1975.

LPs: *Feel The Warm; If She Walked Into My Life* (Enterprise); *My Way; The Prime of My Life* (Motown); *The Legendary Big Band of Billy Eckstine—Together* (Spotlite); *The Soul Sessions, Vol. 6, Newport In New York, '72* (Cobblestone).

EDISON, HARRY (SWEETS),* *trumpet*; b. Columbus, Ohio, 10/10/15. Best known as an alumnus of the Count Basie band (1937-50), Edison in the '60s and early '70s continued to work in many orchestras on TV shows, incl. *Hollywood Palace, Leslie Uggams Show*, specials w. Frank Sinatra etc. He was prominently feat. on the sound track, and in the sound track album, of the film *Lady Sings The Blues.* He continued to play clubs and concerts in the U.S., sometimes leading his own combos, also playing with the bands of L. Bellson, Bill Berry and others. He occasionally rejoined Basie, and was a member of the Swing Masters band led by Benny Carter at Carnegie Hall for NJF-NY, '72.

From '73 Edison frequently acted as Mus. Dir. for Redd Foxx on theatre dates, at concerts and in LV. In '74-5 he was heard in concerts w. Maria Muldaur and the Benny Carter orch. He also pl. in a small group w. Carter in Copenhagen in '75. Edison app. at the Berlin JF, Concord Summer Fest. etc.

LPs: *Home With Sweets* (Vee Jay); duo album w. O. Peterson; *The Trumpet Kings Meet Joe Turner* (Pablo); w. Herb Ellis, Ray Brown (Concord Jazz); *Lady Sings The Blues* (Motown); many others w. Sinatra (Repr.); *Colo. Jazz Party* (MPS/BASF).

EDWARDS, THEODORE MARCUS (TEDDY),* *tenor sax, composer*; b. Jackson, Miss., 4/26/24. In Southern Cal. from late '40s, pl. w. Gerald Wilson off and on from '49 into '70s; w. Max Roach, B. Carter, L. Vinnegar in '50s; S. Manne, B. Goodman, many others in '60s. Comp. & arr. for Lorez Alexandria LP on now-defunct Pzazz label. Activity in late '60s and early '70s chiefly involved with artists named below in LP list. Edwards remained a respected, personal soloist "whose work is particularly identifiable by its deeply plunging pulsation and emotional engagement." (Nat Hentoff).

Film and soundtrack for *They Shoot Horses, Don't They?*; soundtrack for *Any Wednesday.* Concerts at Pilgrimage Th., Hollywood, 1972-3 w. M. Jackson-Ray Brown, and '74 w. own quintet. Concord Fest. '73 w. Jackson-Brown; '74 w. Bill Berry.

LPs: Reissues of own 1947 sessions on *The Foremost!* and *Central Ave. Breakdown* (Onyx); 1960-61 sessions, *Together Again!* w. H. McGhee, *Teddy's Ready!, Good Gravy* (Contemp.). Others as leader: *It's All Right* (Prestige); *Feelin's* (Muse). As sideman: *Hello Benny* w.

Goodman (Cap.); *Bluesmith* w. J. Smith (Verve); M. Jackson-R. Brown (Impulse); *Memphis Jackson* w. M. Jackson (Impulse); Sarah Vaughan w. J. Rowles Quintet (Mainstream); Bill Berry (Beez); several w. G. Wilson (Pac. Jazz, World-Pac.).

ELDRIDGE, DAVID ROY (LITTLE JAZZ),* *trumpet, fluegelhorn, singer, leader*; b. Pittsburgh, Pa., 1/30/11. The former Teddy Hill, Fletcher Henderson, Gene Krupa and Artie Shaw star, after working with Coleman Hawkins; Ella Fitzgerald; and his own quintet in first half of the '60s, joined Count Basie in July '66. He left in September to reform his quintet feat. tenor man Richie Kamuca. They pl. together, off and on, to '70 incl. stints at the Half Note, NYC. Eldridge took over as house leader at Jimmy Ryans in '70 and has appeared there from that time. During the late '60s and in the '70s, however, he has continued to tour as a single and with various packages to Europe such as *Jazz From a Swinging Era*, '67; JATP and other Norman Granz tours in the '70s. Fest: MJF, '71; NJF-NY '73 in *Salute to Ella Fitzgerald*, and w. own gp. at dedication of Louis Armstrong Stadium; MJF '74; Montreux '75 w. D. Gillespie, C. Terry. TV: NJF-NY '73, NET; *Just Jazz*, PBS, '71; episode on *Route '66* w. Ethel Waters, Jo Jones, C. Hawkins. "He still has a gladiatorial view of performance," wrote Benny Green in his notes to one of Eldridge's albums, "the professional's fierce pride in his own ability . . . Roy is one of those players whose transcribed solos would never give more than half an indication of their effect, for they are built on the broad rich tone and the characteristic phrasing."

Won DB Critics Poll, TDWR; elected to DB Hall of Fame, '71.

LPs: *Nifty Cat; Nifty Cat Strikes West* (Master Jazz); *Oscar Peterson & Roy Eldridge; Happy Time; The Trumpet Kings at the Montreux Jazz Festival 1975; Trumpet Kings Meet Joe Turner; Jazz at the Philharmonic at the Montreux Jazz Festival 1975* (Pablo); w. *Buddy Tate & His Buddies* (Chiaro.); Ella Fitzgerald, *Newport Jazz Festival 1973* (Col.); *Earl Hines and Roy Eldridge at the Village Vanguard* (Xanadu); w. Miriam Klein (MPS).

ELLINGTON, EDWARD KENNEDY (DUKE),* *composer, leader, piano, lyricist*; b. Washington, D.C., 4/29/1899. Though he led various combos in Washington while still in his teens, Ellington's career as a leader really got under way in New York, late in 1923, when he took over from Elmer Snowden as director of The Washingtonians. This five man group gradually enlarged until, by 1927, when it opened at the Cotton Club in Harlem, the band was ten strong. For the next 15 years Ellington enjoyed growing successes in many areas, but his work in the U.S. (except for a single concert in 1932 at Columbia U.) was confined entirely to night clubs, vaudeville theatres, dance halls and an occasional movie.

During his first European tours in 1933 and 1939, however, Ellington was recognized as a composer and artist of concert stature. In 1943 he began a series of annual concerts in Carnegie Hall, premiering *Black, Brown &* *Beige*, the first of many extended works written especially for the concert hall.

Notable events in the 1950s were the premiere of *Night Creature* at Carnegie Hall, for which Ellington played with the Symphony of the Air; a triumphant appearance at the 1956 Newport Jazz Festival; his own color TV special, *A Drum Is A Woman*, on CBS in 1957; and the composing and recording, with the orchestra, of his first film score, *Anatomy of a Murder*.

The 1960s found Ellington visiting Europe annually. He became more active as a lyricist, and as writer of words and music of Sacred Concerts, the first of which was performed in 1965 at Grace Cathedral in SF. This work was heard the following year at Coventry Cathedral. Also in 1966 Ellington was the centerpiece in specials for National Educational Television. The band represented the U.S. at the World Festival of Negro Arts in Dakar. In 1967 Billy Strayhorn, Duke's close writing associate since 1939, died; in his memory, the orchestra recorded an album of Strayhorn's compositions, *And His Mother Called Him Bill*, which some critics believe to have been the band's greatest album during the final decade of Ellington's life.

Another superb LP was taped during a Jan. 1968 performance at Yale U. A second Sacred Concert program, with Alice Babs as principal vocal soloist, was introduced later that year at the Cathedral of St. John the Divine. In September, the band toured Latin America and Mexico.

On Ellington's 70th birthday, Apr. 29, 1969, he was the guest of honor at a banquet, dance and jam session held at the White House. President Nixon awarded Ellington the Presidential Medal of Freedom. The band did not take part, but an all-star group gave a recital of Duke's music, after which many jazz celebrities played or sang.

On New Year's day, 1970, the orchestra began a tour of Australia, Southeast Asia and Japan. To celebrate this precedent-setting visit, Ellington composed the *Far East Suite* (rec. on RCA). In July the band returned to Europe. Saxophonist Johnny Hodges, the most famous of Ellington's musicians, died in November.

Ellington was honored in 1971 as a newly elected member of the Swedish Academy of Music. At Newport, in July, he premiered his Africa-inspired suite *Togo Brava*. In Sept. the orchestra left on a triumphant five-week tour of the Soviet Union.

During the first six weeks of 1972, Duke undertook a second Oriental tour. Concerts were given in Japan, Manila, Hong Kong, Bangkok, Mandalay, Ceylon, Kuala Lumpur, Singapore as well as Australia. Toward the end of that year Ellington went to Los Angeles for the taping of a TV special entitled *Duke Ellington—We Love You Madly*. Ellington's band was not used; however, the orchestra assembled by Quincy Jones included several notable former Ellington sidemen.

Immediately after the taping, Ellington was hospitalized, but soon afterward he was on the road again. He visited Paris alone for a TV special; finished work on his Third Sacred Concert, and introduced it at Westminster

Abbey in Oct. of 1973. Also during that year Ellington was awarded the French Legion of Honor.

Early in 1974 Ellington's health showed signs of deterioration, and he was obliged to let the band travel without him during most of the month of January. He rejoined his musicians off and on during February and March. Hospitalized again in New York, he promised that his band would honor a commitment to play in Bermuda toward the end of May. He spent his 75th birthday in a hospital bed. During the next few weeks his condition became desperate, and in the early hours of Friday May 24, he died, a victim of pneumonia and primarily of lung cancer.

On Monday, May 27, memorial services were held at the Cathedral of St. John the Divine. The next day, under the leadership of Mercer Ellington, the band flew to Bermuda to fulfill the promise he had made. During the next year the orchestra reestablished itself under the direction of Duke's son (see ELLINGTON, MERCER).

Of the many tributes and events dedicated to Ellington's memory, one of the most significant was the formulation of plans for a Duke Ellington Center in New York City.

Publs: *The World of Duke Ellington*, by Stanley Dance (Chas. Scribner's Sons, 1970); *Music Is My Mistress*, By Duke Ellington (Doubleday & Co., 1973).

Comps: A virtually complete list of Ellington's works, listed chronologically in order of their copyright dates, appears in *Music Is My Mistress*. Among his later extended works were *La Plus Belle Africaine*, '67; *The Second Sacred Concert*, '68; *Latin-American Suite*, '68-9; *The River* (ballet), '70; *New Orleans Suite*, '71; *Afro-Eurasian Eclipse*, '71; *Togo Brava Suite*, '73; *Third Sacred Concert*, '73.

LPs: The following were listed in U.S. catalogues as available in late 1975: *Black Brown & Beige*, w. Mahalia Jackson (CSP); *Collages*, Ellington w. Ron Collier Orch. rec. in Canada (BASF); *Duke's Big 4*, w. Joe Pass, Ray Brown, L. Bellson; *This One's For Blanton*, duos w. Ray Brown; *The Greatest Jazz Concert In The World*, w. E. Fitzgerald et al (Pablo); *Echoes of an Era* w. Armstrong (Roulette); *Ellington at Newport; Ellington Indigos; First Time*, w. Basie; *Jazz at the Plaza*, Vol. II (Col.); *Ellington '65; Greatest Hits; Will Big Bands Come Back* (Repr.); *Ellingtonia-Reevaluations, The Impulse Years; Ellingtonia*, Vol. 2; *Meets Coleman Hawkins;* w. Coltrane (Imp.); *The Golden Duke; Second Sacred Concert* (Pres.); *Great Paris Concert; New Orleans Suite; Recollections of the Big Band Era* (Atl.); *It Don't Mean A Thing*, w. Teresa Brewer; *My People* (Fl. Dutchman); *Latin-American Suite; The Pianist; Yale Concert* (Fant.); *Nutcracker Suite/Peer Gynt* (Odyssey); *70th Birthday* (Solid State); *Togo Brava Suite; Money Jungle*, w. Ch. Mingus, M. Roach (UA); *Blues Summit*, w. J. Hodges (Verve); *Eastbourne Performance*, last live LP; *Third Sacred Concert* (RCA); *Continuum*, The Ellington Orchestra under the direction of Mercer Ellington (Fant.).

ELLINGTON, EDWARD II, *guitar*; b. New York City, 8/8/44. Grandson of Duke Ellington; son of Mercer Ellington. Sister, Mercedes, a dancer. Began as electrical engineer for RCA. Studied at Berklee Coll. of Music, May '72-May '74: guitar & arranging w. Mark French; theory w. Lennie Johnson. Joined Duke Ellington orch., '74. Infl: Bill Harris, Quincy Jones, Mundell Lowe, Kenny Burrell. TV: Mike Douglas Show w. Ellington band. LP: *Continuum* (Fantasy).

ELLINGTON, MERCER KENNEDY,* *leader, trumpet, composer*; also *saxophone*; b. Washington, D.C., 3/11/19. Own bands, off and on, from '39. Pl. w. father's orchestra briefly in '50. Rejoined the band in '65, after three years as dj on WLIB, NYC. Doubled as trumpeter-road manager until he assumed the leadership following Duke's death in May, '74. European tour, fall '74. TV: Super Bowl, NO, '74; Belmont Race Track; Mike Douglas Show, '75. Fest: Ravinia w. Sarah Vaughan, '74. Co-composer of *The Three Black Kings* w. father. Writing biographical work about Duke Ellington for Houghton Mifflin.

Mercer brought new, young players (incl. his son Edward (q.v.) into the band. He also sought to reactivate older Ellington material that had not been played for quite some time. Many of these pieces are included in the first recording under his aegis, *Continuum* (Fantasy). Two Coral albums of his late-'50s band have been reissued as a double LP, *Black & Tan Fantasy* (MCA).

ELLIOTT, DON (Don Elliott Helfman),* *composer, mellophone, vibes, trumpet*; b. Somerville, N.J., 10/21/26. Active in jazz chiefly in early '50s w. G. Shearing, T. Wilson, T. Gibbs, B. Goodman, B. Rich, and often with own quartet from '54. During '60s, found great success as comp. and prod. of thousands of national radio and TV commercials, also music for TV game shows and specials. Several of his commercials won awards. Also, won prize at Atlanta Film Fest. for documentary for U.S. Postal Service. The Don Elliott "Voices" (multi-voice overdubs) were used by Q. Jones for motion pic. sound tracks in *The Pawnbroker; $; Heat of the Night; The Hot Rock; The Getaway*. As many as 20 voices, all Elliott, were heard backing Roberta Flack in *Smiling*. Comp., scored and prod. soundtrack for film, *The Happy Hooker*; scores for shows, *Tobacco Road; The Opposite Sex*. Owns and operates two 16-track rec. studios. Made first personal app. in 15 years as guest soloist w. NYJRC's tribute to Q. Jones at Carnegie Hall, '75. Coll. concerts, gigs at Stryker's Pub, NYC, '75; also w. N.Y. Jazz Ensemble at Carnegie Hall, and w. G. Mulligan, Westport Country Playhouse, '74.

LPs: *The Don Elliott Ensemble* (Col.); *In The Heat of The Night*, w. Q. Jones (UA); *$*, w. Q. Jones (Repr.); sound track album of *The Happy Hooker*.

ELLIS, DONALD JOHNSON (DON),* *trumpet, drums, composer, leader*; b. Los Angeles, Ca., 7/25/34. After extensive experience as sideman (notably w. Maynard Ferguson, Geo. Russell) and academic work as both student and teacher, Ellis became semi-permanently active as a big band leader in '65, occasionally working with small groups. In the late '60s and early '70s the band achieved a measure of international popularity due to Ellis' many initiatives. He claims, generally with demonstrable justification, to have had the first big band involved in the following innovations: extensive use of odd time signatures; electric string quartet; vocal quartet used as instrumental section; rec. of extended solo using echoplex; use of quarter tones for solos, and for passages by entire trumpet section; fusion of Indian music in jazz; employment of Fender-Rhodes piano, clavinet, ring modulator and phaser etc.

Ellis played most of the major jazz fests. and clubs with his own band; led an all star orch. at the Berlin JF, '68. He has made more TV apps., with or without his band, than the vast majority of jazz artists. TV special, *Birth of a Band*, was built around his Berlin app. He also app. on a Concord, Cal. TV spec., '69; his band played all Ellis' own music for a Soupy Sales spec. Other TV apps. in Hollywood, Hamburg, Paris, Montreal, Antibes etc.

Teaching: theory, composition and trumpet in NYC and LA; courses in arranging etc. at UCLA; *Introduction to Jazz* at San Fernando Valley State Coll. Writer of several articles publ. in DB, '65-9. Commissions: *Synthesis* for S. Kenton's Neophonic Orch.; *Contrasts for Two Orchestras & Trumpet* for Zubin Mehta and the LA Phil.; *Bird of Paradise* for Charlie Byrd; *Reach*, a cantata for chorus and orch., for Berlin JF; *Mind Flowers*, a choral work for Willamette U. Movie Scores: *Moon Zero Two*, filmed in London, '69; *French Connection*, '72.

Based in LA, Ellis' career from '65-75 was extremely eventful, marked by sudden changes of policy, of instrumentation, musical concept and direction. As a consequence he had no single image or identifiable style; nevertheless, as an aggressive proselytizer for new musical developments, he established himself as an important figure and gained a substantial following, the only leader of a big band to do so other than Thad Jones and Mel Lewis with their orch. in NYC.

In the spring of '75 Ellis suffered a serious heart attack and after a long period of recuperation he began writing for various studios. By the end of the year he was playing the "superbone," a combination valve-slide trombone made originally for Maynard Ferguson.

Publs: Various—details obtainable from (Ellis Music Enterprises, 5436 Auckland Ave., N. Hollywood, Ca. 91601).

LPs: *Don Ellis Orchestra at Monterey; Live In 3 2/3/4* (Pacific Jazz); *Electric Bath; Shock Treatment; Autumn; The New Don Ellis Band Goes Underground; Don Ellis at Fillmore; Tears of Joy* (Col.); *Haiku; Soaring* (BASF); w. Geo. Russell, in *Encyclopedia of Jazz*, Vol. 5 (MCA).

ELLIS, MITCHELL HERBERT (HERB), *guitar, composer*; b. Farmersville, Texas, 8/4/21. Though principally involved in studio work in bands on Steve Allen, Joey

Bishop, Della Reese and other shows (more recently w. Merv Griffin), Ellis continued to play frequently in jazz settings. From '72-4 he pl. many concerts, night clubs and coll. seminars in a guitar duo w. Joe Pass. Later formed duo w. B. Kessel, touring Australia and app. at Playboy Club etc. Fests: four years at Concord Mus. Fest.; annual jazz parties at Colorado Springs and Odessa, Tex.

LPs: *Seven Come Eleven; Jazz Concord*, both w. Pass; *Rhythm Willie* w. Freddie Green (Concord Jazz); *Two For the Road*, w. Pass (Pablo); *Hello Herbie*, w. O. Peterson (MPS); *Soft Shoe*, w. Ray Brown; *After You've Gone; Great Guitars*, w. Kessel, Ch. Byrd (Concord); w. Bill Berry (Beez).

ELLIS, LLOYD, *guitar*; b. Pensacola, Fla., 1/25/20. Self-taught. Infl. by D. Reinhardt, C. Christian. Ellis remained unknown in jazz circles until he moved to Las Vegas in '70, when he spent two years with the Red Norvo Trio at the Tropicana Hotel, and came to the attention of many local and visiting musicians. Among them was B.B. King, who in an interview selected Ellis as one of his ten favorite guitarists. Ellis had previously worked w. Stuff Smith, and was a member of Charlie Teagarden's combo in the '60s. Own LP and LP w. Norvo (Famous Door); also *Fastest Guitar In The World* (Carlton); *So Tall, So Cool, So There* (Trey).

ELMAN, ZIGGY,* *trumpet*; b. Philadelphia, Pa., 5/26/14. The swing era trumpeter, best known for his 1936-40 tenure in the Benny Goodman orchestra, where his big hit was *And the Angels Sing*, was inactive in music during the last few years of his life. He died in Van Nuys, Calif., 6/26/68.

ERRISSON, KING (Errisson Pallman Johnson), *percussion*; b. Nassau, Bahamas, 10/29/41. Self-taught, later stud. w. M. Mahoney in LV, Chuck Flores in LA. Pro. debut at 14; during his teens also he was a pro. jockey. After pl. for three years at the Conchshell, leading Nassau night club, Errisson was discovered by a film producer, who feat. him in the James Bond thriller, *Thunderball*. His talent was also observed by Diana Ross, with whom he traveled in the U.S., pl. at Waldorf-Astoria and Basin St. in NYC, Frontier Club in LV etc. Settling in LA in late '60s, he found himself in constant demand by a wide range of artists. Quincy Jones, for whom he rec. several albums, observed: "Errisson has a fantastic sense of time and dynamics. He is one of the greatest artists in his field." Frequently using five conga drums, Errisson is an exceptional performer on congas, bongoes and all percussion. As composer, he wrote the song *Darling Come Back Home*, a hit for Eddie Kendricks. Many TV shows in Japan, also own educ. spec. in U.S. '74.

LPs: *The King Arrives* (Canyon); *Life* (UA); *Drums of Nassau* (Bohemian); others w. D. Byrd, *Blackbyrd; Street Lady* (BN); w. H. Alpert (A & M); w. O.C. Smith (Col.); w. Jerome Richardson (RCA); Percy Faith; The Fifth Dimension (Bell); Chas. Kynard (Mainstr.); Groove Holmes (Liberty); Lou Rawls (Cap.); Clara Ward (Cap.);

also many on the Motown label, with various artists.

ERSKINE, PETER, *drums*; b. Somers Point, N.J., 6/5/54. Father an ex-bassist, now a psychiatrist. Attended S. Kenton National Stage Band Camps at age six; continued for several summers, stud. w. Alan Dawson, Dee Barton. Extensive other studies, incl. Interlochen Arts Acad., Indiana U., after which he joined Stan Kenton orch. July 1972, touring U.S., Europe, Japan, teaching at Kenton Clinics. Favs: Elvin Jones, Mel Lewis, Billy Cobham, Grady Tate; infl. Kenton.

LPs w. Kenton (Creative World).

ERVIN, BOOKER TELLEFERRO JR.,* *tenor saxophone, composer*; b. Denison, Tex., 10/31/30. Prominent in NYC w. Ch. Mingus, '58-62. Worked in Europe '64-6, and again in '68; intermittently leading own groups in U.S. On 7/31/70 Ervin died in a NYC hospital of a kidney ailment. He was saluted by fellow musicians for his powerful, typically Texan sound on tenor sax projected into the '60s, and for his superb mastery of both blues and ballads.

Comps: *Mojo; Boo; Uranus; Largo; A Lunar Tune; A Day to Mourn; No Booze Blooze; Eerie Dearie; Number Two; The Trance; Boo's Blues; Groovin' at the Jamboree; East Dallas Special; Exultation; Mooche Mooche; Tune In; Mour; The In Between; The Muse; Sweet Pea; Tyra.*

LPs: *Lament For Booker Ervin* (Enja); *Heavy; The Trance* (Prest.); *The In Between* (BN); *Structurally Sound* (Pac. Jazz); *Booker and Brass* (Liberty); reissue. *That's Right* (Barnaby); w. Eric Kloss, *Land of the Giants* (Prest.); w. R. Weston, *African Cookbook* (Atl.); reissues w. Mingus on Atl., Col., Trip.

ERWIN, GEORGE (PEE WEE),* *trumpet*; b. Falls City, Neb., 5/30/13. Swing era stylist best known for his work w. B. Goodman, T. Dorsey. After '60, on staff at CBS in NYC, along with extensive jazz concert work incl. two tours of Scandinavia, Germany and Britain w. Kings of Jazz, '74. In '67, he produced "Jazz: The Personal Dimension" for Rutgers U. at Carnegie Recital Hall. Other apps. at Dick Gibson and Odessa jazz parties; Kansas City JF; NYJRC; Jazztage, Hanover, '74; Nice, '75. Publs: *Pee Wee Erwin Teaches Trumpet* (Charles Colin Pub. Co., 315 W. 53 St., New York, NY 10019); *A Wee Bit Of Dixie*—duets (Award Music Co., 136 W. 46 St., New York, NY 10036).

LPs: *The Music of Jelly Roll Morton,* w. D. Hyman (Col.); *Satchmo Remembered* w. NYJRC (Atl.); *Happy Times Orchestra,* w. Bob Thiele (Fl. Dutchman); six albums in *Music For Lovers Only* series, w. Jackie Gleason (Cap.)

EVANS, WILLIAM JOHN (BILL),* *piano, composer*; b. Plainfield, N.J., 8/16/29. Continuing as leader of his own trio, which he formed in '56, for recordings (he also toured for eight months in '58 with Miles Davis Quartet), Evans traveled throughout the U.S., S. America, Japan and Europe with the same instrumentation, using Eddie Gomez on bass, '66- , Marty Morell on drums for six years (other drummers were Joe Hunt, Philly Joe Jones

and, after Morell's departure, Eliot Zigmund). Evans continued to win many awards, among them five Grammies: one in '63 for *Conversations With Myself*; a second in '68 for *Live at Montreux*; a third in '70 for *Alone*; and two more in '71 for *The Bill Evans Album*, which won both as Best Jazz Performance by a Soloist, and Best Jazz Performance by a Group. He won *Playboy's* All Stars' All Stars on piano for two years and innumerable DB readers' and critics' polls.

TV: *Camera Three; Jazz Adventures; Jazz Set*; a program for PBS; and countless European TV shows. He app. at Monterey, Newport and all major European jazz festivals. Publs: three books of originals and transcriptions of solos (The Richmond Org., 10 Columbus Circle, New York, N.Y. 10019).

Joseph McClellan in the Washington *Post* wrote that "Evans is one of the great virtuosos in jazz today, and in the contemporary style his real virtuosity is not in his hands (that is taken for granted) but in the mind that works constantly to make each performance a new creation, each rehandling of a motif a new vision."

Comp: *T.T.T (Twelve Tone Tune); T.T.T.T. (Twelve Tone Tune Two); In Memory of His Father, Harry L. Evans; Peri's Scope; Very Early; 34 Skidoo; Comrade Conrad; Funkallero; Waltz For Debby; Re: Person I Knew; One For Helen; Two Lonely People.* LPs: *The Tony Bennett/Bill Evans Album; Intuition; The Tokyo Concert* (Fant.); *The Bill Evans Album; Living Time* w. George Russell (Col.); *Bill Evans at Town Hall; Live at Montreux; Montreux II; What's New; Alone; Further Conversations With Myself; Stan Getz and Bill Evans; Simple Matter* (Verve); *From Left to Right* (MGM); *Symbiosis* (BASF); reissues, *Peace Piece and Other Pieces; The Village Vanguard Sessions* (Mile.).

EVANS, GIL (Ian Ernest Gilmore Green),* *composer, piano*; b. Toronto, Canada, 5/13/12. First renowned through his arrangements for the Claude Thornhill orch. in the 1940s. He was then associated w. Miles Davis' nine-piece outfit that was dubbed the *Birth of the Cool* band in '49-50. He then went on to a series of brilliant collaborations w. Davis in the '57-60 period and became active with his own band for in-person performances and recording in '59-60. In '66 Evans visited Cal., where he appeared at the Monterey and Pacific JF, Shelly's Manne Hole and in concert at Royce Hall, UCLA. In '68 was presented in concert at the Whitney Museum, NYC; w. Davis at the Greek Theatre, U. of Cal., Berkeley.

Occupied principally with writing during the late '60s, Evans formed an ensemble for recording in '69 and began weekly performances at the Village Vanguard the following year. In '71 this group, which had now grown into an orch., toured Europe appearing in Holland, Copenhagen at Club Montmartre, and on radio and TV in Denmark, Sweden and West Germany. Evans conducted an evening of his own compositions at the Berlin Jazztage. In the summer of '72, the orchestra played weekend concerts at the Westbeth Cabaret, located in Westbeth, an artistic community where Evans lives, in lower Manhattan. The orch. also app. at the Long Island JF, Henry St. Settlement House, Slug's Cafe, and received funding from CAPS.

Evans was named a founding artist of the John F. Kennedy Center for the Performing Arts, taking part in a concert and broadcast there. He also toured Japan with his orch., '72. He made periodic apps. w. orch. at Village Vanguard, '73-5. As one of the musical directors of the NYJRC in its initial season, Evans participated in three programs under its auspices with his orch.: *Jazz In The Rock Age; Gil Evans Retrospective; The Music of Jimi Hendrix.* A European tour incl. Denmark, Sweden, Switzerland, Germany, July '74.

Film scores: D. Nogata's *Fragments*, '67; A. Gittler's *Parachute To Paradise*, '69; O. Lee's *The Sea In Your Future*, '70. TV/Radio: Cond. and arr. TV and radio broadcasts w. Swedish Radio Orch., '73; concert-broadcasts from Village Gate, Town Hall, '74; hour concert at Brooklyn Coll. for WNYC-TV, spring '75.

Fests: NJF-NY-SF-LA, '73; Montreux; Antibes; Umbria, '74; Yale-New Haven, Conn., '75. Awards: Guggenheim Fellowship in Composition, '68; N.Y. State Council on the Arts Composer Commission, '74; won DB Readers' and Critics' polls as arranger, '66, '74; band won DB Critics poll TDWR, '73-4. Comps: *Las Vegas Tango; Flute Song; El Toreador; Isabel; Barracuda; Proclamation; Variations on the Misery; Anita's Dance; Spaced; So Long; Makes Her Move; Zee Zee.* With M. Davis: *Hotel Me; General Assembly; Eleven.*

By utilizing electric piano, bass and guitar along with synthesizers and various percussion instruments, French horn, tuba and flute, while retaining the more conventional reeds and brasses of the jazz ensemble, Evans achieved, according to Gary Giddins, "a cohesive marriage of his own musical personality with the most compelling results of the jazz and rock revolutions of the past decade."

LPs: *There Comes a Time; Music of Jimi Hendrix* (RCA); *Svengali* (Atl.); *Gil Evans* (Ampex); *Gil Evans Orchestra, Kenny Burrell and Phil Woods*, previously unreleased material from '63-4 (Verve); *Arranger's Touch*, previously issued as *Big Stuff* (Pres.).

EVANS, MARGIE, *singer*; b. Shreveport, La., 7/17/41. Stud. voice, piano and guitar w. several teachers. Infl. by Willie Dixon, Johnny Otis, Donald Byrd, Big Joe Turner, Eddie Vinson, T-Bone Walker, Lowell Fulson, Mahalia Jackson. App. in high school production, but during adolescence sang mainly in church. Moved to LA, '58; began recording '63 and achieved her first measure of prominence on joining Otis, with whom she toured intermittently '69-72. Various jobs in '70s; in concert w. W. Dixon, Freddie King, Papa John Creach, Mike Bloomfield, Lowell Fulson, Canned Heat. An exceptionally capable blues shouter in the Bessie Smith tradition. Fests: Monterey, '71, w. Otis.

LPs: *Louisiana Woman* (UA); *Cuttin' Up*, w. Otis (Epic); *Stepping Into Tomorrow*, w. Byrd (BN).

EVANS, SUE, *percussion*; b. New York City, 7/7/51. Not related to Gil Evans, but worked with him often from 1969-75. Perc. & dr. study w. Warren Smith, Morris Lang, Montego Joe in '60s; Sonny Igoe '71-2. Drums w. Judy Collins in US and Europe, 1968-72; perc. w. Steve Kuhn Quartet, midwest, '72-4; Jazz Composers' Orch.; also worked w. Coleridge Perkinson, rec. w. James Brown, Bobby Jones, D. Amram, Roswell Rudd, Billy Cobham, Blood Sweat & Tears and pl. in several off-Broadway shows.

Favs: Tony Williams, Elvin Jones, Max Roach, Airto, Billy Higgins; also Gil Evans, Ornette Coleman. Ms. Evans described herself in 1975 as a percussionist equipped for every setting, from pop, classical and jazz to r & b and free music.

LPs w. Gil Evans (Ampex, Atlantic, RCA); S. Kuhn (ECM); Bobby Jones (Cobblestone).

FADDIS, JON, *trumpet, fluegelhorn, piccolo trumpet*; also *piano*; b. Oakland, Calif., 7/24/53. One sister sings; other is a pianist. Began on trumpet at age eight w. private teacher and in grammar school but didn't really show great interest until 11 or 12. At 15 stud. w. Bill Catalano who introduced him to the music of Dizzy Gillespie. Later studied w. Carmine Caruso; at Manhattan Sch. of Mus. w. Mel Broiles, '72-3. Piano, harmony, theory w. Sanford Gold, '75.

Experience w. r & b bands at age 13 in Oakland. Then Catalano took him to SF to sit in w. rehearsal bands of Rudy Salvini; Cus Cousineau; Don Piestrup. Grad. high school '71 and joined Lionel Hampton for six mos. from that summer. To NYC w. Hampton where he then became a member of Thad Jones-Mel Lewis from Feb. '72-Sept. '75, incl. Russian tour. During this time also worked w. Gil Evans, '72; C. Mingus, concert '72; European tour, summer '73. Concerts w. Chuck Mangione from '72. Pl. w. D. Gillespie gp. at Vanguard; Half Note, '74; big band at Buddy's Place, '75. Won TDWR, DB Critics poll, '74-5. Gillespie's "musical son," Faddis, with his great range and fire, is one of the most promising of the young crop of musicians to come to light in the '70s. As he moved toward a more personal expression his potential seemed vast.

Infl: Gillespie, C. Parker, Snooky Young, Bill Chase, Ellington, Armstrong. Film: documentary w. Gillespie for John Hubley. TV: Lionel Hampton Special in Canada, '71; w. Geraldo Rivera's *Good Night America*, ABC; Sammy Davis show, NBC, '75. LPs: *Oscar Peterson & Jon Faddis* (Pablo); *Jon and Billy*, co-leader w. Billy Harper (Trio); w. Randy Weston, *Tanjah* (Poly.); *Mingus & Friends* (Col.); *Mingus at Carnegie Hall* (Atl.); w. C. Earland (Prest.); w. Jones-Lewis, *Suite For Pops* (Horizon); Swedish Radio Jazz Group, *Greetings and Salutations* (Four Leaf Clover).

FAGERQUIST, DONALD A. (DON),* *trumpet*; b. Worcester, Mass., 2/6/27. Prominent in LA during '50s as one of the first and best trumpeters of the West Coast school, Fagerquist died 1/27/74 in LA of a kidney disease. He had worked with the bands of G. Krupa, W. Herman, Les Brown, A. Shaw, and rec. w. S. Manne, John Graas and Dave Pell.

FALZONE, SALVATORE JOSEPH (SAM), *saxophone, flute, clarinet, composer*; b. Buffalo, N.Y., 12/20/33. Stud. clarinet '47-51. Air Force band '52-5; U. of N.Y. at Fredonia; B.S. mus. educ. w. saxophone major, '56-60; also stud. mus. educ. at U. of Buffalo. In '64 while teaching instrumental music in public schools of N.Y. state, met Don Ellis and worked with him during most of the next decade, incl. Hindustani Jazz Sextet, '65; European tour, Antibes Jazz Fest. etc. '68. Freelance work in LA from '68, also w. Buddy Rich band, '68. Film and TV sound track work for *The French Connection; Dial M for Music.* Comp. and arr. *Get It Together; Go Back Home* for Ellis band. Latter was publ. by Objective Mus. Co., Cal. Arr. *Put It Where You Want It* for Ellis' *Connection* album. Favs. Ch. Parker, S. Rollins, J. Coltrane, Miles Davis, D. Ellis.

LPs: *Live at the Fillmore; Autumn; Tears of Joy,* w. Ellis (Columbia).

FAME, GEORGIE (Clive Powell),* *singer, organ, bandleader*; b. Leigh, Lancashire, England, 6/26/43. First prominent through hit single *Yeh Yeh,* '65. Winner of British polls as top male jazz singer. In '66, gave Festival Hall concert and rec. album w. Harry South band, incl. Ronnie Scott, Tubby Hayes. Presented his own first West End theatre production in London, Dec., '66. In '68 headlined a season at Mayfair Theatre, in a two-hour one man show. Later that year toured continent w. C. Basie orch. Also sang w. Jon Hendricks and Annie Ross, '68 at Berlin JF. Made first US app. May '70 with group known as Shorty. LPs on British labels.

FARLOW, TALMADGE HOLT (TAL),* *guitar*; b. Greensboro, N.C. 6/7/21. Came out of semi-retirement to play a two-month stint at a NYC club called The Frammis, '67 and to rec. w. Sonny Criss for Prestige. Fest: NJF, '68-70; NJF-NY, '72. The '69 app. was w. George Wein's All Stars with whom he also played club and concert gigs on east coast and St. Louis, reunited w. his old leader Red Norvo within the group. For some years Farlow has lived on the New Jersey coast where he does some teaching, pl. occasional engagements in local clubs, colleges and schools. Instruction book, *Tal Farlow Method,* publ. by (Guitar Player Prod., P.O. Box 615, Saratoga, Ca. 95070).

Farlow employs a divider of his own devising which enables him to add another line when he is playing single notes. "It sounds roughly as if I'm playing octaves on a piano," he says. As might be expected, the naturally talented guitarist uses it with restraint and good taste.

LPs: *Fuerst Set* (Xanadu); *Tal Farlow—Guitar Player* (Prest.); *Up, Up And Away,* w. Criss (Prest.); *George Wein's Newport All Stars* (Atl.).

FARMER, ARTHUR STEWART (ART),* *fluegelhorn, trumpet*; b. Council Bluffs, Iowa, 8/21/28. Best known as trumpeter in early '50s w. Lionel Hampton, later w. H. Silver, G. Mulligan and as co-leader w. Benny Golson of the Jazztet, 1959-62. During the '60s he played in partnership w. Jim Hall, worked with increasing frequency in Europe, and switched permanently from trumpet to fluegelhorn. In '68 he moved to Vienna, working with the house band for the Austrian Broadcasting System, but continued to appear throughout Europe in concerts and clubs. In '72 he toured the Orient and Europe with NJF in a group led by organist Jimmy Smith. Though still living in Vienna, he returned often to the U.S., app. at NJF, '73 and '74, and working with local rhythm sections in NYC, LA and other key cities.

Though a product of the bebop era, Farmer was influenced by L. Armstrong, L. Young, Ellington, Nance, Rex Stewart et al, as well as by Gillespie and Parker. He evolved a style of rare lyricism; his solos invariably show a superb sense of construction and his rich tone quality on the fluegelhorn is unequaled in jazz.

LPs: *Gentle Eyes,* with strings; *Homecoming* w. J. Heath (Mainstream); *Portrait of Art* (Contemporary); *Farmer's Market; Early Art* (Prestige); *Farmer-Golson Jazztet* w. Tyner (Cadet). Early LPs as leader, some now unavailable, on ABC-Paramount, UA, Mercury, Atl., Col., Scepter. *What Is There To Say,* w. G. Mulligan (Col.).

FARRELL, JOE (Joseph Carl Firrantello), *tenor sax, flutes*; also all reeds except bassoon; b. Chicago Heights, Ill., 12/16/37. Brother-in-law, Carmen Guierino, who worked commercial jobs around Chi. in late '30s and '40s, started him on clar. in '48. Stud. tenor sax w. Joe Sirolla at Roy Knapp music school in Chi. '53; Majored in flute at U. of Ill. under Charles DeLaney. B.S. in Mus. Ed. '59. Pl. w. Ralph Marterie '57 and many jam sessions w. Ira Sullivan, Nicky Hill and other Chi. musicians. To NYC '60. W. Maynard Ferguson '60-1; Slide Hampton '62; Tito Rodriguez '62-64; George Russell sextet, incl. European tour. Oct. '64; Jaki Byard '65; three yrs. w. Thad Jones-Mel Lewis from '66; at the same time w. Elvin Jones trio '67-70. Also short stints w. Woody Herman '65, Horace Silver in late '60s, Herbie Hancock. In '70s pl. w. Chick Corea, incl. European and Japanese tours w. his Return To Forever group. Own quartet '74-75. NJF w. Ferguson '60; E. Jones '68, 72; as soloist '73-74; Molde, Pori JFs '71-2; George Wein European tour '64; European tour w. E. Jones '68; own group at Berlin JF '73. Comps: *Moon Germs, Great Gorge, Ultimate Rejection.* Insp. & infl: Charlie Parker, Sonny Rollins, John Coltrane, Bud Powell, Ira Sullivan, Johnny Griffin, Jaki Byard, Elvin Jones. American & BBC TV apps. w. E. Jones '68; Canadian TV w. C. Mingus '65 and own group '74; NET w. Don Ellis '62. Won DB Int. Critics Poll as new star on tenor '68; flute '69; DB Readers Poll on sop. sax '69; *Melody Maker* '68.

Farrell, in addition to being a very active jazzman, has also, in the late '60s and the '70s, been one of the busiest of the New York studio men, recording w. Santana, Billy Cobham, the Rascals, the Band, Aretha Franklin, James Brown, etc. Clinician for Selmer Co. '75.

"Mr. Farrell," wrote John S. Wilson, "builds broiling, jabbing solos that flow in an essentially melodic fashion despite a steady interjection of startling turns and quirks. At times, his lines pile up in such quicksilver fashion that he sounds like an entire band in himself."

LPS; *Outback; Moon Germs; Penny Arcade; Upon This Rock; Canned Funk* (CTI); w. Maynard Ferguson (Roulette); *Asia Minor* w. Dizzy Reece (New Jazz); *Live at Lennie's* w. Jaki Byard (Prestige); *Explosion* w. Slide Hampton (Atlantic); w. Thad Jones-Mel Lewis (Solid State); *Puttin' It Together, The Ultimate* w. Elvin Jones (Blue Note); *Strings* w. Pat Martino (Prestige); *Sunday Afternoon at the Village Vanguard* (Solid State); *Return to Forever* w. Chick Corea (ECM), *Light As a Feather* w. Corea (Polydor); *Mingus Revisited* w. C. Mingus (Trip).

FARROW, ERNEST (ERNIE),* *bass*; also *drums, piano*; b. Huntington, West Va., 11/13/28. Raised in Detroit. Active w. Terry Gibbs, Stan Getz, Yusef Lateef in '50s; also own trio in Detroit, '58; Red Garland trio, '60. In 1964 Farrow again returned to Detroit. He formed a quintet for work in local clubs and a 10 piece band, the Big Sound; also app. as sideman w. Jack Brokensha, Harold McKinney, etc. In '69 he reinstituted a jazz policy at the legendary Bluebird and was playing there with his quintet until a tragic swimming pool accident took his life on 7/14/69. LPs: *Lateef; Blues For the Orient,* w. Lateef (Prestige); *The Many Faces of Yusef Lateef* (Milestone).

FATOOL, NICHOLAS (NICK),* *drums*; b. Milbury, Mass., 1/2/15. Swing era veteran heard in early years w. Goodman, Shaw, Bob Crosby. Worked w. P. Fountain at his club in NO, '67-9. Crosby, Phil Harris in LV, '69-73; gigs w. M. Matlock, Dick Cary, Peanuts Hucko. Fests: Sacramento each year; also Aspen; Concord; San Diego. Fatool, since '72, has been a professional golf teacher.

LPs: *The Swing Era* series (Time-Life); others w. Matlock (WB); Fountain (MCA).

FAVORS, MALACHI, *bass*; also *banjo, zither, bells, gongs, log drum, whistles, bicycle horns, ballophone, singer*; b. Chicago, Ill., 8/22/37. Father a pastor and family very religious. Initially inspired by Charlie Parker, Oscar Pettiford, then Wilbur Ware. Started pl. after high school. Recorded w. Andrew Hill, '58 and pl. w. him for two yrs. Worked gigs w. pianists and organists in lounges. Met Roscoe Mitchell in fall, '61, and Richard Abrams soon after, pl. w. Abrams' big Experimental Band throughout the early '60s. By '65 it evolved into the AACM w. Joseph Jarman and Roscoe Mitchell and, a year later, Lester Bowie. When Jarman joined the Roscoe Mitchell Art Ensemble it eventually became the Art Ensemble of Chicago which lived and played in France, June '69-April '71. Writer Arnie Passmun, reviewing the AEC in '73, called Favors ". . . without peer among avant-garde modern American Black Music bassists."

Comp: *Tutankhamen; Illistrum.*

LPs: see Art Ensemble of Chicago; others w. Mitchell; Jarman; Bowie.

FELD, MOREY,* *drums*; b. Cleveland, Ohio, 8/15/15. The prominent swing era drummer, who worked often w. B. Goodman and E. Condon, moved to Cal. in '68, then joined Peanuts Hucko in Denver and was the orig. drummer w. World's Greatest Jazzband. He died 3/28/71 in a fire at his home in Denver.

LPs: w. Goodman (Col.); WGJ (Project 3).

FELDER, WILTON LEWIS,* *tenor saxophone, electric bass, composer*; b. Houston, Texas, 8/31/40. Originally gained popularity as tenor saxophonist w. Jazz Crusaders (later known simply as The Crusaders), Felder during the '60s took to doubling on fender bass and soon found himself in constant demand for hundreds of pop, rock, r & b and jazz rec. sessions in this capacity. He continued to work frequently as a regular member of The Crusaders.

LPs: w. Crusaders (Blue Thumb).

FELDMAN, VICTOR STANLEY (VIC),* *piano, vibes, percussion, composer*; b. London, England, 4/7/34. To U.S. '55, toured w. Woody Herman; C. Adderley; based in LA from '51; occasional overseas tours w. B. Goodman; June Christy et al. In '63 he rec. and gigged w. Miles Davis for whom he wrote *Seven Steps To Heaven.*

In recent years, Feldman has been confined mainly to commercial studio work, principally as a percussionist. Has composed for several doc. films; in '75 completed score to a ballet *Encounter Near Venus*, by Leonard Wibberly, collaborating w. George Russell on the music. Perf. in Apr. '75 by Ballet Pacifica in So. Cal. Feldman's jazz gigs in the '70s often feat. him w. Tom Scott, John Guerin, Chuck Domanico. This quartet is heard in a Feldman album on Choice Records. He traveled across Canada in the first Canadian Jazz Fest., '74.

Other LPs: *Bag of Blues*, w. A. Blakey, B. De Franco (Veejay); *Seven Steps To Heaven* w. Miles Davis (Columbia); *Colorado Jazz Party* (MPS/BASF). Publs: *All Alone By The Vibraphone* (Gwyn Publ. Co. P.O. Box 5900, Sherman Oaks, Ca. 91413); *Musicians Guide to Chord Progression* (Try Publ. Co. 854 Vine St., Hollywood Ca. 90028).

FERGUSON, MAYNARD,* *trumpet, leader, baritone horn, valve trombone*; b. Verdun, Quebec, Canada, 5/4/28. Although he began working some jobs w. a sextet in '65, he didn't break up his big band until the fall of '67. Toured England at the head of a band billed as the Anglo-American Jazz Orchestra. He met trumpeter Ernie Garside, owner of the Club 43 in Manchester, who helped him form an English band. Then Ferguson spent six mos. w. his wife and children at the Rhishi Valley School near Madras, India. Back in England he again put together a big band. An album, *M.F. Horn*, was issued on Columbia in the summer of '71 and the band toured the northeastern US beginning w. an Oct. concert at Town Hall, NYC. By the fourth tour, after mutual agreement with immigration authorities and the union, the personnel became decidedly less British in character. By then, the band had app. in Western and Eastern Europe and had also shrunk from 16 men to 13, the size of Ferguson bands of the '50s and '60s. This outfit applied the hyper-intense brassy energy of Ferguson's Kenton legacy to today's pop-rock material such as Herbie Hancock's *Chameleon*, as well as some recycled Ferguson chestnuts. Baritone saxophonist Bruce Johnstone called the orch. "sort of a violent band . . . The whole evening starts out at a high intensity level and builds." By '74 Ferguson had moved back to the US and was living in Calif. Fest: NJF-NY '74-5. LPs: *Chameleon; M.F. Horn; M.F. Horn, Two; M.F. Horn III; M.F. Horn 4+5/Live at Jimmy's; Maynard Ferguson in London* (Col.); w. Gustav Brom (Supraphon); reissues, Trip; Main.

FERRIS, GLENN ARTHUR, *trombone, composer*; b. Los Angeles, Cal., 6/27/50. Stud. w. several trombone teachers, '59-68; jazz theory and improv. w. Don Ellis, '64-6; J. Klemmer, '69. Pl. w. Ellis, '66-70; Beach Boys, Tim Buckley, '71; Revival, '69-71; F. Zappa & Mothers of Invention, '72; Harry James, '73-4, Billy Cobham, '74-.

Comps: *Neurock n' Roll; Adventures of Gunga Din In His Youth; Dwan; I Like It*. Fests: Newport, Antibes, Monterey, '68; Concord, '69-70; Kongsberg, Montreux, '74.

LPs: w. Ellis, *Autumn; Goes Underground; Live At Fillmore* (Col.); w. Cobham, *Total Eclipse; Shabazz* (Atl.).

FIELDER, ALVIN, *drums*; b. Meridian, Miss., 11/23/35. Began pl. in '48 under infl. of friend. After high school pl. w. local band of Duke Otis. Went to Xavier U., NO, to study pharmacy and met Earl Palmer, Ed Blackwell and was strongly infl. by latter. Did studio work for Duke Records in Houston. Pl. w. Eddie Vinson sextet. To Chicago to take degree in Manufacturing Pharmacy. Met Sun Ra and pl. w. him before becoming part of the AACM in late '60s. Returned to Meridian to run family pharmacy. Received grants for teaching young students and importing musicians such as Roscoe Mitchell, Lester Lashley, John Stubblefield, Malachi Favors, Muhal Richard Abrams and Clifford Jordan for concerts. LP: w. Mitchell, *Sound* (Delmark).

FINNERTY, BARRY, *guitar, composer*; also *piano, electric bass*; b. San Francisco, Cal., 12/3/51. Stud. classical piano at age 5; guitar lessons at 13; attended Berklee Coll. briefly, '71, but mostly self-taught. To NYC to play jazz professionally, '73 and joined Chico Hamilton in April of that year. Also worked with Airto Moreira and Flora Purim Apr.-Nov. '74. Joined Joe Farrell quartet Jan. '75, still app. occasionally w. Hamilton. Finnerty has also perf. w. H. Laws, Tower of Power and Beefy Red. His comp. *Chants To Burn* was recorded by Raul de Souza in the latter's Fantasy album *Colors*. Other comps: *African Visions; In View*. Fests: Montreux w. Hamilton, '73; Monterey w. Moreira, '74. Infls: Miles Davis, J. Coltrane, Julian Bream, E. Dolphy, D. Reinhardt, several contemp. classical composers.

LPs: *Funk Factory* w. Michal Urbaniak (Atco); *Peregrinations* w. Hamilton (Blue Note).

FISCHER, CLARE,* *composer, piano, organ*; b. Durand, Mich., 10/22/28. Prominent since mid-60s as a freelance

musician and composer in LA, Fischer app. in concerts at the Pilgrimage Theatre, and in such clubs as Donte's and The Times etc. Though orig. better known as a pianist, he gained great respect for his unusually resourceful employment of a specially built Yamaha organ, and the Fender-Rhodes electronic piano. Usually feat. with a trio or quintet, he devoted a substantial amount of his playing time to compositions in the Brazilian idiom, to which he is sensitively attuned.

LPs: *Songs for Rainy Day Lovers* (Col.); *Reclamation Act of 1972; Easy Livin'; One—To Get Ready: Four To Go; Great White Hope* (Revelation).

FISCHER, WILLIAM S., *composer, conductor, saxophones, flute, clarinet, keyboards*; also *synthesizer, trombone, percussion, viola, cello, oboe, contrabass, voice*; b. Shelby, Miss., 3/5/35. Grandfather, Robert Fischer, pl. banjo & violin on riverboats out of NO, 1900-15. Began on piano at 7; saxophone w. Kermit Holly Sr. in Jackson, Miss. at 13 and w. Wm. Davis at Jackson Coll. at 15; at Xavier U. in NO at 16. Comp. w. Clifford Richter at 17. Theory major w. B.S. in mus. ed, '56. M.A. in theory & comp. w. Albert Seay at Colo. Coll., '59-62, summers in Aspen. Research in electronic mus. & opera w. Gottfried Von Einem in Vienna at Acad. of Mus., '65-6. As saxophonist went on the road w. Smiley Lewis, '50. Pl. w. Muddy Waters, '51; Joe Turner, Guitar Slim, '52-3; Ray Charles, '53, pl. baritone sax on Charles' first recs., made in NO; Ivory Joe Hunter, '54-5. Formed bands w. John Fernandez, Alvin Batiste and others in NO, '52-6.

Fischer, who between '68-73 participated in more than 70 albums as a free-lance arr.-comp., for such companies as A&M, Blue Note, Prest.-Fant. and RCA. From '68-70, while mus. dir. at Atl., he wrote arrs. for J. Zawinul, David Newman, W. Pickett, R. Flack, H. Mann and Y. Lateef. Wrote orig. mus. for UA films and stage prod. from '71- . Cond. major orchs. in recs. in Berlin, Cologne, Toronto, LA & NYC. Assoc. Prof. of Music at Xavier U., '62-6. Artist-in-residence at Newport Coll. of Art, Newport, Wales, and Cardiff Coll. of Art, Cardiff, Wales, '66; Bost. U. theater div.; U. of Mich., '70; Norfolk State Coll., '71. Visiting lect. at major coll. & univ. in U.S. Early infl: Ray Charles, Guitar Slim, Smiley Lewis, Sonny Stitt, Gene Ammons, Lee Konitz. TV: cond.-arr. for Fr. Norman O'Connor's *Dial M For Music*, CBS. Fests: Berlin JF, '68; MJF, '69-70. Awards: Rockefeller Commission; Fulbright Grant; Nat. Council for the Arts; NY State Council on the Arts; Austrian Govt. Grant; Pan-American (OAS) Grant. Publ: *Analysis of Arnold Schoenberg's 4th String Quartet*, showing technique of the dodecaphonic system (Colo. Coll. Press, '62). Comps: opera, *Jesse*, '66; *Experience in E for Jazz Quintet & Orch.; Suite for Jazz Quintet & Orch.; Quiet Movement for Orch.* Most of Fischer's comps. are publ. by (Ready Prods., 1365 St. Nicholas Ave., New York, N.Y. 10033); and (Bote & Bock, Berlin).

LPs: as perf.-writer w. Zawinul (Vortex); *Experience in E* w. C. Adderley (Cap.); as writer for N. Adderley (A&M); Andy Bey (Atl.); own album (Embryo); *Suite* for *Jazz Quintet* (Atl.); *Quiet Movement* (Desto); *Electronic Music* (Arcana).

FITZGERALD, ELLA,* *singer*; b. Newport News, Va., 4/25/18. After appearing in concerts at home and abroad since 1951 under the aegis of Norman Granz, frequently in his Jazz at the Philharmonic shows, Fitzgerald in 1968 began to tour Europe as a solo act, frequently accompanied by orchestras such as Duke Ellington and Count Basie. In 1971 her career was interrupted as a result of serious eye trouble. She underwent eye surgery in Boston in August of that year, and from then until 1973 cut down somewhat on her working schedule.

Her concert with the Boston Pops in 1972 marked her first appearance with a symphony orchestra. The following years saw an upsurge in demand for similar appearances, and by 1975 she had appeared with more than 40 symphony orchestras throughout the U.S. In October of '75 she toured Europe with Count Basie and Oscar Peterson.

Fitzgerald continued to lead the *down beat* Reader's Poll annually from 1953 through '70, as well as many other polls.

Her television appearances included two specials with Frank Sinatra, a Timex special, and two programs of her own for the BBC in London, as well as appearances on the Carol Burnett show, etc. Festivals: Newport; Nice; Juan les Pins; Baalbek, Lebanon, etc. Though she recorded one or two albums of contemporary songs aimed at the youth market, they were not among her major successes, and she soon returned to her policy, approved by Granz, of singing standard tunes, usually accompanied by outstanding jazz combos and orchestras.

LPs: *At Duke's Place; The Best Of; On The Cote D'Azur*, w. D. Ellington; *Ella & Louis*, w. Armstrong; *History; Mack The Knife* (Verve); *Best Of, Vol. 2* (MCA); *Carnegie Hall, Newport Jazz Fest.* (Col.); *Ella; Things Ain't What They Used To Be* (Repr.); *Ella Fitzgerald* (Arc. Folk); *Ella Fitzgerald* (Pick.); *Ella Loves Cole* (Atl.); *In London*, w. Flanagan, Pass; *Take Love Easy*, w. Pass; *at the Montreux Jazz Festival 1975; Greatest Jazz Concert in the World; Live at the Santa Monica Civic* (Pablo); *Watch What Happens* (BASF).

FLACK, ROBERTA, *singer, piano, songwriter, arranger*; b. Black Mountain, N.C., 2/10/40. Father pl. piano. Stud. from age 12 w. Hazel Harrison, a concert pianist. At age 13 won second place in statewide contest for black students, playing a Scarlatti sonata.

A brilliant student, Flack graduated from high school at 15, and from Howard U. with a BA in Mus. Ed. at 19. She then took up a career as a school teacher. During the next five years taught English literature in Farmville, N.C., then singing and classical music in junior high schools in Washington, D.C. In '62 she doubled as accompanist for a group of opera singers at a restaurant in Washington. By '65 her evolution into popular music as pro. singer and pianist had begun to take shape. During a long stint at Mr. Henry's Club in Washington, she was heard by Les McCann, who recommended her to Atl. Records. Her first album was an immediate hit and by

'70 she was a major new artist. The next few years saw her transcend the jazz and pop fields to become a superstar, whose repertoire incl. material by B. Bacharach, Leonard Cohen, B. Dylan, songs in French and Spanish, and original works. Among her early successes were Gene McDaniels' *Compared To What*, and Ewan MacColl's *The First Time Ever I Saw Your Face*. The latter rec. was used on the sound track of a motion pic., *Play Misty For Me*, as a result of which Flack's fame grew substantially. In '73 her album and single entitled *Killing Me Softly With His Song*, arr. by E. Deodato, again brought her to the top of the pop charts, though she retained her hold on jazz and soul audiences.

Formerly married to bassist Steve Novosel, Flack is an exceptionally well qualified musician who shifts easily from one idiom to another. She was once quoted as saying, "I've been told I sound like Nina Simone, Nancy Wilson, Odetta, Barbara Streisand, Dionne Warwicke, even Mahalia Jackson. If everybody said I sound like *one* person, I'd worry, but when they say I sound like them all, I know I've got my own style."

Comps: *Go Up Moses; Be Real Black For Me; Moody*. Flack has won many awards, among them Grammies for Record of the Year, '72, '73; Best Pop Vocal Performance by a Duo (w. D. Hathaway), '72; Best Pop Vocal Perf., Female, '73. Won DB Readers Poll, '71-3.

LPs: *First Take; Chapter 2; Quiet Fire; Roberta Flack & Donny Hathaway* (Atl.).

FLANAGAN, TOMMY LEE,* *piano*; also *clarinet, alto sax, tenor sax, bass, vibes*; b. Detroit, Mich., 3/16/30. Veteran of many bebop groups in '40s and '50s. Best known in later years as accompanist, serving as musical director for Tony Bennett, '66; regularly w. Ella Fitzgerald from Sept. '68. When not with Fitzgerald, worked as freelance studio and nightclub musician; played at Bradley's in Greenwich Village as duo w. Wilbur Little, '73-'74. Comps: *Dalarna; Minor Mishap; Solacium; Beat's Up; Little Rock; Eclyspo*. LPs: *Tommy Flanagan Overseas*; T. Flanagan Trio (Prestige); *Tommy Flanagan Trio* (Moodsville); *The Tommy Flanagan Tokyo Recital* (Pablo); Trio and sextet w. K. Dorham (Onyx). LPs as sideman w. Coleman Hawkins, *Today and Now* (Impulse); J. Coltrane, *Giant Steps* (Atlantic); *Ella Fitzgerald in London; at Montreux JF 1975* (Pablo); *Ella Fitzgerald at Carnegie Hall* (Col.); *Kenny Dorham Memorial Album* (Xanadu); *Jazz at the Philharmonic at Montreux JF 1975; Dizzy Gillespie Big 7 at Montreux JF '75* (Pablo).

FLAX, MARTY (Martin Flachsenhaar),* *baritone saxophone*; b. New York City, N.Y., 10/7/24. Flax, who pl. w. D. Gillespie on the latter's 1956 State Dept. tours, also worked w. W. Herman, L. Jordan, B. Rich and C. Thornhill. From the late '60s, he was heard in hotel and lounge bands in LV. He died 5/3/72 in LV. LPs w. Gillespie (Verve).

FLORY, MEREDITH (MED),* *alto sax, arranger, clarinet, tenor & baritone saxes*; b. Logansport, Ind., 8/27/26. After many years in big bands and studio work, based first in NYC and from '56 in LA, Flory became less active in music. He concentrated on acting and was seen in many film and TV dramas (*Mannix; Lassie; Bonanza; Policewoman* etc.); also wrote and doctored many motion picture scripts. Early in 1972, with Buddy Clark (q.v.), he developed the concept of Supersax. The group rehearsed frequently during the year but did not make its public debut until Nov. 1972 at Donte's in North Hollywood.

Using many arrangements written by Flory, who transcribed Charlie Parker solos from old recordings and airchecks, the group reached an unexpectedly wide audience with its first album, *Supersax Plays Bird*, which was a 1973 Grammy award winner.

Supersax appeared at Newport West Festival in LA; Concord and Monterey, '73; Orange Coast Fest., '74. Cross-Canada tour, summer '74; Japanese tour Jan. '75.

LPs: *Supersax Plays Bird; Salt Peanuts; Supersax Plays Bird With Strings* (Cap.).

FOLDS, CHARLES WESTON (CHUCK), *piano*; b. Cambridge, Mass., 5/4/38. During adolescence in Evanston, Ill. stud. w. piano teachers from Northwestern Univ. Music courses at Yale, '57-60. Piano stud. in early '60s w. Richard McClanahan in NYC. Mostly self-taught in jazz. First prof. job w. Yale jazz band '56; managed band in senior year. W. Danny Alvin at Basin St. in Chi., Summer '57; next three summers in Europe w. college jazz bands; concerts w. Chet Baker, Kenny Clarke, Stan Getz. After grad. went to NYC where he worked w. Joe Thomas; Ruby Braff; Pee Wee Russell; Max Kaminsky at Eddie Condon's and the Metropole. Toured w. Village Stompers in '63-4; then w. Peanuts Hucko; George Wettling '64; Metropole w. Shorty Baker; Conrad Janis; Red Allen '65. Left music business full-time to work as editor for American Heritage Pub. Co., '65-9. Also gigged w. Bob Crosby; Tony Parenti in '60s; Wild Bill Davison; Hucko; Jimmy McPartland; Buck Clayton-Maxine Sullivan; Bobby Hackett in '70s. March '71-July '73 w. Roy Eldridge at Jimmy Ryan's; other NYC jobs w. the Countsmen; Joe Venuti; Jimmy McPartland; Buddy Tate; Maxine Sullivan; Bobby Hackett, '73-4. Solo piano in weekly "Jazz By Sunlight" series at The Cookery from '73. Infl: Ellington, Tatum, Wilson, Hines, Waller, Donald Lambert. Fest: Virginia Beach w. Kaminsky '62; NJF-NY w. Eldridge '73. LPs: *It's Ragtime* (Jazzways); own trio and one w. Countsmen on Brit. RCA.

FONTANA, CARL,* *trombone*; b. Monroe, La., 7/18/28. Toured with Woody Herman several times in 1950s and '60s, incl. State Dept. tour of Africa in '66. During the following decade he was based in Las Vegas, pl. lead trombone w. Paul Anka and working in local show bands, but took time out for various jazz jobs, inc. gigs and/or records w. Benny Goodman, jazz parties in Colorado and Odessa, Texas; Supersax, Louis Bellson. Co-led combo with Jake Hanna 1975. Toured Japan w. Geo. Auld. Gigs and albums w. World's Greatest Jazzband. Despite the limited quantity of his jazz work due to his LV residency, Fontana was regarded by many fellow-musicians as the most fluent and innovative trombonist

since J.J. Johnson. LPs w. Hanna-Fontana (Concord Jazz); World's Greatest Jazzband (Project 3, World Jazz); *Salt Peanuts* w. Supersax (Capitol); *Concerto for Herd* w. Herman (Verve); *Colorado Jazz Party* (MPS).

FORD, RICHARD ALLEN (RICKY), *tenor saxophone*; b. Boston, Mass., 3/4/54. Studied at New England Conservatory of Music; during this time, worked with Jaki Byard combo. Joined Duke Ellington orchestra under direction of Mercer Ellington, August '74 and drew critical acclaim as a hard-driving, creative soloist blending contemporary characteristics with traditionalist roots. Left Ellington to join Charles Mingus, May '76. LP: w. Mercer Ellington, *Continuum* (Fantasy).

FORD, ROBBEN LEE, *guitar*; also *saxophone, piano*; b. Woodlake, Cal., 12/16/51. Father c & w guitar and harmonica player in Wyoming. Stud. sax at age 11 in high school; self-taught on guitar at 13. Infls. range from Coltrane to Ravi Shankar to Stravinsky. Prof. debut, '70 w. Charlie Musselwhite Blues Band; with brothers, Charles Ford Band, '71; Jimmy Witherspoon, '72-3; Tom Scott L.A. Express and Joni Mitchell, Jan.-Sept. '74; George Harrison, Oct.-Dec. '74. MJF, '72; NJF, '73. App. on Educ. TV prog, *One Of A Kind*. LPs: w. Charles Ford Band (Arhoolie); w. Joni Mitchell, *Miles of Aisles* (Elektra-Asylum); w. T. Scott, *Tom Cat* (Ode); w. Jimmy Witherspoon, *Spoonful* (BN).

FORREST, JAMES ROBERT (JIMMY),* *tenor sax*; b. St. Louis, Mo., 1/24/20. Pl. w. Jay McShann; Andy Kirk in '40s; Duke Ellington, '49-50. Led own gps. in '40s, '50s. Pl. w. Harry Edison, '58-60. After living and playing in St. Louis and LA for periods of time, he joined Count Basie in '73, bringing with him his earthy, big-toned, driving tenor style. LPs: *All the Gin is Gone* (Delmark); w. Basie (Pablo).

FORTUNE, SONNY, *alto saxophone*, also *flute*; b. Philadelphia, 5/19/39. Stud. at Wurlitzer's and Granoff Sch. of Mus., also privately w. Roland Wiggins. Local work w. r & b groups, Chris Columbus, Betty Burgess before coming to NYC in 1967. After 2½ months w. Elvin Jones, was member of Mongo Santamaria band, 1968-mid 1970; Leon Thomas latter part of '70; McCoy Tyner '71-mid '73; Roy Brooks, summer-fall '73. After leading his own group for a while, pl. w. Buddy Rich March-August 1974, then joined Miles Davis.

Fortune is skilled on all the saxophones and has shown his stylistic adaptability, gigging and/or recording w. Lloyd Price, Melvin Sparks, Geo. Benson, Roy Ayers, Oliver Nelson, Pharoah Sanders, Horacee Arnold, as well as Brooks, Rich and Davis.

LP: Strata-East; *Awakening* (Horizon); also *Stone Soul* w. Santamaria (Col.); *Other Side of Abbey Road* w. Benson (A & M); *Sahara* w. Tyner (Milestone).

FOSTER, PAUL ALEXANDER (ALEX), *saxophones, clarinets, flutes*; b. Oakland, Calif., 5/10/53. Brother, Frank (no relation to tenor saxophonist), classical violinist living in Calif. Studies at SF Conserv. of Mus.; Curtis Inst. of Mus., Phila.; Inst. for Advanced Mus. Studies, Valais, Switz. During '73 worked w. Duke Pearson, Clark Terry, Thad Jones-Mel Lewis big bands; Chico

Hamilton, '73-4; Jack DeJohnette Directions from Nov. '74; Paul Jeffrey Octet, '75. Infl: Parker, Coltrane, Rollins, M. Davis, C. Adderley, DeJohnette, European classical music. Pl. alto sax and clarinet in film *Rico* w. Dean Martin, MGM. Fest: MJF; Concord; Montreal; Ahus; Schaeffer Mus. Fest. Represented as composer and player on *Cosmic Chicken* w. Jack DeJohnette Directions (Prest.).

FOSTER, FRANK BENJAMIN,* *tenor, soprano saxophones, composer, educator*; also *flute, clarinet, alto & baritone saxes, piano*; b. Cincinnati, Ohio, 9/23/28. From '53-64 a mainstay of the Count Basie orch. as tenor soloist and arranger. Own big bands and small gps. from '65; also gigs w. W. Herman; Lloyd Price; L. Hampton; Duke Pearson; Peter Duchin; Basie. Toured Europe as guest soloist w. local gps., '68. Joined Elvin Jones, June '70, touring in England and Germany w. him, Oct. '70. Cond. Jazz Interactions' Young Musicians' Clinic in a tribute to Louis Armstrong, Alice Tully Hall, NYC, Dec. '71. Continued to play w. E. Jones, off and on through '74, incl. State Dep't.-sponsored tour of So. America, fall, '73. Concerts: w. NYJRC; CBA; '74; w. Buddy Rich, Feb. '75; Oliver Nelson, at Bottom Line, NYC, June '75. Cond. for Redd Foxx on tour of Eastern U.S. feat. B. Eckstine, in July; then Scandinavian; U.S. and Japanese tours w. Thad Jones-Mel Lewis orch. as arr. and feat. soloist. During '75 also app. w. his own "Loud Minority" and "Living Color"; quintet co-led w. Charli Persip.

TV: Represented Jazz & People's Movement w. own sextet on *Today Show*, NBC; w. Elvin Jones, *American Musical Heritage*, CBS, '71; Joe Franklin, '72. Fest: w. E. Jones, NJF '70; NJF-NY '74; NY Musicians' JF '72-3; Ohio Valley w. Jones-Lewis '72; NJF-NY '73. Awards: CAPS; NEA, '74. Music Consultant, NYC Public Schools, '71-2; Assist. Prof. SUNY at Buffalo, '72-3; Adjunct Prof., CUNY at Queens Coll, N.Y., from '74. Foster has also cond. seminars, workshops, etc., at New Eng. Cons.; Wesleyan U., Conn.; Oakland U., Pontiac, Mich.; Howard U., Wash., D.C. Board member of Jazz Interactions. Comp: *Disapproachment; Ural Stradania; Simone; Raunchy Rita; Cecilia is Love; The Loud Minority; Requiem for Dusty; Ithaca Suite.* LPs: *The Loud Minority* (Main.); *Manhattan Fever* (BN); *Fearless Frank Foster; Soul Outing* (Prest.); w. Duke Pearson; Elvin Jones; Donald Byrd (BN); E. Jones & Richard Davis (Imp.); w. Thad Jones-Mel Lewis, *Suite For Pops* (Horizon).

FOSTER, GARY, *saxophones, flute, clarinet*; b. Leavenworth, Kansas, 5/25/36. Graduated U. of Kansas with BM woodwinds and mus. ed., '61. Settling in Cal., he became active in all major film studios, doubling as woodwind expert. Big bands: Clare Fischer, '65- ; L. Bellson, '68-9; Mike Barone, '69-70; Toshiko, '73- ; Ed Shaughenssy, '74- . Combos: Fischer, '65- ; Jimmy Rowles, '68; Warne Marsh, '68-73; L. Almeida, '74- . Woodwind teacher in LA area. Founded Nova Music Studios, a group of pro. teacher-performers in Pasadena,

'74. Instructor of jazz studies at Pasadena City Coll. Fests: Monterey, '74 w. Fischer; San Diego, Monterey, '75 w. Toshiko.

LPs: *Subconsciously; Grand Cru Classe* (Revelation); *Ne Plus Ultra,* w. Marsh (Revelation); *Thesaurus,* w. Fischer (Atl.).

FOSTER, GEORGE MURPHY (POPS),* *bass*; b. McCall, La., 5/19/1892 (date uncertain). Raised in New Orleans; prominent in 1920s and '30s w. Luis Russell and Louis Armstrong bands. Still active in 1960s, he toured Europe w. all star group of NO veterans in '66. To Chi. in '68 to tape a TV program w. Art Hodes. Living in San Francisco, Foster died there 10/30/69. One of the first musicians to popularize the string bass in jazz, he was best represented on recordings with Armstrong (Col., MCA).

Publ: *The Autobiography of Pops Foster, New Orleans Jazzman,* as told to Tom Stoddard (Univ. of Cal. Press, 1971). The book, reprinted in paperback in 1973, includes a selected bibliography, and a comprehensive discography from 1924-40 by Brian Rust.

FOUNTAIN, PETER DEWEY JR. (PETE),* *clarinet*, also *alto, tenor saxes*; b. New Orleans, La., 7/3/30. Most of his time spent pl. at his own club at 231 Bourbon St. in NO but he also has done nine wks. a year for seven yrs. at the Tropicana in Las Vegas as well as numerous apps. at concerts and fairs. Pl. NO Jazz Fest., Calif. JF. TV apps. w. Lawrence Welk, Ed Sullivan, Andy Williams, Bob Hope, Bing Crosby, Kraft Music Hall, Danny Kaye, Johnny Carson, Bob Crosby. Film short: *Pete's Place* (MCA). Won *Playboy* award 14 times. Book, *A Closer Walk: The Pete Fountain Story* pub. by Henry Regnery, Chi. LPs: most recent on MCA; also Coral, Decca.

FOWLER, BRUCE, *trombone*; b. Salt Lake City, Utah, 7/10/47. Father is noted music educator Dr. William C. Fowler (see below). Stud. w. Ned Meredith early '60s; NTSU; '67-9; U. of Utah, '65-7, '70-2. Worked w. W. Herman, '68, '69; Power Circus, '69-70, F. Zappa and Mothers of Invention, '72-5. Infl.: F. Rosolino, C. Fontana, J.J. Johnson et al. Comps: *Habondia* for six trombones; several other pieces for trombone sections and for jazz-rock groups. LPs: *Lab '68* w. NTSU; *Roxy and Elsewhere,* w. Zappa (Discreet).

FOWLER, DR., WILLIAM L.,* *educator, guitar*; b. Salt Lake City, Utah, 7/4/17. Ph.D. in composition from U. of Utah, '54. Emerged as major figure in jazz education in '60s, director/public relations for National Stage Band Camps, Intermountain Jazz Fest., '67-75; jazz prog., U. of Utah, '68-72. Westminster Coll. '72-4. He was also dir. of guitar prog. for U. of Colorado at Denver, '74-5; coordinator, Visiting Jazz Faculty Prog. U. of Utah, '68-72; Westminster Coll.; '72-4; U. of Colo., '75. Has given many illustrated lectures on history of jazz and history of guitar for Music Educators National Conference. Won Mr. Mobile Music Award, Mobile, Ala., '74.

Comps: *The Pearl; The Great and Marching Words;*

Micat In Vertice. Dr. Fowler has also served as education editor for DB, and is author of several books on guitar published by C. G. Conn, Ltd.

FOWLKES, CHARLES BAKER (CHARLIE),* *baritone sax*; b. Brooklyn, N.Y., 2/16/16. Member of Count Basie band 1951-1969. After a knee injury, left band and remained in New York, playing at Westbury Music Fair etc.; rejoined Basie June 1975.

FRANCIS, DAVID A. (PANAMA),* *drums*; also *bongos, conga*; b. Miami, Fla., 12/21/18. An active big band drummer in NYC w. R. Eldridge, L. Millinder, Willie Bryant, C. Calloway in '40s and '50s; also house drummer at Central Plaza in '50s and busy studio man w. Sy Oliver, Perez Prado, Tony Bennett, R. Charles, C. McRae, '50s and '60s. Dinah Shore's personal drummer, '67-70. Moved to LA, '68, where he played in studios and also at Hong Kong Bar w. Joe Williams, T. Wilson and Calloway. Moved back to NYC, '73, joining Oliver. Toured England w. Warren Covington orch.; France, Spain, Belgium, Switzerland w. group incl. Tiny Grimes, Arnett Cobb, '74. Nice JF, '74. Charter member of NYJRC; guest mus. dir. for prog. recreating music of the Savoy Ballroom at Carnegie Hall, May '75. App. in film *Lady Sings The Blues.* TV: *The Jazz Show*, KNBC, '71. Colorado Jazz Party, '74-5.

LPs: w. Tiny Grimes; Arnett Cobb; Big Nick Nicholas; Milt Buckner; Earl Hines (Black & Blue); also for *Music Minus One.*

FRANKLIN, ARETHA,* *singer*; b. Memphis, Tenn., 1942. With her shift to the Atlantic label in Nov. '66 she soon moved into the realm of pop, blues and soul star. By '73 she had six gold LPs and 14 gold singles, each signifying 1,000,000 records sold. In May '68 she made a European tour, visiting seven major cities in England, France, Germany, Holland, Sweden and France. In Feb. '68 she appeared in concert at Cobo Hall in her "home" city of Detroit on what was proclaimed "Aretha Franklin Day" by the mayor. She was presented with a special Southern Christian Leadership Council Award by Rev. Martin Luther King on that evening.

Through the late '60s and '70s she performed at the LA Forum, Houston Astrodome, Boston Garden, Latin Casino, Apollo Theater, Hollywood Bowl, Radio City Music Hall. In '73 she appeared at African drought benefit, St. John the Divine; in '75 at the Sickle Cell Anemia benefit, Beverly Hilton. Two-week summer tour of Australia '75. TV: specials w. Duke Ellington; Flip Wilson; Mac Davis; Dinah Shore; Bob Hope; *Tonight Show.* Received Honorary Doctor of Laws degree from Bethune-Cookman Coll., '75. Won Grammy Awards in '68, '70-2. TDWR, DB Critics poll, '68. LPs: *You; With Everything I Feel in Me; Let Me in Your Life; Hey Now Hey; Amazing Grace; Young, Gifted and Black; Live at Fillmore West; Spirit in the Dark; The Girl's in Love With You; Soul '69; Aretha in Paris; Aretha Now; Lady Soul; Aretha Arrives; I Never Loved a Man the Way I Love You.* (Atlantic).

FREEMAN, LAWRENCE (BUD),* *tenor saxophone*; b. Chicago, Ill., 4/13/06. As a charter member of the World's Greatest Jazzband, pl. with them for six years before moving to London in late '74, lecturing and pl. at univs. throughout Gt. Britain. He was honored by NYJRC in a tribute program in which he participated, '74. Pl. with Friends of Eddie Condon at NJF-NY, '72. Publs: *You Don't Look Like A Musician* (Balamp Publ., 7430 Second Blvd., Detroit, Mich. 48202).

Freeman, who in '74 celebrated 50 years of playing, remains a vigorous, joyful artist. Comps: *That D Minor Thing; Song of the Dove; Out of My Road, Mr. Toad; Uncle Haggart's Blues; The Eel.* LPs: *The Compleat Bud Freeman* (Monmouth-Evergreen); w. Lee Wiley; *The Music of Hoagy Carmichael* (Mon-Ev.); w. World's Greatest Jazzband on Project 3, Atl., World Jazz; duo album w. Jess Stacy (Chiaroscuro); *Superbud* (77).

FREEMAN, RUSSELL DONALD (RUSS),* *piano, composer*; b. Chicago, Ill., 5/28/26. Originally a member of Shelly Manne's group, Freeman confined his activities during the '60s and '70s to the Hollywood studios, as well as acting as mus. dir. for many night club acts, app. in LV and all over the U.S. Was mus. dir. for *Laugh-In* TV show, '67-73; Tony Orlando & Dawn, '74- . Comp. main title for Mitzi Gaynor Spec., and orig. music for *Letters to Laugh-In.*

FREEMAN, EARL LAVON (VON), *tenor saxophone, composer*; b. Chicago, Ill., 10/3/22. Brothers are guitarist George; drummer Bruz. Studied under Capt. Walter Dyett at Du Sable High. where Gene Ammons and Bennie Green were schoolmates. Pl. w. Horace Henderson; US Navy Hellcats; Sun Ra; Milt Trenier. Had band w. his brothers and Andrew Hill, '51. Most of his work has been confined to the small clubs of Chicago and environs. Pl. w. Dexter Gordon for Joe Segal's Charlie Parker Month concerts, Aug. '70. Terry Martin, writing of him said: "The harmonic and rhythmic innovations of the boppers, particularly Parker, and the later modal players, have been absorbed into a style that, while it builds on the foundation of Hawkins' power and arpeggiated convolutions, and Lester's melodorhythms, emerges as something quite unique." There are times when there is a parallel with the keening qualities found in the wailing of Johnny Griffin but some listeners are put off by Freeman's intonation.

Comps: *Have No Fear, Soul is Here; Doin' It Right Now; White Sand; Portrait of John Young; Catnap; Brother George.* LPs: *Have No Fear* (Nessa); *Doin' It Right Now* (Atl.); w. Charlie Parker, *An Evening at Home With the Bird* (Savoy); w. George Freeman, *New Improved Funk* (Gr. Merch.); *Birth Sign* (Delmark).

FREUND, WALTER JAKOB (JOKI),* *tenor, soprano saxes*; also *clarinet, trumpet, trombone, violin, accordion, sousaphone, piano, vibes*; b. Hochst, Germany, 9/5/26. Piano w. Gunter Hinz, '45; Carlo Bohlander, '48. First jazz job w. Gerry Weinkopf's big band, '49-50, out of which grew Germany's first important modern jazz group, the Joe Klimm Combo, marked by the sound of Freund's tenor lead over trumpet and trombone. W. Jutta Hipp quartet, '52-4; then own group, the first jazz unit to tour Yugoslavia, '54. Own sextet from '62; also member of Radio Frankfurt (Hessicher Rundfunk) as player-arr. and same for Erwin Lehn's big band at Radio Stuttgart. Sousaphone w. Two Beat Stompers, '55-67. Infl: Parker, Coltrane, Konitz. TV: 13 shows, *Variationen in Jazz.* Fests: Second Polish Jazz Fest., '57; Comblain-La-Tour, '60; Frankfurt, '53-'72.

Comps: *Domicile; Four Temperaments* (suite); *Sopran Lament; Pigeon Suite; Concertino for Tenor-Saxophon and Orchestra; Tree Characters; Moon Over Schwalbach; Street Stories.* Voted top arr. in all German jazz polls, '57-'75; second place as tenor sax, '54-'75; top soprano sax in *Podium* poll, '68-'71. LPs: *Yogi Jazz; Wild Goose; Color in Jazz* (MPS); *Four Temperaments* (Brunswick); *Amerika Ich Rede Dich An* (Electrola); German All Stars (Columbia).

FRIED, ALEXEJ, *trumpet, composer*; also *piano, violin*; b. Brno, Czech., 10/13/22. Studied w. Prof. Theodor Schafer at Brno State Conserv. '45-7; w. Prof. Emil Hlobil, Prague State Conserv. '47-8; w. Prof. Pavel Borkovec, U. of Arts, Prague, '48-53, Bach. of Comp. Pl. trumpet in own big band, Alex's Boys, '38-41; arr. for Gustav Brom, Ladislav Habart, Karel Vlach Orchs. '45-8. In '51 led J. Jezek orch. for Czech. radio and Supraphon recs. From '70 has led own bands and composed for FOK Symph. orch., Prague, and Brom big band. One of the founding members of the Int. Jazz Fest. of Prague and its artistic manager of the AUSVN, military artistic corps., '64-7. Prof. of composition at U. of Arts, Prague. Infl: Ellington, Stravinsky, Picasso, folk songs & spirituals. Film: *The Little Bears* for U.S. TV, '65. TV: *Clarinet Concert,* Prague '75; jazz festival composition, *Act,* pl. by Brom, Prague '70. Fest: comp. pl. by Brom at Prague, '71-2; Warsaw '72. Among his many works are the scores for four musicals. Other comp: *Reeping; Triple Concert; Solstice; Jazzconcert;* also arrs. of *Caravan; Blue Skies; Solitude.* LPs: *Bohemian Jazz, 1920-1960; Swing Festival; Jazz Concertos,* w. Brom; *Moravian Wedding; Solstice* (Supraphon); comp. *Sidonia* on Don Ellis' *Soaring* (MPS/BASF).

FRIEDMAN, DAVID, *vibraphone*; also *drums, percussion, piano*; b. New York, N.Y., 3/10/44. Father amateur violinist. Stud. drums w. Stanley Krell, '55; marimba, xylophone, '60. Perc. major at Juilliard; at same time stud. w. Saul Goodman and Moe Goldenberg; then w. Teddy Charles and Hall Overton. Infl. Luciano Berio, Bill Evans, Milt Jackson. During early '60s played extra w. N.Y. Phil., Met. Opera; much contemporary music perf. w. Berio in Europe and U.S. Subsequently w. Tim Buckley, Horace Silver, H. Laws, Horacee Arnold, W. Shorter, Joe Chambers, Don Sebesky et al. Vibes and jazz improv. clinician for Ludwig Drum Co. in clinics and concerts in U.S. and Europe. On faculty of Manhattan School of Music; and Inst. for Advanced Musical Studies, Montreux, Switzerland. App. at NJF w. H.

Laws, H. Arnold, '73. In '75 rec. and concert tours with vibes-marimba duo, playing orig. works. Winner DB poll, TDWR, vibes, '74; tie w. Karl Berger, '75.

Publ: *Vibraphone Technique Dampening & Pedaling* (Berklee Press, 1140 Boylston St., Boston, Mass.). Own LP: *April Joy* (East Wind); w. H. Arnold, *Tribe* (Columbia); w. Laws, *In The Beginning; Live At Carnegie Hall* (CTI).

FRIEDMAN, DONALD ERNEST (DON),* *piano, composer*; b. San Francisco, Ca., 5/4/35. After west coast work, pl. with many groups around NYC, '58. Worked w. Chuck Wayne trio, 66-7; Clark Terry big band, '67; European tour w. Jimmy Guiffre, concerts and clubs in Germany with Attila Zoller, '68; frequently feat. at Half Note, '69, also began small band work w. C. Terry.

In '70 Friedman started teaching jazz piano at N.Y.U., continuing through '73. In 74-5 he joined a commercial trio for steady work in and around NY area and continued teaching. J. Berendt cites Friedman as one of the most important pianists of the '60s and '70s for whom the innovations of Bill Evans were a significant point of departure.

Comps: *Circle Waltz; Spring Signs; Ochre.* LPs: *Metamorphosis* (Prest.); w. Clark Terry (Etoile).

FRISHBERG, DAVID L. (DAVE),* *piano, composer, lyricist*; b. St. Paul, Minn., 3/23/33. An exceptionally eclectic musician, heard with Dixieland and mainstream groups, accompanying singers, writing lyrics and music to songs rec. by Blossom Dearie, Cleo Laine and others. In late '60s worked in NYC w. A. Cohn/Z. Sims, B. Hackett, Ch. Shavers; solo piano at E. Condon's; house pianist at Half Note. In '71, solo pianist and mus. dir. for *Scenes From American Life,* Lincoln Center Rep. Theatre. Moved to LA. Wrote music and lyrics for *Funny Side* NBC-TV series.

'72-3 night club and studio work, incl. gigs with own trio and as sideman w. J. Sheldon, J. Pass, B. Berry. '74-5, traveled and rec. w. Herb Alpert's Tijuana Brass. Continued club and studio jobs. Music and lyrics: *Van Lingle Mungo; The Wheelers and Dealers; One Horse Town; Peel Me A Grape;* also lyrics to *I'm Hip* (mus. by Bob Dorough); *Long Daddy Green* (mus. by Dearie). Frishberg's multiple talents are reflected in his witty lyrics as well as in his versatile playing. Present favs: J. Rowles, Hank Jones, Zoot Sims.

LPs: *Oklahoma Toad* (CTI); *Dave Frishberg,* solo and trio (Seeds); w. J. Rushing, *Livin' The Blues* (ABC); *The You and Me That Used To Be* (RCA); w. Bill Berry (Beez).

FRUSCELLA, TONY,* *trumpet, composer*; b. Orangeburg, N.J., 2/14/27. Pl. briefly w. Lester Young; Gerry Mulligan; Stan Getz in '50s. Often associated w. trumpeter Don Joseph for sessions, etc. From the late '50s he was only intermittently active, hampered by personal problems. Hospitalized for three months in the spring and summer of '69, he had been released for a few weeks when he died from cirrhosis and heart failure at the apartment of a friend in NYC, 8/14/69. His work on LP

w. S. Getz (Verve), and w. his own gp. on Atlantic were deleted long before '75. A session w. Brew Moore for Atl. remained unissued. Dan Morgenstern's DB obituary called him, "a poet of the trumpet with a veiled, haunting sound . . .". Comp: *Moatz* (for Mozart); *Baite* (for Beethoven), latter rec. by Moore (Sonet).

FUKUMURA, HIROSHI, *trombone*; b. Tokyo, Japan, 2/21/49. Brother, Yoshikazu Fukumura, cond. of Kyoto City Symph. Orch. Lessons w. Sadao Watanabe, '70-72. Pl. w. Watanabe's quintet, March '72-Jan. '74. Had own quintet from Jan-Aug. '74. Studied at New England Cons. in Boston, Mass. Holds degree in economics from Nippon Univ., '71. Infl: S. Watanabe, J.J. Johnson, Coltrane. Pl. all major fests. in Japan. Won SJ Readers Poll, '73-4. LPs w. S. Watanabe incl. *Open Road* (CBS/Sony); as leader, *Quintet* (Three Blind Mice); *Live* (Trio).

FULLER, CURTIS DUBOIS,* *trombone, composer*; b. Detroit, Mich., 12/15/34. One of the many players to come out of Detroit to NYC in the '50s, he worked w. the Jazztet; several tours of duty w. A. Blakey's Jazz Messengers in '60s. After leaving Blakey in '65 he freelanced in NYC with a variety of gps., incl. Jimmy Heath in the '70s, until joining Count Basie in '75. Toured Europe w. D. Gillespie Reunion Big Band, '68; Tribute to Charlie Parker, '75. Fest: NJF-NY Radio City jam session, '73; w. Basie, '75. Comp: *Smokin'; Jacque's Groove; Sop City; People, Places and Things.* LPs: *Crankin'; Smokin'* (Main.); w. Albert Heath, *Kwanza*; w. Jimmy Heath, *Love and Understanding* (Muse), w. H. Mobley, *A Caddy For Daddy* (BN).

FULLER, JESSE,* *singer, guitar*; b. Georgia, 1897. Well-known in the SF Bay area for his performances on a home made, one-man-band instrument, the fotella, he had toured in the U.S. and appeared in Europe. Owned a shoe shine parlor in Oakland. Confined to a wheelchair after breaking a hip in '75, he died 1/28/76. LPs: *Brother Lowdown* (Fantasy); others on Good Time Jazz; Arhoolie.

GAFA, ALEXANDER (AL), *guitar*; b. Brooklyn, N.Y., 4/9/41. Self-taught. From 1964-9 worked as a studio musician in NYC; also w. groups of Kai Winding, Sam Donahue; concerts w. M. Legrand. Pl. w. orch. acc. Sammy Davis, '69-'70; mus. dir. and acc. for Carmen McRae, '70-1. Joined Dizzy Gillespie, '71. Infls: Coltrane, Segovia, Wes Montgomery, Johnny Smith. Fests: Newport; Monterey; Chateauvallon; also toured w. Gillespie in *The Musical Life of Charlie Parker* throughout Europe, fall '74. Many TV apps. w. Gillespie. Comps: *Dirty Dog; Behind a Moonbeam; Barcelona.* LPs: *Just A Little Lovin'* w. Carmen McRae (Atl.); *Matrix; The Awakening* w. Mike Longo (Main.); *The Phantom; How Insensitive* w. Duke Pearson (Blue Note).

GALBRAITH, JOSEPH BARRY,* *guitar, educator*; b. Pittsburgh, Pa., 12/18/19. Best known for his work w. Claude Thornhill orch. in the '40s and in recording studios in '50s, he did studio staff playing in NYC from '47-70. Private teaching and faculty member at City College, CUNY, '70-5.

GALES, LAWRENCE BERNARD (LARRY),* *bass, composer*; also *cello*; b. New York City, 3/25/36. Worked w. T. Monk, '65-9; also w. Mary Lou Williams. In '69 Gales moved to Cal., and was heard with Erroll Garner, Willie Bobo, Joe Williams, Red Rodney, Harold Land, H. Edison from '69- . Also during this period worked w. own trio at clubs in LA area. In '74 rec. w. Jimmy Smith and toured U.S. w. Benny Carter, incl. concert at LA Museum of Art. With Bill Berry LA Big Band, '73-4. Gales has also been active in school and coll. concerts and clinics and has received many awards in this field, incl. a citation from LA Mayor Tom Bradley. Comps: *Rosa Mae; Adrien June; Syl'lo'gism.* Fests: all major fests while w. Monk; San Diego, w. M.L. Williams, '74. App. in TV movie *The Morning After*.

LPs: w. Monk, *Monk's Blues* (Col.); w. J. Smith *Paid In Full* (Mojo); w. S. Criss, *Crisscraft* (Muse).

GALPER, HAROLD (HAL), *piano, keyboards, composer*; b. Salem, Mass., 4/18/38. Classical training, 1945-8; Berklee Sch. of Musc., '55-8; also pvt. studies w. Ray Santisi, Jaki Byard, Herb Pomeroy, Margaret Chaloff. Worked in Boston w. Pomeroy big band and combo, Sam Rivers Quartet, Tony Williams; later w. Chet Baker; European festivals w. Bobby Hutcherson-Harold Land, Joe Henderson, Stan Getz, Randy Brecker, Attila Zoller. Acc. many singers incl. Joe Williams, Anita O'Day, Chris Connor, Jackie Paris-Anne Marie Moss, Dakota Staton. Came to general public attention after replacing George Duke in Cannonball Adderley Quintet. Equally at home in orthodox jazz, r & b and free jazz contexts. With L. Konitz, '75. Infls: Red Garland, H. Hancock, Bill Evans, C. Corea, piano; O. Coleman, Miles Davis, Wayner Shorter (composers).

LPs: Mainstream; also w. Adderley (Fantasy); *A New Conception* w. Sam Rivers (Blue Note); *Score* w. R. Brecker (UA); *Baby Breeze* w. Chet Baker (Limelight).

GARBAREK, JAN, *saxophones, flute*; b. Norway, 3/4/47. Self-taught. Worked w. own groups in Norway; occasionally w. Geo. Russell; Chick Corea; Don Cherry; Keith Jarrett; and other Scandinavian all star groups. Infl. by Coltrane, Russell, Miles Davis and Jarrett. Has app. at most major European jazz fests. Frequent apps. at Student City Jazz Club on Oslo Univ. campus are central to club's success. According to Joachim Berendt, Garbarek " 'spiritualizes' rock phrases in terms of free jazz, perceptibly stimulated by study of George Russell's Lydian system." LPs: *Afrique Pepper Bird; Sart; Triptykon; Witchi-tai-to* (ECM); w. Jarrett (ECM); Russell.

GARE, LOU, *tenor saxophone*; b. Rugby, Warwickshire, England, 6/16/39. From '63-5 pl. w. Mike Westbrook band; then primarily w. AMM (duo w. Eddie Prevost, q.v.) from '65- . With AMM, Gare gives lecture-demon-

Terry Gibbs (*Veryl Oakland*)

Dizzy Gillespie and Jon Faddis (*Veryl Oakland*)

Red Norvo, George Benson, Benny Goodman and Milt Hinton

Dexter Gordon

Dusko Goykovich (*G.C. Roncaglia*)

George Gruntz and Joachim Kühn
(*Randi Hultin*)

Jimmy Hamilton and Duke Ellington (*Sam Shaw*)

Jim Hall (*Veryl Oakland*)

Charlie Haden (*David D. Spitzer*)

Herbie Hancock (*Veryl Oakland*)

John Handy III (*Veryl Oakland*)

Billy Hart (*David D. Spitzer*)

Roland Hanna (*Veryl Oakland*)

Billy Harper (*David D. Spitzer*)

Hampton Hawes (*Veryl Oakland*)

Barry Harris (*David D. Spitzer*)

Woody Herman (*Veryl Oakland*)

Roy Haynes (*David D. Spitzer*)

Joe Henderson (*Randi Hultin*)

Eddie Henderson (*Veryl Oakland*)

Billy Higgins (*David D. Spitzer*)

Jon Hendricks and
Maynard Ferguson
(*Veryl Oakland*)

Helen Humes

Eubie Blake and Earl "Fatha" Hines (*Ed Lawless*)

Bobby Hutcherson (*Veryl Oakland*)

Milt Hinton (*Veryl Oakland*)

Paul Horn (*Veryl Oakland*)

Freddie Hubbard (*Veryl Oakland*)

Milt Jackson (*Veryl Oakland*)

Howard Johnson (*David D. Spitzer*)

Budd Johnson (*Veryl Oakland*)

Bob James

Jo Jones (*David D. Spitzer*)

strations, recital-discussions and practical workshops. The group, which started out in '65 as a quartet, was one of the early "free music" organizations in Gt. Britain.

LPs: *AMM Music* (Elektra); *Live Electronic Music* (Mainstr.); *AMM at the Roundhouse* (Incus); *To Hear and Back Again* (Emanem).

GARLAND, JOSEPH COPELAND (JOE),* composer, tenor sax; also *soprano & bass saxes, clarinet*; b. Norfolk, Va., 8/15/07. Leader of nine-piece band with brother, trumpeter Moses Garland, made up of former big band players of the Swing Era, for club dates in NY-NJ area. Degrees from three photography schools incl. NY Inst. of Photography and is an active color photographer. Comps: *Leap Frog; Serenade to a Savage*; and *In the Mood*. The latter, first popularized by Glenn Miller in 1939, won a Grammy award as sung by Bette Midler in 1974. LP: one track w. Baron Lee in *The World of Swing* (Columbia).

GARLAND, EDWARD B. (MONTUDIE), bass; b. New Orleans, La., correct date of birth, 1/9/1885. Worked in NO bands until 1912, then left for Chicago. Pl. w. King Oliver, '16-21. Active in LA with own groups for many years; worked w. Kid Ory off and on from '44-54, later w. E. Hines, Turk Murphy in SF, Andrew Blakeney in LA. App. in *A Night in New Orleans* at Wilshire Ebell Theatre, LA, '73 and '74. In '74 joined Barry Martyn's Legends of Jazz, touring US and Europe. App. on TV w. Legends on Dinah Shore show, '75. Garland was honored by Pres. Ford, Gov. Reagan and Mayor Bradley of LA as the oldest living jazz sideman during a *Night in New Orleans* concert celebration Sept. '74.

LPs: *The Legends of Jazz; Barney Bigard and the Legends of Jazz* (Crescent Jazz).

GARLAND, WILLIAM M. (RED),* piano; b. Dallas, Tex., 5/13/23. An important member of the Miles Davis quintet of the mid-'50s, he returned to Dallas in mid-'60s and, for the most part, has worked there from '66 at Club Arandas and Woodmen Auditorium. To NYC May '71 for recs. and more than a month of weekends w. own trio at Pegleg's. Back to Dallas, June '71. Comp: *Old Stinky Butt*. LPs: *Auf Wiedersehen; The Quota* (MPS); reissues, *Jazz Junction*; others w. M. Davis; J. Coltrane (Prest.).

GARNER, ERROLL LOUIS,* piano, composer; b. Pittsburgh, Pa., 6/15/23. To NYC, '44. Winner of many awards since '46. In late '60s Garner headlined the International Television Fest. in Montreux, for which he was commissioned to compose the festival's theme music. Around this time he was the only U.S. artist to app. at the ROTF Eurovision Gala.

In '71 Garner was the subject of a spec. TV half hour in the *Just Jazz* series. He continued to app. as soloist with major symph. orchs., having made his debut with the Cincinnati Symph. in '57. In '74-5 season he perf. with the National Symph. in Washington; others in Honolulu, Louisville, Indianapolis, Detroit. In early '75 he contracted a severe case of pneumonia which incapacitated him for the remainder of the year. He was convalescing in California, Jan. '76.

Garner has become one of the most popular jazz artists as a concert and fest. attraction, pl. at Antibes in '70, and a series of concert galas on the French Riviera, '73-4. In '70 he made his first tour of S. Amer., and in '72 his initial excursion to the Far East. He re-recorded his best known comp., *Misty*, for use in the film *Play Misty For Me*. Other comps: *Gaslight; Up In Erroll's Room; Mood Island; Solitaire; Feeling Is Believing*, the title tune of an LP that was voted the best jazz piano album of 1970 in the *Jazz and Pop* Critics' Poll. Lyrics were added by Sammy Cahn under the new title *Something Happens*. He won an award from ASCAP, '75, for a hit recording of *Misty* by c&w performer Ray Stevens.

LPs: *Deep Purple* (Pick); *Feeling Is Believing* (Merc.); *Gemini; Magician* (London); *Misty* (Merc.); *Play It Again, Erroll* (Col.).

GARNETT, CARLOS, tenor sax, composer; also *alto, soprano, baritone saxes, flute, ukulele, campana (bell)*; b. Red Tank, Panama Canal Zone, 12/1/38. Self-taught on tenor from age 16. To US '62, working w. various rock 'n' roll gps. Serious self-study of "science of music" from '65. Joined Freddie Hubbard, Dec. '68, rec. first album w. him. With Art Blakey from middle of '69-70; Ch. Mingus for four mos., '70. In Oct. formed own gp., Universal Black Force, working w. it to '72. Also pl. and rec. w. Mtume in same period. Six mos. w. Miles Davis, '72; Norman Connors, '72-5. Reformed own gp., pl. Bottom Line, NYC, Aug. '75.

Infl: Coltrane, H. Mobley, H. Land, Rollins, W. Shorter. TV: *Soul*, NET, w. Mtume; Andrew Hill. Fest: NJF w. Blakey, '69; NJF-NY w. Connors, '74. Comp: *Mother of the Future; Holy Waters; Carlos Two; Ebonesque; Journey to Enlightenment; Caribbean Sun; Chana; Let This Melody Ring On; Samba Serenade; Panama Roots*. Own LPs: *Let This Melody Ring On; Journey to Enlightenment; Black Love* (Muse); w. Connors, *Saturday Night Special; Slew Foot; Dark of Light; Love From the Sun; Dance of Magic* (Buddah/Cobble.); w. Davis, *On the Corner; In Concert; Big Fun; Get Up With It* (Col.); w. R. Kenyatta, *Terra Nova*; w. Hubbard, *Soul Experiment* (Atl.); w. P. Sanders, *Black Unity* (Imp.); w. Mtume (Strata-East); A. Hill (BN); Blakey (Japan. Victor Nivico).

GARRETT, GLEN, alto saxophone, composer; also *tenor, soprano, flute, oboe, clarinet* etc.; b. Salt Lake City, Utah, 5/15/48. BM from U. of Utah, '73; MA from Cal. State U., Northridge, '75. Extensive teaching experience, assisting Dr. William Fowler at U. of Utah, '70-2. Taught own theory class from '72-3; assisted Gerald Wilson in his classes at Cal. State Northridge, '73-5. During '70s pl. w. Gary Pack combo; Mayo Tiana big band; Pat Williams; also w. G. Wilson from Jan. '74- . Infls: C. Adderley, J. Hodges, J. Coltrane, C. Corea, Thad Jones.

GARRISON, JAMES EMORY (JIMMY),* bass; b. Miami, Fla., 3/3/34. An important member of John Coltrane's group from '61, he left in the summer of '66. Soon after he co-led a small group w. Hampton Hawes for about six mos. Toured, incl. Europe, w. Archie Shepp,

'67-8; w. Elvin Jones trio, '68-9. In '70-1 he taught at both Bennington Coll. and Wesleyan U., pl. as soloist at Bennington graduation ceremony. Pl. w. Alice Coltrane, '72. Rejoined E. Jones, '73-4. Trouble with a hand hampered him in the latter half of '74 and a lung operation curtailed his activities in '75 but by the end of that year he was counseling ex-drug addicts and alcoholics as house supervisor for Project Create, and planning to resume playing sometime in '76. On 4/7/76, however, he died of lung cancer. TV: *Like It Is* w. Shepp. Film: videotape w. 360 Degree Experience. Fest: NJF w. Jones; NJF-NY w. Shepp, '73. Comp: *Tapestry in Sound; Sweet Little Maia; What is This?; Ascendant; Sometimes Joie.*

LPs: Elvin Jones/Jimmy Garrison Sextet, *Illumination* (Imp.); w. Jones, *Puttin' It Together; The Ultimate* (BN); w. Alice Coltrane; John Coltrane; Archie Shepp (Imp.); w. Shepp, *There's a Trumpet in My Soul* (Arista); w. 360 Degree Experience, *From Ragtime to No Time* (360 Degree Music).

GASCA, LUIS (Louis Angel Gasca), *trumpet, composer*; b. Houston, Tex., 3/3/40. Stud. Jefferson Davis H.S., Houston, '55-8; Berklee, '59-60. To Japan w. Perez Prado, '60; pl. w. S. Kenton, '61; M. Ferguson, L. Hampton, '63-4; W. Herman, incl. European tour, '67. Then w. Mongo Santamaria, Janis Joplin, Santana (incl. Euro. tour). In '70s worked w. C. Basie, C. Tjader, Joe Henderson, Geo. Duke.

Infl. by Miles Davis, Coltrane, C. Adderley, D. Gillespie, Ch. Parker, Gasca is one of the most versatile of the jazz-oriented Latin trumpet players. Arr. and pl. on *Canyon Lady* album for Joe Henderson (Milest.); Comps: *Dr. Gasca; I Was Born To Love You; Samba Para San Francisco.* Pl. in film score: *Che* w. L. Schifrin. TV: Dick Cavett, Tom Jones shows w. Joplin; Ed Sullivan show w. Kenton. Fests: Monterey w. Herman; Newport, Atlanta w. Santamaria; Santa Barbara, '75.

LPs: *Little Giant* (Atl.); *For Those Who Chant* (Blue Thumb); *Born To Love You* (Fant.); *Canyon Lady*, w. Henderson.

GASKIN, RODERICK VICTOR (VIC),* *bass*; also *guitar, cello*; b. Bronx, N.Y., 11/23/34. Played w. Paul Horn, Jazz Crusaders, Harold Land in LA before joining Les McCann, '64. With Cannonball Adderley, '66-9; T. Monk, '69; Duke Ellington, '69-70; Harlem Philharmonic, '70; Chico Hamilton, '71; John Mayall, '71-3; New World Symph., many small gps. in NYC, '73-5; NY Jazz Quartet, '75. TV: w. Ellington, Ed Sullivan *Salute to Beatles*, CBS '69; Montreux JF w. O. Nelson; C. Hamilton; L. Thomas, '71-2. Other fest: w. C. Adderley, NJF '67; MJF '68; w. Mayall, NJF-NY '73.

From '74 Gaskin, an accomplished photographer, has been an assistant to Chuck Stewart, shooting rec. sessions, album covers, Navy recruiting ads for *Jet, Ebony,* etc.

LPs: w. C. Adderley, *74 Miles Away*; N. Adderley, *Live at Memory Lane* (Cap.); Monty Alexander (Pac. Jazz); Duke Ellington, *70th Birthday* (SS); Hal Galper; Buddy Terry (Main.); A. Zoller, *Gypsy Cry* (Embryo);

Mayall (Poly.); w. O. Nelson; L. Thomas (Fly. Dutch.).

GASLINI, GIORGIO,* *piano, composer*; also *spinetta, synthesizer*; b. Milan, Italy, 10/22/29. Rejecting the type of musician closed in an inaccessible isolation or by a specialist mentality, Gaslini says "One must make music *with* the people more than for the people." Practicing his creed of the "total musician," he played during the '70s in a variety of settings: in the squares of populated areas; in factories and psychiatric hospitals, as well as universities, cinemas and large concert halls. His quartet, formed in Milan in '63, has perf. over 1000 concerts and participated in many fests., films, radio and TV broadcasts. Taught a *Course In Jazz Music* at the Santa Cecilia Conserv., Rome, '72-3. Wrote first Italian jazz opera, *Colloquio Con Malcolm X*, perf. by the Teatro Comunale of Genoa and rec. by P.D.V. Records, '70. App. w. Ellington, Miles Davis, Cecil Taylor, M. Roach, G. Barbieri, D. Cherry, S. Lacy, Bill Evans, J.L. Ponty, Sun Ra.

Comps: *New Feelings; La Stagione Incantata; Grido; Jazz Mikrokosmos; Jazz Makrokosmos; Africa; La Terra Urla; The Woman I Love; Message; Fabrica Occupata; Concerto Della Liberta.* Publ: *Musica Totalie,* Ed. Feltrinelli, Milan.

LPs: *Africa; Fabbrica Occupata* (P.A.); *New Feelings; Message* (BASF).

GAUDRY, MICHEL,* *bass*; b. Normandie, France, 9/23/28. Paris accompanist of Billie Holiday, Carmen McRae in '50s; pl. w. Bud Powell at Blue Note in '60s. In late '60s and '70s occupied mostly w. studio work and as accompanist to pop singers. Pl. in duo w. Jimmy Gourley at Bilboquet, '74. Wrote articles on the bass for *Jazz Magazine* and *Jazz Hot.* Also works as a cartoonist. TV: apps. w. All European Big Band, '67 for BBC; w. S. Grappelli; K. Clarke; H. Geller; J. Griffin; France; Wes Montgomery, Germany '67. Fest: Antibes; Cartagine; Stuttgart; Hamburg; Comblain-la-Tour. LPs: w. Billy Strayhorn, *The Peaceful Side* (UA); Duke Ellington and Alice Babs (Reprise); Barney Kessel; Sonny Criss (Polydor).

GELLER, HERBERT (HERB),* *alto sax, flute, composer*; also *misc. reeds, flutes*; b. Los Angeles, Cal., 11/2/28. After leading his own gps. and working w. small combos on the West Coast in the '50s, he moved to Germany in the '60s, pl. first w. the SFB Broadcasthouse band in Berlin; then w. Nord Deutscher Rundfunk orch. in Hamburg from Nov. '65. In Nov. '74 he recorded an album using electric keyboard and synthesizer for which he wrote the music and lyrics and simultaneously pl. two sopranos, alto and two tenor saxes through overdubbing. Fest: Berlin '73. TV: Bill Evans Jazz Workshop, NDR; Berlin JF; Peter Herbolzheimer band. Comp: *Rhyme and Reason Time; Sudden Senility; The Power of a Smile; Space a La Mode.* Also comps. for NDR Worship series. LPs: *Rhyme and Reason* (Atl.); w. Herbolzheimer; *Alpine Power Plant* w. George Gruntz, the Ambrosettis, D. Humair (MPS); w. Baden Powell, *Grandezza on Guitar* (CBS); w. Lucifer's Friend, *Banquet* (Passport). Reissues:

Gin For Fluegelhorns; Jam Session; Best Coast Jazz (Trip).

GERASIMOV, ANATOLE, *tenor sax, flute, composer*; b. Moscow, U.S.S.R., 10/8/45. Studied clarinet from age 12; attended music school. Pl. w. Gherman Lukjanov, '59; w. Nikolaj Gromin; Alexei Koslov; Rickov, '62-6; Jurii Saulskij big band, '68; Alexander Pitshikov, '69; many concerts and fests. at end of '60s. In '70s participated in jam sessions w. visiting Americans from Ellington, Jones-Lewis bands; Toots Thielemans, Bob James, Milt Hinton, Ben Riley. In '73 had own quartet; then left USSR in August for Italy where he pl. w. Romano Mussolini, etc. To NYC, pl. w. Attila Zoller. From end of '74 w. Mercer Ellington orch. Comp: *Cats and Rats; Blue Train.* LP: w. M. Ellington, tenor solo on *All Too Soon* in *Continuum* (Fantasy).

GETZ, STANLEY (STAN),* *tenor saxophone*; b. Philadelphia, Pa., 2/2/27. Featured with name bands from early '40s; after two years w. W. Herman, formed his own quartet and has worked as a leader ever since that time. During the '50s, the great popularity he had enjoyed as an innovator began to wane; however, his career was revived when he became the first American musician closely identified with the bossa nova movement. He continued to tour with a quartet, also rec. in a variety of orchestral settings.

From '69-72, in addition to living in NYC, Getz maintained a second residence near Marbella, Spain, working frequently throughout the Continent. For two years during this period, he led a European group feat. Eddie Louiss, organ; Rene Thomas, guitar; and Bernard Lubat, drums. This group made a successful rec. of *Didn't We.* Getz also rec. with the Clarke-Boland orch. in '71.

Late in '71 Getz met Chick Corea in London and commissioned him to write a series of original comps. for a new group he planned to organize. This combo made its debut Jan. '72 at the Rainbow Grill, NYC; shortly afterward its first album, *Captain Marvel*, was recorded, though it was not released until '75. The personnel incl. Corea, Stanley Clarke on bass; Tony Williams on drums, and Airto Moreira on percussion. The group remained together, with Hank Jones later replacing Corea. Other pianists incl. Kenny Barron, Albert Dailey. Getz continued to pl. Newport JF annually, and in late '74 toured the Continent w. G. Wein's NJF in Europe package. During that year he pl. for Princess Grace at the Palace in Monaco.

In '75 Getz broadened his base of activities by arranging to produce a "Stan Getz Presents" series for Columbia. He rec. albums w. Jimmy Rowles, Joao Gilberto, produced his own concert at Avery Fisher Hall, and in Dec. '75 took part in the Showboat 4 JF cruise to the West Indies, heading a quartet w. Joanne Brackeen on piano; Clint Houston on bass, and Billy Hart on drums.

While making few, if any concessions to the changes in contemporary music brought about by electronics and the advent of jazz-rock, Getz during the mid-70s managed to establish a broad base of support among younger fans,

appearing successfully at such rock clubs as the Roxy in LA. His style remained basically unaltered; in the view of most critics and fellow musicians, he was still one of the most melodically creative innovators in the history of the tenor saxophone.

LPs: *Captain Marvel* (Col.); *Classics; Stan Getz* (Prest.); *Dynasty; History; Communications*, cond. by M. Legrand; *Stan Getz and Bill Evans* (Verve); w. Clarke-Boland, *Change of Scene* (Euro. Verve); *Newport in New York '72, The Jam Sessions, Vols. 1&2* (Cobble.).

GIBBS, MICHAEL (MIKE), *composer, trombone*; also *piano*; b. Salisbury, S. Rhodesia, 9/25/37. Priv. piano instruc. from age seven for 10 yrs.; trombone, age 17-24. From '59-63 at Berklee, and Boston Conserv. Received Bach. Mus. and a Prof. Diploma in arr. & comp. Attended School of Jazz at Lenox, Mass., '61; Tanglewood Summer Sch., '63 on scholarships; also stud. priv. w. Gunther Schuller, '62. In early '60s pl. trombone w. Herb Pomeroy band. Living in England from '65 pl. w. Johnny Dankworth-Cleo Laine; Tubby Hayes; formed own big band for BBC concert, '68. Ret. to U.S. as comp.-in-res. at Berklee, Sept. '74 until May '76. Infls: Gil Evans, Charles Ives, Olivier Messiaen. Fest: Belfast, w. Gary Burton. Polls: *Melody Maker* as comp., arr., big band, '73-4.

Comps: *Sweet Rain; Family Joy, Oh Boy; Feelings and Things; Tanglewood '63; And On The Third Day; Blue Comedy; Four or Less; Nonsequence.* Orchestrations for Mahavishnu's *Apocalypse* (Col.); *Stanley Clarke* (Nemperor). Film scores: *Madam Sin; Secrets; Intimate Reflections.*

Gibbs, associated with Burton from '61 has contributed to several of Burton's albums incl.: *In The Public Interest* (Poly.); *Seven Songs for Quartet & Chamber Orch.* (ECM); *Throb* (Atl.). Burton says of him "(Gibbs) . . . has been writing for me since we went to school together in Boston . . . I've watched his talent expand and deepen through the years. In the dozen or more pieces he has written for the quartet, he has contributed greatly to our musical personality."

Gibbs' own LPs incl. *Just Ahead*, a double album rec. live at Ronnie Scott's in London; *The Only Chrome Waterfall Orch.* (Bronze).

GIBBS, TERRY (Julius Gubenko),* *vibes, percussion, composer, leader*; b. Brooklyn, N.Y., 10/13/24. One of the first great bop vibraphonists, he was a contemporary of Milt Jackson in the mid-40s, later working w. W. Herman and leading numerous groups of his own after moving to LA in '57. Has also directed big bands off and on since '59 and has made innumerable apps. w. Steve Allen, for whom he has served as musical director, composer and conductor. Led orch. and wrote all original music for TV series, *Operation Entertainment.*

Gibbs has organized small combos for many night club bookings, has appeared on Johnny Carson and Mike Douglas TV shows, *The Jazz Show* on KNBC-TV, '71. LPs: *Explosion; Live from The Summit* w. big band

(Mercury); *Terry Gibbs Big Band Recorded Live From The Summit* (Verve) *Take It From Me, Band Sounds* (Trip) w. quartet (Impulse); *Bopstacle Course* (Muse); *Big Band Sounds* (Trip).

GIBSON, RICHARD DERBIN (DICK), *promoter;* b. Mobile, Ala., 10/20/25. An investment banker, Gibson in 1962 formed the company that made the Water Pik, and in 1967 engineered its sale for millions of dollars; soon after, he went into the business of promoting jazz, helping organize the World's Greatest Jazzband in 1968. He was later instrumental in the launching of a jazz policy at the Downbeat and the Roosevelt Grill in NYC.

Gibson is best known among musicians for the private, three-day marathon jazz parties he has staged since 1963, in September of each year. Based in Denver, he and his wife Maddie held five parties in Aspen, three in Vail and from 1971 staged the events in Colorado Springs. Catering to 500 paying guests, the parties at first were traditionalist-oriented but later incorporated mainstream and modern musicians handpicked by Gibson and playing in a variety of groupings. A few sets from the 1971 party were issued in an LP, *Colorado Jazz Party* (MPS-BASF).

GIFFORD, HAROLD EUGENE (GENE),* *composer, guitar;* b. Americus, Ga., 5/31/08. The arr. for the Casa Loma orch. during the '30s, composer of such early riff tunes as *Black Jazz; White Jazz; Casa Loma Stomp.* Later retired from music, but during the last year of his life became a music teacher in Memphis, Tenn., where he died 11/12/70.

GILLESPIE, JOHN BIRKS (DIZZY),* *trumpet, composer, singer, leader;* also *conga, piano;* b. Cheraw, S.C., 10/21/17. The man who came out of the big band experience of the Teddy Hill, Cab Calloway and Earl Hines bands to help forge a musical revolution-evolution in the mid-'40s with the Billy Eckstine band and his own combos and big bands, continued to enhance his reputation as one of the most creative musicians of the 20th century. In the late '60s he appeared with the quintet he had put together in Jan. '66: James Moody, reeds and flute; Kenny Barron, piano; Frank Schifano, electric bass; and Candy Finch, drums. In Dec. '66 Mike Longo became the pianist and a principal contributor to the repertoire until he left in '73. When Moody went on his own at the end of the '60s, he was replaced by a guitar, first George Davis and then, in '71, Al Gafa, thereby changing the sound of the group with Gillespie the lone horn. With Longo's departure the unit became a pianoless quartet. When Gillespie hired Schifano in the mid-60s he became one of the first leaders to use the electric bass in a jazz group. Russell George continued on the Fender after Schifano; Phil Upchurch and Chuck Rainey both recorded on this instrument with Dizzy. In the '70s, after a short term by Alex Blake, the regular bassist, also electric, was Earl May. David Lee held the drum spot in '70, succeeded by Mickey Roker from '71.

On several occasions Gillespie returned to his love, the big band. There are few leaders as dynamic and colorful as he; in front of an orchestra he really opens into full

flower. In '68 a "Reunion" band toured Europe and was recorded at the Berlin Jazz Festival. There were Gillespie alumni like Sahib Shihab, Cecil Payne, in the reed section along with Moody; Curtis Fuller and Gillespie band veteran of the '40s Ted Kelly among the trombones; and Jimmy Owens and Dizzy Reece as trumpet sectionmates. The band was put together by Gil Fuller, Gillespie's '40s arranger.

In '75, former Gillespie saxophonist and musical director, of the mid-'50s, Billy Mitchell, helped organize a New York-based orchestra which played several engagements at Buddy's Place and a September *Tribute to Dizzy Gillespie* at Avery Fisher Hall in which Gillespie paid himself the highest tribute through his absolutely brilliant performance, in the midst of all his guest stars: Stan Getz, Lalo Schifrin, Max Roach, Percy Heath, John Lewis, James Moody and Buddy Rich.

Gillespie, the world traveler, continued to tour outside the US annually. Some of his voyages took him to St. Croix, Virgin Islands in '73; a tour of Eastern and Western Europe with the *Musical Life of Charlie Parker* package in '74; and a concert tour of Europe and the Mediterranean, incl. Israel and Tunisia, '75. In 1971-2 he took time off from his regular group to travel in Europe, Japan and the US with The Giants of Jazz, an all star line-up incl. Sonny Stitt and T. Monk.

He appeared at all the major festivals, playing a particularly vital role at Monterey on a regular basis (often sitting-in with almost everyone), and also being featured in special events at Newport and Newport-New York such as a *Tribute to Louis Armstrong;* or a Sacred Concert in '72 with All-City Choir directed by John Motley. People have learned to expect the unexpected from Gillespie as when he stepped out on the stage during the middle of a film and duetted with his screen image at the NJF-NY in '75.

His TV appearances included a trumpeter's special with Al Hirt but when he played on the late-night talk shows such as *Tonight* he was also valued by his hosts as a conversationalist. He wrote and played the score and co-starred in a speaking role with Maureen Stapleton in John and Faith Hubley's animated short film, *Voyage to Next.*

British trumpeter Ian Carr, in an appreciation of Gillespie, wrote: "He has a very extensive knowledge of theory and at the same time his instrumental execution matches his thought in its power and speed. He has lightning reflexes and a superb ear. . . He is concerned at all times with swing. Even when he's taking the most daring liberties with the pulse or beat, his phrases never fail to swing . . . The whole essence of a Gillespie solo is cliff-hanging drama. The phrases are perpetually varied. Fast demisemiquaver runs are followed by pauses, by huge interval leaps, by long, immensely high notes, by slurs and smears and bluesy phrases. He is always taking you by surprise, always shocking you with a new thought."

Gillespie won the DB Critics poll, '71-5. Among his

many awards are an honorary Doctorate from Rutgers Univ. in '70; the Handel Medallion from NYC in '72; and Musician of the Year from the Institute of High Fidelity, presented to him by Miles Davis in SF, April '75. Late in the year he was named an External Consultant in Ethnomusicology by the SF School Board to conduct a series of workshops in that city's public schools.

A follower of the Bahai faith which teaches that one day all mankind will be united in peace, Gillespie says, "Baha 'u 'llah is the head of my religious faith . . . he said music is a form of worship. I believe it, because in this music you must rid yourself of the hangups of racialism and things like that . . ."

As a composer he is well-known for his '40s works like *Salt Peanuts; Groovin' High; Blue 'N Boogie; Woody'n You; A Night in Tunisia; Bebop; Dizzy Atmosphere; That's Earl Brother* and the collaborations with Charlie Parker, *Anthropology* and *Shaw 'Nuff.* Later compositions of note are *Con Alma* and *Kush.* In the '70s his works included *Brother King,* written for the late Rev. Martin Luther King Jr., and *Olinga,* dedicated to a Bahai brother. The earlier *Manteca* also became known as *I'll Never Go Back to Georgia* because of its chanted opening refrain.

LPs: *The Giant* (Prest., orig. issued as two separate albums on the America label in France); *Big 4; Big 7 at Montreux JF 1975; Oscar Peterson and Dizzy Gillespie; Oro, Incienso y Mirra* w. comp. by Chico O'Farrill (Pablo); *Swing Low, Sweet Cadillac* (Imp.); *The Real Thing* (Perception); *My Way; Jazz For a Sunday Afternoon* (SS); *Dizzy Gillespie Reunion Band* (MPS); w. Mitchell-Ruff Duo (Main.); *Trumpet Kings at Montreux JF 1975; Trumpet Kings Meet Joe Turner* (Pablo); *Giants of Jazz* (Atl.); *Giants* w. M.L. Williams, B. Hackett (Percept.); reissues, *Greatest Jazz Concert Ever* w. C. Parker, B. Powell, Mingus; *In the Beginning,* '40s big band and combos (Prest.); *Newport Years* (Verve); *Something Old, Something New* (Trip).

GILMORE, JOHN,* *tenor sax, drums;* b. Summit, Miss., 1931. The long-time Sun Ra sideman continued to be one of the key men in the Arkestra, featured on tenor sax but also playing the drums in what often becomes a percussion ensemble. Originally infl. by Rollins and Coltrane he was cited by Coltrane as having infl. him (Coltrane) through certain elements in his playing. Vladimir Simosko talks of Gilmore's solo on *Shadow World* w. Sun Ra as "consisting principally of a well modulated squeal from the horn's freak register, punctuated by a few well placed blats from the bottom of the horn, unaccompanied during the last segment, and surely one of the most hair raising and powerful solos on record."

LPs: see Sun Ra; also w. Freddie Hubbard; McCoy Tyner (Imp.); Elmo Hope, *Sounds From Riker's Island* (Aud. Fid.); Andrew Hill (BN); Pete La Roca, *Turkish Women at the Bath* (Douglas), same album issued under Chick Corea's name, *Bliss* (Muse); Dizzy Reece (Futura); reissue material on *Blowing Sessions* (BN).

GILSON, JEF (Jean-Francois Quievreux),* *piano, composer;* also *clarinet;* b. Guebwiller, Alsace, France, 8/25/26. Made rec. debut w. Jean-Luc Ponty, '62. Led big band '62-7. Worked as singer, arr. w. Double Six of Paris, '65-6. Toured Africa, Madagascar, '68-70. Publ: a journal, *L'Independant Du Jazz* (available from 86 rue du Faubourg St. Denis, Paris, France 75010). Gilson founded Palm Records in April '75, prod. albums w. Byard Lancaster, Baikida, Bill Coleman et al. Fests: Juan-les-Pins, '65; San Remo, '66; Terre Des Hommes, Montreal '72.

Comps: *Chant Inca; L'oeil Vision* for Ponty; *Je Me Souviens Encore Du Grand Orchestre De Dizzy Gillespie; Chakan.* Gilson has also been active as a sound engineer from '51.

LPs: *L'Oeil Vision; Gaveau; 16 Years of Jazz* (SFP); w. Bill Coleman, *Jazz Pour Dieu* (Unidisc); *Swing Low, Sweet Chariot* (Concert Hall); others w. Philly Joe Jones (Vogue); Sahib Shihab (Futura); *New Call From France* (MPS); w. Ponty, *Malagasy* (Palm); *Soul of Africa,* w. Hal Singer (Chant Du Mond).

GIUFFRE, JAMES PETER (JIMMY),* *composer, clarinet;* also *tenor sax, flutes;* b. Dallas, Texas, 4/26/21. During the late '60s and early '70s, Giuffre was very active as a composer and educator, as well as making concert apps. He did not begin to play in clubs again until '75, when he worked at St. James Infirmary and Tin Palace, NYC. He cont. his clarinet studies w. Arthur Bloom, '61-4; reed-making and clarinet w. Kal Opperman, '66-9; flute w. Jimmy Politis, '68-72. Holds teaching positions at New School, N.Y.U., Livingston Coll.; presided over student jazz workshop at own studio, '72. Lecture at Wagner Coll., *Exploring Art in N.Y.,* '68. Performed *The Castle,* a ballet w. Jean Erdman at N.Y.U., U.C.L.A., '67. Pl. concerts at U.C.L.A., '67, '74; Guggenheim Museum, '73; Smithsonian Inst., '74. Commissioned by St. Luke's Church, NYC, to write *Life's Music* for Men and Boy's Choir. Awarded Guggenheim Fellowship, '68. Voted number one clarinet in *Melody Maker* poll, '68; won several *Jazz Podium* (Germany) polls in '60s. TV: *Sunday,* NBC, '74. Comps: *Hex,* orig. written for Orchestra U.S.A., was used as part of ballet, *Manikins,* by Joffrey Ballet Co., '66; *Orb,* for clarinet and string quartet, perf. at Whitney Museum, NYC, by Giuffre and Carnegie Quartet, '69. Scores for films: *This Island; Sighet-Sighet; Smiles; Discovery In a Landscape.* Publ: *Jazz Phrasing and Interpretation* (Associated Music Pub., 866 Third Ave., N.Y., N.Y. 10022); *Sketch-Orks* (Criterion Music, 6124 Selma Ave., Hollywood, Ca. 90028). LP: *Music For People, Birds, Butterflies and Mosquitoes; River Chant* (Choice).

GLADDEN, EDWARD (EDDIE), *drums;* b. Newark, N.J., 12/6/37. Feat. w. many groups in the Newark area since mid-60s, among them Freddie Roach, Larry Young, Johnny Coles, Woody Shaw, Buddy Terry, Mickey Tucker. Also worked w. K. Dorham, Grant Green, J. Moody, J. McGriff. In '74-5 was a member of Shirley

Scott trio feat. Harold Vick. LPs: w. L. Young, *Contrasts, Heaven on Earth* (Blue Note); w. B. Terry, *Soul-Natural* (Prestige); w. Moody, *Never Again* (Muse); w. Tucker and R. Hanna, *The New Heritage Keyboard Quartet* (Blue Note); *Triplicity* w. Tucker (Xanadu); w. McGriff, *The Main Squeeze* (Groove Merchant).

GLEASON, RALPH J., *critic*; b. New York City, N.Y., 3/1/17; d. Berkeley, Calif., 6/3/75. Educ. Horace Greeley H.S., Chappaqua, N.Y.; Columbia Coll., Columbia U., '38. Jazz reviewer, columnist, *Columbia Spectator*, '35-8; founder and editor *Jazz Information*, '39-40; jazz critic *College Years*, '40; *Down Beat* corresp., critic, Assoc. Ed., columnist, '47-60; Contr. Ed., critic *Stereo Review*, '58-63; columnist, critic, *San Francisco Chronicle*, '51-75; syndicated jazz columnist world wide, '57-70; founder, editor, *Jazz* quarterly, '58-60; *Variety* corresp., '53-7; articles on jazz in *Esquire, Saturday Review, Show Bus. Illus.*, NY *Herald Tribune*, LA *Times*, Chicago *Sun-Times*, NY *Post*, London *Times*, *Lithopinion etc*; *Rolling Stone* (a founder and editor, '67-75); 26 half hour jazz shows, *Jazz Casual*, NET, '60-70; TV NET films: *Anatomy of a Hit*, '64; *Love You Madly*, '68; *Sacred Concert*, '69; *Monterey Jazz Fest.*, '69. Books: *Jam Session* (Putnam's '57); *Jefferson Airplane & The San Francisco Sound* (Ballantine, '68); *Celebrating the Duke and Other Heroes* (Atlantic Monthly Press, '75); Member of advisory board Lenox School of Jazz; U.C. Jazz Festival; Monterey JF; Stanford Jazz Year. Lecturer on jazz: Stanford U.; U.C. Berkeley; Sonoma State Coll. Exec. Prod. *Payday*, '73; Documentary perf. TV film NET, '70, *Go Ride The Music, Night at the Family Dog*. Awards: Sun Reporter Citizen of the Year, '64; Deems Taylor Award American Society, Composers, Authors & Publs., '62, '73; White House Enemies List, '73 (this last an honor of which he was particularly proud).

As the first jazz critic to take rock music seriously and to write about it extensively, Gleason earned the admiration of young fans as well as that of his contemporaries. He believed passionately in everything to which he devoted his time and his typewriter. His final book, *Celebrating the Duke*, provided a fitting memorial to a fearlessly honest man, who for 40 years fought relentlessly for his beliefs.

GLENN, EVANS TYREE,* *trombone, vibes*; b. Corsicana, Tex., 11/23/12. The swing trombonist who had worked in the bands of Benny Carter, C. Calloway, Don Redman and many others died 5/18/74 of cancer in Englewood, N.J. He had been pl. w. L. Armstrong from '65 until Armstrong's death in '71, and subsequently led his own combo. His death occurred only six days before that of Duke Ellington, in whose orch. he had pl. from '47-51.

LPs: *Newport in N.Y. '72* (Cobblestone) others w. Ellington (Col.); Armstrong (various labels). Glenn was survived by two sons, both musicians: Tyree Jr., who plays vibes and tenor sax, and Roger, a flutist and vibraphonist.

GOLSON, BENNY,* *composer, tenor saxophone*; b. Philadelphia, Pa., 1/25/29. Worked with many jazz orchs.; co-led Jazztet w. Art Farmer in early '60s, then gave up playing to concentrate on composing and arranging. In '67, moving to LA, began working at Universal Studios as composer. From '68 wrote for various artists in LA: Peggy Lee, Lou Rawls, Nancy Wilson, Sammy Davis Jr., Cal Tjader, Diana Ross, O.C. Smith et al. Began writing TV and radio commercials. Wrote music for M*A*S*H TV series, '73-5. In '75, composed theme and additional music for Karen Valentine Show. Rec. album in Hollywood with A. Farmer, F. Rosolino, Chuck Domanico, Mike Wofford, and Golson's son Reggie, for EastWind Records of Tokyo. Comp. *Yesterday's Thoughts* for Charlie Parker Concert; lyrics later written by Peggy Lee. Work was played at concert in Tokyo feat. Sadao Watanabe.

In May '75, Golson was the central figure in a concert of his comps. at Town Hall. Among his consistently attractive comps. are *I Remember Clifford; Whisper Not; Stablemates; Along Came Betty; Blues March; Five Spot After Dark; Are You Real*.

GOMEZ, EDGAR (EDDIE),* *bass*; b. Santurce, Puerto Rico, 10/4/44. Early experience w. Newport Youth Band; then pl. w. M. McPartland; Paul Bley; Gary McFarland. From '66 almost continuously w. Bill Evans, where his amazingly articulate and sensitive horn-like lines have been an inseparable part of the trio's sound. During these years he has also been closely associated w. Jeremy Steig; and Lee Konitz, w. whom he performed in tandem at Stryker's, NYC, '74. Own gp. at Sweet Basil, NYC, '75. LPs: see Evans; also w. Steig, *Monium* (Col.).

GONSALVES, PAUL (MEX),* *tenor saxophone*; b. Boston, Mass., 7/12/20. A member of the Duke Ellington orch. since '50, Gonsalves died 5/14/74 in London, only ten days before the passing of Ellington. Gonsalves had been in poor health for some years. He was one of several major losses to tenor saxophone jazz of what is generally known as the Coleman Hawkins school. Though his style was closer to Ben Webster's than to Hawkins', all three men had much in common with one another, as well as with Don Byas, Flip Phillips and Lucky Thompson.

Despite the reputation he gained as a creator of excitement, mainly as a consequence of his solo on *Diminuendo and Crescendo in Blue* during an Ellington appearance at the NJF, Gonsalves was greatly admired for the warmth and intimacy of his ballad work.

LPs: *Just A-Sittin' And A-Rockin'* w. Ray Nance (Black Lion); others w. Lawrence Brown, Johnny Hodges; also see ELLINGTON, DUKE.

GONZALES, BABS,* *singer*; b. Newark, N.J., 10/27/19. Led his vocal-instrumental gp., Babs' Three Bips and a Bop, which incl. Tadd Dameron, in mid-'40s. Managed and sang w. James Moody in '50s, Active as a single in '60s, '70s w. annual summer visits to Europe. In summer, '75, app. at Montreux, Hammerfeld, Laren, Cologne and Gothenberg fests.; small Euro. clubs; six dates w. Lionel

Hampton. Gave 17 concerts at universities in Holland in which his performance incorporated a 20 minute anti-drug lecture. U.S. fest: NJF-NY at Fordham U., '74.

Wrote two books about his life in jazz: *I Paid My Dues*; and *Movin' On Down De Line*, which he publ. himself (Expubidence Publ. Corp., 94 Milford Ave., Newark, N.J. 07108). His recordings are available on the Expubident label at the same address.

GOODMAN, BENJAMIN DAVID (BENNY),* *clarinet, leader*; b. Chicago, Ill., 5/30/09. Although not playing on a full-time basis Goodman, heading a variety of small groups (usually including Zoot Sims, Urbie Green, Bucky Pizzarelli, etc.), became more active in the '70s for concerts and performances at theatres-in-the-round. In addition he continued to tour in Europe. He played at the Rainbow Grill on several occasions in the 60s and '70s. and made guest appearances with the Chicago Symphony in '66, with Morton Gould conducting; and '67, with conductor Jean Martinon.

In January '68 he celebrated the 30th anniversary of his famed Carnegie Hall concert with a party and reunion. When he appeared in concert at Carnegie in September of '74, John S. Wilson wrote in the New York Times: ". . . the old fires may be banked but can still be stirred into flame."

Tom Scanlan, in reviewing a Goodman performance at Wolf Trap Farm in June '74, made note of "that gorgeous tone . . . that complete authority, that improvisatory genius with proper notes in proper places and in brilliantly unexpected places as well, with that very sound and approach that was unmistakably Benny Goodman."

In '70 Goodman toured Europe with a 16-piece band, including stops in Italy and Romania. The following year he returned to Europe to tour with an English band, making several guest appearances on TV; as soloist with symphony orchestras and chamber groups; and for a concert at Royal Albert Hall, London.

The sextet toured Europe in '72, recording in Copenhagen and taping a special for Swedish TV. Goodman also organized a big band for Canada's National Exposition and played with his original quartet for the Harvest Moon Ball at Madison Square Garden. In '73 the sextet played in Australia and England and he appeared with the original quartet (Lionel Hampton, Teddy Wilson and Gene Krupa) at the Newport Jazz Festival in New York.

Other festivals have included Comblain-La-Tour, '66; Schaefer Summer Fest., NYC, '72. TV: *Bell Telephone Hour*, '66; *Tonight*, '66; Merv Griffin, '68; Timex Swing Special, '72; BBC-TV, '73; NBC Special, '74; *Tribute to John Hammond*, PBS, '75. Goodman won the DB Readers poll, '73. Other awards include the Handel Medal from New York City, '66; LLD from Illinois Institute of Technology '68; first cultural award given by the State of Connecticut, '73; Citation "for exceptional and distinguished service" from Mayor John Lindsay of NYC, '73. A bio-discography, *B.G. On Record*, was published in '69 (see bibliography).

LPs: *On Stage*; *Today* (London); *The King in Person, Benny Goodman in the 70's* (Time-Life); reissues—

Giants of Swing (Prest.); *Greatest Hits* (Col.); *The Complete Benny Goodman, Vols. 1-3* (Bluebird).

GOODWIN, WILLIAM R. (BILL)* *drums*; also *percussion*; b. Los Angeles, Calif., 1/8/42. After pl. w. Leroy Vinnegar-Mike Melvoin trio, Paul Horn quintet, '66, w. Roger Williams; Gabor Szabo, '67; G. Shearing, '68. Joined Gary Burton, '69, moving to NYC, '70 and remaining w. Burton until Aug. '71. With Toshiko, '71; S. Getz, '72; G. Mulligan, '73-4; Al Cohn-Zoot Sims, '74. From '73 also pl. w. National Jazz Ensemble (charter member); Chamber Jazz Quintet; from '74 w. Children of All Ages; Phil Woods quartet. In '75 gigs w. Mose Allison w. whom he had app., off and on, from '68; Bill Evans. Lives in Pocono Mts. in Pa. near Bob Dorough, P. Woods, A. Cohn. Likes to sit in at local clubs w. John Coates Jr., Steve Gilmore. TV: *Tonight* Show w. Shearing; Tony Bennett Special w. Horn; *Homewood* Show w. Burton on PBS; *Jazz Adventures* w. Evans. Fest: NJF w. Szabo, '67; Burton, '69; Burton & K. Jarrett, '70; NJF-NY w. Mulligan, '73-4. LPs: w. Horn, *Cycle* (RCA); w. Burton & Jarrett; Burton & Grappelli; others w. Burton (Atl.); w. Jack Wilkins, *Windows*; w. Hal Galper, *Wild Bird; Inner Journey* (Main.); w. L. Tabackin, *Let the Tape Roll* (Victor Nippon); w. Dorough, *Multiplication Rock* (Cap.).

GORDON, DEXTER KEITH,* *tenor, soprano saxophones, composer*; b. Los Angeles, Calif., 2/27/23. Prominent w. the Billy Eckstine band and on 52nd St. in the '40s and in LA w. Wardell Gray in late '40s-early '50s as one of the most influential saxophonists of the bop era. Reestablished himself in the '60s w. a series of recs. for Blue Note. Moved to Copenhagen, '62, and has been heard most often at its leading jazz club Montmartre. Pl. clubs, concerts, fest. in Europe; periodic trips to US for recs., clubs, fests. Japanese tour, fall '75. He continued to display his warm, vitally swinging saxophone mastery in small gp. settings; and in a large orchestral context, incl. strings (w. arrs. by Palle Mikkelborg), entitled *More Than You Know* in '75.

Teaching for Worker's Cultural Foundation, Malmo, Sweden; for Jazz & Youth Society, Vallekilde, Denmark, '68. Fest: NJF, '70; NJF-NY, '72; Tangier, '72; Montreux, '73; also Molde; Ossiach, Austria. Won DB Critics poll, '71. TV: *Just Jazz*, PBS, '71. Comp: *Antabus; Candlelight Lady; The Apartment; Ernie's Tune; Tivoli; The Girl With the Purple Eyes; The Rainbow People; Montmartre; Boston Bernie; Fried Bananas; Mrs. Miniver; Valse Robin; The Panther; Stanley the Steamer.* LPs: *More Than You Know; The Apartment; The Meeting; The Source* both w. J. McLean (Steeple.); *Tower of Power; More Power; The Panther; The Jumpin' Blues; Generation; Blues A La Suisse; Tangerine; Ca' Purange* (Prest.); *Montmartre Collection* (Bl. Lion); *A Day in Copenhagen* (BASF); *Charlie Parker Memorial* (Chess); *Newport in New York, The Jam Sessions, Vol. 3&4* (Cobble.); *The Foremost* (Onyx); *Gettin' Around'*; re-issue anthology (BN); w. Miriam Klein (MPS).

GOURLEY, JAMES PASCO JR. (JIMMY),* *guitar, singer, composer*; b. St. Louis, Mo., 6/9/26. Playing and living in Paris from '57 w. own gps. and w. Kenny Clarke. From '66 worked w. Clarke in trio, first w. Lou Bennett, later w. Eddy Louiss as organist. Helped found Half Note club in Canary Islands, fall '70, playing there until April '72 when jazz policy was dropped and he ret. to Paris. Own quartet at Club St. Germain; duo at Bilboquet, '74; singing and pl. solo guitar at Caveau de la Montagne, '75. Solo at Sweet Basil, NYC, summer '75. App. w. Clarke in Elizabeth Taylor-Warren Beatty film, *The Only Game in Town*. Fest: Rencontres International de la Guitare (Arles, France) '73; w. own quartet, Bergamo '74; Middleheim '75; w. Clarke, Bergamo '75. Comps: *Comon' Ovah; Tafira Alta; Tats*; w. NYC lyricist Carol Bernstein, *Graffiti; Truth Game; Never Explain; Wrong Man Blues; Horoscope Blues; Tomorrow Just Flew By; Lost and Found*. LPs: *Comon' Ovah* (Futura); w. S. Grappelli, *Satin Doll* (Festival); *Eddy Louiss Orgue*, vols. 1&2 (America); *Clifford Brown in Paris* (Prest.).

GOYKOVICH, DUSKO (Dusan Gojkovic), * *trumpet, composer*; b. Jajce, Yugoslavia, 10/14/31. Played in many European bands before studying at Berklee Coll., '61-3. In U.S. w. M. Ferguson, '63-4; W. Herman, '64-6. Back to Europe, '66, played for eight months w. Sal Nistico in International Jazz Quintet; then w. Mal Waldron, Jimmy Woode, Philly Joe Jones; also w. Clarke-Boland big band until it broke up in '73. From '67, living in Munich, leading own quintet, composing and arranging. Taught trumpet, improvisation and arranging at Swiss Jazz School in Berne, also at Munich Jazz School. '74-5 co-led, with Slide Hampton, a 12 piece band called Summit, feat. American and European musicians.

In 1975 Goykovich observed: "I am trying to achieve originality through melodic and rhythmic use of Yugoslavian folklore in jazz. I am writing original tunes and playing them with my quintet and big band."

Favs: R. Eldridge, D. Gillespie, K. Dorham, Clifford Brown, M. Davis. Publ: *Introduction for Jazz Trumpet Improvisation* (Jazz Studio, B. Schott's Soehne-Mainz, Germany). LPs for various European labels incl. Enja, Philips, Ensayo, MPS-BASF. Earlier LPs w. Clarke-Boland (Blue Note); Herman (Columbia).

GRAHAM, EDWARD B. (EDDIE), *drums*; b. New York City, 11/18/37. Stud. w. George Lawrence Stone, NYC; Vincent Mott, Miami; U. of Miami, '56-9; Berklee Coll., '59. Pl. w. many commercial groups, also Village Stompers, '68-9; Trummy Young in Hawaii; '70-1; freelance in LV, '72-4; traveled w. Earl Hines combo, '75. Favs: B. Rich, Rollo Laylan.

GRANZ, NORMAN, * *producer*; b. Los Angeles, Ca., 8/6/18. After selling his Verve Record Co. to MGM in '61, Granz continued from his Geneva base to import jazz concert tours on a large scale: Ray Charles, Basie, Fitzgerald, Peterson et al. In '67, for the first time in a decade, he assembled a Jazz at the Philharmonic unit to tour the U.S. At the end of the tour, he announced that he would never again undertake such an enterprise in the U.S., and with the exception of a concert at the Santa Monica Civic '72 and "Tribute to Norman Granz" night

at the MJF, he made no further appearances in the U.S. However, in '73 he returned to the record business, starting his own label, Pablo. For this company he recorded Duke Ellington's final studio sessions, various albums feat. E. Fitzgerald, O Peterson (both of whom he continued to manage) and many w. Joe Pass, D. Gillespie, Joe Turner, C. Basie and other mainstream artists. A tape recorded live during his '67 JATP tour was released on Pablo as *The World's Greatest Jazz Concert*. In July 1975 at Montreux and in October '75 on a European tour, Granz presented a series of programs that were known as Pablo Jazz Festivals but were identical in style of presentation to the original JATP. The Montreux '75 programs were released on Pablo.

GRAPPELLI, STEPHANE (Grappelly), * *violin, piano*; b. Paris, France, 1/26/08. First renowned as a member of the Quintet of the Hot Club of France, 1934-39, Grappelli continued to build his reputation as one of the jazz violin greats with his own groups. In the late '60s and '70s he was still extremely active with apps. in clubs like Le Toit de la Paris Hilton, '69; Ronnie Scott's, '73; Buddy's Place, NYC, '74. His undiminished talents received a standing ovation at a Carnegie Hall concert, fall '74. TV apps. in Europe, U.S., Australia. Fests: Newport, Montreux et al. A more than capable pianist, he names as his originals infls., Beiderbecke ("at the piano"), Armstrong and Tatum. The soundtrack of the Louis Malle film *Lacombe, Lucien*, utilizes recordings of the original Quintet of the Hot Club of France. LPs: *I Remember Django; Just One of Those Things* (Black Lion); *Violinspiration; Afternoon in Paris; Violin Summit* (MPS/BASF); w. Reinhardt, *First Recordings of the Quintet of the Hot Club of France; Django Reinhardt and the American Jazz Giants* (Prestige); w. Yehudi Menuhin (Angel); w. O. Peterson (Prestige); w. Venuti, *Venupelli Blues* (Byg).

GRAVES, MILFORD ROBERT, * *drums, percussion*; b. Jamaica, N.Y., 8/20/41. Prominent in NY avant-garde circles in '60s w. Giuseppi Logan; NY Art Quartet; JCOA. Worked w. Paul Bley, '65; Albert Ayler, '67. From '65 closely associated w. reedman-pianist Hugh Glover in own ensemble utilizing only original works. In '75 working w. Glover on developmental project using music as a therapeutic means to assist psychological problems. To further this research formed Institute of Bio-Creative Intuitive Development.

Self-evolved style of tonal percussion, infl. most significantly, he feels, by tabla teacher, Wasantha Singh, w. whom he stud. North Indian music, '65. Film: *Lord Shango*, '74. TV: *Positively Black; Inside Bed-Stuy; Martin Luther King Special*, Metromedia. Fest: NJF, '67; '73-4; Autumn Fest., Paris, '74; Antwerp; Laren, '73. Won DB Critics Poll, TDWR, '67. Comp: *Transmutations*. LPs: Graves-Don Pullen, *Nommo; Live at Yale U.* (SRP); co-leader w. Andrew Cyrille, *Dialog of the Drums* (IPS); w. Albert Ayler (Imp.); Sonny Sharrock (Vortex); NY Art Quartet; JCOA (Font.).

GREEN, BENNIE, * *trombone, baritone horn*; b. Chicago, Ill., 4/16/23. After gigging around NYC with a quintet from '68, Green joined the D. Ellington orch. in June '69, replacing Buster Cooper. Working across country to LV, pl. there until late Sept.; left the band the following month and settled in LV, where he became a member of hotel bands pl. along the Strip, generally those of Joe Guercio and Jimmy Mulidore. TV: *Duke Ellington Sacred Concert*, St. John's Cathedral. Fests: NJF, '69; NJF-NY, '72.

Though well known internationally as a competent bop-influenced soloist, Green by late '75 had still never played overseas. Publ: *Be Bop Trombone Solos* (Belwin Mills Publ., NYC).

LPs: w. S. Stitt, *Pow* (Prest.), *My Main Man* (Cadet); *Newport in N.Y., The Jam Sessions*, Vols. 1&2 (Cobble.); *The George Benson Cookbook* (Col.).

GREEN, BERNARD (BENNY),* *writer, saxophones*; b. Leeds, Yorkshire, England, 12/9/27. During the '60s this brilliant writer virtually retired from playing to concentrate on his literary activities. Publs. incl. two novels with musical settings: *Blame It On My Youth; 58 Minutes to London*; two books of music criticism: *Jazz Decade; Drums In My Ears*, the latter publ. in the U.S. by Horizon Press. Book and lyrics for musical biography of G.B. Shaw, starring Cleo Laine, John Neville, with music by J. Dankworth, '69; wrote libretto for London revival of *Showboat*, '71. Co-devised Cole Porter revue, *Cole*. Literary critic for *Spectator*, '70- ; film critic for *Punch*, '72- .

TV: Three documentaries on London; biography of Irving Berlin. Radio: eight one-hour shows w. Ella Fitzgerald; 13 one-hour shows w. Fred Astaire. Artistic dir., New Shakespeare Co. Chief annotator for the Pablo label.

GREEN, FREDERICK WILLIAM (FREDDIE),* *guitar*; b. Charleston, S.C., 3/31/11. His impeccable rhythm guitar continued to set the time and sound for Count Basie's band as it has for so many decades. LPs: See Basie; w. Herb Ellis, *Rhythm Willie* (Concord).

GREEN, GRANT,* *guitar*; b. St. Louis, Mo., 6/6/31. Pl. w. Jimmy Forrest in St. Louis in '50s; w. organists Sam Lazar; Jack McDuff. Began rec. for Blue Note in '60s as leader, and as sideman w. H. Mobley; H. Hancock; L. Morgan. Inactive due to personal problems, '67-9, then resumed rec. for BN, later for Verve. Living in Detroit, '74. Performed music for the film, *The Final Comedown*. LPs: *Live at the Lighthouse; Shades of Green; Goin' West; Carryin' On; Alive; Visions* (BN); *Iron City* (Cobble.); *Cantaloupe Woman* (Verve).

GREEN, THURMAN ALEXANDER, *trombone*; b. Longview, Tex., 8/12/40. Educ: Longview H.S., '54-8, Compton Coll. '58-61, U.S. Navy School of Mus., '61-2, West LA Coll., '69-71. Pl. w. Roger Spotts, '65-7, Horace Tapscott, '66-9. Gerald Wilson, '67-74, Francisco Aguabella, '70-1, Teddy Edwards, '72-5, Harold Land, 73-4, Willie Bobo, '74-5. Pl. on sound track *They Shoot Horses, Don't They?* Favs: Ch. Parker, J.J. Johnson, G. Wilson.

LPs: w. G. Wilson, *Live and Swinging; Everywhere, California Soul; Equinox* (Pacific Jazz); *Things Ain't*

What They Used To Be, w. Ella Fitzgerald (Reprise); *Adam's Apple* w. Doug Carn (Black Jazz).

GREEN, URBAN CLIFFORD (URBIE),* *trombone*; b. Mobile, Ala., 8/8/26. Former Gene Krupa, Woody Herman and Benny Goodman sideman led his own big band in '66 after having fronted the Tommy Dorsey orch. In '67 he again led the Dorsey band at the Riverboat, NYC. Own band, using amplifying, octave-expanding devices in a mainstream-rock mix, at Riverboat, '69. From '71 own small gps. at London House, Blues Alley, Royal Box. Occasional tours w. Goodman. Soloist and clinician in Wisc., Minn., No. Dak., Buffalo, N.Y. and Laramie, Wyoming. Featured soloist w. U. of Cincinnati band. Annual participant in Music Educators Convention, San Antonio. Played at White House for Duke Ellington's 70th birthday party. Fest: NJF-NY; Colo. JP; Mobile Collegiate JF; Loosdrecht (Holland). TV: *Dial "M" for Music*; Mike Douglas; *The Main Event* w. Sinatra.

His brand of versatile excellence is marked by a gorgeous, mellow-brassy sound, marvelous control in all ranges of the horn, and overall ease of delivery. Married to his vocalist Kathy Preston. Raises Charolais beef cattle on a farm in Pennsylvania.

LPs: *21 Trombones, Vol. 1; Vol. 2; Green Power; Bein' Green; Big Beautiful Band* (Project 3); *Colorado Jazz Party* (MPS); w. John Bunch (Famous Door).

GREENE, BOB, *piano*; b. New York City, 9/4/22. An early student of traditionalist jazz, he absorbed this music in NO, pl. w. Geo. Lewis at Preservation Hall. Mainly self-taught through listening to Jelly Roll Morton records. Made first important record session w. Sidney De Paris for Blue Note in '52. After working w. Baby Dodds in '50s, Z. Singleton in '60s et al, he org. a recreation of Morton's 1927 Red Hot Peppers band, feat. mostly younger musicians, but incl. Tommy Benford, one of Morton's orig. drummers. The band gave three successful concerts at New York's Lincoln Center and later toured the U.S. and Canada. Fests: NO; Newport; Nice; St. Louis Ragtime Fest.

LPs: *Bob Greene's World of Jelly Roll Morton* (RCA); *Bob Greene and the Peruna Jazzband* (Danish FC Records); *Bob Greene-Don Ewell* (FC); *Dixieland Today* (Circle); *The St. Peter Street Strutters; Johnny Wiggs at Preservation Hall* (Pearl).

GREENE, BURTON (NARADA), *piano, composer*; b. Chicago, Ill, 6/14/37. Classical training at Fine Arts Academy, 1944-51; stud. modern jazz w. Dick Marx '56-8. Co-founded Free Form Improvisation Ensemble w. Alan Silva, '63. Member Jazz Composers Guild '64-5. First quartet, '65, w. Marion Brown, Rashied Ali and Henry Grimes. During '67-9, app. at many jazz and rock clubs NYC; Sam Rivers, Byard Lancaster or G. Barbieri worked with him.

In June '69 Greene left for Europe, where he enjoyed continuous success as composer and performer. Commissions: *Holiday Suite* for Danish Radio; ORTF concerts for trio and quartet; *Depth*, for ten musicians, premiered on AVRO, Hilversum; *Improvisations for Three Pianos* w. Paul Bley for VPRO; Frankfurt Radio concert w.

John Tchicai; Perfs. at Maisons des Jeunes Culturelles, France; East and West Trio and *Shanti Om* suite, perf. by sextet, '74. Fests. in France, Belgium, Germany, Holland. Wrote score for animated film *Birth of a Mountain*.

Greene analyzes his music as "a reflection of my origins and experiences in our Western culture. As an eclectic composer my work exists independently of categories. The music is highly structured, but allows great personal initiative; for example, you have the rhythm and improvisational freedom of jazz contrasted against the precise forms of either Western classical music (fugues and song form etc.) or Eastern classical music (ragas)."

In 1975 Greene toured with a trio featuring cello and table drums, the latter pl. by Indian musician Zamir Ahmed Khan,; also worked with sextet, mainly composed of American musicians living in Amsterdam, Greene's home base. Recordings in Europe: *Burton Greene Quartet; Burton Greene Trio on Tour; Patty Waters Sings* (ESP); *Presenting Burton Greene* (CBS); *Aquarians* (Byg); *Celesphere* (Futura); *Mountains, Trees* (Button-Nose Records); *At Different Times* (Group Music I).

GREENWICH, SONNY, *guitar;* b. Hamilton, Ontario, Canada, 1/1/36. Self-taught. Played w. John Handy in U.S., '66-7; own band, incl. Jimmy Garrison, Jack DeJohnette at Village Vanguard, '68; also worked w. Miles Davis in Toronto. Retired from music for several yrs. to "follow spiritual pursuits," returning to active pl. in late '72. Infl: Rollins, Coltrane, M. Davis, Hindemith, Ravel, Debussy, Bartok. Comps: *Starlight; Peace Chant; Parting; Lily; Loving.* LPs: *The Old Man and the Child* (Sack.); *Sun Song* (CBC); w. Handy in *Spirituals to Swing, 30th Ann'y* (Col.); w. Jimmy Dale, *Soft and Groovy* (Cap.); w. Don Thompson, *Love Song for a Virgo Lady* (Sack.); w. Moe Koffman, *Solar Explorations* (GRT); w. Lee Gagnon, *Jazzzz* (Barclay).

GREER, WILLIAM ALEXANDER (SONNY),* *drums;* b. Long Branch, N.J., 12/13/03. The percussionist w. Duke Ellington's band from 1919 to March '51; worked w. J. Hodges, Red Allen and T. Glenn in '50s and freelanced in NYC during the '60s. Weekends w. own trio, incl. Haywood Henry and Ray Tunia, at Garden Cafe, fall '71. Subbed for Sam Woodyard w. Brooks Kerr at Churchill's, Mar. '74. Joined Kerr's trio at Gregory's w. Russell Procope, May '74 after app. w. Kerr at NYJRC birthday tribute to Ellington in Apr. Fest: NJF-NY '72. Movie: *Sonny,* an 11-minute film issued by Signet Prod., '68. TV: *Today Show,* '74. LPs: *Soda Fountain Rag* w. Kerr (Audiofidelity); *Once Upon A Time* w. Earl Hines (Impulse); many reissues w. Ellington (Decca, Columbia, RCA).

GREY, ALBERT THORNTON (AL),* *trombone;* b. Aldie, Va., 6/6/25. After working w. Benny Carter, J. Lunceford, L. Hampton, D. Gillespie, became known internationally as member of C. Basie orch., '57-61, and again frequently from '64 on. While w. Basie, or during absences from band, he did studio rec. w. Q. Jones, L. Armstrong, J. Hodges, Randy Weston. Led own combo and served as mus. dir. of jazz night club in Phila. Toured Europe several times, with JATP, and as member of

Kansas City Seven, also as a single with all star show. Motion Picture: sound track w. Q. Jones for *Last of the Mobile Hotshots.* TV: Timex show etc.; Oscar Peterson show in Canada; several others in England, France etc.

Grey played the baritone horn (euphonium) on Cadet album feat. a group he co-led w. Billy Mitchell, which won a DB Critics Poll as No. 1 combo. Grey himself also won poll as trombonist.

LPs as leader: *Shades of Grey* (Tangerine); as sideman: *Gula Matari,* w. Q. Jones (A & M); Count Basie-Frank Sinatra at the Sands (Reprise); *Ella Fitzgerald at Carnegie Hall* (Col.); *Jazz At The Santa Monica Civic* (Pablo); *The Newport Years* (Polydor); many others on numerous labels w. Basie.

GRIFFIN, JOHN ARNOLD III (JOHNNY),* *tenor sax;* b. Chicago, Ill., 4/24/28. With Art Blakey; Thelonious Monk in '50s; co-leader w. Lockjaw Davis in early '60s. Moved to Europe Dec. '62, pl. all over the Continent. Lived in Paris in late '60s but moved to Holland, where he has his own farm, in '70s. Prominently featured at the Montreux Jazz Festival '75, he can be heard in three LPs recorded on that occasion: *Count Basie Jam Session; Dizzy Gillespie Big 7; Highlights of the Montreux Jazz Festival 1975* (Pablo). Other LPs: *Blues For Harvey* (Steeple.); quartet (Horo); reissue (Milest.); w. Bud Powell, *Bud in Paris* (Xanadu); w. *Passport et al/Doldinger Jubilee '75* (Atl.); reissue material on *Blowing Sessions* (BN).

GRIMES, LLOYD (TINY),* *guitar;* b. Newport News, Va., 7/7/17. Played w. Cats and a Fiddle; Art Tatum; then own gp., the Rocking Highlanders, '40-50s. In early '60 worked in Harlem, Greenwich Village. Toured France w. Milt Buckner, '68; J. McShann, '70. In '70s pl. w. own gps. at the Cookery; West End Cafe; gigs w. the Countsmen; also w. Earl Hines for a few mos. in late '72. Fest: Kennedy Center Jazz Fest., Wash., D.C.; NJF-NY, '73-4. Took part in all star guitar concert at Town Hall, '71 and appears on an LP taped that night, *The Guitar Album* (Col.). Own LPs: *Profoundly Blue* (Muse); (Black & Blue).

GROSSMAN, STEVEN, *saxophones;* b. Brooklyn, N.Y., 1/18/51. Alto sax from '59. Stud. w. brother Hal, who was later a teacher at Berklee Coll. of Music. Took up soprano sax at 16 and tenor a year later. Late in '69 he made his first record date w. Miles Davis, and from March to Sept. '70 was a member of Davis' group. Pl. w. Lonnie Liston Smith May to Dec. '71; Elvin Jones, '71-3; Stone Alliance w. Gene Perla, '75. Infl: Coltrane, Shorter, Rollins. Own LP: *Some Shapes to Come* (P.M.); LPs: w. Davis, *Jack Johnson; Live-Evil; Miles Davis at Fillmore* (Col.); w. Jones, *Merry-Go-Round; Live at the Lighthouse* (BN); others w. C. Corea; Terumasa Hino (released in Japan).

GROVE, RICHARD DEAN (DICK),* *composer, piano, educator;* b. Lakeville, Ind., 12/18/27. Played in jazz combos and bands in early '60s before graduating into extensive activities writing for TV and records; also led own big band at Donte's, '67. Started educational publ. co., featuring his own improvisation course, '71. Many apps. with own quintet at coll. concerts and fests. Book: *Arranging Concepts*, publ. '73. Comp. 15 min. jazz suite for U. of Fla. under grant from Nat'l Endowment For the Arts, '73. Founded Dick Grove Music Workshops in Studio City, Cal., '73. By '75 the school had grown to 700 students studying some 25 different subjects.

Publs: *Encyclopedia of Basic Harmony & Theory Applied to Improvisation on All Instruments*, Vols. I, II and III; (this, and abovementioned *Arranging Concepts*, publ. by First Place Music Publs. Inc., 12754 Ventura Blvd., Studio City, Ca. 91604).

LPs: *Big, Bad and Beautiful* (FPM); w. Buddy Rich, *Best of Buddy Rich; The New One; Feeling Kind of Blues* (Pacific Jazz).

GRUBBS, CARL GORDON, *alto sax, composer;* also *piano;* b. Philadelphia, Pa., 7/27/44. Brother of Earl Grubbs (see below). Cousin Naima was married to John Coltrane. Studied at Phila. Community Coll.; privately w. Coltrane, Harry Johnson, Owen Marshall. Was given a horn by Eric Dolphy. With brother Earl formed a group called The Visitors which is Phila.-based but pl. in NYC at Folk City during time of NJF-NY, '72. Apps. at Coltrane Memorial concert, Phila. '67; Angela Davis speech at Temple Univ. Nov. '74. Joe Klee described The Visitors: "Compositionally, their originals bring to mind the Trane . . . just after *A Love Supreme*, a transitional period . . ." Additionally infl. by Charlie Parker, Pharoah Sanders, Earl Grubbs. Comps: *Pisces; The Visit; Mood Seekers; Glad To Be Sad; China.* LPs: *Neptune* (Cobblestone); *In My Youth; Rebirth* (Muse).

GRUBBS, EARL DELCI, *tenor, soprano saxes, composer;* also *piano;* b. Philadelphia, Pa., 7/13/42. Studied at City Coll. of N.Y., Phila. Community Coll.; privately w. Owen Marshall, Harry Johnson, Coltrane. Worked w. Coltrane; Pharoah Sanders; and w. brother Carl in The Visitors. Infls: Parker, Coltrane, Sanders, Carl Grubbs. Comps: *In My Youth; Love Is Magic; Joy; A Touch of Warm; Gone Are the Days; Two Wives; China.* The Visitors' album *Neptune* was reviewed by Matt Damsker as having an "elevated . . . continually peaking quality, an altitude that invites comparison with the Mahavishnu Orchestra." Their music reflects the peace and love messages of Coltrane's later work. LPs: see Carl Grubbs.

GRUNTZ, GEORGE,* *piano, composer;* b. Basel, Switzerland, 6/24/32. Winner of several prizes at Zurich jazz festivals in '50s; major jazz fests. around world incl. US from late '50s through '60s. Member of Phil Woods' original Rhythm Machine quartet in Europe, 1968-9. From '70, mus. dir.-in-chief of Zurich Playhouse; in Jan. '72 appointed director of the Berlin Jazz Festival (Berliner Jazztage).

In 1971 Gruntz created a European cooperative of pianists, known as Piano Conclave. Its personnel, which varied from concert to concert, was drawn from a pool of leading European and US artists on piano, elec. piano, harpsichord, synthesizer etc., usually employing six keyboard soloists plus a rhythm section.

LPs: on Atl., MPS-BASF, Philips, Decca, HMV; w.

Franco Ambrosetti, *Steppenwolf* (PDU); also see Woods, Phil.

GRUSIN, DAVE,* *composer, piano;* b. Denver, Colo., 6/26/34. Frequent associate of Q. Jones from '60. While married to singer Ruth Price, acc. her in clubs; arr., prod. recs. for S. Mendes, Peggy Lee. To Brazil w. Mendes, '68, '75; Japan, '73 w. Jones. Grusin has also pl. off and on w. Tom Scott; in '73-4 w. G. Mulligan; '74 w. Lee Ritenour. Arr. and rec. w. Jones, S. Vaughan, C. McRae, Jon Lucien, R. Flack, Aretha Franklin.

His many feat. film credits incl. *Three Days of the Condor; Tell Them Willie Boy Is Here; The Heart Is A Lonely Hunter; The Graduate; Divorce American Style* etc. TV credits: *Trial of Chaplain Jenson; Good Times; Maude; Dan August; Bold Ones; The Name of the Game* etc.

GUARALDI, VINCENT ANTHONY (VINCE),* *composer, piano;* b. San Francisco, Calif., 7/17/28. Early exp. w. Cal Tjader, Woody Herman in 1950s. From 1963, principally active writing and playing music for *Peanuts* TV series, for which he produced the sound track. Nominated for Academy Award for music in feature film *A Boy Named Charlie Brown.* Continued to play concerts and occasional clubs engagements in SF Bay Area until his death of a heart attack, 2/6/76, in Menlo Park, Cal. No LPs since three for Warner Brothers in late 1960s.

GUARNIERI, JOHN A. (JOHNNY),* *piano, composer;* b. New York City, 3/23/17. During the late '60s Guarnieri became intensively involved with the use of 5/4 time, rec. an album of standards and originals using this meter. Perf. piano concerto in 5/4 at Wilshire Ebell Theatre, LA, '70; spent most of early '70s at Tail O'The Cock restaurant in N. Hollywood, Cal., but took time out to tour Europe with Slam Stewart, '74, and w. all star program of jazz pianists, '75. Rec. album of Harry Warren tunes for Detroit Hot Jazz Society. Fests: Concord, '70; NJF-NY, '74; Nice, '75. In '75 working on a book, *From Ragtime to Tatum*, dealing with 75 pianists, with musical and recorded illustrations, for publ. by Schirmer Books.

LPs: *Plays Harry Warren* (Jim Taylor Presents); *Piano Dimensions* (Dot).

GUERIN, JOHN PAYNE, *drums;* also *tenor saxophone;* b. Hawaii, 10/31/39. Family settled in San Diego when he was three. Self-taught; learned by pl. w. Count Basie records. His teenage gp. won college jazz fest. at Lighthouse, '57. Joined Buddy De Franco, '59, for a year. Moved to LA, '63, joined Geo. Shearing, '65 for year and a half. Worked w. T. Monk, D. Byrd, R. Kellaway, V. Feldman, F. Zappa, Howard Roberts, Jimmy Smith and, from '68, thousands of artists in TV, film and rec. studios. From '74, involved in co-op gp., L.A. Express, bridging rock and jazz elements; also branched out into producing, comp., arr.

Guerin, who won a Most Valuable Player award from NARAS in '74 and '75, is a completely adaptable musician who has distinguished himself in every type of setting. Comps: *Mr. & Mrs. America and All The Ships At Sea*, for L.A. Express; *Mauro*, for H. Roberts. Infls: B. Rich, Tony Williams, Miles Davis, J. Coltrane, Gil Evans, Ch. Parker. Fests: Monterey, w. Monk, Tom Scott, B. Bryant; Newport w. L.A. Express; Caracas Music Fest. w. L.A. Express. Publ: *Jazz + Rock = John Guerin* (Gwyn Publ. Co., 14950 Delano St., Van Nuys, Ca. 91601).

LPs: w. L.A. Express (Ode); w. Monk, *Sphere* (Col.); w. Zappa, *Hot Rats* (Bizarre); w. Pat Williams, *Threshold* (Cap.); w. Joni Mitchell, *Court & Spark* (Asylum).

GUERIN, ROGER,* *trumpet*; b. Saarebruck, Saar, France, 1/9/26. Played w. Django Reinhardt. Newport International Band, '58. With Q. Jones, D. Gillespie bands in Europe in '60s. From '66 to '70 studio work in Paris; also worked with Paris Jazz All Stars, '66-8; tours w. Jack Dieval Quartet for Jeunesses Musicales de France, '68-70. From '68-70 he also taught jazz at the Conservatoire Claude Debussy in St. Germain en Laye. From '71 teaching jazz at the Maison des Jeunes et de la Culture, St. Germain en Laye, rehearsing an amateur big band each Monday and pl. concerts in other M.J.Cs. From '70 leading an 18-piece band at the Casino de Paris for Roland Petit, Zizi Jeanmaire. TV apps. w. Dieval and Georges Jouvin as both trumpeter and producer. Fest: Antibes w. own quintet '67; Nice w. Dieval '70; Avignon w. Andre Hodeir '74; Paris JF w. St. Germain Big Band; Antibes w. Eddy Louiss '75. Plans to open jazz school w. Parisian jazzmen at M.J.C. of St. Germain en Laye. LPs: *Trumpets of Paris* w. Georges Jouvin, Roger Delmotte; many albums w. Dieval "but just for the backgrounds with disc-jockeys."

GUIN, FRANCOIS (FRICK), *trombone*; also *flute*; b. Contres, France, 5/18/38. Guin, whose main insp. and infl. is D. Ellington, formed a group in Paris called The Swingers in Oct. '68. Until Mar. '69 app. nightly at the Club St. Germain; from Apr. to Dec. '69 at the Caveau de la Huchette. In Nov. '69, Guin subbed in the Ellington band at the Paris JF; a month later the Swingers, also the Four Bones, a four trombone unit directed by Guin, perf. at the Grande Nuit du Jazz, Paris. App. w. Swingers at Antibes Fest; Duke Ellington 70th Anniv. Celebration at Alcazar, Paris, '69; Claude Bolling Radio Show, Frankfurt, '70; Eiffel Tower show; Zurich, Prague and Warsaw Fests., '71. Maurice Cullaz, pres. of the Academie du Jazz said of The Swingers: "They have the bad luck to be French and not colored." As a result they found it was necessary to tour in West Africa, '71, where they met w. different native combos to mix African rhythms with their own improvs. Also toured in Czechoslovakia, Poland, Switzerland, Turkey, Balearic Islands, Morocco, New Caledonia and Congo, '72-3. Toured southwest and south of France for Jeunesse Musicale Francaise, '73. In '70 Guin won the Jazz Hot poll as number one French trombonist, received the Prix Django Reinhardt as Musician of the Year from the Académie du Jazz.

The Swingers play a program of the history of jazz encompassing material from early spirituals through the comps. of Ch. Mingus, with a heavy concentration on the

Ellington repertoire. Several LPs on the Riviera label, one of which feats. P. Gonsalves. *Three Generations of Jazz* w. Bill Coleman (77 Records).

GULLIN, LARS GUNNAR VICTOR,* *baritone sax, composer*; also *piano*; b. Gotland, Sweden, 5/4/28. Many records with Swedish and U.S. musicians during '50s. Toured Italy w. Chet Baker, '59; from '60 concentrated mainly on solo work and writing, sometimes reforming his band for concerts and records. Won annual government artists' award as leading Swedish jazz musician, '68. Has won many awards on baritone including Swedish newspaper *Expressen's* prize, '73. Made TV film, *Danny's Dream*, '68-9, about his life as a composer, musician and human being. Many fests. throughout Scandinavia, England and Italy. Died 5/17/76 of a heart attack in Vissefjärda, Sweden. His last work *Areos Aromatic Atomica Suite*, was recorded by Swedish Radio Jazz Group in March '76; Comps: *Concerto for Piano and Orch.; Danny's Dream; Aesthetic Lady; Portrait Of My Pals; Jazzamour-Affair Suite; Bluesport*; also music for a TV drama.

LPs: Gullin Quartet, *Dream* (MG); Gullin octet (Atl.) *The Artistry of Lars Gullin* (Sonet); *Portrait of My Pals* (SSX); *Jazz Amour Affair* w. symph. orch; *Like Grass; Bluesport* (Odeon); *Danny's Dream* (Metronone); also w. *S. Getz and his Swedish Jazzmen* (Verve); w. Brew Moore (Fant.); Z. Sims, J. Moody, Q. Jones (Pres.).

GUMBS, ONAJE ALLAN, *piano, composer*; b. New York City, 9/3/49. Cousin, Fernando Gumbs pl. bass w. Exuma. Piano lessons at age seven. Stud. at Music & Art High Sch., '63-7; grad. w. Bach. of Mus. from SUNY at Fredonia, '71. Additional stud. at Indiana U. w. David Baker; Famous Arr. Clinic in LV, July '70. Pl. trombone in high sch. band and orch.; piano at church functions and variety shows. First prof. experience w. Andrew Langston Latin Jazz Quintet. After grad. guitarist-composer Leroy Kirkland helped get him started in mus. business. Worked w. Natural Essence, '72-4; Norman Connors, April-Oct. '73. Special concerts of Black music w. Buffalo Phil., summer '73; Zimbabwe National Rhythm Troup, Buffalo '72-4; also pl. w. Kenny Burrell; Mtume; CBA Ensemble; Betty Carter; Dakota Staton; Jimmy Owens; Carlos Garnett; Frank Foster; Dee Dee Bridgewater. App. w. Nat. Jazz Ensemble at Wolf Trap Farm, Va.; NYJRC in Feb. '75 *Tribute to Miles Davis*. Infl: H. Hancock, H. Silver, K. Jarrett, M. Tyner, B. Taylor; H. Mancini; G. McFarland, W. Shorter, D. Baker, B. Byers. TV: Villanova JF, '68; *Jazz Adventures; Positively Black; Like It Is*. Fests: NJF-NY w. Natural Essence; Norman Connors, '73-4. Comps: woodwind quartet, *Four in Miniature; Prelude to the World* for chamber orch.; *Dark of Light; Are They Only Dreams; Up the Street, Round the Corner, Down the Block; Batuki*. Arrs: *Love From the Sun; Dindi; Maiden Voyage; Skindiver*, all for Connors; *Stella By Starlight* for NYJRC's M. Davis tribute. LPs: w. Connors, *Dark of Light; Love From the Sun; Saturday Night Special* (Buddah); w. Woody Shaw, *Moontrane*; w. Garnett, *Black Love*; w. Buster Williams, *Pinnacle* (Muse);

w. L. Ridley, *Sum of the Parts;* w. C. Sullivan, *Genesis;* w. C. McBee, *Mutima* (Strata-East); w. Lenny White, *Venusian Summer* (Nemperor); w. R. Ayers, *A Tear to a Smile* (Poly.).

GUMINA, THOMAS JOSEPH (TOMMY),* *accordion;* b. Milwaukee, Wis., 5/20/31. Co-leader w. B. De Franco in the early '60s of a quartet that feat. his accordio-organ, Gumina later withdrew almost entirely from jazz activity in order to concentrate on the designing and merchandising of musical instruments.

GUY, FRED,* *guitar;* b. Burkeville, Ga., 5/23/1899. A regular member of the Duke Ellington orch. from the mid-20s until '49, Guy was heard first as a banjoist, and from '33 as a guitarist. In later years he managed a ballroom in Chicago. He committed suicide 11/22/71.
LPs: w. Ellington (Col., RCA).

HABIB, DONALD (DON), *bass, composer;* also *trumpet, piano, percussion;* b. Montreal, Canada, 4/21/35. From a musical family. Studied six yrs. at Provincial Cons., Mont.; one yr. of brass w. Carmine Caruso; Benny Baker, NYC; one yr. bass w. Fred Zimmerman of NY Phil.; comp. w. J. Giuffre; improvisation w. Adolphe Sandole, Phila.; cond. w. Mike Perrault, Mont.; arr. and orchestration, '72-4, w. Rayburn Wright and Manny Albam at Eastman Sch. Worked w. C. Mariano; Toshiko; Michel Legrand; J.J. Johnson; Skitch Henderson; P. Bley; S. Stitt; Rene Thomas; M. Ferguson. Infl: C. Baker, Clifford Brown; Ray Brown, S. LaFaro, Richard Davis; Gil Evans, Muzio Clementi, Tchaikowsky. TV: Mont. Fest: Mont.; Toronto; Ottawa; Montreux. Wrote children's series, variety shows, documentaries for CTV network; arrs. for CBC shows; commercials. LPs: w. Yvan Landry (Can. Cap.); w. Jerry DeVillers (Trans-Can.).

HACKETT, ROBERT LEO (BOBBY),* *cornet;* b. Providence, R.I., 1/31/15. Was guitarist, occasionally heard on cornet, w. Glenn Miller band in '41-2. Since then has led own combos, also making wide impression as soloist in Jackie Gleason series on Capitol in '50s. Moved to Cape Cod, '69, where he was often feat. at Dunfey's. Quintet w. Vic Dickenson pl. two months at Roosevelt Grill, NYC, '70, and toured in U.S., incl. NJF. Many apps. at Colorado Jazz Party, NJF-NY, guest shots w. WGJ; tour of England, Sept. '74; Apps. in Mass. and at Michael's Pub, NYC, '75; confined to a hospital for two weeks at the end of May '76, he was able to play an engagement on June 4 after his release, but died of a heart attack in Chatham, Mass., 6/7/76. Hackett, who said "I've been working steady since I was 14" was one of the jazz perennials, a cornetist with a beautifully burnished sound and a consistent habit of unceremoniously putting

all the notes in the right place at the right time; capable of playing comfortably with Dizzy Gillespie, Zoot Sims or the Eddie Condon alumni. His hobby was sound equipment. TV: *Just Jazz* w. Dickenson, PBS, '71. LPs: *Live at the Roosevelt Grill* (Chiaroscuro); *Plus Vic Dickenson; That Midnight Touch; Time For Love* (Project 3); *Live at the Royal Box* (Hyannisport); *What A Wonderful World; Strike Up the Band* (Fly. Dutch.); w. Mary Lou Williams, *Giants* (Perception); w. WGJ (World Jazz).

HADEN, CHARLES EDWARD (CHARLIE),* *bass, composer;* b. Shenandoah, Iowa, 8/6/37. Rejoined Ornette Coleman in '66 and has cont. to pl. w. him in addition to working w. the JCOA and Keith Jarrett. Haden has also perf. or rec. w. a wide spectrum of musicians incl. Archie Shepp, Tony Scott, Roswell Rudd, Red Norvo, Pee Wee Russell, Alice Coltrane, Mose Allison and John McLaughlin. Fests: NJF w. Shepp, '66-67; w. Don Cherry '73; W. Coleman: MJF '66-67; NJF '70-72; NJF European tour '71; Ann Arbor Blues Fest. '73; many European fests. w. Coleman, Jarrett. Films: *Last Tango in Paris* w. Barbieri; *The Holy Mountain* w. Cherry. Comps: *Song For Che; Circus '68-69.* Won DB Critics new star award '61. His first LP as a leader, *Liberation Music Orch.*, first rec. in '69 was reissued in Oct. '73 after winning awards from *Melody Maker, Swing Journal* and the Grand Prix Int. du Disque Academie. Haden was given grants in comp. by the Guggenheim Foundation '70; the National Endowment for the Arts '73. LPs: *Liberation Music Orch.; The Bass; College Concert* w. Pee Wee Russell, Red Allen (Impulse); *Science Fiction* w. Coleman (Columbia); *Escalator Over the Hill* w. Carla Bley; *Relativity Suite* w. Cherry (JCOA); *The Elements* w. Joe Henderson, Alice Coltrane (Milestone); *Expectations* w. Jarrett (Columbia); *Death and the Flower* w. Jarrett (Impulse); *Tribute* w. Paul Motian (ECM).

HAGGART, ROBERT SHERWOOD (BOB),* *bass, composer;* b. New York City, 3/13/14. The former Bob Crosby bassist-arranger was on staff at NBC and a regular on the *Tonight Show* orch. in '66-67. In '68 he and Yank Lawson (q.v.), with whom he had been associated in the Crosby band and in the '50s in a series of LPs, formed the World's Greatest Jazzband. The band toured the U.S. and Brazil '69; reopened the Roosevelt Grill, NYC, '70; toured Gr. Brit. '71; Hawaii '73; Gr. Brit., Germany, Scandinavia; Rainbow Grill '74. Haggart's *My Inspiration* is the WGJ's theme song and his other comps., *What's New; South Rampart Street Parade; Big Noise From Winnetka; Dogtown Blues;* and *I'm Prayin' Humble,* are prominently feat. in the band's library. In addition has contributed new originals and arrs. of contemporary pop material like *Up, Up and Away,* etc. App. at NJF '69, '72 w. WGJ; w. Friends of Eddie Condon '74. TV: *Today Show; Sunday,* both on NBC. Publ: *Bob Haggart Bass Method* (Robbins Music Corp. 1775 Broadway, New York, N.Y. 10019). LPs: w. WGJ on Project 3, Atlantic. Later albums on their own World Jazz label (4350 E. Camelback Rd., Phoenix, Ariz. 85018).

HAHN, JERRY DONALD, * *guitar*; b. Alma, Neb., 4/21/40. Orig. member, John Handy group, '65-7; toured w. 5th Dimension, '68; Europe, Japan, Canada, U.S., incl. Carnegie Hall recital w. Gary Burton, '68-9. In '70 formed Jerry Hahn Brotherhood, touring U.S. and Bahamas, rec. one album on Columbia. From '72-5 concert tours w. own quartet; from '72 full time prof. at Wichita State U. and clinician for C.G. Conn Ltd. Instr. Co. App. MJF w. Handy, '65 and '66; w. Burton, '68; Berlin J.F. w. Burton, '68; NJF, w. Burton, '69; own quartet at Wichita JF '74-5. In '74-5 had regular monthly column in *Guitar Player Magazine*. LPs: Fantasy, Columbia, Arhoolie; w. Burton on RCA, Atl.; w. Handy on Col.

HAIG, ALLAN W. (AL), * *piano, composer*; b. Newark, N.J., 7/22/24. An important player with Dizzy Gillespie, Charlie Parker in '40s; Stan Getz in '50s. During the '60s he worked for the most part in NYC eastside cocktail lounges, rarely playing jazz, but in the '70s he experienced a renaissance, pl. w. his own duo at Bradley's '73; solo and trio at Gregory's '74-5; trio at Sweet Basil, '75. In '73 he visited Europe for gigs at the Bilboquet; Chat Qui Peche in Paris; the Montmartre in Copenhagen. While there he gave concerts on French and Danish radio. In Nov. '74 he was reunited w. his associate from the bop era, Jimmy Raney for a concert at Carnegie Recital Hall. Haig wrote a Piano & String Quartet in '75.

LPs: *Al Haig-Jim Raney, Strings Attached* (Choice); *Invitation*, rec. in England (Spotlite); *Trio & Quintet* (Prest.).

HAKIM, SADIK (Argonne Dense Thornton), * *piano, composer*; b. Duluth, Minn., 7/15/22. The pioneer bop pianist, who pl. w. Ch. Parker, moved to Canada in the '60s, also spending six months in Europe in '72. Led own trio and quartet at Expo '67 and '68. Many radio shows in Montreal. Heard at Ronnie Scott's Club in London; Montmartre in Copenhagen; Randy Weston's club in Tangier, Morocco. Rec. w. own sextet for CBC, '72. Concerts, clubs in Toronto, Montreal, '74-5. Comps: *The London Suite; Liliane; A Prayer for Liliane*.

LPs: *Duke Ellington Memorial; The London Suite* (CBC); reissues w. Lester Young (BN); Charlie Parker (Arista).

HALL, ADELAIDE, * *singer*; b. Brooklyn, N.Y., 1909. Sang wordless vocals on Ellington records, '27; toured in many black revues in '30s. Settled in England in '38 after appearing at Drury Lane Theatre in *The Sun Never Sets*. Toured extensively throughout Europe during '40s; app. in *Kiss Me Kate* at London Coliseum, '51; *Love From Judy*, London, '53; *Jamaica* w. Lena Horne, NYC '57. Remained occasionally active in later years, living in London. In '74, at church of St. Martin's-In-The-Field, took part in memorial service for Ellington singing *Creole Love Song*, which she had originally rec. with him in '27.

LP: for EMI (England); others w. Ellington.

HALL, EDMOND, * *clarinet*; b. New Orleans, La., 5/15/01. Pl. in '40s and '50s w. Red Allen, Teddy Wilson, E. Condon, L. Armstrong. Toured Europe frequently in '60s, visiting there for the last time in '66. Shortly after playing a Carnegie Hall concert, Hall died of a heart attack in Boston, 2/11/67.

LPs: *Celestial Express*; w. Art Hodes, Original Blue Note Jazz, Vol. 1 (BN); w. Armstrong (various labels).

HALL, HERBERT L. (HERB), * *clarinet, reeds*; b. Reserve, La., 3/28/07. Brother of Edmond Hall. Mainly associated w. Don Albert in '30s, '40s; toured Europe w. Sammy Price in '50s; worked at Eddie Condon's in late '50s. Pl. in US and Canada w. Wild Bill Davison Jazz Giants, '67-9; Don Ewell trio in Canada, '70; Saints & Sinners, '72; Bob Greene, '73 and again in fall '75 for coll. and civic centers in south & midwest. From '74 w. Balaban & Cats; at new Eddie Condon's w. Balaban '75. Fest: Manassas, Va.; Detroit-Windsor, Ont.; NJF-NY w. Greene; Louis Armstrong Stadium dedication, '73; Nice, '75. LPs: *Clarinet Wobble* w. Joe Muranyi (Fat Cat Jazz); *Old Tyme Modern; The Jazz Giants* (Sack.); w. Greene, *The World of Jelly Roll Morton* (RCA); w. Balaban, *A Night at the New Eddie Condon's* (Classic Jazz).

HALL, JAMES STANLEY (JIM), * *guitar*; b. Buffalo, N.Y., 12/4/30. Played w. Chico Hamilton, J. Giuffre in late '50s; Lee Konitz, Sonny Rollins, Art Farmer, early '60s. Hall then decided (in '65) to give up touring, settled in NYC and took a job with the Merv Griffin TV show. Own small groups from '66, incl. duos w. such bassists as Jack Six and Ron Carter; in mid '70s devoting much time to solo playing. Pl. for Duke Ellington's birthday party at White House, '70; concerts for Smithsonian Inst.; feat. soloist w. Nat. Jazz Ens. at New School, '75. Teaching privately, '66-'73. Toured in Japan and Europe; apps. on Swedish, German, Spanish TV. Fests: Berlin, '69; Concord, '73; MJF, '74; NJF, '68, '70, '72-3, '75. Won DB Critics' Poll, '74; *Playboy* All Stars' All Stars, '69, '71-2. Comp: *Careful; Piece For Guitar and Strings*.

Whitney Balliett, in a 1975 profile of Hall in *The New Yorker*, attributed to him "a grace and inventiveness and lyricism that make him preeminent among contemporary jazz guitarists and put him within touching distance of the two grand masters—Charlie Christian and Django Reinhardt."

LPs: *Jim Hall Live!* (Horizon); *It's Nice To Be With You* (MPS/BASF); *Where Would I Be; Alone Together* (Milestone); w. Rollins, *The Bridge* (RCA).

HALL, JOE, *bass*; b. Washington, D.C., 11/9/52. Both parents musical. Pl. piano before taking up bass at 14. Began bass studies, '71. Enrolled at Howard U. as string bass major and became a founder member of the Blackbyrds, a student group sponsored by D. Byrd, who was then Chairman of the Dept. of Jazz Studies at Howard. The group pl. w. Byrd and perf. in concert along w. Sly Stone; M. Gaye; Earth, Wind and Fire and other pop stars.

LPs: *Flying Start; The Blackbyrds* (Fantasy).

HALLBERG, BENGT, * *piano, composer*; b. Gothenburg, Sweden, 9/13/32. Stud. piano w. Sixten Eckerberg in Gothenburg, '44-6; comp. w. Lars-Erik Larsson and counterpoint w. Ake Udden at Royal Academy of Mus.

in Stockholm, '54-7. Worked w. Thore Jederby, Kenneth Fagerlund in late '40s. Attained international recognition when he acc. Stan Getz on the saxophonist's Swedish tour and rec. w. him, '50. In '53 Hallberg also rec. w. Clifford Brown & Art Farmer. He led his own trio and was closely assoc. w. Lars Gullin and other top Swedish jazzmen. From '69 he has been a member of the Swedish Radio Jazz Group and the Arne Domnerus sextet with whom he pl. in NYC at the Swedish Embassy, '74. Infl: Teddy Wilson, Bud Powell, Lennie Tristano, Keith Jarrett. He became increasingly active as a composer from the late '50s beginning with a string quartet, '57; *Collabortion* for string quartet and piano, bass and drums, '63; *Kain,* a ballet for symp. orch. and rhythm section for Royal Swed. Opera, '64; Concertino for piano & string orch., '65; ballet for Swedish TV, '66; *Lyrisk Ballad* for two jazz pianists & orch., '68; *Froken Ensam Hemma,* a children's opera for Royal Swed. Opera; *Music for Jazz Combo & Symph. Orch,* '69; *Icelandic Souvenir; Spelet on Job* (lyrics from the Book of Job—Old Testament) for choir and jazz group, '70; *Beat Rondo,* '71; string trio; *Hallristningar,* '74; *We Love You Madly* (Duke Ellington in memoriam), '75. Publ: *Modern Jazz Piano* (Westin & Co., Brannryrragat. 84, Stockholm, Sweden); *Beginner's Course,* with recorded instr. (Reuter & Reuter Publ., Brahegatan 12, Stockholm, Sweden).

LPs: *P Som i Piano; Collaboration* (EMI); *At Gyllene Cirkeln* (Metronome); as arr: *Alice and Wonderband,* Alice Babs w. Domnerus (Decca); Swedish Radio Jazz Group, *Greetings and Salutations* feat. Thad Jones, Mel Lewis (Four Leaf Clover); as comp: *Spelet on Job* (Swed. Radio); *We Love You Madly* (Philips); feat. soloist in *Du Gladjerika Skona,* music by Jan Johansson (Swed. Radio).

HAMEL, PETER-MICHAEL, *keyboards*; also *singer*; b. Munich, Germany, 7/15/47. Grand-aunt a prominent classical pianist in Germany. Stud. comp. at Munich music high school; jazz piano w. Mal Waldron in conjunction w. French composer Luc Ferrari and German composer Carl Orff; stud. w. Morton Feldman in Berlin; Afro-Latin rhythms w. Jeff Biddeau in Trinidad; Indian classical music w. Imrat Khan and Pandit Patekar; Tibetan instruments and vocals in North India '73-74. Pl. concerts w. Between, an international group comprised of black conga players, classical oboeist and Argentinian guitarist during Olympic games, Berlin '72; avant-garde festivals, Berlin '72, Donaueschingen '73; Munich JF '74; pl. w. vibraphonist Tom Van Geld '74. Awarded several comp. prizes at Beethoven Fest. competition, Bonn '74. Comp. *Dharana; Samma Samadhi; Diaphainon; Maitrya;* and many pieces for Between. Music for theatre and films: *Wallenstein; Schwejk; The Violincello.* TV: *My Friends and Me; Mr. Gringo.* Pub: *Music and Meditation* (Barth Verlag, Munich). Infl. & insp: John Coltrane, Terry Riley, Steve Raich, John Cage, African, Indonesian & Indian music.

LPs w. Between, *Einsteig; And the Waters Opened* (Philips-Phonogram); *Dharana* (Philips-Phonogram); *Hesse-Between-Music,* prod. by J.E. Berendt). Solo LPs:

Hamel; The Voice of Silence (Philips-Phonogram); *Buddhist Meditation* (MPS).

HAMILTON, FORESTSTORN (CHICO),* *drums, composer*; b. Los Angeles, Cal., 9/21/21. After leading own groups off and on from '56 until mid-60s, Hamilton, based in NYC, started his own company, successfully writing jingles, music for movies, radio, TV. During the '70s he gradually returned to public playing. App. at Montreux JF, '72, '73. Formed new combo, '74. During Cal. tour in '75, he took part in a TV spec., *Reunion,* w. Buddy Collette and Fred Katz, both original members of Hamilton's 1950s quintet, for NET in San Diego.

Film scores: *Mr. Rico; Coonskin.* Many TV specs: *Ski Ski; Portrait of Willie Mays; Bellevue* etc. Many commercial spots for IBM specs. on TV. Comps: innumerable for new gp., incl. *Peregrinations; Sweet Dreams Too Soon; Everybody's; Morning Side of Love.*

LPs: *Peregrinations* (BN); *Best Of; Chic Chic Chico; Dealer; El Chico; Further Adventures; His Great Hits; Man From Two Worlds; Passin' Thru* (Imp.); *Head Hunters* (SS); *The Master* (Enterprise).

HAMILTON, JIMMY,* *clarinet, tenor sax*; b. Dillon, S.C., 5/25/17. A key member of the Duke Ellington orchestra for 26 years, mainly as clarinet soloist, also as occasional arranger, Hamilton left the band in the summer of 1968 to free-lance in NYC. He subsequently moved to the Virgin Islands to play and teach. LPs: see Ellington, Duke; also sessions w. Mercer Ellington (MCA); Billie Holiday, Teddy Wilson (Col.), various small group dates with Ellington associates.

HAMMER, JAN,* *piano, electric keyboards, synthesizer, drums, composer*; b. Prague, Czechoslovakia, 4/17/48. Played in Junior Trio w. Miroslav and Alan Vitous during high school. Won int. mus. competition in Vienna, '66, and won scholarship to Berklee Coll. of Music. Studied classical comp. and piano at Prague Conservatory. Played at Warsaw Jazz Jamboree w. Stuff Smith, '67; gigged in Munich, summer '68, leaving for US when Russians invaded Czechoslovakia. Worked around Boston from Nov. '68; in house gp. at *Playboy* Club for a yr. Joined Sarah Vaughan in early '70 for 13 months, touring in US, Canada and Japan. Settled in NYC, working w. Jeremy Steig; Elvin Jones. With Mahavishnu orch. from May '71 through Dec. '73. Then w. B. Cobham's Spectrum to fall '75; recs. w. Jerry Goodman; Stanley Clarke; John Abercrombie.

To record his album w. Goodman, *The First Seven Days,* he composed, using pianos, synthesizers, digital sequencer, Mellotron and drums, employing a multi-track tape machine; he then added background, edited and mixed. Of the Hammer-Goodman collaboration, *Like Children,* Alan Heineman said: "The session is astonishingly complex but almost never pretentious; the playing is virtuoso without seeming egotistical; and the mood is simultaneously warmly relaxed and nervously exploratory."

Comp: *Sister Andrea; Earth in Search of a Sun; Sixth Day—The People; The Seventh Day.*

LPs: *The First Seven Days; Like Children;* w. Stanley

Clarke; Tommy Bolin (Nemp.); w. Mahavishnu; w. J. McLaughlin/C. Santana, as drummer, *Love, Devotion, Surrender* (Col.); w. Cobham (Atl.); w. Abercrombie (ECM); w. Steig (Cap.); w. E. Jones (BN).

HAMMOND, JOHN HENRY, * *record producer*; b. New York City, 12/15/10. Best known for his role in launching the careers of B. Goodman, C. Basie, Meade Lux Lewis, C. Christian, B. Holiday et al, Hammond in the late '60s and early 1970s was still producing albums at CBS Records in NYC, helping to draw the attention of the public to such artists as George Benson, Don Ellis, Bruce Springsteen and Bill Watrous, as well as providing a forum for veteran talents not heard on records in some years, notably Helen Humes, whose return he arranged in '75. Rec. John Lewis for CBS, 1975. Also during that year Hammond was honored in LV as "Man of the Century" by a group of representatives of the rec. industry. In Sept. '75 in Chicago, an educational TV program, *A Tribute to John Hammond*, presented personalities with whose careers Hammond had been involved: Geo. Benson, Benny Carter, Bob Dylan, Leonard Feather, Benny Goodman, John Hammond Jr., Milt Hinton, Helen Humes, Jo Jones, Goddard Lieberson, Benny Morton, Mitch Miller, Red Norvo, Sonny Terry, Jerry Wexler, Marion Williams, Teddy Wilson and others. The show was nationally syndicated on educational stations. Film clips of Bessie Smith, Billie Holiday and Count Basie were included.

HAMMOND, JOHNNY (JOHN ROBERT SMITH), * *organ, piano*; b. Louisville, Ky., 12/16/33. Was formerly known professionally as Johnny "Hammond" Smith. Left Louisville at 18. Living in Cleveland, pl. w. Jimmy Hinsley, Willie Lewis. Switched from piano to organ, worked w. Nancy Wilson, '58, then w. Chris Columbus. Led own combo in NYC. Through '60s pl. many small clubs such as Count Basie's, Minton's, The Shalimar, and rec. frequently. Signed w. Kudu Records, '71, and made a series of commercially successful soul-jazz albums, one of which, *Breakout*, served to introduce Grover Washington Jr. Hammond found an exciting, rhythmically sensitive groove that worked well both musically and commercially. Comp: *Fantasy*. LPs on Kudu, Prest., Mile.

HAMPEL, GUNTER, *vibraphone*; also *clarinets, saxophones, flutes, piano etc., composer*; b. Goettingen, W. Germany, 8/31/37. Grandfather was a Bohemian street musician who entertained on 16 different instruments. Stud. music from '48, also stud. architecture. Led own band from '58, touring throughout Europe, with frequent radio and TV apps. in Germany and other countries. Wrote music for films. Hampel has perf. in U.S. (mainly in and around NYC), but is best known for his work in Europe, Africa, Asia, S. America. He toured for the Goethe Inst. In addition to many LPs under his own name, he has rec. w. Marion Brown and Jeanne Lee. Infls: L. Armstrong, J. Noone, Ellington, Monk, Mingus, Anton Webern, Hans Werner Henze. Fests: Berlin; Donaueschingen; Tunisia; Paris; Holland; Frankfurt and countless others.

Joachim Berendt has called Hampel the most radical among the newer vibraphonists, a musician who has also distinguished himself as a sensitive artist on several other instruments. Barry Tepperman, writing of Hampel's Galaxie Dream Band, said: "His music is unashamedly poetic, romantic in a subtle, timeless manner that Gary Burton and various others have tried for but never quite obtained. He is aware of the full potential harmonic and tonal ranges of all his instruments, and makes use of the possibilities where they can best be integrated into the overall structure of his music." Publ: *Songbook*, Vol. I (Birth Records, 34 Gottingen, Philipp Reis Str. 10, W. Germany).

LPs: *Gunter Hampel* (ESP); others, released in Europe, incl. *The 8th of July*, feat. A. Braxton, Jeanne Lee; *Ballet Symphony-Symphony No. 6; People Symphony; Spirits; Familie; Waltz for 3 Universes Celebrations* (all feat. J. Lee); *Espace* (Duo); *Angel; Broadway; I Love Being With You; Unity Dance; Out From Under; Journey To The Song Within*, all w. Galaxie Dream Band (Birth).

HAMPTON, LIONEL, * *vibes, piano, drums, leader*; b. Louisville, Ky., 4/12/13. After rising to stardom with Benny Goodman in the late '30s he formed his own big band in the early '40s and led it almost continuously to the mid-60s when he formed a smaller group called the Jazz Inner Circle. Except for special big band reunions with his alumni, such at the NJF in the late '60s and NJF-NY in '72, he has stayed in the small band context. At NJF-NY '73 he was again reunited in concert with Goodman, Teddy Wilson and Gene Krupa. In '74 his NJF-NY appearance, with Wilson, Milt Hinton and Buddy Rich was one of the artistic highlights of the festival, reminding people that Hampton had lost none of his intensely swinging skills.

He was an active campaigner for President Nixon and Gov. Rockefeller, pl. quite often in their behalf. Rockefeller aided him and his late wife, Gladys, to form the Lionel Hampton Development Corp. which erected housing at 131st Street and Eighth Avenue in NYC, where some day he would like to add a university in which Hampton hopes "young black kids could learn to be doctors, lawyers, IBM technicians . . . even musicians."

Mayor John Lindsay of NYC appointed him as his goodwill ambassador to the Far East and presented him with The George Frederick Handel Medallion, the city's highest cultural award. In '75 he was made an honorary doctor at Pepperdine Coll. in Calif. TV: produced a spectacular in Toronto '71 w. R. Eldridge, Krupa, Rich, Mel Torme, Z. Sims, G. Mulligan, etc. LPs: *Transition* w. Rich (Gr. Merch.); *Them Changes* (Bruns.); big band at Newport; small gp. reissue, *Stompology* (RCA); *Lionel; Hamp's Big Band* (Aud. Fid.).

HAMPTON, LOCKSLEY WELLINGTON (SLIDE), * *trombone, tuba, composer*; b. Jeannette, Pa., 4/21/32. The former M. Ferguson trombonist and arr. went to Europe in '68; toured England w. W. Herman; pl. concerts in Paris, then settled in Berlin, where he undertook radio staff orch. assignments in addition to working frequently w. various jazz combos and bands, incl. a big orch. of his own. He did not return to the U.S. except for occasional brief visits, declaring himself convinced that there was more freedom of musical expression on the European jazz scene.

LPs: *Umea Big Band at Montreux* (Gazell); w. Dexter Gordon, *A Day In Copenhagen*; w. Miriam Klein, *Lady Like* (BASF); w. Barry Harris, *Luminescence* (Prest.).

HANCOCK, HERBERT JEFFREY (HERBIE) (MWANDISHI),* *keyboards, composer*; b. Chicago, Ill, 4/12/40. First prominent as composer of *Watermelon Man*, popularized by M. Santamaria, which he also rec. with his own group. Traveled w. Miles Davis combo, '63-8. During his tenure w. Davis, Hancock established himself as a composer and instrumentalist far more sophisticated than the simple melody of his song hit had indicated. Among his better known works rec. by Davis were *The Sorcerer; Madness; Riot.*

While with Davis, Hancock continued to rec. with other groups, incl. various combos of his own. Among the works that gained attention were *Canteloupe Island*, rec. on a Hancock quartet date; *Maiden Voyage* and *Dolphin Dance*, which he wrote for a quintet session in '65; and most notably *Speak Like A Child* and *Riot*, both products of a sextet session that feat. fluegelhorn (Thad Jones), bass trombone (Peter Phillips) and alto flute (Jerry Dodgion). At the time of the release of that album late in '68, Hancock described his music: "The harmonies in these numbers are freer in the sense that they are not so easily identifiable chordally in the conventional way. I'm more concerned with sounds than with definite chordal patterns. I tried to give the horns notes that would give color and body to the sounds I heard. Some of this way of thinking and writing comes from listening to Gil Evans and Oliver Nelson, and from having worked with Thad Jones from time to time."

Almost simultaneously with the release of the *Speak Like A Child* album, Hancock left Davis and formed a sextet, feat. trumpet, trombone and Bennie Maupin on reeds. More and more he turned to electronics as a source of energy and communication in his music. An album, *Mwandishi*, whose title he had taken as his Swahili name (the word means composer) marked a turning point in its extensive use of these electronic devices. On this and subsequent LPs the instrumentation was augmented to incl., at one time or another, electric guitar, electric bass, electric piano, echo-plex, phase shifter, synthesizer, and additional percussion.

Hancock moved to Los Angeles in Dec. 1972. While his records enjoyed fairly substantial success and he continued to win innumerable honors, he found it was not economically feasible to retain the sextet. In June, '73 he dissolved the group, formed a quartet, feat. only one horn (Maupin), and concentrated on heavy electronic effects. Explaining his change in direction, he said: "I realized that I could never be a genius in the class of Miles, Charlie Parker or Coltrane, so I might just as well forget about becoming a legend and just be satisfied to create some music to make people happy. I no longer wanted to

write the Great American Masterpiece." Hancock added that he was impressed by the big commercial success of Donald Byrd, who had originally brought him to New York in '61.

With the release in the fall of 1973 of Hancock's first LP by the new group, the album itself (*Headhunters*) and the hit single from it, entitled *Chameleon*, both enjoyed unprecedented sales and elevated Hancock's stature to the point where he was able to attract r & b, pop and rock audiences. He headlined in major concert halls throughout the U.S., Europe and Japan, and for two months in late '74 had four albums on the best selling popular album list: *Headhunters*; the followup, *Thrust; Treasure Chest*, an anthological collection of his works; and the sound track album of the music he had written for Dino De Laurentiis' film *Death Wish*.

Hancock's music by '75 was firmly established as indicative of the heights to which a jazz musician could aspire by adjusting his orientation. He won innumerable awards, among them the DB Readers Poll as Jazzman of the Year; #1 Synthesizer '74; other awards from *Cash Box* (#1 r & b Artist); *Playboy* (Best Instrumental Combo in All-Stars' All-Stars Poll); *Black Music Magazine* (Top Jazz Artist, '74) etc.

In addition to his writing for records, Hancock composed and conducted jingles; wrote the score for Michelangelo Antonioni's picture *Blow-up*, and composed and performed music for Bill Cosby's TV special entitled *Hey, Hey, Hey! It's Fat Albert* (preserved in the album *Fat Albert Rotunda*).

LPs: *Empyrean Isles; Best of Herbie Hancock; Maiden Voyage; Prisoner; Speak Like a Child; Succotash; Takin' Off* (Blue Note); *Crossings; Mwandishi; Treasure Chest; Fat Albert Rotunda* (WB); *Headhunters; Sextant; Thrust* (Col.); w. Miles Davis, *Miles Davis In Europe; E.S.P.; My Funny Valentine; Seven Steps To Heaven; Filles de Kilimanjaro; Miles Smiles; Sorcerer; Bitches' Brew; Nefertiti; Miles Davis' Greatest Hits; Miles In The Sky; In A Silent Way; Live-Evil; Big Fun; On The Corner* (Col.); w. Eddie Henderson, *Realization; Inside Out* (Capricorn).

Hancock has also appeared as sideman on *Happenings; Components* w. B. Hutcherson (BN); w. Wayne Shorter, *Native Dancer* (Col.); *Speak No Evil; All Seeing Eye; Adam's Apple* (BN); *Salt Peanuts* w. Pointer Sisters (Blue Thumb); w. Wes Montgomery, *Going Out Of My Head* (Verve), *Day In The Life* and three others (A & M); w. Paul Desmond, *Summertime; Bridge Over Troubled Water* (A & M); w. F. Hubbard, *Red Clay; Straight Life*; w. Joe Farrell, *Penny Arcade; Moon Germs*; w. M. Jackson, *Sunflower* (CTI); w. Norman Connors, *Dark of Light; Dance of Magic* (Cobblestone); *Love From The Sun* (Buddah); w. George Benson, *White Rabbit; Shape of Things To Come* (CTI); others w. Jon Lucien (Col.); Johnny Nash (Epic); Stevie Wonder (Tamla).

HANDY, CAPT. JOHN, *alto saxophone, clarinet*; b. Pass Christian, Miss., 6/24/00. Living in NO from about 1918, Handy (not related to John Richard Handy III) pl.

w. Kid Rena, Kid Howard and many other bands of the '20s and '30s. Still active during the '60s, when he toured Europe and Japan, he pl. w. the Preservation Hall Jazz Band, app. with this gp. at the '70 NJF. Handy died 1/12/71 in his hometown.

HANDY, JOHN RICHARD III,* *alto, tenor saxes, sax-ello, educator;* also *flute, oboe, piano, singer, shakuhachi, baritone sax, percussion;* b. Dallas, Tex., 2/3/33. After pl. w. Charles Mingus and Randy Weston gps. in NYC in '58-9, formed own gp. Toured Scandinavia as a single in early '60s, then returned to SF and put together new gp. w. violinist Mike White which was hit of MJF '65. Played 36-college tour of western states w. Mont. All Stars, '66; *Spirituals to Swing,* Carnegie Hall; Gunther Schuller opera *The Visitation,* SF, '67. New band w. Mike Nock and White, '68. Led first jazz gp. (octet) to appear at SF Opera House; premiered his *Concerto for Jazz Soloist and Orchestra* w. SF Symphony, '70. In '71 inaugurated a series of collaborations in jazz and North Indian music w. sarodist Ali Akbar Khan; duets w. tabla players Shankar Ghosh and Zakir Hussein. Handy also pl. his *Concerto* w. the Stockton Symph., and was soloist w. the SF State Univ. Symphonic Band in the premiere of Roger Nixon's *Dialogue,* '71. Appeared in *Concerto* w. NO Symph., '72. Judge for Monterey HSJF, '73-4; concerts w. Cabrillo Coll. Symph.; for Cazadero Music Camp; Carnegie Hall w. Mingus; Coll. of Marin w. Khan, '74; for the International Historical Sciences Convention, SF, '75. Also apps. w. local big bands; and at Stern Grove; SF State Univ.

From '68 Handy has taught courses at SF State Univ. in jazz history; from '70 in black music and improvisation; same subjects at Univ. of Calif., Berkeley, '69; Cal. State Univ.; Stanford, '70; SF Conserv. of Mus., '69, '73-. Saxophone instructor, Golden Gate Free Univ., '70. Member of Mayor's Interim Arts Advisory Committee, SF.

TV: *Jazz Casual* w. Ralph Gleason, '65; Bell Telephone Hour, '66; *The Visitation,* Westinghouse, '67; w. SF Symph., KQED, '70. Fest: MJF, '67; NJF; Antibes; Univ. of Calif; Seattle, '68; MJF; Concord, '70; w. Ali Akbar Khan: MJF; U. of Cal.; SF State, '71; Berlin, '72; Bumbershoot (Seattle); Reno, '73; Cazadero 100th Concert Fest., '74.

Comp: soundtrack for Swedish movie *Boo's Ups and Downs;* industrial film for Dayton Corp., Minneapolis; *A Portrait of Birgitta; Dance to the Lady; Scheme No. 1; Scheme No. 2.* LPs: *Live at Monterey Jazz Fest.; The 2nd John Handy Album; New View; Projections; Spirituals to Swing, 30th Anniversary* (Col.); w. Mingus (Atl.; Fant.; Col.; UA).

HANNA, JOHN (JAKE),* *drums;* b. Roxbury, Mass., 4/4/31. Well known in Boston before attaining national stature w. M. McPartland, '59-61, W. Herman, '62-4. Starting in '64, spent 10½ years as member of staff orch. on Merv Griffin TV series, with occasional leaves of absence. Toured Europe, '67, w. C. Terry, B. Brookmeyer, M. Ferguson. Moved to LA, '70 w. Griffin show, playing locally w. Bill Berry band, Herb Ellis-Joe Pass, Supersax.

Went to USSR briefly Nov. 74, on aborted tour w. O. Peterson trio. Despite his many years in the studios, Hanna remained a superbly disciplined and powerful drummer, equally at home in jazz combos and big bands. Publ: *Syncopated Big Band Figures Vol. I (Solo) Vol. II (Duets)* (Try Publ. 854 Vine St., Hollywood, Ca. 90038).

LPs: w. Supersax (Capitol); Herb Ellis-Joe Pass; H. Ellis-Ray Brown; Hanna-Fontana band (Concord Jazz).

HANNA, SIR ROLAND P.,* *piano, composer;* also *cello;* b. Detroit, Mich., 2/10/32. In '67 became regular pianist w. T. Jones-M. Lewis orch, touring Europe and Japan in that year, and Soviet Union, '72. Perf. solo concerts at Olympia Theatre, Paris, for two months, '68; gave benefit tour in Africa for young African students, '69, and was knighted by the late Pres. of Liberia, William Tubman, for humanitarian interests and the furtherance of the education of young Africans, '70. Member of B. Rosengarden orch. on Dick Cavett show, ABC-TV, '73. Left Jones-Lewis band '74. Also in '70s active in NYC as solo pianist at The Cookery, other clubs and college concerts, often w. Z. Sims. His main area of jazz concentration, however, has been with the NY Jazz Quartet with whom he toured Europe and Japan, '74-5. The highly versatile pianist has taught privately from '60. TV: *An Evening With Carmen McRae and The Roland Hanna Trio,* NET. European fests. and NJF-NY w. NY Jazz Quartet, '74; solo concert at Montreux, '74.

Comps: *Midtown Suite; Sonata for Cello and Piano; Perugia; Child of Gemini Suite; Mediterranean Seascape; Song of the Black Knight; Morning.* LPs: solo album, *Sir Elf* (Choice); *Child of Gemini* (MPS-BASF); *Perugia* (Arista); *The New Heritage Keyboard Quartet* (BN); *Let It Happen,* Jazz Piano Quartet (RCA); *Potpourri,* w. Jones-Lewis (Phila. Int'l.); *All Blues; Spanish Blue,* w. Ron Carter (CTI).

HARA, NOBUO (Nobuo Tsukahara), *tenor, soprano, alto saxophones, clarinet, composer, leader;* b. Toyama Pref., Japan, 11/19/26. Started on trumpet at age 14. In 1943 joined Navy band, pl. saxophone, stud. classical music. In '45 he turned to jazz. From '52 Hara was leader of the Sharps and Flats, which soon became estab. as the outstanding big band in Japan, winning the *Swing Journal* Readers' Poll annually from '56-72. The band made innumerable motion picture and TV apps., was seen at the World Jazz Fest. in Tokyo, '64 and at NJF, '67, as well as almost all other fests. in Japan. Insp. by D. Ellington, C. Basie, Hara assembled a tightly knit unit notable for its ensemble precision. The orch. has made about 100 records for Nippon Col., King, CBS/Sony etc. Comps: *Koto; Humpty Dumpty; Flaming Sun.*

HARDEE, JOHN,* *tenor sax;* b. Texas, ca. 1919. In the mid-70s, the big-toned, hard-swinging tenor man was the band instructor at Oliver Wendell Holmes Junior High School in Dallas, where he still gigs. Played at Nice Festival, '75. LP: own quartet (Black & Blue).

HARDMAN, WILLIAM FRANKLIN JR. (BILL),* *trumpet;* b. Cleveland, Ohio, 4/6/33. With Art Blakey's Messengers; Horace Silver; Ch. Mingus in '50s. Joined Lou Donaldson at end of '59 and was w. him, off and on, into '66. Worked w. Lloyd Price big band, '63. With Blakey again, '66-9; Mingus, '69-70. Rejoined Blakey '70 and also formed own gp., The Brass Co., an ensemble incl. Lonnie Hillyer, Eddie Preston, Harry Hall, trumpets; Kiane Zawadi, trombone; Bob Stewart, tuba. Active w. both gps. from '71. Won DB Critics Poll, TDWR, '73. Fest: NJF-NY w. Mingus, '73; w. Blakey, '75. LPs: w. The Brass Co., *Colors* (Strata-East); w. Blakey, *Live at Slugs* (Trip); w. Donaldson, *Fried Buzzard* (Cadet); w. Curtis Fuller, *Crankin'* (Main.); w. Eddie Jefferson, *Come Along With Me* (Prest.).

HARDWICKE, OTTO (TOBY),* *alto, bass saxophones*; b. Washington, D.C., 5/31/04. A childhood friend of D. Ellington, Hardwicke worked with him in Washington and later in NYC, leaving in '28, but rejoining in '32. He remained with Duke until '45 and soon after retired from music. He died 8/5/70 in Washington, after a long illness. Hardwicke's unique, singing tone on alto was a key element in the early Ellington records. He was co-composer of *Sophisticated Lady.*

HARLEY, RUFUS, *bagpipes, saxophones, flute, oboe*; b. Raleigh, N.C., 5/20/36. Family moved to Phila. when he was an infant. Shined shoes and sold newspapers so he could buy a saxophone and pl. in high school band. At 16 was forced to drop out of school and go to work. Several yrs. later began studying w. Dennis Sandole. Canada's Black Watch Bagpipe Band intrigued him as he was watching the funeral of John F. Kennedy on tv in Nov. '63 and, after failing to reproduce the sound on the tenor sax, bought a used set of bagpipes from a New York pawnshop. Stud. and practiced for four mos. under Sandole and began playing it prof. In mid and late '60s st. leading own quartet in clubs, concerts and rec. Infl: Rollins, Coltrane. TV: *To Tell the Truth; What's My Line; I've Got A Secret; Tonight Show.* Film: as Pied Piper in *You're A Big Boy Now.* Fests: Newport, Laurel, Berlin; Montreux '74. "The trick in playing the pipes is not the musical technique," says Harley, "but the mental outlook. . . . There is a long history and a powerful philosophy behind the pipes which is quite different from our Western musical culture."

LPs: *King/Queens* (Atlantic); w. Rollins, *The Cutting Edge* (Mile.).

HARPER, BILLY R., *tenor sax, flute, singer, composer*; b. Houston, Tex., 1/17/43. Parents sing; uncles and aunts sing and pl. piano. Sang along while listening to Ella Fitzgerald on radio at age one; later sang solo, and in choir, at church. One of his first teachers of improvisation was uncle, Earl Harper. Began on saxophone at 12. Instruction from James Williams at Emmett Scott Jr. High in Tyler, Tex., '57. Returned to Houston and at Evan E. Worthing H.S. played in marching and jazz band under Sammy Harris, '59-61. Inspiration from saxophonist Richard Lillie and his wife, Vernell Lillie, Harper's drama instructor. Received Bach. of Mus. from No. Tex. State U., '61-5. Major in saxophone; minor in theory. Also majored in special program for students who were particularly interested in jazz. Began grad. work. Pl. in No. Tex. Big Band that won first prize at KC JF.

Pl. w. r&b bands; as sideman w. James Clay. To NYC '66. From '67 w. Gil Evans; worked w. Art Blakey, '68-70, incl. tour of Japan. From '71 w. Thad Jones-Mel Lewis orch. incl. European tour '73. Other jobs and rec. w. Max Roach; Lee Morgan; Elvin Jones; Donald Byrd, '71-3. Harper, who had led a gp. of his own on occasion in the early '70s, took a quintet to Europe in the summer of '75, app. in Norway, Finland, Holland, Belgium, Denmark, Sweden, France and Italy.

Taught privately during '65-73; taught improvisation at 15 NJ high schools under grant from NJ Council for the Arts, '73; college clinics w. Jones-Lewis., '73-4; private sax and flute instr. at Livingston Coll., New Brunswick, N.J., '75. Infl: Clay, Rollins, Coltrane, G. Evans but says, "I have been inspired by many, but mainly by the 'true life force' that they found in music . . ."

TV: *The Big Apple*, NBC documentary, '66; w. Blakey, BBC-, London '68; w. Jazz & People's Movement on Dick Cavett show, ABC, '70; *Soul*, PBS, w. Roach, '71; Morgan, '72; Euro. TV & radio w. own quintet, '75. Fest: voted "most promising saxophonist" at Notre Dame JF, '64, where he app. w. own sextet; Tangier JF, '72; many fests. w. Evans; Jones-Lewis. Member of the NYJRC. Received comp. grants from NEA, '70, '73; CAPS, '74. Won DB Critics' poll, TDWR, '74-5.

Chuck Berg wrote in DB: "Harper's playing represents a fusion of the Rollins and Coltrane traditions, tempered with the spirituality derived from his childhood religious experiences."

Comp: *Capra Black; Cry of Hunger; Thoroughbred; Croquet Ballet; Soulfully, I Love You; Dance Eternal Spirits, Dance; Call of the Wild and Peaceful Heart.* LPs: *Black Saint* (Black Saint); *Capra Black* (Strata-East); *Jon and Billy,* Harper & Jon Faddis (Trio); w. G. Evans (Ampex, Atl., RCA-Japan); w. Jones-Lewis, (SS); w. Roach (Atl.); L. Morgan (BN); J. Owens (Poly.); C. Earland (Prest.); R. Weston (Poly., Arista); L. Armstrong (Fly. Dutch.); Art Blakey, *Live!* (Trip).

HARRIOTT, ARTHURLIN (JOE),* *alto, baritone, tenor sax, composer*; b. Jamaica, BWI, 7/15/28. Emigrated to England, '51; pl. in many small groups; formed own combo in '60. Throughout the '60s his activities were mostly involved in the area of the fusion of jazz and Indian music; also a member of Michael Garrick's group which featured jazz and poetry. Traveled as a freelance soloist, working in many varied contexts. Harriott died in Southampton, England, 1/2/73.

Own LPs on Brit. Col., Melodisc; others w. Sonny Boy Williamson (Marmalade); Garrick (Argo); Acker Bilk, Stan Tracey, Laurie Johnson (Brit. Col.).

HARRIS, BARRY DOYLE,* *piano, composer*; b. Detroit, Mich., 12/15/29. After moving to NYC from Detroit in early '60s, pl. w. Yusef Lateef; then Coleman Hawkins, off and on, '65-9. Led own trio, quintet from '60s; also worked w. Charles McPherson, his sometime sideman, in latter's gp. With Lateef again, '70, incl. European gigs. Own duo at West Boondock, '67; Port of Call East, '69; Digg's Den, '71; duo at Jimmy's for a yr. and a half, '73 through Feb. '74; Bradley's, '75. Concert

w. trio, trios of C. Walton, Walter Davis, Cami Hall, Nov. '74. TV: w. Hawkins, PBS, '69; w. Lateef, Holland, '70. Fest: Montreux '70 w. Lateef; Radio City Jam Session, NJF-NY, '73; solo piano, NJF-NY, '75. Wrote six arrs. for strings for Ch. McPherson concert, Detroit '74. Working on first symphony. A brilliant interpreter of the music of Parker, Monk, Dameron, etc. Comps: *Luminescence; Like This; Nicaragua; Even Steven; You Sweet and Fancy Lady; Rouge; Just Open Your Heart; Sun Dance.* LPs: *Plays Tadd Dameron* (Xanadu); *Luminescence; Bull's Eye; Magnificent* (Prest.); *Vicissitudes* (MPS/BASF); w. David Allyn; Jimmy Heath; Sam Noto; Al Cohn; Sonny Criss (Xanadu); w. Sonny Stitt (Cobble.; Muse); James Moody; I. Jacquet; Dexter Gordon (Prest.); Cohn-Moody (MPS/BASF); C. McPherson (Prest.; Main.); Lee Morgan (BN); Red Rodney (Muse); C. Hawkins (Pablo); Y. Lateef (Atl.).

HARRIS, WILLIAM GODVIN (BEAVER), *drums*; also *percussion*; b. Pittsburgh, Pa., 4/20/36. Mother was dancer who also pl. piano. Stud. w. Stanley Leonard at Carnegie Tech.; piano and comp. w. Charles Bell; w. Kenny Clarke and Dante Augustini at Premier Drum School and Clinic, Paris; percussionist Richard Fitz, and Marshall Brown, NYC. Nickname derives from early days as a baseball player. Pl. ball as member of Special Services while in Army; also began gigging while at Ft. Knox; then local groups around Pitts. after discharge. To NYC, '63, working w. Sonny Rollins, T. Monk, Joe Henderson, F. Hubbard, etc. Joined Archie Shepp, '67, touring Europe w. him and also pl. there w. Albert Ayler. At the end of the '60s formed the 360 Degree Experience w. Grachan Moncur, Dave Burrell, and has perf. w. it, off and on, from that time. He also pl. in Haiti w. Lee Konitz, Eddie Gomez and Jim Hall; NJF tour of Japan w. Shepp, Konitz, G. Barbieri, '73. Worked w. Lee Konitz-Marshall Brown; Shepp; Chet Baker; Warren Chiasson, '74. Music Dir. for Black and Puerto Rican Culture Program funded by NYS Council for the Arts. Pl. for stage prods., *Slave Ship,* '71; *Lady Day,* '72, at Brooklyn Acad. of Music. Infls: K. Clarke, Max Roach, Roy Haynes, Musa Kaleem, Rollins. Comp: *African Drums*; lyrics for *Money Blues; Attica Blues; Ballad For a Child*; all for Shepp albums. All orig. music for *From Rag Time to No Time,* an album on the 360 Degree Music Company label (269 West 72nd St., NYC 10023). Other LPs w. Shepp on Impulse, MPS; w. Ayler, *Live at the Village Vanguard & the Village Theatre* (Imp.); w. Roswell Rudd, Moncur (JCOA); w. Barbieri, *The Third World; The Legend of* (Fly. Dutch.); w. Marion Brown, *Three For Shepp* (Imp.).

HARRIS, WILLARD PALMER (BILL), * *trombone*; also *guitar*; b. Philadelphia, Pa., 10/28/16. One of the definitive trombone stylists of the '40s, he was best known for his work w. W. Herman orch., '44-6, later for his tours w. N. Granz's JATP. After living in LV in the '60s, Harris moved to Florida, leaving there only occasionally. One of his last major jazz apps. was at the MJF. He died 9/19/73 in Hallandale, Fla.

Winner of many awards in the '40s and '50s, Harris was considered by some musicians to be the most creative artist on his instrument since the advent many years earlier of J. Teagarden and J.C. Higginbotham.

LPs: w. Herman (Col. etc.); Flip Phillips, *A Melody From The Sky* (Bob Thiele Records); C. Ventura (Trip).

HARRIS, WILLIE (BILL), * *guitar*; also *guitorgan, piano*; b. Nashville, N.C., 4/14/25. From '66 continued activities in night clubs and concerts in the Washington area, incl. *From Bach to the Blues* at St. Johns Church, '67; Watergate Barge w. Underground Quintette; Gospel Truth concert w. own trio, '69; National Society of Classic Guitar, '74. Harris, who specializes in unaccompanied, unamplified, six-string Spanish guitar, using no pick, operates his own studio in Washington, where from '71 he has annually prod. the Kenny Burrell Guitar Seminar. Harris' students have incl. Orville Saunders (q.v.), Ed Ellington (q.v.). His son, bassist-guitarist Joe Harris, after pl. w. Marvin Gaye and the Temptations, now works in Washington and teaches with his father.

App. at Django Reinhardt Memorial Concert, Samois, France; also seen on French TV, '73. Was awarded Jazz Composer Fellowship by the Nat'l Endowment for the Arts, '72. Comps: *Blue Medley; Watergate Blues*; score for film, *Sincerely The Blues.* In a review of his concert at the Library of the Performing Arts at Lincoln Center, J.C. Thomas wrote: "*The Wes Montgomery Suite,* Harris' own composition, penned in homage to the late guitarist, was a wry but bouncing evocation of Montgomery's single note style. It was so accurate that, as Laurence Olivier *becomes* Shylock when he plays the role, Harris *was* Montgomery."

Publs: *The Harris Touch; Guitar Arrangements of Classic Jazz; Instant Guitar* (Bill Harris Studio, 2021 Hamlin St., N.E. Washington, D.C. 20018).

LPs: *Down In The Alley; Bill Harris Rhythm* (Black & Blue); *Caught in the Act; Harris in Paris* (Jazz Guitar, own label).

HARRIS, DON, *violin*; also *bass, piano, organ, synthesizer, singer*; b. Pasadena, Cal., 6/18/38. Formerly known by the nickname Sugar Cane. Sang and pl. piano w. The Squires, five piece group, '57-63; during same period had duo partnership with Dewey Terry under the name Don & Dewey. During mid-60s appeared frequently w. Johnny Otis blues shows; subsequently came to prominence w. F. Zappa, toured extensively w. John Mayall in U.S. and abroad; was member of rock group, Pure Food & Drug Act, and rec. a series of albums, mainly as violinist, under his own name.

J. Berendt has observed that Don Harris is the dominant violinist of the contemporary world. His roots are in the blues and his style seems to have derived, at least partially, from Stuff Smith, though Harris names as his main influences and inspirations Little Walter, B.B. King, Ray Charles, John Coltrane.

LPs: w. Don & Dewey (Specialty); w. J. Otis, *Cuttin' Up* (Epic), *Cold Shot* (Kent); Own LPs: *Sugarcane* (Epic); *Cup Full of Dreams; Fiddler On The Rock; I'm On Your Case; Sugarcane's Got the Blues* (BASF).

HARRIS, EDDIE,* *tenor saxophone, electric piano, organ, reed trumpet, singer, composer*; b. Chicago, Ill., 10/20/36. Big hit with the theme from the movie *Exodus* established him as combo leader. With the Atlantic label from '65 he delved into the electronic world when he introduced the Varitone attachment to his tenor sax in '67. In the '70s he began singing through a synthesized saxophone and his guitarist, Ronald Muldrow, used the guitorgan, a Hammond-organ sounding guitar that is touched rather than strummed or picked. Harris, whose music has moved more in an r&b and rock direction (he recorded w. British rock players such as Jeff Beck, Stevie Winwood, Rick Grech, etc. in England—*E.H. in the U.K.*) says: "A lot of musicians are suspicious of electronics. . . . They call it gimmickry, but I can understand that because you always have opposition upon change. Change breeds contempt because whatever your beliefs are you have to go back and examine them. . . . Amplification will add ten years to your life span because you don't have to exert yourself as much. The unit I use is a pre-amp unit, which can emulate different woodwind sounds. At the press of a button it can sound like a bassoon or a tuba or an oboe or whatever they have concocted upon the chassis system."

Fest: Montreux w. Les McCann, '69; NJF. Played in Ghana at celebration of 14th year of independence, '70. Publ: *How to Play Reed Trumpet; The Intervalistic Concept for All Single Line Instruments.* Comp: *Eddie Sings the Blues; Walk With Me; Please Let Me Go; Ten Minutes to Four; Drunk Man; Renovated Rhythm; Recess; Freedom Jazz Dance.* LPs: *Bad Luck is All I Have; I Need Some Money; E.H. in the U.K.; Excursions; Sings the Blues; Instant Death; Live at Newport; Free Speech; High Voltage; Silver Cycles; Plug Me In; The Tender Storm; The Electrifying Eddie Harris; Mean Greens*; Harris-McCann, *Swiss Movement; Second Movement* (Atl.).

HARRIS, EUGENE (GENE),* *piano, keyboards, synthesizer*; b. Benton Harbor, Mich., 9/1/33. From '66-74 cont. to play clubs and coll. dates across the U.S. w. The Three Sounds. Formed own sextet, '74, app. in major U.S. cities. Fests: Kansas City; Wichita.

LPs: *Astral Signal; Gene Harris of The Three Sounds; Elegant Soul* (BN).

HARRIS, JOSEPH ALLISON (JOE),* *drums, percussion*; b. Pittsburgh, Pa., 12/23/26. The one-time Dizzy Gillespie drummer, who settled in Stockholm in 1956, moved to Germany to play on Radio Free Berlin from '61-66, during which time he also rec. w. Clarke-Boland band. Ret. to Pittsburgh '66; moved to LA '67 where he worked at Playboy Club; Donte's w. Benny Carter; taught drums at Eubanks Sch. of Music. Toured w. Ella Fitzgerald '68. Ret. to Germany '70, locating w. Max Greger orch. in Munich for TV work. Pl. jazz workshop, Hamburg, various studio jobs w. Greger '71; also at Club Domicile in Munich w. various groups led by Jimmy Woode, Fritz Pauer, Peter Herbolzheimer in same year. Again ret. to Pitts. '72; house drummer at Walt Harper's Attic backing Joe Williams, Carmen McRae, etc. and

teaching courses in jazz history and total percussion at Univ. Pitts. App. at Pitt. JF '72. Film: *They Shoot Horses Don't They?* '69. Harris is a tennis pro in Pitts. and conducts 10-week, summer clinics all over the city. He also won the musicians' union Local 471/60 golf tournament '67. LPs: timbales on *My Kind of Sunshine* w. Herbolzheimer (MPS); Clarke-Boland (Atl.).

HARRIS, BENJAMIN (LITTLE BENNY),* *trumpet, composer*; b. New York City, 4/23/19. A minor figure in the early bebop movement, he gained some recognition as comp. of *Reets and I; Little Benny* (also known as *Crazeology* and *Bud's Bubble*); and co-composer of *Ornithology.* Also wrote *Wahoo*, based on *Perdido.* Pl. briefly w. Earl Hines, Benny Carter, C. Hawkins et al in '40s; sporadically active in later years. Died in SF, 2/11/75. LPs: w. Charlie Parker (Verve); w. Don Byas in Harlem series (Arista).

HART, WILLIAM W. (BILLY), *drums*; b. Washington, D.C., 11/29/40. Grandmother was a concert pianist. Self-taught; first inspired to become interested in jazz when he heard several Ch. Parker records given him by Buck Hill, a saxophonist. Pl. for three-and-a-half years w. singer Shirley Horn; Jimmy Smith, '64; Wes Montgomery until the latter's death in '68. For a year he worked intermittently w. Eddie Harris and Pharoah Sanders. After pl. clubs w. Marian McPartland, he joined Herbie Hancock, remaining with him for three years. Then spent a year w. McCoy Tyner trio, before joining S. Getz early in '74. Hart's infls. were Harry Stump Saunders, Louis Hayes, Max Roach, A. Blakey, Shadow Wilson, Big Sid Catlett, Philly Joe Jones, Vernel Fournier. Won DB Critics poll, TDWR, '74.

LPs: w. Hancock, *Sextant* (Col.); *Crossings* (WB); others w. Getz (Col.); Joanne Brackeen (Choice).

HARTMAN, JOHN MAURICE (JOHNNY), *singer*; also *piano*; b. Chicago, Ill., 7/3/23. Began piano and singing at eight. Received scholarship to Chicago Musical Coll. where he studied voice, '39. Sang w. Earl Hines for three or four mos., '47; then w. Dizzy Gillespie, '47-8. From that time app. as a single. Rich, smooth baritone in what was originally an Eckstine-derived style. Infl: Eckstine, Sinatra. TV: Sammy Davis; *Tonight; Today*; specials in Australia; Europe. Fest: London, '59; Japan, '63; Australia, '68; NJF-NY, '75. LPs: Impulse; Perception; w. J. Coltrane (Imp.).

HAVENS, ROBERT L. (BOB),* *trombone*, also *vibes*; b. Quincy, Ill., 5/3/30. W. Geo. Girard, Al Hirt in late '50s, then joined Lawrence Welk, 1960. Featured soloist on Welk's weekly TV series. Often seen at trad. jazz clubs around U.S., w. Bob Crosby at Disneyland, freelance studio work etc. Pl. at LA Shrine Auditorium w. Doc Evans in 70th birthday tribute to Louis Armstrong, July 1970. A bona fide sheriff of LA County, Havens also plays in a unique group called the Los Angeles County Sheriffs' Rhythm Posse Band.

Festivals: Monterey, 1966, w. Dick Cary; Sacramento, '74; Ojai w. Abe Most, '75; Indianapolis Dixieland Fest. w. J. McPartland, '75.

LPs: Welk's 25th Anniversary (Ranwood); *The Enter-*

tainer w. Myron Floren (Ranwood); Blue Angel Jazz Club jam session albums, 1969-70, on BAJC's own label.

HAVERHOEK, HENDRIK (HENK), *bass*; also *clarinet, tenor sax, piano*; b. Shoorl, Holland, 2/11/47. Began on clar., '57. Att. Cons. of Arnhem to stud. clar. '65, but switched to bass, '66 under Henk Guldemond and rec. degree as symphonic bassist and teacher in '72. Also took correspondence course from Berklee. From '68 a member of the Rein de Graaff-Dick Vennik quartet. Pl. several tours since '71 w. Mal Waldron; Dexter Gordon; Horace Parlan; Johnny Griffin. With Rene Thomas, '72-4; Don Byas, '72; Duke Jordan; Ben Webster; Bobby Jones-Dusko Goykovich quintet, '73; Pony Poindexter; Jimmy Owens, '74; Red Rodney; Tete Montoliu, '75. Also one-nighters w. G. Ammons, Al Haig, Thad Jones, Frank Rosolino, Joe Henderson, Dizzy Reece, Slide Hampton, Carmell Jones, Leo Wright, Babs Gonzales, Ray Nance, Joe Pass, Lee Konitz & Art Farmer in Holland, Belgium & Germany. Infl: Dexter Gordon, "among many others." Fests: Pescara w. Gordon; Laren (Holl.) w. de Graaff-Vennik; Hammerfeld (Holl.) w. Griffin, Gordon, Konitz, '73; Middleheim (Belg.) w. Thomas, '74. Comp: *Departure; Firestoned*. LPs: *Last Concert* w. Webster (Bovema); *A Little Bit of Miles* w. Waldron (Freedom); *Departure* w. de Graaff-Vennik (BASF); w. Thomas (Vogel); w. Gordon, *Dexterity*.

HAWES, HAMPTON, * *piano, composer*; b. Los Angeles, Cal., 11/13/28. After working a long club stint w. Red Mitchell in LA and spending eight months in SF, Hawes co-led a group w. Jimmy Garrison in '66. He then took a sabbatical; between Sept. '67 and June '69 he toured the world, picking up engagements and making rec. sessions wherever the opportunity presented itself. Back in LA, he worked as duo w. Leroy Vinnegar for eight months. Led trio in London, Paris, Copenhagen, '71. During next three years worked at local LA clubs, pl. fests. at Montreux, Nice etc. During most of '74 was co-featured in a trio w. bassist Carol Kaye. When that group disbanded, Hawes led a quartet for a while; he then met Joan Baez and rec. and pl. concerts with her.

During the '70s Hawes' style underwent a radical change as he devoted much time to electric keyboards and contemporary modal concepts. Throughout this time he was in increasing demand for coll. clinics, lectures and concerts. TV: *Festival In Black*, '74; *Midnight Special* w. Baez, '75. Publ. *Raise Up Off Me*, w. Don Asher, an autobiography (Coward, McCann & Geoghegan, Inc.). Comps: *Blues for Walls; Josie Black; Drums for Peace; Hamp's Collard Green Blues*.

LPs: *The Challenge* (Japanese RCA); *Hampton Hawes Jam Session* (Col.); *Seance; I'm All Smiles* (Contemp.); *Universe; Blues For Walls; Live at Montreux* (Prest.) w. D. Gordon, *A La Suisse*; w. G. Ammons, *Playing in the Yard* (Prest.); *The East/West Controversy* (Xanadu).

HAWKINS, COLEMAN, * *tenor sax*; b. St. Joseph, Mo., 11/21/04. Pl. w. Fletcher Henderson, 1923-34; freelance in Europe, 1934-9; rec. *Body and Soul* in NYC soon after return in '39. Led big band late '39 until early '41, then various small combos, many tours w. Norman Granz

incl. the final American tour of JATP in '67. Last European tour w. Oscar Peterson in '68.

By this time Hawkins' health was declining, heavy drinking had taken its toll, and he was regarded by many as a venerated father figure rather than as the vital force he had been for more than three decades. In mid-April of 1969 he appeared on an educational TV program in Chicago but was so frail he had to play sitting down; his performance revealed only remnants of a style that had set the entire course for the tenor saxophone. A month later, 5/19/69, he died of bronchial pneumonia at Wickersham Hospital in NYC.

Though others have been far more extensively written about (because their impact reached a peak during an era when jazz had become the subject of widespread discussion to the print media), it remains beyond dispute that Hawkins was the most influential figure in the evolution of the tenor saxophone, and one of a very small number of musicians who all but monopolized his chosen field. (Others were Harry Carney on baritone sax and, in his early years, Louis Armstrong.) He was the first jazz soloist to apply his creativity, with unprecedented artistic as well as commercial success, to the refashioning of a ballad. Though *Body and Soul* was by far the best known, the style had begun to crystallize as far back as 1929, when he recorded, as a member of a pickup group called the Mound City Blue Blowers, what may have been the first genuine jazz ballad solo: *One Hour* (based on the song *If I Could Be With You One Hour Tonight*). Both this recording and the original *Body and Soul* can be found in *Body and Soul—A Jazz Autobiography—Coleman Hawkins* (RCA).

Unlike many musicians whose styles were formed during the pre-swing and swing years, Hawkins continued to show an interest in new developments, was an early associate both on records and in person of the bop pioneers, and so updated his style that certain of his solos, if speeded up from 33 1/3 to 45 r.p.m., bore an amazing resemblance to those of Charlie Parker.

In his Grammy award winning notes for *The Hawk Flies*, a two-volume album that contains the products of various sessions rec. between 1944 and 1957, Dan Morgenstern wrote: "Coleman Hawkins was a legend in his own time: revered by younger musicians, who were amazed and delighted at his ability to remain receptive to their discoveries; loved by his contemporaries, who were equally astonished by his capacity for constant self-renewal. He was one of those who wrote the book of jazz."

TV: acting role in episode of *Route 66*. LPs: The number of albums in which Hawkins is heard as leader, co-leader or sideman seems almost limitless, but the following are among the most important and many may still be available: *On The Bean* (Continental); *The Big Sounds of Coleman Hawkins & Ben Webster* (Bruns.); *Coleman Hawkins & Lester Young—Classic Tenors* (Contact); *Body & Soul* (RCA); *Bean & The Boys* (Pres.); *Hollywood Stampede* (Cap.); *A Documentary* (two-LP interview) (Riverside); *The Tenor Sax: C. Hawkins & F.*

Wess (Commodore); *Duke Ellington Meets Coleman Hawkins* (Imp.); *The Hawk In Holland* (GNP); *The High and the Mighty Hawk* (Master Jazz); *The Newport Years*, feat. Hawkins, Eldridge et al (Verve); *The Hawk Flies* (Milestone); *Reevaluations: The Impulse Years* (Imp.); *C. Hawkins & The Trumpet Kings* (Trip); *Hawk & Roy: 1939* (Phoenix); *Jam Session In Swingville*, feat. Hawkins & Pee Wee Russell (Prest.); *Hawk In Germany*, feat. Bud Powell (Black Lion); *Sirius* (Pablo); also several tracks on *Esquire's All-American Hot Jazz* (RCA); *The Greatest Jazz Concert in the World* (Pablo).

HAWKINS, ERSKINE RAMSAY,* *trumpet, leader*; b. Birmingham, Ala., 7/26/14. Led one of the best and most popular bands of the Swing Era. From the '60s leading his own quartet in Catskill Mountains resort area in New York state. Appeared in NYJRC concert which paid tribute to Savoy Ballroom, '74. LP: *Reunion*, a regrouping of some of his former sidemen (Stang).

HAYES, CLARENCE LEONARD (CLANCY),* *banjo, singer*; b. Caney, Kansas, 11/14/08. Settled in SF in late '20s. Popular from late '30s w. traditionalist bands, incl. Lu Watters, Bunk Johnson, Bob Scobey, Turk Murphy. He was an original member of the World's Greatest Jazzband and took part in its first record session, but was in failing health and died of cancer 3/13/72 in SF. Hayes rec. under his own name for Good Time Jazz, Delmark and ABC. He was composer of the hit song *Huggin' & A'Chalkin'*.

HAYES, ISAAC, *keyboards, composer, singer*; b. Covington, Tenn., 8/20/42. Raised in Covington, later moved to Memphis, where his first major hit album, *Hot Buttered Soul*, was released in '69. He subsequently became one of the top stars in soul music and in '72 won the Motion Picture Academy's Oscar award as the creator of the title song and score for the film *Shaft*. Though he has occasionally sung blues, Hayes' connection with jazz is peripheral. LPs on Stax, ABC.

HAYES, LOUIS SEDELL,* *drums*; b. Detroit, Mich., 5/31/37. Toured w. Y. Lateef '55-6; H. Silver, '56-9; C. Adderley, '59-65; O. Peterson, '65-7; F. Hubbard, '70-1. Rejoined Peterson for a year, and in '72 organized his own quintet. In '75-6 co-led quintet w. Junior Cook, touring Europe early '76.

An adaptable and sensitive drummer insp. by Philly Joe Jones, Hayes has been heard on records w. J. Coltrane, J.J. Johnson, Phineas Newborn, W. Montgomery, L. Morgan, Ravi Shankar, Dexter Gordon, S. Stitt, Cedar Walton, Chris Jordan, Lucky Thompson, Terry Gibbs, Joe Henderson.

Own LP, *Breath of Life* (Muse); many others with groups listed above.

HAYES, EDWARD BRIAN (TUBBY),* *tenor saxophone*; also *vibes, flute, baritone* and *alto saxophones*; b. London, England, 1/30/35. Led own groups in England from '50s. Made first U.S. app. at Half Note, NYC, '61; again in '62, '64; Jazz Workshop, Boston, '64; Shelly's Manne Hole, '65. Many international tours with own group, as well as apps. w. symph. orchs. From '69-71 he was almost inactive due to illness. In '71 he returned to

work, but was intermittently ill until he died in a hospital in London while undergoing a heart operation, 6/8/73. Although chiefly known for his tenor saxophone work, Hayes pl. vibes with great sensitivity, and was a composer of rare talent.

Many LPs on British labels, as well as one rec. in U.S. w. Clark Terry et al (Epic).

HAYNES, ROY OWEN,* *drums, leader*; b. Roxbury, Mass., 3/13/26. Worked w. Stan Getz, w. whom he had been associated, off and on, from '50, and Gary Burton but was mainly occupied at the head of his own Hip Ensemble from '70. Appeared at NYC clubs such as Mikell's, Top of the Gate, Five Spot and Tin Palace; Gulliver's in NJ. Toured in Europe, incl. Belgium, Holland '74. Several apps. for Joe Segal's annual "Charlie Parker Month" presentations in Chicago incl. '75 w. L. Konitz, Milt Jackson, Barry Harris. "52nd Street" concert w. Billy Taylor at Town Hall, NYC, '75. TV: Merv Griffin; *Soul*, NET; *Positively Black*, NBC. Fest: Notre Dame, as judge and player, '72-3; NJF-NY; Berlin; Newport International; Colo. Jazz Party. Named by *Esquire* as one of America's best-dressed men. An extremely versatile drum master, at home in a wide spectrum of styles. LPs: *Senyah; Hip Ensemble* (Main.); w. Burton, *Tennessee Firebird; Duster* (RCA); w. L. Coryell, *Barefoot Boy* (Fly. Dutch.); w. C. Corea, *Now He Sings, Now He Sobs* (SS); w. D. Jordan (Steeple.); Sonny Stitt (Muse).

HAYTON, LEONARD GEORGE (LENNIE),* *composer, piano*; b. New York City, N.Y., 2/13/08. First known as an associate of Bix Beiderbecke, F. Trumbauer, J. Venuti, E. Lang and others, Hayton later led his own dance band and was musical director at MGM studios in the '40s. He married Lena Horne in '47 and often served as her musical director. He died 4/24/71 at a hospital in Palm Springs, Cal.

LPs: w. Beiderbecke et al (Col.); Lena Horne (various labels).

HAYWOOD, CEDRIC,* *piano*; b. Houston, Tex., ca. 1914. Played w. Milt Larkins; Lionel Hampton; Sidney Bechet; Illinois Jacquet; Kid Ory. Worked w. Brew Moore in SF in early '60s, moving back to Houston in summer '63. Led own big band at Club Ebony from '64 until his death from a stroke 9/9/69. LPs w. Ory (GTJ).

HAZEL, ARTHUR (MONK),* *drums, cornet, mellophone*; b. Harvey, La., 8/15/03. Prominent in New Orleans from 1920s w. Abbie Brunies et al, later in NYC and LA, Hazel later was assoc. for many years w. Sharkey Bonano. He died in New Orleans Apr. 1968.

HEARD, JAMES CHARLES (J.C.),* *drums*; also *conga*; b. Dayton, Ohio, 10/8/17. After ret. from four years in the Orient, '53-57, he pl. in NYC w. C. Hawkins & R. Eldridge; Lester Lanin; and his own group. Cont. to lead quartet LA area, Las Vegas. Americana Hotel, NYC w. Dorothy Donegan '62 and thereafter for several years. To Detroit '66 where he again led his own trio, pl. and singing. Went out as a single in Feb. '75 to Syracuse, Pitts., Wash., D.C.; to Europe in April w. all-star band.

TV: *Mike Douglas Show*, '64. Fest: Arts Festival, Birmingham, Mich. w. all-star band of Billy Mitchell, Oliver Nelson, Sandy Mosse, Clark Terry, Joe Newman, Al Grey, Wynton Kelly, Toots Thielemans, Joe Kennedy, '60. LP: *Basie Picks the Winners* (Verve).

HEATH, ALBERT (TOOTIE or KUUMBA),* *drums, composer*; also *tympani, flute*; b. Philadelphia, Pa., 5/31/35. Played w. J.J. Johnson in late '50s; Cedar Walton; Jimmy Heath in '60s before traveling to Europe w. George Russell. Worked w. Russell; Friedrich Gulda in Europe while based in Sweden from '65-8. House drummer at Montmartre in Copenhagen, pl. w. Kenny Drew trio; Dexter Gordon quartet. Returned to US and joined Yusef Lateef quartet; became staff teacher for Jazzmobile. Studied flute and arranging w. Lateef; piano at Manhattan Sch. of Mus.; tympani w. Peter Terrace. Trips to Europe w. Lateef. Flew to Denmark to record as sideman for SteepleChase label '74. Moved back to Sweden '74 but in '75 became part of new Heath Bros. gp. w. siblings Percy and Jimmy. A versatile, strong drummer who, after his return from Europe in '69 had become a mature, thoroughly confident percussionist, brimming with explosive vitality. Dexter Gordon said, "Tootie is very loose. You can play anything with him."

His Woodwind Quintet was presented at Manhattan Community Coll. '73. Received grant from NEA to compose a work for 20-piece ensemble, '74. Awarded Jazz Honor Citations from Jazz at Home Club in Phila., '65, '74. Comp: *A Notion; Dr. JEH; Dunia; Sub-Set*, all rec., along w. *Tafadhali* from Woodwind Quintet, in *Kwanza* (Muse); other LPs: *Kawaida* (Trip); w. Lateef (Atl.); J. Heath; K. Barron (Muse); D. Gordon (Prest., Steeple.); K. Drew; A. Braxton; T. Montoliu (Steeple.).

HEATH, JAMES EDWARD (JIMMY),* *tenor sax, soprano sax, flute, composer*; b. Phila., Pa., 10/25/26. Early exp. w. Howard McGhee, Gillespie, M. Davis, Gil Evans, Donald Byrd. Co-leader of quintet w. Art Farmer '65-8. Worked for Jazzmobile in NYC for more than ten years as instructor. Played jazz-lecture concerts w. Billy Taylor and own group. From '67 on, wrote and rec. for many radio stations in Europe. Stage band arrs. for Y. Lateef, C. Terry, B. Taylor, '72-3. Began teaching woodwinds at CCNY, '73. Received N.Y. State Council of the Arts grant, '74; member of N.Y. Jazz Rep. Co., '74. Completed comp., *Afro-American Suite of Evolution* under CAPS grant, '75. App. w. brothers Albert and Percy as Heath, Heath & Heath in trio perfs., then w. brothers and Stanley Cowell in Heath Bros. Quartet, '75, incl. 5-wk. European tour in fall.

LPs: *Picture of Heath* (Xanadu); *The Gap Sealer* (Cobblestone); *Love and Understanding* (Muse); *Olinga*, w. M. Jackson (CTI); *Kwanza* w. A. Heath; *These Are Soulful Days* w. Don Patterson (Muse); *The Quota* w. Red Garland (MPS); *Kawaida* w. A. Heath (Trip).

HEATH, PERCY,* *bass, viola da gamba*; b. Wilmington, N.C. 4/30/23. Came out of the Dizzy Gillespie group of the early '50s to help found the Modern Jazz Quartet, playing with it for more than two decades before its breakup in July '74. During annual summer vacations from the MJQ pl. gigs w. brother Jimmy. In '75 worked briefly w. Sarah Vaughan, app. w. her at NJF-NY; formed Heath Bros. gp. with Jimmy, Tootie and Stanley Cowell. Noted for his counterlines and strong, subtle underpinning for the MJQ. Countless TV, fest. apps. w. MJQ. Comp: *Oops!.* LPs: *The Last Concert* w. MJQ (Atl.); others w. MJQ on Atl.; Little David; w. Albert Heath, *Kwanza* (Muse).

HEATH, EDWARD (TED),* *leader, trombone*; b. Wandsworth, London, England, 3/30/00. Trombonist in name bands from mid-1920s; Led own band in concerts at London Palladium from 1945, and during the next two decades dominated the field in England with a well-trained, popular dance band that included several first rate jazz soloists and some jazz arrangements. Heath's records sold well in the US, enabling him in 1956 to make the first of several successful American tours. Tadd Dameron was on Heath's arranging staff in the mid-'50s. Among the band's more successful jazz-oriented LPs was Fats Waller's *London Suite* (London).

After five years' illness (during which time the band carried on without him), Heath died 11/18/69 at Virginia Water, Surrey. LPs: *Big Band Themes Revisited; Glenn Miller Salute* etc. (London).

HECKMAN, DONALD J. (DON),* *alto sax, composer, critic*; also *soprano sax, clarinet, tarogato*; b. Reading, Pa., 12/18/35. Concerts, rec. w. the Don Heckman-Ed Summerlin Improvisational Jazz Workshop; comp. for TV, theatre and documentary films, '66-70. Music reviewer for various magazines, jazz critic for *Village Voice*, Contributing Editor to *Stereo Review*, '68-71. Rock critic for New York *Times*, Recordings Editor for Sunday *Times*, '71-72. Vice-president, East Coast A&R, RCA Records '73-74. From '74 functioning as a free-lance writer, critic, rec. prod., mus. and comp. TV: *Look Up and Live; Christmas Eve Special*, CBS; *Love; Work; Leisure*—three shows for CFTO, Canada. Comp: theme music for *Children's Film Fest.*, CBS-TV; orig. mus. for *The Dutchess of Malfi; Heartbreak House; Robin Hood; U.S.A.; Pinocchio* on Caedmon Records. Articles and essays anthologized in *Jazz Panorama* (Crowell-Collier); *The Urban Adventurers* (McGraw-Hill); *Black Americans* (Voice of America Forum Lectures). Taught jazz history at City College, CUNY, in early '70s. LPs: *Heckman-Summerlin Imp. Jazz Work.* (Ictus); *Avant-Slant* (Decca); *Ring Out Joy* (Avant-Garde); *Saturday in the Park* (Camden). Heckman received Gold Rec. for his productions of *Blood, Sweat & Tears IV* and *B,S&T's Greatest Hits* (Columbia). Heckman believes "Hindemith's dictum that a musician should be able to play, compose, arrange, criticize and function in all areas of his craft."

HEFTI, NEAL,* *composer, trumpet, piano*; b. Hastings, Neb., 10/29/22. Best known in '40s as composer and trumpeter w. W. Herman; in '50s as composer of many originals w. C. Basie, incl. *Li'l Darlin'*; in '60s as writer of TV and motion pic. scores, among them *Barefoot In The Park* and *The Odd Couple* (both films and TV series); Fred Astaire TV spec; film, *The Last of the Red Hot Lovers.* In '73-5 Hefti took a sabbatical from the studios to undertake concert tours, personal apps. with his own orch. He also lectured at leading univs. Comps: *Girl Talk; Batman Theme; Barefoot in the Park; The Odd Couple; Fred.*

LPs: sound track albums, *Harlow* (Col.); *Barefoot In The Park; The Odd Couple* (Dot); *Duel at Diablo* (UA); *Batman Theme* (RCA).

HEMPHILL, JULIUS, *alto sax, composer*; b. Fort Worth, Tex., ca. 1940. Studied clarinet w. John Carter in early '50s. First prof. job w. Independent Boogie Agency in early '60s. With US Army Band, '64; various Texas bands; Ike Turner. Moved to St. Louis '68 and became a member of BAG w. Oliver Lake, Lester Bowie. During this time also studied at No. Texas State; Lincoln U. Formed gp. w. pianist John Hicks and toured US coll., '71. Pl. w. Anthony Braxton in Chicago; performed in Paris, Sweden, '73. Worked w. Paul Jeffrey Octet in NYC, '74. Film: *The Orientation of Sweet Willie Rollbar,* '72. He presented a stage version of this work at Ornette Coleman's Prince Street loft, '73. His *Kawaida,* a mixed media presentation of instrumental music, voices, dance and drama was premiered at Washington U., St. Louis, '72. *Obituary: Cosmos for 3 Parts* was debuted at Space Life Center, NYC, Dec. '74. Comp: *Lonely Blacks; Skin 1; Skin 2; Lyric; Reflections; The Hard Blues.* Hemphill is also a poet-lyricist. In '72 he formed his own rec. co., Mbari, and released two albums, *Poem For Blind Lemon;* and *Dogon A.D.* The latter was scheduled for re-release on Arista, the label which produced his LP, *'Coon Bid'ness.* Other LPs: w. Braxton, *New York, Fall* 1974 (Arista); Bowie, *Fast Last* (Muse); Kool and the Gang, *Hustler's Convention* (UA).

HENDERSON, WILLIAM RANDALL (BILL),* *singer*; b. Chicago, Ill., 3/19/30. Recorded w. H. Silver, '58; O. Peterson, '63. Toured as Basie vocalist, '65-6. Settling in LA area, spent most of his time as an actor and singer in motion pics. and on TV. Among his movie credits were *Trouble Man,* '72; *Hit The Open Man,* '74. Acting apps. on the Bill Cosby show, '70-1; also roles in *Ironside; Happy Days; Sanford & Son.* Sang on TV shows, *Dial M For Music; Tonight; Midnight Special,* and the Steve Allen, Della Reese and Nancy Wilson shows, all during '72-5. Henderson is a strongly jazz-oriented singer with an original and piquant timbre.

LPs: *Please Send Me Someone To Love; Bill Henderson Sings* (Veejay Int'l.); w. Horace Silver; Jimmy Smith (Blue Note); w. Hank Jones (Riverside); w. O. Peterson (MGM); w. Basie (Verve).

HENDERSON, BOBBY (Jody Bolden) Robert Bolden Henderson),* *piano, trumpet*; b. New York City, 4/16/10. Billie Holiday's first accompanist in '33, he spent most of his career in upstate New York, living during the late '60s in Albany, where he died 12/9/69. LPs: *Home in the Clouds; Last Recordings* (Chiaro.).

HENDERSON, DR. EDWARD JACKSON (EDDIE), *trumpet, fluegelhorn, composer*; b. New York City,

10/26/40. Father sang w. Charioteers; mother was dancer at Cotton Club. Trumpet at elementary school from age 10 to 14. To SF 1954; theory, tpt. at SF Conservatory, '54-7. Spent '58-61 in Air Force, not playing. Became interested in jazz when Miles Davis, then staying with his parents, gave him encouragement and informal instruction.

From 1961 Henderson pursued his dual ambitions, studying at U.C. Berkeley, grad. w. B.S. in zoology, '64; M.D. in medicine '68 at Howard Univ., Washington, D.C. During summers, from '64, pl. w. John Handy. Gigs w. Handy, Big Black, Philly Joe Jones, '68. Joined Herbie Hancock 1970 and toured with Hancock's sextet until it disbanded in '73. Through this period he also worked with Pharoah Sanders, Joe Henderson et al.

Traveled w. Art Blakey's Jazz Messengers for six months in '73; late that year, returned to SF, then played with Azteca for a year. From late '74, active mainly leading own combo, but worked w. Norman Connors in Japan summer '75.

Henderson continued to practice medicine intermittently to supplement his income, both in general practice and psychiatry. Henderson was praised by critics for his full, round tone, exceptional technique and attention-riveting ideas.

Infl: Miles Davis, F. Hubbard, Lee Morgan, J. Coltrane.

TV: Several programs while w. Hancock. Fests: NJF-NY w. Hancock and Blakey; many others during several visits to Europe.

LPs: *Realization; Inside Out* (Capricorn); *Sunburst* (BN). w. Hancock: *Mwandishi; Crossings* (WB); *Sextant* (Col.); five albums w. Norman Connors (Buddah); others w. Ch. Earland (Fantasy); Pete Yellin; Buddy Terry (Mainstream).

HENDERSON, JOSEPH A. (JOE),* *tenor sax, composer*; also *soprano sax, flute*; b. Lima, Ohio, 4/24/37. First prominent w. Kenny Dorham, '62-3; Horace Silver, '64-6. Co-led Jazz Communicators w. Freddie Hubbard, Louis Hayes. Pl. w. Herbie Hancock sextet, '69-70. From that time has led own groups except for four months in '71 when he was affiliated w. Blood, Sweat & Tears. Eugene Chadbourne, writing in the Calgary *Herald,* said: "Henderson is a part of an historical process that's extremely important in American music—the process of improvisation. This is where the real American classical music is . . . When Henderson launches into one of his many lengthy improvisations—each one is almost like a jewel, polished and multidimensional—you can hear the tenor as it came down through the years. And through that tenor, you can hear all the changes improvised music has gone through in America in more than four decades."

By the mid-70's Henderson had moved to Calif. and had become active doing college clinics. Comp: *Recorda Me; Black Narcissus; Soulution; Inner Urge; Isotope; El Barrio; The Bead Game; Tetragon; Afro-Centric; Power to the People; Afterthought; Caribbean Fire Dance; If You're Not Part of the Solution, You're Part of the*

Problem; Junk Blues; Out 'n In; Gazelle; Black Miracle; Immaculate Deception. Won DB Critics poll, TDWR '67.

LPs: *The Kicker; Tetragon; Power to the People; If You're Not Part of the Solution, You're Part of the Problem; In Pursuit of Blackness; Black is the Color; Joe Henderson in Japan; Multiple; The Elements* w. A. Coltrane; *Canyon Lady; Black Miracle* (Milest.); *Inner Urge* (BN); w. K. Burrell, *Ellington is Forever* (Fant.); w. Mose Allison, *Hello There, Universe* (Atl.), w. A. Coltrane, *Ptah the El Daoud* (Imp.).

HENDERSON, MICHAEL, *bass, guitar*; b. Yazoo City, Miss., 7/7/51. Played cello in high school, but later switched to guitar; learned rudiments of guitar and bass at Grinell's music store in Detroit. From then on has been self-taught. First professional job, '66, w. Rudy Robinson band, which also backed the Detroit Emeralds and the Fantastic Four. Pl. w. Motown artists Stevie Wonder, Martha Reeves and the Vandellas, Four Tops, The Supremes, Gladys Knight and the Pips, The Temptations, '66-8. On the road w. Aretha Franklin for year, '68; w. S. Wonder, '69 to late '70, when he joined Miles Davis. Infls: Davis, Franklin, Wonder, M. Gaye. Fests: Montreux, Ann Arbor, Newport, Monterey. TV apps. w. Davis. Comps: for albums by Michael Shrieve (Col.), G. Bartz (Pres.).

LPs: *Jack Johnson; Live at the Fillmore; Live-Evil; On The Corner; Get Up With It,* w. Davis (Col.); numerous dates w. Motown artists.

HENDERSON, WAYNE MAURICE,* *trombone, euphonium, composer*; b. Houston, Texas, 9/24/39. Best known through the '60s as a member of the Jazz Crusaders. The name of the group was later changed to The Crusaders (see HOOPER, STIX). Henderson also enjoyed considerable success as a producer of albums by other artists.

LPs: w. Crusaders (Blue Thumb).

HENDRICKS, JOHN CARL (JON),* *songwriter, singer*; also *drums*; b. Newark, Ohio, 9/16/21. Key member and principal lyricist with Lambert, Hendricks & Ross, the trio that popularized the concept of setting lyrics to jazz melodies and to improvised solos transcribed from records. Original trio broke up in '62, but lasted for two more years with replacements; from '66 Hendricks worked as a single and in Feb. '68 moved to London. Later that year he was voted number one jazz singer in the *Melody Maker* poll. He worked throughout Europe and Africa, performing on English TV with Lulu, M. Ferguson, and various others; app. in French TV movie, *Hommage a Cole Porter,* which won a prize at Cannes.

Teaming up with his wife, Judith, in the role formerly occupied by Annie Ross, and sometimes adding his daughter, Michelle, Hendricks again began making trio apps. He also staged his *Evolution of the Blues* presentation, originally seen at the MJF in 1960. Returning to the U.S., Hendricks settled in Mill Valley, Cal., embarking on a number of ventures, among them a job as jazz critic for the San Francisco Chronicle, '73-4. In the fall of '74

he put on a new version of *Evolution of the Blues* at the Broadway Theatre in SF, which enjoyed a long run into '75.

He signed with Arista Records to make his first Amer. album in 10 years. He also taught classes on Jazz in American Society at Cal. State, Sonoma and U.C. Berkeley. One of those rare jazz singers in whom wit and humor are elements just as important as rhythmic sensitivity, Hendricks has been an untiring propagandist for jazz. Among the jazz works to which Hendricks has contributed lyrics are *Along Came Betty; Bijou; Charleston Alley; Cloudburst; Cousin Mary; Desafinado; Down For Double; Fiesta In Blue; Four; Little Niles; Little Pony; Moanin'; Now's The Time; Sermonette; Sack O' Woe; Shiny Stockings; Walkin'; Watermelon Man.*

Own LP; *Blues for Pablo* (Arista); early albums made by Hendricks were deleted, but were on Col., Reprise and Smash. LPs w. Lambert, Hendricks & Ross on Col., Impulse, Odyssey.

HERBERT, GREGORY DELANO, *composer, alto, tenor saxophones*; also *clarinets, flutes* etc.; b. Philadelphia, Pa., 5/19/47. Priv. lessons, '61; Granoff School of Music, '62; worked briefly w. D. Ellington, '64. In Sept. '64 entered Temple U., remaining there as music and saxophone major until '68. Joined W. Herman Oct. '71 and toured with him internationally until Jan. '75. Favs: J. McLean, C. Adderley, J. Coltrane, S. Rollins et al. A fervently expressive tenor soloist, particularly effective on ballads, but no less skillful on up tempos.

LPs: w. Herman, *The Raven Speaks; Giant Steps; The Thundering Herd; The Herd Live at Montreux; Children of Lima* (Fantasy); w. Pat Martino, *Baiyina* (Pres.); w. Johnny Coles, *Katumbo* (Main.).

HERMAN, WOODROW CHARLES (WOODY),* *leader, alto, soprano saxophones, clarinet, singer*; b. Milwaukee, Wis., 5/16/13. Led own band from '37 and continued to tour with various personnels; sometimes with small combo in late '50s. Organizing a new band in '60, he enjoyed a resurgence of popularity, touring frequently overseas.

In '67 Herman toured Africa and Iron Curtain countries under U.S. State Dept. auspices. In Sept. '67 he app. at the MJF, introducing Bill Holman's three-movement *Concerto For Herd.* Soloists then in the band incl. Luis Gasca, Carl Fontana, Sal Nistico, Albert Dailey, Cecil Payne. Other foreign tours: England, '68, '70, '72. In '74, starred at Montreux JF and toured France, Belgium, Germany, Sweden, Turkey. In '74 the orch. toured the U.S. for two months w. F. Sinatra, and app. with him on a TV spec., *The Main Event.* Other TV: many apps. on Merv Griffin, Mike Douglas shows etc.

Hiring primarily young musicians and making increasing use of contemporary pop material, Herman recorded a series of successful albums for Cadet in '69-70, and for Fantasy from '71- . In '74 he introduced Alan Broadbent's *Variations On A Scene* and *Children of Lima,* both perf. by the orch. together with the Houston Symph.

Herman continued to discover exciting solo talent.

Heard with him during the '70s were trumpeters Tony Klatka, Bill Stapleton, Gary Pack; trombonists Jim Pugh, Bob Burgess; saxophonists Greg Herbert, Frank Tiberi, Frank Vicari; pianists, Broadbent, John Hicks; bassists Gene Perla, Al Johnson; drummers Ed Soph, Joe LaBarbera; composer-arrangers Richard Evans, Broadbent, Klatka, Nat Pierce, Gary Anderson, Pugh, Stapleton; and innumerable others.

By playing compositions and arrangements that covered a vast spectrum, from his early hits such as *Four Brothers* and *Caldonia* to works by Coltrane, F. Zappa, Stanley Clarke, Chick Corea, Thad Jones and Billy Cobham, Herman succeeded in not only retaining and expanding his audience, but in keeping up the high musical level of the orchestra's performances.

A Grammy winner in '63, Herman won again in '73 for his *Giant Steps* album and in '74 for the *Thundering Herd* album. Fests: Newport six times; Monterey three times; Concord twice, during decade from '66-75. In '75 Herman founded the Woody Herman-Sister Fabian Scholarship Fund in Milwaukee. He gives a concert and seminar annually, donating the proceeds to benefit young musicians, and to award scholarships. By '75 half of the band's engagements were played in colleges and high schools. Many of the band's arrangements are available through Hal Leonard Publ. in Milwaukee.

LPs: *Concerto for Herd*, live at Monterey, '67 (Verve); *Woody*, feat. Broadbent's arr. of *Blues in the Night; Heavy Exposure; Light My Fire* (Cadet); *Brand New; The Raven Speaks; Herd at Montreux; Children of Lima*, w. orch. and Houston Symph.; *Giant Steps; Thundering Herd* (Fant.).

Reissues: *The Best of Woody Herman*, 1939-43 (MCA); *Early Autumn*, 1948-50 (Cap.); *Woody Herman, '63* (Trip).

HEYWOOD, EDDIE JR.,* *piano, composer*; b. Atlanta, Ga., 12/4/15. From 1966-69 a partial paralysis of the hand, similar to the ailment which had curtailed his career in the late '40s, greatly hampered his playing ability. He devoted his main efforts toward comp. and arr. while living in Vineyard Haven, Mass. Ret. to active pl. at the Cookery, NYC, April '72. App. at Newport-NY JF, '74; concerts on Martha's Vineyard '70, '73-74; also school, coll. concerts. Citation of Achievement from BMI '69; second award from BMI for over 1,000,000 broadcast perf. of his comp. *Canadian Sunset*. 750 Award from radio station WSB, Atlanta, Ga., '73. Comp: *Portrait of Martha's Vineyard; Golden West*. LPs: *As You Remember Them; The Swing Era: One More Time* (Time-Life).

HIGGINBOTHAM, JACK (J.C.),* *trombone*; b. Social Circle, Ga., 5/11/06. First prominent in the bands of Luis Russell, F. Henderson and L. Armstrong, Higginbotham later was teamed for many years w. trumpeter Red Allen. He remained occasionally active in the late '60s and app. in '72 at the NJF-NY in an all star E. Condon group. He died 5/26/73 in Harlem hospital, NYC.

Higginbotham was one of the most original and force-

ful trombone soloists of the swing era.

LPs: *Comes Home!* (Jazzology); others w. Allen (RCA); Armstrong (Col.).

HIGGINS, BILLY,* *drums*; b. Los Angeles, Calif., 10/11/36. One of the charter members of the Ornette Coleman gp. of the late '50s. Active NY free-lance in '60s w. S. Rollins, H. Mobley, L. Morgan et al. Continued to work w. Coleman, off and on, in '60s and '70s; also w. Bill Lee Brass Company in Brooklyn, '72-3; Chris Anderson, '73-4. From '70 his main associations have been w. Cedar Walton and Clifford Jordan in trios and quartets incl. European, Japanese tours. Fests: NJF-NY w. Jordan '73; Basel; Verona w. Jimmy Heath '74. Comp: *Inja; Buster Henry*. A subtle drummer of unflagging swing as at home with Coleman as with Dexter Gordon.

LPs: w. O. Coleman, *Science Fiction* (Col.); w. C. Jordan, *Glass Bead Games; Colors* w. Brass Company (Strata-East); w. D. Gordon (Steeple.); *Generation* (Prest.); w. J. Heath; J. Raney (Xanadu); Hilton Ruiz (Steeple.); w. Pat Martino, *The Visit* (Cobble.); w. Barry Harris, *Bull's Eye* (Prest.); w. C. McPherson; C. Fuller (Main.); Mal Waldron (Enja).

HILL, ANDREW,* *piano, composer*; b. Port au Prince, Haiti, 6/30/37. Early experience in Chicago w. G. Ammons; J. Griffin; Ira Sullivan. On the road w. Dinah Washington; in LA w. R.R. Kirk, '61; to NYC '63 where he began rec. for Blue Note, and leading own gps. Music co-ordinator for Leroi Jones' Black Art Repertory Theatre, '65. From '66-8 pl. colleges, clubs, and concerts across the US; active creating and performing extended comps. Composer in residence at Colgate U., '70-1, where he received his doctorate. Perf. at various rural art centers, such as the Ohio River Arts Fest., Evansville, Ind.; cond. symposiums at Wayne U., Lafayette U. of NO; organized at co-ordinated NY Musicians' JF; toured cultural centers and penal systems for the NY State Council for the Arts, '72. Audited programs for the NYSCA, '72-3. Own quartet for University of the Streets, NYC, '73. Toured US on the Smithsonian Heritage Program, '73-4. Awarded a Smithsonian Fellowship, '75.

Considered to be in the second wave of avant gardists who followed in the wake of Ornette Coleman, Cecil Taylor and John Coltrane, Hill declared, "The whole energy school of playing isn't valid for the '70s, as far as I'm concerned. It's time to become proficient on your instrument. All this noise . . ."

Roger Riggins called his work, "at the core, a popular music. If anyone has heard such tunes as *Tired Trade* or *Limbo*, they'll know what I mean. He is popular and 'high' art, if you want to call it that, at the same time."

TV: score for *Lenox Avenue Sunday*, CBS Repertory Theatre, '67; *Soul*, PBS, '70; *Black Arts*, CBS, '72. Comp: *String Quartets #1 & 2; Brass Quartet; Golden Spook*, an opera; *Laverne* for organ and piano, co-composed w. his wife, organist Laverne Gillette. All Hill's music is available from Jazz Fund Publ., P.O. Box 1244,

New York, N.Y. 10009. Hill uses the money, quite literally, as a jazz fund to help needy musicians. LPs: *Invitation* (Steeple.); *Spiral* (Arista); *Hommage* (Ai Music); *Smokestack; Grassroots; Lift Every Voice; One For One* (BN).

HILLYER, LONNIE,* *trumpet*; b. Monroe, Ga., 3/25/40. Best known for his work w. C. Mingus; Barry Harris; C. McPherson in '60s, he continued to appear w. them into '70s. Also teaching trumpet students in NYC. Fest: w. Mingus, NJF '71; NJF-NY '72. LPs: w. McPherson, (Main.); *The Quintet/Live* (Prest.); w. Mingus, *Let My Children Hear Music; Mingus and Friends in Concert* (Col.).

HINES, EARL KENNETH (FATHA),* *piano, composer*; b. Duquesne, Pa., 12/28/05. After his triumphant return at the three Little Theatre concerts in NYC, '64, Hines began to tour on a world-wide basis as leader of a small group and solo pianist. He played in Europe, '67-8, '70, '73-5; Japan, '68, '72, '74; Australasia, '72; Latin America w. Oscar Peterson, '69; w. Teddy Wilson, Marian McPartland and Ellis Larkins, '74. Don Schlitten wrote that Hines "still thinks he is at the Grand Terrace in Chicago leading his sensational big band, only there is no band, there is only Earl Hines playing the piano as if he was the band. He uses his left hand sometimes for accents and figures that would only come from a full trumpet section. Sometimes he will play chords that would have been written and played by five saxophones in harmony. But he is always the virtuoso pianist with his arpeggios, his percussive attack, and his fantastic ability to modulate from one song to another as if they were all one song and he just created all those melodies during his own improvisations."

TV: Dick Cavett; Johnny Carson; Merv Griffin; Mike Douglas. Fest: NJF-NY; MJF; Montreux; Nice. Won DB Critics poll '66-7; '69-73. Comp: *Rosetta; You Can Depend On Me; My Monday Date; Blues In Thirds; I Can't Trust Myself Alone; A Night in Trinidad; Blue Fox; Pianology.* LPs: solo, *Earl Hines at Home* (Delmark); *Hines '65; Plays Duke Ellington, Vols. I, II, III* (Master Jazz); *Tour De Force* (Bl. Lion); *Hines Does Hoagy; Hines Comes in Handy; My Tribute to Louis* (Audiophile); *Quintessential Earl Hines; Quintessential Continued* (Chiaro.); combos, *Once Upon a Time* (Imp.); *Blues & Things* w. J. Rushing (Master Jazz); *An Evening With Earl Hines; Back On the Street* w. Jonah Jones; *Live at the Overseas Press Club* w. Maxine Sullivan (Chiaro.); *Father & His Flock On Tour* (MPS); *Earl Hines and Roy Eldridge at the Village Vanguard* (Xanadu); reissues, *The Father Jumps*, big band '39-45 (Bluebird); *A Monday Date*, '23 band & '28 solos (Milest.); *Another Monday Date*, '55-6 solos (Fant.); *The Mighty Father*, '64-6 solos (Fly. Dutch.); *Louis Armstrong and Earl Hines 1928* (Smithsonian Collection); other partial reissue of Armstrong-Hines recs. (Col.).

HINO, MOTOHIKO, *drums*; b. Tokyo, Japan, 1/3/46. Brother of Terumasa Hino; father, Bin Hino, pl. trumpet.

Pro. debut in '63 w. Takao Kusagaya; worked w. Tokyo Union Orch.; Hiroshi Watanabe & His Stardusters; various other Japanese combos in addition to rec. w. J.L. Ponty, Joe Henderson, G. Peacock, and acc. numerous visiting jazzmen from the U.S. and other countries. Member of Terumasa Hino quintet, '74- . Infls: Terumasa Hino, Tony Williams, Elvin Jones. Fests: Berlin, '71; Newport/N.Y. w. T. Hino, '73; plus about ten fests. annually in Japan. Won *Swing Journal* readers' poll annually as number one drummer, '71-5.

LPs: *Motohiko Hino First Album* (Jap. Col.); as sideman on all T. Hino albums.

HINO, TERUMASA, *trumpet, fluegelhorn, composer*; b. Tokyo, Japan, 10/25/42. Father, Bin Hino, was tap-dancer before World War II. After war took up trumpet and is still pl. in clubs. Brother is drummer Motohiko Hino. Father taught him tap-dancing at age four; trumpet at nine. Hino writes: "Besides studying by myself, copied M. Davis, C. Brown, L. Morgan, F. Hubbard, etc., and played with and was taught by many foreign artists during their visits to Japan."

Made pro. debut as second trumpeter at a U.S. camp, '55; pl. at several base camps, '57-60. Third trumpet w. Hiroshi Watanabe & Stardusters; joined Takao Kusagaya & Crescendo Six, pl. U. S. camps and dance halls in Tokyo; then w. Jiro Inagaki, quintet touring Indonesia '61. Joined Hideo Shiraki Combo; led own gp. '64-5 and rec. *Hinology*, which won two awards incl. Golden Disc. Pl. w. Shiraki at Berlin JF, '65; w. his own gp., Berlin '71; NJF-NY '72, Yugoslavia and other Euro. fests. '73. In the summer of '75 he app. w. the Jackie McLean septet at the Five Spot, NYC. Infl: Coltrane, M. Davis, Clifford Brown, R. Workman. Films: *Daytime Attack* (Toho MP), '69; *One-legged Ace* (Toho MP), '72. TV: *Jazz in Japan* (NHK); *Music Fair* (Fuji). Comps: 40 to 50 pieces incl. *Alone, Alone, And, Alone; Fuji (Wistaria).* Won SJ Jazz Disc Award-Jazz of Japan Special Award, '69; Jazz of Japan Award, '72, '74; SJ Readers Poll, '67-74. Hino plays in a hard, brassy style reflecting his infls. and elements of free jazz. LPs: *Fuji* (Japan. Victor); *Journey Into My Mind* (Japan. CBS); *Speak to Loneliness* (East Wind); *Vibrations; Taro's Mood* (Enja); *Hideo Shiraki in Berlin* (MPS/Saba).

HINTON, MILTON JOHN (MILT or JUDGE),* *bass, composer, educator*; b. Vicksburg, Miss., 6/23/10. From '66 continued to be one of the busiest musicians in NYC with recs., transcriptions, studio work such as ABC staff w. B. Rosengarden orch. for Dick Cavett show; Broadway prod., *Music, Music.* Toured East, Middle East & Africa w. Pearl Bailey; Puerto Rico, Mexico, Fla. & LV w. Paul Anka; LV w. Barbra Streisand. House bassist at Michael's Pub, NYC, from '74, backing soloists such as Red Norvo, Teddy Wilson, Flip Phillips, Terry Gibbs, Joe Venuti, Bobby Hackett, Dick Wellstood, etc.

Fest: Colo. JP from '67; Odessa, Tex. JP from '68; Concord JF from '72; NJF-NY w. B. Rosengarden; Radio City jam session, '72; w. Bob Greene; Cab Calloway reunion; Radio City jam, '73; Teddy Wilson; L.

Hampton, '74; Benny Carter; Jazz Hall of Fame, '75. Concert and jazz party in Moscow, '73. Taught at Concord, Calif. Summer Music Camp; conductor of Hunter Coll. Jazz Workshop, NYC. Member of Jazz Panel of National Foundation of the Arts from '70. Pl. White House w. Pearl Bailey several times; guest there for Duke Ellington's 70th birthday. One of the most popular men in jazz, Hinton has been made an Honorary Citizen of NO, '69; Odessa, '72; Concord, '73. Deacon of St. Albans Congregational Church; actively involved w. community and neighborhood youth.

Comp: *Beefsteak Charlie's; Mona's Feeling Lonely; Walk Chicken With Your Head Picked Bald to the Bone; Ebony Silhouette; Blues For the Judge; Sometimes I Wonder.* LPs: *Here Swings the Judge;* others w. Bill Watrous; Danny Stiles; Zoot Sims; John Bunch; Red Norvo (Famous Door); Z. Sims-B. Pizzarelli (Gr. Merch.); *Soprano Summit* (World Jazz); Buck Clayton; J. Venuti (Chiaro.); Bob Greene (RCA); w. Dick Hyman; C. Mingus (Col.); B. Leighton (Mon.-Ever.); E. Garner (MGM).

HODEIR, ANDRE, *composer, critic;* b. Paris, France, 1/22/21. Prominent since mid-1950s as musicologist, author of several scholarly books on jazz. In 1970s continued leading orchestra, writing scores for films; from 1961-8 worked on book, *The Worlds of Jazz,* publ. in US 1972. Won Grand Prix Du Disque, '72, for his work *Anna Livia Plurabelle.* Subject of *A Jazz Portrait,* French television film, 1971.

Publ: *The Worlds of Jazz,* Grove Press Inc., NYC.

LPs: *Anna Livia Plurabelle* (Philips), *Bitter Ending* (Epic), both based on James Joyce's *Finnegan's Wake.*

HODES, ARTHUR W. (ART),* *piano;* b. Nikoliev, Russia, 11/14/04. Raised in Chicago, where he worked in pioneer jazz groups, incl. Wolverines, '26. Well known for many years as musician, disc jockey, journalist and lecturer. Pl. w. dixieland group at Disneyland, '67. Voted Citizen of the Year, Park Forest, Ill., '68. Pops Foster-Art Hodes TV show, '69; Toured Denmark, '70; Stars of Jazz concert tour in U.S. w. Condon, Davison, Bigard, '71; 17 weeks of concerts in '73 w. J. McPartland in spirituals, blues and jazz show. Cont. to app. at occasional fests., toured w. combo from '73. Jazz host on six national educ. TV shows, '69-72. App. w. Davison on *Just Jazz,* PBA, '71. In Dec. '72, Esquire mag. publ. an article by Hodes called *Jazz: The Sweet, Slow Comeback.* Hodes won Emmy award in Chi. for half hour solo TV show.

Comps: *Plain Ol' Blues; Blues Yesterday, Today, Tomorrow; Pagin' Mr. Jelly.* LPs: *Plain Ol' Blues,* duo w. Truck Parham (Mercury); *Rompin' 'n' Stompin'* (RCA); *Stars of Jazz,* vols. 1-3 w. Condon, Davison, Bigard (Jazzology); w. Bigard, *Bucket's Got a Hole in It* (Delmark); solo piano, *The Art of Hodes* (Euphonic); *Sittin' In; Funky Piano; Original Blue Note Jazz,* vol. 1 w. Edmond Hall (Blue Note).

HODGES, JOHN CORNELIUS (JOHNNY or RABBIT),* *alto sax, composer;* b. Cambridge, Mass., 7/25/06. A member of Duke Ellington's orchestra from 1928-51 and again from 1955, Hodges died in NYC after suffering a heart attack 5/11/70.

Hodges brought to jazz a sound that had neither precedent nor successor. His warm, sensuous timbre, always at its most persuasive in ballads and blues, was a quintessential part of the Ellington ensemble's tonal palette. He shared with Benny Carter the honor of being one of the definitive alto sax pioneers in the great formative years of jazz, primarily the 1930s and '40s. In the early years he occasionally doubled on soprano saxophone, modeling his style after that of his idol, Sidney Bechet. During those days, too, his work was notable for up tempo solos characterized by a surging, rhythmically perfect fluency.

In the early 1950s Hodges led his own band, feat. other Ellington alumni incl. Harold Baker, Lawrence Brown, Sonny Greer; he enjoyed modest success for a while, but his talent was never more appropriately displayed than in the big band setting, or in the various small Ellington splinter groups, many of them under his own name, starting with the first Johnny Hodges record session in 1937.

As composer Hodges was credited, or co-credited with Ellington, for *Jeep's Blues; I'm Beginning to See the Light; Hodge Podge; Wanderlust; It Shouldn't Happen to a Dream; Squatty Roo; Good Queen Bess; The Jeep is Jumpin'; Mama Knows; Bustin' With Buster; Away From You; Blues A-Plenty, Juice A-Plenty; Sir John* and dozens more.

LPs: *Ellingtonia!* (Onyx); *Johnny Hodges; Hodges & Hines—Swing's Our Thing; Mess of Blues,* Hodges-Wild Bill Davis; *Rippin' & Runnin'; Blue Notes; Blues A-Plenty; Stride Right,* Hodges-Earl Hines; *The Eleventh Hour; Hodges w. Billy Strayhorn Orch.; Don't Sleep In The Subway; Blue Hodge; Blues Summit,* Hodges-Ellington (Verve); *Triple Play; Things Ain't What They Used To Be,* Hodges-Rex Stewart (RCA); *Lawrence Welk & Johnny Hodges* (Dot); *Hodge Podge,* feat. Ellington (Epic); some tracks in *The Greatest Concert in the World* (Pablo); *Esquire's All-American Hot Jazz* (RCA).

HOLLAND, DAVID, *bass;* also *piano, guitar, cello, bass guitar;* b. Wolverhampton, England, 10/1/46. Stud. bass with James E. Merrit at Guildhall School, London, '65-8. In the same years he perf. classical music in orchestral and chamber concerts in and around London; held principal bass chair in coll. orch. Began in jazz with Dixieland bands, then pl. with a variety of groups which incl. such musicians as Ronnie Scott, John Surman, Humphrey Lyttelton, Evan Parker, Kenny Wheeler and Tubby Hayes. Miles Davis heard him in London and was sufficiently impressed to invite him to join his group. Holland moved to NYC and pl. w. Davis from '68-71. In '71-2 he was a member of Circle w. C. Corea, B. Altschul and A. Braxton, during which time the group used London as its home base for Continental engagements. Worked w. S. Getz, '73-4 and has also perf. w. S. Rivers, Joe Henderson, T. Jones-M. Lewis orch., T. Monk, Roy Haynes, Paul Bley, Karl Berger, J. DeJohnette, Carla Bley (JCOA), L. Konitz. With Braxton, '75.

Holland, equally adept on upright or electric bass, was named by writer Bill Cole as one of "the astonishing number of excellent bassists to have developed during the last decade . . . his tone is as big and round as a struck gong. His intonation is perfect, and he works all positions and stops flawlessly." Holland's infls. incl. Django Reinhardt, Ray Brown, Ch. Mingus, S. LaFaro, G. Peacock, P. Chambers, Davis, J. Coltrane, Monk, Bach, Webern, Schoenberg, Charles Ives, Bartok, Ellington and E. Dolphy. Fests: Newport, Monterey and numerous European apps. Won Melody Maker poll, '69; DB Critics' TDWR, '73. Since '73 active as teacher both privately and in workshops and univs. around the world.

LPs: *Conference of the Birds; Circle in Paris; Music From Two Basses*, w. Barre Phillips; *Music for Cello and Guitar* w. Derek Bailey (ECM); w. Corea, *A.R.C.* (ECM); *Song of Singing* (Blue Note); w. M. Davis, *Filles de Kilimanjaro; In A Silent Way; Bitches Brew; Live at the Fillmore* (Col.); *Town Hall '72*, w. Braxton (Trio).

HOLLEY, MAJOR QUINCY JR. (MULE), * bass; also *tuba, violin;* b. Detroit, Mich., 7/10/24. Worked w. Woody Herman, Kenny Burrell, C. Hawkins, R. Eldridge, Q. Jones, A. Cohn-Z. Sims. With D. Ellington, '64, then free-lanced in NYC until '67 when he taught for three years at Berklee Coll. in Boston. Ret. to NYC, '70, pl. w. James Moody, Pepper Adams at Half Note. Became house bassist at Jimmy Ryan's, first w. J. McPartland, then w. Eldridge. Also pl. Sunday nights at Bradley's w. Jaki Byard. Toured France, Belgium, Switzerland w. Helen Humes; Scandinavia, Germany, England w. Kings of Jazz in mid-70s. Fests: NJF-NY w. Eldridge, '73 at Louis Armstrong Stadium, televised on PBS; Jazzfest, Hanover, Germany; Colorado Jazz Party. Comps: *Mule; Major and the Minor.* Has also worked w. Drug Abuse Program in NYC; Phoenix House; Harlem Teams for Self Help. When Holley bows a solo he sings what he is playing in a manner reminiscent of Slam Stewart but different in that Stewart sings an octave higher than his own bowing. LPs: *Mule* (Black & Blue); w. Helen Humes (Col., Black & Blue); w. Cohn-Sims, *You 'N Me* (Trip); w. Buddy Tate, *The Texas Twister* (Master Jazz); w. L. Konitz, *Chicago* (Groove Merchant).

HOLLOWAY, JAMES L. (RED), * tenor saxophone; also *clarinet, flute, piccolo, piano, bass, drums, violin;* b. Helena, Ark., 5/31/27. Professional since '47, mainly known as tenor saxophonist, based in Chicago from '40s to '67, when he moved to LA. For six years he served as talent coordinator and leader of house band at the Parisian Room, LA. Toured Canada and U.S. w. Jimmy Dean Show, '67. International tours w. John Mayall combo, '73, '74, incl. Australia, Europe, Canada. Various LA apps. w. S. Stitt, Ray Brown, Sweets Edison et al. Pl. on sound track of film *Lady Sings The Blues.* Perf. at commemorative concert celebrating jazz week in LA Dec. '74.

Holloway is capable of generating great excitement with his big sound and hard driving mainstream-modern style. He rec. many of his own comps. for a series of albums on Prestige. Comp: *Kriss Kross*, written w. organist Art Hillery, rec. by J. Moody.

LPs: *Sax, Strings and Soul; The Burner* (Pres.)

HOLMAN, WILLIS (BILL), * composer; b. Olive, Cal., 5/21/27. Well known in '50s, early '60s for his tenor work as well as his writing, Holman discontinued playing in '66 as a result of illness, but made many contributions as composer-arranger. His originals included *Concerto For Herd* for W. Herman, premiered at MJF; *A Separate Walking*, commissioned by Cal. State U., Northridge Jazz Ensemble; *The Daily Dance* for S. Kenton; *Time Being* for Buddy Rich.

Film orchestrating for J. Mandel, G. Mulligan, '66; instrumental arrs. for The Association and 5th Dimension vocal groups, '67-8; TV series: *Operation Entertainment* w. T. Gibbs, '68; Della Reese show w. Pete Myers, '69; Pearl Bailey show w. L. Bellson, '70. Arrs. for Klaus Weiss orch. in Germany, '71. In '72 was involved in formation of LifeLine Music Press (P.O. Box 338, Agoura, Ca. 91301), for printing and distribution of music for school jazz ensembles. Led own 18 piece band in LA area, '74-5. Throughout this period Holman composed and/or arranged for B. Rich (for whom his arr. of *Norwegian Wood* earned a Grammy nomination), S. Kenton, Ed Shaughnessy, Peggy Lee, S. Vaughan and several college ensembles. A writer of broad experience, he reflects in his work the disciplines and guidelines established by the best swing era arrangers.

LPs: as arr. with above mentioned bands.

HOLMES, RICHARD ARNOLD (GROOVE), * organ; b. Camden, N.J., 5/2/31. On the road w. his own gp. from '62, he had a hit single of Erroll Garner's *Misty* from his Prestige album, *Soul Message.* It sold more than 300,000 copies in '69. Holmes rec. 10 more albums for Prest. before shifting to Groove Merchant where he rec. on his own and also teamed w. Jimmy McGriff in the studio and in live concert recordings. Naturally left-handed he was infl. by Paul Chambers and Ron Carter and developed one of the strongest bass lines of all the organists.

LPs: *$6,000,000 Man; Onsaya Joy* (Fly. Dutch.); *Misty* (Prest.); *New Groove; Night Glider;* w. Jimmy McGriff, *Come Together; Giants in Concert* (Gr. Merchant).

HONDA, TAKASHI (TAKEHIRO), piano; b. Iwate Prefecture, Japan, 8/21/45. Brothers-in-law are saxophonist Sadao Watanabe; drummer Fumio Watanabe. Music lessons from childhood. Stud. w. Kazuko Nagamine while in high school and at univ. Began pl. w. fellow students during campus fest. at Kunitachi Univ. Helped form Kazunori Takeda quartet; joined Fumio Watanabe gp. After two yrs. w. Watanabe, pl. w. Mashiko Togashi gp. Following this he formed his own trio and soul gp., pl. mainly at jazz spots in Tokyo, incl. Taro, Pit-in, and concerts in various districts. Acc. singer Mieko Hirota. In '72 pl. w. Terumasa Hino for three mos. but most of his apps. are w. own band or w. Sadao Watanabe. Infl: Sadao Watanabe, Marvin Gaye. Fests: NJF, '70; Montreux, '73, w. S. Watanabe. Won SJ Readers Poll, '74. LPs: *Salaam Salaam* (East Wind); another on Trio; w. S. Watanabe (Japan. CBS).

HOOD, ERNIE, guitar, composer; also *zither, keyboards;* b. Charlotte, N.C., 6/2/23. Brother of baritone saxophonist Bill Hood. Rec. w. C. Barnet, '45; pl. w. W. Manone; Lucky Thompson septet. After many years as comp. and studio musician, scoring for commercial films, Oregon Pops orch., also jazz groups in Portland area, he app. as a zither player w. Flora Purim in the albums *Butterfly Dreams* and *Stories To Tell.* Comp. *Mountain Train* heard in *Stories To Tell.*

Own LP: *Neighborhoods* (Thistlefield Records, c/o Ernest Hood, P.O. Box 123, West Linn, Oregon 97068); w. Purim (Mile.).

HOOD, WILLIAM H. (BILL),* *baritone saxophone, composer;* b. Portland, Ore., 12/13/24. Freelancing in LA, Hood also traveled w. F. Sinatra and toured Japan w. B. Bacharach, and w. Q. Jones. Arr. and pl. on Della Reese TV series; many other TV credits. Studio work w. Tom Scott, D. Grusin, Jack Elliot. Recreated the sound of Adrian Rollini on bass sax for period music in movie, *The Fortune,* '75.

HOOPER, LOUIS STANLEY (LOU), *piano, composer;* also *organ, violin, viola;* b. North Buxton, Ont., Canada, 5/18/1894. Father a violinist in Canada, 1870's-93; brothers Fred, trumpet; Arnold, violin. Began as choir boy and became soloist at St. Luke's Episcopal Church in Ypsilanti, Mich. Piano lessons at 10. Grad. from Detroit Conserv. '16. Postgrad. stud. w. La Verne Brown; Minor White; Prof. F.L. York. Bach. of Mus., '20. Stud. at Teacher's Coll., Columbia U., '23-4. w. Mr. Mohler; Prof. Dykema. Pl. w. Hooper Bros. Orch., Ypsilanti, '06; at New Koppin Theatre, Detroit, '09. Led small concert-party in France during WWI, '18. To NYC '21, pl. in pit orch. of Franklin Theatre w. Mildred Franklin. Worked w. Elmer Snowden until the latter joined Ellington. Then rec. w. Bubber Miley; Louis Metcalf; Johnny Dunn; Ethel Waters; Ma Rainey and pl. stage shows w. Bessie Smith. In orch. for Broadway review, Lew Leslie's *Blackbirds of 1928-29.* Acc. Paul Robeson for six mos. With Myron Sutton's Canadian Ambassadors when they reopened Connie's Inn, Montreal, '39, backing Billie Holiday. Enlisted in Canad. Artillery '39, serving overseas in Europe until '45, in charge of Canadian Concert Parties.

Rediscovered living in Montreal in '62. Member of Montreal Vintage Music Society. In '73 was feted by Int. Assn. of Record Coll. during their convention in Montreal where he performed. He also pl. for and prod. an evening of his works from '18-70, sponsored by the Benny Farm Tenant's Assn. and his old 5th Medium Artillery buddies for the benefit of the Quebec Paraplegic Assn. Moved to Prince Edward Island, '75. Infl: B. Goodman, C. Christian, Bix Beiderbecke, James P. Johnson, Ralph Sutton, Ellington, Louis Armstrong. Comp: *Ruth,* an oratorio; music to *The Congo* by Vachel Lindsay; *Wanderlust; Cakewalk; South Sea Strut; Undecided Rag; Rainy Day Rag; Sunny Day Rag,* last three written in '75. In NYC days taught classical piano at Martin-Smith Music School a subsidiary of the Damrosch Inst. which later became Juilliard Sch. of Music.

LPs: solo piano (Canadian Broadcasting Corp., Mon-

treal); w. *The Jolly Miners* w. Snowden, Bob Fuller (Historical).

HOOPER, NESBERT (STIX),* *drums, leader, composer;* b. Houston, Tex., 8/15/38. Leader of a group known in 1950s as Modern Jazz Sextet, later as Nite Hawks; from 1960 as Jazz Crusaders, and from '72 as the Crusaders. By that time the group had concentrated on a jazz/rock and r & b style that earned substantially increased record sales and national popularity. Hooper told Dennis Hunt of the LA *Times,* "Most of our fans have only been following us for about three years; a lot of them don't even know that we used to be associated with jazz . . . the hard core jazz fans never really accepted us anyway. . . . Now we can play what we like and get money and recognition for it. You can't beat that."

In addition to leading the combo, Hooper busied himself with a variety of free-lance activities in LA and became one of the area's most successful drummers.

LPs w. Crusaders (Blue Thumb, Chisa); w. Jazz Crusaders (Pac. Jazz).

HOPE, ELMO (St. Elmo Sylvester Hope),* *piano, composer;* b. New York City, N.Y., 6/27/23. A childhood friend of Bud Powell, whose style his own closely paralleled, Hope pl. w. Clifford Brown, S. Rollins in NYC, and later w. Harold Land, L. Hampton in LA. Irregularly active owing to poor health in later years, he died 5/19/67. A pianist and composer of rare harmonic acuity and very personal interpretation. He can be heard on several albums, among them one for Blue Note, one for HiFi Jazz, two for Riverside, one for Audio Fidelity. As a sideman he rec. w. Brown, Rollins, Lou Donaldson (BN); J. McLean and F. Foster (Prest.); *Elmo Hope Memorial Album* (Prest.); trio (Contemp.).

HOPKINS, CLAUDE,* *piano, leader;* b. Washington, D.C., 8/3/03. One of the popular big band leaders of the 1930s, worked mostly as leader and sideman within a small group context during the '60s and '70s at such places as the Dinkler Motor Inn, Syracuse, N.Y.; Top of the Plaza, Rochester, N.Y.; Bourbon St. and the Colonial Inn, Toronto. Pianist w. R. Eldridge at Jimmy Ryan's for several years, then gigging at numerous clubs in N.J. Hopkins is also an aircraft mechanic who was very active during the second world war at the General Motors plant in Linden, N.J. Fests: Concord, Cal., '73; Andernos, Spain, '74; Nice, Manassas, '74. TV: Nice, '74; WGBH, Boston, '75. Comps: *Crying My Heart Out For You; Safari Stomp; Late Evening Blues; Crazy Fingers; Blame It On A Dream.* LPs: solo albums on Chiaroscuro and Sackville; trio on Black and Blue; w. Herb Hall quartet; Jazz Giants on Sackville; w. Wild Bill Davison, *Live at the Rainbow Room* (Chiaroscuro).

HOPKINS, LINDA, *singer, organ, piano;* also *drums;* b. New Orleans, 12/14/25. As a child, was discovered by Mahalia Jackson. Spent 11 years touring w. Southern Harp Singers, a spiritual group. Directed youth choir in Richmond, Cal., singing in church and on radio. Began her show business career after auditioning at a local night club.

In 1960, because of her physical and vocal resemblance to Bessie Smith (whom she had seen once in person), and because she was asked to portray a 'big name' in a cabaret show, Hopkins began to evolve an act partially based on Bessie's songs and style, touring with this concept in Europe, 1960. After studying with Stella Adler, she was seen on the stage in *Purlie* and *Inner City*; her performance in the latter earned her Tony and Drama Desk awards.

Long familiar with the blues and with other material employed by Bessie Smith, she developed an entire presentation entitled *Me and Bessie*, enjoying great success during long runs in NYC and LA, 1974-5.

Involved w. Evangelistic Chorus, Greater Central Baptist Church, NYC. TV: Johnny Carson, Dinah Shore, Merv Griffin, Dick Cavett, Mike Douglas, many other shows. Comp: *Listen Women; Doggin' Blues; The Man's All Right; I'm a Happy Child, Running Wild.*

A superb performer in the classic blues tradition as well as in a more light-hearted vein, Hopkins for many years was poorly represented on records, with sessions for Savoy, Federal, Atco and Brunswick that involved songs such as *Danny Boy; Rock and Roll Blues; When the Saints Go Marching In* etc. In 1975 she signed with Columbia and recorded an album of excerpts from *Me and Bessie*. Other LPs: RCA; *Inner City* (RCA); *Purlie* (Ampex).

HORN, PAUL,* *flute, alto saxophone, clarinet, composer*; b. New York City, 3/17/30. Leader of popular LA based quintet in early '60s. Between '66 and '69, while involved in studio work, continued to play concerts and clubs, but went to India in '67 and '68, studying with Maharishi Mahesh Yogi at Academy of Meditation, and himself became a teacher of Transcendental Meditation. Rec. two albums in India in '67; Played solo flute in Taj Mahal, '68. Toured w. Concert Ensemble feat. four flutes, '69.

In '70 Horn moved to Victoria, B.C., where he enjoyed success in several areas of activity; pl. concert tours throughout Canada w. newly formed Canadian quintet, scoring films for Nat'l Film Board of Canada, and heading his own weekly half-hour TV series, The Paul Horn Show. Won CINDY award for music score of *Island Eden*, film for gov't. of B.C. Horn has continued to travel extensively as soloist and clinician at colls. and high schools throughout the U.S. and Canada. Publs: *Paul Horn/Inside*, flute solos (Edward B. Marks Music, 136 W. 52nd St., New York, N.Y. 10019).

LPs: *Here's That Rainy Day* (RCA); *Paul Horn In Kashmir; Paul Horn In India* (Wor. Pac.); *Inside; Inside II; Visions* (Epic); *A Special Edition* (Island).

HOROWITZ, DAVID, *piano, synthesizer, composer*; also *vibes*; b. Brooklyn, N.Y., 7/29/42. Brother, Marc Horowitz, is studio musician on guitar, banjo. Studied comp. & theory w. Mischa Portnoff, '63-7; comp., theory, piano, improvisation w. Hall Overton, '64-6; improv. w. Lennie Tristano, '65-6. Led own gps., '62-6.

Active as studio musician, NYC, from '68. Pl. w. Tony Williams Lifetime, '72-4; w. Gil Evans from '70. In the Evans orch. his synthesizer supplies an underlining with various colors and leitmotifs.

Infl: Overton, Miles Davis, Coltrane, Bartok, G. Evans, T. Monk, Ornette Coleman. Fest: w. Evans, NJF-NY, Montreux, Berkeley. Movie: score for *Human*, French film w. Jeanne Moreau, Terrance Stamp, '75. Comp: *Encounters I* for soprano and chamber orch., commissioned by "Music in Our Time;" *Encounters II* for string quartet and jazz orch., comm. by JCOA. LPs: w. Evans, *The Music of Jimi Hendrix; There Comes a Time* (RCA); *Svengali* (Atl.); w. J. Henderson, *Black is the Color* (Mile.); w. T. Williams, *The Old Bum's Rush* (Poly.).

HOUSTON, CLINTON JOSEPH (CLINT), *bass*; b. New Orleans, La., 6/24/46. Father pl. classical piano as a youth. Family moved to Washington, D.C., when Houston was an infant, then to NYC, '53. Stud. keyboard, harmony at Queens Coll., Long Island. Stud. bass in high school. For some years he was undecided whether to take up a career in mus. or in graphic art. He grad. from Cooper Union in the latter, in addition to studying for two years ('64-6) at Pratt Inst.

Houston worked briefly w. Roy Haynes, '69; also w. Nina Simone, then resumed his art studies. In '71 he decided to become a musician on a full time basis. During that year he pl. w. Roy Ayers at Montreux JF, moved to Germany and spent a year pl. electric and upright bass with Kurt Edelhagen in Cologne.

Back in NYC, he was active on the rec. scene, worked for a while with Herbie Mann, and spent a year and a half w. Chas. Tolliver, visiting Japan with him. Houston moved to Cal. in '74. While working w. Kai Winding, he was heard by S. Getz, who hired him for his quartet in Feb. '75. During the next year, touring w. Getz, he revealed an extraordinary technique and the ability to weave guitar-like lines on the upright bass that placed him among the handful of preëminent new bassists of the '70s.

Houston names as his infls. Scott LaFaro and Ron Carter; he stud. w. Carter for two years.

LPs: w. Tolliver, *Live in Tokyo* (Strata-East); w. Woody Shaw, *Blackstone Legacy* (Contemporary); w. Sonny Greenwich (Sackville); Getz-Gilberto (Col.); w. John Abercrombie and others, *Friends* (Oblivion).

HOWARD, DARNELL,* *clarinet*; b. Chicago, Ill., 1892. Prominent from '20s, he worked w. King Oliver, E. Hines. Lived in SF Bay Area for many years, pl. w. M. Spanier, Jimmy Archey, Hines; visited Europe w. NO group in '66. Died in SF, 9/2/66.

HOWARD, NOAH, *alto saxophone, composer*; b. New Orleans, La., 4/6/43. From the age of about 17, under the influence of Ornette Coleman. Schooled in free-jazz through association in San Francisco with Byron Allen, Sonny Simmons, Dewey Redman among others. Formed first group there with English trumpeter, Ric Colbeck. Went to Europe for a jazz and pop festival staged by a record company, and found the local interest in free jazz so strong that he remained for two months. For the next six years he went back and forth frequently between the US and Europe.

Howard has worked with Sun Ra, Archie Shepp, Albert Ayler, Rashied Ali, Milford Graves, Bill Dixon, Art Taylor, Dave Burrell, Ornette Coleman, Sonny Sharrock, Frank Lowe, Sirone, Jimmy Garrison, Norman Connors, Ted Daniel, Ed Blackwell and the Art Ensemble of Chicago. According to Valerie Wilmer he is "one of the best alto saxophonists around . . . whatever he does, he always retains his technical skill and what the critics term 'taste.' " *Swing Journal* of Tokyo characterized Howard as "one of the most representative musicians of the post-Coltrane era." He was consistently praised by critics throughout Europe during his many concerts there.

LPs: *Noah Howard Quartet; Noah Howard at Judson Hall* (ESP); *One for John* (Byg); *Church No. 9* (Calumet); *From Down to Planet X* (Bovema); *Uhuru Na Umoja; Space Dimensions* (Musidisc); *Black Art; Patterns; Live at the Swing Club Turin* (Altsax); *Black Ark; Live at the Village Vanguard* (Polydor); *Snow & Sunshine* (EMI); w. Shepp, *Black Gypsy* (Musidisc); w. Ayler, *Don Ayler* (Jihad).

HOWELL, MICHAEL, *guitar, composer*; b. Kansas City, Mo., 10/8/43. Introduced to guitar at age seven by his father and by Herley Dennis, a local musician. Degree in Mus. Ed. from Lamar Jr. College in Colorado, 1961. First formal guitar studies at Music and Arts Inst. in SF, with a student of Andres Segovia. Played w. Bobby Hutcherson-Harold Land in SF, 1971; Art Blakey, Jan. '73; Sonny Rollins-John Handy concert, '73; Woody Shaw, fall and winter, '73-4; Guitar Summit at MJF, '74; w. D. Gillespie at MJF and Great American•Music Hall in SF, '75. Infls: Ch. Parker, Ch. Christian, Clifford Brown, Wes Montgomery, D. Ellington, Miles Davis, John Coltrane. Comps: *Through the Looking Glass; A Day In San Francisco; Michelino; The Call; Ebony King; Althea; Circles.* LPs: *Looking Glass; In The Silence* (Milestone); w. Blakey, *Buhaina*; w. G. Ammons, *Brasswind* (Prestige).

HUBBARD, FREDERICK DEWAYNE (FREDDIE),* *trumpet, fluegelhorn, composer, piano*; b. Indianapolis, Ind., 4/7/38. First prominent w. Art Blakey in early '60s; also pl. w. Q. Jones, Friedrich Gulda; led various groups, first on records, later in person.

From 1966-70 Hubbard was contracted to Atlantic Records. During that time, except for one LP called *Soul Experiment* in which he switched from jazz to rock, he maintained the high standards for which he had been known throughout the decade. Experts predicted that he would be "the Miles Davis of the '70s."

Hubbard successfully toured Japan and the US with his own combo and with Nancy Wilson. His recordings for CTI, later for Col., though commercially oriented, retained a splendid level of musicianship and showed him to advantage in his own compositions such as *Red Clay; Delphia; Sweet Sioux; The Intrepid Fox; Sky Dive; Povo; First Light; Spirits of Trane; Destiny's Children; Brigitte;*

Keep Your Soul Together; Gibraltar; Baraka Sasa; Liquid Love; Kuntu; Put It In The Pocket.

In 1972 Hubbard moved from New York to North Hollywood, Calif. Two years later he signed a contract with Columbia Records. His first two albums for that company indicated that he intended to adhere to a set of principles he had outlined in a 1973 interview: "It's very difficult to stay out of rock and make a living . . . After Miles Davis went into that electronic rock bag, everybody started sounding like Miles, trying to sound weird. That's why I'm attempting to stick to something kinda grass roots, keep my feet on the ground; because with everyone using that Fender Rhodes piano and stuff, they'll all sound alike. . . . Not so long ago a lot of young trumpeters were following Miles; now they're trying to play what I'm playing. They hear me constantly searching for new ideas, but keeping enough musicality in there so people can understand where it's at."

Motion picture soundtrack work: *Blowup* (scored by Herbie Hancock); *The Bus Is Coming; Shaft's Big Score*, in which Hubbard was prominently heard.

Hubbard's album *First Light* won a Grammy award in 1972 as the best jazz performance of the year by a small group. As soloist he won DB Readers' Poll 1973-4.

By late 1975 Hubbard had adjusted his stance with respect to the use of electronics. He not only had an electric piano and electric bass in his combo, but was himself using an amplified horn and playing music that seemed to be leaning more heavily in an r & b or rock direction.

LPs: *High Energy; Liquid Love* (Col); *Baddest Hubbard; First Light; Keep Your Soul Together; Red Clay; Sky Dive; Straight Life*; w. S. Turrentine, *In Concert* (CTI); *Art of F. Hubbard; Backlash; Black Angel; High Blues Pressure*; w. Ilhan Mimaroglu, *Sing Me A Song of Songmy* (Atl.); *Artistry of Hubbard; Body & Soul; Reevaluation Impulse Years* (Impulse); *Blue Spirits; Breaking Point; Goin' Up; Hub-Tones*; w. Lee Morgan, *Night of the Cookers* Vols. 1 & 2; *Ready for Freddie* (Blue Note); *Hub of Hubbard* (BASF). Innumerable others as sideman, esp. on Blue Note.

HUBBLE, JOHN EDGAR (ED),* *trombone; also baritone horn*; b. Santa Barbara, Calif., 4/6/28. Active in small gp. traditional music from '40s w. Bob Wilber, Billy Maxted, Phil Napoleon, Don Ewell. Worked w. Dukes of Dixieland, '66; w. Dick Wellstood, Kenny Davern at Ferry Boat in Brielle, N.J., '67; Jimmy Ryan's w. Max Kaminsky, '68. Joined World's Greatest Jazzband '69, touring w. it in England, Alaska, So. America before leaving at the end of '73. Toured Europe w. Kings of Jazz (Pee Wee Erwin, Kenny Davern), '74; w. NYJRC Tribute to Louis Armstrong, fall '75. Pl. weekends at Last Chance Saloon in Poughkeepsie, N.Y. w. Johnny Windhurst, '75. Joined His Farm, a Christian Community Dairy Farm in NY state, working and living there between music jobs.

Fest: Nice; NJF-NY; Colo. JP; Odessa JP. LPs: w. WGJ (World Jazz).

HUCKO, MICHAEL ANDREW (PEANUTS),* *clarinet, tenor sax*; b. Syracuse, N.Y., 4/7/18. The former J. Teagarden and L. Armstrong clarinetist, heard often at Condon's club in NYC, '63-6, was feat. annually at concerts in Denver, Colo., '66-8 with a group called The Nine Greats of Jazz, which later evolved into The World's Greatest Jazzband. From Sept. '70 through June '72 he was jazz soloist on Lawrence Welk's TV series. From 1/16/74 through 9/15/74 toured as conductor of Glenn Miller orch. While in Tokyo, rec. there with Japanese group, *Peanuts Meets Shoji Again*, a reference to his reunion with Japanese clarinetist Shoji Suzuki with whom he had a best seller in '60.

After leaving the Miller band, Hucko settled in Denver, leading a quartet feat. his wife, former Harry James vocalist Louise Tobin. In '75 his sidemen incl. Ralph Sutton, Gus Johnson. Opened own jazz room at Sheraton Inn, Denver, Apr. '75. Hucko's frequent apps. at jazz parties and on TV reflected his undiminished stature as one of the best clarinetists in the B. Goodman mold.

Comps: *First Friday; A Bientot; Tremont Place; Home Sweet Suite; Raggedy Ann; Lullaby of Love; Mata Ai Masho* (Japanese for *See You Again*). Rec. an LP, *Peanuts in Everybody's Bag* (American Artists Records); other LPs w. L. Welk (Ranwood); *Big Band Cavalcade on Tour*, w. Bob Crosby (RCA).

HUGHES, LANGSTON, *lyricist, author, poet, playwright*; b. Joplin, Mo., 2/1/02. The internationally celebrated playwright, some of whose poems dealt with jazz, and one of whose books was a jazz history for children, died of a heart attack in NYC, 5/22/67. An album in which Hughes read his poetry to a background of music by Charles Mingus and Leonard Feather was rec. in '57 for MGM (deleted). An album of gospel songs by Hughes and Jobe Huntley, sung by Porter Sisters in a Harlem church, was released on Folkways.

HUMES, HELEN,* *singer*; b. Louisville, Ky., 6/23/13. Worked w. C. Basie, '38-42. As single, had hit record *Bebaba-Leba*, '45; toured and gigged w. Red Norvo in mid-50s; occasionally active in '60s, spending a year in Australia, '64-5.

After a period of sporadic work and while living in LA, she returned home to Louisville, '67, remaining there until July '73, when she took part in tributes to C. Basie and L. Armstrong at the NJF-NY, then toured France, Switzerland, Spain. In Feb. '74, toured France again for six weeks, rec. two albums for Black and Blue. In summer of '74 played Newport and Montreux fests., a few other jobs incl. Half Note, NYC. Began engagement at Cookery, NYC Jan. to Apr. '75, and during that time made her first Amer. album in many years. On Mar. 2, '75 she was given an official tribute in Louisville and received the keys to the city. While at the Cookery she earned unprecedented acclaim from the critics. Whitney Balliett, in *The New Yorker,* called her "one of the best and most durable of American popular singers who . . . bears easy comparison with Mildred Bailey and Billie Holiday . . . (she) is singing better than ever . . . sharing with us a style of singing and of performing that is almost gone . . ."

LPs on Contemporary; Columbia; also two tracks in *Singin' The Blues* (MCA); two tracks in *Super Chief,* w. C. Basie (Columbia).

HUMAIR, DANIEL,* *drums, composer*; b. Geneva, Switzerland, 5/23/38. Winner of a contest for young amateurs, Humair in '62 became France's number one drummer, both in talent and in popularity. He played with the Swingle Singers in the early '60s and app. at numerous European fests., also w. P. Woods, JATP, H Mann, L. Konitz, A. Braxton, R. Eldridge, Stephane Grappelli, Joachim Kuhn and his own group. He was a sideman for *Last Tango In Paris; The Process* and many other films. From '65 he was also pro. painter. Won DB Critics' poll, TDWR, '69. During visits to U.S. app. at MJF, NJF. Comps: *Sunday Walk; Gravenstein; Out of the Sorcellery; Witch Stitch.* LPs: *Alpine Power Plant*; Jim Hall Trio; Ray Nance; *This Way Out* w. Kuhn; *Sunday Walk* w. J.L. Ponty (MPS); w. Grappelli (Barclay); HLP Trio (CBS); w. L. Konitz (RCA); *Phil Woods in Frankfurt* (Atl.); w. Franco Ambrosetti, *Steppenwolf* (PDU).

HUMPHREY, BARBARA ANN (BOBBI), *flute*; also *piccolo, alto sax*; b. Marlin, Tex., 4/25/50. Cousin a former Ellington trumpeter, Eddie Preston. Stud. Lincoln high school, Dallas, '64-8; Texas Southern U., '68-70; Southern Methodist U., '70-1. Moving to NYC in '71, she sat in with Ellington, Rahsaan Roland Kirk, C. Adderley, D. Gillespie, but the first group with which she worked officially was Herbie Mann's, in July of that year. She stud. privately w. Hubert Laws, and received a rec. contract of her own during her second week in NYC. She has won the *Ebony* mag. music poll as number one flutist. Infls: Laws, Mann. Fests: Newport; Montreux; Schaefer Mus. Fest. Humphrey, who started playing flute in high school, matured very fast on the instrument and displayed potential as a jazz artist, though her albums are primarily aimed at the soul-r & b market.

LPs: *Bobbi Humphrey; Blacks & Blues; Dig This; Satin Doll* (BN).

HUMPHREY, PAUL,* *drums, composer*; b. Detroit, Mich., 10/12/35. Prominent in Cal. groups incl. L. McCann, '63-5, H. James orch. '65-6. Mostly commercial and studio work since then, incl. tour with Chuck Berry, '69; records and gigs w. T-Bone Walker, '70. Formed own first rock group, Cool-Aid Chemists, '70. Toured w. group and had hit record, *Cool-Aid*, '71. Overseas tour w. Sammy Davis Jr., '72. Concerts w. his second group, The Funky Thumbs, '73. Records, TV, tours etc. during '74 with Maria Muldaur, Diahann Carroll, Davis, and own second group. In '75, worked on Smothers Brothers TV show and formed third group.

Publ: *No. 1 Soul Drums*, book & cassette (Gwyn Publ. Co. P.O. Box 5900, Sherman Oaks, Ca. 91413). Comps: *Super Mellow; Walk A Mile For A Smile; Chin Music.*

LPs: *Lizard* (Blue Thumb); w. Q. Jones, *Body Heat* (A & M); *Night Blooming Jazzmen* (Mainstream); Joe Cocker (A & M).

HUMPHREY, RALPH S., *drums*; also *clarinet*; b. Berkeley, Cal., 5/11/44. Educ. Castro Valley Unified School, '56-62; Coll. of San Mateo, '62-64; San Jose State U.,

'64-7; UCLA, '68; Cal. State Northridge, '68-9 where he received Masters degree in perc. perf. Worked w. Don Ellis orch. '69-73, touring extensively at home and abroad, appearing at Newport, '69; Antibes, '69; Monterey; Concord, '70; and on Ed Sullivan Show and Tanglewood Fest. on TV, '69. Played on sound track for *The French Connection* and *Kansas City Bomber* movies. Wrote chapter, *The Role of the Drummer in the Modern Rhythm Section*, in *New Rhythms* by Ellis (Ellis Music Ent., Inc., 5436 Auckland Ave., N. Hollywood, Ca. 91601).

During '73-4 Humphrey toured U.S., Europe and Australia with Frank Zappa; as freelance musician in LA provided backing for various artists such as Tony Bennett, Joe Williams, Carmen McRae, Clare Fischer, John Klemmer et al. LPs w. Ellis (Columbia); w. Zappa (Discreet).

HUNDLEY, CRAIG, *piano, organ, synthesizer*; b. Hollywood, Ca., 11/22/53. Stud. w. Xenia Chasman, Dave MacKay, Gary David, and at Stan Kenton Clinic. After three years of classical study, took up jazz in '66, organized trio, which was soon voted best combo in teenage Battle of the Bands at Hollywood Bowl. Pl. Shelly's Manne Hole, Donte's, MJF, Village Gate. Throughout his teens, enjoyed simultaneous career as TV actor, playing major roles in *Star Trek; Kung Fu; Flying Nun; Lassie.* By early '70s Hundley was less active in jazz, working briefly as musical director for Pat Boone on tour. Own LPs: *Arrival of a Young Giant; Hundley Plays with the Big Boys* (World Pacific).

HUNTER, IVORY JOE, *singer, piano*; b. 1912. A rhythm and blues favorite of the '50s, Hunter comp. many r & b songs as well as country and western material. His best known hit was *Since I Met You Baby.* After several months' illness he died of cancer 11/8/74 in a Memphis, Tenn. nursing home.

LPs: *Ivory Joe Hunter* (Archive of Folk & Jazz); w. J. Otis, *Live at Monterey* (Epic).

HUTCHENRIDER, CLARENCE BEHRENS,* *clarinet*; also *tenor, alto sax*; b. Waco, Tex., 6/13/08. Best known for his pl. w. Glen Gray's Casa Loma Orch. in the '30s, he led his own trio at the Gaslight Club, NYC, '58-68; Bill's Gay Nineties, '68-May '73; then club dates in NYC, Long Island, concerts in NJ. LPs w. Bobby Hackett (Flying Dutchman); Glen Gray (Epitaph).

HUTCHERSON, ROBERT (BOBBY),* *vibes, marimba*; b. Los Angeles, Cal., 1/27/41. First prominent in LA and SF with various small combos, later in NYC in the mid-50s, Hutcherson returned to the West Coast, where from '69-71 he co-led a quintet w. Harold Land Sr. After they went their separate ways, Hutcherson, based in SF, remained a leader in his own right, rec. regularly and becoming increasingly active as a marimba soloist. TV: *The Jazz Show*, KNBC-Los Angeles, '71.

Over the past decade Hutcherson has continued to mature and explore new directions. In his own words, "Our public is always looking for something new. Our group is searching around to find that something new, an extension of the evolution that we have had, of all the music

that happened before. They'll know when we find it."

LPs: *Dialogue; Components; Happenings; Stick-up; Total Eclipse; Now; San Francisco; Head On; Natural Illusions; Cirrus; Linger Lane* (BN).

HUTSON, DAVID LAURENCE, *alto saxophone, clarinet, leader*; b. Chicago, Ill., 4/18/38. B.M. in music at U. of Illinois, where fellow students were Joe Farrell, Denny Zeitlin, with whom he has worked occasionally. Early exp. w. Ira Sullivan, Ralph Marterie. Army, '61-3; during that time gigged w. Otis Johnson band. In NYC, '63-5, pl. w. Dizzy Reece, D. Cherry, C. Corea and dixieland groups. In Japan and Korea, '66-8. Civilian entertainment dir. for Army Spec. Servs. Based in Detroit, '68-75, organizing the New McKinney's Cotton Pickers in '72. Comp. or arr. most of the material for this band. Prod. *Jazz Yesterday* radio series for two years. Played at Bix Memorial Fest., '73 and '74; Newport-New York, '74-5; Breda (Netherlands) Jazz Fest. '75.

LPs: w. New McKinney's Cotton Pickers (Bountiful, 15772 13 Mile Rd., Roseville, Mich. 48066).

HYMAN, RICHARD ROVEN (DICK),* *piano*; also *organ, harpsichord, synthesizer, arranger, conductor, composer*; b. New York City, 3/8/27. Stud. w. Teddy Wilson and others. Played w. Tony Scott, R. Norvo, late '40s; B. Goodman, '50. From early '50s, spent next two decades dividing his time between commercial studio work and jazz. In '66-7, recorded as pianist, organist w. Toots Thielemans, C. McRae, Sam "The Man" Taylor; arranger/conductor for C. Basie, Bobby Hackett, C. Cole, D. Severinsen. Began working in electronics, '68, and from '69 rec. a series of LPs feat. Moog synthesizer. During '69-70 pl. w. Jimmy Hamilton, Thad Jones-Mel Lewis, co-led quartet w. Thielemans; rec. own piano concerto, first public perf. at Eastman School.

In '71 he arr. for Enoch Light's big band series; premiered his comp. *Event*, w. Kostelanetz and Winnipeg Symph; led own trio weekly at Jimmy Weston's. '72-5: regular Sunday night solo gigs at The Cookery, NYC. From '72, began giving lecture-concerts on history of jazz piano. In '73, with the revival of interest in early jazz and ragtime, he rec. a solo ragtime album, an orchestral Jelly Roll Morton LP etc. (see below). Organizer and arranger for Jazz Piano Quartet, '74; musical director of N.Y. Jazz Repertory Co., '74-5; Rec. complete piano works of Scott Joplin, '75.

Hyman in '72 was voted the most valuable keyboard player by the N.Y. chapter of NARAS. At that time he was heavily involved in TV work, as musical director with various David Frost specials; organist on *Beat The Clock*; composer of scores for ABC documentary progs. etc.

Hyman in recent years has enjoyed increasing critical acclaim for his multi-faceted contributions to jazz as instrumentalist, composer and arranger. His exceptional eclecticism has enabled him to recreate the styles of every era from ragtime to contemporary with the perfect blend of technical, intellectual and emotional requirements.

Jazz Fests: Newport-N.Y. w. E. Condon, '72; Dick Gibson jazz parties annually from '67. Comps: Piano concerto (*Concerto Electro*); *The Minotaur* and other works for Moog; co-writer w. Seymour Reiter of an operetta *Joan And The Devil*. Publs: *Songs From the Plays of Shakespeare* (General Music Publ. Co., Irvington, N.Y. 10533); *The Happy Breed*, organ solos; *Scott Joplin for Organ; Jazz Sampler*, piano solo, (Edw. B. Marks Music, 1790 Broadway, N.Y. 10019); *SynthaSound Suite*, synthesizer and organ (Canyon Press, Cincinnati, Ohio 45200); *Grandpa's Spells* and other J.R. Morton piano solos edited by Hyman (Hansen-Edwin Morris, 1370 6th Ave., N.Y. 10019); *Modern Piano Solos* by L. Feather, arr. Hyman; *Modern Duets (Duets for Six Valves); Down Home Melody*, piano solo & concert band arr.; *Bardolino*, piano solo (all Belwin-Mills, 16 W. 61st St., New York, 10023); *Concerto Electro, Duets in Odd Meter and Far-out Rhythms; The Minotaur*, and other works (Eastlake Music Inc., 144 W. 57th St., N.Y. 10019); stage band and small groups comps (Creative Jazz Composers, Box 467, Bowie, Md. 20715).

LPs: *Traditional Jazz Piano, Solo Piano Fantomfingers* (Project 3); *Genius At Play* (Monmouth-Evergreen); *Jelly Roll Morton Orchestral Transcriptions* (Columbia); *The Electric Eclectics of Dick Hyman; Pieces for Moog* (Command); *Shakespeare, Sullivan and Hyman*, w. Maxine Sullivan (Monmouth-Evergreen); *Let It Happen*, by Jazz Piano Quartet w. R. Hanna, M. McPartland, H. Jones (RCA); *Soprano Summit*, w. B. Wilber, K. Davern (World Jazz); *Satchmo Remembered*, a live tribute to L. Armstrong at Carnegie Hall (Atl.); *Colorado Jazz Party* (MPS/BASF).

IND, PETER,* *bass*; b. Uxbridge, England, 7/20/28. In US from 1951, stud. w. L. Tristano, pl. w. Lee Konitz, Coleman Hawkins, B. Rich, P. Bley, Red Allen. After spending three years in Big Sur, Calif., 1963-6, he returned to England, where he became active in teaching, playing, and running his own company, Wave Records, for which he has made several LPs. Addr: 11 Swakeley Drive, Ickenham, Middlesex, England. LP w. Jimmy Raney, *Strings & Swings* (Muse).

INOMATA, TAKESHI, *drums*; b. Hyogo Pref., Japan, 2/6/36. Stud. w. father, a classical oboist from '48; priv. lessons from Roy Harte in LA and Alan Dawson in Boston; also P. Humphrey and others. Member of Hot Penguins in Kyoto, '52-3. Moved to Tokyo, '56. Joined Konosuke Saijo & West Liners, of which he was leader from '58-68. After visiting U.S. in '68, returned to Japan to form Sound L.T.D. In '75 working as studio musician with this group. Publ: *Yamaha Drum Mate Course School; Drum School of Nemu Music Academy* (Yamaha Shuppan); *T. Inomata Drum School* (Nichion).

LPs: *Stravinski Spring Festival; The Third Vol. 1 & 2* (Toshiba); *T. Inomata Drum School; Anniversary*

Record (Nippon Col.); *Exciting Drums; Alpha Ray; Drum Shot Tact* (Tact Series).

INZALACO, ANTHONY (TONY), *drums*; also *vibes*; b. Passaic, N.J., 1/14/38. Studied at Manhattan Sch. of Mus., '56-60. Bachelor's in Percussion; Master's in Mus. Ed. Pl. w. Billy Taylor; Johnny Smith; Buddy Rich; Vinnie Burke; Morris Nanton, '59-61; Maynard Ferguson; Jim Hall; Roger Kellaway; New York Jazz Sextet, '61-5; Chris Connor; Donald Byrd-Duke Pearson; Morgana King; Ben Webster; Jaki Byard; Lee Konitz; Benny Powell, '65-8. Moved to Europe '68 where he has worked w. Webster; D. Byas; Leo Wright; J. Griffin; A. Farmer; Slide Hampton; K. Clarke-F. Boland; Carmell Jones; O. Peterson; K. Drew; Jimmy Woode; Benny Bailey; I. Sulieman; D. Gillespie; C. McRae et al. A regular member of Dexter Gordon's "West European" rhythm section. Infl: "All the drummers from Chick Webb to Elvin Jones." TV: *Dial "M" For Music*, CBS; w. Webster; Peterson, Germany; w. McRae, Holland. Fest: Frankfurt; Berlin; Pori; Loosdrecht; Laren. LPs w. Ferguson, *The Big 'F'* (Main.); w. Clarke-Boland, *Latin Kaleidoscope*; S. Getz w. Clarke-Boland, *Change of Scenes* (MPS); D. Gordon (Steeple.).

ISAACS, CHARLES E. (IKE),* *bass*; also *cello*; b. Akron, Ohio, 3/28/23. Played w. Earl Bostic, many other small groups, and toured w. Carmen McRae while married to her in late '50s. Toured Sweden w. Basie, '62. Pl. w. and managed Gloria Lynne, '62-4. After leading trio accompanying Lambert, Hendricks & Ross, toured Europe and U.S. w. Erroll Garner, '66-70. Living in LA from '64; led trio at Pied Piper where, along w. O.C. Smith, he stayed for three years. Has also worked w. Sweets Edison, Chubby Jackson's big band, C. Terry. Was co-owner or manager of clubs in LA area. Seen in movie *They Shoot Horses, Don't They?* Fests: Monterey, '59, '61 w. L.H.& R.; Newport, '62-3, w. Lynne.

LPs: w. L.H. & R., *Hottest New Group In Jazz; L.H. & R. Sings Ellington* (Col.); w. Garner, *Up In Erroll's Room* (MGM); w. Jack Wilson, *Song For My Daughter* (BN); *Joe Williams Live at Birdland; Basie in Sweden* (Roul.).

ISRAELS, CHARLES H. (CHUCK),* *bass, composer, conductor*; b. New York, N.Y., 8/10/36. Best-known as member of the Bill Evans trio from fall of '61 until early '66. Studied comp. w. Hall Overton, '66-71. Formed own rehearsal band '66 and appeared at Vanguard, Half Note into '68. Associate cond. for *Promises, Promises*, '68-71. Traveled to Europe to play own comps. w. Nord Deutscher Rundfunk orch.; Danish Radio Band, '69-70; Swiss radio, '70. From '73 Assistant Prof. in charge of Jazz Studies at Brooklyn Coll. School of Performing Arts.

In '73 formed the National Jazz Ensemble to present, with the breadth and variety of symphony concerts, the masterpieces of jazz from Jelly Roll Morton and Duke Ellington through Monk and Gil Evans to George Russell and Ornette Coleman. Basic personnel incl. Jimmy Maxwell, Danny Hayes, Tom Harrell, trumpets; Sal Nis-

Elvin Jones (*David D. Spitzer*)

Thad Jones (*Veryl Oakland*)

Hank Jones (*David D. Spitzer*)

Quincy Jones (*Andy Kent*)

Clifford Jordan (*Strata-East Records*)

Stan Kenton (*Veryl Oakland*)

John Klemmer (*Impulse Records*)

Rahsaan Roland Kirk
(*Warner Bros. Records*)

Cleo Laine (*V. J. Ryan, Ltd.*)

Yusef Lateef (*Veryl Oakland*)

Jackie Cain and Roy Kral (*Veryl Oakland*)

Harold Land

Moe Koffman (*Bernie Senensky*)

Arnie Lawrence (*Bob Klein*)

Azar Lawrence (*Veryl Oakland*)

Mel Lewis (*David D. Spitzer*)

Dave Liebman (*Veryl Oakland*)

Hubert Laws (*Veryl Oakland*)

Mike Longo (*David D. Spitzer*)

Shelly Manne *(Veryl Oakland)*

John Lewis (*David D. Spitzer*)

Albert Mangelsdorff (*Veryl Oakland*)

Chuck Mangione (*Veryl Oakland*)

Pat Martino (*Veryl Oakland*)

Ronnie Mathews (*Ed Snider*)

Benny Maupin (*Veryl Oakland*)

John Mayall (*Veryl Oakland*)

Jimmy Maxwell (*Bill Spilka*)

Marian McPartland & Janice Robinson

Roy McCurdy (*Veryl Oakland*)

Jimmy McGriff (*David D. Spitzer*)

Al McKibbon
(*Veryl Oakland*)

John McLaughlin
(*Veryl Oakland*)

Jimmy McPartland

Grachan Moncur III (*David D. Spitzer*)

Charles McPherson (*David D. Spitzer*)

Benny Morton & Benny Carter

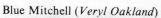

Blue Mitchell (*Veryl Oakland*)

Carmen McRae (*Veryl Oakland*)

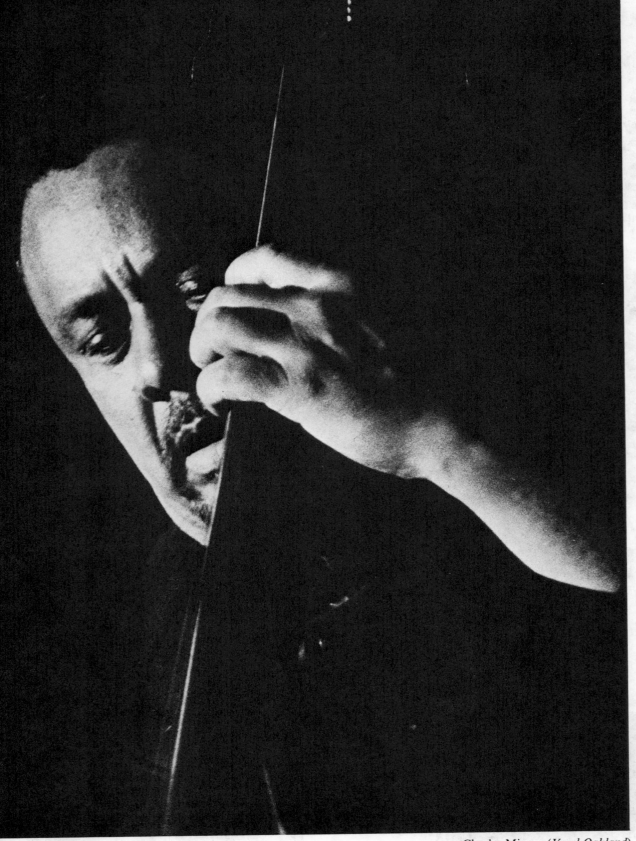

Charles Mingus (*Veryl Oakland*)

Gerry Mulligan (*David D. Spitzer*)

George Mraz (*David D. Spitzer*)

Airto Moreira (*Veryl Oakland*)

Alphonse Mouzon (*Veryl Oakland*)

Zbigniew Namyslowski
(*Duarte Mendonca*)

Jimmy Owens (*Bob Klein*)

Joe Newman & Al Cohn (*Randi W. Hultin*)

Sal Nistico (*Bob Klein*)

Niels-Henning Orsted Pedersen (*Veryl Oakland*)

Cecil Payne (*David A. Spitzer*)

Art Pepper (*Veryl Oakland*)

Sam Jones, Lisle Atkinson, Richard Davis, Milt Hinton
(*David D. Spitzer*)

tico, tenor saxophone; Jimmy Knepper, Rod Levitt, trombones; Bill Goodwin, drums. Guest soloists have been L. Konitz; Bill Evans, R. Eldridge; H. Hancock; and Phil Woods. The Ensemble appeared at Wolftrap Farm, '73; Alice Tully Hall, '74; The New School; Smithsonian Institution, '75.

Comp. grants: Croft Fellowship, '71, stud. w. G. Schuller and Bruno Maderna at Tanglewood (Lenox, Mass.); CAPS, '72; National Endowment, '71, '73. Fest: NJF-NY w. G. Mulligan, '73. Comp: *Extract I*, publ: (Opus Music, 612 No. Michigan, Chicago, Ill. 60611); *Lyric Suite for Fluegelhorn and Jazz Ensemble; Solar Complexes; Pacemaker for Brass Quintet*, perf. by NY Brass Society, '71. Arrs. of *Nardis; All Blues*, orchestrations of transcribed performances of B. Evans trio expanded for big band.

LPs: *National Jazz Ensemble, Vol. 1* (Chiaro.); w. B. Evans, *Town Hall Concerts* (Verve).

IZENZON, DAVID,* bass, composer; b. Pittsburgh, Pa., 5/17/32. Active with the Ornette Coleman trio in the mid-'60s, he cont. w. the saxophonist's group and then led his own quintet in the New York area. Also worked w. Perry Robinson, Jaki Byard. From '72 he has limited his playing because of his young son's brain injury which requires intensive home therapy.

Izenzon, who taught music history at Bronx Community Coll. from '68-71, received a Ph.D. in Psychotherapy in '73 and now operates a private practice. Completed a book on human emotions and their relationships, '75. Film: acted and played in *Solo Bass and Stripper*, unreleased. Comp: jazz opera, *How Music Can Save the World; Hymn to Endlessness; A Tribute to Bass Players*. Fest: NJF-NY '73; N.Y. Musicians Fest. Won DB critics poll, TDWR, '67. LPs: *At the Golden Circle*, Vols. 1&2 w. Coleman (Blue Note); *Chappaqua Suite* w. Coleman (CBS); *Sunshine of My Soul* w. Byard (Prestige).

JACKSON, BRIAN ROBERT, piano, composer; also flute, synthesizer, keyboards, singer; b. Brooklyn, N.Y., 10/11/52. Studied piano w. Mrs. Hepzibah Ross, '59-66; theory w. Fred Simmons at MUSE, '68-9; chord theory w. Jaki Byard, '69. Self-taught on flute. Jammed w. local musicians in Brooklyn, '67-9; worked w. local gps. while at Lincoln U. in Penna., '69-71. Met Gil Scott-Heron at Lincoln, '69 and began writing and pl. w. him. Has also pl. w. Airto; Roy Ayers; Stevie Wonder; Frank Foster; Jimmy Lyons; Stanley Clarke; Pharoah Sanders; Mtume; Ndugu; Lawrence Killian. TV: *Midnight Special; Saturday Night Live; Interface; Harambee; Black News; David Eaton Show*. Fest: Berkeley JF, '73, '75. Infl: H. Hancock, M. Tyner, A. Jamal, A. Bey, H. Silver, Wynton Kelly, John and Alice Coltrane, Miles Davis, Scott-Heron, C. Taylor, A. Hill, W. Shorter, Taj Mahal. Comp: *I Think I'll Call It Morning; Free Will; Speed*

Kills; Pieces of a Man; A Very Precious Time; Offering; Must Be Something. Writing a film score w. Scott-Heron, *Baron Wolfgang Von Tripps*. Would like to get into arranging. Writes lyrics, too, and plans to publish some. "I like to play and I like to write," he says, "but it would *really* trip me out to hear other *artists* do our songs."

LPs: w. Scott-Heron, *Winter in America* (Strata-East); *Pieces of a Man; The Revolution Will Not Be Televised* (Fly. Dutch); *From South Africa to South Carolina; The First Minute of a New Day* (Arista).

JACKSON, CHARLES MELVIN (CHIP), bass; b. Rockville Centre, L.I., N.Y., 5/15/50. Educ. Staples high school, Westport, Conn., '65-8; Berklee College, '70-3. Pl. w. Herb Pomeroy, J. La Porta, '72; G. Burton, '72-3; J. Steig, J. Abercrombie, '73. Joined W. Herman Sept. '73 and remained for 11 months, touring Europe and Canada and app. at numerous fests. Joined C. Mangione quartet, Sept. '74. App. with him on Nancy Wilson TV show, '75. Insp. by Ron Carter, S. Swallow, S. La Faro, P. Chambers, G. Burton.

LPs: *Thundering Herd; Live at Montreux*, w. Herman (Fantasy); *Chase The Clouds Away*, w. Mangione (A & M).

JACKSON, GREIG STEWART (CHUBBY),* bass; b. New York City, 10/25/18. Award-winning bassist during his years w. W. Herman in late '40s. During '60s led combos and big band in Miami, Fla. Org. another orch. in NYC, '69. Summer season in Aruba leading quintet feat. his son Duffy on drums, '70. Had his own jazz disc jockey show in Miami Beach. Moved to Hollywood, '71 and for next four years alternated between LA and LV, pl. w. Urbie Green, Edie Adams and others. Briefly ran own jazz club in N. Hollywood, '73. Participated in Herman reunion at NJF-NY, '72.

Comps: *Girl Child; Have A Nice Forever*. LPs: *Newport in New York, The Jam Sessions, Vol. 1&2* (Cobble.); many earlier albums w. Herman (Col.); reissue of band he took to Sweden in '47, *Bebop Revisited, Vol. 1* (Xanadu).

JACKSON, CLIFTON LUTHER (CLIFF),* piano; b. Washington, D.C., 7/19/02. The veteran pianist, one of the early Harlem stride and boogie woogie specialists, died NYC, of heart failure, 5/23/70. His last regular job was at Jimmy Ryan's in NYC; after leaving because of ill health, pl. occasional concerts with his wife, singer Maxine Sullivan.

JACKSON, DUFF CLARK (DUFFY), drums; also piano, bass, vibes, singer; b. Freeport, L.I., N.Y., 7/3/53. Son of bassist Chubby Jackson. Stud. at age four w. Don Lamond, later w. Roy Burns. Throughout his school days, app. mostly with his father's group, as well as on many TV shows. At age 14, worked a summer season w. Flip Phillips in Florida. In senior year at high school, became drummer for musical show *Hair* in Coconut Grove, Florida. After graduating from Miami Beach High School in June '71, opened at Shelly's Manne Hole in Hollywood with Milt Jackson-Ray Brown quintet.

Later pl. w. K. Winding, T. Gibbs, W. Herman, Monty Alexander Trio, Urbie Green. App. in Japan w. Benny Carter, Aug. '73. Toured for three months w. Lena Horne. Worked regularly for Sammy Davis Jr. in person and on TV series, '74-5. Fests: Dick Gibson Jazz Party, '71; Concord, '73-4. Jackson is highly regarded as a versatile, modern drummer, insp. by L. Bellson, B. Cobham, Burns, Lamond et al.

LP: *Here Comes The Sun*, w. Alexander (MPS-BASF).

JACKSON, MAHALIA,* *singer*; b. New Orleans, La., 10/26/11. Long known as the foremost gospel singer, Miss Jackson was intermittently ill from '64, and was hospitalized with heart trouble in '67, and again in '71. Despite her frail condition, she visited Japan, Europe and India in '71, but was soon hospitalized and died 1/27/72 in Evergreen, Park, Ill.

Though she was reluctant to be identified with jazz, the quality inherent in Mahalia Jackson's sound had much in common with that of the great jazz and blues singers. One of her most memorable performances brought her together with the Duke Ellington orch. at the NJF in '58, when she sang a special treatment of *The Twenty-Third Psalm*, as well as Ellington's *Come Sunday* from *Black, Brown & Beige*. She was heard again at Newport in a birthday tribute to Louis Armstrong, with whom she sang several numbers.

Dan Morgenstern observed in DB: "Her art, projected with immense dignity and vital power through the magnificent instrument of her voice, is one of the glories of black American music in this century, and it reached and touched untold millions." In 1975 a large and comprehensive biography, *Just Mahalia, Baby*, by Laurraine Goreau, was publ. by Word Books, Waco, Tex.

LPs: *Best Of* (Kenwood); *Bless This House; Best-Loved Hymns of Dr. King; Garden of Prayer; Great; Great Gettin' Up; Greatest Hits; I Believe; In Concert; Mighty Fortress; My Faith; Power and The Glory; Recorded in Europe; Right Out of the Church; What The World Needs Now* (Col.).

JACKSON, MILTON (MILT or BAGS),* *vibes*; also *piano, singer, guitar*; born Detroit, Mich., 1/1/23. A member of the original Modern Jazz Quartet (see Lewis, John), Jackson decided in 1974 to leave the group in order to form a combo of his own. The MJQ disbanded in July of that year, was reunited for a concert in the fall; during most of the next year Jackson worked as a single, fronting local rhythm sections in NYC, LA etc. App. in own gp. and w. other stars at Montreux JF, '75.

His career as a leader of various ensembles on records gained in impact during the 1970s; albums such as *Olinga* enjoyed some commercial success. Jackson's style remained basically unchanged, though some students claimed that his playing was freer under conditions less formalized than those of the MJQ.

Before leaving the MJQ, Jackson often co-led a group with Ray Brown during the quartet's annual summer hiatus.

LPs: *Milt Jackson* (BN); *Bags & Flute; Bags & Trane; Ballad Artistry; Plenty Plenty Soul* (Atl.); *Big Band Bags* (Milestone); *Complete Milt Jackson; Opus de Funk* (Pres.); *Goodbye; Olinga; Sunflower* (CTI); *Impulse Years; Jazz 'n' Samba; Milt Jackson Quintet; Statements* (Impulse); w. MJQ, *At Music Inn; The Art of MJQ; The Best of the MJQ; Blues at Carnegie Hall; Blues on Bach; Collaboration; Comedy; European Concert; Fontessa; Legendary Profile; Live at the Lighthouse; Lonely Woman; Modern Jazz Quartet; One Never Knows; Plastic Dreams; Porgy & Bess; Pyramid; The Sheriff; Third Stream Music* (Atl.); *First Recordings; For Lovers* (Pres.); *In Memoriam* (Little David); *On Tour* (SS); w. Ray Brown, *Memphis Jackson; Just The Way It Had To Be; The Way It Is* (Impulse); Montreux '75 series w. own *Big Four*; w. D. Gillespie; C. Basie; O. Peterson (Pablo).

JACKSON, OLIVER,* *drums*; b. Detroit, Mich. 4/28/34. With Earl Hines quartet '66-9. On leaving Hines, formed the JPJ Quartet w. Hines-mates Budd Johnson and Bill Pemberton, adding Dill Jones on piano. In '71 the Johns-Manville Corp. sponsored the quartet for a series of high school concerts in cities where their plants were located. This community relations project, called "New Communications in Jazz," played to over 300,000 students. Jackson has also freelanced w. O. Peterson, E. Garner, C. Shavers, R. Eldridge, C. Hawkins, K. Burrell and many others. European tours w. Hines, '67; *Jazz From A Swinging Era*, '68; JPJ, '71. Fests: Monterey, '67; Newport, '68, 72-5; Yugoslavia, Montreux, '71; Colo. Jazz Party, '73. TV w. JPJ, Montreux '71. Comps: w. Budd Johnson, *Tribulations; Montreux '71; OJBJ Blues; Oliver's Twist*. LPs: *New Communications in Jazz; Montreux '71* w. JPJ (Master Jazz); *Grand Reunion* w. Hines (Limelight); *The Blues, That's Me* w. I. Jacquet (Pres.); *The Tender Gender* w. Burrell (Cadet); *The Last Session* w. Shavers (Black and Blue); w. Herb Hall-Joe Muranyi; Lou McGarity (Fat Cat's Jazz); Tony Parenti (Jazzology).

JACKSON, PRESTON,* *trombone*; b. New Orleans, 1/3/04. Played with many Chicago bands in '20s; L. Armstrong, '31-2. Inactive as musician for many years, but returned in '40s, continued to work occasionally until '60. Came back on record date with Lil Armstrong, Sept. '61. In later years played mostly with Franz Jackson All Stars (from '66), concerts w. Clyde Bernhardt, Little Brother Montgomery, Art Hodes et al. European tour w. Kid Thomas Valentine, '73; also with New Orleans Joy Makers, '74.

Rec. in Sweden with own band, made films in Paris, London. Played at Preservation Hall in New Orleans with Percy Humphrey band, '74. Still playing w. F. Jackson, Montgomery and teaching, '75.

LPs: w. F. Jackson (Pinnacle); Barry Martyn (Crescent Jazz).

JACKSON, QUENTIN LEONARD (BUTTER),* *trombone*; b. Springfield, Ohio, 1/13/09. After touring w. Q. Jones band in *Free and Easy*, '59-60, joined Count Basie until the fall of '62; then worked w. C. Mingus. Rejoined

Duke Ellington briefly in spring '63. NYC studio work; house band at Copacabana, '64. Gigs w. NYC bands assembled for engagements w. Louis Bellson, '64; Gerald Wilson '66. Much Broadway pit orch. work. With Thad Jones-Mel Lewis orch. until illness curtailed his activities in '75. Member of NYJRC. LPs w. Jones-Lewis; Basie.

JACKSON, WILLIS (GATOR), *tenor sax, composer*; also *soprano sax, Gator horn*; b. Miami, Fla., 4/25/32. Began studying at 10; piano, then clarinet. Prof. debut at 14 on tenor sax w. local bands; schoolmates and bandmates incl. C. Adderley, Blue Mitchell. Studied theory and harmony at Fla. A&M. Worked w. Cootie Williams, '50-5. Rec. own comp. *Gator Tail* w. Williams and acquired nickname Gator. Touring US from '55 w. own group, very often in R&B package w. Dinah Washington, The Ravens, Jackie Wilson, etc. For eight yrs. married to Ruth Brown who sang w. him during this time. Pl. summer gig annually at Club Harlem, Atlantic City, N.J. from '63. His r & b associations have led some people to underestimate his abilities as a jazz player but he is a very effective communicator in the Illinois Jacquet vein with touches of Gene Ammons. Infl: C. Hawkins, L. Young, Herschel Evans, Ben Webster, Ch. Parker. TV: Ed Sullivan in '50s; Mike Douglas in '60s; *Dial "M" For Music* w. Father O'Connor. Comp: *Cookin' Sherry,* which won French Grand Prix du Disque, '59; *This'll Get to Ya; Miss Ann; Brother Elijah; On My Own; West Africa; The Head Tune.*

Jackson's Gator horn, a saxophone of his own design, is used for ballads. It hangs almost to the floor, has a round ball with a small opening for the bell and sounds, he explains, "between soprano and alto and French horn and clarinet."

LPs: *West Africa; Headed and Gutted* (Muse); *The Way We Were* (Atl.); many others on Prest.; reissues on Trip; w. J. McDuff; Bill Jennings (Prest.).

JACQUET, JEAN BAPTISTE ILLINOIS,* *tenor saxophone, bassoon*; b. Broussard, La., 10/31/22. The former L. Hampton star, who helped popularize JATP, was active in European tours and fests. with own trio incl. Milt Buckner and Jo Jones; own groups in US, app. at Buddy's Place, NYC, '74; also w. B. Rich group at same club, '74. Talking about the particular brand of *macho* tenor sax that Jacquet fostered, Dan Morgenstern wrote: ". . . but no matter what others may have wrought from his prescriptions, he himself has remained musical and swinging." Fests: NJF-NY w. L. Hampton reunion, '72; Tribute to Ben Webster, '74; Monterey. LPs: *How High The Moon; Bottoms Up; Soul Explosion; The King; The Blues, That's Me* (Prest.); *Genius at Work* (Black Lion); *The Last Blues Album* w. Rich (Groove Merchant); w. B. Tate (Chiaroscuro).

JAMAL, AHMAD,* *piano, composer*; b. Pittsburgh, Pa., 7/2/30. Continued to lead his trio, which for many years incl. Jamil Nasser, bass; and Frank Gant, drums. Jim Szantor wrote in *down beat*: "Jamal's charming, personal brand of space music . . . has always appealed to me. His work is somewhat more aggressive than in the *But*

Not For Me—Tangerine phase of his career circa 1957 . . . He captures the essence of a tune and bases his bravado runs, embroideries, and driving riff-like figures around it—sometimes weaving in and out of the melody, sometimes leaving space for the opinions of his accompanists." Pl. on cruise, *Showboat 4,* Dec. '75. Comp: *Eclipse; Pastures; Spanish Interlude; Death and Resurrection; Swahililand.* LPs: *Jamal Plays Jamal; Jamalca; '73* (20th Century); *The Awakening; Poinciana Revisited; Freelight; Tranquility; Outertimeinnerspace* (Imp.); *Bright, Blue and Beautiful; Cry Young; Heatwave* (Cadet).

JAMAL, KHAN (Warren Robert Cheeseboro), *vibes, marimba, composer, percussionist*; b. Jacksonville, Fla., 7/23/46. Grew up in Philadelphia. First infl. was mother, pianist Willa Mae McGee. Studied at Granoff Sch. of Mus.; Combs Coll. of Mus.; privately w. Bill Lewis; Abraham Howard Jr. Performed w. Frank Lowe; Noah Howard; Grachan Moncur III; Dave Burrell; Archie Shepp; Norman Connors; Byard Lancaster; Sam Rivers; Stanley Clarke; Gary Bartz; Sun Ra; Larry Young; Calvin Hill; Sounds of Liberation; Ted Daniel; Jerome Cooper, etc. App. at NY Mus. Fest.; NJF-NY; Studio Rivbea; Ornette Coleman's Artist House; Studio We; Phila. Mus. Fest.; Phila. Black Arts Fest; Village Vanguard; Chat Qui Peche. Toured western European countries, '75. Mus. Dir. of Phila. Jazz Foundation (Vernon House, Vernon Park, Pa. 19144). Co-leader w. Sunny Murray of Untouchable Factor. Resident artist, LaSalle Coll. of Urban Studies. Infl: Milt Jackson, Lem Winchester, Bobby Hutcherson, Walt Dickerson, Bill Lewis, Roy Ayers, Cecil Taylor, Monk, Tyner, Coltrane, Dolphy, Rufus Harley, A. Ayler, L. Armstrong. Comp: *Pure Energy; Clint; 35,000 Feet Up; Give the Vibes Some.* LPs: *Give the Vibes Some* (Palm); *Inside Out; Straight Ahead* (Live); *Drum Dance to the Motherland; New Horizon* w. Sounds of Liberation (Dogtown); *Back Streets of Heaven* w. Sounds of Lib. & B. Lancaster, unreleased.

JAMES, ROBERT (BOB),* *piano, composer*; also *organ, synthesizer*; b. Marshall, Mo., 12/25/39. Served as accompanist-musical director-arranger for S. Vaughan, '66-8. Staff composer for Association of Producing Artists Repertoire Co. in NY, where he wrote scores for *Pantagleize; Cock-A-Doodle-Dandy* and others, '67-8. Studio work, NYC, arr. and perf. w. Q. Jones, D. Warwicke, R. Flack, Morgana King, '68-72. In '73 James was signed as exclusive arranger for CTI Records and wrote albums for Eric Gale, G. Washington, H. Crawford, Johnny Hammond, Idris Muhammad, Gabor Szabo and S. Turrentine. In '74 James continued to arr. albums for Crawford, Washington and M. Jackson and was also signed by CTI as a rec. artist. His first album, *Bob James One,* with its interpretation of Moussorgsky's *Night On Bald Mountain,* enjoyed a large measure of acclaim, and was followed by the even more popular *Bob James Two.* He also arr. for and perf. w. R. Flack, Paul Simon; arr. and cond. the music for motion pic., *Serpico.*

Comps: score for Broadway musical, *The Selling of the*

President; Valley of the Shadows; Nautilus; Soulero; Piece of Mind. LPs: *Bob James One; Bob James Two* (CTI); *Soul Box; Inner City Blues; Mister Magic* w. Washington (Kudu); *She Was Too Good To Me* w. Chet Baker (CTI); *Walking In Space* w. Q. Jones (A & M).

JAMES, HARRY HAAG,* *trumpet, leader*; b. Albany, Ga., 3/15/16. Formed first band '39 after gaining national fame during two years w. B. Goodman. In late '60s and early '70s still based in Las Vegas, but made frequent U.S. and European tours and continued to combine commercial style with jazz oriented material, using arrs. by Thad Jones, Neal Hefti, Ernie Wilkins. App. in NYC for NJF, at Roseland Ballroom and Carnegie Hall, '74, Carnegie Hall '75. Publs: *Harry James Trumpet Method; Harry James Studies and Improvisations* (Robbins Music). Own LPs: Readers Digest, Longines Symphonette.

JAMES, NEHEMIAH (SKIP),* *singer, guitar, piano*; b. Yazoo County, Miss., 1902. Active in the '20s around Jackson and Vicksburg, he dropped his career from '32-38 but resumed in '38-'40 w. a gospel gp. Rediscovered by young blues enthusiasts in '64 he app. at the Newport Folk Fest. that year and toured Europe w. the American Folk Blues Festival '67. His song, *I'm So Glad*, was recorded by Cream. He died at Univ. of Penn. Hospital, Phila., 10/3/69.

JAMES, STAFFORD LOUIS, *bass, composer*; also *cello*; b. Evanston, Ill., 4/24/46. Brother, Don, pl. reeds in Ill. Studied violin ages seven to 11. While in service stud. bass in NO w. Richard Payne, Chuck Beatty. Further stud. w. Rudolf Fahsbender at Chi. Conserv., '67-8; Julius Levine at Mannes Coll. of Mus., NYC, '73-4. First pl. prof. in NO, '66 w. Trevor Koehler trio. To NYC late '68, working w. Monty Alexander. Pl. w. Pharoah Sanders; Rashied Ali; Joe Lee Wilson; Lonnie Liston Smith; Archie Shepp; Alice Coltrane, '69-70; Danny Mixon from '70; Melba Moore, '71; Charles Sullivan, '71-2; Bobby Timmons, '72; Roy Ayers, '72-3; John Hicks from '73; Gary Bartz; Art Blakey, '73-4; Betty Carter from '73; Cecil, Dee Dee, Ron Bridgewater, '74; Al Haig; Chico Hamilton, Hannibal; Barry Harris, '75. Taught bass at U.N. School, '74-5. Designed church architecture w. Barry Byrne in Chi. Plays chess, draws and rides horses. Infl: NO bassists Payne & Beatty, Ravel, McCoy Tyner, Oscar Pettiford, Paul Chambers, Scott LaFaro, Ron Carter, Eddie Gomez, Richard Davis, Jimmy Garrison. TV: w. Betty Carter, *AM America*; ABC; *Interfaith*, PBS, '75; w. Shepp, *Free Time*, '71; w. Bartz, Montreux JF; *Congress of African People*, Calif. Educ. TV; *It's About Time*, SF. '73. Fest: Notre Dame, '68; w. Bartz, Kongsberg, Montreux, '73; w. Blakey, Perugia, Pescara, NJF-NY, '74; w. Hannibal, Berlin '75; w. Enrico Rava, Umbria, '75; w. Betty Carter, MJF, '75. Comps: *Costa Bruciata Suite*, dedicated to Charles Clark; *Bertha Baptist; City of Dreams; Neptune's Child; Sachia-Nova.* Publ. (Staja Publ., 133 St. Felix Street, Brooklyn, N.Y. 11217). LPs: own quartet (Horo); w. Hannibal (BASF); w. Oliver Lake. *Heavy Spirits*; w. Andrew Cyrille, *Spiral*

(Arista); w. R. Kenyatta, *Nomosa* (Muse); w. Bartz, *I've Known Rivers* (Prest.); w. R. Ali, *New Directions* (Survival).

JARMAN, JOSEPH, *sopranino, soprano, alto, tenor, bass saxophones, bassoon, oboe, flute, clarinets, piccolo, composer*; also *conga, bells, gongs, accordion, vibes, marimba, ballophone, singer*; b. Pine Bluff, Ark., 9/14/37. Moved to Chicago at a very early age. Studied drums at Du Sable High w. Capt. Walter Dyett; saxophone, clar. in Army. Further education at Wilson Jr. Coll.; Chicago City Coll.; and Chi. Cons. of Mus. Began performing w. AACM '65. Played his comp. *Imperfections in a Given Space* w. John Cage, '65. Premiered theater pieces *Tribute to the Hard Core*, spring '66; *Indifferent Piece for Six*, fall '67. Guest lecture for the Contemporary Music Society of the U. of Chi., '67. Lecturer, director of music and theater workshop at Circle Pine Center, Delton, Mich., summer '68, where he perf. his comp. *Gate Piece*. Joined the Art Ensemble of Chicago, April '69. pl. w. it in France, and the US from that time. Comps: *Sorry to Make the Sun Come Up; As If It Were the Seasons; Song for Christopher; Fanfare for the Warriors; What's to Say.*

LPs: see Art Ensemble of Chicago; *Song For; As If It Were the Seasons; Together Alone* (Delmark).

JARRETT, KEITH,* *piano, composer*; also *soprano sax*; b. Allentown, Pa., 5/8/45. After pl. w. Art Blakey in '65, he joined Charles Lloyd in '66 and began to build an international reputation through many European tours, incl. Russia in '67. While w. Lloyd also pl. and recorded w. own trio. In '70-1 he was a member of the shifting Miles Davis personnel and on leaving again formed his own group w. his old section mates, Charlie Haden and Paul Motian, adding reedman Dewey Redman. Besides his quartet performances Jarrett also performs in concert as a solo artist. In the '70s he appeared in both contexts in the US, Europe and Japan and at many of the major festivals. Solo at NJF-NY, '74.

Jarrett first recorded w. his trio for Atlantic's Vortex label but these have been out of print for some time. Then the quartet recorded for Atlantic and Columbia. His recording arrangement in the mid-'70s is unique: his Impulse albums place him in the small group format; for the European ECM label he is taped in solo piano recitals or in orchestral settings. Stephen Davis, in the New York *Times* wrote: "Jarrett's work in Europe seems to differ from that in his own country. While rooted in American jazz lore and tradition, he seems to find greater inspiration when playing in Germany and Scandinavia." In describing his *Köln Concert*, Davis states: "Themes are introduced and mistily evaporate while Jarrett's relentless left hand drums out tense recreated patterns; there is a trance-like quality in his use of repetition but then he will go abruptly into a bluesy improvisation that soars into finely crafted treble runs. A signature specialty has the left hand padding out a melody while the right rolls off swooping liquid patterns. The general effect is something like Chopin and Art Tatum streaming together downriver in a canoe."

An avowed opponent of electric music in a period rife with heavily-amplified jazz-rock Jarrett says: "I could go into the philosophical aspects of it and make it almost an objective argument whereby playing electric music is bad for you and bad for people listening, which I do believe."

On the other hand Jarrett has been known to strum the piano's strings like a harp; use it's top for percussive effects; and accompany himself with falsetto singing, grunts and groans. His gyrations on the piano bench turn off some of his critics who also find him pretentious.

Won DB Critics poll, TDWR, '67; '74 (tie), '75. Comp: *Coral; Gypsy Moth; Pardon My Rags; El Juicio; Piece For Ornette; (If the) Misfits (Wear It); Fort Yawuh; De Drums; Still Life, Still Life; Birth; Markings; Remorse; Spirit; Mortgage on My Soul; Forget Your Memories (And They'll Remember You).*

LPs: *The Koln Concert; Facing You; Bremen/Lausanne; In the Light; Luminessence;* w. Jan Garbarek, *Belonging;* w. Jack DeJohnette, *Ruta and Daitya* (ECM); *Backhand; Treasure Island; Fort Yawuh; Death and the Flower* (Imp.); *Expectations* (Col.); *Birth; The Mourning of a Star; El Juicio; Gary Burton and Keith Jarrett* (Atl.); *Somewhere Before; Restoration Ruin; Life Between the Exit Signs* (Vortex); w. Davis, *Live-Evil; Live at Fillmore East* (Col.); w. Lloyd (Atl.).

JARVIS, CLIFFORD, *drums, percussion;* b. Boston, Mass., 8/26/41. Father, a musician, encouraged him to take up drums at 10. Studied w. Alan Dawson at Berklee from ages 12-17. To NYC in late '50s. Has worked w. Barry Harris; Yusef Lateef; Sun Ra; Grant Green; Randy Weston; R.R. Kirk; in '70s w. Pharoah Sanders; Sirone; Clifford Thornton; also app. as guest instructor at U. of Mass. and other New England area colls. Infl: M. Roach, R. Haynes, PJ Jones, Ed Blackwell, Barry Harris, Sun Ra. Fest: NJF-NY w. Sanders, '72. LPs: w. Huey Simmons (Contemp.); Sanders (Imp.); Lateef (Trip); Sun Ra (ESP); F. Hubbard (BN); R. Weston (UA); B. Harris (River.).

JARZEBSKI, PAWEL, *bass;* b. Poznan, Poland, 4/21/48. Worked w. Michal Urbaniak, '70-2; Zbigniew Namysowski, '73. Toured U.S. w. Urbaniak's Fusion, '74, app. at NJF-NY, then rejoined Namyslowski, app. w. him at Cascais JF, '74. Infls: Miles Davis, Bill Evans, M. Vitous, Jan Garbarek. Many apps. on Polish and Finnish TV. LP: w. Namyslowski, *Winobranie* (Muza).

JCOA. See Mantler, Mike; Bley, Carla.

JEFFERSON, EDGAR (EDDIE),* *singer, dancer;* b. Pittsburgh, Pa., 8/3/18. Pioneer in technique of setting lyrics to improvised jazz solos, the best known of which was based on James Moody's *I'm In The Mood For Love.* Worked w. Moody off and on from '53 as manager and singer.

During '67 and part of '68, Jefferson app. as tap dancer. He rejoined Moody in '68 and remained with him until late '73; then joined forces w. Roy Brooks, touring with their group, Artistic Truth, '74-5. Won DB Critics poll, TDWR, '75. Fest: NJF '69.

LPs: *Body and Soul; Come Along With Me* (Prestige); *Charlie Parker Memorial* album (Chess); *Things Are*

Getting Better (Muse). Earlier LPs with Moody.

JEFFERSON, HILTON,* *alto saxophone;* b. Danbury, Conn., 7/30/03. One of the outstanding lead saxophonists, who also played excellent solos in a style infl. by Frank Trumbauer, died NYC, 11/14/68, after a long illness. He worked with the bands of Claude Hopkins, King Oliver, Chick Webb, Benny Carter, Fletcher Henderson, and spent the entire decade of the '40s w. C. Calloway and was w. Duke Ellington, '52-3. From '54, until his hospitalization in Sept. '68, he continued to gig on weekends w. his own gp. or w. Fats Greene.

JEFFREY, PAUL H., *tenor sax, composer;* also *clarinet, flute, oboe, bassoon;* b. New York City, 4/8/33. Studied music at PS 157, NYC; Kingston (N.Y.) HS; Ithaca (N.Y.) Coll. Worked w. own gp. in Atlantic City, N.J., '56; Wynonie Harris, Big Maybelle in Detroit, St. Louis, '57; I. Jacquet in Winston-Salem, N.C., '58; Florida and other southern states w. B.B. King, '60; NYC w. Sadik Hakim, '61; Johnny Brown, '64; Howard McGhee quartet & big band, '66; Toured Europe w. D. Gillespie's Reunion big band, '68; Billy Gardner trio, '69; a month w. C. Basie, '70. From '70 pl. w. Thelonious Monk; from '72 w. own octet. Infl: Monk, Ellington, Dameron. TV: Sammy Davis special w. Johnny Brown, '66; documentary on Sonny Rollins, NET '68; D. Gillespie on Euro. TV, '68; Monk, NET '72. Fest: NJF jam session, '69; NJF-NY: w. Mingus, '72; own gp. in NY Mus. Fest., '73, and at Fordham U., '74; w. Monk, '75; Newport in Japan, '70. Cond. NYJRC orch. for Monk concert, '74.

Saxophone instructor at Teachers Coll., Columbia U.; on faculty of Jersey State Coll. as lecturer in jazz history; arr. courses; teaching Jazz Ensemble Workshop at U. of Hartford; clinician for Yamaha Co. Own jazz radio show on WFUV (Fordham U.) from '73. Comp: *I.F.U.; Immigration; Ina; Kim; Rodan; Bianca; Ecclesiology; A.V.G.; The Dreamer; Green Ivan; Bondage; Moon Madness; My Son; Brand X; Brand New Day; Geometric Blues; Love Letters; Acirema.* LPs: *Family; Watershed; Paul Jeffrey* (Main.); *Electrifying Sounds* (Savoy); w. Gillespie, *Reunion Big Band* (MPS); w. Monk (Express).

JENKINS, LEROY, *violin, viola, composer, educator;* b. Chicago, Ill., 3/11/32. First violin teacher was O.W. Frederick; then stud. w. Bruce Hayden; basic musicianship w. Walter Dyett, band dir. at Du Sable High; learned blues from Edward Pratt. B.S. in Mus. Ed. from Florida A&M, '61. Taught string inst. in Mobile, Ala. school system, '61-5; inst. music in Chi. school system, '65-9; string-instr. instructor for Chi. Urban Poverty Corps, '69. One of the important players to emerge from the AACM, he worked w. it, '65-69. Creative Construction Co., '65-69. Pl. w. O. Coleman in Paris, '69; Cecil Taylor, '70; Anthony Braxton, '69-72; Albert Ayler, '71; Cal Massey, '70-3; Alice Coltrane, '71-2; Archie Shepp, '69, '70-4; Mtume, '72-4. Formed Revolutionary Ensemble w. Sirone and Jerome Cooper in '71 and has perf. with it since in coll., Shakespeare Fest. Public Theatre, O.K. Harris Gallery, and Museum of Contemporary Art, Chi. Infl: Charlie Parker, Jascha Heifitz, Eddie South, Ornette Coleman, Bruce Hayden, John Coltrane, Braxton,

Roscoe Mitchell, Leo Smith. App. as actor in film, *Borsalino* w. Jean-Paul Belmondo, Alain Delon. Fests: Ann Arbor w. Revolutionary Ens., '73; NJF-NY w. Dewey Redman, '74. Comp: *National Baptist Convention; Vietnam I-II; Simple Like; For Players Only; Bandana Sketches; Muhal; Collegno.* Awarded a grant in comp. from National Endowment for the Arts, '73; CAPS, '75. Won DB Critics' Poll, TDWR, on violin, '74. Nat Hentoff wrote: "Jenkins has so expanded the range and conceptual dimensions of improvisatory violin and viola that he is, as Duke Ellington might have said, 'beyond category.'" LPs w. Revolutionary Ensemble: *Vietnam I-II* (ESP); *Manhattan Cycles* (India Navigation); w. Anthony Braxton, *3 Compositions*; w. Richard Abrams, *Levels and Degrees* (Delmark); w. Archie Shepp, *Things Gotta Change*; w. Alice Coltrane, *Universal Consciousness; Reflection on Creation and Space* (Impulse); w. R. Kirk, *Rahsaan, Rahsaan* (Atlantic).

JEROME, JERRY,* *tenor saxophone, flute, conductor; also clarinet;* b. Brooklyn, N.Y., 6/19/12. The former Goodman and Shaw sideman, after leaving his post as musical director of WPIX-TV, concentrated on composing, arranging and producing radio and TV commercials for national products. Also active playing club dates and jazz concerts in and around eastern U.S., incl. a series for C.W. Post Coll. An avid golfer, he won the Senior Championship tournament of the North Shore C.C. His LPs on ABC-Paramount, Stinson and MGM are no longer available.

JOBIM, ANTONIO CARLOS,* *composer, guitar, piano;* b. Rio de Janeiro, Brazil, 1927. Best known as composer of songs widely feat. by jazz musicians: *Desafinado; One Note Samba; Girl From Ipanema; Quiet Nights (Corcovado).* Comp. of music for movie *The Adventurers,* '69. App. in TV spec. w. Frank Sinatra, E. Fitzgerald, '69. Among his later comps. are *Wave; Triste; Waters of March; Lamento; Mojave.*

Publs: *Wave; Stone Flower,* song folios (Corcovado Music Corp., 4 W. 56th St., New York, N.Y. 10019).

LPs: *A Certain Mr. Jobim* (WB); *Wave; Tide* (A & M); *Stone Flower* (CTI); *Jobim* (MCA); *Frank Sinatra & A.C. Jobim* (Repr.).

JOHANSEN, EGIL, *drums, composer;* b. Oslo, Norway, 1/11/34. Self-taught; started pl. piano at age 6; drums, '50. Main insps. Parker, Gillespie, Roach, Ellington, Tatum. Pl. with many visiting Americans incl. Gillespie, Dolphy, S. Getz, Lucky Thompson, Teddy Wilson; also w. Danish trumpeter Palle Mikkelborg. Many motion pic. and TV apps. As composer, his most important work was a comp. for a TV film, feat. two jazz drummers, conga and percussion.

LPs: w. Swedish Radio Jazz Group, *Greetings and Salutations* feat. Thad Jones, Mel Lewis (Four Leaf Clover); Arne Domnerus; Jan Johansson; Bengt Hallberg; Rolf Ericson; German Jazz Workshop All-Stars; Svend Asmussen.

JOHNSON, ALBERT J. (BUDD),* *tenor, soprano, alto, baritone saxes, clarinet, composer;* b. Dallas, Texas, 12/14/10. Best-known first for his key role as sax-

ophonist-arranger w. Earl Hines, '34-42, he was a catalytic figure in the modern jazz movement w. Billy Eckstine, Dizzy Gillespie. After pl. w. Count Basie and Quincy Jones bands in '60s rejoined Hines in small gp., touring w. him in US, Russia, So. America '66-9 on tenor and soprano. After leaving Hines, formed JPJ Quartet, for which he is mus. dir., w. O. Jackson, B. Pemberton, D. Jones. Appeared in clubs such as the Half Note, Jimmy Weston's; presented concert-"rap sessions" and seminars for more than 300,000 high school students under the auspices of Johns-Manville, mainly in the US but also in Europe during a summer tour, '71.

Johnson also worked intermittently w. Sy Oliver's band in mid-'70s. In '74 he was mus. dir. for NYJRC's *Musical Life of Charlie Parker*, premiered at NJF-NY '74. Toured with it in Europe, fall '74. Guest mus. dir. for NYJRC's second season, '74-5, touring Russia with Louis Armstrong tribute, summer '75. Active as lecturer-demonstrator at U. of Conn.; Rutgers; pl. in Smithsonian Inst. concert series, '75. To KC, Sept. '75, pl. for documentary film on KC jazz style. TV: w. JPJ, Montreux JF '71, NET; film made at high school performance in Green Cove Springs, Fla. seen on many local outlets in US. Fest: w. JPJ, Montreux; Lubljana, '71; NJF-NY '72; NJF-NY jam session '73; Nice Grand Parade du Jazz, '74-5; Colo. Jazz Party, '71-5. Transcribing music from recs. w. co-editor David Baker for Smithsonian "classic jazz" project.

Comps: *Tag Along; You Dirty Old Man; Mr. Bechet; Blues for Sale; Tribulations; Montreux '71.* LPs: *Blues A La Mode* (Master Jazz); w. JPJ (Eng. RCA); also *New Communications in Jazz; Montreux '71* (Master Jazz); w. Hines (Black & Blue); reissue w. Hines (Bluebird); w. Milt Hinton (Famous Door); w. Buck Clayton (Chiaro.); w. R. Eldridge (Master Jazz); J. Rushing (RCA Victor); Red Richards (Eng. RCA); *Newport in New York '72, The Jam Sessions*, Vols. 3&4 (Cobble.); *Colorado Jazz Party* (MPS/BASF).

JOHNSON, GUS,* *drums, composer;* b. Tyler, Texas, 11/15/13. The veteran ex-Jay McShann and Count Basie drummer joined the World's Greatest Jazzband in 1969, replacing the late Morey Feld. He traveled with the band, which recorded his composition *Under The Moonlight Starlight Blue,* until the fall of 1974, when he settled in Denver, Colorado. Worked in Denver with such residents of that city as Peanuts Hucko and Ralph Sutton, and played at Dick Gibson's jazz parties in Colorado Springs. Rejoined WGJ occasionally for records. Won DB Critics poll, TDWR, '71. LPs w. WGJ (Project 3, Atlantic, World Jazz).

JOHNSON, HOWARD LEWIS, *baritone sax, tuba; also composer, arranger, fluegelhorn, clarinets, bass sax etc.;* b. Montgomery, Ala., 8/7/41. Self-taught; started on bari. sax in '54, tuba, '55. Came to NYC Feb. '63, pl. tuba w. Ch. Mingus, '64; road tour on bari. w. Hank Crawford, '65; back w. Mingus July '65 to Apr. '66; also w. A. Shepp for several months in '66. Intermittently w. Gil Evans orch., pl. various instruments, from '66 through mid '70s. After pl. w. B. Rich band in '66, spent most of

'67 in L.A. working w. Gerald Wilson, Big Black, O. Nelson. Back in NYC Sept. '67, worked often w. Evans, Shepp and numerous other groups, incl. own Substructure. In '70s made several apps. annually at Colorado Jazz Parties. Fests: Newport, '66, 68 w. Shepp; Newport-N.Y. w. Evans; Montreux and Antibes w. Evans, '74.

Johnson, who names Clifford Brown, Mingus, Evans, D. Ellington and Herb Bushler as musicians who have insp. or infl. him, is a performer of extraordinary versatility who seems equally at home and capable of first class solos whether in a traditionalist, mainstream, modern or avant garde context. As an arranger he has written charts for Taj Mahal, Paul Butterfield's *Better Days* dates, Geoff Muldaur, Gil Evans and B.B. King.

LPs w. Evans (Ampex, Atl., RCA).

JOHNSON, JAMES LOUIS (J.J.),* *composer, trombone*; b. Indianapolis, Ind. 1/22/24. Won Esquire New Star Award as trombonist, '46. Innumerable other awards in many countries as recently as '75, though by that time he had all but totally given up playing to concentrate on a career as composer, arranger and conductor. After moving to Cal. in '70, Johnson wrote scores for movies *Man and Boy; Top of the Heap; Across 110th Street; Cleopatra Jones; Willie Dynamite.* He was partial orchestrator for *Shaft* and *Trouble Man.* In television, he wrote the music for the series *Barefoot In The Park*, as well as episodes for *Mod Squad; The Bold Ones; Chase; Harry-O* etc.

Studied with and orchestrated for Earle Hagen during those years; app. as jazz trombonist on LP for first time in several years in *The Bosses* w. C. Basie, Joe Turner (Pablo). Arr. LP for Raoul De Souza (Fantasy), '75. Own early albums: *Proof Positive* (Impulse); *The Eminent J.J.* (Blue Note); others on RCA, Columbia etc. Trombone duos w. Kai Winding: *Israel; Betwixt and Between* (A&M); *Stonebones*, done for the same label was released only in Japan.

JOHNSON, FREDERIC H. (KEG),* *trombone*; b. Dallas, Tex., 11/19/08. Heard with many name bands from the late '20s, among them Benny Carter, F. Henderson, C. Calloway, Lucky Millinder; also Gil Evans, '60. Johnson during the '60s toured w. the Ray Charles orch. pl. bass trombone. He died suddenly in Chicago 11/8/67. He was an older brother of saxophonist/arranger Budd Johnson.

JOHNSON, LONNIE,* *singer, guitar*; b. New Orleans, La., 2/8/1889 (date disputed). One of the first great jazz guitarists, Johnson in the late '20s rec. several brilliant guitar duets w. E. Lang and pl. on sessions w. L. Armstrong and D. Ellington. In the mid '60s he settled in Toronto, where he became popular with local blues fans. Inactive after suffering injuries in an accident March '69, Johnson died of a stroke in Toronto, 6/16/70.

LPs: a few tracks on *The Duke Ellington Story*, Vols. 1,2 (Col.); many other recs. w. Armstrong (Col.); J. Dodds, J. Noone, A. Ammons et al, all deleted, as were his own LPs on Prest.

JOHNSON, MANZIE ISHAM,* *drums*; b. Putnam, Conn., 8/19/06. Prominent w. Don Redman band, '31-

40; later w. F. Henderson, James P. Johnson et al, Johnson died 4/9/71 at a hospital in the Bronx, N.Y.

JOHNSON, HAROLD (MONEY), *trumpet, fluegelhorn, singer*; b. Tyler, Texas, 2/23/18. When he was 15, a friend gave him an old cornet. Studied w. Leonard Parker and soon was pl. w. Eddie and Sugar Lou; then in Dallas w. his cousin Red Calhoun's band. After two yrs., went with Skunny Thompson to Tip Top Club in Okla. City, '36, where he jammed w. Charlie Christian and saxophonist Henry Bridges. Joined Nat Towles band, '37, remaining for seven yrs. working out of Omaha. Saxophonist Lee Pope, who used to borrow from him, gave him his nickname. To NYC w. Horace Henderson. When band broke up, pl. w. Bob Dorsey in Rochester for two yrs. Rejoined Towles briefly; then to NYC again w. Count Basie. Pl. w. Cootie Williams '46; Lucky Millinder and Williams '47; then w. Lucky Thompson; Sy Oliver; Herbie Fields; Bull Moose Jackson. To So. America w. Panama Francis, '53; several yrs. w. Reuben Phillips' house band at the Apollo Theater, NYC; then work in the rec. studios; gigs w. Buddy Johnson's small band; Mercer Ellington; show bands at Basin Street East; Copacabana.

State Dept. tour of Russia w. Earl Hines, '66; Euro. tour w. Hines, '68. Pl. NJF and LV w. Duke Ellington, '68; replaced Cat Anderson w. Ellington, June '69. Infl: Armstrong; Nat Towles.

LPs: see Ellington; *Buck Clayton Jam Session #2* (Chiaro.).

JOHNSON, PETE,* *piano*; b. Kansas City, Mo., 3/24/04. The pioneer boogie woogie pianist who, with Albert Ammons and Meade Lux Lewis, helped to bring this style to national attention in the late '30s, was musically active in Buffalo, N.Y. until suffering a heart attack in '58. He was intermittently ill during the next decade, making his final public appearance at a *Spirituals To Swing* concert at Carnegie Hall in Jan. '67, when he was reunited with his Kansas City partner, singer Joe Turner. Johnson died 3/23/67 in Buffalo.

LP: *Spirituals To Swing, 30th Anniversary* (Col.).

JOHNSON, PLAS JOHN JR.,* *tenor sax, flute* etc.; b. New Orleans, La., 7/21/31. Came to prominence in 1966 as featured soloist with H. Mancini in *The Pink Panther* film and LP. Joined staff band on Merv Griffin TV show in LA, 1970. During '70s, stepped up his jazz activities, subbing in Bill Berry band and pl. jobs w. Ray Brown, Herb Ellis, own gp. at Baked Potato etc. Rec. own first album as leader Oct. '75 for Concord Jazz label. Underrated musician with hard-swinging style and warm, full sound.

JOHNSON, SIVERT BERTIL (SY), *composer, piano*; b. New Haven, Conn., 4/15/30. Studied w. Lucy Greene, Hall Overton; Rayburn Wright, in NYC and at Eastman School *Arranger's Holiday*; Juilliard. In high school was introduced to records of Gillespie, Parker, Bud Powell by Roger Brousso (an owner of the Half Note in the '70s) and co-led band w. him. While w. USAF '51-5 in bands w. Donald Byrd, John Pisano, John Williams. After discharge to LA with law career in mind. Sold charts to

Basie; Med Flory rec. his *Jonah and the Wail*. Met Paul Bley and Ornette Coleman. To NYC '60, pl. briefly w. Mingus at Showplace. Wrote for Newport Youth Band, Ruby Braff, Marshall Brown, G. Mulligan Concert Jazz Band; led trio at Chuck's Composite. Then went into commercial arr. until he became pianist-arr. for Yolande Bavan from '66. Increased writing activity from '71 w. Mingus' *Let My Children Hear Music* album. Arrs. for Thad Jones-Mel Lewis; Quincy Jones. In '75 writing regularly for Lee Konitz Nonet; finishing a blues suite for Mingus; preparing a gp. of new comps. for Guggenheim Fellowship application.

Infl: Maurice Rocco, Teddy Wilson, Basie, Lester Young, C. Parker, M. Davis, Ellington, Rollins, Mingus. Fest: NJF w. Rod Levitt. Johnson is also a photographer-journalist who is the jazz editor of *Changes* and a contributor to the NY *Times, New York, Esquire Book of Jazz*. Comp: *Wee* (not to be confused w. Denzil Best's *Wee*); *For Harry Carney; I Should Have Kissed Her More*. Arrs. for Mingus (Col., Atl.). LPs: w. Rod Levitt (Riverside, RCA); Wes Montgomery, *Road Song* (A&M).

JOLLY, PETE (Peter A. Ceragioli),* *piano, keyboards, accordion*; b. New Haven, Conn., 6/5/32. In '65 was one of the orig. pianists to open the N. Hollywood jazz room, Donte's, and has app. there sporadically ever since. From '66-75 mainly engaged in TV and movie studios, working w. such composers as N. Hefti, J.J. Johnson, B. Byers, Don Costa, Anita Kerr, Artie Butler, Earle Hagen. Made several rec. dates with Herb Alpert's Tijuana Brass. In '74 took part in clinic at N. Texas State U. w. Ray Brown, Herb Ellis, L. Bellson, and in '75 conducted workshop series at the Dick Grove School in LA. Continued to play club dates w. own trio.

LPs: *Herb Alpert Presents Pete Jolly; Give A Damn; Seasons* (A&M).

JONES, BOBBY, *tenor, soprano saxes, clarinet, composer; educator*; b. Louisville, Ky., 10/30/28. Started on drums, his father's instrument, switching to clarinet at eight. First prof. job at 10. Father had him listen to recs. of jazz greats; arranged for him to sit-in w. local black combo for important early jazz experience. Later stud. w. Simeon Bellison, Joe Allard, Charlie Parker, G. Russell. While pl. in local sextet was hired by Ray McKinley, spring '49, remaining w. him until mid-'50. Six mos. w. Hal McIntyre, then rejoined McKinley before going into Army where he met Cannonball and Nat Adderley, Junior Mance, Kenny Dennis; led own combo at Officer's Club. After service, worked w. and arr. for Boyd Bennett and his Rockets for two and a half yrs., pl. hillbilly, then rock & roll. Briefly with Boots Randolph to Cleveland, remaining to do clubs, TV, radio and teach privately. Rejoined McKinley again, '59 to Feb. '63 when he went to Woody Herman. Left in Sept. to work in NYC. Joined Jack Teagarden in NO on Christmas Eve. When Teagarden died in Jan. '64, Jones ret. to Louisville. Started Louisville Jazz Council; later became woodwind instructor at Kentucky State Coll. To NY '69. Sat-in w. C.

Mingus at Top of the Gate Nov. '70, and eventually became band member, touring Europe and Japan, '70, Europe '72. Left Mingus, settling first in Belgium, then Holland. To Munich '73, forming quintet, Summit, w. Dusko Goykovich, Horace Parlan. Own trio, '74. Won DB Critics Poll, clarinet TDWR, '73. Thoroughly schooled, he has followed what Charlie Parker told him: "First you master your instrument, then you master the music, and then you forget about all that shit and just play." Comp: *Thanks to Trane; Ballad for Two Sons; 'Stone Bossa; Blues for the Brown Buddha; Waltz for Joy; As the Crow Flies; Hill Country Suite; Only Blue; Lady Love; The Gospel Truth*. LPs: *Hill Country Suite* (Enja); *The Arrival of Bobby Jones* (Cobble.); *Mingus and Friends* (Col.); w. Herman (Philips); Jimmy Raney, *Strings & Swings* (Muse).

JONES, CARMELL,* *trumpet, composer*; also *fluegelhorn, valve trombone*; b. Kansas City, Kans., 1936. Worked w. Harold Land, Horace Silver in early '60s before moving to Germany, Aug. '65, where he joined SFB TV and radio orch. in Berlin. Jones has also pl. extensively in German clubs and all over Europe incl. Berlin Jazz Days, Prague JF and with Paul Kuhn, leader of SFB band, in Moscow and Leningrad. Appeared in German cigarette commercial. Won DB Critics' Poll, TDWR, '64. Comps: *Jayhawk Talk; Dance of the Night Child; Beepdurple; Stellisa; Give Me a Chance; Black Forest Waltz; Sad March; Shadows; Where Did the Time Go; If Love Should Come; I Think of Love*. An amateur carpenter and electrician, he does upholstering and cabinet-making, repairs cars and has built his own mixing board for recording. LPs: w. Annie Ross-Pony Poindexter; *Hip Walk* w. Nathan Davis (MPS); *More Than Meets the Ear* w. Jean-Luc Ponty (Euro. Liberty).

JONES, DILLWYN OWEN (DILL), *piano*; b. Newcastle Emlyn, Wales, 8/19/23. Became interested in jazz by hearing Fats Waller record on radio in '30s. After serving w. the Royal Navy, '42-6, stud. at Trinity Coll. of Music in London, '46-8. Later stud. w. Richard McClanahan, '62-3, and Luckey Roberts, '65, in NYC. While in Navy was encouraged by former Ellington reedman Rudy Jackson in Colombo, Ceylon, '45. A leading figure in post-WWII jazz circles in London, he established himself w. own trio; also pl. w. Ronnie Scott; Humphrey Lyttelton; Stephane Grappelli; George Chisholm. Took part in British tour of JATP. Hosted BBC Jazz Club on radio for many yrs.; first to introduce jazz on BBC-TV. Acc. Louis Armstrong in Hungarian Relief Fund concert at Hammersmith Hall, '57.

Visited US as ship's pianist on Queen Mary, '50. Ret. on many occasions in '50s but did not settle in NYC until '61. Worked w. Yank Lawson '62; Peanuts Hucko and Max Kaminsky at E. Condon's; Roy Eldridge; trio w. Bob Wilber, Carl Kress; Jimmy McPartland in mid '60s; Gene Krupa, '67-8; Dukes of Dixieland, '68. Charter member of the JPJ Quartet w. Budd Johnson, Oliver Jackson and Bill Pemberton, '69, and in next four yrs. toured US for Johns-Manville in high school concert-seminars; pl. several long engagements at Jimmy Weston's, NYC; European dates. Left in '74 to free-lance. Solo piano at several clubs incl. Condon's; gigs w. WGJ; w. Earle Warren, Taft Jordan at West End Cafe; w. M. Kaminsky; R. Eldridge; J. McPartland at Jimmy Ryan's, '74-5; also w. Countsmen, off and on, from '73. Infl: Luckey Roberts, Joe Sullivan, Ellington, Beiderbecke, James P. Johnson, Fats Waller, Willie "The Lion" Smith. Fest: NJF-NY w. JPJ, '72; w. NYJRC Tribute to Bix, '75; Monterey, solo w. John Lewis Piano Forum; Montreux; Lubljana w. JPJ, '71. Comp: *West of the Wind; Something For Luckey; Celtic Twilight.* Versatile, accomplished performer in Harlem stride, Bixian impressionism and mainstream modern. LPs: *Davenport Blues: Dill Jones Plays Bix and Others* (Chiaro.); *Up Jumped You With Love* (77); w. JPJ, *New Communications in Jazz; Montreux '71* (Master Jazz); w. H. Hall-J. Muranyi, *Clarinet Wobble*; w. L. McGarity, *Jazz Master* (Fat Cat's Jazz); w. T. Parenti (Jazzology); w. E. Warren (Eng. RCA).

JONES, ELVIN RAY,* drums, leader; b. Pontiac, Mich., 9/9/27. Following six years w. John Coltrane he formed his own group in '66 and has led small combos of varying sizes from that time. A quartet w. Joe Farrell, pianist Billy Greene and Wilbur Little evolved into a pianoless trio. Jimmy Garrison replaced Little. In the '70s he had saxophonists like Frank Foster, Steve Grossman, Dave Liebman and Azar Lawrence, sometimes using two reeds in the same gp. Other gp. members at different times have incl. Roland Prince, guitar; Gene Perla, David Williams, bass. In addition to clubs and concerts, Jones gives clinics, plays for schools and free concerts in prisons. His gp. tours regularly in Europe and Japan; South America for USIA, '73. '75. App. at most major fests. Whitney Balliett described his style thusly: "The center of Jones' beat shifts continually. Sometimes it is in his constantly changing ride-cymbal strokes and sometimes he softens these and bears down heavily on his high-hat on the afterbeat. Sometimes swift, wholly unpredictable bass-drum accents come to the fore and sometimes the emphasis shifts to left-hand accents on the snare, which range from clear single strokes to chattering loose rolls. Jones' hands and feet all seem to have their own minds, yet the total effect is of an unbroken flow that both supports and weaves itself around the soloists."

Film: drumming and acting role in *Zachariah.* Won DB Critics poll, '66-75; DB Readers poll, '66, '68-9. Comp: *Three Card Molly; Keiko's Birthday March; Elvin's Guitar Blues.* LPs: *New Agenda* (Vang.); *Live at the Village Vanguard* (Enja); *On the Mountain; Live* (PM); *Live at the Lighthouse; Merry Go Round; Genesis; Mr. Jones; Puttin' It Together; Ultimate* (BN); *Dear John C.; Heavy Sounds* w. Richard Davis; *Illuminations* w. J. Garrison (Imp.); w. Coltrane (Imp.); w. Jaki Byard, *Sunshine of My Soul* (Prest.); Joe Farrell, *Outback* (CTI).

JONES, ETTA,* singer; b. Aiken, S.C., 11/25/28. Active w. Buddy Johnson's band, J.C. Heard gp. in '40s; Earl Hines sextet, '49-52. Made comeback in '60 w. Gold Record single, *Don't Go to Strangers,* on Prestige. Toured Japan and Korea w. Art Blakey, '70. App. on *Jazz Cavalcade '72* at John F. Kennedy Center for Perf. Arts along w. G. Ammons, S. Stitt, B. Rich, etc.

Concert at Town Hall w. Billy Taylor; app. at Left Bank Jazz Society, Balto. Md., '75. Toured the club & concert circuit w. the Houston Person trio, '75. TV: Nipsey Russell's *Voices of America* show. LPs: *Etta Jones '75* (20th Century/Westbound); *Etta Jones Sings* (Roul.); others on Prest.; w. Person, *The Real Thing* (Eastbound).

JONES, HENRY (HANK),* piano, composer; b. Pontiac, Mich., 7/31/18. After close to 20 years as a staff musician at CBS he began to free-lance in '75. While still at CBS he also was the first pianist w. the Thad Jones (his brother)-Mel Lewis band in '66; toured w. Benny Goodman. Pl. w. Stan Getz in early '70s; in mid-'70s he app. at the Vanguard in a trio w. Ron Carter and Tony Williams, and other NYC clubs w. Carter and Ben Riley. He was supposed to perform at a concert dedicated to the music of Charlie Parker in August '75 but it was cancelled. The group, with Jackie McLean, Tommy Potter and Max Roach, did appear, however, on ABC-TV's *Like It Is.* Jones also led a trio in an episode of the CBS-TV soap opera *Love of Life.* Fest: NJF-NY; Colo. JP. Comp: *A' That's Freedom.* Own LP: *Happenings* (Imp.); LPs: w. Elvin Jones, *Dear John C.*; w. B. Hutcherson (BN); w. Jones-Lewis, *Presenting* (SS); w. Dexter Gordon (Prest.); w. Bobby Hackett; w. Bucky Pizzarelli-Bud Freeman (Fly. Dutch.).

JONES, HAROLD J.,* drums; b. Richmond, Ind., 2/27/40. Lived in Chicago from 1958. Stud. w. Jack Kurkowski from age 13 to 18; w. James Dutton at Amer. Conserv. of Mus., 18 to 23. In early '60s pl. w. Eddie Harris, D. Byrd, Bunky Green. Toured internationally w. Paul Winter, '61-2. Joined Count Basie Dec. '67 and remained for five years, then moved from NYC to LA, where he freelanced extensively in night clubs, rec. studios and TV, w. E. Fitzgerald, Tony Bennett, S. Davis Jr. TV series w. Nancy Wilson, '74-5. Rejoined Basie briefly in '74. Sweden, Caribbean cruise, Japan w. Carmen McRae, '75.

Insp. by Elvin Jones, M. Roach, A. Blakey, Roy Haynes, Tony Williams, Mel Lewis, L. Bellson, Jones was acknowledged to be one of the steadiest and most propulsive drummers ever to work for Basie. Won DB Critics Poll, TDWR '72.

LPs: w. Basie, *Straight Ahead; Standing Ovation* (Dot).

JONES, JONATHAN (JO),* drums; b. Chicago, Ill., 10/7/11. The star drummer of the Count Basie band of the '30s and '40s pl. w. JATP and Illinois Jacquet in late '40s; Lester Young; Joe Bushkin; Ella Fitzgerald-Oscar Peterson; JATP again in '50s; own gp. in NYC, '57-60. In the '60s he continued to lead his own gps.; also worked w. Teddy Wilson; Claude Hopkins; and Ray Bryant who had been the pianist in his trio. Made several tours of Europe w. JATP. Pl. in Europe w. Milt Buckner '69;

again in '70s. With Joey Bushkin at Michael's Pub '76. Fest: NJF-NY w. Benny Carter's Swingmasters, '72; M. Buckner and tap dancers; also Gretsch Greats, '73; Friends of Eddie Condon and Ben Webster, '74; Newport Hall of Fame, '75; Euro. fests. TV: acting role in *Route 66* episode w. Ethel Waters, Coleman Hawkins, Roy Eldridge; Tribute to John Hammond, PBS, '75.

LPs: *The Drums*, a two-record set in which Jones plays, talks about his life, other drum greats and drumming (Jazz Odyssey); w. Willie "The Lion" Smith; w. Zutty Singleton; w. Milt Buckner (Jazz Odyssey); w. Buckner, *Plays Chords* (MPS); w. Slam Stewart (B&B); reissue w. Basie, *Super Chief* (Col.); w. Jacquet, *How High the Moon* (Prest.).

JONES, ROBERT ELLIOTT (JONAH),* *trumpet*; b. Louisville, Ky., 12/31/08. Continued to lead his own quartet in nightclub engagements. Toured overseas in '70. In residence at Rainbow Room, Sept.-Oct. '75. LPs: w. quartet (Cap.; Decca; Motown); Jonah Jones & Earl Hines, *Back On the Street* (Chiaro.).

JONES, JAMES HENRY (JIMMY),* *composer, conductor, piano*; b. Memphis, Tenn., 12/30/18. Frequent associate of D. Ellington and E. Fitzgerald; acc. the latter, '67-8. Arr. for TV show, *The Strolling Twenties*, CBS, '66. From '69, resident musician and arr. in LA, writing for record dates, TV shows and occasional acc. singer Joe Williams. TV: arr. for *Duke Ellington . . . We Love You Madly*, '73; *Cotton Club '75*. Wrote some arrs. for movie *Shaft's Big Score*. Pianist w. K. Burrell's group, '75; gigs w. guitarist John Collins. Though primarily active as a writer of rare skill, Jones is greatly underrated as a pianist whose gentle touch and harmonic imagination have a character all their own.

LPs: w. C. Adderley, *Big Man; Love, Sex and the Zodiac* (Fant.); w. Burrell, *Ellington Is Forever* (Fant.); w. Harold Ashby, *Born to Swing* (Master Jazz).

JONES, JOSEPH RUDOLPH (PHILLY JOE),* *drums*; also *saxophone, bass; piano, timbales*; b. Philadelphia, Pa., 7/15/23. A key figure in modern drumming w. the Miles Davis quintet of the mid-'50s, he then led his own gp. and free-lanced on both coasts. After pl. the Berlin Fest. w. Sarah Vaughan and Erroll Garner, '67, decided to remain in Europe. Living in London, '67-9, he was prevented from pl. by the British musicians union but taught more than 40 students per week at own school in Hampstead. Moved to Paris '69 to teach w. Kenny Clarke. Own gp. for seven weeks at Chat Qui Peche; free-lance rec. Worked throughout Europe w. Slide Hampton, Dizzy Reece et al incl. Scandinavia, Vienna TV workshop; then toured w. trio opposite Clarke-Boland orch. in England; on own in Italy; Holland; Yugoslavia w. D. Goykovich. To Stuttgart for clinics; own quintet in Munich nightclub, then three mos. dubbing pictures for film company. Radio shows w. Franz Black orch. in Cologne. Ret. to Phila. '72 and led own quintet. Formed jazz-rock gp. Le Gran Prix, '75 w. Byard Lancaster, pl. for Miss Black America Pageant, Sept. '75, televised by ABC-TV. Fest: Austria w. D. Gordon, B. Webster; Holland. Publ: *Brush Artistry* (Premier Drums). "I love handling rock,"

he says. "My English students gave me something in return for my teaching them to play modern and read like hell." LPs: *Trailways Express* (Bl. Lion); w. H. Mobley, *No Room for Squares; The Flip* (BN); A. Shepp; M. Waldron (Byg); w. T. Dameron, *The Arrangers' Touch*; w. M. Davis, *Workin' and Steamin'* (Prest.); tracks w. own gp. in *The Big Beat* (Milest.).

JONES, QUINCY DELIGHT JR.,* *composer, leader, trumpet, keyboards*; b. Chicago, Ill., 3/14/33. From the mid-60s Jones extended his work in the areas of film and TV writing. Among his best known movie scores were *The Getaway; The New Centurions; The Hot Rock; $; The Anderson Tapes; They Call Me Mister Tibbs; Cactus Flower; John and Mary; The Out of Towners; Bob & Carol & Ted & Alice; MacKenna's Gold; The Split; For Love of Ivy; In Cold Blood; In The Heat of the Night; Banning*. Animated films: *Eggs; Of Men and Demons*, both for John and Faith Hubley. TV: themes for many shows incl. *Sanford & Son*; themes and other music for Bill Cosby shows. One of Jones' most celebrated credits was the CBS special, *Duke Ellington . . . We Love You Madly!*, presented in early '73.

Jones was arranger and conductor for the 43rd Annual Academy Awards presentation in '71. He won the Oscar for Best Original Score, *In Cold Blood*, '67. Many other awards and nominations, among them Grammies for *Walking In Space*, as best jazz performance by a large group, '69; *Smackwater Jack*, best instrumental, pop, rock or folk performance, '72; *Summer in the City*, best instrumental, '73. Other awards from Johnson Publ., DB Critics Poll. Billboard, Dutch Edison award for *Walking In Space*, '69; Antonio Carlos Jobim Award for best arranger, Brasil International Song Festival, '67.

After many years in the studios, Jones emerged to make intermittent personal appearances, sometimes with Roberta Flack, also on his own, leading an orchestra with vocal group. His music gradually became more concerned with the use of electronics and with the incorporation of r & b and soul elements. In '74 his album *Body Heat* was designated a gold record, representing sales of over $1,000,000.

In the fall of '74 Jones suffered two brain aneurisms. Two serious operations kept him on the sidelines until March '75, when he reassembled an orchestra and toured Japan.

Jones and his friend Ray Charles, whom he had known since they were both teenagers in Seattle, in '71 brought to reality a longstanding ambition as Jones introduced an orchestral piece, *Black Requiem*, showing the struggle of blacks in the U.S. from the days of the slave ships into the late 20th century. The work was performed with the Houston Symph. Orch., Ray Charles and an 80 voice choir.

LPs: *Gula Matari; Body Heat; You've Got It Bad Girl; Smackwater Jack; Walking In Space* (A & M); *Great Wide World; Live at Newport 1961* (Trip); *Mode* (ABC); *Quintessence* (Imp.); film scores *For Love of Ivy* (ABC); *In Cold Blood* (Colgems); *In The Heat of the Night* (UA).

JONES, ISHAM RUSSELL II (RUSTY), *drums*; b. Cedar Rapids, Iowa, 4/13/32. Greatnephew and godson of bandleader Isham Jones. Parents both were pro. musicians. Stud. at U. of Iowa, '60-5. While in school pl. w. J.R. Monterose. In Chicago w. pianist Judy Roberts, '68-72. Joined Geo. Shearing quintet Jan. '72 and remained with him through '75. Also pl. brief stints w. L. Konitz, M. Allison, Monty Alexander, Ike Cole, Eddie Higgins.

LPs: w. Shearing, *As Requested* (Sheba); *The Way We Are; Continental Experience* (MPS); *Get Off In Chicago* w. Judy Roberts (Ovation); *Quartescence*, w. Warren Chiasson (Van-Los Music, Canada).

JONES, SALENA (Joan Shaw),* *singer, songwriter*; b. Newport News, Va., 1/29/30. Well known under the name of Joan Shaw in r & b, pop and jazz circles in U.S. from late '40s until mid '60s, when she moved to England, changing her name to Salena Jones. In Britain and on the continent she enjoyed fuller acceptance as a jazz artist. Pl. Birmingham, England JF; Jazz at the Maltings, '68; winner of song fests. at Knocke, '70, representing America, and at Gmunden, Austria, rep. Britain, '72. Star guest at Golden Orpheus Song Fest., Bulgaria, '73; concert at Royal Albert Hall, London, '75. TV: many programs for BBC and ITV, incl. *Variety Artist of the Year; Jazz At The Mill*; George Melly show; Les Dawson show etc.

LPs: none available in U.S. except one track on *Singin' The Blues* (MCA); in Europe, *The Moment of Truth; Everybody's Talkin' About Salena Jones; Platinum* (CBS); *Alone & Together; This & That* (RCA).

JONES, SAMUEL (SAM),* *bass, cello, composer*; b. Jacksonville, Fla., 11/12/24. Played w. C. Adderley; D. Gillespie; T. Monk in '50s. Rejoined Adderley in late '59 and remained w. him until early '66 when he replaced Ray Brown in the Oscar Peterson trio. World tours w. Peterson incl. JATP. Left in '69 to settle in NYC. Gigs w. B. Timmons; W. Kelly in early '70s; Thad Jones-Mel Lewis quintet. With Bass Choir from '69; Cedar Walton trio and quartet from '71. Many TV apps. w. Peterson; Bass Choir; C. Terry. Fest: NJF-NY; major European events. Won a Musician of the Year award in Copenhagen, '69. Comp: *Seven Minds; Blues For Amos; Miss Morgan; In Walked Ray; Unit 7; Lillie; Del Sassar*. Excellent accompanist with strongly walking lines full of apt, powerfully resilient notes; adept soloist on both bass and cello. Own LP: *Cello, Again* (Xanadu); LPs: w. Peterson, *The Greatest Jazz Concert in the World* (Pablo); *Mellow Mood; Motions & Emotions; The Way I Really Play* (MPS); w. C. Jordan, *Glass Bead Games* (Strata-East); w. S. Stitt, *Constellation; Tune Up* (Cobblestone); *The Champ; 12*; w. C. Walton, *A Night at Boomer's*, vols. 1&2; *Breakthrough* (Muse); w. C. McPherson, *Siku Ya Bibi*; w. M. Longo, *Matrix* (Main.); w. R. Garland, *Auf Wiedersehen* (MPS); w. L. Thompson, *I Offer You* (Groove Merchant); w. J. Heath (Xanadu).

JONES, WILMORE (SLICK),* *drums*; b. Roanoke, Va., 4/13/07. The former Fletcher Henderson, Fats Waller sideman was active in the New York area w. Scoville Brown, Eddie Durham in early and mid-'60s. He survived a serious illness in '64 to play again but died in NYC, 11/2/69.

JONES, THADDEUS JOSEPH (THAD),* *fluegelhorn, cornet, trumpet, composer, leader*; b. Pontiac, Mich., 3/28/23. With Count Basie '54-'63; Gerry Mulligan; George Russell, '64. Wrote for Harry James, Basie in '60s. In '65 formed a quintet w. Pepper Adams and in December put together an orchestra with Mel Lewis made up of some of the best New York-based jazzmen, ones who were mainly employed as busy studio players, much in demand in the then, very busy NY recording scene. Although the band had, and continues to have fun, its intent from the beginning was serious in the sense that it was not planned as merely a rehearsal outfit designed to meet once a week to let its members get their kicks. It did meet once a week—Monday night at the Village Vanguard to be specific—and soon acquired a loyal following which packed the club each time it appeared. Recordings widened the audience and the Jones-Lewis orch. began to play college dates and fests. out of NYC. Eventually it graduated to extended engagements, both at the Vanguard and in California; five European and three Japanese tours; one to USSR, '72.

The early personnel included Adams, Jerome Richardson, Jerry Dodgion, Joe Farrell and Eddie Daniels, reeds; Richard Williams, Snooky Young, Jimmy Nottingham and Marvin Stamm, trumpets; Bob Brookmeyer, Garnett Brown, Tom McIntosh, Cliff Heather, trombones; Hank Jones, piano; Richard Davis, bass; and Sam Herman, guitar. Roland Hanna took over the piano bench by the band's second album and remained until '74; Eddie Bert was in the trombone section for several years and so was Quentin Jackson until he became ill in '75. Seldon Powell and Frank Foster were heard on tenor sax.

In '75 veterans Dodgion, Adams, Heather and trombonist Jimmy Knepper were still aboard along with players such as Jon Faddis, Cecil Bridgewater, trumpets; Janice Robinson, Bill Campbell, trombones; Billy Harper, Ron Bridgewater, Ed Xiques, reeds; Walter Norris, piano; and George Mraz, bass. Dee Dee Bridgewater was the featured vocalist in the '70s until Juanita Fleming replaced her in '75.

Although writers like Garnett Brown, Tom McIntosh and, particularly, Brookmeyer, helped build the book in the band's first years, the majority of the charts are originals by Jones, an extremely personal writer and a master of subtle voicings who uses flutes, reeds and muted brass ingeniously. "I try to write for each individual and think of the musicians personally," says Jones. "You have to gear your writing to two different people and still retain your overall technical sound."

Jones leads the band, interspersing his piquant, harmonically rich fluegelhorn solos among the arranged segments to advantage. Miles Davis once said, "I'd rather hear Thad Jones miss a note than hear Freddie Hubbard make twelve." In between the orchestra's engagements, Jones and Lewis sometimes lead a small group for gigs in the NYC area.

TV: stereo simulcast produced by KCET on Channel

28 and KBCA-FM in LA, '75.

Jones won DB Critics poll as arranger, TDWR, '67. Jones-Lewis Orch. won DB Critics poll, TDWR, '66; best band, '74-5; DB Readers poll, '72-5; *Playboy* All Stars' All Stars, '75.

Comp: *Mean What You Say; Bossa Nova Ova; No Refill; Once Around; Three and One; Don't Ever Leave Me; Little Pixie; Don't Git Sassy; Mornin' Reverend; Kids Are Pretty People; The Waltz You "Swang" For Me; Say It Softly; The Second Race; 61st and Rich' It; Forever Lasting; Love to One; Greetings and Salutations; Fingers; A Child is Born; Dedication; Us; Tiptoe; It Only Happens Every Time; Ahunk Ahunk; Consummation; Tow Away Zone; Quietude; Big Dipper; Central Park North; Suite For Pops; Yours and Mine; Quiet Lady; Blues in a Minute; All My Yesterdays.* LPs: w. Jones-Lewis, *Potpourri* (Phila. Int.); *Suite For Pops* (Horizon); *Consummation* (BN); *Central Park North; Monday Night; Live at the Village Vanguard; Presenting* (SS); *Thad Jones-Mel Lewis,* double-album reissue of material from above LPs (BN); Thad Jones-Pepper Adams, *Mean What You Say* (Mile.); Thad Jones w. Swedish Radiojazz Group, *Greetings and Salutations* (Four Leaf Clover); w. Dexter Gordon (Prest.); Kenny Burrell (Fant.).

JORDAN, CLIFFORD LACONIA,* *tenor sax;* also *piano, flute;* b. Chicago, Ill., 9/2/31. To NYC from Chicago in late '50s, working w. Horace Silver; in '60s w. K. Dorham; M. Roach; Mingus. Toured Europe as soloist and cond. own music for radio and studio orchs there, '66; toured West Africa and Middle East for US State Dept., '67. In '68 formed Frontier Records; rec. Wilbur Ware, Pharoah Sanders, Cecil Payne, Charles Brackeen, Ed Blackwell and their gps. Moved to Europe, '69, pl. there and in Africa during that yr. Returned to US, '70, and led own gp. in clubs. Completed prod. of '68 recs. and released them in the Dolphy Series on Strata-East label. In the '70s he cont. to lead his own gp.; also gigs w. Cedar Walton trio. Toured Western Europe, Scandinavia; NYC public school concerts, '75. Taught reed instrs., flute and cond. bands for Jazzmobile School; participated in lecture-concert series in NYC public schools for Jazz Interactions. Music consultant for MUSE, '67; Mus. Dir. of first Dancemobile, '68. Faculty member at Henry St. Settlement. Played the role of Lester Young in *Lady Day: A Musical Tragedy* at Brooklyn Acad. of Mus., '72. TV: *Jazz Adventures,* '75. Fest: NJF, '73. Won award from *Art Direction* magazine for album cover design, '74. Does portrait photography of musicians. Comps: *Prayer to the People; The Highest Mountain; Vienna.* Writing music for animated TV feature, *Sofro's Great Adventure.* LPs: *Firm Roots* (Steeple.); *Night of the Mark IIV; A Night at Boomer's, Vol. 1&2* (Muse); *In the World; Glass Bead Games* (Strata-East); reissue material on *Blowing Sessions* (BN).

JORDAN, IRVING SIDNEY (DUKE),* *piano, composer;* b. Brooklyn, N.Y., 4/1/22. Played w. Charlie Parker quintet in '40s; Stan Getz quintet in '50s. In '70s occupied mostly w. duo gigs at a variety of NY area clubs such as Gerald's; Bradley's; Golden Fleece; and Churchill's. Toured in Norway, Denmark, Sweden and Holland, '73 and '74. Pl. concert w. Al Haig in Belgium, '74. Concert w. own quintet at Cami Hall, NYC, '75. One of the most individual of the pianists to come out of the bebop era. In a time when most were overwhelmed by Bud Powell, he stood out with his own touch and rhythmic attack while working in a similar harmonic area. An excellent accompanist and a master at introductions. TV: Sweden. Comp: *Jordu,* which has become a jazz standard; *No Problem; Flight to Jordan; Two Loves; Tall Grass; Flight to Denmark; Lady Dingbat; Night Train From Snekkersten; Do You Want to Be Wu'tless; Subway Inn; 32nd Street Love.* LPs: *Flight to Denmark; Two Loves* (Steeple.); *Murray Hill Caper* (Spotlite); *Brooklyn Brothers* w. Cecil Payne (Muse); *Jordu* (Prest.); w. Clark Terry (Vang.); S. Stitt (Muse); Charles McPherson (Xanadu); Reissues w. C. Parker (Spotlite).

JORDAN, KEVIN, *trumpet;* b. Chicago, Ill., 2/26/51. Entire family active in gospel music. Stud. at high school and coll. in Chicago. BME from Northwestern U., '73; also stud. w. D. Byrd, '73; Bunky Green, '73-4, and pl. w. Green summer of '73 in Montreux. Traveled w. S. Kenton orch. Jan. '74- . Jordan names Green as his greatest insp. but was also infl. by Clifford Brown, D. Gillespie, F. Hubbard.

LPs: w. Kenton, *Chicago; Fire, Fury and Fun* (Creative World).

JORDAN, LOUIS,* *singer, alto saxophone;* b. Brinkley, Ark., 7/8/08. One of the first outstanding musicians to gain popularity as an entertainer and r & b personality, Jordan continued working intermittently, living in LA and leading a new version of his Tympany Five combo until Oct. '74, when he was sidelined by a heart attack while working in Sparks, Nev. He died 2/4/75 in his LA home after suffering a second attack.

Some of Jordan's world-renowned hit recordings were incorporated into an album of new interpretations, made for the Blues Spectrum label two years before his death. Among them were *Choo-Choo-Ch'Boogie; Caldonia; Let The Good Times Roll; Saturday Night Fish Fry; Ain't Nobody Here But Us Chickens; I'm Gonna Move to the Outskirts of Town.* Jordan rec. a similar album, using some different songs, for the Black and Blue label during a visit to France in Nov. '73. The orig. versions of many of his best recordings, made in the '40s and early '50s, were reissued in a two-pocket LP on MCA 2-4079. App. at NJF-NY, '74.

JORDAN, SHEILA (Sheila Dawson),* *singer;* b. Detroit, Mich., 11/18/29. Stud. piano '40-1; harmony and theory w. L. Tristano, '51-2. Sang during school years; later, strongly infl. by C. Parker, she was part of a trio that made up words for many of Parker's tunes. During '50s she was married to pianist Duke Jordan. Discovered by George Russell, she made her first LP in '63. Won DB Critics Poll, TDWR, '63. Pl. NYC clubs, also records and concerts w. Russell. Toured Europe, '65-6, again '69-

70, appearing in many concerts, clubs, radio and TV shows. During '67-8, back in NYC, she perf. in concerts w. Don Heckman jazz group, rec. TV commercials etc. Starting '65, she perf. special worship services (jazz liturgies) at many churches and college chapels, also sang at Cornell, Princeton, N.Y.U. and many other univs.

In 1972 she did the sound track for CBS *Look Up and Live* prog., made apps. w. Lee Konitz, Roswell Rudd. Continued working w. Rudd off and on, '73-5. Artist-in-residence at City Coll., CUNY, '74, teaching course in jazz singing.

Better known in Europe than in the U.S., Jordan has been praised by critics for her flexibility, emotional projection and jazz feeling. LPs: *Portrait of Sheila* (Blue Note); *Flexible Flyer* w. Rudd (Arista); *Escalator Over The Hill* w. Carla Bley (JCOA); *Outer Thoughts* w. Russell (Mile.).

JORDAN, JAMES TAFT,* *trumpet, singer*; b. Florence, S.C., 2/15/15. Featured prominently w. Chick Webb in '30s; Ella Fitzgerald; Duke Ellington in '40s; Benny Goodman in '50s. Free-lancing in NYC from '60s. Pl. for Broadway musical, *Hello Dolly*. Took part in *Salute to Ella Fitzgerald* at NJF-NY '73; Louis Armstrong Tribute w. NYJRC, '74. Pl. once a week at West End Cafe w. Earle Warren, '75. LPs: in *Swing Today* series for Albert McCarthy (Eng. RCA); E. Fitzgerald at Newport (Col.).

JPJ QUARTET. see Jackson, Oliver; Johnson, Budd.

KAMINSKY, MAX,* *trumpet*; b. Brockton, Mass., 9/7/08. After pl. w. own gp. at Metropole, Eddie Condon's in mid-'60s, he app. often at Jimmy Ryan's in late-'60s. Visited London, '70. Subbing on Sundays for Roy Eldridge at Ryan's in mid-'70s. LP: *Max Kaminsky, USA, Meets Barrelhouse Jazz Band, Vienna* (Kurier).

KAMUCA, RICHARD (RICHIE),* *tenor, alto saxophone, flutes*; also *clarinet, oboe, English horn*; b. Philadelphia, Pa., 7/23/30. Pl. w. S. Kenton, W. Herman, M. Ferguson, '50s; Shelly Manne in Hollywood, '60-1, then spent nine years in NYC. Worked with R. Eldridge quintet, '66-71, also w. G. McFarland, G. Mulligan band, Z. Sims-Al Cohn, J. Rushing.

Returned to LA in '72, as member of Merv Griffin TV show orch. Became active again in local jazz circles app. w. B. Berry LA Big Band, occasionally led combos at jazz concerts and co-led quintet w. Blue Mitchell in '75. Visited NYC, briefly, to play w. Lee Konitz, spring '75.

LPs: w. G. McFarland (Impulse); S. Manne (Contemporary); Bill Berry (Beez).

KAROLAK, WOJCIECH, *organ, piano*; b. Warsaw, Poland, 5/28/39. Professional debut, '58, pl. saxophone w. Jazz Believers; later switched to piano w. J. Matuszkiewicz quintet. Led own trio from '62, backing most foreign artists who visited Poland during next three years. Lived in Sweden from '66-72, pl. dance music. Returning

to jazz, as organist, freelanced around Europe, pl. w. Red Mitchell, Putte Wickman, drummer Leroy Lowe and others. In Dec. '72 he moved to Switzerland, joined Michal Urbaniak's Constellation; pl. clubs, fests. in West Germany, Scandinavia, Beleluk countries. After a year returned to Poland to form cooperative trio. In '74 went to U.S. to work w. Urbaniak's new group, Fusion. Back in Poland, co-led a group, Mainstream, w. J.P. Wroblewski. Member of Polish Radio Studio Jazz Orch. as soloist and composer-arranger. Infls: Ch. Parker, Ellington, Miles Davis, Gil Evans. Fav. organist: Larry Young. Fests: Newport-NY, '74; Cascais, '74 w. Z. Namyslowski; numerous others throughout Europe, incl. Jazz Jamboree in Warsaw, from '58. Publ: *Jazz Comps, for Piano* (Polish Music Publ. Co., Cracow, Poland).

LPs: *The Karolak Trio* (Muza); *Moving South* (Record Club of a Polish Jazz Soc'y.); *Easy!*; *Mainstream* (Polskie Nagrania/Polish Recording Company); others w. Don Ellis, Annie Ross, Urbaniak, Wickman et al.

KATZ, RICHARD AARON (DICK),* *piano, composer, producer*; b. Baltimore, Md., 3/13/24. Pl. w. O. Pettiford; K. Dorham; J.J. Johnson-Kai Winding in '50s; Philly Joe Jones; Orch. USA; Helen Merrill in '60s. In '66 freelanced w. Roy Eldridge; Bobby Hackett; founded Milestone Records w. Orrin Keepnews. From '67-71 worked at Milestone as producer and/or A&R man; cont. to free-lance as pianist. Left Milestone to return to full-time play., although he prod. two Jim Hall albums for the company: worked w. Lee Konitz quintet, '72. In July '73 joined R. Eldridge sextet at Jimmy Ryan's and has pl. w. him there from that time. Toured Japan w. Konitz under NJF aegis, '73. Pl. w. Konitz trio at Gregory's, '74-5; toured Europe w. Konitz-Kai Winding quintet, '74.

Taught jazz history course at New School for Social Research, '73-4. TV: CBS News at opening of Saxophone exhibit at Jazz Museum, NYC, March '74 w. Budd Johnson, Kenny Davern, Sonny Stitt, etc.; Berlin JF w. Konitz-Winding, Oct. '74. Other fest: NJF-NY w. Konitz, '73-4; w. Teo Macero all star saxophone ensemble, '74.

Wrote essay on Art Tatum for booklet acc. *Smithsonian Collection of Classic Jazz*; liner notes for Milestone; Atl. Comp: *Checkerboard; Second Thoughts; Something to Sing; Peacemeal*. Wrote many arrs. for Helen Merrill and all star group. LPs: w. Merrill, *The Feeling is Mutual; A Shade of Difference*; w. Konitz, *Lee Konitz Duets; Peacemeal; Satori* (Mile.). Katz also produced these albums.

KAWASAKI, RYO, *guitar, composer*; also *piano, electric bass*; b. Tokyo, Japan, 2/25/47. Grandfather renowned as a genius of the Japanese bamboo flute. Self-taught. Before coming to the U.S. in '73 he had his own group for more than five years and also was active in studio work. He has since pl. w. Gil Evans, Chico Hamilton, Howard Johnson's Substructure, Joe Lee Wilson, Cedar Walton, Grady Tate, Horacee Arnold, Archie Shepp, and

Tarika Blue. Own duo at Sweet Basil, July '75. Infls: Wes Montgomery, K. Burrell, Jim Hall, J. Hendrix, Mike Bloomfield, Miles Davis, Coltrane, Gil Evans. Designed and constructed his own synthesizer, Feb. '75, which he uses for unusual effects as contrast with a very swift, driving single line. Comps: *Agana; Joni; Nogie; Sweet Tears.* LPs: *Prism* (Easy Wind); *Gil Evans Plays the Music of Jimi Hendrix; There Comes a Time* w. Evans; *Mobius* w. Walton (RCA).

KAY, CONNIE,* *drums*; b. Tuckahoe, N.Y., 4/27/27. With MJQ from '55 until its disbandment in '74. A tasteful drummer, subtle yet authoritative, also noted in the MJQ for his use of triangles and other percussive accouterments. From '74 free-lancing in NYC. Worked w. Balaban & Cats at Eddie Condon's, fall '75. LPs: w. MJQ (Atl., Little David); w. Paul Desmond, *Pure Desmond* (CTI); w. B. Wilber-K. Davern, *Soprano Summit* (World Jazz).

KAYE, CAROL (**Carol Louise Smith**), *electric bass*; also *guitar, mandolin, bass guitar, banjo, composer*; b. Everett, Wash., 3/24/35. Father was dixieland trombonist; mother, pianist, still playing at 81. Stud. guitar for four months in '48, but says "I've been an active teacher and player ever since." Switched to electric bass in '65. During '50s pl. w. Henry Busse, The Saints, Hampton Hawes, B. Collette, Curtis Counce, H.B. Barnum, O. Coleman. Throughout '60s was in increasing demand for studio work with hundreds of pop, jazz and rock artists. Her full, clear sound and exceptional technique were occasionally heard in strict jazz settings. In '74 she co-led a trio w. Hawes. Later formed her own somewhat more rock-oriented group, Smoke Company, w. drummer Spider Webb. Insp. by C. Christian, B. Kessel, Miles Davis, Jamie Jamison, Ray Brown.

For several years Kaye has had her own very successful publ. company, printing instruction books and folios written by numerous well known musicians, on virtually all instruments.

Publs: *How To Play Electric Bass; Electric Bass Lines No's. 1, 2, 3, 4, 5; Personally Yours; Carol Kaye Electric Bass Cassette Course (Gwyn Publ. Co. Inc., 14950 Delano St. Van Nuys, Ca. 91601).*

LPs: w. Hawes, *Northern Windows* (Pres.); w. G. Ammons, *Brasswind* (Pres.).

KEEPNEWS, ORRIN, *record producer*; b. New York City, 3/2/23. Graduated Columbia College '43; Air Force '43-45. A fan and record collector; first pro. involvement with jazz in '48 as editor and writer for *The Record Changer*, published by his college classmate Bill Grauer. The two produced a 10-inch LP reissue series for Victor's "Label X" ('52-'53); founded Riverside Records in '53 with reissue rights to '20s Paramount and Gennett sides (Armstrong, Morton, Oliver, Beiderbecke, Ma Rainey, etc.). First artist he produced was Randy Weston in '54. Riverside rose to prominence with signing of Thelonious Monk in '55. Grauer became business head, with Keepnews as jazz producer. (He also wrote countless liner notes for the label's voluminous album output; wrote for magazines; collaborated with Grauer on *A Pic-*

torial History of Jazz.) Launched the recording careers of Bill Evans, Wes Montgomery and others, and worked closely with Cannonball Adderley, Monk, Sonny Rollins, many others. When business problems led to bankruptcy of Riverside in mid-'64, following the death of Grauer in Dec. '63, he free-lanced for a while, then established Milestone Records in '66, eventually signing Rollins, McCoy Tyner, Joe Henderson, Lee Konitz, Gary Bartz. In Oct. '72 joined what is now Fantasy/Prestige/Milestone Records, which later also acquired rights to Riverside masters, making him (as v.p. and director of jazz A&R) "one of the very few to last long enough to reissue material I produced in the first place." Considers his major achievement to be "constant association with and contributing to the careers of more than a few true musical geniuses—Monk, Evans, Montgomery, Rollins, Tyner, and many others—and to still be at it in a multi-track electronic era that is a long way from the monaural studios I started in."

KELLAWAY, ROGER,* *piano, composer*; also *bass*; b. Waban, Mass., 11/1/39. After extensive experience as pianist, bassist, composer in NYC, where he worked with every type of group from dixieland to contemporary, Kellaway settled in LA in '66, where he spent nine months with the Don Ellis band. Mus. Dir. for Bobby Darin, '67-9. Scored first feat. film, *The Paper Lion*, '68. Pl. w. LA Neophonic, Apr. '68.

In '69 Kellaway began writing for the cello quartet, a unique group feat. the classical cellist Edgar Lustgarten, with which he appeared in occasional concerts. He was also associated off and on for several years w. Tom Scott, Howard Roberts, Chuck Domanico and John Guerin in small combo jazz work. In '70 he orchestrated *Beaux J. Poo Boo* for L. McCann and the Cincinnati Symph. Wrote ballet commissioned by George Balanchine and the NYC Ballet Co., and premiered in '71. Comp. *Remembering You*, the closing theme for *All In The Family* TV series, '71, and in '72 played, arr. and co-produced the album on which the star of that series, Carroll O'Connor, recorded the song.

The year '73 saw the first rec. of a classical comp. by Kellaway, *Esque*, for trombone and double bass; rec. dates w. G. Mulligan, Tom Scott and others and an app. with the cello quartet at the Ojai Festival. The following year he toured for four months w. Joni Mitchell and T. Scott's LA Express, throughout U.S., Canada, England. In '75 he wrote arrs. for *Supersax Plays Bird with Strings* album; prod., cond. and arr. for C. McRae's first Blue Note album, *I Am Music.*

Kellaway, who from '72 appeared annually at Dick Gibson's Jazz Parties in Colorado Springs, has shown continual growth in the many areas with which he has found time to become associated, in every facet of jazz, pop and classical music. Since his first solo album, *Stride*, recorded in '66, he has demonstrated the capacity for extraordinary excitement combined with phenomenal technique and great sensitivity. As a composer he is best represented in the unique cello quartet albums, which include such original works as *Jorjana #2; Jorjana #7;*

Jorjana #8; Esque; Morning Song; Ballade; Come to the Meadow; Invasion of the Forest; On Your Mark Get Set Blues.

Fests: Ojai, '73; Concord, w. Ellis, '74; Hawaii, w. cello quartet, '75.

LPs: *Center of the Circle; Cello Quartet; Come To The Meadow* (A & M); *Spirit Feel* (Pac. Jazz); *A Jazz Portrait* (Regina); *The Trio* (Prest.); w. S. Rollins, *Music From Alfie*; w. Tom Scott, *Hair to Jazz* (Imp.); w. Melanie, *Born To Be* (Buddah); *Gather Me; Stone Ground Words* (Neighborhood); w. Scott, *Great Scott*; w. G. Mulligan, *Age of Steam*; also w. Baja Marimba Band and other artists (A & M); w. Maria Muldaur, *Waitress in a Donut Shop* (WB); w. Geo. Harrison (Dark Horse).

KELLY, WYNTON,* *piano, composer*; b. Brooklyn, N.Y., 12/2/31. Came to prominence in early '50s w. L. Young, D. Gillespie. Worked w. Miles Davis, '59-63. His trio backed W. Montgomery in person and on records. Later he worked in clubs in NYC, also w. R. Nance quartet. Kelly died 4/12/71 in Toronto, Canada, probably of an epileptic seizure.

Bill Evans said of Kelly: "When I heard him in Dizzy's big band, his whole thing was so joyful and exuberant; nothing about it seemed calculated. And yet, with the clarity of the way he played, you know he had to put this together in a very carefully planned way—but the result was completely without calculation, there was just pure spirit shining through the conception."

LPs: *Full View; Keep It Movin'* (Mile.); *Smokin'* (Trip); w. Dexter Gordon, *The Jumpin' Blues* (Prest.); w. Cecil Payne, *Zodiac* (St.-East); w. Clark Terry, *Cruising* (Mile.); Davis (Col.); Montgomery (Verve).

KELTNER, JIMMIE LEE (JIM), *drums*; also *trumpet*; b. Tulsa, Okla., 4/27/42. Stud. briefly w. Ch. Westgate in Tulsa at age 13, and w. Forrest Clark of LA Philharmonic at age 19. Pl. w. Albert Stinson in Modern Jazz Proteges, '62; Clare Fischer, '64; D. Randi, '65; Afro-Blues Quintet, '66-7; Red Norvo, '66; G. Szabo, '66-70; John Handy, '67. The rest of his playing career has been primarily in the rock and roll area. Films: *Mad Dogs and Englishmen*, w. Joe Cocker, '70; *Concert for Bangla Desh*, '71.

Keltner says, "I'm just a rock and roll drummer who started out wanting to be a jazz musician, and quit when I heard Tony Williams on *Seven Steps To Heaven*."

LP: w. Jack Bruce, *Out of the Storm* (RSO).

KENNEDY, JOSEPH J. JR. (JOE),* *violin, composer, educator*; b. Pittsburgh, Pa., 11/17/23. Ahmad Jamal's chief arr. in the early '60s, he participated in workshops and concerts at Hampton Inst., '68-9 and took part in the Artists Recital Series at Virginia State Coll., '71-2. In '73 Kennedy, who had been the chairman of the music dept. at Maggie L. Walker H.S. in Richmond, Va., was appointed as Supervisor of Music for the Richmond public school system and also as staff member of the Afro-American Studies Dept. at Virginia Commonwealth U. He became a National Board member of the American Youth Symph. and Chorus, '74, and a member of the Educational Committee of the WJA, '75. Comps: *The Fan-*

tastic Vehicle; Illusions Opticas; Dialogue for Flute, Cello and Piano. The latter work was premiered by the Trio Pro Viva and feat. at Fisk U. Arts Fest., '73, and Minnesota Black Composers Symposium, '75. Wrote arrs. for *downbeat* Music Workshop Pub., '70-1. He cont. to pl. w. the Richmond Symph. but has not done any jazz rec. since '65.

KENTON, STANLEY NEWCOMB (STAN),* *leader, composer, piano*; b. Wichita, Kan., 2/19/12. Cal. based bandleader since '41. Became active in jazz educ., '59. Winner of many awards as number one bandleader and for his albums *West Side Story* and *Adventures in Jazz*, both of which won Grammies. Organized series of concerts w. LA Neophonic Orch. at LA Music Center, '65-6. Also in '66 app. as guest conductor of the Danish Radio Orch. in Copenhagen; organized first Kenton clinic for music students at Redlands U., Cal. Estab. Creative World Music Publications to make the Kenton library available to schools.

In '67 Kenton appeared at the Senate Sub-Committee hearings in an attempt to secure revision of music copyright laws. The band toured during the summer and he lectured at major univs., judged at many music fests. Pl. third Neophonic season in '68.

In '70 Kenton estab. Creative World Records as direct mail outlet for Kenton recs., and subsequently for those of many other jazz artists. His band continued to tour. He was sidelined by a serious illness in '71 and again in '72, but the band pl. various engagements under the direction of others.

In '71 Kenton set up a Jazz Orchestra In Residence prog., taking his band to schools for periods ranging from one day to one week. By '75 he was conducting at least 100 clinics annually, as well as four week-long summer clinics on coll. campuses. From '72-5 the band toured Europe and Japan. Kenton app. at NJF-NY, '72, '74, '75. The band was at Monterey JF (during Kenton's illness; it was conducted by arr. Ken Hanna). Honors: Doctorate of Music awarded by Villanova U., '67; Doctorate of Humane Letters, Drury Coll., '74. Named Jazz Band of the Year by Society for the Appreciation of Big Bands, '74.

The Crusade For Jazz, an hour long TV spec., prod. by Kenton in '68, has been widely used. *The Substance of Jazz*, a film designed for educ. was prod. in '69. Kenton also has made many TV apps. as guest on talk shows. Despite many economic reverses due to conditions affecting all big bands, Kenton in the mid '70s still led an ensemble that had a loyal int'l following. Though he has experimented with various instrumentations, the band's basic sound has remained substantially the same in recent years, with arrs. by Hank Levy, Hanna, Bob Curnow. Usually feat. a 10 man brass section, in which five trombones keynote the band's style with their somber sonorities, Kenton has maintained an effective balance between old favorites from his repertoire from the '40s and '50s, and original material, some of it using 5/4 and other meters, some employing Afro-Cuban variations of old numbers such as the original theme *Artistry In Rhythm*, all pl. with a high, spirited bravura.

Publ: *Kenton Straight Ahead* by Carol Easton (William Morrow & Co., N.Y., '73). In addition to providing a well researched history of the Kenton bands through the years, this is a frank and penetrating examination of Kenton as musician, leader and human being.

LPs: Much of the entire recorded output of the various Kenton orchs. has been reissued on the Creative World Label (1012 S. Robertson Blvd., Los Angeles, Ca. 90035). Among the best of his more recent works, Kenton cites: *Live at Redlands University; Live at Brigham Young Univ.; Live at Butler Univ.; National Anthems of the World; Birthday In Britain; 7.5 On The Richter Scale; Solo: Stan Kenton Without His Orchestra; Stan Kenton Plays Chicago; Fire, Fury And Fun.*

KERR, BROOKS (Chester Brooks Kerr Jr.), *piano*; also *clarinet*; b. New Haven, Conn., 12/26/51. Studied piano from age seven, mostly self-taught until lessons w. Russell Repa in New Haven, '61-3. Further stud. in NYC w. Sanford Gold, '64-72; Willie "The Lion" Smith, '69-73; theory at Manhattan School of Music and Juilliard, '70-2; also summer stud. w. Phil Woods, Chris Swansen, Norm Grossman at Ramblerny, '67; w. Valerie Capers at Camp Usdan, '68. Own group at Dalton School, NYC, '66-70; solo piano at Don's East, '71, Vogue Cafe, '72. Led own combo at Churchill's, Feb. '73-April '74 w. shifting personnel incl. Ray Nance, Matthew Gee, Francis Williams, Paul Quinichette, Paul Gonsalves, Bob Mover, Sam Woodyard and vocalists Annie Hurewitz, Betty Roché; at West End Cafe w. similar trios, Jan.-July '74; trio w. Russell Procope and Sonny Greer at Gregory's from May '74. Pl. w. and assisted Duke Ellington at one-week seminar, Univ. of Wisc., July '72; duets w. Willie "The Lion" Smith at Village Gate, Jan. '73; solo at NJF-NY '73. Kerr, an extremely knowledgeable student of the Ellington repertoire, app. at birthday tributes to Duke at the New School '73, and Carnegie Hall w. the NYJRC, '74. He subbed for Duke in the Ellington orch. at the Third Concert of Sacred Music at Central Presbyterian Church, April '74. Infl: Armstrong, Willie "The Lion", Ellington, Tatum, James P. Johnson, Waller. Comp: *A Portrait of Johnny Hodges; Miss Linda; Pepsi Cola Time; A.C.; The Lion's Gait.* LPs: *Soda Fountain Rag*, a duo w. Greer (Chiaroscuro); *Prevue*, feat. Paul Quinichette (Famous Door).

KESSEL, BARNEY,* *guitar, composer*; b. Muskogee, Okla., 10/17/23. Worked w. name bands in early '40s; toured w. O. Peterson '52-3 and has occasionally reunited with him for recordings and concerts. Since late '50s mainly active as freelance studio musician, periodically returning to jazz. Cont. studio work until '68; then went w. Geo. Wein on European tour as member of "Guitar Workshop" w. J. Hall, Geo. Benson, L. Coryell, Elmer Snowden. In '69 moved to London, living there for 14 months, working all over England and continent. Returned to LA late '70, resumed studio work, and working w. own group, moving away from traditional style, experimenting with use of rock infls., but shortly abandoned group and concept. During '70 he began taking short trips all over U.S. and Europe, still continuing in studio work. Very little activity w. own gp., and began spending at least six months a year in Europe for TV, radio, seminars (some of which were sponsored by local gov'ts.), concerts, clubs, fests. Developed open end series of instruction books called *Barney Kessel Personal Manuscript Series*, incl. text as well as music (Publ: Windsor Music Co., P.O. Box 2629, Hollywood, Ca. 90028). TV: Pl. on *The Odd Couple; Love American Style.* Films: pl. on four Elvis Presley movies for Paramount. In '75 spent one month in S. Africa with own gp., also toured internationally as part of *Great Guitars* package. Fests: Concord, '73-4-5; Carnegie Hall, Kennedy Center w. *Great Guitars*, '74-5; Comps: *Swedish Pastry; Salute to Charlie Christian; Down in the Swamp; Sea Miner; From My Heart; Free Wheelin'.*

LPs: *Kessel's Kit; Reflections in Rome* (both rec. in Rome on RCA); three w. S. Grappelli (Polydor); one w. strings, incl. Kessel's arr. of *Nuages* (Phillips); guitar/bass duo w. Red Mitchell, *Two Way Conversation* (Sonet); *The Great Guitars; Barney Plays Kessel* (Concord Jazz); w. Venuti-Grappelli (Byg).

KEYS, CALVIN, *guitar, composer*; b. Omaha, Neb., 2/6/42. His uncle, blues singer St. Louis Jimmy, comp. *Goin' Down Slow.* Stud. at U. of Nebraska. Joined Preston Love in Omaha, '62. After working w. several Hammond organ trios, led by Frank Edwards, Jackie Ivory, Jackie Davis, Jack McDuff, Groove Holmes, Keys settled in LA. He attended LA School of Mus., pl. w. D. Byrd, Ch. Kynard and several singers incl. Gloria Lynne, Damita Jo.

Toured U.S. and Europe w. Ray Charles for a year, '73-4. Moving to SF, he led his own combos and pl. w. John Handy, B. Hutcherson, Johnny Hammond, H. Crawford. Worked w. A. Jamal briefly at Troubadour in LA, '73 and rejoined him on a permanent basis in Jan. '75.

An original and adventurous guitarist, Keys also has shown promise as a composer. Infls: W. Montgomery, K. Burrell, Grant Green, B. Kessel; also Ch. Parker, J. Coltrane et al. Comps: *Shaw-neeq; Gee-gee; BK; Aunt Lovey; Renaissance; Proceed with Caution.*

LPs: *Shaw-neeq; Proceed with Caution* (Black Jazz).

KIKUCHI, MASABUMI, *piano, composer*; b. Tokyo, Japan, 10/19/39. Began piano and theory study in April '45; ten yrs. later entered the comp. dept. of Senior H.S. attached to the Musicology Dept. of the Tokyo Univ. of Art. After grad. in March '58 made debut w. own trio. Pl. w. L. Hampton for concert tour, '62; gave first recital in Tokyo, '64; made tour of Japan w. S. Rollins, '68. In Sept. of that yr. he att. Berklee on a *down beat* scholarship, study. comp. w. Wm. Maroof; musicology and arr. w. Herb Pomeroy. Ret. to Japan and formed trio, later sextet, both w. bassist Gary Peacock, '69. Was guest pianist w. Woody Herman, '70; toured for a month w. Mal Waldron; acc. Joe Henderson, '71. In Jan. '72 he again visited the U.S., joining Elvin Jones, with whom he had pl. at the NJF '70, for four weeks of gigs in NYC & Toronto, and a rec. date. Pl. concerts in Tokyo w. Gil

Evans, McCoy Tyner; acc. Johnny Hartman on tour, '72. Recital, *Sayonara, Poo-sun*, Jan. '73 in Tokyo. Rejoined Elvin Jones in May '73, remaining w. him until Jan. '74, incl. So. Amer. tour for USIS. With Sonny Rollins, Boston, March '74. Concert tour in Japan, June-July '74 w. mixed Japanese-American gp. incl. Terumasa Hino, Joony Booth. Member of NYJRC in its first session. Won first place as pianist in *Swing Journal* readers poll, '68; jazzman of the year, '71; both these categories, combo, and record of the year, '72; best piano; jazzman of yr., '73. Two of his comps. pl. by G. Evans at Carn. Hall, Jan. '74. LPs: Japan Phonogram; Philips; w. E. Jones (BN).

KILLGO, KEITH, *drums, singer*; b. Baltimore, Md., 1/30/54. Began pl. drums at age 9; also stud. w. R. Flack for three years. After graduating from high school, attended Bradley U. in Peoria, Ill. where he majored in mus. theory. While attending Howard U. as mus. educ. major, pl. with such guest musicians as M. Davis, B. Timmons, S. Getz, Woody Shaw, J. Henderson, Rollins. In '73 he became founder member of the Blackbyrds, a coll. group sponsored by D. Byrd. Killgo was feat. as lead singer and drummer. Comp: *Love Is Love*. LPs: *Flying Start; The Blackbyrds* (Fantasy).

KING, RILEY B. (B.B.),* *guitar, singer*; b. Itta Bena, Miss., 9/16/25. The advent of rock which brought about a new interest in and awareness of blues by white audiences gave new popularity to King. He appeared at major pop fests. in US and Canada and played many dates at large colls. during '68-9. In November of that year his band made a 14-city tour of the US w. the Rolling Stones. In the '70s he has made apps. on a world wide basis, playing at both jazz and pop fests.; Las Vegas hotels; and rec. commercials for large corps. and manufacturers. Moved to Las Vegas, '75.

"Thousands of people came to the Rolling Stones concert and discovered B.B. King," wrote Ralph J. Gleason. "They joined the thousands of others led to his music by his disciples, by Mike Bloomfield and Eric Clapton, by Elvin Bishop, and a host of other guitarists whose inspiration and main influence B.B. King has been. All the guitar players in town pay homage to the master of the blues guitar."

Won as Best Blues Instrumentalist; Best Blues Male Singer; and Best Blues Album, *To Know You Is to Love You* (ABC), in *Ebony Magazine* poll, '75. LPs: ABC; Bluesway; one track each in *Newport in New York '72, The Soul Sessions, Vol. 6; Jimmy Smith Jam, Vol. 5* (Cobble.).

KING, FREDDIE, *singer, guitar*; b. Longview, Tex., 9/30/34. Family moved to Chicago in '50, where he worked in local taverns and was associated with the harmonica player and singer, Little Sonny Cooper. Began rec. in '56 for a small independent company; made his first major session for King Records Aug. '60. A guitar solo entitled *Hide Away* became a typical Chicago blues hit in '68. King also made numerous sessions w. pianist Sonny Thompson.

LP: *Burglar* (RSO).

KING, MORGANA,* *singer, actress*; b. Pleasantville, N.Y., 6/4/30. Continued to play supper clubs such as the Maisonette, NYC, but also app. in the motion pictures *The Godfather; The Godfather II*. LPs: Reprise; Main.; Trip.

KIRK, RAHSAAN ROLAND,* *tenor sax*; also *manzello, flute, clarinet, strichophone, trumpet, composer*; b. Columbus, Ohio, 8/7/36. His new name, Rahsaan, came to him in a dream, just as the idea to play three instruments simultaneously had revealed itself previously. Kirk led his Vibration Society in clubs, concerts and festivals throughout the U.S., Canada, Europe, Australia and New Zealand. Fest. apps. incl. NJF, NO Jazz & Heritage, Berlin Jazz Days. He won the DB Critics' Poll, '72-3; DB Readers' Poll, '68, '71, '74; *Playboy* Poll, '71, '73; *Playboy* All Stars' All Stars, '74. TV: *Soul*, '72; *Tempo*, BBC, London, '67. Comp: *Expansions; Saxophone Concerto; Volunteered Slavery; Bright Moments; Dem Red Beans and Rice; Carney and Bigard Place; Blacknuss; The Seeker; Baby, Let Me Shake Your Tree; Lady's Blues; The Inflated Tear; The Black and Crazy Blues*. Although his multi-horn forays, once skeptically viewed as gimmickry, are now taken for granted, Kirk is an amazing improviser, on one, two or three instruments, who embodies the entire spectrum of the music from early New Orleans roots through to the avant garde of the '70s.

In late '75 Kirk suffered a stroke which paralyzed his side. At the onset of his recuperation he began therapy to regain his essential dexterity. LPs: *The Case of the 3-Sided Dream in Audio Color; Bright Moments; Prepare Thyself to Deal With a Miracle; Blacknuss; Rahsaan, Rahsaan; Volunteered Slavery; Left and Right; The Inflated Tear; The Art of Roland Kirk; The Best of Roland Kirk; A Meeting of the Times* w. Al Hibbler; *Mingus At Carnegie Hall* (Atlantic); *The Jaki Byard Experience* (Prest.); reissues: *Kirk in Copenhagen; Domino; We Free Kings* (Trip); *Newport in New York, The Jam Sessions, Vols. 3&4* (Cobble.).

KITAMURA, EIJI, *clarinet, bass clarinet, soprano, alto, tenor saxophones*; b. Tokyo, Japan, 4/8/29. Self-taught. Pl. w. Saburo Nanbu, '51-3; own Cats Herd group, '54-7; Mitsuru Ono & His Six Brothers, '57-60. Led own quintet '60- . From '59 was annual winner of *Swing Journal* readers' poll as number one clarinetist. Infls: B. Goodman, T. Wilson, E. Hines. From '68, Kitamura pl. in the house band of NET-TV *Morning Show*.

LPs: *Operation Benny Goodman*, w. Sharps & Flats (King); *Swingin' Clarinet*, E. Kitamura Quintet (Gramophone); *Immortal Swing Jazz Spirits*, E. Kitamura & All Stars (Teichiku); *Teddy Wilson Meets Eiji Kitamura; Live Session Teddy & Eiji; Teddy Wilson/Eiji Kitamura Swing Special* (Trio); *Right-Oh*, Kitamura & Kazuo Yashiro (Audio Lab.).

KLATKA, ANTHONY J. (TONY), *trumpet, composer*; b. Southampton, England, 3/6/46. Began pl. prof. at age 11; stud. at Colo. St. Univ. '64-66; Berklee '71-3. Arrs. and trumpet for Wayne Cochran '67; Woody Herman '68-71. While at Berklee pl. in Boston w. many acts incl. Tony Bennett, Dionne Warwicke, 3 Degrees. W. Herman again, spring '73 until Feb. '74, when he joined Blood, Sweat & Tears. Infl: Mike Gibbs, Gil Evans, Ellington, Beethoven, Thad Jones, Miles Davis, Jack Sheldon, Coltrane, Clifford Brown, Chick Corea. Fest: w. Herman, Monterey '70, NJF-NY '73. Comp: *South Mountain Shuffle; Look Up; Thinking of You; She's Coming Home; Blues For Poland*; arrs. for Herman: *La Fiesta; Naima; Watermelon Man; Bass Folk Song*. LPs: w. Herman, *Woody* (Cadet); *Brand New; Thundering Herd* (Fant.); *Mirror Image* w. B,S,&T (Col.); *Ridin' High*, all writing by Klatka, w. Cochran & C.C. Riders (Chess).

KLEIN, MIRIAM, *singer*; b. Basel, Switzerland, 3/27/37. Became involved with jazz at age 16. An admirer of Bessie Smith, Billie Holiday, L. Young, Clifford Brown and Frankie Newton, she spent some time in Paris, where she was heard w. D. Byas and Art Simmons. On returning to Switzerland, she married trumpeter Oscar Klein; the next several years were given over to the birth and raising of four children. During this time she began singing again, working with her husband's group, '64-70. In early albums she sang blues and standards w. O. Klein and Albert Nicholas. Little was heard of her until June '73, when she recorded for MPS-BASF an album entitled *Lady Like*. Backed by R. Eldridge, D. Gordon, S. Hampton and others, she rec. some of B. Holiday's hits with a style and timbre amazingly like Holiday's. The album was provocative, some critics dismissing it as a second rate imitation, while others, incl. Eldridge and other musicians, were greatly impressed by the authenticity of Klein's recreations. Fests: Montreux; Heidelberg; Frankfurt; Munich; Zurich; Copenhagen.

KLEIN, OSCAR, *trumpet, guitar, composer*; b. Graz, Austria, 1/5/30. Self-taught. Insp. by Cootie Williams, Wild Bill Davison, R. Eldridge, and by guitarists Eddie Condon, Blind Blake, Lightnin' Hopkins. Pl. w. Fatty George band, '53-7; Tremble Kids, '58-60; Dutch Swing Coll. Band, '60-3. From '64 led various groups, also pl. w. Mezz Mezzrow, Wild Bill Davison, Albert Nicholas, M. Spanier, J. Venuti. In recent years active mainly as businessman, but still gigging, writing and teaching as a sideline. Married to singer Miriam Klein. TV series, *Pickin' The Blues*, '75. Fests: San Remo, Comblain La Tour, Frankfurt, Dortmund. Publ: *Pickin' The Blues*, finger style instruc. book (Caesar Perrig Editions, Basel).
  LPs: *Chicagoan All Stars; Hats Off Eddie Condon; Lady Like* (MPS); *Wild Capricorn*, w. Wild Bill Davison; *Pickin' The Blues* (Intercord).

KLEMMER, JOHN, *tenor, soprano saxes, flute, composer*; also *clarinet, piano*; b. Chicago, Ill., 7/3/46. Began on alto sax at age 11. Led concert and stage band in high school. Stud. at S. Kenton clinics, '60-5; priv. studies w. Joe Daley, '62-9; orchestration and film scoring w. Albert Harris in LA, '70-4. After working w. various bands and combos spanning dixieland, bebop and avant garde, began rec. at age 19. Two years later he moved to LA to join Don Ellis orch., with which he toured the east and west coasts and Europe. Rec. three albums w. Ellis, that feat. solo work and own arrs. During this time he also pl. w. O. Nelson in a State Dept. sponsored tour of French

West Africa in late '68, and rec. various albums w. Nelson.
  Signed w. ABC/Imp. Records in '70 and during this time became increasingly well known as a practitioner of jazz-rock and innovator in experiments with echo-plex, ring modulator, wah-wah attachments, which he considers to be an integral part of his saxophone sound. "These are not gimmicks," he has said, "but rather instruments in themselves. They are new tools of expression."
  Klemmer, many of whose scores have been publ., feels that writing and arranging are just as important to his development as playing the saxophone. One of his major ambitions is to become extensively involved in motion pic. scoring. Infls: Rollins, Coltrane, M. Davis, Debussy, Ravel. TV: *Dial M For Music; Live From Tanglewood*, both in '68 w. Ellis; *Featuring John Klemmer*, a half hour spec. on WTTW, Chicago, '68.
  Fests: Newport, Antibes, '68 w. Ellis; Monterey, '70, w. Ellis; Montreux as leader, '73. Comps: Klemmer has written material for all his albums, close to 100 works, among which are *My Love Has Butterfly Wings; Here Comes The Child; Prelude and Waterfalls*. Big band arrs. for Ellis: *The Old Man's Tear*; for B. Bryant, *The Beauty of Her Soul*. Publs: big band charts (Creative World Publs., 1012 Robertson Blvd., LA, Cal. 90048).
  LPs: *Involvement; And We Were Lovers; Blowin' Gold; All The Children Cried; Eruptions* (Cadet); *Constant Throb; Waterfalls; Intensity; Magic and Movement; Fresh Feathers*; (Impulse); *Don Ellis at Fillmore; Autumn*, w. Ellis; *Don Ellis Goes Underground* (Columbia); w. O. Nelson, *Soulful Brass; Black, Brown and Beautiful* (Fl. Dutchman); *Born in Mississippi*, w. J. Lee Hooker; *Swahili Strut*, w. B. Bryant (Chess).

KLOSS, ERIC, *saxophones, composer*; also *piano, drums*; b. Greenville, Pa., 4/3/49. Studied saxophone at Western Penn. School for Blind Children, '59-'67; w. Robert Koshan, Henry Marconi, Tom McKinley in Pittsburgh. Grad. cum laude from Duquesne U. with philosophy major, May '72. First pro. app. w. Bob Negri trio at age 12 in Pitts. and pl. there w. Negri at Three Rivers Art Fest., June '62. App. in concert w. Charles Bell at Pitt. Carnegie Music Hall, '62 and '63. Feat. w. Walt Harper during winters of '65, '66, '67. Made rec. debut '65 and has since led own groups; also clubs and concerts w. Pat Martino, Frank Cunimondo. Infls: C. Parker, O. Coleman, Dolphy, Coltrane, Bill Evans, Miles Davis. Many apps. on Pitts. TV, incl. documentary film on his life, '66. Fests: NJF-NY, '73; Pitts. JF. Comps: *In a Country Soul Garden; Sock It To Me Socrates; Cynara; Waves; Quasar; Libra; Licea; Affinity*. LPs: *Essence; One, Two, Free* (Muse); *Doors* (Cobble.); *Consciousness; To Hear Is to See; In the Land of the Giants; Sky Shadows; We're Going Up; Life Force; First Class Kloss; Grits and Gravy* (Prestige).

KNEPPER, JAMES M. (JIMMY),* *trombone*; also *bass trombone, baritone horn, composer*; b. Los Angeles, Ca., 11/22/27. Prominent w. Ch. Mingus, '57-61; USSR w. B. Goodman, '62. From mid-60s played in orchs. of many Broadway shows. Gigged and toured w. Thad

Jones-Mel Lewis orch., incl. USSR, Japan, Europe. Also pl. w. Gil Evans, L. Konitz, N.Y. Jazz Ensemble. Arr. & pl. w. Lee Konitz Nonet in NYC clubs, 1975. An exceptionally gifted soloist, he has been accorded insufficient recognition in jazz circles. Some of his best solos were on the Mingus album, *Tijuana Moods*, reissued on RCA in '75. Other LPs with Mingus (Atl., Col. etc.); G. Evans (Impulse); also see Jones-Lewis.

KOEHLER, TREVOR CURTIS, *baritone sax, composer*; also *soprano sax, flute*; b. Minneapolis, Minn., 7/9/36. Mother pl. country fiddle for square dances. Stud. trumpet, trombone and euphonium at Anchorage (Alaska) Junior high school; then tenor sax at Anchorage High, '50-4; tenor sax and composition at Cons. of Music, Coll. of the Pacific in Stockton, Ca., '54-7. Pl. w. Don Keller & the Blue Notes, '54-7; house band at Jimbo's Bop City in SF, an after-hours where visiting musicians came to sit-in. Took up baritone sax and pl. w. Billy Taylor, Arnett Cobb, Dizzy Gillespie, Hampton Hawes and Anita O'Day there, '57-8. With U.S. Army Band, Stanley Willis Jr. Duo, '58-9; Sonny Simmons sextet, Pharoah Sanders quartet, '60-1. Own groups and various gigs in Bay Area incl. Big Mama Thornton, '62-6. On the road, '66-8, w. Lionel Hampton in NO; midwest territory bands; Eddy Arnold in Tex.; Tenessee Ernie Ford in Little Rock. W. Insect Trust, an eclectic rock band based in NYC, '68-70. Also began working w. Gil Evans at this time. In the '70s continued w. Evans while also pl. w. Sam Rivers, Albert Dailey and on his own, before ending his life 2/26/75 in NYC. Infl: M. Davis, Coltrane, Ch. Parker, O. Coleman, Copland, Debussy. Fest: Memphis Country Blues Fest. '70; European fests., incl. Montreux, and NJF-NY w. Evans '72-4. Won Jazz & Pop poll '70; received a jazz composers' grant from National Endowment For the Arts '72. Comp: *Recourse & Night Flight* for Nat. Endow.; *Amadama; Train Won't Wait; Charlie Chaplin; Ducks; Glade Song.* LPs w. Evans: *Svengali* (Atl.), *Plays Jimi Hendrix* (RCA); *Insect Trust* (Cap.); *Hoboken Saturday Night* (Atco).

KOFFMAN, MOE,* *flute*; also *piccolo, saxophones, clarinets*; b. Toronto, Ontario, Canada, 1/28/28. Pl. w. big bands in U.S., '50-5, incl. Sonny Dunham, B. Morrow, J. Dorsey, C. Barnet, T. Beneke. Ret. to Toronto and rec. hit, *Swingin' Shepherd Blues*, '57. Own quintet for concerts, coll. dates. Mus. dir. and house group leader at George's Spaghetti House. Active as contractor for TV, rec., jingles, films. Group feat. at Expo '67; Maple Mus. Junket, Montreal, summer '72; Fest. Canada, '73; Belvedere "King-Size" JF, '74; Ontario Place Forum, '75. Koffman was guest soloist w. B. Goodman & Q. Jones at C.N.E. '73; w. W. Herman & D. Gillespie, C.N.E. '75; w. Toronto Symph. Apr. '75. TV: guest soloist w. Johnny Carson on six occas.; L. Hampton Special; *Playboy After Dark* tribute to Tony Bennett; mus. dir. for own show, *Everything Goes*, '74. LPs: *Plays Bach; Four Seasons; Master Sessions; Solar Explorations; Best of; Live at George's* (GRT); *Tales of Koffman* (UA).

KOIVISTOINEN, EERO, *saxophones, composer*; b. Helsinki, Finland, 1/13/46. Studied at Sibelius Academy;

Berklee Coll. of Mus. Own trio, '67-9; quartet, '69-71; co-led quartet w. Heikki Sarmanto, '71-3; own Music Society (quartet) from '73. Won Finnish Jazz Musician of the Year, '67. Received three-year State grant for Artists, '70. Infl: Ellington, Gil Evans, Coltrane. Led quartet at Montreux JF '69 and won international competition which led to app. at NJF the same year. LPs: *Odysseus; For Children* (Otava); *Third Version; Wahoo!* (RCA Victor).

KOLLER, HANS,* *tenor & soprano saxes*; also *clarinet, sopranino, alto & baritone saxes*; b. Vienna, Austria, 2/12/21. One of the leaders in post-World War II German jazz circles, he continued at the head of his own groups in the '60s and '70s. From '70 it has been called Hans Koller's Free Sound. Originally influenced by Lennie Tristano and Lee Konitz, he later was inspired by John Coltrane. Many apps. on German TV and at European Fests. Won Austrian jazz poll on tenor, soprano and for group, '72. Comp: *Blues Suite; Berlin Suite; Homage A Cocteau; Nicolas De Stael; Circle; Phoenix; Impressions of Vienna; Ulla M; Painter's Lament; Vision.* Publ: *Saxophon-Schule* (Solisten Verlag, Vienna). Since 1957 Koller has also been active as an abstract painter with exhibitions in West Germany, Austria and Paris. LPs: *Exclusiv; Zoller-Koller-Solal; Vision; Relax With My Horns; Phoenix; Kunstkopfindianer* (MPS/BASF).

KOMEDA, KRZYSZTOF (Krzysztof Trzcinski), *composer, piano*; b. Poznan, Poland, 4/27/31. Youngest student at the Poznan Conservatory; later took private piano lessons and stud. mus. theory. From '50 closely associated w. jazz; co-creator of the Polish jazz movement. Played w. own gp. as well as Moscow; Kongsberg; Bled; jazz clubs in Sweden and Denmark.

Composed for ballet, musical theater and films incl. directors such as Jerzy Skolimowski, Henning Carlsen and Roman Polanski. Those with the latter incl. *Knife in the Water; The Vampire Killers; Cul-de-Sac;* and *Rosemary's Baby.* Active in jazz-poetry fusion. As songwriter won special award at National Song Fest., Opole, '64.

Komeda, who was injured in an accident in Hollywood in January '69, underwent brain surgery in LA but never regained consciousness. Flown to Warsaw in April, he died a few days later, 4/23/69. The 15th Int. Warsaw Jazz Jamboree, '73, honored him with an entire concert of his music. LP: *The Music of Krzysztof Komeda, Vols. 1-4* (Muza).

KONITZ, LEE,* *alto saxophone*; also *soprano, tenor saxes*; b. Chicago, Ill., 10/13/27. After a brief reunion in '64 for nightclub and concert work w. Lennie Tristano, his mentor and main associate of the '40s and '50s, he worked at the head of his own gps. Also active as a teacher, often utilizing tape for lessons via mail. Played in England and on the Continent '69, and several times during the '70s. In '74 he began playing in two NYC clubs, Gregory's and Stryker's, a few nights apiece on a weekly basis with a trio at the former and a duo at the latter. In the summer of '75 the Stryker's group became a unique nine-piece band which also performed at the Tin Palace.

Konitz remains a highly individualistic improviser, one

who learned from Charlie Parker in the '40s but had his own way even then in a time when everyone was completely under Bird's influence. His playing in the '70s reflects the further development of an already mature style.

Won DB Critics' Poll, TDWR, '69. Films: soundtracks for *A Place for Lovers; Desperate Characters; Cops & Robbers.* Fest: Newport in Japan, '72; NJF-NY '73; Berlin; Basel; Rotterdam, '73; Antibes, '74. Comps: *Hymn; 4th Dimension; Dorian Fanfare; Minor Blue.* Publ: *Jazz Lines* (William H. Bauer, 121 Greenway Place, Albertson, L.I., N.Y.). LPs: *Duets; Spirits; Peacemeal; Satori* (Milest.); *Alto Summit* (BASF); *Altissimo* (Japan. Victor); *Chicago* (Gr. Merch.); *I Concentrate on You; Lone-Lee* (Steeple.); *Stereo Konitz* (Ital. RCA); w. Andrew Hill, *Spiral* (Arista); reissue, *Ezz-thetic* (Prest.).

KONOPASEK, JAN, *baritone sax, flute, composer*; also *reeds, flutes, piano*; b. Prague, Czech., 12/29/31. Great grandfather a music teacher. Grandfather dir. of music school. Mother pl. concert violin and piano; father violin & piano. Classical piano study w. private teacher '38-51. Studied at Berklee Coll. on scholarship, '71-3. Worked w. Karel Krautgartner orch., Studio 5, S&H Quartet and Quintet in Czech., '57-65; w. radio & TV Jazz Orch. of Station Free Berlin, '68-71. Member of Stan Kenton's "Berlin Dream Band," '69; Oliver Nelson's "Berlin Dream Band," '70. In '73-4 w. Woody Herman in U.S., Canada, Europe & Asia. Moved to NYC July '75. Sat-in w. Thad Jones-Mel Lewis Orch. Infl: Krautgartner, Jancy Korossy, H. Silver, G. Mulligan, S. Rollins, Clifford Brown, Thad Jones, J. Henderson, Laco Deczi, Leo Wright, H. Pomeroy, Mike Crotty. Film: *Prague Blues.* TV: w. Woody Herman, London '74. Pl. background music for cartoon shorts by Gene Deitch. Fest: Lanscrona, Sweden, '63-4; Copenhagen; Bled; Budapest; Berlin Jazz Days w. Kenton '69, Nelson '70; MJF w. Herman '73. Montreux, Pori, Trans-Canada w. Herman '74. Comp: *Anchee Suite; Granma's Inventions; Herbes, Pommes & Roi; Deuce Bleuce; Tropic of Cancer; What Happened at the Picture Gallery.* These led to the Richard Levy award for arr. & comp. at Berklee, '73. LPs: many on Supraphon label in Czech. as leader and sideman, late '50s-early '60s; w. Nelson, *Berlin Dialogue for Orchestra* (Fly. Dutch.); w. Herman, *Thundering Herd; Herd at Montreux* (Fant.).

KOVERHULT, TOMMY, *tenor sax*; also *flute, alto, soprano, baritone saxes*; b. Stockholm, Sweden, 12/11/45. Self-taught. Began pl. prof. in '67, app. w. Don Cherry, Eje Thelin and others. With Bernt Rosengren from '67, app. annually on TV, incl. film *A Place to Play At.* Fests: many in Sweden; also Molde; Antwerp w. Thelin; Warsaw w. Jan Wallgren's Orch. Won two awards from *Orkester Journalen.* Does a little teaching. LP: *Notes From Underground* w. Rosengren.

KRAL, IRENE,* *singer*; b. Chicago, Ill., 1/18/32. Former W. Herman and M. Ferguson band vocalist. Living in LA, she freelanced occasionally in S. Cal. during '60s and '70s and was heard on several records (see below). Married to trumpeter Joe Burnett. Singer Jackie Cain is

her sister-in-law and Roy Kral is her brother.

LPs: *Where's Love,* acc. by Alan Broadbent (Choice); *Better Than Anything,* acc. by Junior Mance Trio (Ava; deleted); *Wonderful Life* (Mainstream); *My Fair Lady,* w. S. Manne; *Guitar from Ipanema,* w. L. Almeida (Cap.).

KRAL, ROY JOSEPH,* *singer, piano, composer*; b. Chicago, Ill., 10/10/21. In '74 celebrated silver anniversary with wife, Jackie Cain (q.v.). Their professional association began in '46 before joining C. Ventura combo, '48. Left April '49 to form own group, Jackie & Roy. Kral prod., wrote and sang in many TV commercials, '62-9. In '60s and '70s active w. wife in clubs, fest. and TV apps. Comps: *The Way We Are; Niki's Song; Good And Rich; Waltz For Dana; A Wilder Alias,* all incl. in LP, *A Wilder Alias* (CTI). For other LPs see Jackie Cain.

KROG, KARIN,* *singer*; b. Oslo, Norway, 5/15/37. Active in clubs, TV and festivals throughout Europe. Pl. and rec. w. Don Ellis Orch. and Clare Fischer trio in LA, '67; concerts w. European All Stars at World-Expo, Osaka and other cities in Japan. State Grant Study tour of USA, incl. perfs. in NY and Mass., '70. Concerts at Illini JF, U. of Illinois, '72. Concert tour of Norway, '73, England and Scotland with Synthesis and Richard Rodney Bennett. In '74 took course in TV production, doing free-lance work for Norwegian TV; produced various jazz progs. for them, and three jazz workshops for NDR-Hamburg. Won DB Int'l Critics' Poll, TDWR, '69. Her *Some Other Spring* was voted Best Vocal Jazz Record of the Year in Japan, '71. Inspired by Billie Holiday and others, she has developed into one of Europe's most original jazz singers. Worked briefly in Hollywood May '75.

Own LPs: *Jazz Moments; Joy; Some Other Spring* (Sonet); *Open Space* w. European All Stars (MPS); *Gershwin + Krog; You Must Believe In Spring; We Could Be Flying* (Polydor).

KRUPA, GENE,* *drums*; b. Chicago, Ill., 1/15/09. First achieved fame in B. Goodman band, '35-8. Led own big band almost continuously from '38-51, after which he usually worked as leader of a trio or quartet, occasionally rejoining Goodman for special concerts and TV shows.

One such reunion took place during the NJF-NY, '73. By this time Krupa, whose health had been frail for years, was suffering from leukemia. He died 10/16/73 at his home in Yonkers, N.Y.

Krupa, without question, was the first musician in jazz history to attract mass popular attention to the role of the drummer. Quoted in DB, Max Roach said: "The kind of exposure that he gave to the instrument opened up the door for people to look at men like Chick Webb . . . he was more than just another student of black music, like most folks are; he was also a contributor." Teddy Wilson, long an associate of Krupa in the Goodman trio and quartet, said: "He was undoubtedly the most important jazz drummer in the history of jazz music. He made the drums a solo instrument, taking it out of the background." Buddy Rich, Roy Haynes and many others, including drummers such as Beaver Harris who represented a much later school, joined in tribute to Krupa as a powerful force whose musicianship and personality remained unique throughout his career.

LPs: *Drummin' Man* (Col.); *Gene & His Orch; Sidekicks* (CSP); *Essential; Verve's Choice* (Verve); w. A. O'Day, R. Eldridge (Col.); others w. Goodman (RCA); *Jazz at the New School* (Chiaro.).

KUDYKOWSKI, MIROSLAW, *guitar*; b. Ludwigsburg, Germany, 9/20/48. To US in 1949. Raised in Linden, N.J. Stud. w. Harry Leahy. Freelanced in NYC, sometimes with own groups; worked w. Lonnie Youngblood, 1969-71; toured as member of Les McCann group, Mar. 74- . Fests: Newport, Berkeley. LPs: *Another Beginning* w. McCann (Atl.).

KUHN, JOACHIM KURT, *piano, composer*; also *alto sax*; b. Leipzig, E. Germany, 3/15/44. Brother is clarinetist Rolf Kuhn. Stud. piano and comp. w. Arthur Schmidt Elsey '49-61. Debut concert '49 playing music of Robert Schumann. Continued to give classical concerts until '61 when he became professional jazz musician with the S & H Quintet; own trio '62-6; co-led quartet w. brother in Hamburg, '66-9; own group in Paris '69-71. Pl. w. Jean-Luc Ponty Experience, '71-2; Joachim Kuhn-Eje Thelin group '72-3; Association P.C. '73-4, incl. TV and radio, and tours of Asia, N. Africa, Portugal, Spain. Apps. w. own group and as soloist, '74. Fests: Newport, Montreux and many others throughout Europe. Inspired by Franz Schubert, Miles Davis, John Coltrane. Won *Jazz Forum* poll from '70. Comps: *Paris 71/72* for piano and orch.; *Piano Solos,* 1-12. LPs: *Boldmusic; Piano; This Way Out; Chinemascope; Open Strings* w. J.L. Ponty; *The Association Plus Jeremy Steig; Mama Kuku; Connection 74* w. R. Kuhn (MPS); *Impressions of New York,* Rolf & Joachim Kuhn (Imp.).

KUHN, STEPHEN LEWIS (STEVE),* *keyboards, composer*; b. Brooklyn, N.Y., 3/24/38. After pl. w. K. Dorham, Coltrane and Getz in early '60s, joined Art Farmer in July '64 and worked w. him and w. own trios through '66. From '67 to May '71 lived in Stockholm and pl. w. own trio for concerts, TV, radio, rec. throughout Europe. Ret. to NYC, May '71, working w. own quartet. Also rec. jingles, etc. Fests: Pori, Finland; Molde, Norway; Stockholm; Berlin. Comp: *Silver; The Child is Gone; A Change of Pace; Life's Backward Glance; Thoughts of a Gentleman; The Baby; The Sand House; Something Everywhere; Memory; Pearlie's Swine.* LPs: *October Suite* (Imp.); *Trio '67* (Prest.); *Live in New York* (Cobble.); *Trance; Solo Piano* (ECM-Poly.).

KUNSMAN, ROMAN, *alto, tenor saxes, flute*; b. Kuibishev, U.S.S.R., 12/7/41. Studied at various music schools and, from age 17, alto sax w. Gennady Goldstain. Lead alto w. Anatolij Kroll big band, '62-3. Pl. at Leningrad jazz club, '64; own gp. at Leningrad JF, '69. Left Soviet Union for Israel '70 and has led his own Platina Jazz Group from that time, app. at NJF-NY, '74. Infl: C. Parker, S. Rollins, J. Coltrane, Goldstain. LP on the Israel label.

KYNARD, CHARLES E.,* *organ, composer*; also *piano, tuba*; b. St. Louis, Mo., 2/20/33. Freelance work in LA

during '60s. Kansas City JF; cross-country jazz and religious concert tour, '67-8. Scored mus. for film, *Midtown Madness,* '69. Mus. supervisor and actor in movie, *Love Sweet Love,* '74. For more than a decade Kynard has been teaching mentally retarded children for the county of LA, while continuing his career in many night clubs and touring annually for both jazz and religious audiences.

"Kynard will be around long after many of the organ glamour boys are gone"—DB, '73.

Own LPs on Mainstream, Pres.; as sideman w. *Night Blooming Jazzmen*; Blue Mitchell; Paul Jeffrey (Mainstream).

LA BARBERA, JOSEPH JAMES (JOE), *drums*; also *piano*; b. Dansville, N.Y., 2/22/48. Parents musical. Pl. w. father and brothers, Pat and John (q.v.) in family band. Father taught him drums, saxophone and clarinet which he pl. through high school. Stud. drums w. Alan Dawson at Berklee, '66. First prof. job w. Sam Noto-Joe Romano quint. in Buffalo, '66; Chuck Israels trio, '66; Frankie Randall '67. After Army duty, '68-70, was w. Gap Mangione for six mos. in '70 before joining Woody Herman in '71 for a year. With Chuck Mangione, '72- . Infl: M. Davis, Coltrane, Shelly Manne, B. Evans, C. Mangione. TV: *A Day in the Garden* w. C. Mangione, PBS. Fest: NJF-NY w. Herman '73; NJF-NY, MJF, Pori, Pescara w. C. Mangione. LPs: *The Raven Speaks* w. Herman (Fant.); *Land of Make Believe* w. C. Mangione (Merc.); *Chase the Clouds Away* w. Mangione (A&M); *Once I Loved* w. Esther Satterfield (Sagoma); w. Gerry Niewood (Sagoma).

LA BARBERA, JOHN, *trumpet, piano, composer, arranger*; b. Warsaw, N.Y., 11/10/45. Brother of Joe and Pat (q.v.). Started pl. at five w. family band. Stud. incl. Berklee Coll., Eastman Sch. of Musc. Led 18 pc. college band. Tpt. w. Buddy Rich band '68. Toured England w. Tony Bennett. Tpt., pno. w. Glenn Miller band under B. De Franco, touring Europe, Far East. During this time studied and transcribed old Miller band arrangements. After leaving De Franco, became B. Rich's principal arr. for three years. In 1975, writing for Rich, W. Herman, C. Basie, B. Watrous, L. Biviano., also marketing high school and college stage band music through Life Line Press of Agoura, Cal. Teaching jazz arr. course at Alfred U., Alfred, N.Y., and writing book on arr. techniques.

Insp. by Clifford Brown, Kenny Dorham and arrs. Gil Evans, Bill Holman, LaBarbera in the early '70s became one of the most respected new arrangers, solidly rooted in the jazz orchestral tradition. Comps: *A Piece of the Road Suite* and *Sassy Strut,* rec. by Rich; *Dichotomy* rec. by Watrous.

LPs: *A Different Drummer; Rich in London; Stick It* w. Rich (RCA); *Roar of '74* w. Rich (Groove Merchant); *Manhattan Wildlife Refuge* w. Watrous (Col.).

LA BARBERA, PASCEL (PAT), *tenor sax, soprano, alto, clarinet, flute*; b. Mt. Morris, N.Y., 4/7/44. Brother of John, Joe (see above). Stud. w. father from '52; Berkelee, '64-7; also w. J. LaPorta, J. Henderson, other priv. teachers. Best known as soloist w. B. Rich band, '67-73; also pl. w. L. Bellson, W. Herman and own group. W. Elvin Jones from '75. Many TV apps. w. Rich in U.S., London and continent. Fests. w. Rich incl. Monterey, Newport, Concord. Living in Toronto in '75. Infl. by Coltrane, Rollins, Henderson, I. Sullivan, J. Romano. LPs: w. Rich, *Different Drummer; Stick Up; Rich In London* (RCA); *Keep The Customers Satisfied* (World Pacific); *The Roar of '74* (Groove Merchant).

LACY, STEVE (Steven Lacritz), * *soprano saxophone, composer*; b. New York, N.Y., 7/23/34. Played w. Cecil Taylor; Gil Evans in '50s; Thelonious Monk; then own gp. in NYC during '60s. Moved strongly into free improvisation in mid-'60s in Europe, Buenos Aires, NYC, Germany. From '67 has spent three yrs. in Rome; five yrs. in Paris w. trips to Portugal, Holland, Italy, Japan. Has led own trios, quartets, sextet, big bands (briefly) and quintet. Also gave solo concerts in France, Italy, Germany, England. Some teaching and lecturing. Films: shorts in Rome; *Free Fall*, US; *Alfred R*, Zurich. Fest: Amougies; Louvain; Ghent; Toulouse; Nancy; Rotterdam; San Remo; Nurenberg; Moers; Krefeld; Berlin '71. Pl. Jazz in the Garden at Museum of Modern Art, summer '67. *Melody Maker* wrote that he "has always been a deceptively straightforward kind of player, making brilliant use of clean lines and economy . . . in any company . . ."

Comp: *Tao*, cycle for voice and quintet; *The Woe*, melodrama for quintet and tape; *Garden Variety*, ballet for gp. and tape; *The Sun*, litany for sextet and voice; *Clangs*, five songs for two voices and sextet; *Shots*, eight pieces for sextet. LPs: *The Gap* (America Musidisc); *Avignon Solo; The Crust* (Emanem); *Scraps; Lapis; Dreams* (Saravah); *Flakes* (Italian RCA); *The Forest and the Zoo* (ESP); w. Cecil Taylor, *In Transition* (BN); w. Mal Waldron, *Hard Talk* (Enja).

LAINE, CLEO, *singer*;* b. Southall, Middlesex, England, 10/27/27. Name at birth Clementina Dinah Campbell. Prof. debut with John Dankworth Seven, then w. his big band from '53. Married Dankworth '58. Firmly established from 1956 as a *Melody Maker* poll winning singer, she left the band in '58 to branch out in theatrical ventures as actress, opera and musical comedy singer. First stage app. was in *Flesh To A Tiger*. Title role in Ibsen's *Hedda Gabler*; starred w. Robert Morley in *A Time to Laugh*; played both Hippolyta and Titania in West End prod. of *Midsummer Night's Dream*. Took over role from the ailing Lotte Lenya in Brecht-Weill *Seven Deadly Sins* at Edinburgh Festival, also playing this part at Sadlers Wells.

In addition to one acting part in the film *The Roman Spring of Mrs. Stone*, Laine sang on soundtracks for *The Servant*, *The Criminal* and other films. Though continuing to win jazz polls, she gave Lieder recitals, was starred w. London Symphony Orch., and from 1971-3 played Julie in the London revival of *Showboat*.

She and Dankworth continued to appear together intermittently, but never in the U.S. until the fall of 1972, for a concert at Alice Tully Hall. Each subsequent appearance in America was played to bigger audiences in larger halls, incl. Carnegie Hall, Santa Monica Civic Aud., '73; Hollywood Bowl, '74 etc. The Dankworths made their night club debut at the Rainbow Grill in the fall of '73. Early in '75 they taped a TV special at Royce Hall in UCLA, Los Angeles. They also appeared at NJF-NY, '75.

Concurrent with the U.S. concerts, Laine's albums began to be released in the U.S. Her popularity grew as critics in London, New York and Los Angeles hailed her not only as an astonishingly original jazz artist, but as the greatest living all-around singer.

John S. Wilson of the New York Times attributed to Laine a voice "richly colored in the lower range, brilliantly articulate when she tops into falsetto and fantastically agile in the areas between. She went from exuberant jazz vocalizing to whirlwind duets with Dankworth's saxophone (with a precision that was several steps removed from the casual solo scat singing of Sarah Vaughan or Ella Fitzgerald) to the very varied demands of poems, set to Dankworth's music, by Eliot, Donne, Shakespeare, Spike Milligan (the English comedian) and Ogden Nash. She sang Bessie Smith and Noel Coward, back to back, giving each a warm understanding but coloring both with something that was herself."

The consummate artistry of Cleo Laine gained invaluable support from the collaboration of her husband in the roles of musical director, alto saxophonist, clarinetist etc. (see DANKWORTH, JOHN). Along with her incomparable musicianship, she brings to her work, when it is appropriate, the rare qualities of humor and satire.

LPs: *I Am A Song; A Beautiful Thing; Live At Carnegie Hall* etc. (RCA); *Day By Day* (Stanyan); *Cleo's Choice* (GNP-Crescendo).

LAINE, GEORGE VITELLE (PAPA JACK), * *drums*; b. New Orleans, La., 9/21/1873. Laine, a drummer and blacksmith, whose career was interrupted when he fought in the Spanish-American war in 1898, was active in pre-jazz NO music and counted Nick LaRocca of the Original Dixieland Jazz Band among his many proteges. Laine continued in music until the late '20s. The subject of a '64 show on national educ. TV, he died of pneumonia 6/2/66 in NO.

LAIRD, RICHARD QUENTIN (RICK), *bass*; b. Dublin, Ireland, 2/5/41. Began pl. in Auckland, N.Z., 1959. Moved to Sydney, Australia, pl. w. Don Burrows, Erroll Buddle (Austr. Jazz Quartet), Mike Nock. Later, in London, stud. at Guildhall Sch., '63-4; free-lanced w. J. Dankworth, T. Hayes, Ronnie Scott; house band at Scott's club '64-6. Emigrated to US, stud. at Berklee Coll. '66-8. Worked in Boston w. Ch. Mariano, Phil Woods, Z. Sims. Toured w. B. Rich band for 1½ yrs. 1969-70, then returned to London. Joined John McLaughlin June 1971 to form Mahavishnu orch., remaining until it disbanded 12/31/73. Free-lancing in NYC '74-5 w. J. Abercrombie, Nock, etc.

Favs: R. Brown, P. Chambers, P. Heath, S. La Faro. Though a fine upright bassist, Laird switched to elec. in 1968 "for practical reasons." First rec. comp.: *Stepping Stones* w. Jan Hammer, on *Like Children* (Nemperor).

LPs: *Inner Mounting Flame; Birds of Fire* w. Mahavishnu (Col.); B. Rich, *Live* (Liberty); Horacee Arnold (Col.).

LAKE, OLIVER, *alto saxophone, composer;* also *flute; synthesizer;* b. Marianna, Ark., ca. 1944. Family moved to St. Louis when he was one. Interested in music at very early age. Played cymbals and bass drum in drum & bugle corps. Became involved w. alto sax, '60, after hearing Paul Desmond record. First strong infl. was Jackie McLean. In '68 his band evolved into BAG, the Black Artist Group which is a St. Louis parallel of Chicago's AACM. Worked in Paris '72. Gigs w. Ambrose Jackson; Leo Smith. To NYC, '74. Experimenting w. synthesizer. Comp: *While Pushing Down Turn; Owshet; Heavy Spirits; Movement Equals Creation; Altoviolin; Intensity; Rockets.* LPs: *Heavy Spirits* (Arista); Paris rec. (New Music Dist. Services).

LAMARE, HILTON (NAPPY),* *guitar, banjo, elec. bass, singer;* b. New Orleans, La., 6/14/10. Best known as member of original Bob Crosby orch. and of many reunion groups w. Crosby since band broke up in 1942. In late '60s and early '70s, occasional work w. Crosby, Abe Most, John Best; banjo in combos at Disneyland and on soundtrack for film *The Great Gatsby.* Concerts at Wilshire Ebell Th., LA, w. Legend of Jazz. Soundtrack work for commercials and Phil Harris feature at Disney studios, 1974-5.

LAMBERT, DAVID ALDEN (DAVE),* *singer, vocal arranger;* b. Boston, Mass., 6/19/17. A pioneer in bebop vocals, and in the art of scoring vocal group arrangements based on jazz comps. and solos, Lambert was best known as a member of the Lambert, Hendricks & Ross trio, which achieved national prominence in '58. They remained together until '63, when Yolande Bavan replaced Annie Ross. Lambert left the group two years later, briefly led a quintet of his own, and starred in a short jazz film, *Audition.* He was killed in an accident near Westport on the Connecticut turnpike 10/3/66.

LPs: see HENDRICKS, JON.

LANCASTER, WILLIAM BYARD (THUNDERBIRD), *saxophones, flute;* also *bass clarinet, trumpet, piano, singer;* b. Philadelphia, Pa., 8/6/42. Sister, Mary Ann Tyler, has Doctor's in Mus. Ed. from Univ. of Pitts. Studied at Shaw Univ., '60-1; Berklee Coll. of Mus., '61-3; Boston Conserv., '62-4. Stud. mus. ed., '75. Worked w. J.R. Mitchell-Byard Lancaster Experience, from '55; Sunny Murray, '65-7; Burton Greene; Bill Dixon, '66; Sun Ra, '69; McCoy Tyner, '70; own gp., Sounds of Liberation, '71-3; Walt Miller & Co.; Le Gran Prix, co-led w. Philly Joe Jones, '75. Played in France, England, Holland and Belgium in '70s. His gp. pl. at Freedom Games track meet. Le Gran Prix supplied the music for Miss Black America competition, '75; the finals were seen on national TV. Infl: Stanley Clarke, Sonny Sharrock, Darryl Brown, Jeffrey Johnson, Khan Jamal, Bill Meeks.

Comp: *Sweet Evil Miss,* ballet-opera in five movements, incorporating solo piano, a rock band and 120-piece orch. LPs: *New Horizons* w. Sounds of Liberation (Dogtown); *It's Not Up to Us* (Vortex); *Us* (Palm); w. S. Murray (ESP); Byg); Burton Greene (Col.); Larry Young, *Heaven on Earth* (BN); Bill Dixon (RCA); Marzette Watts (ESP).

LAND, HAROLD C. JR., *piano, composer;* b. San Diego, Cal., 4/25/50. Father is noted tenor saxophonist Harold Land Sr. Stud. classical music w. priv. teachers; Los Angeles City Coll. '68-70, perf. in coll. band. First pro. engagement at Club Tropicana in LA with own quintet, '66-7. Then w. Wayne Henderson's Freedom Sounds; concerts w. Gerald Wilson orch., '67-8. Continued w. Wilson 68- ; began working in quintet and sextet w. father, app. locally; also w. Kenny Burrell. U.S. tour w. Pharoah Sanders, '75. Land was seen briefly in the movie *Uptown Saturday Night,* and made his first fest. app. at Concord w. Wilson '75. Infls: H. Land Sr., McCoy Tyner, Herbie Hancock, Darryl Clayborn.

LPs: w. Henderson, *People Get Ready* (Atl.); w. Land Sr. *Shoma* (Mainstr.); w. Paul Humphrey, *America Wake Up* (Blue Thumb).

LAND, HAROLD DE VANCE,* *tenor sax, flute, composer;* b. Houston, Tex. 2/18/28. First nationally prominent while touring w. Max Roach-Clifford Brown Quintet, 1954-5. Whenever possible, pl. w. Gerald Wilson orch., 1955- ; the band in recent years also incl. his son, pianist Harold C. Land (see above).

From 1969-71 Land co-led a quintet w. Bobby Hutcherson. Three tours throughout US; clubs throughout US, college campuses US and Canada. Land also pl. annually from '71 w. Tony Bennett in LV. Featured in Bennett-Lena Horne show at Shubert theatre, LA, 1975. Led own quintet, incl. son, from 1972, mostly in and around LA. Awarded a fellowship grant from Nat. Endowment for the Arts to compose a jazz suite, 1975. Still a strong individualist on tenor, Land has also been heard to splendid effect in past few years as a flutist.

Films: *Seven Days in May; They Shoot Horses, Don't They?* TV: *The Jazz Show,* LA, 1971. Festivals: Antibes, Pori, '69; Tunis, Molde, '70; Verona, '72; Bay Area, '74-7.

Comps: *Ode to Angels; De-Liberation; Short Subject; Mtume; A New Shade of Blues; Damisi; Step Right Up To The Bottom; Choma; Peace Maker; Forty Love; Stylin'; The Aquarian.*

LPs: *New Shade of Blue; Choma; Damisi* (Mainstr.); w. Hutcherson, *Head On; Now; Total Eclipse; San Francisco* (BN); *Brown & Roach Inc.-1954* (Trip).

LANDRUM, RICHIE PABLO, *African drums, percussion;* also *African string instruments;* b. New York City, 7/18/39. Mother pl. piano; brothers pl. sax and guitar. Studied percussion at Juilliard. Received music teaching license. Private studies in Afro-Cuban drumming w. Julito Collazo, Patato Valdes, Francisco Aguabella; Haitian drumming w. Tiroro, Alphonso Cimber; Brazilian w. Jose Paulo, Carmen Costa; jazz w. Louis Hayes, Max Roach, Elvin Jones, Charli Persip; African drums w. Saka Acquaye, Ladji Camara, Solomon Ilori, Olatunji.

Worked w. Katherine Dunham; Fred Astaire; Arthur Murray; Roland Wingfield; Bernice Johnson; Laroque Bey; Syvilla Fort; Pearl Primus. App. w. Arundel Opera Theatre, Kennebunk, Maine; Negro Ensemble Co.; Black Arts Theatre, Chicago. Fest: NJF; MJF; w. Randy Weston, Tangier Fest. '72. Infl: Weston. TV: *Soul* w. Leon Thomas; Pharoah Sanders; Merv Griffin; Dick Cavett; Johnny Carson; *Black Perspective*; *Black News*; *Like It Is.* Taught at Leroy and Gloria's Dancing School, St. Croix, V.I.; Laroque Bey Sch. of Dance; in '67, Harlem Y.M.C.A.; Mt. Morris Park Assoc.; Haryou Act Summer Prog., '67-71; Neighborhood Youth Board, Brooklyn, '68-72; Guggenheim Museum Children's Summer Prog., '70-2; NY Board of Educ., '70-2. Makes own African drums and would like to open drum making school in future. LPs: w. Pucho; Groove Holmes; George Braith; Johnny Hammond (Prest.); John Patton (BN); Freddie Hubbard; Stanley Turrentine; Hubert Laws (CTI); Kenny Barron (Muse); Leon Thomas; Gato Barbieri; T-Bone Walker-Joe Turner (Fly. Dutch.); Dinizulu, *Songs and Dances of West Africa; Mystical Africa* (Eurotone).

LANG, MICHAEL ANTHONY (MIKE),* *piano, keyboards, synthesizer, composer*; b. Los Angeles, Cal., 12/10/41. Pl. w. Paul Horn 1964-5. Own trio off and on from '67. MJF w. Don Ellis '67 and Tom Scott '68. From late '60s through mid-70s Lang was constantly in demand for motion picture, TV and recording work in LA area with, to name a few among hundreds, Lalo Schifrin, Q. Jones, Bill Plummer, O. Nelson, J. Klemmer, R. Kellaway, P. Rugolo, Bud Shank, N. Hefti, B. Golson, Dee Barton, J. Mandel. Wrote TV scores for ABC Suspense Theatre, PBS Hollywood TV Theatre. Comps: *Karen's World*, rec. w. P. Horn; *Rural Still Life* rec. w. Tom Scott. LPs: w. Klemmer, *Constant Throb; Fresh Feathers* (Imp.); w. Don Ellis, *Electric Bath; Shock Treatment* (Col.); w. Tom Scott, *Rural Still Life*; B. Plummer & Cosmic Brotherhood (Imp.).

LA PORTA, JOHN D.,* *composer, saxophones, clarinet*; b. Philadelphia, Pa., 4/1/20. Extensive background in jazz and classical music, playing w. W. Herman, C. Mingus, Leonard Bernstein, Igor Stravinsky, Teo Macero. Starting in '59 at the Berklee School (now College) of Music, he gave evening faculty concerts at the Summer Jazz Clinics in addition to playing jazz concerts in the New England area w. Herb Pomeroy. As a teacher, from '62, he was in charge of the instrumental performance dept., with 600 students under his aegis. In '75 La Porta was engaged in a large work called *Tonal Organization of Improvisational Techniques*, combining text and demonstration records.

Publs: *Developing the Jazz Band; A Guide to Jazz Phrasing*, books and records; *Developing Sightreading Skills in the Jazz Idiom; Rock Band Arrangements* (all publ. by Berklee Press, 1140 Boylston St. Boston, Mass. 02215).

LPs: *Berklee Saxophone Quartet* (Berklee Records); *A Jazz Journey*, w. Rusty Dedrick (Monmouth-Evergreen).

LARKINS, ELLIS LANE,* *piano*; b. Baltimore, Md., 5/15/23. Prominent in 1940s at Blue Angel, Cafe Society, NYC. After many years of relative obscurity, Larkins enjoyed renewed recognition in late '60s and early '70s. Acc. Joe Williams, '68, '69 (entertained troops in Germany) and again '72. Worked long engagements at New York clubs, restaurants incl. Gregory's, '72-4; Michael's Pub, The Cookery, '74-5; Tangerine, '75. Toured South America in piano show w. T. Wilson, M. McPartland, E. Hines, '74. Concerts: Left Bank Jazz Society, Baltimore, '72; NY Town Hall, '73; NYU, '74.

Larkins has made many TV appearances with, among others, Father N. O'Connor, Art Linkletter, Joe Franklin, Merv Griffin, Mike Douglas, Rosie Grier, Pat Collins. Festivals: NJF-NY, Baltimore, Seattle, Monterey, '73; Hudson riverboat concerts summer '73, '74.

A favorite of virtually every singer he has accompanied, Larkins works equally well alone or with a rhythm section. His articulation is exceptionally delicate, his harmonic taste is perhaps unmatched, his left hand style subtly rhythmic. He is one of the masters of the acoustic piano, extolled for many years by such admirers as John Hammond, who was associated with many of his recordings, and John S. Wilson.

LPs: *Ellis Larkins Plays the Bacharach and McKuen Songbook* (Stanyan); *Lost In The Wood*, others for McKuen, Sylvia Syms (Stanyan); Helen Humes (Col.), *Stardust* w. S. Stitt (Roulette), *Grand Reunion* w. R. Braff (Chiaroscuro), *Ella Fitzgerald Live at Carnegie Hall* (Col.), and many earlier solo albums for Decca, since deleted.

LATEEF, YUSEF,* *tenor sax, flute, oboe, composer, educator*; also *shennai, bamboo flutes*; b. Chattanooga, Tenn., 1921. After leading own gp., pl. w. C. Mingus; B. Olatunji; C. Adderley in early '60s. From mid-'60s has again led his own bands, touring in the US, Europe, and Japan. Fest: NJF; Bilzen; Kongsberg; Tokyo. Majored in flute and received an M.A. in Music Education at Manhattan Sch. of Mus. Doctorate in Education from U. of Mass., Sept. '75. Associate Professor of Music at Manhattan Community Coll.

Lateef did not want to be included in this book because it is an encyclopedia of jazz and not an encyclopedia of music. This points up two things: that American society has not given the jazz writers and performers the respect and recognition commensurate with their art; and that many of these artists, especially among the black composers and players, are strongly affected by this attitude despite their high degree of artistic achievement. Lateef's music is wide-ranging, encompassing areas long identified with jazz and those associated with "serious" music (an inadequate terminology which further underlines the dichotomy), and "pop" points in between. In whatever directions his many talents are manifest, his exclusion from this volume would be conspicuous.

Publ: stage band arrs.; *Trio for Flute, Piano & Cello; Duet for Two Flutes; Solo for Flute*; book of improvised solos for flute, oboe & saxophone; *Flute Book of the Blues #2*; quartet arr. of *Psychicemotus* (Fana Music, P.O. Box 393, Amherst, Mass. 01002). He also collaborated with Kenny Barron, Bob Cunningham and Albert

Heath in *Something Else*, a book of poetry, philosophical essays, short stories, etc.

Comp: *I Be Cold; Yusef's Mood; Symphonic Blues Suite; Nocturne; Down in Atlanta; Buddy and Lou; Destination Paradise; Kongsberg; Brother; The Poor Fisherman; Below Yellow Bell.* LPs: *The Blue Yusef Lateef; Yusef Lateef's Detroit; Suite 16; The Diverse Yusef Lateef; The Gentle Giant; Hush 'N Thunder; Part of the Search* (Atl.); reissues on Prest.; Imp.; Trip.

LAWRENCE, ARNIE (Arnold Lawrence Finkelstein), *alto & soprano saxophones, composer*; also *tenor & baritone sax, flute, clarinet, conga*; b. Brooklyn, N.Y., 7/10/38. Pl. w. Mat Mathews quartet, '55-6; Rusty Dedrick, '65; Urbie Green quintet; D. Hyman, '65-8; F. Foster band; W. Chiasson-J. Garrison quartet, '66; Doc Severinsen sextet, orch., '65-72; Duke Pearson band, '67-8; Johnny Richards, '68; Chico Hamilton, on and off, from '67- ; NBC Orch., '67-72; Joe Newman quintet, '69-70; Les De Merle, '69; Rod Levitt, '74-5; Blood, Sweat & Tears, '74; Lawrence has been associated w. Clark Terry from '70 when he began pl. w. the trumpeter's small group. He has been w. Terry's Big Bad Band from '73 and has also continued to record and appear w. a group called Children Of All Ages from '66.

Lawrence whose alto work is sometimes reminiscent of Cannonball Adderley, is also capable of playing in a free-jazz style. Infls: Clifford Brown, Johnny Richards, Ch. Parker, Coltrane, Art Tatum. Comps: *Contentment; Gonna Get Some Right Now; Meeting of Two Worlds; Laotian Lament; Universe is God's Sanctuary; Look Toward the Day of Man's Awakening; Swinging on a Sitar; Tell It Like It Is.* Fests: w. Terry, many Euro., '73, incl. Montreux; NJF-NY, Monterey, '74; NJF midwest mini-tour, summer '75. LPs: *You're Gonna Hear From Me; Look Toward a Dream* (Proj. 3); *Inside An Hourglass* (Embryo); w. Hamilton, *The Dealer* (Imp.); *El Exigente* (Fl. Dutch.); w. Severinsen on ABC, RCA, Command; *Mirror Images* w. B,S&T; w. Genya Ravan (Col.); w. Richards, *Aqui Se Habla Espanol* (Roulette); w. Children Of All Ages (Differant Drummer, Embryo).

LAWRENCE, AZAR, *tenor, soprano saxes, composer*; b. Los Angeles, Cal., 11/3/53. Began on violin at five; took up alto at 12 and "became serious at 16." Pl. w. pianist Herbert Baker; Watts Fest.; Dorsey HS jazz band & jazz workshop; after hours pl. w. Candy Finch. In LA worked w. Ike & Tina Turner; from Dec. '72 w. Watts 103rd St. Rhythm Band until he joined Elvin Jones, Feb. '73. Left Apr. '73 and the next month went w. McCoy Tyner. With the pianist's quartet from that time, Lawrence attracted enough attention, as his style became more personalized under the tent of Coltrane's influence, that he soon became a recording leader in his own right. Bob Blumenthal, reviewing *Bridge Into the New Age*, wrote: "The music exemplified by this album is to John Coltrane what hard bop is to Charlie Parker. That's no criticism, for hard bop is some of my favorite music; but once again a younger generation is digesting and simplifying the discoveries of a daring father figure, arriving in the process at a music that is more predictable, more easily

comprehensible to the audience, and more overtly rooted in the Afro-American community."

Infl: Coltrane, Rollins, Lateef, Shorter, Black Arthur, Ray Straughter. Lawrence, in acknowledging his points of origin, adds "but my main influence was my parents, who helped me to get instruments and allowed me to practice all night."

Fest: NJF-NY; Montreux; other major fest. w. Tyner. TV: Montreux '73 w. Tyner, NET. Comp: *From the Point of Love; From the Point of Light; Summer Solstice.*

LPs: *Bridge Into the New Age; Summer Solstice* (Prest.); w. Tyner, *Sama Lucaya; Enlightenment; Atlantis* (Mile.); w. E. Jones, *New Agenda* (Vang.).

LAWS, HUBERT,* *flute, composer*; also *saxophones, guitar, piano*; b. Houston, Tex., 11/10/39. After establishing himself in NYC during the mid-'60s w. a variety of top musicians and singers, he reached prominence w. his own group through a series of recordings for Atlantic and CTI and annual Carnegie Hall concerts '73-5. Laws, a member of the Metropolitan Opera orch. '68-73 and an alternate w. the N.Y. Philharmonic '71-4, has recorded works by Bach, Mozart, Ravel, Stravinsky and Satie in a unique manner which reflects his expertise in several areas. He explains that "The classical feeling in my music is more a result of personal taste than educational background."

Concert tours in Europe, Japan, Hawaii, Africa and Canada as well as the U.S. Fests: Berkeley, '72; Newport, '73. Won DB Readers' Poll, '71-4; Ebony Music Poll, '74; Playboy Poll, '75. Comps: *What Do You Think of this World Now?; Let Her Go; No More; A Strange Girl; Shades of Light.* Publ: *Flute Improvisation* (Hulaws Music, 66 W. 94th St., New York, N.Y. 10025).

LPs: *At Carnegie Hall, Crying Song, In The Beginning, Morning Star, Afro-Classic, Rite of Spring* (CTI); *Wild Flower, Flute By-Laws* (Atl.); w. Q. Jones, *Body Heat; Walking In Space* (A & M).

LAWS, RONALD (RONNIE), *tenor saxophone*; also *soprano saxophone, flute*; b. Houston, Tex., 10/3/50. Stud. Steven F. Austin State U.; Texas Southern U. Left Houston, settling in LA, '71. Pl. w. Q. Jones, H. Masekela, K. Burrell; gigged and rec. w. Walter Bishop Jr., Doug Carn. Spent year and a half as member of Earth, Wind & Fire. Formed his own quintet, '75, and during that year began rec. as a leader for Blue Note. An outstanding musician inspired by his brother, Hubert Laws, and by J. Coltrane.

LPs: *Pressure Sensitive* (BN); w. H. Laws, *In The Beginning* (CTI); w. Earth, Wind & Fire, *Last Days And Time* (Col.); w. Bishop, *Keeper of My Soul;* w. Carn *Adams Apple* (Black Jazz).

LAWSON, RICHARD HUGH JEROME,* *piano, composer*; b. Detroit, Mich., 3/12/35. Came to NYC w. Yusef Lateef gp. in late '50s. From '60-8 also worked w. S. Rollins; R. Eldridge; G. Coleman; C. McPherson; Grady Tate; S. Turrentine. From '68 pl. w. Lockjaw Davis; Joe Williams w. Harry Edison-Jimmy Forrest; Joe Henderson; McPherson; Lateef. One of the founding members of the Piano Choir, '72. Own trio from '75; also w. C. Mingus, touring Europe w. him, fall '75. Fest: Watts '70 w. Lateef. Taught comp. and jazz improvisation at Henry St. Settlement House; Nassau County In School Jazz Ensemble, '75. Comp: Watts Fest. theme, '70; *Jaboobie's March; Ballad For the Beasts*; writing *Doom and Gloom*, a piece for seven electric keyboards on grant from NEA. LPs: w. Piano Choir, *Handscapes; Handscapes 2* (Strata-East); w. Roy Brooks (Jazz Workshop); Kenny Burrell, *God Bless the Child*; S. Turrentine (CTI).

LAWSON, JOHN (YANK),* *trumpet, leader*; b. Trenton, Mo., 5/3/11. Many big band assoc. in '30s, '40s w. B. Pollack, B. Crosby, T. Dorsey, B. Goodman. During '50s, co-led Lawson-Haggart Jazz Band for series of LPs. Mainly involved in studio work on staff at NBC in NYC, '50s and through '68, but with frequent jazz jobs at Condon's Club etc. In 1965 a wealthy jazz fan, Dick Gibson, helped organize a group, presented as the Nine Greats of Jazz, for a party at Elitch's Gardens, Denver. Personnel was nucleus of what became, two years later, the group known as the World's Greatest Jazzband of Yank Lawson and Bob Haggart. The band made its first appearance outside Denver in Nov. '68 at the Riverboat in NYC. Members at that time included B. Butterfield, L. McGarity, C. Fontana, B. Wilber, Bud Freeman, R. Sutton, Morey Feld. At concerts, singer Maxine Sullivan was often added.

While some critics found the group's name pretentious, others, among them John S. Wilson, contended that the WGJ, as it was often called, made a viable attempt to justify it. Arrangements, most of them written by Haggart, some by Wilber, gave the band a personal flavor in its original format (nine or ten men); during this period the group enjoyed great successes at concerts, festivals, and in Dec. '71 on its first visit to England. The band also pl. throughout Europe, Mexico, Brazil, Virgin Islands. Financial difficulties over the years led to a reduction to eight and later seven men; by early 1975, after increasingly frequent turnover, death or defection had taken the original members and only the leaders were left; sidemen now were G. Masso, trombone; J. Muranyi, clarinet; Al Klink, tenor; Dill Jones, piano; Bobby Rosengarden, drums.

LPs: Project 3, Atlantic. Later albums on their own World Jazz label (4350 E. Camelback Rd., Phoenix, Ariz. 85108).

LEE, WILLIAM FRANKLIN III (BILL), *educator, piano*; also *trumpet, bass*; b. Galveston, Tex., 2/20/29. B.M., '49, M.S., '50, NTSU, M.M., Ph.D., '56, U. of Tex; also stud. at Eastman School of Music and in France w. Nadia Boulanger. Extensive prof. exp. w. G. Krupa, Ch. Parker, A. Shaw, L. Young, H. McGhee, G. Mulligan and many others. Principally known as one of the foremost figures in the jazz education movement.

Dir. of mus., Sam Houston State U., '56-64; Dean, School of Mus., U. of Miami, '64- ; President, NAJE, '72-4. Dr. Lee, recipient of many awards and honors, is the composer and/or author of numerous published

works. Among them are *Music Theory Dictionary; The Nature of Music; Modern Musical Instruments; The Art and Science of Music* (Charles Hansen Pubs., 1842 West Ave., Miami Bch., Fla. 33139); *Mini-Suite for Trumpet and Piano; Interlude for Classical Guitar; Alamjohoba* for concert band (U. of Miami Pubs.); *Suite for Brass* and several other works (Collier-Dexter, Ltd., London); *Spring Carnival* and *Festival* for piano (Southern Music Co., 1740 Broadway, New York, 10019).

LEE, WILLIAM JAMES EDWARDS (BILL), *bass, composer*; b. Snow Hill, Ala., 7/23/28. Mother, Alberta G. Lee, retired concert pianist; father, Arnold W. Lee, trumpet & cornet. Began pl. drums in family band w. brothers and sisters at age eight. Flute at 11. Studied at Snow Hill Inst. In '47 went to Morehouse Coll. in Atlanta, study w. musicologist Willis James; Kemper Harold; bassist "Pepper." Took up bass '50. To Chicago '52. Israel Crosby recommended him for job w. Buster Bennett. Pl. w. Johnny Griffin, Billy Wallace, Clifford Jordan, Andrew Hill, Vernell Fournier, John Gilmore, George Coleman, Frank Strozier et al. To NYC '59 where he worked w. Philly Joe Jones, Phineas Newborn, Ray Bryant and many folk and blues gps. incl. Josh White, Odetta, Theodore Bikell, Judy Collins. Leader-founder of NY Bass Violin Choir '68; co-leader w. B. Hardman & B. Higgins of The Brass Company from '72. Mus. dir. for Muriel Winston's A Fresh Viewpoint. Leader of Descendants of Mike and Phoebe, a family band named for his ancestors from the 1800s and incl. Consuela Lee Morehead, piano; A. Grace Lee Mims, vocals; A. Cliffton Lee, trumpet. Lee has written five folk-jazz operas, parts of which have been performed at the NJF, and for NET: *The Depot; One Mile East; Baby Sweets; The Quarter; Little Johnny* (children's opera). Wrote music for Broadway prod., *Hand is On the Gate*. Comp: *The Rabbi; Monica; Juan Valdez*. Infl: Jimmy Blanton; Consuela Lee Morehead; Charlie Parker. TV: *Today*; Harry Belafonte specials. Fest: NJF, '71; all the Newport Folk Fest.; house bassist for Phila. Folk Fest. LPs: The Descendants of Mike and Phoebe, *A Spirit Speaks*; The Brass Company, *Colors*; w. Muriel Winston; Clifford Jordan, *Glass Bead Games* (Strata East); w. Richard Davis, *Philosophy of the Spiritual* (Buddah), *With Understanding* (Muse).

LEE, DAVID JR., *drums, percussion, composer*; b. New Orleans, La., 1/4/41. Three brothers in NO are musicians: Robert, flute and percussion; Adam, percussion; Joseph, congas and percussion. Started pl. at age 12. Stud. w. Charles Speres in elem. sch.; Yvonne Bush in junior h.s.; Ernest Sacheray; Solomon Spencer in h.s. First prof. job w. Spencer's band, '54. Pl. in NO w. a wide variety of musicians incl. Snooks Eaglin; Nat Perrilliat; George Davis; Alvin Batiste; Earl Turbinton; also 4th Army Band in Texas; 8th Army Band in Korea. In '60s worked w. Willie Tee and the Souls. Co-founded NO Jazz Workshop, '69. To NYC, joining Dizzy Gillespie at Jazz Workshop in Boston, Dec. '69. With Roy Ayers for seven mos., '71; Sonny Rollins, '72-5; Joe Newman from '73; formed own quintet '75.

Infl: Paul Barbarin, Ed Blackwell, Max Roach, Elvin Jones; inspiration: George Davis, Gillespie, Rollins, Coltrane, Joe Newman. TV: w. Willie Tee; Gillespie; Rollins; Ayers; Joe Williams, etc. Fest: NJF-NY; MJF; Nice; Pescara; Kongsberg; Berlin; Middleheim; Antwerp; also toured Italy w. Chet Baker, '75. Drum instructor for Jazz Interactions, '75; also teaching privately. Lectures, seminars and concerts, U. of Conn., Feb. '73. Comp: *In His Presence Searching; Evolution.* LPs: *Evolution,* w. own company (Supernal Records, 62 West 87th St., #3F, New York, N.Y. 10024); w. Rollins (Mile.); Gillespie (Perception); Joe Zawinul; Gary Burton-Larry Coryell (Atl.); R. Ayers (Poly.); Lonnie Liston Smith; Leon Thomas; Harold Alexander (Fly. Dutch.); Pete Yellin (Main.); A. Dailey (Col.); C. Rouse (Strata-East); Alan Braufman (India Navigation Co.); F. Wess (Enterprise); Richard Landry (Chatham Square).

LEE, PEGGY (Norma Deloris Egstrom),* *singer, composer*; b. Jamestown, N.D., 5/26/20. Continued to play major showrooms and concert halls, incl. Kennedy Center and Royal Albert Hall, '71; guest solos with Boston Pops, '74; concert tour of Japan, Apr. '75. Won Grammy award 1969 as best contemporary female vocalist for record of *Is That All There Is?* TV: *A Man and a Woman* w. Anthony Quinn, '72 (was also given screen credit for the concept); Petula Clark, Julie Andrews shows in London; numerous U.S. network variety and talk shows. Comps: lyrics for *The Shining Sea*, music by John Mandel; theme for movie *The Russians Are Coming; The Heart Is A Lonely Hunter; Nickel Ride*, both with music by David Grusin; *Then Was Then and Now Is Now*, music by Cy Coleman; *So What's New*, music by John Pisano.

Lee was awarded a Doctor of Music Honoris Causa degree from N. Dakota State U., '75. A talented artist, she was commissioned by Sylvania to do four paintings for its *Sights & Sounds of the Seventies*, '70; was one of 11 artists whose paintings were included in the Franklin Mint Gallery of American Art Exhibition at Lincoln Center, '73.

LPs: *Is That All There Is?; Make It With You; Where Did They Go?; Bridge Over Troubled Water; Norma Deloris Egstrom* (Cap.); *Let's Love* (Atl.).

LEEMAN, CLIFFORD (CLIFF),* *drums*; b. Portland, Maine, 9/10/13. Veteran of swing era bands, later pl. in many dixieland groups at Eddie Condon's etc. Toured Japan in '67 w. Condon, J. Rushing and group; again in '70 w. R. Norvo, J. Venuti, R. Braff. Pl. w. several groups org. by Dick Gibson at Roosevelt Grill in NYC w. P. Hucko, Venuti, Hackett, Teddy Wilson; also pl. annual jazz parties for Gibson in Colorado and Dr. O.A. Fulcher in Odessa, Tex.; NJF-NY, '74. W. Balaban & Cats at Eddie Condon's, '75. Also worked in Sweden, Iceland, Germany, England, Scotland. LPs: w. Bobby Hackett, *Live at the Roosevelt Grill;* w. Wild Bill Davison, *Live at the Rainbow Room;* w. Venuti-Zoot Sims (Chiaroscuro); *Colorado Jazz Party* (MPS/BASF); w. Condon (Col.); early rec. w. Ch. Barnet (RCA).

LEGRAND, MICHEL,* *conductor, composer, piano, singer*; b. Paris, France, 2/24/32. Began composing for films in late '50s. Received Oscar for *Windmills of Your Mind*, Best Song, '68; second Oscar for Best Original Dramatic Score, *Summer of '42.* During the '60s and early '70s, though principally known as a writer for TV and movies, Legrand occasionally app. in clubs and rec. with jazz groups. His film credits incl. the score for *Lady Sings The Blues.* He is a competent jazz pianist and fair singer who has indulged in a few wordless vocals. Having scored more than 50 motion pictures, many of which have been released in sound track albums, Legrand has nearly 100 LPs to his credit, a few of which are of some jazz interest: *The Umbrellas of Cherbourg*, sound track (Philips); *Legrand Jazz*, feat. Miles Davis (Col.); *Brian's Song* (Bell); *The Windmills of Your Mind* (UA); *Recorded Live at Jimmy's*, feat. P. Woods (RCA); *At Shelly's Manne Hole* (Verve); w. S. Vaughan (Mainstream); *Stan Getz Communication '72* (Verve); P. Woods, *Images* (RCA).

LEONHART, JAMES C. (JAY), *bass*; b. Baltimore, Md., 12/6/40. Brother Bill Leonhart, jazz and classical guitarist, works in SF. Stud. at Peabody School, Baltimore; Berklee, '61-2; Oscar Peterson's Advanced Sch. of Contemp. Mus. '62. Private bass study w. Wm. Curtis, Ray Brown, Orin O'Brien. Began pro. w. brother in banjo duo, '51-5; bass w. Pier Five Jazz Band in Baltimore, '55-9. Took up electric bass. Worked w. Buddy Morrow, '61; Mike Longo, '62-3; free-lance in Baltimore, also acc. Ethel Ennis, '63-7. To NYC '68 pl. w. Urbie Green, '68-70; Marian McPartland, '70-1; Tony Bennett, '71-3; Jim Hall, '73-4; also Thad Jones-Mel Lewis, Barbara Carroll, Zoot Sims, Leslie Uggams, Lee Konitz, B. Rich, G. Bertoncini, Tal Farlow, Sylvia Syms and John Bunch.

Infls: Ray Brown, O. Peterson, Clifford Brown, Bill Evans, Jim Hall, Chuck Rainey, Gil Evans. Comps: *Radials; Kentucky Wild Flower.* TV: *Today* Show w. M. McPartland, Carroll; *Tonight* Show w. James Brown; NET w. Green; staff work on NBC, CBS. Fests: Milwaukee Arts w. McPartland, '73; NJF-NY, Concord w. Hall, '73; NJF-NY '74 w. B. Eckstine; NJF-NY '75 w. S. Syms. LPs: *Delicate Balance* w. McPartland (Halcyon); *Urban Renewal* w. Green (Proj. 3); *Summer of '42* w. Bennett; *Time to Fly* w. David Pomeranz (Col.); *One More Time* w. S. Syms (Atl.).

LEVEY, STAN,* *drums, composer*; b. Philadelphia, Pa. 4/5/25. One of the influential bop drummers of the '40s, Levey was very busy as accompanist to many singers during the '50s and '60s. Apart from writing the scores for a number of educational films, he has now virtually given up the music business to concentrate on photography, and operates his own studio.

LEVIEV, MILCHO, *piano, keyboards, synthesizer, composer*; b. Plovdiv, Bulgaria, 12/19/37. Grad. 1960 from Bulg. State Cons. in Sofia. Leader, comp. & arr. Bulgarian Radio-TV Big Band, '62-6; led jazz quartet, '65-8; to W. Germany, worked w. A. Mangelsdorff '70-71. Emigrated to US Feb. '71. Keyboards, comp., arr. for Don

Ellis orch. '71-4, also Willie Bobo combo Nov. '73-Mar. '74; B. Cobham from March '74. Pl. w. C. McRae, J. Klemmer, Airto, T. Vig, Lee Ritenour et al.

Leviev app. as pianist-conductor w. Sofia Philharmonic '63-8, worked on numerous Bulgarian TV shows and scored nine movies, one of which, *A Hot Noon*, was first Bulgarian jazz film score, '63. Another, *Detour*, won first prize at Moscow film fest. '68. He won medal for comp. at International Comp. Contest, Vienna Youth Festival, '59.

Comps: *Music for Big Band and Symphony Orch.* ('65); *Concerto for Jazz Combo & Strings* ('65; US premiere '72, LA, w. members of Don Ellis band and Westside Symph.). Symphonic, chamber music, many jazz and theatre music works. Publ: *Odd Meters in Bulgarian Folk Music* in *The New Rhythm Book* (Ellis Music Enterprises, 5436 Auckland Ave., N. Hollywood, Cal.).

Leviev writes: "I immigrated to the U.S. seeking the authentic jazz idiom, which I consider the most vital element in music today. I tried very hard to establish jazz in Bulgaria, but without encouraging results. I was president of the Sofia Jazz Club 1967-8. Jazz in Europe—as a movement, not individual musicians—is still more of a snobbery than real necessity."

LPs: *Jazz Focus '65* (MPS); w. Ellis, *Tears of Joy, Connection,* (Col.), *Soaring* (MPS); *Virginland* w. Airto (Salvation-CTI); *Total Eclipse* w. Cobham (Atlantic).

LEVIN, MARC LEONARD, *cornet, flute, composer*; also *fluegelhorn, mellophone, piccolo, Indian flutes, percussion, melodica, voice, violin*; b. Bayonne, N.J., 8/6/42. Studied trumpet w. Melvin Thompson, '56-7; Alan Jacobs, '57-8; John Ware of N.Y. Phil., '58-9; John Martel, '59-60; William Gerstenberger at Rutgers U., '62-3; theory w. Hall Overton at New School, '64; brass techniques w. Carmine Caruso, '67. From '65-9 stud. trumpet and comp. w. Bill Dixon, whom he considers his greatest influence. Other infl: Clifford Brown, Mingus, Monk, Booker Little, Calo Scott, Christian Kyhl. Worked w. Alan Silva, '65; Dixon, '66-9; Ed Curran, '66-7; Perry Robinson; Burton Greene, '66; own ensemble, '65-73. Moved to Copenhagen, '73, where he leads own group; also pl. w. Cyclamium, '73-4; Annette Peacock, '74. Collaborated w. Mal Waldron in Germany and Scandinavia, '75. MA in Psych. from New School. Works as a consultant in Copenhagen drug programs. Comps: *The Dragon Suite; Songs, Dances and Prayers; Letter to Richard Nixon re: The Chile Affair; Blues For George and Henry,* dance score; *Buttons; The Swing,* film scores. LPs: *Songs, Dances and Prayers* (Sweet Dragon); *The Dragon Suite* (Savoy, Byg); w. Bill Dixon (RCA Victor); Ed Curran (Savoy).

LEVITT, ALAN, *drums*; b. New York City, 11/11/32. Played w. S. Getz; L. Tristano. L. Konitz, P. Bley in early '50s; w. Bechet; Solal in Paris, '56-58, before returning to U.S. where he worked w. Toshiko, J. McLean, Chris Connor, Dick Haymes. Toured U.S., Europe and Asia w. L. Hampton, '66. Worked in LA w. Georgie Auld; Joe Albany; Teddy Edwards, '67. In '68 rec. for ESP w. members of his family: wife Stella, vocals; son,

Sean, guitar, etc. Acc. singers Jackie Paris & Ann Marie Moss, '69; C. Connor; David Allyn, '70. Pl. w. L. Konitz; Z. Sims, '71; C. Mingus, '72. In '73 to Las Palmas, Canary Islands w. family to work at Half Note club. Worked at Whiskey Jazz club in Madrid w. Pedro Itturalde; Lou Bennett; Donna Hightower; toured Spain w. own gp., '74. Moved to Paris '75. Toured Holland w. Peter Ind; concerts w. Slide Hampton; toured Holland, Belgium, England w. Warne Marsh. TV: Holland, Spain w. Lionel Hampton, '66; *To Tell the Truth* w. his family, '68; *Today* w. D. Allyn, '70. App. in film, *Take a Hard Ride,* '75. Fest: San Sebastian w. Itturalde; Newport Fest. in Madrid, '74. LP: *We Are the Levitts* (ESP).

LEVY, HENRY J. (HANK), *composer, baritone saxophone*; b. Baltimore, Md., 9/27/27. Stud. Baltimore City Coll.; Navy School of Mus.; Wm. & Mary; Peabody Conserv.; Catholic U.; Towson State Coll. With S. Kenton band on baritone, '53. Wrote for Sal Salvador orch., '60-2. Many arrs. for Don Ellis, '66- ; Kenton, '69- . Gov't grant to write work, *Opus for Overextended Jazz Ensemble,* premiered by Baltimore Symph., '71.

In '68 Levy sold the family retail business and began a teaching career at Towson. Has also busied himself with many of the Kenton clinics. His coll. band won the Notre Dame fest. '70-1-2; Quinnipiac, '71-2-3, '75. Levy is a scholarly and highly skilled writer, insp. by J. Richards and Don Ellis, who has been particularly effective composing and arranging works in unusual meters. Comps: for Ellis, *Chain Reaction; Whiplash; Passacaglia & Fugue;* for Kenton, *Indra; Ambivalence.* Publ: *A Time Revolution* (Creative World, 1214 S. Robertson Blvd., Los Angeles, Ca. 90035).

LPs: w. Ellis, *Live at Monterey; Live in 3 2/3/4 Time* (Wor. Pac.); *Electric Bath; Connection; Tears of Joy* (Col.); *Soaring* (BASF); w. Kenton, *Live at Redlands; Fire, Fury & Fun; Live at Brigham Young U.; Live from London; Birthday in Britain* (Creative World).

LEVY, LOUIS (LOU),* *piano*; b. Chicago, Ill., 3/5/28. Best known as accompanist for E. Fitzgerald, Peggy Lee for many years and as freelance jazz musician mainly in LA. Worked off and on for Nancy Wilson from '66; jobs w. B. Goodman in late '60s. Joined Supersax New Year's Eve, '73, and was still working with the group in '75.

LPs: w. Supersax, *Salt Peanuts; Supersax Plays Bird With Strings* (Cap.); w. F. Sinatra, *My Way* (Repr.); many P. Lee albums through '73 (Cap.); w. N. Wilson, *Broadway My Way; Hello Young Lovers* (Cap.); w. Chubby Jackson in *Bebop Revisited, Vol. 1* (Xanadu).

LEWIS, GEORGE,* *clarinet*; b. New Orleans, La., 7/13/00. Active as co-leader with Red Allen of own group, and w. Eureka Brass Band in '20s. After a decade of inactivity, he was rediscovered in '42 and became a key figure in NO jazz revival, making several tours of Europe and Japan. Returning home he worked intermittently in NO until shortly before his death there, 12/31/68.

LPs: *Easy Riders Jazz Band; In Japan,* Vols. 1/3; *Ragtime Stompers* (GHB); *George Lewis* (Archive of Folk & Jazz Music); *In Concert* (BN).

LEWIS, JOHN AARON,* *composer, piano, educator*; b. La Grange, Ill., 5/3/20. Prominent in Dizzy Gillespie orch. of mid-'40s; important contributor to Miles Davis nonet '49. Formed Modern Jazz Quartet with Milt Jackson, Percy Heath and Kenny Clarke in '52. In its 22 years (Clarke was replaced by Connie Kay in '55), under Lewis' direction, it became one of the premier units in jazz. During the group's existence it was in the habit on disbanding each year for a summer hiatus but in July '74 the MJQ was permanently dissolved, reuniting only for a concert at Avery Fisher Hall in November. "There really has never been a combination in jazz like the fusion created by the MJQ," wrote Nat Hentoff. "The delicate, almost evanescent lyricism, the sometimes grave, sometimes playful polyphony; and the sure sense of the roots of jazz."

Lewis, a member of the Board of Trustees of the Manhattan School of Music has been teaching at the Davis Center for Performing Arts at City College, CUNY, from '74. In the summer of '75 he taught at Harvard U. He is also a member of the panel for Jazz, Folk & Ethnic Music for the NEA.

TV: Flip Wilson; Helen Reddy; Dick Cavett; *Camera 3*; English & Australian programs. Fest: Tunisia; Gulbenkian Music Fest., Lisbon; Baalbek Music Fest., Lebanon; Geneva; Avignon; Nice; Milan; Pescara. Lewis has also been the music coordinator for the Monterey JF from its inception, working closely w. producer Jimmy Lyons. In '75 he appeared as a solo pianist at NJF-NY, demonstrating his subtle but effective rhythmic thrust and deep feeling for the blues.

Wrote the score for *Cities For People*, a film, shown on KPBS, San Diego, which won a first prize at the SF Film Fest., '75. Other comps: *In Memoriam; Jazz Ostinato; Mirjana of My Heart; Lyonhead; Beach Head*. The last three pieces are included in Lewis' Columbia album *P.O.V.* in which he utilizes violin, cello, flute, piano and percussion in a chamber-like setting. Other LPs: w. MJQ, *Blues on Bach; Plastic Dreams; Live at the Lighthouse; Legendary Profile* (Atl.); *In Memoriam* (Little David).

LEWIS, MEL,* *drums, leader*; b. Buffalo, N.Y., 5/10/29. Worked w. Gerry Mulligan band, Dizzy Gillespie group in '60s. In Dec. '65 he and Thad Jones formed the Thad Jones-Mel Lewis Orchestra, which in the following ten years established itself as what many observers feel is the best big band in the world. (For personnel, polls, etc. see Jones, Thad.) He and Jones also co-led a small group on occasion in NYC area clubs during the '70s.

Lewis is able to swing a big band with a minimum of fuss and a maximum of taste. His abilities as a consummately musical drummer were placed in bold relief when he played unaccompanied in a NJF-NY concert called *Drum Shtick*, '73.

LPs: see Jones, Thad; w. Jones-Pepper Adams, *Mean What You Say* (Mile.); w. Jones and Swedish Radiojazz Group (Four Leaf Clover); w. Al Cohn-Zoot Sims, *Body and Soul* (Muse); w. Jimmy Rushing, *The You and Me*

That Used to Be (RCA); w. Bobby Hackett (Fly. Dutch.).

LEWIS, TED (Theodore Leopold Friedman),* *leader, clarinet*; b. Circleville, Ohio, 6/6/1892. The veteran bandleader, some of whose records in the '30s feat. B. Goodman, F. Waller and J. Teagarden, died 8/25/71 of a heart attack at his home in NYC.

LIEBMAN, DAVID (DAVE), *tenor, soprano saxes, flute*; b. Brooklyn, N.Y., 9/4/46. Private studies w. Joe Allard, '62-6; Charles Lloyd, '66-8; Lennie Tristano, '67-8. Worked w. Ten Wheel Drive, '70; Elvin Jones, '71-3; Miles Davis, '73-4. Formed own group, Lookout Farm, '74. Co-founder, in '71, of musicians' co-operative, Free Life Communication, funded by N.Y. State Council on the Arts. Infl: Coltrane, Rollins, M. Tyner, E. Jones, M. Davis, Wayne Shorter. TV: *In Concert* w. Davis, ABC. Fest: Montreux w. Davis; Newport in U.S. and Europe w. Davis; Jones. LPs: *Sweet Hands* (Horizon); *Lookout Farm; Drum Ode* (ECM); *Open Sky* (P.M.); *My Goals Beyond* w. John McLaughlin (Douglas); *Live at the Lighthouse; Genesis* w. Jones (Blue Note); *Get Up With It* w. Davis (Columbia).

LINCOLN, ABBEY,* *singer, actress*; b. Chicago, Ill., 8/6/30. Prominent in late '50s and '60s as collaborator with Max Roach. Starred in film, *For Love of Ivy*, '68. Divorced Roach and moved to LA, 1970. Continued her career as actress and singer, app. on segments of *Mission Impossible; Name of the Game; ABC Movie of the Week*; singing on *Flip Wilson Show; Hollywood Palace* etc. Active in community affairs, also taught drama at Cal. State U., Northridge, 1974. In '75 she assumed a new name, Aminata Moseka. The first name was bestowed on her by the president of Guinea during a visit to that country; Moseka by the Minister of Information in Zaire. Occasional apps. at Parisian Room, other clubs in LA, SF.

LINDBERG, NILS, *piano, composer*; also *organ*; b. Uppsala, Sweden, 6/11/33. Grew up in Dalarna as a member of a long-standing musical family incl. legendary fiddler Kruskorpf Mats Olsson and uncle, Oscar Lindberg, composer, and prof. at the Royal Academy of Music. Stud. music at Uppsala U., '52-6; counterpoint and comp. at Royal Academy, Stockholm, '56-60. While at the Academy perf. as pianist with jazz groups. Lindberg has also app. with the Swedish Radio Symph. and Hanover Symph. during '70s. He was Judy Garland's pianist for her last Scandinavian tour. App. w. D. Ellington's orch. at Malmo and Copenhagen, Oct. '73. Accompanist for Alice Babs in concerts and recs. First made his reputation with arrs. for four saxophones and rhythm sec. on LP *Sax Appeald*, '60, but became more widely known with a suite in three movements entitled *Trisection*, one of the first major Swedish works written for jazz orch. w. soloists, '62. His main infl. is Swedish folklore which he combines w. jazz in his comp. *7 Dalecarlian Paintings*, rec. in '72-3. Other comps. incl. *Lapponian Suite* for clarinet, rhythm sec. and symph. orch., commissioned by Norddeutscher Rundfunk; *Noah's Ark; Dialogue*. Arr.

Far Away Star for Babs' perf. w. Ellington. App. at Stockholm JF, '71 and '73. TV: Five progs. w. Babs; *Concerto 63* for jazz group and symph. orch. commissioned by Eurovision and shown all over Europe. His music for an LP by Jan Allan was awarded the Grammis, Swedish equivalent of the Grand Prix du Disque, '70.

LPs: *Trisection* (EMI); *Jan Allan with Music By Nils Lindberg; Sax Appeald* (Telestar); *7 Dalecarlian Paintings; Music with a Jazz Flavor; Alice Babs Serenading Duke Ellington* (Swedish Society Discofil).

LINN, RAYMOND SAYRE (RAY),* *trumpet*; b. Chicago, Ill., 10/20/20. Veteran of T. Dorsey, Herman, Shaw, Raeburn bands in '40s. Freelance studio work for many years in LA; also lead trumpet w. Lawrence Welk, '66; Pat Boone TV show, '67; lead trumpet/arr. w. Paul Smith orch. on Steve Allen show, '68-9. Toured as lead trumpet/arr. w. Big Band Cavalcade nostalgia show, '72. Led own dixieland band, the Chicago Stompers, in many local clubs, '73- .

LISTON, MELBA DORETTA,* *composer, trombone*; b. Kansas City, Mo., 1/13/26. Prominent in 1940s, early '50s w. C. Basie; D. Gillespie; again w. Gillespie '56-7; Quincy Jones '59-61. Many sessions as arr. for Randy Weston. During 1960s returned to LA, where she had lived during '40s; free lanced as arr. To NYC where she co-led Clark Terry big band and wrote for Duke Ellington; Jon Lucien; Solomon Burke; Tony Bennett; and Buffalo Symphony Orch., '67. Taught trombone at Pratt Institute Youth-In-Action Orch. in Brooklyn, and Harlem Back Street Youth Orch., '68. In '70s divided her time between work w. youth orchs. in Watts, Calif., and arr. for Count Basie, Abbey Lincoln, Diana Ross and Ellington. Moved to Jamaica, where she became teacher at Univ. of West Indies; dir. of popular music studies, Jamaica Institute of Music, Kingston. Film: comp. & arr. music for *The Marijuana Affair*. Fest: NJF-NY w. Weston, '73. LP: w. Weston, *Tanjah* (Polydor); '40s sides w. Dexter Gordon reissued on *Bebop Revisited, Vol. 1* (Xanadu).

LITTLE, WESTON WILBUR, *bass*; b. Parmele, N.C., 3/5/28. Benny Golson is a distant cousin. While in service w. Army Air Corps on Guam, '46, started pl. piano, then switched to bass. Pl. w. small combo in service clubs. In '49 to Washington, D.C. where he worked in Dept. of Interior and pl. w. small gps. incl. Sir Charles Thompson, Leo Parker. Toured and rec. w. Griffin Bros., Margie Day, '49-51; Paul Williams, '51-3. Returned to Wash., and w. own trio backed visiting hornmen such as Miles Davis, K. Dorham, Coltrane, '53-5. Studied w. Joe Willens of Nat. Symph. Pl. w. J.J. Johnson '55-8, touring U.S. and Europe, then back to Wash. again for government work and free-lance pl. w. Sonny Stitt, Shirley Horn; Nina Simone; Roland Kirk, etc., '58-66. During this time also pl. for Left Bank Jazz Society in Baltimore. To NYC, working w. Elvin Jones, off and on, '67-70. Then free-lancing w. Junior Mance; Frank Foster; K. Dorham; K. Burrell. From '70 pl. w. George Coleman-Danny Moore; Tommy Flanagan; Barry Harris; Al Haig. W. Clark Terry, '74; Ellis Larkins, '75. A resource-ful soloist and an accompanist capable of pulling his weight in a duo or a big band and anyplace in between. Infl: Ray Brown. TV: *Dial "M" For Music* w. E. Jones; *Like It Is* w. Lucky Thompson, '72; E. Larkins, '75. Film: soundtrack for *The Female Response*. Fest: NJF w. E. Jones; NJF-NY w. C. Terry, '74; Newport in Europe w. Lee Konitz, Kai Winding, etc. Comp: *Whew!*; *Soul Mama*. LPs: w. E. Jones, *Poly-currents; Coalition* (BN), *Live at the Vanguard* (Enja); w. C. Terry (Vanguard); w. J. Mance (Atl.); earlier ones, most likely deleted, w. J.J. Johnson (Col.); *Tommy Flanagan Overseas* (Prest.); Randy Weston (UA); recent ones w. Konitz; Haig for foreign labels, unreleased.

LLOYD, CHARLES,* *saxophones, flutes, composer*; also *synthesizer*; b. Memphis, Tenn., 3/15/38. Played with Chico Hamilton, '61-4; Cannonball Adderley, '64-5; then own groups. Lloyd was the first jazz musician invited by Russian People's Group to make a tour of the Soviet Union, in '67. Between '66 and '69 he was also seen at fests. in Poland and Czechoslovakia and at MJF. First jazz musician to play the Fillmore Auditorium, '67. Toured Far East for U.S. State Dept., '68. In '69 Lloyd was the subject of an award-winning, 60-minute documentary film, *Charles Lloyd—Journey Within*, by Eric Sherman, seen at the N.Y. Film Fest., Museum of Modern Art, NYC, and on educ. TV. During '70 and '71 his combo pl. concerts in over 100 colleges. From '70-4 he did doctoral work at Cal. Tech., where he was also artist-in-residence, '72-3. In '73 he played the Newport JF in NY. He took part in a poetry-and-music reading in Santa Cruz, Cal., in '74 with Gary Snyder, Allen Ginsberg, Lawrence Ferlinghetti. Toured Canada, '74. Wrote scores for various documentary films, TV commercials, educational film strips.

In addition to playing and teaching music, and continuing to give lectures and workshops at colleges and prisons, Lloyd became a teacher of transcendental meditation. Much of his music in the '70s took on a high energy coloration that proved popular with rock audiences. In '75 Lloyd was living in Malibu, Cal. Comps: *Forest Flower; Sombrero Sam; Passin' Thru'; Transfusion; T.M.* LPs: *Geeta; Waves* (A & M); *Moonman; Warm Waters* (Kapp); *Dream Weaver; Forest Flower; Love-In; Journey Within; Soundtrack; In Europe* (Atl.); *Discovery; Of Course, Of Course* (Col.); earlier LPs w. Hamilton (Repr., Col., Imp.).

LOCKE, EDWARD (EDDIE), *drums*; b. Detroit, Mich., 2/8/30. Studied at Miller HS. Met Oliver Jackson and formed duo, Bop and Lock, singing, dancing and drumming in theaters in and around Detroit. Encouraged by Cozy Cole they app. on bill opposite Arnett Cobb at Apollo, NYC, '54. Remained in NYC and began gigging around. Pl. w. Tony Parenti, Dick Wellstood at Metropole; then w. Roy Eldridge. Worked w. Coleman Hawkins and Eldridge at Metropole, '58. Most often w. Hawkins until his death in '69. In '70s w. Eldridge at Jimmy Ryan's. He credits Roy w. helping him to shape his feature solo on *Caravan*. Has also worked w. Ray Bryant; Red Allen; Teddy Wilson; Kenny Burrell; Earl

Hines. Main infl: Jo Jones. "Locke was too young to have experienced the best days of the Swing Era," wrote Stanley Dance, "but he is unusual in his ability to comprehend and adjust to the requirements of two of its greatest figures, Roy Eldridge and Coleman Hawkins."

TV: *Dial M For Music; Tonight*; Mike Douglas. Fest: NJF-NY. LPs: w. Hawkins, *Today and Now* (Imp.); *Live at the Village Gate* (Verve); w. Eldridge, *Happy Time* (Pablo); w. Lee Konitz, *Chicago* (Gr. Merch.).

LOFTON, LAWRENCE ELLIS (TRICKY),* *trombone*; b. Houston, Tex., 5/28/30. Pl. in school from 1941; high sch. band '43-7; Army band '48-'53. Toured w. Joe Liggins, '53-5; T-Bone Walker, Lowell Fulson, '55-6; Big Joe Turner, many r & b gps incl. Bill Doggett '58; Richard Groove Holmes '61. Toured w. J. McGriff '71-2. Free lancing in LA, w. Bill Berry band '72- , also in SF with Jon Hendricks' *Evolution of the Blues* show. Infls: Hendricks, J.J. Johnson, J. Cleveland, J.C. Higginbotham, Tricky Sam Nanton. Seen briefly in film *Blazing Saddles* w. C. Basie. LPs: *Tricky Lofton Brass Bag* (PJ); w. Doggett, *All Blue* (King); Richard Groove Holmes (PJ); Bill Berry, *Hot & Happy* (Beez); J. Hendricks, *Tell Me The Truth* (Arista).

LONGO, MICHAEL JOSEPH (MIKE), *piano, composer*; also *electric keyboards*; b. Cincinnati, Ohio, 3/19/39. Mother is piano teacher and was church choir dir.; father was bass player active in club-dates. Began playing at age three, taught by mother. Bachelor of Mus. degree from Western Kentucky U., '59. Stud. counterpoint w. Frank Gaskin Fields, NYC, '67-8; composition w. Hall Overton, '71-2. First pro. job with father's band in Fla. at age 15. Worked w. C. Adderley while attending high school in Ft. Lauderdale; various r & b groups in So. Fla. With Hal McIntyre orch., '57; house pianist at Metropole, NYC w. Henry Red Allen, C. Hawkins, Geo. Wettling et al, '60-1. To Toronto Oct. '61 to study w. O. Peterson, working various clubs there until he formed his own trio and returned to NYC, Mar. '62 for jobs at Basin St. E., The Embers, Hickory House etc. Acc. various singers, '62-6. Own trio at Embers West from June '66, backing R. Eldridge, Z. Sims, C. Terry and others. D. Gillespie heard trio and hired Longo, Dec. '66. Became mus. dir. for Gillespie, writing much of the group's repertoire from '68-73. During this period also freelanced in NYC; worked frequently w. J. Moody quartet. Formed own group, '73. Early infls: Sugar Chile Robinson, Basie, Peterson, Garner, Tatum. Many TV and fest. apps. w. Gillespie, incl. Newport, Monterey, Mexico Fest. of the Arts, and throughout Europe and Japan. Won DB Hall of Fame scholarship, '59. Comps: *Shack o Mack; Lay'in It Down* (both rec. by B. Rich); *Soliloquy; Piece of Resistance; The Awakening; 900 Shares of the Blues; Matrix; Ding-a-Ling; Soul Kiss*; string quartet under grant from Nat'l Endowment for the Arts. Publ: *Consolidated Artists Newsletter* (290 Riverside Dr., #11D, New York, N.Y. 10025).

LPs: *900 Shares of the Blues; Funkia* (Gr. Mer.); *Jazz Portrait of Funny Girl* (Clamike); *Matrix; The Awakening* (Mainstr.); w. Moody, *Heritage Hum*; w. Astrud Gil-

berto, *Now* (Perception); and others w. Gillespie on Imp., Perception, MPS-BASF, Pablo.

LOUISIANA RED (Iverson Minter), *singer, guitar, harmonica*; b. Vicksburg, Miss., 3/23/36. Self-taught. Rec. for Roulette in '62, but did not come into prominence until '70s. Insp. by Muddy Waters and Elmore James, he app. at the Phila. Folk Fest. and in '75 at Montreux. Comps: *Sweet Blood Call; The Whole World* (collab. w. Kent Cooper); *Too Poor to Die*.

LPs: *Lowdown Back Porch Blues* (Roul.); *Louisiana Red Sings The Blues* (Atco); *Sweet Blood Call* (Blue Labor).

LOUISS, EDDY (Edouard Louise), *organ*; also *piano, trumpet, singer*; b. Paris, France, 5/2/41. Father, who came from the Antilles, pl. his ethnic music and jazz w. own dance band in Paris. Mother taught him piano; pl. in father's band. Formed first gp. w. teenage friends. Appeared at Chat Qui Pêche. With Double Six of Paris in early '60s. Active in studio work. Pl. w. Kenny Clarke; Johnny Griffin; Jean-Luc Ponty; Rene Thomas; Stan Getz. Infl: Miles Davis; John Coltrane. TV: France; Germany; BBC. Fest: Antibes; Bergamo; Lugano; Montreux. Won DB Critics Poll, TDWR, '68, '71-4; *Jazz Forum* readers poll, '71-2, '74. Comp: *Our Kind of Sabi*. LPs: Musidisc; MPS; America; w. Ponty (Col.); w. Gillespie & Double Six (Philips); w. Getz, *Dynasty* (Verve).

LOWE, FRANK, *tenor saxophone*; also *soprano sax, bass clarinet, flute, piccolo*; b. Memphis, Tenn., 6/24/43. Wife, Carmen Lowe, is flute student. Vocal and piano instruction in elementary school; instrumental music studies w. Tuff Green, band dir. at Melrose Jr. high. Attended U. of Kansas, '61-3; moved to SF where he stud. theory and harmony under Pete Magadini at SF Conservatory of Music. Worked for Stax Records as salesman, music student and part time songwriter, '59, but made switch from r & b to jazz through listening to O. Coleman, Coltrane and Cecil Taylor. Met Sonny Simmons, Dewey Redman and bassist Donald Garrett in SF. The latter instructed him in "the music I had been searching for." To NYC, '66, where he worked w. Sun Ra, eventually returning with him to SF and further studies at the Conserv. With A. Coltrane in NYC from early '70 through '73. When Ms. Coltrane moved to Cal., he remained in NY working w. D. Cherry, Sunny Murray, C. Bley, M. Graves, Rashied Ali, and with own groups. Infls: J. Coltrane, O. Coleman, C. Taylor, E. Dolphy, L. Young, Ch. Parker, Paul Hindemith. Collaborated w. Cherry in the music for Alexandro Jodorowsky's film, *Holy Mountain*; prod. and arr. own film, *Street Music*. Fests: Berkeley, Ann Arbor, w. A. Coltrane; NJF-NY, w. Cherry and own group. Won DB Critics Poll TDWR, '74.

LPs: *Black Beings* (ESP); *Fresh* (Arista); *Alternatives* (Circle); F. Lowe-R. Ali, *Duo Exchange* (Survival); w. Noah Howard, *Live at the Village Vanguard* (Freedom); w. Cherry, *Relativity Suite* (JCOA); three albums w. A. Coltrane (Imp.).

LOWE, MUNDELL,* *composer, guitar*; b. Laurel, Miss., 4/21/22. Originally well known as jazz guitarist, he settled in LA, Dec. '65, working as comp. for films, TV shows etc., among them *Love on a Rooftop; I Dream of Jeannie; The Iron Horse; Wild, Wild West; Hawaii 5-0.* In '69 he served as music supervisor for educ. TV station KCET, comp. most of the music for Hollywood Television Theater; co-produced *Jazz In The Round* for PBS network, also cond. the band, '70; comp. and cond. music for the highly successful motion pic. *Billy Jack*, '72. Left KCET to do extensive freelancing. In '73-4 he arr. and prod. several albums, also resumed playing guitar on jazz gigs around LA, and participated in school clinics and teaching on a visiting faculty basis. Worked in Europe with singer Betty Bennett, '74-5. Night club dates w. R. Kamuca, '75. Pl. at MJF, '71-4.

LP: *California Guitar* (Famous Door).

LUCIE, LAWRENCE (LARRY),* guitar; also *banjo, mandolin, clarinet;* b. Emporia, Va., 12/18/14. The veteran big band guitarist (Benny Carter, F. Henderson, C. Hawkins, Louis Armstrong) was still active in the '70s. Pl. in reconstituted Chick Webb band at NJF-NY, '74; tributes to Armstrong, '74-5; tributes to Basie and Lucky Millinder at Carnegie Hall, '73. A charter member of NYJRC, he also remained busy as a studio guitarist and teaching at the Borough of Manhattan Community Coll. in NYC. Publ: *Lucie's Special Guitar Lessons* (Playnote Music Publishing, 306 West 51st St., New York, N.Y. 10019).

LUCIEN, JON (Jon Lucien Harrigan), singer, songwriter; also *bass; guitar; synthesizer; clavinet;* b. Tortola, Brit. Virgin Islands, 1/8/42. Raised on St. Thomas. Father, a blind musician, started him and brothers in music; learned scat singing from mother who sang to him when he was a baby. Further self-studies on ukulele, guitar and bass while in reform school from ages nine to 16. Worked w. British comp.-pianist, Marty Clark, who taught him "all the right things."

To NYC '62, pl. clubs, weddings, bar-mitzvahs, Catskill Mt. hotels. Rec. singles for Col., Cap. which went generally unnoticed. Rec. LP for RCA, '70 but it was second album, *Rashida*, which moved him into the public consciousness. Parlayed a two-week engagement at the Village Gate into 15 weeks, then made successful tour of clubs in Boston, Phila., Baltimore, Wash., D.C. Concerts at Philharmonic Hall, '74; Carnegie Hall, '75. App. at NJF-NY, '75. Infl: Jesse Belvin, Nat Cole, Miles Davis, John Coltrane. Lucien says: "I just listened to the horns and the way Miles used to phrase *Funny Valentine*, you know how hecantakeoneworddanddothreenoteswithit but still make the one word mean something. As if he were reciting a poem."

Rafiq Abrahim wrote: "He is jazz. He is calypso. He is classical. He is now. His music is a well balanced fusion of these categories and more. He is the synthesis of the Seventies."

TV: Mike Douglas; Merv Griffin; Dinah Shore. Comp: *Find Yourself a Lover; Soul Mate; Creole Lady; Song For My Lady; Follow Your Heart.*

LPs: *Song For My Lady* (Col.); *I Am Now; Rashida; Mind's Eye* (RCA).

LUCRAFT, HOWARD,* composer, leader, guitar; b. London, England, 8/16/16. The musician-journalist continued to write compositions for foreign TV as well as jazz articles for *Crescendo; Overture; Melody Maker; LA Times.* Music editor of *Daily Variety*, 1972-3. Jazz radio shows on KCBH; KPFK; KBCA. Teaching jazz style at schools throughout LA County. From '74, active again leading 20 piece orch. in Cal., Arizona; also comp. for jazz septet which, in '75, rec. LPs, *Potpourri* (Bosworth) and *Americana* (Glendale).

LYONS, JAMES (JIMMY),* alto sax, flute; b. Jersey City, N.J., 12/1/32. Best known for his association w. Cecil Taylor from '60. In '69 pl. concerts at Maeght Foundation in France w. him; also made first rec. as leader for Byg Records in Paris. Taught music for Narcotic Addiction Control, '70-1. From '71-3 artist-in-residence w. Taylor at Antioch Coll., Ohio where he was orch. director for Black Music Ensemble. Toured Japan twice w. Taylor. US and European tours for club and concert app., '74. Composer-instrumentalist, dir. Black Music Ens. at Bennington Coll., Vermont, '75. Did two films in France, one for Maeght Found. w. Taylor. Fest: Antibes; Willisau; Perugia, '75. Comp: *Aztec Nights* for 25 pieces at Antioch, '72; *Something's the Matter*, Bennington, '75. LPs: *Other Afternoons* (Byg); w. Taylor, *Spring of Two Blue-J's* (Unit Core); *Unit Structures; Conquistador* (BN); for the Maeght Found. (Shandar).

LYONS, JIMMY, producer; b. Peking, China, 11/18/16. Began career in 1941, presenting S. Kenton band live from ballroom in Balboa Beach, Calif. In early '40s wrote, produce radio progs. for NBC's Thesaurus Division. During W.W. II he prod. *Jubilee*, jazz progs. for Armed Forces Radio. In '46 he broadcast from San Diego, Tijuana. Worked for Woody Herman, '47. Moved to SF, '48, broadcasting on KNBC for five years. His *Jazz at Sunset* concerts in 1953 from Carmel, Cal. feat. E. Garner, E. Fitzgerald, G. Shearing, D. Brubeck et al. This led to his founding the Monterey Jazz Festival in 1958. Lyons also broadcast live from SF Hangover Club; was on KGO '57-8; KFRC '61-5, both in SF. Appointed to Calif. Arts Commission, '64; chairman '67-8; exec. sec. '68-9. Member of U.S. State Dept. Cultural Presentations Committee. In '72 established annual Calif. High School Jazz Band Competition, winners appearing at MJF. Lyons influenced careers of many jazz artists, notably Dave Brubeck and Gerry Mulligan; Brubeck's *The Lyons Busy* and Mulligan's *Line for Lyons* were written for him.

LYSTEDT, LARS, valve trombone, critic; b. Umea, Sweden, 12/12/25. Played trumpet '42-52, then valve trombone; mainly self-taught. His quintet, which he led from '58-72, became (in '60) the first Swedish band to perf. behind the Iron Curtain, at Warsaw Jazz Jamboree. The quintet won the city of Umea Cultural Prize in '68, and in that year was voted the best int'l group at the Zurich JF. From '68 led the Umea Big Band; originated and org. the Umea JF, biggest of its kind in Sweden. Favs: Bill Harris, L. Armstrong, D. Gillespie.

Lystedt has had a parallel career as a writer, contributing to the magazine *Orkester Journalen* since '50, and acting as Swedish correspondent for DB from '69. He won several awards for music journalism in the early '70s.

LPs: Lars Lystedt Quintet, *Fanfar!* (Jazz Records); Sextet, *Jazz Under the Midnight Sun* (Swedisc); *Umea Big Band in Montreux*, feat. Slide Hampton (Sonet); *Jazz In Umea* (Caprice); Umea Big Band, *Swingtime Festival* (Hitachi).

LYTELL, JIMMY (James Sarrapede),* clarinet; b. New York City, 12/1/04. A member of the Orig. Memphis Five during the '20s, Lytell re-formed the group, '49, and again in the mid-50s. He continued to work occasionally, leading his own groups on Long Island, until he was sidelined by a long illness. He died 11/26/72 at Kings Point, L.I. Lytell, one of the first and most prominent dixieland clarinetists, had worked in the Original Dixieland Jazz Band as a replacement for Larry Shields in '22.

LYTLE, JOHN DILLARD (JOHNNY),* vibes, composer; also drums; b. Springfield, Ohio, 10/13/32. Continued to tour with own trio from '66, incl. apps. in concerts w. W. Montgomery, Nancy Wilson, Miriam Makeba, Ray Charles. Many coll. dates, incl. Battle of the Vibes w. Roy Ayers at Central State Coll. Fests: Albion, Mich.; October Fest., Clairton, Pa., Black Expo, Phila. Comps: *The Village Caller; The Man; The Loop; Libra; Sister Silver and the Moore Man; Happy Ground.* Lytle has received awards from the Urban League and Buffalo U., and the key to the city of Springfield, where he is dir. of the Davey Moore Arts Cultural Center and Davey Moore Foundation. Also received an Outstanding Musician award from the foundation.

LPs: *People and Love; Soulful Rebel* (Milestone); *Man and Woman; Close Enough; Be Proud* (SS).

LYTTELTON, HUMPHREY,* trumpet, leader, composer; b. Windsor, England, 5/23/21. Frequently leader of own band from '50s, originally in traditionalist style, later led swing type, Ellington-influenced small group. Annual visits to Germany, Switzerland, Austria. TV: *In Concert*, BBC-2, '75; Michael Parkinson, BBC-1. Many comps. incl. *Big Ol' Tears; Sprauncy; Lion Rampant; Madly*, for Duke Ellington Tribute concert. Own radio prog., *Humphrey Lyttelton Plays Best · of Jazz on Record.* Many other radio, TV apps., incl. panel shows etc.

Publ: *Take It From The Top* (Robson Books). LPs: *Take It From The Top; Kansas City Woman*, feat. Buddy Tate and comps. written specially for Lyttelton by Buck Clayton (Black Lion).

MABERN, HAROLD JR.,* piano, composer; b. Memphis, Tenn., 3/20/36. Moved from Chi. to NYC in early '60s, working w. L. Hampton, the Jazztet, J.J. Johnson. Acc. Joe Williams, '66-7; also many other singers, incl. Sarah Vaughan, Dakota Staton, Irene Reid, Arthur Pry-

sock. Gigged w. R.R. Kirk; Rollins; Hubbard; L. Morgan; R. Haynes; Wes Montgomery in late '60s. In '73-4 worked w. Walter Bolden trio at the Cellar, NYC; also w. George Coleman; Danny Moore; Keno Duke; Billy Harper; Clark Terry; Joe Newman. Member of the Piano Choir, a seven-piano group under the direction of Stanley Cowell; and a workshop band at Project Create. TV: *Soul* w. Lucky Thompson, Ossie Davis, Ruby Dee; Lee Morgan; Bobbi Humphrey. Fests: NJF w. Johnson; Williams; Young-Holt; Morgan; Hubbard in '60s; as solo pianist, NJF-NY, '75. Comps: *Rakin' and Scrapin'; Waltzing Westward; Such Is Life; I Remember Britt; Aon; Strozier's Mode; A Few Miles From Memphis; For Big Hal; In What Direction Are You Headed.* Received grant from CAPS to write a suite for seven pianos. LPs: *A Few Miles From Memphis; Rakin' and Scrapin'; Greasy Kid Stuff* (Prestige); *Handscapes* w. the Piano Choir; *Sense of Values* w. K. Duke (Strata-East); w. Blue Mitchell, Hank Mobley, Lee Morgan, Hubbard (BN); Johnson (Imp.); Buddy Montgomery (Mile.); Stanley Turrentine (CTI); Frank Foster (Main.).

MACKAY, DAVID OWEN (DAVE), piano, composer; b. Syracuse, N.Y., 3/24/32. Stud. Trinity Coll., Hartford, '50-4; Boston Univ. School of Mus., '56-9; also w. L. Tristano. Pl. w. B. Hackett, S. Stitt, C. Mariano, Bob Wilber, Serge Chaloff in Boston; Jim Hall and own gps. in NYC; own gp. in Chicago. Settling in LA, pl. many local clubs leading own gp. w. wife, the late Vicky Hamilton; also gigged w. Don Ellis, S. Manne, Paul Horn, Chet Baker, Emil Richards, Joe Pass et al. Fests: Monterey; Costa Mesa, both w. Ellis. Comps: *Samba For Vicky; Peek-A-Boo; Here; Like Me; Silent; Now.*

LPs: *Dave Mackay & Vicky Hamilton* (Imp.); w. Ellis, *Live at Monterey; Live in 3 2/3/4 Time* (Pac. Jazz); w. Richards, *Live at Donte's; Journey To Bliss* (Imp.).

MAGRUDER, JOHN DECKER BOYD, saxophones, composer; also flutes, clarinet, oboe, bass; b. Greenwich, Conn., 11/19/25. B.S. (cum laude) mus. ed., '49; M.A. in music, '50, NYU. Received Cal. Community Coll. Credential, '72. Worked w. Horace Silver in Conn., '47-50; had own quartet, '51-9; Don Ellis orch., '65-8; writing for and perf. with his own 17 piece big band, the Magruder Machine, '73- , and own quintet, '75- . Mus. educator in LA City school system from '59- ; Santa Monica Coll. '72-4; Chairman, Mus. Dept. at Univ. High School, W. LA. Received spec. award from LA Mayor Thomas Bradley for work with youth in the field of music, '74. Infls: Getz, Parker, Coltrane, Goodman, DeFranco, Gerald Wilson, Gil Evans, Thad Jones and a variety of modern classical composers. Fests: app. w. own jazz group at 1939 World's Fair, NYC; Monterey, '67-8; Tanglewood, '68; Newport, '67-8; Nice, '68. TV: Don Ellis Special.

Magruder has written TV commercials, music for the Amer. Film Inst., two musical comedies: *The Village Square* and *A Fair Wind to Belford*; symphonic comps; for educ. purposes, and originals for Ellis incl. *Zim.* LPs: w. Ellis, *Live at Monterey; Live in 3 2/3/4 Time* (Pac. Jazz); *Shock Treatment; Electric Bath; Autumn* (Col.).

MAHAVISHNU. see McLaughlin, John.

MAHONES, GILDO,* *piano, composer;* b. New York City, 6/2/29. Prominent from '59 as accompanist for Lambert, Hendricks & Ross. During '60s backed many other singers, among them O.C. Smith for a year in LA, '66; followed by three and a half years as musical director for Lou Rawls. Subsequently worked at many LA clubs either leading own trio or as sideman for Joe Williams, J. Witherspoon, Esther Phillips, King Pleasure, Abbey Lincoln, Leon Thomas; also S. Stitt, J. Moody, A. Farmer, S. Criss, Jim Hall, T-Bone Walker, B. Bryant. Concerts in Cal. and Yamaha Jazz Fest. in Japan, w. Benny Carter, '73; also at Monterey and Newport JF. Musical director and pianist for two shows: *Don't Bother Me I Can't Cope* and *Charlatan.* Mahones' comps. include *The Most Happy Fella* for Bunions Bradford band; *Art's Revelation* for A. Blakey.

LPs: *I'm Shooting High; Gildo Mahones Soulful Piano* (Pres.); w. Lambert, Hendricks & Ross (Col.); w. Lambert, Hendricks & Bavan (RCA); w. J. Hendricks (Wor. Pac., Col., Repr.); w. Witherspoon (Pres., ABC); w. Booker Ervin (Pres.); w. Rawls (Cap.); w. Frank Wess; Ted Curson (Pres.); w. F. Foster; Bennie Green (BN).

MAIDEN, WILLIAM RALPH (WILLIE),* *saxophones, composer, clarinet, piano;* b. Detroit, Mich., 3/12/28. Wrote and/or played for M. Ferguson band from '52 to '65. In '66 worked for Ferguson's sextet and for C. Barnet orch. In '67-9, pl. casual gigs in S. Cal. Became part time teacher at Cerritos Jr. Coll. and continued comp. and arr. From '69-73 he was w. S. Kenton orch. as saxophonist and arr. In '73-4 was assoc. prof., teaching contemp. comp. at the U. of Maine at Augusta. He received a federal grant to present jazz to rural areas and made two tours to fulfill this objective. Died in LA, 5/29/76. Comps: *Little Minor Booze; Height of Ecstasy; Boilermaker; Kaleidoscope; No Harmful Side Effects; April Fool,* all rec. by Kenton.

LPs: w. Kenton, *Birthday in Britain; Live at Brigham Young University; Live at Butler; Live at Redlands;* w. C. Barnet, big band (Creative World).

MAINIERI, MICHAEL JR.,* *vibes;* also *synthi-vibe, keyboards, percussion;* b. Bronx, N.Y., 7/24/38. Came to prominence w. B. Rich in early '60s; own groups from '63. Pres. of Gnu Music Inc., NYC, a music prod. company servicing and supplying comps. and arrs. for TV, radio and record prod. projects. Also busy as studio musician, '67-71. Prod. and arr. an album for 17 piece band called White Elephant, '71. Invented new instrument of his own design called a synthi-vibe, a vibe "controller" which allows him to play electronic sounds through any synthesizer. A five octave instrument, it replaces the keyboard on any synthesizer and allows him to trigger its oscillator with mallets instead of fingers.

Lives in Woodstock, N.Y. where he has his own rec. studio in converted barn. Formed new quartet, '75. Won ASCAP award for Best New Arranger-Composer, '69. Wrote music for film *St. Petersburg Race,* '71; NBC-TV spec. *Of Men and Women,* '74.

Comps. and arrs. for White Elephant; Nick Holmes album. LPs: *White Elephant; Soulful Crooner* w. Holmes (Just Sunshine); others w. Wes Montgomery (CTI); Tim Hardin, Paul Simon (Col.); Don McLean (UA).

MAKOWICZ, ADAM (Matyszkowicz), *piano, keyboards, composer;* also *fender bass;* b. Czechoslovakia, 8/18/40. Stud. w. mother, a piano teacher, later Chopin Secondary School of Music in Cracow, Poland. Started pl. jazz w. Tomasz Stanko in Cracow in '62. Moving to Warsaw in '56, led own trio; toured extensively w. Zbigniew Namyslowski and w. NOVI singers throughout Europe, Cuba, India, New Zealand. Pl. w. B. Webster, Idrees Sulieman, Jan Garbarek. In '71 he joined Michal Urbaniak group, with which he pl. many fests., concerts, concerts and recorded several albums. Took part in "Piano Conclave" app. by leading European pianists, '74, then org. similar meeting on Polish TV, using local keyboard artists. Favs: Tatum, Peterson, K. Jarrett, H. Hancock. Fests: Jazz Jamboree, Warsaw, '64- ; many others in West Germany, Montreux, etc. Comps: *For Pia; Chassing; Live Embers; Blues for Michal;* music for two short films.

Makowicz is best known in the U.S. for his duo album, *Newborn Light* (Col.) w. Urbaniak's wife, singer Urszula Dudziak. Many other LPs for European labels w. Urbaniak, Namyslowski, Jazz Jamboree, NOVI, Tallinn International Jazz Fest. etc.

MALACHI, JOHN, *piano;* b. Red Springs, N.C., 9/6/19. Self-taught. Pl. w. Trummy Young, '43; B. Eckstine big band, '44-5; accomp. for Eckstine, '47; Illinois Jacquet, '48. Accomp. for many singers, incl. Pearl Bailey in LA, '50; D. Washington, '51; S. Vaughan, '52-4; Al Hibbler, '55-8; Dakota Staton, G. Lynne, Joe Williams et al. Pl. w. short-lived Louis Jordan big band in '51. Infls: T. Wilson, A. Tatum, L. Young, D. Gillespie, Ch. Parker, B. Eckstine, S. Vaughan.

Because of his residence in Washington, D.C., where he freelanced for many years, Malachi did not earn the recognition he deserved as one of the first completely qualified bop-influenced pianists.

LPs: w. Vaughan, *Swingin' Easy* (Trip); Eckstine (Spotlite); w. T.J. Anderson, *Classic Rags and Ragtime Songs* (The Smithsonian Collection).

MALONE, THOMAS HUGH (TOM), *trombone;* also *tuba, trumpet, piccolo, flute, saxophone, electric bass, synthesizer;* b. Honolulu, Hawaii, 6/16/47. Studied at Univ. of Southern Mississippi, '65-7; w. Leon Breeden at No. Texas State, '67-9, where he received BS in Psych.; graduate work at New School, NYC, '70. Worked w. Lee Castle-Jimmy Dorsey orch., '67; W. Herman, '69; Duke Pearson, '70; D. Severinsen; Louis Bellson, '72; BS&T '73; Gil Evans, '73- ; B. Cobham, '75; B. Watrous, '71-5. Infl: J.J. Johnson, U. Green; Watrous, Bruce Fowler, C. Fuller, H. Hancock, F. Hubbard. TV: *Tonight Show* w. Severinsen, '72; *Midnight Special; Rock Concert* w. BS&T, '72. Fest: Montreux w. Evans, '74; Cobham, '75. Malone, who plays 14 instruments prof., has written arrs. for Evans: *Crosstown Traffic; Angel;* and for BS&T: *Empty Pages; No Sweat.* Publ: *Alternate Position Sys-*

tem for Trombone (Synthesis Publs., 306 W. 92nd St., New York, N.Y. 10025). LPs: w. Herman, *Heavy Exposure* (Chess); w. Ten Wheel Drive, *Peculiar Friends*; w. James Brown (Poly.); w. BS&T, *No Sweat* (Col.); w. Evans, *Plays Jimi Hendrix; There Comes a Time* (RCA); also w. Cobham (Atl.); Stanley Clarke (Nemp.); M. Santamaria (Fania); Dave Sanborn (War. Bros.).

MANCE, JULIAN C. JR. (JUNIOR),* *piano, composer*; b. Chicago, Ill., 10/10/28. After acc. Joe Williams, '62-4, cont. to tour w. own trio until his activity became limited due to Meniere's disease, a malady of the middle and inner ear, '66-7. In '68 he resumed with a new trio on a full time basis playing clubs and college concerts. Toured France, '70; England, '74. TV apps. on *Someone New; Black Book; Tonight Show; Tillmon's Tempo; Kennedy at Night; Black Dimensions; Positively Black.* Fests: Montreux, '70; NJF-NY, '73. Comps: *Harlem Lullaby; That Mellow Feeling; Jubilation; The Uptown; Junior's Tune; Playhouse; Big Chief; Happy Time; Down the Line; Letter from Home; Zabuda.*

LPs: *Harlem Lullaby; I Believe To My Soul; Live At The Top; With A Lot of Help From My Friends* (Atl.); *The Junior Mance Touch* (Poly.); w. G. Ammons, *The Boss Is Back; Brother Jug* (Pres.); w. A. Franklin, *Soul '69* (Atl.).

MANCUSO, RONALD BERNARD (GUS),* *baritone horn, piano*; also *bass, trumpet, vibes*; b. Rochester, N.Y., 1933. Traveled with B. Eckstine throughout U.S. and Orient, '66; own groups in LV, '67-8 incl. Carl Fontana, Sam Noto, Sal Nistico. In '69 joined S. Vaughan as bassist, later made world tour w. G. Wein's Jazz Expo '70. From '70-3 worked mainly in LV w. comedian-musician Pete Barbutti, in Dottie Dodgion trio. Toured w. Peter Nero. In '74 moved to LA, gigging at clubs, mostly on piano, w. T. Vig, Carol Kaye, A. Pepper, D. Ellis.

LP: w. Buck's Band (MCM).

MANDEL, HARVEY, *guitar*; also *bongo, conga drums*; b. Detroit, Mich., 3/11/45. Self-taught, starting at age 16. Pl. in Chicago w. Bobby Dee and the New Breed, '62-4; Barry Goldberg Blues Band, '65-6; Charlie Musselwhite, '67-8. Later toured w. several rock groups, among them Canned Heat, '69-70, which played at Woodstock and visited Europe; J. Mayall, '70-1 (two U.S., one European and one Japanese tour); Pure Food And Drug Act, '71-3. Led own band, '74- touring U.S., England, Continent, Canada. Infl. by Sugar Cane Harris, B.B. King, Mayall, E. Clapton, Jon Hendricks and many other rock, blues and jazz artists, Mandel also has done some arranging and produced a few albums.

Solo albums: *Cristo Redentor; Righteous; Games Guitars Play* (Phillips); *Baby Batter; Snake; Shangrenade; Feel The Sound; Best of Harvey Mandel* (Janus); *Fiddler on the Rock,* w. Sugar Cane Harris (BASF); *Future Blues; Live In Europe* w. Canned Heat (Liberty); *USA Union; Back to the Roots* w. Mayall (Polydor); others with Graham Bond, Pure Food & Drug Act, Rolling Stones etc.

MANDEL, JOHN ALFRED (JOHNNY),* *composer*; b. New York City, 11/23/25. No longer a part of the jazz scene, Mandel continued to enjoy great success as a writer of music for motion pictures and TV. Some of his tunes, most notably *The Shadow of Your Smile* and *Emily,* were popular among jazz musicians and singers during the 1970s.

MANGELSDORFF, ALBERT,* *composer, trombone*; also *guitar*; b. Frankfurt am Main, Germany, 9/5/28. Continued to tour with his own groups on a worldwide basis, incl. fests. in Newport, '67, '69; New Orleans, '68; Tokyo Summer Jazz; Osaka, '70; Comblain La Tour; Antibes; Prague; Warsaw; Bled, Yugoslavia. Won DB Critics' Poll, TDWR, '65; German jazz polls from '54. By simultaneously singing and blowing, he is able to play several notes at once, thereby producing a band-like effect, examples of which may be heard on his LP, *The Wide Point.*

Publ: *Jazz Improvisation on Trombone* (Ed. Schott, Mainz, Germany). Mangelsdorff is a prolific composer, fully represented on his own LPs: *Tension; Folkmond and Flower Dream* (CBS); *Now Jazz Ramwong* (CBS and Pac.); *Animal Dance* (Atl.); *The Wide Point; Albert and His Friends; Never Let It End; Trombird; Birds of Underground* (MPS); *Albert in Tokyo* (Enja).

MANGIONE, CHARLES FRANK (CHUCK),* *fluegelhorn, trumpet, piano, composer*; b. Rochester, N.Y., 11/29/40. After leading group with brother Gap (see below), went to NYC in '65; pl. w. W. Herman, K. Winding, M. Ferguson. Joined A. Blakey's Jazz Messengers fall of '65 and remained until '67.

From '68-72 Mangione was dir. of the jazz ensemble of the Eastman School of Music in Rochester, N.Y. He formed the Chuck Mangione quartet in '68. In '70 he app. as guest conductor with the Rochester Phil. A recital on that occasion, entitled *Friends and Love,* was televised as a PBS spec. and released as an album. An unusual and successful blending of jazz, folk, middle-of-the-road pop and classical influences, the album was widely acclaimed and achieved substantial commercial acceptance. The best known comp. to emerge from the album was *Hill Where the Lord Hides,* which became a hit single. Mangione followed this initiative with another collaboration with the Rochester Phil. in '71, entitled *Together,* also a PBS spec. From '72 he toured with his quartet, made apps. with the Phil. orchs. of Oakland, Cal.; Edmonton, Alberta and Hamilton, Ont. He app. at numerous fests: Montreux; Newport; Concord, Monterey; Pescara, Italy; Pori, Finland; Kansas City and Niagara Falls.

In '74 Mangione formed his own recording company, Sagoma, in order to present individually several of the artists who had app. with him in concert and on records, among them Gap Mangione, Gerry Niewood and Esther Satterfield. He also published a choral series of his own comps. designed for high school choruses.

Mangione's comps. have been recorded by many pop and jazz artists incl. Cannonball Adderley, Herb Alpert, Ray Bryant, Percy Faith, Mark Murphy, Superfunk.

Comps: *Hill Where The Lord Hides; Friends and Love; Legacy; Land of Make Believe; Feel of a Vision; Sunshower; El Gato Triste*; and all other orig. material on his albums.

LPs: *Friends and Love; Together; Land of Make Believe* w. Hamilton Phil.; w. quartet, *Alive; Chuck Mangione Quartet* (Merc.); *Chase The Clouds Away* (A & M); as cond. w. Gap Mangione (Merc.).

For details of publs. and records: Sagoma Records, Sagoma/DGM Inc., 270 Midtown Plaza, Rochester, N.Y.

MANGIONE, GASPARE CHARLES (GAP),* *piano, composer*; b. Rochester, N.Y., 7/31/38. Brother of Chuck Mangione (see above). Pl. w. Chuck in Jazz Brothers in early '60s. Active from '65 w. own gp. and as teacher in Rochester. Appears as part of the expanded cast for his brother's concert performances.

LP: *She and I* (A&M).

MANN, HERBIE,* *flute, composer, leader*; also *tenor sax*; b. Brooklyn, N.Y., 4/16/30. A leader of his own group from '59, Mann continued to explore new avenues of expression in the late '60s and '70s, shifting personnel in relation to the material. Already having incorporated Afro-Latin, Brazilian, and Middle Eastern elements, by '69 he had rec. w. Memphis r&b studio men along w. his regulars, Roy Ayers, Sonny Sharrock, Larry Coryell and Miroslav Vitous. In '71 he recorded the album *Push Push*, using rock guitarist Duane Allman. By '73 his group had evolved into what is called The Family of Mann w. Pat Rebillot on keyboards and David Newman on tenor sax and flute. Certainly his involvement with blues and soul had begun years before (he acknowledged this in a tribute LP to Ray Charles, *The Inspiration I Feel*) but when he was finished with the Memphis funk, he moved more toward a "New York sophisticated rock," as he called it. In '74 he rec. in England w. British rockers and followed this with a reggae album done w. Tommy McCook, the leader of reggae star Jimmy Cliff's band. In '75 the Family of Mann had a "disco" hit in *Hi-Jack*. Explaining that he did not want to be confined by the narrow definition of "disco" and that "people have been dancing to my music since I started playing," Mann came full circle on *Waterbed* by redoing *Comin' Home Baby*, his success of '62; Charles' *I Got a Woman*; and the kind of Latin number which in its '70s incarnation is called "salsa."

Fest: NJF; NJF-NY; "Newport" fests. all over US; Montreux '72; other Euro. fests. Numerous TV apps. Won DB Readers Poll, '66-70. Comps: *Memphis Spoon Bread and Dover Sole; High Above the Andes; Mediterranean; Paradise Music; Body Oil*. As a producer he recorded artists such as Ron Carter, Miroslav Vitous and Attila Zoller for his own Embryo label (distributed by Atlantic) in '70. LPs: *Waterbed; Discotheque; Reggae; London Underground; Turtle Bay; Hold On, I'm Comin'; Evolution of Mann; Mississippi Gambler; Best of Herbie Mann; Concerto Grosso in D Blues; Live at the Whiskey A Go Go; Memphis Underground; The Inspiration I Feel; Windows Opened; The Wailing Dervishes;*

The Beat Goes On; Impressions of the Middle East; Monday Night at the Village Gate (Atl.); *Stone Flute; Push Push; Memphis Two-Step; Muscle Shoals Nitty Gritty* (Embryo).

MANNE, SHELDON (SHELLY),* *drums, composer*; b. New York City, 6/11/20. The former Kenton and Herman drummer continued as a busy freelance musician in LA in the '60s and '70s. He operated his own jazz club, Shelly's Manne Hole, from Nov. '60 through Sept. '72. Reopened at a new location in LA, Oct. '73; closed Apr. '74. During much of this time Manne led a small jazz group whenever possible, sometimes at his own club. He played the Concord Fest., '68 and '74; concerts in Italy, '70; Ronnie Scott's in London, and many other European apps. In '74 he became a member of a group known as the L.A. Four, along w. Ray Brown, L. Almeida and B. Shank, seen in clubs and concerts, mostly around LA.

As composer, wrote score for *Daktari* TV series; motion pictures *Young Billy Young; Trial of the Catonsville Nine*; scored Center Theater Group's prod. of *Henry IV*, Part I at Mark Taper Forum, LA Music Center. He also taped a series of 13 half-hour lessons, for Cable Network TV, entitled *Let's Play Drums*. A book of the same name, publ. (Chappell Music, 609 5th Ave., New York, N.Y. 10017). LPs: *Alive in London; Gambit; At The Black Hawk; At The Manne Hole; Bells Are Ringing; Checkmate; Concerto for Clarinet & Combo; Li'l Abner; More Swinging Sounds; My Fair Lady; My Son The Drummer; Outside; Peter Gunn; Proper Time; Son of Gunn; Sounds Unheard Of; 2, 3, 4* (Contemp.); *Mannekind* (Mainstr.); *Manne That's Gershwin* (Cap.); w. Bill Evans, *A Simple Matter of Conviction* (Verve); others w. J. Klemmer (Imp.); L.A. Four (Concord); w. Sonny Criss (Prest.); Sonny Stitt (Fly. Dutch.).

MANONE, JOSEPH (WINGY),* *trumpet, singer*; b. New Orleans, La., 2/13/04. Virtually inactive in recent years, he appeared at the Nice Festival in the summer of '75. LP w. Papa Bue (Storyville).

MANTLER, MICHAEL,* *composer, trumpet*; also *valve trombone*; b. Vienna, Austria, 8/10/43. Associations in early '60s with Cecil Taylor, Carla Bley; in '65, w. Bley, introduced Jazz Composers Orchestra at Newport JF and at Museum of Modern Art. Toured Europe w. Bley and Steve Lacy as co-leader of Jazz Realities Quintet. App. in many Western European cities, on radio, TV in Hamburg, Amsterdam etc. Film music for two documentaries in Rome; rec. album in Holland. Returned to U.S. Feb. '66. Worked on consolidation of JCOA. During fall of '66 made second tour of Europe w. quintet. Took part in RCA rec. of C. Bley's "Dark Opera Without Words," *A Genuine Tong Funeral*, w. G. Burton quartet and orch.

Completing a series of comps. for orch. in early '68, he rec. them w. JCO, feat. C. Taylor, Pharoah Sanders, R. Rudd, D. Cherry, G. Barbieri and L. Coryell. In '69 took part in Charlie Haden's Liberation Music Orchestra LP; gave premiere of new works in concert at Electric Circus, NYC, feat. Taylor, Sanders, Cherry. '70-1, comp. extended piece for two orchs. and piano. New orchestral work with words by Samuel Beckett, '71-2. Prod. rec. of opera, *Escalator Over The Hill*, by C. Bley and Paul Haines. Took part in TV workshops in Hamburg and Vienna, Jan. '72.

Mantler continued extensive administrative work for JCOA and its division JCOA Records, and the New Music Distribution Service, estab. '72 (6 West 95th St., New York, N.Y. 10025). Perf. w. JCO during its week-long presentation of Cherry's *Relativity Suite* at N.Y.U. Started (together w. C. Bley) own record label, Watt Works. Completed work on two-orch. piece. Began work on new extended piece. Received CAPS grant in '74. Participated in rec. of C. Bley's *Tropic Appetites*, '73-4.

Among awards received for *The Jazz Composer's Orchestra*, a two record set feat. the comps. of Mantler, were Jazz Album of the Year, Sixth Int'l Jazz Critics Poll, Jazz & Pop Mag., '68; Grand Prix, Academy Charles Cros, France, '68; Album of the Month, various Canadian, English, French, German, Japanese mags.

Mantler has earned the respect and admiration of his peers, not only for his work as composer and conductor, but for his ongoing contributions as activist for the JCOA.

In addition to LPs mentioned above, Mantler can be heard on other JCOA and Watt Works albums.

MANUSARDI, GUIDO, *piano, composer*; b. Chiavenna, Italy, 12/3/35. Worked in Sweden, 1960-66; Romania, '67-71, then Italy and throughout Continent, acc. Joe Venuti, Don Byas, Dexter Gordon, Slide Hampton, Art Farmer et al. From Sept. '74 pl. in duo w. Red Mitchell. Favs: Bill Evans, McCoy Tyner. Many fest. app. acc. Bobby Hackett, Roy Eldridge, Venuti. Long stay in Romania made lasting impact on his style. LPs w. own gps. CBS (Italy), BASF (Germ.), Amigo (Sweden), Dire (It.), Oscar (It.); w. all star gp. *Tribute to Louis*, live at San Remo (CBS-It.).

MARCUS, STEPHEN (STEVE), *tenor, soprano saxophones*; b. New York City, 9/18/39. Stud. privately, also Berklee School, '59-61. Pl. w. S. Kenton; '63, D. Byrd; '65, W. Herman from '67 off and on; H. Mann, '67-70; L. Coryell, '71-3; own group, Count's Rock Band, '73-5. Feat. w. B. Rich band, '75. Infls: Coltrane, Rolling Stones, Beatles, Miles Davis. Fests: Newport, '63, '68, '69, '70; Montreux, '70.

LPs: *Count's Rock Band; Tomorrow Never Knows* (Vortex); w. Coryell *Barefoot Boy* (Fl. Dutchman); *Offering* (Vanguard).

MARIANO, CHARLES HUGO (CHARLIE),* *alto saxophone, electronic saxophone, nagasuram*; b. Boston, Mass., 11/12/23. Prominent in Kenton band, later touring with his, then, wife Toshiko Akiyoshi; taught at Berklee. In Malaysia under sponsorship of USIA, teaching music to members of State Radio Orchestra, '66-7. To Japan, summer '67, rec. several LPs there. Back at Berklee, Aug. '67 until late '68, but made one return trip to Japan during this time. In '67, he formed a jazz-rock group, Osmosis.

Mariano left the U.S. in '71, pl. in Holland, lived in Belgium and formed a group, Ambush, for eight months. Returned to U.S. to rec. an Atl. LP, *Mirror*. Spent last four months of '72 in Zurich for a theatre production of play *Marat/Sade*. In '73 in India for four months studying the nagasuram, a flute-like wooden instrument, which he has feat. ever since. Later in '73 pl. on continent and in London with Dutch pop gp. Supersister. After leaving this combo he pl. and rec. in Finland for several months, joined the German pop gp. Embryo, and from Feb. '74 worked w. a small combo known as Pork Pie, which pl. several major European fests. Living in The Hague, Holland, for most of '75 but returned to US in the fall to teach once again at Berklee.

Other LPs: *Iskander*, w. Supersister (Polydor); *We Keep On*, w. Embryo; *Transitory*, w. Pork Pie (MPS); *September Man*, w. Philip Catherine (Atl.); *Altissimo* (Japanese Victor); under his own name, *Cascade* (Keytone); (Horo).

MARKEWICH, MAURICE (REESE),* *piano, flute, piccolo*; b. Brooklyn, N.Y., 8/6/36. Markewich, who received his M.D. from the N.Y. Medical Coll., '70, attended the Manhattan Center for Advanced Analytic Studies from '71- . He is ass't psychiatrist at Beth Israel Medical Center, instructor in psychiatry at the Mt. Sinai School of Medicine, and is in priv. practice as psychiatrist-psychoanalyst.

Markewich has not been active in the '70s as a pro. musician, but has written several books on music: *The Definitive Bibliography of Harmonically Sophisticated Tonal Music; The New Expanded Bibliography of Jazz Compositions Based On The Chord Progressions of Standard Tunes; Inside, Outside: Substitute Harmony In Modern Jazz and Pop Music; Jazz Publicity II: Newly Revised and Expanded Bibliography of Names and Addresses of Hundreds of International Jazz Critics and Magazines* (all available from 39 Gramercy Park North, New York, N.Y. 10010).

LPs: *New Designs in Jazz* (Modern Age); w. Nick Brignola *This Is It* (Priam).

MARRS, STELLA (MS. SOFT SOUL), *singer*; b. New York City, 3/22/32. Active as a singer from '58, as single and w. gps., big bands. Toured w. Lionel Hampton, July-Oct. '69; April, '72; Jan. '73. Has worked in LV, Houston, Fla., NJ; many coll. concerts; NYC clubs such as Rainbow Grill, Plaza Nine, Boomer's, Jimmy Weston's, etc. Backed by own trio in mid-'70s. In theater app. w. New Heritage Repertory Workshop; also wrote, produced and performed in *I A Black Woman*. Numerous apps. as extra, sometimes w. speaking lines, in movies *Cotton Comes to Harlem; Angel Levine; The Landlord; Where's Poppa*, etc. Has performed for Jazz Interactions; Jazz Vespers; Festival on the River. TV: Sydney, Australia, '68; Joe Delaney show, LV; hostess on own show, Telepromter Cable TV, Channel D. Radio: jazz DJ on WHBI; then, in '75, on WRVR, NYC. LPs: *Anyone Can Whistle* (Grenider); w. Duke Pearson, unreleased (BN).

MARSALA, MARTY,* *trumpet, drums*; b. Chicago, Ill., 4/2/09. Younger brother of Joe Marsala, in whose combo he pl. during the late '30s. Marsala later lived for many years in SF, where he pl. w. Earl Hines and led his

own group. In '62 he returned to Chicago, leading a dixieland band at Jazz Ltd. He died in a Chicago hospital,
4/27/75.

MARSH, WARNE MARION, * tenor sax, clarinet, flute;
b. Los Angeles, Calif., 10/26/27. Early associate of Lennie Tristano in NYC. Moved to LA, 1966. Began teaching full time '68. Formed quartet, also worked w. Clare
Fischer orch. Joined Supersax during its rehearsal days in
summer of '72. In addition to working with this group,
occasionally led quartet '74-5 with Lou Levy, Jim Hugh-
art, Frank Severino. Pl. in Europe, '75. Wrote arrs. of
Salt Peanuts, Ornithology for Supersax.

LPs: *Ne Plus Ultra; Art of Improvising* (Revelation);
w. Clare Fischer, *Thesaurus* (Atl.); w. Art Pepper, *The
Way It Was* (Contemp.); w. Supersax, *Supersax Plays
Bird; Salt Peanuts; Supersax Plays Bird With Strings*
(Capitol).

MARSHALL, JACK WILTON, * composer, guitar; b. El
Dorado, Kans., 11/23/21. The versatile west coast artist,
who had been active as a composer, arranger, conductor,
as lecturer at USC, and musical director for Capitol
Records, died suddenly of a heart attack in Huntington
Beach, Cal., 9/2/73. A Jack Marshall scholarship fund
was set up for young guitarists to enable them to sustain
their education at USC.

LPs: *Sounds Unheard Of* (Contemporary).

MARTINEZ, LUIS (SABU), percussion; b. New York
City, 7/14/30. Self-taught. Pl. w. D. Gillespie, Ch.
Parker, C. Basie, B. Goodman in late '40s; A. Blakey, off
and on, '49-61; H. Silver, '57; Tony Bennett, '57-63.
Moving to Europe pl. w. radio jazz group of Stockholm,
'68-73; also w. Peter Herbolzheimer's Rhythm Combina-
tion & Brass, '72. From '73, led own group, New Burnt
Sugar, in Sweden. Credits the Lecuona Cuban Boys of
the '40s as his "musical fathers." Also infl. by Parker,
Blakey, Gillespie.

Publ: *Conga Lesson's Book* (Air Skandinaviska Music,
Stockholm, Sweden). Own LPs: *Palo-Congo* (Blue Note);
Safari With Sabu (RCA); *Sorcery* (Col.); *Jazz Espagnole*
(Alegre); *Afro Temple* (Grammofonverket); *New Burnt
Sugar Live at Hall Prison* (Ton I Ton, Sweden); *Wide
Open; Wait A Minute; Live at Ronnie Scott's; Latin Ka-
leidoscope* w. Clarke-Boland (MPS); *Orgy In Rhythm;
Holiday For Skins,* w. Blakey (Blue Note).

MARTINO, PAT (Pat Azzara), guitar, composer; b. Phil-
adelphia, Pa., 8/25/44. Father, a singer, encouraged him
to get guitar; guitarist cousin gave some instruction.
Stud. w. Dennis Sandole. On road at age 15 w. Willis
Jackson; Red Holloway; Sleepy Henderson; four mos. w.
S. Stitt. Worked w. Lloyd Price, then Jackson again.
Made rec. debut w. him, '63. During '60s pl. in many or-
ganist's combos incl. Jimmy Smith; Jack McDuff;
Groove Holmes; Jimmy McGriff; Don Patterson; Trudy
Pitts. Returned to Phila. '66. Eight mos. w. John Handy
'66. Leading own gp. from late '60s; also teaching priva-
tely. Infl: D. Sandole, Billy Bean, Johnny Smith, Charlie
Christian, Wes Montgomery. Comp: *Strings; Lean
Years; Mom; Querido; Trick; Baiyina; Where Love's a
Grown Up God; Israfel; Distant Land; The Visit; Special*

*Door; The Great Stream; Passata on Guitar; Willow; On
the Stairs.* Pete Welding called his playing ". . . probing, imaginatively controlled musical clarity and co-
herence—fleet as the wind when required but always
easy, fluid, full of gracefully virtuosic touches (to remind
you of the control behind the ease)—imperturbable, su-
premely cool, and quietly intense."

Won DB Critics poll, TDWR, '69; tie, TDWR, '72.

LPs: *Strings; East; Baiyina; El Hombre; Desparado*
(Prest.); *The Visit* (Cobble.); *Live!; Consciousness*
(Muse); w. Ch. McPherson; Groove Holmes; Don Patter-
son; Willis Jackson (Prest.); Eric Kloss (Prest.; Muse);
Bobby Pierce (Cobble.).

MARTYN, BARRY (KID), drums, singer; b. London,
England, 2/23/41. Professional debut 1955; visited New
Orleans, '60, stud. drums w. Cie Frazier; produced LP of
New Orleans music, '61, played on album there, '63,
after becoming the only white member of the black musi-
cians' local union. During '60s brought U.S. musicians to
Europe to play with his band. In '68-9 pl. at NO Heritage
Jazz Fest. Played at Louis Armstrong tribute concert in
LA, '70; moved there permanently, '72, formed and
played in The Legends of Jazz, '73. Organized production
company, record label; promoted local concerts. Or-
ganized Louisiana Shakers Band, '74. Returned to
Europe for tour w. band, spring '75.

Martyn has rec. w. Jim Robinson, George Lewis, B.
Bigard, Chris Barber and many other traditionalist musicians. He has written extensively on NO jazz and in '75
completed taping a biography of B. Bigard.

Own LPs: *The Legends of Jazz; The Legends of Jazz
With Barney Bigard* both on Crescent Jazz Productions,
(P.O. Box 60244, Los Angeles, Ca. 90054).

MASON, HARVEY JR., drums, percussion, composer;
also piano, bass, trumpet; b. Atlantic City, N.J.,
2/22/47. Started on drums at age four under guidance of
father, who at that time was in Army band. Stud. at
Berklee, New England Conserv. (on full scholarship) concentrating on theory, tympani, mallets etc. to complete
Bach. of Ed. from New England Conserv. While there,
led quintet w. Jan Hammer, Geo. Mraz. Traveled w. E.
Garner for four months in late '69; joined Geo. Shearing,
'70 and remained for 13 months.

Since '71, based in LA, Mason has been in increasing
demand as a studio musician, and as sideman for dozens
of jazz and rock groups, in addition to pl. with several
symph. orchs. Pl. w. D. Ellington, Q. Jones, R. Norvo,
H. Laws, G. Mulligan, Chet Baker, R. Braff, Herbie
Hancock, F. Hubbard, Gunther Schuller. Comps: co-
writer w. Hancock of *Chameleon;* writer/arr., *Man What
You Did* for D. Byrd LP; many arrs. for Sylvers; rearranged *Watermelon Man* for Hancock. TV: *Bobbie
Gentry Show; Bill Cosby Show,* w. Q. Jones, etc.; acting
role in drama, *The Most Deadly Game,* '70.

LPs: w. D. Byrd, *Black Byrd; Street Lady;* w. Bobbi
Humphrey, *Blacks & Blues; Satin Doll;* Moacir Santos,
Saudade (BN); Shearing, *Trio; Quartet; George Shearing*
(Sheba); Chas. Earland, *Leaving This Planet* (Fant.);
Mulligan, *Reunion* at Carnegie Hall (CTI); B. Hutcher-

son (BN); J. Klemmer; Hubbard; Hancock (Col.).

MASSEY, CAL, *composer, trumpet*; b. Philadelphia, Pa., 1/11/28. Son, Zane, pl. tenor sax; cousin, Billy Massey, trumpet. Raised in Pittsburgh. Began on trumpet at 13. Infl. and encouraged by Freddie Webster whom he met a yr. later. Studied for short time at Pitt Institute. On the road at 17 w. various bands incl. J. McShann. To Phila. in mid-'40s, pl. w. Jimmy Heath's big band; also worked w. Philly Joe Jones; toured briefly w. Billie Holiday. Later pl. w. Eddie Vinson; G. Shearing big band; B.B. King; led own combos. From mid-'50s devoted the majority of his time to writing. His comps. were rec. by C. Parker; J. Coltrane; M. Tyner; J. McLean; F. Hubbard; L. Morgan; A. Shepp. In '69 he became closely associated w. Shepp, touring Europe and No. Africa w. him. Formed the ROMAS orch. w. arr.-cond. Romulus Franceschini, '70, for concerts, educ. TV. Comp: *Fiesta; Bakai; Nakatini Suite; Love Song; Message From Trane; Toyland; Demon's Dance; Assunta; Father and Son; What Would It Be Without You; Quiet Dawn; Goodbye Sweet Pops; The Black Liberation Suite; Looking For Someone to Love.* The last was among several songs and arrs. he wrote in '72, for *Lady Day: A Musical Tragedy*, a play about Billie Holiday w. music also by Shepp and Stanley Cowell. He had been in poor health for some time and, after attending a preview performance on the previous night, died of an apparent heart attack at his home in Brooklyn, N.Y., 10/25/72.

LPs: one track w. own gp. in anthology, *The Jazz Life* (Candid), is unavailable; his writing is represented on albums by the artists named above. His '70s collaborations w. Shepp are on Impulse and Black Saint.

MASSO, GEORGE, *trombone, composer*; also *piano, vibes*; b. Cranston, R.I., 11/17/26. Stud. Boston U., Mus. M., '59; also Electronic Music Workshop. Pl. w. Jimmie Palmer band, '44-5; Army band, '45-6; J. Dorsey, '48. Masso taught mus. in New England public schools for 18 years, the last seven at U. of Connecticut. Gave lecture-demonstrations on history of jazz for various institutions in northeastern U.S. Took leave of absence from U. of Conn., '73 and resigned in '74 to resume work as full time musician. Pl. w. B. Goodman sextet incl. European tour, '73; B. Hackett quintet, '74; World's Greatest Jazzband, '75.

Favs: Lou McGarity, Jack Teagarden, Trummy Young, T. Dorsey et al. TV: Commentator and perf. w. own quintet in history of jazz program in Providence, R.I. Fests: Groton, '68; NO, '72; New London, '73; Meadowbrook w. Goodman, '73. Comps: *Make Up Your Mind* (jazz piece for stage band); *Fantasy in Syncopation* for U. of Conn. band; several other major works for brass, voices etc.

LPs: w. World's Greatest Jazzband (World Jazz); others w. Wild Bill Davison (Jazzology); *Mood in Mink*, feat. soloist on tromb. and vibes, w. Jack Quigley orch. (Seeco).

MASTREN, CARMEN NICHOLAS,* *guitar*; also *banjo, mandolin*; b. Cohoes, N.Y., 10/6/13. With T. Dorsey orch. in late '30s; Glenn Miller AAF band during WWII.

Active in studios from '46, joining NBC in '53. Remained through '70, doing *Today; Tonight*; and *Say When*, a morning game show for which he wrote and pl. most of the music. Rec. many jingles during this time and '70-3 when he left NBC to free-lance. App. in Broadway musical *Over Here* w. Andrews Sisters, '74. Played w. NYJRC for Louis Armstrong, Jelly Roll Morton; *Seventy-Five Years of Jazz* concerts, '74-5. Film: banjo and guitar for *The Wild Party*. LPs: w. NYJRC, *Satchmo Remembered* (Atl.).

MASUDA, MIKIO, *piano, composer*; b. Osaka, Japan, 8/14/49. Self-taught. Took up bass at 16; later switched to piano, pl. in Osaka. In '69 moved to Tokyo and pl. w. Hiroshi Suzuki quintet and Isao Suzuki quartet at jazz clubs. With Terumasa Hino, '73. Moved to NYC '73 and worked w. Art Blakey '74. Infl: Coltrane, McCoy Tyner, Ellington, Herbie Hancock. Fest: many in Japan; NJF-NY, '72; Altena Free Jazz Meeting '73 w. Hino; Yugoslavia & other Euro. fests. Comp: *Mickey's Trip; Song for Bumiji; Prayer; Add Some; Hard Luck; Black Daffodil.* LPs: *Traces* (East Wind); w. Hino, *Fuji* (Japan. Victor); *Hartman Meets Hino* (Toshiba EMI); *Journey into My Mind; Into Eternity* (CBS/Sony).

MASUO, YOSHIAKI, *guitar*; b. Tokyo, Japan, 10/12/46. Chosen to pl. w. Sadao Watanabe band while at Waseda Univ., Dec. '68. Went to U.S. June '71. Pl. w. Lee Konitz, '72-Feb. '73. With Sonny Rollins from April '73, app. in clubs, concerts and fests. such as Montreux, Kongsberg '74; NJF-NY, '74-5. Other fests: NJF '68, Montreux, '70 w. Watanabe. Infl: Wes Montgomery, Watanabe, Rollins. Won SJ Readers Poll, '70-1. A strong, technically adroit and creative soloist, rooted in bop. Own LPs: *24 Yoshiaki Masuo; Winds of Barcelona* (Japan. CBS); w. Elvin Jones, *Merry Go Round* (BN); w. Rollins, *The Cutting Edge* (Milestone); *111 Sullivan Street* (East Wind).

MATLOCK, JULIAN CLIFTON (MATTY),* *clarinet*; also *saxophones, flute*; b. Paducah, Ky., 4/27/09. Veteran of Bob Crosby band; often reunited with him for dates such as Rainbow Grill, NYC, 1966-7; Merv Griffin TV show, '72. Pl. w. Phil Harris at Lake Tahoe, Las Vegas, '67. Many gigs in LA area incl. Disneyland w. Ray McKinley, '70. Went to Europe, April '72, playing in England w. Alex Welsh. Feat. at annual Dick Gibson Jazz Parties, 1966-70. Other jazz parties for Dr. O.A. Fulcher in Odessa, Tex. and Dr. Wm. McPherson in Pasadena, Calif. Arranged and played on Disney film track '74 feat. Phil Harris.

LPs: *Paducah Patrol* (WB); early work w. Bob Crosby (MCA); *Bud Meets Eddie* w. Eddie Miller (Fontana); several LPs from Dr. McPherson's parties (Blue Angel).

MATHEWS, RONALD ALBERT (RONNIE),* *piano, composer*; b. Brooklyn, N.Y., 12/2/35. Joined the Max Roach gp. in '63 and was with him, on and off, to '68. Pl. w. Freddie Hubbard, '65-6; Art Blakey, '68-9, touring Europe w. him '68; Japan, '68 and, again, in '75. After free-lancing in NYC area, '70-1, he ran a Jazz Workshop and did private tutoring at Long Island U. From '72 has worked w. Louis Hayes sextet; from '74 w. Clark Terry quartet and big band. He also counsels New York high school students in a drug prevention program which incorporates music as a positive social alternative. Fest: NJF-NY w. Terry. Comp: *Jean-Marie.*

LPs: *Trip to the Orient* (East Wind); w. L. Hayes, *Breath of Life* (Muse); *Clark Terry & His Jolly Giants* (Vang.); Charles Davis (Strata-East); Art Blakey (Trip); Max Roach (Atl.).

MATTHEWS, DAVID, *composer, piano;* also *French horn, valve trombone;* b. Sonora, Ky., 4/3/42. Studied at Louisville Acad. of Mus., '58-60: French horn w. Wm. Sloan; jazz and comp. w. Don Murray and Sam Denison. College Conserv. of Music of U. of Cinn., '60-4, study. w. Felix Labunski, BM in Comp. Att. Eastman Sch. of Mus., stud. w. Rayburn Wright, Manny Albam, summers, '71, '73-4. Arranger and conductor for James Brown band, '70-3. Led own band on Monday nights at Five Spot, NYC, from '74. Gigs at Bradley's w. Sam Brown-Dave Matthews trio, '74-5. Likening his work to Gil Evans and, occasionally, Thad Jones, Dan Morgenstern wrote: "But Matthews is not derivative; he just makes good use of a still vital tradition."

Infl: Miles Davis, Bill Evans, Ellington, Gil Evans, Bartok, Stravinsky, Alban Berg. Comp: *Theme from King Heroin;* suite: *Black Light; Blue Night; Flight,* rec. by David Sanborn; *Prayer; Overture To My Brother,* for symph. orch. LPs: *Live at the Five Spot* (Muse); as arr.-co-prod: w. Mark Murphy, *Bridging a Gap; Mark II; Mark Murphy Sings* (Muse); as arr.-comp: w. Blue Mitchell, *Many Shades of Blue* (Main.); as arr.-co-comp: w. James Brown, *Sho' Is Funky Down Here* (People); as arr.: w. D. Sanborn (WB); T-Bone Walker (Repr.); Hank Crawford; Ron Carter (Kudu); Paul Simon (Col.).

MATTHEWS, ONZY D. JR., * *arranger, singer, piano;* b. Fort Worth, Tex., 1/15/36. Led big band in LA during '60s; arr. and cond. for many singers. From 1969-72 worked in St. Thomas, V.I., St. Maarten, Aruba and Curacao, singing and pl. piano for Sheraton Hotel chain. Collab. as composer w. Duke Ellington '73-4, also subbing for him during Duke's illnesses. Arrs. for Earl Hines and his singer Marva Josie, '73-4. Led 17-piece band at NJF-NY 1973. Rearranged early Ellington hits such as *Drop Me Off In Harlem; Squeeze Me; It Don't Mean a Thing* for the Ellington band '74. LPs: w. Lou Rawls, *Tobacco Road; Black & Blue* (Cap.).

MAUPIN, BENNIE, *tenor saxophone;* also *flute, bass clarinet, soprano saxophone, saxello;* b. Detroit, Mich., 8/29/46. Stud. at Garfield Jr. high school w. Alfred Hickman, '54; Northeastern High School w. Rex Hall, '55-8; also privately w. Larry Teal Jr. and Sr.; Detr. Inst. of Musical Art w. Dr. Fillmore, '60-2; priv. lessons w. Carmine Caruso and Joe Allard, NYC. Pl. w. Roy Haynes, '66-8; H. Silver, '68-70; in 70s w. Lee Morgan, Miles Davis, McCoy Tyner, F. Hubbard; joined H. Hancock, '71. Maupin, who names among his infls. Y. Lateef, W. Shorter, J. Coltrane and S. Rollins, is a versatile multi-reedman who has emerged as one of the most accomplished players of the post-Coltrane period. His tenor is a personal extension of his influences, and his dark-

toned bass clarinet is particularly persuasive. TV: *Midnight Special; New Year's Eve Special* w. Hancock. Fests: Newport, Monterey, Nice, Pori, and drum fest. in Japan.

Comps: *Neophilia; Quasar; Water Torture; The Jewel In The Lotus; Anua; Ensenada.* Own LP: *Jewel In The Lotus* (ECM); *Afternoon of a Georgia Fawn,* w. Marion Brown (ECM); *Bitches Brew* w. M. Davis (Col.); w. Hancock, *Mwandishi; Crossings* (WB); *Sextant; Head Hunters; Thrust* (Col.).

MAXWELL, JAMES KENDRICK (JIMMY), *trumpet;* also *bagpipes;* b. Stockton, Calif., 1/9/17. Grandfather, cornetist in Spanish-American War, pl. French horn in Walla Walla Symph. from ages 65-85. Father, clarinetist in Navy Band. Mother was violinist. Her brother pl. cornet w. Paul Whiteman, '19. Self taught from age four but "really got serious in '32 by copying Louis Armstrong." Studied w. Herbert Clarke for two yrs.; Lloyd Reese, two yrs; Benny Baker, eight yrs.: all in '39-49 period. Self taught in harmony and theory copying recs. of Ellington, Stravinsky, Debussy and Ravel. Played w. Gil Evans, '32-6; J. Dorsey, '36-7; Maxine Sullivan, '37; Skinnay Ennis, '38-9; Benny Goodman, '39-43. During this period also pl. w. Raymond Scott, '40; Paul Whiteman, '43, '46; CBS staff, '43-45; also month w. C. Basie; Perry Como Show, '45-65; NBC Symph., '48-9; Great Neck (L.I.) Symph., '52-6. Subbed for Cat Anderson w. Ellington for three wks., '61. On staff at NBC, '60-74, doing *Tonight Show,* '65-73. In '58-66 also worked w. bands of Quincy Jones; Oliver Nelson; Gerry Mulligan. Toured USSR: w. Goodman, '62; w. NYJRC Louis Armstrong Tribute, summer '75. W. NYJRC Armstrong Tribute to Europe, fall '75. Played w. Ellington band again, May-Dec., '74. Has also copied recordings of classic numbers for the band to replace missing scores and parts. Pl. w. National Jazz Ensemble from '75; Dave Berger Experimental Orch., '73-5.

Lectures for NY Brass Conf.; Aspen Music Camp; Nat. Brass Conf. in Denver, '73; Hartt Coll., Hartford, Conn., '74; Vermont Summer Music School, '73, '75. Film: *Powers Girl* w. Goodman; background for Ethel Waters in *Cabin in the Sky;* trumpet solo of theme for *The Godfather.* Fest: NJF w. Shearing, '59; Q. Jones, Judy Garland, '61.

Played bagpipes in St. Patrick's Day parades, '58-64; also for Shakespeare in the Park, *Richard II,* '62; on rec. w. John Lennon; and several jingles incl. Peter Sellers for TWA; in NYC on Channel 13, '64.

Son played guitar in Russian rock gp., summer of '70 in Leningrad; teaches Russian at Tufts U. Maxwell, himself, studied Japanese language and culture at Col. U., '41-5; also taught himself to read Chinese.

Although renowned as a lead player, he participated in many jam sessions, '39-45, in Harlem, Greenwich Village and on 52nd St. w. Eldridge, Hawkins, Webster, T. Wilson, C. Christian, etc.

Infl: Armstrong, Eldridge, Berigan, Cootie Williams, Ellington, Strayhorn. Also admires Clifford Brown, Clark Terry. Own fav. solo: *Struttin' With Some Bar-*

becue w. Nat. Jazz Ens. (Chiaro.). Feat. on *I Know That You Know; After You've Gone; Ramona*; one version of *The Man I Love* w. Goodman (Col.); *Happiness is Just a Thing Called Joe* w. Manny Albam in *Brass on Fire* (SS).

MAY, E. WILLIAM (BILLY), *composer*; b. Pittsburgh, Pa., 11/10/16. Former big band arranger for Ch. Barnet. Wrote arrs. and conducted for Frank Sinatra-Duke Ellington album, but generally confined his activities to TV and film composing. Arr. and cond. reconstructed versions of old swing era hits for Time-Life album series.

LPs: *The Swing Era*, 15 volumes (Time-Life).

MAYALL, JOHN, *singer, harmonica, guitar, piano, composer*; b. Macclesfield, Cheshire, England, 11/29/33. Self taught from age 13. Formed one of the first important British blues bands, the Powerhouse Four, in 1956. Organized the Bluesbreakers, 1962 in London, but did not become a full time pro. mus. until '63. Experimented with electric blues sounds until 1967, when he recorded *The Blues Stone*. In 1969 he organized a softer-sounding, more acoustically oriented group that recorded the *Turning Point* album.

From 1970 Mayall spent about half of each year living in Hollywood and half in England. He organized a series of small blues groups, some of which leaned primarily toward rock while others employed leading jazzmen incl. Blue Mitchell, Ernie Watts, Victor Gaskin, Freddie Robinson, Don Harris. Among the alumni of his British groups are Eric Clapton, Aynsley Dunbar, Mick Fleetwood, Mick Taylor, Keef Hartley, Jack Bruce, Jon Mark, Johnny Almond.

Mayall, sometimes called "the grandfather of British blues," established his importance mainly as a catalyst and discoverer of talents who went on to individual recognition. He appeared in *Don't Look Back*, the movie about Bob Dylan. Pl. at NJF '69. Infl: Big Maceo, Sonny Boy Williamson, Otis Rush, Django Reinhardt.

LPs: Polydor, Blue Thumb, London.

MAYERS, LLOYD G., *piano, keyboards, violin*; b. Brooklyn, N.Y., 11/11/29. Began on violin but, helped by younger sister who is pianist, switched to that instr. when he entered High School of Performing Arts. BA from Manhattan School of Mus. First pro. job w. Eddie Vinson, '49. Worked w. Bennie Green, '54; D. Washington, '54-5; Josephine Baker, '59-60; Nancy Wilson, '62-3; Johnny Griffin-Lockjaw Davis, '64; Joe Newman, '65-6; Sammy Davis Jr., '67-72. Mayers, who was also active in NYC studio scene from early '60s, wrote arrs. for Redd Foxx's prod. co., '73, and then became member of D. Ellington orch., under dir. of Mercer Ellington, following Duke's death. Infls: Tatum, Bud Powell, Wynton Kelly, Hancock, Corea; composers, Ellington, O. Nelson. TV apps. w. Davis. Arrs. for Gloria Lynne, Davis, Ruth Brown, Charlie Rouse, Ellington orch.

Mayers rec. two albums as leader: *Taste of Honey* (UA); and one with trio (Merc.) but neither are available; as sideman w. Nelson, Newman, Green, Griffin-Davis (Pres.) also deleted. He can be heard on reissue, *Live at Count Basie's*, w. Newman (Trip). LP w. M. Ellington, *Continuum* (Fant.).

MAYL, GENE, *bass, tuba, singer*; b. Dayton, Ohio, 12/30/28. Began on acoustic bass, '44; tuba while in France, '48; occasionally plays elect. bass. Worked with the bands of Claude Luter, Claude Bolling and D. Byas in France, '48-9. Founded his own Dixieland Rhythm Kings in '48 and has worked with them from that time except for two years w. Bob Scobey's Frisco Jazz Band; two months w. Muggsy Spanier, and short tours w. Billy Maxted, Pee Wee Hunt and the Dukes of Dixieland. Mayl has also app. in concert alongside musicians such as Geo. Brunis, Wild Bill Davison and Clancy Hayes, and has pl. w. all star groups at the Bix Beiderbecke JF, Davenport, Iowa; Detroit JF; Manassas JF. The Dixieland Rhythm Kings have toured the U.S. and Canada and app. at the following fests: NO, where they were the first non-NO band to perf; West Virginia Water Fest.; Burlington, Iowa Steamboat Days Fest. From the late '60s, they have pl. annually on the steamer *Delta Queen*. Comps: *Koor's "29"; Put-In Blues*.

LPs: *On Parade* (Red Onion, Box 366, Dayton, Ohio 45401); *Trip to Waukesha* (Blackbird); *Swinging Saloon Dixie* (Jazzology); w. Brunis (Jazzology); *Bix's Gang Lives* (Fat Cat's Jazz).

MAYS, LYLE DAVID, *keyboards, composer*; b. Marinette, Wis., 11/27/53. Stud. at U. of Wisconsin, '73; NTSU, '74-5. Instructor at Nat'l. Stage Band camps, summer '74. Led sm. groups in coll., winning two jazz fest. competitions. After leaving NTSU, he joined W. Herman. Infls: Bill Evans, F. Zappa, I. Stravinsky. Comps: *Sir Gawain & The Green Knight; Overture to the Royal Mongolian Suma Foosball Festival*.

MAYUTO (Mailto Correa), *percussion*; also *guitar, piano, composer, singer*; b. Sao Goncalo, Rio de Janeiro, Brazil, 3/9/43. Professional debut at age 12 in night club. After working with many bands in Rio, he formed a samba show that became very popular, winning first place at local festivals. At one point Mayuto started medical school, but gave it up in order to concentrate on music. Worked in Mexico w. Tamba Four, '70. Moving to Cal., he pl. w. Ch. Lloyd, '71; toured w. G. Szabo, '71-2; H. Masekela, '72. Took part in Song Festival w. Santana in Rio, '72. Troubadour Club, LA w. C. Adderley, '73; traveled w. F. Hubbard, '73-4; concerts w. K. Burrell, G. Barbieri, H. Belafonte, D. Byrd, D. Ellis, C. Tjader, '74. Wrote music for two plays, *Orpheus*, presented in Philadelphia, '73; and *Sortilege*, seen at the Inner City Cultural Center, LA, '75. TV specials w. Belafonte, Nancy Wilson, Bola Sete. Film: sound tracks, *Cinderella Liberty; Lost In The Stars; Trouble Man; Sarava*. Fests: Mexico, '71, w. Sete; Concord, '71 w. Szabo; Newport, '74 w. Hubbard.

Along with his other talents, Mayuto has written several hundred songs and poems. Gabor Szabo called him "a fiery percussionist, full of lyricism and romantic beauty."

LPs: w. Burrell, *Up The Street, Round The Corner, Down The Block* (Fant.); w. Adderley, *The Happy People* (Cap.); w. Tjader, *Tambu* (Fant.); w. Lloyd, *Waves* (A & M); w. Howard Roberts *Equinox Express Elevator* (ABC); w. Szabo, *Spellbinder* (Blue Thumb); w. Moacir

Santos, *Saudade* (BN); w. Hubbard, *Liquid Love* (Col.); w. H. Mancini, *Symphonic Soul* (RCA).

M'BOOM RE: PERCUSSION. see Roach, Max.

McBEE, CECIL, *bass, composer*; b. Tulsa, Okla., 5/19/35. Began on clarinet in high school. Performed duets w. sister, Shirley, at concerts and w. marching bands on statewide basis. Took up bass at 17 and began to pl. at local night clubs. At Central State in Wilberforce, Ohio he stud. bass and jazz comp. before being inducted into the Army where he spent two yrs. at Ft. Knox, Ky. as cond. of the military band. Moved to Det., '62 where he pl. w. Paul Winter, '63-4, moving to NYC w. the group in '64. He worked w. Grachan Moncur '64; Jackie McLean, '65; Wayne Shorter, '65-6; Freddie Hubbard, Miles Davis, '66; Charles Lloyd, '66-7; Yusef Lateef, '67-9; Bobby Hutcherson, '69; Pharoah Sanders; Alice Coltrane, '69-72; Charles Tolliver, '70; Lonnie Liston Smith, '72-3; Sonny Rollins, '73; Michael White, etc. In July '75 formed own gp. and pl. the Tin Palace, NYC.

Fest: NJF-NY '73 w. Sam Rivers; Montreux '73. The *Montreux Riviera* wrote: "During the last few years bassists have explored the possibilities long unimaginable on this instrument, but McBee almost entirely renews it."

Infl: Pettiford, Ray Brown. Award: NEA Grant for composition, '75. Comp: *Song of Her; Felicite; Wilpan's; Love; Morning Changes; From Within; Voice of the Seventh Angel; Life Waves; Mutima; A Feeling; Tulsa Black.* LPs: *Mutima;* w. Tolliver, *Music Inc.; Live at Slugs* (Strata-East); w. McLean; Moncur; Shorter (BN); Andrew Hill (BN, Arista); w. Lateef; Lloyd (Atl.); w. Sanders; Alice Coltrane; Sam Rivers; John Klemmer (Imp.); w. Leon Thomas; Lonnie Liston Smith (Fly. Dutch.); Norman Connors (Buddah).

McBROWNE, LEONARD LOUIS (LENNY),* *drums*; b. Brooklyn, N.Y., 1/24/33. Busy freelance musician in NYC from early '50s. Pl. w. Randy Weston, '66; toured w. Booker Ervin for most of the next three years. Worked in Blue Mitchell group. After rec. as sideman on several Prest. albums, joined Geo. Wein's Newport All Stars, late '69. To Japan w. all star guitar group, '70. On return to U.S. pl. Newport JF. Back to Japan w. T. Monk; during this trip, rec. w. Helen Merrill, Teddy Wilson.

McBrowne spent most of '71-4 w. K. Burrell. He moved to SF in '72 but continued to work w. Burrell as well as with the locally based Vernon Alley trio. Attended Laney Coll., Oakland, '72-3. Pl. in show, *Me and Bessie* w. Linda Hopkins in SF, '75. Fests: Monterey, '66; Newport, '67, '70, '71 and various other cities under Newport auspices.

LPs: w. Randy Weston, *African Cookbook* (Atl.); w. Barry Harris, *Luminescence;* w. Sonny Criss, *Up, Up and Away;* w. Teddy Edwards, *It's All Right* (Prest.); w. Booker Ervin, *Booker and Brass* (Liberty); *The In Between* (BN); w. Red Garland, *The Quota* (MPS); w. Burrell, *Both Feet On The Ground; Up The Street, Round the Corner, Down The Block* (Fantasy); w. Sam Noto, *Entrance* (Xanadu).

McCANDLESS, PAUL, *oboe, English horn, bass clarinet, composer*; b. Indiana, Pa., 3/24/47. Oboe major at Duquesne U. and Manhattan Sch. of Mus.; studied w. Robert Bloom and Bernard Z. Goldberg. Appeared w. the Duquesne Wind Symph.; Manhattan Orch.; New College Fest. Orch.; New Haven Symp.; Pittsburgh Symph.; Springfield Symph. Pl. w. the Winter Consort, '68-73, app. at Fillmore East & West; Tanglewood; Schaefer Fest.; Chautauqua; many coll. dates. With Oregon from its formation out of the Winter Consort in the early '70s. Won Pittsburgh Flute Club Award. Voted outstanding soloist at Villanova Intercollegiate JF, '67. Finalist in English horn auditions for NY Phil., '71. Infl: Coltrane, Schoenberg, Berg, Webern, Debussy, Stravinsky, Bartok, yoga. Comp: *All the Mornings Bring; Undertow; Fond Libre; The Swan; St. Philomene.* LPs: w. Oregon, *Winter Light; Distant Hills; Music of Another Present Era;* w. Ralph Towner & Glen Moore, *Trios & Solos* (ECM); w. Winter Consort, *Road* (A&M).

McCANN, LESLIE COLEMAN (LES),* *piano, keyboards, synthesizer, composer, singer*; b. Lexington, Ky., 9/23/35. Began recording with trio, '60. Internationally known after app. at Antibes JF, '62. In the late '60s and early '70s McCann broadened his musical scope. As a singer, he enjoyed success with the ballad *With These Hands,* as well as such social message songs as *Compared to What?* His app. in '69 w. E. Harris at the Montreux JF produced a best selling album, *Swiss Movement,* in which they were feat. as co-leaders. McCann was responsible for the discovery and presentation of R. Flack (q.v.).

In '69, McCann's combo began experimenting extensively in electronics, with the leader pl. elect. piano, clavinet and Arp synthesizer. McCann participated in the motion picture *Soul To Soul,* for which he was one of a group of black American artists who went to Accra, Ghana for the filming. Other movie or TV apps: Nancy Wilson show; *Interface* (PBS); *Positively Black* (NBC-NY); *Playboy* show; Mike Douglas show. Some of his photographs were shown on Bill Cosby's NBC-TV spec. In '75 an exhibition of McCann's photographs was held in the Studio Museum of Harlem.

The group pl. concerts at Lincoln Center w. Mahalia Jackson; Carnegie Hall w. Nancy Wilson, and app. in seminars at many coll. campuses, '70-5. App. in an all star Black Music Show, '72-3-4. Since '71, McCann and his wife have been working as volunteer teachers to a group of children in Mezcales, a small agrarian community near Puerto Vallarta, Mexico.

Among McCann's comps. are *A Little 3/4 For God & Co.; Kathleen's Theme; Beaux J. Poo Boo; The Song of Love; The Morning Song; Some Day We'll Meet Again; Shorty Rides Again.* As arr. he was responsible for the music on Lou Rawls' album, *Stormy Monday* (Cap.). Has been regular participant in Jazzmobile in NYC ghettos.

LPs: *Another Beginning; Comment; Invitation to Openness; Layers; Live at Montreux; Much Les; Talk To* the People (Atl.); *Bag of Gold; More or Les; New From The Big City* (Pac. Jazz); w. Harris, *Swiss Movement* (Atl.).

McCLURE, RONALD DIX (RON),* bass; also *piano, accordion*; b. New Haven, Conn., 11/22/41. Continued his studies with Hall Overton in NYC, '65 and worked w. Wynton Kelly trio backing Wes Montgomery and afterward, '65-6. Joined Charles Lloyd and was part of that group when it became first American outfit to play a Soviet jazz festival, '67. Helped form The Fourth Way in '69, pl. and rec. in U.S. and Europe into '70 when he joined Joe Henderson. With Dionne Warwicke for three mos., '70; also Gary Burton, Mose Allison. Taught at Berklee Coll. of Music, '71-2 and free-lanced w. Thelonious Monk, Tony Bennett and Keith Jarrett. To SF where he rec. w. the Pointer Sisters, Jerry Hahn, Julian Priester and Cal Tjader. Pl. w. Freddie Hubbard, Morgana King and was briefly reunited w. Mike Nock and Eddie Marshall of the old Fourth Way. Returned to NYC, Jan. '74 to join Blood, Sweat & Tears. Insp. & infl: Miles Davis, Bill Evans, Scott LaFaro, Paul Chambers, Charles Ives, Hall Overton. Fest: NJF, Montreux, Monterey w. Fourth Way; NJF-NY w. Airto '73. Comp: *Farewell, Goodbye; Skiffling* for Fourth Way; *Mirror Image* for B,S&T. LPs: *Charles Lloyd in the Soviet Union* (Atl.); *Sun & Moon* w. the Fourth Way (Cap.); *In Pursuit of Blackness* w. Henderson (Milestone); *Mirror Image* w. B,S&T (Col.); Pointer Sisters (Blue Thumb).

McCRACKEN, ROBERT EDWARD (BOB),* clarinet, tenor sax; b. Dallas, Tex., 11/23/04. Pl. w. F. Trumbauer, J. Venuti in '30s; B. Goodman, Russ Morgan, '40s; L. Armstrong, J. Teagarden, '50s; K. Ory, Red Allen, '59. During '60s, managed an apartment building in LA, but still played occasionally, rejoining Teagarden in '62, and working w. Wild Bill Davison in '67. McCracken died in LA 7/4/72.

McCURDY, ROY WALTER JR.,* drums; b. Rochester, N.Y., 11/28/36. A full time member of the Cannonball Adderley quintet from the mid-60s, McCurdy traveled internationally with the group, incl. a particularly successful tour of S. America in '72. In his spare time he did studio work for NBC Movies of the Week, and was feat. on various rec. dates. When Adderley was sidelined by illness in July, '75, McCurdy toured w. Kenny Rankin. He also pl. on commercial jingles w. B. Golson, and gigged locally w. both Golson and Jerome Richardson. LPs: w. Adderley (Cap.; Fant.); Nat Adderley (Atl.; Milest.); w. Joe Williams; G. Ammons (Fant.); D. Axelrod (Cap.); w. J. Zawinul (Vortex).

McDUFF, BROTHER JACK (Eugene McDuffy),* organ, composer; also *piano, bass*; b. Champaign, Ill., 9/17/26. Continued to tour w. his own gp., app. at NJF-NY, 74-5. LPs: *The Fourth Dimension; Heatin' System* (Cadet); others on Cadet, Blue Note.

McEACHERN, MURRAY,* trombone; b. Toronto, Ontario, Canada, 1915. A swing era veteran who pl. trombone w. B. Goodman in '36, alto sax and trombone w.

Glen Gray in '38, McEachern later freelanced in LA. He joined D. Ellington in '73, remaining with the band a few months. In '74 he was appointed leader of the newly organized Tommy Dorsey "ghost" band under the auspices of Dorsey's estate.

LPs: *Music for Sleepwalkers*, Vols. I, II, III (Archives Records).

McFARLAND, GARY,* composer, vibes, singer; b. Los Angeles, Cal., 10/23/33. The respected composer-arranger, an important contributor to many albums from the '60s, died 11/3/71 of a heart attack in NYC. He was one of the founders of the short-lived but artistically successful Skye Records, for whom he recorded his suite *America The Beautiful*, one of his outstanding works.

LPs: *Point of Departure; Profiles; Simpatico; Tijuana Jazz* (Imp.); *How To Succeed in Business Without Really Trying* (Verve).

McGARITY, LOU,* trombone; also *violin, singer*; b. Athens, Ga., 7/22/17. Pl. two long stints w. B. Goodman in '40s; Raymond Scott, '42-3; west coast w. Red Nichols, then back in NYC, '47. McGarity worked w. E. Condon, the Lawson-Haggart band, rec. w. Cootie Williams, M. Spanier, N. Hefti, Wild Bill Davison; toured Orient w. Bob Crosby in '64 and became a charter member of World's Greatest Jazzband in '67, leaving in '70 owing to ill health. He remained intermittently active and was working a job in Washington when he suffered a heart attack. He died 8/24/71 in Alexandria, Va. McGarity was a powerful soloist in the Jack Teagarden tradition. LPs: *Jazz Master* (Fat Cat's Jazz); w. WGJ (Project 3).

McGHEE, WALTER (BROWNIE),* singer, guitar, composer; b. Knoxville, Tenn., 11/30/15. Partner of Sonny Terry from April 1939. Continued to tour on full time basis: folk and blues festivals throughout US and Canada, '66; England and Continent, '67; six week tour of schools in Scandinavia, '68; British tour w. B.B. King, Fleetwood Mac, '69; subsequent blues, folk and jazz concerts and festivals in England, Germany etc. New Zealand and Australia, 1974-75, taking part in the first blues festivals ever held there. Back to England and Continent '75.

LPs, Films, TV etc.: see Terry, Sonny. Comps: *Life is a Gamble; Tell Me Why; Blues Had a Baby (And They Called It Rock and Roll); Walk On; Hole in the Wall; I Couldn't Believe My Eyes; My Father's Words; Watch Your Close Friend; Rainy Day.*

Living in Oakland, McGhee late in 1975 was working on his autobiography. He then had seven children, eight grandchildren and one greatgrandchild.

Publ: *Brownie's Many Ways of Playing Guitar* (Oak Publications, 33 W. 60th St., NYC 10023).

McGHEE, HOWARD,* trumpet, composer; b. Tulsa, Okla., 3/16/18. Played w. Andy Kirk, Charlie Barnet bands; Coleman Hawkins combo; JATP in '40s; own gps. into '50s at Birdland, etc. After a period of relative inactivity in late '50s made comeback w. own quartet. In the spring of '66 formed a big band and has alternated between small and large ensembles from that time; also as a single for concert apps. In late '60s-early '70s often associated w. singer Joe Carroll. Pl. Hudson River boatrides in '70s; Stryker's, NYC; Three Sisters, West Paterson, N.J. w. quintet, '75. Concerts, Shrewsbury, N.J., '74-5. From '60s playing Jazz Vespers for St. Peter's Lutheran Church; Christmas show on NBC-TV for Rev. John Gensel, '67. Toured Europe w. Newport package, '67. Fest: NJF-NY, Radio City jam, '72; w. big band at Apollo Theater, '73. Comp: *Born On This Day; The Search; Bless You*, written for George Tucker. LPs: *Newport in New York, The Jam Sessions, Vols. 3&4* (Cobble.); w. Don Patterson, *Boppin' & Burnin'* (Prest.); Fats Navarro reissue (BN).

McGRIFF, JIMMY,* *organ*; b. Phila., Pa., 4/3/36. Continued to travel around the US w. his group for clubs and concerts. Pl. in Jazz in the Garden series at Museum of Modern Art in '60s. Recorded twice w. Richard "Groove" Holmes, once in concert. LPs: Groove Merchant; Solid State; w. Holmes, *Come Together; Giants in Concert*; w. Junior Parker, *Good Things* (Gr. Merch.).

McINTOSH, LADD, *composer, educator, reeds*; b. Akron, Ohio, 7/14/41. Father pl. tenor sax in '30s; mother a piano teacher. Stud. Ohio State U. School of Mus., '59-70 intermittently; BM in comp., MM woodwinds. As a student, won outstanding composer awards at five major coll. jazz fests.

McIntosh is one of the leading jazz educators to whom an entire chapter was devoted in Allen Scott's book, *Jazz Educated, Man.*

Comps: *Bravo, Picasso; In Memoriam; The Fallen Warrior*, commissioned by Jimmy Lyons, dedicated to John F. Kennedy; *Illicit Debauchery (and How to Cultivate It); Groupies; The Incredible Mr. Ellington; Music for a Different Planet, Dying In Another Time* (12-tone jazz comp.).

McIntosh was the only dir. to take a winning band to the Nat'l. Amer. Coll. Jazz Fest. from more than one school: Ohio State, '67; U. of Utah, '71 and '72; Westminster Coll., '73.

McINTOSH, THOMAS S. (TOM),* *composer, trombone*; b. Baltimore, Md., 2/6/27. In addition to working w. T. Jones-M. Lewis band, '66-9, McIntosh organized the New York Jazz Sextet, touring East Coast colleges, and feat. his jazz suite, *Whose Child Are You?* In '69 he moved to the West Coast, where he gave up his instrumental activity in order to concentrate on comp. or arr. for motion pics. Among the films with which he was associated were *The Learning Tree*, '69; *Soul Soldier*, '71; *Shaft's Big Score*, '72; *Slither*, '73; *John Henry*, '74. Comps: *Malice Toward None; Cup Bearers; Great Day.* LPs: w. N.Y. Jazz Sextet (Scepter); Jones-Lewis (SS).

McINTYRE, EARL P., *bass trombone, composer*; also *trombones, tubas*; b. New York, N.Y., 11/21/53. Stud. at High School of Mus. & Art; Mannes Coll. of Mus.; priv. w. Alan Raph, John Clark, Jack Jeffers, Benny Powell. Pl. w. Ch. Mingus, Billy Taylor, Taj Mahal, T. Jones-M. Lewis, Natural Essence, Howard Johnson, C. Terry big band, James Spaulding, Paul Jeffrey, S. Rivers.

In '75 writing for Chas. Rouse, Alex Blake, Walter Booker, and pl. in B. Taylor band in *Black Journal* series. Infls: H. Hancock, Milton Nascimento, W. Shorter, J.J. Johnson, Howard Johnson.

Comps: *Impressions of an African Rain Forest; Overkill Horn; Variations on Last Night; Ivan The Terrible; Song of the Valdez Diamond.* LPs: *In Search of Happiness* w. Natural Essence (Fant.).

McINTYRE, KENNETH ARTHUR (KEN),* *alto saxophone, composer*; also *flute, oboe, bass clarinet, bassoon, piano*; b. Boston, Mass., 9/7/31. Made his rec. debut, '60 and from that time was an important and active member of the decade's avant garde, through club apps., fests. and further rec. From '67-9 taught theory, instrumental music, history of jazz, and cond. the Lab Band, for which he also comp., at Central State U. in Ohio; Ass't. Prof. at Wesleyan U., '69-71; visiting lecturer in African-American Music History and Improvisation in the African-American Tradition, Smith College, '71- . Dir. of Music and Dance, Prof. of Humanities at State U. of N.Y. Coll. at Old Westbury, '71- . Received Nat'l Endowment for the Humanities Summer Stipend award for research in *The Concept of Time in Ghanaian Music*, '71. Ed.D. from U. of Mass., '74.

Apps. w. Harlem Phil. Orch. and Bridgeport Symph. Orch. Film scores: *How Wide Is Sixth Avenue; Miracle on the BMT.* TV: *Dateline Boston* w. John McLellan, WHDH; *Profiles of the Arts*, w. N. Hentoff, WNBC. Fests: Hampton, '68; Newport, '66, '73; N.Y. Musicians Fest., '72. LP: *Hindsight* (SteepleChase).

McKENNA, DAVID J. (DAVE),* *piano*; b. Woonsocket, R.I., 5/30/30. Continued his longtime association w. Bobby Hackett by pl. w. him on Cape Cod. He also was in residence w. his own group in that section of Massachusetts in the '70s. In Oct. '74 pl. at Michael's Pub, NYC. Gigged w. Jake Hanna-Carl Fontana in LA, July '75. Writing about a McKenna performance Whitney Balliett remarked that "the rhythmic impetus he developed summoned up highballing freights . . . but the slow numbers were just as hypnotic."

An elegant, two-handed player, particularly effective as an unaccompanied soloist, a role he filled during the NJF-NY, '73. Appeared at Colorado JP many times in late '60s and '70s. LPs: *Cookin' at Michael's Pub; Solo Piano; Quartet* feat. Z. Sims (Chiaro.).

McKIBBON, ALFRED BENJAMIN,* *bass*; b. Chicago, Ill. 1/1/19. Living in LA; staff musician at NBC from mid-1960s, also jobbing extensively in clubs and concerts w. combos, and w. singers incl. Joe Williams, F. Sinatra, Diahann Carroll. Recorded w. Ray Charles. Toured with Giants of Jazz, an all-star group of bop musicians, in US and Europe, '71-2. Mainly working w. Sammy Davis '75. LPs: *Giants of Jazz* (Atl.); w. Monk (Black Lion).

McKINLEY, RAY,* *drums*; b. Fort Worth, Tex., 6/18/10. Popular swing era figure heard w. J. Dorsey; co-leader of band w. Will Bradley, then own band. Took over direction of Glenn Miller AAF band jointly w. Jerry Gray. Led Miller style band under sponsorship of Miller's estate from '56 until Jan. '66. Hosted U.S. Treasury

Show *Bring Back The Bands*, '67-8. Own small combo at Rainbow Grill, NYC, '68, '69 with such sidemen as Bernie Privin, trumpet; Lenny Hambro, clarinet. Musical consultant for Disney World, '71. Since then, part time activity heading big dance bands.

LPs: *Ray McKinley's Greatest Hits* (Dot).

McKINNEY, HAROLD WALTON (HAL), *piano, composer, singer*; also *violin, oboe, vibes*; b. Detroit, Mich., 7/4/28. He is the second of seven brothers and three sisters, among whom is the trombonist known as Kiane Zawadi. Stud. w. mother; priv. teachers, '35-42; BA from Morehouse Coll., '52. Early exp. pl. gospel music in church. Insp. by Ch. Parker, Bud Powell, Ellington, Gershwin and classical composers. Led own groups at clubs in Detroit. Traveled w. G. Krupa, W. Montgomery; pl. w. K. Burrell, S. Stitt, Louis Smith; acc. Carmen McRae, other singers. Worked in husband/wife duo w. Gwen McKinney. After many years of formal and informal studies, he became a teacher and authority on Afro-American music, serving as mus. dir. of Detroit's Metropolitan Arts Complex, and a local TV series. Wrote articles for Michigan Chamber of Commerce magazine, Mich. Chronicle and Negro History Bulletin. Was assoc. with the first jazz studies sponsored by Wayne U. Toured Detroit public schools and colls. throughout Mich. under aegis of Cultural Enrichment Division, '67-8, and Mich. State Council for the Arts, '69-70.

Comps: *Ode to Africa* for chorale and band; *Blue Job* (based on the 14th chapter of the Book of Job); *Sonata in C# Minor* (based on jazz and blues, and set in sonata form); *Heavenese*, original music and lyrics. LPs: *Voices and Rhythms of the Creative Profile* (Tribe); as singer, *Something In The Wind* w. Paul Winter (A & M); *Bohannon*, w. Hamilton Bohannon (Dakar).

McLAUGHLIN, JOHN, *guitar, composer*; also *piano, synthesizer*; b. Yorkshire, England, 1/4/42. Mother a violinist. Self-taught except for a few piano lessons. First pro. job in late '50s w. Big Pete Deuchar and his Professors of Ragtime; other jobs in England w. Graham Bond, Herbie Goines, Brian Auger. Emigrating to the U.S. in '68, he worked w. Tony Williams' Lifetime; pl. w. Miles Davis, rec. *Bitches' Brew; In a Silent Way*. Formed own group, the Mahavishnu Orchestra, '71, taking the name given by his guru, Sri Chinmoy.

McLaughlin drew his original inspiration from blues artists such as Muddy Waters, Big Bill Broonzy and Leadbelly, as well as such jazz stars as Django Reinhardt, Tal Farlow and Barney Kessel. In his own group these elements were synthesized into a pan-idiomatic style that reflected a rare sense of spirituality. McLaughlin was heavily influenced by his spiritual master, Sri Chinmoy but left him in late '75, dropping the name Mahavishnu. Fests: Montreux; Festival at Orange, France, '75. Comps: *Meetings of the Spirit; Dawn; The Noonward Race; A Lotus On Irish Streams; Vital Transformation; The Dance of Maya; You Know You Know; Awakening; Birds of Fire; Celestial Terrestrial Commuters; Thousand Island Park; Sanctuary; Open Country Joy; Resolution; Power of Love; Vision Is A Naked Sword; Smile of the Beyond; Wings of Karma; Hymn to Him; Eternity's Breath; Life's Dance; Can't Stand Your Funk; Cosmic Strut; Earth Ship; On The Way Home To Earth*, etc.

Some of the sidemen who have pl. w. Mahavishnu incl. Billy Cobham, Khalid Yasin (Larry Young), Armando Peraza, Jean-Luc Ponty, John Surman, Tony Oxley, et al.

Jim Schaffer wrote in DB, 4/26/73, "Mahavishnu's exotic sound is among the finest to arise from the musical experimentation of the past decade. The technical achievement inherent in *Birds of Fire* verges on the edge of credibility when combined with the unique oneness that gives the Mahavishnu Orchestra its own place in the jazz world."

LPs: w. Mahavishnu Orch., *The Inner Mounting Flame; Birds of Fire; Between Nothingness and Eternity; Apocalypse; Visions of the Emerald Beyond*; John McLaughlin-Carlos Santana, *Love Devotion Surrender* (Col.); McLaughlin, *Extrapolation* (Polydor); *Devotion; My Goals Beyond* (Douglas); w. Miles Davis, *Bitches Brew; In A Silent Way; Tribute to Jack Johnson; Live/Evil* (Col.); w. Tony Williams (Poly.).

McLEAN, JOHN LENWOOD (JACKIE),* *alto sax, flute, composer, educator*; b. New York City, 5/17/32. After playing w. Charles Mingus, Art Blakey and app. in the Off-Broadway prod. of *The Connection*, toured Europe and Japan w. own gp. and pl. in US clubs while living in NYC, '66. In '67 began to study flute and took job as bandmaster and counselor for State Correction Dept. Stopped pl. in clubs. Began to commute to Connecticut and took part time teaching position at U. of Hartford, '68-9. Cont. teaching there in '70-1 and moved to Hartford, also counseling drug addicts. From '72 teaching full time at Hartt Coll. of Hartford U., developing Afro-American Music Dept. Instrumental in forming a culture program for inner city children (adults also attend) called *The Artist Collective*, teaching music, dance, visual arts and drama. From '72 McLean also traveled to Denmark to teach at Vallekilde, a summer music school. While there he pl. at Montmartre as a soloist and w. Dexter Gordon and rec. for the SteepleChase label. In '75 he appeared at the Five Spot, NYC, w. own band that incl. his son, Rene, on tenor sax.

Acted and pl. in film version of *The Connection*; many TV apps. w. Gil Noble on *Like It Is*, ABC; local TV in Hartford. Fest: Chateauvallon, France. A product of the bop generation's second wave, McLean is capable of playing convincingly and originally in a number of contemporary grooves with the same searing passion and invention that has marked his work from the time he was a teenage sensation. Comp: *Little Melonae; Dr. Jackle; Dig; Minor March; Quadrangle; Marie Caveau; Day of Absence*, a play for Robert Hooks; *The Gimmick*, play for Roger Furman. LPs: *New York Calling; Antiquity; Live at Montmartre; Ode to Super* w. G. Bartz; *The Meeting; The Source*, both w. D. Gordon (Steeple.); *Jacknife; Demon's Dance; 'Bout Soul; New and Old Gospel* (BN).

McLEOD, ALICE. see Coltrane, Alice.

McNAIR, HAROLD, * *flute, alto, tenor saxophones*; b. Kingston, Jamaica, 5/11/31. Heard in Europe from '59 w. K. Clarke and Q. Jones, McNair was prominent on the British scene for his work w. Donovan and Ginger Baker. He died in London 3/7/71.

McPARTLAND, JAMES DUGALD (JIMMY), * *cornet*; b. Chicago, Ill., 3/15/07. Veteran of early Chicago jazz; pl. w. Ben Pollack, '27-9. Was married, '45, to Marian Page, and has occasionally app. with her during and since the 20 years of their marriage. Visited Durban, S. Africa, '71, '72; toured w. Art Hodes, '73; NJF and Nice JF, '74. Plays Jimmy Ryan's club, NYC, every year as leader. Co-leader of combo w. Buddy Tate at Americana Hotel, NYC. Concerts and workshops in schools with own group, and w. Marian McPartland, '74-5.

McPartland remained one of the best cornetists in the Bix Beiderbecke tradition. Publs: *Sounds of Dixieland* for Combos; *Dixieland Series*, w. Dick Cary (Edw. B. Marks Music Corp., 1790 Broadway, N.Y. 10019).

LPs: *Jimmy McPartland's Dixieland* (Harmony); *The McPartlands Live at the Monticello* (Halcyon); *On Stage*, w. Maxine Sullivan (Jazzology).

McPARTLAND, MARIAN, * *piano, composer*; b. Windsor, England, 3/20/20. To U.S. '46, with husband Jimmy McPartland. After working with him in Chicago, she started with her own trio with which she played during the '50s, most often at the Hickory House in NYC. During the '60s she diversified her activities, returning several times to England, touring briefly w. B. Goodman sextet in '63, and writing such compositions as *Twilight World* (rec. by Tony Bennett in '73).

McPartland also has served on the committees of various jazz orgs. and arts councils; has worked as a disc jockey, journalist and record producer. She started her own Halcyon label in '69. Alec Wilder wrote 20 piano pieces for her, six of which she rec. on Halcyon. She wrote music for an educ. film, *The Light Fantastic Picture Show* in '74, obtainable from Films Inc., 1144 Wilmette Ave., Wilmette, Ill. 60091.

Also during '74 she undertook a nine week pilot project teaching jazz to children in predominantly black public schools in Washington, D.C., with D. Ellington among her guest performers, shortly before his death. She toured South America in a piano package with E. Hines, Teddy. Wilson and Ellis Larkins. Concert and workshop apps. at Harvard and Howard U's. Her comp. *Ambiance* was rec. by the Thad Jones-Mel Lewis orch. Played solo piano at NJF-NY, '74.

Marian McPartland has progressed over the years from a competent but derivative British import to a mature artist of complete self-assurance. At an unaccompanied concert in 1975 in Los Angeles, she impressed the audience with the rhythmic agility of her left hand, and the skilfull way with which she used it, sometimes to accompany, more often to complement and correlate what was going on in the right. She is an exceptionally lyrical ballad performer, enriching and expanding the harmonic and melodic essence of every theme.

Own LPs on Halcyon; also *Let It Happen* by Jazz Piano Quartet w. D. Hyman, R. Hanna, Hank Jones (RCA).

McPHERSON, CHARLES, * *alto sax*; b. Joplin, Mo., 7/24/39. Although he formed his own group in '66, he also cont. his assoc. w. Barry Harris and Ch. Mingus, touring in Europe w. the latter in '72. Occasionally lecturing at colls., demonstrating *Jazz and the Saxophonist* in '70s. Fests: NJF, '69, '71; NJF-NY, '73-4; Eastern and Western Europe, incl. Berlin Jazztage, Cascais JF, Portugal, w. *Musical Life of Charlie Parker* tour, fall '74. App. many times w. own quintet at Boomer's, NYC, '74-5. Won DB Critics' Poll TDWR, '67. A strong interpreter and extender of the Parker idiom with a particularly singing tone.

Comps: *Horizons; Night Eyes; Charisma; She Loves Me.* LPs: *Beautiful* (Xanadu); *Today's Man; Siku Ya Bibi* (Mainstream); *Horizons; From This Moment On; Live at the Five Spot* (Prest.); *Charles Mingus and Friends in Concert* (Col.); w. Mingus (Fant., Prest.); w. Bobby Jones (Cobble.).

McRAE, CARMEN, * *singer, piano*; b. New York City, 4/8/22. A solo vocalist since '54, McRae continued to tour, enjoying particular popularity in Japan, which she visited five times between '64 and '75. She moved to Beverly Hills, Cal. in '67 and was frequently seen at LA and Hollywood clubs. She had a role in the film *Hotel.* Other overseas visits included Holland and Denmark, '73; Ronnie Scott's Club, London, '74; Sweden, June '75, followed immediately by an appearance on *Showboat 3*, the jazz festival cruise.

Though occasional demands were made by recording producers to give her a so-called contemporary direction, McRae for the most part remained loyal to her credo of interpreting top quality songs in a style mirroring her jazz experience, her talent as a musician (she continued to play piano from time to time in her act) and her rare ability to bring to life even the most mundane of lyrics. Festival appearances included Monterey almost every year, as well as Newport, Concord, Brussels etc. TV: *Merv Griffin; Tonight Show; Mike Douglas Show; Soul; Like It Is; Pearl Bailey Show; Hollywood Palace; Jonathan Winters Show.*

LPs: *I Am Music* (BN); *Great American Song Book; Sound of Silence; Just A Little Lovin'; Portrait of Carmen; For Once In My Life* (Atl.); *It Takes A Whole Lot of Human Feelings; Ms. Jazz* (Groove Merchant); *Carmen* (Temponic); *Carmen McRae; Carmen's Gold; Live and Doin' It; Alive!; In Person; I Want You;* (Mainstr.). An album entitled *Carmen Alone*, in which she sang and played piano, was recorded in Tokyo.

McSHANN, JAY (HOOTIE), * *piano, singer, composer*; b. Muskogee, Okla., 1/12/09. (Note: McShann states that this date, given in all ref. books, is incorrect, and that he was born 1/12/16.) Prominent bandleader, often in KC in late 1930s and early '40s; sidemen incl. Ch. Parker. Enjoyed renaissance of interest in late '60s, touring as single or w. small gps. Toured Europe, '68; Spain and France, '69; London, Continent, '70; Spain, France,

'71; annual tours since then incl. seven East Europe cities in '74 w. *Musical Life of Charlie Parker*. TV apps. in Barcelona, '69-70-71; Paris, '73; Montreux, '74. Motion picture: *The Last of the Blue Devils*, 60 minute documentary on Kansas City jazz, '74. Fests: Kansas City, '71; Monterey, Zurich, Montreal, '72; Orange, France, NJF-NY, '73; Montreux, NJF-NY, '74, etc.

Publs: *Boogie Woogie & Blues Piano Solos & Instructions; The Book of the Blues* (MCA Music). Comps: *Confessin' the Blues; Hootie Blues; Yardbird Waltz; Dexter Blues; Jumpin' Blues*; 60 others.

LPs: *Going to Kansas City* (Master Jazz); *Man From Muskogee* (Sackville, Canada); *Kansas City Memories* (Black & Blue, Paris); *McShann's Piano* (Cap.).

MEHEGAN, JOHN,* *piano, teacher, writer*; b. Hartford, Conn., 6/6/20. Mehegan has a distinguished career as music instructor, occasional critic, and writer of a series of books on jazz improvisation, publ. by Watson-Guptill. From '68 he was jazz teacher at the U. of Bridgeport, Conn. Jazz instruc. series for *Clavier Magazine*, '69. Clinics at many univs. Comp. and played TV sound track for Arthur Miller's *Story of Two Mondays*, '73. Lecturer in jazz at Yale U., '74-5. App. at clinic in Trondheim, Norway, sponsored by Northern Piano Teachers Union, '74. Series of clinics in Scandinavia, '75.

MENDES, SERGIO,* *piano, composer*; b. Niteroi, Brazil, 2/11/41. Resident in U.S. since mid-60s, leading the popular group known as Brasil '65, later Brasil '66. The group toured w. F. Sinatra and B. Rich band, '67, pl. w. National Symphony in Washington, '68, app. at White House, '70. Many TV specs. w. Bob Hope, Fred Astaire et al. The group's name was changed in '69 to Brasil '77. Mendes moved toward a sound with greater mass appeal, using an extra percussionist in a style once described as "electro-bossa-rock-pop-good-time-music." Comps: *So Many Stars; Song of No Regrets*.

LPs: *Vintage 74*, w. A.C. Jobim as guest star (Bell); reissue of Mendes Trio, *So Nice* (Pickwick Int'l.); *Foursider; Pais Tropical* (A & M); *Sergio Mendes* (Elektra).

MENZA, DON, *tenor saxophone, composer*; also *saxophones, clarinets, flutes*; b. Buffalo, N.Y., 4/22/36. Stud. sax in high school, '53-4; also State U. of N.Y. in Fredonia. Self-taught as composer-arranger. Pl. in Stuttgart w. 7th Army Jazz Band w. D. Ellis, Leo Wright, E. Harris, Cedar Walton, Lanny Morgan, '56. After discharge, pl. w. Al Belletto, '59. Won Best Tenor Sax and Best Soloist awards at Notre Dame JF. Toured w. M. Ferguson, '60-1; led quintet w. Sam Noto in Buffalo, '62-3. From '64-8 Menza worked in Munich w. Max Greger's TV band; also was co-leader of Bavarian radio jazz ensemble which won top honors at the first Montreux JF in '67. Returned to U.S., joined B. Rich, '68. After leaving Rich, settled in LA and became very active pl. in bands for all three major TV networks and many rec. companies, as well as jingle recs. Feat. soloist in films, *The Savage Is Loose; The Organization; Taking of Pelham 1-2-3; Play Misty For Me*. Freelance work w. several big bands in LA area, incl. L. Bellson. He app. in concert w. Buffalo Phil. perf. two of his orig. works.

Comps: *Groovin' Hard; Acid Truth; Time Check*, for Rich; *Inferno; Spanish Gypsy; Back Home*, for Bellson; *One for Otis; Straight Out; Statements & Reflections* etc. for Ferguson; *Morning Song; Devil's Disciples; Cinderella's Waltz; Spanish Boots*, for own album.

Menza is a hard driving tenor soloist infl. mainly by S. Rollins, and a composer-arr. in the mainstream-modern tradition, insp. by B. Holman, O. Nelson and Al Cohn. He was awarded a Federal grant from the National Endowment For the Arts to write three pieces for coll. workshop jazz bands.

LPs: *Morning Song* (MPS); w. Ferguson, *Straight Away; Maynard '62; Maynard '63; Message from Maynard; Si Si MF* (Roul.); w. Rich, *Live at Caesar's Palace* (Liberty); w. Bellson, *Explosion* (Pablo); w. F. Strazzeri, *Taurus* (Creative World); w. Jack Daugherty, *Class of '71* (A & M); w. Greger, *Maximum* (Poly.).

MERRILL, HELEN,* *singer*; b. New York City, 7/21/30. Freelance work as night club vocalist in late '40s and '50s; active mainly in Europe and Japan, '59-67. Settled in Tokyo, '67, where during next five years she made 12 LPs for Japanese Victor, as well as many TV and concert apps. Travels incl. return to U.S. for Milestone LP, '68; jazz fest. in Ljubljana, Yugoslavia, '69. Toured Japan w. Nobuo Hara's Sharps and Flats, '69. Conducted interviews on own show, English language radio station in Tokyo, '70; taught singing '71.

After living in Hong Kong for several months, Merrill returned to the U.S., settling in Chicago in late '72. She worked with local musicians, formed a ten piece band w. Kenny Soderblom and in '75 rec. her first U.S. album in six years, and sang in NYC clubs. She was listed as top vocalist in *Swing Journal*, Tokyo, annually from '67-72.

LPs: *The Feeling Is Mutual; A Shade of Difference* (Milestone). Among the Japanese albums not released in the U.S. are one w. Teddy Wilson and one w. Gary Peacock.

MEZZROW, MEZZ (Milton Mesirow),* *clarinet, saxophones*; b. Chicago, Ill., 11/9/1899. The controversial clarinetist, who had been living in Paris since 1951, died there of arthritis 8/5/72. Though a limited instrumentalist, he was an indomitable propagandist for NO style jazz. His autobiography, describing his experiences not only in music, but also as a user and seller of drugs, provided the basis for a somewhat fictionalized but highly readable book, *Really the Blues* (Random House).

MICHEL, EDWARD M., *producer*; b. Chicago, Ill., 8/20/36. After graduating UCLA (Psych.) 1956, worked as asst. at Pac. Jazz Records. Produced first album in '58. Served in Army Resrve; worked for N. Granz, Val Valentin at Verve Rec. In Europe for Interdisc. To NYC '61 for Riverside as asst. to Bill Grauer, O. Keepnews. To LA, 1966. Joined Impulse Rec. '69. With engineer Bill Szymczyk, explored use of quadraphonic technique in connection with developing free musical forms. Produced LPs by G. Barbieri, Marion Brown, Alice Coltrane, Keith Jarrett, Dewey Redman, Sam Rivers, Pharoah Sanders, Sun Ra, Michael White. Late in '75 he moved to A & M's new Horizon label.

MIKKELBORG, PALLE, *trumpet, composer, conductor;* also *piano;* b. Copenhagen, Denmark, 3/6/41. Self-taught as trumpeter, composer; stud. cond. at Royal Music Cons. in Copenhagen. Began pl. at Club Vingaarden in Copenhagen, '61-4; w. Danish Radio Jazz Group, '64-70, last four yrs. as leader; Danish Radio Big Band, '65-70; Alex Riel-Mikkelborg quintet, '67-8; own quartet, '65-7; Octet, '67-9; Peter Herbolzheimer big band, '70- ; own septet, '72- . Mikkelborg has also worked for varying periods w. G. Russell, D. Gordon, Joachim Kuhn, Eje Thelin, Jan Garbarek, Dollar Brand, Johnny Dyani, Philip Catherine, C. Mariano, M. Ferguson, Ed Thigpen, Tootie Heath, Don Cherry, Bernt Rosengren, Ben Webster, Y. Lateef and, "for one unforgettable night," the Gil Evans orch. Infl: A. Ayler, G. Evans, M. Davis, Clifford Brown, G. Russell, B. Evans, Don Cherry, Charles Ives, Olivier Messiaen. TV: Has comp. mus. for several TV plays and film mus.; TV prod. w. Bill Evans trio & symph. orch., '70; Gordon & strings, '71; app. several times w. own gps., '67, '69, '71, '73-4; TV portrait of his music, '75. Has performed at most major European fests. incl. Montreux where he won a first prize, '68. Was voted Jazzman of the Year in Denmark, '68; number one trumpet in *Jazz Forum*, '69; received Cultural Government Scholarship, '69. Mikkelborg, who states that he is strongly guided by Yoga philosophy, is highly regarded as one of Europe's most creative writer-players. Comps: for big band, *Te Faru; Tempus Zncertum Remanet; Mess-Ra; Salamander Dance; Good Morning Sun; Ashoka Suite; The Mysterious Corona;* for symph. orch. & big band plus soloists, *Maya's Sloer; KMO.* LPs: *The Mysterious Corona;* Danish Radio Jazz Group (Debut); *Brownsville Trolley Line* (Sonet); *My Kind of Sunshine; Wait A Minute; Live at Ronnie's* (MPS); *September Man* (WB); *Live at Onkel Po* (Poly.); *Action-Re-Action* w. Thigpen (Sonet); *You Must Believe in Spring* w. Karin Krog (Poly.); *More Than You Know* w. D. Gordon (Steeple.); *Rhyme and Reason* w. H. Geller (Atl.).

MILES, BARRY, *composer, piano, keyboards, drums;* b. Newark, N.J., 3/28/47. Very early pro. start, app. on TV shows in '58. Best known orig. as drummer, later mainly as pianist-composer. Toured Europe on "People to People" program, won award as outstanding musician at festival in Düsseldorf. Stud. at Princeton U. '69. Awards from Nat. Endowment for Arts, '73-4. TV: *Fusion Suite* (PBS); several others on PBS. Publ: *Twelve Themes and Improvisations* (Belwin-Mills).

LPs: *White Heat; Scatbird* (Mainstream); *Silverlight* (London), earlier albums on Venture, etc. deleted.

MILES, CHARLES J. (BUTCH) (Charles J. Thornton, Jr.), *drums;* also *percussion;* b. Ironton, Ohio, 7/4/44. Began at age 9 on snare drum. Stud. privately at music store in Charleston, West Va. w. Frank Thompson, '60-1; major in music at West Va. State Coll., '62-6. Pl. w. various small gps. in West Va. and then went on road w. trio throughout the midwest in '59-69 period; also keyboard percussion w. Charleston Symph. '64-6. With Austin-Moro big band in Detroit, '70-1; Mel Torme, '71-4.

Joined Count Basie in Jan. '75. Infl: Rich, Krupa, Bellson, Morello, Alla Rahka, Jo Jones, Cobham, Sonny Payne, Beethoven, Basie, Ellington. Film: *Snowman* w. Torme. TV: *Bandstand*, CBC, Toronto, '73; *On the Town*, Australia, '74. Fest: Concord, '73; NJF-NY; KCJF; Montreux; Antibes, '75. An energetic, spirited drummer with a driving pulse. LPs: w. Basie (Pablo); w. Torme, *Live at the Maisonette* (Atl.).

MILLER, EDDIE,* *tenor saxophone, clarinet;* b. New Orleans, 6/23/11. Best known as key member of Bob Crosby orch. late '30s, early '40s. Rejoined Crosby for frequent guest apps. in '50s, '60s. Toured England as soloist accom. by Alex Welsh orch. March '67. Later that year he went to New Orleans to join Pete Fountain at the latter's club, and was still there in '75, also app. at NOJF. Other fest: NJF-NY w. Crosby; Colo. Jazz Party, '75. Comps: *Lazy Mood; March of the Bob Cats.* LPs: several with Fountain (MCA); *Portrait of Eddie* (Blue Angel); *The Tenor of Jazz*, rec. in London w. Ben Webster, Lockjaw Davis, Bud Freeman (English Fontana).

MILLER, ERNEST (KID PUNCH),* *trumpet, singer;* b. Raceland, La., date uncertain, probably June 1889. The pioneer New Orleans jazzman, who worked with Kid Ory and later with many bands in Chicago, was still playing in his native town during his last years. He died 12/4/71 in New Orleans.

MILLINDER, LUCIUS (LUCKY),* *leader;* b. Anniston, Ala., 8/8/00. Popular in the '30s and '40s, when his band incl. Red Allen, Buster Bailey, John Kirby, Sweets Edison, Dizzy Gillespie and dozens of others who later achieved individual fame, Millinder died 9/28/66 of a liver ailment at Harlem Hospital. Two tracks feat. Wynonie Harris and Sister Rosetta Tharpe, both of whom sang in his band in the '40s, were reissued in *Singin' The Blues* (MCA).

MINASI, DOMINIC (DOM), *guitar;* also *bass;* b. Queens, N.Y., 6/3/43. Stud. w. Joe Geneli, eight yrs.; Sal Salvador, three yrs.; Dan Duffy, one yr.; Jim Hall, six mos.; and majored in music in h.s. Pl. w. Les & Larry Elgart, '69; B. Rich, '72; R. Hanna, '73; Jimmy Heath; Ray Nance; Louis Hayes; Arnie Lawrence; George Coleman; J. Nottingham; Sonny Dallas; Bud Shank; Ernie Wilkins; own gp., '74-5. Infl: Johnny Smith; Coltrane, M. Davis, R. Kellaway. Won partial scholarship to Berklee, '63. Wrote all arrs. on first album, *When Johanna Loved Me.* Publ: *Musicians Manual for Chord Substitution* (Sunrise Artistries, 64-24 Grand Ave., Maspeth, N.Y. 11378). LPs: *When Johanna Loved Me; I Have the Feeling I've Been Here Before* (Blue Note).

MINCE, JOHNNY (John Henry Muenzenberger),* *clarinet, saxes;* b. Chicago Heights, Ill., 7/8/12. Prominent with many swing bands incl. T. Dorsey, Bob Crosby; then spent 20 years as member of CBS radio house band on Arthur Godfrey show, '46-66. Replaced Buster Bailey w. L. Armstrong, Apr. '67. Soon afterward, became active playing club dates in the NYC area; played Dick Gibson's annual jazz parties in Colo. for three years; Odessa, Tex. jazz party for two years; jazz fest. in Hanover, Germany, '74. Toured England w. Kings of Jazz, late '74. Mince is a swing style clarinetist insp. by Goodman, Dodds, I. Fazola.

LPs: *Back Home In Indiana*, w. Lee Wiley; *Greatest Song Hits of Walter Donaldson* (Monmouth-Evergreen); *What a Wonderful World*, w. B. Hackett (Flying Dutchman).

MINERVE, HAROLD (GEEZIL), *alto sax, clarinet, flute, piccolo*; b. Havana, Cuba, 1/3/22. Raised in Orlando, Fla. from age two. Father pl. clarinet, flute and banjo. Took up clarinet at seven but not seriously until private lessons at 12. Pl. in high school band. In '40 left home w. band from Ohio led by drummer Jeff Gilson. After completing school went out on road show pl. alto sax in band backing Ida Cox. Pl. in NO band formerly led by Joe Robichaux but fronted by Joan Lunceford (no relation to Jimmie Lunceford) of Mobile, Ala. Then w. Clarence Love; Ernie Fields. From '43 spent three yrs. in military service. Back w. Fields until '50 when he joined Buddy Johnson. Left in '57 to gig in NYC. With Mercer Ellington at Birdland, '60; Ray Charles, '62-4. Musical dir. for Arthur Prysock. Became member of Duke Ellington organization Sept. 7, '71. Infl: Bechet, Goodman, Shaw, Bigard, Benny Carter, Hodges. Fav. lead alto, Willie Smith. LPs: see Ellington (Duke and Mercer).

MINGUS, CHARLES,* *bass, composer, piano, leader*; b. Nogales, Ariz., 4/22/22. Prominent in LA and SF in '40s; NYC '50s and '60s. From late '50s led series of Jazz Workshop bands that served as forums for such musicians as John Handy, Booker Ervin, Eric Dolphy, Jimmy Knepper, Ted Curson, Clifford Jordan, Charles McPherson, Rahsaan Roland Kirk, J. McLean, Paul Bley, Jaki Byard and many others.

Despite the great importance of his work as leader, catalyst and instrumentalist, Mingus, after the mid '60s, went into semi-retirement, partly due to ill health, and was heard from infrequently. Taking up residence in New York's East Village, he worked on an autobiography, *Beneath the Underdog* (Alfred A. Knopf), published in '71. This spurred renewed interest in his music. He began recording again, and in Feb. '72 made a comeback concert at Philharmonic Hall, NYC, leading a 20-piece orch. Soon afterward, several Mingus albums were released, incl. reissues.

Mingus toured Europe leading a quintet in the fall of '72; again in fall '75. He was also seen in such Village clubs as the Five Spot and Top of the Gate. He was presented in concert at Carnegie Hall in Jan. '74, joined by Kirk.

In addition to annual apps. at Newport, he has been heard in recent years at Antibes, Montreux and fests. in Italy and Japan. He was elected to DB Hall of Fame. Received Guggenheim Fellowship, '71. Among his best known comps. are *The Black Saint and the Sinner Lady; Thrice Upon A Theme; Revelations; Tijuana Table Dance; Fables of Faubus.*

LPs: *At The Jazz Workshop; At Monterey; Chazz; My Favorite Quintet; Quintet Plus Max Roach; Town Hall Concert* (Fantasy); *Charlie Mingus & Friends; Better Git It In Your Soul; Let My Children Hear Music; Mingus Ah Um* (Col.); *Art of Charlie Mingus; Best of Charlie Mingus; Blues and Roots; Mingus Moves; Oh Yeah; Mingus at Carnegie Hall; Changes One; Changes Two* (Atl.); *Black Saint and the Sinner Lady; Mingus, Mingus, Mingus; Charles Mingus Plays Piano*-solo; *Reevaluation, the Impulse Years* (Imp.); *Tijuana* Moods (RCA); *Great Concert* w. E. Dolphy; *Reincarnation of a Lovebird* (Pres.); *Mingus Moods; Mingus Revisited* (Trip); *Town Hall Concert* (SS); *Wonderland* (UA). As sideman in *Newport in New York, The Jam Sessions, vols. 1&2* (Cobblestone).

MITCHELL, BILLY,* *tenor, alto, soprano saxophones, flute, clarinets, composer, educator*; b. Kansas City, Mo., 11/3/26. One of the many talents to emerge from the Detroit jazz scene of the '40s. Pl. w. Woody Herman, '49; Dizzy Gillespie, Count Basie in '50s. Left Basie in '61 and formed gp. w. Al Grey which was together '62-4. Returned to Basie, mid-'66-mid-'67. Music dir. for Stevie Wonder; along w. Slide Hampton wrote music for Wonder's first night club performance. In '70 returned to Europe for tour w. Clarke-Boland Big Band, of which he had been a founder-member in '63. Pl. alto sax and was mus. dir. for Dizzy Gillespie orchestra which appeared twice at Buddy's Place and for tribute to Dizzy at Avery Fisher Hall, '75. From the late '60s has served as consultant to the Nassau County Office of Cultural Development, one of the largest and most successful organizations of its kind. From '70 very active teaching and performing in educational institutions at all levels. Staff member of major Jazz Workshops in NYC area: Jazzmobile; Jazz Interactions; Henry Street Settlement Music School. In '73 formed Billy Mitchell Incorporated (407 Yale Ave., Rockville Centre, N.Y. 11570), which makes available his Jazz Ensemble or Dizzy Gillespie's group for a combination concert-"rap-session"-clinic-workshop-and tandem concert with the school band for high schools and colleges. Mitchell conducted such seminars at New York Inst. of Tech. and Hofstra U., '75; and took part in a saxophone seminar at Yale. His company also produced a film, *The Marijuana Affair*, with a score by Melba Liston. Mitchell played on the soundtrack.

Comp: *J&B; Bops; Comeback, Baby; Sweet and Basie.* LPs: w. Clarke-Boland, *Off Limits* (Poly.); Bobby Pierce, *New York*; Eddie Jefferson, *Things Are Getting Better* (Muse); Roland Prince (Vang.).

MITCHELL, RICHARD ALLEN (BLUE),* *trumpet*; also *fluegelhorn*; b. Miami, Fla., 3/13/30. After leaving H. Silver, with whom he played from '58-64, maintained similar group under his own leadership w. Junior Cook, C. Corea and Al Foster to '69. Toured w. R. Charles, '69-71; John Mayall, '71-3. From '74, freelance work in LA mainly w. Bill Berry, Bill Holman, Jack Sheldon, L. Bellson, Richie Kamuca. Canadian cross-country tour w. Bellson, '74.

Own LPs on RCA, Blue Note, Mainstream; w. Silver (Blue Note); *Night Blooming Jazzmen* (Mainstream);

Mayall (Polydor); Bill Berry (Beez).

MITCHELL, ROBERT E. JR. (BOB), *trumpet, fluegelhorn, valve trombone*; b. Birmingham, Ala., 5/23/35. Attended Juilliard School 1964-7; stud. tpt. w. Wm. Vacchiano, then first tpt. w. NY Philharmonic. Other teachers: Leo Demers, Jimmy Stamp, Louis Maggio. Worked with Earl Hines, 1969-71; free-lanced in LA until he joined Count Basie, late 1974. Infls: Gillespie, Miles Davis, Rafael Mendez, Clifford Brown, Woody Shaw, Maynard Ferguson, Clark Terry. Feat. solo on *Freckle Face* in Basie LP on Pablo, 1975.

MITCHELL, GEORGE,* *trumpet*; b. Louisville, Ky., 3/8/1899. The celebrated trumpeter and cornetist, who pl. on some of the best known sessions w. Jelly Roll Morton in the '20s, lived in retirement for many years and died 5/27/72 in Chicago. LPs: w. Morton (RCA).

MITCHELL, GROVER,* *trombone, euphonium, composer*; b. Whatley, Ala., 3/17/30. Heard as lead trombonist w. Basie, Oct. '62 to May '70. Moved to LA June '70. Since then, engaged primarily in TV and movie work; also rec. w. S. Vaughan, Nancy Wilson, B. Eckstine, E. Fitzgerald, Diana Ross, Maria Muldaur, Cass Elliott et al. Films: seen, also heard in solo on sound track of *Lady Sings The Blues*. Comp. *Magna; Fat Cat* for R. Callender's *Basin Street Brass* album (Legend).

Mitchell, who has worked with such major composer-conductors as O. Nelson, Q. Jones, H. Mancini, B. May, M. Legrand, recently has been stressing the writing aspects of his career.

LPs: *Have a Nice Day*, w. Basie (Daybreak); *Michel Legrand and Sarah Vaughan* (Mainstream); *Nifty Cat Strikes West* w. R. Eldridge (Master Jazz); *Now and Then* w. B. Collette (Legend).

MITCHELL, KEITH MOORE (RED),* *bass*; also *piano, cello, bass guitar*; b. New York City, 9/20/27. Prominent in LA for many years, often working with Hampton Hawes, Mitchell was briefly w. D. Gillespie in '68, but was unable to work full time as a jazz musician. In July '68 he decided to leave the U.S. He pl. at Cafe Montmartre in Copenhagen w. Phil Woods; then in a trio w. Bobo Stenson and Rune Carlsson in Switzerland. Settling in Stockholm, he became one of Europe's busiest free-lance musicians, both in European groups and with many of the principal visiting American soloists. Formed new gp. w. Scandinavian musicians, Communication; rec. in Stockholm 1975.

LPs: w. S. Asmussen-T. Thielemans (A & M); w. L. Konitz, *I Concentrate On You* (Steeple.); w. Al Cohn, *Broadway/1954* (Prest.).

MITCHELL, ROSCOE, *soprano, alto, tenor, bass saxophones, flute, piccolo, oboe, clarinet*; also *tambourine, drums, bells, gongs, whistles, steeldrum, bell lyre, bike horns, singer*; b. Chicago, Ill., 8/3/40. First infl. as a child by recs. of Billie Holiday, Louis Armstrong, Billy Eckstine, and by the church of his uncle, Charles Commodore Carter, a popular preacher, artist and mystic, he began to sing, dance and create his own compositions. Pl. baritone sax in high school band; alto in senior yr. Both inst. in Army w. Headquarters USARA Band in Heidel-

berg, Germany. Discharged from Army July '61; pl. in Art Blakey-style gp. w. Henry Threadgill. Infl. at the time by Wayne Shorter but had already heard Ornette Coleman while in service. Joined Richard Abrams' Experimental Band and became associated w. Joseph Jarman, Anthony Braxton and others who led into the formation of the AACM. His own gp., the Roscoe Mitchell Sextet rec. for Delmark in Aug. '66. With Jarman, Lester Bowie and Malachi Favors formed Art Ensemble of Chicago after pl. concerts under the names Joseph Jarman & Company and the Lester Bowie Quartet. Pl. and lived in France, June '69-April '71. Comp: *Odwalla; Sound; Ornette; The Little Suite; Tkhke; The Key; Congliptious; Old; Tnoona; Nonaah.*

LPs: see Art Ensemble of Chicago; also *Sound* (Delmark); *Congliptious* (Nessa).

MIXON, DANIEL ASBURY (DANNY), *piano, composer*; also *trombone*; b. New York City, 8/19/49. From age three tap dancing w. the Ruth Williams Dance Studio, performing annually at Carnegie Hall until age 14. From 15-17 attended H.S. of Performing Arts stud. ballet, tap and drama w. intention of becoming prof. dancer but took up trombone at 15 and pl. in all-borough orch. Grandfather and grandmother who pl. by ear taught him piano. At 17 left home to pl. w. Patti and the Bluebells in Atlantic City. Abandoned dance career. Acc. Joe Lee Wilson, '67-70; Betty Carter, '71-4, to whom he was married during most of this period. For two yrs. in this time did only formal stud. of piano w. Roland Hanna. Worked w. Grant Green; Art Blakey; Carlos Garnett; Rufus Harley; Big Maybelle; Joe Williams; Eddie Jefferson; Dee Dee Bridgewater; Roy Brooks; Frank Foster. For a while typed as a singers' accompanist he has branched out in recent years. Own trio from '72. In '75 working w. Bob Cunningham trio; Pharoah Sanders. Has also pl. w. Piano Choir which rec. his *Main Extensions*.

Infl: Art Tatum, Erroll Garner, Ahmad Jamal, McCoy Tyner, Ravel, Dvorak, Stravinsky, Bartok. TV: documentary on *Three Generations of Jazz* concert done at NYU w. Eubie Blake, Roland Hanna; *Someone New* w. own trio, NBC, '69; *Woman Alive* w. D. Bridgewater, PBS, '75. Fest: NJF-NY w. own trio, '73; Reims w. P. Sanders, '75. LPs: w. Piano Choir, *Handscapes* (Strata-East); w. Betty Carter (Bet-Car).

MIYAMA, TOSHIYUKI, *clarinet, alto saxophone, leader*; b. Chiba Pref., Japan, 10/31/21. Joined Navy band, '39, remaining until 1945. Pl. for U.S. Forces camps in Japan as member of Lucky Puppy band, '46-7. In '50 he formed his own band, the Jive Aces, a ten piece group that pl. mainly at Johnson Air Base. In '58 he augmented to 16 pieces, changing the name to New Herd Orch. Two years later he expanded to 18 pieces.

The New Herd pl. extensively in concerts, on TV, radio and at Air Bases. Miyama names Woody Herman, S. Kenton, Thad Jones-Mel Lewis orch., D. Gillespie, Ch. Parker, Q. Jones as his sources of inspiration. Fests: NJF in Tokyo (pl. w. T. Monk); MJF, '74; at the latter the band enjoyed unanimous acclaim and was heralded as the surprise success of the entire fest.; also NJF, '75. New

Herd won a special Jazz Disc Award from *Swing Journal* in '69; Jazz of Japan Award, '70, '71; voted best big band in SJ, '73-4.

LPs: *Modern Jazz Ten Players Collection; New Herd Modern Jukebox; Perspective; Poetry to Libra; Poetry to Aries* (Col.); *Four Jazz Compositions; Yamatai'Fu* (Toshiba EMI); one rec. live at Monterey JF (Trio).

MOBLEY, HENRY (HANK),* tenor sax, composer; b. Eastman, Ga., 7/7/30. Most important associations w. Horace Silver, Art Blakey in '50s; Miles Davis in '60s. In the mid-'60s co-led gps. w. Lee Morgan; Kenny Dorham. App. at Ronnie Scott's for seven wks., '67; then toured Europe. To Paris '68 to pl. at Chat Qui Peche w. Slide Hampton; then as soloist in Munich; Rome; Poland; Hungary; Yugoslavia. Returned to NYC in mid-'70, worked at Slugs and pl. other jobs w. a band he co-led w. Cedar Walton. Played in Chicago summer '73. In '75 he was living and pl. in Philadelphia. Fest: NJF-NY, Radio City jam session, '73. Comp: *Breakthrough; Early Morning Stroll; The Morning After; Ace Deuce Trey; 3rd Time Around; A Caddy For Daddy; The Dip; The Vamp; Ballin'; East of the Village; My Sin; Straight Ahead (Kismet); Pat 'N Chat.*

LPs: Cedar Walton/Hank Mobley quintet, *Breakthrough* (Cobble.); *Reach Out; Hi Voltage; Caddy For Daddy; The Turnaround; The Flip; Dippin'* (BN); w. E. Jones, *Midnight Walk* (Atl.); reissue, *Blowing Sessions* (BN).

MODERN JAZZ QUARTET. see Lewis, John.

MOFFETT, CHARLES MACK,* drums, trumpet, orchestra bells, composer, educator; b. Fort Worth, Tex., 9/11/29. Active in NYC in '60s w. Ornette Coleman, Sonny Rollins. Made Euro. tour w. Coleman; rec. w. A. Shepp; Coleman; Charles Tyler. Pl. w. bassist Ron Brooks gp., drums and trumpet, sometimes simultaneously. Living in SF area in mid-'70s, app. w. the Charles Moffett Family incl. his sons Charles Jr., tenor sax; Mondre, trumpet; and Codaryl, percussion. Played at the Keystone Korner, March '75. LPs: *The Charles Moffett Family, Vol. 1* (LRS Records, 212 Bishop Ave., Point Richmond, Cal. 94801); *Gift* (Savoy).

MONCUR, GRACHAN III,* trombone, composer; b. New York City, 1937. After working w. Ray Charles, the Jazztet and Jackie McLean, he played w. Archie Shepp, '67-9. Also w. Warren Chiasson in late '60s; then charter member of the 360 Degree Experience. After serving as music director of a drug rehabilitation program in Harlem he became the director of the Creative Black Musicians Workshop in Newark, N.J., the city where he co-led a quartet w. organist John Patton.

Shepp recorded his composition *Hipnosis* but his major work of the '70s was *Echoes of Prayer* on the JCOA label. For this recording he conducted a 22-piece orch. which incl. a percussion ensemble from Brazzaville in the Congo. Evocative of Martin Luther King, Marcus Garvey and the social struggle in America, it mixes West Indian, Latin and European classical influences. It was recorded in April '74, following a performance at New York Univ. Other LPs: w. Shepp, *Way Ahead; For Losers; Kwanza* (Imp.); *Live at the Donaueschingen Festival* (MPS/BASF); *New Africa* (Byg).

MONK, THELONIOUS SPHERE,* piano, composer; b. Rocky Mount, N.C., 10/10/17. Continued to lead quartet through second half of the '60s. When Charlie Rouse left in '70 he was replaced, first by Pat Patrick and then by Paul Jeffrey. In '71-2 Monk toured w. Dizzy Gillespie, Sonny Stitt et al in a group called The Giants of Jazz, playing all over Europe and appearing at the NJF-NY '72. Due to illness his activities were severely curtailed and when he performed with the NYJRC in a concert of his music on April 6, 1974, it was his first public engagement in over a year. Another rare concert was given with his quartet at the NJF-NY '75, one of the artistic triumphs of the festival. Despite his limited activity he is still looked upon as a father figure by today's musicians, up to and including the avant garde. At Newport-NY his quartet included his son, Thelonious Monk Jr. on drums.

In the '70s his earlier compositions such as *'Round Midnight, Well You Needn't* and *Straight No Chaser* were still being played and recorded. *Nutty* was done with a rock beat by Blue Mitchell in '75. *The Ballad of Thelonious Monk*, recorded by Carmen McRae with its composer, Jimmy Rowles, utilizes the titles of many Monk songs in its lyrics. LPs: *Monk's Blues; Straight No Chaser; Underground; Who's Afraid of the Big Band Monk* (Col.); *Something in Blue; The Man I Love* (Black Lion); w. *Giants of Jazz* (Atl.); reissues on Milestone, Prestige, Blue Note.

MONTGOMERY, CHARLES F. (BUDDY),* piano, vibes, composer; b. Indianapolis, Ind., 1/30/30. Toured country for several years with brothers Monk and Wes until the latter's death. Moved in Jan, 1969 to Milwaukee, Wis., where he became involved in a variety of enterprises. In addition to pl. concerts and clubs, he worked annually with Wisconsin's *Summerfest*; was music consultant and instructor for inner city youth in Racine; produced concerts for prisons; taught jazz at Wis. Coll. Conservatory; was judge or clinician at university workshops, etc. From June 1974 he led his own trio at the Marc Plaza Hotel's Bombay Bicycle Club in Milwaukee. Comps: *This Rather Than That; Rosebud; Blues For David; Probin'.*

LPs: *This Rather Than That* (Impulse); *Two Sides of Buddy Montgomery; Best of Wes Montgomery & Friends* (Milestone). Earlier albums w. brothers were on Riv., Fant., Pac. Jazz.

MONTGOMERY, WILLIAM HOWARD (MONK),* bass, composer; b. Indianapolis, Ind., 10/10/21. A pioneer of the electric bass, which he introduced to the public while w. Lionel Hampton's orch. in '51. Pl. w. Mastersounds, '57-Jan. '60. During '60s worked w. his brothers Buddy and Wes, and various small combos in LA and SF, incl. C. Tjader. Pl. in bands cond. by Bill Cosby from '69; led own quartet, '69. From '70-2 was member of Red Norvo trio in Las Vegas lounge. Settling in LV, he initiated a crusade for the use of jazz and contemporary music in that city. Late in '74 assembled a 12 piece ensemble to tour S. Africa with singer Lovelace Watkins, the first U.S. jazz band to travel in that country. In '75 he became one of the founders and principal activists in the World Jazz Assn., organizing an affiliated group in LV.

Comps: *Close Your Face; Sister Lena; Bass Odyssey.* LPs: *It's Never Too Late; Bass Odyssey* (Chisa); *Reality* (Phila. Int'l.); *Two Sides of Buddy Montgomery* (Mile.); others with Buddy and Wes Montgomery (q.v.).

MONTGOMERY, JOHN LESLIE (WES),* guitar, composer; b. Indianapolis, Ind., 3/6/25. Self-taught. First prominent w. Mastersounds, 1958, a group co-led by his brothers Buddy and Monk. Later led own trio and in '65 teamed for a year w. Wynton Kelly's trio. From '65 rec. a series of major pop-jazz hits. In 1966 his *Goin' Out of My Head* won a Grammy as best instr. jazz perf. of the year. He won numerous other awards incl. DB critics' poll 1960-63, '66-7; DB readers' poll, '61-2, '66-7; *Playboy* All Stars' All Stars for six consecutive years.

Montgomery, who used his thumb instead of a plectrum, and who had developed a much imitated parallel-octaves style that established him as the most original and most imitated guitarist since Charlie Christian, was at the height of his fame when he died suddenly of a heart attack at his Indianapolis home, 6/15/68.

LPs: *The Best Of; Best of Vol. II; Bumpin'; California Dreamin'; Goin' Out of My Head; Movin' Wes; Return Engagement; Smokin' At The Half Note; Tequila; Willow Weep For Me* (Verve); *And Friends; While We're Young* (Milestone); *Best of* w. brothers (Fant.); *Day In The Life; Down Here On The Ground; Greatest Hits; Road Song* (A & M).

MONTOLIU, VINCENTE (TETE), piano; b. Barcelona, Spain, 3/28/33. Blind from birth. His father, who pl. English horn in Barcelona Symph. wanted him to become a concert pianist; but in '40 his mother bought him some Ellington records and he became interested in jazz. Three years later Don Byas lived in the Montoliu home and acted as his informal teacher. For many years Tete remained almost unknown, because of the lack of jazz activity in Spain. He staged Sunday morning jam sessions at a small Barcelona theatre. As word of his talent spread, he began to appear around the continent backing Roland Kirk in many European countries during the latter's '64 tour. He also pl. w. Archie Shepp at the Montmartre in Copenhagen for two months, and w. D. Cherry for three weeks, but didn't feel completely at ease with their music. Montoliu in the late '60s and '70s gradually gained acceptance as a gifted soloist with an extremely inventive right hand and an original but adaptable style.

LPs: *Catalonian Fire; Music for Perla; Tete!* (Steeple.); *Songs for Love* (Enja); w. A. Braxton, *In the Tradition* (Steeple.); w. Dusko Goykovich (Enja).

MOODY, JAMES,* saxophones, flute, composer; b. Savannah, Ga., 3/26/25. Known for long associations with D. Gillespie, in the latter's big band in late '40s and small combo in early '60s. Leader of own small combos and participant in saxophone battles with Gene Ammons, Sonny Stitt et al. In late '60s Moody was based in NY but

toured frequently in US and Europe. Pl. at Dick Gibson's Colorado Jazz Party, '71-2. During '72 he made LA his home, but traveled extensively in the Far East and in Europe, as part of an all star group. Took up residence in Las Vegas June 1974. Featured artist on *Showboat 1*, the first jazz festival cruise from NY to West Indies, June '74. Resident member of house band at Hilton Hotel in LV. Reunited w. Gillespie at tribute concert to latter in NYC, Oct. 1975. A driving, powerful tenor player, supple alto saxophonist and one of the most original jazz flutists. TV: *Just Jazz*, PBS, '71. Comp: *Vezzioso; Never Again; Hear Me; Don't Look Away Now; Feeling Low; Everyone Needs It; Savannah Calling; Last Train From Overbrook; Darben the Redd Foxx.* LPs: Vanguard; *Feelin' It Together; Never Again!* (Muse); *Don't Look Away Now*; many reissues w. '40s, '50s gps (Prest.); other reissues on Cadet; Trip; *The Blues and Other Colors; The Brass Figures* (Mile.); *Heritage Hum; The Teachers* (Perception); *Sax & Flute Man* (Paula); w. Gillespie, *The Real Thing* (Percept.); *Swing Low Sweet Cadillac* (Imp.); w. Dexter Gordon, *Tower of Power; More Power*; w. Eddie Jefferson, *Body and Soul* (Prest.); w. Al Cohn, *Too Heavy For Words* (MPS); *Colorado Jazz Party* (MPS/BASF); w. C. Mingus and Friends (Col.).

MOONEY, JOE,* singer, keyboards; b. New Jersey, 1911. Best known when he played accordion and led a quartet in NYC in the late 1940s, Mooney later switched to Hammond organ and worked for many years in Florida. He died 5/12/75 in Ft. Lauderdale, Fla. LPs: *The Greatness of Joe Mooney; The Happiness of Joe Mooney* (Columbia).

MOORE, WILLIAM JR. (BILLY),* composer, piano; b. Parkersburg, W. Va., 12/7/17. Came to prominence when he replaced Sy Oliver as arranger for the J. Lunceford band, '39. Living in Europe since early '50s. writing for French bands, touring w. Peters Sisters, '53-60, working for Berlin radio band, then spending several years acc. Delta Rhythm Boys, after which he became relatively inactive in music, living in Copenhagen and taking up movie script writing.

MOORE, MILTON AUBREY (BREW),* tenor saxophone; b. Indianola, Miss., 3/26/24. Active on NY scene in late '40s-early '50s; then to SF; Europe. From March '65-to Nov. '67 he was based in Copenhagen but then returned to the US, app. in NYC at Joey Archer's Sports Corner, '67-8; Half Note, '68-9. Session for Jazz Interactions; Duke Ellington Society concert w. Ray Nance, '69. Pl. w. Johnny Robinson combo at Limelight in Greenwich Village, '70. To Half Note Club in Canary Islands, '70, then Scandinavia, where he once again took up residence. In '72 he again came back to the US when his father died, living in Mississippi until August '73 when, after stopping momentarily in NYC, he went to Copenhagen. Approximately 10 days later, 8/19/73, he lost his life in a fall down a flight of stairs.

Originally inspired by Lester Young, Moore incorporated elements of the stylistic innovations introduced by Charlie Parker without radically altering his basic style:

romantic, emotional, floating and hard-driving swing. Fest: NJF, '69. Comp: *Brew's Stockholm Dew's; Ergo; No More Brew.*

LPs: *Brew's Stockholm Dew* (Sonet); w. R. Nance, *Body and Soul* (SS); reissue w. Cal Tjader (Fant.).

MOORE, DANIEL WILLIAM (DANNY), *trumpet*; also *piano, violin*; b. Waycross, Ga., 1/6/41. After grad. from Center HS in Waycross, attended Florida A&M U. Toured w. Paul Williams in US, '62. Played w. Art Blakey, '64; five mos. w. C. Basie, '66; also w. Quincy Jones in '60s. A regular member of the Thad Jones-Mel Lewis orch., '69-72; with Aretha Franklin from '71. Often associated in gps. w. George Coleman as co-leader from '72, pl. w. him and Harold Mabern at Boomer's, '75. Worked w. D. Gillespie big band, '75. Infl: Clifford Brown, Thad Jones. Fest: Montreux '73 w. Oliver Nelson. Comp: *A Song for Cherry Hill.* Authoritative as both lead player and soloist. LPs: w. Jones-Lewis, *Central Park North; Live at the Village Vanguard* (SS); w. Q. Jones, *Gula Matari* (A&M); w. O. Nelson, *Swiss Suite* (Fly. Dutch.); w. Johnny Hammond, *Breakout* (Kudu); w. Wes Montgomery (Verve).

MOORE, GLEN R., *bass, composer*; also *violin, piano, flute*; b. Portland, Ore., 10/28/41. Piano lessons in childhood; bass at 13. Stud. w. James Harnett in Seattle; Gary Karr in NYC. Began prof. w. show, *The Young Oregonians*, '56. Pl. w. Jim Pepper, NYC '67; Zoot Sims; Nick Brignola '68; Airto; Paul Bley, Annette Peacock in '68-71; also w. Tim Hardin '68-9; Winter Consort '70-1; Chico Hamilton '72; Benny Wallace '74; Jeremy Steig, on and off, '67-75. From '70, however, main association has been Oregon, a group which mixes many elements into its musical olio. Infl: S. LaFaro, G. Peacock, D. Reinhardt, R. Towner, Jan Hammer, Bartok, J.S. Bach. Fests: Bergamo '74; Molde; Pori '75; NJF-NY '74-5. Comps: *Land of Heart's Desire; At the Hawk's Well; Deer Path; Belt of Asteroids; Three Step Dance; Your Love; Mary's New Bloom; With the Light.* LPs: w. Oregon, *Music of Another Present Era; Distant Hills; Winter Light* (Vang.); *Trios & Solos* (ECM); *This is Jeremy Steig* (SS); *Paul Bley Synthesizer Show* (Milest.); w. Winter Consort, *Road* (A&M).

MOORE, PHIL JR., * *composer*; also *vocal coach, singer, piano*; b. Portland, Ore., 2/20/18. After many years in New York, Moore returned in Jan. 1974 to Los Angeles, where in the 1940s he had been a staff arr. and cond. at MGM studios. He served as assoc. mus. dir. for the TV special *Duke Ellington: We Love You Madly*; composer for TV drama *Sty of the Blind Pig*, 1974; comp., mus. dir., cond. of stage revue *$600 And A Mule*, 1974; mus. dir. *Cotton Club '75*, TV special. Many arrs. for pop artists, also for Quincy Jones.

MORELL, JOHN, *guitar, composer*; b. Niagara Falls, N.Y., 6/2/46. Self taught on guitar, but instructed in orchestration by Albert Harris. Grandfather, father, brother all guitarists. Worked w. Les Brown, '67-70; S. Manne, '70-4; own group, '75- . Also active in rec. field w. H. Mancini et al; many clubs and concerts in LA area.

Made several fest. apps. while w. Manne in Europe, '70. Also at Berkeley Fest. w. Gil Evans-Miles Davis, '68. Morell is a highly sensitive and skilled guitarist, as well as a prolific composer. Many of his compositions have been recorded by Manne, incl. *Seance; Witch's; Pink Pearl; Three On A Match; Don't Know.* During '75 Morell was a member of the band on the Dinah Shore TV show. Infls: Gil Evans, John Coltrane, Miles Davis.

LPs: *John Morell Plays Hits of the '70s* (Cap.); w. Manne, *Alive in London* (Contemp.); *Mannekind* (Mainstr.).

MORELL, MARTY, *drums*; b. New York City, 2/15/44. Studied piano and clarinet before he took up drums at age 12. Percussion studies at Manhattan School of Music at 16. Gained experience w. symphony orch. Pl. w. Al Cohn-Zoot Sims before joining Bill Evans trio in '68 and remaining until the spring of '75. LPs: see Evans; w. Jeremy Steig, *Monium* (Col.).

MORELLO, JOSEPH A. (JOE), * *drums, educator*; b. Springfield, Mass., 7/17/28. A key member of the Dave Brubeck quartet from '56 until its breakup in Dec. '67. From that time conducting clinics for Ludwig Drums around the US; teaching privately and at Dorn & Kirschner Music in Union, N.J. Gigs at Gulliver's in West Paterson, N.J. Instruction books publ: (Ludwig Industries, 1728 No. Damen Ave., Chi., Ill. 60647). LPs: own gp. (Ovation); w. Brubeck (Col.).

MORGAN, LEE, * *trumpet, composer*; b. Philadelphia, Pa., 7/10/38. Best known for his tours with the D. Gillespie orch., '56-8; w. A. Blakey, '58-61 and again '64-5; and with his own combo, Morgan was shot and killed at Slugs', the club in NYC where his quintet was performing, 2/19/72, after a quarrel with a woman who had been his companion for some years.

Morgan had enjoyed commercial success with a record of his comp. *The Sidewinder* in '65. Much of his recorded work, especially in the earlier years, showed a remarkable resemblance to the style of the late Clifford Brown, though later he developed an exceptionally individual identity marked by an excellence of conception, tone and phrasing.

One of his earliest solos was *Night in Tunisia*, which he played as a featured sideman w. Gillespie on a Verve album. He rec. prolifically from '56 as a leader in his own right: *Cooker; Cornbread; Gigolo; At The Lighthouse; Rumproller; Search for the New Land; Sidewinder; 6th Sense* (BN); *Date With Lee; One of a Kind; Speedball; Two Sides of* (Trip); *Genius* (Tradition); others with many small groups for Vee Jay; also *Blue Trane* w. J. Coltrane (BN); *Freedom Rider; Jazz Corner of the World, Vols. I & II; Meet You At The Jazz Corner; Night In Tunisia*, w. Blakey (BN).

Along with his contribution as a musician, Morgan is remembered as an activist and member of the Jazz and People's Movement who, in '70-1, protested media neglect of and indifference to jazz artists.

MORGAN, HOWARD (SONNY), *African and Latin percussion, flute*; b. Philadelphia, Pa., 7/17/36. Studied at

Granoff School of Music. Flute w. Henry Zlotnick; John De Matties; American perc. w. Ellis Tollin; Jimmy Nichols; Dave Levine. From '50-60 stud. rhythms and music of Ghana under Saka Acquaye; rhythms of Haiti w. Maya Deren; music and dances of Caribbean countries w. John Hines; Sydney King; Geoffrey Holder; Katherine Dunham; Syvilla Fort; Walter Nicks. From '63-71 studied Yoruba language, music and drumming w. Michael Olatunji. Toured major colls. w. him, in charge of lecture-demonstrations. Before leaving Phila., performed on flute and perc. w. own band, '53-60, incorporating African melodies and rhythms. Has worked w. Willie Bobo; Harry Belafonte; G. Holder; Montego Joe; Duke of Iron; Mongo Santamaria; Mary Lou Williams; Leon Thomas; Jose Paulo; Carmen Costa; Max Roach; Joe Mensah. With Negro Ensemble Co., arr. drum gp. for *Kongi's Harvest*, playing leading drum, Dun Dun (or African squeeze drum), and actual Orikis of the Yoruba lang.; arr. music for drums, steel pan, flute and singers for *Ballet Behind the Bridge*; pl. flute and drums for *Dream on Monkey Mountain*. For New Lafayette Theatre, wrote and arr. music for *We Righteous Bombers*, many other prods. Became active in film rec. through New Lafayette. Did sound track rec. for *The Slaves*. One of the most respected of the conga-bongoists by young percussionists. Infl: Saka Acquaye, Mongo Santamaria, Julito Collazo, Jose Paulo. Fest: NJF; MJF; Berlin; Holland; Montreux. LPs: w. Leon Thomas; Count Basie; Gato Barbieri; Oliver Nelson (Fly. Dutch.); Kenny Barron (Muse); Milford Graves (ESP); has also rec. w. Max Roach; Ch. Earland; Art Blakey; Olatunji; Montego Joe; Les Baxter; Belafonte; D. Gillespie.

MORTON, HENRY STERLING (BENNY),* *trombone*; b. New York City, 1/31/07. The former Fletcher Henderson, Don Redman, Count Basie sideman of the '30s, and a regular w. Teddy Wilson, Edmond Hall and his own band, at Cafe Society in the '40s, did much Broadway pit work in the '50s, and free-lanced in NYC during the '60s. Europe w. Top Brass tour '67. Played at the Roosevelt Grill w. B. Hackett '70, replacing Vic Dickenson; also subbed at Roosevelt w. Buck Clayton; Eddie Condon. Worked w. World's Greatest Jazzband, '73-4 incl. Europe '74. Gigging w. Countsmen, '75. Fest: Colo. JP; Nice. LPs: w. Roy Eldridge, *The Nifty Cat* (Master Jazz); w. WGJ (World Jazz).

MOSES, ROBERT LAURENCE (BOB), *drums, composer*; b. New York City, 1/28/48. Took up drums at 10. Mostly self-taught. Played Latin gigs in the Bronx; then w. early jazz-rock gp., Free Spirits w. Larry Coryell, '66. Worked for a short time w. R.R. Kirk, '67; two yrs. w. Gary Burton, '67-8. In '69-73 free-lanced in NYC w. Coryell, Steve Marcus; Free Life Communication w. Dave Liebman, Randy Brecker; Compost w. Jack De Johnette. Toured England w. Mike Gibbs' big band, '74. Burton and Steve Swallow did one show w. them in London and, as a result, Moses was reunited w. Burton, touring w. him from '75. Charles Mitchell in *down beat* wrote: "Bob's compositions reflect the spirit of his drums: a constant search for new colors, inflections, ways

of dealing with tone and rhythm, free travel 'inside' and 'out.' At the kit, Moses plays sonic alchemist, constantly, quietly keeping the cauldron at a low, intense boil. Swing is a strong implication—enough so that finger-snappers are seldom disappointed with a Gary Burton ensemble performance—but no on-the-beat obsession limits the range of Moses' percussive expression."

Infl: Roach, Mingus, Kirk, Ellington, Tatum, Roy Haynes, Elmo Hope, Andrew Hill, Edgar Bateman. Fest: major European fests. w. Burton. Comps: *Our Life; The Dancing Bears; Bittersweet in the Ozone; Stanley Free; Arb Om Souple; Mfwala Myo Lala*. The last two titles are part of the language of Castaluquinga, according to Moses "a visionary sphere that has come to me at various times . . . I acquired certain information about the language; I started to see a plane of reality that had its own culture, music, style. There are other people who seem to have received messages from there, too, so its not just my imagination or something that exists just within me."

LPs: *Bittersweet in the Ozone* (Mozown, 415 Central Park West, New York, N.Y. 10025); w. Gibbs, *The Only Chrome-Waterfall Orchestra* (Bronze); w. Burton, *In the Public Interest* (Poly.); *In Concert* (RCA); w. Open Sky, *Spirit in the Sky* (PM).

MOST, ABRAHAM (ABE),* *clarinet, saxes, flute*; b. New York City, 2/27/20. Prominent LA studio musician for many years. His versatility enabled him to reproduce the styles of many jazz clarinetists in the series of Time-Life recordings that began in 1970. Featured clar. soloist in film *Slither* '72. From '71 app., in occasional concerts w. orch. similar to Time-Life gp. Comps: *Miniature Suite; Triple Fugue for Saxophone Quartet and Piano; Theme and Variations for Woodwind Quintet.*

Publs: *Jazz Improvisations for Treble Clef Instruments; Jazz Improv. for Bass Clef Instruments* etc. (Gwyn Publ. Co., P.O. Box 5900, Sherman Oaks, Calif. 91413).

MOST, SAMUEL (SAM),* *clarinet, flute*; *also saxes, etc.*; b. Atlantic City, N.J., 12/16/30. One of first jazz flutists in early 1950s, he pl. w. Buddy Rich, L. Bellson, Red Norvo in '60s, has own gps. from time to time, but mainly a studio musician in LA, also in house bands at LV, Lake Tahoe casinos. Publ: *Jazz Flute Conceptions* (Gwyn Publ. Co., P.O. Box 5900, Sherman Oaks, Calif. 91413).

LPs: *Thunderbird* w. Bellson (Impulse); *That's Him & This Is New* w. Frank Strazzeri (Revelation).

MOTIAN, STEPHEN PAUL,* *drums, percussion, composer, piano*; b. Philadelphia, Pa., 3/25/31. Pl. w. Bill Evans, 1959-63; Paul Bley, '64; Keith Jarrett, off and on, '66-9; again '71-5. Other work in late '60s w. Mose Allison, Arlo Guthrie, Ch. Lloyd (incl. tour of Asia), Karl Berger, Morgana King. Very active w. JCOA in '70s. Comp. and rec. music for two short films by Stan Vanderbeek, 1970. Worked w. Roswell Rudd, Gato Barbieri, Don Cherry, '73; toured Japan w. Jarrett '74. Fests: NJF-NY, Montreux w. Barbieri. NJF-NY also w. Allison, Jarrett.

Comps: *Conception Vessel; Tribute*, both rec. on ECM. LPs: *Escalator Over The Hill* (JCOA); others w. B. Evans (Verve); Bley (ECM); Ch. Haden Liberation Orch. (Impulse); Jarrett (Atl.).

MOUZON, ALPHONSE, *drums*; also *keyboards, composer, arranger, vocals*; b. Charleston, S.C., 11/21/48. Attended Bonds-Wilson H.S., S. Carolina, pl. in band, under director Lonnie Hamilton, with whom he took lessons; also drum leader in school marching band. Won several awards on perc. in S.C. Grad. '66, moved to NYC. Stud. medicine and worked in a NYC hospital, also pl. with Ross Carnegie society orch. on weekends. Student at NY City Coll., '67-9; at same time pl. in orch. for *Promises, Promises* on Broadway. Freelanced w. R. Ayers, Gene McDaniels, Roberta Flack et al. In '70 went on road w. Ayers for a year. With Weather Report, '71-2; McCoy Tyner, '72-3; Larry Coryell's Eleventh House, '73-5. Moved to Cal. late '75.

Mouzon made his first album date at age 19 w. Gil Evans (Ampex). Fests: Norway JF, '73; Montreux, w. Tyner, '73; Coryell, '75; Newport, w. Tyner, '73; all star big band, '75; Berlin JF, '75. Mouzon stud. acting for 2½ years, and is pursuing an acting career simultaneously with music. Mouzon says: "Jazz/rock drummers like myself, Billy Cobham and Lenny White bring jazz polyrhythms to a rock pulse."

Comps: *Virtue*, recorded by Bobbi Humphrey and M. Santamaria; *Just Like The Sun; Nyctophobia*, rec. by Coryell; *Essence of Mystery; New York City.*

LPs: *Essence of Mystery; Funky Snakefoot; Mind Transplant; The Man Incognito* (BN); w. Coryell, *Introducing Eleventh House* (Vanguard); *Level One* (Arista); w. Les McCann, *Invitation to Openness* (Atl.); w. Doug Carn, *Spirit of the New Land* (Black Jazz); *Weather Report* (Col.); w. Tyner, *Sahara; Song For My Lady; Song of the New World; Enlightenment* (Milest.); w. McDaniels, *Headless Heroes of the Apocalypse*; w. Flack, *Feel Like Making Love*; w. Robin Kenyatta, *Stomping at the Savoy* (Atl.); w. Jeremy Steig, *Temple of Birth* (Col.); w. Wayne Shorter, *Odyssey of Iska* (BN).

MOVER, ROBERT ALAN (BOB), *alto sax, composer*; also *soprano sax*; b. Boston, Mass., 3/22/52. Father, Jimmy, played trumpet w. T. Dorsey, Charlie Spivak, etc. in '40s; mother sang professionally; sister, Joy, is singer in Miami. Studied guitar, drums briefly. Took up alto sax in '65, studying w. Ted Rosen in Miami. Pl. w. high school all star band, '67. Studied w. Phil Woods at Ramblerny in Pennsylvania, summer '67. Learned further from pl. w. Ira Sullivan in Miami, '68. From '69 into early '70s living between NYC and Boston, pl. a variety of music jobs and sitting in. With Charles Mingus for five months, '73; Chet Baker '74. Pl. in Rio de Janeiro for six mos. w. Lucio Alves; Johnny Alf, '74. Rejoined Baker for nine mos. in '75 incl. NJF-NY, Nice, Laren, Middleheim fests. Own gp. in '76 at Tin Palace, NYC. Infl: C. Parker, L. Young, B. Powell, Konitz, Rollins, Ira Sullivan. Comps: *Muggawump; Saudade do Brooklyn; Survival of the Sickest; Falsidade; Night Dance of the Little*

People. LP: w. Yoshiaki Masuo, *111 Sullivan Street* (East Wind).

MOYE, DON, *drums, congas, bongoes, bass marimba, ballophone, misc. percussion, whistles, horns, singer*; b. Rochester, N.Y., 5/23/46. Took some percussion classes at Wayne State U. in Detroit, '65-6. Learned from trumpeter Charles Moore and pl. w. Detroit Free Jazz. Met Joseph Jarman at Artist's Workshop in Detroit. Went to Europe in May '68 w. DFJ, pl. in Switzerland, Italy, Yugoslavia, Scandinavia. Pl. w. Steve Lacy in Rome, then in Paris. Also pl. there w. The Gospel Messenger Singers, Sonny Sharrock, Dave Burrell, Gato Barbieri, Pharoah Sanders, Alan Shorter. Met Art Ensemble of Chicago members at the American Center for Students and Artists in '69 and was invited to join the group. Returned with it to US in April '69. Peter Occhiogrosso called Moye, "a percussionist who can do just about anything without sounding ostentatious" and added that he provides "the kind of connective tissue that keeps the Ensemble together through their most abstract forays."

Received NREA Grant for composition, '73. Artist-in-residence at Michigan State U., '73.

LPs: see Art Ensemble of Chicago; w. Randy Weston, *Carnival* (Arista).

MRAZ, GEORGE (JIRI), *bass*; b. Pisek, Czechoslovakia, 9/9/44. Stud. Prague Conserv., '61-6. Pl. w. Jan Hammer trio. Moved to West Germany '66 where he worked for a year in Munich w. Pony Poindexter, Hampton Hawes, Benny Bailey. To U.S. in late '60s where he stud. at Berklee before pl. w. Dizzy Gillespie. Toured w. Oscar Peterson '72; Ella Fitzgerald, summer '72; then joined Thad Jones-Mel Lewis orch. with which he remained, making many fest. and concert apps. throughout U.S. and overseas during next four years. Took time out to work w. Stan Getz, Sept. '74 to Jan. '75. Duo w. Walter Norris at Bradley's, spring '75. Mraz has been praised highly by all the musicians he has worked with since his arrival in NYC. His beat is firm; his sound is exceptionally clean and clear, and his improvisational ideas are consistently creative. LPs: w. Jones-Lewis (Phila. Int.); Peterson (BASF); Horacee Arnold (Col.); Norris (Enja); Buddy De Franco (Famous Solos); Jimmy Smith (Verve); Zoot Sims (Pablo).

MUHAMMAD, IDRIS, (Leo Morris), *drums*; b. New Orleans, La., 1939. Father a banjo player; brothers all drummers. Pl. first job at ten. On grad. from high school, joined Larry Williams band. After working w. guitarist Joe Jones, Dee Clark, began doing dates in NYC w. Lloyd Price in early 1960s. Spent almost four years in each of three jobs: w. Jerry Butler, for whom he was mus. dir.; Lou Donaldson; and the house band for *Hair*, in which he worked from 1968-72. During that time he also worked as consultant on another play, *Indians*, for which he designed the drums.

After *Hair* closed Muhammad went to India for six months, returned to US and resumed playing, on tour w. Emerson, Lake & Palmer and soon after with the backup group for Roberta Flack. He signed in 1974 with Creed

Taylor's Kudu record label and gained some prominence in his own right.

Muhammad says: "The rock beat was created in New Orleans, and I was one of the drummers who first brought that kind of beat to New York." LPs: Prestige, Kudu; w. Donaldson (Blue Note).

MUKAI, SHIGEHARU, *trombone*; b. Nagoya, Japan, 1/21/49. Pl. w. Doshisha Univ. Modern Jazz Group and the Third Orch.; then w. quintets of Yoshio Otomo; Fumio Itabashi; Ryo Kawasaki; Hiroshi Fukumura; Seiichi Nakamura; Terumasa Hino. Formed own quintet; also working w. SMC Orch. Infl: J.J. Johnson, Coltrane, Slide Hampton, Wayne Henderson, Terumasa Hino. App. at various Japanese JF. In Oct. '74 won Shinjuku JF Award. Won 2nd trombone in SJ Readers Poll, '74. Own LP: *For My Little Bird* (Nippon Col.); w. H. Fukumura, *First Flight* (Trio); quintet (Three Blind Mice); w. S. Nakamura, *First Contact* (King); w. T. Hino, *Journey Into My Mind* (CBS/Sony).

MULDAUR, MARIA (Maria Grazia Rosa Domenica d'Amato), *singer, blues fiddle*; b. New York City, 9/12/42. Self-taught, helped by informal music appreciation sessions with extensive blues and jazz collections of Jim Kweskin and Geoff Muldaur. Toured w. Even Dozen Jug Band, '63; Kweskin Jug Band, '64-9. She and Muldaur, who had worked w. Kweskin together, then made two LPs for Reprise. After their divorce she app. as a single during '72, attaining national prominence with her record of *Midnight at the Oasis* which became a hit on radio and part of a best selling LP in '73.

Though her accompaniments and her style of singing have crossed over into many areas incl. rock, pop, spiritual, gospel and blues, Muldaur was best known in jazz circles, from late '74, through a series of concerts with an all star band directed by Benny Carter, who wrote the arrangements and pl. alto sax.

Some critics heard in Muldaur a remarkable resemblance, in the lightness of timbre and jazz-oriented phrasing, to Mildred Bailey. Others found her mannered and shallow. Among the artists who have inspired her are Bailey, D. Ellington, Bessie Smith, D. Reinhardt, Memphis Minnie, Claude Jeter, Mavis Staples, B.B. King.

In the summer of '75 Carter assembled a new band which pl. at the NJF, at a concert in tandem w. Muldaur. He then app. with her at the Montreux JF. Muldaur was later heard at Ronnie Scott's Club in London.

Among singers whose appeal is primarily to the young pop/rock audience, Muldaur is unique, not only for her sensitivity toward jazz, but for her use of arcane material such as the old Danny Barker r & b hit *Don't You Feel My Leg*, Ellington standards such as *Prelude To A Kiss* and other ballads, incl. *Lover Man*, all of which she performs with a conviction not common to singers of her generation.

Muldaur was named as number one new female vocalist of '74 in several music trade publications.

LPs: early sessions w. Kweskin Jug Band (Vanguard); pl. blues fiddle and sang backup on two Paul Butterfield LPs (Bearsville); own solo albums, *Maria Muldaur* (which incl. *Midnight at the Oasis*); *Waitress in a Donut Shop* (Reprise).

MULLIGAN, GERALD JOSEPH (GERRY or JERU),* *baritone, soprano saxes, clarinet, composer, piano*; b. New York City, 4/6/27. After switching from his 13-piece Concert Jazz Band to a small gp. format in '66, he began a series of tours as guest soloist with Dave Brubeck's group from '68. In '72 he recorded a new large ensemble he called *The Age of Steam* and appeared with it at the NJF-NY '73. He also pl. at the new Half Note w. a small gp. using the same generic title. A successful reunion concert w. Chet Baker in '74 and subsequent albums of the event, led to a repeat performance, again in NYC, '75. In the summer of '74 he played in Italy and France. He also spent time as artist-in-residence at Miami U. in that year. Film: pl. on soundtrack of *Hot Rock* for Quincy Jones. Fest: several apps. at NJF-NY; MJF; Montreux; Midem, etc. Played curved soprano sax at *Salute to Zoot* concert; w. own sextet at Hopper's, NYC, Dec. '75.

"With Gerry," says Brubeck, "you feel as if you're listening to the past, present and future of jazz all at one time, and it's with such taste and respect that you're not quite aware of the changes in idiom. Mulligan gets the old New Orleans two beat going with a harmonic awareness of advanced jazz, and you feel not that tradition is being broken, but rather that it's being pushed forward."

Won DB Readers poll on baritone, '66-75; critics poll, '74-5.

Comp: *K-4 Pacific; Golden Notebooks; Maytag; Country Beaver; It's Sandy at the Beach; A Weed in Disneyland; Grand Tour; Song For An Unfinished Woman; Song For Strayhorn. By Your Grace*, rec. on album w. Beaver & Krause, *Ghandarva* (War. Bros). Own LPs: *Age of Steam* (A&M); Carnegie Hall Concerts w. Baker (CTI). LPs w. Astor Piazzolla, *Summit* (Carosello, Ital.); w. Brubeck, *Compadres; Blues Roots; at Berlin Philharmonic* (Col.); reissues, w. Baker (Prest.); *Revelation*, w. Lee Konitz (BN).

MURANYI, JOSEPH PAUL (JOE),* *clarinet, soprano sax, singer*; b. Martins Ferry, Ohio, 1/14/28. Well known for work with Max Kaminsky, J. McPartland and numerous other Dixieland groups. Toured world w. Louis Armstrong 1967-71. On leaving Armstrong (he was the band's last regular clarinetist), became resident musician at Jimmy Ryan's, NYC, w. Roy Eldridge. In 1975, also worked gigs on sop., clar. w. World's Greatest Jazzband. Increased activity on soprano and vocals 1974-5. LPs: *Clarinet Wobble*, clar. duet w. Herb Hall (Fat Cat Jazz); Joe Muranyi Quartet, unreleased.

MURPHY, MARK HOWE,* *singer*; b. Syracuse, N.Y., 3/14/32. After app. in jazz clubs, at NJF, '62 etc., Murphy settled in London, which was his base throughout the balance of the decade. He returned to NYC briefly in '73 to record an album, *Mark II.* Murphy, in addition to working in London in night clubs and on records, began a career as an actor. He made a pilot film in Spain for British TV, in which he pl. Jesus Christ. In the words of Peter Keepnews, "He remains little known in his native land except among a small coterie of jazz lovers."

LPs: *Bridging A Gap; Mark II* (Muse); w. Herb Geller, *Rhyme and Reason* (Atl.).

MURPHY, MELVIN E. (TURK),* *trombone, composer, leader;* b. Palermo, Cal., 12/16/15. Pioneer of traditionalist jazz in the Bay Area since the late '30s. Co-owner with pianist Pete Clute, since September '60, of Earthquake McGoon's in SF. Murphy, unlike many New Orleans stylists, avoids most of the old jazz standards, preferring to play relatively unknown material from the turn of the century, obscure songs of the '20s by King Oliver, Kid Ory et al, and original compositions. He was a key figure in the West Coast ragtime revival, many years before Scott Joplin's music was used in the film *The Sting.* His band toured Australia in the summer of '74, and played four European countries in Nov-Dec. that year.

LPs: *Jazz Band* (Merry); *Many Faces of Ragtime* (Atl.); *Vol. I; Vol. II* (Motherlode).

MURRAY, DAVID, *tenor sax, composer;* also *soprano sax, flute;* b. Berkeley, Calif., 2/19/55. Father pl. guitar in church; mother was nationally famous as pianist in the Sanctified Church. Both were big infl. on him. Grew up in SF Bay area. Pl. in Missionary Church of God and Christ. At 12 became interested in r&b and led gps. as teenager. Met Stanley Crouch and was introduced by him to Bobby Bradford and Black Arthur. Own gp. w. trumpeter Butch Morris in Bay Area during coll. vacations. Piano lessons from Margaret Kohn at Pomona Coll. where he stud. music for two yrs. before leaving for NYC, '75. Led own gps. at Sunrise Studio, Studio We, Studio Rivbea, Yale U. and performed solo. Sat-in w. Cecil Taylor; Don Cherry; A. Braxton; worked w. Sunny Murray in Phila. Infl: Parker, Rollins, Shepp, Ayler, Coltrane, Ellington, Webster, Hawkins, B. Bradford, Black Arthur, Crouch. Interested in "exploring the areas of music Albert Ayler opened up as far as new or unusual saxophone techniques are concerned . . . working on a study of Paul Gonsalves' improvisational approach. I have been particularly impressed by him and feel he never got the credit he was due."

Played lead in a play by Crouch entitled *Saxophone Man.* TV: short film w. Verta Mae Grosvenor. Fest: w. Abbey Lincoln, Oakland '74; own gp., Studio Rivbea '75. Comp: *Flowers For Albert; Miss Sweet; Suite For Yellowman Warrior; Low Class Conspiracy; Shout Song; Dewey Circle; Ballad For a Decomposed Beauty; Welcome to the Set; S.B. and C. Follies;* w. B. Morris, *Don't Enter Me.* LPs: w. S. Crouch, unreleased.

MURRAY, JAMES ARTHUR (SUNNY),* *drums, composer;* b. Valliant, Okla., 9/21/37. Established himself as one of leading avant drummers, playing and recording w. Cecil Taylor; Albert Ayler; Archie Shepp; Gil Evans in '60s. Active in France in late '60s-early '70s. Performed in Sweden, Denmark, Norway, Finland, Holland, Austria, Belgium, Switzerland, Italy; Pan-African Fest. in Senegal. Pl. concerts and clubs in NYC, SF, Phila.; many coll. dates. Co-leader w. Khan Jamal in The Untouchable Factor.

"In a radical fashion," wrote Joachim Berendt describing Murray's rhythmic approach, "the marking of the meter is here replaced by the creation of tension over long passages . . . It swings without beat and measure, meter and symmetry . . . simply by virtue of the power and flexibility of its tension-arcs."

Treasurer and National Advisor for Phila. Jazz Foundation. Won DB Critics poll, TDWR, '66. Grants from CAPS, '70, '73. Comp.-arr. scores for films: *In the Beginning* (Nigeria); *Walking Woman* (Canada); *The Party* (France); plays: *June Bug Graduates Tonight; Barabbas.* LPs: *Sunny's Time Now* (Jihad); *Homage to Africa; Sunshine; Never Give a Sucker An Even Break* (Byg); *ORTF Concerts* (Shandar).

MUSSELWHITE, CHARLES DOUGLAS III (CHARLIE), *harmonica, guitar, composer;* b. Kosciusko, Miss., 1/31/44. Father pl. guitar, harmonica. Mainly self-taught. Worked in the streets and Chicago bars in mid-1960s w. Johnnie Young Blues Band. Duos w. Big Joe Williams, John Lee Granderson; also pl. w. blues bands of J.B. Hutto, Mike Bloomfield, Barry Goldberg, and w. South Side Sound System. App. on TV w. Goldberg in Chi. 1966, later w. own band in Detroit. Pl. in the first Ann Arbor Blues Festival, also St. Cloud, Minn. Folk Festival. Living in San Jose, Cal., 1975. Comps: *Taylor's Arkansas; Up & Down the Avenue; Takin' My Time; Louisiana Fog; Leavin'; Fell On My Knees; Finger Lickin' Good; 39th and Indiana; Highway Blues; Fat City,* many others.

LPs: *South; Takin' My Time; Goin' Back Down* (Arhoolie); *Tennessee Woman; Stone Blues; Stand Back* (Vanguard); *Louisiana Fog* (Cherry Red); *Memphis, Tennessee* (Paramount).

MUSSO, VIDO WILLIAM,* *tenor sax, clarinet;* b. Carrini, Sicily, 1/16/13. Mainly known for his work w. S. Kenton in '40s. Living in Las Vegas since '57; led own group at Desert Inn, '67-70; Sands Hotel, '70-5, also backing Sonny King. Worked w. Tony Martin, Tony Bennett at local casinos as soloist in their backup bands. Reunited briefly w. Kenton in '68. LPs w. Kenton (Creative World).

MYERS, HUBERT MAXWELL (BUMPS),* *tenor sax;* b. Clarksburg, W. Va., 8/22/12. Best-known for his work w. Benny Carter in the '40s, he worked mostly in the rec. studios in the '50s. Played briefly w. Horace Henderson in '61-2. Bad health curtailed his activities during the yrs. prior to his death in LA, 4/8/68.

NAMYSLOWSKI, ZBIGNIEW, *alto saxophone, composer, leader; also flute, cello, trombone, piano;* b. Warsaw, Poland, 9/9/39. Uncle led society band. Piano at four; regular music lessons at six. Took up cello at 12; studies, incl. theory, at High School of Music in Warsaw. Pl. trombone w. Witold Krotochwil trad band; cello w. Krzysztof Sadowski Modern Combo, '56. Gained recognition at Sopot Fest.; toured in Denmark w. Polish All Stars; France w. Krotochwil. Worked w. New Orleans Stompers. Switched to alto sax '60 and joined Andrzej Trzaskowski's Jazz Wreckers w. whom he toured US and Europe before leaving to form own quartet, '63. Pl. in Europe, India, Australia, New Zealand and USSR. Also pl. w. Krzysztof Komeda gps. for concerts, film soundtracks, recs.; Novi Singers' tours; half year in Italy w. Polish rock singer Czeslaw Niemen. Pl. w. George Arvanitas in Paris for six wks., summer '70. From '71 leading own quintet and pl. w. Polish Radio Jazz Studio Band. Infl: C. Parker, J. Coltrane, S. Rollins. TV: Poland; Germany; Australia; BBC. Fest: NJF w. Wreckers, '61; all Warsaw Jazz Jamborees; Molde; Kongsberg; Tallin; Frankfurt; Comblain-la-Tour; Bologna; Prague; Cascais. Comps: *Piatawka; Siodmakwa; Nieprzespana Noc; Bez Wyciszenia; Winobranie (Wine Feast); Kuyawiak Goes Funky.* Has also written for radio, TV, film soundtracks, orchestras.

A special aspect of Namyslowski's success is that in addition to effectively utilizing elements of contemporary jazz and rock, he has also incorporated and thoroughly integrated Polish folk music (as in *Winobranie*) into his music.

LPs: *Quartet; Wine Feast; Kuyawiak Goes Funky* (Muza); *Lola* (Decca); *Pop Workshop,* vols. 1&2, w. Tony Williams and others (EMI); w. Novi Singers, *Novi in Wonderland* (Saba); w. K. Komeda, *Astigmatic* (Muza); *Jazz and Poetry* (German Electrola).

NANCE, WILLIS (RAY),* *cornet, violin, singer;* b. Chicago, Ill., 12/10/13. The Duke Ellington alumnus played w. Henri Chaix in Switzerland, '67 but was mainly occupied in Sol Yaged's gp. at the Gaslight Club, NYC, '66-9. Pl. in Scandinavia in early '70s. Filled in w. Ellington band at various times in '70s. Pl. w. Brooks Kerr at Churchill's, NYC, Feb.-May '73. Toured in England w. Chris Barber '74. Appeared w. own band for Duke Ellington Society concert at New School, NYC, May '69. Concert apps. w. B. Bigard, L. Bellson at Wilshire-Ebell, LA, '75; K. Burrell at Town Hall, NYC, Dec. '75. Pl. at Sonny's Place; The Penthouse, L.I. '75; Barbara's, Greenwich Village, Jan. '76. Nance, ill with kidney trouble that forced him to use a dialysis machine several times weekly from late '75, died 1/28/76 and jazz lost one of its great artist-entertainers. TV: Just Jazz, PBS, '71. Comp: *Wild Child; Ray's Blues.* LPs: *Body and Soul* (SS); *Huffin' and Puffin'* (MPS); *Jaki Byard With Strings* (Prest.); w. Jimmy Rushing, *The You and Me That Used to Be* (RCA); *Just a Sittin' and a Rockin'* w. P. Gonsalves (Bl. Lion); *Jazz For a Sunday Afternoon* (SS).

NAPOLEON, MARTY,* *piano;* b. Brooklyn, N.Y., 6/2/21. Pl. w. Louis Armstrong 1952-4; rejoined him '66 and during the next five years toured the world with him (for details see Armstrong). Led own trio at Playboy Club, NYC, '71; concerts w. Gene Krupa. Pee Wee Erwin, Chris Griffin, '71-2; NJF-NY, solo piano at Cookery, '73, etc. Comp. & arr. *Louis' Dream* (co-written w. Armstrong), rec. in LV, Feb.

'67. Commissioned to write series of piano instruction books for Ch. Hansen Publ., '75.

LPs: w. Armstrong (Mer., MCA, Disneyland, ABC-Par. etc.).

NASSER, JAMIL SULIEMAN,* *bass;* b. Memphis, Tenn., 6/21/32. From '64 to the early '70s a member of Ahmad Jamal trio. In '75 w. Al Haig trio at Gregory's, NYC, on Sundays. LPs: w. Haig-Jimmy Raney (Choice); also see Jamal.

NATIONAL JAZZ ENSEMBLE. See Israels, Chuck.

NAUGHTON, ROBERT (BOBBY), *vibes; also piano;* b. Boston, Mass., 6/25/44. Self-taught. In late '60s and early '70s worked in groups w. Perry Robinson, Sheila Jordan; perf. with JCOA, '72. Pl. w. Leo Smith group and leading own unit, incl. percussionist Randy Kaye. Infls: Thomas Tallis, T. Monk, Bill Evans, Walt Dickerson, G. Russell, Carla Bley, Hans Richter. Comp. piece for *Everyday,* a film by Richter, originally shot in '29 but completed in '71, starring Sergei Eisenstein and Jean Hans Arp. Other comps: *Snow; Ordet; Fancy Free.* App. N.Y. Musicians JF, '72-3.

LPs: *Nature's Consort; Understanding* (Otic Records, also available on Japo Records, Gleichmannstr. 10, Munchen, W. Germany.).

NAURA, MICHAEL, *piano;* b. Memel, Lithuania, 8/19/34. Self-taught. Started Shearing style quintet, Berlin, 1953. Later insp. by Bill Evans, MJQ. Traveled around Europe w. own gp. '56-63. Later worked as editor of mus. progs. for Norddeutscher Rundfunk (radio), Hamburg; since '72 head of that station's jazz dept, also pl. w. own quartet, embracing some elements of free jazz. Associated off and on for 20 years with vibraphonist Wolfgang Schlüter. LPs (in Germany): MPS-BASF; Intercoed; ECM.

NDUGU (Leon Chancler), *drums, percussion;* b. Shreveport, La., 1/7/52. Stud. at Gompers High; Locke High, LA; also w. step-brother Reggie Andrews. Further studies at Cal. State Coll., '70-2. Musically self-taught, starting in '67 in Jr. H.S., pl. w. Jazz Prophets, Executives. Worked w. Harold Johnson, Larry Nash, '68-9; Pepperdine Coll. orch., Willie Bobo, Locke High Jazz Workshop, '69-70. On grad. from school, worked w. Gerald Wilson, Hugh Masekela, H. Hancock, '70; T. Monk, F. Hubbard, E. Harris, Harold Land-Bobby Hutcherson, Miles Davis, Joe Henderson, '71; in '72 pl. w. Hampton Hawes, Harold Land, George Duke and was co-leader of Ujima ensemble. Freelance studio work in LA, '72-4; toured w. Santana, '74- . Insp. by Red Holt, Art Blakey, Bruno Carr, H. Hancock, Stix Hooper, Art Taylor, Jack DeJohnette, Reggie Andrews. Fests: Watts, '70-1; Newport in Europe.

One of the most dependable and promising of the new generation of percussionists, specializing in congas, vibes, timbales etc.

LPs: w. Weather Report, *Tale Spinnin';* w. Santana, *Borboletta* (Col.); w. Jean-Luc Ponty, *Upon The Wings of Music;* w. E. Harris, *Excursions* (Atl.); w. Duke, *Feel; Faces In Reflection; The Aura Will Prevail* (MPS); w. Hawes, *Universe; Blues For Walls* (Prest.); w. Land, *Damisi; Choma* (Mainstr.).

NEAPOLITAN, RAY, *bass; also guitar, sitar;* b. Chicago Ill., 8/30/40. Educ. Chicago Conserv. of Music, '57, then w. private teachers, Jerry Lofstrom in Chi.; Ralph Pena, Peter

Mercurio, Carol Kaye in LA. Began working with Terry Gibbs group, '62 and has since appeared w. Shelly Manne, Louie Bellson, Buddy Rich, Carmen McRae, Eddie "Lockjaw" Davis, Mose Allison, Don Ellis, Gabor Szabo, Roger Kellaway, Maynard Ferguson, Oliver Nelson, Frank Sinatra et al. On sound track for movies *Play Misty For Me; French Connection; Rosemary's Baby;* Burt Bacharach, F. Sinatra, B. Streisand TV Specs. W. D. Ellis at MJF, '66, '67, '68, Antibes Fest., '68; NJF, '68. Neapolitan is greatly respected in both studio and jazz circles.

LPs: w. Ellis (Pacific Jazz); w. Emil Richards (Limelite, Impulse); Barbara Streisand (Columbia).

NEIDLINGER, BUELL, * bass; b. Westport, Conn., 3/2/36. Early associate of Cecil Taylor. Pl. w. symph. orchs. in Houston, '62-4; Boston, '68-70. Prof. of Music, Cal. Inst. of Arts, '71- . Ojai Fest., '74.

LPs: Cecil Taylor-Buell Neidlinger (Barnaby); *Jean-Luc Ponty Plays Frank Zappa* (Wor. Pac.).

NELSON, OLIVER EDWARD, * composer, saxophones, flute; b. St. Louis, Mo., 6/4/32. Extensive background as composer in jazz, pop and classical fields in NYC before moving to LA, 1967. Though primarily working as composer for TV and films, he still played saxophone from time to time, notably on a tour of French West Africa under the aegis of the U.S. State Dept. in 1969, for which he led a small band.

TV credits: orig. theme and background music for *Matt Lincoln; Longstreet; Six Million Dollar Man;* episodes for *Ironsides; It Takes a Thief; Name of the Game.* Educational film: *Encounter and Response,* for Lutheran Church of America. Feature films: *Death of a Gunfighter; Skullduggery; Zig Zag; Trans Europe Express.*

Nelson assembled a big band for an engagement at the Bottom Line in NYC, June '75, and the following week headed a West Coast personnel for a brief booking at the Grove, LA. These were his final appearances. He taped a recording for *Million Dollar Man,* 10/27/75, and died the following morning after suffering a heart attack at his Los Angeles home.

Despite his acceptance in the studio world and the numerous honors awarded him, Nelson never quite achieved the recognition he deserved, for two main reasons: he was obliged to divide his time between commercial studio work and the serious writing he preferred, and was similarly forced to restrict himself to writing on many occasions when he would rather have been playing.

Publ: *Patterns for Saxophone* (Noslen Music Co., P.O. Box 705, Hollywood, Calif., 90028).

Commissions: *Concerto for Xylophone, Marimba and Vibraphone,* for Amer. Wind Symph. Orch., '67. *Jazzhattan Suite,* for BMI, '67. *Septet for Winds,* for Amer. Wind Symph., '68. *Dialogues for Orchestra,* for Berliner Jazztage Fest., '70. *Suite for Narrator, String Quartet and Jazz Orchestra,* for Mayor Carl B. Stokes of Cleveland, '70.

LPs: *Main Stem; Afro-American Sketches* (Prest.); *Berlin Dialogue; Black, Brown & Beautiful; Oliver Nelson In London With Oily Rags; Swiss Suite; Skull Session* (Fl. Dutchman); *Blues and the Abstract Truth; Live From Los Angeles; Michelle; More Blues; Musical Tribute to JFK; Sound Pieces* (Imp.); w. Leon Thomas, *In Berlin* (Fl. Dutchman); w. *Sound of Feeling* (Verve).

NESTICO, SAMUEL L. (SAM), *arranger, trombone;* b. Pittsburgh, Pa., 2/6/24. His name at birth was Sal Nistico—the same as that of his first cousin, the tenor saxophonist who pl. w. C. Basie in 1965. Put in a total of 20 years in the service: three years during World War II, then (after several years on staff at ABC studios in Pittsburgh) 17 more years, switching from Air Force to Marines and retiring in March '68 as chief arr. for U.S. Marine Band in Washington, D.C. He then moved to Los Angeles.

While in the service Nestico pl. briefly w. T. Dorsey, W. Herman. During his civilian years he was with Ch. Barnet, '46, and G. Krupa, '48.

Through trombonist Grover Mitchell, an old friend from Pittsburgh, Nestico began writing regularly for the Count Basie band in '68. His many original comps. for Basie's LPs were published for school bands in a special Basie-Nestico series.

Simultaneously Nestico has had a busy career orchestrating at many movie studios, arranging and orchestrating for TV series, and arranging for the Time-Life swing band recreation series, '69-73. In '75 he wrote three works performed in concert 4/19/75 by the Basie band and the Baltimore Symphony.

Publ: More than 300 works in educ. field, primarily concert band, symphony orch. and stage band pieces, publ: (Kendor Music Inc., Delavan, N.Y., 14042; Hal Leonard Music, 6525 Bluemound Rd., Milwaukee, Wis., 53213; Studio P/R, 224 S. Lebanon St., Lebanon, Pa., 46052). LPs: all the writing for *Basie Big Band* (Pablo); other arrs. for Basie on various labels.

NEWBORN, PHINEAS JR., * piano, composer; b. Whiteville, Tenn., 12/14/31. Played w. his own trio in NYC in late '50s, and w. Charles Mingus. Visited Europe briefly in '58 and '59. In the '60s he appeared sporadically in LA area clubs but was inactive professionally for long periods due to illness. In Nov. '75 he did two numbers at the World Jazz Association's first concert in LA. Earlier in the year a new album, *Solo Piano,* was released on Atlantic. Other LPs: *Please Send Me Someone to Love; Touch* (Contemporary).

NEWMAN, DAVID (FATHEAD), * saxophones, flute; b. Dallas, Tex., 2/24/33. Featured sideman w. Ray Charles orch., '54-64, he also led his own rec. gps. from '59. To NYC '66 working w. own gp. and w. King Curtis and the Kingpins. By '68 he had rec. three albums for Atlantic and added soprano sax to his reed lineup. Gigged in Dallas and rec. in NYC in late '60s. Rejoined Charles temporarily in '70-1. With H. Mann's Family of Mann, '72-4. Back to Dallas, '75. Pl. on rec. sessions w. Aretha Franklin; Nikki Giovanni; Cornell Dupree; Kate Smith; Greg Allman; T-Bone Walker; Shirley Scott, etc. LPs: *Newmanism; The Weapon; Lonely Avenue; Best of David Newman; The Many Facets of David Newman; Bigger and Better; House of David* (Atl.); *Capt. Buckles* (Cotillion); w. Mann (Atl.).

NEWMAN, JOSEPH DWIGHT (JOE), * trumpet; b. New Orleans, La., 9/7/22. First well-known for his featured role in the Count Basie orch., '52-61, he became active in early '60s in NYC w. Jazz Interactions, a non-profit organization dedicated to fostering a greater interest in and deeper understanding and appreciation of jazz. (His wife, Rigmor, is executive director.) Leading instrumentalists teach in its Young Musicians Clinic. It also has given many lecture-concert series in the schools; a lecture series at Hunter Coll. and the St. Peter's Church Center, in which Newman has delivered talks on Louis Armstrong; and monthly sessions at various NYC clubs. It publishes a weekly listing of who is playing in the clubs (527 Madison Ave., Suite 1615, N.Y., N.Y. 10022) and maintains Jazzline, a telephone service which informs in the same manner (212-421-3592). After serving as vice-president, Newman has been president from '67. That year he conducted the JI Orch. in Oliver Nelson's *Jazzhattan Suite;* in '72 he conducted the premiere performance of Thad Jones' tribute to Louis Armstrong, *Suite for Pops.* He teaches in the JI Workshop and also gives private master classes. Additionally he has led his own gp. from the time he left Basie, app. several times in the mid-'70s at Boomer's. Closely allied w. Rev. John Gensel of St. Peter's Lutheran Church, he collaborated w. him on two religious works, *O Sing to the Lord a New Song,* in the '60s; and *The Story of Pentecost,* '72. A member of the NYJRC he participated in the program devoted to the music of Louis Armstrong, '74, and toured w. it in Russia, summer '75, and Europe, fall '75.

TV: *Positively Black.* Broadway: *Promises, Promises,* '69-72; *Raisin,* '73-5. Fest: NJF; NJF-NY; Molde; Nice; Zurich; Berlin; Cascais; Umea; Warsaw; also in Italy; France; NO; Colo. JP. In '75 pl. club dates in Geneva, Munich, Vienna. Conducted seminars at many univs. incl. Pitts., Hartford, Vermont. One of the most consistent and spirited trumpeters, blending elements of swing and bop. LPs: w. S. Stitt (Muse); I. Jacquet (Prest.); J. Moody (Vang.); w. NYJRC, *Satchmo Remembered* (Atl.); w. Basie; Colo. Jazz Party (MPS); *Newport in New York, The Jam Sessions, Vols. 3&4* (Cobble.); reissue w. own gp. (Trip).

NEWSOM, THOMAS PENN (TOMMY),* *saxophones, flute, clarinet, composer;* b. Portsmouth, Va., 2/25/29. NBC staff musician from '62, pl. on Tonight show under Skitch Henderson and later Doc Severinsen. In '68 switched from second tenor sax in the band to first alto sax and assistant conductor. Comps: *Puddintane,* for Ed Shaughnessy band; *Suite for Trumpet* for Severinsen; *La Boehm; Titterpipes* for B. Goodman. Publ: *Tommy Newsom's Standard & Popular Solos* (Armstrong Edu-Tainment, Box 769, New York, N.Y. 10019).

LPs: w. Severinsen (RCA); w. C. Byrd, arrs. for *Brazilian Byrd* (Col.).

NEW YORK BASS CHOIR. see Lee, Bill.

NEW YORK JAZZ REPERTORY COMPANY. see Wein, George.

NICHOLAS, ALBERT (AL),* *clarinet;* b. New Orleans, La., 5/27/00. One of the last of the trend-setting NO clarinetists; one time member of the K. Oliver, Luis Russell and L. Armstrong bands, Nicholas lived in Europe from the early '50s, settling in Switzerland in '70. He died 9/3/73 in Basel.

LPs: w. Armstrong (Col.); own album; w. A. Hodes (Delmark); w. Jelly Roll Morton (RCA); w. B. Bigard (RCA); many on European labels, Supraphon, etc.

NIEHAUS, LEONARD (LENNIE),* *composer, alto saxophone;* b. St. Louis, Mo., 6/1/29. Active mainly in commercial work in recent years, arr. for night club artists, TV shows

etc. Commissioned by LA Valley Coll. to write extended jazz works.

Publs: *Basic Jazz Conception for Saxophone;* (Try Publ. Co., 854 N. Vine St., Hollywood Ca. 90038). Eighteen original stage band comps. (Life Line Music Press, Box 338, Agoura, Ca. 91301); three orig. stage choir compositions (Vortex Music Inc.).

NIEWOOD, GERRY (Gerard J. Nevidosky), *saxophones, flutes, composer;* b. Rochester, N.Y., 4/6/43. Received B.S. degree in Industrial Relations from U. of Buffalo in '75, but decided in '66 to change careers. Grad. of Eastman School of Music, Rochester, N.Y., '70. Stud. sax w. William Osseck, flute w. John Thomas. Pl. w. B. Rich and L. Bellson bands. Came to prominence as member of C. Mangione quartet and ensemble, '71-   . Infl. or insp. by J. Coltrane, S. Rollins, S. Stitt, Clifford Brown, C. Corea, Miles Davis, Joe Romano, Mangione. Fests: Newport, Concord, Monterey, several in Europe. Won DB Critics poll, TDWR, soprano sax, '74. Comps: *Floating; Homage; Semitique.*

A versatile, melodically inventive artist on all his instruments, he played a central role in the success of the Mangione group.

Own LP: *The Gerry Niewood Album* (Sagoma/DGM); w. Mangione, *Friends & Love; Together; The Chuck Mangione Quartet; Alive; Land of Make Believe* (Merc.).

NIMITZ, JACK JEROME,* *baritone saxophone;* also other *saxophones, clarinets, flutes;* b. Washington, D.C., 1/11/30. Mainly studio musician in LA, but has continued to work in jazz whenever possible. Pl. on sound track of film *Lady Sings The Blues.* Worked w. O. Nelson at Marty's, LA, '67; gigs w. B. Berry band. Was a founder member of Supersax, '73, touring Japan with the group in '75. Fests: Monterey, '64, w. Ch. Mingus; Newport/West, w. L. Bellson, '73; Concord w. C. Mangione, '74; Monterey, Canada, many others w. Supersax.

LPs: many sessions for *Time-Life* swing band recreation series; w. O. Nelson, *Sound Pieces; Black Brown & Beautiful* (Fl. Dutchman); Berry LA Band (Beez); K. Burrell; G. Ammons (Fant.); Supersax (Cap.).

NIMMONS, PHILLIP RISTA (PHIL),* *clarinet, composer, conductor, educator;* b. Kamloops, Brit. Columbia, Canada, 6/3/23. From '66 led band for CBC jazz radio shows; toured Armed Forces bases in Can., Europe, Middle East, Africa & India, sponsored by CBC and Canad. Govt. Arr. & orchestrated O. Peterson's *Canadiana Suite* for own group, Nimmons 'N' Nine Plus 6, w. Peterson as feat. soloist at Beaverbrook Playhouse, Fredericton, N.B., '70. Pl. inaugural concert at Ontario Place, '71; annual apps. Wrote and premiered *Suite P.E.I.* for Prince Edward Island centennial, '73; wrote *Palette A Deux* for World Saxophone Congress, '73. Premiered *Atlantic Suite* on concert tour of Atlantic Provinces, '74; orchestrated and arr. selection of Ellington songs for O. Peterson perf. w. Vancouver Symph., April '75. Orchestrated & arr. Peterson's thematic material for Ontario Place film, *Big North,* '75. Annual participant at Univ. of New Brunswick Jazz & Chamber Mus. Fest; dir. of summer jazz course at Niagara Coll., '73; appointed dir. of jazz prog. at Univ. of Toronto, '75. Won BMI award for best orig. jazz comp., '68; citations from Canad. govt., '67, '69, '71-2.

Comps: *Opus UNB; Friendly Encounter; Under a Tree; Chips 'N Gravy; Kernel Strange; Poly-Rock; Dorian Way; Arf; Eee-Suave* (Ellington tribute). LPs: *Take Ten; Mary Poppins Swings; Strictly Nimmons* (Canad. RCA); *Nimmons Now; Suite P.E.I.; Canadiana Suite* (CBC transcription service & Canadian Collection); *Atlantic Suite* (Nimmons 'N' Music Ltd.).

NISTICO, SALVATORE (SAL),* *tenor saxophone;* b. Syracuse, N.Y. 4/2/40. First prominent w. Chuck and Gap Mangione, '60-1. For rest of decade alternated between bands of W. Herman ('62-5, '66, '68-70) and Count Basie ('65, '67). During '70 worked in LA w. Don Ellis and others; rejoined Herman, '71. From '72-5 freelanced around NYC, w. Tito Puente, various small groups, Chuck Israels' National Jazz Ensemble; toured Europe w. Slide Hampton. Pl. w. Buddy Rich combo at Rich's club, '74.

A powerful soloist who by the early '70s had developed a style of his own compounded of elements he had found in C. Parker, G. Ammons and S. Rollins, Nistico is well represented in many albums, most notably w. Herman, *Woody Herman 1963; Woody Herman 1964; Encore* (Philips); *Woody's Winners* (Columbia); *Concerto for Herd* (Verve); *Heavy Exposure; Woody; Light My Fire* (Cadet); *Comin' On Up* w. Sal Amico, Barry Harris (Riverside); own quintet on Italian label, Horo.

NOCK, MICHAEL ANTHONY, *piano, elec. keyboards, synthesizer;* b. Christchurch, N.Z., 9/27/40. First lessons from father, '51, for six months; then mainly self-taught until he stud. at Berklee Coll. under a scholarship, '61. Led trio in Australia, '59-60. House pianist at Lennie's in Boston, '62-3, working w. C. Hawkins et al. Toured w. Y. Lateef, '64-5, then freelanced in NYC w. Booker Ervin, S. Turrentine and others until joining John Handy mid-'67, moving to SF where he formed the Fourth Way in Sept. '68. After orig. Fourth Way disbanded in June '71, became involved in electronic music and freelance work as leader and sideman in SF.

Nock has had wide exp. in nearly every jazz style. Living in NYC he worked with groups led by Wild Bill Davison, S. Stitt, A. Blakey, Sam Rivers, F. Hubbard. Fests: Newport, '67 w. Steve Marcus; Monterey, '68, Montreux '70 w. Fourth Way. Comps: *Quartet for Saxophone* ('66); *Steps,* for jazz group, string quartet and electronic sound, written in '71 under NEA grant; *Love Waltz; Projections; Eros; Colours; Becoming.* LPs: *Between or Beyond* (MPS); w. Lateef, *1984* (Impulse); w. Handy, *Projections* (Columbia); w. Marcus, *Count's Rock Band* (Vortex-Atl.); *The Sun and the Moon Have Come Together* w. Fourth Way (Harvest-Capitol).

NORMAND, EMILE R. (CISCO), *drums;* also *piano, vibes, composer;* b. Windsor, Ont., Canada, 11/21/36. Mother, Germaine, was pianist who led dance band in '50. Studied w. Holy Rosary Sisters of St. Joseph, '44-7; Windsor U., '48-53. Played w. Yusef Lateef, Terry Pollard at Club 12, Detroit, '56. From '60 in Montreal for jazz radio shows and TV, CBC. Pl. for Montreal Jazz Society '60-1; La Porte St. Jean Jazz Concerts, Quebec City '60-3; with Claude Leveille, a French-Canadian composer who was once a protege of Edith Piaf, in Quebec, Russia, Latvia, Estonia & Lithuania, '68-70. With *Hair,* Montreal, '70-1; Les Grands Ballets Canadiens; *Tommy* in Chicago, Detroit, NYC, '72. Infl: Lateef, Charles

Coleman, Miles Davis, T. Monk, MJQ. Many TV apps. as guest vibes soloist. Fest: Laval U., Quebec City; Western U., London, Ont.; Montreal U.; Concordia U. JF, Montreal. Normand is also a painter, under contract to Eaton's of Canada. LPs: *Emile Normand Canada;* w. Pierre Nadeau Trio (RCI); *Information: Concert Pierre Leduc* (Elysee); with N. Ayoub, *The Montreal Scene* (RCA Victor, Can.).

NORRIS, WALTER,* *piano, composer;* b. Little Rock, Ark., 12/27/31. Stud. w. John Summers in Little Rock, '36-50; Heida Hermanns in NYC, as piano major at Manhattan Sch. of Mus., '64-9. Pl. w. Howard Williams big band, Little Rock '44-50. After discharge from service, w. Jimmy Ford in Houston, '52-3; own trio in Las Vegas, '53-4. To LA, '54, where he worked w. own trio and w. Frank Rosolino, Jack Sheldon, Zoot Sims, Teddy Edwards, Sonny Criss. Toured w. Shorty Rogers-Bill Holman quintet '57; Stan Getz in SF '58; Ornette Coleman, LA '58; Johnny Griffin, SF '59. To NYC where he pl. w. Hal Gaylor and Billy Bean in "The Trio," '61. From July '63 through April '70 was mus. dir. at NYC Playboy Club, where he app. w. own combos. Taught piano, theory and cond. in NYC, April '70 until June '74, when he joined Thad Jones-Mel Lewis orch., touring Europe w. them in summer of that year. Continued w. Jones-Lewis in '75; also duo w. George Mraz at Bradley's, NYC spring '75. Infl: Parker, Gillespie, Tatum, Teddy Edwards, Bud Powell, Dinu Lipatti, Vladimir Ashkenazy. Fest: MJF w. Leroy Vinnegar-Teddy Edwards '58. Comp: *Drifting; Nota Cambiata; Space Maker; Rose Waltz; Thumbs Up; D&D; Scramble.* LPs: *Drifting* (Enja); *Something Else* w. Ornette Coleman (Contemporary).

NORVO, RED (KENNETH NORVILLE),* *vibraharp, xylophone;* b. Beardstown, Ill., 3/3/08. First jazz pioneer on mallet instruments, prominent from early '30s w. Paul Whiteman; own band w. wife Mildred Bailey as singer. Settled in Cal., '47; led own trio in '50s. Moved to Las Vegas and for 12 years spent at least half of each year at the Sands Hotel. Led new trio at Tropicana, '70-2 but was in complete retirement July '72-July '73, after which he resumed occasional playing in LV, NYC etc.

TV: Benny Goodman, Frank Sinatra specs., Dinah Shore; Merv Griffin; J. Carson shows etc. Fests: Newport, Montreal, Berlin, Nice, Monterey, Concord, all in late '60s or '70s; also Dick Gibson Jazz Parties in Colo. As film comp. wrote incidental music for *Kings Go Forth* and six numbers for *Screaming Mimi.*

Despite a series of private traumas incl. severe trouble with his hearing from the late '60s, Norvo continued to provide a light, gently swinging brand of music that was entirely personal.

LPs: *Vibes a la Red* (Famous Door); *Back to the Roots* w. K. Starr (GNP-Crescendo).

NOTO, SAM,* *trumpet;* also *fluegelhorn;* b. Buffalo, N.Y., 4/17/30. The former Kenton, Bellson, Basie sideman formed his own quintet in Buffalo, '65. Opened own coffee house called Renaissance and pl. there w. his gp. for a yr. After the demise of the club, Noto left for Las Vegas where he worked in the show bands at the Flamingo & other hotels, '69-75. While there he met Red Rodney who recommended him to prod. Don Schlitten. In '74 Schlitten taped an album w. the two trumpeters for Muse and in '75 rec. Noto for his own Xanadu label. Encouraged by these events and frustrated by the stultifying LV scene, Noto moved to Toronto in the summer of '75 and became active in the studio and club scene. Known as a powerful lead man and high-note specialist w. Kenton, he revealed himself in the '70s as a virtuosic soloist inspired chiefly by Clifford Brown. Comp: *Last Train Out; Entrance; Jen-Jen.* LPs: *Entrance!* (Xanadu); *Superbop* w. Rodney (Muse).

NOTTINGHAM, JAMES EDWARD JR. (JIMMY),* trumpet; also fluegelhorn, Latin percussion; b. Brooklyn, N.Y., 12/15/25. Many name bands from mid-40s, incl. Hampton, Barnet, Basie, Gillespie, R. Charles. Lead and solo trumpet w. T. Jones-M. Lewis, incl. their first tour of Japan. Pl. on their recs. for band's first five years of existence. Lead and spec. effects w. C. Terry's big band, '74-5. For many years Nottingham also was a staff musician at CBS, until '73. In '70 opened own club, Sir James Pub in St. Albans, N.Y., feat. himself and many prominent jazz guests. Fests: Newport-N.Y. w. B. Carter, '73, '75; Nassau County Jazz w. Gillespie; West Point, N.Y. w. B. Goodman sextet, etc. LPs w. Jones-Lewis, incl. Joe Williams w. Jones-Lewis (United Artists); Teresa Brewer and Ellington Orch. (Fly. Dutch.).

O'BRIEN, FLOYD,* trombone; b. Chicago, Ill., 5/7/07. A frequent associate of the so-called "Austin High Gang," O'Brien later pl. in NYC with many name groups incl. G. Krupa, Bob Crosby, J. Teagarden; later he moved back to Chicago, pl. w. Art Hodes and others. He died in Chicago, 11/18/68. He was heard on records w. E. Condon, M. Mezzrow, F. Waller, Red Nichols in '30s and '40s and later w. groups led by Albert Nicholas, Hodes and others.

O'DAY ANITA,* singer; b. Chicago, Ill., 12/18/19. Best known for her work w. Gene Krupa band in '40s. In the '60s she was still prominent on the jazz scene, touring Japan in '63 and '66; to England, '70, European tour, '71. Played small role as jazz singer in '71 movie, *Zig-Zag,* and again in movie, *The Outfit,* '74. Started own record company, '72. Jazz fests: Berlin, '71; Newport, '73; Monterey, '74. Also during '74 played Carnegie Hall and N.Y. supper clubs. In '75 Ms. O'Day's performances confirmed her undiminished stature as one of the definitive, fact-finding jazz singers. Among her most personal characteristics are a uniquely personal timbre, a manner of skipping in front of and behind the beat, and the extensive use of melisma. She enjoyed something of a comeback in '74-5, appearing frequently at Ye Little Club in Beverly Hills, and occasionally returning to N.Y. for engagements at Reno Sweeney's.

LPs: *Hi-Ho Trailus Boot Whip* (Bob Thiele Music) feat. her first recs. as soloist; *Gene Krupa-Anita O'Day,* feat. R. Eldridge (Columbia) spanning 1941-5; *Anita O'Day & Berlin JF '70* (MPS-BASF); *Once Upon a Summertime; Anita and Rhythm Section* (Box 422, Hesperia, Ca. 92345).

OEHLER, DALE DIXON, composer, arranger, piano; b. Springfield, Ill., 10/1/41. Father played piano w. J. Dorsey, Lee Konitz in '40s. Extensive studies from '48-69. MA from U. of Iowa. Worked with local groups in the Springfield-Chicago area while at Northwestern U. '58-63.

Oehler, who names as his influences Igor Stravinsky, Luciano Berio, Edwin Hawkins, Gil Evans and Quincy Jones, earned awards as best pianist and best arranger at Notre Dame Jazz Fest., '66. During early '70s he became a successful arranger for many jazz, pop and fringe-jazz LPs. Among those on which he participated as arr. and/or pianist are: *High Energy* w. F. Hubbard (Columbia); *Natural Juices* w. Gene McDaniels (Ode); *The Other Side,* sound track album *Shaft's Big Score* (MGM); *Inside Bugsy,* w. Bugsy Maugh (Dot); *Trouble Man* w. Marvin Gaye (Tamla); *Who's This Bitch Anyway* w. Marlena Shaw (Blue Note); and many others for Moacir Santos et al.

O'FARRILL, ARTURO (CHICO),* composer, arranger; b. Havana, Cuba, 10/28/21. First prominent in NYC as arr. for B. Goodman, D. Gillespie. Moved to Mexico late '50s, returned to U.S. in '65, resumed writing frequently for C. Basie, also for Glenn Miller orch. under B. De Franco. Arrs. for C. Tjader LP, '67; comp. suite for Clark Terry, introduced at Montreux, '70. From '71 became increasingly involved in composing and arranging and production of radio and TV commercials. His *Symphony #1* was premiered in Mexico City, '72. Wrote extended work for S. Kenton, also arrangement for Candido LP, '73; arrs. for F. Wess, G. Barbieri albums, '74. Conducted concert at Avery Fisher Hall, NYC, with Machito orch. and Joe Newman, '74; cond. new work, *Oro, Incienso y Mirra,* w. Gillespie and Machito at St. Patrick's Cathedral, '75.

Comp: *Ramon Lopez* for S. Kenton orch. LP (Creative World); Arr: *High Voltage; Basic Basie,* for Basie LPs (MPS-BASF); *Chapter Three; Viva Emiliano Zapata* for Barbieri LP (Impulse). Own LPs: *Spanish Rice* (co-leader w. C. Terry); *Nine Flags* (AVC-Impulse); *Married Well* (Verve); w. Gillespie, *Oro, Incienso y Mirra* (Pablo).

OGERMAN, CLAUS,* composer, piano; b. Ratibor, Germany, 4/29/30. To U.S., '59. Has enjoyed continuous success as arranger-conductor for hundreds of albums by pop, jazz and r & b artists. Comps: *Some Times,* a symphonic jazz-ballet, premiered 7/14/72 at Lincoln Cent., NYC by American Ballet Theatre; *Symbiosis; Elegia; A Face Without A Name,* all rec. by Bill Evans; *Time Present and Time Past,* symphonic dances, pl. by various symph. orchs.

LPs: w. F. Sinatra, *Francis Albert Sinatra & A.C. Jobim* (Repr.); w. O. Peterson, *Motions & Emotions* (MPS); w. W. Montgomery, *Tequila* (Verve); w. B. Evans, *With Symphony Orchestra* (Verve); w. S. Getz, *Voices* (Verve); w. A. C. Jobim (MCA); others w. D. Byrd, J. Hodges, K. Winding, Jimmy Smith, Jackie & Roy, Astrud Gilberto (Verve); S. Vaughan (Merc.); B. Goodman (RCA-Readers Digest); Urbie Green (Project 3); David Clayton-Thomas (Col.).

OLAY, RUTH,* singer; b. San Francisco, Cal., 7/1/27. After living for many years in LA, moved to Copenhagen, '73, working there at Montmartre, commuting to U.S. frequently

Oscar Peterson (*David D. Spitzer*)

Flora Purim

Hannibal Marvin Peterson (*Veryl Oakland*)

Esther Phillips (*Veryl Oakland*)

Julian Priester (*Veryl Oakland*)

Jean-Luc Ponty

Buddy Rich (*Bob Klein*)

Jerome Richardson
(*Veryl Oakland*)

Larry Ridley
(*Bob Klein*)

Sam Rivers
(*David D. Spitzer*)

wey Redman (*David D. Spitzer*)

Ben Riley (*Veryl Oakland*)

Sonny Rollins (*Veryl Oakland*)

Max Roach (*Veryl Oakland*)

Perry Robinson (*David D. Spitzer*)

Jimmy Rowles

Roswell Rudd (*David D. Spitzer*)

Charles Rouse (*Bob Klein*)

Pharoah Sanders (*Veryl Oakland*)

Wayne Shorter (*Veryl Oakland*)

Linda & Sonny Sharrock

Bud Shank (*Veryl Oakland*)

Archie Shepp (*David D. Spitzer*)

Horace Silver (*Veryl Oakland*)

George Shearing & Dave Brubeck (*Veryl Oakland*)

Sonny Stitt (*Veryl Oakland*)

Zoot Sims (*Veryl Oakland*)

Gabor Szabo (*Veryl Oakland*) Lew Soloff (*Veryl Oakland*) Sonny Simmons (*Veryl Oakland*)

for spec. apps. TV in Oslo; app. at Hebrew Univ. in Jerusalem. Worked at Mr. Kelly's in Chicago w. E. Garner, Feb. '75. Fests. in Denmark, Sweden, summer of '75. In Dec. '74, she sang at Ye Little Club in Beverly Hills, where she had been its opening attraction 18 years earlier.

LPs: *Live at Mr. Kelly's* (UA); *Soul In The Night* (ABC).

OLIVER, MELVIN JAMES (SY),* *composer, leader, singer, trumpet;* b. Battle Creek, Mich., 12/17/10. Prominent as an arranger-performer w. J. Lunceford in '30s and arr. for T. Dorsey in '40s. During '60s busy as a free-lance arr. in NYC but in '70s began leading his own band on a fairly regular basis, pl. the music of Lunceford which he helped create, Ellingtonia and other classics from the Swing Era. The band app. at the NJF-NY for dances at Commodore Hotel, '72, Roseland, '74; for the Duke Ellington Society at the New School; at the Riverboat; and, in '75, in two separate, lengthy engagements at the Rainbow Room. Oliver was one of the four musical directors for the NYJRC in its first season, '74, concentrating on programs of Lunceford, Dorsey, Ellington, Fletcher Henderson, etc.

LPs: *Yes Indeed* (Black & Blue); Stang.

OREGON. see Moore, Glen; Towner, Ralph.

ORSTED PEDERSEN, NIELS-HENNING,* *bass;* b. Osted, Denmark, 5/27/46. A prodigy who pl. w. Danish gps. at age 14; two yrs. later he was pl. & rec. w. Bud Powell and soon had enhanced his growing reputation through gigs w. R. Kirk, B. Evans and S. Rollins. Later he pl. w. Oscar Peterson, toured w. JATP and was house bassist at Copenhagen's Club Montmartre where he pl. w. all the visiting Americans, most notably Dexter Gordon and Kenny Drew. Formed duo w. Drew in '70s; also member of Danish Radio Big Band; perf. w. own gp. Polls: Won DB Int. Critics poll, TDWR, '68; no. 1 European bassist in *Jazz Forum*, '74-5. Orsted Pedersen's exceptional talent makes him one of the leading bass virtuosos of the contemporary scene. Lennie Tristano says: "He may be the best bassist in the world." LPs: *Duo; Duo 2* w. Drew; *Paul Bley/NHOP; Two's Company* w. Joe Albany; *Dark Beauty* w. Drew; *Catalonian Fire* w. T. Montoliu; others w. Jackie McLean; D. Gordon; Anthony Braxton (SteepleChase); w. O. Peterson, *The Trio;* also many albums rec. at Montreux JF '75 incl. *The Trumpet Kings; Milt Jackson Big Four; Dizzy Gillespie Big 7; Court Basie Jam Session; Oscar Peterson Big 6; The Montreux Collection* (Pablo).

ORTEGA, ANTHONY ROBERT (TONY),* *saxophone, clarinet, flute;* b. Los Angeles, Cal., 6/7/28. Continued to work w. Gerald Wilson, whose band he joined in '64; also w. L. Schifrin, D. Gillespie at the Hollywood Bowl in '67; F. Zappa, '72; O. Nelson; N. Riddle. TV: acting role on *Lucille Ball Show; Ironsides,* w. Q. Jones. Film; *Change of Habit,* w. E. Presley.

LPs: *New Dance* (Revelation); others w. Wilson (Pac. Jazz).

ORY, EDWARD (KID),* *trombone, composer;* b. La Place, La., 12/25/1886. After moving to Hawaii in '66, Ory went into semi-retirement. He returned to NO in '71 to app. at the jazz fest., but in his few subsequent apps. was able only to sing. On 1/23/73 he died in Hawaii of heart failure and pneumonia.

Ory earned his most lasting fame as composer of *Muskrat Ramble,* which he rec. in Feb. '26 w. L. Armstrong and His Hot Five. One of the first musicians identified with the "tailgate" trombone style, he is represented on innumerable recordings, among them his own LPs: *Tailgate!; Creole Jazz Band* (3 albums, '54, '55, '56); *This Kid's The Greatest; Favorites* (Good Time Jazz); others w. Armstrong (Col.); Jelly Roll Morton (RCA).

OSBORNE, MARY,* *guitar, singer;* b. Minot, North Dakota, 7/17/21. Insp. by Charlie Christian, became one of the first elec. guitarists, prominent through NYC record dates w. Mary Lou Williams, C. Hawkins, M. Ellington and own trio. Jack Sterling radio show daily, '52-63; freelance gigs and teaching '64-7. Moving to Bakersfield, Cal., '67, worked with local groups and was partner with husband, Ralph Scaffidi, in Osborne Guitar Co., manufacturing guitars, amps, PA systems. Occasional concerts and club work in LA, incl. Donte's, Pilgrimage Theatre; Palace of Fine Arts, SF w. Joe Venuti, '69; fests. for George Wein in Berkeley and at Hollywood Bowl, '73.

LPs: w. Tyree Glenn; also Louie Bellson/Gene Krupa (Roulette).

OSTLUND, PETUR DAVID (ISLAND),* *drums;* b. New York City, 12/3/43. Lived in NYC until age seven, then spent four years in Trois Rivieres, Quebec, after which he was a resident of Reykjavik, Iceland until age 26, then moved to Stockholm. Stud. w. Gene Stone, '58-60; Reykjavik Conservatory of Mus., '66-9; Ingesund Mus. School, Sweden, '72-3. Winner of Icelandic poll annually, '62-9; Icelandic Musician of the Year, '66. Has pl. w. A. Farmer, D. Byrd, Ch. Tolliver, K. Winding, Y. Lateef, Booker Ervin, Dexter Gordon, Lars Gullin, Dave Pike, Barney Kessel. Member of Red Mitchell's sextet, '74-5; also teaching at Royal Academy of Mus., Stockholm.

LPs: *Communication,* w. Mitchell; *A Sleeping Bee,* w. Farmer (Gramofonverket); *Happy New Year* w. Wickman, Mitchell et al; *Like Grass,* w. Gullin (EMI); *Rumanian Impressions,* w. Guido Manusardi (Amigo).

OTIS, JOHNNY,* *piano, vibes, leader, composer;* b. Vallejo, Cal. 12/28/21. After a period of almost total inactivity in music, Otis gradually returned to casual gigs and record production in the late '60s. In '69 the album *Cold Shot* (Kent) rekindled his career. He has been traveling nationally with his show since '70, often feat. his son, Shuggie Otis (q.v.). Toured Far East, '71; Europe, '72; Africa/Europe '74. TV: own series '56-61; Barrel House show, '70. Movies: *Jukebox Rhythm,* '58; *Play Misty For Me,* '71. Fests: Monterey, '70; Antibes, '74. Comps: *Every Beat of My Heart; So Fine; Dance With Me Henry; Hand Jive; Oxford Grey. Listen to the Lambs,* a colorful and highly readable autobiography, was publ. in '66 by W. W. Norton.

LPs: *Cold Shot* (Kent); *Johnny Otis Show Live at Monterey; Cuttin' Up* (Epic); *R & B Blues* (Blues Spectrum).

OTIS, JOHNNY JR. (SHUGGIE),* *guitar;* also *bass, drums, keyboards, singer, composer;* b. Los Angeles, Cal., 11/30/53. Stud. guitar w. Burdell Mathis; arr. and comp. w. Albert Harris; general mus. educ. w. father. Became member of the Johnny Otis Show in '67, remained until '73 and worked with the show again in '75, in addition to leading his own group.

Other jobs w. F. Zappa, Billy Preston, Preston Love, Al Kooper, Gene "Mighty Flea" Conners.

An unusually sensitive and prodigious musician, Otis was only 15 when the first album feat. him with his father's gp., *Cold Shot,* app. on the Kent label in '69. He names among his infls. T-Bone Walker, B.B. King, K. Burrell, Jimi Hendrix, Sly Stone, Debussy, Stravinsky, Beethoven, Johnny Otis Sr. Comps: *Freedom Flight; Barrelhouse Blues; Gospel Groove; Shuggie's Boogie; Purple; Rainy Day.* Fests: Monterey, Newport, '70; Berkeley, Newport/LA, '73.

LPs: *Here Comes Shuggie Otis; Freedom Flight; Johnny Otis Show Live at Monterey* (Epic); also, with his father, a series of albums with various blues artists under the title *Great R & B Oldies* (Blues Spectrum).

OTSUKA, KEIJI (GEORGE), drums; b. Tokyo, Japan, 4/6/38. Self-taught. After playing w. Tony Scott gp., Sadao Watanabe quartet, and Sleepy Matsumoto quartet, formed own gp. Infl: Tony Williams, Miles Davis, Roy Haynes, Jack DeJohnette. Fests: World JF, '64; Four Big Drummers Fest. w. Haynes, DeJohnette, Mel Lewis, '70; Expo '70 and other major Japanese fests. Won SJ Jazz Disc Award '68; SJ Readers Poll, '68-9. Own LPs: *Page 1; Page 2; Page 3* (Nippon Col.); *Chris Connor & George Otsuka* (Japan. Victor); *Jackieboard* w. DeJohnette; *Groovin With My Soul Brothers* w. Haynes (Trio).

OTT, HORACE, composer, arranger; also *piano, organ, trombone, tympani, vibes;* b. St. Matthews, S.C., 4/15/33. Priv. piano lessons from '44. Began writing arrs. while in 11th grade, continued while student at S. Carolina State Coll. One year of teaching school (band director); two years of army, incl. spec. serv. stints; a year of writing for rehearsal bands prior to entering prof. rec. career, in which he became very active in pop, r & b and jazz circles. Among artists he has comp., arr. and/or conducted for, mainly on rec. are Joe Williams, Nat King Cole, Betty Carter, C. Basie, R. Flack, Groove Holmes, B. Rich, J. Witherspoon, L. Donaldson. Arr. music for film *Gordon's War;* comp. *Prove It,* rec. by Aretha Franklin; *Sassy Soul Strut* for L. Donaldson (Blue Note); arr. four albums for Nina Simone, incl. some of his own comps; also *Worth Waiting For* LP by J. Williams (Blue Note).

OUSLEY, HAROLD LOMAX,* tenor saxophone, composer; also *alto sax, flute, clarinet;* b. Chicago, Ill., 1/23/29, Worked w. Machito; Howard McGhee; Joe Newman; Clark Terry in first half of '60s; Also led own combos at Birdland; Club Baron; Count Basie's. Cont. w. own gp. from '66-73, '75- . Toured in Caracas; Puerto Rico w. Machito, '69. Pl. w. L. Hampton, '70; C. Basie, '73-4, incl. Europe and Japan. Concert-lecture, *A Historical Resume of Jazz,* on St. Thomas, St. Croix and St. John, West Indies, in late '60s; from that time in US. *Jazz Mass* in various churches; jazz seminars in Music Therapy at Groves Therapeutic Counseling Service, Jamaica, N.Y. Film: *Cotton Comes to Harlem;* wrote and rec. theme for *Not Just Another Woman.* TV: *Like It Is; Jazz Adventures; Sight and Sound; The Night People; Black Pride.* Fest: Columbia U. Concert at NJF-NY, '72. Comp: *Return of the Prodigal Son; The Kid; Aquarian Melody; Son of Man; The People's Choice; Code Name Thunder Walk.* LPs: *The*

Kid (Cobble.); w. Jack McDuff, *Walk On By* (Prest.); w. Grassella Oliphant, *The Grass is Greener* (Atl.).

OVERTON, HALL F.,* composer, piano, teacher; b. Bangor, Mich., 2/23/20. Overton, who distinguished himself as a classical musician along with his jazz activities, and who taught at Juilliard from '60, was well known for his association w. Th. Monk, for whom he orchestrated a number of the latter's compositions for concert presentation. Overton died 11/25/72 of a ruptured esophagus at Roosevelt Hospital in NYC. As jazz pianist, he was heard on recs. in the '50s w. Jimmy Raney, S. Getz, O. Pettiford, Phil Woods Teddy Charles and others, and in a piano duo session w. Dave McKenna for the long defunct Bethlehem label; also a classical album, *Pulsations* (CRI); *Who's Afraid of the Big Band Monk* (Col.).

OWENS, CHARLES M. (Charles M. Brown), tenor saxophone, composer; also *flute;* b. Phoenix, Ariz., 5/4/39. Stud. sax at San Diego State Coll. and while in U.S. Air Force; also w. Joe Viola at Berklee, '64-5. Pl. w. B. Rich, '67-9; M. Santamaria, '69 to May '70; Bobby Bryant; Paul Humphrey. With J. Mayall, '72- European tour w. F. Zappa, pl. flute and piccolo; Patrice Rushen in SF, '75; G. Wilson, '74-5. Infls: O. Nelson, Dolphy, Coltrane. TV: *Dial M For Music; The Jazz Show,* KNBC. Comps: *Night Cry; Black Pride; I Stand Alone.* Arr. *Ode to Billy Joe* in Rich album, *Live at Caesar's Palace* (Pac. Jazz). LPs: *Motherlode* (Vault); w. Henry Franklin, *The Skipper at Home* (Black Jazz).

OWENS, JAMES ROBERT (JIMMY),* trumpet, fluegelhorn, composer; b. New York City, 12/9/43. Early experience in the '60s w. L. Hampton, Mingus, etc. W. Herbie Mann, '65-6. One of the orig. members of the Thad Jones-Mel Lewis orch.; also pl. w. Clark Terry's big band; the New York Jazz Sextet; the Symphony of the New World; and the Billy Taylor band for the David Frost TV show. European tours w. Dizzy Gillespie reunion band, '68; Young Giants of Jazz, '73. Other European tours in '67, '69, '72, '74, pl. w. radio orchs. in Germany, Holland.

Owens, who is an extremely active NYC freelancer, is on the Board of Governors of the New York chapter of NARAS; the Board of Dir. for the NYJRC, serving as one of its mus. dirs. for the 1974-75 season; on the Jazz/Folk/Ethnic Music Panel of the Nat. Endowment for the Arts; and one of the founders of the Collective Black Artists. He is also a member of the Nat. Jazz Ens. He teaches and lectures for the CBA and for Jazzmobile. Won DB Critics' Poll, TDWR, '67. Fests: many European apps. incl. Berlin, Loosdrecht, Bologna, Helsinki; also Monterey, Newport. In '74, Owens led the CBA orch. in a tribute to Dizzy Gillespie at Fordham U. as part of NJF-NY. Comps: *Complicity; Milan Is Love; Git the Money Bluze; You Had Better Listen; The Jazz Jaleo; Lo-Slo-Bluze; Never Subject to Change; Funk-A-De Mama; We're Going up.*

LPs: *No Escaping It* (Polydor); *You Had Better Listen* (Atlantic); *Newport in New York, the Jam Sessions,* Vol. 1 (Cobblestone); w. Leon Thomas, *Full Circle* (Fly. Dutch.); w. Taylor, *O.K. Billy* (Bell); w. Billy Harper, *Capra Black* (Strata-East); w. A. Shepp, *The Way Ahead; For Losers*

(Imp.); *The Dizzy Gillespie Reunion Band* (MPS); w. B. Timmons, *Got to Get It;* w. Gary Bartz, *Libra* (Milest.); w. Teddy Edwards, *It's All Right;* w. Eric Kloss, *First Class Kloss; Life Force; We're Going Up;* w. Booker Ervin, *Heavy* (Prestige).

OXLEY, TONY, *drums, percussion, electronics;* b. Sheffield, Yorks., England, 6/15/38. From '57-60 in Black Watch Military band. Own quintet in Sheffield, '60-4; collaborated w. guitarist Derek Bailey, '64-7. Moved to London, '67 to work at Ronnie Scott's Club, continuing there into the early '70s, acc. such visiting American jazzmen as Sonny Rollins, Bill Evans, S. Getz, L. Konitz, C. Mariano et al. Formed own sextet for clubs, concerts throughout Europe. In '71 started Incus record label w. Bailey and other musicians; also joined Jazz Composer Orch. Received commission from Arts Council of Gt. Britain for LJCO, '72. In '73 organized and taught at Barry Summer School, course in Jazz and Improvised Music. Oxley has worked for many Amer. mus. in Europe incl. Rollins, J. Griffin, Art Farmer, Joe Henderson, Charles Tolliver et al. Also played w. John McLaughlin, Giorgio Gaslini, Michel Portal, Barry Guy orch. Formed own new gp., The Angular Apron, '74. Won MM polls in percussion category, '68, '70-1; six comp. awards from Arts Council of Gt. Britain. Worked w. George Gruntz on music for film *Steppenwolf,* prod. by Gruntz. Oxley names many classical composers as his main infl., as well as Dolphy, Blakey, Elvin Jones, Coltrane, Bill Evans.

LPs: *Baptised Traveller; Four Compositions for Sextet* (CBS); *Ichnos* (RCA); *Tony Oxley, 71-4;* w. Howard Riley, *Synopsis* (Incus).

PACK, GARY LEE, *trumpet, fluegelhorn, valve trombone;* b. Los Angeles, Cal., 10/17/50. Stud. w. Forrest Ray, Long Beach, Cal., '61; Dr. Herbert D. Patnoe, '68-9; Claude Gordon, Bill Green, '70; Jerry Coker, Dan Haerle, U. of Miami, '72. Much early exp. in coll. jazz groups, incl. Jack Wheaton's Junior Neophonic Orch. Joined D. Ellis, '70; left to work w. S. Kenton for nine months in '71. After three months back with the Ellis band, he left for Miami in '72 to teach in summer jazz-rock seminar at U. of Miami. After working w. M. Torme, Ira Sullivan and others in the Miami area, returned to Kenton band for six months. Pl. in SF w. Don Piestrup. Led Foothill Coll. jazz ensemble, '74. Toured w. W. Herman Feb. to Nov. '74, incl. concerts and TV w. F. Sinatra. Returned to LA, pl. w. Ellis octet, '74-5. Fests: Montreux; Belvedere, Canada, w. Herman '74; Concord, w. Kenton, '71. Infls: I. Sullivan, J. Coltrane, F. Hubbard, Clifford Brown et al.

LPs: w. Kenton, *Live at Brigham Young University; 7.5 On The Richter Scale* (Creative World); w. Herman, *Herd at Monterey; Children of Lima* (Fantasy).

PAGE, NATHEN, *guitar;* also *bass, piano;* b. Leetown, W. Va., 8/25/37. Brother, Henry Page, is drummer in Tampa, Fla. Self-taught. Played w. Jimmy Smith; Roberta Flack;

Herbie Mann; Tony Williams; Doug Carn; in '75 w. Sonny Rollins, incl. NJF-NY; Jackie McLean at Five Spot, NYC.

Infl: Coltrane, Miles Davis, C. Adderley, H. Hancock, Tyner, Clifford Brown, C. Parker, Ahmad Jamal. Movie: *Soul to Soul.* TV: Mike Douglas; Steve Allen; *Tonight;* Merv Griffin; *Harambee; Nine in the Morning;* David Frost; *Morning Show from Virginia Beach.* Fest: NJF; NJF-NY; Houston; Dallas; Hampton, Va.; Laurel, Md.; MJF; Canada.

Comp: *Knapp Time.* LPs: w. J. Smith, *The Boss* (Verve); w. Doug Carn, *Revelation; Adams Apple* (Black Jazz); w. R. Flack, *Soul to Soul* (Atl.); w. Rene McLean, *What It Is* (Steeple.).

PALMER, EARL C. SR.* *drums;* b. New Orleans, La., 10/25/24. To LA, '57; continuously busy for many years as studio musician doing commercials, TV, movies, pop record dates etc., and occasional jazz apps. w. Benny Carter and own group. Past VP of NARAS.

LPs: w. Maria Muldaur, Carter, *Waitress in A Donut Shop* (Repr.).

PALMIER, REMO (formerly Palmieri),* *guitar;* b. New York City, 3/29/23. Prominent in '40s w. C. Hawkins, R. Norvo, B. Holiday, Mildred Bailey, and on early D. Gillespie records. Won *Esquire* New Star Award, '45. Palmier became inactive in jazz after joining the CBS staff in '45, where he worked on the Arthur Godfrey show continuously until '72. He then returned to jazz, starting a quartet w. Hank Jones; also pl. night club dates w. B. Hackett. In '74 he pl. a series of jazz concerts w. B. Goodman.

LPs: *Bobby Hackett and Vic Dickenson at the Royal Box* (Hyannisport).

PANASSIÉ, HUGUES, *critic;* b. Paris, France, 2/27/12. Founder of the Hot Club of France in '32, Panassié in '34 wrote a book, *Le Jazz Hot,* one of the first scholarly volumes on jazz to appear in any country. A long time champion of traditionalist and NO jazz, he became the center of a controversy when he strongly opposed bop and other new developments beginning in the '40s. From '50 he edited and wrote a monthly bulletin for the Hot Club of France. Panassié died 12/8/74 of a heart attack at his home in Montauban, France. He was well remembered for a series of recordings he made during a visit to New York in 1938. In '49 he visited NO to see L. Armstrong crowned King of the Zulus. Armstrong, E. Hines, L. Hampton, and particularly clarinetist Milton Mezz Mezzrow had been among his closest musician friends.

PARENTI ANTHONY (TONY),* *clarinet, saxophones;* b. New Orleans, La., 8/6/00. The veteran NO jazzman, who had worked for many years as a studio musician in NYC, later became a regular at E. Condon's and led the house band at Jimmy Ryan's from '63-9. He died 4/17/72 in NYC.

LPs: *Jean Kitrell; Night at Jimmy Ryan's; Ragtime; The Great Tony Parenti; Ragtime Jubilee* (Jazzology).

PARKER, EVAN, *tenor, soprano saxes;* b. Bristol, England, 4/5/44. Studied saxophone w. James Knott, '58-62. Played w. Spontaneous Music Ensemble, '66-68; Tony Oxley sextet, '69-72; Pierre Favre, '69-71; Music Improvisation Company, '69-72; Peter Brotzmann Octet; Chris McGregor Sextet, '70; Globe Unity Orchestra; Alexander Von Schlippenbach trio/

quartet from '70; Evan Parker-Paul Lytton duo from '72; Brotherhood of Breath from '73. Infl: Coltrane, Dolphy, Derek Bailey. TV: *Aquarius*, TV Arts program for LNTV w. Lytton. Fest: many Euro. fests. incl. Bilzen, '69; Donaueschingen; Berlin, '72; Antibes, '75; Baden-Baden, '68-9, '75. Co-director w. Derek Bailey, Tony Oxley of Incus Records. Member of Musicians' Co-operative. Publ: *New/ Rediscovered Musical Instruments* (Quartz/Mirliton). LPs: *Topography of the Lungs; Collective Calls; Saxophone Solos; Evan Parker & Paul Lytton at the Unity Theatre* (Incus); *The Music Improvisation Company* (ECM); *Pakistani Pomade; Three Nails Left* (FMP).

PARLAN, HORACE LOUIS,* *piano*; b. Pittsburgh, Pa., 1/19/31. First active on NY scene w. C. Mingus in '50s; pl. w. Booker Ervin; Lockjaw Davis-Johnny Griffin; R.R. Kirk. In '73 he moved to Copenhagen, working from that time in Scandinavia w. local musicians, incl. Dexter Gordon, and American visitors such as Al Cohn-Zoot Sims; Red Rodney. LP: w. own trio & quintet, *Arrival*; w. D. Gordon. (Steeple.).

PARLATO, DAVID CHARLES, *bass*; also *piano*; b. Los Angeles, Cal., 10/31/45. Father, Charles Parlato, is trumpeter and singer who has worked in the bands of Kay Kyser, Horace Heidt et al. Educ. Valley State Coll., '66-8; then priv. study w. Nat Gagnursky (classical); Monty Budwig (jazz); Jr. Neophonic w. S. Kenton. Made first pro. app. w. D. Ellis orch., '67; then worked with the combos of Frank Strazzeri, '69; Warne Marsh, '70; Paul Horn '68-71; Gil Melle, '69-71; Tim Weisberg, '70-2; John Klemmer, '72-4; Frank Zappa, '72; Ashish Khan-Alla Rakha-Emil Richards-Don Preston, '73; Gabor Szabo, '74-5. Infls: Miles Davis, J. Coltrane, Gil Evans. Fests: w. Ellis, Monterey, '67-8; Newport, '68; w. Weisberg, Monterey, '70.

LPs: w. Ellis, *Electric Bath; Shock Treatment* (Col.); w. Strazzeri, *That's Him and This Is New*; w. Marsh, *Ne Plus Ultra* (Revelation); w. Horn, *The Concert Ensemble* (Ovation); *A Special Edition* (Island); w. Melle, *Waterbirds* (Nocturne); others w. Weisberg (A & M); Klemmer (Imp.).

PARNELL, JACK,* *drums, leader*; b. London, England, 8/6/23. First popular w. Ted Heath; formed own big band, '51. Mus. Dir. for ATV from '57; also for Independent TV Corp. in U.S. MD for many TV specs. starring L. Horne, Tony Bennett, other pop stars. Won Emmy as Mus. Dir. for Barbra Streisand Spec., '74. Other awards for comp. TV themes. Only occasionally active in jazz in recent years.

LPs: *Music of the Giants*; two albums of TV and film themes (Cap.)

PASCOAL, HERMETO, *piano, flute, guitar*; b. Lagoa da Canoa, Brazil, 6/22/36. Worked with several small groups in Brazil, his most notable association being Quarteto Novo w. Airto. To NYC, '72; rec. w. Miles Davis, Duke Pearson; later went to Cal. Named by Flora Purim as one of her most important influences. Arr. *Little Church; Nem Um Talvez* on Davis' *Live/Evil* album, and pl. flute, organ. Other LPs: *Hermeto* (Buddah); w. Airto, *Natural Feelings; Seeds on the Ground* (Buddah); A.C. Jobim, *Stone Flower* (CTI).

PASS, JOE (Joseph Anthony Passalaqua),* *guitar*; b. New Brunswick, N.J., 1/13/29. Came to prominence in early '60s w. Gerald Wilson, Bud Shank, Bobby Troup, many other LA recording and club groups. After touring w. G. Shearing,

'65-7, worked mainly in TV and rec. studios in LA, also playing jazz gigs in Donte's etc. and rec. w. Sinatra, B. Eckstine, S. Vaughan, Joe Williams, C. McRae. To Germany, '70 to make two LPs for MPS-BASF, one with own trio and one w. A. Van Damme. Several fest. apps. from '66 at Monterey; Concord and Newport-N.Y., '73. Toured Australia with B. Goodman, '73. Formed successful two-guitar partnership w. Herb Ellis for clubs and records, '72-4. Enthusiastically supported by Norman Granz, he worked in '73-4 w. Ella Fitzgerald and O. Peterson, both managed by Granz, and rec. with them. Played first London solo gig at Ronnie Scott's Club, '74.

Pass is regarded by many musicians who have heard him as an incomparable modern jazz artist, a total virtuoso of the instrument, capable of swinging fiercely at fast tempos and of exceptional harmonic imagination on ballads. Many examples of his work have been published: *Joe Pass Guitar Style; Chord Book; Chord Solos; Jazz Guitar Solos; Jazz Duets* (Gwyn Publishing, P.O. Box 5900, Sherman Oaks, Ca. 91413).

LPs: *Virtuoso; Joe Pass at the Montreux JF 1975*, solo albums; *The Trio* w. O. Peterson; *Peterson & Pass à Salle Pleyel; Peterson Big Six at Montreux; Portrait of Duke Ellington*; w. Ellington, *Ellington's Big Four; Two For the Road* w. H. Ellis; *JATP at Montreux*; w. E. Fitzgerald, *Take Love Easy; Ella in London* (Pablo); w. H. Ellis, *Seven Come Eleven* (Concord Jazz); w. Carmen McRae, *Great American Song Book* (Atl.). Own LPs on World Pacific: *Catch Me; Sign of the Times; Simplicity; Stone Jazz*; also on World Pacific w. Gerald Wilson; Richard "Groove" Holmes; Chet Baker; Jazz Crusaders.

PASTOR, TONY (Antonio Pestritto),* *tenor sax, singer*; b. Middletown, Conn., 1907. A key member of Artie Shaw's band from 1936-40, Pastor led his own orchestra in the '40s and '50s, then formed a vocal act with three sons. Retired in 1958; died 10/31/69 at his home in Old Lyme. Conn. LP: *The Complete Artie Shaw*, Vol. 1 (Bluebird).

PATTERSON, DON,* *organ, composer*; b. Columbus, Ohio, 7/22/36. Pl. and rec. w. Sonny Stitt, Gene Ammons in '60s. Formed own gp. for touring club circuit. In early '70s working in and around Gary, Ind. Comp: *Jesse Jackson; Little Angie; My Man String; Funk in ¾; Opus De Don; Dem New York Dues; Freddie Tooks Jr.*

LPs: *These Are Soulful Days: The Return of Don Patterson* (Muse); *Boppin' & Burnin'; Funk You; Opus De Don; Four Dimensions* (Prest.).

PAUER, FRITZ, *piano, composer*; b. Vienna, Austria, 10/14/43. Stud. priv. w. Cissy Faber in Vienna, '48; at LBA, '57-60; priv. cons., '60-1. Worked w. Hans Koller, '60-2; own trio at Dug's and Jazz Galerie in Berlin backing soloists such as Art Farmer, Leo Wright, Carmell Jones, Don Byas, D.Gordon, B. Ervin, '62-8. With Eric Kleinschuster Sextet; teacher at Vienna Jazz Cons., '68. From '70, member of the ORF Radio Big band; lead. own trio. Infl: M. Tyner, Bud Powell, J. Zawinul, F. Gulda, O. Nelson, Ellington, T. Monk, B. Evans. TV: *Piano Conclave*, Vienna '73; Fests: Bled, Yugo., '62; Frankfurt, '66; Berlin; Prague, '69; Montreux, '70-1; Warsaw, '72. Won first prize as best pianist, Modern Jazz Competition, Vienna, '66. Publ: *Modal*

Forces, Domicile Jazzseries No. 4; *Mythologie,* Domicile Jazzseries No. 5 (Ernst Knauff, Siegestrasse 19, Munich, Germany); *Meditationen/Three Poems* (Papgeno Musikverlage, Neulerchenfelderstrasse, Vienna, Austria). Comp: *Concert for Big Band and Symph. Orch.* LPs: *Mythologie; Fata Morgana; Live at the Berlin Jazz Galerie; Power By Pauer* (MPS/BASF).

PAVAGEAU, ALCIDE (SLOW DRAG),* *bass;* b. New Orleans, La., 3/7/1888. The pioneer jazz bassist, who played with Geo. Lewis and Bunk Johnson in the '40s, died in NO 11/8/68.

PAYNE, CECIL McKENZIE (ZODIAC),* *baritone sax, flute, clarinets, alto sax;* b. Brooklyn, N.Y. 12/14/22. one of first baritone sax stars of bop era. Traveled w. Machito orch. 1963-6; Woody Herman '66-7, then lived in Brussels for a year, working as single. Back to US Nov. '68, but returned to Continent a month later as member of Dizzy Gillespie reunion band. Joined Count Basie '69; left '71 and formed Jazz Zodiac Quartet. Joined NY Jazz Repertory Orch. '74. Toured Europe w. *Musical Life of Charlie Parker* unit late '74. Played *Showboat 2* jazz festival Caribbean cruise, Dec. 74, w. sister Cavril Payne as vocalist.

Comps: *Cerupa; Flying Fish; Brookfield Andante; Martin Luther King, Jr.*

LPs: *Brooklyn Brothers* (Muse); *Zodiac* (Strata-East); *Brookfield Andante; Cecil Payne Spotlite II* (Spotlite); w. Cavril Payne, *Teasin' Tan* (Cepp).

PAYNE, PERCIVAL (SONNY),* *drums;* b. NYC, 5/4/26. Joined Count Basie early 1955, remaining for ten years; led own trip and pl. w. Frank Sinatra before rejoining Basie Dec. '65 for several months. After a long tenure w. Harry James, returned to Basie again, and left for the third time in '74. Toured with a combo, Don Cunningham & Co., '75. LPs: see Basie.

PEARSON, COLUMBUS CALVIN JR. (DUKE),* *composer, arranger, piano;* also *trumpet* b. Atlanta, Ga., 8/17/32. In addition to a long assoc. w. Donald Byrd, who recorded Pearson's comp. *Cristo Redentor,* worked as pianist w. Nancy Wilson and other singers. From '63-70 was a & r asst. to Alfred Lion at Blue Note Records in NYC. Also led own big band intermittently. On music faculty at Clark Coll., Atlanta, Ga., '71. Accompanist to Carmen McRae, '72; Joe Williams, '73; accomp., arr. and mus. dir. to Ms. Hollon Milburn, '73-5.

In '70 Pearson was the only non-Ellington alumnus to perf. for the Duke Ellington Society; also arr. and cond. music for Ellington's 74th birthday party and Honorary Doctorate at Clark Coll., '73.

Comps: *Cristo Redentor; Jeannine; New Girl.* Fav. arrs: *Time After Time* from his big band album; also *New Girl.* LPs: Early small groups (Prestige, Blue Note); later, larger groups: *How Insensitive,* w. Flora Purim and vocal ensemble; *Now Hear This,* with big band; *Introducing Duke Pearson's Big Band; It Could Only Happen With You,* w. F. Purim. LPs w. D. Byrd *At Half Note Cafe; The Cat Walk; I'm Trying To Get Home,* brass with voices; *A New Perspective* (Blue Note).

PEIFFER, BERNARD,* *piano, composer;* also *keyboards, synthesizer;* b. Epinal, France, 10/23/22. To U.S., '54, working primarily in Phila. area. From '66 pl. night clubs, concert

tours and involved with teaching privately and at Wilmington School of Mus., '68; Jenkintown Music School, '73-4; also coll. lectures. Apps. on French TV, '66; *Capt. Kangaroo,* CBS-TV, '67.

Peiffer's career was temporarily halted by a serious illness in '69, but he resumed in '70, pl. in LA for a short period in July of that year at Donte's. Often a guest on the *Mark of Jazz* TV show in Phila., '70-4. Fests: Antibes; Comblain-La-Tour; Middlekerke, Belgium, '66; Bicentennial Continental Congress, Phila., '74; NJF-NY, '75. Wrote music for *Grit,* voted best promotional film of the year, Atlanta Int'l. Film Fest., '68; *Red Light, Green Light* for CBS-TV; other comps: *Poem For A Lonely Child; Rondo; Black Moon; Blues for Django; Manege; Homage To J.S. Bach; Exodus; Prelude Fugue on Lullaby of Birdland.*

LPs: *Bernard Peiffer Plays Lullaby of Birdland* (Poly.)

PEMBERTON, WILLIAM McLANE (BILL),* *bass;* b. Brooklyn, N.Y., 3/5/18. Played w. Frankie Newton in '40s; then built solid reputation w. Rex Stewart; Sy Oliver; Cootie Williams; Tony Scott. Acc. such pianists as Eddie Heywood, Mary Lou Williams, Ellis Larkins, Marian McPartland, Art Tatum; singers Sarah Vaughan, Ella Fitzgerald, Carmen McRae, Lee Wiley, Lena Horne, Pearl Bailey, Josh White, Bobby Short, Sammy Davis Jr. Occupied mainly w. studio work in NYC, '60-6. Member of Earl Hines quartet, '66-9, incl. Russian, So. American tours. Formed JPJ Quartet w. Budd Johnson, Oliver Jackson (q.v.) after the three left Hines. TV, fests., clubs, tours w. JPJ from '69. Also gig w. Bobby Hackett at Roosevelt Grill, '70; *Grande Parade Du Jazz* for G. Wein, Nice '75. Comp: *I Need You.* LPs: w. JPJ (Master Jazz; English RCA); w. Herb Hall-Joe Muranyi; Lou McGarity (Fat Cat's Jazz); John Hardee; Vic Dickenson for French labels.

PENA, RALPH,* *bass;* b. Jarbridge, Nev., 2/24/27. Played in many West Coast gps. w. Shorty Rogers, Ben Webster, Pete Jolly; toured w. Geo. Shearing, Frank Sinatra. Pena was in Mexico to score a film when he was hit by a car; two weeks later, 5/20/69, he died in a Mexico City hospital.

PENLAND, RALPH MORRIS,* *drums, composer;* b. Cincinnati, Ohio, 2/15/53. Stud. at high school, '69-71; stud. and taught at New England Conservatory. Pl. w. Webster Lewis, Boston and Europe, '71-3; Freddie Hubbard, U.S. & Canada, '73-4; Ch. Lloyd, Los Angeles, '75; other gigs in LA w. Eddie Harris, Kenny Burrell, Harold Land. Debut of own unit, Penland Polygon, at Pilgrimage Theatre, Hollywood, Sept. 1975. Infl: Tony Williams, Elvin Jones, Miles Davis, John Coltrane. LPs w. Hubbard (CTI, Col.), Eddie Harris (Atl.).

PEPPER, ARTHUR EDWARD (ART),* *alto saxophone;* also *tenor, soprano saxes, clarinet, flute;* b. Gardena, Cal., 9/1/25. Pl. w. Benny Carter orch. at age 18; briefly w. S. Kenton, '43-4, then again off and on until '52. Problems with narcotics kept him off the scene intermittently for long periods. In '66 he was released from San Quentin after serving three years. During next year, in his own words, "I was scuffling and sitting in with rock bands, playing tenor." For several months in '68 he played lead alto w. B. Rich and was feat. on the ballad *Alfie.* Hospitalized with ruptured spleen, late '68. Rejoined Rich in '69 and traveled with the band across country, but illness soon ended this association. After leaving a hospital, he entered Synanon, the rehabilitation center in Santa Monica, Cal. He remained there three years, occasionally playing with visiting groups.

Bet. '72 and '75 he worked as a bookkeeper in Venice, Cal. Invited to the U. of Denver as jazz clinician on clarinet; soon afterward he was hired by Norlin Music to conduct clinics at high schools, colleges and univs. throughout the U.S. During this time was also completing his biography.

Contrary to previous statements, Pepper feels that his most powerful influences were Lester Young, Zoot Sims, Coltrane, rather than Ch. Parker and Konitz.

LPs: *Gettin' Together; Art Pepper Plus Eleven; The Way It Was* (Contemporary); *Omega Man* w. Carl Perkins (Onyx).

PERAZA, ARMANDO,* *bongos, conga drums, composer;* b. Havana, Cuba, 5/30/24. The former Shearing sideman worked w. C. Tjader from '69. In '70 he joined Mongo Santamaria, visiting Europe with him and pl. at Monterey JF. Pl. in SF w. Azteca combo, '71. Toured w. Santana '71- , incl. trips to Europe in '72, '75; Asia, '72, '74; Central, S. America, '72. Movies: sound track w. L. Schifrin for *Che Guevara,* '69.

LPs: w. Santamaria (Prest.); Santana; New Riders of the Purple Sage (Col.); Creedence Clearwater (Fant.).

PERCIFUL, JACK T.,* *piano;* also *organ;* b. Moscow, Idaho, 11/26/25. With Harry James, '58-74. With Red Kelly in Tumwater, Wash., '75. Made two European tours w. James and app. with him at NJF-NY, '74.

LPs: w. James, *Double Dixie* (Dot); *In A Relaxed Mood* (MGM); w. Corky Corcoran, *Something* (RCS).

PERKINS, WILLIAM REESE (BILL),* *saxophones, clarinets, flutes;* b. San Francisco, Calif., 7/22/24. Ex-Herman, -Kenton. Recording engineer in Hollywood studio 1961-9. Free-lance woodwind player in studios from 59- . TV: Della Reese series on lead alto, '69; alternate sax chairs on *Tonight* show '68- . Was member of Supersax for the first year of its existence. Gigs and records w. Toshiko Akiyoshi orch. 1974-5.

LPs w. Toshiko (RCA); Clare Fischer, *Thesaurus* (Atlantic); w. Paul Chambers, *The East/West Controversy* (Xanadu).

PERLA, GENE AUGUST, *bass, composer,* also *trombone, piano;* b. Woodcliff Lake, N.J., 3/1/40. From ages five to 15 studied w. Czech classical pianist Anca Seidlova. Pl. trombone in high school. Attended Sch. of Engineering, U. of Toledo, '58. In '62 entered Berklee Coll. of Mus. and Boston Conserv. simultaneously. Took up bass in '64. Pl. w. Willie Bobo in NYC and Calif., '67. Toured w. Nina Simone, '68; Woody Herman, '69; w. Sarah Vaughan in US, Canada, Japan and So. America, '70. Beginning in '71, w. Elvin Jones for two and one half yrs. incl. Europe, So. America; Sonny Rollins, '74-5. Formed Stone Alliance w. Steve Grossman, and percussionist Don Alias, '75. Infl: Ted Heath, Miles Davis, Bill Evans, Charlie Haden, Gary Peacock, Elvin Jones. Fest: NJF-NY; Oakland; MJF, all w. Jones. TV: Johnny Carson; Mike Douglas; Merv Griffin; Dick Cavett, w. Vaughan; Billy Eckstine syndicated show. Comp: *P.P. Phoenix; Tergiversation; Eberhard; Nanuri.* Perla has his own label, P.M. (20 Martha St., Woodcliff Lake, N.J.

07675) and has issued records by Elvin Jones; Steve Grossman; and Dave Liebman. LPs: w. Jones, *On the Mountain* (P.M.); *Merry-Go-Round* (BN); w. Simone, *Here Comes the Sun* (RCA); w. Mickey Tucker (Xanadu).

PERSIP, CHARLES LAWRENCE (CHARLI),* *drums, percussion;* b. Morristown, N.J., 7/26/29. Best-known as drummer w. Dizzy Gillespie big band in mid-'50s. Led own gp. which incl. Freddie Hubbard, Roland Alexander, Ron Carter and was busy NYC freelance in early '60s. Toured Japan w. Newport Festival Drum Panorama that also feat. B. Rich, L. Bellson, PJ Jones, '65. Joined Billy Eckstine as accompanist and assistant mus. director, Sept. '66, remaining w. him for seven yrs. In the mid-'70s pl. w. CBA; Archie Shepp; Frank Foster; NYJRC.

During his yrs. w. Eckstine, conducted drum clinics for Brockstein's Drum Shop, Houston; Moe's Drum Shop, Las Vegas; Organization of Drummers, Sydney, Australia. Lectures and seminars at New Eng. Conserv., U. of Mass, Claremont U. Teaching for Jazzmobile; member of staff of music dept. of Henry St. Settlement House, NYC; also private instruction. Book: *How Not to Play Drums.* TV: *Tonight; Mike Douglas; Just Jazz,* all w. Eckstine; *Look Up and Live* w. Mary Lou Williams. Fest: NJF-NY w. Eckstine, '72; tribute to Gillespie w. CBA Ensemble, '74. LPs: w. Eckstine, *Newport in New York, The Soul Session* (Cobble.); w. R.R. Kirk (War. Bros); *We Free Kings* (Trip); w. Gil Evans, *Out of the Cool* (Imp.).

PERSON, HOUSTON, *tenor saxophone;* b. Florence, S.C., 11/10/34. At So. Carolina State Coll. studied w. band director Aaron Harvey. In Army in Germany pl. w. Eddie Harris, Don Menza, Lanny Morgan, Leo Wright, Don Ellis and Lex Humphries. After service attended Hartt Coll. of Music, Hartford, Conn. Went on the road w. organist Johnny Hammond for two yrs.; then formed own gp. In '73 teamed up w. singer Etta Jones for clubs, concerts. They had worked together intermittently from '68. Dan Morgenstern called his playing, "warm, straightforward, unaffected and swinging." Infl: Illinois Jacquet, Gene Ammons, Sonny Stitt, Hank Mobley, Harold Land. LPs: *Get Outa My Way* (Westbound); *Broken Windows, Empty Hallways; Blue Odyssey; Person to Person; Trust in Me; Goodness!; Houston Express; Chocomotive;* w. Don Patterson, *Four Dimensions* (Prest.); w. Tiny Grimes, *Profoundly Blue* (Muse).

PERSSON, AAKE,* *trombone;* b. Hassleholm, Sweden, 2/25/32. Greatly respected during '50s and '60s as possibly Europe's leading jazz trombonist, he played with many visiting Americans, incl. Q. Jones, C. Basie, D. Gillespie; also in Swedish radio studio orch. Rec. w. Clifford Brown, S. Getz, Lars Gullin, H. Mann, Bengt Hallberg and many others. Persson died 2/4/75, reportedly driving his car off a bridge in Stockholm, where he was visiting. He had been living and working in Berlin. LPs w. Clarke-Boland Orch. (Atlantic, BASF, Black Lion, Col.).

PETERSON, HANNIBAL MARVIN CHARLES, *trumpet, composer;* also *koto;* b. Smithville, Tex., 11/11/48. Mother is pianist "of the Earl 'Fatha' Hines school." First instruction from James Wilson in harmony, theory, '62-5. Pl. in Booker T. Washington concert band; Texas City High Sch. band directed by Robert Renfroe, '63. Stud. at North Texas State,

'67-9. Led own Soul Masters, '61. Worked w. Chuck Jackson; T-Bone Walker, '65-7. To NYC '70 where he pl. w. Roy Haynes; Gil Evans; Elvin Jones; Pharoah Sanders; Archie Shepp; Rahsaan Roland Kirk into '74 when he formed the Sunrise Orch. Infl: Coltrane, Malcolm X, Ellington, Leos Janacek, B.B. King, Sun Ra, Cecil Taylor, Leadbelly. TV: w. Texas City Symphonic Band; several Euro. apps. Fest: NJF-NY; Galveston; Berlin; Japan. Comp: *Children of the Fire; The Voyage; Symphony African.* Publ: *The Ripest of My Fruits* (Sunrise Publs., Box 527, Planetarium Station, New York, N.Y. 10024).

Hannibal's playing is full of dramatic energy, and power in the upper register. Gil Evans calls him ''a very special, serious, schooled musician. When you hear the way he writes for strings on his record, *Children of the Fire,* you will realize that.''

LPs: *Children of the Fire* (Sunrise); *Hannibal* (MPS); w. Evans, *Svengali* (Atl.); *There Comes a Time; Plays the Music of Jimi Hendrix* (RCA); w. Richard Davis, *Epistrophy & Now's the Time; Dealin';* w. Eric Kloss, *Essence* (Muse); w. E. Jones, *Live at the Village Vanguard* (Enja).

PETERSON, OSCAR EMMANUEL,* *piano;* also *organ;* b. Montreal, Que, Canada, 8/15/25. Came to U.S. in '49; under management of Norman Granz, travelled regularly with JATP and in concert tours of his own, visiting Europe annually, through the 1950s & 60s. In later years he extended his overseas activities, working frequently in Japan, Australia, South America, Mexico, and taking part in college lectures and seminars throughout the U.S. and Canada.

In 1972 Peterson abandoned his trio format to appear for a while exclusively as a solo recitalist in concerts. He later resumed using the trio, dividing his time at concerts between solo and trio work. His sidemen changed more frequently than in earlier years. They included Bobby Durham, Ray Price on drums; Joe Pass on guitar; George Mraz, Niels-Henning Orsted Pedersen on bass. He was also reunited for occasional concerts and recordings with sidemen who had worked for him in the 1950s, among them guitarists Herb Ellis and Barney Kessel and bassist Ray Brown.

In 1974 Peterson had his own television series in Canada. Entitled *Oscar Peterson Presents,* it featured leading jazzmen and singers as guests. The series was awarded a plaque at the 17th International Film and TV Festival in New York. In 1975 Peterson's album *The Trio* won a Grammy award. Other awards: Toronto Civic Medal, 1971; Honorary Doctorate of Laws from Carleton University, 1973; Medal of Service of the Order of Canada, 1973; Late in '74 Peterson went to the USSR, with Orsted Pedersen and drummer Jake Hanna; however, their projected tour of the Soviet Union was abruptly cut short following disagreements about conditions. By the mid 1970s Peterson had won the *Playboy* ''Musicians' Musicians'' award ten times, and continued frequently to win other magazine awards at home and abroad. For a five-year period starting in the late 1960s Peterson made all his records in Germany while under contract to MPS-BASF. He subsequently recorded for Granz's new label, Pablo, incl. five duo albums made respectively w. D. Gillespie; H. Edison; J. Faddis; C. Terry; and R. Eldridge. Also sessions from Montreux JF, '75.

Publications: *Jazz Exercises and Pieces; Oscar Peterson New Piano Solos* (Hansen Publications, Inc., 1842 West Avenue, Miami Beach, Fla. 33139).

LPs: *Affinity; Collection; Newport Years; Night Train; Night Train, Vol. 2; Return Engagement; Something Warm; O.P. Trio; Very Tall,* feat. M. Jackson; *West Side Story* (Verve); *Exclusively For My Friends; Great Connection; Hello Herbie,* feat. Ellis; *In A Mellow Mood; In Tune,* feat. Singers Unlimited; *Reunion Blues; Tristeza on Piano; Walking the Line;* (BASF); *Featuring Stephane Grappelli* (Pres.); *History of an Artist; The Trio; The Greatest Jazz Concert in the World;* w. Joe Pass *À Salle Pleyel; Satch and Josh* w. Basie (Pablo).

PETROVIC, BOSKO, *vibes, composer;* b. Bjelovar, Yugoslavia, 2/18/35. Violin at seven; accordion, piano, drums at 15. Took up vibes in '66, and four years later founded Zagreb Jazz Quartet, which for the next decade was widely considered to be the best combo in Yugoslavia. From '70, led new quartet, known as B.P. Convention. Has pl. w. John Lewis, S. Getz, G. Mulligan, A. Farmer, many other American musicians, as well as Albert Mangelsdorff, Svend Asmussen, Michal Urbaniak. Also occasionally leads Bosko Petrovic Nonconvertible All Stars. Infls: Ch. Parker, D. Gillespie, L. Hampton, D. Ellington. Style of playing strongly infl. by Yugoslavian folk music. Comps: *With Pain I Was Born; Sigurd's Garden; Blue Sunset.*

LPs: w. Zagreb Jazz Quartet, *Feel So Fine,* feat. Buck Clayton, Joe Turner; *With Pain I Was Born* (Fontana); w. B.P. Convention, *Green Mood;* w. Nonconvertible group, *Swinging East* (MPS); w. O. Nelson, *Swiss Suite* (Fl. Dutchman).

PHILLIPS, ESTHER (Esther Mae Jones),* *singer;* b. Galveston, Texas, 12/23/25. First successes singing w. Johnny Otis Band, '49-52, billed as ''Little Esther.'' Made comeback in mid-'60s and, after another smaller career setback, rebounded again beginning w. app. on *Tonight Show,* '69. Reunited w. Otis on several occasions incl. Monterey JF. A series of recs. for the Kudu label served to establish her w. a new audience as well as put her in touch w. old following. In '73 she was nominated for a Grammy Award for ''Best R&B Performance by a Female Vocalist.'' The winner, Aretha Franklin, gave her trophy to Miss Phillips.

Vernon Gibbs wrote in *Essence:* ''Her voice has a raunchy fullness which compares with the best gospel singers, a boldly swinging quality which testifies to the influence of those singers who come from the ballad-blues or big band swinging traditions . . .''

LPs: *From a Whisper to a Scream; Alone Again, Naturally; Black-Eyed Blues; Performance; What A Difference a Day Makes* (Kudu).

PHILLIPS, JOSEPH EDWARD (FLIP),* *tenor saxophone;* also *bass clarinet;* b. Brooklyn, N.Y., 2/26/15. The former star of Woody Herman's first Herd, and JATP, took up residence in Pompano Beach, Fla. in the '60s, managing a condominium and working w. own gp. In '70s he began traveling again for apps. at Colo. Jazz Party, annually from '70, and Pasadena Jazz Fest. Took part in W. Herman alumni reunion at NJF-NY, '72. Early in '75 he relinquished the managerial job and returned to music full time. Played w. Teddy Wilson at Michael's Pub. NYC, Aug. '75, revealing he had lost none of his warm-toned, vibrant skill. LPs: *Flip in Florida* (Onyx); *A Melody From the Sky* (Bob Thiele Music); *Colorado Jazz Party* (MPS-BASF); *Newport in New York, The Jam Sessions,* vols. 3&4 (Cobblestone); w. B. Butterfield (DCS).

PIANO CHOIR. see Cowell, Stanley.

PICHON, WALTER (FATS), * *piano, composer;* b. New Orleans, La., 1906. Long active at the Absinthe House in NO, Pichon cont. to work sporadically during the '60s. He died in Chi., 2/25/67.

PIERCE, WILHELMINA GOODSON (BILLIE), * *piano, singer;* b. Pensacola, Fla., ca. 1905. Living in NO from '30, Pierce and her husband DeDe worked together for many years and were among the local musicians who benefited from the traditionalist revival of the '60s. They rec. for Atl., Riverside and various independent companies, and were often heard at Preservation Hall in NO, as well as on hundreds of coll. campuses and at jazz fests. She died 9/29/74 in NO. LP: *New Orleans Legends—Live, Vol. 15* (Jazzology).

PIERCE, BOBBY, *organ, piano, singer;* b. Columbus, Ohio, 1942. Mother plays piano. Lessons at age four. By the time he was eight infl. by Don Patterson who is six years older. Own bands, off and on, from age 16. Played organ w. S. Stitt, G. Ammons, J. Moody. With Clarence Wheeler, '72, then began rec. w. own gp. Infl: Tyner, Coltrane, O. Peterson; Ray Charles, O.C. Smith, Bill Withers. Comps: *I Remember Ray; To Newport With Love; New York; Children Are the Creator's Messengers; Sleep Baby.* LPs: *Introducing Bobby Pierce* (Cobble.); *New York* (Muse).

PIERCE, JOSEPH DE LACROIS (DEDE), * *trumpet, cornet;* b. New Orleans, La., 2/18/04. Still active locally and in concert apps. in other cities during the '70s, Pierce died 11/23/73 in NO. LP: see Pierce, Billie.

PIERCE, NAT, * *piano, composer;* b. Somerville, Mass., 7/16/25. Pl. w. Woody Herman Sept. 1951-June '55; rejoined as arr. & road mgr. spring '61-June '66. From that time, has cont. to write occ. for Herman, but mainly active in and around LA pl. & arr. for C. McRae, L. Bellson, Bill Berry; also many arrs. for C. Basie, Anita O'Day, Earl Hines, J. Rushing, Sweets Edison, B. Tate; and as pianist w. Z. Sims, Ch. Barnet et al. Subbed for eight weeks in S. Kenton band '72 during Kenton's illness. Led own band in LA '72 and again in '74-5.

Pierce also has been taking part in high school and college clinics. He has been seen in almost all major U.S. and European festivals, mainly w. Herman. Was subject of two long essays in Stanley Dance's *The World of Swing* (Scribners).

In 1975 Pierce claimed that he was ''now recognized as the second best rhythm pianist in the world—Basie is first; Ellington has passed on.''

LPs (as pianist and/or arr.) w. Herman (Col.); Roy Eldridge (Master Jazz); Rushing (Col.); J. Hodges (RCA); L. Bellson (Pablo); Basie (Roulette).

PIESTRUP, DONALL JAMES, *composer, arranger;* also *piano;* b. Santa Cruz, Cal., 12/19/37. Grad. UC Berkeley, '60, where he was a first-stringer on football team. Led own band from '61 in SF Bay Area. Began arr. for B. Rich band, '66. Moved to LA, '67 and became mainly active in commercial music, writing jingles etc. Also own band at Donte's.

Comps: *New Blues; Goodbye Yesterday; Day's Journey; Group Shot,* for Rich; others for LA Neophonic; M. Ferguson. Early infl: Parker, Gillespie, Shearing; then M. Davis, Coltrane, T. Jones, Q. Jones, O. Nelson, B. Holman, Ellington.

LPs: w. Rich (Pac. Jazz, RCA).

PIKE, DAVID SAMUEL (DAVE), * *vibes, marimba, composer;* b. Detroit, Mich., 3/23/38. Played at Berlin Jazz Fest. 1968 and remained in Europe for five years, leading his Dave Pike Set, a quartet w. German musicians. Worked at numerous jazz festivals, clubs etc. on Continent, then settled in Southern California, where he organized a new group in Orange County. A pioneer in amplified vibes, which he began playing in 1960. During the 1970s Pike's group played almost continuously at Hungry Joe's in Huntington Beach, Calif., visiting Los Angeles for occasional gigs.

LPs: *Infra-Red; Riff for Rent; Salamao* (MPS-BASF); *Pike's Peak* (Epic). Earlier LPs w. H. Mann, Jazz Couriers, Paul Bley.

PISANO, JOHN, * *guitar, composer;* b. New York City, 2/6/31. Came to prominence w. Chico Hamilton quint., '56-8. Joined Herb Alpert and the Tijuana Brass, '65, recording and touring the U.S., Europe, Australia, New Zealand, Japan. In '70 TJB disbanded and Pisano continued freelancing and app. w. own group at local clubs. Rejoined TJB in '74, remaining until early '75. Formed quartet with Barry Zweig for night club engagements, and also toured extensively w. Peggy Lee as her mus. dir. Pisano is a talented composer and several of his works have app. on albums by TJB and Lee. Among them are: *So What's New; Slick; The Robin.* Four TV specs. in U.S., one in England w. TJB; also Newport JF, '68.

LPs: *Quietly There,* w. Bill Perkins Quintet (Riverside); w. TJB; w. Lani Hall (A & M).

PIZZARELLI, JOHN (BUCKY), *guitar;* b. Paterson, N.J., 1/9/26. Uncle, Bobby Domenick, played guitar with name bands. Educ. Central High School in Paterson. Self-taught while sitting in w. Joe Mooney. Army service in Europe and Philippines, '44-6. Toured w. Vaughn Monroe orch. '56-63. Staff musician at NBC, NYC, '54-66. Later on staff at ABC, playing Dick Cavett show w. Bobby Rosengarden orch. European tours w. B. Goodman, '70, '72, '73, '74; rec. 2 LPs w. Goodman in Stockholm. Pizzarelli, who plays a seven string elec. guitar, was feat. for some time in the early '70s as half of a guitar duo w. George Barnes. Playing a solo concert at Town Hall, NYC, '73, he was praised by John S. Wilson, according to whom ''he showed that he could sustain the better part of an hour's program playing unaccompanied and make it a varied and enlivening experience.'' During the concert, Pizzarelli also played a Villa-Lobos work on classical guitar and was joined by his 15 year old daughter, Mary, for a pair of guitar duets in a style estab. during the '30s by Carl Kress and Dick McDonough.

Own duo, often incl. Zoot Sims, at Soerabaja, NYC in '70s.

Publ: *Touch of Class,* guitar book (Keith Perkins Publ., Famous Solos Ent., Box 567, Saddle River, N.J. 07458). LPs: *Nightwings* (Fly. Dutch.); *Green Guitar Blues,* solos; *Bucky Plays Bix & Kress,* five guitars (Monmouth-

Evergreen); *Guitars Pure and Honest,* duets w. Geo. Barnes (A & R); *A Flower For All Seasons* (Choice); *Nirvana,* co-leader w. Z. Sims (Groove Merchant).

PIZZI, RAY, *saxophones, flute, bassoon;* b. Boston, Mass., 1/19/43. Berklee Coll. '61-2; Boston Conserv '60-4; earned Bach. of Ed. & credits towards masters degree on clarinet. Stud. improv. w. Herb Pomeroy; bassoon w. Simon Kovar. From '64-69 teaching mus. in publ. schools in Boston, taking leave of absence during '66 to tour w. W. Herman orch. Moved to Cal., '69, and began working w. L. Bellson in '70, remaining for a year. With Willie Bobo, '72, '73; brief tenures during '73-5 w. F. Zappa, T. Jones-M. Lewis, S. Manne, Ravi Shankar, Moacir Santos, H. Mancini, B. Kessel. Feat. soloist on Dinah Shore TV show, '75. Fests: Newport, '71; Monterey, '73, w. Bellson; Concord, '71, w. Kessel; Monterey, '72 w. Jones-Lewis. Pizzi during the '70s was also busy teaching priv. improv. course. Infls: Ravel, Debussy, Ch. Parker, J. Coltrane, S. Rollins.

LPs: w. Santos, *Maestro; Saudade; Carnival of Spirits* (Blue Note); others w. Shankar (Dark Horse); Luis Gasca (Fant.).

POINDEXTER, NORWOOD (PONY),* *alto, soprano, tenor saxes, clarinet;* b. New Orleans, La., 2/8/26. After working w. accompanying gp. to Lambert, Hendricks & Ross and w. own gp. in early '60s, left for Europe '64 and has been there from that time, pl. clubs and fests. Living in Germany in '70s. Comp: *Sopa Prisa; Talgo; Freeze; It Don't Feel Like It Used to Feel; Movin' On; Lucky Duck.* LPs: *En Barcelona,* w. daughter Dina as vocalist (Spiral); *The Happy Life of Pony; Annie Ross & Pony Poindexter; Alto Summit* (MPS); *Super Sax Section* (French Epic).

POINTER SISTERS, *singers, composers;* b. Oakland, Calif.; **RUTH,** 3/19/46; **ANITA,** 1/23/48; **PATRICIA (BONNIE),** 7/11/50; **JUNE,** 11/30/53. Parents, Sarah and Elton Pointer, both Protestant pastors. The daughters sang gospel music in the church choir when June was seven years old. Early exp. as backup singers w. Cold Blood, later w. Taj Mahal and various other recording artists, incl. Esther Phillips, Elvin Bishop, Dave Mason.

The sisters credit their success to David Rubinson, their manager, who helped to bring them back to San Francisco when they were stranded in Houston, Tex. He rounded out their musical education by playing them jazz records, including those of Lambert, Hendricks & Ross. For some time Ruth was not a member of the group, having had to take a job as a key punch operator. The four sisters organized an act and scored a major success in July 1973 at the Troubadour in Hollywood. Before long they were in steady demand for guest apps. on national television programs.

June Pointer later left the group owing to illness; after the Pointers had worked as a trio for a while, she returned and they continued to enjoy success with a unique repertoire that comprised jazz, r & b., rock, soul and contemporary pop material. (In Nov. '75, June again left the group for reasons of poor health.) As composers, they were partially or wholly responsible for a series of songs such as *Jada; Sugar* (not connected with the old jazz songs of the same names); *Shaky Flat Blues; Fairy Tale;* and *How Long (Betcha Got A Chick on the Side).*

Among their best known jazz performances are *Cloud-*

burst; Little Pony; and *Salt Peanuts.* Opinions concerning the validity of these performances was mixed, some critics feeling that they were not innately jazz-oriented. Others felt that their style and elan transcended category and that their ability to interpret a wide range of material gave them a quality unique in the age of rock groups.

LPs: Blue Thumb; also guest app. singing *Flat Foot Floogee* on Jon Hendricks' *Tell Me The Truth* (Arista).

POLCER, EDWARD JOSEPH (ED), *cornet;* also *vibes;* b. Paterson, N.J., 2/10/37. Studied w. Prof. James V. Dittamo, '44-50; under his direction pl. solo cornet in Paterson Civic Orch. at age 13. Played w. Knights of Dixieland at Hawthorne, N.J., H.S., '50-4; while at Princeton U., '54-8, where he received Engineering Deg., pl. w. Stan Rubin's Tigertown Five, touring Europe twice; all major Eastern colls.; Grace Kelly's wedding, Apr. '56. From '58-69 free-lanced in NY, NJ, Conn., frequently subbing for Max Kaminsky at Jimmy Ryan's. From '69 w. Balaban & Cats. Toured US & Canada w. Benny Goodman, '72; US w. Bob Greene, '75. Has also worked as engineer-purchasing agent, '63-72; dir. of NY Jazz Museum's Touring Program, '75. A melodic, mellow-toned cornetist with an unforced delivery. Infl: Ruby Braff, Louis Armstrong, Bobby Hackett, Muggsy Spanier. Fest: Odessa JP; NJF-NY w. Balaban, '75. LPs: w. Balaban & Cats, *A Night at the New Eddie Condon's* (Classic Jazz); *Bits & Pieces of Balaban & Cats; A Night at the Town House* (Balaban & Cats); w. Big Chief Russell Moore's Pow Wow Jazz Band (Jazz Art Workshop); w. Jane Harvey (Classic Jazz).

POLLACK, BEN,* *leader, drums;* b. Chicago, Ill., 6/22/03. The former drummer, whose band in the '20s incl. B. Goodman, J. Teagarden, Glenn Miller, Bud Freeman, J. McPartland, remained active in music off and on until the mid '60s, when he retired to Palm Springs, running a restaurant there. He committed suicide by hanging himself in his Palm Springs home, 6/7/71.

LPs: *Pick-A-Rib Boys,* w. Teagarden; Ben Pollack-Wingy Manone (Savoy).

POMEROY, HERB,* *composer, trumpet, educator;* b. Gloucester, Mass., 4/15/30. Faculty member at Berklee Coll. of Music., Boston, 1955- . Dir. of jazz bands at Mass. Inst. of Tech. 1963- . Host on own weekly half hour TV series, *Jazz with Herb Pomeroy,* 1965-7. Festivals: Jyvaskyla, Finland, '68; Montreux, '70. Comps: two original scores, *The Road of the Phoebe Snow; Wilderness of Mirrors,* for Boston Ballet Co.; commissioned by Nat. Jazz Ensemble to write extended work, *Jolly Chocolate,* premiered at Lincoln Center, NYC, Jan. '74.

Pomeroy has continued to lead a band in the course of his work at Berklee; many now celebrated jazz artists have passed through its ranks. Berklee has issued annual series of LPs by student bands on its own label. Among the sidemen who have graduated from these groups are Alan Broadbent, Lin Biviano, Joe and Pat LaBarbera, Harvey Mason, Miroslav Vitous, Ernie Watts, Mike Mantler, Gene Perla.

LPs: *Jazz in the Classroom* (Berklee Press Publs., 1140 Boylston St., Boston, Mass., 02215).

PONDER, JAMES WILLIS (JIMMY), *guitar, composer;* b. Pittsburgh, Pa., 5/10/46. Self-taught. Began pl. and singing in junior high school but really got serious after hearing Wes Montgomery, '60. Pl. w. Sam Pearson in Pitts. for two yrs. in mid-'60s. With Charles Earland, '66-9. Sat in w. Jimmy McGriff in Pitts. Moved to NYC '68, pl. briefly w. Fathead Newman. Worked w. Newark tenorman Joe Thomas, '69-72, then formed own gp. In '75 co-led Final Edition w. Grassella Oliphant. Infl: Montgomery, Grant Green, Kenny Burrell, Thornel Schwartz. TV: *Positively Black* w. Irene Reid; Educ. TV w. own gp. Comp: *Peace Movement; Jennifer; Illusions; Sometimes I Get the Blues.* LPs: *Illusions* (Imp.); *While My Guitar Gently Weeps* (Cadet); w. John Patton, *That Certain Feeling;* S. Turrentine-Shirley Scott, *A Common Touch;* Lou Donaldson; Donald Byrd; Lonnie Smith; Reuben Wilson (BN); McGriff (Gr. Merch.); Mickey Tucker (Xanadu); Jack McDuff (Cadet).

PONTY, JEAN-LUC,* *acoustic and electric violins, violectra, composer;* also *keyboards;* b. Arranches, Normandy, France, 9/29/42. Classical violinist until highly successful app. at Antibes Jazz Fest. in 1964. Freelanced all over Europe from '66-9. In 1969 he came to U.S. for recordings and night club and fest. dates w. Geo. Duke trio. Back to France, working w. own group throughout Europe, '70-2. In '73 Ponty emigrated to U.S. Soon began working w. F. Zappa and Mothers of Invention, and in '74 joined the Mahavishnu Orch. Regular winner on violin in DB Critics' and Readers' Polls from '69. Fest. Apps. at Monterey, '67 and '69; Newport, '70, '74, Berlin, '71, Montreux, '72. Composed and arranged all selections on *Ponty-Grappelli* and *Upon The Wings of Music* (Atlantic) albums.

Ponty told Steve McGuire of DB that it took him three or four years to make the mental leap from classical music to jazz: "The amplification and the weird sounds I got helped me make the step. It helped me get away from the classical sound and classical esthetics and forget what the teachers had been teaching me. In the rock experience now I have learned more and more about the use of electronics . . ." Ponty has used a baritone violin with the strings tuned one octave lower than the normal violin. Known as a veritone or violectra, it has a range between viola and cello.

His association with Zappa established Ponty as the first jazz-experienced violinist to make a totally successful crossover into the worlds of rock and electronic music. His technique and creativity have consistently met every challenge that has confronted him while playing in an unprecedented variety of settings.

Own LPs: *Sunday Walk; King Kong* (BASF-MPS); *Live At The Experience* (World Pacific); w. Mahavishnu, *Apocalypse* (Col.); *Violin Summit* (MPS).

PORCINO, AL,* *trumpet;* b. New York City, 5/14/25. After many years on the road w. bands of Krupa, T. Dorsey, Kenton, Basie, Chubby Jackson and W. Herman, settled in LA, pl. w. Terry Gibbs big band, working in studios and touring w. Sinatra, Vic Damone, Eddie Fisher. Roger Miller series on NBC-TV, '66; Hollywood Palace on ABC-TV, '67. Toured w. B. Rich '68, incl. app. at Ronnie Scott's, London, feat. singing & pl. Louis Armstrong's *Jubilee,* which he uses as personal theme song. To NYC '69 where he pl. in pit for *Promises, Promises;* then joined Thad Jones-Mel Lewis and made two European tours w. them. Premiered *Friends and Love,* '70; and *Together,* '71 w. Chuck Mangione. Worked winter season in Miami Beach before joining Herman, '72. Premiered *Land of Make Believe* w. Mangione. Toured col-

leges as clinician for King Instr. Co., '73. His own band backed Mel Torme at the Maisonette, NYC, '74. While working in the show band at the Playboy Club in McAfee, N.J., he revived his band briefly in the summer of '75. Fest: NJF-NY w. Herman '72. William Whitworth wrote of his exceptional ability: "I think Al has been more successful than any other lead player in combining bigness with brilliance . . . put him in a brass section and you hear a projection, a beautiful sound, a pulsing time, and a fiery conception that . . . constitute a landmark in the history of jazz lead playing."

LPs: *The Raven Speaks* w. Herman (Fant.); *Together; Friends And Love* w. Mangione (Merc.); *Mercy, Mercy* w. Rich (Wor. Pac.); *Consummation* w. Jones-Lewis (Blue Note); *Mel Torme Live at the Maisonette* (Atl.); Sinatra-Ellington (Reprise).

PORTAL, MICHEL, *clarinet, saxophone;* b. Bayonne, France, 11/27/35. Stud. clarinet at Conservatoire de Paris. Active in all forms of contemporary music; inspired by Charles Mingus, E. Dolphy, Stockhausen and many others. Led own jazz group heard on French LP *Michel Portal Unit at Chateauvallon.* Other LPs: *Our Meanings and Our Feelings; Splendid Yzlment; Alors!!!*

POTTER, CHARLES THOMAS (TOMMY),* *bass;* b. Philadelphia, Pa., 9/21/18. The one-time bassist w. the Charlie Parker quintet in the '40s, played w. Tyree Glenn, Sweets Edison, Buck Clayton in early '60s. Later free-lancing w. J. McPartland; Buddy Tate; Pervis Hendson. Civil service employee in Brooklyn Hospital recreation department. Own group for club dates, '75. Appeared w. Jackie McLean, Hank Jones and Max Roach, playing and talking about Charlie Parker in a program devoted to Bird on ABC-TV's *Like It Is,* '75. LPs: reissues of Parker's Dial sessions (Spotlite), Savoy sessions (Arista).

POWELL, BENJAMIN GORDON (BENNY),* *trombone;* b. New Orleans, La., 3/1/30. In addition to studio work w. Merv Griffin TV show, Powell pl. w. T. Jones-M. Lewis, '66-70; Duke Pearson, '68-70. From '66-70 he was on the Board of Directors of Jazzmobile; he also served as a teacher in that org., and in '70 was Executive Director of Jazz Interactions.

Moving to LA in '70 w. the Griffin show, he worked on movie sound tracks, and from '72 was co-leader with his wife, singer Petsye Powell, of the combo Life Style. Dir. of lecture-concert programs for LA public schools, '73; helped organize Jazz Nexus lecture-concert series through Local 47 of the Musicians' Union. Many other activities as teacher, concert organizer, along w. gigs in local big bands incl. T. Gibbs, Bill Berry, B. Holman.

Fests: Concord, w. Berry, K. Winding, others; Newport/N.Y., w. M. Legrand, and w. C. Basie reunion band; Monterey, w. Q. Jones.

LPs: w. Donald Byrd, D. Pearson, Jones-Lewis, Moacir Santos (BN).

POWELL, MELVIN (MEL),* *piano, composer;* b. New York City, 2/12/23. No longer a participant in the jazz scene, the former B. Goodman pianist during the '70s was Dean of Music at Cal. Inst. of Arts in Valencia, Cal.

PRATT, BOBBY, *trombone, piano;* b. South Glens Falls, N.Y., 5/23/26. Studied trombone w. his brother, Norman Pratt. Began prof. career in Schenectady, N.Y. pl. in clubs and burlesque at age 15. To NYC '42. Pl. w. Charlie Barnet, '43-4; one nighters w. Tommy Reynolds from East to West Coast, '44. Worked w. Johnny Richards; Georgie Auld, '44; Stan Kenton, '45; Raymond Scott, '45-6; Lennie Lewis, '47; Sam Donahue, '48-9; Johnny Bothwell, '49-50. While dental work was being completed in '50 switched to piano on which he is self-taught. In the '40s and '50s pl. w. C. Parker; B. Webster, C. Hawkins, Big Sid Catlett, Trummy Young, Max Roach, Lester Young, Slam Stewart, Vic Dickenson, Dizzy Gillespie, Eddie Heywood, Billy Butterfield, Sonny Dunham, Wild Bill Davison, George Wettling and Gene Krupa. In the '60s w. Ruby Braff; Billy May; and Jimmy McPartland. From '67 at Jimmy Ryan's: piano, '67-70; trombone from '70; worked w. Max Kaminsky; Tony Parenti; Zutty Singleton; Marshall Brown; J. McPartland; Herman Autrey; and Roy Eldridge. Infl: Vic Dickenson, Trummy Young, Lester Young, Charlie Parker, Eldridge, Billy Kyle, Count Basie. TV: NJF-NY w. Eldridge, PBS, '73; special w. Bobby Hackett, Nicol Williamson. Film: soundtrack for *Book of Numbers*. First rec. w. J. Richards on Musicraft, '44; Lennie Lewis on Queen, '47. LP: w. Eldridge, *Little Jazz and the Jimmy Ryan's All Stars* (DRE, Jimmy Ryan's, 154 West 54th St., New York, N.Y.).

PRESTON, DONALD WARD (DON), *Moog synthesizer; also all keyboards, string bass, composer;* b. Flint, Mich., 9/21/32. Father is resident composer for Detroit Symph. Grad. Cass Tech. High Sch., Detroit, 1950. Prof. debut w. Herbie Mann, '51-3; w. Hal MacIntyre, '57-8; Nelson Riddle, '58. In LA, app. w. Carla and Paul Bley trios, '57-8; duo w. Ch. Haden, '59. All through '60s was involved with experimental jazz w. Don Ellis, Paul Beaver, Emil Richards et al. From '67-74, assoc. w. F. Zappa and Mothers of Invention, touring all over the world. Also European tour and Village Vanguard w. Gil Evans, '71.

Preston, a prolific composer has had commissions from sculptors, dancers etc. One work, *Juice,* for dancer Meredith Monk, was perf. at Guggenheim Museum in NYC. LPs: w. C. Bley, *Escalator Over The Hill* (JCOA); w. Bobbi Humphrey, *Satin Doll* (Blue Note); numerous albums w. Mothers of Invention.

PREVIN, ANDRE,* *piano, composer, conductor;* b. Berlin, Germany, 4/6/29. Comp. and arr. for motion pic. studios from '48, but maintained dual career, frequently recording jazz LPs in '50s and early '60s, the best known being *My Fair Lady,* a hit in '57.

By the mid '60 Previn was inactive in jazz. He conducted the Houston Symph., '67-9, and was principal conductor and artistic director of the London Symph. from '68. Cond. all major orchs. in U.S. and Europe; toured worldwide, appearing mostly at opera houses. Own series on BBC-TV; also interview shows with musician guests. Remained active as pianist, but not in jazz.

Publs: *Andre Previn: Music Face to Face,* (Hamish Hamilton, London, England); *Edward Greenfield: Andre Previn* (Ian Allen, Shepperton, Surrey, England.)

Jazz LPs on Contemporary; also *Joplin: The Easy Winners,* w. Itzhak Perlman (Angel).

PREVOST, EDDIE, *drums;* b. Hitchen, Hertfordshire, England, 6/22/42. Mainly active, since '65, with the group known as AMM (duo w. Lou Gare, q.v.), but also performs w. own sextet. Has app. all over Europe with both groups and participates in lectures, recitals and workshops.

LPs: w. AMM on Elektra, Mainstream, Incus, Emanem.

PRICE, JESSE, *drums;* b. Memphis, Tenn. 1910. The veteran of many Kansas City bands, who worked briefly w. Count Basie in early '30s, mid-40s, and who also pl. w. Stan Kenton for a few months in 1944, was a principal performer in a reunion of KC musicians at the Monterey JF, 1971. By this time he was ailing, and in March 1974, when he went home to Kansas City to take part in a documentary film, he was terminally ill. He died of cancer, 4/20/74 in Los Angeles.

LP w. Harlan Leonard (RCA).

PRIESTER, JULIAN ANTHONY,* *trombone;* b. Chicago, Ill., 6/29/35. Early experience w. Sun Ra in mid-'50s. To NYC '58, joining Max Roach gp. the following year and pl. w. him into the early '60s w. the band that incl. Eric Dolphy, Clifford Jordan, Booker Little, etc. Free-lanced in NYC. Six mos. w. Duke Ellington in late '60s. With Herbie Hancock sextet from '70-3. Living in SF in mid-'70s, pl. w. a gp. of musicians incl. Bayete, Henry Franklin, etc., experimenting w. electronic sounds such as wah-wah pedal. Comp: *Wandering Spirit Song.* LPs: *Love, Love* (ECM); w. Hancock, *Mwandishi; Crossings* (War. Bros.); *Sextant* (Col.); Billy Harper, *Capra Black* (Strata-East); Roach, *Percussion Bitter Sweet; It's Time* (Imp.); Johnny Hammond, *Gears* (Milestone); Art Blakey, *Live!* (Trip).

PRINCE, ROLAND DON MATTHEW, *guitar, composer; also piano;* b. St. John's, Antigua, W.I., 8/27/46. Youngest of 12 children, most of whom studied music. Sisters pl. classical piano; brothers had local bands. Pl. piano at three; stud. for five yrs. while teenager. Self-taught on guitar at 12; pl. w. brother's band. Moved to Toronto at 19, pl. w. local mus.; stud. arr. & comp. w. Gordon Delamont; To NYC, '69. Worked w. Jack McDuff, '69-70; Billy Mitchell, off and on, from '70; Lonnie Smith; Wynton Kelly; gigs w. A. Blakey, '71; S. Turrentine; own trio; Newport All Stars, '73; gigs w. Jimmy Smith, '74; Elvin Jones, '74-5. Infl: Radio Havana (Latin and Calypso music while he was growing up); Nelson Symonds; Nat Cole; Ernest Ranglin; T. Monk; Wes Montgomery; Christian; Parker; Coltrane. TV: w. Lucky Thompson, NET '72; Europe w. E. Jones;. Fest: NJF-NY w. Newport All Stars, '73; w. E. Jones; Euro. fests. w. Jones. Comp: *Red Pearl; Love and Innocence; Antigua (Anti-Calypso); Uriah; Iron Band Dance; Geneva; Stachel's Prayer (Answer).* LPs: own date for Vanguard; w. E. Jones (Vang., East-West); J. Moody (Vang.); J. Hartman (Perception); Larry Willis (Gr. Mer.); Roy Haynes; Pete Yellin; Buddy Terry (Main.); Shirley Scott (Cadet); Earl May; *Compost* w. J. DeJohnette (Col.).

PRITCHARD, DAVID, *guitar, composer;* b. Pasadena, Calif., 3/3/49. Stud. at U.C. Santa Barbara, but mainly self-taught. Led Quintet De Sade, '67-9; toured East Coast and Europe w. Gary Burton quartet, '69; also pl. w. Mike Gibbs band. Perf. jazz and poetry w. Kenneth Rexroth, '70. Perf. and rec. w. Peter Robinson's Contraband group; film work w. G. Melle; freelance activities in NYC, '71-2. From '73 worked in LA w. Don Ellis, Don Preston-Emil Richards group; Oscar Brown Jr., and others. Led own group, Halcyon, at Cellar Theatre, Hungry Joe's, other locations in LA area, '75. Infls: W. Montgomery, G. Szabo, L. Coryell, Miles Davis, Carla Bley, Mike Gibbs, Chick Corea, John Coltrane. Comps: *Henniger Flats,* rec. by Burton on *Throb* (Atl.); *Reverie* for Contraband.

LPs: Contraband, *Time & Space* (Epic); w. Pat Britt (Vee Jay); Quintet De Sade (Absolutely Frank Productions).

PROBERT, GEORGE ARTHUR JR., *soprano saxophone;* b. Los Angeles, Cal., 3/5/27. Pl. w. Bob Scobey, '50-3; Kid Ory, '54; Firehouse Five Plus 2, '55-71. In '72, guest star at concerts in NO and Atlantic; freelance rec. and club work. Formed own Once Or Twice Band, '73, working in LA. Led group for six months on Mondy night dixieland sessions at Concerts by the Sea, Redondo Beach, Cal. Pl. at Manassas JF, '74. In addition to this own band, he gigged w. Fine Time trio, feat. G. Wiggins, piano, and Bill Douglass, drums. Pl. fests. and concerts in France, Belgium and Holland. In '75 toured Europe again; also app. at Sacramento Dixie Jubilee.

Own LPs on Black Panther (Belgium); Nobility; Fat Cat; Jazzology.

PROCOPE, RUSSELL,* *alto, soprano saxes, clarinet;* b. New York City, 8/11/08. Joined Duke Ellington in '45 and was w. the band until Ellington's death in May '74. He then became part of the Brooks Kerr trio, working at Gregory's in NYC from that time. Won DB Critics' poll on clarinet, '70-3. LPs: see Ellington.

PUERLING, EUGENE THOMAS (GENE),* *singer;* b. Milwaukee, Wisc., 3/31/29. The one-time member of the Hi-Lo's, the popular vocal gp. of the '50s, was at the head of another talented vocal gp., Singers Unlimited, in the '70s. LPs: *Singers Unlimited; Four of Us;* w. Oscar Peterson, *In Tune* (BASF).

PUGH, JAMES EDWARD, *trombone;* also *bass trombone, bass trumpet, euphonium;* b. Butler, Pa., 11/12/50. Stud. in Atlanta, Ga., '61-3; Pittsburgh, '63-8; Eastman School, Rochester, '68-72; jazz and arr. w. C. Mangione and others. Pl. w. Eastman jazz combo and Arrangers Orch., '68-72; Mangione, '71-2. Principal trombone w. Rochester Phil., summer' 72. Joined W. Herman Oct. '72 and gained considerable prestige as lead and jazz trombonist in this band, app. at many fests. incl. Newport, '73 and '75; Concord, '73; Montreux, Pori, Pescara, Belvedere (Canada), '74. Comp: *Art for Art's Sake (Concerto for Bass Trombone and Orchestra).*

While studying, Pugh received many citations for his superior performances, including an award from Eastman School. Infls. as player: Urbie Green, Carl Fontana; as composer: Gustav Mahler, Stravinsky, Gil Evans.

LPs: *The Eastman Trombone Choir* (Mark); w. Herman, *Giant Steps; Thundering Herd; Herd at Montreux; Children of Lima* (Fantasy).

PULLEN, DON GABRIEL, *piano, composer;* also *organ;* b. Roanoke, Va., 12/25/44. Father, dancer, guitarist, singer; uncle singer; cousin, Clyde "Fats" Wright, pianist. Studied at Johnson C. Smith U., Charlotte, N.C.; privately w. Muhal Richard Abrams; Giuseppi Logan. Worked w. own gp., '65-70; Nina Simone, '70-1; Art Blakey, '74; Charles Mingus, '73-fall '75. Capable of pl. "inside" or "outside." Infl:

Clyde "Fats" Wright, Ornette Coleman, Eric Dolphy. TV: *Jazz Adventures* w. own gp.; *Black Journal.* Fest: Umbria, '74-5; Montreux, '75; NJF tour, '73-4, national, '75; many Scandinavian fests. Comp: Andredon Music Pub. Co., (c/o Mietus Copyright, 527 Madison Ave., N.Y., N.Y.). LPs: Sackville; Horo; w. Milford Graves, *Nommo; Live at Yale U.* (SRP); w. George Adams; Dannie Richmond (Horo); w. Mingus (Atl.).

PUMA, JOSEPH J. (JOE),* *guitar;* b. New York City, 8/13/27. Left NYC small combo work to tour as accompanist and conductor for Morgana King, Fran Jeffries in the late '60s. Formed duo w. Chuck Wayne, '72, which played NYC clubs such as The Guitar and Stryker's Pub. Faculty member Housatonic Coll., Bridgeport, Conn. teaching applied mus. and guitar. TV: Mike Douglas Show w. M. King; NBC *Sunday* show w. Wayne. Puma and Wayne have also app. in concert at the Jazz Museum; for *Jazz on the River;* and at the NJF-NY, '73. Comp: *Little Joe's Waltz.* LP: *Interactions* (Choice).

PURDIE, BERNARD (PRETTY), *drums;* b. Elkton, Md., 6/11/39. Started playing drums at age six. Gained experience sitting-in until he got own set at 15. Led an otherwise all-white country & western band. First black man to graduate from Elkton High School. Attended Morgan State Coll, for two yrs. To NYC where he rec. w. Mickey & Sylvia; worked for Lonnie Youngblood; Les Cooper. Active making demo recs. for NY studios. By '66 was doing between 15 and 20 dates a week. Generally credited w. developing and popularizing the "boogaloo" beat permeating soul music. "The beat—the bass drum thing," he says, "had been around for a while, but until the engineers learned how to record it properly, nothing happened."

His busy schedule led him to rec. work w. James Brown; the Beatles; Blood, Sweat & Tears; the Isley Bros.; Jimmy Smith. Own band, P.P. Mavins, app. in Conn. and NY metropolitan area. Credits Sticks Evans for teaching him to read fast after he arrived in NYC. Has been active as a teacher; at one time had 60 students until playing time interfered. LPs: own albums (Date); *Purdie Good; Shaft;* w. Johnny Hammond, *Soul Talk* (Prest.); w. Yusef Lateef, *The Diverse Lateef* (Atlantic).

PURIM, FLORA, *singer, guitar, percussion;* b. Rio de Janeiro, Brazil, 3/6/42. Stud. piano, '50-4 with priv. teachers, incl. mother Rachel Purim; guitar, '54-8 w. Oscar Neves; later perc. informally w. Airto Moreira.

Purim's most important work before she left Brazil was a rec. w. a group called Quarteto Novo w. Moreira and Hermeto Pascoal. After arriving in U.S., '67, learned to read and write music under tuition of Moacir Santos in LA. Toured Europe w. S. Getz, '68. Rec. two albums w. Duke Pearson, '69-70. In '71, in addition to rec. w. Airto, whom she later married, Purim worked the whole year w. Gil Evans' band and C. Corea's combo. For two years she toured the U.S., Europe and Japan w. Return to Forever, feat. Corea, Airto, J. Farrell, S. Clarke. She and Airto left the group in '73. A new group was formed w. Airto as leader and Purim as feat. sol-oist, fusing Brazilian, jazz, pop and other idioms.

Besides working w. Airto, Purim made her own first solo

album, *Butterfly Dreams,* in the spring of '74, and a second album a few months later. Shortly after completing the latter she surrendered to begin serving a one to three year prison term at Terminal Island, San Pedro, Cal. She had been arrested in Sept. '71 for possession of cocaine, but had stayed free through a series of appeals. During '75 she was permitted to give a concert from the prison, which was broadcast, and to take leave of absence to study music at college. In December she was released on parole and was working again with Airto, Jan. '76.

Purim won the DB Critics' Poll in '74, TDWR; in Dec. of '74 she displaced R. Flack as number one female singer in the DB Readers' Poll. Films: sang title sang in *Les Biches,* French movie; comp. and pl., w. Airto and S. Clarke, sound track of short film, *Hermetic Triumph,* seen at Cannes Film Fest.

A gifted lyricist, Purim wrote the lyrics to Clarke's *Light as a Feather;* McCoy Tyner's *Search for Peace;* Neville Potter's *San Francisco River;* George Duke's *Love Reborn;* Airto's *Alue;* Hermeto Pascoal's *We Love* and many others. Her unusual success in bridging the gaps between Brazilian, jazz, and American pop music is explained in her philosophy: "My principal instrument is my voice, but I also consider the echo-plex one of my main instruments, because I developed my wordless singing, using this electronic device to distort, change or duplicate the sound as I needed, in order to team up with such instruments as flute, soprano sax, guitar, trombone, and the human sounds of pain or happiness or simple talking."

Own LPs: *Butterfly Dreams; Stories to Tell* (Milest.); w. Corea, *Light as a Feather; Return to Forever* (Poly); w. G. Duke, *Feel* (BASF); w. Airto, *Virgin Land* (CTI); *Seeds On The Ground* (Buddah); w. C. Santana, *Welcome* (Col.); w. D. Pearson, *How Insensitive; It Could Only Happen With You* (BN).

QUINICHETTE, PAUL,* *tenor sax;* b. Denver, Colo., 5/7/16. Known as "Vice-Pres" during his time with the Count Basie Band, '51-3, because of his stylistic resemblance to Lester Young, he pl. in NYC, '53-58 w. his own gps.; Benny Goodman Octet, '55; Nat Pierce big band. Dropped out of music, working as a radiologist, TV repairman, etc., and did not resurface until '73 when he began pl. w. Brooks Kerr at Churchill's, NYC. In April '74 began a series of Saturdays and Sundays at the West End Cafe w. pianist Sammy Price, and Buddy Tate as the other tenor in a group sometimes called Two Tenor Boogie. George Kelly sometimes replaced Tate on occasion and, in '75, Harold Ashby sometimes filled the second reed role. App. on NYJRC tribute to Count Basie, Jan. '75. Comp: *Prevue; Crossfire; Sandstone.*

LPs: w. Brooks Kerr, *Prevue* (Famous Door); w. Buddy Tate (Master Jazz); reissues, (Trip).

RADER, DONALD ARTHUR (DON),* *trumpet, fluegelhorn, composer;* b. Rochester, Pa. 10/21/35. During '60s, pl. w. W. Herman, M. Ferguson, C. Basie, L. Bellson, H. James, T. Gibbs; often w. Les Brown, '67-72, incl. three round the world trips w. Bob Hope. Pl. w. T. Gibbs orch. in *Operation Entertainment,* ABC-TV series, '68-9. On staff of S. Kenton clinics, '68-70. In Tokyo for two months as jazz soloist w. Japanese orch., '71. Concerts, clinics, records w. own quintet, '72-3. Toured as lead trumpet w. Jerry Lewis, Europe, Mexico, '72-3. Feat. soloist in Japan w. Percy Faith, '73-4. Freelance work in Hollywood, w. quintet, TV shows etc., '74-5.

TV: Spec. half hour educ. prog. w. Cerritos Coll. Lab Band, '68. Soloist w. Kenton on 90 minute spec. from Concord JF, PBS-TV, '69.

In addition to playing numerous coll. jazz fests., '68-75, Rader wrote many articles for the National Association of Jazz Educators Journal; a diary of his trip to Viet Nam and Thailand w. Hope and Brown was publ. by DB, Feb. '68. Comps: *Polluted Tears; Greasy Sack Blues; Chicago; Big Sur Echo; Saludita; Now; Viareggio.*

LPs: *Polluted Tears* (DRM); *New Thing,* w. P. Faith (Col.); *Love Story/Sound of Tomorrow* (Express, Japan).

RAE, JOHN (John Anthony Pompeo),* *drums;* also *vibes, timbales;* b. Saugus, Mass., 8/11/34. Traveled w. C. Tjader May '61 to Mar. '66. Led own group in Aspen, Colo. Worked in SF w. V. Guaraldi. After brief stints w. G. Szabo, rejoined Tjader, Aug. '68, remaining until Mar. '70. Freelanced in SF w. Don Piestrup band, W. Wanderley, many others during next four years. Joined Charlie Byrd, Mar. '74. In spare time, worked as disc jockey at KJAZ, Alameda, Cal., repaired drums at Drumland, SF, and took part in clinics at many high schools and colls. Fests: Monterey w. Tjader, L. Schifrin; Concord w. Tjader, '68. Films: Bit apps. w. John Davidson in *Streets of San Francisco;* and w. Robert Redford in *The Candidate.* Publs: *Jazz Phrasing for Mallets* (Belwin-Mills publ., 16 W. 61st St., New York, N.Y.); *Latin Guide for Drummers* (Try Publ., 854 N. Vine St., Hollywood, Ca. 90038).

LPs: *Great Guitars,* w. Byrd, D. Ellis, B. Kessel (Concord Jazz); *Evil Eyes,* w. Mike Vax (Artco); *Cal Tjader Plugs In* (Syke); *For All We Know,* w. Byrd (Col.); *Thundering Herd,* w. Herman (Fantasy); *Art Van Damme in San Francisco* (MPS).

RAINEY, CHARLES W. III (CHUCK), *bass;* also *guitar, piano, trumpet, trombone, composer,* etc.; b. Cleveland, Ohio, 6/17/40. Educ. Lane U., Jackson, Tenn. Toured w. Big Jay McNeely, 1960-61; Sil Austin, '61-2; Sam Cooke, '63; Jackie Wilson, '64; King Curtis, '64-8; Al Kooper, '68; Voices of East Harlem, '69-70; H. Belafonte, '70; Aretha Franklin, '71-5; R. Flack, '72; Q. Jones, '73; Crusaders, '72-3; Ujima, '72; Hamp Hawes, ,74-5. Fests. w. Jones, Flack, Crusaders et al.

Overlapping with these jobs, Rainey was one of New York's busiest musicians in many areas, recording with hundreds of jazz, pop, rock and soul artists (Ray Charles, S. Vaughan, F. Hubbard, D. Byrd, G. McFarland, C. Adderley, G. Ammons), composing and arranging for some sessions, and accumulating dozens of film and TV credits.

Comps: *Genuine John,* rec. by Bernard Purdie and by own gp.; *Got it Together,* rec. by Nancy Wilson; *The Rain Song; Eloise,* rec. by own gp.; *Jamaican Lady,* rec. by Cornell Dupree.

LPs: *Chuck Rainey Coalition* (Cobblestone); *Genuine John* (Capitol). Others: see artists listed above.

RANDI, DON (Don Schwartz), * *piano, composer, keyboards;* b. New York City, 2/25/37. Stud. at LA Conservatory. Made jazz albums in early '60s; later became involved with composing, arranging for films, TV and records. Since '70, has owned nightclub, The Baked Potato in Hollywood, leading a small band there.

LPs: *Live at the Baked Potato* (Poppy); *Love Theme From Romeo & Juliet and Other Motion Picture Themes* (Cap.).

RANEY, JAMES ELBERT (JIMMY or JIM), * *guitar, composer;* b. Louisville, Ky., 8/20/27. Acknowledged as one of the premier guitarists of the '40s and '50s w. Al Haig, Stan Getz and Teddy Charles gps., he rejoined Getz in '62-3 but then worked mostly backing singers and for Broadway shows. Returned to Louisville in late '60s, teaching, working in non-music jobs and also doing some playing. In the summer of '72 he visited NYC, playing at the Guitar; Gulliver's (NJ); and Bradley's. Other trips to NY were for a concert w. Haig at Carnegie Recital Hall, Nov. '74; recs. w. Haig and w. own gp., '75. Raney's playing in the '70s showed that he was still capable of spinning long lines that stretch out in networks of logical beauty. His pure sound, amplifier down, in a day when electric possibilities are almost limitless but so often abused, is perhaps a bit more melancholy, burnished by the passage of time to include aural tears that are sometimes even Djangoesque. Comp: *Suite For Guitar Quintet; Momentum; We'll Be Together; The Flag Is Up; Double Image.*

LPs: *The Influence* (Xanadu); *Momentum* (MPS); Haig-Raney, *Strings Attached,* incl. one track in which his son, Doug Raney, duets w. him (Choice); *Strings & Swings,* one half recorded at concert for Louisville Jazz Council, '69 (Muse).

RANGER, CLAUDE, *drums, percussion;* b. Montreal, Quebec, Canada, 2/3/41. Self-taught. Worked and rec. w. saxophonist Lee Gagnon in mid-'60s; w. saxophonist Brian Barley in trio called Aquarius Rising from late '60s until Barley's death in Toronto, '71. Led own gps. for Radio Canada's *Jazz En Liberte;* also pl. w. S. Greenwich; Jerry Labelle; Pierre Leduc; Ron Proby; Art Roberts. To Toronto where he worked w. Lenny Breau; Herbie Spanier, '72; Doug Riley, Moe Koffman, '74-5. Free-lanced in clubs & concerts w. G. Coleman, Greenwich, J. Moody, Alvin Pall, Fred Stone, Don Thompson, P. Woods. Infl: M. Roach, Tony Williams, E. Jones, O. Coleman. TV: house band for *Music Machine,* CBC. Comp: *Tickle; Le Pingouin.* Called by Barry Tepperman in *Coda,* "indisputably the best drummer on the Canadian scene." LPs: w. Doug Riley, *Dr. Music's Bedtime Story;* w. Koffman, *Solar Explorations* (GRT); w. Barley (RCI); also w. Gagnon; Spanier.

RAVA, ENRICO, *trumpet, composer;* b. Trieste, Italy, 8/20/43. Mother a pianist graduated from Conservatorio di Torino "G. Verdi." Originally self-taught, later studies w. Carmine Caruso, NYC. Pl. w. S. Lacy quartet in Europe, S.

Amer. and U.S., late '60s; also w. M. Waldron, Bill Dixon, JCOA, D. Cherry, Barney Wilen, G. Hampel, in U.S. and Europe; L. Konitz in Italy; Dollar Brand; and Roswell Rudd's Primordial group, NYC. From '70, he has divided his time between NYC, Italy and Buenos Aires, where his wife, Graciela, a film-maker, lives. He has toured in Europe with his own group annually from '72. Infls: Cherry, C. Taylor, M. Davis, Rudd, S. Rollins. TV: specs. feat. his group and comps. in Puerto Rico, '71; Italy, '73-4; Buenos Aires, '74; Hamburg. Fests: many major European events; also Biennale Panamericana, Cordoba, Arg. Comps: score for the Italian film *O.R.G.* in which he also app.; theatre score for Ibsen's *Hedda Gabler,* Buenos Aires, '74. Rava's own albums contain many of his original comps.

LPs: *Il Giro Del Giorno in 80 Mondi* (Fonit-Cetra); others on MPS, RCA, ECM; w. Lacy, *The Forest and the Zoo* (ESP); w. Konitz, *Stereo Konitz* (Ital. RCA); w. Brand, *African Space Program* (Enja); w. C. Bley, *Escalator Over The Hill;* w. Rudd, *Numatik Swing Band* (JCOA).

RAWLS, LOU, * *singer;* b. Chicago, Ill., 12/1/35. A popular jazz and blues singer in the mid-60s. Rawls continued to tour clubs throughout the U.S., frequently app. at casinos in LV. LPs on Cap., MGM, Pickwick Int'l., Bell.

RAZAF, ANDY (Andreamenentania Paul Razafinke-riefo), * *songwriter;* b. Washington, D.C., 12/16/1895. The prolific lyricist, whose songs included *Ain't Misbehavin'; Honeysuckle Rose; Black and Blue* (all w. Fats Waller, his chief collaborator); *Memories of You; Stompin' At The Savoy; In The Mood; Gee Baby Ain't I Good To You,* died 2/3/73 in LA, after being an invalid and almost totally bedridden for 20 years. An album of Razaf's songs was rec. in the '50s by Maxine Sullivan for Period Records, now defunct, but his works are represented on hundreds of recordings by almost every jazz singer.

REBILLOT, PATRICK EARL (PAT), *piano, composer;* also *keyboards, synthesizer;* b. Louisville, Ohio, 4/21/35. Stud. piano and organ at Mt. Union Coll. in Ohio, '49-53; piano w. Jeno Takacs at Cincinnati Conservatory of Mus., where he received a BS in mus. ed. in conjunction with U. of Cinc., '57. Principal church organist from age 12 to 17 in Louisville. Classical acc. at Cinc. Conserv. While in Army spec. Servs. began arr. and toured world with Army entertainers, '58-60. Moved to NYC, and in '60s worked w. Benny Powell, J. Steig, B. Goodman, Paul Winter (incl. tour of Brazil, '65), S. Vaughan. App. many times at Half Note w. Z. Sims, R. Eldridge, J. Moody, J. Rushing. Conductor for *Jacques Brel;* also led own small combos at various Greenwich Village jazz clubs. With G. Burton quartet, '71-2, then joined H. Mann on keyboards and as mus. dir. From late '60s, extensive freelance rec. in NYC. Infls: Waller, Ellington, Monk, M. Davis, Rushing. Fests: Laurel JF w. S. Rollins, late '60s; Newport-NY, 72-4, Concord, '72-3, Montreux, '72, w. Mann; Montreux, '74 w. Airto, F. Purim. Comps: *Thank You, Mr. Rushing; Song For The New Man; The Beautiful Bend Ahead; Free Fall; Let Me Know; In A Melancholy Funk.* Arrs. for Mann LPs.

LPs: *Free Fall* (Atl.); others w. Mann (Atl.); *The Prophet; Journey* w. A. Mardin; *Mirror* w. C. Mariano; *Newmanism,*

w. D. Newman (Atl.); *Nine Flags* w. Chico O'Farrill (Imp.); *Soul Outing* w. F. Foster (Pres.); *Children of All Ages* (Barbeque).

REDISKE, JOHANNES, * *guitar, composer;* b. Berlin, Germany, 8/11/26. Prominent for many years as soloist in radio groups and leader of his own quintet, Rediske, who had been called by some critics the "German Charlie Christian," died in Berlin, 1/22/75.

REDD, ELVIRA (VI), * *alto saxophone, soprano saxophone, singer;* b. Los Angeles, Cal., 9/20/30. In '67 Redd app. for ten weeks at Ronnie Scott's Club in London; feat. w. Max Roach at Montmartre Club in Copenhagen. Returned to U.S. to pl. clubs in SF, LA. Feat. w. D. Gillespie at NJF, '68. Toured Africa, Europe w. C. Basie orch, '68. In '69 she began teaching for Compton Unified Schools, but continued to pl. local engagements, also took part in Ch. Parker Memorial Concerts in Chicago. Taught in LA City schools, '72- . Guest artist w. Rahsaan Roland Kirk at Royce Hall, UCLA, '74.

LPs: own albums for Solid State, Atl. (deleted); *Charlie Parker Memorial Album* (Cadet); *Chase* w. G. Ammons, D. Gordon (Prest.).

REDMAN, WALTER DEWEY, *tenor sax, clarinet, composer, educator;* also *alto sax, musette, auto harp;* b. Fort Worth, Tex., 5/17/31. Although he has no concrete evidence he thinks Don Redman was his uncle. Clarinet at age 13; pl. in Baptist church band during the collection. Several mos. of lessons but mostly self-taught. Pl. in high school marching band. Went to Tuskegee Inst. for a few mos., to study electrical engineering. Ret. to Texas where he attended Prairie View A&M receiving BS '53. Pl. in march. band, swing band, switching to tenor from alto. Masters in educ. from No. Texas State, '59 but did not participate in jazz courses. Taught public school classes, '56-9. To LA '59. Shortly thereafter went to visit SF and stayed for seven yrs., pl. w. Pharoah Sanders; Don Garrett; Smiley Winters; Wes Montgomery; co-led big band w. Monty Waters; after hours jamming at Bop City; own after hours band at Soulville. Left for NYC, '67, pl. w. Sunny Murray before joining his former schoolmate Ornette Coleman. With Coleman to late '74, also working w. Charlie Haden Liberation Music Orch.; own group. With Keith Jarrett from early '70s. Other gigs w. Alice Coltrane; JCOA; Newport All Stars. Infl: "All saxophonists including Bird and Red Connor."

Fest: NJF-NY w. Coleman, '72; Jarrett, '74; many Euro. fests. NYJRC, '74, feat. in concert of John Coltrane's music. John Litweiler has written that Redman "evolves distinct styles for the serious, disparate concepts of Coleman, Jarrett, Dewey Redman and the rest. With Coleman's band, his style is closely akin to Ornette's, but with others it not. He admits to a Coltrane influence, too, but at 43 he's the sum of a lifetime of practicing, listening and selecting. . . . For all his experience, he remains one of the very fresh, bright voices in contemporary music."

Comp: *For Eldon; Interconnection; Boody; Images (In Disguise);* many others in own albums.

LPs: *Coincide; Ear of the Beahearer* (Imp.); *Look for the Black Star* (Arista); *Tarik* (Byg); w. Jarrett, *Death and the Flower; Treasure Island; Fort Yawuh* (Imp.); *Expectations*

(Col.); *El Juicio; Birth* (Atl.); Coleman, *Science Fiction* (Col.); *Friends and Neighbors* (Fly. Dutch); *Crisis; Ornette at 12* (Imp.); *Love Call; New York is Now* (BN); Haden, *Liberation Music Orch.* (Imp.); Carla Bley, *Escalator Over the Hill;* Don Cherry, *Relativity Suite;* Roswell Rudd, *Numatik Swing Band* (JCOA).

REHAK, FRANK JAMES, * *trombone, composer;* also *baritone horn, valve trombone;* b. Brooklyn, N.Y., 7/6/26. Toured w. G. Krupa, C. Thornhill, Herman, Gillespie et al. Sporadically active in '60s but, he says, "My life was at an all time low because of the use of large quantities of heroin and alcohol. In 1969 I left Woody Herman's band, at his request, wieghing 118 lbs. and close to death. He strongly suggested I come to Synanon for help. I did so, and the years since then have been nothing short of miraculous."

As head of the music dept. at Synanon, Rehak has been intensely active leading a chorus, jazz-rock group, teaching adult and children's music classes, composing and programming for the facility's internal radio station, which broadcasts to the various branches of Synanon throughout Calif. He has also lectured at colleges and judged at school and coll. jazz fests. His ambition is "to create a musical environment within Synanon, and then to extend it to the larger society; to record some of my own music, utilizing Synanon people."

In '75 Rehak appeared as leader of a big band, composed partly of Synanon residents, in a concert at the Santa Monica branch. His playing, which had gained him respect of musicians for many years, had reached a new peak of creativity.

Early LPs w. Gillespie (Verve); Geo. Russell (MCA).

RENAUD, HENRI, * *piano, composer, producer;* b. Villedieu (Indre) France, 4/20/25. As leader of own gp. at Tabou Club in Paris in '50s; pianist w. K. Clarke, '61 and house pianist at Trois Mailletz, '62-4, he was one of the leading French musicians, rec. with a variety of visiting Americans. Joined CBS Records as jazz producer in '64, and in '70s put together a series of classic jazz reissues under the title *Aimez vous le Jazz?* From '70-4 prod. jazz programs for three French TV channels; weekly jazz program on national French radio, '72- . Although mainly occupied with the above activities, Renaud still works occasionally as a pianist, leader. Fest: own quintet at Antibes, '68. Publ: *Jazz Classique; Jazz Moderne,* jazz history in two volumes (Casterman Publ., 66 rue Bonaparte, 75006 Paris). Comp. part of the sound track for the Louis Malle film *Murmur of the Heart,* '70, rec. by Roulette.

LPs: *Clifford Brown Quartet in Paris; Sextet in Paris;* w. L. Konitz, *Ezz-thetic; The Oscar Pettiford Memorial Album* (Pres.); w. Al Cohn, K. Winding, T. Farlow, J.J. Johnson, Milt Jackson in *The Birdlanders* (Everest).

RETURN TO FOREVER. see Corea, Chick.

RICH, BERNARD (BUDDY), * *drums, singer, leader;* b. Brooklyn, N.Y., 6/30/17. After leading his own combo in early '60s he rejoined Harry James' orch., '61 but left to form own band in April '66, the first time had had led a large orch. since '51. It was a well-drilled machine with the leader's drums as the focal point and an impressive book with contributions by Bill Holman, Don Piestrup, Bill Reddie, Don Menza, Don Sebesky and John La Barbera, among others. Reddie's arr. of a *West Side Story* medley contains a tour de force for Rich, a 10 minute plus show stopper. Art Pepper was in the reed section for a short periods in the '60s but the only sideman to receive recognition out of the ordinary was tenor saxophonist Pat La Barbera.

In '74 Rich disbanded and organized a small group which went into residence at a club at 64th St. and 2nd Ave. in NYC to which he lent his name, Buddy's Place. When his group, which incl. Sal Nistico, Sonny Fortune, Jack Wilkins and Kenny Barron, traveled to another city, other name gps. were featured there. Late in the club's existence, Illinois Jacquet became part of Rich's combo. In '75 Buddy's Place closed and a new Buddy's Place opened on the site of what had been Gallagher's 33 restaurant near Madison Square Garden. Again lent his name but was not a partner. He reorganized the big band for several engagements there. Not only did Rich reiterate his position as one of the all time drum masters, and perhaps the greatest technician of all, but the sheer swinging power his youthful band brought to bear on the original material and songs from the Beatles, the Doors, Burt Bacharach and Paul Simon, captivated a young audience at that time (the mid and late '60s) heavily swayed by rock.

Rich, whose acid wit was often in evidence on the bandstand, displayed his quick way with a put-down in his many appearances on late-night TV talk shows, particularly with Johnny Carson where in his guest role he also sat-in w. Doc Severinsen's orch.

Fest: numerous apps. w. orch.; also w. L. Hampton, T. Wilson; drum battle w. Blakey, Roach, Elvin Jones at Radio City jam session, both at NJF-NY, '74. Won DB Readers poll, '67, '70-2; Hall of Fame, Reader's Poll, '74; band won DB Critics poll, TDWR, '68.

In '68 *Super Drummer: A Profile of Buddy Rich* by Whitney Balliett was published by Bobbs-Merrill.

LPs: *Big Band Machine; Roar of '74; Last Blues Album, Vol. 1 Very Live;* Buddy Rich & L. Hampton, *Transition* (Gr. Merch.); *Different Drummer; Rich in London,* rec. live at Ronnie Scott's; *Stick It* (RCA); *Keep the Customer Satisfied* (Liberty); *Swingin' New Big Band; Buddy and Soul; Big Swing Face; The New One; Mercy, Mercy* (Pac. Jazz); w. Zoot Sims-Bucky Pizzarelli, *Nirvana* (Gr. Merch.); reissues on Verve; UA.

RICHARDS, EMIL,* *vibraphone, percussion, composer;* b. Hartford, Conn., 9/2/32. First prominent w. G. Shearing, Paul Horn. Worked w. D. Ellis' Hindustani Jazz Sextet, '64-6. In '67-9, in addition to working in movie studios and pl. w. LA Neophonic Orch., led his own group, the Microtonal Blues Band in LA area. In '69 went to India; stud. meditation, Indian music; trip around the world collecting authentic instruments. Joined R. Kellaway cello quartet, also pl. w. Harry Partch percussion ensemble.

In '72 made another world tour; stud. music in Tibet, Bali. Concerts w. F. Sinatra for two months in '74; visited S. Amer. to do more research, later formed six-man percussion group, pl. music of leading film composers. Also in '74 went on two month tour w. Geo. Harrison, Ravi Shankar, perf. in both groups. Continued recording major TV and film scores, '75. His playing is heard on *Kung Fu; Planet of the Apes; Airport '75; Earthquake; Chinatown* etc. Received Most Valuable Player award for perc. from NARAS, '73, '74.

Comps: *It's Ten To Five; Lucky Eleven; The Day After The Night In Tunisia; Bombay Bossa Nova; Alexandria's "Raga" Time Band.* Publs: *Emil Richards World of Percussion,* w. cassettes (Gwyn Publ. Co., P.O. Box 5900, Sherman Oaks, Ca. 91413); *Emil Richards Mallet Exercises in 4/4; Emil Richards Original Jazz Comps. in 3-5-7-9-10-10½-11-13-19* (Try Publ., 854 Vine St. Hollywood, Ca. 90038); *Making Music in Mommy's Kitchen; Making Music Around The Home or Yard* (Award Music Co., 136 W. 46th St. New York, N.Y., 10036). LPs: *New Time Elements, New Sound Elements* (Uni); *Journey To Bliss; Spirit of 1976,* w. Microtonal Blues Band (Imp.); others w. Kellaway (A & M); J. Donato (Blue Thumb); *Harlow* score for Neal Hefti (Col.); Harrison, Shankar (Dark Horse); F. Zappa (Discreet).

RICHARDS, JOHNNY (John Cascales),* *composer;* b. Schenectady, N.Y., 11/2/11. Arranger for many jazz artists in '40s and '50s, incl. Boyd Raeburn, Ch. Barnet, D. Gillespie, S. Vaughan and most notably S. Kenton, with whom he enjoyed a lengthy association. From '58 into the '60s Richards continued writing but occasionally led big bands at Birdland etc. He died in NYC 10/7/68. Among his most important works are *Cuban Fire* and *Adventures in Time,* both for Kenton. Many of his best comps. and arrs. for Kenton and for his own orch., have been reissued on the Creative World label.

RICHARDS, CHARLES (RED),* *piano, singer;* b. Brooklyn, N.Y., 10/19/12. Continued to co-lead Saints and Sinners w. V. Dickenson until the trombonist left the group in '68. Cut down to quintet, later quartet, working Toronto frequently to '72. Quartet w. Herb Hall pl. many times at Dinkler's, Syracuse, N.Y., '72-4. Richards also subbed in World's Greatest Jazzband, Sept.-Dec. '74; solo piano at Eddie Condon's, '75.

LPs: w. own quartet & quintet; w. Eddie Durham; Vic Dickenson (English RCA); w. Saints & Sinners, *Sugar* (MPS); *Saints & Sinners in Canada* (Sackville).

RICHARDSON, JEROME G.,* *saxophones, flutes* etc.; b. Oakland, Cal., 12/25/20. A regular member of the Thad Jones-Mel Lewis orch. in the late '60s, Richardson also pl. in the B. Rosengarden band on the Dick Cavett TV show, '70-1. He moved to LA in late '71 and became heavily involved with studio work along w. occasional jazz jobs. Toured Japan three times: w. Q. Jones, '72, '73; Percy Faith, '74. Gigs w. O. Nelson, Kenny Burrell. TV series w. Carol Burnett. Worked occasionally w. L. Bellson, D. Grusin, the Aldeberts. Led own group in LA clubs and at Santa Barbara fest.

LPs: *Brass Fever* (Imp.); w. Nelson, *Skull Session* (Fl. Dutch.); *Michelle* (Imp.); w. Jones, *Body Heat; Smackwater Jack; Gula Matari; Walkin' In Space* (A & M); *Quintessence* (Imp.).

RICHMOND, DANNIE,* *drums, percussion, vocal;* also *tenor sax;* b. New York City, 12/15/35. Except for occasional side ventures, was best known from '56-70 w. Ch. Mingus. Pl. w. Mark-Almond for three years; also off and on w. Joe Cocker, and one tour w. Elton John; BBC radio w. Danny Thomas; back w. Mingus, '74. When not on the road, Richmond gives drum clinics at colleges and high schools. In '65 he wrote a method book and solo book for publ. in Germany.

Many TV apps. w. Mark-Almond on such rock shows as *In*

Concert and *Midnight Special;* also NET programs w. Mingus. LPs w. Mingus (Columbia, Candid, World Pacific, Impulse, Atl. etc.); also w. Mark-Almond (Columbia).

RIDLEY, LAURENCE HOWARD JR. (LARRY),* *bass, educator;* b. Indianapolis, Ind. 9/3/37. Early assoc. of F. Hubbard. Toured w. dozens of jazz groups in '60s incl. R. Weston, L. Donaldson, C. Hawkins, J. McLean, Art Farmer-Jim Hall, Hubbard, S. Rollins, H. Silver. In late '60s, was heard w. D. Gillespie, T. Monk, McCoy Tyner, JCOA etc.; w. Newport All Stars annually from '68. Original member of N.Y. Bass Violin Choir. Also worked with big bands incl. D. Ellington, T. Jones-M. Lewis. Toured Europe w. Young Giants of Jazz group, '73. Orig. member of NYJRC. Feat. artist at Amer. Coll. JF, '72.

Ridley in the '70s became increasingly active in education. Appointed Asst. Prof. of Music Livingston Coll. of Rutgers U. '71; Chairman of Mus. Dept., '72. Artist in res.: U. of Utah; Creighton U.; Southern U.; Grambling Coll. DB writer John Sinclair said: ''Ridley is committed to making wider and deeper impressions in whatever musical context he finds himself. He is a perfect section mate. He picks lines that are a constant stimulus, creating juggernaut rhythms that move soloists to play into themselves more and to move out from that point to their listeners' ears . . .''

LPs: *Sum of the Parts* (Strata-East); w. Newport All Stars, *Tribute to Duke* (MPS/BASF); *Newport in N.Y. '72, The Jam Sessions, Vols. 3-4* (Cobblestone); w. Dexter Gordon (Prestige); Jackie McLean (Blue Note); *Colorado Jazz Party* (MPS/BASF); w. Al Cohn (Xanadu); *Venuti-Grappelli* (Byg).

RIEDEL, GEORG,* *bass, composer;* b. Karlsbad, Czechoslavakia, 1/8/34. Pl. w. Lars Gullin, '53-4; Arne Domnerus, '55- ; Swedish Radio band, '58-61; radio jazz group, '62- . Many recs. and extensive radio work in Germany, Denmark etc., as well as sound tracks for some 35 motion pics. Comps: *Dizzy* (for Gillespie and big band); choral works, several symphonic works, chamber music; *Kind of Requiem,* in memoriam for Ellington. Insp. by Ellington, Ch. Mingus, Messiaen, Jan Johansson. Won Prix Italia for his TV ballet, *Riedaiglia;* nine gold records for children's music. Many LPs on SR, Philips, Megafon etc.; Swedish Radio Jazz Group, *Greetings and Salutations* feat. Thad Jones, Mel Lewis (Four Leaf Clover).

RIEL, ALEX POUL, *drums;* b. Copenhagen, Denmark, 9/13/40. Stud. in Copenhagen, '55; one semester at Berklee in Boston w. Alan Dawson, '66. Pl. w. NO, swing and bop groups before graduating into the avant garde, working w. John Tchicai, Archie Shepp, Gary Peacock. Co-led group w. Palle Mikkelborg, '67. While in U.S. pl. w. Rahsaan Roland Kirk, Toshiko Akiyoshi, Herb Pomeroy and many others. Worked for several years w. Savage Rose. In '65 Riel was voted Danish Musician of the Year; in '67, the Riel-Mikkelborg quintet won first prize at Montreux JF, and later that year the group was seen at NJF.

LPs: w. B. Webster, *My Man;* w. J. McLean, *A Ghetto Lullaby;* w. McLean-D. Gordon, *The Source; The Meeting;* w. Gary Bartz, *Ode to Super* (SteepleChase); w. Sahib Shihab (Debut, Poly.); *Violin Summit* (MPS); Alex Riel Trio (Vibe-

Fona); w. Savage Rose (Poly.); w. Stuff Smith (Metronome); w. Herb Geller (Nova, Atl.).

RIFKIN, JOSHUA, *piano;* b. New York City, 4/22/44. Extensive studies from '54, incl. composition at Juilliard; w. Karlheinz Stockhausen in Darmstadt, Germany, '61; NYU, '64-6; musicology at Princeton, '67-70. Asst. Prof. of Mus. at Brandeis U., active as musicologist and cond. Rifkin came to prominence with his interpretations of Scott Joplin's ragtime works, which won Record of the Year awards from *Stereo Review* and *Billboard.* His infls. are entirely classical. In '74-5 Rifkin made several apps. on BBC-TV.

LPs: *Piano Rags by Scott Joplin,* Vols. I, II, II (Nonesuch); w. Judy Collins, *Wildflowers* (Elektra).

RILEY, BENJAMIN A. (BEN),* *drums, educator;* b. Savannah, Ga., 7/17/33. With Thelonious Monk, '64-7. Teaching in Wyandanch, L.I. elementary school system, junior college; USDAN summer camp, '68-70. With New York Jazz Quartet (Frank Wess, Roland Hanna, Ron Carter) from '71, incl. Japanese tour '74. Alice Coltrane from '71. Ron Carter quartet, '75. TV: *Positively Black* w. Carter. App. w. NYJQ at NJF-NY, '74. LPs: w. NYJQ, *Concert in Japan* (Salvation); w. A. Coltrane (Imp., WB); w. Monk (Col.); w. Lonnie Smith (BN).

RILEY, DOUGLAS BRIAN (DOUG or DR. MUSIC), *piano, organ, composer;* b. Toronto, Ontario, Canada, 12/4/45. Stud. at the Royal Cons. of Mus., Toronto, w. Lawrence Goodwill, '50-6; w. Paul DeMarky in Mont., '56-60; Royal Cons. w. Patricia B. Holt, '61-4; Univ. of Tor., BM in Comp. w. Prof. John Weinzweig. Deeply interested in ethnomusicology, he has completed one-half of his Master's at the Univ. of Tor. under Dr. Kolinski and has spent two summers on Iroquois Reservations, collecting and transcribing their music on a govt. grant. Worked w. Boss Brass, '69; Dr. Music, '70-4; Moe Koffman quintet; Sonny Greenwich, '74-5; own trio, '73-5. Infl: Ray Charles, B. Evans, G. Evans, B. Powell, A. Tatum, Bach, Bartok, Beethoven, Stravinsky. TV: arr., pianist and/or mus. dir. for *Rolling on the River; Music Machine;* Hart & Lorne Specials; Anne Murray Specials; *Celebration;* Lou Rawls Special. App. at Jazz at the Shaw Fest., July '75. Comp. mus. for feat. films: *Megantic Outlaw; Foxy Lady; Cannibal Girls; The Naked Peacock;* shorts, *Olivia's Scrapbook; Summer in Canada;* ballets, *Lies, Wishes and Dreams; Sessions for Six; Jeux en Blanc et Noir.* Own LP: Dr. Music, *Bedtime Story;* w. Koffman, *Master Sessions; Solar Explorations* (GRT); *Ray Charles Doin' His Thing* (ABC).

RILEY, HERMAN, *tenor saxophone;* also *saxes, clarinet, flutes;* b. New Orleans, La., 8/31/40. Played in high school band, '50-4; U.S. Army reserve band, '53-5. In service, not playing, '55-7. Lived in NYC Apr. to Aug. '57, then in San Diego, where he attended City Coll., remaining there until '63, when he moved to LA. Riley pl. w. Wm. Huston big band, Ivory Joe Hunter, Roy Brown and other blues bands in NO. In LA he was heard w. B. Bryant, C. Basie, S. Manne, Q. Jones, Benny Carter, Joe Williams, Donald Byrd and singers Sammy Davis Jr. and Della Reese. Chosen as Outstanding Solo Artist at the Monterey Coll. JF in '61, he pl. the MJF w. Bryant in '69. For Bryant he composed *A Prayer for*

Peace, heard in Swahili Strut (Cadet). Pl. Concord JF w. Q. Jones, '73. Went to S. Africa w. Monk Montgomery band, '74.

LPs: w. Blue Mitchell (Mainstream); Bryant (Cadet); G. Ammons (Pres.); D. Reese (ABC).

RILEY, HOWARD, *piano, composer;* b. Huddersfield, England, 2/16/43. B.A. and M.A. from Univ. of Wales, '61-6; M.M. from Indiana Univ., '66-7; M. Phil. from York Univ., '67-70. From his arrival in London, '67 has worked with own trio; also w. Evan Parker, J. McLaughlin (duo); Tony Oxley; London Jazz Composers Orch., late '60s, early '70s. Has also app. as solo artist. From '70 has been Prof. at Guildhall School of Mus. and Drama, lecturing in jazz and improv. Fests: Paris Bienniale, '71; Berlin; Donaueschingen, '72; w. own trio. In '69 his group was first non-classical combo to app. at London Proms, Royal Fest. Hall. The trio has broadcast and televised extensively in England, France, Germany. Comps: *Angle; Continuum; Convolution; Rope; Triptych; Zynan; Two Designs.* Riley was one of the first British musicians to be awarded an Arts Council Bursary for jazz comp ('69), and has written many works for string quartet and flute-piano duos.

LPs: *Discussion* (Opportunity); *Angle; The Day Will Come* (CBS); *Flight* (Turtle); *Solo Imprints* (Jaguar); *Synopsis* (Incus); *Singleness* (Chariavari); others w. LJCO (Incus).

RITENOUR, LEE MACK, *guitar;* also *classical guitar, banjo, mandolin, electric bass;* b. Hollywood, Ca., 11/1/52. Stud. privately w. Duke Miller, Joe Pass, Howard Roberts, Christopher Parkening; then to USC School of Music under Jack Marshall. Prof. debut at age 12 w. The Esquires (19 piece orch.); w. Afro Blues Quintet, Craig Hundley Trio, '69. Traveled w. Sergio Mendes and Brasil '77, later freelancing extensively in LA studios. Formed first own group, '73, w. John Pisano; second group w. D. Grusin, '74, for local dates. Began teaching classical guitar at USC in same year and in '75 coordinated new studio guitar program. A prodigious and versatile young musician, Ritenour has rec. w. Herbie Hancock, Gato Barbieri, Mendes, Peggy Lee, Oliver Nelson, Moacir Santos, Carly Simon and many other contemporary artists.

RIVERS, SAMUEL CARTHORNE (SAM),* *tenor sax; composer;* also *soprano sax, piano, bass clarinet, flute, viola;* b. El Reno, Okla., 9/25/30. An important part of the Boston scene in '40s, '50s w. Jaki Byard; Joe Gordon; Herb Pomeroy; and Gigi Gryce. Pl. two mos. w. Miles Davis in summer '64. Moved to NYC and began teaching in Harlem at his own studio, '67. Pl. w. Cecil Taylor, '67-71; six mos. w. McCoy Tyner. In '71, w. his wife Bea, opened Studio Rivbea at 24 Bond Street in lower Manhattan. He continued his teaching and opened it to the public for performances by his own group w. guest artists such as Dewey Redman, Frank Lowe, Charles Tyler, Clifford Jordan and Sonny Fortune. In Jan. '75 he app. as guest soloist w. the SF Symphony. From '68 composer-in-residence for the Harlem Opera Society; lecturer on Afro-American musical history at Connecticut Coll., '72; artist-in-residence at Wesleyan U., '70-3. "There is often a certain austerity to Rivers' music," wrote Robert Palmer. "It isn't cold or forbidding, but it's more or less 'pure,' uncontaminated by programmatic conceits . . . independent of the kind of extramusical imagery so often associated with organized sound."

"The way I see it," says Rivers, "the music of the '70s should be a fusion of the '40s, '50s and '60s."

Fest: NJF-NY; Montreux, '73; Perugia; Molde; Antibes, '74. Won DB Critics poll on flute, TDWR, '75; his album *Streams* won a Best Record award from the French Academie du Disque. Comp: *Dawn; Exaltation; Tranquility; Shades;* also comps: for Harlem Ensemble; Winds of Manhattan, a woodwind gp. LPs: *Sizzle; Hues; Streams; Crystals* (Imp.); *Conference of the Birds* (ECM); *Involution* (BN); w. Don Pullen (Black Saint); w. C. Taylor (Shandar); *Miles Davis in Tokyo,* (CBS, Japan).

RIZZI, TREFONI (TONY),* *guitar;* b. Los Angeles, Cal., 4/16/23. Former name band musician, later on staff for many years at NBC, he has continued to do TV and film work, pl. every stringed instrument. Comp. and played the music on a daily soap opera. In '73, organized a five guitar group that interpreted harmonzied versions of the comps. and improvised solos of Charlie Christian. This combo was heard at Donte's and other clubs in the LA area.

ROACH, MAXWELL (MAX),* *drums, vibes, composer, leader, educator;* b. Brooklyn, N.Y., 1/10/25. One of the key figures in the development of modern jazz in the '40s as the drummer in Charlie Parker's quintet, he emerged as a leader in the '50s and has led small groups from that time. In the '70s they have incl. Cecil Bridgewater, Billy Harper and Reggie Workman. The quartet appeared several times at the NJF-NY in the '70s and pl. a concert in Paris '75. From '72 he has also been involved with the ensemble he conceived, M'Boom Re: Percussion which consists of Roy Brooks, Joe Chambers, Omar Clay, Warren Smith, Freddie Waits and himself. "The basis of M'Boom," says Roach, "is that it utilizes mallet instruments and every kind of percussive instrument. We lean heavily on instruments from the Third World . . . It not only involves powerful and innovative rhythmic aspects, but also moves into new melodic and harmonic variations . . .'' M'Boom performed at campuses such as Adelphi, Swarthmore and Dartmouth; conducted clinics; appeared at NJF-NY '73; and toured Europe that year.

Roach, who had lectured on black music history at Yale, Pittsburgh U., Kalamazoo Coll. and Nassau Community Coll., has, from '72 been Professor of Music at the U. of Massachusetts in Amherst, Mass. He has traveled to Africa to do research and sits on the selection committee of the National Board of the Nigerian Festival.

Film: *Freedom Now Suite,* adapted for film by Gianni Amici and released in '66, won first prize at the 18th International Film Fest. in Locarno. Roach has also written scores for *Black Sun,* Nikatsu Studios, Japan; and *Trail of Tears,* NET Prods.

At the NJF-NY '72 his group combined with the 22-member J.C. White Singers in selections from their Atlantic album, *Lift Every Voice and Sing,* an integration of spirituals and gospel songs with instrumental improvisations. Roach and the White Singers performed together again at NJF-NY, '75. In '74 he not only appeared w. his group but took part in a drum conclave during the jam session at Radio City w. Art Blakey, Buddy Rich and Elvin Jones. Roach's ability to construct solos that are highly musical as well as rhythmically contoured in a most imaginative way was again clearly demonstrated.

Divorced from Abbey Lincoln, '70.

Comp: musical show, *Another Valley;* percussion pieces, *A Love Silent; Attucks to Attica,* the latter written on grant from CAPS; *For Big Sid,* other solo drum pieces.

Most of the selections on *Lift Every Voice and Sing* are dedicated to Martin Luther King, Malcolm X, Medgar Evers, Patrice Lumumba and Paul Robeson. Other LPs: *Members, Don't Get Weary; Drums Unlimited* (Atl.); reissues (Trip).

ROBERTS, CHARLES LUCKEYETH (LUCKEY),* *piano, composer;* b. Philadelphia, Pa. 8/7/1895. An early ragtime soloist and popular society bandleader, was well known as the composer of *Moonlight Cocktail,* 1941, and *Massachusetts,* 1942. In the late 1950s he suffered a stroke and went into almost total retirement. He died 2/5/68 in NYC. Roberts is considered to have represented a significant link between ragtime and the Harlem stride school of jazz piano.

ROBERTS, HOWARD MANCEL,* *guitar, composer;* b. Phoenix, Ariz., 10/2/29. One of the first combo leaders to appear at Donte's in No. Hollywood in late '66, helping to establish it as a jazz club, Roberts continued to work mainly in TV, film and recording studios. He estimated that from '66-76 he appeared on 2000 LPs, of which 2% were jazz records, incl. Tom Scott, O. Nelson, T. Monk, G. Mulligan.

In the '70s Roberts became increasingly active in personal apps., often at guitar seminars throughout the U.S., expanding contemporary guitar education. Comps: originals and arrangements for many of his own albums, the most important of which, in his view, is *Equinox Express Elevator.* From '74 he wrote a regular monthly column for *Guitar Player* magazine. Publs: *Howard Roberts Chord Melody; Howard Roberts Guitar Book; Sightreading by Howard Roberts* (Playback Publ., P.O. Box 4278, N. Hollywood, Ca. 91607).

LPs: *Antelope Freeway; Equinox Express Elevator* (Imp.); *The Movin' Man; The Velvet Groove* (Verve); *H.R. Is A Dirty Guitar Player; Guilty; Spinning Wheel; Jaunty-Jolly; Whatever's Fair; All Time Great Instrumental Hits; Color Him Funky; Out of Sight; Goodies; Something's Cookin'* (Cap.).

ROBINSON, ELI,* *trombone;* b. Greenville, Ga., 6/23/11. A veteran of many bands, incl. Co. Basie, '41-7, Robinson rec. frequently w. Buddy Tate's band in the '50s and '60s. He underwent lung surgery in '69 and died 12/24/72 in NYC.

LP: w. Tate, *Unbroken* (MPS).

ROBINSON, FRED LEROY (FREDDY), *guitar;* also *harmonica, electric bass;* b. Memphis, Tenn., 2/24/39. Stud. at Chicago School of Mus., '59-61. In Chicago pl. with Little Walter, '57; Howlin' Wolf, '60; Jerry Butler, '62. In LA w. Ray Charles, '68; J. Mayall, '71. Rec. w. the Crusaders, S. Turrentine, Groove Holmes, Nancy Wilson, Peggy Lee, Bill Cosby, the Staple Singers, Bobby Bryant, Ray Brown, Milt Jackson, the Impressions. Infls: R. Charles, Little Walter, Howlin' Wolf, Muddy Waters. TV: Midnight Spec. and L. Armstrong Memorial Spec. w. Mayall; TV and radio commercials for wine company, singing and playing solo. Fests: Newport w. Charles, '68; NJF-NO w. Mayall, '73. LPs: *Black Fox* (Wor. Pac.); *Jazz Blues Fusion* w. Mayall (Poly.); w. L. Feather, *Night Blooming Jazzmen* (Main.).

ROBINSON, JAMES (JIM),* *trombone;* b. Deeringe, La., 12/25/1892. New Orleans veteran who pl. w. Bunk Johnson and George Lewis in '40s was a member of the Preservation Hall Jazz Band from '61 until his death from cancer in NO, 5/4/76. He toured with the PHJB in Europe and Japan, pl. concerts there and at major concert halls in the US during the '70s. LPs: *Jim Robinson and his New Orleans Band; Jim Robinson and Tony Fougerat;* w. Orange Kellin; Dede Pierce; Don Ewell (Center); w. Preservation Hall Jazz Band (Atlantic).

ROBINSON, PERRY MORRIS, *clarinet;* b. New York, N.Y., 8/17/38. Father is composer Earl Robinson, who wrote *Ballad for Americans* and *Joe Hill.* Grad. from High School of Music and Art, NYC, '56; attended School of Jazz, Lenox, Mass., '59; Manhattan School of Music, '60-1; further studies w. Eric Simon at Mannes School of Music, NYC; Kalman Black of LA Symph. Toured Spain, Portugal, '59-60; pl. w. Tete Montoliu in Spain, '60. Back in NYC, w. Sunny Murray, Paul Bley, '62; Archie Shepp and Bill Dixon at World Youth Fest. In Helsinki, '67; Roswell Rudd's Primordial Quintet, '68; also trio w. D. Izenzon and Randy Kaye. Apps. w. JCOA in '70s; joined Two Generations of Brubeck, '73 and continued with them while also pl. w. Gunter Hampel and the Galaxie Dream Band. Infls: S. Rollins, Pee Wee Russell, Ch. Parker, Tony Scott. Fests: Frankfurt, '72, '74; Newport, '73; Baden Baden Free Music Symposium, '74. Won DB Critics Poll TDWR, '67; *Jazz and Pop,* '69; *Jazzwerld,* Holland, '70. Comps: *Ragaroni; Walk On; Margareta.* Robinson is also a professional magician.

LPs: *Funk Dumpling* (Savoy); *The Call* (ESP); *Escalator Over The Hill,* w. Carla Bley (JCOA); *Brother, The Great Spirit Made Us All,* w. Brubeck (Atl.); *Spirits* w. Gunter Hampel-Jeanne Lee (Birth).

ROBINSON, PETE, *piano, keyboards, synthesizer, composer;* b. Chicago, Ill., 3/3/50. Moved to Vancouver, B.C., '53. Piano lessons from '56. To SF, '62. Pro. debut w. rock bands. At 15 was DB scholarship winner to Berklee. Moved to LA, '66, joined Don Ellis, while studying w. Michael Tilson Thomas. After two years w. Ellis, spent a year w. S. Manne. In '72, comp. electronic music for Shakespeare Society of America. Concerts, seminars and recs. w. Phil Woods, '73-4. Extensive experience in producing for Playboy Records. Film scores: six documentaries.

Robinson, who operates his own multitrack studio for production work in electronic music, has also pl. w. Gil Melle (Alaska Fest. of Mus.), J. Klemmer, O. Nelson, Q. Jones, Ernie Watts. He has invented hybrid instruments, including electronic drums, polystrings etc.

LP w. own group, Contraband, *Time and Space* (Epic); also *dialogues for Piano and Reeds* (Testament); w. P. Woods (Testament); w. Manne, *Outside* (Contemporary); w. Melle, *Waterbirds* (Nocturne); Ellis, *Autumn* (Col.).

ROCCISANO, JOSEPH LUCIAN (JOE), *alto, soprano saxophones;* also *flute, clarinet, piccolo, tenor saxophone;* b. Springfield, Mass., 10/15/39. Stud. priv. w. Harry Huffnagle, '56; Ascher Slotnik, '57; Albert Harris, '74. At Potsdam State U., '59-63, received B.S. in mus. ed. First por. engagement w. Warren Covington, '57-9. Pl. local gigs until '63, then traveling w. Sam Donahue until '64. To Cal.,

'66, working w. Ray Charles, '67-8. Busy freelance player, writer in LA, w. B. Holman, T. Gibbs, Don Ellis, W. Herman, L. Bellson, Don Menza-Don Piestrup, Bobby Bryant et al; also own 12 piece band. App. at MJF and NJF with Ellis; also at World Jazz Festival, Japan, '64. Infs: P. Woods, C. Parker, Coltrane, Rollins. Comps: *Seven-Up* (for Ellis orch.); *Time Will Tell* (for Holman); *Inside-Outside; He Was All Of Us;* also many arrs. for Bellson, Ellis and Doc Severinsen. Publ: *Stage Band Arr. & Comp.* (Life Line Music Press, Box 338 Agoura, Ca. 91301).

LPs: w. Ellis, *Live in 3 2/3/4 Time* (Pac. Jazz); *Electric Bath* (Col.); w. D. Rader, *Polluted Tears* (DRM).

ROCCO, MAURICE JOHN,* piano, singer; b. Oxford, Ohio, 6/26/15. Known primarily for his boogie woogie performances while standing at the keyboard, he was a popular entertainer in U.S. clubs and Hollywood musicals during the '40s. He lived in Paris and Hong Kong before moving to Bangkok, Thailand in the early '60s and was a fixture at the Bamboo Bar of the Oriental Hotel until knifed to death in his apartment, 3/24/76.

ROCHLIN, IRVIN (IRV), piano; also percussion; b. Salem, Ohio, 4/14/26. Mother was pianist for silent movies. Stud. voice & piano w. Carl Gronemeyer in Chi., '38-42; percussion w. Lou Singer, '37-43; harmony & comp. at LA City College, '63-5; piano w. Erica Zador, '64. Worked as vocalist on CBS radio in Columbus, Ohio, '47; then as pianist in Chi. w. Anita O'Day, '48-9; Ike Day, '49; Chubby Jackson, '49-50; Georgie Auld, '51; Joe Daley, late '40s-early '50s; Jay Burkhart big band, '48-50; Ira Sullivan, off and on for 10 yrs. in late '40s-early '50s; Mary Ann McCall, '52; Z. Sims, '50; S. Getz, '57; Jimmy Cook big band, '60; J. Griffin, late '40s-early '50s; Jimmy Gourley, off and on for 25 years, beginning in Chi. After a period in LA, Rochlin, who was also known as Irv Craig during his Chi. yrs., left for Las Palmas, Canary Islands in '69 to play at the Half Note club, at the time partially-owned by Gourley. He pl. there w. Sims; Brew Moore; D. Gordon; Harold McNair, '70. In '71-3 he worked w. Ben Webster in Europe after settling in Amsterdam, '71. He also pl. w. Bobby Jones, '74 and cont. to work w. Gordon through '75. Infl: Teddy Wilson, Bud Powell, Wynton Kelly, Bill Evans; J. Mandel, Cole Porter, Ellington. French TV w. Gourley, '72. Comps: *The Nature of Things,* rec. by B. Evans; *Pepito's Rib,* rec. by Gordon. LP: *The Last Concert* w. Webster (Bovema).

RODIN, GILBERT A (GIL),* saxophone, trumpet, flute; b. Chicago, Ill., 12/9/06. Rodin, who helped organize the Bob Crosby band in '35, and who from the '60s was a successful TV producer, retired in '73 in order to write his autobiography. Before the project was completed he died 6/10/74 of a heart attack in Palm Springs, Cal.

RODNEY, RED (Robert Chudnick),* trumpet, fluegelhorn; b. Philadelphia, Pa., 9/27/27. Featured soloist w. bands of Thornhill, Krupa and Herman in '40s, and Charlie Parker quintet '49-50, he was based mainly in Las Vegas during the '60s, pl. in show bands backing the personalities who appear at the gambling capital. Moved to LA, pl. at Donte's, '72; jam session at Radio City Music Hall, NJF-NY, '73. A serious blood ailment slowed his comeback but he recovered sufficiently to tour w. G. Wein's *Musical Life of Charlie Parker* in Europe, fall '74. Rodney remained on the Continent until April '75, pl. clubs and concerts in Denmark, Sweden, Portugal, Belgium, Holland and England. Fest: Cascais, '74; Bergen, '75; Colo. Jazz Party '75. TV: many European apps. Comp: *Superbop; The Red Arrow; Box 2000; The Danish Jazz Army; Aarhus Express.* LPs: *Superbop; Bird Lives* (Muse); *The Red Arrow* (Onyx); w. Bebop Preservation Society (Spotlite); w. Danish Radio Orch. (Storyville); reissue, w. C. Parker (Verve).

RODRIGUEZ, ALEX, trumpet, fluegelhorn; b. Los Angeles, Cal., 8/26/40. Toured w. L. Hampton, '62-3; M. Ferguson, '64; W. Herman, '65; Gerald Wilson, '66- . While living in NYC, '69-70, pl. w. Frank Foster, P. Sanders, R.R. Kirk, Roy Haynes. Back in Calif., resumed gigging w. G. Wilson, also pl. w. H. Land quintet, and in Oct.-Dec. '73, toured U.S. and Canada w. S. Kenton. Pl. Watts Fest. w. Wilson, '71-4. Infls.: Coltrane, Clifford Brown, Booker Little.

LPs: *Live and Swinging; Everywhere; California Soul* w. Wilson (Pac. Jazz).

ROKER, GRANVILLE WILLIAM (MICKEY),* drums; b. Miami, Fla., 9/3/32. Busy freelancer in the mid '60s, he acc. Nancy Wilson, '65-7, and w. Duke Pearson's big band, '67-9, while continuing to work w. a variety of groups in NYC. With Lee Morgan from '69 into '71 when he joined D. Gillespie. TV apps. on the *Today* show w. Gillespie, Mary Lou Williams. All major fests. in Europe and U.S. w. Gillespie.

LPs: *Dizzy Gillespie's Big 4* (Pablo); *Live at the Lighthouse,* w. Morgan; *Speak Like a Child,* w. H. Hancock; *Now Hear This,* w. Pearson (BN); *Olinga,* w. Milt Jackson (CTI); *Zoot Sims Party* (Choice); *The Arrival of Bobby Jones* (Cobble.).

ROLAND, GENE,* composer, trumpet; also tenor saxophone, piano; b. Dallas, Tex., 9/15/21. Writing for Ib Glindemann radio orch. and pl. w. Papa Bue band at Vin Garten club, Copenhagen, Feb-Jun. '67. Trumpet at Jimmy Ryan's, '74; piano at Gregory's, '75. In the '70s, leader of own 21 piece and eight piece bands in NYC, pl. the Wine and Cheese Fest., '73. His assoc. w. S. Kenton, begun in the summer of '44 and renewed intermittently, was reactivated when he traveled with the band in '73. Comps: *Country Cousin; Blue Gene,* in Kenton album *7.5 On The Richter Scale* (Creative World).

ROLLINS, THEODORE WALTER (SONNY),* tenor, soprano saxophones, composer; b. New York City, 9/7/29. Prominent from '57, when he won the DB Critics' Poll as New Star. Pl. intermittently after voluntary inactivity, '59-61, Rollins again was in retirement from '68-71. During that period he visited Japan and India, stud. yoga, zen and the theories of Ghita. His retreat ended in June '71 and by the following year he was working with some regularity, touring Europe, pl. college concerts, composing a concerto under a Guggenheim Fellowship awarded him in '72. From '73 he visited Europe annually, also pl. in Japan in '73. Fests: Newport, '72-3-5; Chateauvallon, '73; Montreux, Antibes, Kongsberg, '74. TV: hour-long spec. for BBC, filmed live at Ronnie Scott's Club and at various locations around London, '74. His best known comps. are *Alfie's Theme* (from the movie *Alfie*); *Sonnymoon for Two; The Cutting Edge;* and his adaptation of the West Indian melody, *St. Thomas.*

His album *The Cutting Edge* was awarded the Grand Prix du Disque, a French award similar to the American Grammy. Working with various small instrumental groups, incl. promising musicians he had discovered, among them the guitarist Masuo, Rollins also has made unaccompanied performing a valuable part of his artistic approach. As Hollie I. West observed, "No other jazzman approaches him in sustaining the creativity and esthetic balance of solo work . . . Rollins has performed entire concerts by himself in brilliant style as if he were accompanied by a large orchestra."

Rollins is also noted for his ability to take the most unlikely of themes, such as *Happy Days Are Here Again,* and make thme meaningful through odd rhythmic patterns, long bursts of linear improvisation, and touches of sardonic humor. Won DB Critics poll, '67-70, '72-5; Readers poll, '72-5; Hall of Fame, '73.

LPs: *The Bridge* (RCA); *Alfie; East Broadway Rundown; Reevaluation: The Impulse Years* (Imp.); *Nucleus; The Cutting Edge; Freedom Suite; Horn Culture; Next Album* (Milest.); *First Recordings; Jazz Classics; Plays for Bird; Saxophone Colossus; Saxophone Colossus & More; Sonny Rollins; Tenor Madness; Three Giants; Worktime* (Pres.); others on BN.

ROMANO, JOSEPH (JOE), *tenor, alto saxes;* also *clarinet, flute;* b. Rochester, N.Y., 4/17/32. Studied alto sax at eight; clarinet at Eastman School from ages 10-12; tenor for a yr. Began professionally pl. w. local bands in Roch. at 14. Air Force at 17, pl. w. bands in Alaska, Texas and New York state. Joined Woody Herman in Calif. '56 and pl. w. him, off an on, to '66. Worked in Las Vegas, '60-1; also two yrs. w. Chuck Mangione in Roch. in '60s. Member of Sam Noto quintet in Buffalo, '66-7. Buddy Rich, off an on, '68-70. Remained in Cal., pl. two weeks w. S. Kenton; then Les Brown, '70-2. Also w. L. Bellson during this period. Rejoined Rich '72-4. Free-lance in Roch., '74-5. To NYC Feb. '75. Pl. w. Chuck Israels' National Jazz Ensemble; subbed in Thad Jones-Mel Lewis orch. Infl: Charlie Parker, Sonny Rollins, Bud Powell, Coltrane, C. Hawkins, L. Young. TV: Pearl Bailey, Bob Hope shows w. L. Brown, '70-2. Fest: Monterey w. Herman, '60s; Bellson, '71; NJF, KCJF w. Herman. LPs: w. Noto, *First Act* (Xanadu); w. Rich, feat. on *God Bless the Child* in *Stick it* (RCA Vict.); *Buddy and Soul* (Pac. Jazz); w. Mangione, *Recuerdo* (Jazzland); w. Herman (Philips); w. Gus Mancuso, *New Faces* (Fantasy).

ROSENGARDEN, ROBERT M. (BOBBY), *drums, percussion;* b. Elgin, Ill., 4/23/24. Mother a pianist for silent movies. Two sons musicians: Mark, drummer w. Herbie Mann; Vince Guaraldi; Neal, trumpeter, pianist for jingles, rec. Pirvate instruction from age five. Stud. w. Oliver Coleman in Chi. at 11 for two yrs.; Roy Knapp through high school. Music scholarship to U. of Mich. where he stud. w. Dr. Wm. D. Revelli '42-3. Pl. w. 75th Inf. Band, Ft. Leonard Wood, Mo., '43; 502nd Air Force Band, Keesler Field, Miss., '44-5; Teddy Phillips, '45; Henry Busse, '45-6. To NYC '46 where he worked w. Charlie Spivak; Raymond Scott; bands at the Copacabana, Bill Miller's Riviera; Alvy West's Little Band, '46-8; Skitch Henderson, '48 incl. NBC radio. Regular member NBC staff, incl. symphony, '49-68. Cond. band for Dick Cavett show, ABC-TV, '69-74; also mus. dir. for

Waldorf-Astoria's Empire Room, '73. Pl. w. Benny Goodman, off and on, from '65; WGJ, intermittently, from '73, incl. European tour, '75. Member of NYJRC in second season; toured Russia, other European countries with its Louis Armstrong program, '75. Gigs w. Joe Venuti; Peanuts Hucko at Michael's Pub, '75. Extremely busy studio man, rec. w. Ellington; Lena Horne; Billie Holiday; J.J. Johnson-Kai Winding; Joe Williams; Doc Severinsen; Frank Sinatra; Ella Fitzgerald; Tito Puente; Dick Hyman; N.Y. Philharmonic, etc. Concerts w. Miles Davis-Gil Evans in '50s. Infl: Chick Webb, O'Neil Spencer, G. Krupa, B. Rich, Jo Jones. Film: *C-Man* w. Conrad Nagel; also many soundtracks. Fest: NJF-NY w. own band, '72; NJF; Nice; Concord; KC; Colo. and Odessa jazz parties. Comp: co-author w. Phil Kraus of Cavett show theme, *Meet the Girls.* Often thought of in the past as a top studio man, he has proven himself to be a versatile, spirited jazz drummer as well. LPs: *Colorado Jazz Party* (MPS/BASF); w. Jimmy Smith, *Peter and the Wolf; Hoochie Coochie Man* (Verve); w. A. C. Jobim, *Wave* (A&M); w. B. Goodman, Stravinsky, *Ebony Concerto* (Col.); w. Tony Mottola (Command; Proj. 3); w. C. Byrd; D. Brubeck (Col.); J. Venuti (Chiaro.).

ROSOLINO, FRANK,* *trombone, singer;* b. Detroit, Mich., 8/20/26. Early exp. w. G. Krupa, S. Kenton, H. Rumsey. Recording, TV and club work in later years. Several jazz clinics for Conn Instrument Co. since mid-1960s. Toured and featured w. Maria Muldaur and Benny Carter orch. '74. During '73-75, made individual recordings and personal appearances in Italy, Holland, England and Canada. Occasionally worked as soloist with Supersax. Recorded with Q. Jones and appeared w. him in concerts in U.S. and Japan. TV: featured soloist on Merv Griffin show. Movies: sound track of *Hot Rock* w. Q. Jones. Jazz festivals: Monterey, Concord; Charlie Parker Memorial in KC with Supersax; annual Dick Gibson Colorado jazz parties. Comp: *Blue Daniel* recorded by C. Adderley, S. Manne. LPs: own quintet (Horo); *Conversation* w. C. Candoli (Ital. RCA); w. Frank Strazzeri, *Taurus* (Revelation); *Supersax with Strings* (Capitol); w. Q. Jones, *Body Heat* (A&M); *Hotel,* soundtrack (Warner Bros.); *Brass Fever* (Imp.).

ROSS, ANNIE (Annabelle Short Lynch),* *singer, songwriter;* b. Mitcham, Surrey, Eng., 7/25/30. Member of Lambert, Hendricks & Ross Trio 1958-62. Living in England, ran own nightclub in mid-60s; took part in jazz festivals all over Europe. One woman show at Hampstead Theater Club, London. Frequent acting experience since then, including role of Polly in *Threepenny Opera* with Vanessa Redgrave; Weill & Brecht's *7 Deadly Sins* at Covent Garden with Royal Ballet; Royal Chichester Prod. of Pirandello's *Tonight We Improvise.*

Ross also appeared w. A. Previn at the Royal Festival Hall in a concert of K. Weill's music. Motion pictures: *Straight On 'Till Morning,* for which she composed and sang lyrics and music of the title song; *Alfie Darling,* sequel to *Alfie,* w. Alan Price. LPs: *Handful of Songs* (Ember), *Facade* w. Cleo Laine, J. Dankworth (RCA); reissues, *The Bebop Singers* (Prest.); w. Lambert, Hendricks & Ross (Col.).

ROSS, ARNOLD,* *piano, keyboards, composer;* b. Boston, Mass., 1/29/21. Name band musician in '40s, also acc. to many singers from early '50s. In recent years Ross has confined his work mainly to TV and rec. studios, w. N. Riddle, P. Weston, Johnny Mann, also touring occasionally w. singers (Edie Adams, Jane Russell, Frances Wayne Hefti) as cond.-acc. In '73 he made a trio ablum, his first in many years, for Nocturne Records. TV specs. w. Bing Crosby, F. Sinatra, other pop artists.

LPs: *Arnold Ross Trio; Arnold Ross Trio No. 2* (Nocturne).

ROSS, RONALD (RONNIE), * *baritone saxophone;* b. Calcutta, India, 10/2/33. Worked in England w. Ted Heath, many other English and visiting American groups, incl. W. Herman, '59. With Clarke-Boland band, '65-6; Hans Koller band, '67; BBC-TV w. D. Gillespie. Fest. apps. in Helsinki, Prague etc. w. Slide Hampton band and others. An exceptional performer on all saxophones, clarinets, flutes and piccolo, Ross also has worked with symph. orchs. Led band called 8 to 1 in mid-'70s.

LPs: *Cleopatra's Needle,* w. own sextet (Fontana); others w. Stan Tracey, Fredrich Gulda, Mike Gibbs, Lalo Schifrin, Slide Hampton, Tubby Hayes, George Gruntz; reissue, w. John Lewis, *European Windows* (RCA).

ROUSE, CHARLES (CHARLIE), * *tenor sax;* b. Washington, D.C., 4/6/24. After more than 10 years w. Thelonious Monk's quartet he left in early '70 to appear as a free-lance soloist w. local rhythm sections in Chicago, Wash., D.C., Newark, Phila. and Detroit. Formed own sextet '75 with an emphasis on Brazilian music, appearing at Five Spot; Rust Brown. Fest: NJF; MJF w. Monk; NJF-NY w. own group at New York Musicians Fest., '73. Comp: *Two Is One; Minor Walk.* LPs: *Two Is One* (Strata-East); w. Duke Jordan (Steeple.); Monk (Col.); reissue w. Fats Navarro (BN).

ROWLES, JAMES GEORGE (JIMMY), * *piano, composer;* b. Spokane, Wash., 8/19/18. Veteran of Goodman, Herman, T. Dorsey, Bob Crosby orchs., Rowles during the '60s continued to work as accompanist for many singers incl. Peggy Lee, Carmen McRae et al; also busy in the Hollywood studios and working with his own trio at many different night clubs in the LA area. In '73, at NJF-NY, he took part in a recital at Carnegie Hall which featured 10 pianists, in which he played solo piano in a tribute to Art Tatum. In that same year an album recorded live at Donte's w. C. McRae was issued on Atl. While in New York, 1974 he played a season at The Cookery and at Bradley's. Long engagements at Bradley's '75. Fest: NJF-NY, '74-5.

Long acknowledged as the favorite accompanist of every singer for whom he has worked, Rowles is an artist of consummate harmonic imagination. For many years he has specialized in building a repertoire of Ellington and Strayhorn compositions.

Comps: *The Peacocks; We Take The Cake; Ballad of Thelonious Monk; Morning Star; Frasier.* LPs: *Solo Piano* (Halcyon); *Trio* (Blue Angel); *Zoot Sims Party* (Choice); w. Sarah Vaughan (Mainstr.); B. Kessel (Concord); Kay Starr (GNP-Crescendo); w. C. McRae (Atl.).

ROWSER, JAMES EDWARD (JIMMY), * *bass;* b. Philadelphia, Pa., 4/18/26. Freelanced in NYC w. Al Cohn-Z. Sims et al, '66 until he joined L. McCann Sept. '69, touring worldwide. App. in movie *Soul to Soul,* w. McCann,

filmed in Accra, Ghana, '71. Fests. w. McCann, incl. Montreux, '72.

LPs: w. McCann on Atl.

ROY, THEODORE GERALD (TEDDY), * *piano;* b. Duquoin, Ill., 4/9/05. An associate in the '20s and '30s of Frank Trumbauer, B. Hackett, Pee Wee Russell et al, Roy later pl. solo piano at E. Condon's club, freelanced in NYC and rec. for Commodore with a revived version of the Original Dixieland Jazz Band in the mid-40s. He died 8/31/66 in a NYC hospital.

ROYAL, ERNEST ANDREW (ERNIE), * *trumpet;* b. Los Angeles, Calif., 6/2/21. Worked w. Lionel Hampton, Woody Herman, Duke Ellington, Stan Kenton, Neal Hefti. Member of ABC staff '57-72. From that time an extremely busy freelance in NYC on countless dates incl. Quincy Jones, Oliver Nelson, Gil Evans. Broadway shows: *Raisin; Bubbling Brown Sugar.* Pl. in Europe w. Friedrich Gulda, '68. European tour w. NYJRC '75. A versatile player who is capable of filling a soloist's role but is most often called on for his excellent lead work. TV: Tribute to Duke Ellington w. Quincy Jones, '75. LP: *There Comes a Time,* w. G. Evans (RCA Victor).

ROYAL, MARSHALL, * *alto saxophone, flute* etc.; b. Sapulpa, Okla., 12/5/12. After working with Count Basie from early 1951 until Jan. 1970, Royal settled in LA. For two years he played at the Ambassador Hotel's Grove, where he was contractor and lead alto player, first under Geo. Rhodes, later under Hal Borne. Freelance work incl. clubs, concerts w. Bill Berry LA Big Band. Several tribute concerts honoring Duke Ellington, in whose band he had played in the film *Check and Double Check* in 1930 and on several later occasions.

In the fall of 1974 Royal fronted a band assembled by Monk Montgomery to tour South Africa with singer Lovelace Watkins.

Films: *Lady Sings the Blues; Blazing Saddles,* w. Basie; *Lepke* (all on camera as well as sound track); *Mame.*

LPs: *Jack Daugherty and the Class of 1972* (A & M); many sessions of swing era recreations for series on Time-Life Records.

RUDD, ROSWELL HOPKINS JR., * *trombone, composer;* also *French horn, piano, conga;* b. Sharon, Conn. , 11/17/35. Extensive studies incl. Yale U., '54-8. Throughout '60s worked with traditional and mainstream bands, despite his close identification with avant garde music and with such musicians as A. Shepp, John Tchicai and Milford Graves in NY Art Quartet, and the so-called Primordial Groups w. Chas. Davis, Karl Berger, Perry Robinson, R. Kenyatta, Ch. Haden; also Roswell Rudd & Friends, feat. Sheila Jordan, Beaver Harris et al. Fests: Newport, '65 w. JCOA, '66 w. Shepp. Movies: app. in *The Hustler* as Dixie musician. Won research grant from National Endowment for the Arts, Performance Grant from NY State Council. Taught world music and jazz improvisation at Bard Coll., '73-5. Three months at St. James Infirmary, NYC, leading combo, winter of '74-5. Dutch radio spec., Apr. '75; also app. in Amsterdam w. Theo Loevende.

Long involved in the study not only of traditional European

music and its evolution but also of the jazz tradition and other musical idioms, Rudd in '64 began working as a staff musicologist with the folklorist-ethnomusicologist Alan Lomax. According to Rudd, ''This helped to fill a noticeable gap in my formal education. The work has given me immeasurable insights into the elements of ancient music, which I've been able to apply to my activities as a composer and performer.''

Rudd has written a number of extended works, many of which for economic reasons could not be recorded or presented publicly. For many years he was unable to make a consistent living in music and was forced to take other jobs. Michael Cuscuna wrote: ''Roswell Rudd is an extraordinary trombonist and composer and ethnomusicologist whose work has yet to reach full public recognition . . . a man whose musical elements make him one of the most unusual artists of our time.''

Comps: *Bop City Dues; Sky Above, Mud Below; Moselle Variations; Heartbreak & Reformulation;* symphonic works, *Blues for the Planet Earth; Springsong; Numatik Swing Band;* operas, *The Gold Rush; Taki 183.*

Own LPs: *Numatik Swing Band* (JCOA); *Flexible Flyer* (Arista); *Everywhere* (Impulse); w. A. Shepp, *Live At The Donaueschingen Music Festival* (BASF-MPS).

RUIZ, HILTON, *piano, composer;* b. New York City, 5/29/52. Studied classical w. George Armstrong; Latin w. Prof. Messorana; jazz w. Mary Lou Williams, '71- ; Cedar Walton, '72; Harold Mabern at Jazz Interactions Young Musicians Workshop, '72-3; Chris Anderson, '75. At age eight perf. in solo recital at Carnegie Recital Hall; at nine pl. in accordion symphony at Biviano School. Has pl. w. Latin soul bands, Ismael Rivera; Ralph Robles from age 13; at 14 rec. w. Ray Jay and the East Siders. Braodcast w. Latin bands on radio station WHOM.

Worked w. Frank Foster's big band and small gp., '70; Joe Newman, '71; Cal Massey big band, '71-2; Freddie Hubbard; Joe Henderson, '72; Clark Terry band and gp.; Jackie McLean, '73; subbed for two wks. w. Mingus, '73. From Nov. '73 pl. w. Rahsaan Roland Kirk, off and on, touring Europe, Australia, New Zealand, Canada. Worked w. Roy Brooks' Artistic Truth; concerts w. CBA big band, '72-4; Betty Carter, '74; Rashied Ali, '74-5. Infl: Coltrane quartet w. McCoy Tyner, C. Parker, T. Monk, Waller, Tatum, D. Gordon, D. Byas, early H. Hancock. TV: as child, Sandy Becker show, ABC; *Jazz Adventures* w. Baby Laurence. Fest: Montreux w. Kirk. Promising young pianist with much facility and fire.

Comp: *Arrival; One For Hakim.* LPs: *Piano Man* (Steeple.); w. Brooks, *Ethnic Expression* (Im Hotep); w. Kirk, *Case of the 3-Sided Dream in Audio Color* (Atl.).

RUMSEY, HOWARD,* *bass, club owner;* b. Brawley, Cal., 11/7/17. Original Kenton band member in early 1940s. Inaugurated jam session policy at Lighthouse in Hermosa Beach, Cal., 1949, remaining there as co-owner and manager, until '71. Secured new premises in Redondo Beach, Cal., and in '72 opened Concerts by the Sea, a plush, acoustically excellent jazz room, presenting the top jazz artists from all over the country.

RUSHEN, PATRICE LOUISE, *piano, composer;* also *flute;* b. Los Angeles, Cal., 9/30/54. Stud. at U. of S. Cal., Music

Preparatory Division. Early piano lessons w. Earl Hultburg, '60-3; Dorothy Bishop, '63-72. First prominent when she won awards as member of Locke High School band in LA. While still in her teens, she toured w. Leslie Drayton, Melba Liston, Abbey Lincoln, The Sylvers; has worked w. Gerald Wilson orch.; D. Byrd. Pl. at Monterey JF, '72. TV: *Black Omnibus.*

Rushen, who names H. Hancock, McCoy Tyner, K. Jarrett, Thad Jones, Gil Evans, J. Henderson and O. Peterson as her influences, is a musician of prodigious talent who, while still in high school, already showed a rare degree of maturity and technical command at the piano. Her comps. incl. *Shortie's Portion; 7/73; Traverse.*

LPs: *Prelusion; Before the Dawn* (Pres.); also w. J.L. Ponty (Atl.); Stanley Turrentine (Fant.).

RUSHING, JAMES ANDREW (JIMMY),* *singer;* b. Oklahoma City, Okla., 8/26/03. Featured with the Basie band from '35-50. Rushing later sang his blues hits w. B. Goodman, toured Australia w. E. Condon, and freelanced in and around NYC. In '69 he had an acting role in the film, *The Learning Tree.* Rushing's last album, *The You And Me That Used To Be,* made in '71, feat. many popular songs and standards, was voted Record of the Year in the '72 DB Critics' Poll. Rushing was also voted number one male singer in the same poll. Before the results were announced, he contracted leukemia and died 6/8/72 in NYC. In his last years he app. frequently at the Half Note, NYC, backed by A. Cohn-Z. Sims. Also seen at KC JF, '72, where he was inducted into the KC Jazz Hall of Fame.

Rushing's ebullient delivery and rhythmic drive established him not only as an outstanding blues singer (probably the first ever to become a key member of name bands), but also as a warm, personal interpreter of non-blues material.

LPs: *Listen to the Blues; Essential Jimmy Rushing* (Vanguard); *Gee Baby; Who Was It Sang That Song* (Master Jazz); *The You And Me That Used To Be* (RCA); also w. Basie (RCA, Col.); D. Ellington (Col.).

RUSSELL, GEORGE ALLAN,* *composer, piano, educator;* b. Cincinnati, Ohio, 6/23/23. With his sextet which he had formed in '60, he toured Europe as part of George Wein package '64 and then remained in Scandinavia, playing, writing and teaching his Lydian Chromatic Concept of Tonal Organization, a method praised by John Lewis, Ornette Coleman, Gil Evans and David Baker, among others. In '69 he returned to the US to teach his concept as a member of the faculty at the New England Conservatory in Boston. He also taught in Finland, '66, '67; Norway, Sweden, Denmark, '68; Tanglewood, Mass., summer '70; Denmark, summer '71. Performed several times a year for Scandinavian Radio in Oslo, Stockholm and Copenhagen, '65-71. Fest: Bologna, '69; Tanglewood, '70; Berlin, '70; Kongsberg, '71. Comp: *Othello Ballet Suite; Electronic Organ Sonata No. 1; Electronic Sonata for Souls Loved By Nature; Now and Then; Concerto for Self-Accompanied Guitar; Listen to the Silence; Events I-VIII.* The latter were part of a large work for pianist Bill Evans and big band commissioned by Columbia Records and recorded in '72. A concert performance w. Evans was given at Carnegie Hall in '74 under the auspices of the NYJRC.

From '67 *The Lydian Chromatic Concept* has been an official text at the U. of Indiana Music School. Kare Kolberg, president of the Norwegian Branch of the Int. Soc. for Contemporary Mus., called it "the wallbreaker which opened the way out of the '50s closed way of thinking . . . poetic, demanding without being binding, open without being anarchistic, precise without being petty."

Awards: NEA Grant, '69; Guggenheim Fellowships, '69, '72. Publications and LP, *Listen to the Silence* (Concept, New Music Distribution Service, 6 West 95th St., New York, N.Y. 10025). Other LPs: *Othello Ballet Suite/Electronic Organ Sonata No. 1; Essence of George Russell* (Sonet); *Electronic Sonata for Souls Loved By Nature* (Fly. Dutch.); w. Bill Evans, *Living Time* (Col.); reissues on Milestone; MCA; BASF.

RUSSELL, CHARLES ELSWORTH (PEE WEE),* *clarinet;* b. St. Louis, Mo., 3/27/06. Played with Bix Beiderbecke in Frank Trumbauer's band in St. Louis. Later worked in NYC w. Red Nichols, Ben Pollack, Louis Prima, B. Hackett, Bud Freeman in '30s; many Dixieland groups organized by E. Condon, Geo. Wein and others in '40s. Despite serious illnesses, he continued to work through the '50s and '60s, gradually attaining the stature of a legend, and experimenting with more contemporary approaches. After a brief illness he died 2/15/69 at a hospital in Alexandria, Va.

Russell was one of the foremost individualists of jazz history, his sound totally personal and unorthodox by academic clarinet standards. Late in his career he also showed a remarkable talent as a painter. He is represented on many albums as a leader: *Ask Me Now; College Concert; Spirit of 67* (Imp.); *Memorial Album* (Pres.); *Pee Wee Russell* (Archive of Jazz and Folk); *A Legend* (Mainstr.); *New Groove* (Col.); *Jazz Reunion*, Russell-Hawkins (Candid); w. E. Condon-Bud Freeman, *The Commodore Years* (Comm.); *Eddie Condon Concerts* (Chiaroscuro). *Eddie Condon's World of Jazz* (Col.).

RUSSELL, WILLIAM EUGENE (GENE), *piano, composer;* b. Los Angeles, Cal., 12/2/32. Cousin of guitarist Ch. Christian. Stud. Westlake Jr. Coll; Fine Arts Conserv; LA City Coll. in '50s; priv. lessons w. H. Hawes. Insp. by Hawes, A. Jamal, Gene Harris, Carl Perkins, Sonny Clark. Russell became an active musician, combo leader and composer in LA during '60s, writing some of the music for several movies in '67-8; theme for TV show, *Doin' It,* '72; app. as actor in *Black Gestapo.* Worked as actor and musician in *The Young and the Restless,* CBS TV, '75.

Russell is best known as the founder of Black Jazz Records, for which he has recorded as a leader in addition to producing sessions with many other artists. He is also pres. of G.R. Productions and Aquarican Records. Russell has pl. in the groups of Rahsaan Roland Kirk; Zoot Sims; L. Vinnegar; D. Gordon; Wardell Gray; Miles Davis in concerts in LA and NYC; and subbed for Gene Harris in The Three Sounds for three months when the latter was ill.

Fests: Monterey, '68 w. own trio; J. Coltrane Memorial Fest., '70; Fest. in Black, '71; Cal State JF, '74.

LPs: *Up, Up and Away* (Decca); *Taking Care of Business* (Dot); *New Directions; Talk To My Lady* (Black Jazz); w. Joe Cocker, *Feelin' Alright* (A & M).

RUTHERFORD, ELMAN (RUDY), *clarinet, baritone, alto saxes, flute;* b. Detroit, Mich., 1912. Played w. L. Hampton, '43; Count Basie, '44-7; Ted Buckner's band in Detroit, '47; Basie again, '51. In '50s and '60s app. w. own combos at Count Basie's, other NYC area clubs, Ramapo Country Club. Worked w. Ram Ramirez trio, '59; Buddy Tate, '64; also w. Wilbur De Paris. Joined Earl Hines '75. Film: app. w. Chuck Berry in *Jazz On a Summer's Day* at NJF. Feat. on clarinet w. Basie on *High Tide* in mid-'40s. LPs: w. De Paris (Atl.).

RYPDAL, TERJE, *guitar, flute, soprano saxophone, composer;* b. Oslo, Norway, 8/23/47. Father, Jakop Rypdal, captain in military band. Wife, Inger-Lise, pop singer and actress. Stud. piano from age five, guitar at 13. After working as a pop musician, Rypdal in the late 1960s played with Jan Garbarek's group, also w. George Russell Sextet and big band. Stud. Lydian Concept with Russell. First break as guitar soloist in free-jazz festival at Baden-Baden, Germany, 1969. Pl. w. Violin Summit at Baden-Baden, '71; own trio at Berlin Jazz Festival '72. Started new group, Terje Rypdal Odyssey, which in late '75 played its first concert in England. An important contemporary composer, Rypdal has written many works for his own group as well as such extended pieces as *Eternal Circulation,* for symphony orch. and jazz musicians; *Symphony No. 1,* 1973; *Electric Fantasy; Tension;* and music for theatre. LPs: *Bleak House* (Polydor); *Whenever I Seem to Be Far Away; What Comes After; Odyssey* (ECM).

SADI, FATS (Lallemand Sadi),* *vibraphone, bongos, singer, composer;* b. Andenne, Belgium, 10/23/26. In '40s and '50s worked w. D. Reinhardt, Andre Hodeir, M. Legrand; lived in Paris '50-61; toured for three years w. Caterina Valente. Settled in Brussels, leaving occasionally to work w. Clarke-Boland band. From '72 had own TV show in which he sang, played bongos and acted. LPs for Vogue; Pallette; Manhattan; Saba labels; also w. L. Thompson, Christian Chevallier, Raymond Fol.

SAFRANSKI, EDWARD (EDDIE),* *bass;* b. Pittsburgh, Pa., 12/25/18. The former poll winning bassist, a member of S. Kenton's orch. '45-8, spent most of the late '60s and early '70s gigging in LA with mainstream and traditionalist groups. He died in LA, Jan. '74.

SAMPLE, JOSEPH LESLIE (JOE),* *piano;* also *electric keyboards, organ;* b. Houston, Tex., 2/1/39. From 1954 was assoc. w. Stix Hooper, Wayne Henderson, Wilton Felder in the combo eventually known as the Crusaders. Was still working with them in '70s, but beginning in '67 this job overlapped with various others as he started a career as a

Billy Strayhorn and Duke Ellington (*Sam Shaw*)

Cecil Taylor (*David D. Spitzer*)

Clark Terry
(*Veryl Oakland*)

...higpen, Danny Richmond,
...Higgins and Norman Connors (*Randi Hultin*)

Billy Taylor (*Bob Klein*)

Stanley Turrentine (*David D. Spitzer*)

Toots Thielemans (*Veryl Oakland*)

Joe Venuti (*Veryl Oakland*)

Leone Thomas (*Veryl Oakland*)

McCoy Tyner (*Veryl Oakland*)

Sarah Vaughan (*Veryl Oakland*)

Cedar Walton (*David D. Spitzer*)

Eddie "Cleanhead" Vinson
(*David D. Spitzer*)

Grover Washington, Jr.

Harold Vick (*David D. Spitzer*)

Bill Watrous (*Veryl Oakland*)

Chuck Wayne (*Bob Klein*)

Lenny White (*Veryl Oakland*)

Frank Wess (*Veryl Oakland*)

Ernie Wilkins (*Bob Klein*)

Tony Williams (*David D. Spitzer*)

Mary Lou Williams (*Veryl Oakland*)

Joe Williams (*Veryl Oakland*)

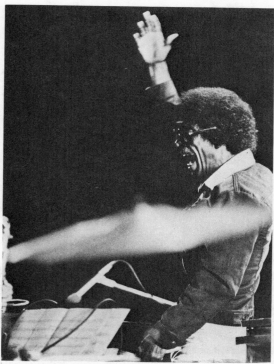

Gerald Wilson (*Veryl Oakland*)

Jimmy Witherspoon (*Veryl Oakland*)

Phil Woods (*Veryl Oakland*)

Sam Woodyard (*Krzysztof Zagrodski*)

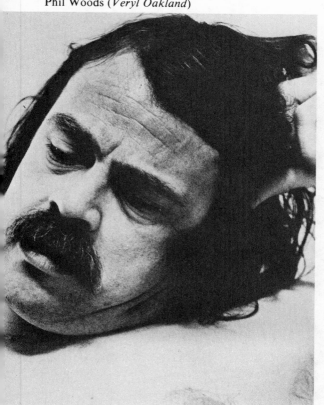

Joe Zawinul (*Veryl Oakland*)

The World's Greatest Jazz band; front, Yank Lawson and Bob Haggart; second row (from left), Ed Hubble, Bud Freeman, Gus Johnson, Vic Dickenson; back row, Bob Wilber, Ralph Sutton, Billy Butterfield.

Denny Zeitlin

Hollywood studio musician. He became a regular Motown session man, rec. w. Diana Ross, the Jackson 5 and many others. Rec. w. Joni Mitchell, Joan Baez and many other pop singers. Jazz records and gigs w. Harold Land-Bobby Hutcherson, O. Nelson, Q. Jones.

Early in '73 Sample went to Caracas as a member of the Tom Scott quartet. This group was the nucleus of what became known as the L.A. Express with which he was feat. in a series of successful recordings.

Comps: *Adventurers in Paradise* (comp. for and w. Minnie Riperton); *A Ballad for Joe Louis; A Search for Soul; A Shade of Blues; Put It Where You Want It.*

LPs: w. Crusaders (Pacific Jazz, Blue Thumb); w. L.A. Express (Ode); w. H. Land-B. Hutcherson, *San Francisco* (Blue Note).

SAMPSON, EDGAR MELVIN, * *composer, saxophones;* b. New York City, 8/31/07. Though he enjoyed his greatest fame as an arranger for the Chick Webb and B. Goodman orchs. in the '30s, Sampson later resumed playing saxophone, leading his own group, '49-51. He pl. w. several Latin bands, gigged w. Harry Dial and led combos of his own until the early '60s, when a serious illness inactivated him. He died 1/17/73 at his home in Englewood, N.J.

As composer and arranger of such classics as *Don't Be That Way; Stompin' At The Savoy; If Dreams Come True; Blue Lou; Lullaby In Rhythm,* Sampson developed a style that was prototypical of the swing era. Though he was not as prolific as Fletcher Henderson, everything he wrote was graced with a rare symmetry and melodic charm. An excellent and underrated soloist, he was heard playing violin on an early Henderson rec., *House of David Blues;* clarinet on a date w. Bunny Berigan in the mid-30s; alto on many sessions w. Webb, and baritone on *Ring Dem Bells,* on a famous L. Hampton date for RCA, heard in a since-deleted LP entitled *Swing Classics.*

SANBORN, DAVID WILLIAM (DAVE), *alto saxophone, flute;* b. Tampa, Fla., 7/30/45. After spending time in an iron lung during a childhood bout w. polio in St. Louis he was advised by a doctor to take up a wind instrument as physical therapy. Pl. alto sax in grade school band. At 14 gigged at "teen town" youth centers backing Albert King; Little Milton; pl. w. small combos in high school. Left St. Louis to study music at Northwestern U., '63-4. Got more heavily into blues in Chicago. After additional studies at U. of Iowa, '65-7, went to West Coast where drummer Philip Wilson brought him into the Paul Butterfield band. Played and rec. w. them, '67-71; lived in Woodstock, N.Y. for a yr. and resumed w. Butterfield '72. Worked w. Stevie Wonder, '72-3, touring w. him on Rolling Stones package '72. With Gil Evans from '74. Toured US w. David Bowie '74. Pl. w. Brecker Brothers '75. Forming own gp. for traveling after rec. first album. Gil Evans says: "He's got the technique but he's also got an emotional sound—that 'great cry.'"

Inf: Hank Crawford, Jackie McLean, Charlie Parker. TV: Euro. & US w. Evans; w. Butterfield; David Frost w. Wonder; Dick Cavett w. Bowie; *Saturday Night Live* w. Paul Simon, NBC. Fest: Woodstock w. Butterfield; Juan-Les-Pins w. Evans '75. Rec. hit disco single of *The Bottle* w. Joe

Bataan (Salsoul). LPs: *Taking Off* (WB); w. Evans, *Svengali* (Atl.); *Music of Jimi Hendrix; There Comes a Time* (RCA); w. Joe Beck; Esther Phillips (Kudu); Brecker Brothers (Arista); Hubert Laws (CTI); others w. Wonder; James Taylor; Bowie.

SANDERS, FARRELL (PHAROAH), * *tenor, soprano saxes, composer;* b. Little Rock, Ark., 10/13/40. With John Coltrane from '66. After Coltrane's death in '67 he continued to tour and record w. Alice Coltrane until '69 when he formed his own group which incl. Leon Thomas and Lonnie Liston Smith through '71. David Baker talked of his "strong, lean lyricism unencumbered by romantic excesses, the economy of materials, the wide range of musical expressivity, the absolute control of his instrument over a staggering three-octave range, and the remarkable fluency . . ."

On the other hand, Joachim Berendt who described him "as others among the newer tenorists, he extends the range of the tenor sax, by means of 'overblowing,' into the highest registers of the soprano," opined: "It is regretful that Sanders within a few years stereotyped and banalized a way of playing that had initially given rise to the highest hopes."

Sanders' framework has ranged from swirling, rasping, guttural explosions to pastoral, spiritual, pan-African expressions. He has played many fests. in US and abroad. Comp: *Tauhid; Upper Egypt; Thembi; Love is Everywhere; To John; The Creator Has a Master Plan; Colors; Hum Allah, Hum Allah.* LPs: *Black Unity; Elevation; Jewels of Thought; Karma; Live at the East; Love in Us All; Summun Bukmun Umyum; Tauhid; Thembi; Village of the Pharoahs; Wisdom Through Music* (Imp.); *Izipho Sam* (St.-East); w. Alice Coltrane; John Coltrane (Imp.); Don Cherry (BN).

SARDABY, MICHEL, *piano, composer;* b. Martinique, 9/4/35. Father was classical pianist. Self-taught from age five. As a child traveled a lot w. parents between NYC and other parts of U.S. From age 12 pl. w. various gps. at different places on Caribbean islands. At 17 formed his own 18-piece band. Left Martinique for Paris '53, studying at Ecole Boulle as parents did not want him to become a professional musician without receiving a diploma. From '56 pl. at Paris clubs such as Blue Note, Jazzland, Club St. Germain, Living Room, Le Chat Qui Peche; also other European clubs w. Albert Nicholas, Don Byas, Ben Webster, Stuff Smith, Chet Baker, Sonny Criss, Kenny Clarke, J. J. Johnson, Clark Terry, Johnny Griffin, Dexter Gordon, etc. Early infl.: Ellington, Waller, Tatum, Nat Cole. His rec. *Michel Sardaby /a New York* received the prize of the Academy of Paris. Played NJF in Paris; concerts in Paris at the Salle Pleyel and American Culture Center; Europe and Israel. His own LPs in which he is represented as composer include *Michel Sardaby à New York* w. Billy Cobham, Richard Davis and Ray Barretto; *Night Cup* w. Percy Heath and Connie Kay; *Gail* w. Davis, Billy Hart, Leopoldo Fleming; *Blue Sunset* (Debs); *Five Cat's Blues* (President).

SARMANTO, HEIKKI, *pianist, composer;* b. Helsinki, Finland, 6/22/39. Private studies at age 13. Stud. at Helsinki U. and Sibelius Academy. Received grant to study at Berklee Coll., '68-72. While in Boston stud. privately w. Margaret Chaloff. Worked w. own gp. in Scandinavia;

USSR; Switzerland. Has also pl. in Boston and NYC. Worked or sat in w. S. Rollins; A. Farmer; C. Terry; J. Henderson; G. Russell; C. Mariano. Early infl: Tatum, Bud Powell, Clifford Brown, Bartok, Debussy, Chopin. Won Best Finnish Jazz Musician '70; Best Pianist, Montreux JF '71. Composed music for radio, TV, modern dance. Comp: *Opuscule; Hymn to Jazzland; Theme for Christer; Jungle Flute; October Suite; Marat; Jazz Vesper;* over 100 vocal works for Finnish poetry, 30 vocal works for English poetry, '74-5. LPs: *Flowers in the Water; Onnen Aika* (EMI Col.); *Like a Fragonard; Everything Is It* (EMI Odeon).

SATO, MASAHIKO (Satoh), *piano, composer;* also *synthesizer;* b. Tokyo, Japan, 10/6/41. Violin lessons w. Hiroshi Hatoyama, '47-50; piano w. Fusako Uenuma, '47-51; Hiroshi Ito, '51-6. Stud. at Berklee, '66-8. Pl. w. Jiro Inagaki quintet, '63-4; own trio, '64-8. Pl. w. Clark Terry, Charlie Mariano et al, mainly in Boston, '66-8; then formed own trio which in the '72-4 period was called Garando. Own quartet, The Shadow Mask, from '74. Won Best Player Award at Art Fest., '71-2; SJ Readers Poll on piano, '70-1; as comp.-arr., '71-3. Infl: Yuji Takahashi, Olivier Messiaen, Akira Miyazawa. Fests: Berlin '71; Montreux, '73. Comps: *Yamataifu,* for big band; *Xenogamy* for orch. & Jazz combo. LPs: *Palladium* (Toshiba EMI); *Trinity* (Enja); *Sosho* (Trio); *Y. Takahashi & M. Sato; Four Compositions* w. Anthony Braxton (Nippon Col.); *Samadhi* w. Gary Peacock; *Yamataifu* w. Miyama & New Herd (Toshiba EMI).

SAUNDERS, ORVILLE, *guitar;* b. Washington, D.C. 6/2/54. Attended McFarland junior school. Stud. w. Bill Harris and worked w. K. Burrell at the latter's annual seminar, '74. Pl. w. Billy Hart, H. Hancock, G. Benson, Larry Ridley. A guitar major at Howard U, he joined the Blackbyrds in '75. LPs: *The Blackbyrds; Flying Start* (Fant.) others w. Richard Groove Holmes et al.

SCHIFRIN, BORIS (LALO),* *piano, composer;* b. Buenos Aires, Arg., 6/21/32. Toured w. D. Gillespie, '60-2. Since then has worked mainly as writer of film and TV scores. Cond. LA Neophonic Orch., '66. Scored *The Cincinnati Kid,* incl. vocal by Ray Charles on sound track, '66. Won two Grammies for *Mission: Impossible* TV music, '67. In '69 he was commissioned by C. Adderley to write a Third Stream work, *Dialogues for Jazz Quintet and Orchestra,* perf. at UCLA. Took part in LA Music Fest. cond. his *Jazz Suite on the Mass Texts,* feat. Paul Horn, '69. *Pulsations,* a Third Stream work commissioned for the LA Phil., was premiered in '70, cond. by Zubin Mehta.

During the '70s, Schifrin has continued to be very active in the fields of TV and motion pictures. Some of his scores, such as *Bullitt; Mannix; Dirty Harry,* are jazz-oriented; some include authentic jazz selections such as *Black Widow Blues* from *The Hellstrom Chronicle.* In '73, Schifrin made a rare personal app., playing at Shelly's Manne Hole. He has taken part as judge at song fests. in Rio, '70; Mexico City, '71. Taught composition at UCLA, '68-71. App. at Tribute to Dizzy Gillespie, Avery Fisher Hall, NYC, '75.

Some of his themes have become popular songs and have been rec. by such singers as Peggy Lee, C. McRae, Lou Rawls, Tony Bennett. Among them are *The Right To Love; Down Here On The Ground; The Fox; The Love Cage.*

LPs: *Marquis de Sade* (Verve); w. Gillespie, *A Musical Safari* (Booman); *Dialogues,* w. Adderley (Cap.); *The Other Side* (Audio Fidel.).

SCHLITTEN, DON, *producer, photographer;* b. Bronx, N.Y., 3/4/32. Began serious interest in jazz at age 13; art studies at High School of Music. Commercial artist until 1960. Prod. first LP for Signal Records, '57. Joined Pres. Records, '60 as art dir.—his photographs app. on hundreds of albums; later became creative activities VP. During next 10 years prod. over 150 LPs, incl. Pres. Historical Series, Spoken Word series (James Mason, Burgess Meredith, Norman Mailer). Became freelance a & r man in '70; prod. Vintage reissue series and J. Rushing's *The You and Me That Used To Be* for RCA, voted Record of the Year in DB Critics' Poll, '72; 12 LPs, incl. *Colorado Jazz Party,* for MPS; 16 LPs incl. first NJF-NY LPs for Buddah-Cobblestone; 36 LPs for Muse and 21 Onyx releases, incl. two that won Grammies for best jazz perf: Art Tatum, *God Is In The House; Charlie Parker, First Recordings!,* '74.

Schlitten states that his biggest infl. as producer, "other than the music," is Norman Granz. I. Gitler wrote in DB that Schlitten's "intensity, creativity, emotional involvement, keen perception and extraordinarily analytical ear make his productions truly unique. He really lives his work."

Among the many artists whose records he has produced are J. Moody, D. Gordon, S. Stitt, Booker Ervin, J. Raney, Jaki Byard, J. Heath, S. Criss, Barry Harris, P. Martino, E. Kloss, Red Rodney. In '75 he formed his own company, Xanadu Records Ltd.

SCHNITTER, DAVID BERTRAM, *tenor saxophone;* also *soprano, alto saxes, clarinet, flute;* b. Newark, N.J., 3/19/48. After grad. from Irvington H.S. attended Jersey City State Coll. majoring in clarinet. Participated in orch., stage band and other ensembles. During coll. yrs. also worked locally in Newark area. In '72 began visiting NYC for jam sessions, rehearsal bands, commercial work w. Latin bands. Sat in w. Joe Newman, Frank Foster, Howard McGhee; then began working w. Ted Dunbar; Wilbur Little, '73. Led own gp. at Boomer's three nights weekly for a year, '73-4. Joined Art Blakey Nov. '74. Also gigs w. own gp. at the Cellar, NYC, '74; Three Sisters, NJ, '75. Pl. in Japan and England w. Blakey.

Infl: Rollins, Dexter Gordon, Coltrane, Clifford Brown, Charlie Parker. TV: *Jazz Adventures,* Feb. '75. Fest: NJF-NY w. Blakey '75. LP: *Sonny Stitt with Art Blakey and the Jazz Messengers* (Polydor).

SCHOEBEL, ELMER,* *piano, composer;* b. E. St. Louis, Ill., 9/8/1896. Best known as comp. or co-comp. of such dixieland hits as *Bugle Call Rag; Farewell Blues; Nobody's Sweetheart,* Schoebel lived in Florida from '55, pl. occasionally w. local bands. He died 12/14/70 in Miami, Fla.

SCHOOF, MANFRED, *trumpet, composer;* also *piano;* b. Magdeburg, Germany, 4/6/36. Stud. at Music Akademie, Kassel, '55-8; trumpet, piano, theory, counterpoint at Cologne Musikhochschule (coll.). Pl. w. Gunter Hampel, '63-5;

leading own gp. from '65; also from time to time w. A. Mangelsdorf; Geo. Russell, '69 and '71; Clarke-Boland orch., '69-72. In Feb.-Apr. '75, Schoof's sextet and critic J.E. Berendt toured Asia under the auspices of the Goethe Institution in a prog. combining musical perf. and lectures. Infls: Miles Davis, J. Coltrane. Fests: Berlin, '66-7, '69, '70-1, '74; Prague, '66; Antibes; Lugano; Warsaw, '67; Belgrade, '71; Ljubljana, '73. Schoof has written for orch., combo, film and TV: *Ode* for Globe Unity Orchestra was perf. at the Donaueschingen Fest., '70; *Kontraste & Synthesen* for Globe Unity Orch. and choir at NDR, '74. Has won German jazz polls on trumpet from '67.

LPs: *Voices* (German CBS); w. Barney Wilen, Keshau Sathe trio, *Jazz Meets India;* w. New Jazz Trio, *Page One; Page Two* (MPS); w. S. Getz, Clarke-Boland, *Change of Scene* (Euro-Verve); w. Mal Waldron, *Hard Talk* (Enja).

SCHROEDER, EUGENE CHARLES (GENE),* *piano,* b. Madison, Wis., 2/5/15. The veteran of many Eddie Condon groups in the 1940s and '50s died 2/16/75 in Madison, Wis. LPs w. Condon (Col., Chiaroscuro).

SCHULLER, GUNTHER,* *composer, conductor, educator;* b. Jackson Heights, N.Y. 11/11/25. A French horn player w. the Metro. Opera Orch. for 10 yrs, he became associated w. jazz in the Miles Davis Nonet of '49-50. Later closely allied w. John Lewis, he was involved with the classical-jazz fusion called "Third Stream." Pres. of the New England Conservatory in Boston from '67, he formed the New Eng. Cons. Ragtime Ensemble for a Fest. of Romantic American Music. Reworking the arrs. of Scott Joplin rags from the famous New Orleans Red Back Book of Rags, he presented them w. the Ensemble and rec. for Angel what became a best-selling album. These arrs. were pl. in film *The Sting,* which won an Oscar for scoring in '74 for Marvin Hamlisch.

He also formed the New Eng. Conserv. Jazz Repertory Orch. for which he transcribed Ellington works with plans to incorporate arrs. from bands such as Earl Hines, Benny Moten, McKinney's Cotton Pickers, Paul Whiteman, Sam Wooding and Jim Europe. Two works of his were premiered in '75: *Triplum 2* by the Baltimore Symph.; *Four Sound Scopes* by the Hudson Valley Phil. Publ: *Early Jazz,* a history-analysis with mus. examples up to early '30s (Oxford Univ. Press, '68).

SCHULMAN, IRA, *flute, tenor saxophone, clarinet;* also *piccolo, alto flute, bass clarinet, saxophones;* b. Newark, N.J., 1/12/26. Stud. mus. at Senn H.S., Chicago, '41-5; Northwestern U.; Midwestern Conserv. of Mus., '45-7; clarinet w. Buck Wells, Jerome Stowell; saxophone w. Santy Runyon; flute at Northwestern. In h.s. pl. w. L. Konitz, Bill Russo, then w. bands of Jimmy Dale, Jay Burkhart and Russo. Also worked w. legendary drummer Ike Day in Chicago. Moved to Cal., '59, pl. w. Onzy Matthews. Joined orig. Don Ellis orch. in '64, staying with it for four years, then w. Dave Mackay-Vicky Hamilton for two years. In '70s, pl. in LA grammar and high schools, colls., as well as concerts for the City Parks and Mayor's Bureau of Mus. w. Baroque Jazz Ensemble. The format is a history of Amer. jazz incorporated into a program of baroque classic jazz and includes works of Bach, Mozart, Debussy, Ellington, Parker, Monk, Clifford Brown. Schul-

man has also worked and rec. w. T. Vig, and has been active as a teacher of woodwinds since coll. Infls: L. Young, D. Reinhardt, Basie, Billie Holiday, Ch. Parker, Fats Waller, T. Monk, B. Powell, Sid Catlett, M. Roach, Bach, Mozart, Segovia. Fests: Monterey, '66-8; Newport, '67-8; Cannes, '68, all w. Ellis.

LPs: w. Ellis, *Electric Bath; Shock Treatment* (Col.) *Live in 3⅔/4 Time* (Pac. Jazz); w. Mackay-Hamilton, *Rainbow* (Impulse).

SCOTT, RONNIE,* *tenor saxophone, leader;* b. London, England, 1/28/27. Gained early exp. w. Ted Heath, Cab Kaye, J. Parnell. Formed first band '53. Since '59 proprietor of Ronnie Scott's Club, presenting visiting Amer. artists, among whom have been the big bands of B. Rich, T. Jones-Mel Lewis, W. Herman, S. Kenton, as well as soloists S. Getz, O. Peterson, T. Monk, R.R. Kirk et al. Scott cont. to pl. w. his own trio, app. at his own club, as well as making frequent tours of Europe, incl. Poland and Hungary. From early '60s member of Clarke-Boland big band, app. on all its LPs.

In '74 the trio toured Australia, followed by engagements in NYC, incl. Carnegie Hall; their app. in Rochester, N.Y. was televised by ABC-TV. Scott has been seen on English TV constantly since the '60s; many shows feat. local and Amer. jazzmen have been taped for TV and radio from the club.

Though now principally identified with the club, Scott has made a substantial contribution as one of England's foremost jazz soloists, and has remained active in this capacity.

LP: *Scott at Ronnie's* (RCA).

SCOTT, SHIRLEY,* *organ;* b. Philadelphia, Pa., 3/14/34. Toured and rec. w. husband S. Turrentine until '71 when they separated musically and matrimonially. Continued to tour with own group; new edition formed in '74 feat. saxophonist Harold Vick. Frequent apps. on local NY and Phila. TV shows with her trio. NJF-NY, w. Vick amd Geo. Coleman, '74. Comps: *What Makes Harold Sing?; Big George; Do You Know A Good Thing When You See One?; You Can't Mess Around With Love.* LPs: *One For Me* (Strata-East); *Lean On Me* (Chess); others w. own trio (Impulse); w. Turrentine (Pres.); *Cookbook* w. Lockjaw Davis (Pres.).

SCOTT, THOMAS WRIGHT (TOM), *tenor saxophone;* also *saxes, flutes, miscellaneous woodwinds, composer;* b. Los Angeles, Cal., 5/19/48. Mother, the late Margery Wright, was a pianist. Gained early experience observing his father, Nathan, a noted TV and motion picture composer *(Dragnet; My Three Sons),* working in the studios. First interested in folk music, then in big bands, mainly Goodman and Shaw. Played clarinet in high school, and during that time wrote score for a high school film. Self-taught as composer-arranger.

In '65 his Neoteric Trio won the combo division in the Teenage Battle of the Bands at the Hollywood Bowl. Also, while still in his teens, he learned all the saxophones and flutes, played with Don Ellis and Oliver Nelson bands, Roger Kellaway and Howard Roberts groups, and in orchestras on TV shows such as *Ironsides* and *Good Morning World.* At 19 he recorded his first LP as a leader, *The Hon-*

eysuckle Breeze. This included one of his first and best known compositions, *Blues for Hari*. He was barely out of his teens when he followed his father into the TV studios as a writer, his credits including a Burt Reynolds show, *Streets of San Francisco; Cannon; Baretta*. Movie scores for *Conquest of the Planet of the Apes; Uptown Saturday Night*. During the '70s he became closely associated with a group of gifted and protean Hollywood musicians, among them Kellaway, John Guerin, Chuck Domanico, Roberts, Max Bennett, Victor Feldman. His gigs, night club work and concerts with musicians of this caliber led to the formation of his own group, the L.A. Express. While heading this combo, he was leading a triple life as studio musician and composer, jazzman in night clubs, and concert artist on tour with singer Joni Mitchell. His music represents a synthesis of innumerable elements: the John Coltrane influence, French and German classical impressionism, rock artists such as the Beatles and the Mothers of Invention, soul stars Aretha Franklin and Ray Charles, and Indian music reflecting his year of studies with Hari Har Rao. Infl: G. Mulligan, Coltrane, C. Adderley, C. Parker, P. Woods, George Coleman, King Curtis.

By '75 Scott had become one of the most popular and commercially successful young musicians of his generation, appealing to the pop and rock audience as well as maintaining certain jazz elements in his music. TV: *Midnite Special*, '75. Fest: MJF, '68; Montreux, '70; *Onda Nueva*, (Caracas); NJF-NY, '73. Awards: DB Critics, TDWR, '70; *Jazz & Pop* '70; NARAS MVP '73-4; Grammy '74.

Comps: *Blues for Hari; King Cobra; Refried; Love Poem; Liberation; Malibu; Visions off the Highway; Mantra; Boss Walk; Lookin' Out For Number Seven; Head Start; Freaky Zeke; Rural Still Life; With Respect to Coltrane; Freak In; Court & Spark; Miles of Aisles*. LPs: *Tom Cat; Tom Scott & The L.A. Express* (Ode); *Great Scott* (A & M); *Tom Scott in L.A.; Hair to Jazz* (Fl. Dutchman); *Rural Still Life; The Honeysuckle Breeze* (Impulse); w. Mitchell, *Court & Spark; For The Roses; Miles of Aisles* (Elektra-Asylum); w. G. Mulligan, *Age of Steam* (A & M); w. Pat Williams, *Threshold* (Cap.); w. Carole King, *Jazzman* (Ode); w. O. Nelson, *Live in Los Angeles* (Imp.).

SCOTT, TONY,* clarinet, baritone sax, composer; also piano; b. Morristown, N.J., 6/17/21. This world traveler spent the first half of the '60s in the Far East, returning to NYC in '65. Pl. w. own gp. at Dom, Half Note. Concert of Indian-influenced jazz, w. Collin Walcott on sitar and tabla, for Museum of Modern Art's *Jazz in the Garden* series, '67. Living in Italy in '70s, working in Rome w. the gp. led by pianist Romano Mussolini. Toured US w. Mussolini on circuit of Italian-American clubs, '72. LP: *52nd Street, Vol. 1* (Onyx).

SCOTT-HERON, GIL, singer, lyricist, poet, writer; b. Tennessee, ca. 1948. After a childhood in rural Tennessee was raised in the Chelsea section of Manhattan. Sang in high school R&B gp. At 19 wrote a novel, *The Vulture;* two yrs. later a second novel, *The Nigger Factory,* was published. He also wrote a book of poetry, *Small Talk at 125th and Lenox.* At Lincoln U. in Pennsylvania '69 met Brian Jackson. Influenced by listening to Imamu Baraka (Leroi Jones) they be-

gan, according to Scott-Heron, "with some simple premises that related to the traditional African delivery of poetry, through voice and conga. It seemed practical within a system where very few of our people can read with the type of interpretive perception that's necessary to deal with poetry."

In the '70s he and Jackson performed w. their nine-piece unit called Midnight. Sheila Weller, in a *Rolling Stone* piece, described the material in Scott-Heron's albums as "original poems and songs which speak with extraordinary insight, anger and tenderness of the human condition, political deceit, the black experience, cultural roots and rape. Verbalizing the spirit and message of the new black music in a more widely accesible framework, he can be placed—on the pop/jazz continuum—somewhere between Leon Thomas and Donny Hathaway. But his statements—often delivered as strong, exhortative oral poetry—cut much deeper. And the eloquent literacy of his melodic songs make him far more than a jazz balladeer."

Comp: *The Bottle; H₂figate Blues; The Revolution Will Not Be Televised; Ain't No New Thing; Winter in America; No Knock; Lady Day and Coltrane; The King Alfred Plan.* LPs: *The First Minute of a New Day; From South Africa to South Carolina* (Arista); *Small Talk at 125th and Lenox; Pieces of a Man; The Revolution Will Not Be Televised* (Fly. Dutch.); *Winter in America* (Strata-East).

SEAMAN, PHILLIP WILLIAM (PHIL),* drums; b. Burton-on-Trent, Staffordshire, England, 8/28/26. The outstanding British drummer, who had rec. w. Dizzy Reece, Tubby Hayes, J. Deuchar, Ronnie Scott and Joe Harriott among others, died 10/13/72 in Lambeth, London, England.

SEBESKY, DONALD J. (DON),* composer; also trombone, piano; b. Perth Amboy, N.J., 12/10/37. First recognized as a writer in the '60s for the M. Ferguson band, in which he also pl. trombone. He gave up playing to concentrate on arr.-cond. With Verve he recorded as a leader and wrote for W. Montgomery, Astrud Gilberto, many others. He has also arr. material for B. Rich, Peggy Lee, D. Warwicke, R. Flack, S. Stitt, but scored his greatest artistic and commercial successes with a series of albums written for various artists on the A & M and CTI labels. By drawing on both his jazz and classical knowledge, Sebesky has placed these featured artists in orchestral settings that reflect many hues and timbres, thereby making their music readily accessible to a wider ranging audience. Film score: *The People Next Door;* TV score: *F. Scott Fitzgerald And The Last of the Belles.* Publ: *The Contemporary Arranger* (Alfred Music, 75 Channel Dr., Pt. Washington, N.Y. 11050).

LPs: *Rape of El Morro; Giant Box* (CTI); *Jazz-Rock Syndrome; Distant Galaxy* (Verve); for Montgomery, *California Dreamin'* (Verve); *A Day In The Life; Down Here on The Ground; Road Song* (A & M); for H. Laws, *Morning Star; Rite of Spring;* for F. Hubbard *First Light; Sky Dive;* for Jackie & Roy, *Time And Love;* others for G. Benson, P. Desmond (A & M, CTI); Chet Baker, Milt Jackson (CTI).

SEIFERT, ZBIGNIEW, violin; also alto sax; b. Cracow, Poland, 6/6/46. Studied violin at Chopin Sch. of Mus. in Cracow; grad. from Cracow Higher Sch. of Mus., '70. At Chopin Sch. he had also stud. saxophone w. Alojzy Thomys. Formed own quartet '65. It won Best Modern

Combo at Wroclaw Jazz on Oder Fest '69 and repeated at Nagykoros, Hungary in the same year. Seifert also won top soloist award. At that time he was Coltrane-oriented saxophonist. After pl. Polish Jazz Jamboree he joined Tomasz Stanko gp. Pl. at Berlin Jazztage; Jazz Jamboree, '70; West Berlin Free Music Workshop; Altena Int. Jazz Meeting, etc. Member of Polish Radio Jazz Studio Orch. from '70. With Stanko began to play violin, gradually featuring it more than the saxophone. Pl. w. Bosko Petrovic at Ljubljana JF '71; rec. for Czech label w. Jiri Stivin, Barre Philips, '72. Beginning in '73 app. at many Euro. fests. w. Hans Koller, and as soloist. Then pl. w. Joachim Kuhn. Wrote 25-minute concerto for violin, orchestra and jazz gp., commissioned by Radio Hamburg. *Jazz Forum* described him as ''a violinist (who) endeavors to get beyond the sonorous material imposed by the conventional manual capabilities of the instrument.'' LPs: *Variousspheres;* rec. in Holland; w. Stanko, *Music for K; Jazz Message From Poland; Purple Sun* (Muza); w. Stivin, *Petran Do Cepice* (Supraphon); w. Koller, *Kunstkopfindianer;* w. Kuhn, *Chinemascope;* w. Volker Kriegel, *Lift* (MPS).

SELDEN, FRED LAURENCE, *alto saxophone;* also *soprano, tenor, baritone saxes, sopranino, piccolo, flutes, clarinets;* b. Los Angeles, Cal., 1/22/45. BA in mus. from UCLA, '66; Stud. comp., arr. w. Shorty Rogers, '61-6; saxophone w. B. Shank et al; film scoring w. L. Schifrin, Earle Hagen. Pl. lead alto w. Don Ellis orch. '69-74, and w. H. Mancini on *Mancini Generation* TV show. Jobs around LA w. L. Bellson, B. Holman and own sextet. Comps: *The Magic Bus Ate My Donut; Spirit Lady; Euphoric Acid; Love for Rent; Tyme Cube.* Publs: *Magic Flute Solos; Far Out Flute Solos* (Chas. Hansen Music, 1860 Broadway, New York, N.Y. 10023); *Lennon & McCartney/Flute, Rock & Jazz Style; Lennon & McCartney/Eb, Bb, C Combo Books* (Chappell Music Co., 810 7th Ave., New York 10019).

LPs: w. Ellis, *Tears of Joy; Don Ellis at Fillmore; Connection; The New Don Ellis Band Goes Underground* (Col.); *Soaring* (MPS).

SENENSKY, BERNARD MELVYN (BERNIE), *piano, composer;* also *organ, synthesizer, keyboards;* b. Winnipeg, Manitoba, Canada, 12/31/44. Stud. piano priv. w. Clara Perlman from age nine to 16; then w. jazz pianist Bob Erlendson. Accompanied visiting players at Bourbon Street and The Colonial in Toronto, incl. Joe Williams, A. Farmer, Z. Sims, P. Woods, B. DeFranco, S. Stitt, etc. in mid-'70s. Leads own trio; also active in studio work. Visited Israel, Oct. '73, and pl. w. Platina Jazz Group for troops. Infl.: K. Jarrett, M. Tyner, B. Evans, C. Corea, Coltrane. TV: guest app. on Oscar Peterson Presents, CTV '74.

Comps: *Poochie; Beloved Gift; New Life Blues; Ronnie; B.B.; Little Waltz for a Little Boy; Reunion; Catching Up; Capricorn Dance; Up N' Down; Another Gift; Silvertrane.* LPs: *Beloved Gift;* w. Fred Stone; Herbie Spanier (RCI).

SETE, BOLA (Djalma de Andrada),* *guitar, lutar, composer;* b. Rio de Janiero, Brazil, 7/16/28. Moved to U.S. '60; pl. w. D. Gillespie, '62; own group and w. Vince Guaraldi trio from '63. After leading own trio through '69, Sete retired, but was active again in '71, leading a quintet. During next few years he concentrated mainly on playing solo guitar and lutar, an instrument of his own design, at coll. concerts. TV: *The Jazz Show,* KNBC, LA. One of the most innovative and eclectic guitarists in jazz history, Sete was insp. as much by Reinhardt, Geo. Van Eps and Andres Segovia as by C. Christian, B. Kessel and Tal Farlow. Wrote orig. music for film *The Monster Buoy,* which won the International Independent Film Makers Award in '66.

LPs: *Ocean,* solo guitar (Takoma); *Going to Rio* (Col.).

SEVERINSEN, CARL H. (DOC),* *trumpet; leader;* b. Arlington, Ore., 7/7/27. A member and assistant conductor of the orch. on the *Tonight* show, which he joined Oct. 1, 1962, Severinsen worked under the leadership of Skitch Henderson for four years, Milton DeLugg for one year, before taking over direction himself 10/9/67.

Following a farewell concert at Philharmonic Hall, NYC, Apr. '72, Severinsen moved with Johnny Carson and the *Tonight* show to the NBC-TV studios in Burbank, Cal., starting from 5/1/72. A few key sidemen came with him from NYC but the West Coast band consisted mostly of local musicians. Though not feat. extensively on the show, the rotating personnel usually included some or all of the following: Snooky Young, Conte Candoli, John Audino, trumpets; Lew Tabackin, Ernie Watts, Pete Christlieb, Dick Spencer, saxophones; Ross Tompkins, piano; John B. Williams, bass; Ed Shaughnessy, Louie Bellson or Colin Bailey, drums.

Severinsen continued to app. frequently as a brass clinician, pl. as soloist with various symph. orchs., and worked many weekends throughout the U.S. as leader of his own organization, The Now Generation Brass, which incl. some members of the *Tonight* show orch. He occasionally made other TV apps. incl. host of Timex jazz spec. for NBC.

Awards: First place as bandleader and trumpeter in *Playboy* magazine poll. LPs: *Brass Roots; Rhapsody For Now* (RCA); *Fever* (Command); *I Feel Good* (Juno); *16 Great Performances* (ABC).

SHANK, CLIFFORD EVERETT JR. (BUD),* *alto, baritone saxophones, flute, composer;* b. Dayton, Ohio, 5/27/26. Still an important figure on the West Coast jazz scene, during the late '60s and early '70s, Shank confined himself mainly to freelance movie and TV studios, but making apps. at local LA clubs such as Donte's every two or three months with a jazz quintet. He also participated in many coll. concerts and clinics throughout the U.S. In Apr. '74 he helped found the L.A. Four with drummer Shelly Manne, bassist Ray Brown and guitarist Laurindo Almeida. This group made two visits to Mexico, one to Australia and New Zealand, two to Canada, and played many club and concert dates on the West Coast.

Shank has composed countless jingles and TV spots and was heard in solo spots in the movies *The Thomas Crown Affair; Assault on a Queen; Sandpiper; Charley; Summer of '42.* App. at Concord JF w. L.A. Four, '74-5.

LPs: *Michelle; California Dreaming; Bud Shank & The Sax Section; Let It Be* (Wor. Pac.); w. L.A. Four (Concord).

SHARROCK, LINDA (Linda Chambers),* *singer;* b. Phila., Pa., 4/3/49. While an art student in coll. in Phila. heard Coltrane's music and Sonny Sharrock while he was pl. at Showboat in Phila. in '68 w. Byard Lancaster. She already knew and loved modern classical music. Moved to NYC to attend the Arts Students League but instead studied theory w. Giuseppi Logan and started singing. She also learned from Sharrock w. whom she toured nationally in Herbie Mann's gp., '69-70. Worked w. Sanders on east coast, '70-1. From '73 the Sharrocks have app. w. their own gp. in Europe and US. In a review of *Paradise*, Lars Gabel wrote: "Her voice colorings are endowed with the warmth and feeling that were absent on her earlier albums . . . and even though there are traces now and then of undigested influences from such diverse sources as Yoko Ono and classical coloratura singing . . . *Paradise* indicates that Linda Sharrock may be one of our more controlled radical vocalists."

Infl: Coltrane, Sanders, Sharrock, Albert Ayler. Fest: Antibes Jazz-Pop Fest., '71. Co-composed music for *Another Place* (see Sonny Sharrock). LPs: *Paradise* (Atco); *Black Woman* (Vortex); w. S. Sharrock; *Monkey, Pokie, Boo* (Byg).

SHARROCK, SONNY, *guitar, composer;* also *pedal steel guitar, banjo;* b. Ossining, N.Y., 8/27/40. Singing in rock and roll gp., '54-9. Began listening to jazz in '58. Got first guitar and started playing at age 20. Studied for a yr. w. Bob Evans. Attended Berklee, Sept. '61-Feb. '62. Studied comp. w. Rheet Taylor, NYC, Feb.-May '63. Moved to NYC '65. Pl. w. Olatunji, Oct. '65; Byard Lancaster, June '66-Sept. '67; Pharoah Sanders, Sept. '66-Sept. '67; Sunny Murray, Feb. '67; Herbie Mann, Oct. '67-April '73, incl. world tours. Pl. w. Don Cherry, Berlin, '68; Miles Davis, summer '69; Cannonball Adderley, Jan.-March '70. From '73 he and his wife, Linda, have toured in the US and Europe w. their own gp. Sharrock, whose infl. include Coltrane, Blind Willie Johnson, Little Richard, Tchaikovsky, Ornette Coleman, Fats Domino, Linda Sharrock and Miles Davis, says he "became the first guitarist to play free jazz. (No changes, no time.) Can notate but not read music. Do not know any standard tunes or any other musicians' licks."

Joachim Berendt called him "the free-jazz guitarist *par excellence*," who "plays clusters, sounding all the notes imaginable simultaneously (as do modern concert pianists) with the ecstatic vitality of harmonically unchained free jazz."

Fest: NJF-NY; NJF; Berlin; NY Musicians; many others US and Euro. Co-composed music and pl. for *Another Place*, a short film by Sadat Pakay based on the James Baldwin work. Other comp: *Black Woman; Peanut; 1953 Blue Boogie Children; Gary's Step*. Won DB Critics poll, TDWR, '70; *Jazz Podium* (Germany); *Jazz* (Holland) polls. LPs: *Paradise* w. Linda Sharrock (Atco); *Black Woman* (Vortex); w. M. Davis, *Jack Johnson*, (Col.); P. Sanders, *Tauhid* (Imp.); W. Shorter, *Super Nova* (BN); many w. Mann (Atl.; Embryo).

SHAUGHNESSY, EDWIN THOMAS (ED),* *drums;* also *tabla, composer;* b. Jersey City, N.J., 1/29/29. From '48 was active with many jazz groups as well as studio orchs. Joined *Tonight* TV show orch. '64; though this was still his principal job in '75, in that year he also introduced his own 17 piece band, Ed Shaughnessy Energy Force. Pl. Maryland JF w. R. Eldridge, C. Hawkins, '69. From '66, stud. Indian rhythms w. Alla Rakha, Ravi Shankar's tabla player, also

continuously busy as a drum clinician at colleges and high schools.

Comps: *Nigerian Walk; Blues Detambour*. Publs: *The New Time Signatures in Jazz Drumming* (Belwin Co., 250 Maple Ave., Rockville Centre, N.Y. 11570) *Big Band Drummers Reading Guide* (Energy Force Pub., 5414 Shirley Ave., Tarzana, Ca. 91356). LPs: *Rhapsody For Now*, w. Severinsen (RCA); *Afro American Sketches*, w. O. Nelson (Prestige); *Broadway Basie's Way* and others w. Basie (Command); *Ravi Shankar and Friends* (Dark Horse).

SHAVERS, CHARLES JAMES (CHARLIE),* *trumpet, singer, composer;* b. New York City, 8/3/17. Famous as a member of John Kirby sextet, '37-44, Shavers gained widespread recognition during more than a decade off and on w. T. Dorsey orch. He was later heard w. the Dorsey "ghost" band led by Sam Donahue, and worked on several occasions w. B. Goodman. He toured Europe on his own in '69, '70, made a guest app. w. Budd Johnson's JPJ Quartet in May '71, but was hospitalized soon afterward and died 7/8/71 (two days after Louis Armstrong's death) in the Bronx, N.Y.

Shavers was one of the most vital and versatile trumpeters who came to prominence during the swing era. As a composer-arranger, he was the key figure in the Kirby band, which was the most brilliant and subtle small group of its day. Shavers' most famous comp. was *Undecided*.

LPs: *The Last Session* (B&B); C. Ventura; C. Hawkins (Trip); Dorsey (RCA); own LPs, deleted, incl. *The Complete Charlie Shavers* (Bethlehem); *Excitement Unlimited* (Cap.); *Charlie Shavers at Le Crazy Horse Saloon In Paris* (Everest).

SHAW, ARVELL,* *bass, singer;* b. St. Louis, Mo., 9/15/23. Renewed association w. Louis Armstrong in '64 and remained with the band through a tour of Eastern Europe, '66. S. Amer. tour w. B. Goodman, '67. Own trio at Shepheard's, NYC, and for Hilton hotel chain in U.S. and Puerto Rico. Rejoined Armstrong for Waldorf-Astoria engagement, '70. Gigs w. Dorothy Donegan, Teddy Wilson, '72-4; own sextet for school and coll. perf.-lecture program in Nassau and Suffolk counties on L.I. and upstate N.Y. communities, funded by N.Y. State Council on the Arts and the National Endowment for the Arts. Own quartet, '75. Films: *New Orleans; High Society; The Glenn Miller Story; Je Suis de la Revue*, w. Fernandel. TV: *Timex Swing Festival*, WNBC, '72; Fests: Fest. of the Arts, Sullivan County, N.Y. w. own sextet; NJF-NY, '73-4; Nice, '74. Comp: *They Are People*.

LPs: *Nice Festival All Stars;* Claude Hopkins (Black & Blue); *Jazz Giants;* Herb Hall (Sackville); also see L. Armstrong.

SHAW, MARLENA (Burgess), *singer, songwriter;* b. New Rochelle, N.Y., 9/22/44. An uncle taught her chords at the piano, but her musical education was mainly informal. First pro. job with Howard McGhee in New Bedford, Mass., '64. Spent a year in Catskill Mtns. resorts; coll. concerts, mostly in the South, also concert dates w. M. McPartland et al. Began rec. for Cadet, '66. After working at a series of Playboy clubs, she joined the Basie orch., staying off and on from '68-70, mainly for a European tour, '68, and residencies in Las Vegas hotels, after which she moved to LV.

Fests: Onda Nueva, Caracas, Venezuela; also Montreux, '73. Infls: Ray Charles, Stevie Wonder, Michel Legrand et al. Comps: *Woman of the Ghetto; Street Walkin' Woman; You*. Shaw's early albums, and her work with Basie (she did not record with the band) revealed her as a potentially important jazz singer, but on signing with Blue Note Records in '72, she diversified her repertoire and style to aim at the pop and r & b market.

LPs: *Who Is This Bitch, Anyway?; From The Depths of My Soul; Marlena* (BN); *Out of Different Bags; Spice of Life* (Cadet).

SHAW, WOODY, *trumpet;* b. Laurinburg, N.C., 12/24/44. Raised in Newark, N.J. where his father was a member of a gospel gp., the Jubilee Singers. Took up trumpet in sixth grade, '55. Pl. w. school bands; then gigged w. Larry Young, Tyrone Washington. In early '60s pl. w. Eric Dolphy. Then went to Paris where he pl. w. Kenny Clarke; Bud Powell. In '64 he and Larry Young worked at the Chat Qui Peche; also in Belgium, Germany. Replaced Carmell Jones in Horace Silver gp. in '65. Jamming w. Hank Mobley, Donald Byrd, Jackie McLean, '66-7 which was also a period of much practicing. Pl. w. McCoy Tyner from, '68 off and on into '70s; Gil Evans, '72; Art Blakey, '73; then own gps. for clubs, recs.; featured w. Junior Cook-Louis Hayes Quintet '76. Originally infl. by Gillespie, M. Davis, Clifford Brown; later, by Booker Little, Freddie Hubbard, Donald Byrd, Lee Morgan. Many observers noted his resemblance to Hubbard but he has become more personal in the mid-'70s, as he moved away from purely chordal playing and into a controlled freedom. In October '72 he said: "After two choruses I get tired of playing the changes, and I think that's the difference in today's music and say 10 years ago, or maybe a little earlier than that. I like to superimpose harmonically. I like to play it deliberately in another key and resolve it."

Tied with Kenny Wheeler for trumpet, TDWR, in DB Critics poll, '70.

Comp: *Song of Songs; The Goat and the Archer; Love: For the One You Can't Have; The Awakening*. LPs: *Blackstone Legacy; Song of Songs* (Contemp.); *The Moontrane* (Muse); w. Silver, *Song For My Father;* w. McLean, *'Bout Soul; Demon's Dance* (BN); w. Blakey, *Buhaina; Anthenagin; Child's Dance* (Prest.); w. Joe Henderson (Mile.); w. Buster Williams, *Pinnacle* (Muse); w. C. Corea, *Inner Space* (Atl.).

SHEARER, RICHARD BRUCE (DICK), *trombone;* b. Indianapolis, Ind., 9/21/40. Stud. at LACC, '60; Bob Edmondson, Dick Nash and other priv. teachers. Pl. w. Claude Gordon, '59; Perez Prado, '60; Si Zentner, '60-1; Billy May, '61; then with various show groups. Joined Tex Beneke, '64; Righteous Bros., '64-5; Louie Bellson, '65. From '65 Shearer began a long assoc. w. S. Kenton orch. As first trombonist and asst. dir., he also led the band when Kenton was sidelined by illness. Favs: Bill Harris, Bob Burgess, Don Lusher, Dick Nash.

Fest: Monterey, '71; Newport, '71, '73. LPs: *Stan Kenton Live at Redlands; Live at Brigham Young; Live At Butler; Stan Kenton Plays Chicago, Fire Fury Fun,* and many others w. Kenton (Creative World).

SHEARING, GEORGE ALBERT, *piano, composer;* b. London, England, 8/13/19. Continued to work mainly with the quintet instrumentation he had inaugurated in '49. In addition, occasionally pl. jobs in trio context, and in '74 toured with *Big Band Cavalcade* show backed by orchestral arrangements. In '67, and annually since '73, gave week-long jazz workshops at Chautauqua, N.Y., conducting piano and jazz ensemble seminars.

Shearing has pl. with several of the major symph. orchs., incl. those in Houston, Atlanta, Detroit, SF, Milwaukee, Baltimore, Cleveland, usually combining a classical concerto with a program featuring the quintet backed by the orch.

Traveling up to 10 months annually, Shearing played clubs and hotels throughout the U.S. and in Europe and Japan. Many of his dates were community concerts. In June of '74 he went to Germany to record three new albums for the MPS label. Previously, after a long association with Capitol, he had been recording for his own company, Sheba.

In May '75, Shearing received an honorary Ph.D. in music from Westminster Coll., Salt Lake City, Utah. Comps: *Lullaby of Birdland* and about 100 others; music for Emmy award winning TV special about the Foundation for the Junior Blind. Publs: *Shades of Shearing* (Bayes Music, Box 2120 N. Hollywood, Ca. 91602). LPs: *The Best Of* (Cap.); *Light, Airy & Swinging; The Way We Are; Continental Experience* (MPS); *As Requested; Heart & Soul* w. Joe Williams and several others (Sheba Records, Box 2120, N. Hollywood Ca. 91602).

SHELDON, JACK, *trumpet, singer;* b. Jacksonville, Fla., 11/30/31. Still doubling as musician and TV actor, sometimes seen in commercials, Sheldon was best known during the '70s as a member of Mort Lindsey's orch. on the nightly Merv Griffin TV show, in which he was frequently seen as comedian, singer and soloist. During the summer of '74 he led his own small group for an extended engagement in Monterey, Cal. He continued also to make occasional apps. at Donte's and other LA clubs.

SHEPP, ARCHIE, *tenor, soprano saxes, composer, leader educator;* b. Ft. Lauderdale, Fla., 5/24/37. First important work w. Cecil Taylor in '60. He then became involved w. Don Cherry and John Tchicai in the New York Contemporary Five in US and Europe. From mid-'60s has led own groups. His playing attitudes in that period included anarchic, shrieking protest music; tender, Ben Websterized Ellington ballads; marching band segments inserted among his most stormy passages; and parodies of popular songs such as *The Shadow of Your Smile*.

In '69 he became associated with Cal Massey, playing his compositions and in '72, a musical on which they had collaborated, *Lady Day: A Musical Tragedy,* was performed at the Brooklyn Academy of Music. While in Paris in '69 Shepp played with other musicians ordinarily associated with the bop movement, Hank Mobley and Philly Joe Jones. He was later heard playing *Hankerin',* an early-'50s Mobley piece and it seemed that this eclectic, with his fingers in drama, poetry and sociology, was becoming even more diversified in his musical outlook. Barry McRae noted his "attempt to introduce an element of Africanism into his work

. . . with the *Magic of Ju Ju* . . . His concern with a return to Africa has hardly helped, and he has also worked in the presence of less distinguished talents such as Burton Greene and Noah Howard. His superb playing on titles like *Marmarose* and *Huru* (Byg) confirms his undiminished talent, but there is again the suspicion that Shepp—the traditionalist—is trying to prove he is not.''

In the '70s Shepp embarked on a new aspect of his career, that of college professor, teaching at the Univ. of Buffalo and, then, at Univ. of Massachusetts in Amherst, Mass., where he was in residence in '75.

His mid-'70s group, like his mid-'60s edition had a trombone in the front line but Charles Majid Greenlee (known as Harneefan Mageed w. Dizzy Gillespie in the '40s) was a different sound and style from either Roswell Rudd or Grachan Moncur. But Gordon Kopulous still characterized Shepp's style with ''the guttural, raspy vocal tone; yelps in the middle of a scale; melodic all the time.''

Shepp makes no distinction between folk and art music. ''I don't,'' he says, ''because I don't believe in the word 'art.' It's, to me, not functional, it's passive. It's bourgeois in the sense that art develops at a point when people have leisure time . . . So art music is something that I don't really subscribe to. I think essentially the same way the music is played and enjoyed in the black community.''

Yet Shepp is typical of the wave of musicians who emerged in the '60s who essentially do not perform for ''inner city'' audiences. His brand of emotional-cerebral music has had far more impact on white intellectuals than on ghetto residents.

In addition to many European tours, he played in North Africa, '69. Many festival apps. incl. NJF; NJF-NY '72; NJF-NY '73 where he led his own group w. Grachan Moncur III and Dave Burrell; took part in the dedication of Louis Armstrong Stadium; and participated in the Radio City jam session.

Comps: *A Sea of Faces; I Know 'Bout the Life; New Africa; The Wedding; Mama Too Tight; Portrait of Robert Thompson; Rest Enough; Attica Blues; Call Me By My Rightful Name; Samba da Rua; It Is the Year of the Rabbit.* LPs: *A Sea of Faces* (Black Saint); *There's a Trumpet in My Soul* (Arista); *Attica Blues; Cry of My People; For Losers; In San Francisco; Kwanza; Magic of Ju Ju; Mama Too Tight; On This Night; Things Have Got to Change; Three For a Quarter; Way Ahead* (Imp.); *Live at the Donaueschingen Festival* (MPS); *Black Gypsy; Coral Rock* (Prest.); own gp. w. Philly Joe Jones (Fant.); w. Grachan Moncur III, *New Africa* (Byg).

SHEW, BOBBY (Robert Joratz), *trumpet; also fluegelhorn, slide, piccolo & pocket trumpets;* b. Albuquerque, N.M., 3/4/41. Self taught with the exception of a few lessons at age 13. Pl. in h.s. concert bands and All-State bands and orchs., but learned mre from casual dance jobs. Attended U. of N.M. for one year, majoring in commercial art, with some music classes. While in Army assigned to NORAD band, where he mixed with many professionals, receiving impetus toward a career in music. Attended S. Kenton clinics at Indiana U. under Johnny Richards, S. Donahue, John LaPorta, '59-60. Pl. w. T. Dorsey orch. under Donahue, '64-5; W.

Herman, '65; Della Reese, also LV house bands, '65-6; B. Rich, Apr. '66-Jun. '67; LV hotels, '67-Jan. '68. He joined T. Gibbs big band, '68 on *Operation Entertainment,* ABC-TV, until Sept. '68, when he became lead trumpet for Robert Goulet, remaining until July '69.

Through Jan. '73 he occupied himself mainly with work in LV, but also toured as lead trumpet w. Tom Jones, P. Anka, '71. Moved to LA, Jan. '73 and has since been associated with the bands of L. Bellson, N. Hefti, D. Menza, Gibbs and Ed Shaughnessy's Energy Force. In '74 he also pl. with the quintets of B. Shank, A. Pepper. Busy studio musician, also active as priv. teacher, jazz clinician. Infls: Farmer, Gillespie, Don Fagerquist, C. Candoli, K. Dorham. Fests: French Lick with all star band from Kenton Clinics, '59; Antibes w. Herman, '65; Pacific Jazz, w. Rich, '67; Concord and Belvedere, w. Bellson, '74.

LPs: w. Bellson, *Louie Rides Again* (Pablo); w. Rich (Pac. Jazz); w. Herman (Col.); w. Toshiko-Lew Tabackin (RCA-Japan); *Symposium* w. Edith Hill and the Children of Selah (Peppered Snowfall).

SHIHAB, SAHIB (Edmund Gregory),* *baritone saxophone; also bass clarinet, flutes, alto, soprano saxophones, composer;* b. Savannah, Ga., 6/23/25. Spent more than a decade in Europe, playing frequently with Clarke-Boland band until 1972; taught music at Polytechnic High School in Copenhagen, '73. Returned to US late '73, settling in LA, where he led his own group in clubs and worked w. Quincy Jones orch. LPs with Clarke-Boland (BASF, Black Lion, Co., Atl.).

SHOEMAKE, CHARLES EDWARD (CHARLIE), *vibes; also piano;* b. Houston, Tex., 7/27/37. Piano major at SMU, Dallas for one year, mostly self-taught from age six. From '59-63 worked w. many local groups in LA area incl. Ch. Lloyd, A. Pepper, Lighthouse All Stars. In '63 began acc. singers, such as Sue Raney, Eddie Fisher et al. Took up vibraharp seriously in '65, working extensively in studios w. L. Schifrin, Q. Jones, N. Riddle, J. Mandel. In '67 he joined Geo. Shearing quintet, traveling throughout the U.S., until '73. In that year Shoemake opened his own teaching studio and from '73- made apps. at Donte's, Pilgrimage Theatre with own group and Tony Rizzi Five Guitars. Infls: Ch. Parker, Bud Powell, S. Rollins. Numerous fest. apps. w. Shearing.

LPs: w. Shearing, *Shearing Today; Fool on the Hill* (Cap.); *As Requested* (Sheba).

SHORT, ROBERT WALTRIP (BOBBY),* *singer, piano;* b. Danville, Ill., 9/15/26. Made his original reputation at the Blue Angel, NYC, the Haig in LA, and the Gala in Hollywood in late '40-early '50s;- then pl. engagements in London and Paris; NYC supper clubs. From '68 the Carlyle Hotel in NYC has been his main base of operation w. his own trio. Many apps. at NJF incl. NJF-NY '72 on Ellington program. Whitney Balliett calls him ''one of the last examples (and indubitably the best) of the cafe singer or the supper-club singer or 'troubadour,''' and describes his piano style as having a ''a loose, enthusiastic resemblance to Art Tatum's—it is florid and arpeggioed and slurred . . .''

LPs: *K-R-A-Z-Y for Gershwin; Live at Cafe Carlyle; Mad About Noel Coward; The Mad Twenties; Very Best* (Atl.); w.

Mabel Mercer, *At Town Hall; Second Town Hall Concert* (Atl.).

SHORTER, WAYNE,* *soprano, tenor saxophones, composer;* b. Newark, N.J., 8/25/33. Primarily known as a tenor saxophonist while with Art Blakey ('59-63), and during his early years with Miles Davis, whom he joined in '64, Shorter gradually transferred the emphasis of his performance to soprano sax. During his years with Davis, he further consolidated his reputation as a composer of highly sophisticated contemporary works. Notable among them were *E.S.P.; Iris; Orbits; Footprints; Dolores; Limbo; Vonetta; Prince of Darkness; Masqualero; Nefertiti; Fall; Pinocchio; Paraphernalia; Sanctuary.*

In the spring of '70, Shorter left Davis. Later that year Joe Zawinul quit the Cannonball Adderley group, and together the two men organized Weather Report (see ZAWINUL, JOE). Shorter, however, continued what was in effect a dual career, recording from time to time albums under his own name that were less abstract and more tonal than his work with Weather Report, and often touched with a Latin-American influence. A typical example was *Native Dancer,* released in '75, in which the Brazilian singer and guitarist Milton Nascimento participated as composer and performer on several tracks.

An earlier album, recorded just before the formation of Weather Report, was *Odyssey of Iska,* in which it was observed that "To study the evolution of Wayne Shorter as an individualist in music, compositionally or improvisationally, is to follow in large measure the path pursued by jazz as a whole during the past five or six years. The jazz idiom as we have known it, once a central rhythmic and harmonic facet of Shorter's identity, now has become one of many elements that have reached far beyond the purlieus of any one pigeonholed music. To put it in more basic terms, jazz is no longer his sole bag; it is rather one of many tools in a larger and more capacious bag that is cosmic in its scope."

As a soprano saxophonist, Shorter found this instrument even more compatible to his highly individual style than tenor. The latter, however, remained a consummately expressive voice, capable both of understated beauty and of powerful energy bursts evoking the John Coltrane legacy.

Comps: aside from the above works recorded with Davis, Shorter wrote most or all of the music for the LPs under his own name. Among them are: *The All Seeing Eye; Genesis; Chaos; Face of the Deep; Mephistopheles; Down In The Depths; Powder Keg; Calloway Went That-A-Way; Peaches and Cream; Dead End; Black Diamond; Seeds of Sin; Scourin'; Pay As You Go; Second Genesis; Mr. Chairman; Tenderfoot; The Albatross; Super Nova; Swee-Pea; Water Babies; Capricorn; More Than Human; Adam's Apple; El Gaucho; Teru; Chief Crazy Horse; Diana; Ana Maria; Beauty and the Beast; Wind; Storm; Calm; Joy; Moto Grosso Feio; Montezuma; Antigua; Iska.*

With Weather Report he composed and recorded: *Mysterious Traveller; Blackthorn Rose; Scarlet Woman; Tears; Eurydice; The Moors; Surucucu; Non-Stop Home; Manolete; Freezing Fire; Lusitanos;* w. Zawinul, *Milky Way; Umbrellas.*

Fests: With Davis and/or Weather Report, Shorter has appeared in virtually every major jazz fest. around the world. Annual first place winner on soprano sax in DB polls since '69. Along with his music, Shorter has found time to show his literary and artistic talents as writer and painter.

LPs: *The All Seeing Eye; Super Nova; Adam's Apple; Odyssey of Iska; Moto Grosso Feio* (BN); *Wayne Shorter* (GNP Crescendo); *Second Genesis* (V.J.); *Native Dancer* (Col.); w. Davis, *E.S.P.; Miles Smiles; Nefertiti; Miles In The Sky; Filles De Kilimanjaro; The Sorcerer; In A Silent Way; Bitches Brew;* w. Weather Report, *Mysterious Traveller; I Sing The Body Electric; Sweetnighter; Weather Report* (Col.).

SILVER, HORACE WARD MARTIN TAVARES,* *piano, composer;* b. Norwalk, Conn., 9/2/28. From '56 led own instrumental quintet feat. trumpet, tenor sax, bass, drums and himself. From '69 he became increasingly interested in lyric writing. During the '70s many of his albums presented an expanded group with guitar and singers. Among them was a trilogy of albums under the generic title *The United States of Mind,* subdivided into Phase I, *That Healing Feeling;* Phase II, *Total Response;* Phase III, *All.* In evaluating this project, Silver observed: "We have endeavoured to write memorable melodies and words about the mind, body and soul . . . dedicated to that spiritual part of us that flows through the mind, body and soul, the real self, the spiritual self, which when acknowledged and allowed to operate through us, leads to health, happiness, love and peace." This philosophy was mirrored both in Silver's perennially attractive melodies and his words, which were sung by Andy Bey, Salome Bey, Gail Nelson, Jackie Verdell and Silver himself.

Silver continued to enjoy international popularity. In the fall of '68 he toured Europe and pl. at Ronnie Scott's club. To Italy and Finland, summer of '73, Brazil concert tour, Oct. '73; NJF, '73; European tour, Aug-Sep. '74, after which Silver took up residence in LA and retired temporarily, forming a new group in the summer of '75.

Among many awards, he received the keys to the city of his home town in '68. TV: numerous apps. in U.S., London and continent; hour-long music and talk show in Brazil, '73. In '75 Silver made his first album as leader of a 13 piece band, for which Wade Marcus collaborated with him effectively on the orchestrations. Among the new Silver works introduced on this LP were *Barbara; Dameron's Dance; Sophisticated Hippie* (a tribute to Duke Ellington); *Mysticism.* His earlier works incl. *Senor Blues; The Preacher; Doodlin'; Nica's Dream; Sister Sadie; Filthy McNasty; Strollin; Peace; Song For My Father; Opus De Funk; Home Cookin; Come On Home; The Tokyo Blues.*

LPs: *Song for my Father; The Cape Verdean Blues; You Gotta Take a Little Love; Serenade to a Soul Sister; The United States of Mind,* Phases I, II, II; *In Pursuit of the 27th Man; Silver 'N Brass* (BN).

SIMMONS, JOHN,* *bass;* b. Haskell, Okla., 1918. Although largely inactive in music since the early '60s, Simmons in '75 was still living in LA, contrary to rumors (some of which were printed) that he had died. Some of Simmons' early records, incl. those w. B. Holiday on Commodore, were reissued in the '70s.

SIMMONS, HUEY (SONNY),* *alto saxophone, composer;* also *English horn, heckelphone, tenor saxophone;* b. Sicily Island, La., 8/4/33. Insp. by Ch. Parker, Simmons became well known in avant garde circles through his partnership in the early '60s w. Prince Lasha. From mid-60s worked clubs throughout N.Y. and Cal. Family moved to Woodstock, N.Y., where he pl. concerts and clubs w. group feat. his wife, trumpeter Barbara Donald. Together they started the Woodstock Music Festival. Returned to Cal., '70; concerts in Bay Area; more gigs w. Lasha. TV in Sacramento; made movie in Woodstock, '69. Nairobi JF. w. B. Hutcherson and Lasha, '71. Comps: *City of David; Zarak's Symphony; Interplanetary Travelers; Dolphy's Days; Burning Spirits; Coltrane in Paradise; Seven Dances of Salome; Ruma Suma; Reincarnation; Back to the Apple; Things And Beings.*

Simmons, who in '75 wrote that he had been "spending a lot of time studying and writing some new music that has not been introduced to this planet," is one of the most forceful and convincing composers and soloists in his field, having developed beyond the original influences of Parker and Ornette Coleman.

LPs: *Staying On Watch; Music of the Spheres* (ESP); *Manhattan Egos* (Arhoolie); *Ruma Suma; Burning Spirits* (Contemporary); w. Lasha, *The Cry; Firebirds* (Contemporary); w. Elvin Jones, *Illuminations* (Impulse); w. Dolphy, *Iron Man* (Douglas); *Eric Dolphy Memorial Concert* (V.J.); w. Smiley Winters, *Les Oublies De Jazz Ensemble* (Touche).

SIMON, MAURICE,* *alto saxophone;* also *tenor, baritone saxophones, flute, clarinet;* b. Houston, Tex., 3/26/29. For many years divided his time between name bands, cabarets and groups backing singers. In '60s led combo in LV for Damita Jo, and LA for Milt Trenier, Micki Lynn. Pl. bari. sax. w. Ray Charles orch., '67. TV series, *Here's Lucy,* under direction of Marl Young, '69. In '70s pl. w. Roy Porter, Fats Domino, Hal Borne; in '74 joined D. Ellington orch. under direction of Mercer Ellington, pl. first tenor, then baritone and later alto. Fests: Monterey w. Jesse Price, '72.

LPs: w. M. Ellington (Fantasy).

SIMONE, NINA (Eunice Waymon),* *singer, piano, arranger;* b. Tryon, N.C., 2/21/33. Continued to tour, playing clubs, concerts and festivals into the '70s at the head of her own group. Appeared several times at NJF-NY, the last time in *An Evening with Nina Simone* '74. From that point she entered a self imposed hiatus. Ralph J. Gleason called her "a singer, an actress, a preacher and a religious symbol . . . her very presence inspires to achievement, to art, and ultimately to life itself."

LPs: *It is Finished; Here Come the Sun* (RCA); *Gifted and Black* (Canyon); reissues on Philips.

SIMPKINS, ANDREW (ANDY),* *bass;* b. Richmond, Ind., 4/29/32. Best known through association with pianist Gene Harris in the Three Sounds, from 1957. Moved to LA 1966; continued to tour w. Three Sounds until early '68, then free-lanced. Joined George Shearing 1968, touring extensively with him; to Germany for rec. sessions with him in '74. Between jobs w. Shearing, he also pl. on film sound track scores, worked w. Carmen McRae, Joe Williams, and

gigged w. Clare Fischer, David Mackay and others. LPs w. Shearing (MPS-BASF, Sheba); Kenny Burrell (Fantasy).

SIMS, JOHN HALEY (ZOOT),* *tenor saxophone;* also *soprano, alto sax, clarinet;* b. Inglewood, Cal., 10/29/25. Joined Bobby Sherwood's band at 17, then put in a year w. B. Goodman, with whom he was reunited many times over the next 30 years. Famous as one of the "Four Brothers" sax section w. W. Herman, '47-9, and from '57 as intermittent partner in two tenor team w. Al Cohn, who had also been in the Herman band. In '67 Sims was feat. in N. Granz' JATP tour of U.S. and Europe. Working mostly as solo performer with local rhythm sections, he was seen often in NYC, LA, Toronto, Boston, Washington, Dick Gibson's annual jazz parties in Colorado, Ronnie Scott's Club in London.

In '72, at NJF-NY, Sims rejoined W. Herman for a concert at Philharmonic Hall. For six weeks during that year he again toured Europe w. Goodman, and in March '73 they toured Australia. During the summer of '74 Sims again played with Goodman for concerts throughout the U.S. Toured Scandinavia w. Cohn, fall '74; Norman Granz Euro. tour, '75. many apps. w. Bucky Pizzarelli at Soerabaja, NYC in '70s. Featured in "Salute to Zoot" concert at NYU Loeb Student Center, Dec. '75.

Though Lester Young was his early infl., Sims for many years has shown a totally distinctive sound and style, marked by a natural sense of swing, perfect structural concepts and a melodic creativity that seems equally intense in up tempo and ballad performances. In recent years, he has taken to doubling effectively on soprano sax. TV: B. Goodman special; O. Peterson shows in Canada. Fests: Newport, '72, '73, '74. Comps: *Red Door; Dark Cloud; Nirvana.*

Sims has made more than 40 LPs under his own name, among them *Body and Soul* w. A. Cohn (Muse); *First Recordings!* (Prestige); *At Ease* (Famous Door); *Otra Vez* w. J. Raney (Mainstream); *Waiting Game* (Impulse); *Zoot Sims Party* w. J. Rowles (Choice); *Nirvana* w. B. Pizzarelli (Groove Merchant); *Joe and Zoot* w. J. Venuti (Chiaroscuro); *Encounter* w. Pepper Adams (Prestige); *Zoot Sims and the Gershwin Brothers* (Pablo); LPs as sideman: *The Bosses* w. C. Basie, J. Turner (Pablo); *The You and Me That Used To Be* w. J. Rushing (RCA); *Transition* w. B. Rich-L. Hampton (Groove Merchant); w. Dave McKenna (Chiaroscuro); Phoebe Snow (Shelter); *Colo. Jazz Party* (MPS/BASF); *The Greatest Jazz Concert in the World* (Pablo).

SINATRA, FRANCIS ALBERT,* *singer;* b. Hoboken, N.J., 12/12/15. Sinatra continued his activities until '71, when he announced his retirement. He returned gradually, beginning with concert appearances in '73, and made a triumphantly successful tour in '74 acc. by Woody Herman. Late in '75 he starred in a series of apps. at the Uris Theatre in NYC, followed by a week in London, for both of which he headed a show that also feat. the Count Basie orch. and (in London) Sarah Vaughan.

TV: Special, *The Main Event.*

A book entitled *Sinatra: Twentieth Century Romantic,* by Arnold Shaw, was publ. in '68 by Holt, Rinehart and Winston.

LPs: Reprise; Capitol.

SINGER, HAROLD (HAL),* *tenor saxophone;* b. Tulsa, Okla., 10/8/19. Name band musician since the early '40s; Singer settled in Europe in '65. He pl. in the big bands of Johnny Dover and Slide Hampton; w. his own gp. in Paris clubs; and was seen at numerous fests in Poland, Hungary and throughout western Europe. Film: *The Only Game in Town* w. Kenny Clarke. TV and radio in many European countries. LPs: *Blues and News* (Futura); *Blue Stompin'* (Pathe Marconi); *Milt and Hal* (Black & Blue); *Paris Soul Food* (Poly.); *Soul of Africa* (Chant du Monde); w. Buck Clayton (Poly.); Milt Buckner; Eddie Vinson; T-Bone Walker; Johnny Letman (B&B); Kitty White (Barclay).

SINGLETON, ARTHUR JAMES (ZUTTY),* *drums;* b. Bunkie, La., 5/14/1898. The pioneer NO drummer, who played w. L. Armstrong in Chicago and NYC in the '20s, worked at Jimmy Ryan's, NYC, '60-6, and freelanced until a stroke rendered him inactive in '69. In '73 he received a Certificate of Appreciation from the City of New York; won Gene Krupa Award, '74, and in '75 was voted into the NARAS Hall of Fame for his participation in the Hot Five records made w. Armstrong in '28. Singleton died 7/14/75 in NYC.

LPs: w. Cozy Cole, Jo Jones (Jazz Odyssey); reissues w. Armstrong (Col.).

SIRONE (Norris Jones), *bass, composer;* also *trombone, drums, cello;* b. Atlanta, Ga., 9/28/40. Studied theory & comp. from ages five to seven w. Dr. Raymond Carver, band dir. at Clark Coll.; trombone from ages seven to 12 w. Ralph Mays; 12-17 w. Alfred Wyatt incl. concert mus.; bass w. Dr. Thomas Howard, '57-65. Worked w. Sam Cooke, '60; Jerry Butler, '61-2. Local Atlanta gigs w. cooperative band, The Group, which incl. George Adams, '57-61. Moved to NYC '65, pl. w. Noah Howard; Sunny Murray; Sonny Sharrock; Albert Ayler; Marion Brown; Archie Shepp; Dave Burrell; Pharoah Sanders; Gato Barbieri; Roswell Rudd; Cecil Taylor; Sun Ra; Bill Dixon; Rashied Ali; Don Cherry; Jackie McLean. From '70-5 has worked w. Dewey Redman; Ornette Coleman; Rudd; Taylor; and Ali. Main association from '70, however, has been w. Revolutionary Ensemble, a trio w. Leroy Jenkins and Jerome Cooper. Infl: Jimmy Blanton, Tommy Potter, Slam Stewart, Paul Chambers, Oscar Pettiford, A. Shepp, Sun Ra, Coltrane, Ellington, C. Taylor, O. Coleman, Beethoven, Bartok.

TV: Educ. TV w. The Group, Atlanta; *Soul* w. P. Sanders; *Jazz Set* w. Ali. Fest: Stockholm '75, Ann Arbor w. Revol. Ens.; Amougies, Belg. w. D. Burrell, Steve Lacy, Robin Kenyatta, '70; NJF w. S. Murray; NJF-NY w. Redman. Publ: (Re Publ. Co., P.O. Box 838, Peter Stuyvesant Station, New York, N.Y. 10009). Sirone feels that "we are the interpreters of Nature's Music. We find that everything on the earth contributes to its harmony." Comp: *Hu Man; Involution Evolution; The People's Republic; Configuration; Peace; Ishi.* LPs: w. Revolutionary Ensemble, *Manhattan Cycles* (India Navigation); *Viet Nam 1&2* (ESP); *The People's Republic* (A&M); *Psyche* (Re); w. Marion Brown (Imp., ESP); w. Noah Howard; Barbieri (ESP); w. L. Jenkins, *For Players Only;* R. Rudd (JCOA); Sanders (Strata-East); Redman (Imp.); C. Taylor, *Spring of Two Blue J's* (Unit Core).

SIVUCA (Severino D'Oliviera), *guitar, accordion, piano, singer, composer;* b. Itabayana, Brazil, 5/26/30. Older brother studied accordion; Sivuca was self-taught on the instrument from age nine. Took up guitar in later years. Left home at 15 to play professionally. Formed gp., The World on Fire, w. two other accordion-playing albinos, '49. Established as a major artist in Brazil w. recordings *Feijoada* and *Vasorina,* '50.

Appointed Ambassador of Musical Goodwill by Brazilian Gov't, '58, he led a gp. on European tour and was honored at Brussels International Fair. Remained in Europe after '59 tour, returning for brief visit to Brazil before moving to US, '64. Worked w. Miriam Makeba, '65-9; then w. Oscar Brown Jr. in show *Joy,* '69. Touring w. Harry Belafonte in '70s; also apps. w. own gp. at Top of the Gate, etc. Philharmonic Hall concert and Jamaican tour w. Makeba, '73.

Comp. score for NBC White Paper *Cry Help!,* '70; six documentary films for Pepsico Int. on the soccer star Pele, '73. TV: *Sivuca and his Music, Camera III,* CBS, '73.

A versatile performer who blends his Brazilian roots with many other elements including classical and jazz. Ira Mayer wrote in the *Village Voice:* "To call Sivuca a great musician is understating the case. His manner of scat singing is to bossa nova what Ella Fitzgerald's is to American jazz."

John S. Wilson said that "he projects an unquenchable sense of joy both visually and musically."

LPs: *Sivuca; Sivuca Live at the Village Gate* (Vanguard); w. Belafonte (RCA).

SIX, JACK, *bass;* also *trumpet;* b. Danville, Illinois, 7/26/30. Stud. trumpet with various teachers in Chicago, LA, NYC, 1945-55; composition major at Juilliard, '55-6; bass w. Wendell Marshall, Ruby Jamitz, '59; Homer Mensch, '60-2. Worked with many big bands incl. C. Thornhill, '58; W. Herman, '59-60. Combos: H. Mann, '59-64; Don Elliott, '60-64; Jimmy Raney, '61; Dukes of Dixieland, '64. Six became internationally known as bassist during his frequent tours w. D. Brubeck, '68-74. When not with Brubeck, he freelanced extensively w. G. Mulligan, Joe Williams and other singers and combos around NYC.

Fests: Newport, Berlin, Monterey, Mexico etc. w. Brubeck. Comps: *Five Piano Sketches; Debbie's Dance; Cello Sonata; Clarinet Sonata.* LPs w. Brubeck (Col., Atl.).

SJOSTEN, LARS, *piano;* b. Oskarshamn, Sweden, 5/7/41. Grandfather a violinmaker; aunt a violinist; mother taught piano. Studied piano and harmony privately; later studies w. George Russell. Settled in Stockholm, '60, and pl. w. Eje Thelin, Lars Gullin. Became house pianist at Golden Circle club where he pl. w. Dexter Gordon, Art Farmer, George Russell, Sonny Stitt, Steve Lacy, Borje Fredriksson and Gullin. In late '60s active in radio and recording. Toured Sweden w. Rolf Ericson's big band; Czechoslovakia w. Bernt Rosengren quintet. From '70 working w. own trio and quartet and w. Gullin. Awarded first Jan Johansson Scholarship '69. Infl: Dexter Gordon, Rolf Ericson, Gullin, Tadd Dameron. Many fest. app. in Sweden and Norway. Comp: *Tidigt; Ladislav; Gazoline, My Beloved; Pledge; Kong Fredrik's Blues.* LPs: *Lars Sjosten, Jazz Pianist; Club Jazz* on Swedish label; w. Gullin on SSX, Odeon; Brew Moore, (Sonet); others w. Rolf Ericson; Bernt Rosengren.

SKIDMORE, ALAN RICHARD JAMES, *tenor saxophone;* also *soprano sax, concert flute, alto flute, drums;* b. Kingston on Thames, Surrey, England. 4/21/42. Father, Jimmy Skidmore, is a saxophonist. Took course of lessons on theory and reading from Leslie Evans, but basically self taught. Infls: J. Skidmore, Ellington, Coltrane, Rollins, Monk et al. Worked w. Alexis Korner, Mike Westbrook, Eric Delaney, John Dankworth, Tubby Hayes, Mike Gibbs; also w. visiting Americans, incl. M. Ferguson, C. Corea. Had own show on BBC TV jazz series, '69; Jazz Workshops, German TV, '69, '70, '71, '72. No. 1 tenor saxophonist in *Melody Maker* poll, '71-2-3-4. Won Press Award at Montreux Fest. '69 for best band and best soloist.

In '75 Skidmore had own group w. John Surman. Comps: *Free for Al; Red Lady; T.C.B.; Safety First; Signal.* Own LPs: *Once Upon A Time* (Decca); *T.C.B.* (Phillips); w. Mike Gibbs, *Just Ahead* (Polydor); John Warren, *Tales of the Algonquin* (Decca); Norma Winstone, *Edge of Time* (Decca); Rolf Kuhn, *Devil In Paradise;* V. Kreigel, *Missing Link* (on MPS/BASF).

SMALLS, CLIFTON ARNOLD (CLIFF), *piano, arranger;* also *trombone;* b. Charleston, S.C., 3/3/18. Father started him on piano and trombone. While playing w. Carolina Cotton Pickers, attended KC Conservatory. During the '40s, while w. Earl Hines orch. as trombonist and second pianist, attended Chicago Conservatory. Was staff arr. for Carolina Cotton Pickers; also for Hines for whom he wrote charts on *Wagon Wheels; Blue Skies; Cottage for Sale,* all unrecorded. Worked w. Lucky Millinder; Bennie Green. Cond. & arr. for Billy Eckstine, '48-50. Served in same capacity w. Clyde McPhatter in early '50s; Brook Benton, '50s-'60s. Also worked w. Reuben Phillips band. Piano acc. for Ella Fitzgerald; Roy Hamilton, '60s; piano, cond., arr. for Smokey Robinson and the Miracles. In mid-70s w. Sy Oliver orch. and a member of the NYJRC. During his career also appeared w. Earl Bostic; Hal Singer; Tiny Grimes; Purvis Henson; Palmer Davis.

Infl: Art Tatum, Earl Hines. Film: sound track for Ella Fitzgerald in *Let No Man Write My Epitaph.* TV: *Mike Douglas Show* w. Benton; Robinson. Fest: NJF-NY; Concord. LPs: tracks in *Master Jazz Piano, Vol. 2;* w. Buddy Tate, *The Texas Twister;* w. Julian Dash (Master Jazz); w. Sy Oliver, *Yes Indeed* (Black & Blue); *Take Me Back* (Ilac); w. Ella Fitzgerald, *Live at Carnegie Hall* (Col.); w. Bennie Green (Prest.); w. S. Robinson (Tamla).

SMITH, CLADYS (JABBO),* *trumpet, trombone, singer;* b. Claxton, Ga., 1908. Although he continued to live in Milwaukee, the former Ellington and Charlie Johnson trumpet star was virtually inactive in music. Honored at the NJF-NY Hall of Fame concert, '75, he appeared on stage with his horn but did not solo. Two volumes of his early work were reissued on Biograph under the title, *Jazz Ace of the Twenties.*

SMITH, JAMES HOWARD (JIMMIE), *drums, percussion;* b. Newark, N.J., 1/27/38. Stud. Al Germansky School for Drummers, Newark, '51-'54; Charlie Perry, '51-54; Juilliard School of Mus., '59-60. From 1960 he worked w. E. Garner, B.B. King, L. Hampton, Richard Groove Holmes, Lambert, Hendricks & Ross, Jimmy McGriff, B. Webster,

Sweets Edison, Herb Ellis, Art Pepper, Joe Pass, Jimmy Smith (the organist) in clubs throughout the U.S.; also in clubs, concerts and fests. In Europe, Australia, New Zealand, Japan. Wrote arr. of *Misty* for Holmes for album *Soul Message* (Pres.). App. at NJF, MJF, Concord JF.

LPs: *Forrest Fire,* w. J. Forrest; *Gumbo,* w. Pony Poindexter (Pres.); *Salud,* w. J. Hendricks (Repr.); w. Garner, *Up in Erroll's Room* (MGM); *Gemini* (Poly.); w. Jack Wilson, *Song For My Daughter* (BN); w. O.C. Smith, *Live* (Col.); w. Richard Boone, *I've Got A Right To Sing* (Nocturne); w. Lambert, Hendricks & Bavan (RCA).

SMITH, JAMES OSCAR (JIMMY),* *organ;* b. Norristown, Pa., 12/8/25. Since '56, when his first recordings established him, Smith has been the best known and most influential jazz organist, winning innumerable awards in many countries. Though best known for his exciting r & b performances, he recorded an all ballad album for Verve in '70. In '72 he was selected as Honorary Director-Advisor to board of Amateur Organists Association International. In Sept. '72, he toured Portugal; the following year his suite, *Portuguese Soul,* on which he was backed by the Thad Jones-Mel Lewis orch., was released on Verve. In Apr. '74 Smith formed his own company, Mojo Records. In Sept. of the same year he was married to his manager, Lola Ward. Shortly afterward, he toured Israel for the first time. After leaving June '75 for an extensive European tour, Smith announced that he would be going into semi-retirement, restricting his performances to concerts, festivals and recordings.

Films: *Get Yourself a College Girl; Where the Spies Are.* TV: *Black Omnibus; Mike Douglas; Dating Game.* Fests: Newport, San Diego, many in Europe; toured w. Geo. Wein concert package, fall of '72, leading all star group w. C. Terry, A. Farmer, K. Burrell et al.

LPs: *Paid in Full; Jimmy Smith '75* (Mojo); *Bluesmith; Portuguese Soul; The Best Of; Blue Bash; Dynamic Duo* (w. W. Montgomery); *Further Adventures; Respect* (Verve); *Back at the Chicken Shack; Bucket; The Incredible Jimmy Smith; Plain Talk* (BN); *Jimmy Smith Jam, Newport in New York* (Cobble).

SMITH, LEO, *trumpet, fluegelhorn, piccolo trumpet, composer;* also *African flute, Indian flute, koto, Gamelan keyboards, percussion;* b. Leland, Miss., 12/18/41. Father, Alex "Little Bill" Wallace, was blues singer-guitarist who rec. and performed on radio w. Willie Love in early '50s. Studied blues w. Wallace, summer '55. At Lincoln High School stud. w. Earl Jones, '55-6, pl. in HS band. Organized own ensemble for improvising. Studied trumpet w. Henderson Howard, '57-61, incl. pl. Ellington arrs. Further stud. at Army Sch. of Mus., Ft. Leonard Wood, Mo., '62; Sherwood Sch. of Mus., Chi., '67-8, trumpet w. Wm. Babbcott, theory, harmony; Wesleyan U. (World Mus. Dept.), '74-5, African, Indonesian and Gamelan, Japanese, South Indian musics. Joined AACM in Chi., '67. Played w. Creative Construction Company (A. Braxton, L. Jenkins) in US and France, '67-70; Integral w. Henry Threadgill, Lester Lashley, '70; Creative Improvisation Ensemble w. Marion Brown in US, Germany, Austria, '70-2. From '71 w. New Dalta Ahkri w. Threadgill, Oliver Lake, etc. Infl:

Armstrong, Joe Smith, M. Davis, Navarro, Cherry, Booker Little, Don Ayler, Lester Bowie, the AACM. Film: *See the Music,* documentary w. Marion Brown by German dir. Theodor Kotulla, '70. TV: France, '68; Germany, '70. Fest: Amougies, '69; Radio Fest., Holland '71; Ann Arbor, '72. Publ: *Notes; Rhythm* (Leo Smith Pub. Co., P.O. Box 102, New Haven, Conn. 06501). Comp: *Creative Music-1; Ending EP-2; The Bell; Silence; Manhattan Cycles; Reflectativity; t wmukl-D; Ellington; Celebration Pieces; Eelo, sjz II, III, & IV; Seven Improvisations for Creative Orchestra.* LPs: *Creative Music-1; Reflectativity* (Kabell, same address as above); w. Muhal Richard Abrams (Delmark); Leroy Jenkins (JCOA); A. Braxton (Delmark; Sackville).

SMITH, LONNIE LISTON, *piano, electronic keyboards, composer;* also *tuba, trumpet;* b. Richmond, Va., 12/28/40. Father, Lonnie Liston Smith Sr., a member of the Harmonizing Four, a spiritual quartet, for more than forty years. Brother, Ray, sang with the Jarmels; brother, Donald, sang w. U. of Illinois Jazz Band and w. Lonnie's gp., the Cosmic Echoes.

Graduated from Armstrong HS in Richmond where he pl. trumpet in marching band; sang bass and baritone in choirs. Played tuba in marching band and piano in orchestra at Morgan State College where he grad. w. BS in Mus., '61. Worked w. Royal Stage Band; acc. Ethel Ennis, '61-2. Moved to NYC, pl. w. Betty Carter, '63-4; Rahsaan Roland Kirk, '65; Art Blakey, '66-7; Joe Williams, '67-8; Pharoah Sanders, '69-71; Gato Barbieri, '71-3; Miles Davis, '73-4; then formed the Cosmic Echoes.

Infl: Fats Waller, Art Tatum, Jelly Roll Morton, Ellington, Miles Davis, Cecil Taylor, Coltrane, Eubie Blake, Sun Ra, James P. Johnson, Lester Young. TV: *Jazz Set,* '71; *In Concert* w. M. Davis, '73; *Soul* w. P. Sanders; Montreux JF w. Barbieri. Fest: NJF w. Max Roach, '65; w. Sanders, Calif. JF '68; Nice '68, '71; w. Barbieri, Colombes, Montreux, '71; Berlin, Nice, Milan, Hammerveld, Dusseldorf, Copenhagen, '72. Comp: entire score for P. Sanders' *Jewels of Thought;* also *Let Us Go to the House of the Lord; Astral Traveling; Morning Prayer; Imani* (Faith); *Aspirations; Rejuvenation; In Search of Truth; Cosmic Funk; Beautiful Woman; Peaceful Ones; Summer Days; Expansions; Shadows; Desert Nights; Voodoo Woman.* LPs: *Visions of a New World; Astral Traveling; Cosmic Funk; Expansions* (Fly. Dutch.); w. Sanders, *Karma; Jewels of Thought; Thembi; Summum, Bukmun, Umyun* (Imp.); w. Barbieri, *Third World; Fenix; El Pampero; Under Fire; Bolivia* (Fly. Dutch); w. Kirk, *Here Comes the Whistleman* (Atl); *Please Don't Cry, Beautiful Edith* (Verve); w. M. Davis, *On the Corner; Big Fun* (Col.); w. Sonny Simmons, *Burning Spirits* (Contemp.); w. Norman Connors, *Slew Foot* (Buddah); w. Leon Thomas, *Spirits Known & Unknown* (Fly. Dutch); w. S. Turrentine, *Sugar* (CTI).

SMITH, MABEL: see BIG MAYBELLE.

SMITH, MICHAEL JOSEPH, *piano, keyboards, synthesizer, composer;* b. Livingston County, Ky., 8/13/38. Self-taught except for a few lessons w. David Baker and Ran Blake. First solo concert at age six. Served in Navy, '55-9. Priv. stud. of electronic music and perfs. w. synthesizers, '60-5. Relocated to Boston. Between '66-9, lectures, comp. and perf. in NYC, Boston. '70-1: involvement w. New Eng-

land Conserv. and Juilliard; first concert tour in Europe. Settled in Paris, '73, rec. various albums and comp. and app. at jazz fests. in Italy, Holland, Finland, West Berlin. Wrote score for U.S. film, *No Place to Hide.* Living in Sweden, '75. Comps: *Symphony for Geomusic;* also more than 150 works in contemp. music, avant garde jazz, piano concertos, ¢etudes, string quartets etc.

LPs: *Geomusic 2; Geomusic 3* (Saravah); *Preparation for a Descent Into Hell* (Ricordi Int'l); w. S. Lacy, *Flakes* (RCA); *Scraps* (Saravah).

SMITH, SONELIUS LAREL, *piano, composer;* b. Hillhouse, Miss., 12/17/42. Family sang, pl. piano by ear. Moved to Memphis at age six. Took up piano at nine, private lessons through high school. Studied piano & theory w. Josephus Robinson at Arkansas A,M & N, Pine Bluff, Ark., '62-9. Formed gp. w. reedman John Stubblefield at coll., pl. Intercollegiate JF at Kiel Auditorium, St. Louis, several times in late '60s. To Europe for month '69 w. Campus at Sea, sponsored by Indiana U. In NYC '69, pl. w. K. Dorham; Roy Brooks. Wrote arrs. for Bob Crewe at Saturday Music. Worked w. R.R. Kirk for nine mos. from Nov. '69. From '70 has gigged w. Frank Foster, H. Vick, D. Byrd, Elvin Jones, R. Kenyatta, A. Shepp, F. Hubbard, A. Blakey, L. Hampton. From '72 w. Piano Choir.

Infl: Tatum, Bud Powell, Ramsey Lewis, Jamal, H. Hancock, Tyner. TV: Italian documentary w. Shepp; *Today;* Ed Sullivan w. Kirk; *Positively Black* w. Kenyatta. Fest: Hampton, Va. w. Kirk. Teaches piano and voice privately. Wrote 13 songs for *Ark,* a play by Nancy Fales presented at Theatre La Mama, '74. Wrote three-movement work, *New York Blues.* Other comps: *The Need to Smile; Sanctum Saintorium* (for seven pianos); *Mellow in the Park; The World of Children;* over 100 songs. LPs: w. Shamek Farrah, *First Impressions;* w. Piano Choir (Strata-East); w. Kenyatta, *Stompin' at the Savoy;* w. Kirk, *Rahsaan, Rahsaan,* etc. (Atl.).

SMITH, HEZEKIAH LEROY GORDON (STUFF),* *violin, singer;* b. Portsmouth, Ohio, 8/14/09. First prominent at the Onyx Club on 52nd Street in NYC, where he and his combo created a sensation with their novelty tune, *I'se A-Muggin',* Smith was the first musician to make successful use of an electrically amplified violin. After living for some years in Cal., he left in '65 for bookings in Scandinavia and throughout Europe, but soon became seriously ill and performed only occasionally during the final year of his life. He died 9/26/67 in Munich, Germany.

LPs: *Black Violin* (MPS-BASF); *Memorial Album* (Prest.); *Have Violin Will Swing; Stuff Smith* (Verve); *Swingin; Stuff* (Emarcy); *Stuff Smith,* feat. S. Grappelli (Everest); *Violin Summit* (MPS).

SMITH, TALMADGE (TAB),* *alto, tenor saxophones;* b. Kingston, N.C., 1/11/09. Well known for his work in the '30s and '40s w. L. Millinder, T. Wilson and his own combo. Lived in St. Louis in '50s and '60s, continuing to play occasionally. Smith died 8/17/71 in St. Louis.

LPs: w. Billie Holiday; C. Basie (Col.); tracks in *Jazz Giants, Reeds, Vol. 2* (Trip); *Harlem Odyssey* (Xanadu).

SMITH, WARREN DOYLE,* *trombone;* b. Middlebourne, W. Va., 5/17/08. Prominent as a member of the Bob Crosby orchestra 1937-40, Smith later worked in California w. Pete

Daily, Joe Darensbourg and many other Dixieland jazz groups. He was active until shortly before his death in Santa Barbara, Calif., 8/28/75.

SMITH, WARREN, *percussion, composer, teacher;* b. Chicago, Ill., 5/14/34. Father, Warren Smith Sr., was reedman w. Noble Sissle, '27-33, incl. European travels; w. Jimmie Noone, Tiny Parham in Chi. Had inst. repair shop '30s-50s; taught Johnny Griffin, Gene Ammons among others. Mother pl. harp and piano prof. Many aunts, uncles, cousins perform prof. Uncle, Frank Derrick, led band at Great Lakes Naval Station during World War II.

Stud. reeds w. father; harp w. mother; drums at age six w. Buddy Smith and, later, w. Oliver Coleman. Percussion w. Paul Price at Ill. Univ. (BS in Mus. Ed. '57); Manhattan Sch. of Mus. (Masters in Percussion '58). Also stud. briefly w. Eddie Baker, piano & theory; snare drum w. Harold Farberman; vibes w. Jack Jennings; comp. w. Coleridge Perkinson.

Began gigging w. uncles when he was 15. Worked w. Gil Evans at Jazz Gallery, '58; Johnny Richards; Aretha Franklin; Nina Simone; Lloyd Price. Mus. dir. of Price's club, Turntable, '68. Toured Europe w. Negro Ens. Co.; served as Janis Joplin's mus. dir. for Euro. tour, '69; percussionist w. Tony Williams Lifetime '71. Pl. w. Evans again '74; NYJRC, '74-5; Sam Rivers, '75. Leads own gp. Composers Workshop Ensemble. Member of M'Boom re:percussion w. Max Roach, Roy Brooks et al. A hardswinging trap drummer, he is a wizard w. mallets, tympani, gong and miscellaneous percussion.

Broadway shows: *West Side Story; Three Penny Opera; Lost in the Stars; Golden boy; Raisin,* etc. TV: ABC staff for Jimmy Dean, Les Crane shows, '64-7; numerous apps. w. others artists. Charter member of Symph. of the New World; pl. under Stokowski w. American Symph. Orch. Many guest artist, speaker and clinician apps. at colls. from '69. Summer artist-in-residence at Dartmouth, '75. Taught elementary, junior high and high school in NYC, '58-68; Third St. Settlement School, '60-67; Chairman, of Dept. of African American Studies, Adelphi U., '70-1; Assoc. Prof. of Music at SUNY at Old Westbury; instructor at Adelphi.

Infl: Roach, Philly Joe Jones, Elvin Jones, Tony Williams; Ellington, Mingus, Gil Evans, Frank Derrick. Fest: Montreux w. T. Williams, '71; NJF-NY; Laren; Antibes; Toulon w. M'Boom, '73; Montreux; Antibes; Perugia w. G. Evans, '74. Comp: *Love In the Open; I Know the Scenery By Heart; Miles Whale;* other works perf. in *Music in Our Times* series, '70-2. Publ: *Beginning Rhythmic Notation; Professional Percussion Workshop; Five Pieces* (for mallet instruments); *Rhythmic Exercises for Lab Band* (Miff Music Co., 151 W. 21st St., New York, N.Y. 10011). LPs: *Composers Workshop Ensemble; We've Been Around* (Strata-East); w. J. Richards, *My Fair Lady* (Roul.); w. G. Evans, (RCA); w. Dave Sanborn (War. Bros.).

SMITH, WILLIAM HENRY JOSEPH BERTHOL BONAPARTE BERTHOLOFF (WILLIE THE LION),* *piano; composer;* b. Goshen, N.Y., 11/25/1897. A major infl. in NYC in the '20s, Smith in later years app. at many jazz fests., pl. at Dick Gibson's Jazz Party in Colo. Springs, and in Jan. '73 gave a duo recital with a young protege,

Brooks Kerr. This was Smith's last public app; after a brief illness he died 4/18/73 in a NYC hospital.

Smith's autobiography, *Music On My Mind* (Doubleday) was publ. in '64. Though identified with ragtime and particularly with stride piano, he was a maverick, one of whose most delightful and durable compositions was the simple and melodic *Echoes of Spring.*

LPs: *Willie "The Lion" Smith* (GNP); *Live at Blues Alley* (Chiaroscuro); *Pork & Beans* (Black Lion); *Music On My Mind* (Saba); *The Memoirs of Willie The Lion Smith* (RCA); *Grand Piano*—duets w. Don Ewell (Exclusive); *The Lion Roars* (Dot); *A Legend* (Mainstream); *Piano Solos By Willie Smith* (Commodore).

SMITH, WILLIAM McLEISH (WILLIE),* *clarinet, alto saxophone, singer;* b. Charleston, S.C., 11/25/10. Gained recognition as one of the principal soloists in the J. Lunceford band, with which he pl. from '29-42. Spent most of the next 20 years w. Harry James, except '51-3 when he was w. D. Ellington and B. May. In mid-60s worked w. Johnny Rivers in LV; also briefly w. Charlie Barnet early '67. He died in LA 3/7/67. Smith's exuberant sound on alto and relaxed, good humored singing earned him long lasting respect and popularity.

LPs: w. Lunceford, *Rhythm Is Our Business; Harlem Shout; Jimmie Lunceford & His Orch.* (Decca); *Lunceford Special* (Col.); *The Original Jimmie Lunceford Orch.* (Perception); *Jimmie Lunceford in Hi-Fi* (Cap.); also small gp. dates w. Nat Cole, Teddy Wilson, Jazz at the Philharmonic et al. Own LPs: *The Best of Willie Smith* (GNP-Crescendo); *Alto Artistry, Jazz Giants Reeds, Vol. 2* (Trip).

SNOW, PHOEBE (Phoebe Laub), *singer, composer, guitar;* b. Teaneck, N.J., 7/17/52. Piano lessons from early childhood, but at age 15 switched to guitar and became seriously interested in music. During her late teens she was introduced to jazz and related forms of music by a friend near her home; after writing poetry for some time she began around 1971 to put her verses into song form. In 1972, while performing in an amateur night show at the Bitter End in NYC, she was approached by a record producer to make a session, but nothing came of this, and in November, when her friend committed suicide, she went into an extended period of mourning.

Snow resumed composing in 1973, and early the following year recorded her first album, for Shelter Records. On one track, *Harpo's Blues,* the accompaniment included Zoot Sims and Teddy Wilson. The album became a gold-record best seller and Snow was acclaimed as one of the most important new vocal stars of the year.

During 1974 she was prevented from recording owing to a legal dispute, but meanwhile she appeared successfully in concerts and clubs. She signed with Columbia Records, and her first LP for that label, *Second Childhood,* appeared in Feb. 1976. As on the first album, there were occasional indications of a jazz influence in her style, and her backing on some tracks featured Jerome Richardson, Ron Carter and Grady Tate.

SNOWDEN, ELMER CHESTER (POPS),* *saxophone, guitar, banjo;* b. Baltimore, Md., 10/9/00. An early associate of Duke Ellington, first in Washington in 1919, later in NYC in '24, where Ellington took over direction of the Washingtonians, a group Snowden had earlier led. In the '60s Snowden was still playing intermittently in Phila.; toured Europe in '67 with the Newport Guitar Workshop. He had been planning to open a guitar school when he died suddenly 5/14/73 in Phila.

LP: *Harlem Banjo* (Riverside); *The Jolly Miners* (Historical).

SOLAL, MARTIAL,* *piano, composer;* b. Algiers, N. Africa, 8/23/27. Prominent since '40s in Paris. Wrote background scores for motion pictures incl. many industrial films. Several visits to U.S. to app. at Monterey and other fests. From '69, pl. concerts throughout Continent with regular trio, feat. bass and drums; from '69-71, concerts with a new trio feat. two bassists and no drummer. From late '71 solo concerts. In '75 became active as teacher, staging a week long seminar in Nice. Solal recorded many LPs for Pathe-Marconi, '66-9 and for French RCA, '71-2. Later, freelancing, he recorded two albums in Italy; one w. L. Konitz for Milestone in NYC; and one, for Spotlite, in LA; also one for MPS-BASF. Comps: *Rhythmical Escape* (30 minute suite for oboe, cello and jazz trio); *Fluctuat nec Mergitur; Etudes for Piano.*

LPs: as listed above; also M. Solal-H. Hawes Quartet (Byg).

SOLOFF, LEWIS MICHAEL (LEW), *trumpet;* also *fluegelhorn, piccolo trumpet;* b. New York City, 2/20/44. Father, Buddy Soloff, was a soft shoe dancer in a vaudeville team known as Bud & Buddy. Mother a vaudeville violinist. Stud. ukulele with father at age five; piano age five to 13. Took up trumpet in fifth grade in Lakewood, N.J., later stud. priv.; attended Juilliard Prep. Dept., '55-61; Eastman School, '61-5 graduating with Performer's Cert. in trumpet and B.M. in Applied Trumpet and Mus. Ed. Further studies at Juilliard, '65-6, w. Edward Treutel; also w. Carmine Caruso and players from Rochester, N.Y., Philadelphia and Chicago symphonies. His '65 performer's recital, *The Feel of a Vision,* was written by C. Mangione.

First pro. experience pl. in Catskill Mtns. show bands for seven summers from age 15½. From Sep., '65 to May '68 he pl. and/or rec. w. Machito, Tito Puente, Vincent Lopez, M. Ferguson, Joe Henderson, K. Dorham, C. Terry, Barry Miles, Gil Evans, Thad Jones-Mel Lewis, Radio City Music Hall orch., Chuck Jackson, Mangione, Urbie Green, Slide Hampton, Orch. Harlow, H. McGhee, D. Pearson, Frank Foster. From May '68 through Aug. '73 was feat. w. Blood, Sweat & Tears, touring worldwide incl. Eastern Europe. Soloist on *Feel of a Vision* w. Symphony of the New World; Rochester Phil. and Utica Symph; *Concerto for Trumpet and Orch.* by Alexandra Pakhmutova w. NO Symph. From Sept. '73 has been mainly associated w. Gil Evans orch; also app. on Mangione concerts as feat. soloist. Formed quintet, Salt & Pepper # 3, w. Jon Faddis, '75. Active as clinician for Bach trumpet. Infls: Parker, Gillespie, Miles Davis, Dorham, Hubbard, Clifford Brown, C. Terry, Faddis, Gil Evans. Many TV apps. w. B.S.&T. Fests: NJF, Montreux w. B.S.&T.; Montreux; Antibes; Perugia w. Evans, '74.

Soloff, a fine all around technician with a remarkable range, is an exceptionally capable lead man and strong soloist.

LPs: w. Evans (RCA); B.S.&T. (Col.); Gerry Niewood (Sagoma); Robin Kenyatta (Atl.).

SOPH, EDWARD B., *drums;* b. Coronado, Cal., 3/21/45. Influenced by Baby Dodds, Zutty Singleton, Danny Richmond, Roy Haynes et al. Stud. w. Elder Mori, Houston, Tex., '60-3; North Texas State U., '63-8, pl. w. Lab band under Leon Breeden. In '60s worked locally in Texas w. Jimmy Ford, Arnett Cobb, Don Wilkerson. Joined S. Kenton in summer of '66; W. Herman, '68, '70, '71. In '74-5 freelanced w. C. Terry, Bill Watrous and Chris Connor. Fests: Newport, '68, '70, '71; Monterey, '70, Concord, '71. Soph is a member of the faculty of the National Stage Band Camps.

Though heard to great advantage on his work w. Herman, Watrous et al, Soph says, ''I would like to rid myself of the stigma of being a big band drummer. I prefer small groups, with two exceptions: Woody and those bands at N. Texas.''

LPs: w. Herman, *Giant Steps* (Fantasy); Watrous, *Manhattan Wildlife Refuge* (Columbia); C. Terry, *Big Bad Band at Wichita Jazz Fest. '74; and his Jolly Giants* (Vang.).

SOUCHON, EDMOND II, M.D. (DOC),* *guitar, banjo, singer;* b. New Orleans, 10/25/1897. The prominent surgeon, avocationally a jazz musician and leading champion of New Orleans jazz, died while taking part in a jam session in NO 8/24/68. He had given lectures, made records, and for years was editor of the *Second Line,* official publication of the NO Jazz Club. *New Orleans: A Family Album,* a collection of biographies and photographs, by Souchon and Al Rose, was publ. in 1968 by Louisiana State Univ. Press.

SPANIER, HERBERT ANTHONY CHARLES (HERBIE),* *trumpet, composer;* also *fluegelhorn, piano, bass, percussion;* b. Cupar, Sask., Canada, 12/25/28. Pl. w. C. Thornhill, P. Bley in NYC, mid-'50s; LA, LV, '58-9. Ret. to Canada and was active in Montreal through '69. Own quintet for concerts at Laval, Mont., Sherbrooke Univs.; *Jazz en Liberté* on CBC radio. Moved to Toronto, '70. Own quartet at George's Spaghetti House, several times annually; also member of Phil Nimmons big band. Orig. infls: Gillespie, Davis. TV: many apps. on CBC. Fests: American Mus. Fest., Lewiston, N.Y. Art Park w. D. Amram; Fest. of Jazz & Chamber Mus. w. Nimmons in Fredericton, N.B., '75. Wrote mus. for film, *Via Montreal,* which won prize in So. America. Received Senior Arts Grant from Canada Council for research into Brass Acoustical Innovations, '68. Comps: *Northland Blues; Precis En Bleu; Prelude; Waltz No. 4; Dimensions in Blue; Open Door; Equivalence; Bird Talk; Forensic Per Tur Bations; Ballade for Gina.* Own LP: on Radio Canada Int.; w. Galt McDermott (Laurentian); w. Nimmons (Nimmons' N Mus. Ltd.).

SPANIER, FRANCIS JOSEPH (MUGGSY),* *cornet;* b. Chicago, Ill., 11/9/06. A member of many name bands from the '20s incl. Ted Lewis, Ben Pollack, Bob Crosby, Spanier later lived in SF. After apps. at NJF, '64 he retired owing to ill health and died in Sausalito, Cal. 2/12/67.

SPANN, OTIS,* *piano, singer;* b. Jackson, Miss., 3/21/30. Reputed to be a ''half-brother'' of Muddy Waters. Respected as a powerful pianist, highly personal singer and strong accompanist, Spann worked w. Howlin' Wolf, Buddy Guy, James Cotton, Big Mama Thornton, Bo Diddley, toured Europe several times with Waters and others (his association with Waters had begun in 1947, when he moved to Chicago). Spann died 4/25/70 in a Chicago hospital. LPs w. Waters on various labels; rec. under own name for Candid, Prestige, Testament, BluesWay, London, BluesTime, Vanguard. During the weekend of Sept. 8-10, 1972 a series of concerts, held in Ann Arbor, Mich., celebrated the formal dedication there of Otis Spann Memorial Field. A two-volume album, w. Howlin' Wolf, Dr. John, Koko Taylor, Willie Dixon, Freddie King, Sippie Wallace and others, was released on Atlantic Records.

SPARGO, TONY (Anthony Sbarbaro), * *drums, kazoo;* b. New Orleans, La., 6/27/1897. Member of Original Dixieland Jazz Band, 1914, Spargo in the '60s was the only surviving member of that gp. He pl. w. Phil Napoleon during the '50s, became inactive during the '60s and died 10/30/69 in Forest Hills, N.Y. LPs: w. ODJB (RCA).

SPAULDING, JAMES RALPH (JIMMY), * *alto, tenor saxes, flute;* b. Indianapolis, Ind., 7/30/37. Worked w. Sun Ra in Chicago in '50s; Freddie Hubbard; Max Roach; Randy Weston in NYC in first half of '60s. Pl. w. Roy Haynes, '66; Hubbard; Roach, '67; Bobby Hutcherson, '70; Weston in early '70s; also w. Leon Thomas; Art Blakey; Horace Silver; Pharoah Sanders; G. Wein's Newport All Stars. In '75 worked w. Duke Ellington orch. under the dir. of Mercer Ellington. As a leader of his own small gp. pl. concerts at Loeb Student Center, NYU, '68; NYC Community Coll., '69; The East, Brooklyn '69-70; Cornell U. series, '69-70; Jazzmobile; MUSE, '70; Vassar, Utica, Manhattan Colls; Left Bank Jazz Society, '71. TV: NET; *Dial M For Music* w. Hubbard; *Positively Black* w. Leon Thomas. Fest: NJF w. Thomas, '70; NJF-NY w. Wein, '73. Received BA from Livingston Coll., '75; candidate for Masters at Rutgers U. Participated in Jazz Workshops at Rutgers, '75, w. Budd Johnson; C. Terry; Weston; S. Rollins; Jo Jones; Milt Hinton; Milt Jackson; Bob Wilber; Charles Davis. LPs: w. Hubbard, *Backlash; High Blues Pressure; Black Angel;* w. Roach, *Drums Unlimited* (Atl.); *New Wave in Jazz* (Imp.); w. Silver, *The Jody Grind* (BN); *Louis Armstrong and Friends;* w. Thomas; Rosko (Fly. Dutch); S. Turrentine; Larry Young (BN); Duke Pearson (Atl.).

SPINOZZA, DAVID, *guitar;* also *piano, drums, trumpet;* b. Portchester, N.Y., 8/8/49. Stud. theory in high school; classical guitar w. Leonid Bolotine; orchestration w. Ariadno Mikeshina; "Listened to all of the Wes Montgomery records." An extremely active NYC studio player who has rec. w. R. Flack, M. Legrand, John Lennon, Paul McCartney, James Taylor, Carly Simon, H. Mann, C. Mariano, M. Mainieri, Stevie Wonder, Howard Johnson, M. Stamm, Mike and Randy Brecker, Aretha Franklin. Infls: Montgomery, Segovia, Bolotine, Lionel Chamberlain. Has written arrs. for Taylor, Richard Davis and Paul Williams; app. w. Williams on *Tonight* show. Fest: NJF-NY w. Les McCann.

LPs: *Hard Mother Blues* w. E. Wilkins (Mainstream); w. Arif Mardin, *Journey* (Atl.); w. Franklin, *I'm In Love* (Atl.); w. Lennon, *Mind Games* (Apple); w. Dr. John, *In The Right Place* (Atco).

SPROLES, VICTOR, *bass;* b. Chicago, Ill., 11/18/27. Studied under Walter Dyett at Du Sable High in Chi., '42-6;

pl. in band w. 16th A.E.F. during WWII. Gigged w. Coleman Hawkins in Milwaukee, '52. Member of house rhythm section at French Poodle in Chi., '52-3, pl. w. Ira Sullivan; from '54-7 he filled the same role at the Beehive, backing visiting stars like Lester Young, Sonny Stitt, Charlie Parker. From '58-60 worked w. Johnny Griffin-Lockjaw Davis quintet; then w. Norman Simmons in Chi., Nevada, Calif. and Arizona. Acc. Carmen McRae, '62-4, incl. trips to Switzerland, England. With Art Blakey, '65-6, incl. Japanese tour. From '69-72 was most often at Half Note in NYC w. Al Cohn-Zoot Sims, Anita O'Day, Jimmy Rushing and James Moody. Also pl. w. Hazel Scott, '70. In '69 he began pl. w. Clark Terry incl. Montreal Expo and '75 summer tour of Europe. Infls: Junior Raglin, Slam Stewart, Wilbur Ware, Paul Chambers, Ray Brown, Richard Davis, Bill Lee, Chubby Jackson. TV apps. w. Blakey, McRae, Scott and Johnny Hartman. MJF w. McRae, LPs: w. Wardell Gray in *The Foremost* (Onyx); w. C. Terry (Vanguard, Etoile); w. Lee Morgan, *The Sixth Sense; The Rumproller* (BN); w. B. DeFranco, *Free Sail* (Choice); w. Sun Ra, *Supersonic Jazz* (Saturn); w. Ira Sullivan (Delmark); w. J. Griffin, *Big Soul* (Mile.); w. C. McRae (Time).

STABULAS, NICHOLAS (NICK), * *drums;* b. Brooklyn, N.Y., 12/18/29. Heard w. many gps. in NYC, incl. L. Tristano, A. Cohn & Z. Sims, Urbie Green, Chet Baker, Stabulas was killed in an automobile accident, 2/6/73.

LPs w. Gil Evans; M. Allison (Prest.); Jimmy Raney, *Strings & Swings* (Muse).

STACY, JESS ALEXANDRIA, * *piano;* b. Bird's Point, Mo., 8/4/04. In 1918 the family moved to Cape Girardeau, Mo. Stacy earned fame as pianist in B. Goodman band '35-9. During '40s led own big band, also back w. Goodman, and on west coast w. J. Teagarden. Worked locally in LA during '50s, but became inactive in music in '60, taking a day job, then retiring.

Stacy was persuaded to emerge for the '74 NJF where his perf. was acclaimed by critics. As a consequence, he made occasional live apps., returned to records, and did sound track work for *The Great Gatsby.*

In Feb. '75 he won the New Jersey Jazz Society's Jazz Musician of the Year award, presented at their annual Pee Wee Russell Memorial Concert. Like Earl Hines, Stacy showed that he had survived and transcended the many changes in jazz piano styles and that his incisive, firmly swinging work remained effective with or without a rhythm section.

Comp: *Ec-Stacy; Complainin'; Burning The Candle At Both Ends; Ain't Going Nowhere; Ramblin'; The Sell Out; Lookout Mountain Squirrels; Doll Face; Miss Peck Accepts.* LPs: *Jess Stacy Piano Solos* (Swaggie); *Stacy Still Swings* (Chiaroscuro); *The Great Gatsby* (Paramount). Early LPs with Goodman (RCA).

STADLER, HEINER, *composer, piano;* b. Lessen, Poland, 9/4/42. Studied harmony w. Rudolf Lerich in Hamburg, '68-70; piano w. Juergen Sonnenschmidt; harmony w. Peter Hartman; composition w. Walter Steffens, '60-4. To NYC in mid-60s. Infl: T. Monk, Ch. Parker, George Russell, Edgard Varese, Walter Steffens. Comp: *Three Problems; Love in the Middle of the Air; Six Pieces for Quartet; The Fugue 2; No*

Exercise; Chained; Blues For Sister Sally; Clusterity; Homage to Bird and Monk, six pieces by Monk and Parker recomposed for sextet. Arr. of *Main Stem* for J. Moody in *The Blues and Other Colors* (Milestone). LPs: *Brains On Fire,* vols. 1&2; *Ecstasy* w. Steffens; *No Exercise* (Labor Records, 106 Haven Ave., New York, N.Y. 10032).

STAHL, DAVID, *trumpet, fluegelhorn, cornet;* b. Reading, Pa., 1/23/49. Stud. w. Walter Gier in Reading; Penn State U. 1966-70, B.S. in Mus. Ed. After college, pl. in US Army Band in Washington, Aug. '70-Aug. '73. Also during this time pl. lead tpt. in Catholic Univ. of America Jazz Band dir. by Hank Levy. Joined Woody Herman 8/3/73, playing lead tpt. through 1/9/75, again from 2/10-4/24/75; the next day, he joined Count Basie. Concerts with F. Sinatra while w. Herman in '74 and again while w. Basie in Sept. '75. Favs: M. Ferguson, Bill Chase, Conrad Gozzo, Don Jacoby. TV: BBC show with Herman, Jan. '74. Fests: Concord, Montreux, Pori w. Herman; Montreux, Antibes, Kansas City w. Basie. LPs: *Herd at Montreux* w. Herman (Fantasy).

STAMM, MARVIN LOUIS,* *trumpet, fluegelhorn;* b. Memphis, Tenn., 5/23/39. Played w. S. Kenton, '60-2; W. Herman, '65-6; then settled in NYC becoming heavily involved in studio work, rec. with such artists as Q. Jones, O. Nelson, G. McFarland, F. Foster, M. Albam, D. Pearson, M. Legrand, Pat Williams, Bob James, D. Sebesky, W. Montgomery, Deodato, Grover Washington Jr. et al. With T. Jones-M. Lewis orch. '66-70, incl. European tour, '69. Guest soloist-clinician at many univs., high schools and colls. throughout U.S.; concerts w. B. Goodman septet; Legrand, James and Sebesky; U.S. and overseas tours w. F. Sinatra, '74. TV: feat. soloist w. C. Mangione and Rochester Phil., PBS. Fests: Monterey w. Jones-Lewis, '71; Newport w. Legrand, '75.

LPs: *Machinations* (Verve); w. Foster, *Manhattan Fever; Introducing the Duke Pearson Big Band* (BN); w. Jones-Lewis, *Consummation; Jazz Wave Tour* (SS); w. Williams, *Threshold* (Cap.); w. Legrand, *Twenty Songs of the Century* (Bell); w. Mangione, *Friends & Love* (Merc.); w. Nelson, *Jazzhattan Suite* (Verve); w. McFarland, *Scorpio and Other Signs* (Skye); w. Bob Freedman, *The Journeys of Odysseus* (Milest.).

STANKO, TOMASZ, *trumpet, fluegelhorn, composer;* b. Rzeszow, Poland, 7/11/42. Father gave him first violin lessons. Studied violin and piano at elementary music school. From '59 studied trumpet at Cracow Secondary and Higher Sch. of Music, grad. from latter in '69. First heard jazz at Dave Brubeck concert '58. Formed gp. w. Adam Makowicz '62. From '63 also pl. w. Krzysztof Komeda; from '65-9 w. Andrzej Trzaskowski. Took part in his Hamburg Workshops and Manfred Schoof's Trumpet Summit in Nuremberg. In '70 pl. w. A. Von Schlippenbach Globe Unity Orch. at Donaueschingen Jazz Days; Warsaw Jazz Jamboree; Berlin; Baden-Baden Free Jazz Meeting. Pl. w. Don Cherry, A. Mangelsdorff, Gerd Dudek in European Free Jazz Orch. at Donaueschingen '71. Many Euro. fests. in '70s. Toured Switzerland, '72. Winner of Polish polls from '65. Joachim Berendt called him "the first musician in Europe to translate Ornette Coleman into his own language." LPs: *Astigmatic; Twet; Music for K;* w. Komeda; Trzaskowski; Wroblewski (Muza).

STAPLETON, WILLIAM JOHN (BILL), *trumpet, fluegelhorn, arranger/composer;* also *trombone;* b. Blue Island, Ill., 5/4/45. Father, a professional pianist, and mother both teach music at home. Stud. at No. Texas St. Univ., Sept. '63-May '67 and Jan.-May '71; trumpet w. John Haynie. Pl. w. No. Tex. Lab Band, '63-7, and, after Army service, again in '71. During his No. Texas St. days, also pl. w. Joe Reichman, Teddy Phillips, Ralph Marterie, Buddy Morrow, Don Jacoby, did studio work in Dallas. App. at LA Music Center w. No. Texas Lab Band and S. Kenton Neophonic, '66. With Woody Herman, '72-March '74; Neal Hefti, '74; Bill Holman, '74-5. Active as clinician; summer teaching at National Stage Band Camp. Infl: Clifford Brown, Terry, Hubbard, Hackett, Gillespie, C. Baker, Mulligan, Holman. Comp: *Bill's Blues,* five arrs. in Herman's Grammy Award winning *Giant Steps.* LPs: w. Herman, *Giant Steps; The Raven Speaks; The Thundering Herd* (Fantasy); North Texas Lab Band, '67, '71.

STATON, DAKOTA,* *singer;* b. Pittsburgh, Pa., 6/3/32. Continued club and concert apps. such as new Half Note, NYC, '73; jazz cruise on *Showboat I,* May '74. LPs: '67 (London); *Ms. Soul; Madame Foo-Foo; I Want a Country Man* (Groove Merchant).

STEIG, JEREMY, *flutes;* b. New York City, 9/23/42. Father is prominent artist William Steig; mother Liza, sisters Lucy and Maggie also are artists. Steig, who has illustrated his own album covers, has had one-man shows in White Plains and Woodstock, N.Y. Played recorder at age six. Took up flute at 11, studying w. Paige Brook, '53-6. Attended HS of Mus. & Art. Began pl. in Greenwich Village coffee houses at 15. Pl. w. Paul Bley, Gary Peacock, '61. Worked w. jazz-rock gp. backing Tim Hardin, '66-7. Formed Jeremy and the Satyrs in the latter yr. and has had own gps. ever since. Early associates in these gps. were Warren Bernhardt, Mike Mainieri, Donald McDonald, Eddie Gomez. In '70 was associated w. Jan Hammer. A motorcycle accident in '62 paralysed the right side of his face and left him deaf in one ear for six months. For a year's time he had to place a wooden block in his mouth in order to play but he overcame these ailments to prove himself as a soulful jazzman with a particularly forceful, gutsy attack, beginning with his debut album, *Flute Fever* (Col.), '63. With the advent of the Satyrs he became involved with jazz-rock and by '75 his performances made use of such electronic devices as the ring modulator, wah wah pedal echo machines, etc. Chuck Berg in *down beat* said: "One can only conclude Steig is a virtuoso. His command of tongueing techniques (from flutter to triple), his variety of tone colors (from the classical sound-ideal to a raging howl), his mastery of the flute family (from bass to piccolo), his ability to hum and sing along with the articulated notes from his flute, and his success in integrating electronics combined with the harmonic, rhythmic and melodic imaginativeness, all stamp him as an original."

Orig. infl: Coltrane, Rollins, Miles Davis, Monk, Bill Evans. Won DB Critics poll, TDWR, '67, '73-4. TV: *Camera Three* w. B. Evans; and w. own gp.; *Jazz Set,* NET, '71; PL. Berlin JF several times in '70s incl. Art Blakey's *Orgy in Rhythm,* '72; Association P.C., '74. Toured Europe w. own quartet on Sonny Lester package, '69-70. Pl. Germany and Switz. w. own quintet, Nov.-Dec. '75. Comp: *Come With*

Me; Belly Up; co-composed w. E. Gomez, *Dream Passage; Djinn Djinn.* LPs: *Temple of Birth; Monium* (Col.); *Fusion* (Gr. Merch.); *Energy* (Cap.); *Wayfaring Stranger* (BN); *Legwork; This is Jeremy Steig* (SS); *Flute Summit* (Atl.); *Mama Kuku* (MPS); *Jeremy & the Satyrs* (Reprise); w. Bill Evans, *What's New;* w. Richie Havens, *Something Else Again* (Verve).

STEVENS, LEITH,* *composer, conductor;* b. Mt. Moriah, Mo. 9/13/09. Stevens, who scored dozens of films, many of them with a jazz background or theme, incl. *The Gene Krupa Story; The Five Pennies; The Wild One,* died 7/23/70 in Hollywood, Cal.

STEVENSON, GEORGE EDWARD,* *trombone;* b. Baltimore, Md., 6/20/06. The name band veteran (F. Henderson, C. Hopkins, L. Millinder, Cootie Williams, R. Eldridge), who in later years pl. with small gps. in NYC, died there 9/21/70.

STEWART, JAMES OTTO (JIMMY), *guitar;* also *banjo, mandolin, composer;* b. San Francisco, Cal., 9/8/37. Stud. at Coll. of San Mateo, Chicago School of Mus., Berklee. Pro. debut at age 15. Arr. for many pop singers, cond. on TV in U.S. and Australia. Guitarist w. many jazz combos incl. three years w. Gabor Szabo. Edited Wes Montgomery jazz guitar method; co-author *This Is Howard Roberts;* wrote numerous articles for music periodicals and comp. such works as *Concertina for Electric Guitar and Orch.; 12 Homages for Classic Guitar;* works for string quartets etc. Publs: *Homage to the Spirit of the Guitar* (Guitar Player Prods., P.O. Box 615, Saratoga, Ca. 95070); *Wes Montgomery Jazz Guitar Method* (Robbins Music, 1775 Broadway, New York); *This Is Howard Roberts* (Playback, P.O. Box 4562, N. Hollywood, Ca. 91607). Fests: Monterey, '67-8; Newport, '68; UCLA w. G. McFarland, '68. Stewart, an exceptionally experienced and able artist on all plectrum instruments, attributes his inspiration to a range of influences from Segovia and Bartok to Charlie Christian and L. Almeida.

LPs: w. Szabo, *The Sorcerer; More Sorcery; The Best Of* (Imp.); *Bacchanal; Dreams* (Skye); *Rod McKuen Grand Tour 1971* (WB).

STEWART, REX WILLIAM,* *cornet, composer;* b. Philadelphia, Pa., 2/22/07. A veteran of such name bands as those of Fletcher Henderson, Horace Henderson, Luis Russell, Benny Carter, Stewart was best known for his work w. the D. Ellington orch. with which he pl. almost continuously from late 1934 until '45. After working extensively in Europe and Australia, pl. a year at Eddie Condon's club, and as a musician and disc jockey in LA during the '60s, Stewart died suddenly in LA, 9/7/67. His best known accomplishment was the use of the squeezed tone, half-valve effect, which he introduced in *Boy Meets Horn,* co-composed w. Ellington and rec. in '39. This tonal device was imitated by countless trumpeters in later years.

Stewart in the last few years of his life was successfully active as a journalist, writing a series of witty and perceptive articles for *down beat* and other publications. He was the author of a collection of his pieces issued under the title *Jazz Masters of the '30s* (Macmillan), publ. posthumously.

LP: *The Ellingtonians* (Trip).

STEWART, LEROY (SLAM),* *bass;* b. Englewood, N.J., 9/21/14. As member of Slim and Slam duo, '38, was first to popularize technique of improvising jazz solos on bowed bass and humming in octave unison. Countless concert and fest. apps., overseas tours, '50s and '60s, incl. Australia, '66; Europe, '71, England and continent w. Benny Goodman sextet, '73-4; France, Belgium, Switzerland w. own quartet, '75.

In '71 Stewart became a member of the faculty of the State Univ. of Binghamton, N.Y. He also conducted workshops and seminars at Yale U. Along with these activities, he app. in clubs and concerts w. various small groups, incl. his wife, Claire Stewart. Guest artist w. Binghamton Symph. In Nov. '70 he gave premier perf. of *La Reve Symphonique pour Slam,* comp. for him by Jack Martin and pl. by Stewart with the Indianapolis Symph.

In '71-2 he pl. w. C. Terry, Milt Buckner, Tyree Glenn, Jimmy and Marian McPartland, Buddy Tate, Zoot Sims-Al Cohn. In June '73 he rejoined Goodman, for whom he first worked in '44, and was heard with him in various groups during the next two years. Also pl. workshops at Yale U. w. Dwike Mitchell and Willie Ruff; Carnegie Hall concert w. NYJRC in tribute to A. Tatum w. B. Taylor, Tiny Grimes; concerts at Lincoln Center and Princeton U. w. Dr. Frances Cole, harpsichord, in baroque and string concerts. Publ: *Styles in Jazz Bass* (Morris & Co.).

LPs: *Slam Stewart Trio; Slamboree;* w. Joe Turner; w. Gene Rodgers (Black & Blue); others rec. in Europe in '75; and earlier albums w. Tatum (MCA); Goodman (Col.) etc.

STINSON, ALBERT FORREST JR. (AL),* *bass;* b. Cleveland, Ohio, 8/2/44. Worked in Calif. w. Terry Gibbs, Frank Rosolino, Chico Hamilton, Charles Lloyd. He was touring w. Larry Coryell's group when he died 6/2/69, of unknown causes, apparently in his sleep, in Boston, Mass. He was considered an exceptional bassist with a brilliant technique and adventurous ideas. LPs w. Hamilton, Joe Pass et al.

STITT, EDWARD (SONNY),* *tenor, alto saxes;* b. Boston, Mass., 2/2/24. In the late '60s and '70s he continued to tour w. his own gps., as a single w. local rhythm sections, and record prolifically. He was also a member of The Giants of Jazz w. Dizzy Gillespie, T. Monk, K. Winding which toured the world in '71-2; and part of *The Musical Life of Charlie Parker* which opened the NJF-NY in June '74 and toured eastern and western Europe in the fall of the year. Dan Morgenstern, in the liner notes for *Tune-Up,* said: "He has at his finger tips every lick and trick in the book, and if he wants it that way, he can just coast along on his experience and get away with it every time. But when Stitt is inspired and means business, he is awesome . . ." The last sentence can be well applied to his work on *Constellation* and with the Giants of Jazz, as well as *Tune-Up.* Comp: *Blues For Prez and Bird; The Eternal Triangle.* LPs: *Tune-Up; Constellation* (Cobble.); *12!; The Champ; Mellow* (Muse); *Parallel-A-Stitt* (Roul.); *Sonny Stitt with Art Blakey and the Jazz Messengers* (Poly.); *Previously Unreleased Recordings* (Verve); *Pow;* w. G. Ammons, *We'll Be Together Again* (Prest.); *Giants of Jazz* (Atl.); *Newport in New York, The Jam Sessions, Vols. 3&4; The Soul Session, Vol 6* (Cobble.); reissues, *Genesis* (Prest.).

STIVIN, JIRI, *flute, alto sax, composer;* also *soprano sax, recorder, bass clarinet;* b. Prague, Czech., 11/23/42. Stud. flute privately w. M. Munclinger; J. Valek; in John

Dankworth's jazz class at Royal Acad. of Mus., London, '69. In Prague pl. w. Jazztett, '62; Jazz Q, '63; Army Quintet, '65; SHQ w. Karel Velebny, '67; Quax Ensemble, a grp. for electronic music, '68; w. C. Cardew's Scratch Music, in London, '69; Steven & Co. Jazz System, '70; System Tandem w. Rudolf Dasek from '72. Stivin has also pl. w. the Czech radio big band; Gustav Brom; as soloist with Danish radio big band & in many European jazz groups. Infl: Coltrane, O. Coleman, M. Davis, J. Surman, Barre Phillips, S. Rollins, D. Brubeck Quartet, B. Evans, G. Mulligan, G. Russell, C. Cardew. Comp: *Dog's Suite;* many comp. for Czech. films & TV. Fest: Ljubljana, Prague, San Sebastian, Warsaw, Zurich, Pori, Altena, Berlin, Budapest, Copenhagen. Stivin finished film high school in Prague '65 and his first occupation was as a cameraman. He and Dasek were invited to perform at NJF-NY '75 but he was unable to attend because of a sudden illness. LPs: *Stivin & Co. Jazz System* (Supraphon; Panton); *SHQ,* w. Velebny (ESP); *Nonet SHQ & Woodwinds* (Saba); w. System Tandem (RCA Victor; Japo).

STONE, FRED, *fluegelhorn, trumpet;* also *synthesizer, piano, composer;* b. Toronto, Canada, 9/9/35. Father a conductor, alto player, 1920-60. Fred Stone stud. w. several Toronto teachers from age 12. At 16, made pro. debut in father's orch. During late '50s and early '60s, pl. as lead trumpet in CBC symph. orch. Wrote several books and papers relating to jazz and creativity. Received six awards for solo instrumental perfs. and contemporary comp. from Canada Council beginning in '67. Feat. soloist and/or composer on a number of albums including two w. D. Ellington, in whose orch. he toured in '70. Canadian columnist for *Jazz Forum* magazine in Europe from '70. Comps: approx. 100 original jazz works for own big band, '65- ; *Maiera,* suite for fluegelhorn and Ellington orch., rec. in Milan, '70; *Leah* for Ellington.

Stone has made many TV apps. as soloist, conductor; pl. on scores for numerous films. Fests: Casa Loma JF, '65-9; 21 fests. throughout world w. Ellington. Publs: *Treatise on Improvisation* (Humber Coll. Productions, Toronto, Ontario); *Jazz & Concentration; Jazz In Canada; Creativity: Jazz Composition* (publ. by Stone's own company, 65 Fisherville Rd., Willowdale, Ontario, Toronto). In '75 Stone was Prof. of Music at Humber Coll. in Toronto.

LPs: w. Ellington, *New Orleans Suite* (Atl.); w. Ellington/Ron Collier Orch., *Collages* (MPS); own LPs on RCA, CBC, Sackville.

STRAND, LES (Leslie Roy Strandt),* *electric organ, piano, pipe organ;* b. Chicago, 9/15/24. Played in Chicago clubs, mainly as soloist in '50s; early '60s. Stopped pl. publicly in '64 and began teaching. Returned to school and received BA, major in music theory, from Roosevelt Coll., '67. Moved to Wash., D.C. w. wife, former DB associate editor Pat Harris. Some clubs, concerts in stores but mostly teaching. Won first prize at Eighth Yamaha Int. Electone Fest., Nemu-no-sato, Japan, '71. Jimmy Smith has called Strand the "Art Tatum of the organ." LP: *The Winners: Les Strand & the Yamaha* (Yamaha); earlier albums on Fantasy, now deleted.

STRAYHORN, WILLIAM (BILLY or SWEE'PEA),* *composer, piano;* b. Dayton, Ohio, 11/25/15. The closest

writing associate of Duke Ellington from the time he joined the band in '39, Strayhorn composed *Take the A Train; Lush Life* (lyrics and music); *Chelsea Bridge; Day Dream; Raincheck; Passion Flower; A Flower is a Lovesome Thing; Johnny Come Lately.* In addition, he collaborated w. Ellington on the composing and arranging of hundreds of other works, among them *Suite Thursday* and the adaptation of Tchaikovsky's *Nutcracker Suite.* Over the years he occasionally played piano in the band, and in the various splinter groups. Strayhorn became ill in '66 and died 5/31/67 in a New York hospital.

In a eulogy on Strayhorn, Duke Ellington wrote, "He was the biggest human being who ever lived, a man with the greatest courage, the most majestic artistic stature, a highly skilled musician whose impeccable taste commanded the respect of musicians and the admiration of all listeners." A posthumously released album of Strayhorn's compositions played by the Ellington orch. was issued under the title . . . *And His Mother Called Him Bill* (RCA).

Albums under Strayhorn's own name include *!!!Live!!!* (Roul.) *The Peaceful Side* (UA); *Echoes of an Era* (Roul.); *Cue For Sax* (Master Jazz). A session of Ellington-Strayhorn duets is incl. in *The Golden Duke* (Prest.). Strayhorn plays in three tracks on *Esquire's All American Hot Jazz* (RCA). He is represented as composer in the vast majority of collections of records made by Ellington from 1939 on and reissued on LPs (see Ellington, Duke).

STRAZZERI, FRANK JOHN,* *piano, composer;* also *tenor saxophone, flute, baritone horn, organ, vibes;* b. Rochester, N.Y., 4/24/30. First widely known for his rec. w. Carmell Jones and Bud Shank in '60s; has since served as mus. collaborator for Johnny Cash TV show; pl. w. Doc Severinsen sextet for Johnny Carson at theatre-in-the-round; O. Nelson big band; Kai Winding quartet and tour w. Elvis Presley. In mid-70s most consistent association w. C. Tjader quintet; also periodically w. A. Pepper, Chet Baker, Joe Pass, Herb Ellis, T. Gibbs, Mundell Lowe, Z. Sims, F. Rosolino, C. Candoli, Harry Edison. TV: w. Les Brown on Bob Hope specs.; w. Presley at Madison Sq. Gdn. spec; World Satellite spec. from Hawaii. Fests: Concord twice w. Brown, Winding and Tjader; Monterey w. Tjader. Comps: *Jo Ann; My Lament; Strazzatonic; Taurus; Lazy Moments; Calcutta; Sphinx; View From Within;* also arrs. for Les Brown band. Publs: *Jazz Piano Solos* (Try Publ. Co. 854 Vine St., Hollywood, Ca. 90038); *Jazz Piano Method, "Strazzatonic"* (Gwyn Publ. Co. Inc., 14950 Delano St., Van Nuys, Ca. 91601). LPs: *View From Within* (Creative World); *That's Him and This Is New* (Revelation); *Frames* (Glendale); w. C. Tjader, *Last Night While We Were Young* (Fant.); others w. Nelson (Imp.); Presley (RCA).

STROZIER, FRANK R., *alto sax, flute, composer;* also *clarinet, piano;* b. Memphis, Tenn., 6/13/37. To Chicago in '54, pl. w. MJT +3. Moved to NYC, '59, working w. Roy Haynes, Miles Davis in '60s. In '65 settled in LA and became part of Shelly Manne's gp. Moved back to NYC at beginning of '70s. Pl. w. Keno Duke's Jazz Contemporaries. Member of NYJRC in first season '74. Comp: *Tiburon; D.R.T.* Won DB Critics poll, TDWR, on also sax '71. LPs: w. Duke, *Sense of Values* (Strata-East); w. Bobby Pierce, *New York* (Muse).

SUDHALTER, RICHARD MERRILL (DICK), *cornet;* also *alto horn, fluegelhorn, piano;* b. Boston, Mass., 12/28/38. Father, Al Sudhalter, was well known alto saxophonist in '30s. Graduated '60 from Oberlin Coll.; stud. trumpet w. Louis Davidson, Armando Ghitalla. In '60 Sudhalter left the United States for Austria, then lived in Germany, Great Britain and other countries. His life was divided equally between music and journalism. From '64-72 he was a correspondent for UPI, covering events in Britain, Germany, Yugoslavia, and the invasion of Czechoslovakia. He became a regular contributor to *Jazz Journal* and other publications. As a musician, he worked with artists of every school, among them Matty Matlock, Ben Webster, Dexter Gordon, Pee Wee Russell, Steve Kuhn, Vic Dickenson, Roger Kellaway, Bill Rank.

In '74 Sudhalter completed work on *Bix: Man & Legend,* in collaboration with Philip R. Evans, the definitive study of the life and times of Bix Beiderbecke, published in the U.S. by Arlington House. Among Sudhalter's infls., along with Bix, he names Bobby Hackett, Ruby Braff, L. Young, F. Trumbauer, Benny Carter, Bing Crosby and many others.

TV: British and German specs.; Bix Commemorative program, April, '75. Pl. & narrated Bix program for NYJRC at Carnegie Hall '75. Fest: Nice JF, '75. Came to NYC to lead quartet at the Riverboat, December '75.

LPs: *Sudhalter and Son,* I & II (77 Records); *Sweet and Hot—Anglo-American Alliance* (EMI); *New Paul Whiteman Orchestra* (Mon. Evergreen).

SUGANO, KUNIHIKO, *piano;* b. Tokyo, Japan, 10/13/35. Wife, Junko Kimura, pl. piano at Birdland club in Tokyo. Grad. from Gakushuin Univ.; took lessons from Yuriko Nemoto. After grad. worked for a yr. at Ishifuku Kinzoku K.K. Began in prof. music w. gp. of Osamu Hashimoto; w. Tony Scott, '59; Jun Yoshiya, Sleepy Matsumoto. Formed own trio. Infl: Linton Garner, E. Garner, W. Kelly, O. Peterson, H. Silver, H. Hawes, A. Previn, P. Newborn, Johnny Williams. LPs: *Finger Popping* (Columbia-Tact); *Music; Portrait; World of Kunihiko Kanno* (Audio Lab); *Live* (Trio); *Love Is a Many Splendored Thing* (Three Blind Mice).

SULIEMAN, IDREES DAWUD,* *trumpet, fluegelhorn;* also *alto sax;* b. St. Petersburg, Fla., 8/7/23. One of the earliest of the "modern" trumpeters of the '40s. Settled in Stockholm in the early '60s, after having toured in the Middle East and pl. in Cairo. A member of the Clarke-Boland Big Band until it broke up in '73. Living in Copenhagen in '70s. LPs: see Clarke-Boland; w. Horace Parlan, *Arrival;* Dexter Gordon, *More Than You Know* (Steeple.).

SULLIVAN, CHARLES HENRY, *trumpet, fluegelhorn, composer;* b. New York City, 11/8/44. Uncles, Hubert and Herman James, trumpeters in NY area. Lessons from Hubert in '54 for two yrs., then stopped pl. until '61 when he again stud. w. him. Further stud. w. Cecil Collins at Manhattan Sch. of Mus., '62-7, grad. w. BA. Pl. for an Off-Broadway prod. of *The Exception and the Rule* and *The Prodigal Son,* '65. Toured Europe for five mos. w. Donald McKayle Dance Co., '67. Worked w. Lionel Hampton, '68; Roy Haynes, '69; Count Basie, '70; Lonnie Liston Smith, '71; Sy Oliver, '72; Norman Connors, '73; Sonny Fortune,

'73- . Upstate NY tour of Jazzmobile w. Billy Taylor, summer '75. Own quartet at Boomer's, '75. Theater: pit bands for *Promises, Promises,* '68; *Salvation,* '69; *Rainbow,* '71. Fest: NJF-NY w. Connors. TV: NJ educ. channel w. L.L. Smith; *Black Journal* w. B. Taylor, PBS, '75. Member of NYJRC; JCOA. Infl: Lee Morgan, Coltrane. Comp: *Genesis; Evening Song; Now I'll Sleep; Goodbye, Sweet John.* LPs: *Genesis;* w. S. Fortune, *Long Before Our Mothers Cried* (Strata East), *Awakening* (Horizon); w. Carlos Garnett (Muse); Dollar Brand (Enja).

SULLIVAN, IRA BREVARD,* *trumpet, fluegelhorn, saxophones, flute, composer;* also *percussion;* b. Washington, D.C., 5/1/31. One of the important Chicago modernists of the late '40s and up until he moved to Florida in the early '60s. Working in Ft. Lauderdale and Miami from that time. In addition to pl. clubs and concerts he also has brought his gp. into elementary schools, churches and junior colls. In '71 he pl. at the Miami Jazz Fest.; Kennedy Center JF, Wash., D.C. Musical contractor-percussionist for Miami production of *Hair,* '72. A member of large jazz ensemble, the Baker's Dozen, in Miami. Originally inspired by the music of Charlie Parker and other bop giants, he incorporated elements of Coltrane, post-Coltrane and rock into his '70s performances. Comp: *Nineveh; E Flat Tuba G.*

LPs: *Horizons;* w. Eddie Harris, *Come On Down* (Atl.); *Nicky's Tune* (Delmark); reissue, w. Red Rodney, *The Red Arrow* (Onyx).

SULLIVAN, JOE (Dennis Patrick Terence Joseph O'Sullivan),* *piano;* b. Chicago, Ill., 11/5/06. An associate of the so-called "Austin High Gang" along w. E. Condon, B. Freeman, F. Teschemacher et al, Sullivan was well known in the '30s when he rec. a solo session for John Hammond and toured w. Bob Crosby's band. After long periods of semi-inactivity, he app. at the MJF in '63 and NJF, '64. He died 10/13/71 in a hospital in SF. Sullivan's best known comps. incl. *Little Rock Getaway* and *Gin Mill Blues.*

Own LP on Folkways; also some tracks in *A Jazz Holiday* (MCA).

SULLIVAN, MAXINE, *singer;* also *valve trombone, trumpet;* b. Homestead, Pa., 5/13/11. Achieved overnight fame with swing-style rec. of *Loch Lomond* 1938. Married to John Kirby 1937-41; sang w. him on radio series. Movies, night clubs from 1930s to mid-50s, then inactive for much of next decade except for occ. concerts, LPs. Worked as nurse; busy in community affairs in Bronx. Founder, director of House That Jazz Built, non-profit recreation center.

Made comeback '67 at Town Hall concert; Dick Gibson Jazz Party in Colorado '68. W. Bobby Hackett at Riverboat, NYC, '69; many clubs, concerts and nine countries overseas w. World's Greatest Jazzband, '69-75, incl. Newport, Nice fests. At the age of 64 she was still singing with the same light, gently swinging quality that had established her in the swing era. Own LPs, also LPs w. Bob Wilber, Dick Hyman (Monmouth-Evergreen); w. World's Greatest Jazzband at Carnegie Hall (World Jazz).

SUMMERLIN, EDGAR E. (ED),* *saxophone, composer, educator;* b. Marianna, Fla., 9/1/28. A pioneer in the liturgical jazz field, he wrote and cond. for religious TV show, *Look Up and Live* in early '60s. Pl. w. Don Ellis; co-led sextet w. D. Heckman. From '71 director of jazz program at City Coll. of N.Y. while continuing to be active as writer for church councils; American Guild of Organists; TV; stage; film; and dance groups; adjudicator and cond. for high schools; performer and lecturer at Int. Congress on Communication of Culture Through Art, Architecture and Mass Media, '70, in Europe, U.S. colleges. One of three American artists invited to conference on Salvation Today in Bangkok, Thailand, '72. Mus. consultant to playwrights' unit of Actors' Studio, '71. Mus. Dir. for Hamm & Clov Stage Co., NYC. Film: Comp. music for *Ciao,* only full-length American film chosen for Venice Film Fest., '67. TV: wrote and perf. mus. for Christmas Eve program on CBS, '66; *Come Along,* CBS, '72. Stage: music for *Felix,* Actors' Studio, '72; *Darts,* Hamm & Clov, '74. Dance: *Traveling Through Three; The Continuing Saga of the Bouncing Ball* for Brenda Bufalino Dance Co., New Paltz, N.Y., '73. Perf. *Varieties in Jazz* at City Coll. Center for Perf. Arts, '74. Comps: *Evensong: A Jazz Liturgy* for First Int. JF; *Christ Lag In Todesbonden or Where Do We Go From Here; Bless This World; Slippin' Through Time; Excursions.* Publ: *Heavy Hymns* (Hope Pub. Co., Carol Stream, Ill.). LPs: *Ring Out Joy* (Avant Garde); *Jax or Better* w. Heckman/Summerlin sextet (English Jazz Workshop); *Saturday in the Park and Other Songs Made Famous by Chicago* (RCA Camden).

SUN RA (Herman "Sonny" Blount) (Le Sony'r Ra), *piano, electric keyboards, synthesizer, Roksichord, Sun harp, composer, leader;* b. Birmingham, Ala., May (under Gemini), ca. 1915. His Solar Arkestra, Space Arkestra or Intergalactic Myth-Science Arkestra, as it has been variously known, is in certain ways a "family," many of its members having been with him for a long time. Some, like reedmen John Gilmore, Marshall Allen and Pat Patrick, began with him in '56. In the '70s a typical Arkestra consisted of three brass; six reeds; five or six percussion; bass; and the leader on an assortment of keyboards. With the dancers and vocalists often employed there are often more than 20 performers on stage during a presentation dressed in colorful costumes (heavy on the gold lamé) and headgear, ranging from Sun Ra's Egyptian space helmet to turbans, burnooses and Robin Hood caps. Films, shown on a screen behind the band, are common to his performances, often depicting the leader and his Arkestra. Even a fire-eater has been incorporated into what are theatrical performances embodying myriad elements.

Many observers have felt that these trappings and the "space" oriented titles that he places on his compositions are merely "show biz," "jive" and one big "put-on" or that he is a naif. "But naivete does not exist where black art is concerned," says critic Joachim Berendt.

Imamu Baraka (Leroi Jones) wrote: "Sun Ra more validly than anybody else performs classical contemporary Black Music of Ancient Black Tradition."

Sun Ra states: "I paint pictures of infinity with my music, and that's why a lot of people can't understand it . . . Intergalactic music concerns the music of the galaxies. It concerns intergalactic thought and intergalactic travel, so it is really outside the realms of the future on the turning points

of the impossible. But it is still existent, as astronomy testifies."

Film: *Space is the Place.* The Arkestra won DB Critics poll, TDWR, '71-2; Sun Ra won on organ, TDWR; and synthesizer, '75. Fest: NJF-NY '73. Two month tour of Mexico, early '74.

Comp: *Space is the Place; Rocket Number Nine; Sea of Sounds; Hidden Spheres; Astro Black; The Cosmo-Fire; Black Myth; Watusi; Shadow World; The Stargazers; Outer Spaceways Inc.*

LPs: *It's After the End of the World* (MPS); *Nothing Is; Heliocentric Worlds* (ESP); *Angels and Demons at Play; Crystal Spears; Magic City; Nubians of Plutonia,* etc. (Imp., orig. issued on Sun Ra's own label, Saturn); *Pictures of Infinity* (Bl. Lion); *Space is the Place* (Blue Thumb).

SUPERSAX. see Clark, Buddy; Flory, Med.

SURMAN, JOHN, *baritone saxophone;* also *soprano, bass clarinet, synthesizer;* b. Tavistock, England, 8/30/44. Educ. London Coll. Mus./London Univ., '60-4. First pl.w. Mike Westbrook '59-64; then various groups inc. Mike Gibbs, Graham Collier, Chris McGregor, Dave Holland, John McLaughlin, '64-8, in England. The Trio, w. Stu Martin, Barre Phillips in W. Europe/E. Europe, '69-72. "SOS" w. Alan Skidmore, Mike Osborne, Europe, '73- . Surman has app. at most of the major European jazz fests., as well as on European and Japanese TV. He won the *Melody Maker* poll, '68-74 on bari., sop. saxes; DB poll, TDWR, '69. Infls: Johnny Dodds; Harry Carney; Ellington; Parker; Coltrane; Rollins; Bach; Ravel; Bartok and many others. Surman is VP of Jazz Centre Society, London. Comp. ballet music for *Sablier Prison* for Paris Opera.

LPs: *How Many Clouds* (Decca); *Westering Home* (Island); *The Trio* (Pye); *SOS* (Ogun); *Citadel* w. Westbrook (RCA); *Live at Woodstock,* Surman/Martin (A.T.V.).

SUTTON, RALPH EARL, *piano;* b. Hamburg, Mo., 11/4/22. First prominent w. J. Teagarden in late '40s; popular in NYC, where he pl. for several years at Eddie Condon's. Moving to SF, pl. at clubs in the Bay Area, Monterey JF, '61. To Aspen, Colo. '64, where his wife had a supper club, Sunnie's Rendezvous, at which he worked. In '66 he pl. in NYC w. Bob Crosby. Every summer, starting in '65, pl. in Denver with the Ten Greats of Jazz, which evolved into the World's Greatest Jazzband. Sutton toured with the group through Sept. '74, when he settled in Pine, Colo. and worked w. P. Hucko and Gus Johnson at a Denver hotel. Fests: Monterey, Newport etc. w. WGJ; Colorado Jazz Party. Publ: *Piano Man, The Story of Ralph Sutton* by James D. Shacter (Jaynar Press, P.O. Box 3141, Merchandise Market Plaza, Chicago, Ill. 60654).

Once wrongly identified as exclusively a ragtime pianist, Sutton is an artist of exceptional skill, originally inspired by Fats Waller and James P. Johnson, playing impeccably with a powerful left hand and an excellent rhythmic and harmonic sense, in a broad range of styles.

LPs: w. WGJ (Atl., Project 3, World Jazz); *The Compleat Bud Freeman* (Mon. Ev.); two on Blue Angel Jazz Club.

SUZUKI, ISAO, *bass; also cello, vibes, piano;* b. Tokyo, Japan, 1/2/36. Pl. w. Sleepy Matsumoto quartet, '61-4; Sadao Watanabe quartet, '64-5; formed own gp. and worked at Club Five Spot in Tokyo, '65-9; w. Art Blakey's Jazz Messengers in U.S., '69-70. Ret. to Japan in '70 and resumed w. own gp. Infl: Jim Hall. Won *Swing Journal Jazz Disc Award, Jazz of Japan Award*, '73. LPs: *Blow Up; Blue City; All Right* (Three Blind Mice).

SWALLOW, STEPHEN W. (STEVE), * *bass, bass guitar, composer;* b. New York City, 10/4/40. Pl. w. Paul Bley; George Russell; J. Giuffre; A. Farmer; A. Cohn-Z. Sims in '60s; Stan Getz, '65-7. Joined Gary Burton, '67 and was w. him to '70 when moved to Bolinas, Calif. where he spent three years writing, and playing in SF w. pianists Art Lande; Mike Nock. With Burton again from '73; also played and rec. w. Mike Gibbs and, intermittently w. Steve Kuhn. Original list of favs. should have incl. Red Mitchell. A composer of grace, wit and imagination, his abilities in this direction are also strongly indicated in his electric bass (bass guitar) solos. In addition his supporting lines are a strong factor in the lustrous power of the Burton ensemble. Comp: *Hotel Hello; Chelsea Bells; Hullo, Bolinas; Portsmouth Figurations; Domino Biscuit; Sweet Henry; Sweeping Up; The Green Mountains; Arise, Her Eyes; Eiderdown; I'm Your Pal; Falling Grace; General Mono's Well Laid Plan.* LPs: *Hotel Hello* w. Burton; w. S. Kuhn, *Trance* (ECM); w. M. Gibbs, *The Only Chrome-Waterfall Orch.* (Bronze); *In the Public Interest* (Poly.); w. Mike Mantler (Watt); w. Burton, *Ring* (ECM); *Duster; In Concert; A Genuine Tong Funeral* (RCA); Burton-Grappelli, *Paris Encounter* (Atl.).

SWARTZ, HARVIE, *bass, composer;* also *piano;* b. Chelsea, Mass., 12/6/48. Began as pianist but switched to bass in '67. Studied w. Orrin O'Brien of NY Phil. Freelanced in Europe in '70 w. D. Gordon; K. Drew; Art Taylor; Brew Moore; J. Heath; J. Griffin. In Boston worked w. Mose Allison; Al Cohn-Zoot Sims; C. Shavers; Chris Connor; Jaki Byard. Moved to NYC '73, gigging w. Mike Abene; Jackie Paris-Ann Marie Moss; L. Konitz; Jackie & Roy. Later free-lanced w. Steve Kuhn; Thad Jones-Mel Lewis; Gil Evans; Chet Baker; Hubert Laws; Jack Wilkins; Arnie Lawrence; B. Watrous; Sheila Jordan. TV: *Today* w. Jackie & Roy. Fest: NJF-NY w. Baker '75. Comp: *I've Touched Your Soul; Islands; Truce.* LPs: w. D. Friedman (East Wind); Barry Miles (London); David Matthews; Eric Kloss; Mark Murphy (Muse); Jackie & Roy (CTI); Paris-Moss (Diff. Drum.).

SWOPE, EARL, *trombone;* b. Hagerstown, Md., 8/4/22. Prominent in 1940s w. bands of Boyd Raeburn, Geo. Auld, Buddy Rich, Woody Herman, and in '50s w. Elliott Lawrence, Joe Timer (in Washington, D.C.), Jimmy Dorsey, Swope returned to Washington, freelanced, then worked for a while with Louie Bellson in 1959. He was playing in the Bob Cross band in Washington when he died 1/3/68 after a brief illness. LPs w. Herman (Col., Cap.); Sonny Berman (Onyx); Stan Getz (Prestige); many others w. Bill Potts, Willis Conover et al, now deleted.

SZABO, FRANK J., *trumpet, fluegelhorn;* b. Budapest, Hungary, 9/16/52. Stud. w. Tom Scott, 1962-9; also at Van Nuys High Sch. and LA Valley College. Pl. in LV and on road w. Harry James, '70 and '71; two month tour w. Frank Sinatra Jr. Orch., early '71; rest of '71 touring USA, Europe, Japan w. Ray Charles. Tours, clubs w. L. Bellson,

Feb. '72-Oct. '74. Joined Count Basie Dec. '74 and toured internationally with him through 75; also gigged with Sweets Edison. Infls: M. Ferguson, F. Hubbard, Rafael Mendez, Al Porcino, Doc Severinsen, J. Coltrane, Ch. Parker. LPs w. Ray Charles (Tangerine); Bellson, Basie (Pablo).

SZABO, GABOR, * *guitar, composer;* b. Budapest, Hungary, 3/8/36. To U.S., '56. After pl. w. C. Hamilton, G. McFarland, C. Lloyd, formed own group, traveled extensively, '66-8. In '68, in partnership w. C. Tjader and McFarland, organized and recorded for Skye Records, a short-lived company. In '69 he disbanded, taking six months to plan a new, more heavily rock and blues oriented combo; also rec. an album acc. Lena Horne. Since '70 has led various quartets, based in LA. In '75 he decided to form a new gp. consisting of musicians all of whom at one time or another had been a part of his previous units, representing a complete progression from chamber-like classically oriented music to hard jazz-rock sounds. He called this group The Perfect Circle.

Comps: *Lady Gabor; Gypsy Queen; Mizrab; Spellbinder; Bacchanal; Divided City; The Fox; Lilac Glen; Time; The Director; Rising.* Film music for Roman Polanski's *Repulsion;* Gabor Kalman's *Farm Boy of Hungary* and several educational shorts. Though his career in the late '60s and early '70s seemed to lack a clearly defined direction, Szabo at his best continued to reflect the almost limitless variety of influences to which he had been exposed both in Hungary and the U.S.

Fests: Monterey, '67-8, '70; Newport, '67; Concord, '71. TV: Lena Horne Spec.; Flip Wilson show; color TV spec: *Gabor Szabo (U.S.A.) Jazz Podium,* filmed in Budapest, 90 minutes of music and interviews and travel around the city with dialogue in English and Hungarian.

LPs: *Mizrab; Rambler; Skylark* (CTI); *Bacchanal; Dreams; Gabor Szabo 1969; Lena & Gabor* (Skye); *The Best of; Gypsy '66; Spellbinder; Jazz Raga; Simpatico; The Sorcerer; Wind, Sky & Diamonds; More Sorcery; His Greatest Hits* (Imp.); *Magical Connection; High Contrast; Live with Charles Lloyd* (Blue Thumb).

TABACKIN, LEWIS BARRY (LEW), *tenor saxophone, flute;* b. Philadelphia, Pa., 5/26/40. Stud. during high school years, '55-8; BM with flute major, Phila. Conserv. of Mus., '58-62. Moved to NYC, '65, working there w. M. Ferguson, C. Calloway, Urbie Green, B. Rosengarden, C. Terry, Duke Pearson, T. Jones-M. Lewis, Joe Henderson, Chuck Israels, Doc Severinsen; also small gp. apps. w. D. Byrd, Elvin Jones, Attila Zoller, Don Friedman, Toshiko Akiyoshi. Had own trio '68-9. In '69 pl. Hamburg Jazz Workshop w. Israels, feat. w. Danish Radio Orch., and toured Switzerland.

Married to Toshiko Akiyoshi, he toured Japan with her in '70 and again in '71. In '72 they moved to LA, where Tabackin continued to work as a member of Severinsen's band on the *Tonight* show, and w. Severinsen's Now Generation gp. for in-person apps. Occasionally he co-led a quartet, and a big band, both with Toshiko. The orch. rec. in Hollywood for release on Japanese RCA.

Tabackin is an exceptional tenor saxophonist in a tradition clearly inspired by Sonny Rollins, though he also acknowledges his debt to Lester Young, Coleman Hawkins, Ben Webster, Don Byas, Chu Berry, Coltrane. He is also a flutist of rare distinction. Fests: Laurel, Baltimore, '68; Newport, '69; Expo. '70; San Diego, '75.

LPs: Toshiko Akiyoshi-L. Tabackin big band, *Kogun*(RCA Japan); Lew Tabackin Trio, *Let The Tape Roll*(RCA Japan); *Now Hear This*; *Introducing Duke Pearson Big Band,* with Pearson (BN); *Electric Byrd,* w. D. Byrd (BN); w. Akiyoshi, *Top of the Gate* (Takt, Japan); *Jazz in the Personal Dimension*; *Personal Aspect in Jazz* (RCA, Japan); w. Attila Zoller, *Gypsy Cry* (Embryo).

TAKAS, WILLIAM J. (BILL),* *bass*; b. Toledo, Ohio, 3/5/32. Active in second half of the '50s w. Z. Sims; Tal Farlow; Marian McPartland; Pee Wee Russell. Pl. w. Gerry Mulligan Concert Jazz Band '60; Paul Anka; Gene Krupa, '61-2, Vic Damone, '63-4; Judy Collins; Theodore Bikel; Anka, '65; Doc Severinsen, '66, at which time he took up Fender bass; B. Goodman, '67; house man at the Half Note backing Sims, Al Cohn, K. Winding, J. Rushing, B. Brookmeyer, Anita O'Day; also w. Ten Wheel Drive, '68-9. NBC staff w. Severinsen; own gp. in modern opera *Elephant Steps,* '70. Cond. band for musical, *Dr. Selavey's Magic Theatre,* '72-3. In '74-5 Takas, on Fender bass, acc. a variety of mus. at Bradley's, NYC, incl. Al Haig, Jimmy Rowles, Jimmy Raney, Mike Longo, Barry Harris and Bob Dorough. Pl. w. Dorough in LA, SF; also gigs w. Manhattan Transfer, '75. TV: wrote and arr. music and pl. w. International Ooba-Ooba Band for NBC Special *Earth Year One,* '71. Fest: Hollywood Bowl; NJF w. Mulligan. LPs w. Mulligan (Verve); *Children of All Ages* (Differant Drummer); others w. La Belle; Ten Wheel Drive; Buzzy Linhart.

TANNER, PAUL,* *educator, trombone*; b. Skunk Hollow, Kentucky, 10/15/17. Tanner's career as a jazz educator, which had begun when he gave courses at UCLA in '58, continued to expand throughout the '60s and '70s. By '75 he was teaching 1200 students a day in his history of jazz classes.

Tanner wrote and narrated TV shows concerning jazz history, wrote music and script for educational film entitled *Discovering Jazz* for Bailey Film Associates, an affiliate of CBS. The film was shown around the world. He is the author of innumerable music instruction books, the latest in '75 was *The Complete Practical Book for Tenor Trombone,* publ. by Holly-Pix (Western International, 13115 Morrison St., Sherman Oaks, Ca. 91423). Tanner's text book, *A Study of Jazz* (Wm. C. Brown, 2464 Kerper St., Dubuque, Iowa), was fully revised and reissued in '73. In the mid-'70s it was in use for history of jazz courses in more than 300 colleges. Tanner's knowledge of the subject stemmed partly from his directorship of the Curriculum for Higher Education for the National Association of Jazz Educators.

Early in '75, Tanner, along with Hal Cook and KBCA radio personality Bob Summers, conceived the idea for the

World Jazz Association. Tanner was appointed Exec. Dir., of the WJA, headquartered at Suite 4C, 10966 Rochester Ave., Los Angeles, Cal. 90024.

In addition to his many other activities, Tanner continued to play trombone professionally whenever possible.

TAPSCOTT, HORACE, *piano, composer*; b. Houston, Tex., 4/6/34. Stud. from age six with mother, a pianist. Early exp. w. Monroe Tucker gp. To LA 1945. At Jefferson High Sch. pl. in Swing Band w. Don Cherry, E. Dolphy, S. Criss, Art Farmer, Dexter Gordon, 1948-52. Also worked w. Dolphy in Gerald Wilson orch. ca. '50-51. In service, pl. in AAF band '53-7. Formed own group, '58. Toured w. Lionel Hampton '59-61; lived in NYC for a while, then returned to LA and formed a small unit which, with changing personnel, he has led ever since; members incl. Azar Lawrence and Black Arthur Blythe. Wrote music for poet Elaine Brown for Vault and Black Forum LPs, also pl. on albums w. Lou Blackburn for Imperial.

Tapscott, who says "Our music is contributive, not competitive," is highly regarded by Stanley Crouch and other West Coast observers. Crouch wrote that "this is a new Black music, but new only because, as an African writer once said, it recognizes 'time is flow.' Tapscott and his men know that all of the time, if it's carrying the feeling of the people, it is new, is free." Comps: *Sonny's Dream*; *This Is For Benny*; *The Golden Pearl*.

LPs: *The Giant Is Awakened* (Fl. Dutchman); also comps. and arrs. for Sonny Criss album, *Sonny's Dream* (Prest.).

TATE, GEORGE HOLMES (BUDDY),* *tenor sax*; also *soprano, alto, baritone, clarinet, flute*; b. Sherman, Texas, 2/22/15. After ten years with Count Basie, formed own small band. By early 1970s divided time between quartet and septet, making several overseas tours of Europe and Japan. Annual apps. at NJF, other festivals at Nice and throughout Continent. Awarded prize by Academie du Disque Francais for best jazz record of 1968 with LP featuring himself, Milt Buckner and Wallace Bishop. Made film for Roger Vadim in Paris, Jan. 1974. Playing w. P. Quinichette in Two Tenor Boogie at West End Cafe, NYC, '75.

One of the most able survivors of the warm-toned, Hawkins-inspired school of Texas tenor saxophonists, Tate found a wider audience than many of his contemporaries, continuing to play the Sheraton Hotel chain annually, many college concerts, Dick Gibson's jazz party etc.

LPs: *The Texas Twister*; *Swinging Like Tate* (MJR); *Unbroken* (BASF); *Buddy Tate & His Buddies* (Chiaroscuro); *Very Saxy* w. Lockjaw Davis, Coleman Hawkins, Arnett Cobb; *Kansas City Nights* w. Buck Clayton (Prestige); *When I'm Blue*; *Midnight Slows* (Black & Blue).

TATE, GRADY,* *drums, singer*; also *percussion*; b. Durham, N.C., 1/14/32. His work w. Quincy Jones band in early '60s led to many assignments as free-lance studio musician in NYC through '66. He cont. in the studios '67 but toured w. Peggy Lee who also gave him opportunity to sing. From '68-74 a member of orch. for *Tonight Show,* NBC. During this period he launched vocal career which intensified in activity from '72. At the same time remained active as a drummer. Sings both blues and ballads effectively in throaty baritone style. TV: Joey Bishop; Merv Griffin; *Black Journal*; Joe Franklin. Fest: NJF-NY; Col. JP; many other imp. fests. LPs: *By Special Request* (Buddah); *Movin' Day*; *She Is My Lady* (Janus); *Windmills of My Mind*; *Feeling Life*; *After the Long Ride Home* (Skye); w. Q. Jones (A&M); Jimmy Smith (Mojo; Verve); w. S. Getz, *Sweet Rain* (Verve); w. Aretha Franklin (Atl.).

TAYLOR, WILLIAM (BILLY),* *piano, composer, educator*; also *electric keyboards, synthesizer*; b. Greenville, N.C., 7/24/21. One of the most active and articulate people in jazz, both in and around the music, Taylor was musical director of the David Frost television show from '69-72. During this period he did less work with his trio but took the 11-piece Frost band, which incl. Frank Wess, Hubert Laws and Jimmy Owens, out for weekend concerts at colleges. In '72 he was part of Black Communications Corp. (incl. Ben Tucker) which purchased radio Station WSOK in Savannah, Ga. He also returned, for a short time, as general manager of WLIB, NYC, where he formerly had been a deejay.

From '73 Taylor has appeared w. his trio (Bob Cranshaw, then Larry Ridley, bass; Bobby Thomas, drums) on an intermittent basis but his other projects are multifarious. He is president of Billy Taylor Productions (119 West 57th St., New York, N.Y. 10019) which creates radio and TV commercials and publishes folios of his compositions under Duane Music and Castion Music. Other of his works are publ. by Charles Hansen (1860 Broadway. New York, N.Y. 10023).

As an educator he is a Yale Fellow at Calhoun College where he had conducted seminars; has taught a special course in the history of jazz piano at the Manhattan Sch. of Mus.; from '72 jazz history at C.W. Post Coll.; and designed a jazz program for the Wash., D.C. school system. In '75 he instituted a lecture series under his name at Howard U. which incl. clinics for credit. He received his Doctorate in Mus. Ed. (dissertation on History of Jazz Piano) in Sept. '75. Still active w. Jazzmobile, which he helped found, reshaping workshop with Dave Bailey.

He was a musical director of the NYJRC during its first two seasons. Board member of the National Council on the Arts; NARAS. In Oct. '75 replaced Harold Arlen on Board of Dir. of ASCAP. Played at White House State dinners for Pres. Nixon, '74; Ford, Feb. '75.

Fest: NJF; NJF-NY; MJF. Comp: *Suite For Jazz Piano and Orchestra*, performed w. Utah Symph. in Mormon Tabernacle, Jan. '73, and also perf. w. Minneapolis & Oakland Symphs.; National Symph.; Wash., D.C.; *Impromptu*; *I Wish I Knew How It Would Feel to Be Free*; *Theodora*; special material for *Sesame Street* and *The Electric Co.* TV: *Friends of Langston Hughes*; *Over 7 (Rainbow Sundae)*, ABC, *Black Journal Tonight*, PBS: mus. dir. of 18-piece band and featured artist, '75; added host duties, '76. LPs: *I Wish I Knew How It Would Feel to Be Free* (Tower); *O.K. Billy*; *Merry Christmas from David Frost and Billy Taylor* (Bell).

TAYLOR, CECIL PERCIVAL,* *piano, composer, educator*; b. New York City, 3/15/33. The avant of today's avant garde, Taylor has been leading his own group from the '50s. Jimmy Lyons has been its alto saxophonist from '60; Andrew Cyrille the drummer from '64. A tour of Europe in

'69 incl. Sam Rivers on tenor saxophone in the unit; at times during the '70s he added Sirone on bass. Taylor continued to perform in concert as a solo pianist as he did at NJF-NY '72 and the Montreux JF '74. His group played for the Maeght Foundation in France, '69; and at the Metropolitan Museum of Art, NYC, '72. Club appearances were not that frequent but he played two engagements at the Five Spot in '75.

In the '70s Taylor also became involved in academia, teaching a course in *Black Music 1920-1970* and directing the Black Music Ensemble at the University of Wisconsin in '70-1. He left there when, after failing two-thirds of his students for lack of seriousness in their work, a faculty committee changed his gradings to "satisfactory" and he resigned in protest. He then went to Antioch College in Yellow Springs, Ohio, where he taught for two years, and Glassboro State College, in New Jersey.

"Despite the fact that Taylor was around long before Coltrane recorded *Giant Steps* or Coleman came to New York," wrote Gary Giddins, "and despite the fact that he has long had a passionate coterie of admirers and influenced dozens of more accepted musicians (including Chick Corea and Steve Kuhn), he remains the outermost concentric circle of the avant garde. . . . Yes, his music is heavily rhythmic, but no, you can't tap your foot to it; yes, his music is intensely lyrical, but no, you won't be humming it after one hearing; yes, his music is richly harmonic, but no, he does not employ chord changes."

Film: for Bureau of Research, ORTF (French Radio/TV), '66. Awarded Guggenheim Fellowship, '73. Won Record of the Year for *Silent Tongues*, and was elected to Hall of Fame, DB Critics poll '75.

Comp: *Conquistador*; *With (Exit)*; *Unit Structure*; *Tales (8 Whisps)*; *Indent*; *Lono*; *Student Studies*; *Amplitude*; *Niggle Feuigle*; *Spring of Two Blue-J's*; *Colors Are Marchin'*; *Baptism Dances*; *Huddlin'* and *Hollow Heart*; *Chimes*.

LPs: *Silent Tongues*, solo piano at Montreux '74 (Arista); *Indent*; *Spring of Two Blue-J's* (Unit Core Records, 96 Chambers St., New York, N.Y. 10007); *Unit Structures*; *Conquistador* (BN); *Bulu Akisakila Kutala* (Trio); w. Jazz Composers Orch. (JCOA); *Nuits de la Fondation Maeght* (Shandar); reissue, *In Transition* (BN).

TAYLOR, CREED, *producer*; b. Lynchburg, Va., 5/13/29. Bach. degree in psychology from Duke U., where he pl. trumpet in marching band and in Duke Ambassadors Dance Orch. In '54 became a & r head at Bethlehem Records. In '56 joined ABC-Paramount, where he started the Impulse label. Joined Verve, '62, producing the Grammy award-winning, million-selling Getz-Gilberto album; also Ch. Byrd's and Getz's *Jazz Samba*, generally credited with starting the bossa nova trend.

In '67 Taylor moved to A & M records, where he enjoyed great success with Wes Montgomery's *A Day in the Life* and others for whom he found a successful commercial jazz direction. In '70 he started his own companies, CTI, Kudu and Salvation Records, recording Hubert Laws, Freddie Hubbard, Stanley Turrentine, Joe Farrell, Deodato, George Benson, Esther Phillips, Chet Baker and Jackie & Roy, with Don Sebesky as chief arranger. CTI was voted # 1 jazz company by Billboard in '74.

TAYLOR, CALVIN EUGENE (GENE),* bass; b. Toledo, Ohio, 3/19/29. Raised in Detroit. Came out of that fertile jazz environment to play w. Horace Silver quintet, '58-64, then w. Blue Mitchell in mid-'60s. In the '70s worked very often w. Judy Collins in folk field; Duo w. Duke Jordan at Bradley's; various duo and trio gigs w. Barry Harris in NYC. LPs: *Barry Harris Plays Tadd Dameron* (Xanadu); w. E. Kloss, *Doors;* w. Neal Creque (Cobble.); w. Eddie Jefferson, *Come Along With Me* (Prest.).

TAYLOR, KOKO, singer; b. Memphis, Tenn., 1938. Insp. by records of B.B. King, Sonny Boy Williamson, Howlin' Wolf and Elmore James, she began singing blues after moving to Chicago in '53. Gigged in local Southside and Westside taverns; made her first record date for USA label in '63. Under sponsorship of Willie Dixon she later signed w. Chess Records and scored a major success w. Dixon's comp. *Wang Dang Doodle,* which became her theme song and estab. her as a popular figure in black-oriented night clubs and on radio stations. Later became a favorite in Europe, where she toured extensively, sang at Montreux JF, rec. in France. She also app. w. Muddy Waters, Mike Bloomfield, Johnny Winter, Buddy Miles and Dr. John on the Nat'l Public TV prog. *Sound Stage.* One of the better latterday singers in the early blues tradition.

LP: *I Got What It Takes* (Alligator); *Basic Soul* (Chess).

TEAGARDEN, CHARLES (CHARLIE),* trumpet; b. Vernon, Tex., 7/19/13. Brother of the late Jack Teagarden. After working at Silver Slipper in LV, '61-4, he did relief band work in Strip hotels. Elected to the Exec. Board of Local 369 of the Musicians' Union in LV, '63, he became one of the President's assistants in '68 and at that point gave up an active career in music.

LPs: some tracks in *A Jazz Holiday* (MCA).

TEMPERLEY, JOSEPH (JOE),* baritone sax; also tenor, soprano saxes, bass clarinet, flute; b. Fife, Scotland, 9/20/29. From '60-65 he continued w. the Humphrey Lyttelton band w. which he had toured the U.S. in '59. Moved to NYC and pl. w. Woody Herman '66. Worked and/or rec. w. Buddy Rich, Thad Jones-Mel Lewis, Clark Terry, Duke Pearson, Joe Henderson, Deodato, New York Jazz Composers Orch. between '67 and Oct. '74, when he replaced the late Harry Carney in the Duke Ellington band. App. in English film, *What Makes Sammy Run.* TV w. Herman, Rich, Terry, Lyttelton, Jimmy Rushing, Big Joe Turner, Eric Dolphy. LPs: *Central Park North* w. Jones-Lewis (Solid State); *Let My Children Hear Music* w. Charles Mingus (Columbia); *Big Bad Band* w. Terry (Etoile); *Buck Clayton Jam Session* (Chiaroscuro); *East & West* w. Herman (Col.); *Continuum* w. Mercer Ellington (Fant.).

TERRY, CLARK,* trumpet, fluegelhorn, singer, leader; b. St. Louis, Mo., 12/14/20. Continued to play in the NBC orch. for the *Tonight Show* until the spring of '72 when Johnny Carson shifted his base of operations to LA. Led own combos and big band for clubs, concerts and fests. He also appeared as a soloist for George Wein; Norman Granz tours in Europe. Active as a clinician. An effervescent brassman who combines technical wizardry with flair, and unrelenting swing; and a humourous, highly-entertaining vocalist in his patented "mumbles" style. Big band won DB Critics poll, TDWR, '75.

Fest: NJF-NY '72; MJF; Montreux; Molde; Pori; Nice; NO; Wichita; Odessa, Tex.; Colo. JP from '69. Publ: *Let's Talk Trumpet (From Legit to Jazz) Books 1,2&3;* co-author w. Phil Rizzo, *The Interpretation of the Jazz Language* (C.J.C. Inc., P.O. Box 467, Bowie, Md. 20715). Comp: *Sheba; Samba de Gumz; Tee Pee Time; Electric Mumbles.* LPs: *and his Jolly Giants; Big B-a-d Band Live at the Wichita Jazz Festival 1974* (Vang.); *Big Bad Band at Carnegie Hall 1970* (Etoile); *It's What's Happenin'; Spanish Rice* (Imp.); others w. Terry-Bob Brookmeyer Quintet (Verve; Main.); *Oscar Peterson-Clark Terry; The Trumpet Kings at Montreux '75; JATP at Montreux '75* (Pablo); *Newport in New York '72: The Jam Sessions, Vols. 3&4; The Jimmy Smith Jam, Vol. 5* (Cobble.); *Colorado Jazz Party* (MPS).

TERRY, SONNY (Saunders Teddell),* harmonica, composer, singer; b. Durham, N.C., 10/24/11. Partner of Brownie McGhee (q.v.) from 1939. Continued to work 11 months out of each year, touring overseas approx. twice annually. Motion picture soundtrack work for *Book of Numbers; Buck and the Preacher; Cisco Pike.* TV: Mike Douglas show; *Midnight Special* etc. In fall of '75, went to Chicago to take part in special PBS televised tribute to John Hammond Sr., who had been responsible for his coming to NYC for the *From Spirituals to Swing* concert in '38. Terry sang a duet on this TV show with John Hammond Jr.

Comp.: *Mean Woman Blues; These Women Are Killing Me; Hootin' the Blues* (used as prelude for Broadway show *Finian's Rainbow); I'm A Burnt Child; Jet Plane Blues; Motorcycle Blues; Long Way From Home.*

LPs w. McGhee (Mercury, BluesWay, A & M, Fantasy, etc.).

THARPE, SISTER ROSETTA (Rosetta Nubin),* singer, guitar; b. Cotton Plant, Ark., 3/20/21. Though trained in religious music, Sister Tharpe gained popularity as a vocalist with the bands of C. Calloway and L. Millinder. Later, feat. as a soloist, she maintained her reputation for many years, touring the U.S. and Europe. She died in 1973.

THELIN, EJE, trombone; b. Jonkokping, Sweden, 1938. First important job w. Joe Harris, '58-9. Had own group from '61-5. Pl. at Jazz Hus Montmartre, Copenhagen '63 with George Russell, at Montmartre '64. Soloist at Montmartre '66. In '73-4 played with John Surman in Europe; in '75 w. drummer Leroy Lowe in Sweden and U.S. From late '60-72 engaged at Graz Jazzinstitute as teacher. In mid-'70s occupied w. teaching, playing with various groups, and involved w. electronic experiments w. own quartet. TV: Sweden and the Continent. Fest: Antibes fest. in Juan-les-Pins '63; w. Barney Wilen, Roy Brooks, Palle Danielsson, Jazzjambouree, Warsaw '66; and most major European fests. from '63. LPs: *Eje Thelin Group* (Riks); *Candles of Vision* (Calig); *So Far; At the German Jazz Festival.*

THIELE, ROBERT (BOB), producer, songwriter; b. Brooklyn, N.Y., 7/27/22. An amateur clarinetist who evinced an early interest in jazz, he was a radio announcer on jazz record shows, 1936-44; editor and publisher, *Jazz Magazine,* '39-41. Owned and ran Signature Records 1940-48, rec. many sessions w. Pee Wee Russell, Coleman Hawkins, Art Hodes, James P. Johnson et al. In the 1950s he was an a & r director for Coral Records; then w. Dot, '59-

60; president, Hanover-Signature, '60-63; a & r producer at Roulette, '63-4.

From 1965-69 Thiele was responsible for the production of a great number of important albums as a & r director for Impulse, most notably those of John Coltrane, in whom he was a staunch believer; Oliver Nelson, Pharoah Sanders, Archie Shepp and many others. In 1969 he formed his own company, Flying Dutchman. For that label as well as his others, Amsterdam, Bob Thiele Music and Contact, he has recorded or reissued important works by both avant garde and traditional jazz artists. Married 10/24/72 to Teresa Brewer (q.v.).

Comps: lyrics to Duke Ellington's *C Jam Blues,* under the title *Duke's Place;* also *What A Wonderful World,* rec. by Louis Armstrong.

LPs: *20's Score Again* w. New Happy Times Orch. (Signature). Hundreds of others as producer, on above-listed labels.

THIELEMANS, JEAN (TOOTS),* *harmonica, guitar, whistler, composer;* b. Brussels, Belgium, 4/29/22. After working as a staff musician in NYC in the mid-60s, Thielemans from '69 was closely associated w. Quincy Jones, playing on sound tracks of several films, as well as on Jones' records, and at MJF, '72. In Nov. '72, he toured USSR with a quartet (Bob James, Milt Hinton, Ben Riley). Revisiting Belgium about twice a year as a single, Thielemans commuted between Europe and U.S., also, in his own words, ''commuted between my love for jazz and the more commercial work.''

Motion Pictures: *Midnight Cowboy; Getaway; Cinderella Liberty; Sugarland Express.* As comp., songs and background for Swedish animated film, *Dunderklumpeu.* TV: theme music for *Sesame Street.* Comps: his best known work is *Bluesette,* which he re-recorded in a new version with Jones in '75. Fest: Montreux '75.

LPs: *Toots & Svend,* w. S. Asmussen (A & M); *Captured Alive* (Choice); w. Jones, *Walking In Space; Gula Matari; Smackwater Jack; You've Got It Bad Girl; Mellow Madness* (A & M); w. O. Peterson at Montreux (Pablo); others w. J.J. Johnson, Z. Sims.

THIGPEN, BEN, *drums;* b. Laurel, Miss., 1909; d. St. Louis, Mo. 10/5/71. Prof. debut at 15 w. Bobby Boswell. Worked w. dance team, later settling in Chi., where he stud. w. Jimmy Bertrand. Best known for his long tenure in Andy Kirk orch., '30-47. Later, in St. Louis, led own groups and pl. w. Singleton Palmer's band throughout '60s. Father of Ed Thigpen (see below).

THIGPEN, EDMUND LEONARD (ED),* *drums;* also *percussion;* b. Chicago, Ill., 12/28/30. Pl. w. Bud Powell, Billy Taylor trios in '50s; then w. Oscar Peterson, '59-65, before settling in Toronto. Joined Ella Fitzgerald, '66. Moved to LA, '67, working w. Pat Boone, Johnny Mathis, Peggy Lee, Andy Williams, Oliver Nelson, Gerald Wilson and freelancing in the studios. Rejoined Fitzgerald '68 and remained w. her until July '72. In Sept. '72 moved to Copenhagen, working as a free-lance and teaching. Formed group w. Svend Asmussen, '73; also toured w. Sylvia Vrethammen in Sweden. From '74 teaching at Music Conservatory in Aarhus, Denmark; perf. w. own new group, Action Re Ac-

tion. Fests: Montreux w. Fitzgerald, '69; also NJF, Verona, Kongsberg, Pori & other major Euro. events. Comp: music & lyrics for *Denise; Illusions,* a suite. Publ: *Talking Drums; Be Our Guest* w. Ray Brown (c/o Sonet Records, Torsvikksvangen 7A, Lidingo, Sweden). LPs: *Ed Thigpen's Action Re Action* (Sonet, GNP-Crescendo); *Out of the Storm* (Verve); *Jazz at Santa Monica* w. E. Fitzgerald, C. Basie & all stars (Pablo); w. Horace Parlan; Duke Jordan; Johnny Griffin; Dexter Gordon (SteepleChase); w. O. Nelson, *At Marty's On The Hill* (Imp.); w. Major Holley, *Mule* (Black & Blue).

THOMAS, JOSEPH LEWIS (JOE),* *trumpet;* b. Webster Groves, Mo., 7/24/09. The lyrical trumpet player continued to work in the NY metropolitan area in various settings. App. with own group at Leaves, an East Side night club; coll. dates '67-8. Toured w. own group feat. his wife, vocalist Baby Mathews, for Job Corps, '69-71. Colls., jazz clubs, private parties, '72. Also w. Mike Burgevin group at Brew's, and Jim Andrews group at O'Connors (Watchung, N.J.) '73. Pl. at dedication of L. Armstrong Stadium at NJF-NY, '73, an event filmed for NET.

Comps: *Swingtime Up In Harlem; No Better For Ya; He's Got So Much; Blues For Baby.* LPs: w. A. Tatum, *Masterpieces* (MCA); w. Vic Dickenson All Stars (British RCA); w. C. Cole, R. Norvo, *Jazz Giants* (Trip).

THOMAS, LEONE (Amos Leon Thomas Jr.), *singer, lyricist;* also *miscellaneous percussion;* b. East St. Louis, Ill., 10/4/37. Studied music at Lincoln HS w. Daisy O. Westbrook, ''who taught by rote, increasing the ear's capacity.'' Two yrs. at Tenn. State. While in junior high school sang w. drummer Ben Thigpen; in high school w. Grant Green; Jimmy Forrest. To NYC Feb. '59 where immediately he replaced Austin Cromer as vocalist on show at Apollo which incl. Dakota Staton, Ahmad Jamal, Nipsey Russell, Art Blakey's Messengers. Toured w. this package on black theater circuit: Howard; Regal, Royal, etc. Worked w. Randy Weston; R.R. Kird; Mary Lou Williams, rec. live w. her at Town Hall. Took the place of Joe Williams in Count Basie orch. '61 and later was replaced by Ocie Smith and Irene Reid. After Army service rejoined Basie, and was w. him '64-5. He sang at the inaugural balls of Presidents Kennedy and Johnson w. Basie. With Pharoah Sanders, '69-72; still pl. occasional gigs w. him in mid-'70s. Own gp. before working w. Santana '73. Resumed as leader '74. A more than capable blues singer, sometimes reminiscent of Joe Williams, Thomas emerged with Sanders as a lyricist and also a scat singer, further coloring his performances with a form of yodeling he learned by listening to the music of Central African pygmy tribes. Added second ''e'' to Leon, '76. Infl: Ellington, Monk, Coltrane, Gillespie, Milton Nascimento, King Pleasure, Eddie Jefferson, Betty Carter. Won DB Critics poll, TDWR, '70; DB Readers poll, '70-3. TV: *Like It Is; Soul; Inside Bed-Stuy; Mike Douglas Big Band Festival.* Fest: NJF; MJF; Berlin, '70; Montreux, '70-1. Wrote lyrics to Sanders' *The Creator Has a Master Plan; Colors; Hum Allah, Hum Allah;* also *Straight No Chaser; Cousin Mary; Bags' Groove.* LPs: *The Leon Thomas Album; Full Circle; Spirits Known and Unkown; Blues and the Soulful Turth; Facets;* w. Oliver Nelson *In Berlin* (Fly. Dutch);

Louis Armstrong and Friends (Amsterdam); w. Sanders, *Karma*; *Jewels of Thought* (Imp.), *Izipho Sam* (St.-East); w. Santana, *Welcome*; *Santana Lotus—Live in Japan* (Col.); w. Basie, *Pop Goes the Basie* (Reprise); *Basie Picks the Winners* (Verve); w. Mary Lou Williams, *Praise the Lord in Many Voices* (Avant Garde); w. R.R. Kirk, *A Meeting of the Times* (Atl.).

THOMAS, RENE,* *guitar*; b. Liége, Belgium, 2/25/27. Lived in Montreal, '58-63, visiting NYC in '58 and rec. w. Toshiko and S. Rollins. Ret. to Europe, toured w. Lou Bennett, K. Clarke, and many other groups, incl. duo w. drummer Han Bennink. With Stan Getz, '69-72, incl. tour of Mexico. Returned to Montreal, '73, to visit relatives, but continued to work around the Continent until his sudden death of a heart attack in Santander, Spain, 1/3/75. Thomas was described by Rollins in 1958 as "better than any of the American guitarists on the scene today." In Europe, he was respected as one of the greatest guitarists to have emerged on the Continent since Django Reinhardt, who was his original inspiration. In later years Thomas was infl. by Jimmy Raney. He won DB poll, TDWR, 1967. Comp: *Ballad for Leo.*

LPs: *Dynasty* w. Getz (Verve); *A Songbook in Europe* w. Lucky Thompson (MPS); *TPL* (Vogel). European LPs w. Eddy Louiss, Jacques Dieval, Lou Bennett et al.

THOMPSON, DONALD WINSTON (DON),* *bass*; also *piano, vibes, drums*; b. Powell River, B.C., Canada, 1/18/40. After leaving John Handy group w. which he played in mid-'60s, he worked mainly in the studios of Vancouver and Toronto. Member of house rhythm section at Bourbon St. in Toronto, backing F. Rosolino, J. Hall, P. Desmond, B. Kessel, J. Moody, Blue Mitchell, C. McPherson. Comp: *Pluto & Mercury* on *Solar Explorations* LP by Moe Koffman; *Bilbo*; *Country Place*; *Don't*; *Echoes From Before* on *Koffman Live at George's.* He also pl. on both albums (GRT). Own LP: *Love Song to a Virgo Lady* (Sack.); other LPs: w. John Handy, incl. *Spirituals to Swing 30th Anny.*

THOMPSON, ELI (LUCKY),* *tenor, soprano saxes, composer*; b. Detroit, Mich., 6/16/24. Active on the LA scene during the '40s w. Charlie Parker, Dodo Marmarosa, Boyd Raeburn's orch. he pl. w. Kenton in the mid-'50s and then pl. and lived in Europe, '57-62 before returning to NYC. Back to Europe in late '60s, coming back to US again in '71. Taught for a year at Dartmouth U. from Sept. '73, and recorded two albums for Groove Merchant, *Goodbye Yesterday* and *I Offer You.* Reissue of earlier material w. Oscar Pettiford, Jimmy Cleveland from the '50s, *Dancing Sunbeam* (Impulse). Rec. for MPS in Europe.

THOMPSON, CHARLES PHILLIP (SIR CHARLES),* *piano, organ, composer*; b. Springfield, Ohio, 3/21/18. While w. I. Jacquet in '47 composed *Robbins' Nest*, a jazz standard; later led organ trio in many clubs. Toured Europe, '59; w. C. Hawkins at Berlin JF, '64. Sporadically active during next few years, he underwent major surgery in NYC in '74. Living in LA, he made a comeback concert June '75 at the Pilgrimage Theatre.

LPs: *Hey There* (Black and Blue); *Kansas City Nights* w. B. Clayton & B. Tate (Prest.); tracks in *Master Jazz Piano*, vol. 2 (Master Jazz).

(Col.); w. Sonny Greenwich, *Old Man & the Child* (Sack); *Sun Song* (Radio Canada Int.); w. J. McShann, *Man From Muskogee* (Sack.); w. Jim Hall (Horizon).

THORNTON, CLIFFORD EDWARD III, *cornet, composer, educator*; also *valve trombone, shenai, African percussion*; b. Philadelphia, Pa., 9/6/36. Grandfather, a reed player, founded and dir. Wissahickon Concert Band and Happy Six Jazz Band in Germantown, Pa. Uncle, Jimmy Golden, pianist w. Philly jazz gps.; aunt, Alease Golden, church organist in Wilmington, Del. Studied at HS of Music & Art, NYC, '51-4; Temple U. '54-6; Morgan State Coll. '57; privately w. Donald Byrd, NYC, 57; Webster Young, SF, '61; Bavarian State Conserv., Wurzburg, W. Germany, '64-5; Juilliard, '66-8; Wesleyan U., '69-70; Manhattan Sch. of Mus., '72-4. Worked w. Ray Draper, '56-7; US Army Band, '58-61, in Korea, Japan; Phil Moore Jr; Sonny King, SF, '61-3; Sun Ra; Pharoah Sanders, '63-7; John Tchicai, '66; own gps., '66-9; Archie Shepp, '69-72; own gps., in NYC, Europe, '72-5. Instructor at New York Sch. of Mus., '65; Assistant Professor of Music, Wesleyan U., '69-75. Infl: Clifford Brown; D. Byrd, Webster Young, John Gilmore, Sun Ra, Jimmy Golden. TV: scored film for ORTF, Paris, '71; Antibes Fest. w. A. Shepp, BRT, '70; educational TV in NYC, NJ, Conn., '70-2. Fest: Amougies, '69; Carthage, Antibes, '70; Ghent, '71; Etudes et Rencontres Artistique, Geneva, '72-3; NY Jazz Musicians Fest., '72. Comp: *The Gardens of Harlem.* LPs: *Freedom and Unity*; *Communications Network* (Third World); *Ketchaoua* (Byg); *The Panther and the Lash* (America); *The Gardens of Harlem* (JCOA).

TIBERI, FRANK, *tenor saxophone*; also *bassoon, flute, clarinet*; b. Camden, N.J., 12/4/28. Started in 1936 with private lodge organization. Played in marching street band. Private teacher on clarinet; self-taught on sax and flute. Stud. bassoon w. Sol Schoenbach. Played in clubs from age 13, joined Bob Chester at 17. Worked in musical show doubling on many instruments. In mid-50s played w. B. Goodman quintet, Urbie Green; TV shows and movie sound tracks as sideman. In '69 joined W. Herman orch. on lead and jazz tenor, also playing jazz bassoon and conducting rap sessions at coll. seminars. Fests. w. Herman: Newport, Monterey, Tokyo, Concord, Montreux and many others in Europe.

Influenced by Ch. Parker, Lester Young, J. Coltrane, Dennis Sandole, Gil Evans and many classical composers, Tiberi proved to be a major force with his tenor work in the Herman band, and one of the handful of effective soloists on jazz bassoon.

LPs w. Herman: *Woody Brand New* (Cadet); *Giant Steps*; *Thundering Herd* (Fantasy).

TIMMONS, ROBERT HENRY (BOBBY),* *piano, vibes, composer*; b. Philadelphia, Pa., 12/19/35. Well known as composer of *Moanin'*, written while he was w. A. Blakey in '58, and *Dis Here* and *Dat Dere*, written and rec. while he was w. C. Adderley, '59-60, Timmons pl. at Greenwich Village bars and restaurants during the late '60s and early '70s. He died 3/1/74 of cirrhosis of the liver in a NYC hospital.

" 'Laid-back swagger' pretty well describes the way he played piano. . . ," wrote Peter Keepnews, "with a right hand effortlessly capable of the fleet lyricism of a Bud Powell and a left hand not averse to the earthy rumblings of a Meade Lux Lewis. It was the same kind of mixture of the urbane and the down-home that characterized the style of one of his predecessors in the Messengers' piano chair, Horace Silver. If anything, it was even further *down,* closer to the black church experience that had been a vital part of Bobby's growing up. . .''

LPs: *Moanin'*; *Got To Get It*; *Do You Know The Way* (Milest.); *Soulman*; *Chicken & Dumplin's*; *Chun-king*; *Little Barefoot Soul*; *Soul Food*; *Workin' Out* (Prest.); others w. Adderley (Riverside); Blakey (BN).

TIZOL, JUAN, * valve trombone, composer; b. San Juan, Puerto Rico, 1/22/00. Pl. w. Duke Ellington, 1928-44; Harry James, '44-51; Ellington, 51-3; James, '53-60; Ellington, '60. Retired, in LA, reappearing only once for a record session in 1964 w. Louie Bellson. Best known comps: *Perdido, Caravan.* LPs: *Big Bands!,* 1964, w. Bellson (Onyx); others w. Ellington (various labels).

TJADER, CALLEN RADCLIFFE (CAL), * vibes; also *drums, composer;* b. St. Louis, Mo., 7/16/25. A former Brubeck and Shearing sideman, in the late '50s Tjader led his own combo, continuing to do so during the '60s and '70s. He confined himself to app. mostly on the West Coast where he makes his home, w. occasional trips to Phoenix, Tucson, Seattle etc. for clubs and concerts. Active in coll. clinics. Has played several summer fests in Central Park, NYC, as well as various ballrooms and Madison Sq. Gdn. Tjader was recording continuously for the Fantasy label, but in 1968, together with Gabor Szabo and the late Gary McFarland, he formed Skye Records, which was in operation until '70, at which time he returned to Fantasy. In Nov. '74 he was feat. in an Irving Granz prod. at Arizona State U. w. Ella Fitzgerald. He plays the Monterey and Concord fests. annually.

LPs: *Puttin' It Together*; *Primo*; *Last Night When We Were Young*; *Last Bolero in Berkeley*; Cal Tjader & Charlie Byrd, *Tambu* (Fant.).

TOLLIVER, CHARLES, * trumpet, composer; b. Jacksonville, Fla., 3/6/42. Influenced by Clifford Brown; early gigs w. J. McLean, Joe Henderson, A. Blakey while based in NYC. Went to LA '66 w. Willie Bobo; while there, joined Gerald Wilson orch. for one year. Left LA May '67, returned to NYC, joined M. Roach group for two years.

In May '69, Tolliver formed his own first combo, naming it Music, Inc. He took it to Europe, and while there made his first recording of the quartet. Since '69 the group has become internationally respected for its innovative approach, touring North and South America, Europe and Japan. Won DB TDWR award on trumpet, 68.

Fests: Newport, '67 w. Max Roach; many fests., TV apps. in Europe.

In '71 Tolliver became co-founder, Chairman and chief officer of Strata-East Records, Inc., a label owned entirely by artists. He is composer of *Singin' Wid a Sword In Ma Han,* performed in adaptation by Roach with the latter as soloist at Montreux Jazz Fest., '71; also *Collection Suite,* played by N.Y. Jazz Repertory orch., Carnegie Hall, '74.

Of all the trumpeters to come to prominence in the '60s,

Charles Tolliver was perhaps the most sensitive to the necessity of swinging. Michael Shera observed: "He is one young musician who refuses to run blindly up the alleyways of musical anarchy in search of a mythical freedom, as too many of his contemporaries are doing. If the freedom they are seeking involves the opportunity to be creative, inventive and original, they will find there is a lot to be learned from the method of Charles Tolliver."

LPs: w. Jackie McLean, *It's Time*; *Jacknife*; *Action* (Blue Note); Booker Ervin, *Structurally Sound*; Gerald Wilson, *Live & Swinging* (Pacific Jazz); Roy Ayers, *Virgo Vibes*; *Stoned Soul Picnic* (Atl.); Horace Silver, *Serenade to a Soul Sister* (Blue Note); Max Roach, *Members Don't Git Weary* (Atl.); McCoy Tyner, *Song For My Lady* (Milestone); Doug Carn, *Spirit of the New Land* (Black Jazz). Own LPs: *Paper Man* (Arista); *Music Inc./The Ringer*; *Charles Tolliver & All Stars* (Polydor); *Live at Loosdrecht Festival*; *Music Inc. & Big Band*; *Music Inc/Live at Slugs, Vol. I*; *Music Inc/Live at Slugs, Vol. II*; *Music Inc/Live in Tokyo* (Strata-East, 156 Fifth Ave., New York, N.Y. 10010).

TOMPKINS, ROSS, piano, composer; also *keyboards, synthesizer*; b. Detroit, Mich., 5/13/38. Stud. privately and at New England Conserv. Active in NYC during '60s, he joined NBC staff orch pl. Tonight show, '67- . In addition, he had a busy jazz career working with K. Winding, '60; E. Dolphy, '64; J.J. Johnson. Pl. w. many gps. at Half Note, NYC, incl. W. Montgomery, '66; B. Brookmeyer-C. Terry; Joe Newman; I. Jacquet, '67; R. Eldridge; A. Cohn-Z. Sims frequently, '68-72; many jobs w. B. Hackett, '65-70; B. Goodman, '68; gigged w. James Moody, NYC and Cal. In '71 he moved to Cal. remaining a member of Doc Severinsen's *Tonight Show* band. He continued to make frequent local apps. with jazz combos and bands, incl. L. Bellson orch.; has also led own small combos from time to time at Donte's and elsewhere. Tompkins, who names Ellington, Armstrong, E. Hines and Fats Waller as the sources of his inspiration, is an eclectic, technically outstanding mainstream-modern soloist. Fests: Newport; Concord; annual apps. at Colorado Jazz Party.

LPs: *Ross Tompkins Trio* (Roulette); w. K. Winding-J.J. Johnson, *Stonebones*; *Israel* (A & M); w. Bellson, *Explosion* (Pablo); *Breakthrough* (Proj. 3); *Louie Rides Again* (Percussion Power); *Colorado Jazz Party* (BASF); w. Eddie "Lockjaw" Davis, *Lock the Fox* (RCA); w. Herb Ellis-Freddie Green (Concord).

TONEY, KEVIN, keyboards, composer, singer; b. Detroit, Mich., 4/23/53. Piano lessons from age five; stud. at Cass Tech. High and at Howard U. School of Music, where he became a protege of Donald Byrd, who was then Chairman of the Dept. of Jazz Studies. Joining with a group of other students at Howard, Toney in '73 became leader of The Blackbyrds. While remaining a full time student, Toney traveled whenever possible, w. Byrd himself, and independently with the Blackbyrds. The group's first album became a soul and pop hit in addition to gaining a jazz audience. The first single release, *Do It Fluid,* became a gold record (one million sales). After the issue of their second album and several changes in personnel, the Blackbyrds completed a movie sound track for *Hit The Open Man.*

Toney, who during his years a student pl. w. such visiting guests as Woody Shaw, Gerald Wilson, S. Rollins, J. McLean, was majoring in jazz studies and comp. in '75. Comps: *Future Children, Future Hopes*; *Spaced Out*. LPs: *Flying Start*; *The Blackbyrds* (Fantasy).

TORME, MELVIN HOWARD (MEL),* *singer, composer, piano, drums, producer* etc.; b. Chicago, Ill., 9/13/25. From the mid-'60s Torme wrote all his own arrangements. He continued to tour regularly, often playing in LV, visiting Australia almost annually; app. on British TV. Writer of articles for various magazines, essays for N.Y. *Times,* and a book about Judy Garland, *The Other Side of the Rainbow,* publ. by Wm. Morrow, '70. Torme has written many orig. TV scripts, prod. TV specs., and app. as actor in numerous dramatic series. Pl. title role in movie, *Snowman*. He continued to maintain his reputation as one of the few artists of his generation to retain a jazz and quality/pop image in his singing, his choice of material and his own arrangements.

LPs: *Live at the Maisonette* (Atl.).

TOWNER, RALPH N., *guitar, piano, French horn, composer*; b. Chehalis, Wash., 3/1/40. Mother a piano teacher and church organist; father pl. trumpet. Improvising at the piano from age three. Trumpet at five. Studied theory and comp. at the U. of Oregon, '58-63; graduate work, '64-6. Stud. classical guitar w. Karl Scheit at Vienna Acad. of Mus., '63-4, '67-8. Pl. trumpet in dance band at age 13 in Bend, Ore.; lute and guitar w. Elizabethan Consort and the Eugene (Ore.) Chamber Ensemble, '64-6. Replaced Larry Coryell in Chuck Mahaffay band, Seattle '66. To NYC '69, jamming w. John McLaughlin, Airto; gigs w. Tamba Four. Pl. w. Jimmy Garrison, '69-70; Jeremy Steig, '69-71; Winter Consort, '70-1; Weather Report, '71; Gary Burton, '74-5. From '71 occupied mainly w. Oregon, a gp. which grew out of Winter Consort, and which includes Paul McCandless, Collin Walcott and Glen Moore. "The band is equally at home with baroque counterpoint, Indian raga, harmonically advanced improvising, rock rhythms and contemporary classicism," said Robert Palmer in *Rolling Stone*.

Milo Fine wrote: "Towner has an uncanny knack for harmonic overtones, and the quickness to carry them out. He also probes into areas of dissonance and thick harmonies."

Won DB Critics Poll, TDWR, '74. Infl: Bill Evans, Scott La Faro, Paul Bley, Keith Jarrett, Julian Bream. Fest: Woodstock w. Tim Hardin; Tanglewood, Chatauqua, Schaefer Fest. w. Winter Consort; solo at NJF-NY, '73; w. Oregon, '74-5; Pori, Bergamo, Molde, Berlin. Comp: over 60 instrumentals incl. *Distant Hills*; *Icarus*; *Ghost Beads*. LPs: *Diary*; w. Burton, *Matchbook*; *Solstice*; w. Jarrett, *In the Light* (ECM); w. Oregon, *Music of Another Present Era*; *Distant Hills*; *Winter Light* (Vang.); w. Weather Report, *I Sing the Body Electric* (Col.); w. Winter Consort, *Road* (A&M).

TRACEY, STAN,* *piano, composer*; b. London, England, 12/30/26. Early work w. Jack Parnell, Ted Heath, Ronnie Scott; house pianist at Scott's club from its opening, '60-68. Local and continental gigs with quartet and big band, '69-71. In '72 formed duo w. Mike Osborne; teaching at City Literary Inst., London. Played many concerts in England and on continent with ten piece band, quartet, trio, duo,

solo, '73. Comp. and perf. Southwark Cathedral Shakespeare's birthday concert; soloist in Ellington remembrance service; British tour spons. by Arts Council, '74. Regular winner of *Melody Maker* polls from '66 in composer, arranger, piano and best album categories.

Numerous LPs with own groups on Col., Philips and various European labels.

TRISTANO, LEONARD JOSEPH (LENNIE),* *piano, composer, educator*; b. Chicago, Ill. 3/19/19. As he had in the '50s and '60s, Tristano devoted himself to teaching, playing in public only at the Half Note in '66, and in concert at the Art & Science Fest., Leeds, England in the summer of '68. In '73 the French TV Network brought its cameras to his house for an interview that contained minimal playing. That same year he sponsored a concert at Carnegie Recital Hall for one of his students, pianist Connie Crothers. He also held private recitals of his students at his Queens studio. At the end of '75 he was preparing to record for a Japanese label, East Wind. LP: a reissue of his late '40s sextet w. Lee Konitz and Warne Marsh, *Crosscurrents* (Capitol).

TRUNK, PETER,* *bass*; also *trumpet, cello*; b. Frankfurt-am-Main, Germany, 5/17/36. First prominent in '50s as member of Albert Mangelsdorff combo, Trunk, who also pl. in Germany w. many visiting Americans, was killed 12/31/73 in a traffic accident in NYC.

TRZASKOWSKI, ANDRZEJ, *piano, composer*; b. Cracow, Poland, 3/23/33. Stud. piano, musicology, contemp. and electronic mus. w. various teachers from '50s through '74. In '51 he formed Melomani, which he claims was the first authentic Polish jazz group. In '58 was mainstay of the Jazz Believers w. Krzysztof Komeda and Jan Wroblewski. In '59 formed the Wreckers, a group heard in '62 on a two month tour of the U.S., taking part in Washington and Newport Fests. The group was later renamed the Andrzej Trzaskowski quintet; personnel incl. M. Urbaniak and Z. Namyslowski. Toured Euro., rec. for radio, TV. Trzaskowski later developed an avant garde orientation. In '65-6 the personnel of the group incl. Ted Curson.

Trzaskowski has pl. and rec. w. S. Getz, A. Farmer, P. Woods, Nathan Davis, D. Pike; worked regularly w. Hamburg Radio station, '65-71. From Jan. '75, art director and conductor for Polish radio and TV orch. feat. the country's leading jazz and studio musicians. Winner of awards as best Polish jazz musician; also *Jazz* and *Jazz Forum* polls in best composer, pianist, leader categories. Comps: *Nihil Novi*; *Synopsis*; *Bluebeard*; *The Quibble*; *Posters*; *Epitaph for K.K.*; *Double*; *The Blocks*; *Magma*; *His Better Feelings*; *Vision*; also scores for about 30 films.

LPs: *The Wreckers and Andrzej Trzaskowski Trio* (Muza); *The Andrzej Trzaskowski Quintet*; *The A.T. Sekstet feat. Ted Curson*; *Stan Getz in Poland*—with Andrzej Trzaskowski Trio (Polskie Nagrania).

TUCKER, MICHAEL B. (MICKEY), *piano, keyboards, composer*; also *oboe, English horn*; b. Durham, N.C., 4/28/41. Raised in Pittsburgh until he was 13, then moved back to Durham. Private piano lessons at age six. Att. Morehouse Coll. in Ga.; taught at Roosevelt HS in Lake Wales, Fla.; Miss. Valley State Coll., Itta Bena, Miss. Worked w. Damita Jo '65; Timmie Rogers, '66-7; Anthony

& the Imperials, '67-8; James Moody, '69-71; three mos. w. Thad Jones-Mel Lewis, late '73; Eddie Jefferson; Frank Foster; Sonny Red; Willis Jackson; Cecil Payne; Roy Brooks, '73-5; Final Edition, '75. A very fresh keyboard talent in that he finds new ways to extend the jazz tradition within that tradition's basic tenets, not the least of which is vibrant swinging.

Infl: Fats Waller; Art Tatum; Hamp Hawes; Phineas Newborn, Oscar Peterson, Herbie Hancock (acoustic piano). TV: Mike Douglas; Ed Sullivan; w. Final Edition on educ. Ch. 50, NJ. Fest: NJF-NY w. Moody. Comp: *State of Affairs*; *A Little 3 for L.C.*; *Something About Bean*, dedicated to Coleman Hawkins; *Suite* for *Eight Hands*, for two pianos, two perc.; *This One's For You*.

Benjamin Gray, a pianist from Inkster, Mich. interested him in two-piano collaborations which he explored w. Roland Hanna in *New Heritage Keyboard Quartet* (BN). Own LP: *Triplicity* (Xanadu); w. Moody, *Never Again*; Eric Kloss, *Essence*; E. Jefferson, *Things Are Getting Better*; Willis Jackson, *West Africa* (Muse); R.R. Kirk, *Blacknuss* (Atl.).

TURNER, JOSEPH VERNON (BIG JOE),* *singer, composer*; b. Kansas City, Mo., 5/18/11. Living in LA in '60s and '70s, the veteran blues singer app. in local clubs, as a single, and with J. Otis show. Many visits to Monterey JF; also Newport, Ann Arbor Fests. In March '74 he took part in the filming, along w. C. Basie, Jay McShann and others, of *Last of the Blue Devils*, a retrospective dealing with early Kansas City jazz. Comps: *TV Momma*; *Cherry Red*; *Wee Baby Blues*; *Roll 'Em Pete*; *Squeeze Me Baby*; *Piney Brown Blues*; *Mrs. Geraldine*.

LPs: *Singin' The Blues*; *Roll 'Em* (Bluesway); *Big Joe Is Here* (Atl.); *Big Joe Turner Turns on the Blues* (Kent); *Great R & B Oldies*, Vol. 4 (Blues Spectrum); *The Bosses—Count Basie/Joe Turner*; *The Trumpet Kings Meet Joe Turner* (Pablo); some tracks on *Art Tatum Masterpieces* (MCA); w. Papa John Creach, *Filthy* (Grunt).

TURNER, JOE,* *piano*; also *singer*; b. Baltimore, Md., 11/3/07. After World War II returned to Europe where he earlier toured w. Adelaide Hall. From '62 was fixture at Calavados club in Paris. In January '76 pl. long engagement at the Cookery, NYC. during which time Gary Giddins wrote: "Unlike most of the stride players, Turner has an authentic feeling for the blues, both as a pianist and as a singer." LPs: *Joe Turner Trio* w. Slam Stewart, Jo Jones (B&B); *Stride By Stride* (77); *Smashing Thirds* (MPS).

TURNEY, NORRIS WILLIAM, *alto saxophone*; also *tenor, soprano saxes, clarinet, flutes, piccolo, piano*; b. Wilmington, Ohio, 9/8/21. Stud. piano from age 10-12; saxophone in '35 under Mrs. Inez Jones, wife of Wilmington H.S. mus. dir., Luther Jones; clarinet under George Carr of Cincinnati Cons; harmony & theory w. Artie Matthews, Cosmospolitan Sch. of Mus., Cinci. Began flute stud. in '65 in NYC w. Henry Zlotnick; later w. Harold Bennett. Pl. briefly w. Fate Marable out of St. Louis. With A.B. Townsend band at Cotton Club, Cinci. '41-3; Jeter-Pillars orch. in St. Louis, Chi. and at Apollo Theater, NYC. Joined Tiny Bradshaw in early '45 and moved to NYC. With Billy Eckstine band from late '45 for two yrs.

before ret. to Ohio for teaching, pl. w. gps incl. own. Back to NYC '51 for a yr. of free-lance; Phila., one yr. w. Elmer Snowden; two yrs. w. Johnny Lynch in Atlantic City, N.J.; a yr. w. Bull Moose Jackson. Ret. to NYC, '59, working rock gigs on tenor; club dates; Catskill Mts.; and a yr. w. Machito. Took part in many rehearsal bands around NYC incl. F. Foster, Clark Terry, Duke Pearson, H. McGhee and one he co-led w. Danny Small. In '67 joined Ray Charles for a year. Toured w. Duke Ellington '68-72, distinguishing himself as a versatile multi-reedman-flutist. Working in pit band for hit Broadway musical *Raisin,* free-lancing and rehearsing his own small gp. Infl: Ellington, Goodman, Sy Oliver, Hodges, Carter, Willie Smith, Parker. TV: U.S. & Europe w. Charles, Ellington incl. Ed Sullivan, Timex shows. Fests: NJF w. Ellington, Charles, Sy Oliver, Wild Bill Davis; many Euro. fests. Won TDWR awards in DB Critics poll as flutist, '70-1. Comp: *Checkered Hat,* dedicated to Johnny Hodges, in Ellington's *Togo Brava* album. LPs: *Boys From Dayton* (Master Jazz); w. Ellington, *New Orleans Suite* (Atl.); *Togo Brava Suite* (UA); *70th Birthday Concert* (SS); w. R. Weston, *Tanjah* (Poly.).

TURRE, STEVE, *trombone*; also *electric bass*; b. Omaha, Neb., 12/8/49. Stud. at NTSU, '68-9; in SF w. Norman Williams, '70. Pl. w. R.R. Kirk in SF, '70; Van Morrison, '71; bass trombone w. R. Charles, '72; Charles Moffett, A. Blakey, '73; Thad Jones-Mel Lewis, '73; Woody Shaw in NYC, '74; toured w. C. Hamilton, '74- . Movie sound tracks, educ. TV w. Hamilton; TV in Euro. w. Charles, Jones-Lewis. Fests: Monterey, '73 w. Jones-Lewis. Comp: *Sanyas*.

LPs: w. Hamilton, *Peregrinations* (BN); w. Woody Shaw, *Moontrane* (Muse).

TURRENTINE, STANLEY,* *tenor sax*; b. Pittsburgh, Pa., 4/5/34. Continued to lead gp. w. wife, organist Shirley Scott through the '60s until '71 when they parted company musically and matrimonially. He had led his own gps. from that time, also rec. w. larger ensembles for CTI which brought him to a wider, pop audience. In '75 he moved to the Fantasy label for albums produced and arranged by Gene Page in even more of a pop soul vein. Due to the settings his albums made the charts for he was playing in the same blues-inflected, naturally funky style that had been his trademark for many years. Of his new-found success as a "crossover" artist Turrentine said: "It's a natural thing for me. I hear Stevie Wonder tunes, or Marvin Gaye tunes, on the radio all the time. If I like the tune, I'll do it—no matter who wrote it. I just want *lots* of people to hear my music! I want to make records that will sell—to everybody."

Fest: NJF-NY, etc. Many TV apps. Comp: *Sugar*.

LPs: *Have You Seen the Rain*; *Pieces of Dreams*; *In the Pocket* (Fant.); *Sugar*; *Don't Mess With Mister T*; *Salt Song*; *Cherry* (CTI); reissue anthology (Blue Note); reissue, *Yester You, Yester Me* (Trip).

TYNER, ALFRED McCOY (Sulaimon Saud),* *piano, composer*; b. Philadelphia, Pa., 12/11/38. After leaving John Coltrane's group in Dec. '65, he formed own trio with which he appeared around NYC in '66. He also worked as a sideman w. Ike and Tina Turner; Jimmy Witherspoon. Recorded for Blue Note in late '60s-70 but not all the material was released until later. In '72 he began rec. for Milestone and his album *Sahara* won the *down beat* Critics poll as Record of the Year. First his group included Sonny Fortune but in '73 he was replaced by reedman Azar Lawrence who bore a striking stylistic resemblance to Coltrane. The LP *Enlightenment*, rec. at the Montreux Fest. in '73 won the Montreux Jury's Diamond Prize as the year's best recording.

From the time *Sahara* was issued Tyner began to receive long overdue recognition and began to tour extensively with his group, both in the US and in Europe and Japan. Eschewing electronics and fashionable trends he has fashioned an expression within a body of music that is contemporary but apart from the monotony of obvious hitseekers or the more fallow members of the avant garde.

Whitney Balliett wrote that "Tyner spent five years as a sideman baking in John Coltrane's oven and by the time he left Coltrane most of the ingredients now rampant in his work . . . had risen: the continually shifting modal patterns, the racing, almost glissando arpeggios, and the hammering, enfolding chords."

Garry Giddins made analogies with art and literature: "McCoy paints with the opulence of Africa, the Orient, and the Middle East, which is why his lustiness is manifested in stirring dynamics and coloration rather than melody. Tyner's craggy pulse can inspire and invigorate. Like Conrad, he wants to make us see."

Fest: NJF-NY, incl. solo concert, '74; many U.S., Euro. fests.

Tyner tied for first place with Keith Jarrett in the DB Critics poll, '74; won the DB Readers poll, '74-5; Jazzman of the Year, '75. Comp: *Land of the Lonely*; *Celestial Chant*; *Elvin (Sir) Jones*; *The Discovery*; *Folks*; *Enlightenment Suite*; *Presence*; *Nebula*; *Walk Spirit, Talk Spirit*; *Sama Lucaya*; *Above the Rainbow*; *La Cuba 5na*; *Desert Cry*; *Paradox*; *Makin' Out*; *Pursuit*; *Love Samba*; *Atlantis*.

LPs: *Atlantis*; *Enlightenment*; *Sama Layuca*; *Song of the New World*; *Song for My Lady*; *Sahara*; *Echoes of a Friend*, piano solos dedicated to J. Coltrane; *Trident*, trio w. R. Carter, E. Jones (Mile.); others on BN; Imp.

Groove Holmes, B.B. King, Dizzy Gillespie. Drafted 1965; in Special Services, Germany, pl. in jazz club w. trio. Back on recording scene '67, many dates w. Richard Evans, Grover Washington, C. Adderley et al. In 1970 joined Ramsey Lewis, changing gp. from trio to quartet for first time.

Playing Calif., Upchurch decided to settle there, working w. Quincy Jones on movie soundtracks etc., but says "The earthquake of Feb. 1971 sent me scurrying back to Chicago." Rejoined Q. Jones to tour Japan 1972. Co-leading quintet w. Tennyson Stephens and rec. album for CTI, 1975.

Upchurch won NARAS Governors' Award 1975 for contributions to Chi. music scene. He was subject of book, *What It's Like To Be a Musician*, by Arthur Shay, publ: (Reilly & Lee Books, 114 West Illinois St., Chi., Ill. 60610).

Own LPs: Cadet, Milestone, CTI. LPs w. Q. Jones, *Body Heat* (A & M); *Grooving With the Soulful Strings* (Cadet); *Bad Benson* w. Geo. Benson (CTI).

URBANIAK, MICHAL, *violin, composer*; also *soprano, tenor saxophone*; b. Warsaw, Poland, 1/22/43. Stud. at Academy of Music in Warsaw. Pl. w. The Wreckers in Poland and USA, '62-4; K. Komeda quintet, '64; Jazz Rockers, also in Poland. Forming his own group in '65, he worked in Scandinavia, Switzerland, West Germany, Benelux etc. In '74-5 his new group, Michal Urbaniak Fusion, toured in the US, and Urbaniak made his home in NYC. He plays a custom made five-string violin and violin synthesizer. Favs: Coltrane, Miles Davis, Komeda, Z. Namyslowski, Lutoslawski. Film score for *On The Road*. Many TV apps. incl. Prague, '64-6; Berlin, and a dozen other cities. Fests: In Warsaw almost every year from '62-72; Prague, '64, '69, '72; Newport, '62, '74; Montreux, '74; Molde and Kongsberg (Norway), '71. In that same year he was declared the best soloist at the Montreux JF (Grand Prix) and was awarded a scholarship to Berklee Coll. of Mus. Won *Jazz Forum* Musician of the Year award, '72 and '73; his combo was voted best of the year in '73. Married to singer Urszula Dudziak (q.v.).

LPs: *Fusion*; *Atma* (Columbia); *Traction* (Intercord); *Constellation* (CBS); *Constellation Live* (Muza); w. Arif Mardin: *Journey* (Atlantic).

UNDERWOOD, .RUTH KOMANOFF, *marimba, percussion*; also *piano*; b. New York City, 5/23/46. Stud. w. many teachers; Ithaca Coll. of Mus., '62-5; Juilliard, '65-8. Best known for her work w. Frank Zappa's Mothers of Invention; also with her husband, Ian Underwood.

LPs: w. Zappa, *Uncle Meat* (Bizarre/Reprise); *Apostrophe*; *Mothers—Live At Roxy and Elsewhere*; *One Size Fits All* (Discreet).

UPCHURCH, PHIL, *guitar, fender bass, composer*; b. Chicago, Ill., 7/19/41. Father, a pianist, introduced him to ukulele '52, two years later bought him elec. guitar, on which he was basically self-taught. Came up in r & b scene '58-62, touring w. groups. Settled down in Chi. as studio musician, rec. w. S. Getz, Ramsey Lewis, Woody Herman,

VALDAMBRINI, OSCAR, * *trumpet, fluegelhorn, composer*; b. Turin, Italy, 5/11/24. With tenor saxophonist Gianni Basso continued to lead the Basso-Valdambrini quintet which, from '55-60, pl. at the Taverna Mexico in Milan w. sitters-in such as G. Mulligan, C. Baker, L. Gullin, S. Getz, M. Davis and C. Candoli. Valdambrini guested w. L. Hampton and also pl. w. M. Ferguson. In '67 & '68 was part of D. Ellington band for concerts at Lyric Theatre, Milan. App. at all Italian fests. from '56 and 30 concerts annually at theatres and universities. In '62 the Basso-Valdambrini band won a contest organized by a men's toiletry company and visited the U.S. as the prize. Awarded two Gold Records and the ''Golden Diapason.'' Voted top Italian trumpeter '74. Insp. & infl: Armstrong, Gillespie, Parker, C. Baker.

LPs: thirteen albums w. Basso for Italian labels, two of which were issued on Verve; *Buddy Collette in Italy w. Basso-Valdambrini* (Ricordi); *The Best Modern Jazz in Italy* (Italian RCA).

VANCE, RICHARD THOMAS (DICK),* *composer, arranger, trumpet*; b. Mayfield, Ky., 11/28/15. From mid-30s played and/or wrote for many swing bands incl. F. Henderson, C. Webb, Don Redman, C. Barnet, D. Ellington, Glen Gray. Still active in '60s and '70s, playing for several years in Radio City Music Hall orch. through '65; Broadway shows: *Hallelujah Baby,* '67; *No, No Nanette,* '71-2; *Seesaw,* '73; played at NJF, Carnegie Hall, '73. Conducted band for Jazz Dance Theatre, touring Africa for State Dept., '69. From '70, member of music faculty at Manhattan Community Coll., teaching musicology; and Jazz Performance Workshop. Made one of the later arrs. of *Black and Tan Fantasy* for D. Ellington; arr. *Yearning For Love* for M. Ellington.

Own LP: *Like Dixie* (Sue); LP w. Eddie Barefield's Bearcats (Major-Minor).

VAN EPS, GEORGE,* *guitar*; b. Plainfield, N.J., 8/7/13. Appeared at Colorado Jazz Party in '60s and w. own gp. at Downbeat, NYC, in late '60s. Relatively inactive after suffering a heart attack, he pl. occasionally at Donte's in LA early '70s.

VAUGHAN, SARAH LOIS,* *singer*; b. Newark, N.J., 3/27/24. An early associate of the pioneer bop musicians, with whom she worked in the Earl Hines and Billy Eckstine bands and on small group record sessions, Vaughan from the mid-1940s was a solo artist, internationally known for her unique qualifications as a singer capable of incomparable jazz performances yet qualified to be an opera singer. Over the years her range and scope, along with the warmth and communicative values of her performances, continued to expand. In the 1960s and early '70s she appeared in more than 60 countries, from small, intimate night clubs to stadiums with a capacity of 100,000, with backings that ranged from a jazz trio to symphony orchestras with vocal groups. She was heard with the Boston Pops, the Cleveland Symphony, LA Philharmonic, San Francisco Symphony and many others.

Vaughan enjoyed the unusual distinction, while touring internationally with consistent success, of doing so without the help of recordings. For a five-year period she had no record contract, returning early in 1972 when she signed with the Mainstream label. Later that year an album of Michel Legrand's compositions, for which she was accompanied by a large orchestra with Legrand as arranger and conductor, was moderately successful commercially.

TV: *Wolftrap,* seen on 241 PBS stations, '75; many guest apps. w. Sammy Davis, Johnny Carson, Mike Douglas, Merv Griffin, Glen Campbell et al.

Festivals: Newport, Monterey; others in Belgium, Holland, Tunisia, etc.; Charlie Parker Festival, KC; Ravinia Fest., Chicago. In Dec. '74 she took part in *Showboat 2,* a jazz festival aboard the S.S. *Rotterdam* cruising to the West

Indies; immediately afterward she flew to Martinique to sing at a banquet in honor of President Ford and President Giscard d'Estaing of France.

LPs: Many early albums reissued on Trip, Roulette; *A Time In My Life*; *Send in the Clowns*; *Sarah Vaughan/Michel Legrand*; *Sarah Vaughan Live In Japan*; *More From Japan*; *Sarah Vaughan & Jimmy Rowles Quintet* (Mainstream).

VAUGHN, THOMAS WADE (TOM), *piano, composer*; b. Benton, Ky., 10/14/36. Family moved in 1947 to Pontiac, Mich., where he had early contact w. Thad, Elvin Jones. Stud. classical music, pl. jazz in clubs during seven years in college (BA magna cum laude, Eureka, Ill., '61; Bachelor of Sacred Theology, Yale Divinity School, '64); was heard by Geo. Wein sitting in w. G. Krupa in Detroit club and, with Wein's help, went to NYC, rec. live at Village Gate, and pl. at NJF '66. That he was an Episcopalian priest who played jazz piano earned him considerable publicity as Father Tom Vaughn; however, he later dropped this billing and appeared in clubs and concerts as Tom Vaughn.

Infl: Tatum, Gershwin, O. Peterson, J.S. Bach, Alfred Newman, Palestrina, Bartok, J. Coltrane, V. Horowitz. His early LPs reflect strong impact of the funk-soul movement. After moving to Southern Calif. July '68, he continued to gig occasionally. In 1975 he was associate rector at St. Martin's In The Fields, Canoga Park, Calif.

Comps: *Angela*; *Mr. Cholly*; *Moonwalk*; *Wanda*; *Motor City Soul.* LPs: RCA, Capitol.

VAZ, FRANCOIS R., *guitar, banjo*; b. Paris, France, 6/19/31. Priv. studies in France, '49-53. At 18 was successful actor in France, in addition to leading own band, pl. mostly dixieland, '46-50. Inactive in music, '53-9. Moved to LA, '60, began to gain prominence acc. singers, among them Arthur Prysock, Della Reese, Lou Rawls, Esther Phillips, Lorez Alexandria, Carmen McRae, Lena Horne, Ray Charles. Also pl. w. G Szabo, '67; Jimmy Smith, Willie Bobo, '70; F. Hubbard, '74. Comp. *Little Boy Dear,* rec. by Rawls (Cap.). Infls: D. Reinhardt, J. Raney, T. Farlow, Ch. Parker, Coltrane, Bill Evans. TV: six months in band on Barbara McNair series; jazz shows in Boston, SF etc. Many fests. incl. KC, '67; Berkeley and Monterey, '68; Oakland, '72.

LPs: w. Szabo (Skye); Alexandria (Pzazz); McRae (Atl.); Pat Britt (Vee Jay).

VENTURA, CHARLIE,* *saxophones*; b. Philadelphia, Pa., 12/2/16. The popular combo leader and frequent G. Krupa sideman, lived in LV from '58-61, later moved to Denver, where he worked with Johnny Smith, then to Minnesota. After a long illness, he settled in LV again from '70-2, conducting a disc jockey show. From '72-5 he pl. gigs as house leader at Sheraton Tobacco Valley Inn in Connecticut w. B. Hackett, Dave McKenna and others and made his home in Windsor, Conn. Pl. w. Teddy Wilson at Michael's Pub, NYC, late '74. Still active on freelance basis in '76.

LPs: *Charlie Boy—Charlie Ventura '46* (Phoenix); reissue of '40s big band and small gps. (Trip); many pop albums w. Jackie Gleason (Cap.).

VENUTI, GIUSEPPE (JOE),* *violin*; b. Lecco, Italy, 4/4/98. The first great jazz violinist of the '20s was confined to playing lounges in Los Angeles, Las Vegas and Seattle (his home base) in the '60s. In '67 he played at Dick Gibson's Colorado Jazz Party in Vail, the first of many apps. he has made at these annual affairs through '75. He was featured at the NJF '68 where his performance served to reveal that he had lost none of his prodigious skill and that age had not dampened his fiery swing either. To London for Jazz Expo, '69. He survived a severe illness in April '70 to resume working later in the year and has been active from that time, leading a quartet at the Roosevelt Grill, '71. He has also played engagements several times at Michael's Pub and appeared at major fests. in US and Europe. In '75 he filled an important role in the NYJRC tribute to Bix Beiderbecke at NJF-NY; at same fest. he was honored by the Newport Hall of Fame.

LPs: *Once Again With Feeling* (Ovation); *Plays Gershwin*; *Plays Jerome Kern* (Golden Crest); two albums w. Zoot Sims; *Joe Venuti Blue Fours* (Chiaro.); *The Daddy of the Violin* (MPS); *Venupelli Blues* w. S. Grappelli (Byg); w. B. Pizzarelli, *Nightwings* (Fl. Dutch.).

VESALA, EDWARD, drums; b. Mantyharju, Finland, 2/15/45. Studied at Sibelius Academy. Pl. w. Jan Garbarek trio, '72-4. Has also performed w. Joachim Kuhn; Tomasz Stanko; Archie Shepp; Paul Bley; Peter Brotzman. Voted Finnish Jazz Musician of the Year, '72. Infl: Billie Holiday, John Coltrane. Com: *Areous Vlor Ta*; *Nan Madol*. LPs: *Nan Madol* (Japo); *Nana*; *I'm Here* (Blue Master); w. Stanko, *Twet* (Muza); w. Garbarek, *Triptykon* (ECM).

VICK, HAROLD EDWARD,* tenor sax; also alto, soprano saxes, flute, bass clarinet, oboe; b. Rocky Mount, N.C., 4/3/36. After graduating from Howard U., toured w. r&b bands, settling into small group work in NYC in the early '60s. With the Jean Erdman Theatre Co., pl. recorders and percussion as well as his usual reeds, '66-7. Pl. w. Walter Bishop, Grant Green, '67; own quintet, '67-8; Negro Ensemble Co., incl. European tour, '69; Dizzy Gillespie big band; King Curtis, '69-70; lectures and demonstrations on jazz history in NYC public schools w. Benny Powell for Jazz Interactions, '70; Aretha Franklin, '70-4; Compost, '71-3; Shirley Scott, '74; Jazzmobile w. George Coleman Octet, '74. In April '74, Vick suffered a massive heart attack, but was miraculously back playing in August of that year. Film: App. as actor in *An Even Chance*, produced for the Foundation for Change, for which he composed music and pl. saxophone, '71. TV: Composed music for *Epitaph*, prod. w. a grant from the Ford Foundation in cooperation w. the Henry St. Settlement, '70. Co-founder and organizer of the Black Experience Family Repertory Co., for which he composed music for a full-length stage prod. under a grant from the NYS Council for the Arts, '70. Awarded comp. grant from the National Endowment for the Arts, '73. Comp: *Our Miss Brooks*; *Night Flight*; *Out Of It*; *Melody For Bu*; *The Ripper*; *Seventh Period*; *Buzzard Feathers*; *Don't Look Back*; *Keep On Movin' On*. LPs: *Don't Look Back* (Strata-East); *Commitment* (Muse); *Straight Up*; *Watch What Happens*; *Caribbean Suite* (RCA); *Steppin' Out* (BN); under pseudonym Sir Edward for *The Power of Feeling* (Encounter); w. Compost, *Life is Round* (Col.); w. Joe Chambers, *The Almoravid*; w. Bu Pleasant, *Ms. Bu* (Muse); w. S. Scott, *One For Me* (Strata-East).

VIG, TOMMY,* vibes, drums, composer; b. Budapest, Hungary, 7/14/38. Left Hungary during 1956 revolt; in U.S. stud. at Juilliard, worked for many groups in NYC. Living in Las Vegas from mid-60s, he led a 56 piece orch. at Music Educators' Nat'l Conference, '67, in a concerto for tenor saxophone and orch. feat. Charlie McLean. Vig was guest soloist w. LA Neophonic, '68. Concerts at Tropicana, LV, some feat. Don Ellis. In '69 Vig moved to LA, where he concentrated mainly on studio work but continued to comp. and perf. in a big jazz orch. context as well as pl. drums or vibes in groups led by Red Rodney, T. Gibbs, Cat Anderson, Joe Pass, John Collins et al. Since the mid-60s has given annual jazz concert at Caesar's Palace in LV. In '75 he conducted his own work, *Music For a Tschopp Exhibit*, at Brand Library, commissioned by painter Stanley Donald Tschopp, feat. Ellis. Vig scored several films, mixing modern classical music with jazz. Won DB Critics' Poll, '67, on vibes, TDWR. Comps: *Just For You*; *For Mia*; also four movement symphonic work, *Instruments*, dedicated to Zubin Mehta. Vig's infls. range from Bartok, Miles Davis, Ellington to Albert Ayler, George Ligeti and Kryzysztof Penderecki.

LPs: *The Sound of the Seventies* (Milestone); *Tommy Vig in Budapest* (Mortney Records).

VINNEGAR, LEROY,* bass, composer; b. Indianapolis, Ind., 7/13/28. Established from '54 in LA as outstanding exponent of "walking" bass style. Continued to freelance in Hollywood during '70s; Fests. at Concord, Montreux, Monterey. Vinnegar's best known comps. are *For Carl* (dedicated to the late pianist Carl Perkins) and *Hard To Find*. Others incl. *My Mom*; *Twila*; *Hey Mon*. Own LPs: *The Kid* (PBR); *Glass of Water* (Legend); *Leroy Walks* and *Leroy Walks Again* (Contemporary); *Swiss Movement* w. L. McCann-E. Harris (Atl.); *High In The Sky* w. H. Hawes (Vault); *Live At The Lighthouse*, '66 w. Crusaders (World Pacific); *Bluesmith* w. J. Smith (Verve); w. S. Criss (Xanadu).

VINSON, EDDIE (CLEANHEAD),* singer, alto saxophone; b. Houston, Tex., 12/18/17. First prominent w. Cootie Williams orch., '42-5; own group, '45-9. Spent two years in and around Omaha, '60-2; Kansas City, '62-4, working in big bands and combos. First trip to France, '67 for fest. and rec. In late '60s and early '70s, based in LA, but toured frequently incl. Europe w. Basie. Gigs w. J. Otis in LA. Fests: Newport-NY, '71-4; Monterey, '70, '72-3-4; Ann Arbor, '70, '73; Montreux, '71, '74; Nice, '72; Paris, '68.

Vinson in '75 was still rooted in the mainstream of the blues, both as singer and saxophonist. There were few if any changes in his repertoire, which included such early hits as *Cherry Red*; *Kidney Stew Blues*; *Old Maid Boogie*; *Tune Up*. Stanley Dance wrote: "Vinson commands your attention. He communicates emotion and humor."

LPs: *You Can't Make Love Alone* (Mega); *Cleanhead's Back In Town* (Fl. Dutchman); *Jazz Greatest Names* (Black & Blue); w. O. Nelson, *Swiss Suite* (Fl. Dutchman).

VIOLA, ALFONSO ALFRED (AL), guitar; b. Brooklyn, N.Y., 6/16/19. Mainly self-taught, but stud. harmony, theory at Cal. Acad. of Music; also private classical guitar lessons. Insp. by C. Christian, W. Montgomery, O. Peterson, Coltrane, B. Collette. Toured w. Page Cavanaugh trio, '47-9; Bobby Troup trio, '50-4; Ray Anthony, '55-6; Harry James, '57; B. Collette quintet from '57, off and on, to date; Les Brown intermittently to date. Acc. Julie London at Command Perf. for John F. Kennedy in Washington, '61. International tour w. F. Sinatra, '62; White House concert w. Sinatra, '73. Neophonic concerts w. Stan Kenton in '60s. Numerous movies and TV series.

Own LP: *Alone Again* (Legend); w. Collette (Legend); many others, now mostly unavailable. Publ: *Guitar Lament* (MCA Music).

VITOUS, MIROSLAV LADISLAV, *bass, guitar, composer*; b. Prague, Czechoslovakia, 12/6/47. Father, a saxophonist, stimulated his interest in music. Studied violin from age six, piano from nine-14, then took up bass. While at Prague Conservatory, pl. w. Junior Trio feat. Jan Hammer, piano, and his brother Alan Vitous on drums; also worked w. Dixieland gp. Won first prize at an international contest in Vienna sponsored by Friedrich Gulda; this entitled him to a scholarship at Berklee College of Music in Boston.

Vitous arrived in the U.S. 8/10/66. Though offered a job by C. Adderley, he remained at Berklee for eight months. To NYC summer of 1967; befriended by Walter Booker, he soon worked w. Art Farmer, F. Hubbard and the Bobby Brookmeyer-Clark Terry Quintet. Heard in this combo by Miles Davis, he worked w. Davis briefly before joining Herbie Mann, remaining with Mann for two years. Toured w. Stan Getz '70, then rejoined Mann for almost a year. Back w. Davis briefly, then became a founder member of Weather Report, remaining until late '73.

During '74 and '75, except for an appearance with Airto, Vitous remained off the scene, living near Los Angeles and practicing a new instrument made specially for him, a double-necked combination guitar and bass. In late 1975 he recorded with an all star gp. incl. H. Hancock, Airto, Jack De Johnette (Col.). Made first apps. leading own combo, early '76.

Influenced mainly by Scott La Faro, also by Ron Carter and Gary Peacock, Vitous shortly after his first American jobs gained the respect of fellow musicians as an extraordinary technician and creative artist on both upright and fender bass.

Comp: *Mountain in the Clouds*; *Epilogue*; *Cerecka*; *Infinite Search*; *I Will Tell Him On You*; *When Face Gets Pale*.

LPs: His first album as a leader, *Infinite Search*, in '70, on the now defunct Embryo label, was widely praised. It was reissued w. an added track as *Mountain in the Clouds* (Atl.). Others w. Weather Report (Col.); w. C. Corea, *Now He Sings, Now He Sobs* (SS).

VON OHLEN, JOHN (BARON), *drums, composer*; b. Indianapolis, Ind., 5/13/41. Stud. w. Bob Phillips. Toured w. Billy Maxted and his Manhattan Jazz Band, '67-8; W. Herman, '69-70; S. Kenton, '70-2. Later, based in Indiana, he co-led a 17 piece orch. w. former Kenton baritone saxophonist Chuck Carter. Comps: *A Walk Through Bombay*; *Red Man*.

LPs: *Baron Von Ohlen Quartet*; w. Kenton, *Live at Redlands*; *Live at Brigham Young*; *Stan Kenton in London* (Creative World); w. Herman, *Concerto for Herd* (Verve).

VON SCHLIPPENBACH, ALEXANDER (ALEX), *composer, piano*; b. Berlin, 4/7/38. Stud. composition, piano at school in Cologne; jazz piano with Francis Coppieters. Joined Gunter Hampel quintet in Paris, '63; toured w. Manfred Schoof quintet, '64-7. Many important concerts w. Globe Unity Orchestra in Berlin, Donaueschingen, Tokyo, '66-70. From '70 on led own quartet feat. Evan Parker. Fest: Berlin, Antibes, Montreux, Warsaw, Molde etc. Infl. by Arnold Schoenberg, B.A. Zimmermann, Charlie Parker, Hartwig Bartz, Thelonious Monk, Cecil Taylor.

Von Schlippenbach is a leading figure on the continental free music scene. His LPs for various European labels incl. *Heartplants*; *Globe Unity* (Saba); *Glockenbar* (Wergo); *Payan* (Enja); *The Living Music*; *Pakistani Pomade*; *Globe Unity 73* (all on FMP); *Voices* (CBS).

WADENIUS, GEORG, *guitar*; also *electric bass*; b. Stockholm, Sweden, 5/4/45. Mother, a concert pianist who had her own jazz quartet for 25 years, now is teacher, forming big bands, choirs and small groups among her students. Learned by listening to his mother, rehearsing classical works and playing evergreens and songs from American musicals in clubs. His high school studies were directed more toward music than regular academics. After high school, stud. medicine, but relinquished ambitions to become a doctor in favor of a musical career. First professional job with a trio called Made in Sweden, '68; w. Solar Plexus quartet, '71. Came to USA Jan. '72 to join Blood, Sweat & Tears and toured extensively with the group, incl. Montreux JF. TV: *Midnight Special*, w. B.S.&T. Comp. *Save Our Ship*; *My Old Lady*; *Are You Satisfied*; *She's Coming Home*, all rec. by B.S.&T.; parts of *Concerto Grosso* for Symphony Orch. and Four Piece Rock Group; songs for a children's album, *Hello Hello*, which won an award in Sweden. Insp. by J. Hall, W. Montgomery, Jimi Hendrix, J. McLaughlin, B.B. King.

LPs: w. B.S.&T., *New Blood*; *Mirror Image* (Col.).

WAITS, FREDERICK DOUGLAS (FREDDIE), *drums*; also *percussion, flute*; b. Jackson, Miss., 4/27/43. Worked w. Kenny Dorham; Curtis Fuller; Cedar Walton; Sonny Rollins in '60s. Pl. w. NY Jazz Sextet, '66-7; McCoy Tyner, '67-70; toured w. Ella Fitzgerald, '67; '68 in Europe. Between '67-70 gigged w. F. Hubbard; R. Bryant; W. Bishop; Betty Carter; Joe Williams; Gary Bartz. A member of M'Boom re: percussion from '71. Worked w. L. Morgan; Novella Nelson; Milt Jackson; Jazzmobile; Melba Moore; Carmen McRae; Nancy Wilson; Billy Taylor, '71-2. App. w. E. Fitzgerald and Boston Pops Orch., '73; Toured Europe and Africa w. Mercer Ellington; Europe w. Roland Hanna; drum instructor for Jazzmobile; school concerts w. Elvin Jones; concerts at prisons and detention houses in NYC, '74. Pl. w. Stan Getz; Cecil Bridgewater; Grady Tate; Billy Taylor, '75. Member of NYJRC, '74-5. A resourceful drummer with fire and taste.

TV: Musical dir., contractor, drummer w. Al Green for

Soul; apps. w. many other artists incl. McRae; Morgan; Fitzgerald. Super Bowl half-time w. M. Ellington; *Dial M for Music*; *Sunday Live* w. B. Taylor and Captain Kangaroo. Fest: w. M'Boom re, Live at the Delacorte, '72; Laren; NJF-NY, '73. Also NJF-NY w. Fitzgerald; K. Barron; B. Hackett; Gretsch Greats; Radio City jam session, '73; Laren w. Hanna and NY Jazz Quartet, '74. Forming own gp. incorporating own music. Comp: *Inner Passions*; *Al Kifah*. Theater: w. NY Shakespeare Fest., *Sambo*, '70; *Ti Jean and His Brothers*, '72.

　　LPs: w. K. Barron; J. Moody; R. Davis (Muse); L. Morgan; M. Tyner; A. Hill (BN); H. Laws (CTI); P. Sanders (Imp.); G. Bartz (Mile.); B. Maupin (ECM); J. Zawinul (Vortex); Bobby Jones (Enja); E. Fitzgerald (Col.).

WALCOTT, COLLIN, *tabla, sitar*; also *congas, drums, percussion, clarinet*; b. New York City, 4/24/45. Mother, a classical pianist, is trustee of Hartt Sch. of Mus. in Hartford, Conn. Stud. violin for two yrs. in grammar sch.; snare drum w. Walter Rosenberger of N.Y. Phil., '57-9; pl. timpani and sang madrigals at Putney School, Putney, Vt.; stud. percussion w. George Gaber, Indiana U., '63. From '67 stud. sitar w. Ravi Shankar; tabla w. Alla Rakha. Worked w. Tony Scott, '67-9; w. Peter Walker as intermission mus. at Cafe Au Go-Go, '67-8; congas for Eric Mercury; then w. Tim Hardin, '68-9. Joined Paul Winter Consort, '70; Oregon, '71. Infl: Shankar, Rakha, Ali Akbar Khan, Mongo Santamaria, Herbie Hancock. Films: *Raga*; *Such Good Friends*. Fest: NJF-NY, '74-5; Pori; Molde; Bombershoot Fest. in Seattle, '75. Comp: *Sail*; *Margueritte*; *Cloud Dance*; *Night Glider*; *Prancing*; *Easter Song*. LPs: *Cloud Dance* (ECM); *Winter Light*; *Distant Hills*; *Music of Another Present Era* (Vang.); *Drum Ode*; *Trios & Solos* (ECM); *Tale of the Exonerated Flea* w. Horacee Arnold (Col.); *Music for Yoga Meditation* w. Scott (Verve); *Rainy Day Raga* w. P. Walker (Vang.).

WALD, JERRY, * *clarinet, leader*; b. Newark, N.J., 1/15/19. Leader of a popular swing band in the '40s, Wald pl. clarinet in a style modeled after A. Shaw. After leading various small groups, he settled in LV, where he died Sept. 1973.

WALDRON, MALCOLM EARL (MAL), * *piano, composer*; b. New York City, 8/16/26. Best known for early work with C. Mingus, Billie Holiday, E. Dolphy. After visiting Europe in '65, settled in Italy, '66, playing his first free-jazz concert there opposite G. Barbieri group. The following year moved to Munich, also touring Poland, Switzerland, Germany, Italy. From that point on Waldron became an internationally active figure, playing innumerable fests., TV shows, writing music for albums and films, and enjoying particular success in several visits to Japan starting in '70, recording there with singer Kimiko Kasai, '71. Won Japanese *Swing Journal*'s Jazz Disc Silver Award, '69; Album of the Year Award, '71. During '74, a year typical of his activities, Waldron toured Scandinavia, Germany, Holland, Belgium and Austria, playing fests. in Zagreb, Nuremberg and Bergen. He remained in Munich as home base, occasionally playing there in clubs.

　　Comp: *Russian Melody*; *Hard Talk*; *Soul Eyes*; *Left Alone*; *Snakeout*; *All Alone*; *Dee's Dilemma*; and the film scores for *The Cool World*, '63, and *Sweet Love Bitter*, '65.

　　Publs: *Secret Agent Suite for Big Band* (Editions Modern, Munich, Germany); *Reflections in Modern Jazz* (Sam Fox Music Publs.); *Left Alone* (Edw. Marks Music Publs.).

　　LPs: Many for various European and Japanese labels. Two for Black Lion, '72; *Free At Last* (ECM); *Reminiscent Suite* (Victor); *Mal Waldron With Steve Lacy Quintet* (America Disc); *All Alone* (G.T.A.); *Blues For Lady Day* (Arista); *Up Popped the Devil*; *Black Glory*; *Hard Talk* (Enja); *Mal Waldron on Steinway* (Paula); reissue, *The Great Concert of Eric Dolphy* (Prest.).

WALKER, AARON (T-BONE), * *singer, guitar*; b. Linden, Tex., 5/22/09 (date disputed). Long a resident of California, Walker from the late '60s was irregularly active, slowed down by illness. He app. occasionally w. J. Otis and on his own in Cal. clubs, and continued recording intermittently. He was hospitalized 12/31/74 and died 3/17/75 in LA.

　　LPS: *I Want A Little Girl* (Delmark); *Funky Town*; *Stormy Monday Blues*; *Dirty Mistreater* (Bluesway); *Every Day I Have The Blues* (Blues Time); *The Truth* (Bruns.); *T-Bone Blues* (Atl.).

WALLACE, VINCE (Vincenzo Gambino), *tenor saxophone, composer*; also *drums, piano*; b. Ft. Worden Army Base, Port Townsend, Wash., 6/15/39. Early experience in SF Bay Area and in Long Beach, Cal., w. S. Manne, Gene "Mighty Flea" Connors, D. Gordon, Shorty Rogers, Hal Stein, Vi Redd. Has led various groups of his own. App. in J. Coltrane Memorial concert at Both/And, SF, '67. Moving to S. Cal., he pl. regularly at the Studio Cafe in Balboa from summer of '75; gigs at Donte's, '75. Comps: *World Peace Symphony*; *Bombay Calling*; *The Devil's Workshoppe*; *Confrontation in East Oakland*; *Rainclouds over Coltrane Valley*; *Scotland Yard*.

　　LP: *Vince Wallace Plays Vince Wallace*; *Live At The Studio Cafe* (AMP).

WALLIN, BENGT-ARNE, * *composer, trumpet, fluegelhorn, leader*; b. Linkoping, Sweden, 7/13/26. Pl. w. Arne Domnerus gp., '53-5. Quit playing to concentrate on writing. Scores for many films and TV series, best known being the motion picture, *Dear John*. Other comps: *Symphony For Solo Trumpet/Fluegelhorn*. Took up horns again in '75. Many TV apps. as soloist throughout Europe. Greatly admired by Q. Jones and Clark Terry, Wallin wrote *The Four Leaf Clover* dedicated to Terry. Won award for best jazz record, '62; also many polls in *Orkester Journalen* as best trumpeter, composer/arranger.

　　:LPs: *Old Folklore in Swedish Modern*; *Adventures in Jazz and Folklore* (Dux); w. Harry Arnold Big Band (Metronome); w. Domnerus Orch. (Metronome, Elektra).

WALRATH, JACK ARTHUR, *trumpet, fluegelhorn, composer*; b. Stuart, Fla., 5/5/46. Started pl. trumpet in '55. Won contests through junior h.s. and h.s. in Montana. Att. Arranger's Stage Band Camp in Calif., '63 & '64. Berklee Coll. from '64, grad. '68. Pl. in rec. band. Also led various gps. around Boston while in school which incl. Miroslav Vitous, Pat and Joe La Barbera. Worked many r&b gigs w. Drifters; Platters; Jackie Wilson, etc. Member of Change, an avant garde r&b band w. Billy Elgart, Gary Peacock, for which he wrote most of the music. Moved w. gp. to LA, '69. Led Avant Garde quartet, Revival, w. Glenn Ferris, '69-71. Worked w. King Errison; Preston Love & Motown

Orch.; Luis Gasca. On the road w. Ray Charles, remaining for a yr. Left band in SF '72; pl. and wrote for Chris Poehler band at Great American Music Hall; short stay w. Cold Blood. To NYC '73, becoming involved in Latin scene for a yr. w. Louie Cruz band. Led own band for a few gigs before joining Paul Jeffrey Octet for five mos. With Charles Mingus from Oct. '74, touring Europe in '75.

Infl: Louis Armstrong, Nat Adderley, Dizzy Gillespie, Sonny Rollins, Eric Dolphy. Walrath says: "Lately in my composition I have been employing devices which I think are of my own invention. I have yet to find a name for this concept but it consists of making the melody the harmony and vice versa. I think I have been influenced in this direction by the music of Bartok, or at least my conception of it. The music that seems to interest me right now is that of Iannis Xenakis."

TV: own gp. on Herb Pomeroy's program in Boston; in Europe w. R. Charles; Mingus; US w. Paul Jeffrey. Fest: Boston Globe fest. w. Berklee Band, '68; LA w. Revival, '70; Bologna w. R. Charles, '71; NJF-Oakland, '72; numerous fests. in Italy, Scandinavia, Spain, etc. w. Mingus. Comps: *Black Bats and Poles*; *Dracula*; *Innocence*; *You Don't Know My Mammy Like I Know My Mammy Who Lives in a Cold Water Flat 3 Blocks Down and to the Left, Jackson*; *Autumn on Neptune*; *Alone*; *The Dance After the Feast*; *Chrono-Synclastic Infundibulum*; *Hog Breath*. LPs: own quintet (Waverly); w. Mingus, *Changes I, Changes II* (Atl.); R. Charles, *Jazz II* (Tangerine); Dannie Richmond (Horo); Errison, *The King Arrives* (Canyon).

WALTON, CEDAR ANTHONY,* *piano, composer*; b. Dallas, Tex., 1/17/34. First important jobs were w. J.J. Johnson in late '50s; the Jazztet, '60-1. After leaving Art Blakey, w. whom he worked from '61-4, free-lanced in NYC, acc. Abbey Lincoln and pl. w. a variety of gps. incl. Eddie Harris, Blue Mitchell, Kenny Dorham, Lee Morgan, Freddie Hubbard, Jimmy Heath, Milt Jackson and Art Farmer. Formed own trio and became "house" rhythm section for Prestige Recs. in late '60s. Rejoined Blakey as mus. dir. for Japanese tour in Feb. '73; pl. in Europe, Nov. '73 as member of Young Giants of Jazz w. Newport JF tour. His trio has app. at Boomer's in Greenwich Village many times during the mid-70s. Gordon Kopulos called him "on both acoustic and electric piano . . . a melody maker with few peers. His tone, even on acoustic piano, is ringing and powerful without being loud. His solos are warm yet structured neatly. As an 'accompanist,' Walton is a rarity. He feeds chordal lines that are full but also unobtrusive, leaving the soloist with openings to authentically complement the chord structure of a song." Fests: NJF-NY in Radio City midnight jam, '73; solo piano, '75; Kongsberg; Ljubljana, '75. Comps: *Mosaic; Fantasy in D* (a.k.a. *Ugetsu*); *Plexus*; *Mode For Joe*; *Soho*; *The Loner*; *I'm Not So Sure*; *Shoulders*; *Bolivia*; *Firm Roots*; *Suite Sunday*; *Holy Land*.

LPs: *Mobius* (RCA); *A Night at Boomer's*, vols. 1 & 2 (Muse); *Breakthrough* (Cobble.); *Cedar!*; *Spectrum*; *Soul Cycle* (Prest.); w. Houston Person; Sonny Criss; A. Blakey (Prest.)

WANZO, MEL, *trombone*; b. Cleveland, Ohio, 11/22/30. Pl. in Army band along w. Adderley brothers and Junior Mance, '52-4. Later, in '50s, worked w. Big Joe Turner, Ruth Brown, r & b bands. TV staff musician in Cleveland, '60-3; Glenn Miller orch., '63; W. Herman, '66-8; C. Basie, '69-. Mainly known as lead trombonist on such Basie albums as *Have a Nice Day* (Daybreak); *Songs of Bessie Smith*, w. Teresa Brewer; *Afrique* (Fl. Dutchman).

WARD, CARLOS N., *alto sax*; also *clarinet, flute, piccolo, soprano sax*; b. Panama Canal Zone, 5/1/40. Names his aunt, pianist Avinal Ward, as his first important influence. Stud. clarinet, trumpet rudiments at high school in Seattle, '53-6; clarinet, saxophone w. John Jessen, '56-60; harmony at Garfield high school; clarinet at U.S. Naval School of Mus., '60. Infl. by Parker, Rollins, O. Coleman, Coltrane, Dolphy, C. Adderley and r & b artists. Member of many groups from early '60s, among them those of Don Cherry, Dollar Brand, Sam Rivers, Pharoah Sanders, Sunny Murray, Cal Massey, McCoy Tyner, Bill Barron, David Izenzon, Rashied Ali, Norman Connors, Clifford Thornton, Roy Brooks, Jazz Composers Orchestra; also the J. Coltrane octet '65. Pl. at NJF, '69 w. Murray and '73 w. Cherry; Berlin JF w. Cherry and Brand, '73; w. Karl Berger, 73; B.T. Express, 75, at NJF-NY. Seen on NET TV shows w. Ali's quartet.

LPs: *New Directions In Modern Music* w. Rashied Ali quartet (Survival); *From Now On*; *Karl Berger & Co.* w. Berger (Milestone); *Gardens of Harlem*, w. Thornton; *Relativity Suite*, w. Cherry (JCOA); *Third World Underground* w. Brand-Cherry (Trio Pat); *African Space Program*, w. Brand (Enja).

WARD, CLARA,* *singer*; b. Philadelphia, Pa., 4/21/24. Leader of the Clara Ward Singers, one of the best known gospel groups, and daughter of Gertrude Ward, who had started the Ward Singers in the '20s. Clara Ward died 1/16/73 in LA. The Ward Singers, in addition to appearing in concert halls throughout the U.S. and overseas, were seen frequently on TV, made more than 50 LPs and app. twice before Pres. Lyndon Johnson.

LPs: *Hang Your Tears Out To Dry* (Verve); *Gospel Concert* (Roul.).

WARREN, EARLE RONALD,* *alto sax, singer, composer*; b. Springfield, Ohio, 7/1/14. In the spring of '67 he returned briefly, for a London date, to the Count Basie orch., the band in which he established his reputation in the '30s and '40s. Earlier that year toured 11 European countries with *Jazz From a Swinging Era*. Musical dir. for the Platters, '69; the Drifters, '70. Own band at the Lorelei, NYC, '71-2. From '72 has headed the Countsmen, a mainstream gp. that usually incl. Buddy Tate, Doc Cheatham, Dill Jones and, sometimes, Benny Morton or Vic Dickenson. The name derives in part from some members' past association w. Basie but it also signifies, Warren says, "that these should be counted." They began by pl. concerts at City Coll., Columbia U. and NYU and have cont. to pl. at colls. and for jazz organizations in the NY metropolitan area. From '75 has also led a quartet, the Warren Court, one night a week at the West End Cafe w. Taft Jordan and Dill Jones.

Film: *Born to Swing* by John Jeremy, '72. Cond. NYJRC orch. in tribute to Basie, Jan. '75. Fest: NJF-NY w. Benny Carter, '75; Nice '75; Belfast, Kew Gardens, London, Nov. '75. Comp: *We're Rollin'* ; *You Know It Too*; *Smiley's Blues*. LPs: *Earle Warren*; *The Countsmen* (Eng. RCA); *Buck Clayton Jam Session, Vols. 1&2* (Chiaro.).

WARREN, PETER, *bass, cello, composer*; b. New York City, 11/21/35. Educated at Adelphi Coll. and Juilliard School of Music. Cello debut at Carnegie Hall at age 17. Performed mainly as a classical musician until '59 when he worked in Las Vegas, leaving there w. T. Dorsey orch. Accompanied Dionne Warwicke, '65-7. Pl. w. Herbie Mann, '68. In '69-70 worked w. Blues Project II; his own gp., Interchange; and the N.Y. Bass Revolution w. David Izenzon. To Europe '70, remaining until '74 and working with a variety of musicians incl. Charlie Mariano and Stu Martin in Ambush; Jean-Luc Ponty; Don Cherry; Anthony Braxton; Chick Corea, John Surman; Albert Mangelsdorff; Terumasa Hino. Returned to U.S. '74, joining Jack DeJohnette's Directions in '75 for tours in U.S. and Canada. Conducted workshops at the Creative Music Foundation, a school funded by NY State Council on the Arts. Infl: Gary Peacock, Stu Martin, Jack DeJohnette. Fest: Baden Baden, Hamburg TV Workshop, Antibes, Berlin, Bilsen, Chateauvallon, Donaueschingen. Comp: *Subrahar*; *Phallic Dance*. NEA Grant to compose and perform works on the cello, '76. LPs: *Bass Is* (Enja); w. DeJohnette, *Cosmic Chicken* (Fant.); w. Steve Kuhn, *This Way Out*; *Interchange*; *Going to the Rainbow* (MPS); w. T. Stanko, *TWET* (Muza); w. J.L. Ponty, *Open Strings* (MPS); w. Braxton, *Donna Lee* (America); w. T. Hino, *Vibrations*; w. H. Sato, *Trinity*; w. A. Mangelsdorff, *Spontaneous* (Enja); w. Carla Bley, *3/4* (Watt); w. Cherry, *Donaueschingen Contemporary Music Festival* (Philips).

WARWICK, CARL,* *trumpet*; b. Belmar, N.J., 10/27/17. Veteran with many name bands from mid-'30s incl. B. Berigan, W. Herman, L. Millinder, B. Rich; State Dept. tours w. D. Gillespie, '56-7. Dir. of Mus. for all penal institutions in N.Y., '66-. During vacation toured w. Sammy Davis Jr., '72. In March '74 he presented the idea to Exprinter Tours for a jazz cruise at sea, and was instrumental in lining up talent for the cruises, which left from NYC twice a year with such stars as Gillespie, Fitzgerald, Basie, Vaughan et al. Fests: Newport, '58 w. Gillespie; '73 w. Benny Carter.

LPs: w. Gillespie (Verve); Herman (Col.); feat. on *Baby Baby All the Time* w. Rich (Merc.).

WASHINGTON, GROVER JR., *tenor saxophone*; also *alto, soprano, baritone saxophones, clarinet, electric bass, piano*; b. Buffalo, N.Y., 12/12/43. Father pl. tenor; mother sings in choir; one brother is an organist in church choirs; youngest brother, Darryl, pl. drums w. Richard "Groove" Holmes. Father bought him saxophone at 10. Lessons at Wurlitzer Sch. of Mus. Pl. in high school band; for two yrs. was member of All City H.S. Band as baritone player. Stud. chord progressions w. Elvin Shepherd. Left Buffalo at 16 w. Four Clefs, based in Columbus, Ohio but on the road five and six mos. at a time. Group broke up in '63; joined organist Keith McAllister for two yrs. While in Army at Ft.

Dix, N.J. for two yrs, Washington worked in Phila. w. organ trios and rock groups; also in NYC for Jazz Interactions w. Billy Cobham. After service, pl. w. Don Gardner's Sonotones in Phila., '67-8. Worked for local rec. distributor, '69-70; ret. to full-time pl. w. Charles Earland, '71. Rec. w. (guitarist) Joe Jones, Leon Spencer, Johnny Hammond. As a result of Hammond album he was signed to his own rec. contract by Kudu. Infl: Coltrane, Joe Henderson, Oliver Nelson. TV: Canada; Japan; *Perspective Minorities*, WPVI, Phila.; *Dedication of Louis Armstrong Stadium* at NJF-NY, '73, PBS. Fests: Berkeley JF, '71; Olympic JF, London to Germany, '72; CTI concert tour of Japan, Hawaii, '74; CTI Calif. concert tour, '75. Comp: *Loren's Dance*; arr. of *It's Too Late* for Johnny Hammond. Commercially oriented, versatile musician, who enjoyed great popular success from '75.

LPs: *Mister Magic*; *All the Kings Horses*; *Inner City Blues*; *Soul Box* (Kudu); w. J. Hammond, *Breakout* (Kudu); w. D. Sebesky, *Giant Box*; w. R. Weston, *Blue Moses* (CTI).

WATANABE, KAZUMI, *guitar*; b. Tokyo, Japan, 10/14/53. Stud. jazz guitar w. Sadanori Nakamura, '69-70; jazz theory w. Makoto Uchibori, '70-1; Sadao Watanabe (no relation), '71-2; jazz guitar w. Masayuki Takayanagi, '72-4; classical guitar, harmonics w. Tamaki Shimizu, '70-1. Pl. w. Sadanori Nakamura at Club Evans; Masaru Imada at Pit-in, '70-1; own trio & quartet at Naru, '71; Isao Suzuki quartet at Club Five Spot, '72; own gps. at 86, As Soon As clubs; also w. Yoshio Otomo quintet, I. Suzuki quartet, Shigeharu Mukai quintet, Eiji Toki quartet at same clubs as well as Pit-in, Taro and Junk. Formed two-guitar gp. w. Masahiro Ikumi, '73-4. Pl. w. Takehiro Honda gp. at Nemu Jazz Inn and Pit-in, '74; Sadao Watanabe quintet at Pit-in, '75. Infl: Jim Hall, Wes Montgomery, H. Hancock, Coltrane, Nakamura, Takayanagi, Sadao Watanabe, I. Suzuki, Julian Bream, L. Coryell. Pl. numerous jazz fests. in Japan. LPs: *Infinite* (Toshiba EMI); w. I. Suzuki, *Blue City*; *All Right* (Three Blind Mice).

WATANABE, SADAO,* *alto saxophone, flute, sopranino*; b. Tochigi Pref., Japan, 2/1/33. In 1956 took over leadership of Toshiko Akiyoshi's quartet, when latter left to study at Berklee in Boston. In '62, Watanabe himself left Japan to attend Berklee. In '65 he worked w. G. McFarland and C. Hamilton. Back to Japan, '65; launched jazz school for young musicians, Feb. '66. A record he made w. Charlie Mariano won an award from *Swing Journal*, and as Best Japanese Jazz Album in '68. That summer he made his first app. at the NJF. In March, '69, Watanabe app. at *Swing Journal* workshop concert, Salute to Charlie Parker. In '70 he was heard at the Montreux and Newport fests. Pl. in Africa, '72. His first solo album was selected as Best LP by *Swing Journal* in '73. In June of that year he again app. at Montreux. He comp. the score for the African film *The Ujama* in '74. On returning from Africa, he gave a series of recitals in major Japanese cities. Publ: *Jazz For Myself*, autobiography (Arachi Publ. Co.).

Naming Charlie Parker and Gary McFarland as his sources of inspiration, Watanabe developed into one of the most individual and versatile artists to emerge from the Japanese jazz scene, winning awards at one time or another in six different categories for his records, combo leading, playing, composing and arranging.

LPs: *Sadao Watanabe* (King); *Iberian Waltz* (Tact); *Round Trip*; *Pastoral* (CBS/Sony); w. G. Szabo, *Gypsy '66* (Imp.); w. McFarland, *The In Sound* (Verve); w. Hamilton, *El Chico* (Imp); *Jazz in the Classroom*, Vol. 1-10 (Berklee Records).

WATERS, BENJAMIN (BENNY),* *tenor saxophone, clarinet*; b. Brighton, Md., 1/23/02. Prominent in name bands from '26, including seven years w. Charlie Johnson; later w. F. Henderson, C. Hopkins in '30s; J. Lunceford, '41; several years in Cal. After traveling w. Roy Milton's band, returned to NYC,'50, pl. clarinet, sop. sax w. Jimmy Archey, whose band went to Europe in '52. Waters remained on the continent, joining Bill Coleman, then settling in Paris, where, for 15 years, he was with the band of trumpeter Jacques Butler. Waters took over leadership of the band in '67. From '69 he spent most of his time freelancing throughout Europe.

LPs: Coronet; D.S.C.

WATERS, ETHEL,* *singer*; b. Chester, Pa., 10/31/00. A recording star in the '20s, she later became even more widely known as an excellent actress on Broadway and in Hollywood. TV and public apps. in '70s w. evangelist Billy Graham. Featured in one program of TV series *Route 66* along w. Jo Jones, Coleman Hawkins and Roy Eldridge. LP: *Ethel Waters' Greatest Years* (Columbia).

WATERS, MONVILLE CHARLES (MONTY), *alto sax, composer*; also *soprano sax, flute, piano*; b. Modesto, Calif., 4/14/38. Mother and aunt taught him piano; later took lessons on piano, sax w. private teacher. Had own band in SF. Pl. w. Jon Hendricks there '65-8; also gigs w. King Pleasure; Miles Davis. To NYC Feb. '68 w. Hendricks. Worked w. Elvin Jones; Joe Lee Wilson; Philly Joe Jones; George Coleman; Woody Shaw; Sam Rivers; Jimmy Garrison; Roy Brooks; Andrew Hill; Erroll Parker; Eddie Jefferson; and own gp. Infl: Charlie Parker, Tadd Dameron, Dizzy Gillespie, James Moody, Coltrane, Gil Fuller, Ornette Coleman, Louis Armstrong, Sidney Bechet. TV: special in SF w. own big band; *Like It Is*; *Free Time*; *Jazz Set*, all w. Joe Lee Wilson. Fest: Pacific JF; MJF w. Hendricks; NJF-NY w. Wilson; Earl Cross, '73. Comp: over 500 comps. incl. *That Day*; *Parting*; also arrs. for own bands; K. Pleasure; J.L. Wilson; Hendricks; P.J. Jones. Publ: (Deep Waters Pub. Co., 185 E. 3rd St. 2H, New York, N.Y. 10009). LPs: own quartet for Japanese label; w. J.L. Wilson (Survival); Ronnie Boykins (ESP).

WATERS, MUDDY (McKinley Morgenfield),* *singer, guitar*; b. Rolling Fork, Miss., 4/4/15. A mainstay on the Chicago blues scene in the '50s, he became an important figure in the traditional blues revival of the '60s, influencing young white musicians in the U.S. and England. His *Rollin' Stone*, recorded in the '50s, later inspired Bob Dylan's *Like a Rolling Stone* and helped name a British rock group and an American rock journal. As a result of the rise in popularity of rock music Waters' career also took an upward turn. An auto accident in '69 crushed his pelvis and nearly killed him but he resumed touring with his band a year later. Played England and the Continent; in '73 did concert tour of New

Zealand and Australia incl. national TV special for Austr. Broad. Corp. Won DB Critics poll for Best R & B Group, '68; Grammy Awards for *They Call Me Muddy Waters*, '71; *The London Muddy Waters Sessions*, '72; elected to *Ebony* Black Music Hall of Fame, '73. *Time* wrote: "Muddy Waters is the king of dirty blues, down home blues, funky blues or straight blues—most properly known as delta or country blues. Of them all, Muddy Waters remains the purest, the most loyal to where he has been and what it has cost him." Fests: Newport Folk Fest., '67; NJF-NY, '72; Ann Arbor Fest., '69.

LPs: *Electric Mud*; *After the Rain* (Cadet); *Super Blues* (Checker); *The Blues, A Real Summit Meeting* (Buddah); *Ann Arbor Blues & Jazz Fest.* (Atl.); *Down on Stovall Plantation* (Testament); *The London Muddy Waters Sessions*; *They Call Me Muddy Waters*; many others (Chess).

WATROUS, WILLIAM RUSSELL II (BILL), *trombone, composer*; b. Middletown, Conn., 6/8/39. Father, Ralph J. Watrous, pl. w. name bands in 1920s. Stud. harmony w. Richard Benvenuti at New London High Sch., then went into service for four years and recorded with hundreds of major artists through 1960s. Played w. Roy Eldridge, Kai Winding, Quincy Jones, Woody Herman, Johnny Richards, Count Basie, and worked as studio musician on staff at CBS 1967-9, also ABC for Dick Cavett show 1968-70. Was a member of Ten Wheel Drive in '71; left to form his own big band, which he called Manhattan Wildlife Refuge.

Watrous, who has also played baritone horn, bass trumpet and drums, is a mainstream-modern soloist of extraordinary skill. He credits John Hammond, producer of his first big band album, with helping him achieve success as a leader. Among his favs. and infl. he named Clifford Brown, Ch. Parker, Carl Fontana, Vic Dickenson, Johannes Brahms and Dizzy Gillespie.

Appeared at NJF-NY annually from '72, in jam sessions, as sideman w. Bobby Rosengarden and in 1975 as leader; also MJF in '73, Quinnipiac JF annually '70-73; Colo. Jazz Party '74-5.

LPs: *Bone Straight Ahead*; *In Tandem* (Famous Door); *Manhattan Wildlife Refuge*; w. MWR, *Tiger of San Pedro* (Col.).

WATTS, ERNEST JAMES (ERNIE), *saxophones*; b. Norfolk, Va., 10/23/45. Family moved to Detroit two years later, and in '57 to Wilmington, Del., where he became interested in music while at high school. He was awarded a *down beat* scholarship to study at Berklee in Boston, and during his second year there was offered a job with B. Rich, in whose band he toured for nearly two years, '66-8. Settling in LA, he played w. Gerald Wilson, Toshiko, Wayne Henderson, and toured Africa w. a seven piece group led by O. Nelson. Subsequently he joined the *Tonight Show* band and concentrated on commercial work. A well rounded musician who plays all the saxophones, clarinets, flutes, oboe and English horn, he was infl. by Coltrane and Miles Davis.

Own LPs on World Pacific; w. B. Rich, *Big Swing Face* (World Pacific); *Night Blooming Jazzmen*; *Freedom Jazz Dance* (Main.).

WATTS, TREVOR, *alto, soprano saxophones*; b. York, Yorkshire, England, 1939. Joined RAF School of Mus., '58. Five years in RAF band in Germany. In London, '63, pl. w. New Jazz Orch.; left in '65 to concentrate on free group improv. With John Stevens started Spontaneous Music Ensemble, Britain's first avant garde jazz group. Led own band, Amalgam, '67. Also pl. w. Splinters (along w. Phil Seamen, Tubby Hayes, Stan Tracey, Stevens); Bobby Bradford quartet; London Jazz Composers Orch. Concerts w. Steve Lacy; rec. w. S. Swallow, Rashied Ali. With Stevens ran The Little Theatre Club, home of Britain's free jazz scene, '65-74.

LPs: w. SME, *Challenge* (Eyemark); *Oliv* (Marmalade); *The Source* (Tangent); *S.M.E. for C.N.D. for Peace For You To Share* (A Records); *Birds of a Feather* (Byg); *So What Do You Think?* (Tangent); *S.M.E. Plus Bobby Bradford* (Freedom); *Face to Face S.M.E. In Concert* Part 1 & Part 2 (Emanem); *S.M.E. a S.M.O.* (A Records); w. Amalgam, *Prayer for Peace* (Transatlantic); *Amalgam Play Blackwell and Higgins*; *Ripple* (A Records).

WAYNE, CHUCK, * guitar; b. New York City, 2/27/23. Active on 52nd St. in the '40s as one of the first guitarists in the bop movement, he later gained prominence in the most celebrated of the George Shearing quintets, '49-52. A CBS staff member from '60-9, he pl. for the Garry Moore, Carol Burnett, Ed Sullivan shows, etc., led own trios and duos in NYC clubs. Free-lance recs. w. Steve Lawrence-Eydie Gorme, Barbra Streisand; jingle dates; *The Nervous Set, Copper and Brass* on Broadway. Rejoined CBS to pl. the Merv Griffin Show, '71-2. Formed guitar duo w. Joe Puma at the St. Regis Hotel, '73; pl. clubs and concerts w. Puma. Comps: originals for LPs listed below; score for documentary film *The Mugging*. Fest: Radio City jam session, NJF-NY, '72; w. Puma, NJF-NY, '73. Publ: *Arpeggio Dictionary* w. Ralph Pat (Belwin Music). Wayne also pl. classic guitar for several yrs. in the '70s. He and Puma gave some public seminars at the Guitar, a NYC club, in '74. LPs: *Interactions* w. Puma (Choice); tracks in *Guitar Town Hall Concert* (Col.); w. Duke Jordan (SteepleChase).

WAYNE, FRANCES, * singer; b. Boston, Mass., 8/26/19. Sang w. Ch. Barnet; earned fame w. Woody Herman '43-5. Married Neal Hefti, '45; to Cal., semi-retired, '46. Toured in Hefti band '52-3, retired again, emerging for gigs at Donte's, N. Hollywood, late 1974; also w. new Hefti orch. in '75. LPs: all deleted, but her version of *That Old Black Magic* w. Barnet (she was first singer to record it) was reissued in '75 on MCA.

WEATHER REPORT. See Shorter, Wayne; Zawinul, Joe.

WEBER, EBERHARD, bass, composer; also bass guitar, cello; b. Stuttgart, Germany, 1/22/40. Father teaches cello and piano. Began study of cello w. him at age six. Switched to bass in '55 on which he is self-taught. Worked w. Wolfgang Dauner, '63-71; Dave Pike Set, '72; Volker Kriegel Spectrum, '73-4. Formed own group, Colours, in '75. In the '60s Weber worked for six yrs. in a private film co., directing films for tv. Later freelanced as a dir. in theater & tv but became a full-time pro. mus. in '68. Infl. as comp: Steve Reich. Began comp. in '72. Wrote music for his album *Colours of Chloe*. Also comp. suite for 12 cellos and jazz quartet for Berlin Jazz Fest. '74. Other fest: Pori; Warsaw; Frankfurt. LPs: *Colours of Chloe*; *Ring* w. Gary Burton; *Solstice* w. Ralph Towner (ECM); *The Call* w. Mal

Waldron (Japo); w. Baden Powell on MPS; CBS; *Missing Link* w. Kriegel (MPS); *Dream Talk* w. Dauner (CBS).

WEBSTER, BENJAMIN FRANCIS (BEN), * tenor saxophone; b. Kansas City, Mo., 2/27/09. Though heard with many other name bands, Webster achieved international eminence during his incumbency in the Duke Ellington orch., '39-43. In later years he usually led his own small groups, but after a period of relative inactivity while based in LA in the mid-60s, he moved to Europe, working there somewhat more regularly in clubs and concerts around the Continent. Following a two week hospitalization, he died 9/20/73 in Amsterdam.

Webster's playing from the early years was often aggressive and intensely alive; yet he is best remembered for the extraordinary warmth and soulfulness he brought to his ballad performances, notably *All Too Soon* and *Just A' Sittin' and A' Rockin'* w. Ellington. Along with C. Hawkins, D. Byas, P. Gonsalves, Chu Berry, L. Young, he was one of the handful of great tenor saxophonists in the melodic/ harmonic tradition established before and during the swing era.

Film: *Quiet Days in Clichy,* app. in nightclub sequence.

LPs: w. Ellington (Col., RCA); Mercer Ellington (MCA); own albums, *See You At The Fair* (Imp.); *At Work In Europe* (Pres.); *Atmosphere for Lovers and Thieves*; *Duke's In Bed* (Black Lion); *Meets Don Byas* (BASF); *Ben Webster & Sweets Edison*; *Coleman Hawkins & Clark Terry* (Col.); *Blow Ben, Blow* (Delta); *For The Guv'nor* (Imperial); *The Warm Moods* (Repr.); *The Soul Of Ben Webster*; *Ben Webster & Associates*; *Meets Oscar Peterson* (Verve); *My Man* (Steeple Chase); *Live at Pio's* (Enja); others w. B. Holiday (Verve); T. Wilson-B. Holiday (Col.); many others, deleted but likely to be reissued, incl. sessions w. A. Tatum, B. Rich, C. Terry, J. Hodges.

WEIN, GEORGE THEODORE, * piano, producer; b. Boston, Mass., 10/3/25. As he had from 1954, with the exception of 1961, Wein continued to produce the Newport Jazz Festival at Newport, R.I. until the '71 event was curtailed by an invasion of youths from outside the festival grounds, who, after setting fences afire, proceeded to break chairs and smash the piano on stage.

In '72 the NJF moved to New York City to establish itself as an historic city-wide happening and a trend-setter for urban festivals. In R.I. the fest. generally ran three or four days; in NYC it stretched over 10.

From '70 Wein has produced the New Orleans Jazz Fest. for which he created a companion event, the Jazz and Heritage Fair. He also has an annual summer national touring festival which plays in Oakland, Kansas City, Chicago, Hampton, Va., Atlanta, Cincinnati, Houston and San Diego.

In the summer of '74 he inaugurated La Grande Parade Du Jazz in Nice, France, a festival of more than 100 name musicians representing traditional jazz from New Orleans through the Swing Era.

His European Newport Jazz Festival, an annual tour from '64 has given concerts in every major European country with the exception of Russia. From '66 he presented Duke Ellington in over 200 concerts in Asia, Africa and Europe, including Ellington's final European tour in November '73.

In January '74 Wein founded the New York Jazz Repertory Company of which he is executive director. It is the first major jazz repertory company and is funded by grants from the NYS Council on the Arts; the National Endowment for the Arts; and the Carnegie Hall Corp. in association with the Dept. of Cultural Affairs of the City of N.Y. At the conclusion of its second season in the spring of '75, the NYJRC toured Russia with its programs dedicated to the life and music of Louis Armstrong.

As a pianist, Wein continued to lead his Newport All Stars at his festivals and for nightclub appearances at the Half Note, Michael's Pub, etc. At various times in the late '60s and '70s it has included Red Norvo, Barney Kessel, Ruby Braff, Tal Farlow, James Spaulding, Eddie "Lockjaw" Davis and Larry Ridley.

LPs: Many artists have been recorded "live" at the NJF but in '72 Cobblestone tapped six volumes of the NJF-NY, incl. two double-pocket jam session sets from Radio City; a "soul" set w. Billy Eckstine, Curtis Mayfield, et al; and a Yankee Stadium session w. B.B. King, Zoot Sims, Clark Terry. It was also available as a boxed set. Wein's own LPs: *Newport All Stars* (Atlantic); *Alive and Well in Mexico* (Col.); *Tribute to Duke* (BASF); the latter two also w. Newport All Stars; w. R. Braff, *Plays Louis Armstrong*; w. Venuti-Grappelli (Byg).

WELLS, WILLIAM (DICKY),* *trombone*; b. Centerville, Tenn., 6/10/09. The former stylist with the Count Basie band of the '30s and '40s toured Europe w. Buddy Tate in '68, played at the NO JF in '69 but has been relatively inactive in the '70s. In '71 *The Night People*, a book about his experiences, as told to Stanley Dance, was published by the Crescendo Pub. Co. LP: *Trombone Four-in-Hand* (Master Jazz); *Dicky Wells in Paris, 1937* (Prest.); w. Lester Young in *The Big Three* (Bob Thiele Music), all reissues.

WELLS, MICHAEL JOHN (SPIKE), *drums*; b. Tunbridge Wells, Kent, England, 1/16/46. Largely self-taught on drums, but stud. briefly w. Philly Joe Jones, '67; classical mus. educ. (piano, cello, voice), Canterbury Cathedral Choir School, '55-60; King's School, Canterbury, '60-4. Pl. w. Tubby Hayes '68-73; Humphrey Lyttleton band, '69-70; Roland Kirk; Chas. Tolliver, '69; Ronnie Scott sextet '70, with whom he also app. in Czechoslovakia; Scandinavian tour w. S. Getz, '70. From '69, intermittently house drummer at Ronnie Scott's Club, backing visiting artists such as Johnny Griffin, Dakota Staton, Art Farmer, Z. Sims, Blossom Dearie, L. Konitz, F. Hubbard, Annie Ross. Stephane Grappelli. Infls: Roy Haynes; Elvin Jones; Clifford Jarvis. App. on BBC-TV series, *Jazz Scene* w. Hayes; also on German and Norwegian TV. Hungarian JF w. Maynard Ferguson, '69; Pori, Finland JF, w. Dave Horler, '75.

LPs: *The Orchestra*, w. Hayes; *That's Just The Way I Want To Be*, w. Dearie (Philips).

WELLSTOOD, RICHARD MacQUEEN (DICK),* *piano*; b. Greenwich, Conn., 11/25/27. After pl. w. G. Krupa, '64-6, he worked in the band at The Ferryboat, Brielle, N.J., '66-Sept. '68. Traveled w. the gps. of Roy Eldridge, Jimmy McPartland, Dukes of Dixieland, '69-70. From '70 much work in N.J. but also own gp. at Michael's Pub, NYC,' 73-4; solo piano at Blues Alley, Wash., D.C. & To-

ronto; Bourbon Street, Toronto, '73; six-week Euro. tour w. World's Greatest Jazzband, '74; solo in Hartford, Conn. and eight weeks at Cookery, NYC, '75. Fests: Colorado Jazz Party, '73; Odessa, Tex. Jazz Party; St. Louis Ragtime Fest. '74; Kerrville, Tex. Rag. Fest., '73-4; solo piano at NJF-NY, '74. Comps: *Fucallia*; *South Amboy Highball*; *Dollar Dance*; *George Sanders*. A versatile pianist whose prime interests include ragtime and Harlem stride. Dan Morgenstern has written that Wellstood's "artistic versatility" is "perhaps better described as breadth or depth . . . (he) hears and understands as much music as anyone I know—musician or musicologist, jazzman or classicist."

LPs: *From Ragtime On*; *And his Famous Orch.* (Chiaroscuro); *Alone* (Jazzology); *and his Hot Potatoes* (Seeds); *Walkin' with Wellstood*; *Rapport* w. Butterfield ("77"). Some of his albums contain his own witty liner notes.

WELSH, ALEX,* *trumpet, cornet*; b. Edinburgh, Scotland, 7/9/29. Prominent bandleader since mid-50s. In '66-7 toured Britain acc. many U.S. jazzmen incl. Wild Bill Davison, Eddie Miller, Peanuts Hucko, Ben Webster, Eddie "Lockjaw" Davis. Clubs, concerts all over Britain and Europe. Fests: Barcelona, '66; Antibes, '67; Newport, '68; Jazz Expo, London annually '67-70; Leipzig, '73; Edinburgh, '74; Breda, '75. Also in '75 Louis Armstrong Memorial Concert at Royal Fest. Hall, London, w. Davison, Clark Terry. Voted top small band in Britain, MM poll, '70. Has pl. over 25 TV network shows and 250 radio programs.

LPs: *At Home With Alex Welsh Band*; *Dixieland Party*; *Vintage '69* (Col.); *Louis Armstrong Memorial Album*; *If I Had A Talking Picture of You* (Bl. Lion-Poly.); *Dixieland Party*, Part 2 (Bl. Lion-Transatlantic Recs.).

WESS, FRANK WELLINGTON,* *tenor sax*; also *flutes, saxophones*; *clarinets*; b. Kansas City, Mo., 1/4/22. With C. Basie in '50s-'60s became well known as first of the modern jazz flutists and as tenor and alto soloist. Left Basie in '64 and became very busy free-lancer in NYC studios w. jingles, rec. dates, etc. Also active in teaching, clinics. Pl. in bands for Broadway shows: *The Apple Tree*, '66; *Golden Rainbow*, '67; *Irene*, '72-3. A member of ABC-TV staff orch., '68; w. Billy Taylor band for David Frost show, '69-72. Coll. concerts, clubs, tours, incl. Japan, w. New York Jazz Quartet (R. Hanna, R. Carter, B. Riley), '74-5. Tony Bennett-Lena Horne Show, '75. Concerts w. NYJRC, '74-5. Pl. w. C. Terry big band in '70s. TV: *Black Journal*; Sammy Davis; Howard Cosell, *Saturday Night Live*; many telethons. Fest: Concord; Laren, Holland; Middleheim, Belgium; NJF-NY: w. B. Taylor, '72; *Basie Reunion* band, '73; NYJQ, '74; Benny Carter, '75. Writing jazz flute solo book. Comps: *Placcitude*; *Bay Street*; a 10-minute piece, *Jazzmobile Ups and Downs*. LPs: *Wess to Memphis*; *Flute of the Loom* (Enterprise); *NY Jazz Quartet, Live in Japan* (Salvation); w. C. Terry (Etoile).

WESTON, AZZEDIN NILES, *congas, percussion*; b. Brooklyn, N.Y., 8/12/50. Father is Randy Weston who wrote *Little Niles* for him. Absorbed much music from his father and associates. Piano lessons from Nadi Quamar at age 13; stud. drums in junior high sch. and pl. in school band, '63. Harmony and theory at Mayflower Sch. of Arts, Plymouth, Mass., '64; drums w. Sticks Evans, Lennie

McBrowne, '65. Traveled in 16 African countries w. R. Weston, '66, and was greatly influenced to change to hand drums. Ret. to US '67 and began to pl. congas w. Latin bands incl. Mark Diamond, '68. In the middle of that year went back to Africa, this time living in Morocco w. his father and pl. w. him in countries south of the Sahara. To Tangier late '69; he helped design African Rhythms Club where he acc. R. Weston; also pl. w. Moroccan musicians. Co-led gp., Safari East w. T. Monk Jr. in NYC, '72. Worked w. Ahmad Jamal, '73-4; Pharoah Sanders; Leon Thomas; D. Gillespie big band at Buddy's Place and *Tribute to Dizzy* concert at Avery Fisher Hall; R. Weston in Sicily; Tunisia, '75. Infl: R. Weston, Big Black, Max Roach, West African, North African and Senegalese drummers. TV: *AM America* w. D. Gillespie; *Like It Is*; *Positively Black* w. R. Weston. Fest: w. R. Weston, Tangier '72; NJF-NY '73; Tabarka (Tunis) '75. Comp: *Blues for Senegal*. Strong interest in the music and rhythms of Africa has made him "explore these rhythms and expand myself musically."

LPs: w. R. Weston, *African Rhythms*; Tanjah (Poly.); *Blue Moses* (CTI); *Jamal Plays Jamal* (20th Cent. Fox).

WESTON, RANDOLPH E. (RANDY), * *piano, composer*; b. Brooklyn, N.Y., 4/6/26. In the fall of '66 pl. major Calif. campuses w. own sextet in a history of jazz presentation which Ralph J. Gleason called "a kind of superior lecture-demonstration." Pl. three-month, 14-country tour of West Africa for U.S. State Dept. beginning in Jan. '67; returned to Morocco, Tunisia, Aug.-Sept.; then remained in Morocco, work. in major cities. Lived in Rabat, '67-8, before settling in Tangier and opening own African Rhythms Club there at end of '69. Traveled and pl. in Africa w. Bill Wood, Ed Blackwell, '68. Returned to U.S. in April '72 for piano party at townhouse of Brooks Kerr's mother, NYC. Back in Tangier, summer and org. Fest. of American, African & Moorish Mus., Sept. '72. To NYC for Carnegie Hall concert, Jan. '73; *Uhuru* w. Symph. of the New World at Phil. Hall, Feb. '73; gigs w. group at The Onliest Place, Village Vanguard, Livingston Coll.; 24-hr. tribute to Ellington, '73. App. w. duo at Bradley's; band at Hartford, Conn. concert; African Rhythms prog. at Billie Holiday Theater, Brooklyn, '74; duo concert at Smithsonian Inst., Wash., D.C.; solo concerts in Switz., France, Tunisia, Algeria, Sicily, '75. TV: *Like It Is*, '70; *Positively Black*, '74; many Euro. apps. incl. Spain, Norway, etc. '74. Fests: MJF, '66; NJF-NY, '73; Kongsberg; Christianstaad; Antibes; Montreux, '74; Fest. of American Folk Life, Wash., D.C.; Groningen; Nigeria, '75. Won TDWR award in DB Critics' poll, '72. Comps: *Ganouah*; *Marrakech Blues*; *Night in the Medina*; *Ifran*; *African Cookbook*; *Tangier Bay*. A new work dedicated to Arabic singer, Om Kel Thoum, written for World of Islam Fest., London. Publ: *The Lively Art of Jazz* (Charles Colin, 315 W. 53rd St., New York, N.Y. 10019); other comps: (Charles Hansen, 1860 Broadway, New York, N.Y. 10023).

As a player Weston reflects his early infls., Tatum, Powell, Monk and Ellington in a highly individual manner which Leonard Feather has credited with "a pure jazz essence, overwhelming technical assurance and natural sense of joy." As a composer he has incorporated his first-hand experience with North African themes and rhythms and his Afro-American background to produce startlingly fresh material.

LPs: *Tanjah*; *African Rhythms* (Poly.); *Blue Moses* (CTI); *Blues to Africa*; *Carnival* (Arista/Freedom); *African Cookbook* (Atl.); *Blues* (Trip); solo albums on Black Lion; Chant Du Monde.

WESTBROOK, MICHAEL JOHN DAVID (MIKE), *composer, leader, baritone horn*; b. High Wycombe, England, 3/21/36. Self-taught. Formed first band at Plymouth Art School, '58. Led octet in Plymouth, '60; 11 piece band in London, '62-6; during late '60s had groups of varying sizes between six and 26, playing Ronnie Scott's Old Place, Montreux Fest., BBC, many British fests; '70-2 led several different combos, app. at European fests.; also co-directed, with John Fox, the multi-media group Cosmic Circus, staging events with films, light shows, circus perfs. and music. Later headed five piece group, Mike Westbrook's Brass Band, for outdoor fests., '73; 18 piece orch for concerts, '74-5. John Surman was a frequent associate of Westbrook's beginning in '60.

Comps: *Celebration*; *Marching Song*; *Release*; *Metropolis*; *Tyger* (stage musical commissioned by National Theatre in '71); *Citadel/Room 315* (commissioned by Swedish Radio). Awards: composer, TDWR, DB Critics' Poll, '69; big band, TDWR, DB Critics' Poll, '70. *Melody Maker* Critics' Poll: big band, '69; triple winner in British section as comp., arr., big band, '70. Voted top European comp. by *Jazz Forum*, '72.

LPs in Europe on Deram, RCA, Cadillac labels.

WETTLING, GEORGE, * *drums*; b. Topeka, Kansas, 11/28/07. Best known for his many concert, club and record assignments with Eddie Condon, Wettling in his earlier years pl. w. big bands led by Jack Hylton, Artie Shaw, B. Berigan, Red Norvo, Paul Whiteman. For several years he led a trio at the Gaslight Club, NYC, later toured briefly with the Dukes of Dixieland, and took part in a reunion band of veteran jazzmen at the '65 *down beat* Jazz Festival in Chicago. His last steady job was w. Clarence Hutchenrider's trio at Bill's Gay Nineties in NYC. He died of cancer in NYC 6/6/68. Wettling, a drummer of diverse accomplishments in many contexts, also was a gifted painter and writer, contributing to *down beat* and other publications.

LPs w. Condon (Col., etc.), Berigan, Shaw (RCA).

WHEELER, KENNETH (KENNY or KEN), *trumpet, fluegelhorn, composer*; b. Toronto, Canada, 1/14/30. Father and two brothers active as semi-pro musicians in St. Catherines, Ontario. Studied harmony w. John Weinzweig at Toronto Conserv. in early '50s; counterpoint w. Bill Russo; comp. w. Richard Rodney Bennett in London, Eng., early '60s. Played w. John Dankworth, '59-65; then intermittently w. Ronnie Scott; Joe Harriott; Tubby Hayes; Friedrich Gulda; Clarke-Boland big band. With Mike Gibbs from '69; Globe Unity Orch. from '72. Although he is an important member of London's free-jazz scene and a busy studio musician, he often travels to the US to play and record w. Anthony Braxton with whom he has been associated from '72. Infl: Booker Little, Braxton, Art Farmer, Benny Bailey, Miles Davis, Buck Clayton, L. Konitz, S. Lacy, B. Evans, Bobby Wellins, Evan Parker, Ellington, Jimmy Knepper,

Tony Oxley. Fest: NJF w. Dankworth, '59; Berlin Anti-Fest. w. Globe Unity, '74; Berlin w. Gibbs, '75; Antibes, Montreux w. Braxton, '75. Tied w. Woody Shaw in DB Critics poll, TDWR, '70.

LPs: *Windmill Tilter* w. J. Dankworth (Fontana); *Song for Someone* w. own orch. (Incus); *Gnu High* w. K. Jarrett, D. Holland, J. DeJohnette (ECM): these three albums all comp. & arr. by Wheeler; w. Braxton, *New York, Fall 1974*; *Five Pieces 1975* (Arista); w. Mike Gibbs, *The Only Chrome-Waterfall Orch.* (Bronze).

WHITE, ANDREW NATHANIEL III, *alto, tenor saxes, composer*; also *oboe, English horn, electric bass*; b. Washington, D.C., 9/6/42. Uncle, Addison White, pl. saxes, flute, guitar. Stud. saxophone w. John C. Reed, Nashville, Tenn., '54-60; theory & musicianship w. Brenton Banks, '58-60. Pl. w. Tenn. A&I U. Symph. Band, '58-60. Att. Howard U., Wash., D.C., '60-4, pl. w. U. Band and Symphonetta, and grad w. a B. Mus. in Mus. theory. Received numerous grants for study and perf.

Early experience w. J.D. Chavis; Don Q. Pullen; Hank Johnson; Andrew Goodrich; Brenton Banks, '55-60, on alto, tenor and upright bass. Mus. dir. and saxophonist for the J.F.K. Quintet in Wash., '61-64; tenor w. Kenny Clarke in Paris, '64-5; alto w. New Jazz Trio in Buffalo, '65-6; tenor w. Charlie Hampton, house band at the Howard Theatre in Wash., '66-7; electric bass w. Stanley Turrentine; tenor w. the Cyclones; Otis Redding, '67; electric bass w. Stevie Wonder and principal oboist and English horn player for American Ballet Theatre Orch. of N.Y., concurrently '68-70. With Fifth Dimension as elec. bassist, '70-; elec. bass for *Hair*; bass and saxophones for Bobby Rydell, Thelma Houston, Otis Redding, Wilson Pickett and S. Turrentine.

Infl: C. Parker, M. Davis, Coltrane. In Sept. '73 completed a catalogue of 209 transcribed Coltrane solos, some of which he performed in concerts for NYJRC; CBA. Lectured at Howard and Rutgers Univs. Apart from his jazz works, his comps. incl. *Concerto* for 18 instrs.; and *Concertina* for seven instrs. These, the Coltrane trans. and a *Treatise on Improvisation* are available, along w. 13 albums of his own gps. (see below) from Andrew's Music (4830 So. Dakota Ave., N.E., Washington, D.C. 20017). Writer Peter Ochiogrosso described White's ''prowess as a saxophonist'' as ''beyond question'' and called his trans. of Coltrane's recorded solos ''one of the great contributions to American music this century, doing for Trane what Kirschel did for Mozart some years ago.''

LPs: *Andrew Nathaniel White III*; *Quartet Live at the New Thing*; *Live in Bucharest—Live in the Studio*; *Who Got De Funk?*; *Passion Flower*; *Songs for a French Lady*; *Theme*; *Live at the Foolery*, vols. 1-6 (Andrew's Music); w. McCoy Tyner, *Asante* (BN); w. Weather Report, *I Sing the Body Electric*; *Sweetnighter* (Col.); w. Marion Williams (Atl.); Stevie Wonder (Tamla); Fifth Dimension (Bell). The early J.F.K. quintet Riverside albums are deleted.

WHITE, CHRISTOPHER WESTLEY (CHRIS),* *bass, composer, educator*; b. New York City, 7/6/36. The former Dizzy Gillespie bassist of the first half of the '60s then pl. extensively w. the Billy Taylor trio and has also app. w. J. Moody; Teddy Wilson; Willie ''The Lion'' Smith; Eubie

Blake; Earl Hines; and Thad Jones-Mel Lewis. From the late '60s, however, he has been increasingly active as a lecturer, educator and administrator. In the summer of '67 he was Community Liaison for the Jazzmobile; served as its Executive Director, summer '68; then as member of Board of Dir. Founder ('66) and Exec. Dir. of Rhythm Associates, the only music sch. in NY state staffed entirely by pro. jazz mus.; designer and consultant to MUSE Jazz Workshop, staffed by Rhythm Ass. White is Director of the Institute of Jazz Studies of Rutgers U., Newark Coll. of Arts & Sciences, designing a long range plan for reorganization of its activities; also Instructor in Music at Rutgers, Newark. Member of Mayor's Urban Action Task Force, NYC, '68; Special Assist. to Gov. NY State in Community Relations, '68-9; Ethnic Promo. Dir., National Dance Co. of Ghana, Madison Sq. Garden Center, '68; Exec. Prod. *Black Expo* at City Center, '69; Artistic Dir. *Black on Black,* March-May' 72, at Carnegie Recital Hall. Designer and dir. for mobile arts tours in NY State: *Summer on Wheels,* '68; *Celebrate Yourself,* '70. Consultant: NY State Council on the Arts; Urban Directions; Arts and Humanities NJ Bicentennial Commission. He has lectured on jazz at Wagner Coll.; U. of West Indies, Kingston, Jamaica; Antioch Coll. Publ: articles for *Feet,* NYC; *Jazz Education and the Community*; *Studies in Jazz*; *Discography I* (Institute of Jazz Studies, Newark, N.J.); *Check Yourself*; *American Music*; *From Storyville to Woodstock,* edited by Charles Nanry (Trans-Action Books, New Brunswick, N.J.); contributor to *Grove's Dictionary of Music and Musicians* (Macmillan, London, Eng.); Jazz Editor, *The Black Perspective in Music,* journal edited by Eileen Southern (Foundation for Research in the Afro-American Creative Arts, Inc., Poughkeepsie, N.Y.).

Gave concert (two nights) of original music at Carnegie Recital Hall, '73. Wrote feature film score, *Aggro Siezeman,* released in West Indies, April '75. Comp: suites, *Dana's Basement*; *Fantasy.* Fest: Loosdrecht, '72; NJF-NY, '73-5. LPs: w. Jimmy Owens, *You Had Better Listen* (Poly.); Andrew Hill, *Invitation* (Steeple.); Kenny Barron, *Spirits* (Muse).

WHITE, JOSHUA (JOSH),* *singer, guitar*; b. Greenville, S.C. 2/11/08. The popular folk and blues singer, best known during the 1940s when he app. at such clubs as Cafe Society and the Blue Angel in NYC, became inactive after suffering injuries in a serious automobile accident in 1966. He died 9/5/69 in Manhasset, N.Y., while undergoing heart surgery. One of the first artists to be strongly identified with political and social protest material, White also played a major role in reestablishing such songs as *John Henry* and *The Lass with the Delicate Air.*

LPs: *Chain Gang Songs; Empty Bed Blues; House I Live In; Spirituals & Blues* (Elektra); *In Memoriam* (Tradition); *Josh White* (Archive of Folk & Jazz); *Sings the Blues* (Stinson).

WHITE, LEONARD III (LENNY), *drums*; b. Jamaica, N.Y., 12/19/49. No musical educ. Stud. art at N.Y. Inst. of Tech. Started playing w. Jazz Samaritans, '67; then w. J. McLean for a year, '68. In '69 rec. *Bitches Brew* w. Miles Davis. With J. Henderson, '70; F. Hubbard, S. Getz, L. Gasca, '72; Azteca, '73. Became orig. member of Chick Corea's Return to Forever, '73. App. on many European TV shows w. Corea; also Don Kirshner Rock Concert, U.S. TV. Fest: NJF-NY, '72-4. White, who is an accomplished photographer and painter, cites among his infls. Davis, J. Coltrane, Philly Joe Jones, Tony Williams and Elvin Jones. Comps: *The Shadow of Lo*; *Sofistifunk*; *La Piedra Del Sol*. Own LP: *Venusian Summer* (Nemp.); other LPs: w. Azteca (Col.); *Realization* w. Eddie Henderson (Capricorn); *Red Clay* w. Hubbard (CTI); *Where Have I Known You Before* w. Return To Forever (Polydor).

WHITE, MICHAEL WALTER, * violin, electric violin*; b. Houston, Tex., 5/24/33. Came to public attention w. John Handy quintet at MJF, '65. From late '60s was member of Fourth Way, in addition to rec. and app. w. his own group from '71. White's music combines contemporary jazz patterns with Eastern and classical influences. Dennis Hunt described his performance as "floating, cerebral, exploratory music that cannot be experienced passively." He is clearly influenced by a total spectrum of artists, incl. many non-violinists; among them are J. Coltrane, E. Dolphy, Sun Ra, D. Ellington, Ch. Mingus, T. Monk. At various times White perf. w. Sun Ra, Prince Lasha, Coltrane, Dolphy, Wes Montgomery, Kenny Dorham, Richard Davis. Comps: *Ebony Plaza*; *Blessing Song*; *Father Music/Mother Dance*.

LPs: *Spirit Dance*; *Pneuma*; *Land of Spirit and Light*; *Father Music/Mother Dance*; *Go With The Flow* (Imp.); w. Fourth Way, *The Sun and Moon Have Come Together*; *Werewolf*; *The Fourth Way* (Cap.); w. Handy, *Live at Monterey* (Col.); w. Pharoah Sanders, *Thembi* (Imp.); w. Jerry Hahn (Arhoolie); Sonny Simmons, *Burning Spirits* (Contemp.); McCoy Tyner, *Song For My Lady* (Milest.).

WHITE, QUINTEN (ROCKY), *drums*; b. San Marcos, Texas, 11/3/52. Entered Tex. Southern U. on a scholarship in '71. Remained there for two and a half years; during that time the Univ. jazz ensemble won many awards and was invited to the National Coll. Jazz Festival at JFK Center in Washington, D.C., where White was feat. w. Roy Burns and L. Bellson in a drum specialty. Not long afterward he joined the Duke Ellington orch., remaining with the band intermittently after Duke's death. Under the leadership of Mercer Ellington, he was one of several soloists to instill a new, youthful spirit to the orch. Fests: Longhorn; Notre Dame; National Coll. Jazz Fest in Chicago and Urbana etc.

LPs: *Third Sacred Concert*, w. Ellington (RCA); *Continuum* w. M. Ellington (Fant.).

WHITE, ELLERTON OSWALD (SONNY), * piano*; b. Panama City, Canal Zone, 11/11/17. Heard from late '30s w. Teddy Hill, Benny Carter, other name bands; acc. for Billie Holiday, '39. White later worked w. small gps. in NYC, incl. Hot Lips Page, W. De Paris and three years w. Louis Metcalf. He joined Jonah Jones Apr. '69 and remained w. him for the next two years. White died in NYC, 4/29/71. Reissue, w. Billie Holiday (Atlantic).

WHITEMAN, PAUL, * leader*; b. Denver, Colo., 3/28/1890. The man who was publicized in the 1920s and '30s as "King of Jazz," and who in 1930 was the star of a film by that name, was in semi-retirement in the '50s and '60s but made occasional comebacks. He died of a heart attack 12/29/67 in Doylestown, Pa. Though many great jazzmen, notably Joe

Venuti, Eddie Lang, Bix Beiderbecke, Jack Teagarden, Frank Trumbauer, Red Norvo, the Dorsey Brothers and arranger Don Redman worked for him in the early years, their roles as jazzmen were often subjugated to elaborate interpretations of popular dance music. Despite the misleading nature of the title that haunted him throughout his career, Whiteman was an important contributor to 20th century popular music.

WIGGINS, GERALD FOSTER, * piano*; b. New York City, 5/12/22. Prominent in LA from 1948, first w. Benny Carter; later toured as acc. for Lena Horne, Kay Starr, many other singers. Own trio at Memory Lane, LA, late '60s along with free-lance film studio and recording work. To Las Vegas w. Supremes; gigs w. Teddy Edwards, Leroy Vinnegar. Acc. Eartha Kitt, Helen Humes, '75, pl. w. Humes at Cookery, NYC and various West coast festivals and clubs. Son, J.J. Wiggins, bassist w. Ellington band (see below).

WIGGINS, GERALD FOSTER (J.J.), *bass*; also *trombone, bass horn*; b. Los Angeles, Calif., 4/15/56. Stud. at Henry Grant Studio, also Jr. High Sch., 1968-71 and High Sch., '71-4. While w. Craig Hundley trio, '68, made many concert and TV appearances and won trophy as outstanding instrumentalist at Hollywood Bowl teenage Battle of the Bands, though he was not yet a teenager. Pl. w. own trio, also in trio led by his father, pianist Gerald Wiggins. Joined the Duke Ellington Orch., dir. by Mercer Ellington, Oct. 1974; impressed audiences and particularly musicians with his astonishingly mature technique, intonation and ideas. Infl: Wilfred Middlebrooks, Red Mitchell, Red Callender, Joe Comfort, Curtis Counce, Ray Brown, Chuck Domanico. LPs: w. Ellington (Fantasy); Craig Hundley (World Pac.).

WILBER, ROBERT SAGE (BOB), * clarinet, soprano sax, composer*; also *alto, tenor saxes, bass clarinet*; b. New York City, 3/15/28. Associated with traditional jazz in his teens, he was heard in the groups of E. Condon, B. Hackett and M. Kaminsky in the '50s and early '60s. Worked w. Bob Crosby; Yank Lawson at Condon's; Ralph Sutton in Aspen; also arr. and pl. Ellington's music for Duke Ellington Society concerts, '66-7. In '68 joined the World's Greatest Jazzband, touring w. it throughout the US and in Brazil, Hawaii, Mexico, Canada and Europe (twice). Left in Jan. '75 to form Soprano Summit w. K. Davern, pl. Nice Fest. and touring So. Africa, summer '75. A mus. dir. of the NYJRC for '74-5 season, he wrote, arr., cond. and pl. w. it at Carnegie Hall and toured Russia, '75.

Wilber, who plays the curved soprano, originally was inspired by Sidney Bechet but elements of Johnny Hodges, Lester Young and Charlie Parker surface in a homogeneous, but by no means bland, mainstream style delivered with elegant swing and warmth. TV: Ed Sullivan; *Tonight*; Dick Cavett; Mike Douglas; Steve Allen; *Today*; NET, '68-74 w. WGJB; *Sunday*, NBC; *Roundtable* w. Soprano Summit, '75. Fest: NJF; Concord; Nice; Odessa, Tex.; Colo. Jazz Party. Comps: *A Long Way From Home*; *Crawfish Shuffle*; *Dreaming Butterfly*; *Please Clarify*; *Johnny Was There*. Publ: *50 Jazz Phrases for Saxophone* (Bregman, Vocco & Conn). LPs: *Soprano Summit* (World Jazz); *Music of Hoagy Carmichael* (Mon.-Ever.); numerous sessions for MMO; *Century Plaza* w. WGJ (World Jazz); others w. WGJ (World Jazz; Atl.;

Project 3); w. Rusty Dedrick, *Music of Irving Berlin*; *Music of Harold Arlen*; w. Maxine Sullivan, *Close As Pages in a Book* (Mon.-Ever.).

WILCOX, EDWIN FELIX (EDDIE),* *arranger, piano*; b. Method, N.C., 12/27/07. Regular member of J. Lunceford band from '29 until the leader's death in '47, after which he co-led the band with tenor saxophonist Joe Thomas. The two later split up and Wilcox formed his own orch. which he led until '49. He was subsequently active as arranger and a & r man, writing for many pop hit records. He died in NYC, 9/29/68.
LPs: see Lunceford, Jimmie.

WILDER, JOSEPH BENJAMIN (JOE),* *trumpet, fluegelhorn*; b. Colwyn, Pa., 2/22/22. Left ABC staff after 16 yrs., '73. Pl. in band for Dick Cavett, Jack Paar shows. First trumpet w. Symph. of the New World, '65-71. Pl. four concerts as member of NY Phil., '75. Worked w. T. Bennett-L. Horne; Michel Legrand, '74; Steve Allen-Terry Gibbs, '75. Busy in the rec. studios for Roberta Flack dates, etc., jingles, Wilder is a fine all-around brassman whose jazz abilities have only really been allowed to shine in recent years at the Colorado Jazz Party, '72-5. Film: trumpet solos for the soundtrack of *The Wild Party* w. James Coco, Raquel Welch. TV: Bill Cosby; Sammy Davis; Howard Cosell. An expert photographer. LPs: w. Jane Harvey (Classic Jazz); C. Mingus, *Let My Children Hear Music* (Col.).

WILEY, LEE,* *singer, composer*; b. Port Gibson, Okla., 10/9/15. One of the most successful singers in the pop field in the '30s, she became associated w. Eddie Condon and the players in his circle from '39. During her marriage to Jess Stacy in '40s she toured w. his big band; then as a single in late '40s. She made occasional apps. on TV, in concert and on record in the '50s but was in virtual retirement in the '60s and '70s; her last public performance was at the NJF-NY '72 w. Condon. A TV film, based on her life and featuring Piper Laurie was shown in '63. "Although she sings with devastating sex appeal," George Frazier wrote, "she does so in an exalted way."
She died of cancer in NYC, 12/11/75. LPs: *Back Home Again* (Mon.-Ever.); earlier recs. on Storyville; Col.; RCA.

WILKINS, ERNEST BROOKS (ERNIE),* *composer, tenor, alto, soprano saxophones, flute, piano*; b. St. Louis, Mo., 7/20/22. Pl. w. C. Basie, D. Gillespie in '50s; also arr. for Basie, T. Dorsey, Harry James. From Nov. '66 to Jan. '69 was with Phoenix House, drug addict rehabilitation program, in NYC. Joined Clark Terry's big band, playing, arr. and as mus. dir. Went with Terry to Montreux JF and org. big band of European and African musicians. Resumed free-lance work in New York, writing new arrs. for Basie. Worked as a & r man for Mainstream Records '71-early '73; during that time, gigged w. own combos. In summer of '73, toured Europe w. Terry. Since '73 has spent much time in Europe as comp.-arr.-cond. and player. Wrote arrs. for, and recorded with, Art Farmer in Vienna. Pl. w. Dexter Gordon, Rolf Ericson, Leo Wright, Kenny Drew, Niels Orsted Pederson. TV: two shows in '74 in Yugoslavia, one w. Terry, one w. Yugo. mus. Fests: NJF-NY in Basie reunion band '73; with Terry Quintet '74. Pl. most of important European fests. w. Terry.

LPs: Mainstream; w. Terry (Vang., Etoile); arrs. for Ch. McPherson (Main.); many earlier LPs as arr. and cond. w. Sarah Vaughan, Ernestine Anderson et al. Arrs. for Quincy Jones (Merc.), Joe Newman (Roul.), Jimmy Cleveland (Merc.).

WILKINS, JACK, *guitar*; also *vibes, piano*; b. Brooklyn, N.Y., 6/3/44. Started guitar at age 14; stud. from age 18 w. John Mehegan, classical guitar w. Rodrigo Riera, others. Was part of all-guitar gp. w. Chuck Wayne in '64. Pl. w. Earl Hines at Town Hall, NYC; Buddy Rich at his club and throughout USA and Europe; concerts etc. w. S. Getz, D. Gillespie, Morgana King, Pearl Bailey, Sammy Davis; own trio at Jimmy's on 52nd Street. Pl. at Colo. Jazz Party, '74. Favs: Johnny Smith, Julian Bream, D. Reinhardt, Joe Pass, Wes Montgomery. Fluent soloist in pure modern jazz style.
LP: *Windows* (Mainstream); w. Buddy Rich, *Very Live at Buddy's Place*; w. Rich, L. Hampton, *Transition* (Groove Merchant).

WILLIAMS, CHARLES ANTHONY JR. (BUSTER), *bass*; *composer*; b. Camden, N.J., 4/17/42. Studied piano, drums and bass w. father. Began pl. bass at age 15. Harmony at Combs Coll. of Music, Phila., '59. Worked w. Gene Ammons-Sonny Stitt, '60; Dakota Staton, '61-2; Betty Carter, '62-3; Sarah Vaughan, '63; Nancy Wilson, '64-8; Jazz Crusaders, '65-8; Miles Davis, '67; Herbie Mann; Art Blakey, '69; Herbie Hancock, '69-73; McCoy Tyner, '74; Mary Lou Williams, '75; also has pl. w. Harold Land-Bobby Hutcherson; Lee Morgan; Sonny Rollins; Kenny Burrell; Jimmy Heath. Made an inner-circle reputation among musicians during his yrs. w. Nancy Wilson before moving to NYC. A big, deep sound with a resilient beat; acute intonation and inventive lines.
Infl: Oscar Pettiford, Paul Chambers, Ray Brown, Ron Carter, Bob Cranshaw. TV: Red Skelton; Danny Kaye; Andy Williams shows; *Positively Black*; *Soul*; *Express Yourself*. Broadway show: *Company*. Fest: MJF; NJF; Berkeley; Pori; Antibes. Teaches at Jazzmobile Workshop. Comp: *Firewater*; *Pinnacle*; *The Hump*; *The Emperor*; *Native Dancer*; *Tayamisha*; *Ruby P'Gonia*; *Shadows*. LPs: *Pinnacle* (Muse); w. Hancock, *Mwandishi* (WB); H. Land, *New Shade of Blue* (Main.); Joe Farrell, *Outback* (CTI); Dexter Gordon, *Tower of Power*; *More Power* (Prest.); Hilton Ruiz, *Piano Man* (Steeple.).

WILLIAMS, CLAUDE (FIDDLER), *violin*; also *guitar, bass*; b. Muskogee, Okla., 2/22/08. Pl. w. T. Holder in '20s, remaining when Andy Kirk took over the band. With Count Basie as guitarist, occasionally violin, '36. Pl. on first Decca session. Later worked w. Austin Powell quartet; Roy Milton in early '50s. From '73 touring w. Jay McShann. App. w. him at NJF-NY, '73. Dan Morgenstern called him, "A swing fiddler in the Stuff Smith tradition."
LPs: w. McShann, *The Man From Muskogee* (Sack.); *The Blues: A Real Summit Meeting* (Buddah).

WILLIAMS, CHARLES MELVIN (COOTIE),* *trumpet*; b. Mobile, Ala., 7/24/08. After he had his own big band in the '40s and small groups in the '50s, he rejoined Duke Ellington in '62 after a 22 year hiatus. Until he left the orchestra under the direction of Mercer Ellington in the fall of '75 he was a featured soloist who, in the '70s, played only occasionally in the section. During this period he took short leaves of absence from time to time due to illness. In his mid-60s he was still a vital, personal, classic jazz voice. LPs: see Ellington (Duke and Mercer).

WILLIAMS, DAVID (HAPPY), *bass*; b. Trinidad, West Indies, 9/17/46. Father, Buddy Williams, is well-known bassist in West Indies; brother is also bassist. Sister, a concert pianist studied at the Royal Academy in London. Studied violin in school and bass w. father. Sister encouraged him to come to London at age 15 to study and listen. In June '69 she again encouraged him to visit NYC. He sat in at Nuclear Experience w. Beaver Harris and was hired immediately. Studied w. Ron Carter whom he lists as primary infl. Other infl: Coltrane, Miles Davis. Pl. w. Chuck Mangione in Rochester, late '69-early '70; Roberta Flack, '70-2. Gigs w. Ornette Coleman; Donald Byrd; Charles McPherson; Cedar Walton; Billy Taylor; Donny Hathaway. With Elvin Jones from late '74, incl. eight trips to Europe, So. America. While w. Flack, pl. w. Quincy Jones band on concert w. Ray Brown, Chuck Rainey. Comp: *Many Moods*. LPs: w. Elvin Jones, (Vang.); w. Louis Hayes, *Breath of Life*; w. Kenny Barron, *Peruvian Blue* (Muse); w. Sam Jones, *Cello Again* (Xanadu); w. Archie Shepp; George Adams (Horo); w. R. Flack (Atl.).

WILLIAMS, FRANCIS (FRANC), *trumpet*; b. McConnels Mills, Pa., 9/20/10. Father, a coal-miner, pl. guitar and tuba. Grew up in Toledo, Ohio w. Art Tatum. Took up piano at an early age, switching to cornet at 12. After pl. in Cleveland and Chicago, went to NYC, '38, working w. Fats Waller; Edgar Hayes; Claude Hopkins; Horace Henderson; and Ella Fitzgerald. Pl. w. Sabby Lewis in Boston before joining Duke Ellington in '45. Left in '51 and pl. w. many Latin bands: Alberto Socarras; Machito; Tito Puente; Perez Prado. Pl. for many Broadway shows; Emil Coleman at the Plaza's Persian Room; annual Christmas gig w. Sammy Davis Jr. at Copacabana. Toured US w. Harry Belafonte, '56; Europe '58. Charter member of NYJRC, '74, pl. on European tour w. *Musical Life of Charlie Parker*, fall '74; Bix Beiderbecke tribute at NJF-NY, '75. Own quartet, Swing Four w. Eddie Durham, twice weekly at West End Cafe, '75-6. LPs: w. Ellington, solos on *Three Cent Stomp* in *World of Duke Ellington* (Col.); *Trumpet No End* in *The Golden Duke* (Prest.).

WILLIAMS, JOE,* *singer*; b. Cordele, Ga., 12/12/18. Best known as blues singer with C. Basie, Dec. '54 to Jan. '61, Williams subsequently developed a successful career as a vocalist in night clubs, concerts and jazz festivals, showing himself equally adept at popular songs, but never renouncing his identification with the blues. Concerts and music festivals in USA, Europe, England. Starred w. Duke and Mercer Ellington orchs.; frequent reunions w. Basie; concerts w. B. Rich, L. Bellson etc., Cincinnati Symph. Night clubs, incl. Ronnie Scott's, London; Buddy's Place, NYC; Playboy Clubs in several U.S. cities; MGM Grand Hotel in LV. *Showboat 2* jazz fest. cruise, on SS Rotterdam, Dec. '74.

Williams made one motion picture appearance as an actor in *Moonshine War*, '69. TV: Mike Douglas, Johnny Carson, Merv Griffin shows; Harry Belafonte's *Strolling Twenties,* '66; *Love You Madly,* D. Ellington spec., '73. A regular at the NJF for many years, he was also seen at Montreux, '72;

Monterey etc. Living in LV, Williams has worked there occasionally, but is constantly in demand for engagements around the U.S. and overseas.

LPs: *Presenting Joe Williams with Thad Jones/Mel Lewis Orch.*; *Old New & Blue*; *Worth Waiting For* (BN); *The Heart & Soul of Joe Williams & Geo. Shearing* (Sheba); *Joe Williams With Love* (Temponic); *Live with Cannonball Adderley Quintet*; *Big Man* (Fant.); *A Man Ain't Supposed to Cry* (Roul.).

WILLIAMS, JOHN B. JR, *bass*; b. New York City, 2/27/41. Stud. and pl. drums for eight years. Grew up in a neighborhood among such musicians as S. Rollins, the Heath brothers, Milt Jackson, J. McLean etc. Self-taught on bass while in the Marine Corps. After the service, stud. for two years w. Ron Carter, doubling on elect. bass and cello. Following tours w. H. Silver, '67-9, Williams was heard w. K. Burrell, Leon Thomas, K. Winding, '69, D. Gillespie, Hugh Masekela, '70; also gigged w. C. Terry, Z. Sims, Billy Cobham, C. McRae. In '72 Williams was a regular member of the Doc Severinsen orch. on the *Tonight* TV show. He names Miles Davis, Carter, Paul Chambers, Bob Cranshaw and Severinsen as inspirations and influences. Pl. NJF-USA, '67; Europe, '68.

LPs: w. H. Silver, *You Gotta Take A Little Love*; B. Hutcherson-H. Land, *San Francisco* (Blue Note); Billy Cobham, *Crosswinds* (Atl.).

WILLIAMS, LEROY, *drums*; also *piano*; b. Chicago, Ill., 2/3/37. Started on drums at 15. Self-taught except for two mos. w. Oliver Coleman at age 20. Pl. w. Wilbur Ware; Scotty Holt; Jack De Johnette (w. the latter on piano); John Gilmore; Gene Ammons; Sonny Stitt; Bennie Green. Worked w. Judy Roberts trio, '59-64. To NYC '67 where he has been associated w. Barry Harris from that time; w. Ch. McPherson from '69. Also pl. w. Booker Ervin, '67; Sonny Rollins, '68; Clifford Jordan, '68-9; Wilbur Ware, '69-70; Hank Mobley, '70; T. Monk; Y. Lateef, '71; Ray Bryant, '71-2; James Moody; Stan Getz, '73; Andrew Hill, '74-5. Harris says of Williams: "He can really syncopate. He really feels that off-beat thing."

Infl: Roach, K. Clarke, E. Jones, Philly Joe Jones "and all of 'em." TV: w. Bryant, Trenton, N.J.; w. McPherson; Jordan, *Like It Is*. Fest: NJF w. A. Shepp, '68. LPs: w. Harris, *Magnificent* (Prest.); *Plays Tadd Dameron* (Xanadu); *Vicissitudes* (MPS); w. McPherson (Main.); w. Mobley (BN).

WILLIAMS, MARION,* *singer*; b. Miami, Fla., 8/29/27. Lead singer with Clara Ward '47-58, before forming Stars of Faith. Featured in Langston Hughes' *Black Nativity* in US and Europe, '61-5, then toured Europe as soloist. Sang solo at Yale '67 and by '71 had pl. six solo concerts at Harvard. Many coll. apps. in '70s. TV: *Soul*; Dick Cavett; two CBS specials taped at her church in Philadelphia. Received International Television Prize from Princess Grace of Monaco while touring Europe w. Langston Hughes' *The Prodigal Son*. Honored at Yale as Ellington Fellow. Fest: Dakar Fest. of Negro Arts; Antibes; Bergamo; Montreux; NJF-NY. Made public service tv commercial singing *Standing Here Wondering Which Way to Go*. Hollie West says that "more than any other living singer, Williams possesses the melodic inventiveness of the great jazzmen.''

Comp: *A Pity and a Shame.*

LPs: *Prayer Changes Things; Blessed Assurance; Standing Here Wondering Which Way to Go; Gospel Now; The New Message* (Atl.).

WILLIAMS, MARY LOU (Mary Elfrieda Winn),* *piano, composer;* b. Pittsburgh, Pa., 5/8/10. The reemergence of the former standout of the Andy Kirk orch. of the '30s, begun in the first half of the '60s, abated in the second half. However, encouraged by a young priest, Fr. Peter O'Brien, she emerged once again. Her 18 weeks at the Cookery in Greenwich Village, '70-1, not only inaugurated a jazz policy for that restaurant but firmly established it. She played another long engagement there at the end of '75. During the '70s other club apps. incl. the London House, Blues Alley, Bourbon Street, Cafe Carlyle. In '68 she toured Europe, playing at Timme Rosenkrantz's club in Copenhagen and concerts in Italy; trio concert in London, '69.

The main thrust of Ms. Williams' composing was centered on extended works for the Catholic Church which she had embraced in the '50s. Her first Mass, entitled simply *Mass,* was written while she was teaching at Seton HS in Pittsburgh, and was performed at actual liturgy celebrated by the Bishop of Pitts., John Cardinal Wright in St. Paul's Cathedral, Pitts., '66. In '67 she gave concert at Carnegie Hall, *Praise the Lord in Many Voices* incl. a detailed history of jazz on solo piano, and three sacred pieces: *Thank You Jesus; The Lord's Prayer; Praise the Lord.* Second Mass, *Mass for the Lenten Season,* premiered '68 and pl. for seven consecutive Sundays at Church of St. Thomas the Apostle, NYC. After she performed the Mass in Rome, she received the liturgical texts of the *Votive Mass for Peace* from the Vatican which commissioned her to write third Mass which she did in '69. Originally titled *Music for Peace* it was subsequently named *Mary Lou's Mass.* The work was premiered in concert form at Columbia U., '70. In '71 she rewrote it for the Alvin Ailey City Center Dance Theatre, adding several new sections. She has been represented in the Ailey NYC seasons in '72-3 and by the Ailey Company on tour in the US and Europe, '73. *Mary Lou's Mass* was also performed at St. Paul's in Pitts., '73; w. chorus of NYC school children at St. Patrick's, '75, rec. by NET.

In addition to playing many coll. concerts Ms. Williams was in residence in Toronto, NYC, Wash., D.C., and Rochester during '73, involving trio concerts, classes in history of jazz, training of local choirs for perfs. of *Mary Lou's Mass.* Other concerts for Overseas Jazz Club '70; Smithsonian Institution; Whitney Museum, '75. At the inauguration ceremony of the Charlie Parker Foundation in KC, she had a street, Mary Lou Williams Lane, named for her. Received Guggenheim Fellowship, '72-3; grant from NY State Council on the Arts. Honorary degrees from Fordham U.; Manhattan Coll.; Loyola U., NO. Appointed full professor at the U. of Massachusetts, Amherst, Mass. from fall '75.

TV: *Today; Tonight; Dick Cavett; AM America; Sesame Street; Mr. Rogers' Neighborhood; Lamp Unto My Feet; Black Pride; Dreams and Visions* w. Ailey. Fest: NJF-NY, '71-3; MJF, '71-2. Publ: *Mary Lou's Mass; St. Martin De*

Porres for Chorus (Cecilia Music Publ., P.O. Box 32, Hamilton Grange, N.Y., N.Y. 10031). Comp: *Lamb of God; Zoning Fungus II; Medi I and Medi II; Play It Momma; Joycie; Dirge Blues; Miss D.D. Gloria; The Scarlet Creeper; Blues for John; Ode for St. Cecilia.*

"She is never less than contemporary," wrote John S. Wilson, "and always well out in the vanguard of valid new ideas."

Clive Barnes called *Mary Lou's Mass* "strong and joyful music, with a spirit that cuts across all religious boundaries to provide a celebration of man, God and peace. The gently religious fervor of the music, with its overtones of both jazz and gospel, and its spiritual exaltation make the score perfect—a celebration of life—an assertively happy work—it treats of the special ecstasy of grace—but there is also humor here."

LPs: *Mary Lou's Mass; Zoning* (Mary—addr. same as Cecilia Music); *Praise the Lord in Many Voices* (Avant Garde); *From the Heart* (Chiaro.); *Giants* w. D. Gillespie, B. Hackett (Perception); *Zodiac Suite* (Folk.); trio (Steeple.); *Black Christo of the Andes* (MPS); *Newport in New York, The Jam Sessions, Vols. 1 & 2* (Cobble.); w. Buddy Tate and His Buddies (Chiaro.); reissues w. Andy Kirk (Main.); *Cafe Society* (Onyx); w. Don Byas (GNP, Crescendo, Vogue).

WILLIAMS, PATRICK MOODY (PAT), *composer;* also *trumpet, vibes;* b. Bonne Terre, Mo., 4/23/39. Stud. Duke U., '61; grad. work in comp., Columbia U., '61-3. Twelve tone comp. studies in LA, '69-75. Comp., arr., mus. dir. in NYC studios, '61-7 and in LA, '68- . Though principally known as a successful composer of scores for many feature films, Williams has conducted or judged at jazz fests., has written a *Rhapsody for Concert Band and Jazz Ensemble,* and states: "I am very interested in composing music that intertwines jazz and classical techniques. I feel uncomfortable straying too far from my jazz background." Infls: Ellington, Tatum, Basie; Stravinsky, Richard Strauss, Ravel. Film Credits: *Mrs. Sundance; Ordeal; The Magician; Streets of San Francisco; Terror in the Sky; Evel Knievel; San Francisco International; Don't Drink The Water; A Nice Girl Like Me; How Sweet It Is.* TV Series: *Mary Tyler Moore Show; Bob Newhart Show; Streets of San Francisco.*

LPs: as composer and/or perf., *Shades of Today; Think; Heavy Vibrations* (MGM-Verve); *Threshold* (Cap.); *Carry On* (A & R).

WILLIAMS, RICHARD GENE,* *trumpet, composer;* also *piano, saxophone;* b. Galveston, Texas, 5/4/31. Played w. Charles Mingus; Slide Hampton in early '60s. Joined Thad Jones-Mel Lewis in '66, remaining w. them into '69, touring Europe and Japan. Soloist for Orchestra U.S.A. New York premiere of Gunther Schuller's *Journey Into Jazz.* Soloist for Broadway show *The Me Nobody Knows,* '70-1. European gigs with local musicians, '71 and, as guest of the Belgian government, '72. Pl. w. Gil Evans in Calif., '73. European tours w. Clark Terry band, '73; w. *Musical Life of Charlie Parker,* '74; w. Lionel Hampton, '75. Broadway musicals: *Raisin,* '74; *The Wiz,* '75. NYJRC concert, *The Music of Monk,* '75. Also free-lancing w. own quartet.

Dr. Frederick Tillis of the U. of Mass. wrote trumpet concerto for him, as yet unperformed. TV: show devoted to poetry of Robert Kaufman w. Ossie Davis and Ruby Dee, music by Lucky Thompson. Fest: w. Jones-Lewis, NJF, '67; Orange County, Calif. '68; w. G. Evans, NJF-NY '72; w. C. Mingus, NJF-NY; Bilzen, Belgium, '73; w. C. Terry, Pori, San Sebastian, Verona, '73; w. *Life of Parker,* Portugal, Rumania, Yugoslavia, '74. Comp: *Rogi; Two Bags; Renita's Bounce; Raucous Notes; Blues in a Quandary.* LPs: w. Jones-Lewis, *Presenting; Monday Night; Central Park North; Presenting Joe Williams* (SS); w. Ch. McPherson, *Today's Man* (Main.); w. R.R. Kirk, *Left & Right;* w. G. Evans, *Svengali* (Atl.); w. O. Nelson, *The Mayor and the People* (Fly. Dutch.); w. Booker Ervin, *The In-Between* (BN); w. Bill Evans-George Russell, *Living Time* w. Music, Inc. (Strata-East); w. C. Terry (Vang.).

WILLIAMS, ANTHONY (TONY),* *drums, composer;* b. Chicago, Ill., 12/12/45. Grew up in Boston where he pl. w. Sam Rivers. To NYC '62, pl. w. Jackie McLean. From '63-9 was an integral part of the Miles Davis quintet, establishing himself as one of the young innovators helping to change the face of jazz. After leaving Davis he formed his own gp., Lifetime, w. John McLaughlin and Larry Young, mixing chord-based and free jazz with rock. in an exciting, if albeit, high-decibel amalgam. When McLaughlin formed his Mahavishnu Orch. in '71 he was replaced by Ted Dunbar who app. w. the gp. at the NJF-NY, '72. *The Old Bum's Rush,* an album released in '73, had a different cast incl. the drummer's father, Tillmon Williams, on tenor sax.

In '75 Lifetime was reformed with a new personnel incl. Allan Holdsworth, guitar; and Alan Pasqua, electric keyboards. Robert Palmer, reviewing the album *Believe It* in the New York *Times,* remarked that Williams "is playing much less in terms of color and shading, for at one time he was one of the most poetic drummers in contemporary jazz. But he is playing music which fuses rock energy and improvisational interest without frills and without gratuitous grandstanding."

Comp: *Wildlife; Sangria For Three; Emergency; Beyond Games; There Comes a Time.*

LPs: *Believe It* (Col.); *Emergency; Turn It Over; Ego; Old Bum's Rush* (Poly.); w. Davis, *Miles Smiles; Sorcerer; Nefertiti; Miles in the Sky; Filles De Kilimanjaro; In A Silent Way;* w. *Newport in New York, The Jam Sessions, Vols. 3&4* (Cobble.); w. Gil Evans, *There Comes a Time* (RCA).

WILLIS, LAWRENCE ELLIOTT (LARRY), *piano, composer;* b. New York City, 12/20/40. Voice major at High School of Music & Art; grad. Manhattan School of Music; stud. privately w. John Mehegan. Insp. by B. Evans, W. Kelly, Miles Davis, H. Hancock, Mehegan. Pl. w. J. McLean, '63, H. Masekela, '64, K. Winding, '65-7, S. Getz, '69, C. Adderley, '71, Earl May, '71-2. Accomp. singers incl. Esther Marrow, Gloria Lynne. In '72 Willis joined Blood, Sweat & Tears, appearing with them on TV rock specs., at fests. and concerts. etc. Also free-lancing in NYC clubs as soloist, '75.

Comps: *Inner Crisis; Poor Eric; Megalomania; Journey's End.* Also arr. *So Long Dixie; Mary Miles; Mirror Image; Inner Crisis* for B.S.&T. Own LP: *Inner Crisis* (Groove Merchant); LPs w. McLean, *Jacknife* (Blue Note); Masekela (Blue Thumb); J. Henderson (Milestone); A. Mouzon (Blue

Note); also *New Blood; No Sweat* w. B.S.&T. (Columbia).

WILSON, EDWARD JOHN (ED), *trombone, composer;* b. Sydney, Australia, 6/22/44. Worked as staff musician w. Australian Broadcasting Commission, '65-72. During this period he and Warren Daly (q.v.) organized the Daly-Wilson big band, which enjoyed unprecedented local acceptance. After disbanding late in '69, Wilson toured Australia and New Zealand in '70 with the Glenn Miller orch. under B. De Franco. The Daly-Wilson band was reorganized in '71 and won a gold record for its album *Big Band On Tour.*

Wilson has been responsible for writing most of the band's library, usually in collaboration with Daly. Comps: *Kings Step Out; El Boro; My Goodness; On My Own; Limp Dropper.*

LPs: *Live at the Cell Block* (EMI); *Featuring Kerrie Biddell* (Festival); *On Tour; Featuring Marcia Hines* (WB). All albums released in the U.S. on G.R.C. Elephant label.

WILSON, GERALD STANLEY,* *composer, leader, trumpet;* b. Shelby, Miss., 9/4/18. Continued to record and appear with big band; made five albums between '66-70. Arranged two of his own compositions, *Blues for Yna Yna* and *Collage,* for S. Kenton's Neophonic Orch. In '69 Wilson began arr. for E. Fitzgerald, rec. an album with her in '70. Also in '69 he joined KBCA in LA, where his own radio interview show became a popular daily feature. In the same year he joined the faculty of Cal. State U. at Northridge as lecturer on jazz history, where he acquired an unusually large class and established himself as an outstanding educator.

In '72, Wilson comp. and arr. his first work for symph. orch. Its title, *5/21/72,* denotes the date it was perf. by the LA Philharmonic Orch. conducted by Zubin Mehta, at the Music Center. He has since arr. and orchestrated four more works for the LA Phil. and its 250 voice choir, perf. in '75.

In '71 Wilson's comp. *Viva Tirado,* rec. by El Chicano, became a hit, receiving a BMI award as one of the most popular songs of the year. Other comps. incl.: *Josefina; Jeri; Teri; Nancy Jo; Carlos; The Golden Sword; Lighthouse Blues; Aram; Eric; Sonato for Guitar; The Royal Suite; Teotihuacan; El Viti.* Fests: Berkeley, '67; Tulsa, '68; Kongsberg, '73; Concord, Santa Barbara, '75.

LPs: *Golden Sword; Everywhere; Feeling Kinda Blues; California Soul; Eternal Equinox; Live & Swinging; You Better Believe It* (Pac. Jazz); *Things Ain't What They Used To Be* w. Fitzgerald (Repr.).

WILSON, JACK JR.,* *piano, composer;* also *keyboards, vibes, drums, baritone saxophone;* b. Chicago, Ill., 8/3/36. Extensive freelance work in LA, '62- ; also arr. for his own reh. band. TV: *The Jazz Show,* KNBC, LA; *Repertoire Workshop,* CBS; *Peyton Place,* ABC; *Bob Hope Presents,* ABC. Film: *Bus Riley's Back In Town.* Many apps. at Memory Lane leading trio and acc. O.C. Smith, Esther Phillips, Sam Fletcher and other singers. Publs: Big band arr.; also series of instruction books (Maggio Music, 12044 Vanowen, N. Hollywood, Ca. 91605).

LPs: *Something Personal; Easterly Winds; Song For My Daughter* (BN); *The Jack Wilson Quartet; The Two Sides of Jack Wilson; The Jazz Organs* (Atl.); *Brazilian Mancini; Ramblin'* (Vault); w. Esther Phillips, *Live* (Atl.); *From a Whisper to A Scream* (CTI); w. Gerald Wilson, *Live and*

Swinging; *Everywhere*; *Greatest Hits* (Wor. Pac.); w. Charlie Barnet (Vault); w. Blue Mitchell, *Vital Blue* (Main.).

WILSON, JOSEPH LEE (JOE LEE), *singer*; also *piano, guitar, percussion*; b. Bristow, Okla., 12/22/35. Private piano lessons from ages seven to nine. Voice lessons in LA; voice major at LA Conserv., '55; music major at LACC, '56-7. Began singing prof. '58. Toured on West Coast; Canada; Mexico. In NYC has worked S. Rollins; F. Hubbard; L. Morgan; R. Haynes; M. Jackson; M. Davis; A. Shepp; Rashied Ali; J. McLean; Roy Brooks; P. Sanders; F. Foster; CBA; own band. Infl: Roscoe Weathers, Louis Jordan, E. Jefferson, K. Pleasure, Joe Williams, Sammy Davis, Tony Bennett, Sinatra, E. Fitzgerald, S. Vaughan, C. McRae, Betty Carter. TV: *Like It Is*; *Call Back*; *NBC Showcase 1968*; *Dick Cavett*; *Soul*; *Free Time*; *Jazz Set*. Fest: U. of Mass. Pan-American Fest., '73; NY Mus., '72; NJF-NY, '73; Live Loft JF, '75; Third World Culture Fest., Yale U. '75. App. in musical, *Lady Day*, at Brooklyn Acad. of Mus. Comp: *Come and See (Sparrow Singing Jazz)*; *One (Dedicated to My Father)*. Won DB Critics poll, TDWR, '73. Harvey Siders called him, "a jazz singer in the true sense of the word," who "phrases and attacks in the manner of a J.J. Johnson trombone solo, at the same time pausing thoughtfully throughout his vocal improvisations conjuring up the syncopated silences of Ahmad Jamal."

LPs: *What Would It Be Without You* (Survival); *Mr. Joe Lee Wilson in the Great City* (Power Tree); *Livin' High Off Nickels and Dimes* (Oblivion); w. Shepp, *Attica Blues*; *Things Have Got to Change*; *The Cry of My People* (Imp.); Charles Earland, *Charles III* (Prest.); Billy Gault (Steeple.); Mtume (Strata-East).

WILSON, NANCY, *singer*; b. Chillicothe, O., 2/20/37. A major star throughout the 1960's after her discovery by Cannonball Adderley, Wilson continued to travel throughout the US and overseas.

In '73 she played a concert at the London Palladium, appeared in a 90-minute German TV special, and toured the continent. Later she appeared at the Royal Swazi Hotel in Swaziland. She married Rev. Wiley Burton in April, 1974.

In addition to singing in a jazz-influenced style, she occasionally appeared on television in acting roles on such shows as *Police Story* and *The FBI*. She served as hostess on her own TV series on KNBC in LA from Mar. 1974-Mar. 1975. Her guests were personalities from all professions, including such jazz performers as Airto, Milt Jackson and Ahmad Jamal. The program won an Emmy award.

Very concerned with civil rights, Wilson was associated with the Black Caucus, appeared at seminars and political meetings, after performing for such groups.

LPs: Many commercial albums, though on some she was teamed with such arrangers as Oliver Nelson, Gerald Wilson and Jimmy Jones. While in Japan in '75 she recorded a live album for Toshiba. All of the US LPs on Capitol.

WILSON, PHILLIP SANFORD, *drums, percussion, composer*; also *vibes, piano*; b. St. Louis, Mo., 9/8/41. Grandfather, Ira Kimball, pl. drums on riverboats. Violin lessons in grade school at age nine. Drum corps at 10 through 17, teaching in corps at 14. Met Lester Bowie while in high school. Began pl. prof. at 16. Worked w. organist Don James. At 19

went to NYC w. organist Sam Lazar, working at Minton's w. him for a yr. Returned to St. Louis and pl. blues and rock bands. With Jackie Wilson; Solomon Burke; Motown revue, '62-3. Went to California w. Bowie; Oliver Lake in Burke's group. Pl. w. Julius Hemphill, David Sanborn in St. Louis '64. To Chicago, '65, where he became involved w. AACM. Joined Paul Butterfield '68 and was w. him into '70. Pl. w. Mother Lode in Toronto, '71-2. In SF '72 spent much time practicing; also gigging w. Hemphill. In NYC app. w. Anthony Braxton at Town Hall, May '72. Worked w. Full Moon '73; also pl. percussion w. Chico Hamilton. Studied theory, harmony, piano at Memphis State U. '74. Wrote for Stax Records. Working w. Braxton '76. Infl: Sonny Hamp, Philly Joe Jones, Elvin Jones. Film: *Rico* w. Dean Martin. TV: w. Hemphill at So. Illinois U., PBS. Fest: NJF-NY, '73 w. Paul Jeffrey. Comp: *Selfish People*. LPs: w. Hemphill (Arista); Bowie (Muse); w. Art Ensemble of Chicago, *Old* (Del.); Full Moon (Douglas); Butterfield (Electra); Lazar (Chess).

WILSON, PHILLIPS ELDER JR. (PHIL), *trombone, composer, conductor, educator*; b. Belmont, Mass., 1/19/37. After building an enviable reputation w. W. Herman orch., '62-5, he left to take up teaching position at Berklee where he taught arr. & comp.; headed the trombone dept; founded and dir. the Thursday Night Dues Band and the Jazz Trombone Choir, '65-74. Faculty member Nat. Stage Band Camps from '65; dir. of Mus. Dept., Exeter Acad., '67-71; dir. Choate Sch. jazz-rock summer prog., '72- . Clinician for Conn Inst. Co. from '65; Board of Dir. of Int. Trom. Assoc. from '72; co-founder-dir., Boston Sackbut Week from '73. Appointed by G. Schuller as chairman of jazz division of Afro-American Dept. of New England Conserv., '74. Cond. Bost. Symph. in their children's series, premiering his work, *The Earth's Children*, '72; cond. Westchester Symph. in own comp., *The Left and the Right*, for symph. orch. and Marian McPartland trio, '71. Pl. w. M. McPartland; C. Terry; L. Armstrong; H. Hancock; B. Hackett. Arr. of *Mercy, Mercy, Mercy* for B. Rich; other comps. & arrs. for Herman, Terry, McPartland, D. Severinsen. Infl: Armstrong; O. Peterson; Ellington. Publ: co-author, *Chord Studies for Trombone* (Berklee Press, 1140 Boylston St., Boston, Mass.).

LPs: *The Prodigal Son* (Freeform); *Thurs Night Dues* (SJC); arrs. for Rich (RCA Victor; Pac. Jazz).

WILSON, THEODORE (TEDDY), *piano, composer*; b. Austin, Tex., 11/24/12. One of the personalities to emerge from the Benny Goodman band of the '30s and leader of his own big band in '39-40, Wilson has continued, as he did in the '60s, to appear primarily at the head of his own trios but he also gave solo performances. He played in Europe; Australia; and three times in Japan, '70, '71, '73, where he recorded extensively. He worked often at Michael's Pub, NYC; the trio augmented in the latter part of the set, during certain engagements, by tenor men such as Flips Phillips; and Charlie Ventura.

Fest: Colo. JP, annually, from mid-60s through '73; NJF-NY '72 w. Benny Carter's Swing Masters; Lionel Hampton Tribute; '73 w. B. Goodman quartet; '74 w. own sextet in Salute to Cafe Society; Solo Piano; '75 in Newport Jazz Hall of Fame; Montreux. Dan Morgenstern writing of Wilson in *Jazz People* (see bibliography) says: "At times there is still a spark, a tension, something beyond the always impeccable and pianistically perfect surface.''

LPs: *With Billie in Mind* (Chiaro.); *Striding After Fats*; *Runnin' Wild!*; *Moonglow* (Bl. Lion); *My Ideal* (Jap. Philips); *Jimmy Takeuchi & Teddy Wilson* (Toshiba); Teddy Wilson-Eiji Kitamura, three albums (Trio); Teddy Wilson & Marian McPartland, *Elegant Piano* (Halcyon); reissue, *Teddy Wilson & His All Stars* (Col.); w. Phoebe Snow (Shelter).

WINDING, KAI CHRESTEN, * *trombone, composer, leader*; b. Aarhus, Denmark, 5/18/22. One of the first trombonists in the bop movement of the '40s, pl. w. S. Kenton; C. Parker; G. Mulligan; M. Davis. Two trombone gp. w. J.J. Johnson in '50s. Own gps. from that time. W. Playboy Clubs in '60s incl. post of mus. dir. of NY branch. Active in studios, jingle field; comp. and scoring for industrial films. Co-led World's Greatest Jazzband II w. Eddie Condon at Roosevelt Grill, '69. From '70 in LA as member of staff band led by Mort Lindsey on Merv Griffin TV show. Reactivated four trombone gp. for Concord Fest. and engagement at Hong Kong Bar, '71. Toured world w. Giants of Jazz in '71-2. Euro. tour w. Lee Konitz; solo tour of Scandinavia, '74.

From '73 cond. school clinics; contracting for Pete Rugolo for TV films, feature films. coordinating personnel for Chuck Mangione LA concerts, Calif. tours. Formed own production co., Kaiwin Ltd., rec. own combo. Film: *A Man Called Adam* w. Sammy Davis. TV: Griffin; *Sammy & Co.*; NBC jazz shows w. B. Eckstine; Playboy 20th Anny Special, '75. Fest: NJF world tour, '71; Euro. & U.S., '72; Concord, '70-4; Colo. JP, '68-71; Berlin, '74. Comp: *Danish Blue*; *Concord Blues*. LPs: *Danish Blue* (Glendale); *Solo*; *Dirty Dog*; *Rainy Day*; *More Brass* (Verve); w. *Giants of Jazz* (Atl.); w. J.J. Johnson, *Israel*; *Betwixt and Between*; *Stonebones* (A&M, latter released in Japan only); w. all star brass, *Incredible Trombones*; *Brass Fever* (Imp.); Colorado Jazz Party (MPS/BASF); *Newport in New York, The Jam Sessions, Vols. 3&4* (Cobble.).

WINESTONE, BENJAMIN (BENNY), * *saxophones*; b. Glasgow, Scotland, 12/20/06. The veteran tenor sax star, prominent in London before World War II and subsequently in Canada, where he worked with Maynard Ferguson in 1947-8, later played in a variety of small combos until illness forced him into retirement. He died in Toronto 6/10/74.

WINSTONE, NORMA, *singer*; b. London, England, 9/23/41. Stud. piano at Trinity Coll. Since early '60s has app. in many clubs and concert halls in Britain, incl. Ronnie Scott's. Attended free jazz meetings in Baden-Baden for German radio, '70, '73. Broadcasts for same with own group, Edge of Time, from Rothenburg, '74.

One of England's most original jazz singers, Winstone won the MM poll, '71-3. She is married to British jazz pianist John Taylor. Infls: Sinatra, Fitzgerald, McRae, J. Coltrane.

LPs: as leader, *Edge of Time* (Argo); as guest, *A Symphony of Amaranths* w. Neil Ardley (Regal Zonophone); *Labyrinth*, w. Ian Carr (Vertigo); w. Michael Garrick (Argo); w. Mike Westbrook, *Love Songs* (Deram); w. K. Wheeler *Song For Someone* (Incus).

WINTER, PAUL THEODORE JR., * *soprano, alto sax, composer*; b. Altoona, Pa. 8/31/39. Best known as leader of first jazz group to perf. at the White House, in late '62 for Mrs. John F. Kennedy. Later organized group known as Winter Consort. Perf. ''The Charles Ives Show'' at Kennedy Center, Wash., D.C., '75.

LPs: *Winter Consort, Something In The Wind, Road* (all A& M); *Icarus* (Epic).

WITHERS, WILLIAM HARRISON (BILL), *singer, composer, guitar, piano*; b. Slab Fork, W. Va., 7/4/38. Served in Navy for nine years, worked in an aircraft factory and also as milkman before making his professional start in music at the age of 32. His first album revealed a long neglected talent for fashioning attractive melodies and intelligent lyrics, performing them with impassioned sensitivity. He appeared at Berkeley JF, NO JF and on many TV shows w. Dick Cavett, Bill Cosby, David Frost, Nancy Wilson, Flip Wilson, Mike Douglas et al; also on *The Jazz Show*, KNBC, LA. Insp. by Hal David, Lou Rawls, Aretha Franklin, Little Willie John, Stevie Wonder.

Withers won a Grammy award in '71 for *Ain't No Sunshine*, as best r & b song. Among his other compositions are *Grandma's Hands*; *Lean On Me*; *Harlem*; *Let Me In Your Life*.

LPs: *Just as I Am*; *Still Bill*; *Live at Carnegie Hall*; & *'Justments* (Sussex).

WITHERSPOON, JAMES (JIMMY), * *singer*; b. Gurdon, Ark., 8/8/23. Living in LA, Witherspoon continued to app. in clubs around the US and was frequently seen at the MJF. All through the '60s he made annual periodic visits to sing for the inmates in prisons. In later years he visited Europe approximately once a year. In '73 he toured Japan and the Far East. In '74, Witherspoon went to England to rec. a session which, when released in the U.S., turned out to be his biggest popular success in many years. Entitled *Love Is A Five Letter Word*, it contained little in the way of orthodox blues material, but set his unique timbre in a context that broadened his appeal.

From '72 Witherspoon was feat. on KMET radio in LA, as star of his own blues disc jockey show. Film: title role in *Black Godfather*, '75. TV: *Tonight Show*; *Midnight Special*; *An Evening With Spoon* for educ. TV; others in Boston, Phoenix, Arizona, Washington, D.C. Comps: *I Was Lost*; *Don't Gotta*.

LPs: *Spoonful* (BN); *Love Is A Five Letter Word* (Cap.); *Best of*; *Blues For Easy Livers*; *Spoon in London* (Pres.); *Handbags & Gladrags* (ABC); *Spoon Concerts* (Fant.); others w. G. Mulligan (Archive of Folk & Jazz); Ben Webster (Verve).

WOLFF, MICHAEL B. (MIKE), *piano, composer*; b. Victorville, Cal., 7/31/52. Six months later his family moved to Memphis, Tenn., living there until '61; then to Berkeley, Cal., where Wolff lived until he attended UCLA in '70, majoring in music and studying piano w. Abie Tzerko. After a year and a half at UCLA, transferred to U.C. Berkeley. Joined C. Tjader summer of '72, staying with him for two years. In mid-'74 joined Fingers, the group led by Airto, remaining until it disbanded Nov '74. In Jan. '75 he became a member of the C. Adderley quintet.

Wolff says: ''My true love is the acoustic piano, but I am expanding into electronics: electric piano, clavinet, ring modulator, echo-plex, phase shifter, synthesizer etc.'' He was influenced by his father, Marvin L. Wolff, who played woodwinds in a band in Indianola, Miss., along w. Brew Moore. Comps: *Poppy*; *Waban*; *Sad Eyes*; *Samba de Oneida*. LPs: *Last Bolero In Berkeley*; *Putting It All Together*, w. Tjader; *Tambu* w. Tjader-C. Byrd; others w. Adderley (Fant.).

WONDER, STEVIE, *composer, singer, pianist* etc; b. Saginaw, Mich., 5/13/51. Wonder, whose first album was released when he was 12 years old, became an exceptionally popular performer and writer. Winner of several Grammy awards, he is of interest to the jazz world as the composer of a number of songs extensively used by jazz musicians, most notably *You Are The Sunshine Of My Life*.

WOODE, JAMES BRYANT (JIMMY),* *bass, composer, piano*; b. Philadelphia, Pa., 9/23/29. Leaving Duke Ellington in '60 after five yrs., he moved to Europe, working in Sweden, France and Germany. Lived in Germany and Austria but by '75 was based solely in Munich. With Clarke-Boland Big Band until band broke up in '73. Active w. radio, TV bands and in clubs. Comp: *Now Hear My Meaning*; lyrics for Francy Boland's *November Girl*. LPs: w. Mal Waldron, *Black Glory* (Enja); Clarke-Boland (MPS, Poly., Prest.); Charlie Parker (Phoenix).

WOODMAN, BRITT,* *trombone*; also *baritone horn*; b. Los Angeles, Cal., 6/4/20. Traveled w. D. Ellington, '51-60; later pl. in many Broadway shows, recordings and TV specials. Moved to Cal., Oct. '70. Cont. to freelance, working with the big bands of Bill Berry and Toshiko-Lew Tabackin. Rehearsing w. own eight piece gp. and occasionally app. with Ellington alumni groups in Duke Ellington tributes. Feat. soloist w. T. Vig 32 piece orch., '75. TV: *Brotherhood Special* '74. Fest: Concord, w. Berry, '74.

LPs: w. Chico Hamilton, *The Gamut* (UA); w. Toshiko-Tabackin, *Kogun* (RCA); w. B. Berry (Beez).

WOODS, CHRISTOPHER COLUMBUS (CHRIS), *alto saxophone, composer*; also *baritone sax, clarinet, flute, piccolo*; b. Memphis, Tenn., 12/25/25. First cousin Bob Mabane, tenor sax w. J. McShann in swing era, was early idol and insp. Stud. alto w. Dave Caples in St. Louis, '38-9; clar. w. Mike Zottarelle, St. Louis, '48; flute w. Henry Klein, Brooklyn, N.Y., '68-73; theory & harm. at Music & Arts Univ., St. Louis, '48-51; Brooklyn Conserv., part time '64-73; w. Scott O'Neal, alto as comp., '67-71. Pl. w. Tommy Dean, Jeter-Pillars, George Hudson in St. Louis, '48-51; Ernie Fields, '51; own gp. in St. Louis, '52-62. Moved to NYC and has worked w. D. Gillespie, C. Terry, H. McGhee, S. Oliver, W. Covington, Duke Pearson, B. Rich. Extensive tours of Europe as sideman and soloist, '73-4. Infl: Parker, Hodges, Willie Smith, Young, Hawkins, Joe Thomas. TV: half-hour show w. own gp. for six mos., St. Louis '55; Volkswagen commercial w. C. Terry; *Mark of Jazz* w. B. Rich, Phila. Fests: NJF; Pori; Nancy; San Sebastian. Comps: *Blues for Lew*; *Rhode Island Red*; *Swivel Hips*; *Monsieur LesBois in Paris*; *Love Theme for a Very Special Friend*; *My Lady*; *Portrait of a Golden Angel*; *Scufflin' Along*.

LPs: *Paris Meets Woods* (Futura); *Together in Paris*, Marco DiMarco-Chris Woods Sextet (Modern Jazz); *Big Bad Band* w. Terry (Etoile); *Reunion Band* w. Gillespie, (MPS); *Stickball* w. Charles Williams; *Blood, Sweat & Brass*; *Hard*

Mother Blues w. E. Wilkins (Mainstream); *Yes Indeed* w. S. Oliver (Black & Blue).

WOODS, JOHNNY, *woodwinds, educator*; b. Pittsburgh, Pa., 4/2/30. Wife a Swedish concert pianist. Stud. at U.S. Navy School of Music, '51-2; B.S. in Ed. from Ohio St. Univ., '60; grad. work at Potsdam St., N.Y. '63. Woodwind teacher and big band dir. in N.Y. state; org. 10 bands plus his own and a teachers' octet for first Central N.Y. Stage Band Fest. '61, cont. through '64. Rehearsal leader for Colgate Coll. big band '62-3. In '65 Woods, who had toured Sweden and Finland w. the Int. Jazz Combo, '54-7, moved to Stockholm, where he taught clarinet in city music schools through '73. In free time org. five youth bands in Stockholm; lecturer at Royal Acad. of Music, '69; led Nat. Concert Bureau Wind Ensemble '71. Two big band concerts and jazz lecture at U.S. Cultural Center '71. Director of big band summer clinics in Sweden and Finland and full-time supervisor of Sweden's first jazz school, Jazz Ensemble Workshop, funded by the Swedish government. Contributor to Swedish jazz journals and to *Jazz Forum*.

WOODS, PHILIP WELLS (PHIL),* *alto sax, composer*; also *clarinet, piano*; b. Springfield, Mass., 11/2/31. Established himself as one of top alto players w. Gillespie, Q. Jones, B. Goodman and own groups in '50s and '60s. A busy NYC free-lance, he headed jazz dept. of Ramblerny, a summer arts camp in New Hope, Pa., '66-7. Left for Europe in March '68, making Paris his home base in May and forming European Rhythm Machine for clubs, concerts, radio, TV and fests. all over the Continent. In Dec. '72 moved to Calif., settling in LA for 10 months where he led quartet incl. pianist Pete Robinson on elec. piano. Returned to East Coast Oct. '73 to live in Pennsylvania, form new quartet, write and teach. Feat. soloist w. Michel Legrand for concerts, clubs.

Films: *The Hustler*; *Blow-Up*. Fest: NJF; Montreux; Frankfort; Molde; Berlin; Pori; Stockholm; Palermo; Nervi; Lisbon; Barcelona; Bologna, Aarhus, Col. Jazz Party. Comp: *Round Trip*; *Rights of Swing*; *Four Moods for Alto & Piano*; *Saxophone Quartet*; *Peace*, a ballet for French TV. Publ: saxophone method and band arrs. (Creative Jazz Composers, Box 467, Bowie, Md. 20715).

Polls: won *Playboy* Musicians' Musicians '71; DB Critics Poll, '70-1, '75; Readers poll, '75; combo won Critics Poll, TDWR, '70.

A fiery, passionate, lyrical player, originally out of the Charlie Parker school, Woods has incorporated elements of rock and avant garde into his personal, evolving expression.

LPs: *Musique Du Bois* (Muse); *New Music* (Testament); *Round Trip* (Verve); *Rights of Swing* (Barnaby); *Early Quintets* (Prest.); w. Euro. Rhythm Mach., *At The Frankfurt Jazz Fest.* (Embryo); *At The Montreux Jazz Fest.* (MGM); w. Q. Jones, *You've Got It Bad Girl* (A & M); w. M. Legrand, *Images*; *Live at Jimmy's* (RCA); w. C. Terry (Vang.).

WOODYARD, SAMUEL (SAM),* *drums*; b. Elizabeth, N.J., 1/7/25. Pl. w. D. Ellington orch., '55, remaining with occasional absences for more than a decade. After leaving Ellington, was ill and inactive for several years, living in LA, but returned in early '70s pl. occasionally w. Bill Berry band. Rejoined Duke pl. congas, '73; later pl. congas w. B. Rich. To NYC, '74. Gigs at West End Cafe. From Feb. '75 he spent several months in Europe, pl. Dunkirk JF with Claude Bolling orch., and later working w. Gerard Badini's Swing Machine.

LPs: w. Ellington on various labels; w. Badini (Blue Star); w. Rich, *Roar of '74* (Gr. Mer.); w. Brooks Kerr-Paul Quinichette, *Prevue* (Famous Door).

WORKMAN, REGINALD (REGGIE),* *bass, educator*; b. Philadelphia, Pa., 6/26/37. Worked w. Coltrane; Moody; Blakey; Lateef; H. Mann in '60s, touring Japan w. Mann, '66. Played w. T. Monk; Alice Coltrane; Music Inc. incl. State Dept. concert tour-seminar of Brazil, '72; concert tour, Holland '74; w. Max Roach, two wks. in Italy, '73-4. Workman also toured Japan as an African American Music Consultant for All Art Promotion, Inc., '70.

From '67 teaching bass for in-house music program at the New Muse Community Museum of Brooklyn where he took over for Bill Barron as Director of the Music Workshop Program, '75. He also has directed workshops and/or taught at Samuel Tilden Comm. Center, '67-8; NY Chapter of Young Audience Inc., '67-70; Central Brooklyn Model Cities Summer & Winter Academy, '70; Wilmington, Del. School of Music, '71; Trenton, N.J. Board of Education, '72; U. of Mass., '73-4; Jazz Interactions Music Workshop from '75.

In '70 he had a month's training at the Moog Co., Trumansburg, N.Y., learning how to operate and perform w. Moog Synthesizer. Studied at Manhattan Borough Comm. Coll., '70-1; Lincoln U.; NJ Board of Ed. teacher training courses, '72; U. of Mass., '73-4.

Produced series of cultural presentations at Olatunji's Center for African Culture, '67. From '70 president of Board of Directors of CBA; member of advisory board of the Afro-American Bi-centennial Hall of Fame and Museum, Inc., Youngstown, Ohio. Received grant from CAPS for Comp., '71; Orchard Hill Residential Coll. of U. of Mass. award, '74; El Hajj Malik Shabazz Award '75.

LPs: *Reggie Workman-Dee Dee Bridgewater Duet*; w. Heiner Stadler (Labor); w. Billy Harper; Charles Tolliver (Strata-East); Lee Morgan (BN); H. Mann (Atl.); A. Coltrane; Marion Brown (Imp.); Cedar Walton (Prest.); Mal Waldron (Enja); Johnny Coles (Main.); Roy Brooks (Imhotep); T. Hino (Canyon); T. Honda (Trio).

WORLD'S GREATEST JAZZBAND. see Haggart, Bob; Lawson, Yank.

WRIGHT, EUGENE JOSEPH (GENE or SENATOR),* *bass*; b. Chicago, Ill., 5/29/23. After working w. Basie, Norvo et al, came to international prominence touring w. Dave Brubeck quartet, '58-68. In '69-70 led own ensemble in concerts at black colleges across the country. Pl. w. Monty Alexander trio, '71-4. In '74-5, maintaining homes in Chicago and Beverly Hills, he divided his time between TV and movie work, a night club season w. Jack Sheldon in Monterey, teaching privately and at schools, and writing. Wright is head of the advisory board in the jazz division of the International Society of Bassists; chairman of jazz department, U. of Cincinnati.

Publ: *Modern Music for Bass* (Hansen Pub. Co. 1824 West Ave., Miami, Fla. 33139). LPs: w. Brubeck (Col.); Monty Alexander (BASF).

WRIGHT, LAMMAR, SR.,* *trumpet*; b. Texarkana, Tex., 6/20/12. Lead trumpeter in the '30s and early '40s w. C.

Calloway, later w. many other bands, incl. D. Redman, Cootie Williams, L. Millinder, Wright died 4/13/73 in NYC. His sons, Lammar Jr. and Elmon, both became trumpeters and pl. w. many name bands from '40s.

WRIGHT LEO NASH,* *alto saxophone, flute, clarinet, piccolo*; b. Wichita Falls, Tex., 12/14/33. Feat. w. Dizzy Gillespie quintet, '59-62; free-lanced in Europe, '63-4, then settled in Berlin for work at clubs such as the Blue Note, Dug's. A member of Radio Free Berlin Studio Band for past decade. Pl. at Pori Fest. in Finland '72. Comp: *Ode to a Blossom*; *Pink Bossa Nova*; *Lee'os Blues*.

LPs: *It's All-Wright* (BASF); *Alto Summit* (MPS).

WRIGHTSMAN, STANLEY (STAN),* *piano*; b. Oklahoma City, Okla., 6/15/10. A veteran of the Ben Pollack and Bob Crosby bands, Wrightsman later was heard in many Dixieland combos in the LA area. He died 12/17/75 in Palm Springs, Cal.

WROBLEWSKI, JAN (PTASZYN),* *tenor saxophone, composer*; b. Kalisz, Poland, 3/27P36. After his debut in '56 w. Krzysztof Komeda sextet, led own gps. incl. Jazz Believers; Polish Jazz Quartet; Mainstream, co-led w. Wojciech Karolak. Was first to mix jazz w. Polish folklore. In '58 he visited U.S. w. Newport Youth Band; then started and led Jazz Studio of Polish Radio which he describes as "half workshop, half orchestra". Infl: Sonny Rollins, Gil Evans. Has app. at most of European fests. TV: reg. apps. w. Jazz Studio orch. on Polish network; other Euro. progs. A former vice-pres. of the Polish Jazz Federation, he served as pres. from '72-5. For six yrs., every Wednesday, has presented a radio show, *3 Quarters of Jazz*. Awards: Golden Cross of Merit from State Council; Poland's 30th Anniversary medal. An arr. & comp. for Polish radio from '57, he has also worked in pop music for radio and the Muza Rec. Co. Comps: *Wariant Warszawski* for Polish Nat. Phil. & Jazz Quartet; *K.K.'s Talkin' to the Band*, third prize in Prague Int. contest for jazz comp., '67. Has written over 100 orchestral works.

LPs: *Polish Jazz Quartet*; *Jazz Studio Orch.*; *Sweet Beat*; *Seaweed Sellers*; *SPPT Chalturnik*; *Mainstream* (Muza); *The Music of Komeda* (Metronome).

WYANDS, RICHARD,* *piano*; b. Oakland, Calif., 7/2/28. After establishing a reputation at local SF & Oak. clubs in '50s, he acc. Ella Fitzgerald, Carmen McRae in mid-'50s. Moved to NYC, '58, where he worked w. Roy Haynes, Mingus, J. Richardson, Gigi Gryce. From the mid-'60s through '74 he traveled extensively w. K. Burrell, pl. clubs in major U.S. cities and coll. concerts. Pl. Ronnie Scott's in London w. Burrell, '69; Japanese tour, '72. He also free-lanced around NYC when not working w. JPJ Quartet, the group he joined in '74. TV: *Tonight Show* w. Burrell; *Contemporary Memorial* (for Robert Kennedy) w. Grady Tate, Joe Williams, CBS. Fests: NJF; Montreux, '69; NJF-NY, '72 w. Burrell. LPs: w. Burrell, *God Bless the Child* (CTI); *Night Song* (Verve); *Up the Street, 'Round the Corner, Down the Block* (Fant.); w. F. Foster, *Manhattan Fever* (Blue Note); w. F. Hubbard, *First Light* (CTI).

WYBLE, JIMMY,* *guitar*; b. Port Arthur, Tex., 1/25/22. Many years in LA pl. studios; toured w. B. Goodman, '60 and again in '63; R. Norvo quintet, '61-2. In '64 he was w. Norvo acc. F. Sinatra in Australia and throughout U.S. From

'65-75 freelanced in LA studios, also app. w. a gp. known as Tony Rizzi Five Guitars Plus Four Play Charlie Christian. Publ: *Classical/Country* (Playback Mus. Publ. Co., P.O. Box 4278, N. Hollywood, Ca. 91607). TV: Five years on Flip Wilson show; Kraft Music Hall; Music Scene etc., for all three networks. Films: *The Wild Bunch*; *Ocean's 11*; *Kings Go Forth*.

LPs: w. Norvo, *Windjammer* (Dot); *Red Norvo Plays The Blues* (RCA); *Naturally* (Rave); w. Goodman, *Swings Again* (Col.); *The Sound of Music* (MGM); *The Swing Era, Into the 70s* (Time/Life).

XIQUES, EDWARD F. JR. (ED), *saxophones, clarinets, flutes*; b. Staten Island, N.Y., 10/9/39. Started by father on soprano sax at age eight; self-taught until Boston U., '57, where he received B.M. degree, '62. During that time worked with local bands incl. J. Byard, H. Pomeroy. To NYC, taught school '62-8; also played with commercial bands such as B. Morrow, Les and Larry Elgart, and freelance jazz work w. Duke Pearson, Chris Swansen's N.Y. Improvisation Ensemble on baritone. Made film, *A Tuesday Afternoon*, w. Swansen. Toured w. W. Herman five months in '70. Joined T. Jones-M. Lewis orch., '71 and was still with this band in '75, but also freelanced in NYC and worked w. Bill Watrous; Ten Wheel Drive. NJF and many European jazz fests., mainly with Jones-Lewis.

LPs: w. Jones-Lewis (Philadelphia Int'l.); *Manhattan Wildlife Refuge*, w. Watrous (Col.); w. Ten Wheel Drive (Cap.).

YAGED, SOLOMON (SOL),* *clarinet*; b. Brooklyn, N.Y., 12/8/22. Vet. of many traditionalist groups at Nick's, Metropole etc., Yaged opened in '66 at the Gaslight Club, NYC, and during next decade his quartet there incl. such sidemen as Ray Nance, who worked with him for four years. He continued to app. frequently on TV telethons and in jazz concerts in N.Y. and other eastern states. John S. Wilson observed in the N.Y. Times that "Yaged for more than 25 years has been a masterful exponent of the Benny Goodman style and manner. He even talks like him and bears a slight resemblance to him."

Three LPs: live at Gaslight Club (Lane).

YAMAKI, KOZABURO, *guitar*; b. Tokyo, Japan, 6/18/31. Pl. w. Yasuki Enoshima & Rhythm Mates at Haneda Officers' Club, '53; own group and Grace Six at US base camps in Tokyo. From '56 concert master of Toshiyuki Miyama's New Herd Orch. Infl: Ellington, Gillespie. Fests: w. Miyama, MJF, '74; NJF-NY, '75. Won Best Player Award at Art

Fest., '70, for *Four Compositions*. Comp: *Furisode*; *Senshuraku*; *Nio To Hato (Nio and Dove)*.

LPs: w. New Herd, *Four Compositions* (Toshiba EMI); *Nio To Hato*; *Tsuchinone or Sound of Earth* (Nippon Col.).

YAMASHITA, YOSUKE, *piano*; b. Tokyo, Japan, 2/26/42. Stud. at Kunitachi Music Univ., '62-7. Pl. w. Terumasa Hino, many other groups in Tokyo during '60s; formed own trio, '69, touring Japan. In '73, traveled throughout Europe with the trio app. at several fests. in West and East Germany and Yugoslavia. Author of many essays for several magazines.

LPs: *Frozen Days* (Crown); *Mina's Second Theme*; *Mokujiki* (Victor); *Yosuke Alone* (King); *Dancing Kojiki* (Maro); *Dedicated to Cassius Clay* (URC).

YELLIN, PETER (PETE), *alto sax, composer*; also *flute, tenor sax, clarinet, bass clarinet*; b. New York City, 7/18/41. Father a pianist and former member of NBC staff. Stud. sax w. Joe Allard; flute w. Harold Bennet; Bachelor's degree from Juilliard. Before he began pl. at age 19, Yellin attended Denver U. on a freshman basketball scholarship. Worked w. Lionel Hampton, '63-6; Buddy Rich, '67; Tito Puente, '68-9; Joe Henderson, '70-3. Fest: NJF-NY w. own group, '73; w. Puente, '74; MJF w. Rich, '68. Infl: Parker, Coltrane, Rollins, M. Davis, Henderson. Comps: *Dance of Allegra*; *Esculynn*; *Bird and the Ouija Board*; *Mebakush*; *Norma*; *Tojo*; *It's the Right Thing*. Awarded grant for comp. from National Endowment for the Arts.

LPs: *Dance of Allegra*; *It's the Right Thing* (Mainstream); *Pursuit of Blackness* w. Henderson (Milestone).

YOUNG, LARRY (Khalid Yasin),* *organ, composer*; also *synthesizer, keyboards*; b. Newark, N.J., 10/7/40. After initial experience w. r&b gps. in late '50s he pl. in '60s w. Lou Donaldson; Grant Green; Elvin Jones; Lee Morgan; and Joe Henderson. In the late '60s and '70s continued to evolve into areas of the avant garde and jazz-rock w. John Coltrane; John McLaughlin; Jimi Hendrix; Tony Williams' Lifetime; and Miles Davis. "Musicians suffer when they do that," he says, referring to limiting oneself to any one particular style of music. "There are so many jazz players who could have really made a major influence on rock, but wouldn't because of their attitude towards it."

Jack McDuff called him "the Coltrane of the organ."

LPs: *Larry Young's Fuel* (Arista); *Lawrence of Newark* (Perception); *Unity* (BN); w. McLaughlin, *Devotion* (Douglas); McLaughlin-Santana, *Love, Devotion and Surrender*; w. Miles Davis, *Bitches Brew* (Col.); w. T. Williams, *Emergency*; *Turn It Over*; *Ego* (Poly.).

YOUNG, EUGENE (SNOOKY),* *trumpet*; b. Dayton, Ohio, 2/3/19. The former J. Lunceford trumpeter joined the NBC staff orch. in '62 and worked on the *Tonight Show*, first under Skitch Henderson, and later Doc Severinsen. During this time, until he left with the show for Cal. in '72, he doubled as a member of the T. Jones-M. Lewis orch., of which he became a founder member in '66.

In Cal., in addition to movie sound track work, Young pl. occasionally w. Gerald Wilson, L. Bellson and others. Along with his *Tonight Show* tenure, he pl. regular gigs throughout the U.S. as a member of Severinsen's Now Generation Brass.

LPs: *Boys From Dayton* (Master Jazz); w. Severinsen

(RCA); D. Axelrod; C. Adderley; K. Burrell (Fant.); Bellson (Pablo); also see Jones-Lewis.

YOUNG, JAMES OSBORNE (TRUMMY),* *trombone, singer*; b. Savannah, Ga., 1/12/12. The former J. Lunceford and L. Armstrong soloist, a resident of Honolulu from mid-'60s, made occasional brief visits to mainland U.S. to record recreations of his early Lunceford hits with the Time-Life orch. under B. May's direction; to app. at Dick Gibson's annual jazz parties in Colorado Springs, and to play a concert, *A Night in New Orleans,* at the Wilshire Ebell theatre in LA. He also app. on a segment of the TV series *Hawaii Five-0* w. Nancy Wilson. Mainly active in the '70s pl. nightly at Sheraton Waikiki Hotel, leading his own group.

LPs: *A Man And His Horn* (Flair Records, 2071 S. Beretania St., Honolulu, Hawaii 96814); *Colorado Jazz Party* (MPS).

ZAPPA, FRANK, *singer, guitar, composer*; b. Baltimore, Md., 12/21/40. As a teenager, lived in the desert in So. Cal., attending Antelope Valley H.S. He was almost entirely self-taught musically. Led a small band in Lancaster in early '60s; formed the Mothers of Invention, '64. The group's first LP was released two years later and Zappa shot to fame as one of the focal figures in a bizarre combination of electronic music, avant garde sounds and visual showmanship. Though not himself a jazz musician, he frequently employed among his sidemen musicians with jazz experience. They included violinists Don (Sugar Cane) Harris and J.L. Ponty; George Duke, elect. keyboards; Bruce Fowler, ex-W. Herman trombonist; Ralph Humphrey, formerly w. Don Ellis on drums; David Parlato on bass. One of Zappa's comps. was entitled *Eric Dolphy Memorial Barbeque.*

LPs: *Hot Rats; Chunga's Revenge* (Repr.); *Waka/Jawaka-Hot Rats Grand Wazoo* (Bizarre); *A-Pos-Tro-Phe; Roxy & Elsewhere Over-Nite Sensation* (DisCreet).

ZAWINUL, JOSEF (JOE),* *piano, keyboards, synthesizer, composer*; also *guitar, oud, electric stick, misc. perc.*; b. Vienna, Austria, 7/7/32. To U.S. 1959. Member of Cannonball Adderley group from '61-70. During this period, in addition to recording with various groups of his own, he played a major role in the success of the Adderley group, as composer of such hits as *Mercy Mercy Mercy,* winner of a Grammy for best instrumental performance, '67. He made four albums with Miles Davis, '69-70: *In A Silent Way,* for which he composed the title number; *Bitches Brew; Live-Evil* and *Big Fun.* In '66 he was a judge at the International Jazz Competition in Vienna. Recorded *Concerto for Two Pianos and Orch.* with F. Gulda. In '71 he was co-founder with W. Shorter of a new group, Weather Report; the other original members were Miroslav Vitous, Alphonse Mouzon and Airto Moreira.

Weather Report was based on a conceptually free musical direction, often involving high energy performances, but capable of great lyricism, ranging from tonality to atonality and from strong bursts of rhythm to free flowing interludes, sometimes characterized as space music.

By '75 Zawinul had composed some 130 works. Among them were *74 Miles Away; Riverbed; Lateef Minor 7th; Midnight Mood; Rumpelstiltskin; Hippodelphia; Walk Tall; Country Preacher; The Scavenger; Newk's Time; Dr. Honoris Causa; Pharaoh's Dance; Orange Lady; Nubian Sundance; Boogie Woogie Walk; Unknown Soldier; Milky Way; American Tango; Scarlet Woman; Between The Thighs; Badia;* also *Experience in E for Symphony Orchestra.*

Living in Pasadena, Cal., Zawinul has to his credit many successful world tours, with Adderley and with Weather Report. The latter won the DB Readers' Poll, '72-3-4. The group's first LP was voted Jazz Album of the Year in '71, and *Mysterious Traveler* was similarly acclaimed in '74. There were many other awards for the group and its records in the U.S., Europe and Japan. Movies: Zawinul appeared with Adderley in *Play Misty For Me;* wrote music for *Pin Striped Dream.* TV: Grammy Award show, '67; Don Kirshner Rock Concert with Weather Report.

Though he has become identified in recent years with a highly sophisticated form of music at a level of abstraction far beyond that of his early years with Adderley, Zawinul has remained an extraordinarily flexible musician. All of his works, including such relatively simple pieces as *Mercy Mercy Mercy,* have validity in their own terms. As a pianist, he has shown exceptional talent in the use of electric keyboards and synthesizer, but without sacrificing a facility for playing acoustic piano solos that show astonishing skill and creativity, still reflecting such early influences as Art Tatum.

LPs: w. Weather Report, *Weather Report; Tale Spinnin'; I Sing The Body Electric; Sweetnighter;* w. Adderley, *Live at Shelly's; Mercy Mercy Mercy; 74 Miles Away; Country Preacher; The Cannonball Adderley Quintet & Orch.,* incl. *Experience In E* suite; *In Person* (Cap.); *Planet Earth* (Riv.); own LPs: *Money in the Pocket; Rise and Fall of Third Stream* (Atl.); w. Gulda (Preiser).

ZEITLIN, DENNIS JAY (DENNY),* *piano, keyboards, synthesizer, composer*; also *bass*; b. Chicago, Ill., 4/10/38. Has had dual career in music and psychiatry. Prominent in jazz in mid-60s, when he recorded for Col., app. at Newport and Monterey JF. In '68, he withdrew from the public scene to devote himself to the study of electronic instruments, multiple keyboards, and a synthesis of rock, jazz and classical idioms. Restricted himself mainly to the SF Bay Area, maintaining his private practice in psychiatry, also serving as assistant clinical prof. of psychiatry at U.C.S.F. Formed own record company, Double Helix, '73. His first LP for this label met with favorable critical response; by '75 Zeitlin had stepped up his concert schedule. Comps: *A Scarf In The Air; El Guego de las Montanas; Deja Vu; Mirage; Dormammu; Quiet Now; Stonehenge; I-Thou; Dodecahedron.*

LPs: *Expansion* (Double Helix, P.O. Box 817, Kentfield, Ca. 94904); *Carnival; Zeitgeist* (Col.).

ZOLLER, ATTILA CORNELIUS,* *guitar*; also *trumpet, bass*; b. Visegrad, Hungary, 6/13/27. Came to U.S., '59 and after pl. w. H. Mann '62-5, organized own quartet for club work in NYC. Pl. w. R. Norvo in NYC, Canada, '66; B.

Goodman and own group, '67. From '60 he has made yearly visits to Europe for concerts, radio, TV and rec. Toured Japan w. Astrud Gilberto, '70, and as part of the Guitar Festival w. Jim Hall, K. Burrell, '71. Own summer prog., *Jazz On The Roof,* incl. weekly clinics and weekend concerts in Vermont, '75. App. at Berlin Jazztage, '73.

In '71 a patent was granted Zoller for the Bidirectional Pick-up Device for guitar and elec. bass. Also invented first magnetic pick-up for vibraharp, manuf. by J.C. Deagan.

LPs: *Gypsy Cry* (Embryo); *A Path Through Haze* w. Masahiko Sato trio; *Katz & Maus,* original film score; w. H. Koller, A. Mangelsdorff, *Zo-Ko-Ma*; Zoller-Koller-Solal (MPS).

ZWEIG, BARRY KENNETH, *guitar*; also *violin*; b. Detroit, Mich., 2/7/42. Stud. theory and violin at N. Hollywood high school, grad. 1960; LA Valley Coll. for two yrs. stud. w. Robert MacDonald, Raphael DeCastro, Jack Gothan, violin; Bud Matlock, Horace Hatchett, Johnny Smith, guitar. first road gig w. Leo Diamond, '61; first jazz gig w. Eddie Miller, Nappy Lamare, Charlie Lodice. Drafted into Army, '64, assigned to World Band in Colorado Springs. Pl. for two years w. Bob Shew and others. Joined Buddy Rich, '66, rec. and traveling with band for eight months. From '66-70 freelancing around LA area; also road tours w. Andy Williams, Henry Mancini et al. With Willie Bobo '70-71. From '75- in John Rodby's orch. on Dinah Shore TV show; also member of John Pisano-Barry Zweig Quintet; Tony Rizzi's Five Guitars. Pl. on sound track of Don Ellis' score of *The French Connection.*

LPs: *Do What you Want To Do,* w. Bobo (Sussex); *The Kid,* w. L. Vinnegar (PBR).

ZWERIN, MICHAEL,* *bass trumpet, journalist*; also *trombone*; b. New York City, 5/18/30. The former sideman w. C. Thornhill, M. Ferguson, who pl. w. the Miles Davis Nonet at 18, toured Russia w. Earl Hines for U.S. State Dept., '66. Jazz columnist for *Village Voice,* '66-9; *Village Voice* European Editor, '69-72; free-lance articles for *Rolling Stone, Penthouse, Village Voice,* '73-5. Zwerin, no longer active musically, has been in Europe since '69. Living in the south of France, '75, writing a novel. Publ: *Silent Sound of Needles,* a book about drug addict rehabilitation (Prentice-Hall, New Jersey); *Little Battalions* (Wildwood House, 1 Wardour St., London, Eng.).

Introduction to poll tabulations

The following tabulations of poll winners are intended to serve as a yardstick of the respective opinions of jazz fans, critics and leading musicians. Their inclusion should not be construed to imply that the musicians listed are necessarily the most important or most successful. They are simply the most popular with these groups of voters.

The *down beat* readers' poll is the oldest and best known of all, having been conducted annually since 1936. The same publication has conducted a poll of experts since 1953, to which in recent years more than 50 critics from all over the world have contributed their votes. In this poll, two winners are elected in each category. The first is designated as "Established Talent"; the second, originally known as the "New Star" category, was modified from 1963 to include "Talent Deserving of Wider Recognition." Results of the *down beat* polls from 1960 through 1965 were published in *The Encyclopedia of Jazz in the Sixties.*

	Down Beat Critics' Poll 1966	*Down Beat Readers' Poll 1966*	*Down Beat Critics' Poll 1967*	*Down Beat Readers' Poll 1967*
Record of the Year	*Ornette Coleman at the Golden Circle, Vol. 1* - Blue Note	*Ornette Coleman at the Golden Circle, Vol. 1* - Blue Note	1. *The Popular Duke Ellington* Duke Ellington - RCA (tie with) 2. *Miles Smiles* Miles Davis - Col.	*Miles Smiles* Miles Davis - Col.
Reissue of the Year	*Golden Years, Vol. 2* Billie Holiday - Col.		*Things Ain't What They Used To Be* Ellington Groups - RCA (Hodges-Stewart)	
Jazzman of the Year		Ornette Coleman		Charles Lloyd
Hall of Fame	Charlie Christian	Bud Powell	Bessie Smith	Billy Strayhorn
Band	Duke Ellington *Thad Jones-Mel Lewis	Duke Ellington	Duke Ellington *Don Ellis	Duke Ellington
Combo	Miles Davis *Denny Zeitlin	Miles Davis	Miles Davis *Charles Lloyd	Miles Davis
Composer	Duke Ellington *Carla Bley	Duke Ellington	Duke Ellington *Herbie Hancock	Duke Ellington
Arranger	Gil Evans *Rod Levitt	Gil Evans	Duke Ellington *Thad Jones	Oliver Nelson
Trumpet	Miles Davis *Ted Curson	Miles Davis	Miles Davis *Jimmy Owens	Miles Davis
Trombone	J. J. Johnson *Buster Cooper	J. J. Johnson	J. J. Johnson *Garnett Brown	J. J. Johnson
Alto Saxophone	Johnny Hodges *John Handy, *John Tchicai (tie)	Paul Desmond	Ornette Coleman *Charles McPherson	Paul Desmond
Tenor Saxophone	John Coltrane *Charles Lloyd	John Coltrane	Sonny Rollins *Joe Henderson	Stan Getz
Baritone Saxophone	Harry Carney *Ronnie Cuber	Gerry Mulligan	Harry Carney *Pepper Adams	Gerry Mulligan
Clarinet	Pee Wee Russell *Edmond Hall	Buddy DeFranco	Pee Wee Russell *Perry Robinson	Buddy DeFranco
Misc. Instrument	Roland Kirk, manzello & strich *Jean-Luc Ponty, violin	Roland Kirk, manzello & strich	Roland Kirk, manzello & strich *Michael White, violin	Roland Kirk, manzello & strich
Flute	Roland Kirk *Charles Lloyd	Herbie Mann	James Moody *Jeremy Steig	Herbie Mann

*Talent deserving of wider recognition

	Down Beat Critics' Poll 1966	Down Beat Readers' Poll 1966	Down Beat Critics' Poll 1967	Down Beat Readers' Poll 1967
Vibes	Milt Jackson *Roy Ayers	Milt Jackson	Milt Jackson *Tommy Vig	Milt Jackson
Piano	Earl Hines *Jaki Byard	Oscar Peterson	Earl Hines *Keith Jarrett	Oscar Peterson
Organ	Jimmy Smith *Larry Young	Jimmy Smith	Jimmy Smith *Don Patterson	Jimmy Smith
Guitar	Wes Montgomery *Rene Thomas	Wes Montgomery	Wes Montgomery *George Benson, Jimmy Raney (tie)	Wes Montgomery
Bass	Charles Mingus *Richard Davis	Ray Brown	Richard Davis *David Izenzon	Ray Brown
Drums	Elvin Jones *Sunny Murray	Elvin Jones	Elvin Jones *Milford Graves	Buddy Rich
Male Singer	Louis Armstrong *Lou Rawls	Frank Sinatra	Louis Armstrong *Richard Boone	Lou Rawls
Female Singer	Ella Fitzgerald *Carol Sloane	Ella Fitzgerald	Ella Fitzgerald *Lorez Alexandria	Ella Fitzgerald
Vocal Group	Double Six of Paris	Double Six of Paris	Beatles *Supremes	†Beatles

	Down Beat Critics' Poll 1968	Down Beat Readers' Poll 1968	Down Beat Critics' Poll 1969	Down Beat Readers' Poll 1969
Record of the Year	Far East Suite - RCA Duke Ellington	Electric Bath - Col. Don Ellis	And His Mother Called Him Bill - Duke Ellington - RCA	Filles De Kilimanjaro Miles Davis - Col.
Reissue of the Year	Hodge Podge - RCA Johnny Hodges		V.S.O.P. Vol 1 Louis Armstrong - Col.	
Jazzman of the Year		Gary Burton		Miles Davis
Hall of Fame	Sidney Bechet, Fats Waller (tie)	Wes Montgomery	Pee Wee Russell, Jack Teagarden (tie)	Ornette Coleman
Band	Duke Ellington *Buddy Rich	Duke Ellington	Duke Ellington *Kenny Clarke- Francy Boland	Duke Ellington
Combo	Miles Davis *Gary Burton	Miles Davis	Miles Davis *Elvin Jones Trio	Miles Davis

*Talent deserving of wider recognition
†Name changed in Readers' Poll to Rock/Pop/Blues Group

	Down Beat Critics' Poll 1968	*Down Beat Readers' Poll* 1968	*Down Beat Critics' Poll* 1969	*Down Beat Readers' Poll* 1969
Composer	Duke Ellington *Wayne Shorter	Duke Ellington	Duke Ellington *Mike Westbrook	Duke Ellington
Arranger	Duke Ellington *Tom McIntosh	Oliver Nelson	Duke Ellington *Francy Boland	Duke Ellington
Trumpet	Miles Davis *Charles Tolliver	Miles Davis	Miles Davis *Randy Brecker	Miles Davis
Trombone	J. J. Johnson *Carl Fontana	J. J. Johnson	J. J. Johnson *Lester Lashley	J. J. Johnson
Alto Saxophone	Johnny Hodges *Sonny Criss	Cannonball Adderley	Johnny Hodges *Lee Konitz	Cannonball Adderley
Soprano Saxophone			Lucky Thompson *John Surman	Joe Farrell
Tenor Saxophone	Sonny Rollins *Joe Farrell	Stan Getz	Sonny Rollins *Albert Ayler	Stan Getz
Baritone Saxophone	Harry Carney *Cecil Payne	Gerry Mulligan	Harry Carney *John Surman	Gerry Mulligan
Clarinet	Pee Wee Russell *Eddie Daniels	Pee Wee Russell	Jimmy Hamilton *Roland Kirk	Jimmy Hamilton
Misc. Instrument	Jean-Luc Ponty, violin *Howard Johnson, tuba	Roland Kirk, manzello, strich	Jean-Luc Ponty, violin *Ray Nance, violin	Roland Kirk, manzello, strich
Flute	James Moody *Hubert Laws	Herbie Mann	James Moody *Joe Farrell	Herbie Mann
Vibes	Milt Jackson *Karl Berger	Gary Burton	Bobby Hutcherson *Red Norvo	Gary Burton
Piano	Bill Evans *Roger Kellaway	Herbie Hancock	Earl Hines *Chick Corea	Herbie Hancock
Organ	Jimmy Smith *Odell Brown, *Eddy Louiss (tie)	Jimmy Smith	Jimmy Smith *Lonnie Smith	Jimmy Smith
Guitar	Kenny Burrell *Larry Coryell	Kenny Burrell	Kenny Burrell *Pat Martino	Kenny Burrell
Bass	Richard Davis *Eddie Gomez	Richard Davis	Richard Davis *Niels-Henning Orsted Pedersen	Richard Davis

*Talent deserving of wider recognition

	Down Beat Critics' Poll 1968	Down Beat Readers' Poll 1968	Down Beat Critics' Poll 1969	Down Beat Readers' Poll 1969
Drums	Elvin Jones *Billy Higgins	Elvin Jones	Elvin Jones *Daniel Humair	Elvin Jones
Male Singer	Louis Armstrong, Ray Charles (tie) *Jimmy Witherspoon	Ray Charles	Ray Charles *Jon Hendricks	Ray Charles
Female Singer	Ella Fitzgerald *Aretha Franklin	Ella Fitzgerald	Ella Fitzgerald *Karin Krog	Ella Fitzgerald
Blues/R&B Group	Muddy Waters *Junior Wells	†Beatles	Muddy Waters *Canned Heat, J. B. Hutto (tie)	†Blood, Sweat & Tears

	Down Beat Critics' Poll 1970	Down Beat Readers' Poll 1970	Down Beat Critics' Poll 1971	Down Beat Readers' Poll 1971
Record of the Year	Bitches' Brew - Col. Miles Davis	Bitches' Brew - Col. Miles Davis	New Orleans Suite - Atlantic Duke Ellington	Weather Report - Col.
Reissue of the Year	Blue Note's Three Decades of Jazz, Vol. 1 - Blue Note		Bessie Smith Series - Col.	
Jazzman of the Year		Miles Davis		Miles Davis
Hall of Fame	Johnny Hodges	Jimi Hendrix	Roy Eldridge, Django Reinhardt (tie)	Charles Mingus
Band	Duke Ellington *Mike Westbrook	Duke Ellington	Duke Ellington *Sun Ra	Duke Ellington
Combo	Miles Davis *Phil Woods	Miles Davis	Miles Davis *Art Ensemble of Chicago	Miles Davis
Composer	Duke Ellington *Mike Gibbs	Duke Ellington	Duke Ellington *Carla Bley	Duke Ellington
Arranger	Duke Ellington *Duke Pearson	Quincy Jones	Duke Ellington *Herbie Hancock	Quincy Jones
Trumpet	Miles Davis *Woody Shaw, Kenny Wheeler (tie)	Miles Davis	Dizzy Gillespie *Roy Eldridge	Miles Davis
Trombone	J. J. Johnson *Malcolm Griffiths, Eje Thelin (tie)	J. J. Johnson	Vic Dickenson *Vic Dickenson, Bill Watrous (tie)	J. J. Johnson

*Talent deserving of wider recognition
†Name changed in Readers' Poll to Rock/Pop/Blues Group

	Down Beat Critics' Poll 1970	Down Beat Readers' Poll 1970	Down Beat Critics' Poll 1971	Down Beat Readers' Poll 1971
Alto Saxophone	Phil Woods *Eric Kloss	Cannonball Adderley	Phil Woods *Frank Strozier	Cannonball Adderley
Soprano Saxophone	Wayne Shorter *Tom Scott	Wayne Shorter	Wayne Shorter *Budd Johnson	Wayne Shorter
Tenor Saxophone	Sonny Rollins *Paul Gonsalves, Pharoah Sanders (tie)	Stan Getz	Dexter Gordon *Harold Ashby	Stan Getz
Baritone Saxophone	Harry Carney *Nick Brignola	Gerry Mulligan	Harry Carney *Pat Patrick	Gerry Mulligan
Clarinet	Russell Procope *Frank Chace, Bob Wilber (tie)	Rahsaan Roland Kirk	Russell Procope *Bob Wilber	Rahsaan Roland Kirk
Misc. Instrument	Jean-Luc Ponty, violin *Stephane Grappelli, violin	Rahsaan Roland Kirk, manzello, strich	Rahsaan Roland Kirk, manzello & strich *Russ Whitman, bass saxophone	Rahsaan Roland Kirk, manzello & strich
Flute	James Moody *Norris Turney	Herbie Mann	James Moody *Norris Turney	Hubert Laws
Vibes	Milt Jackson *Dave Pike	Gary Burton	Bobby Hutcherson *Roy Ayres, Karl Berger (tie)	Gary Burton
Piano	Earl Hines *Stanley Cowell	Herbie Hancock	Earl Hines *Jaki Byard, Tommy Flanagan (tie)	Herbie Hancock
Organ	Jimmy Smith *Lou Bennett	Jimmy Smith	Jimmy Smith *Eddy Louiss	Jimmy Smith
Guitar	Kenny Burrell *Sonny Sharrock	Kenny Burrell	Kenny Burrell *Dennis Budimir	Kenny Burrell
Bass	Richard Davis *Miroslav Vitous	Richard Davis	Richard Davis *Miroslav Vitous	Richard Davis
Drums	Elvin Jones *Jack DeJohnette	Buddy Rich	Elvin Jones *Gus Johnson	Buddy Rich
Violin			Jean-Luc Ponty *Michael White	Jean-Luc Ponty
Male Singer	Louis Armstrong *Leon Thomas	Leon Thomas	Louis Armstrong *Richard Boone	Leon Thomas
Female Singer	Ella Fitzgerald *Jeanne Lee	Ella Fitzgerald	Ella Fitzgerald *Betty Carter	Roberta Flack

*Talent deserving of wider recognition

	Down Beat Critics' Poll 1970	Down Beat Readers' Poll 1970	Down Beat Critics' Poll 1971	Down Beat Readers' Poll 1971
Blues/R&B Group	B. B. King *Ike & Tina Turner	†Blood, Sweat & Tears	B. B. King *Soft Machine	†Blood, Sweat & Tears
Pop Musician of the Year		Frank Zappa		Frank Zappa
Pop Album of the Year		Blood, Sweat & Tears		Chase

	Down Beat Critics' Poll 1972	Down Beat Readers' Poll 1972	Down Beat Critics' Poll 1973	Down Beat Readers' Poll 1973
Record of the Year	The You And Me That Used To Be - RCA Jimmy Rushing	Inner Mounting Flame - Col. Mahavishnu Orchestra	Sahara - Milestone McCoy Tyner	Birds of Fire - Col. Mahavishnu Orchestra
Reissue of the Year	Genius of Louis Armstrong, Vol. 1 - Col.		God Is In The House - Onyx Art Tatum	
Jazzman of the Year		Ornette Coleman		Chick Corea
Hall of Fame	Clifford Brown	Gene Krupa	Fletcher Henderson	Sonny Rollins
Band	Duke Ellington *Sun Ra	Thad Jones/Mel Lewis	Duke Ellington *Gil Evans	Thad Jones/Mel Lewis
Combo	World's Greatest Jazz Band *JPJ Quartet	Weather Report	Mahavishnu Orchestra *Art Ensemble of Chicago	Weather Report
Composer	Duke Ellington *Carla Bley	Duke Ellington	Duke Ellington *Chick Corea	Chick Corea
Arranger	Duke Ellington *Alan Broadbent	Quincy Jones	Duke Ellington *Sy Oliver	Quincy Jones
Trumpet	Dizzy Gillespie *Lester Bowie	Miles Davis	Dizzy Gillespie *Bill Hardman	Freddie Hubbard
Trombone	Vic Dickenson *Bill Watrous	J. J. Johnson	Vic Dickenson *Dicky Wells	J. J. Johnson
Alto Saxophone	Ornette Coleman *Gary Bartz	Ornette Coleman	Ornette Coleman *Anthony Braxton	Ornette Coleman
Soprano Saxophone	Wayne Shorter *Joseph Jarman	Wayne Shorter	Wayne Shorter *Kenny Davern	Wayne Shorter
Tenor Saxophone	Sonny Rollins *Gato Barbieri	Sonny Rollins	Sonny Rollins *John Klemmer	Sonny Rollins

*Talent deserving of wider recognition
†Name changed in Readers' Poll to Rock/Pop/Blues Group

POLL TABULATIONS

	Down Beat Critics' Poll 1972	*Down Beat Readers' Poll 1972*	*Down Beat Critics' Poll 1973*	*Down Beat Readers' Poll 1973*
Baritone Saxophone	Harry Carney *Ronnie Cuber	Gerry Mulligan	Harry Carney *Howard Johnson	Gerry Mulligan
Clarinet	Russell Procope *Bob Wilber	Rahsaan Roland Kirk	Russell Procope *Bobby Jones	Benny Goodman
Misc. Instrument	Rahsaan Roland Kirk manzello & strich *Airto Moreira, percussion	Rahsaan Roland Kirk, manzello & strich	Rahsaan Roland Kirk, manzello & strich *Howard Johnson, tuba	Rahsaan Roland Kirk, manzello, strich
Flute	James Moody *Norris Turney	Hubert Laws	James Moody *Jeremy Steig	Hubert Laws
Vibes	Gary Burton *Roy Ayers	Gary Burton	Milt Jackson *David Friedman	Gary Burton
Piano	Earl Hines *Randy Weston	Oscar Peterson	Earl Hines *Jan Hammer	Chick Corea
Organ	Jimmy Smith *Eddy Louiss	Jimmy Smith	Jimmy Smith *Eddy Louiss	Jimmy Smith
Guitar	Kenny Burrell *Tiny Grimes, Pat Martino (tie)	John McLaughlin	Kenny Burrell *George Benson, Attila Zoller (tie)	John McLaughlin
Bass	Richard Davis *Dave Holland	Richard Davis	Richard Davis *Stanley Clarke	Ron Carter
Drums	Elvin Jones *Harold Jones	Buddy Rich	Elvin Jones *Oliver Jackson	Billy Cobham
Violin	Jean-Luc Ponty *Mike White	Jean-Luc Ponty	Jean-Luc Ponty *Mike White	Jean-Luc Ponty
Male Singer	Jimmy Rushing *Richard Boone	Leon Thomas	Ray Charles *Joe Lee Wilson	Leon Thomas
Female Singer	Ella Fitzgerald *Dee Dee Bridgewater, Asha Puthli (tie)	Roberta Flack	Sarah Vaughan *Anita O'Day	Roberta Flack
Blues/R&B Group	B. B. King *Mahavishnu Orchestra	†Mahavishnu Orchestra	B. B. King *War	†Mahavishnu Orchestra
Pop Musician of the Year		Frank Zappa		Stevie Wonder
Pop Album of the Year		*Inner Mounting Flame* Mahavishnu Orchestra		*Birds of Fire* Mahavishnu Orchestra

*Talent deserving of wider recognition
†Name changed in Readers' Poll to Rock/Pop/Blues Group

	Down Beat Critics' Poll 1974	Down Beat Readers' Poll 1974	Down Beat Critics' Poll 1975	Down Beat Readers' Poll 1975
Record of the Year	Solo Concerts - ECM/Poly. Keith Jarrett	Mysterious Traveller - Col. Weather Report	Silent Tongues - Arista/ Freedom Cecil Taylor	Tale Spinning - Columbia Weather Report
Reissue of the year	Monk/Trane - Milestone Thelonious Monk/John Coltrane		1. First Recordings - Onyx Charlie Parker (tie with) 2. Solo Masterpieces - Pablo Art Tatum	
Jazzman of the Year		Herbie Hancock		McCoy Tyner
Hall of Fame	Ben Webster	Buddy Rich	Cecil Taylor	Cannonball Adderley
Band	Thad Jones/Mel Lewis *Gil Evans	Thad Jones/Mel Lewis	Thad Jones/Mel Lewis *Clark Terry	Thad Jones/Mel Lewis
Combo	McCoy Tyner *Ruby Braff-George Barnes Quartet	Weather Report	McCoy Tyner *Oregon	Weather Report
Composer	Duke Ellington *McCoy Tyner	Chick Corea	Keith Jarrett *Randy Weston	Chick Corea
Arranger	Gil Evans *Bill Stapleton	Gil Evans	Gil Evans *Michael Gibbs	Gil Evans
Trumpet	Dizzy Gillespie *Jon Faddis	Freddie Hubbard	Dizzy Gillespie *Jon Faddis	Miles Davis
Trombone	Vic Dickenson *Garnett Brown	Garnett Brown	Roswell Rudd *Bruce Fowler	Bill Watrous
Alto Saxophone	Ornette Coleman *Anthony Braxton	Ornette Coleman	Phil Woods *Sonny Fortune	Phil Woods
Soprano Saxophone	Wayne Shorter *Gerry Niewood	Wayne Shorter	Wayne Shorter *Gerry Niewood	Wayne Shorter
Tenor Saxophone	Sonny Rollins *Billy Harper	Sonny Rollins	Sonny Rollins *Billy Harper	Sonny Rollins
Baritone Saxophone	Gerry Mulligan *Howard Johnson	Gerry Mulligan	Gerry Mulligan *John Surman, Pat Patrick (tie)	Gerry Mulligan
Clarinet	Rahsaan Roland Kirk *Kalaparusha Ara Difda	Rahsaan Roland Kirk	Rahsaan Roland Kirk *Perry Robinson	Rahsaan Roland Kirk
Misc. Instrument	Rahsaan Roland Kirk, manzello & strich *Howard Johnson, tuba	Rahsaan Roland Kirk, manzello & strich	Rahsaan Roland Kirk, manzello & strich *Howard Johnson, tuba	Rahsaan Roland Kirk, manzello & strich
Flute	James Moody *Jeremy Steig	Hubert Laws	Hubert Laws *Sam Rivers	Hubert Laws

POLL TABULATIONS

	Down Beat Critics' Poll 1974	Down Beat Readers' Poll 1974	Down Beat Critics' Poll 1975	Down Beat Readers' Poll 1975
Vibes	Gary Burton	Gary Burton *Karl Berger	Gary Burton *Karl Berger, Dave Friedman (tie)	Gary Burton
Piano	McCoy Tyner	Keith Jarrett, McCoy Tyner (tie) *Muhal Richard Abrams	Keith Jarrett *Dollar Brand	McCoy Tyner
Electric Piano				Chick Corea
Organ	Jimmy Smith *Clare Fischer, Eddy Louiss (tie)	Jimmy Smith	Jimmy Smith *Sun Ra	Jimmy Smith
Guitar	Jim Hall *Ralph Towner	John McLaughlin	Joe Pass *John Abercrombie	Joe Pass
Violin	Jean-Luc Ponty *Leroy Jenkins	Jean-Luc Ponty	Jean-Luc Ponty *Michal Urbaniak	Jean-Luc Ponty
Acoustic Bass	Richard Davis *Stanley Clarke	Ron Carter	Ron Carter *George Mraz	Ron Carter
Electric Bass	Stanley Clarke *Stanley Clarke	Stanley Clarke	Stanley Clarke *Steve Swallow	Stanley Clarke
Drums	Elvin Jones *Billy Hart	Billy Cobham	Elvin Jones *Billy Higgins	Billy Cobham
Synthesizer	Jan Hammer, Paul Bley (tie) *Mike Mandel	Herbie Hancock	Sun Ra *George Duke	Herbie Hancock
Percussion	Airto *Dom Um Romao	Airto	Airto Moreira *Sue Evans	Airto
Male Singer	Joe Williams *Roy Eldridge, Stevie Wonder (tie)	Stevie Wonder	Joe Williams *Eddie Jefferson	Stevie Wonder
Female Singer	Ella Fitzgerald *Flora Purim	Flora Purim	Sarah Vaughan *Dee Dee Bridgewater	Flora Purim
Blues/R&B Group	B. B. King *Jimmy Dawkins	†Frank Zappa and the Mothers of Invention	†B. B. King *Blackbyrds, Otis Rush (tie)	Earth-Wind-Fire
Vocal Group	Pointer Sisters *Pointer Sisters	Pointer Sisters	Jackie & Roy *Jackie & Roy	Pointer Sisters
Pop Musician of the Year		Stevie Wonder		Stevie Wonder
Pop Album of the Year		*Fulfillingness'* First Finale - Tamla		*Blow by Blow* - Epic Jeff Beck

*Talent deserving of wider recognition
†Name changed in Readers' Poll to Rock/Pop/Blues Group

During the decade from 1965-75 the Japanese jazz community emerged as the most important in the world, after that of the United States, in terms of the per capita interest in the music, the variety of idioms appealing to the Japanese public, and the quantity and quality of work opportunities for visiting American musicians.

The importance of Japan on the world scene, and the constantly evolving nature of interest at the fan level, is reflected in the annual polls conducted by *Swing Journal*. This Tokyo-based publication, published monthly, often runs to 350 or 400 pages, elaborately produced and with many full pages photographs in color and black and white, as well as many in depth interviews and record reviews.

The following tabulation shows the results of the *Swing Journal* readers' poll from the first, in 1960, through the 1975 poll.

Note: A dash means that this category had not yet been established. Ditto indicates that the winner was the same as the previous year.

Year	Jazz Man of Year	Hall of Fame	Record of The Year	Big Band	Combo	Trumpet	Trombone	Soprano	Alto	Tenor	Baritone	Clarinet
'60	————	——	————	C. Basie	MJQ	M. Davis	J.J. Johnson	——	C. Adderley	S. Rollins	G. Mulligan	B. DeFranco
'61	————	——	————	"	"	"	"	——	"	J. Coltrane	"	J. Giuffre
'62	————	——	————	"	M. Davis	"	"	——	"	S. Rollins	"	"
'63	————	——	————	"	"	"	"	——	"	"	"	"
'64	————	——	————	D. Ellington	O. Peterson	"	"	——	"	J. Coltrane	"	"
'65	————	——	————	"	Jazz Messengers	"	"	——	"	"	"	"
'66	J. Coltrane	——	A Love Supreme/ J. Coltrane	"	M. Davis	"	"	——	"	"	"	"
'67	O. Coleman	——	Alfie/S. Rollins	"	"	"	"	——	O. Coleman	"	"	B. DeFranco
'68	C. Lloyd	——	Miles in Berlin	"	"	"	"	——	"	S. Rollins	"	P.W. Russell
'69	M. Davis	——	Filles De Kilimanjaro/Miles Davis	"	"	"	"	——	"	"	"	B. DeFranco
'70	"	——	Bitches Brew/ Miles Davis	"	"	"	"	——	"	"	"	"
'71	"	——	Left Alone/ Mal Waldron	"	"	"	"	——	"	"	"	"
'72	C. Corea	——	Chick Corea Solo vol. 1	"	Weather Report	"	"	——	"	"	"	B. Goodman
'73	M. Davis	——	Miles Davis in Concert	Q. Jones	M. Davis	"	"	W. Shorter	P. Woods	"	"	"
'74	M. Tyner	——	Headhunters/ H. Hancock	Thad-Mel Orch.	M. Tyner	"	"	"	S. Stitt	"	"	"
'75	M. Davis	C. Parker	Death & The Flower/K. Jarrett	"	"	"	"	"	"	"	"	"

Flute	Piano	Organ	Vibes	Guitar	Bass	Drums	Misc. Instrument	Male Singer	Female Singer	Vocal Group	Composer, Arranger
B. Shank	T. Monk	——	M. Jackson	B. Kessel	P. Chambers	M. Roach	M. Davis	F. Sinatra	C. Connor	LH&R	B. Golson
H. Mann	"	——	"	W. Montgomery	"	"	"	"	E. Fitzgerald	"	"
E Dolphy	"	——	"	"	"	"	J. Coltrane	"	"	"	G. Evans
H. Mann	"	——	"	"	R. Brown	A. Blakey	"	R. Charles	"	"	"
"	O. Peterson	——	"	"	"	M. Roach	"	"	"	Four Freshmen	D. Ellington
"	"	——	"	"	C. Mingus	"	"	"	"	"	"
"	"	J. Smith	"	"	R. Brown	E. Jones	"	M. Torme	"	"	"
"	B. Evans	"	"	"	"	"	"	"	"	Swingle Singers	"
C. Lloyd	"	"	"	"	R. Carter	M. Roach	R. Shankar	R. Charles	"	"	
H. Mann	"	"	G. Burton	K. Burrell	"	E. Jones	O. Coleman	"	N. Wilson	Sound of Feeling	"
"	"	"	M. Jackson	"	"	"	"	"	"	Swingle Singers	
"	"	"	"	"	R. Davis	"	"	"	"	"	"
H. Laws	C. Corea	"	"	"	M. Vitous	"	W. Shorter	M. Torme	"	"	G. Evans
"	M. Tyner	"	"	J. McLaughlin	S. Clarke	"	A. Moreira	J. Hartman	E. Fitzgerald	"	Q. Jones
"	"	"	G. Burton	K. Burrell	R. Carter	"	"	F. Sinatra	"	Pointer Sisters	G. Evans
"	K. Jarrett	"	M. Jackson	J. Pass	"	"	Mtume	"	"	"	"

Jazz education by Charles Suber

"Jazz Education"—the term implies estrangement from traditional and established "Music Education." The implication is historically accurate.

For all of its considerable current academic status, Jazz Education is not yet considered—by those who determine such matters—an essential part of the musical training *required* by teachers and student musicians. This determination is reflected in the widespread use—in school curricula and echoed by mass media—of such elitist characterizations of European music as "serious" or "good" or "classical" music. Jazz and blues—synonomous terms in the context of this essay—are too often characterized by educational pejorative expressions, such as "popular" or "commercial" or "youth" music.

Jazz Education seems to be, like jazz, a shade too popular, a shade too dark and common to warrant complete integration into the Music Education club.

Then, why—in the face of the schools' unofficial policy of benign neglect—does Jazz Education continue to flourish in isolation? The reasons become clearer as one understands how jazz musicians have learned and developed their art—and their profession—in the past 50 years.

Jazz Education in the Twenties

Take as an arbitrary starting time the twenties and the widening distribution of recorded jazz. Recordings were the first jazz textbooks. Early recordings, regardless of their sound quality, enabled a musician to listen—and thereby study and emulate—another musician's non-written music. Recordings helped to establish the first recognizable elements of a jazz style to which the eager-to-learn musician could add his own individuality.

There were no schools in which a musician could learn—or even hear—jazz. But there were private legit teachers from whom the professional jazz musician could learn advanced instrumental techniques and how to read and write music—skills needed to be competitive in the new music business of recording the first Jazz Age.

School Music in the Twenties

There was a sharp escalation in the number of high school concert and marching bands throughout the U.S. after World War I. The rapid growth of the new school instrumental music was principally motivated by non-academic considerations: larger, consolidated schools fostered by better roads and auto transportation; increased popularity of inter-scholastic football competition; the need to replace music in the community disrupted by WWI—and the availability of professional musicians capable of developing and conducting school bands.

These professional musicians were well schooled players (but not degreed graduates of college music departments) who had been employed in the community bands-in-the-park so popular prior to WWI. Many of these musicians served in military bands during the war and returned to their communities to find a changed professional music market.

People listened to music at home on their new radios and Victrolas. Or they could go out in their new cars and travel on new roads to be entertained at the new Movie Palace. Or they could dance the new steps at the new ballroom or live it up at the new Roadhouse outside of town featuring prohibited gin and wicked jazz.

So, the professional bandsman did what he knew best; he organized and conducted the new school band, gave private lessons to students recommended by the local instrument dealer, and gave band clinics for a band instrument manufacturer—and adapted military band formations to between-the-half marching band shows. He used published Sousa marches and arranged orchestral repertory for student band training. Specially written symphonic school band literature started to become available by 1926-27, the apogee years for regional and national school band contests. The school band director had a lot of music going on, but he was not yet considered a bona fide Music Educator by the traditional orchestra and voice faculty.

Jazz Education in the Thirties

New musical and commercial challenges faced professional musicians in the thirties. Elements of jazz and blues were being incorporated into the popular swing/dance bands and the scores of Broadway and movie musicals. Something new called "Symphonic Jazz" had appeared by the American Composers, George Gershwin and Ferde Grofe—following the lead of European composers such as Ravel, Milhaud, and Stravinsky.

The beginnings of a "studio musician" standard of performance emerged as radio stations hired staff orchestras, the members of which had to be expert in all idioms. (In 1938, for example, Toscanini thought it necessary to hire several brass players with jazz capabilities in the newly formed N.B.C. Symphony.)

(Radio sponsored music was a mixed blessing to the economic well being of the professional musician. "Live" musicians found themselves competing with recordings played on radio without royalty payments to the musicians. The thousands of territory and name bands musicians who played on "remote" broadcasts from hotels and ballrooms were paid little or nothing for their performance.)

Obviously, the ambitious professional musician had to learn new skills to compete in the new job market. The "hot" jazz musician had to learn legit techniques; the legit player had to learn jazz techniques. But just playing was not enough. The most important element of the big swing and dance bands was the arranger. The real big money was in composing music—and holding the copyrights!

Where could these professional musicians learn their trade? There still weren't any schools offering anything like jazz education even though a considerable number of leaders and arrangers did come out of college with a good legit musical education and plenty of campus dance band experience.

(Fletcher and Horace Henderson came out of Wilberforce; Jimmie Lunceford from Fisk, and Erskine Hawkins from 'Bama State. Fred Waring was a Pennsylvanian, and Glen Gray and several Casa Lomans came from Illinois Wesleyan. Johnny Green wore Harvard Crimson, and Les Brown was a Duke Blue Devil.)

The only source of jazz education in the thirties was the private teacher. Many good teachers were available in all the major music cities such as New York, Boston, Philadelphia, Chicago, Detroit, New Orleans, Houston, Denver, and Los Angeles.

Norbert Beihoff, a Milwaukee teacher, was one of the first to explain techniques of jazz improvisation as part of his text, *Modern Arranging and Orchestration*, published in 1935. The following year, two Chicago musicians, Carl Kelley and Russell Brooks, began to teach their system of learning improvisation based on a knowledge of chord structures, passing tones, and blue notes—transcribed from jazz recordings.

The demand by musicians to know more about the business of swing and jazz prompted the initial publication of *down beat* in Chicago in 1934. Its early success helped in-fluence *Metronome*, a New York based magazine for concert band and orchestra musicians since 1897 to change its editorial emphasis to swing and jazz in 1935.

Almost from its first issue, *down beat* published regular columns on various components of jazz education: Arranging by Will Hudson and others; Improvisation and jazz piano stylistic analysis by Sharon Pease; Modern saxophone studies by Dave Gornston; and other instrumental columns . . . as well as transcribed solos of jazz soloists: Coleman Hawkins, Bix Beiderbecke, Harry James, Jack Teagarden, et al.

Paul Eduard Miller wrote and compiled *down beat*'s first *Yearbook of Swing* in 1938. It carried articles on improvisation, arranging and composition, and jazz styles and analysis.

Non-teaching professionals were offering insights to their jazz playing in such method booklets as: *The Gene Krupa Drum Method, Frank Trumbauer's Saxophone Studies,* and *Eddie Lang's Fingerboard Harmony for Guitar.*

While recordings continued to be an important source of study for the aspiring jazz musician, the original recorded arrangements and solo transcriptions became available. Also available were "Acompo Records" that provided "full orchestra accompaniment"—tunes like *I Got Rhythm, Limehouse Blues, Tiger Rag,* etc.—to which the student musician would play along on his own instrument.

The most important influence on professionally oriented jazz education in the thirties was Joseph Schillinger, a brilliant music theorist and teacher, who came to New York City from Russia in 1928.

Schillinger's unique concepts, later embodied in *The Schillinger System of Musical Composition* (Carl Fisher, N.Y., 1941), sharply varied from traditional Conservatory teaching methods. The Schillinger system allowed composers, for the first time, mathematically exact rules that could be used to adapt any component of music—rhythm, harmony, density, counterpoint, etc.—from any musical idiom to jazz-related composition. The system also allowed jazz players to develop their improvisations (spontaneous compositions) along certain, predetermined paths.

Commercial arrangers have said that the best thing about the Schillinger system was that the chart practically wrote itself. You found the melody line, applied the proper mathematical formula, wrote out the notes, and voilá, you met the deadline.

Some of Schillinger's best known students included George Gershwin; Oscar Levant; Benny Goodman; Paul Lavalle; Max Steiner, who paid $5000 for a set of Schillinger's personal notebooks; also Van Alexander and Glenn Miller, who both wrote arranging method books based on the Schillinger system.

Even though Schillinger did teach at several schools in New York—he was asked to leave Teachers' College, Columbia University, for being too far out—his forte was private teaching for which he charged $15 a lesson (show or not).

Schillinger's influence on professional jazz musicians didn't stop with his death in 1943. The Schillinger system as modified and evolved by his students—and coupled with the educational funding supplied by the G.I. Bill—was a major factor in jazz education in the forties and beyond.

School Music in the Thirties

The WWI "war babies" began to enter high school in large numbers in the early thirties. The first crop of college trained instrumental specialists began to enter high school teaching about the same time. High school school administrators were beginning to insist that school band directors be qualified and certificated music educators. State universities and other teacher training schools obliged by making "band" a required subject of study for music education majors.

By the end of the thirties, high school and symphonic college bands were capable of playing a sophisticated repertory. "Pep" bands, with a somewhat smaller instrumentation, would play swing music, or something akin to it, at indoor rallies and basketball games. Virtually every college campus—and many high schools—had at least one student dance band to play for school affairs not prestigous enough to warrant a name band.

Many college dance band leaders went on to the professional big time. A larger number of them played their way through college in order to pay for their education as a doctor, lawyer, engineer, or whatever. (And most of them still carry their musicians' union card.)

But while student musicians were able to swing on campus—or in high school gyms—it was all very extra-curricular. School music departments didn't recognize jazz.

Jazz Education in the Forties

World War II affected everything and everybody. Citizen soldiers, musicians among them, began to be drafted in 1940. Soon every service camp, base, and capital ship had its resident military and dance/jazz bands. (And the black Americans had theirs, and the white Americans had theirs, and the Nisei had none.) The Navy School of Music went so far as to include swing and jazz in their wartime training procedures.

In 1944, the U.S. Congress enacted a piece of legislation that was to allow hundreds of thousands of servicemen to complete and further their education after discharge: The Servicemen's Readjustment Act—the G.I. Bill of Rights.

On the home front, anybody who could lick a reed was a working musician. There wasn't much time or incentive to upgrade one's musical capabilities.

The worldwide facilities of Armed Service Radio broadcast a lot of jazz and swing via transcriptions and records. (So did Tokyo Rose.) Jazz and swing were part of the American dream for which our boys were fighting.

In 1943, Dr. Leopold Stokowski did 50 minutes on KFAC, Los Angeles, on the virtues of jazz. Stokowski said: "Jazz is a vitally important part of our folk music and folk lore. It has no traditions—no limitations—and it will go on forever developing as long as musicians give free rein to their imagination. Jazz is unique—there's never been anything like it. In this kind of music, the United States is second to none in the whole world . . . Duke

Ellington is, in my opinion, one of America's outstanding artists. Ellington's music never imitates the symphony. It seems simple, but it is actually music of great subtlety. His men play as though they were creating the music at the moment by way of freedom of improvisation."

Shortly after Paris fell to the allies, Gertrude Stein was quoted at a Glenn Miller memorial concert: "Jazz is tenderness and violence." Miss Toklas had no comment.

Then rather suddenly the war was over in August, 1945. And the job hunt was on.

Most of the ex-G.I.s who elected to study privately intended to find work as professional players or writers. However, the largest number of returning musicians used the G.I. Bill to finance a college music education degree. (Example: 22-year old Mel Powell, a former pianist with Benny Goodman, came out of an army special service unit in 1945 and headed for Yale to study with Hindemith. Eventually, Powell became Dean of the School of Music, California Institute of the Arts, Valencia.)

College music departments expanded rapidly but the curricula remained pre-war traditional. By the end of the forties, ten colleges were offering jazz courses on a non-credit basis. Only five colleges offered jazz for credit: 1945—Berklee School of Music, then known as Schillinger House (2-year Professional Diploma), Lawrence Berk, director; 1945—Westlake College of Music (2-year Professional Diploma), Alvin Learned, director; 1946—Los Angeles City College (2-year Academic Diploma), Bob McDonald, director; 1947—California State Polytechnic (details not available); 1948—North Texas State College (4-year "Dance Band Major"), M.E. "Gene" Hall, director.

Documentation on high school jazz activities in the forties is sketchy but excerpts from *down beat* provide some clues.

Feb. 15, 1944—"Dr. J.T.H. Mize, head of the music department of the Rye (N.Y.) High School, edits a weekly mimeographed publication, *American Music and Jazz*, distributed to 180 high schools in the country. His book—*Let's Listen—A Thesaurus of American Music*, is a practical guide to teachers and students who want to know about jazz and other music forms. Mize has lectured on 'Jazz in the Classroom' at Yale, Penn State, College of New Rochelle, and U. of Conn."

March 11, 1946—"A recent 'Swing in School' concert by 80 Nassau High School Students was batoned by Long Beach music supervisor, Glenn E. Brown, at Town Hall [N.Y.C.]. The student concert band made a valiant effort in performing Fred Waring and Robert Shaw choral arrangements plus Will Hudson's scoring of Kenton's *Artistry Jumps*. Because the high school's principal didn't authorize this activity, the participating students had to cut classes to make the concert."

There was no shortage of private teachers and studios offering jazz-related music education. Many of the teachers were authorized Regional Representatives of the Schillinger system, such as Maury Deutsch and Rudolf Schramm, Clarence Cox in Philadelphia, and Lawrence Berk in Boston. (Of all the Schillinger alumni, Berk was the most successful in integrating a complete jazz program within a total music curriculum. In 1976, the Berklee College of Music was a fully accredited 4-year college with more than 2200 full time students.)

Not all the private jazz teaching was Schillingerized. In 1945-46, Charlie Colin's New York studio offered "Advance Dance Studies"; Phil Moore was teaching arranging and coaching the likes of Lena Horne; Walter "Foots" Thomas, former Cab Calloway saxophonist, offered a correspondence course in improvisation. Otto Cesana invited musicians to "Study Arranging" at his N.Y. studio or by correspondence.

In the second half of the forties, as paper supplies and copyists became more plentiful, a considerable amount of jazz study materials were published: Van Alexander's *First Arrangement; 30 Studies in Swing* by David Gornston; and "Jam at Home" rhythm records with Nick Fatool, ʾrums, George Van Eps, guitar; Stan Wrightsman, piano; .nd Phil Stephens, bass . . . Frank Skinner's *New Method for Orchestra Scoring* . . . Artie Shaw's *Special Arrangements for Small Orchestra* distributed by the Intercollegiate Syndicate . . . *88 Keys to Fame* by Sharon Pease, "an examination of the styles of 30 jazz pianists, with bios and photos, reprinted from earlier issues of *down beat* (*down beat* was featuring Coleman Hawkins' solos: *I Cover the Waterfront, When Day is Done,* (the immortal) *Body & Soul,* etc.).

March 11, 1946: "Station WOV gives Jazz Scholarship —open to all high school and college students in the NY metropolitan area. Idea of the scholarship is to promote the serious study of jazz by young people gifted in that direction. First place prize: 14 intensive private lessons under Teddy Wilson."

May 6, 1946: "The Carver Club of U.C.L.A. presented a jazz scholarship benefit concert on behalf of improved race relations. Talent donating their services included: Herb Jeffries, emcee; Lester Young, King Cole Trio, Benny Carter, Ray Bauduc, and Red Callender.

Leonard Feather, Robert Goffin and Marshall Stearns lectured on jazz history and development in 1941 at the New School for Social Research.

Jazz Education in the Fifties

The cut off date to apply for G.I. Bill benefits was July 25, 1951, so many schools placed "Hurry, hurry!" ads: Roy Knapp advertised his Chicago School of Percussion as "the oldest yet most modern school of music in America—all instruments—study vibes and improvisation with Margie Hyams" . . . New York's Hartnett Music Studios offered Schillinger system lessons with Sam Donahue and Bobby Byrne on the faculty . . . Rudolf Schramm offered a special 15 week Schillinger system course at New York University . . . Westlake College of Music (Hollywood) advised that "students, including veterans, are trained for professional job demands rather than public school positions."

The first jazz-in-the-summer seminars were begun in 1950 by Marshall Stearns at the Music Inn, Lenox, Mass.

("next door to Tanglewood"). The 1951 session included author-critic, Rudi Blesh; Juilliard piano and improvisation instructor, John Mehegan; ragtime musician and composer, Eubie Blake; and American theater composers, Marc Blitzstein and Leonard Bernstein. Quote of the week: ". . . to keep your musical arteries from hardening, do not label your favorite period as the only true jazz."

About 30 more colleges added jazz courses, on a noncredit basis, during the fifties. About 17 more colleges added jazz courses for credit bringing the national total to about 21. The colleges were not yet responding to the growing demand by high school administrators for new music educators to have stage band experience.

The stage band movement in high school was accelerating in a pattern quite similar to the rapid growth of school concert bands after WWI. The G.I. Bill music education majors were now out teaching in high schools. And like the ex-World War I bandsmen, the WWII veteran did what he knew best. He conducted the required marching and concert bands, but also organized a stage band (a euphemism coined in the Baptist southwest to avoid the sinful aspects of dancing and jazzing) to play *his* music.

This new breed of high school band director knew the advantages of jazz or swing music: greater motivation on the part of the player, increased technical facility in another idiom, increased responsibility for one's part; and more opportunity for individual creativity. The school stage band director did have a major personal advantage over the concert band director. The younger man (and some women) could continue to play on weekends and thereby keep *au courant* with professional standards of performance.

At first, he had difficulty getting arrangements suitable for school swing bands. So he used his professional experience to arrange published stocks. The first charts specially written for school stage bands were published and arranged by Art Dedrick, Kendor Music, Delevan, N.Y. Dedrick published the first set of four tunes in 1954: *Little Brown Jug; Tuxedo Junction; Brown Jump;* and *The Preacher.* In 1955, Dedrick arranged, under a license from Mills Music, school stage band charts of Ellington's *Mood Indigo;* and *Sophisticated Lady.* In 1956, Sammy Nestico, arranger for the Airmen of Note (the official stage band of the U.S. Air Force) began his long association with Kendor, writing mostly Basie-type arrangements.

Dedrick never did study directly with Schillinger (said he couldn't afford the lessons) but he did use Schillinger's book as a basis for his own writing. Art Dedrick's brother, Rusty, and many other New York players and writers studied with a Tom Timothy who had developed a successful modification of the Schillinger system in the late forties.

Other professional arrangers turning out school stage band material during the late fifties included Marshall Brown (his Farmingdale High School Stage Band wowed them at the Newport Jazz Festival in 1957); Neal Hefti with deceptively simple Basie arrangements of *Li'l Darlin'; Sunday A.M.; Cute;* and *The Kid From Red Bank;* Clem DeRosa, a professional drummer who had organized elementary and junior high school students into stage bands; John LaPorta, a former arranger and reed player with Woody Herman; and Ralph Mutchler, whose Northwestern University Jazz Band won first place in the first Notre Dame Intercollegiate Jazz Festival in 1959.

Accompanying the rapid proliferation of high school stage bands were regional high school stage band festivals. (See section on School Jazz Festivals at the end of this chapter.)

Another indication of the interest in school type jazz, was the beginning of the National Stage Band Camps by Ken Morris in 1959 on the campus of Indiana University.

On the faculty of that first stage band camp were many of the pioneer jazz clinicians who were to bring their professional standards to schools throughout the U.S. The faculty included: Stan Kenton, rehearsal techniques; Russ Garcia, arranging; Shelly Manne, drums; Laurindo Almeida, guitar; Don Jacoby, trumpet; Eddie Safranski, bass; Ray Santisi, piano; Matt Betton, theory and pedagogy; and Gene Hall, director and author of curriculum.

Jazz Education in the Sixties

The jazz education activity that began after WWII and quickened in the fifties, emerged in the sixties as a strong force in school music.

In 1960, there were about 5000 high schools in the U.S. with at least one organized "stage band" under the direction of a school music specialist. Most of these bands were not part of the formal school music curriculum but were usually considered a "reward" activity in which students from the concert band or orchestra could participate on the basis of demonstrated deportment, interest, and ability. These stage bands, however, did not admit additional students into school music—a fact that was to become a latent problem of the seventies.

By the end of the sixties, the number of high school stage bands—by then more often called "jazz" bands—doubled to about 10,000. (Actually, there were about 8500 junior and senior high schools with jazz related bands with the more experienced educators organizing two or more ensembles.)

In 1960, there were about 40 colleges offering jazz-related courses; half of these colleges allowed academic credits for jazz courses or ensembles. By the end of the sixties, there were 165 colleges with non-credit jazz courses; 135 gave academic credits.

In 1960, there were about a dozen school stage band (or jazz) festivals; about 75 in 1969. During this ten year period, several regional college jazz festivals were established: Villanova U. (Pa.); Mobile, Ala.; California State U.-Northridge; Elmhurst College (Ill.); Quinnipiac College (Conn.) and U. of Utah—all based on the format of the original Notre Dame festival.

The first national college jazz festival—with participating groups chosen from regional competitions—was in Miami Beach in 1967, sponsored by a beer company, an airline, and a shirt manufacturer. The beer company moved the national event to St. Louis in 1968 and 1969

when it disintegrated because of "conflicting commercial considerations." (The advertising agency wanted rock vocals.)

The first formal jazz seminar sponsored by the Music Educators National Conference was held at its biennial convention in Atlantic City in 1960. (Dave Brubeck, George Wein, and Rev. Norman O'Connor did an informal jazz session at the 1958 M.E.N.C. biennial in St. Louis.) The 1960 seminar starred Billy Taylor—the first of his many appearances as a jazz clinician and teacher of teachers—Hall Overton; Dr. Ralph Pace of Teachers College-Columbia U., who organized the event; Dr. Gene Hall of North Texas State U., whose article on school jazz was the first such piece published in the *Music Educators Journal*; and Charles Suber, moderator. The success of this seminar led to more jazz-related sessions at various state and national M.E.N.C. events during the sixties.

By 1968, the interest in jazz among school music educators resulted in two important events. One was the establishment of the National Association of Jazz Educators (NAJE), chartered as an auxiliary organization of the M.E.N.C. (It became more autonomous in 1973.) The other event was the M.E.N.C. symposium on "Youth Music" at Tanglewood in the summer of 1968. The symposium discussed how school music departments could become more relevant to the needs of students, and how more students could be involved in school music.

In the summer of 1969, a 4-week Youth Music Symposium was held at the U. of Wisconsin-Madison, sponsored by the U.S. Office of Education, the M.E.N.C., and organized by Emmett Sariz, director of the U.W.-Extension Music Dept. This symposium attracted a good deal of attention because of its conclusions: students wanted to create their own music using the expertise of their teachers; youth oriented instruments such as guitar had a place in school music; and that rock and jazz offered more students an opportunity to participate in school music. (Many educators attending the symposium were anxious to embrace rock without knowing anything about its musical roots.)

The sixties saw the evolution of a grade school-college-grade school spiral of jazz education.

A "war baby" born in 1942 arrived in high school during the mid-fifties where he or she had the opportunity to learn stage band music from an ex-professional swing band musician educated by the G.I. Bill. This high school stage band musician wanted to continue with "jazz" in college whether it was offered for credit or not. Then, as was likely, the college jazz musician, majoring in music education, went into secondary school music teaching where he would use the idiom with which he was familiar. Many of these "second generation" jazz-knowledgeable educators organized jazz-type ensembles in middle and junior high schools.

The college jazz programs were a direct result of pressure from the high schools. High school stage band musicians wanted to continue their taste of jazz in college; the high school administrators wanted the new music teachers to be able to teach the music that was making such a hit with the students and their parents. However, despite the pressure—or because of it—college music departments were not giving jazz anything like parity with traditional music. Course credit for jazz study was grudgingly granted and budgets for faculty and materials were skimpy. In virtually every college with a jazz program—Berklee was an exception because of the uniqueness of its original concept—the entire teaching load fell on one person.

That one person recruited and developed the ensembles; begged, borrowed, and stole suitable arrangements, or in many successful programs wrote the book himself. In his spare time, he provided the equivalent of private lessons on instrumental techniques, the elements of improvisation, and hired the bus to take the band to a regional festival "representing the excellence of the _____ University School of Music."

The one-person jazz faculty was—and is—a well-schooled, working professional who has been conditioned to cope with the remoteness and disinterest—and sometimes, outright hostility—of "serious" musicians. The history of jazz education is the record of determined, hard-working professional musicians who were so proud of their music, and so dedicated to the education of their students, that they did whatever had to be done with whatever resources were available.

And so the success of the program at North Texas State University—the only university that offered a "jazz major" in the sixties—rested on the 18 hours-a-day efforts of Leon Breeden (professional clarinetist) who had succeeded Gene Hall (professional saxophonist). At Indiana University, the largest music school in the United States, the first, lonely jazz faculty member was Buddy Baker (professional trombonist) who later helped to establish the jazz program at U. of Northern Colorado with Derryl Goes (professional drummer). Succeeding Buddy Baker at Indiana U. was Jerry Coker (professional saxophonist and arranger), and then in 1966 the incumbent head of I.U.'s 32-hour jazz program, David Baker (professional trombonist and arranger-composer). Roger Schueler (professional trumpet player) built the jazz program at Millikin U. Evan Solat (professional arranger) represented the jazz idiom at Philadelphia Musical Academy; John Garvey (professional string player and conductor) singlehandedly brought jazz into the U. of Illinois; Bob McDonald (professional studio musician) was the jazz department at Los Angeles City College; ditto Dick Carlson at Los Angeles Valley College.

Sometimes, despite his most valiant efforts and the loyal support of his students, the college would refuse to grant jazz any official status. Such was the situation, in the sixties, when Ralph Mutchler (professional pianist and arranger) left Northwestern U. to establish an excellent program at Olympic College (Bremerton, Wash.) Ladd McIntosh (professional saxophonist and arranger-composer) was not encouraged to stay on at Ohio State U., even after his band won top honors at the 1967 national college jazz festival. Bill Dobbins (professional pianist and arranger-composer) left Kent State U. under similar circumstances.

The U.S. State Department sponsored, for several years during the sixties, tours abroad of college jazz ensembles selected at the Notre Dame festival. Two Indiana bands toured the Far East, a combo from West Virginia State College toured North Africa, the U. of Illinois jazz lab band toured Europe; and North Texas State U. toured Mexico. (Jazz bands from Northwestern U. and the U. of Denver were denied the opportunity to tour for the U.S.A. because of vetoes by their respective Deans of Music).

The situation for the average high school stage band director was somewhat different. Because he or she was usually the only instrumental instructor in the music department, there were no musical colleagues to stigmatize jazz as something unfit for the education of young people.

The high school principal's chief concern was that parents and community be pleased with the students' behaviour and musical performance. It was okay if the band director wanted to form—on his own time—something called a stage band if it didn't interfere with the required number of half-time shows, Christmas programs, spring musicals, and graduation ceremonials. Parents were so delighted with their children playing the swing music that "we used to jitterbug to" that they organized candy and cake sales to buy the band director whatever it took to field a winning, swinging band. And—a very important consideration for the support of musical instrument companies—parents were glad to buy a new, professional-type instrument for their professional-type sons and daughters. What had been suitable for eighth clarinet in the concert band was obviously not the kind of instrument a professional needed to play in the front line of a jazz band.

This new market for professional instruments motivated the instrument manufacturers, and their dealers, to co-sponsor school jazz festivals, award scholarships to the National Stage Band Camps, and offer the "clinic" services of professional musicians wherever requested.

Some of the most widely traveled professional jazz "clinicians" in the sixties (and into the seventies) were: trumpets—Dizzy Gillespie, Bobby Herriot, Don Jacoby, Herb Pomeroy, Doc Severinsen, Marv Stamm, and Clark Terry; trombone—Buddy Baker, David Baker, Urbie Green, Frank Rosolino, and Phil Wilson; reeds—Cannonball Adderley, Jerry Coker, Buddy DeFranco, Sam Donahue, Paul Horn, John LaPorta and Charlie Mariano; guitar—Jack Peterson, Howie Roberts, Sal Salvador, and Johnny Smith; piano—Dan Haerle, Marian McPartland, Ray Santisi, and Billy Taylor; bass—Ray Brown, Carol Kaye, Mike Moore, and Eddie Safranski; drums—Louis Bellson, Roy Burns, Alan Dawson, Jack DeJohnette, Clem DeRosa, Elvin Jones, Joe Morello, Charlie Perry, and Ed Thigpen.

While most of these professionals did clinics on jazz techniques relative to their instrument, many of them also provided instruction on ensemble rehearsal techniques, the elements of improvisation, and the use of new, jazz-related materials.

There were also a number of professional leaders and arrangers who traveled the clinic circuit: Manny Albam, Don Ellis, Maynard Ferguson, Woody Herman, Quincy

Jones, Thad Jones, Stan Kenton, Chuck Mangione, Oliver Nelson, and Johnny Richards.

Obviously, the professional players were, in considerable numbers, providing assistance to the professional educators. Sometimes the professional players sought more direct involvement in jazz education. During the sixties Oscar Peterson, Ray Brown, and Ed Thigpen organized a jazz school in Toronto; Phil Woods started a summer jazz camp in New Hope, Pa.; and Stan Kenton established his own summer stage band clinics at which his band was the resident faculty.

The demand for good stage band arrangements produced, during the sixties, professional-type charts—usually with a basic instrumentation of eight brass, five saxes, and four rhythm—from arrangers such as: Manny Albam, Art and Rusty Dedrick, Gil Evans, Dick Fenno, Neal Hefti, John Lewis, Richard Maltby, Sammy Nestico, Lenny Niehaus, Glenn Osser, Pete Rugolo, Bob Seibert, and Ray Wright.

The professionals also authored the method books necessary to advance the level of jazz education. Some of the most important texts authored in the sixties by professional jazz musicians were: ensemble training—John LaPorta's monumental 22-volume *Developing the School Stage Band* (Berklee Press); instrumental techniques—*Developmental Techniques for the School Dance Band Musician* (Berklee Press) by Rev. George Wiskirchen, with the advice of many professional jazz players; *Practice with the (Trombone) Experts* (MCA) by Paul Tanner; *Clarinet LP/Workbook* (Canyon Press) by Leon Breeden; *Flute Book of the Blues* (Alnur) by Yusef Lateef; *Patterns for Saxophone* (Noslen) by Oliver Nelson; and various volumes of *Scale Studies* and *Chord Studies* by Joe Viola and other Berklee faculty members. The most influential book for young jazz drummers during the sixties was Alan Dawson's *Manual for the Modern Drummer* (Berklee Press), assisted by Don DeMicheal. And many tubas were replaced by string basses in stage band rhythm sections because of Bill Curtis' *A Modern Method for String Bass* (Berklee Press).

Most of the new jazz-related materials were published by new companies whose principals were directly involved in school jazz education: Kendor Music (Delevan, N.Y.); KSM (Dallas, Tex.); Today's Music! (Libertyville, Ill.); New Sounds in Modern Music (New York); Berklee Press (Boston); Modern Music School (Cleveland); Cimino Publications (N.Y.); Mission Music (Castro Valley, Calif.); MJQ Music (N.Y.), and Studio P/R (Lebanon, Ind.)

Jazz Education in the Seventies

Jazz education continued its rapid statistical growth into the seventies. By the school year, 1975-76, there were more than 500,000 student musicians participating in jazz-related ensembles and courses supervised by a "jazz educator."

About 60% of the 30,000 junior and senior high schools in the U.S. had an average of 1.2 stage/jazz bands. About 400 colleges were offering at least one jazz ensemble or course for credit. Several universities—Indiana, North Texas State, Wesleyan (Conn.), Eastman School of Music, Northern Colorado, Illinois, New England Conservatory of Music, Miami (Florida)—were offering postgraduate jazz programs.

The technical level of the school jazz musicians was higher than ever. Many of the college jazz bands were as polished as the professional road bands. In fact, Buddy Rich, Woody Herman, Stan Kenton, Maynard Ferguson, and Bill Watrous recruited their sidemen directly from the colleges. The transition was easy. The college musicians were playing the same charts as the recording bands—and had more time to rehearse.

Because of jazz education in the schools, these bands took on new life—working six and seven days a week doing one-niter concert/clinic stands at high schools and colleges. A typical date: Woody Herman and the members of his band would do clinics and demonstrations during the day and a concert at night at a high school for a minimum fee of $2500. The band parents and the student musicians would sell out the 1500 seat school auditorium at $3 per ticket. The net would go back into the school band fund for new instruments, arrangements, sound reinforcement equipment, trips to festivals, etc.

The arrangements played by college bands and many of the high school bands were the same as those recorded by professional jazz and jazz-rock groups. Most colleges and an increasing number of high schools had in-house student arrangers who write custom-tailored charts for their own ensembles.

Jazz educators were increasingly organized—nationally and by states—into NAJE which held its first national convention in Chicago in 1974. Every state, regional, and national music educator meeting was replete with stage band and jazz demonstrations and seminars.

Many jazz educators were gaining the seniority in their college or public school system that might insure the stability and acceptance of their jazz programs.

Universities were bestowing honorary degrees and artist-in-residencies on the likes of Duke Ellington, Benny Carter, Gerry Mulligan, Herbie Hancock, Oliver Nelson, Quincy Jones, Eubie Blake, et al.

There were about 170 school jazz festivals attracting as many as 200 ensembles at one location, including stage bands and jazz combos from elementary and middle schools.

There was an outstanding jazz improvisation program at Washington Elementary School, the lab school for University of California-Berkeley, organized by Dr. Herb Wong for grades K-thru-6. Dr. Wong was able to prove that learning improvisational skills on conventional musical instruments enabled students to improve their academic skills such as reading and mathematical concepts. Teachers who took their practice teaching at Washington Elementary School are furthering that jazz-inspired concept in California grade schools.

With all that activity in the schools, it would seem that jazz education had indeed arrived. But what had arrived where?

Were all those students learning, and performing, jazz?

Were all those schools becoming committed to accepting jazz as part of a music education? The answer to both questions was no, not really.

Take the colleges for example. In the school year, 1975-76, fewer than 20 colleges required any jazz course toward the fulfillment of a music degree. Fewer than 10 colleges required their music education majors—the future school music teachers—to have any jazz competence. Most colleges—even those with a considerable jazz emphasis—did not consider a jazz ensemble to be a "major ensemble" like the concert band or orchestra. With but few exceptions, college jazz departments employed only one full-time person responsible for teaching a variety of jazz courses to 100 or more students. (Even if college administrators wanted to add jazz educators, tight budgets and a tenured, traditionally oriented faculty made such additions very difficult.)

But regardless of college credits or problems with fearful faculty, jazz education in the schools in the seventies faced a fundamental internal challenge. This serious challenge came from the majority of jazz educators who had relatively little professional experience. These teachers whose jazz experience was almost entirely within academia were—sincerely and without malice—academicizing jazz: encompassing it within definitions, codifying its style and form, and standardizing its modes of expression.

The influence of the contemporary, professional jazz musician—so important to the history of jazz education—had been diluted in the expansion of all those stage bands and jazz programs.

Contemporary professionals were the first school jazz educators, clinicians, arrangers, and authors. Contemporary jazz musicians brought to jazz education the professional standards of their peers. The professional knew that jazz could not be defined until and unless it was no longer a living music. The professional knew which criteria distinguish jazz from other musics: improvisation—spontaneous composition; a sense of moving time—swing; and individuality of expression—making your own, personal sound.

The professional knew why jazz contests were nonproductive. Harvey Phillips, the great tuba player and music educator, said it simply: "I tell each student he only has one musician to compete with the rest of his days—himself. And I try to make him understand the ethical responsibility of being a professional musician." (*The New Yorker*, Dec. 15, 1975).

It should not be assumed, however, that jazz education in the schools was dead or was even dying. Like jazz itself, jazz education has had—and will have many premature obituaries. Jazz education in the school in the seventies did have a problem. There were many indications that the problem could be relieved or solved.

Jazz educator with contemporary, professional jazz experience continued to fight for their music and their students. They set an example of teaching improvisation and arranging, organizing small jazz ensembles, and favoring large jazz bands in the Thad Jones/Mel Lewis style.

The working jazz professional did not turn his back on

the students who wanted to learn to play creatively. A new crop of clinicians and campus residents included Herbie Hancock, Billy Cobham, Joe Pass, Bill Watrous, Tom Scott and Gary Burton, as well as the older, still very contemporary jazz players and arrangers.

About 40% of school jazz festivals in 1976 will be non-competitive with the likelihood that jazz ensemble contests will be a rarity by 1980.

There are colleges that—because of professionally experienced jazz musicians on the faculty—are committed to give their students all the available expertise without restricting their modes of expression. Berklee continues to grow without losing its ability to inspire. Eastman is adding faculty and quite rapidly integrating jazz within its excellent total program. Gunther Schuller—with colleagues George Russell, Phil Wilson, Jaki Byard, and Ran Blake—is revitalizing the New England Conservatory. Leon Breeden at North Texas State has demonstrated his concern about improvisation and small ensemble jazz by adding Rich Matteson to the faculty.

It's happening in the high schools too. Combo participation in (non-competitive) festivals is on the increase. Attendance at the Combo/Improvisation Clinics (first established in 1972 by the Summer Jazz Clinics) is surpassing big band camp attendance.

Clinicians specializing in improvisational techniques—such as Jamey Aebersold, David Baker, Dan Haerle, John LaPorta, Joe Henderson, Larry Ridley, Rufus Reid, Ed Soph, Dom Spera—are much in demand. And the number of method books and recordings on improvisational techniques continues to mount. In-depth, self-study texts by David Baker (*down beat* Workshop Publications); Jamey Aebersold (Aebersold Music); John LaPorta (Berklee Press); Dom Spera (Hal Leonard), and others are being purchased, and used, by thousands of students and working musicians.

Ironically, one of the factors helping jazz to become essential to school curricula is its commercial implications. The generally poor state of the economy in the mid-seventies has turned students and their parents to seek an education that is likely to provide a financial return. High schools are doing more career counseling than ever before. Two and four year colleges are rapidly adding vocational music training in an effort to compete for students in the face of declining enrollments.

The music educator most likely to motivate and organize "business of music" courses is the professional jazz musician. He knows the musical and "commercial" value of film scoring, jingle writing, copying, recording arts & sciences, retailing and marketing, publishing, copyright law, management, etc. The jazz educator's professionalism is becoming a financial asset to a school, a fact that may make more rapid "acceptance" of jazz studies.

The overriding reason jazz education—in or out of the schools—is here to stay is the demand by young musicians to create music in the jazz tradition. In general terms, young musicians are following Alvin Toffler's blueprint for the use of education to achieve individuality expressed in *Future Shock*. In specific terms, young musicians will go where they have to go to get what they want.

Most young musicians do not want to be jazz professionals. They will shop for the kind of education that suits their needs. Whatever they do with that education is a plus for themselves and music.

If young musicians want to be professional contemporary musicians—and there is no school that can offer them what they need—they will do what aspiring professionals have done before them. They will play the great records, study the solos, immerse themselves in the music, and go out and play where and whenever anyone will listen. They will seek out good, private professional teachers such as Dick Grove and his great staff of studio musicians in Los Angeles, or Karl Berger and Jack DeJohnette and their colleagues in New York, or study with a Joe Daley or a Willie Pickens in Chicago, an Ira Sullivan in Miami—there is no shortage of professional jazz musicians able and willing to pass on what they know.

Conclusion: jazz will be around as long as people need it. Jazz education will be around as long as musicians need it. Nothing has happened to make us believe that jazz and jazz education will not be around into the eighties and beyond.

ALABAMA

University of Alabama; University, AL 35486. Write: Steve Sample or Director of Jazz Studies, Music Dept.*

ARKANSAS

Arkansas State University; State University (Jonesboro), AR 72467. Write: Chairman, Music Dept.*

Henderson State College; Arkadelphia, AR 71923. Write: Dr. Joe Clark or Director of Jazz Studies, Music Dept.*

ARIZONA

University of Arizona; Tuscon, AZ 85721. Write: Thomas R. Ervin or Director of Jazz Studies, School of Music.*

Arizona State University; Tempe, AZ 85281. Write: Dr. Dan Swaim or Director of Jazz Studies, Music Dept.*

Mesa Community College (2-yr.); Mesa, AZ 85201. Write: Grant Wolf or Director of Music.

Northern Arizona University; Flagstaff, AZ 86001. Write: Director of Jazz Studies, Music Dept.*

CALIFORNIA

Cabrillo College (2-yr.); Aptos, CA 95003. Write: Director of Music.

California Institute of the Arts; Valencia, CA 91355. Write: Mel Powell or Dean, School of Music.*

University of California/Berkeley; Berkeley, CA 94720. Write: Dr. David Tucker, 53 Student Center.

University of California/Los Angeles; Los Angeles, CA 90024. Write: Paul Tanner or Chairman, Music Dept.*

California State Polytechnic University; Pomona, CA 91768. Write: John DeFoor or Director of Jazz Studies, Music Dept.

California State University/Fresno; Fresno, CA 93705. Write: Larry Sutherland or Director of Jazz Studies, Music Dept.*

California State University/Northridge; Northridge, CA 91324. Write: Joel Leach or Chairman, Music Dept.

California State University/San Diego; LaJolla, CA 92037. Write: Director of Jazz Studies, Third College.*

California State College/Sonoma; Rohnert Park, CA 94928. Write: Gail Atkinson or Chairman, Music Dept.

Cerritos College (2-yr.); Norwalk, CA 90650. Write: Don Erjavec or Chairman, Music Dept.

Chaffey College (2-yr.); Alta Loma, CA 91701. Write: Chairman, Music Dept.

Cuesta Community College (2-yr.); San Luis Obispo, CA 93430. Write: Warren H. Balfour or Director of Music.

DeAnza College (2-yr.); Cupertino, CA 95014. Write: Dr. Herb Patnoe or Chairman, Music Dept.

Diablo Valley College (2-yr.); Pleasant Hill, CA 94523. Write: Chris Nelson or Chairman, Music Dept.

East Los Angeles College (2-yr.); Los Angeles, CA 90022. Write: Walter E. Carr or Director of Music.

Foothill College (2-yr.); Los Altos Hills, CA 94022. Write: John Mortarotti, Fine Arts Chairman.

Gavilan Community College (2-yr.); Gilroy, CA 95020. Write: Ronald G. Ward or Chairman, Music Dept.

Long Beach City College (2-yr.); Long Beach, CA 90808. Write: Ron Logan or Director of Music.

Los Angeles City College (2-yr.); Los Angeles, CA 90029. Write: Bob McDonald, Music Dept., 855 N. Vermont Ave.

Los Angeles Valley College (2-yr.); Van Nuys, CA 91401. Write: Richard Carlson or Director of Music, 5800 Fulton Ave.

Monterey Peninsula College (2-yr.); Monterey, CA 93940. Write: Don Schamber or Director of Music, 980 Fremont Ave.

Orange Coast College (2-yr.); Costa Mesa, CA 92626. Write: Dr. Charles Rutherford, Music Dept., 2701 Fairview Ave.

University of the Pacific; Stockton, CA 95204. Write: David Goedecke or Director of Bands.

College of the Redwoods (2-yr.); Eureka, CA 95501. Write: Jack Wheaton or Chairman, Music Dept.

Sacramento City College (2-yr.); Sacramento, CA 95822. Write: Forrest R. Van Ripen or Director of Music, 3835 Freeport Blvd.

San Bernadino Valley College (2-yr.); San Bernadino, CA 92903. Write: Paul Oxley or Director of Music, 701 S. Mt. Vernon Ave.

San Diego State University; San Diego, CA 92182. Write:

Dr. Eddie S. Meadows, or Chairman, Department of Music & Afro-American Studies.

San Jose State University; San Jose, CA 95192. Write: Dwight Cannon or Director of Jazz Studies, Music Dept.

Santa Monica College (2-yr.); Santa Monica, CA 90405. Write: James B. Fugle or Director of Music, 1815 Pearl St.

College of the Siskiyous (2-yr.); Weed, CA 96099. Write: Jerry Edwards or Dean of Students.

Southwestern College (2-yr.); Chula Vista, CA 92010. Write: Jim Merrill or Chairman, Performing Arts, 900 Otay Lakes Road.

COLORADO
University of Colorado; Boulder, CO 80302. Write: Jack Foote or Director of Jazz Studies, School of Music.*

University of Colorado at Denver; Denver, CO 80202. Write: Dean, College of Music.

Colorado State University; Ft. Collins, CO 80521. Write: Otto Werner or Director of Bands, Music Dept.*

University of Denver; Denver, CO 80210. Write: Dr. Roger Fee or Dean, Lamont School of Music.*

Metropolitan State College; Denver, CO 80203. Write: Dr. Jerrald McCollum or Chairman, Music Dept.

University of Northern Colorado; Greeley, CO 80631. Write: Derryl Goes or Director of Jazz Studies, School of Music.*

CONNECTICUT
University of Bridgeport; Bridgeport, CT 06602. Write: Neil Slater or Director of Jazz Studies, Music Dept.*

Quinnipiac College; Hamden, CT 06518. Write: Sam Costanzo or Chairman, Fine Arts Dept.

Wesleyan University, Middletown, CT 06457. Write: Richard Winslow or Chairman, Music Dept., Center for Creative and Fine Arts.

Yale University; New Haven, CT 06520. Write: Willie Ruff or Dean, School of Music.*

DISTRICT OF COLUMBIA
Howard University; Washington, DC 20001. Write: Director of Jazz Studies, School of Music.*

FLORIDA
University of Florida; Gainesville, FL 32601. Write: James Hale or Chairman, Music Dept.*

University of Miami, Coral Gables, FL 33124. Write: Dr. William Lee or Director of Jazz Studies, School of Music.*

Miami Dade Community College/North Campus (2-yr.); Miami, FL 33167. Write: John A. Alexander or Director of Music, 11380 N.W. 27 Ave.

Palm Beach Junior College (2-yr.); Lake Worth, FL 33460. Write: Sy Pryweller or Director of Music.

GEORGIA
Columbus College; Columbus, GA 31907. Write: Paul Vander Gheynst or Chairman, Music Dept.

Fort Valley State College; Fort Valley, GA 31030. Write: George R. Holland or Chairman, Music Dept.

University of Georgia; Athens, GA 30602. Write: Roger L. Dancz or Director of Bands, Music Dept.*

Georgia State University; Atlanta, GA 30303. Write: Jim Progris or Chairman, Music Dept.*

Morehouse College; Atlanta, GA 30314. Write: Ted McDaniels or Chairman, Music Dept.

IDAHO
University of Idaho; Moscow, ID 83843. Write: Richard F. Werner or Dean, School of Music.*

Ricks College (2-yr.); Rexburg, ID 83440. Write: Noel Brown or Chairman, Music Dept.*

ILLINOIS
Chicago State University; Chicago, IL 60621. Write: Bunky Green or Chairman, Music Dept.

DePaul University; Chicago, IL 60604. Write: Dr. Leon Stein or Dean, School of Music, 25 E. Jackson Blvd.*

Eastern Illinois University; Charleston, IL 61920. Write: Dean, School of Music.*

Elmhurst College; Elmhurst, IL 60126. Write: Dr. James Sorensen or Chairman, Music Dept.

Governors State University; Park Forest South, IL 60466. Write: Dr. Warrick Carter or Coordinator, Jazz Studies, College of Cultural Studies.

Wm. Rainey Harper College (2-yr.); Palatine, IL 60067. Write: Bob Tillotson or Director of Music.

University of Illinois; Urbana, IL 61801. Write: John Garvey or Chairman, Jazz Division, School of Music.*

University of Illinois at Chicago Circle; Chicago, IL. 60680. Write: Chairman, Music Dept.

Illinois State University; Normal, IL 61781. Write: Chairman, Music Dept.*

Illinois Wesleyan University; Bloomington, IL 61701. Write: Dr. Thomas Streeter or Dean, School of Music.*

Joliet Junior College (2-yr.); Joliet, IL 60435. Write: Director of Music.

Kaskaskia College (2-yr.); Centralia, IL 62801. Write: Director of Music.

Kennedy-King College (2-yr.); Chicago, IL 60623. Write: Director of Bands, Music Dept.

College of Lake County (2-yr.); Grays Lake, IL 60030. Write: Chuck Banks or Director of Music, 19351 W. Washington St.

Millikin University; Decatur, IL 62522. Write: Roger Schueler or Dean, School of Music.*

North Central College; Naperville, IL 60540. Write: Robert Rollin or Chairman, Music Dept.*

North Park College; Chicago, IL 60625. Write: Dr. Lee Burswold or Chairman, Music Dept.*

Northern Illinois University; DeKalb, IL 60178. Write: Ron Modell or Chairman, Music Dept.

Northwestern University; Evanston, IL 60201. Write: Director of Jazz Studies, School of Music.*

Quincy College; Quincy, IL 62301. Write: Charles Winking or Chairman, Music Dept.*

Southern Illinois University; Edwardsville, IL 62025.

Write: Dr. William Tarwater or Dean, School of Music.*

Thornton Community College (2-yr.); South Holland, IL 60473. Write: Donald F. Kramer or Director of Music.

Triton College (2-yr.); River Grove, IL 60171. Write: Burrell Gluskin or Director of Instrumental Music, 2000 Fifth Ave.

Waubonsee Community College (2-yr.); Sugar Grove, IL 60554. Write: Duane Wickiser or Director of Music, Rte. 47 and Harter Road.

Western Illinois University; Macomb, IL 61455. Write: Robert Morsch or Director of Bands, Music Dept.*

Wilbur Wright College (2-yr.); Chicago, IL 60634. Write: John DeRoule or Director of Adult Education.

INDIANA

Ball State University; Muncie, IN 47305. Write: Larry N. McWilliams or Director of Jazz Studies, School of Music.*

Butler University; Indianapolis, IN 46208. Write: Robert Grechesky or Dean, Jordan College of Music.*

University of Evansville; Evansville, IN 47702. Write: Edwin Lacy or Chairman, Music Dept.*

Indiana University; Bloomington, IN 47401. Write: David Baker or Director of Jazz Studies, School of Music.*

Indiana University Southeast; Jeffersonville, IN 47130. Write: Jamey Aebersold or Chairman, Music Dept.

Indiana State University; Terre Haute, IN 47809. Write: John P. Spicknall or Chairman, Music Dept.*

University of Notre Dame; Notre Dame, IN 46556. Write: George Wiskirchen, C.S.C., or Director of Bands.

Purdue University; Lafayette, IN 47907. Write: Roger Heath or Director of Bands.

Saint Francis College; Ft. Wayne, IN 46808. Write: Richard D. Brown or Chairman, Music Dept.

IOWA

Coe College; Cedar Rapids, IA 52402. Write: Jerry Owen or Chairman, Music Dept.

Cornell College; Mt. Vernon, IA 52314. Write: Dr. Jesse G. Evans or Chairman, Music Dept.*

Grinnell College; Grinnell, IA 50112. Write: Cecil Lytle or Chairman, Music Dept.

University of Iowa; Iowa City, IA 52242. Write: Morgan Jones or Director of Jazz Bands, School of Music.*

Iowa Central Community College (2-yr.); Ft. Dodge, IA 50501. Write: Thomas R. Kruse or Director of Music.

Morningside College; Sioux City, IA 51106. Write: Gary Slechta or Chairman, Music Dept.*

North Iowa Area Community College (2-yr.); Mason City, IA 50401. Write: Henry T. Paine or Director of Instrumental Music, 400 College Drive.

University of Northern Iowa; Cedar Falls, IA. Write: Chairman, Music Dept.*

Westmar College, LeMars, IA 51031. Write: Gerald B. Olson or Director of Music.

KANSAS

Bethany College; Lindsborg, KS 67456. Write: Dean Leon Burch or Dean of Students.*

Bethel College; North Newton, KS 67117. Write: Gary Fletcher, or Chairman, Music Dept.

College of Emporia; Emporia, KA 66801. Write: Frank A. Malambri or Chairman, Music Dept.

University of Kansas; Lawrence, KS 66045. Write: Robert E. Foster or Dean, School of Music.*

Kansas State Teachers College; Emporia, KS 66801. Write: Thomas Wright or Coordinator of Jazz Studies, Music Dept.*

Kansas State University; Manhattan, KS 66502. Write: Phil Hewett or Chairman, Music Dept.*

Wichita State University; Wichita, KS 67208. Write: Dr. J.C. Combs or Dean, School of Music.*

KENTUCKY

Bellarmine College; Louisville, KY 40205. Write: Jamey Aebersold or Chairman, Music Dept.

Morehead State University; Morehead, KY 40351. Write: Walter L. Barr or Director of Jazz Studies, Music Dept.*

LOUISIANA

Louisiana State University; Baton Rouge, LA 70803. Write: Everett Timm or Dean, School of Music.*

Louisiana Tech University; Ruston, LA 71270. Write Joe Sheppard or Chairman, Music Dept.*

Loyola University; New Orleans, LA 70118. Write: Joseph Hebert or Dean, College of Music, 6363 St. Charles Ave.*

Nicholls State University; Thibodaux, LA 70301. Write: Paul Mathis or Chairman, Music Dept., College of Education.

Northeast Louisiana University; Monroe, LA 71201. Write: Robert Eidenier or Dean, School of Music.*

Southeastern Louisiana University; Hammond, LA 70401. Write: Lee Fortier or Chairman, Music Dept.*

Southern University; Baton Rouge, LA 70813. Write: Alvin Batiste or Director of Jazz Institute, Division of Music.*

Southern University in New Orleans; New Orleans, LA 70126. Write: Ed Jordan or Chairman, Music Dept.

University of Southwestern Louisiana; Lafayette, LA 70501. Write: James M. Goodman or Dean, School of Music.*

MAINE

Bowoin College; Brunswick, ME 04011. Write: Marion Brown or Chairman, Music Dept.

MARYLAND

University of Maryland; College Park, MD 20742. Write: Dr. Andrew Goodrich or Chairman, Music Dept.*

Morgan State College; Baltimore, MD 21239. Write: Melvin Miles, Jr. or Chairman, Music Dept.

Towson State College; Baltimore, MD 21204. Write: Hank Levy or Director of Jazz Studies, School of Fine Arts.

MASSACHUSETTS

Berklee College of Music; Boston, MA 02115. Write: Office of Admissions, 1140 Boylston St.

Clark University; Worcester, MA 01610. Write: Director of Admissions.

University of Massachusetts/Amherst; Amherst, MA 01002. Write: Roland Wiggins or Director of Institute of Black Music.*

The New England Conservatory of Music; Boston, MA 02115. Write: Phil Wilson or Director of Admissions.*

Northeastern University; Boston, MA 02115. Write: J.R. Mitchell or Director of Jazz Studies, College of Liberal Arts.

Tufts University; Medford, MA 02111. Write: T.J. Anderson or Chairman, Music Dept.

Westfield State College; Westfield, MA 01085. Write: Dr. Donald J. Bastarache or Chairman Music Dept.

MICHIGAN

Central Michigan University; Mt. Pleasant, MI 48859. Write: Dr. William Rivard or Chairman, Music Dept.*

Henry Ford Community College (2-yr.); Dearborn, MI 48128. Write: Don Lupp or Director of Music.

Thomas Jefferson College (Grand Valley State Colleges); Allendale, MI 49401. Write: Joel Zelnik or Director of Jazz Studies, Music Dept.

The University of Michigan; Ann Arbor, MI 48105. Write: Director of Jazz Studies, School of Music.*

Michigan State University; East Lansing, MI 48824. Write: Burgess Gardner or Director of Jazz Studies, Music Dept.*

Michigan Technological University; Houghton, MI 49931. Write: Donald P. Keranen or Chairman, Music Dept.

Northern Michigan University; Marquette, MI 49855; Write: Ron Caviani or Chairman, Music Dept.*

Oakland University; Rochester, MI 48063. Write: Marvin Holladay or Chairman, Music Dept.

Wayne State University; Detroit, MI 48202. Write: Dr. James Hartway or Chairman, Music Dept.*

Southwestern Michigan College (2-yr.); Dowagiac, MI 49047. Write: Rich Bressler or Chairman, Music Dept.

Western Michigan University; Kalamazoo, MI 49001. Write: Dr. Robert Fink or Chairman, Music Dept.*

MINNESOTA

Gustavus Adolphus College; St. Peter, MN 56082. Write: Mark Lammers or Chairman, Music Dept.*

Hamline University; St. Paul, MN 55104. Write: Paul A. Pizner or Chairman, Music Dept.*

Hibbing Community College (2-yr.); Hibbing, MN 55746. Write: Thomas F. Palmersheim or Chairman, Music Dept.

University of Minnesota/Duluth; Duluth, MN 55812. Write: R. Dale Miller or Chairman, Music Dept.*

Moorhead State College; Moorhead, MN 56560. Write: Dr. Al Noice or Chairman, Music Dept.*

Willmar Community College (2-yr.); Willmar, MN 56201. Write: Dale Wright or Director of Music.

Winona State College (2-yr.); Winona, MN 55987. Write: Gene Anderson or Director of Music.

MISSISSIPPI

Delta State College; Cleveland, MS 38732. Write: Gary Nyberg or Chairman, Music Dept.

University of Mississippi; University, MS 38677. Write Dr. Robert Jordan or Chairman, Music Dept.*

University of Southern Mississippi; Hattiesburg, MS 39401. Write: Raoul Jerome or Coordinator of Jazz Curriculum, Music Dept.*

MISSOURI

Central Missouri State University; Warrensburg, MO 64093. Write: Dr. Wesley True or Chairman, Music Div.*

Drury College; Springfield, MO 65802. Write: Don Verne Joseph, Box 67. School of Humanities.

Meramec Community College (2-yr.); Kirkwood, MO 63122. Write: Ronald E. Stilwell or Director of Music.

University of Missouri; Columbia, MO 65201. Write: George DeFoe or Chairman, Music Dept.*

University of Missouri/St. Louis; St. Louis, MO 63121. Write: Stan DeRusha or Chairman, Music Dept.

Northeast Missouri State University; Kirksville, MO 63501. Write: Dr. Dale A. Jorgenson or Chairman, Music Dept.*

Southwest Missouri State University; Springfield, Mo 65802. Write: Robert M. Scott or Chairman, Music Dept.*

MONTANA

University of Montana; Missoula, MT 59801. Write: Lance R. Boyd or Chairman, Music Dept.*

Montana State University; Bozeman, MT 59715. Write: Carl Lobitz or Chairman, Music Dept.

Rocky Mountain College; Billings, MT 59102. Write: Dr. Wm. L. Waggoner or Chairman, Music Dept.

NEBRASKA

Hastings College; Hastings, NE 68901. Write: John Mills or Chairman, Music Dept.*

University of Nebraska at Omaha; Omaha, NE 68101. Write: Reg Schive or Chairman, Music Dept.

NEVADA

University of Nevada/Las Vegas; Las Vegas, NV 89154. Write: Frank Gagliardi or Chairman, Music Dept.

University of Nevada/Reno; Reno, NV 89507. Write: Dr. John Carrico or Chairman, Music Dept.

NEW HAMPSHIRE

Plymouth State College; Plymouth, NH 03264. Write: Vincent Marinelli or Chairman, Music Dept.

NEW JERSEY

Fairleigh Dickinson University; Rutherford, NJ 07070. Write: Stanley Purdy or Chairman, Music Dept.

Glassboro State College; Glassboro, NJ 08028. Write: John H. Thysen or Chairman, Music Dept.*

Jersey City State University; Jersey City, NJ 07305. Write: Richard Lowenthal or Chairman, Music Dept.

Livingston College of Rutgers University; New Brunswick,

NJ 08903. Write: Larry Ridley or Chairman, Music Dept.

Seton Hall University; South Orange, NJ 07079. Write: Jack McKinney or Chairman, Music Dept., 400 S. Orange Ave.

NEW MEXICO

University of New Mexico; Albuquerque, NM 87131. Write: William E. Rhoads or Chairman, Music Dept.*

NEW YORK

Columbia University; New York, NY 10029. Write: Dr. Marion McGill or Chairman, Music Dept., Teachers College, Broadway and 116th St.

Eastman School of Music, University of Rochester; Rochester, NY 14604. Write: Rayburn Wright or Director of Jazz Studies and Contemporary Music, 26 Gibbs St.*

Five Towns College (2-yr.); Merrick, NY 11566. Write: Dr. Stanley G. Cohen or Director of Jazz Studies, 2350 Merrick Ave.

Ithaca College; Ithaca, NY 14850. Write: Steve Brown or Director of Jazz Studies, School of Music.*

Manhattan School of Music; New York, NY 10027. Write: Lyle "Rusty" Dedrick or Director of Jazz Studies, 120 Claremont Ave.*

State University of New York at Binghampton; Binghampton, NY 13901. Write: Albert Hamme or Director of Jazz Studies, Music Dept.

State University of New York College at Brockport; Brockport, NY 14420. Write: Dr. Ira Schwartz or Chairman, Music Dept.

State University of New York at Buffalo; Buffalo, NY 14222. Write: William H. Tallmadge or Chairman, Music Dept.

State University of New York/College at Old Westbury; Westbury, NY 11568. Write: Chairman, Music Dept., Performing Arts Group.

State University of New York/College at Oswego; Oswego, NY 13126. Write: Hugh G. Burritt or Chairman, Music Dept.

State University of New York/College at Potsdam; Potsdam, NY 13676. Write: R. Shiner or Dean, Crane School of Music.*

State University of New York at Stony Brook; Stony Brook, NY 11790. Write: John Lessard, or Chairman, Undergraduate Studies.

Syracuse University; Syracuse, NY 13210. Write: Stephen Marconi or Director of Jazz Ensembles, School of Music.*

NORTH CAROLINA

Appalachian State University; Boone, NC 26808. Write: Joe Phelps or Chairman, Music Dept.*

East Carolina University; Greenville, NC 27834. Write: George L. Broussard or Dean, School of Music.*

University of North Carolina at Chapel Hill; Chapel Hill, NC 27514. Write: John Harding or Chairman, Music Dept.

University of North Carolina at Greensboro; Greensboro,

NC 27412. Write Raymond Ganglio or Dean, School of Music.*

Mars Hill College; Mars Hill, NC 28754. Write: Wayne Bowman or Chairman, Music Dept.*

Pembroke State University; Pembroke, NC 28372. Write: Harold Slagle or Chairman, Music Dept.

NORTH DAKOTA

Minot College; Minot, ND 58701. Write: Gerald Poe or Chairman, Music Dept.

Valley City State College; Valley City, ND 58072. Write: R.Q. Johnson or Chairman, Music Dept.

OHIO

The University of Akron; Akron, OH 44325. Write: Richard Jackoboice or Chairman, Music Dept.

Ashland College; Ashland, OH 44805. Write: Curt Wilson or Director of Bands.*

Bowling Green State University; Bowling Green, OH 43402. Write: Wendell Jones or Dean, School of Music.*

Capital University; Columbus, OH 43209. Write: Ray Eubanks or Chairman, Music Dept.*

Case Western Reserve University; Cleveland, OH 44106. Write: Philip L. Weinacht or Chairman, Music Dept.*

Central State University; Wilberforce, OH 45384. Write: Stanley D. Kirton or Chairman, Music Dept.*

University of Cincinnati; Cincinnati, OH 45221. Write: Dean, College-Conservatory of Music.*

Denison University; Granville, OH 43023. Write: R.L. Bostian or Chairman, Music Dept.*

Hiram College; Hiram, OH 44234. Write: John M. Burley or Chairman, Music Dept.*

Kent State University; Kent, OH 44240. Write: Dr. Walter Watson or Director of Jazz Studies, School of Music.*

Lakeland Community College (2-yr.); Mentor, OH 44060. Write: Chairman, Music Dept.

Miami University; Oxford, OH 15056. Write: Dr. Charles Spohn or Dean, School of Music.*

Muskingum College; New Concord, OH 43662. Write: J. Terry Gates or Chairman, Music Dept.*

Oberlin College; Oberlin, OH 44070. Write: Dean, Conservatory of Music.*

Ohio State University; Columbus, OH 43210. Write: Tom Battenberg or Director, School of Music.*

Otterbein College; Westerville, OH 43081. Write: Gary Tirey or Chairman, Division of Fine Arts.*

OKLAHOMA

Cameron College; Lawton, OK 73501. Write: Chairman, Music Dept.

East Central State College; Ada, OK 74820. Write: James L. Franklin or Chairman, Music Dept.

Oral Roberts University; Tulsa, OK 74105. Write: Bill Shellenberger or Chairman, Music Dept.

Phillips University; Enid, OK 73701. Write: Dr. Milburn Carey or Director, School of Music.*

Southeastern Oklahoma State University; Durant, OK

74701. Write: Dr. Paul Mansur or Chairman, Music Dept.

Southwestern State College; Weatherford, OK 73096. Write: Terry Segress or Chairman, Music Dept.*

University of Tulsa; Tulsa, OK 74104. Write: Ron Predl or Dean, School of Music.*

OREGON

Mt. Hood Community College (2-yr.); Gresham, OR 97030. Write: Larry McVey or Chairman, Creative Arts Division, 26000 S.E. Stark St.

University of Oregon; Eugene, OR 97405. Write: Stan Fink or Dean, School of Music.*

University of Portland; Portland, OR 97203. Write: Don Camack or Chairman, Music Dept.

Pacific University; Forest Grove, OR 97116. Write: Dr. Albert M. Freedman or Dean, School of Music.*

Portland State University; Portland, OR 97207. Write: Dr. Wm. Stainaker, Music Dept.

PENNSYLVANIA

Lebanon Valley College; Annville, PA 17003. Write: Frank Stachow or Chairman, Music Dept.*

Lehigh University; Bethlehem, PA 18015. Write: James T. McLaughlin or Director of Jazz Ensembles, Box 186.

Mansfield State College; Mansfield, PA 16933. Write: Thomas Ryan or Chairman, Music Dept.*

Philadelphia Musical Academy; Philadelphia, PA 19107. Write: Evan Solot or Director of Jazz Studies, 313 Broad St.*

University of Pittsburgh; Pittsburgh, PA 15213. Write: Dr. Nathan Davis or Director of Jazz Studies, 5619 Kentucky Ave.

Temple University; Philadelphia, PA 19122. Write: James W. Herbert or Director of Bands, College of Music.*

SOUTH CAROLINA

Furman University; Greenville, SC 26913. Write: George Hitt or Chairman, Music Dept.*

University of South Carolina; Columbia, SC 29208. Write: Dr. William Moody or Chairman, Music Dept.*

SOUTH DAKOTA

Huron College; Huron, SD 57350. Write: Chairman, Music Dept.

Northern State College; Aberdeen, SD 57401. Write: David Mauney or Chairman, Music Dept.*

TENNESSEE

Austin Peay State College; Clarksville, TN 37040. Write: Aaron Schmidt or Chairman, Music Dept., College of Education.*

East Tennessee State University; Johnson City, TN 37601. Write: Dr. James E. Stafford or Chairman, Music Dept.

Fisk University; Nashville, TN 37203. Write: Robert L. Holmes or Director of Instrumental Music.*

George Peabody College for Teachers; Nashville, TN 37203. Write: John Legg or Director, School of Music.*

Memphis State University; Memphis, TN 38152. Write:

Dr. Thomas Ferguson or Director of Bands, Music Dept.*

TEXAS

Alvin Junior College (2-yr.); Alvin, TX 77511. Write: Jerry Perkins or Chairman, Music Dept., 3110 Mustang Road.

East Texas State University; Commerce, TX 75428. Write: Tom Wirtel or Chairman, Music Dept.*

Hardin-Simmons University; Abilene, TX 79601. Write: Lawson Hager or Dean, School of Music.*

University of Houston; Houston, TX 77004. Write: Don Elam or Aubrey Tucker, or Dean, School of Music.*

Lamar University; Beaumont, TX 77710. Write: James M. Simmons or Chairman, Music Dept.*

Mountain View College (2-yr.); Dallas, TX 75211. Write: Russ Benzamin or Chairman, Music Dept.

Odessa College (2-yr.); Odessa, TX 79760. Write: Jack Hendrix or Director of Instrumental Music.*

North Texas State University; Denton, TX 76203. Write: Leon Breeden or Director of Lab Bands, School of Music, Box 5038. NTU Station.*

University of Saint Thomas; Houston, TX 77006. Write: Thomas Borling or Chairman, Music Dept., 3812 Montrose Blvd.

St. Mary's University; San Antonio, TX 78228. Write: Herb Schweppe or Director of Instrumental Music.

Sam Houston State University; Huntsville, TX 77340. Write: Dr. Robert Morgan or Chairman, Music Dept.*

Stephen F. Austin State University; Nacogdoches, TX 75961. Write: Dr. M.E. Hall or Chairman, Music Dept.*

Tarleton State University; Stephenville, TX 76402. Write Guy Gamble or Director of Jazz Ensembles, Music Dept.

Tarrant County Junior College (2-yr.); Hurst, TX 76053. Write: Jack Cobb or Director of Music.

Texas A&I University; Kingsville, TX 78363. Write: Dr. Joseph L. Bellamah or Chairman, Music Dept.*

University of Texas at Austin; Austin, TX 78712. Write: Dr. Glen Daum or Undergraduate Music Admissions, Music Dept., College of Fine Arts.*

Texas Southern University; Houston, TX 77004. Write: Lanny Steele or Chairman, Music Dept.

Texas Tech University; Lubbock, TX 79409. Write: Don Turner or Chairman, Music Dept.*

Wharton County Junior College (2-yr.); Wharton, TX 77488. Dr. W.W. Wendtland or Chairman, Music Dept.

UTAH

Brigham Young University; Provo, UT 84601. Write: Chairman, Music Dept.*

University of Utah; Salt Lake City, UT 84112. Write: Henry Wolking or Chairman, Music Dept.*

Utah State University; Logan, UT 84321. Write: Larry Smith or Chairman, Music Dept.

Westminster College; Salt Lake City, UT 84105. Write: Ladd McIntosh or Chairman, Music Dept., 1840 South 1300 East.

VERMONT

University of Vermont; Burlington, VT 05401. Write: Herbert L. Schultz or Chairman, Music Dept.*

VIRGINIA

Hampton Institute; Hampton, VA 23668. Write: Consuela Moorehead or Chairman, Music Dept.*

Shenandoah Conservatory of Music; Winchester, VA 22601. Write: Paul Noble or Chairman, Music Dept.*

Virginia Commonwealth University; Richmond, VA 23220. Write: Dr. Paul Dorsam or Assistant Dean, Division of Music.*

WASHINGTON

Central Washington State College; Ellensburg, WA 98926. Write: John F. Moawad or Chairman, Music Dept.*

Clark College (2-yr.); Vancouver, WA 98663. Write: Dale Beacock or Director of Performing Arts.

Columbia Basin College; Pasco, WA 99302. Write: Don Paul or Chairman, Music Dept.

Highline Community College (2-yr.); Midway, WA 98031. Write: Marius "Butch" Nordal or Chairman, Music Dept.

Olympic College (2-yr.); Bremerton, WA 98310. Write: Dr. Ralph Mutchler or Director of Instrument Music.

Washington State University; Pullman, WA 99163. Write: Michael Olsavsky or Chairman, Music Dept.*

WEST VIRGINIA

Marshall University; Huntington, WV 25703. Write: J.D.Folsom or Chairman, Music Dept.

West Virginia Wesleyan College; Buckhannon, WV 26201. Write David Milburn or Chairman, Music Dept.

WISCONSIN

Carthage College; Kenosha, WI 53140. Write: Fred Riley or Chairman, Music Dept.

Lawrence University; Appleton, WI 54911. Write: Chairman, Conservatory of Music.*

Milwaukee Area Technical College (2-yr.); Milwaukee, WI 53202. Write: Gene Morrissette or Chairman, Music Dept.

University of Wisconsin-Eau Claire; Eau Claire, WI 54701. Write: Dominic Spera or Chairman, Music Dept.*

University of Wisconsin-Green Bay; Green Bay; WI 54302. Write: Lowell Ives or Chairman, Music Dept.

University of Wisconsin-Milwaukee; Milwaukee, WI 53201. Write: Dr. Gerald K. Grose or Chairman, Music Dept.*

University of Wisconsin-Parkside; Kenosha, WI 53140. Write: Robert Thomason or Chairman, Music Dept.

University of Wisconsin-Platteville; Platteville, WI 53818. Write: Tom Richards or Chairman, Music Dept.

University of Wisconsin-Stevens Point; Stevens Point, WI 54481. Write: Donald Chesebro or Chairman, Music Dept.*

University of Wisconsin-Superior; Superior, WI 54880. Write: Henry M. Meredith or Chairman, Music Dept.

University of Wisconsin-Waukesha (2-yr.); Waukesha, WI 53186. Write: Jack Whitney or Chairman, Music Dept., 1500 University Drive.

University of Wisconsin-Whitewater; Whitewater, WI 52190. Write: Dr. Frank Ferriano or Chairman, Music Dept.

A guide to available jazz films
by Leonard Maltin

(Leonard Maltin's jazz writing has appeared in *down beat, The Village Voice, Jazz* magazine, and *Saturday Review.* He has also written scores of articles on film, and six books, including *TV Movies: A Paperback Guide to 10,000 Movies on Television,* and *The Great Movie Shorts.* He teaches at the New School for Social Research in New York.)

The complete chronicle of jazz in films has yet to appear. David Meeker's British paperback *Jazz in the Movies* and Jean-Roland Hippenmeyer's Swiss publication *Jazz sur Films* are excellent beginnings, and the New York Jazz Museum has attempted to collect and catalogue as much jazz film as possible.

But the obscurity of many films, and the lack of interest on the part of the companies that made these movies, create a near-impossible task for anyone who wants to see, acquire, or even document all that has passed.

In recent years, the only real jazz films have come from Europe, while occasional American television shows with modern-jazz figures remain unavailable for re-viewing. Perhaps with the coming of video-discs it will be easier to obtain such material, but with the exception of jazz sound-tracks, the history of jazz on film is largely confined to the 1930s and 40s.

Worse, much of this existing material is not generally available at this time. Three-minute "soundies," produced in the 1940s for coin-operated machines, and five-minute "Snader Telescriptions," made in the early 1950s for TV use, are among the most valuable jazz films extant, but they are no longer available for rental or purchase from any specific source, and jazz collectors happen upon them only by chance. Duke Ellington, Louis Armstrong, Fats Waller, Count Basie, Lionel Hampton, and Gene Krupa are among those who appeared in these films, which one can still find in smaller rental-library catalogues, and occasionally for sale on home-movie lists.

Even lesser-known feature films of the 1930s, which included jazz sequences, are not always available.

Therefore, I have limited myself in this index to films which can currently be rented on 16mm sound in America. And I have limited myself to short-subjects which principally feature jazz musicians. The number of feature films with brief appearances by jazzmen is too great to list here; a handful of key feature films is printed at the end of the short-subject index.

We have gathered as much material as possible on each title; please bear in mind that song numbers may not have been performed by the "star" but by supporting acts included in these short-subjects. Complete addresses for the film-rental companies referred to in each entry will be found at the end of the index.

We can only hope that the growing historical interest in jazz will induce film companies to make more material available, and that by the time of the next *Encyclopedia of Jazz* this list will be ten times as long. Until then, there is much worthwhile material on tap:

A

ALBERT AMMONS
BOOGIE DOODLE (1948). Famous abstract animated film by Norman McLaren set to boogie-piano track by Ammons. McGraw-Hill

LOUIS ARMSTRONG
RHAPSODY IN BLACK AND BLUE (1932). Silly story framework for two band numbers, "I'll Be Glad When You're Dead You Rascal You," "Shine." Ivy; Select; Kit Parker

I'LL BE GLAD WHEN YOU'RE DEAD YOU RASCAL YOU (1932). Betty Boop cartoon featuring Armstrong's rendition. Ivy; Kit Parker

LOUIS ARMSTRONG (1962. A live performance caught on film, with Jewel Brown, Trummy Young, Billy Kyle, and others; half-hour. Kit Parker

B

CHARLIE BARNET

JASPER'S IN A JAM (1946). George Pal Puppetoon in color, with Barnet and Peggy Lee on the soundtrack; "Cherokee," "Pompton Turnpike." Ivy
CHARLIE BARNET AND HIS ORCHESTRA (1947) with Igor and Tania, Della Norell, Rita Shore. "I'll Remember April," "You're a Sweetheart." Universal
CHARLIE BARNET AND HIS ORCHESTRA (1949). "Redskin Rhumba," "Atlantic Jump," "My Old Flame." Available for purchase on Super 8mm of 16mm sound from Blackhawk Films
BRIGHT AND BREEZY (1956) with the Four King Sisters, Romo Vincent. "Skyliner," "Lullaby of Birdland," "Easy Street." Universal

COUNT BASIE

SUGARCHILE ROBINSON, BILLIE HOLIDAY, COUNT BASIE AND SEXTET (1951). "One O'Clock Jump," "Terry Toon," "God Bless the Child," "Now or Never." Universal

EUBIE BLAKE

PIE PIE BLACKBIRD (1934) with Nina Mae McKinney, The Nicholas Brothers. "Memories of You," "China Boy," "Everything I've Got Belongs to You." United Artists

C

CAB CALLOWAY

MINNIE THE MOOCHER (1932). Betty Boop cartoon featuring a cartoon-ized version of Calloway dancing and singing title song. Ivy; Kit Parker
SNOW WHITE (1933). Betty Boop Cartoon, as above. Ivy; Kit Parker
OLD MAN OF THE MOUNTAIN (1933). Betty Boop cartoon, as above. Ivy
PARAMOUNT PICTORIAL (Pictorial Magazine #837). Irving Mills introduces Calloway, Duke Ellington, and Baron Lee in brief musical excerpts. Ivy
CAB CALLOWAY'S HI DE HO (1934). "The Lady with the Fan," other songs. Ivy or Kit Parker Films
CAB CALLOWAY'S JITTERBUG PARTY (1935) with Cotton Club entertainers. Ivy
CAB CALLOWAY AND HIS ORCHESTRA IN HI DE HO (1937). "I Gotta Right to Sing the Blues," "Hi De Ho Miracle Man." United Artists

BENNY CARTER

See NAT KING COLE AND HIS TRIO
See LIONEL HAMPTON: ADVENTURES OF AN ASTERISK

BOB CROSBY

BOB CROSBY AND HIS ORCHESTRA (1938). "Pagan Love Song," "Dixieland Swing," others. Ivy

D

JIMMY DORSEY

JIMMY DORSEY AND HIS ORCHESTRA (1938) with Bob Eberly. "It's the Dreamer in Me," "I Love You in Technicolor." United Artists
JIMMY DORSEY AND HIS ORCHESTRA (1940) with Helen O'Connell, Bob Eberly. "Rubber Dolly," "Only a Rose." Ivy
JIMMY DORSEY AND HIS ORCHESTRA (1948) with The Mellolarks, Dottie O'Brien, Bill Lawrence. "Am I Blue," others. Universal

TOMMY DORSEY

TOMMY DORSEY AND HIS ORCHESTRA (1951) with Charlie Shavers, Frances Irvin, Bob London. "Diane," others. Universal

DORSEY BROTHERS

THE DORSEY BROS. ENCORE (1953) with Gordon Polk, Lynn Roberts, Earl Barton. "Jazz Me Blues," "Ain't She Sweet," "Street Scene," "Yes Indeed," "We'll Git It." Universal

E

ROY ELDRIDGE

SMASH YOUR BAGGAGE (1933) with Smalls Paradise Entertainers, including Eldridge and Dickie Wells. Musical revue, including "Tiger Rag." United Artists

DUKE ELLINGTON

BLACK AND TAN (1929) with Fredi Washington, Hall Johnson Choir. Available for purchase in 16mm sound or Super 8mm sound from Blackhawk.
A BUNDLE OF BLUES (1933) with Ivy Anderson. "Stormy Weather," others. Ivy; Kit Parker Films
PARAMOUNT PICTORIAL (Pictorial Magazine #837). Irving Mills introduces brief sequences of Ellington, Cab Calloway, and Baron Lee. Ivy
SYMPHONY IN BLACK (1935) with Billie Holiday. Features title composition. Ivy
A DATE WITH DUKE (1947). George Pal Puppetoon in color, with Duke on film and on soundtrack. Ivy
SALUTE TO DUKE ELLINGTON (1950) with Ray Nance, Johnny Hodges, Harry Carney, Tyree Glenn. "Things Ain't What They Used to Be," "Violet Blue," "The History of Jazz in Three Minutes." Universal

F

ELLA FITZGERALD

THE TENDER GAME (1958) with the Oscar Peterson Trio. Lovely animated cartoon by John Hubley of two people falling in love to the song "Tenderly." McGraw-Hill; Macmillan

H

LIONEL HAMPTON
LIONEL HAMPTON AND HIS ORCHESTRA (1949) with William Curley Hammer, Lorence Carter, Sonny Parker, Kitty Murray. "The New Look," "Hamp's Gumbo," "Curley's Dance Medley," "Wee Albert." Universal
LIONEL HAMPTON AND HERB JEFFRIES (1956) with Loray White, Vicky Lee. "Black Coffee," "The Bug," "Baby Don't Love Me No More," "Universal stomp." Universal
ADVENTURES OF AN ASTERISK (1956). Fine animated short by John Hubley featuring Hampton and Benny Carter, who wrote the score. McGraw-Hill; Macmillan

WOODY HERMAN
WOODY HERMAN AND ORCHESTRA (1938). "The Shag," "You Must Have Been a Beautiful Baby." United Artists
RHAPSODY IN WOOD (1947). George Pal Puppetoon in color with Herman on-screen explaining origin of clarinet; "Blue Flame." Ivy
WOODY HERMAN AND HIS ORCHESTRA (1948) with The Woodchoppers, The Modernaires, Don and Beverly. "Sabre Dance," "Jingle Bell Polka," "Camptown Races." Universal
HERMAN'S HERD (1949) with The Mellolarks. "Jamaica Rumba," "Tap Boogie," "I've Got News for You," "Lollybop," "Keen and Peachy." Universal

BOBBY HACKETT
SATURDAY NIGHT SWING CLUB (1938) with Leith Stevens and Orchestra, Les Lieber, Nan Wynn, Mel Allen, Eddie Condon. United Artists

BILLIE HOLIDAY
See COUNT BASIE, DUKE ELLINGTON

J

HARRY JAMES
HARRY JAMES AND HIS MUSIC MAKERS (1953) with Gale Robbins, Allan and Ashton. "I've Got a Crush on You," "Trumpet Blues," "Ciribiribin," "Charmaine," "Moaning Low." Universal
RIOT IN RHYTHM (1957) with The DeCastro Sisters, Johnny O'Niel. "Cherry," "Roll 'em," "Heartbreak Hotel." Universal

K

STAN KENTON
STAN KENTON AND HIS ORCHESTRA (1945) with June Christy. "Artistry in Rhythm," others. United Artists

GENE KRUPA
GENE KRUPA AND HIS ORCHESTRA (1941). "Call of the Canyon," "Perfidia." Ivy
GENE KRUPA AND HIS ORCHESTRA (1949) with Bill Black, Dolores Hawkins, Frankie Ross (Frank Rosolino). "Star Burst," "Lemon Drop," "Deep Purple," "Bop Boogie," "Melody in F." Universal

L

JIMMIE LUNCEFORD
JIMMIE LUNCEFORD AND HIS DANCE ORCHESTRA (1937). "Nagasaki," "Rhythm Is Our Business." United Artists

N

RED NICHOLS
RED NICHOLS AND HIS FIVE PENNIES (1950) with June Hutton, The Skylarks. "Do It Again," "Three Blind Mice," "South Rampart Street Parade." Universal

O

ANITA O'DAY
COOL AND GROOVY (1956) with Buddy DeFranco Quartet, Chico Hamilton Quintet, The Hi-Los. "Honeysuckle Rose," "I'll Remember April," "Jeepers Creepers." Universal

P

OSCAR PETERSON
BEGONE DULL CARE (1949). Classic abstract animated film by Norman McLaren set to three themes by the Oscar Peterson Trio. McGraw-Hill
THE TENDER GAME (1958). See ELLA FITZGERALD

R

DON REDMAN
DON REDMAN AND HIS ORCHESTRA (1934). "Ill Wind," "Nagasaki." United Artists.
I HEARD (1933). Betty Boop cartoon featuring "I Heard" and "How'm I Doin'?" Ivy; Kit Parker

BUDDY RICH
BUDDY RICH AND HIS ORCHESTRA (1948) with

Terry Gibbs, Louis DaPron. "Let's Get Away from It All," "Not So Quiet Please," "John Had the Number but No Nickel," "One O'Clock Boogie." Universal
MELODIES BY MARTIN (1956) with Freddie Martin and Orchestra; Rich has solo feature on "Jitterbug Routine." Universal

S

ARTIE SHAW
ARTIE SHAW'S SYMPHONY OF SWING (1939) with Helen Forrest, Tony Pastor, Buddy Rich. "Jeepers Creepers," "Lady Be Good," "Deep Purple." United Artists
ARTIE SHAW'S CLASS IN SWING (1939) with Helen Forrest. "I Have Eyes," "Shoot the Liquor to Me, John Boy." Ivy
NOBLE SISSLE
THAT'S THE SPIRIT (1933) with Cora La Redd, Washboard Serenaders, Mantan Moreland. "Tiger Rag," "St. Louis Blues." United Artists
BESSIE SMITH
ST. LOUIS BLUES (1929). Famous early-talkie short directed by Dudley Murphy. Available for purchase from National Cinema Service; rental from Macmillan; Kit Parker

T

JACK TEAGARDEN
PARAMOUNT PRESENTS HOAGY CARMICHAEL (1939) with Jack Teagarden and his Orchestra. "Small Fry," "Lazy Bones," "Stardust." Ivy; Kit Parker

Y

LESTER YOUNG
JAMMIN' THE BLUES (1944) with Illinois Jacquet, Harry Edison, Marlowe Morris, Sid Catlett, Jo Jones, Red Callender, John Simmons, Barney Kessel, Marie Bryant; produced by Norman Granz, directed by Gjon Mili. United Artists; Macmillan; Kit Parker

FEATURE FILMS OF SPECIAL INTEREST

HOLLYWOOD HOTEL (1937). Captures the Benny Goodman Quartet and Big Band at its best, including "Sing Sing Sing," along with other Busby Berkeley numbers, big cast headed by Dick Powell. United Artists
JAZZ BALL (1957). Compilation of soundies shorts with Louis Armstrong, Cab Calloway, Buddy Rich, Gene Krupa, Peggy Lee, many others. Ivy Films

JAZZ ON A SUMMER'S DAY (1960). Classic Bert Stern color documentary on 1959 Newport festival, with Louis Armstrong, Gerry Mulligan, Thelonious Monk, Anita O'Day, George Shearing, Sonny Stitt, Jimmy Giuffre, many others. New Yorker Films, 43 West 61st Street, New York, N.Y. 10023
JIVIN' IN BEBOP (1947). Feature made for black theaters with Dizzy Gillespie and his Band, Helen Humes, and a host of variety acts. Kit Parker Films
NEW ORLEANS (1947). Contrived "history" of jazz features Billie Holiday and Louis Armstrong together, Woody Herman, all-star New Orleans group, many others. Select Film Library
STORMY WEATHER (1943). All-black musical with Fats Waller, Bill Robinson, Lena Horne, Cab Calloway. Films Incorporated

GENERAL GUIDE TO RENTING HOLLYWOOD FEATURE FILMS

Universal Pictures and pre-1949 Paramount Pictures from Universal 16 (THE GLENN MILLER STORY, THE BENNY GOODMAN STORY, CRAZY HOUSE with Basie, BELLE OF THE NINETIES with Ellington, BIRTH OF THE BLUES with Teagarden, BIG BROADCAST OF 1937 with Goodman, etc.)
MGM, RKO, 20th Century Fox, and post-1949 Paramount Pictures from Films Incorporated (THE STRIP with Armstrong and Teagarden, GIRL CRAZY with Tommy Dorsey, BEAT THE BAND with Krupa, SUN VALLEY SERENADE with Glenn Miller, ST. LOUIS BLUES with Nat Cole, Ella Fitzgerald, Cab Calloway)
United Artists and pre-1949 Warner Brothers films from United Artists 16mm (I WANT TO LIVE with Gerry Mulligan and Shelly Manne, GOING PLACES with Armstrong, BLUES IN THE NIGHT with Lunceford)
Republic and independently-produced features from Ivy Films (THE FABULOUS DORSEYS, I'LL REACH FOR A STAR/HIT PARADE OF 1937 with Ellington, HIT PARADE OF 1947/HIGH AND HAPPY with Woody Herman)
Columbia, post-1949 Warner Brothers, Samuel Goldwyn, and Walt Disney features from various other film companies listed, including Select Film Library, Macmillan Audio Brandon.

Film Rental Companies
(some of these also offer leasing plans for prints)

United Artists 16mm Division, 729 Seventh Avenue, New York, N.Y. 10019
Ivy Films, 165 West 46th Street, New York, New York 10036
McGraw-Hill Films, Princeton Road, Hightstown, N.J. 08520

or 1714 Stockton St., San Francisco, California 94133

Macmillan Audio Brandon Films, 34 MacQuesten Parkway South, Mount Vernon, New York 10550

or 1619 North Cherokee, Los Angeles, California 90028

Universal 16mm, 445 Park Avenue, New York, New York 10022

Select Film Library, 115 West 31st Street, New York, New York 10001

Films Incorporated, 1144 Wilmette Road, Wilmette, Illinois 60091

Kit Parker Films, Box 227, Carmel Valley, California 93924

Film Purchase Companies

Blackhawk Films, Eastin-Phelan Building, Davenport, Iowa 52808

National Cinema Service, 333 West 57th Street, New York, New York 10019

Recomended Recordings
Of The Decade 1966-1975

THE SMITHSONIAN COLLECTION

This new label, under the auspices of the Smithsonian Institution, reissued some highly important material with extensive and authoritative background information and discography supervised by Martin Williams.

The Smithsonian Collection of Classic Jazz contains 84 original recordings culled from the archives of 17 record companies in a boxed collection of 6 LPs. Two-LP sets each of *King Oliver's Jazz Band/1923* and *Louis Armstrong and Earl Hines/1928* were subsequently issued. Also of interest is *Classic Rags and Ragtime Songs* including material by Eubie Blake and Scott Joplin. (The Smithsonian Collection, P.O. Box 5734, Terre Haute, Indiana 47802).

THE ENCYCLOPEDIA OF JAZZ
IN THE SEVENTIES

COMPANION RECORD ALBUM

A specially assembled two-pocket album under the above title, comprising outstanding performances by a broad spectrum of great jazz artists recorded during the period from 1966 through 1975, will be found on the RCA label. It consists of material from the RCA and Flying Dutchman catalogues. Side Two concentrates on the international jazz scene; the other three sides represent a cross section of American combo, big band and vocal styles and idioms. Partial personnels are listed below.

SIDE ONE:
1. Lonnie Liston Smith & The Cosmic Echoes. *Voodoo Woman*. Donald Smith, Cecil McBee, Michael Carvin, Art Gore.

2. Shelly Manne. *Night and Day*. Victor Feldman, Mike Wofford, Tom Scott, Oscar Brashear.
3. Horace Tapscott Quintet. *Dark Tree*. Black Arthur Blythe, David Bryant.
4. Gil Evans Orchestra. *King Porter Stomp*. Dave Sanborn.

SIDE TWO:
1. Gato Barbieri. *Tupac Amaru*. Lennie White III, Joe Beck, Lonnie Liston Smith.
2. John Dankworth and his Orchestra. *Long John*. Don Rendell, Kenny Baker.
3. Cleo Laine. *Music*.
4. Toshiko Akiyoshi-Lew Tabackin Big Band. *Since Perry/Yet Another Tear*.

SIDE THREE:
1. David Amram. *Waltz From "After The Fall."* Pepper Adams, Jerry Dodgion.
2. Nina Simone. *Ain't Got No/I Got Life*.
3. Bob Thiele's Orchestra. *I Saw Pinetop Spit Blood*. Bobby Bryant, Bob Brookmeyer, Chuck Domanico, Mike Wofford, Dennis Budimir. Composed and arranged by Oliver Nelson.
4. Groove Holmes. *Green Dolphin Street*.

SIDE FOUR:
1. Buddy Rich. *Space Shuttle*. Pat LaBarbera.
2. Jazz Piano Quartet. *Maiden Voyage*. Dick Hyman, Roland Hanna, Marian McPartland, Hank Jones.
3. Blue Mitchell. *Collaborations*. Harold Land.
4. Duke Ellington and his Orchestra. *Don't You Know I Care*, Harold Minerve, Harry Carney.

Recommended Records

In order to compile a list representative of various critical viewpoints, it was decided to solicit the additional opinions of several experts other than the authors to compile a list of major contributors to recorded jazz during the period from 1966 through 1975. Voters were advised that big bands, combos, singers and representatives of any and all styles of jazz could be included. Each critic put ten albums by ten different artists or groups in nomination.

If an album received more than one vote, the number of votes is indicated in parentheses after the title.

The list reflects a consensus of the opinions of Philippe Carles, Willis Conover, Leonard Feather, Ira Gitler, Nat Hentoff, Kiyoshi Koyama, Dan Morgenstern, Martin Williams and John S. Wilson.

Art Ensemble of Chicago	*Message To Our Folks*	**Byg**
Count Basie	*Basie Jam*	**Pablo**
	Trio	**Pablo**
Carla Bley	*A Genuine Tong Funeral*	**RCA**
Dollar Brand/Gato Barbieri	*Confluence*	**Freedom**
Anthony Braxton	*New York, Fall 1974*	**Arista**
Gary Burton-Ralph Towner	*Matchbook*	**ECM**
Jaki Byard	*The Jaki Byard Experience*	**Prestige**
Don Cherry	*Complete Communion*	**Blue Note**
	Relativity Suite	**JCOA**
Ornette Coleman	*Crisis*	**Impulse**
	Science Fiction	**Columbia**
	Skies of America	**Columbia**
	The Empty Fox Hole	**Blue Note**
John Coltrane	*Concert In Japan*	**Impulse**
	Ascension (2)	**Impulse**
Chick Corea	*Return To Forever*	**ECM**
Miles Davis	*Bitches' Brew (4)*	**Columbia**
	In A Silent Way (3)	**Columbia**

Urszula Dudziak	*Newborn Light*	Columbia
Duke Ellington	*And His Mother Called Him Bill* (3)	RCA
	Concert Of Sacred Music	RCA
	Far East Suite (2)	RCA
	70th Birthday Concert	UA
Bill Evans	*At The Montreux Jazz Festival* (2)	Verve
Bill Evans-George Russell	*Living Time*	Columbia
John Garvey And The University Of Illinois Jazz Band	*In Champaign-Urbana*	Century
Dizzy Gillespie	*Big Four*	Pablo
	The Giant	Prestige
Dexter Gordon	*The Panther* (2)	Prestige
Herbie Hancock	*Speak Like A Child*	Blue Note
Barry Harris	*Plays Tadd Dameron*	Xanadu
Earl Hines	*The Quintessential Recording Session* (2)	Chiaroscuro
Dick Hyman	*Genius At Play*	Monmouth-Evergreen
Keith Jarrett	*Solo Concerts* (2)	ECM
Jazz Composers Orchestra with Cecil Taylor, Don Cherry, Pharoah Sanders, Roswell Rudd, etc.		JCOA
Thad Jones/Mel Lewis	*Consummation*	Blue Note
	Suite For Pops	Horizon
Lee Konitz	*Duets*	Milestone
	Satori	Milestone
Steve Lacy	*Solo*	Emanem
Charles Mingus	*And Friends In Concert*	Columbia
	Mingus Moves	Atlantic
Modern Jazz Quartet	*Last Concert* (3)	Atlantic
Max Morath	*The Entertainer*	Arpeggio

Zbigniew Namyslowski	*Winobranie*	Muza
New York Jazz Repertory Company	*Presents The Music Of Louis Armstrong*	Atlantic
Joe Pass	*Virtuoso*	Pablo
Joe Pass-Oscar Peterson	*The Trio*	Pablo
Oscar Peterson and Dizzy Gillespie	*(2)*	Pablo
Revolutionary Ensemble	*Manhattan Cycles*	India Navigation
Sonny Rollins	*The Cutting Edge In Japan*	Milestone JVC
Jimmy Rushing	*The You And Me That Used To Be*	RCA
Archie Shepp	*Attica Blues*	Impulse
Zoot Sims	*And The Gershwin Brothers*	Pablo
Zoot Sims-Bucky Pizzarelli	*Nirvana*	Groove Merchant
Sonny Stitt	*Constellation*	Cobblestone
Sun Ra	*It's After The End Of The World*	MPS
Supersax	*Plays Bird*	Capitol
Cecil Taylor	*Indent* *Silent Tongues*	Unit Core Arista
McCoy Tyner	*Echoes Of A Friend* *Sahara*	Milestone Milestone
Sarah Vaughan	*Live In Japan (4)*	Mainstream
Bill Watrous	*The Tiger Of San Pedro*	Columbia
Weather Report	*Tale Spinnin'*	Columbia
Dick Wellstood	*And His Famous Orchestra From Ragtime On*	Chiaroscuro Chiaroscuro
Bob Wilber-Kenny Davern	*Soprano Summit*	World Jazz

Bibliography: Books 1966-1975

ALBERTSON, CHRIS, *Bessie*, (Stein & Day) 253 pp, 1972.

ALLEN, WALTER C., *Hendersonia—The Music of Fletcher Henderson and His Musicians*, A Bio-Discography (Walter C. Allen, P.O. Box 1382, Highland Pk., N.J. 08904) 651 pp, 1973.

AMRAM, DAVID, *Vibrations*, an autobiography (Macmillan) 469 pp, 1968.

BALLIETT, WHITNEY, *New York Notes: A Journal of Jazz, 1972-1975* (Houghton Mifflin) 250 pp, 1976.

BALLIETT, WHITNEY, *Alex Wilder & His Friends* (Houghton Mifflin) 205 pp, 1974.

BALLIETT, WHITNEY, *Such Sweet Thunder* (Bobbs-Merrill) 366 pp, 1967.

BALLIETT, WHITNEY, *Ecstasy at the Onion* (Bobbs-Merrill) 284 pp, 1972.

BALLIETT, WHITNEY, *Super Drummer: A Profile of Buddy Rich*, w. photos by Fred Seligo (Bobbs-Merrill) 120 pp, 1968.

BERENDT, JOACHIM, *The Jazz Book*, translated by Dan Morgenstern & Helmut and Barbara Bredigheit (Lawrence Hill & Co.) 459 pp, 1975.

BERTON, RALPH, *Remembering Bix* (Harper & Row) 428 pp, 1974.

BLESH, RUDI & HARRIET JANIS, *They All Played Ragtime* (Oak Publs.) republished 1966, 347 pp.

BLESH, RUDI, *Combo USA: Eight Lives in Jazz* (Chilton Book Co.) 240 pp, 1971.

BRASK, OLE & DAN MORGENSTERN, *Jazz People* (Harry N. Abrams) 300 pp, 1976.

BUERKLE, JACK J. & DANNY BARKER, *Bourbon Street Black*, The New Orleans Black Jazzman (Oxford Univ. Press) 244 pp, 1973.

CHILTON, JOHN, *Billie's Blues*, The Billie Holiday Story, 1933-59 (Stein & Day) 264 pp, 1975.

CHILTON, JOHN, *Who's Who of Jazz: Storyville To Swing Street* (Bloomsbury Book Shop, London) 447 pp, 1972.

COKER, JERRY, *The Jazz Idiom* (Prentice-Hall) 1975.

COLE, BILL, *Miles Davis: A Musical Biography* (Wm. Morrow & Co.) 256 pp, 1974.

COLE, MARIA, with LOUIE ROBINSON, *Nat King Cole*, An Intimate Biography (Wm. Morrow & Co.) 184 pp, 1971.

COLLINS, MARY, *Oh, Didn't He Ramble*, The Life Story Of Lee Collins (Univ. of Illinois Press) 159 pp, 1974.

CONNOR, D. RUSSELL and WARREN W. HICKS, *B.G. On The Record*, A Bio-Discography of Benny Goodman (Arlington House) 691 pp, 1969.

COOK, BRUCE, *Listen To The Blues* (Chas. Scribner's Sons) 263 pp, 1973.

DANCE, STANLEY, *The World of Duke Ellington* (Chas. Scribner's Sons) 311 pp, 1971.

DANCE, STANLEY, *The World of Swing* (Scribner's) 436 pp, 1974.

EASTON, CAROL, *Straight Ahead*, The Story of Stan Kenton (Wm. Morrow & Co. Inc.) 252 pp, 1973.

ELLINGTON, DUKE, *Music Is My Mistress* (Doubleday & Co. Inc.) 523 pp, 1973.

ERLICH, LILLIAN, *What Jazz Is All About* (Julian Messner) 255 pp, Revised 1975 (Orig. publ. 1962).

FEATHER, LEONARD, *From Satchmo To Miles* (Stein & Day) 258 pp, 1972.

FERNETT, GENE, *A Thousand Golden Horns* (Pendell Co.) 171 pp.

FLOWER, JOHN, *Moonlight Serenade:* A Bio-Discography of the Glenn Miller Civilian Band (Arlington House) 554 pp.

FOUNTAIN, PETE, with BILL NEELY, *A Closer Walk*, The Pete Fountain Story (Henry Regnery Co.) 202 pp, 1972.

FREEMAN, BUD, *You Don't Look Like A Musician* (Balamp Publ., 7430 Second Blvd., Detroit, Mich. 48202) 125 pp, 1974.

GAMMOND, PETER, *Scott Joplin And The Ragtime Era* (St. Martin's Press) 256 pp, 1975.

GARLAND, PHYL, *The Sound of Soul* (Henry Regnery Co.) 246 pp, 1969.

GLEASON, RALPH J., *Celebrating the Duke, And Louis, Bessie, Billie, Bird, Carmen, Miles, Dizzy and Other Heroes* (Little Brown & Co.) 280 pp, 1975.

BIBLIOGRAPHY

GLOVER, TONY (LITTLE SUN), *Blues Harp* (Oak Publ.) 72 pp, 1966.

GONZALES, BABS, *I Paid My Dues: Good Times . . . No Bread* (Expubidence Publ. Corp.) 160 pp, 1968.

GONZALES, BABS, *Movin' On Down De Line* (Expubidence Publ. Corp.) 256 pp, 1975.

GOREAU, LAURRAINE, *Just Mahalia, Baby* (Word Books, Texas) 611 pp, 1975.

GREEN, BENNY, *Drums In My Ears*, Jazz In Our Time (Horizon) 188 pp, 1973.

HAWES, HAMPTON, with DON ASHER, *Raise Up Off Me* (Coward, McCann & Geoghegan Inc.) 179 pp, 1972.

HEILBUT, TONY, *The Gospel Sound*, Good News & Bad Times (Simon & Schuster) 350 pp, 1971.

HODEIR, ANDRE, *The Worlds of Jazz* (Grove Press) 279 pp, 1972.

Jazz Guitarists. Collected Interviews from *Guitar Player Magazine* (Guitar Player Productions) 120 pp, 1975.

JONES, LEROI, *Black Music* (Wm. R. Morrow) hardcover & paper, 1969.

JONES, MAX & JOHN CHILTON, *Louis: The Louis Armstrong Story* (Little, Brown & Co.) 256 pp, 1972.

KEEPNEWS, ORRIN & BILL GRAUER, *A Pictorial History of Jazz*, revised edition (Crown Publs.) 297 pp, 1966.

KEIL, CHARLES, *Urban Blues* (Univ. of Chicago Press) 231 pp, 1967.

KIMBALL, ROBERT & WILLIAM BOLCOM, *Reminiscing With Sissle & Blake* (The Viking Press) 254 pp, 1973.

KINKLE, ROGER D., *The Complete Encyclopedia of Popular Music and Jazz*, 1900-1950 in four volumes (Arlington House) Vol. 1, 464 pp, Vol. 2, 1266 pp, Vol. 3, 2000 pp, Vol. 4, 2644 pp, 1974.

KIRKEBY, ED, in collaboration with SINCLAIR TRAILL & DUNCAN P. SCHIEDT, *Ain't Misbehavin': The Story of Fats Waller* (Dodd, Mead & Co.) 248 pp, 1967.

LONGSTREET, STEPHEN, *Sportin' House: A History of the New Orleans Sinners and the Birth of Jazz* (Sherbourne Press, Inc.) 293 pp, 1966.

McCARTHY, ALBERT, *Big Band Jazz* (G.P. Putnam's Sons) 360 pp, 1974.

MERRYMAN, RICHARD, *Louis Armstrong: A Self-Portrait* (The Eakins Press) 59 pp (cloth & paper) 1972.

MINGUS, CHARLES, edited by NEL KING, *Beneath the Underdog* (Alfred A. Knopf) 366 pp, 1971.

MOORE, CARMAN, *Somebody's Angel Child:* The Story of Bessie Smith (Thos. Y. Crowell Co.) 122 pp, 1970.

NANRY, CHARLES (Ed.), *American Music: From Storyville to Woodstock (Transaction Books) 290 pp, 1972.*

OLIVER, PAUL, *The Story of the Blues* (Chilton Book Co.) 176 pp, 1969.

OTIS, JOHNNY, *Listen To The Lambs* (W.W. Norton & Co.) 256 pp, 1968.

PANASSIE, HUGUES, *Louis Armstrong* (Charles Scribner's Sons) 149 pp, 1972.

PHILLIPS, JANE, *Mojo Hand* (Trident Press) 180 pp, 1968.

PLEASANTS, HENRY, *The Great American Popular Singers* (Simon & Schuster) 384 pp, 1974.

PLEASANTS, HENRY, *Serious Music & All That Jazz* (Simon & Schuster) 256 pp, 1969.

RICHARDS, KENNETH G., *Louis Armstrong* (Childrens Press) 95 pp, 1968.

RIVELLI, PAULINE & ROBERT LEVIN, Eds., *Rock Giants*, Jazz & Pop (World Publ. Co.) 125 pp, 1970.

ROACH, HILDRED, *Black American Music, Past & Present* (Crescendo Publ. Co.) 199 pp, 1973.

ROONEY, JAMES, *Bossmen: Bill Monroe & Muddy Waters* (Dial Press) 159 pp.

ROSE, AL & EDMOND SOUCHON, *New Orleans Jazz: A Family Album* (Louisiana State Univ. Press) 310 pp, 1967.

ROXON, LILLIAN, *Rock Encyclopedia* (Grosset & Dunlap) 613 pp, 1969.

RUSSELL, ROSS, *Jazz Style in Kansas City and the Southwest* (Univ. of Cal. Press) 292 pp, 1972.

RUSSELL, ROSS, *Bird Lives: The High Life and Hard Times of Charlie (Yardbird) Parker* (Charterhouse) 1973.

SACKHEIM, ERIC, *The Blues Line* (Grossman Publs.) 500 pp, 1970.

SANFORD, HERB, *Tommy & Jimmy: The Dorsey Years*, intro. by Bing Crosby (Arlington House) 305 pp, 1972.

SCHAFER, WILLIAM J. & JOHANNES RIEDEL, *The Art of Ragtime* (Louisiana State University Press) 1973.

SCHULLER, GUNTHER, *Early Jazz; Its Roots and Musical Development* (Oxford Univ. Press) 401 pp, 1968.

SCOTT, ALLEN, *Jazz Educated, Man* (Amer. Int'l. Publs.) 133 pp, 1973.

SHACTER, JAMES D., *Piano Man*, The Story of Ralph Sutton (Jaynar Press, P.O. Box 3141 Merchandise Mart Plaza, Chicago, Ill. 60654) 244 pp, 1975.

SHAW, ARNOLD, *The Rock Revolution* (Crowell-Collier Press) 215 pp, 1969.

SHAW, ARNOLD, *The World of Soul* (Cowles Book Co. Inc.) 306 pp, 1970.

SHAW, ARNOLD, *The Street That Never Slept* (Coward, McCann & Geoghegan) 378 pp, 1972.

SIDRAN, BEN, *Black Talk* (Holt, Rinehart & Winston) 201 pp, 1971.

SIMON, GEORGE T., *The Big Bands* (Macmillan) 537 pp, 1967.

SIMON, GEORGE T., *Simon Says: The Sights and Sounds of the Swing Era* (Arlington House) 492 pp, 1972.

SIMON, GEORGE T., *Glenn Miller & His Orchestra* (Thos. Y. Crowell Co.) 473 pp, 1974.

SIMON, GEORGE T., *The Big Bands Songbook* (Thomas Y. Crowell Co.) 356 pp, 1975.

SIMOSKO, VLADIMIR & BARRY TEPPERMAN, *Eric Dolphy*, A Musical Biography & Discography (Smithsonian Institution Press) 132 pp, 1974.

SIMPKINS, C. O., *Coltrane: A Biography* (Herndon House) 287 pp, 1975.

SPELLMAN, A. B., *Four Lives in the Bebop Business* (Pantheon Press) 235 pp, 1966.

STAMBLER, IRWIN, *Encyclopedia of Pop, Rock & Soul* (St. Martin's Press) 609 pp, 1974.

STEARNS, MARSHALL & JEAN, *Jazz Dance*, The Story of American Vernacular Dance (Macmillan) 464 pp, 1968.

STEWART, REX, *Jazz Masters of the '30s* (Macmillan) 223 pp, 1972.

STODDARD, TOM (as told to), *Pops Foster—The Autobiography of A New Orleans Jazzman* (Univ. of Cal. Press) 207 pp, 1971.

SUDHALTER, RICHARD M. & PHILIP R. EVANS, *Bix, Man and Legend* (Harper & Row) 512 pp, 1974.

TANNER, PAUL & MAURICE GEROW, *A Study of Jazz* (Wm. C. Brown) 189 pp, 2nd Edition, 1973.

THOMAS, J. C., *Chasin' The Trane* (Doubleday) 252 pp, 1975.

WELLS, DICKY, *The Night People*, as told to Stanley Dance (Crescendo Publ. Co.) 122 pp, 1971.

WILDER, ALEC, *American Popular Song: The Great Innovators, 1900-1950* (Oxford Univ. Press) 536 pp, 1972.

WILLIAMS, MARTIN, *Jazz Masters of New Orleans* (Macmillan) 287 pp, 1967.

WILLIAMS, MARTIN, *The Jazz Tradition* (Oxford Univ. Press) 232 pp, 1970.

WILLIAMS, MARTIN, *Jazz Masters In Transition 1957-69* (Macmillan) 288 pp, 1970.

WILMER, VALERIE, *Jazz People* (The Bobbs-Merrill Co.) 167 pp, 1971.

WILSON, JOHN S., *Jazz: The Transition Years, 1940-1960* (Appleton-Century-Crofts) 185 pp, 1967.

THE ENCYCLOPEDIA OF JAZZ IN THE SEVENTIES
was photo-composed by
Publishers Phototype, Inc., Carlstadt, N.J.,
and Cemar Graphic Designs Ltd., Rockville Centre, N.Y.